W9-BNG-750

West's Law School Advisory Board

TEACHING MATERIALS ON
ESTATE PLANNING

Fourth Edition

■ ■ ■

By

Gerry W. Beyer

Governor Preston E. Smith Regents Professor of Law
Texas Tech University School of Law

AMERICAN CASEBOOK SERIES®

WEST®

A Thomson Reuters business

Mat #40765049

610 Opperman Drive
St. Paul, MN 55123
1–800–313–9378

Printed in the United States of America

ISBN: 978–0–314–19591–3

To Aloysius A. Leopold—
For his friendship and encouragement.

To Eugene F. Scoles—
For sharing his wisdom.

PREFACE

We have entered a new era of estate planning. Since Congress enacted the modern federal estate tax in 1916, the primary focus of estate planning, and consequently estate planning courses, had been taxation. But estate planning is no longer a process with which only the wealthy need be concerned. Instead, every person regardless of estate value needs a carefully reasoned, prepared, and executed estate plan to cover a wide array of concerns including asset management and disposition, disability planning for property management and health care, and planning for the physical aspects of death, as well as saving taxes. In recognition of this change, a growing number of law schools now offer separate estate planning courses; one in the overall estate planning process and another focusing on wealth transfer taxation.

These materials are designed to provide the student with a comprehensive review of the estate planning process. The book begins by placing estate planning in perspective, that is, what estate planning encompasses, why it should be done, and the reasons so many people forego it. Because estate planning requires many documents, the introductory chapter includes an overview of the drafting process. The student may apply this knowledge when completing the drafting exercises provided throughout the book.

Part One focuses on the law applicable to estate planning beginning with a review of the introductory estates, wills, and trusts course that most students will have taken as a prerequisite to estate planning. Do not dismiss this chapter as merely being repetitive of other courses because the materials stress how to deal with these topics in the broader estate planning context. Because there are many ways to dispose of property other than by a will or via intestacy, the next chapter focuses on probate avoidance techniques such as inter vivos gifts, joint tenancies, multiple-party accounts, and life insurance. Coverage of tax planning comes next. The tax chapter introduces estate and gift tax concepts assuming the student has little or no prior exposure to tax matters; it is not intended as a substitute for a specialized course in wealth transfer taxation. The next three chapters cover planning for disability and the physical aspects of death. If the likelihood of disability and the inevitability of death are not carefully anticipated, there may be no estate left to pass to the decedent's intended beneficiaries.

Part Two concentrates on the estate planning practice such as client contact and the practical problems that arise including ethical considerations, the potential of malpractice, will contest avoidance techniques, and the additional concerns that are raised when a client has a special circumstance (e.g., minor child, creditors to avoid, desire to control property in perpetuity, property in another jurisdiction, or marital problems). Because an estate plan fails if the documents are not properly prepared, executed, preserved, and reviewed, the next chapter covers these matters. The book concludes with a discussion of estate administration, i.e., how the at-death portion of the estate plan is put into action after the client dies.

To receive maximum value from this course, the student is urged to perform the *locate* and *draft* exercises based on the law of the state in which the student intends to practice. Estate planning involves more than understanding the generic principles and policies involved; a person must actually *do* it to appreciate its difficulty and complexity. If the student completes and organizes the *locate* and *draft* materials in an "estate planning notebook," the student will have a valuable resource tool to use when embarking on a career that includes estate planning.

Citations and footnotes of the courts and commentators have been omitted without so specifying and the footnotes that remain may be renumbered. Comments following statutory provisions, especially those of uniform laws, are frequently omitted without indication.

You may access updates to the casebook at http://www.ProfessorBeyer.com. If, as you use this book, you have any suggestions, comments, corrections, or criticisms, I would greatly appreciate your sharing them with me. You may e-mail me at gwb@ProfessorBeyer.com.

Good luck in the course. I urge you to use your estate planning skills to enrich your clients' lives and ease their apprehension of disability and death.

GERRY W. BEYER

Texas Tech University School of Law
November 2012

ACKNOWLEDGEMENTS

The author acknowledges with great appreciation permission to reprint the materials listed below:

ACTEC Commentaries on Model Rules of Professional Conduct (4th ed. 2006), selected provisions. Reprinted with the permission of the American College of Trust and Estate Counsel.

American Arbitration Association, *Arbitration Rules for Wills and Trusts*, 1–2 (2009). Reprinted with the permission of the American Arbitration Association.

Sam E. Beller, *How to Compare Long–Term Care Insurance Policies*, 26 EST. PLAN. 296 (1999). Reprinted with permission of Thomson Reuters and Sam E. Beller.

Frank S. Berall, *Estate Planning Considerations for Unmarried Cohabitants*, 31 EST. PLAN. 307 (2004). Reprinted with permission of Thomson Reuters.

John T. Berteau, *Steps to Avoid Beneficiary Conflicts Over Bequests of Tangible Personal Property*, 12 EST. PLAN. 356 (1985). Reprinted with permission of Thomson Reuters.

Gerry W. Beyer, *Enhancing Self-Determination Through Guardian Self-Declaration*, 23 IND. L. REV. 71, 72–87 (1990). Copyright © 1990, Trustees of Indiana University. Reprinted with permission of the Trustees of Indiana University.

Gerry W. Beyer, *Pre-Mortem Probate*, PROB. & PROP., July/Aug. 1993, at 6, 7–9. First published in Probate & Property, copyright © 1993, American Bar Association. Reprinted by permission.

Gerry W. Beyer & Steven F. Carvel, *Manipulating the Conduct of Beneficiaries with Conditional Gifts*, EST. PLAN. DEV. TEX PROF., June 2001, at 1. Reprinted with permission.

Gerry W. Beyer & Kerri M. Griffin, *The Role of Legal Assistants in the Estate Planning Practice*, EST. PLAN. DEVEL. FOR TEX. PROF., Jan. 2012, at 1. Reprinted with permission.

Chadwick Bothe, *The Stigma of Survival: Medicaid Estate Planning*, 51 S. TEX. L. REV. 815 (2010). Reprinted with permission of Chadwick Bothe.

Alexander A. Bove, Jr., *The Mechanics of Establishing an Offshore Trust*, American Bar Association, Section of Real Property Probate and Trust Law Asset Protection Planning Committee, Spring Symposium April 2005 (revised March 2012). Reprinted with permission of Alexander A. Bove, Jr.

Karen S. Cohen, *The 10 Most Powerful Postmortem Planning Pointers For Trusts and Estates*, J. ACCOUNTANCY, May 2012. Reproduced with permission of the Journal of Accountancy.

Ronald R. Cresswell & Lendy Leggett, *Setting and Collecting Fees*, in State Bar of Texas, Fifteenth Annual Advanced Estate Planning and Probate Course ch. O (1991). Reprinted with permission.

James Crist, *Mediating Probate Disputes*, HENNEPIN LAW., Oct. 22, 2008. Reprinted with permission of James Crist, Partner, Steinhagen & Crist.

A. Kimberley Dayton, Timothy H. Guare, & Molly M. Wood, *Advising The Elderly Client*, § 33:10, Patient Self–Determination Act (2011). Reprinted with permission of Thomson Reuters.

Brian L. Dobben, *Estate Planning: The Initial Client Interview*, 81 ILL. B.J. 261, 261–62 (1993). Reprinted with permission of the *Illinois Bar Journal*, Vol. 81 #5, May 1993. Copyright by the Illinois State Bar Association. www.isba.org.

Stuart B. Dorsett, *International Estate Planning: What To Do When Your Estate Crosses The Border*, Dec. 16, 2010. © 2010, Ward and Smith, P.A. Reprinted with permission.

Toby Eisenberg, *Charitable Tool Box*, in San Antonio Estate Planners Council's Docket Call in Probate Court (2011). Copyright © 2011 Toby Eisenberg. Reprinted with permission.

Lawrence A. Friedman, *Special Needs Estate Planning*, N.J. LAW., August 2010, at 38. This article was originally published in the August 2010 issue of New Jersey Lawyer Magazine, a publication of the New Jersey State Bar Association, and is reprinted here with permission and with the permission of Lawrence A. Friedman, Esq., Friedman Law, Bridgewater, New Jersey, www.specialneedsnj.com.

David Gage & John Gromala, *Mediation in Estate Planning: A Strategy for Everyone's Benefit*, 4 MARQ. ELDER'S ADVISOR, Fall 2002, at 23 Reprinted with the permission of Marquette University Law School Elder's Advisor.

A. Silvana Giner, *GRITS, GRATS, and GRUTS*, Drafting Irrevocable Trusts in Massachusetts, Ch. 9, 2005, 1st Supp. 2009. © MCLE | NE, reprinted with permission, all rights reserved.

Sebastian V. Grassi, Jr., *Key Issues To Consider When Drafting Life Insurance Trusts*, 31 EST. PLAN. 390 (2004). Copyright © 2004 RIA and Sebastian V. Grassi, Jr. Reprinted with permission of Thomson Reuters.

Ardath A. Hamann, *Family Surrogate Laws: A Necessary Supplement to Living Wills and Durable Powers of Attorney*, 38 VILL. L. REV. 103, 103–06, 130–32, 134–37, 160, 162–76 (1993). Copyright © 1993, Villanova University. Reprinted by permission of the Villanova Law Review.

Donna S. Harkness, *Life Care Agreements: A Contractual Jekyll and Hyde?*, MARQ. ELDER'S ADVISOR 39 (Fall 2003). Reprinted with permission of Donna S. Harkness.

Jennifer Hasley, *Avoiding Risk Factors and Understanding the Attorney Grievance Process*. Revised June 2012. Reprinted with permission of Jennifer Hasley.

John Parker Huggard, *Qualified Domestic Trust*, N.C. Estate Settlement Practice Guide § 30:6 (2012). Reprinted with permission of Thomson Reuters.

Robert S. Hunter, *Estate Planning and Administration, The Estate Planning Advisors, Generally*, 7 Ill. Prac., Estate Planning & Admin. § 2:1 (4th ed.). Reprinted with permission of Thomson Reuters.

Robert B. Joslyn, *Use of Plain English in Drafting Wills and Trusts*, 63 MICH. B.J. 612, 612–13 (1984). Copyright © 1984, State Bar of Michigan. Reprinted by permission of the Michigan Bar Journal.

Edward F. Koren, Estate, *Tax and Personal Financial Planning*, 2 Est. Tax & Pers. Fin. Plan. § 15:21 (updated 2012). Reprinted with permission of Thomson Reuters.

Robert J. Lynn & Grayson M.P. McCouch, Introduction to Estate Planning, §§ 1.2, 1.3, 1.5, 3.2, 6.2, 6.6, 7.5, 7.8, 7.9, 13.4 (5th ed. 2004). Copyright © 2004. Reprinted with permission of Thomson Reuters.

Marilyn J. Maag, *The Development of POLST to Honor Medical Treatment Goals at End-of-Life*, ACTEC Summer Meeting, June 2012. Reprinted with permission of Marilyn J. Maag (Porter Wright Morris & Arthur LLP).

John K. McNulty & Grayson M.P. McCouch, Federal Estate and Gift Taxation, §§ 1–3, 50, 80 (7th ed. 2011). Copyright © 2011. Reprinted with permission of Thomson Reuters.

Thane Josef Messinger, *A Gentle and Easy Death: From Ancient Greece to Beyond Cruzan Toward a Reasoned Legal Response to the Societal Dilemma of Euthanasia*, 71 DENV. UNIV L. REV. 175, 175–78 (1993). Copyright © 1993, Denver University Law Review. Reprinted by permission of the Denver University Law Review.

Robert L. Moshman, *Avoiding A GSTT Asteroid: Revisting a Dangerous Adversary: The Generation–Skipping Transfer Tax*, EST. ANALYST (Sept. 2011). Copyright © R. Moshman 2011. Reprinted with permission.

Robert L. Moshman, *Comparing FLPS and LLCS*. Adapted from *FLP vs. LLC & Sam Walton's FLP Estate*, EST. ANALYST (June 2008). Reprinted with permission of Robert L. Moshman.

John K. O'Meara, *Estate Planning Concerns for the Professional Athlete,* 3 MARQ. SPORTS L.J. 85, 85–86 (1992, revised Oct. 2011). Reprinted with permission.

Personal Financial Planning Handbook: With Forms & Checklists, ¶ 14.06 *Planner-Client Communications* (2nd ed. 2011). Reprinted with permission of Thomson Reuters.

Thomas L. Shaffer, *The "Estate Planning" Counselor and Values Destroyed by Death*, 55 IOWA L. REV. 376, 367–86, 388, 393–95, 407–09 (1969). Copyright © 1969, The University of Iowa. Reprinted by permission of the Iowa Law Review.

Thomas L. Shaffer & Carol Ann Mooney, The Planning and Drafting of Wills and Trusts 35, 38–48 (5th ed. 2007). Reprinted with permission of Thomson Reuters.

Martin M. Shenkman, *Estate Planning Strategies For Clients Living With Chronic Illnesses*. Reprinted with the permission of Martin M. Shenkman who maintains the charitable website www.RV4TheCause.org which is a free website he uses to disseminate information on planning for chronic illness.

Uniform Anatomical Gift Act (Revised). Excerpts of this Act have been reprinted through the permission of the National Conference of Commissioners on Uniform State Laws.

Uniform Custodial Trust Act. Excerpts of this Act have been reprinted through the permission of the National Conference of Commissioners on Uniform State Laws.

Uniform Health Care Decisions Act. Excerpts of this Act have been reprinted through the permission of the National Conference of Commissioners on Uniform State Laws.

Uniform Probate Code. Excerpts of this Code have been reprinted through the permission of the National Conference of Commissioners on Uniform State Laws.

Uniform Power of Attorney Act. Excerpts of this Act have been reprinted through the permission of the National Conference of Commissioners on Uniform State Laws.

Uniform Transfers to Minors Act. Excerpts of this Act have been reprinted through the permission of the National Conference of Commissioners on Uniform State Laws.

Andrea Utecht and Abraham C. Reich, *Successful Partnering Between Inside and Outside Counsel*, § 31:29 Multi–Disciplinary Practice. Reprinted with permission of Thomson Reuters.

Thomas S. Word, Jr., *A Brief for Plain English Wills and Trusts*, 14 UNIV. RICH. L. REV. 471, 471–81 (1980). Copyright © 1980, University of Richmond Law Review Association. Reprinted by permission of the University of Richmond Law Review.

Wesley E. Wright, *Medicaid Estate Recovery: When The Government Wants Your Homestead*, Texas State Bar College, Summer School ch. 12 (2004, revised 2012). Copyright © 2012 by Wright Abshire, Attorneys. Reprinted with permission.

* * *

The author wishes to thank the following individuals, listed in alphabetical order, for their stellar assistance in the preparation of the Fourth Edition of this book:

Carly Hardt, 2012 J.D., Texas Tech University School of Law

Justin M. Lopez, 2013 J.D. Candidate, Texas Tech University School of Law

Lauren Munselle, 2013 J.D. Candidate, Texas Tech University School of Law

Kerri Griffin Nipp, 2011 J.D., Texas Tech University School of Law

Whitney Savage, 2012 J.D., Texas Tech University School of Law

Kyle Wolf, 2012 J.D., Texas Tech University School of Law

Summary of Contents

Table of Contents

Page

TABLE OF CASES

The principal cases are in bold type. Cases cited or discussed in the text are in roman type. References are to pages. Cases cited in principal cases and within other quoted materials are not included.

Table of Authorities

When to Hold Up, Know When to Fold Up, 38 U.Kan.L.Rev. 193 (1990), 650
Begleiter, Martin D., The Gambler Breaks Even: Legal Malpractice in Complicated Estate Planning Cases, 20 Ga. St. Univ. L. Rev. 277 (2003), 650
Belgium Passes Death Law, Radio Netherlands Wereldomroep, May 16, 2002 available at http://www.rnw.nl/hotspots/html/bel020516.html, 492
Beller, Sam E., How to Compare Long–Term Care Insurance Policies, Est. Plan. 296 (1999), 398
Berall, Frank S., Estate Planning Considerations for Unmarried Cohabitants, 31 Est. Plan. 307 (2004), 792
Berendt, Emily & Laura Lynn Michaels, Your HIV Positive Client: Easing the Burden on the Family Through Estate Planning, 24 J. Marshall L.Rev. 509 (1991), 802
Berteau, John T., Steps to Avoid Beneficiary Conflicts Over Bequests of Tangible Personal Property, 12, Est.Plan. 356 (1985), 802
Betty White Leaves $5M to Her Pets, San Antonio Star, Nov. 4, 1990, at 25, p. 816
Beyer, Gerry W., Accelerated Life Insurance Payments and Viatical Settlements, Est. Plan.Stud. (April 1998), 405
Beyer, Gerry W., Drafting in Contemplation of Will Contests, American Bar Association, Estate and Trust Litigation: Drafting in Contemplation of Contests; the Trial; and the Judicial Perspective—A View From the Bench (1991), 677, 679, 875
Beyer, Gerry W., Enhancing Self–Determination Through Guardian Self–Declaration, 23 Ind.L.Rev. 71 (1990), 335
Beyer, Gerry W., et al., The Fine Art of Intimidating Disgruntled Beneficiaries With In Terrorem Clauses, 51 SMU L.Rev. 225 (1998), 683
Beyer, Gerry W. & Jessica Jackson, What Estate Planners Need to Know About Firearms, Est. Plan. Dev. Tex. Prof. (April 2010), 852
Beyer, Gerry W. & Jessica Petrini, Lottery Players and Winners: Estate Planning for the Optimistic and the Lucky, Est. Plan. Dev. Tex. Prof. (Aug. 2000), 838
Beyer, Gerry W. & Kerri M. Griffin, Estate Planning for Digital Assets, EST. PLAN. DEV. TEX. PROF., April 2011, at 1, p. 844
Beyer, Gerry W. & Kerri M. Griffin, The Role of Legal Assistants in the Estate Planning Practice, Est. Plan. Devel. for Tex. Prof., Jan. 2012, at 1, 1–4, p. 651
Beyer, Gerry W. & Mikela Bryant, Rewards from the Grave: Keeping Loyalty Program Benefits in the Family, Est. Plan. Dev. Tex. Prof., July 2011, at 1, p. 850
Beyer, Gerry W., Pet Animals—What Happens When Their Humans Die?, 40 Santa Clara L. Rev. 617 (2000), 825
Beyer, Gerry W., Pre–Mortem Probate, Prob. & Prop. 6 (July/Aug. 1993), 689
Beyer, Gerry W., Simplification of Inter Vivos Trust Instruments—From Incorporation by Reference to the Uniform Custodial Trust Act and Beyond, 32 S.Tex.L.Rev. 203 (1991), 359
Beyer, Gerry W., Statutorily Enacted Estate Planning Forms: Development, Explanation, Analysis, Studies, Commentary, and Recommendations (1990), 4, 297, 866
Beyer, Gerry W., Statutory Fill-in Will Forms—The First Decade: Theoretical Constructs and Empirical Findings, 72 Or. L.Rev. 769 (1993), 868
Beyer, Gerry W., Statutory Will Methodologies—Incorporated Forms vs. Fill–In Forms: Rivalry or Peaceful Coexistence, 94 Dick.L.Rev. 231 (1990), 867
Beyer, Gerry W. & Steven F. Carvel, Manipulating the Conduct of Beneficiaries With Conditional Gifts, 825
Beyer, Gerry W., The Will Execution Ceremony—History, Significance, and Strategies, 29 S.Tex.L.Rev. 413 (1988), 877
Beyer, Gerry W., Videotaping the Will Execution Ceremony—Preventing Frustration of the Testator's Final Wishes, 15 St. Mary's L.J. 1 (1983), 894
Beyer, Gerry W., Wills, Trusts, and Estates—Examples and Explanations (5th ed. 2012), 22, 79
Beyer, Gerry W. & William R. Buckley, Videotape and the Probate Process: The Nexus Grows, 42 Okla.L.Rev. 43 (1989), 895
Black's Law Dictionary 589 (8th ed. 2004), 2
Blanton, M. Eldridge III, Who Gets a Dead Man's Gold? The Dilemma of Lottery Winnings Payable to a Decedent's Estate, 28 U. Rich. L. Rev. 443 (1994), 844
Bloom, Susan F., The Need For a Will: Preresiduary Considerations and Common Drafting Errors, 182 PLI/EST 7 (1988), 875
Bos, John E., The Durable Power of Attorney, 64 Mich.B.J. 690 (1985), 296
Bothe, Chadwick, The Stigma of Survival: Medicaid Estate Planning, 51 S. Tex. L. Rev. 815 (2010), 422
Bourne, Claire, Group is On a Mission to Sign Up More Black Organ Donors, USA Today, Aug. 4, 2003, at 6D, 521
Bove, Alexander A., Jr., The Mechanics of Establishing an Offshore Trust, American Bar Association, Section of Real Property Probate and Trust Law Asset Protection Planning Committee, Spring Symposium April 2005 (revised March 2012), 759
Boyer, J. Randall, Gifts of the Heart ... And Other Tissues: Legalizing The Sale of Human Organs and Tissues, 2012 BYU L. Rev. 313 (2012), 522
Brackney, William A., Creditors' Rights in Life Insurance, Prob. & Prop. 52 (Mar./Apr. 1993), 121
Bragg, Rick, Daughter Implicates Mom, Now Will Die, San Jose Mercury News 1A (May 19, 1999), 453

Johnson, Kathryn A. & Adam J. Wiensch, Trustee Selection for Successful Trust Administration, Prob. & Prop. 38 (May/June 1994), 583, 586

Jones, Bill, Practice Building Client Development, 60 Tex.B.J. 1161 (1997), 572

Jorrie, Robert & Mason Standley, The Tax Advantages of Lingering Death, 48 Tex.B.J. 1070 (1985), 452

Joslyn, Robert B., Use of Plain English in Drafting Wills and Trusts, 63 Mich.B.J. 612 (1984), 15

Kamisar, Yale, Who Should Live—or Die? Who Should Decide?, Trial 20 (Dec. 1991), 491

Kao, Ja Lee, Valuing Future Lottery Winnings for Estate Tax Purposes: Estate of Shackleford v. United States, 52 Tax Law. 609 (1999), 841

Kennedy, Daniel B., Designing a Client–Friendly Office, 82 Ill.B.J. 443 (1994), 562

Kenworthy, William P. & W. Douglas Sweet, Planning for Qualified Plan and IRA Distributions, Prob. & Prop. 13 (Nov./Dec. 1995), 127

Kerekes, Robert J., My Child ... But Not My Heir: Technology, the Law, and Post–Mortem Conception, 31 Real Prop., Prob. & Tr.J. 213 (1996), 753

Keydel, Frederick R., Forms Can Streamline Your Estate Planning Practice, Prob. & Prop. 56 (May/June 1988), 561

Kimbrough Street, Practical Guidelines for Selecting an Individual Trustee, 20 Est. Plan. 268, 270 (1993), 580, 583, 584, 586

King, Hamlin C., A Primer to the New Estate Freeze Rules, Ohio Law. 20 (Jan./Feb. 1991), 263

Knox, Richard A., 1 in 5 Doctors Say They Assisted a Patient's Death, Survey Finds, Boston Globe 5 (Feb. 28, 1992), 492

Koch, Victoria J., The Specter of Death—Bereaved Clients Require Sensitivity and Emotional Support From Lawyers, A.B.A.J. 82 (Nov. 1998), 905

Kong, Doloros, Patient Proxy Laws Face Hitches, Boston Globe 29 (Dec. 3, 1992), 393

Koontz, Albert C., Planning for Disability: A Neglected Area of the Estate Planning Process, 72 Ill.B.J. 366 (1984), 296

Koren, Edward F., Estate, Tax and Personal Financial Planning, 2 Est. Tax & Pers. Fin. Plan. § 15:21 (updated 2012), 897

Koren, Edward F., Incentive Trusts and Beyond: Settlors' Intent and the Fiduciary Conundrum (pt. 1), Koren Est. & Pers. Fin. Plan., Apr. 2009, p. 836

Krohm, Carol & Scott Summers, Advance Health Care Directives: A Handbook for Professionals (2002), 362

Kruse, Clifton B., Jr., A Call for New Perspectives for Living Wills (You Might Like it Here), 37 Real Prop., Prob. & Tr. J. 545 (2002), 453

Laffey, Myles J., Common Drafting Errors, 13 Quinnipiac Prob.L.J. 57 (1998), 875

Langbein, John H., Living Probate: The Conservatorship Model, 77 Mich.L.Rev. 63 (1978), 696

Larve, Gerald A., Euthanasia and Religion (1985), 491

Last Laugh—Wills With a Sense of Humor, The, Fam. Advoc., Summer 1981, at 60, 62, p. 823

Ledford, Nita, Note—Intentional Interference With Inheritance, 30 Real Prop., Prob. & Tr.J. 325 (1995), 688

Legal Blank, The, 30 Law Notes 124 (1926), 869

Legal–Malpractice–Lawyers–Attorneys.com, Legal Malpractice Statistics (2002–2004), 650

Lehr, Dick, Death and the Doctor's Hand, Boston Globe 1 (April 25, 1993), 492

Leimberg, Stephan R. & Charles K. Plotnick, A Sample Letter to Clients on Their Duties as Executors and Trustees, Prac.Law. 23 (Sept. 1986), 580

Leimberg, Stephan R. & Thomas P. Langdon, Insurance Planning: Who Should Be the Beneficiary and Owner?, Prob. & Prop. 19 (July/Aug. 1996), 262

Leopold, Aloysius & Gerry Beyer, Ante–Mortem Probate: A Viable Alternative, 43 Ark. L.Rev. 131 (1990), 697

Lerner, Ralph E., Valuing Works of Art for Tax Purposes, 28 Real Prop., Prob. & Tr.J. 593 (1993), 142

Lieberson, Alan D., Advance Medical Directives (1992 and most recent Supp.), 455

Lieberson, Alan D., Natural Death Act Directives, 16 West's Legal Forms 99 (Supp. 1992), 451

Lieberson, Alan D., Overview of Orders Not to Resuscitate, in 16 West's Legal Forms 133 (Supp. 1992), 453

Liebmann–Smith, Richard, Checkups, Amer. Health 13 (July/Aug. 1995), 540

Life Insurance, Part 2, 58 Consumer Reports 525 (1993), 120

Life Insurance, Part 3, 58 Consumer Reports 595 (1993), 120

Living Wills: Tackle the Hard Stuff, Health 20 (July/Aug. 1997), 450

Lotto Texas Heirs Cry For Help With Federal Tax Bills, San Antonio Express–News, July 12, 1996, at 6B, 838

Lowe, Alexandra Dylan, Facing the Final Exit, A.B.A.J. 48 (Sept. 1997), 491

Lustig, Nathan to Entrustet HIWI Blog, Digital Estate Planning: What are Digital Assets? (Apr. 19, 2010), 844

Lynn, Robert J. & Grayson M.P. McCouch, Introduction to Estate Planning (5th ed. 2004), 48, 62, 83, 95, 115, 135, 267

Maag, Marilyn J., The Development of Polst to Honor Medical Treatment Goals at End–of–Life, ACTEC Summer Meeting, June 2012, p. 456

Ng, Peter P.G., Building a Successful Practice at a Small Firm, Tr. & Est. 22 (Sept. 1993), 555

Obade, Claire C., Advance Healthcare Planning Under the New Federal Patient Self–Determination Act, 38 Prac.Law. 83 (1992), 455
O'Connor, John J., Note, The Commercialization of Human Tissue—The Source of Legal, Ethical and Social Problems: An Area Better Suited to Legislative Resolution, 24 Loy.L.A.L.Rev. 115 (1990), 524
Olsen, Jack, Hastened to the Grave (1998), 97
O'Meara, John K., Estate Planning Concerns for the Professional Athlete, 3 Marq.Sports L.J. 85 (1992), 2, 837
Organ Donor Resolution, Prob. & Prop. 6 (Jan. /Feb. 1992), 520
Organ Gift a Blessing, Philadelphia Daily News 53 (June 8, 1989), 520

Palmer, James D., Jr., Medicaid Eligibility—OBRA Raises the Hurdles, Prob. & Prop. 44 (Sept./Oct. 1994), 433
Patients with Living Wills Have Lower Hospital Costs, San Antonio Express–News 2A (March 4, 1994), 452
Patterson, Gina, The Supreme Court Passes the Torch on Physician–Assisted Suicide: Washington v. Glucksberg and Vacco v. Quill, 35 Hous.L.Rev. 851 (1998), 491
Paul II, Pope John, Blood and Organ Donors, 30 The Pope Speaks 1–2 (1985), 521
Perales, Donny J., Rethinking the Prohibition of Death Row Prisoners as Organ Donors: A Possible Lifeline to Those on Organ Donor Waiting Lists, 34 St. Mary's L.J. 687 (2003), 523
Persky, Anna Stolley, Life from Death Row, ABA J., April 2012, at 16, p. 523
Personal Financial Planning Handbook: With Forms & Checklists, Second Edition (2011), 570
Pesoli, Christina, Best Kept Secrets to Keeping Your Client Happy, 61 Tex.B.J. 1002 (1998), 572
Pittman, Larry J., Physician–Assisted Suicide in the Dark Ward: The Intersection of the Thirteenth Amendment and Health Care Treatments Having Disproportionate Impacts on Disfavored Groups, 28 Seton Hall L.Rev. 774 (1998), 491
Poll, Ed, A Bigger Burden: Mandatory Malpractice Insurance Disclosure: Who Benefits?, 25 No. 7 Legal Mgmt. 24 (Nov./Dec. 2006), 650
Polycarpe, Velly B., Examining the Right to Premortem Cryopreservation, 21 Hofstra L.Rev. 1385 (1993), 541
Potts, Gregory, Pampered Pets Prove Profitable, J. Rec. (Oklahoma City), July 6, 1999, p. 815
Powell, Agnes C., The Need for Increased Life Insurance Due Diligence, Tr. & Est. 39 (May 1992), 262
Pratt, David & Elaine M. Bucher, Updated Practical Planning With Crummey Powers, 29 Est. Plan. 73 (2002), 241
Precker, Michael, Fireworks Company Will Help You Go Out In a Blaze of Glory, San Antonio Express–News 10F (Nov. 27, 1998), 540
Psychotherapists Adopt Policy on Witnessing Assisted Suicides, Plain Dealer 5C (Aug. 25, 1993), 492

Rabkin, Jacob A. & Matthew H. Johnson, Current Legal Forms With Tax Analysis ix (1988), 871
Reed, Lawrence W., Encourage Organ Donors With a Little Quid Pro Quo, USA Today, July 24, 2003, at 13A, 524
Regan, John J., Entitlements (rev. ed. 1994), 758
Reidinger, Paul, Lawpoll: Should Active Euthanasia be Legal?, A.B.A.J. 20 (June 1988), 491
Reimer, Christopher M., The Undiscovered Country: Wyoming's Emergence as a Leading Trust Situs Jurisdiction, 11 Wyo. L. Rev. 165 (2011), 777
Rhein, Jennifer L., No One in Charge: Durable Powers of Attorney and the Failure to Protect Incapacitated Principals, 17 Elder L.J. 165, at 174 (2009), 335
Ricker, Darlene, The Vanishing Hourly Fee, A.B.A.J. 66 (March 1994), 580
Robert, Charles R., Estate Planning for Families With Handicapped Children, Compleat Law. 51 (Fall 1986), 754
Robertson, John A., In the Beginning: The Legal Status of Early Embryos, 76 Va. L.Rev. 437 (1990), 754
Roney, Marty, Company Will Load Loved Ones' Ashes Into Ammunition, USA Today, Sept. 30, 2011, p. 542
Rosenfeld, Jeffrey P., To Heir is Human, Prob. & Prop. 21 (July/Aug. 1990), 678
Ross, Eunice L. & Thomas J. Reed, Will Contests (2d ed. 1999 & most recent Supp.), 679
Rudisill, Kenneth M., Jr., Information to Be Considered in Preparing an Estate Plan (Efficiency = Inexpensive), Law Notes 31 (Spring 1984), 561
Russell, L. Mark, et al., Planning for the Future: Providing a Meaningful Life for a Child With a Disability After Your Death (1993), 758

Salasko, Elizabeth R., Beyond Plain Vanilla: The New Flavors of IRAs, Prob. & Prop. 23 (May/June 1998), 127
Sales of Brain Membranes by Hospital Aides Reported, Buffalo News A3 (May 21, 1994), 524
Sandler, Tim, Grave Robbers, The Boston Phoenix 32 (Mar. 12, 1993), 540
Savoie, Joe R., The Commissioners' Model of Ante–Mortem Probate, 37 ACTEC L.J. ___ (2012), 697

Swickard, Joe, Henry Ford's Video Asks No Fuss Over Will, Detroit Free Press 1A (Sept. 24, 1988), 685

Symposium—Physician–Assisted Suicide: Legal Rights in Life and Death, 12 St. John's J.Legal Comment. (1997), 491

Tate, Joshua C., Conditional Love: Incentive Trusts and the Inflexibility Problem, 41 Real Prop. Prob. & Tr. J. 445, Fall 2006, p. 836

Thar, Anne E., Do You Know Your Limits?, 86 Ill.B.J. 227 (1998), 650

Thar, Anne E., Engagement Letters Can Reduce Malpractice Claims, 84 Ill.B.J. 99 (Feb. 1996), 650

Thar, Anne E., Nightmare on Main Street: Estate Planning and Probate Pitfalls, 85 Ill.B.J. 497 (1997), 650

Thar, Anne E., What Do Clients Really Want? It's Time You Found Out, 87 Ill.B.J. 331 (1999), 572

Todorova, Aleksandra, Dead Ringers: Grave Robbers Turn to ID Theft, Wall St. J., Aug. 4, 2009, p. 846

Treaster, Joseph B., Cash Before Death a Growing Trend in Life Insurance, San Antonio Express–News 1L (Oct. 4, 1998), 415

Truss, Lynne, Eats, Shoots & Leaves: The Zero Tolerance Approach to Punctuation (2004), 19

Turano, Guerino J. & Philip H. Ward, Joint Tenancy and Tenancy by the Entirety: The Pros and Cons, 83 Ill.B.J. 309 (1995), 97

Tutelian, Louise, How to Choose a Guardian for Your Child, Good Housekeeping 156 (April 1998), 726

Utecht, Andrea & Abraham C. Reich, Successful Partnering Between Inside and Outside Counsel, 9

Vida, Marie A., Legality of Will–Creating Software: Is the Sale of Computer Software to Assist in Drafting Will Documents Considered the Unauthorized Practice of Law?, 41 Santa Clara L. Rev. 231 (2000), 674

Wade, James R., When Can A Lawyer Represent Both Husband and Wife in Estate Planning?, Prob. & Prop. 13 (Mar./Apr. 1987), 619

Walker, Rob, Cyberspace When You're Dead, N.Y. Times, Jan. 5, 2011, p. 846

Warnock, Harold C., Living Wills—The Need for Uniform State Laws, Prob. & Prop. 52 (May/June 1991), 453

Watson, Thomas J., Estate Planning Work—Not for the Timid, Wis. Law., Dec. 2011, at 30, p. 650

Watters, Jeffrey D., What They Don't Know Can Hurt Them: Why Clients Should Know if Their Attorney Does Not Carry Malpractice Insurance, 62 Baylor L. Rev. 245 (2010), 650

Weigel, Rainer R., Master Probate Checklist, 10 Prob.Notes 78 (1984), 907

Weinberg, Michael D., Split–Dollar: A Dream Come True, Prob. & Prop. 18 (May/June 1995), 122

Weinstock, Harold, Planning an Estate: A Guidebook of Principles and Techniques (3d ed. 1988), 220, 566

Wentworth, Daniel A., Durable Powers of Attorney: Considering the Financial Institution's Perspective, Prob. & Prop., Nov./Dec. 2003, at 37, p. 335

What is Long–Term Care?, Medicare.gov, http://www.medicare.gov/longtermcare/static/home.asp (last updated Mar. 25, 2009), 404

When It's Time to Buy Life Insurance, 58 Consumer Reports 431 (1993), 120

Whitaker, G. Warren & Michael J. Parets, My Client Married an Alien: Ten Things Everyone Should Know About International Estate Planning, Prob. & Prop., Mar./Apr. 2004, at 24, p. 810

Whitcombe, Paul T., Defamation by Will: Theories and Liabilities, 27 J.Marshall L.Rev. 749 (1994), 684

Whitton, Linda S., Durable Powers as an Alternative to Guardianship: Lessons We Have Learned, 37 Stetson L. Rev. 7, 35–36 (Fall 2007), 334

Whitton, Linda S., Everything You Needed to Know About Good Lawyering, You Can Learn from Elder Law, 40 Stetson L. Rev. 73, 82–87 (Fall 2010), 334

Who Owns Your E–Mails?, BBC News, Jan. 11, 2005, p. 845

Williston, Beverly, Gilligan's Lovey Leaves It All to Her Dog, San Antonio Star, Apr. 28, 1991, at 5, p. 816

Willits, Pamela J., Worth the Weighty?, Ohio State, Jan./Feb. 2004, at 19, 21, p. 542

Wingfield, Alan D., Fiduciary Attorney–Client Communications: An Illusory Privilege?, Prob. & Prop., July/Aug. 1994, at 60, p. 638

Wintriss, Lynn, Waiver of REA Rights in Premarital Agreements, Prob. & Prop. 16 (May/June 1993), 127

Wintriss, Lynn & Cristin P. Carnell, A Checklist of Predeath Planning for the Dying Client, Prob. & Prop. 9 (July/Aug. 1987), 561

Wisconsin Gives Tax Break to Organ Donors, USA Today, Feb. 2, 2004, at 6D, 524

Wisenberg, Dinah, Loved Ones Often Make Wrong Medical Prediction, San Antonio Express–News 10B (April 15, 1998), 370

Woodward, M.K. & Ernest E. Smith, III, Probate and Decedents' Estates § 336 (17 Tex. Prac. 1971), 875

Word, Thomas S., Jr., A Brief for Plain English Wills and Trusts, 14 Univ.Rich.L.Rev. 471 (1980), 10

Would-be Donors' Kin Sometimes Refuse Vital Organ Donations, San Antonio Express–News 14A (Aug. 28, 1995), 521

Wright, Wesley E., Medicaid Estate Recovery: When the Government Wants Your Home-

Table of Statutes and Regulations

UNITED STATES

UNITED STATES CONSTITUTION

UNITED STATES CODE ANNOTATED

15 U.S.C.A.—Commerce and Trade

UNITED STATES CODE ANNOTATED

18 U.S.C.A.—Crimes and Criminal Procedure

26 U.S.C.A.—Internal Revenue Code

UNITED STATES CODE ANNOTATED

26 U.S.C.A.—Internal Revenue Code

UNIFORM ANATOMICAL GIFT ACT

UNIFORM CUSTODIAL TRUST ACT

UNIFORM HEALTH CARE DECISION ACT

UNIFORM HEALTH CARE DECISION ACT

UNIFORM PROBATE CODE

UNIFORM PROBATE CODE

UNIFORM STATUTORY FORM POWER OF ATTORNEY ACT

UNIFORM STATUTORY FORM POWER OF ATTORNEY ACT

UNIFORM TRANSFERS TO MINORS ACT

UNIFORM TRUST CODE

VIATICAL SETTLEMENTS MODEL ACT

STATE STATUTES

ALASKA STATUTES

ARIZONA REVISED STATUTES

WEST'S ANNOTATED CALIFORNIA PROBATE CODE

INDIANA PROBATE CODE

LOUISIANA CODE OF CIVIL PROCEDURE

MINNESOTA STATUTES ANNOTATED

NEW JERSEY STATUTES ANNOTATED

NEW YORK, MCKINNEY'S PUBLIC HEALTH LAW

NEW YORK, MCKINNEY'S SURROGATE'S COURT PROCEDURE ACT

OHIO ANTE–MORTEM STATUTES

OREGON DEATH WITH DIGNITY ACT

VERNON'S TEXAS CODE ANNOTATED

Government Code

Health and Safety Code

Transportation Code

TREASURY REGULATIONS

CODE OF FEDERAL REGULATIONS

REVENUE RULINGS

PRIVATE LETTER RULINGS

MODEL RULES OF PROFESSIONAL CONDUCT

IRS NOTICES

TEACHING MATERIALS ON ESTATE PLANNING

Fourth Edition

CHAPTER 1

WELCOME TO ESTATE PLANNING

■ ■ ■

A. BASIC PREMISE

"Death, as the Psalmist saith, is certain to all, all shall die."[1]

Estate planning is based on the undeniable and inescapable fact that each one of us will become metabolically challenged and cease to function as a carbon-based life-form, as well as the 50% chance we have of being physically or mentally disabled for at least ninety days. Should estate planning consequently be shunned just because it is a depressing area of legal specialization?

Absolutely not! Estate planning may be the only area of law that applies to every individual. For example, you can avoid the criminal justice system by obeying the law, you can keep out of family courts by being happily married or staying single and childless, you can bypass the income tax system by being unemployed, and you can usually elude being sued if you do what you promise and always act prudently. But, there is nothing you can do to escape the inevitability of death and the probability of disability. As an estate planner, you have the potential of providing valuable and essential assistance to every person, regardless of the individual's financial or family circumstances.

Estate planning also offers you the tremendous opportunity to engage in the practice of preventative law. You may avert many legal problems and the associated human and financial costs before they arise. By expertly crafting your client's estate plan, the client's personal and property affairs will have a smooth transition from day-to-day life, through times of disability, and finally into death. Court proceedings may be simplified and, in some cases, eliminated entirely.

If you have not already done so, please read the Preface which starts on page v.

1. WILLIAM SHAKESPEARE, KING HENRY IV, Part II, Act III, Scene ii, ll. 35–36, in THE ARDEN EDITION OF THE WORKS OF WILLIAM SHAKESPEARE, THE SECOND PART OF KING HENRY IV 97 (A. Humphreys 1966) (stated by Justice Robert Shallow).

B. GOALS OF ESTATE PLANNING

The term "estate planning" is defined in many ways. Here are some examples to give you an insight into what several writers believe is included within the term's scope.

- "The preparation for the distribution and management of a person's estate at death through the use of wills, trusts, insurance policies, and other arrangements, esp. to reduce administration costs and transfer-tax liability."[1]
- "[T]he accumulation, conservation, and eventual distribution of property according to personal objectives."[2]
- "[T]o accumulate an estate and to secure the greatest benefits of this estate to the taxpayer and to [the taxpayer's] beneficiaries."[3]
- "An arrangement for the devolution of one's wealth * * *."[4]
- "Estate planning is generally defined as the orderly disposition of property, with primary emphasis on family needs. A secondary consideration is a desire to minimize taxes and other costs that may reduce the net assets available for the satisfaction of family needs. A broader definition of estate planning would include the orderly and economical creation of property for the ultimate enjoyment of the estate creator, his or her family and any others he or she may want to benefit."[5]

Succinctly stated, estate planning is a process by which individuals make comprehensive arrangements for their property and personal needs which will remain in effect during disability and after death. This process requires you to ascertain your client's intent regarding estate planning matters and then to take steps to carry out that intent to the greatest extent permissible within legal bounds. In determining your client's wishes, you will pay particular attention to the following items:

Recipients of property—identity. Whom does the client wish to benefit from the client's property, e.g., spouse, children, parents, other relatives, friends, or charities?

Recipients of property—timing. When does the client want the donees to enjoy the property, e.g., immediately, upon the occurrence of a designated condition, upon the client's death, or at some other time? Do any recipients have special needs which must quickly be met while other recipients can benefit by receiving the property later in life?

Use of property. How does the client want the donees to be able to use the property, e.g., an unrestricted outright gift or a gift in trust with limitations or conditions on use?

---

1. BLACK'S LAW DICTIONARY 589 (8th ed. 2004).

2. JOHN J. GARGAN, THE COMPLETE GUIDE TO ESTATE PLANNING 1 (1978).

3. ROBERT S. HOLZMAN, HOLZMAN ON ESTATE PLANNING 2 (1967).

4. A. JAMES CASNER, ESTATE PLANNING 1 (1961).

5. John K. O'Meara, *Estate Planning Concerns for the Professional Athlete*, 3 MARQ. SPORTS L.J. 85, 85 (1992).

Person managing property. Whom does the client want to manage the property now and in the future, e.g., donee, trustee, executor, or agent?

Tax concerns. Is the client's estate large enough, either now or anticipated to be so by the time of the client's death, to necessitate tax planning? If yes, is the client willing to take steps to save taxes even though it removes property from the client's control or otherwise disrupts the client's power to deal with the property without restriction?

Disability planning. What plans does the client wish to make for potential disability regarding property management and health care, e.g., durable powers of attorney, self-designation of guardians, insurance, etc.?

Death planning. How does the client want matters relating to the physical aspects of death handled, e.g., use of heroic medical techniques, implementation of anatomical gifts, and the final disposition of the body?

Once you have determined what your client would like to have happen, you must strive to effectuate that intent. The basic approach to doing so is as follows:

Gather information. You must accumulate all of the relevant information from the client and other appropriate sources.

Conduct research. Solid legal research skills are essential to finding the relevant state and federal law (cases, statutes, and regulations) and helpful secondary authorities (treatises, periodicals, form books, continuing legal education materials, etc.).

Select appropriate techniques. A huge arsenal of techniques are available for your use in preparing the estate plan. You must choose the appropriate tools with great care, e.g., a will, trusts, insurance policies, multiple-party accounts, holding property as joint tenants, etc.

Prepare and execute documents. Many documents may be necessary to carry out the estate plan. It is your responsibility to have the documents correctly and accurately prepared and executed with the necessary formalities, and to supply instructions for their protection.

Review and update estate plan. An estate plan is not a static arrangement. As the client's circumstances change (e.g., marriage, divorce, births, deaths, change in income, etc.) and as legislatures amend federal and state laws, you must review the estate plan and suggest appropriate revisions.

Carry out plan. When the client becomes disabled or dies, you may be involved in the procedures needed to make certain the plan continues to function as your client intended.

NOTE

The economic status of the client may impact the client's estate planning goals. For example, wealthy clients may "[1] want to protect their family from ever being *destitute*. [2] They want to provide *incentives and opportunities* to their family. They hope their descendants will take those opportunities and become productive because of their own sweat and blood. [3] They do *not* want to provide an unearned, nonworking *lifestyle* to their heirs. Giving an heir an unearned healthy annual income often takes away ambition and self worth. [4] Clients want to minimize *intrafamily conflicts*. Family harmony is more important than an inheritance." John J. Scroggin, *Protecting and Preserving the Family: The True Goal of Estate Planning, Part II—Some of the Tools*, PROB. & PROP., July/Aug. 2002, at 34.

C. REASONS PEOPLE FOREGO ESTATE PLANNING

GERRY W. BEYER, STATUTORILY ENACTED ESTATE PLANNING FORMS: DEVELOPMENT, EXPLANATION, ANALYSIS, STUDIES, COMMENTARY, AND RECOMMENDATIONS

Part I, pages 2–9 (1990).

Individuals must take the initiative to acquire comprehensive estate plans, either by themselves or with the aid of an attorney, if they desire to have their intent carried out upon death and procure the other benefits of estate planning. Failure to take affirmative estate planning steps may have unwelcome consequences. Instead of acquiring a plan customized to meet specific needs and circumstances, generic plans may be imposed on individuals and their families.

The most commonly imposed plan is set forth in each state's intestacy or descent and distribution statute. Intestate succession laws provide recipients for property not governed by a valid will or will substitute. These statutes attempt to do what persons would have done with their estates, had they taken the time to consider and properly formalize their desires, by granting inheritance rights to the surviving spouse, children, and other relatives and listing people to serve as managers of property and guardians of children. These legislatively mandated plans are based on the presumed intent of the average person, not the actual intent of the decedent. Accordingly, these schemes often fail to carry out anyone's true desires; they merely represent a "guess" based on an assumption, supported by public policy, that the decedent would have wanted the decedent's property to pass to particular individuals and have certain people serve as executors and guardians. No room exists for the introduction of evidence to show that the decedent actually intended otherwise.

The intestacy statutes apply only to the deceased's probate estate, i.e., property subject to administration. Thus, many of an individual's assets are not included in the probate estate, such as trusts, multiple-party bank accounts, and life insurance. These will substitutes are potentially powerful estate planning techniques. Unfortunately, they are frequently used in a haphazard manner with little or no thought given to a comprehensive plan. Instead, will substitutes are used or acquired primarily for other reasons; their estate planning function is secondary. For example, joint bank accounts with rights of survivorship may serve as an easy method of transmitting wealth to a surviving spouse. When such accounts are opened, however, the primary concern is usually with the ease of paying bills and making deposits. In a like manner, consider employer-supplied retirement and pension plans. These plans are supplied as an incident of employment and death beneficiary designations are made by most employees without appreciating the impact these contractual arrangements may have on their estate plans. * * *

Although state legislatures have granted all competent adults residing in the United States extensive power to control their estates by using wills and will substitutes, most individuals fail to prepare comprehensive estate plans. In fact, the majority of Americans die without even a simple will. There are several reasons why most individuals forego the significant benefits of estate planning. * * *

A. UNAWARE OF IMPORTANCE

Many individuals are naive about the critical importance of estate planning. They either do not know what will happen to their estates during incompetency and upon death or operate under incorrect assumptions about what will occur. Non-legally trained individuals, as well as some attorneys, often fail to appreciate the estate problems they have and the possible solutions. As one commentator noted: "it has been one of the surprises of my life to observe that a man who has accumulated his wealth through ability and foresight will often be found to have been astonishingly neglectful in providing for those he leaves behind."[1]

Even persons who have made estate plans may not realize the necessity of periodically reviewing them. Common changes in circumstances often impact the effectiveness of once satisfactory plans. Many people fail to recognize that events such as births, deaths, adoptions, changes in property owned, marriages, divorces, estate and tax law amendments, and changes in the state of domicile may cause significant distortion in estate plans and be followed by the frustration of expectations.

B. INDIFFERENCE

Apathy is a contributing factor to why some individuals die without preparing estate plans. Believing that "you can't take it with you," some people voluntarily forego arranging for distribution of their property. These individuals may realize the importance of estate planning but simply do not wish to take advantage of their ability to exercise dead-hand control over assets, the naming of fiduciaries, and other matters for which advance planning is available.

---

1. W. AYERS, WHAT YOUR HEIRS CAN NEVER TELL YOU 2 (1943).

C. COST

Obtaining a comprehensive and integrated estate plan is often an expensive process, particularly when extensive use is made of legal counsel. Although some attorneys will provide simple form wills for one-hundred dollars or less, the fees for complete estate plans often run into the thousands of dollars because of the substantial amount of time involved. These expenses place individualized estate plans out of financial reach for many people and increase the reluctance of those with sufficient resources to incur the cost.

D. TIME AND EFFORT

Preparation of a comprehensive estate plan requires significant time and effort. Many people are unwilling or unable to devote time to estate planning matters when the pressures of work and family are more immediate.

Even in a simple estate, a significant investment of time is necessary. The following scenario illustrates the time required. An initial meeting is held with the client which permits the attorney to gather the necessary information to begin work on the estate plan. Additional information is frequently needed from the client, either because the client does not have all of the necessary information and documents or has not organized them in a usable form. Also, the client may need to ponder and decide on various aspects of the plan. At the second meeting, the attorney and client review a rough draft of the will and other estate planning documents and engage in a more detailed discussion of possible options. For simple estates, this meeting may be the one at which estate documents are signed and other aspects of the plan finalized. For more complex estates, additional meetings may be necessary. If the client's transportation and waiting time are included along with preparation and meeting time, it becomes apparent that estate planning requires individuals to sacrifice sizable blocks of time and expend considerable effort.

Procrastination is common among individuals who are interested in estate planning and willing, at some point, to go through the process. There is a "natural preoccupation . . . with the accumulation and present enjoyment of their estate and from the illusion of continued life."[2] Because urgency is typically not present, it is very easy to postpone making a will and taking other estate planning steps.

E. COMPLEXITY

Estate planning is a complex process which continues to grow in intricacy. For example, relevant tax laws constantly change, the availability of will substitutes grows, the nature of assets change, and the needs of clients and their families expand. Most people do not view this complexity as a stimulating challenge; rather, it tends to discourage them from making estate plans.

---

2. 1 PAGE ON THE LAW OF WILLS § 1.6, at 24 (W. Bowe & D. Parker ed. 1960).

F. LACK OF PROPERTY

Lack of property is a commonly cited reason for failure to have an estate plan. Many people are apparently unaware that there are other reasons to have estate plans besides to designate the recipients of property. Even for small estates, especially if there is a spouse and children, it is important to prevent intestacy so the surviving spouse's ability to deal with household items and other property is not subject to claims of the children. Other significant benefits include the nomination of guardians for minor children upon the simultaneous death of the parents or upon the death of the surviving parent, the ability to control the use and disposition of life insurance proceeds, and the selection of an agent to make property and health care decisions during incompetency.

G. ADMISSION OF MORTALITY

In the past, many people believed that they would not live long after executing a will, even if they were then in good health. For many, this belief persists today. Thus, individuals procrastinate the preparation of estate plans as a conscious or unconscious defense against admitting mortality.[3] "[P]ersonal death is a thought modern [persons] will do almost anything to avoid,"[4] and it is easy for individuals to elude such thoughts by postponing (usually indefinitely) the estate planning process.

H. RELUCTANCE TO REVEAL PRIVATE FACTS

To prepare a good will, you must inquire into your client's personal and private matters. For example, you need to know about children born out of wedlock, the value of property, medical conditions, and family situations. Your client may not want to open his or her private life for your inspection.

QUESTIONS

1. Another common reason a person may not want to prepare an estate plan is to avoid revealing personal and family matters which may be embarrassing (e.g., marital discord, a child born out of wedlock, or a medical condition) or legally damaging (e.g., amount/source of income or actual value of property). Can you think of other reasons why someone may not want to prepare an estate plan?

2. What type of estate plan do you have? If you do not have one, are any of these excuses applicable to you? Do you think you can provide good advice to your client about estate planning if you have not even prepared a plan for yourself?

---

3. See T. ATKINSON, HANDBOOK OF THE LAW OF WILLS § 38, at 160 (2d ed. 1953) ("A superstitious prejudice against wills is found in many persons past middle age. Apparently they think that testamentary preparation for disposition of their property at their death may somehow hasten their demise. While this attitude is a foolish one, it frequently cannot be altered by any amount of sound advice."). Perhaps a similar fear prevents people from making arrangements for their own funerals.

4. Shaffer, *The "Estate Planning" Counselor and Values Destroyed By Death*, 55 IOWA L. REV. 376, 377 (1969).

D. PERSONS INVOLVED IN THE ESTATE PLANNING PROCESS

ROBERT S. HUNTER, ESTATE PLANNING AND ADMINISTRATION*

The Estate Planning Advisors, Generally
17 ILL. PRAC., ESTATE PLANNING & ADMIN. § 2:1 (4th ed.).

It is popular to write of the "estate planning team." The term is applied to a group of advisors from the respective fields that engage in estate planning. Normally, they are the lawyer, the accountant, the banker or trust officer, investment counsellor and the insurance agent.

The theory is that, working together smoothly and harmoniously, each provides the client with a steady flow of advice, information and assistance, and that the client emerges with a carefully designed plan suited to his needs and his situation.

The theory is a good one. It is a desirable objective. Certainly, these specialists are all available to the client. Each specialist has much to offer in devising the best possible plan.

Yet, estate planning as a highly professional field is still in its infancy. In large estates, it has become a more general practice to bring in more than two advisors at the same time. In most estates, however, it is the exception when more than the accountant and lawyer or lawyer and life insurance agent is consulted at about the same time.

The various businesses and professions involved have not worked out any practical formula to bring all these specialists together so that each will be furnishing the best advice at a reasonable cost so as to emerge with the perfect plan for the individual client.

It is regrettable that a pattern has not been worked out that would activate the team quickly, complete its work expeditiously and produce everything needed for a sound plan. Until such a pattern is evolved, the advisors and the client must work within the framework of the various resources available, making the most of the assistance at hand.

Much more typical than the team are those regular situations that activate the process of estate planning: the client consults the attorney about a will, or the insurance agent has a prospect who is interested in planning beyond the immediate purchase of an insurance policy, or the accountant is asked by a client what can be done about the staggering taxes.

In those typical situations, it is common for one advisor to consult one or more of the others in related fields of planning either at his own suggestion or upon that of the client. Often, this is not done because of a

* Reprinted with permission of Thomson Reuters.

regular pattern of cooperation but because of a need for assistance on one or several limited points.

ANDREA UTECHT AND ABRAHAM C. REICH, SUCCESSFUL PARTNERING BETWEEN INSIDE AND OUTSIDE COUNSEL*

§ 31:29 Multi–Disciplinary Practice

Multi-disciplinary practice is when lawyers unite with non-lawyers in a single organization to represent the same clients. In 2000, the ABA Commission on Multi-disciplinary Practice recommended that the Model Rules be amended to allow for multi-disciplinary practices. Despite the recommendation, the ABA did not amend the Model Rules. This issue continues to gain in importance as the traditional concept of "the practice of law" has evolved. One concern with providing for multi-disciplinary practices is that lawyers will not be able to maintain their professional integrity and independence. That said, multi-disciplinary practices provide counsel with more resources to provide an increased number of services to their clients. It is already a fact that multi-national consulting firms are hiring law school graduates and practicing lawyers.

While lawyers are bound by the rules of ethics and professional responsibility, non-lawyers are not. Accordingly, any multi-disciplinary practice would also be required to comply with the ethical rules as they apply to the lawyers who work there. Among the possible ethical issues that will arise are: 1) the unauthorized practice of law—the concern that lawyers will be assisting non-lawyers in performing legal tasks which constitute the practice of law; 2) the impermissible sharing of legal fees and forming of partnerships between lawyers and non-lawyers; 3) protection of the lawyer's professional judgment from manipulation by non-lawyer supervision; and 4) possible disclosure of confidential client information and loss of attorney-client privilege.

States, however, have generally not authorized multi-disciplinary practices, though some are still studying the question. A minority of states have adopted ABA Model Rules of Professional Conduct, Rule 5.7, applying the Rules of Professional Conduct to lawyers who provide "law-related services." Despite previously rejecting the rule, Minnesota adopted Rule 5.7, effective October 1, 2005. Pennsylvania, Maine, North Dakota, Indiana, and Massachusetts have also adopted Rule 5.7.6.

"Multi-jurisdictional practice" describes a lawyer's legal work in a jurisdiction in which the lawyer is not admitted to practice law. The ABA's Report on the Commission on Multi-jurisdictional Practice proposed significant amendments and additions to Rule 5.5, which were adopted by the ABA on August 12, 2002. The changes to the rule address circumstances under which attorneys could practice in areas other than those in which they are licensed. The states vary widely on whether in-house corporate

* Reprinted with permission of Thomson Reuters.

counsel must be admitted to the bar in that jurisdiction and at what point, if any, their work would be considered the unauthorized practice of law. As of October 27, 2010, the highest courts of fourteen states have adopted rules identical to Model Rule 5.5. Thirty other states and the District of Columbia have adopted similar rules with exceptions or wording changes. Still other states have created a committee to study ABA MJP recommendations.

QUESTIONS

1. To what extent should you include the client's spouse, children, parents, friends, and spiritual advisors in the estate planning process? What are the potential benefits and dangers of involving these individuals?

2. If the client needs the assistance of another professional, e.g., a life insurance underwriter, financial planner, or accountant, but has not already associated with one, to what extent may you help the client locate a suitable person? Are you limited to general advice such as, "ask your friends" or "look in the telephone book"? Or, may you recommend a competent person with whom you have worked before? What if this person is your relative or a personal friend? May you receive a commission for a referral.

3. What would you do if you were unable to get along with one of the other members of the client's estate planning team? How would you proceed if you discovered that this person was doing a poor job, either because of negligence, incompetence, or wickedness?

4. What is your opinion on multidisciplinary practice? Is any type of multidisciplinary practice allowed in your state?

E. OVERVIEW OF DOCUMENT DRAFTING—PLAIN LANGUAGE

THOMAS S. WORD, JR., A BRIEF FOR PLAIN ENGLISH WILLS AND TRUSTS*

14 UNIV. RICH. L. REV. 471, 471–81 (1980).

We lawyers thrive on disagreement. But on this we are unanimous: clients are precious, hard to get and easy to lose.

A typical citizen asks a lawyer's help but seldom: to buy a house, face a traffic charge, or make a will. The will client comes emotionally charged. [The client] deals with [the client's] most personal concerns: * * * family, * * * wealth, and * * * death. A will is the most personal of writings, save perhaps a love letter. And yet we respond to our client's simply expressed wishes about who gets what with a bewildering instrument that is:

1. Too wordy and redundant;

2. Flooded with lawyerisms, unfamiliar words and inactive verbs; and

* Reprinted with permission of the University of Richmond Law Review.

3. Poorly organized.

A will should be written for the client's eyes. Of course it must be sound technically, but it need not be written in Legalese. By applying plain English principles in our wills (indeed in all our drafting) we can respond to our clients in language they will understand. We will also improve our instruments technically.

The following examples came from wills drafted by Virginia lawyers of high esteem (who, for obvious reasons, will remain anonymous). Compare them to the plain English substitutes, and make your own judgments.

I. TOO WORDY AND REDUNDANT

Last Will and Testament
of
John Quincy Doe

> I, John Quincy Doe, now residing in the City of Richmond, State of Virginia, being of sound mind and memory, do hereby make, publish and declare this to be my last will and testament, hereby revoking, annulling and canceling any and all wills and codicils heretofore made by me.

That's 49 words. Would not the following do as well?

> I, John Quincy Doe, of Richmond, Virginia, make this will, and revoke all earlier wills and codicils.

That's 17 words. They do as much as the 49. The distinction between "will" and "testament" left us long ago. "Publish and declare" should come at the end, in the attestation clause, if at all. Do annul and cancel add anything to revoke? Why waste two bullets on a dead man? Would anyone think we were revoking someone else's will? * * *

One penchant for redundancy—a string of words with the same meaning—has a base in history. At various times the English had two languages to choose from—at first that of the Celts or Anglo–Saxons; later the choice was English or Latin; and still later English or French. Lawyers began using a word from each tongue, joined together, for a single meaning. Thus came legal tautology: free and clear (from Old English freo and French cler), full and complete, good and sufficient, kind and character. * * *

II. LAWYERISMS, UNFAMILIAR WORDS AND INACTIVE VERBS

Lawyerisms in wills are inexcusable. They should be replaced with everyday words, or eliminated entirely. The result will be a document more readable and more technically sound. Consider these "lawyerisms":

said	aforesaid
such	therefor
thereof	to-wit
hereinabove	viz
hereinafter	and/or

If a [drafter] does no more than vow [the drafter] will not use these, [the person's] drafting will improve dramatically.

Consider this provision in a wife's will, designed to express the right of a husband to her furniture for life:

> In the event my *said* husband continues to occupy *said* property, it is my desire, and I so direct, that my furniture remain in the *said* dwelling house while the *same* is occupied by my *said* husband. In the event my *said* husband moves to another dwelling house or an apartment, it is my desire, and I so direct, that he take such of my furniture . . . from the dwelling house to completely furnish the other dwelling or apartment to which he may move. My husband shall have the use and possession of the *aforesaid* articles of personal property for and during the term of his natural life, and at his death I give and bequeath the *same* to the following persons in the following manner, *to-wit:*

Witness nine lawyerisms (the words in italics), not to mention the tautologies (use and possession, for and during the terms of, natural life). Could not the lawyer say as much, and to [the] client's greater satisfaction, with this:

> My husband shall have the right to use my furniture for life. At his death or when he ceases to use any item, I give it as follows:

Some will say that unfamiliar words (technical legal terms) are necessary evils in wills. A few of them, like *per stirpes,* may be. But most unfamiliar words can be replaced with simple, familiar words that say the same thing. Consider these terms and the alternatives:

last will and testament	will
devise	give (or leave)
bequeath	give (or leave)
give, devise and bequeath	give (or leave)
nominate, constitute, appoint	name
corpus	principal (capital)
in the event that	if
prior to	before
issue	descendants (or children and their descendants)

Lawyers seem compelled to use inactive verbs, unfamiliar words and lawyerisms in drafting trust provisions. For example:

> I give, devise and bequeath unto Green National Bank, IN TRUST NEVERTHELESS, [description of the trust assets] . . .
>
> This Trust shall be known as Trust A, and shall be held, administered, managed, controlled, disbursed and paid under and according to the powers, authority and discretion hereinafter given and granted to the Trustee, in the following manner and upon the following terms and conditions.
>
> (1) I direct that said Trustee shall pay unto my wife the net income from this trust, the same to be paid as nearly as possible in

> equal monthly installments so long as she shall live. In the event, however, that my wife shall determine that the income or payments received by her under this clause of my will, and other sources are not sufficient for her proper comfort, maintenance and support, upon her written request the Trustee shall pay unto her such additional sum as she may request, but not to exceed $15,000 in any one calendar year....
>
> (2) In the event my wife shall be in need of additional funds by reason of injury, incapacity, sickness or from any other cause, I give the power and discretion to the Trustee to pay over to her for her benefit such portion of the principal and/or corpus of this trust as the Trustee may deem right and proper, and the Trustee shall have the sole judgment of what amount, if any, will be right and proper to pay under this provision of my will.
>
> (3) I direct that my wife shall have the right and power by her will, referring specifically to my will, to direct how such funds remaining in this trust shall be distributed after her death. In the event my wife shall fail to exercise such power of appointment by her will, designating the beneficiaries to receive any balance or residue of this fund, then such balance or such residue shall be paid into and become a part of the trust set out in clause Third of this will, hereinafter known as Trust "B"....

Had the [drafter] steeled him[-or her]self to eliminate lawyerisms and unfamiliar words, and to use active verbs, [the drafter] might have written:

> I give to my Trustee [description of trust assets] ... The Trust shall be known as Trust "A". I direct the Trustee to manage Trust A as follows:
>
> (1) Pay the income to my wife monthly. Pay to her as much principal as she may request in writing, but not more than $15,000 in any calendar year. In addition, pay to my wife as much principal as the Trustee in its discretion considers necessary to provide for her medical or other needs.
>
> (2) Upon my wife's death, distribute the principal as my wife shall specify in her will, making reference to this power. She may specify to her estate or in any other manner. To the extent my wife does not effectively so specify, add the principal at her death to Trust "B" under this will.

III. ORGANIZATION

Language specialists point out that several factors affect the degree of difficulty in understanding written material, including:

1. The conceptual difficulty of the subject.
2. Information load, or the amount of information in the writing in relation to its length.

3. Readability, or method of presentation. (Two sub-factors influence readability—word familiarity and complexity of writing style).

Aside from using familiar words and simple writing style, we can help our clients' reading comprehension by:

1. Putting the dispositive terms at the beginning.
2. Using introductory headings as signposts.
3. Extracting technical material from the basic dispositive terms, and placing the technical material toward the back. * * *

And now for a confession. Despite what I have said, I do not believe that the typical client can understand fully the technical aspects of a relatively complex will, even when it is written according to plain English principles. But most clients can understand the basic dispositive terms if the technical niceties are extracted and put in separate sections toward the end. (When you send the client a draft for review tell [the client] in the covering letter that the important part is in the first article. With an infirm or obtuse client it may be wise to send the first article alone.)

For example, few clients understand fully a marital deduction formula clause. (The most astute will understand it right after you have explained it, but when they look at the will a year later they will not remember what it means). For this reason, we should remove the marital deduction formula from the dispositive provisions, and put it in a separate article.

Other miscellaneous technical provisions should be extracted from the dispositive terms. A facility of payment clause is a good example. Rather than repeating "pay to or expend for the benefit of, with or without the intervention of a guardian or committee" throughout the dispositive terms of a trust, just say "pay to." Then place a definition of "pay to" in the technical terms section. Do the same with other technical items such as relationships (effect of adoption or illegitimacy), spendthrift provisions, directions against apportionment of income on the death of an income beneficiary, directions for payment of taxes out of the marital deduction trust when the surviving spouse dies, and any specific tax-related directions to the fiduciaries. * * *

V. CONCLUSION

Recent cries for plain English in legal documents and government regulations suggest plain English is something new. It is not. Good writers and good lawyers have practiced and advocated it for a long time. But the public now demands it, under penalty of law.

Wills and trust agreements are consumer documents. They can and should be written in plain English.

Converting your will and trust agreement forms into plain English can be hard work, but it is fun. Give it a try.

ROBERT B. JOSLYN, USE OF PLAIN ENGLISH IN DRAFTING WILLS AND TRUSTS*

63 MICH. B.J. 612, 612–13 (1984).

The use of plain English as a writing style for legal documents has two stated goals—readability and accuracy. * * * Considering that a client's will and trust agreement are the primary (if not exclusive) documents determining the time and manner of disposition of [the client's] wealth, it is vital that their wording provide as much clarity as possible—not just to other professionals (i.e., attorneys, bank and trust officers, court officials, tax authorities, life insurance representatives, stockbrokers, etc.) but also to the client and [the client's] family.

Unfortunately, many of the words and phrases in the probate and trust area are highly technical, thanks to the substantial body of interpretive case law going back to England (residue, intestate, incorporation by reference, etc.), [state probate legislation], and the Internal Revenue Code (e.g., marital deduction, alternate valuation, qualified disclaimers, etc.). Thus caution should be exercised since extensive elimination of perceived legalese may prove disastrous later on when the imprecise or ambiguous provisions of the will or trust must be referred to in the light of a specific factual situation.

GENERAL SUGGESTIONS

Before considering specific examples, I would suggest that certain generalized drafting techniques be employed in preparing wills and trusts.

The first is the use of the present tense whenever possible. Instead of stating:

"The term 'beneficiary' shall be construed to mean . . ."

provide simply that:

"The term 'beneficiary' means . . ."

Another drafting technique is to devote a section to certain defined terms to avoid unnecessary repetition throughout the document. For example, instead of repeating:

"including (without limitation) and by way of illustration"

"individuals, partnerships, trusts, estates, charitable organizations, governmental agencies, and other entities"

"leave, give, devise, and bequeath"

each time, provide for a single, all purpose definition at the beginning or end of the will or trust agreement as follows:

"As used throughout this document—

---

* Reprinted with permission from the July 1984 issue of the Michigan Bar Journal.

> (1) The term 'including' means 'including (without limitation) and by way of illustration'.
>
> (2) The term 'person' means 'individuals, corporations, partnerships, trusts, estates, charitable organizations, governmental agencies, and other entities of any kind, both singular and plural'.
>
> (3) The phrase 'to leave' means 'to leave, give, devise, and bequeath'."

Readability and clarity are also enhanced by using numbered and lettered subparagraphs for listing and categorization purposes. Thus, the following trust provision:

> "The right to remove any then acting family trustee is given to the settlor (as to the original trust) or, if he is then deceased or incapacitated, the settlor's wife (as to each and every trust), or, if she is then deceased or incapacitated, those of settlor's children (as to each and every trust) who are then living and not incapacitated, acting by majority if three or more thereof, acting unanimously if two thereof, acting alone if one thereof, or, if none, the eldest lineal descendant of settlor who has attained at least 21 years of age."

is much easier to understand and construe if it is broken down into parts like this:

> "The right to remove any then acting family trustee is given to the first in order of the following listed persons who is not then deceased or incapacitated:
>
> (1) Settlor, as to the original trust,
>
> (2) Settlor's wife, as to each and every trust,
>
> (3) As to each and every trust, settlor's children:
>
> (A) If three—acting by a majority,
>
> (B) If two—acting unanimously,
>
> (C) If one—acting alone, or
>
> (D) If none—settlor's eldest lineal descendant, provided he or she has then attained at least 21 years of age."

Other drafting techniques to be utilized are (i) avoiding negative sentence structure and (ii) reducing the number of prepositional phrases by using possessive nouns. Instead of drafting this way:

> "Each beneficiary who is not under the age of 30 shall be permitted without restriction to withdraw all of the assets of the trust."

try this:

> "After reaching age 30, each beneficiary may fully withdraw all of the trust's assets."

A final suggestion is to cut out, or at least cut back on, these standard legalese terms:

Avoid	Suggested Alternatives
Hereat	"At this time"
Hereby	"By this," "by means of this," or "as a result of this"
Herein	Eliminate
Heretofore	"Previously"
Herewith	Eliminate
Said	"The," "that," or "those"
Such	"The," "that," or "those"
Whereas	"Since"
Wherein	"In which" or "of which"
Witnesseth	Eliminate

NOTES AND QUESTIONS

1. An advocate of plain English drafting presented a plain language will to several attorneys who agreed it was legally sufficient and did not create ambiguities. "However, a consensus of their views was that many of their clients, who had become used to legalese in their wills, might be uneasy about the 'legality' of plain language. They also thought that some clients might think that their streamlined wills were being deprived of elements of solemnity and dignity that are supposedly found in the sonorous verbosity of the traditional versions." Lawrence X. Cusack, *The Blue-Pencilled Will: What's Wrong With a Will in Plain English?,* TR. & EST., Aug. 1979, at 33, 34. Do you think the concerns of these lawyers are justified? Why or why not? See Wayne Schiess, *What Transactional Drafters Should Know About Plain English*, 39 TEX. J. BUS. L. 515, 514–525 (concluding that beliefs such as "nonlawyers take traditional legal language seriously because it is impressive" and "clients expect and prefer traditional legal language" are myths).

2. "Some lawyers misinterpret the rising call for plain language as a command to write only short, simple sentences. * * * But *plain* does not mean *simpleminded.* Of course, we might simplify legal writing by stubbornly adhering to the myth of the short, simple sentence. That would certainly be better than the opposite tendency. But it would simultaneously strip language of its rhythm and grace. It would also damage our credibility and persuasive power because most readers would consider the writers of such simplistic prose condescending, unintelligent, or uneducated." Beverly Ray Burlingame, *Exploding One Myth About Plain Language,* 56 TEX. B.J. 288, 288 (1993).

3. How effective is plain language in an estate large enough to require planning to reduce the federal estate tax? See Thomas M. Burke, *Plain Language Estate Plan for Dick and Jane,* 59 N.Y. ST. B.J. 38 (1987).

4. Should state legislatures enact provisions requiring estate planning documents to be in plain language as they have done for other types of consumer documents such as apartment leases and consumer credit contracts?

5. To encourage the use of plain English, should attorneys be fined for using archaic language? See David C. Elliott, *A Model Plain-Language Act,* 56

TEX. B.J. 1118 (1993) (suggesting fines for approximately 40 words, e.g., $100 for using "hereby," $150 for "therefore," and $200 for "witnesseth").

6. Plain language instruments can serve as a tool of microeconomic reform to reduce the costs of business. "Millions of dollars are wasted each year because people do not understand legislation, forms, and the many documents published by governments, banks, insurance companies, and other organizations, resulting in needless mistakes and delays." Mark Duckworth & Christopher Blamford, *Proving That Clarity Pays*, 58 TEX. B.J. 394, 394 (1995).

7. Rewrite the following will provisions in "plain" language and resolve ambiguities and other problems raised by these clauses.

a. "Realizing the fragility of life, I hereby make and do now declare and publish the following instrument as my last and final will and testament and that I have full capacity and good memory and that I hereby revoke, cancel, annul, and repeal all wills and codicils which I have previously executed."

b. "In the event that my spouse shall have predeceased me, I leave the hereinabove listed property, both real and personal, to my devoted child, Pat Merrick."

c. "I give, devise, and bequeath my entire collection of 8–track audiotape recordings to Harold Smith."

d. "I leave all my property to my issue."

e. "All reasonable expenses may be paid by the trustee."

f. "The term 'survives me' shall be construed to mean that the beneficiary outlives the testator herein by at least 30 days."

g. "I leave the rest, residue, and remainder of my estate to Juan Cortez."

h. "Should the said Raymond Smith not survive me by thirty days, as aforesaid, I give, devise, and bequeath the said property to my son, Jeffrey Smith, for and during the term of his natural life with the remainder over to his issue as shall be living at the time of his death, in equal shares, share and share alike."

i. "I leave my car to Elizabeth O'Hare."

j. "I leave $25,00 to Gordon West."

k. "I leave my niece, Maria Cortez, the automobile which I am driving at the time of my death."

8. For additional information, see Debra Baker, *Where There's a Will, There's a Way . . . to Make Mistakes (and Here's How to Avoid Them)*, ABA J, May 1998, at 60; Lynn B. Squires & Robert S. Mucklestone, *A Simple "Simple" Will*, 57 WASH. L. REV. 461 (1982) ("A will should clearly communicate a testator's wishes, both to the court and to the testator when the testator reads it outside the lawyer's office." *Id.* at 475.).

9. For an informative and amusing discussion of the proper use of punctuation and how correct punctuation is effective in clarifying the mean-

ing of documents, see LYNNE TRUSS, EATS, SHOOTS & LEAVES: THE ZERO TOLERANCE APPROACH TO PUNCTUATION (2004).

10. For excellent advice such as to "use plain, simple language" and not to kill off the client by inviting clients to set up appointments "to arrange for their execution," see Robert M. Harris, *Drafting Tips for Simple Wills*, PRAC. LAW., Sept. 1995, at 25.

PART 1

THE LAW

■ ■ ■

CHAPTER 2

INTESTACY, WILLS, AND TRUSTS REVIEW*

■ ■ ■

A. INTESTACY

1. WHEN DOES INTESTACY OCCUR?

A decedent dies intestate "as to the person" if the person dies without a valid will. A decedent may also die intestate "as to property" if the person dies with a valid will but the will does not dispose of all of the decedent's property.

QUESTION

What will you do to prevent your client from dying partially intestate when you prepare a will?

2. BASIC IDEA

After the decedent's property is used to pay debts, taxes, funeral expenses, and administration expenses, the remainder, if any, is distributed under the state's law of descent and distribution to the decedent's heirs. Non-probate assets, such as life insurance proceeds and survivorship bank accounts, are not affected. See Chapter 3.

3. THEORY BEHIND DISTRIBUTION SCHEME

In theory, intestacy laws reflect what society views as the "proper" distribution of an individual's property at death. The distribution is supposed to reflect what a person would have written in a will had one been executed. Generally, the closer the familial relationship between the intestate and the survivor, the larger the survivor's share becomes. Of course, the distribution may not reflect the decedent's true intent; the scheme cannot be altered by showing the decedent would have actually wanted a different distribution.

---

* For a comprehensive review of intestacy, wills, and trusts, see GERRY W. BEYER, WILLS, TRUSTS, AND ESTATES—EXAMPLES AND EXPLANATIONS (5th ed. 2012).

4. STATE VARIATIONS

Each state has a different scheme of intestate succession.

LOCATE

What is your state's intestate distribution plan? Note that if you live in a jurisdiction with a community property system, you may find up to four schemes: (1) community property of a married person, (2) quasi-community property of a married person, (3) separate property of a married person, and (4) property of an unmarried person.

DRAFT

Determine your oldest living ancestor. Prepare a chart showing how that person's property would pass if that person were to die today.

5. REAL v. PERSONAL PROPERTY

At common law, real and personal property passed in different ways because of the feudalistic political structure of the Middle Ages. The monarch was in charge of the law governing real property because realty was the most essential element in the political, economic, and social structure of the time. *Descent* refers to the succession of real property.

The church and its courts had authority over laws governing interests in personal property. The monarch allowed this division of control because personal property did not have much value; it was only after the industrial revolution that personal property (e.g., machines, corporate securities, intellectual property, etc.) became a significant factor in the economic and political structure. *Distribution* refers to the succession of personal property.

Most commentators and the drafters of the Uniform Probate Code believe that it is no longer meaningful to make a distinction between real and personal property. In some states, however, there are still vestiges of this distinction.

LOCATE

Does your state have a unified intestate system for property or is there a difference between the succession to real and personal property?

6. PROTECTION OF SURVIVING SPOUSE AGAINST DISINHERITANCE

a. Common Law

The surviving spouse was not considered to be an heir because the spouse was not a blood relative of the decedent. Instead, a widow was entitled to *dower,* i.e., a life estate in one-third of the real property which the husband owned during marriage regardless of whether the property was still owned by the husband at the time of his death. The surviving spouse received only a life interest so the realty would stay in the deceased husband's blood line. The husband could not unilaterally deprive his wife of this interest by conveying the land inter vivos by deed or at death by will. A widower, on the other hand, was entitled to *curtesy,* i.e., a life estate in all of the wife's real property, provided a child was born to the marriage.

b. Modern Law

Both dower and curtesy have been eliminated or greatly altered in most American jurisdictions. Most states make the spouse an heir under descent and distribution statutes. Typically, the spouse will be the only non-blood heir except for adopted individuals.

1) Common Law Marital Property States

Even if the deceased spouse left a will, statutes in common law marital property states grant the surviving spouse the right to *elect to take against the will.* That is, the surviving spouse can obtain a share of the estate even if nothing is given to the surviving spouse under the will. Thus, the surviving spouse will weigh the potential benefits under the will against the amount provided for by statute and select the best deal. These provisions are also called *forced share provisions.*

2) Community Property Marital Property States

In community property states, the surviving spouse is protected against disinheritance because the surviving spouse already owns an undivided one-half interest in the community.

c. Definition of "Spouse"

Traditionally, a surviving spouse was of the opposite sex from the deceased spouse because only individuals of different sexes could marry. There is a growing movement to permit individuals in same-sex relationships to marry and receive all the benefits of marriage, including the right to take under intestacy as a surviving spouse. In 2004, Massachusetts became the first state to make it legal for same-sex couples to marry followed in later years by states including Connecticut, Iowa, Maryland, New Hampshire, New York, Vermont, and Washington, as well as the District of Columbia.

A growing number of individuals are in committed relationships that are not evidenced by a formal marriage. These spousal equivalent relationships may exist between partners of different sexes or of the same sex. Is the surviving partner of one of these relationships entitled to inherit upon the death of the other partner?

If the partners are of opposite sexes, most states provide no inheritance rights to the surviving partner. Some states, however, recognize the concept of a *common law marriage* so that the surviving partner will be treated as a surviving spouse and be entitled to inherit even though the partners were not formally married. The requirements of a common law marriage typically include the partners (1) agreeing to be married, (2) living together as husband and wife, and (3) representing to others that they are married.

In addition, some states, such as California, allow opposite-sex unmarried couples to register as domestic partners if at least one partner is over age 62, which will then entitle the surviving partner to inherit the same share as a surviving spouse.

A few states permit same-sex partners to obtain inheritance rights via other means, such as by entering into a *civil union* (e.g., Delaware, Hawaii, Illinois, New Jersey, and Rhode Island) or registering as a *domestic partner* (e.g., California and Maine) or *reciprocal beneficiary*. If the partners satisfy the statutory formalities, the surviving partner typically is entitled to inherit the same share a surviving spouse would inherit.

LOCATE

1. What type of marital property system does your state have? How does it work?

2. Does your state have any provisions providing inheritance rights of non-marital partners or same-sex partners?

d. Homestead

The surviving spouse may have the ability to occupy part or all of the family home free from the possessory claims of the true title holders as well as to retain it exempt from the claims of some of the deceased spouse's creditors. Jurisdictions vary as to the extent of this right; in some it is limited to a small dollar amount such as $10,000, while in other states, the homestead may be used to shelter an unlimited value. In some states, the size of the homestead is based on an amount of land which may vary depending on whether it is in an urban or rural area.

LOCATE

What right does a surviving spouse have to the homestead in your state? Is the right lost if the couple lived in rental accommodations?

e. Exempt Personal Property

The surviving spouse and minor children are frequently granted the right to retain certain personal property free from the claims of creditors. In some instances, the spouse's or children's claim is superior to the claims of will beneficiaries to whom the items were left. Jurisdictions vary considerably with regard to the type of items which are exempt. Usually, exempt personal property is tangible in nature such as home furnishings, food, clothes, jewelry, firearms, sporting equipment, motor vehicles not used in a business, certain quantities of farm animals, and household pets. In some states, certain types of intangible personal property may also be exempt such as the cash surrender value of life insurance policies and current wages for personal services. The maximum value of the exemption varies widely among the states. For example, UPC § 2–403 imposes a limit of $10,000 while some states protect $50,000 or more of exempt personal property.

LOCATE

What personal property is exempt in your state?

f. Family Allowance

The court may have the authority to grant an allowance for the support of the surviving spouse and minor children for a statutorily provided period of time. Typically, it is the amount necessary to keep them in the style of living to which they were accustomed while the decedent was alive for one year after the decedent's death although some states authorize family allowances to be made until the administration is closed. Some states impose a dollar limit on the family allowance.

LOCATE

How is the family allowance computed in your state?

7. POSTHUMOUS HEIRS

An heir conceived while the intestate is alive but who is not born until after the intestate's death may or may not be able to take in the same manner as an heir who was already born when the intestate died. By use of alternative reproduction technologies, heirs may be born years or decades after the intestate's death. See Chapter 10(B).

LOCATE

How does your state treat posthumous heirs? Does it matter whether the heir is a descendent of the intestate or of a collateral heir of the intestate? Does your state have statutes governing children conceived as a result of alternative reproduction techniques.

8. HALF- AND WHOLE–BLOODED HEIRS

In some states, half-blooded heirs (i.e., individuals who share only one parent in common) take smaller shares than whole-blooded heirs (i.e., individuals who share both parents in common) when they inherit from a collateral relative (e.g., siblings who inherit from a deceased sibling).

LOCATE

How are half-blooded relatives treated in your state?

9. ADOPTED CHILDREN

Adoption was not known to the common law of England. In fact, it did not exist in England until 1926. Most adoption law developed in the United States.

An adopted individual is usually treated the same as a biological child, that is, as part of the adoptive parents' family and thus will inherit from and through the adoptive parents. In some states, an adopted child may also inherit from and through the biological parents. If an adopted child dies intestate, property usually passes to the adoptive family, not the biological family.

LOCATE

How are adopted individuals treated in your state? Does it make a difference if the person was adopted as an adult rather than as a minor?

10. NON-MARITAL CHILDREN

In the past, and to a lesser extent even today, children born out of wedlock have been frowned upon and discriminated against. The law dealing with the ability of children born out of wedlock to inherit from their biological parents reflects this change in social attitudes.

In *Trimble v. Gordon*, 430 U.S. 762, 97 S.Ct. 1459, 52 L.Ed.2d 31 (1977), the Supreme Court held that both children born out of wedlock and children born in wedlock must be treated equally when determining the method of descent and distribution of intestate property. Discrimination against children born out of wedlock was deemed a violation of the equal protection clause of the 14th Amendment. However, in *Lalli v. Lalli*, 439 U.S. 259, 99 S.Ct. 518, 58 L.Ed.2d 503 (1978), the Supreme Court retreated from *Trimble* in a five to four decision. The court held that a state may apply a more demanding standard for children born out of wedlock who seek to inherit from their fathers than from their mothers. The court's justifications for allowing the tougher standard included the more efficient and orderly administration of estates, maintenance of the finality of judgments, avoidance of spurious claims, protection of the decedent's will, and the inability of the father to contest.

States have many different approaches for determining when children born out of wedlock may inherit from their biological fathers. Most jurisdictions permit them to inherit as long as they can prove paternity but many impose higher standards of proof.

LOCATE

How does your state treat children born out of wedlock?

11. STEPCHILDREN

A stepchild is a child of a person's spouse who is not a biological or adopted child of the person. Generally, a stepchild may not inherit from a stepparent.

LOCATE

How does your state treat stepchildren?

12. CRIMINAL CONDUCT

If an heir murders the intestate, the heir will be precluded from taking a beneficial interest in the property either by statute or through the imposition of a constructive trust to prevent unjust enrichment. Other criminal conduct, such as being convicted of a capital offense or adultery, may or may not impact the intestate scheme.

LOCATE

What is the effect of an heir's criminal conduct under the law of your state?

13. SURVIVAL

Many states require that an heir (as well as a beneficiary of a will, beneficiary named in a life insurance policy, or co-owner in a joint tenancy) outlive the intestate (testator, insured, or joint tenant) by a certain period of time. A survival period helps avoid the expense of multiple administrations on the same property within a short period of time as well as court cases to determine the order of death which may involve inadequate or gruesome evidence.

LOCATE

Does your state have a statutory survival period? If yes, what is it? Does your state have a consistent time period for all situations or is it different depending on the situation, e.g., an heir must outlive the testator by 120 hours but a beneficiary need only survive a testator by an instant?

NOTE

For further information, see J. Rodney Johnson, *The New Uniform Simultaneous Death Act,* PROB. & PROP., May/June 1994, at 22.

14. ADVANCEMENT

An advancement is a prepayment of an inheritance while the heir apparent is still alive. The donor intends the irrevocable gift to be an anticipatory distribution in complete or partial satisfaction of the interest of the donee in the donor's estate. In many states, the donee may not inherit from the intestate unless the donee/heir accounts for all advanced property.

LOCATE

How are advancements treated under the law of your state? What type of evidence may be used to prove that the intestate made an advancement to the heir?

15. DISCLAIMER

A property interest cannot be forced on a person who is unwilling to accept it. Thus, an heir, beneficiary of a will, beneficiary of a life insurance policy, etc. may disclaim. Under the law of most states, disclaimed property passes as if the disclaiming person had predeceased the donor.

QUESTION

Why would a person decide to forego "free" property? See Chapter 4(H).

LOCATE

1. How may a person disclaim under the law of your state?
2. Who receives disclaimed property under the law of your state?

16. ESCHEAT

If an intestate dies with no heirs, the property escheats to the state or some other governmental entity.

17. GOVERNING LAW

Personal property is generally controlled by the intestacy laws of the decedent's domicile at the time of death while real property is governed by the law of the situs of the property. See Chapter 10(N).

18. DISINHERITANCE—THE NEGATIVE WILL

Some states allow a person to disinherit an heir without requiring the person to give the property to someone else using a valid will.

LOCATE

Does your state recognize negative wills?

19. LOCATING HEIRS

QUESTION

What would you do to locate the heirs of an intestate person? Would you try to find them yourself or would you hire a professional tracing service?

B. WILLS

State governments grant their citizens the privilege of controlling the passage of their property upon death by making a will. You do not have an inherent right to exercise this dead-hand control; thus, states could take away the privilege at any time. Of course, if legislators did vote to curtail the effect of a will, it is highly unlikely they would be reelected!

Because the ability to make a will is a privilege, a will is ineffective if all requirements are not followed exactly. Only a few states permit courts to evaluate wills with a "substantial compliance" standard. See U.P.C. § 2–503 (granting court dispensing power to excuse a harmless error).

NOTE

For an interesting historical review of wills, see Barbara R. Hauser, *The Tale of the Testament*, PROB. & PROP., Sept./Oct. 1998, at 59.

PART I. WILL VALIDITY

1. TYPES OF WILLS—GENERALLY

There are three basic types of wills. The *formal* or *attested* will which is in writing and witnessed, the *holographic* will which is entirely in the testator's own handwriting, and the *nuncupative* or oral will.

2. REQUIREMENTS FOR A VALID WILL

a. Legal Capacity

A person has legal capacity upon reaching the state's legal age, usually 18. In some states, legal capacity also exists if the person is married, in the military, or has had the disabilities of minority removed.

LOCATE

When does a person have the legal capacity to execute a will in your state?

b. Testamentary Capacity—Sound Mind

Although courts vary in how they define testamentary capacity, it is typical for testamentary capacity to encompass the following elements:

1) Understand Action

The testator must understand the activity in which the testator is engaged, i.e., making a will.

2) Comprehend Effect of Action

The testator must understand the effect of the testator's act in making the will, i.e., to dispose of property upon death.

3) Know the Nature and Extent of Property

The testator must understand the general nature and extent of the testator's property; an exact knowledge is not required.

4) Recognize Natural Objects of Bounty

The testator must know the testator's next of kin and natural objects of the testator's bounty, i.e., the testator must know the identity of family members, e.g., parents, children, etc.

5) Simultaneously Hold Elements in Mind

The testator must be able to collect and hold in the testator's mind the first four elements long enough to perceive their relationship to each other and to form a reasonable judgment as to them.

LOCATE

What are the elements of testamentary capacity in your state?

NOTES

1. An adjudication of incompetency often gives rise to a presumption that the testator lacked testamentary capacity. This presumption may be rebutted by contrary evidence.

2. A sane person may lack capacity at times, e.g., during sleep, while affected by drugs, or after an accident.

3. It is very difficult to determine where in the degeneration process of the human mind that one loses testamentary capacity. See Chapter 10(I) for a further discussion of how to effectively assist clients with questionable capacity.

4. A person is free to leave property in a socially unreasonable manner. However, in these cases, juries are prone to find against a will disinheriting close relatives such as a spouse and children. You must keep this in mind when drafting wills. See Chapter 9(B) for methods of preventing will contests.

c. Testamentary Intent

The testator must intend the very instrument being executed to be the will. For example, a letter to the decedent's attorney explaining what the person would like the will to provide is insufficient.

d. Formalities

Wills must be executed according to certain statutory formalities and these formalities vary among the states. The discussion below is a review of some of the typical requirements for an attested will. Note that about one-half of the states permit a holographic will to be valid without witnesses. In addition, a few states permit nuncupative wills to dispose of certain property under limited circumstances.

1) In Writing

The will must be in writing. Most, if not all, statutes do not specify what the will is to be written with or on.

2) Signed by Testator

The signature requirement usually encompasses any symbol executed or adopted by the testator with present intent to authenticate the will. Most states allow the testator to sign by proxy. Some states mandate a location for the signature, e.g., at the end (foot).

3) Attestation

Most states require the will to be witnessed by at least two individuals. The age requirement of the witnesses varies; some states allow them to be only 14 years old while others require them to be at least 18. Of course, the witnesses must be competent. Most states do not require *publication,* i.e., the witnesses do not need to know they are attesting to a will. It is a good idea, however, for the witnesses to know the nature of the document in case their testimony is needed later. Some states require signatures to be in correct order (i.e., the testator first) while others adopt a continuous transaction approach. Witnesses are less likely than the testator to be able to sign by proxy. Witnesses may be required to attest in the testator's presence. States vary as to whether the testator must sign in the witnesses' presence and whether the witnesses must attest in each other's presence. In some states, if the witness is also a beneficiary, the beneficiary forfeits some or all of the gift.

4) Self-Proving Affidavit

If state law allows it, the testator and witnesses should execute a self-proving affidavit so there is no need to bring the witnesses into court to probate the will. This technique saves a significant amount of time and money.

LOCATE

What are the will formalities in your state? Pay particular attention to the following:

- May the testator sign by proxy?
- Does the testator's signature need to be in any particular location on the will?
- How many witnesses are needed?
- Are holographic wills exempted from the witnessing requirement?
- How old must the witnesses be?
- Is publication required?
- In what order must the testator sign and the witnesses attest?
- May the witnesses sign by proxy?
- Do the witnesses need to attest in the testator's presence?
- Does the testator need to sign in the witnesses' presence?
- Do the witnesses need to attest in each other's presence?
- Where must the witnesses sign the will?
- What is the effect of a witness also being a beneficiary of the will?
- Does your state permit the use of self-proving affidavits?
- Are nuncupative wills recognized? If yes, under what conditions and for what property?

NOTES

1. For details on how to conduct a will execution ceremony, see Chapter 11(F).

2. Section 551 of the Floyd D. Spence National Defense Authorization Act for Fiscal Year 2001 provides that a *military testamentary instrument* is exempt from all state law formalities and has the same legal effect as a will prepared and executed under local state law. The statute sets forth the requirements for military testamentary instruments and how to make them self-proved. Under this legislation, all military lawyers may follow the same procedure without regard to the domicile of their clients. This is especially important when many wills have to be prepared quickly during major military operations. This legislation could be challenged on 10th Amendment grounds because succession matters were not delegated to the United States by the Constitution and thus are reserved to the states. On the other hand, matters regarding the wills of service personnel are tightly connected with the federal government's right to maintain the military. The case to watch for is one in which the will is valid under the federal law but not under state law and the heirs contest the will.

3. CONDITIONAL WILLS AND GIFTS

A will or a testamentary gift may be conditional, i.e., it operates only if a stated event occurs or does not occur. See Chapter 10(P) for a discussion of clients who desire to regulate a beneficiary's conduct with conditional gifts.

4. COMBINATION WILLS

a. Joint Will

A joint will is a single testamentary instrument containing the wills of two or more persons.

QUESTION

An almost universal piece of estate planning advice is never use a joint will. Why not?

b. Reciprocal Wills

Reciprocal wills are wills that contain parallel disposition plans, e.g., the husband leaves everything to his wife, or to their children if his wife predeceases; the wife leaves everything to her husband, or to their children if her husband predeceases.

QUESTIONS

1. Estate planners frequently use these *sweetheart wills*. Why?
2. What are the potential dangers of using reciprocal wills?

c. Contractual Will

A contractual will is one executed as consideration for another act or promise pursuant to a contractual arrangement.

LOCATE

What are the requirements for a contractual will under the law of your state?

QUESTION

Under what circumstances, if any, would you recommend the use of a contractual will?

PART II. CHANGES IN CIRCUMSTANCES AFTER WILL EXECUTION—PROPERTY AND PERSONS

1. ADEMPTION

Ademption occurs when a specific gift fails because the item given in the will is no longer in the testator's estate at the time of death. For example, if the will gives Blackacre to X and the testator sells or gifts Blackacre prior to death, X takes nothing under this provision of the will. In addition, the intended beneficiary does not normally receive the equivalent value via proceed tracing or otherwise. Accordingly, it is important for specific gifts to contain an express statement of the testator's intent if the item is not in the estate. The testator should either (1) explain that ademption causes the intended beneficiary to go home empty-handed, or (2) provide a substitute gift (e.g., other specific property, money, or a greater share of the residuary).

DRAFT

Testatrix wants to leave her wedding ring to her daughter. If the ring is not in her estate, Testatrix wants the daughter to have $10,000 instead. Draft the appropriate will provision.

2. SATISFACTION

Satisfaction occurs when a testamentary gift under the will is given to the beneficiary by the testator between the time of will execution and the time of death (compare advancement in the intestacy context).

Assume that Testator's will gives $50,000 to each of Testator's five grandchildren and the residuary to X. One of the grandchildren enrolled in law school and Testator paid the grandchild's tuition of $15,000 per year for three years. When Testator dies, X will claim that the $45,000 Testator spent on tuition partially satisfied the gift and thus this grandchild should receive only $5,000 from the estate.

LOCATE

What type of evidence may be used under the law of your state to prove that Testator satisfied part of the grandchild's legacy?

DRAFT

Draft the appropriate will provision to solve this problem assuming that Testator does not intend inter vivos gifts to affect testamentary gifts.

3. EXONERATION

Unless otherwise provided in the will, the law of many states mandates that all liens, mortgages, and other debts against specific gifts be paid by other estate property. Unintended exoneration could result in a tremendous frustration of a testator's intent. Assume that Testator owns Blackacre valued at $200,000 with a mortgage balance of $150,000 and various other assets with a combined value of approximately $50,000. To equalize the distribution of the estate to Testator's two children, Testator leaves Blackacre to one child (equity of $50,000) and the residuary to the other child. Upon Testator's death, the specific gift of Blackacre may be entitled to exoneration from the residuary estate and thus one child will receive an equity of $100,000 and the other child will receive nothing. To avoid this unfortunate scenario, the will should expressly indicate whether debts against specifically gifted property are to be exonerated and if so, from what property and to what extent.

LOCATE

If the will is silent, what does your state presume about the exoneration of encumbrances on specifically gifted property?

DRAFT

Draft a will provision which reflects a testator's intent for exoneration not to take place.

4. APPRECIATION AND DEPRECIATION

A change in value of a specific gift is normally irrelevant; the beneficiary receives the item regardless of whether its value has dramatically increased or decreased between the time of will execution and the date of the testator's death.

QUESTION

How is the potential appreciation and depreciation of specifically gifted property important in preparing the estate plan?

5. LAPSE

Lapse occurs if a gift fails because the beneficiary predeceased the testator. The subject matter of the gift normally passes under the will's residuary clause, or, if the lapsed gift was the residuary, via intestacy. If, however, the state anti-lapse statute applies, the gift is saved for the beneficiary's descendants.

To prevent the result of lapse from being governed by rules that may not comport with the testator's intent, each gift should expressly indicate who receives the property should the beneficiary die first. For example, the testator could make an express gift over to a contingent beneficiary, indicate that the gift passes to the descendants of the deceased beneficiary, or merely state that the gift passes under the residuary clause.

LOCATE

How does your state's anti-lapse statute operate?

NOTE

For further information, see John L. Garvey, *Drafting Wills and Trusts: Anticipating the Birth and Death of Possible Beneficiaries,* 71 OR. L. REV. 47 (1992).

DRAFT

Testator wants to leave his heirloom watch to Fred, but if Fred is already dead, the watch should pass to Jason. Draft the appropriate will provision.

6. ABATEMENT

State law specifies the order in which gifts fail if the estate has insufficient property to satisfy all testamentary gifts. This order may or may not be in accordance with the testator's intent. Thus, you must ascertain the relative strength of each gift and make certain the testator's primary beneficiaries receive preferential treatment either under state law or by expressly stating the abatement order.

LOCATE

What is your state's default abatement order?

DRAFT

Assume that local law prefers general gifts to residuary gifts and gives primary preference to specific gifts. Testator wants to leave $200,000 to X, Blackacre to Y, and the residuary to Z. Testator is most concerned about X receiving the $200,000. Draft the appropriate will provision to carry out Testator's intent.

7. APPORTIONMENT OF TAXES

Apportionment refers to whether transfers that occur because of a person's death (e.g., gifts under a will, life insurance proceeds, survivorship accounts) will be reduced by the amount of state or federal estate tax attributable to the transfers. Federal law mandates that life insurance beneficiaries and recipients under a power of appointment shoulder their fair share of the estate tax. I.R.C. §§ 2206 & 2207. States vary significantly on how apportionment is handled with respect to other property in the absence of a will provision on point. Some states impose equitable apportionment while others follow the normal abatement order which places the burden on the residual beneficiaries. A statutory apportionment scheme may or may not reflect the testator's intent. As a result, if the estate may be large enough to have estate tax liability, you must carefully question the testator regarding tax apportionment desires and draft accordingly.

LOCATE

Does your state have a statutory provision dealing with the apportionment of taxes? If yes, how does it operate?

NOTES AND QUESTIONS

1. Why do some estate planners call an apportionment clause a dispositive provision in disguise?

2. See generally Mark Mathewson, *Tax Apportionment: Playing Fair With Your Heirs,* 82 ILL. B.J. 269 (1994); Mark A. Segal, *Tax Apportionment: Who Picks Up the Tab,* PROB. & PROP., July/Aug. 1994, at 33.

PART III. REVOCATION

1. REVOCATION BY OPERATION OF LAW

a. Marriage

1) Common Law Marital Property States

The surviving spouse is entitled to a *forced* or *elective* share of the deceased spouse's estate. The amount of this share varies according to the jurisdiction. The surviving spouse is entitled to this share regardless of the provisions of the deceased spouse's will. In some states, the size of the share depends on the number of children or the length of the marriage.

It is very important for you to remember the potential of the surviving spouse electing a forced share when drafting a will which may not be favorable to the surviving spouse. The spouse may elect to take the forced share rather than under the will and thus disrupt the testator's plan.

NOTE

See Susan N. Gary, *Share and Share Alike: The UPC's Elective Share,* PROB. & PROP., Mar./Apr. 1998, at 19.

2) Community Property Marital Property States

Marriage after will execution does not normally impact property disposition. The surviving spouse simply owns one-half of the community.

LOCATE

1. Does marriage automatically revoke a pre-marriage will in your state?

2. How is the surviving spouse's forced share or community share computed in your state?

3. Can the spouse's right to a forced share or community share be waived in an ante-or post-nuptial agreement?

b. Divorce After Will Execution

Many states have statutes voiding all provisions in favor of an ex-spouse upon divorce. Note, however, that automatic voiding normally does not occur because of the mere filing of a divorce action. Thus, anytime your client has serious marital difficulties, prompt changes to the estate plan are vital. See Chapter 10(J).

LOCATE

What is the effect of divorce on a will in your state?

c. Lapse

See the discussion in Chapter 2(B)(Part II(5)).

d. Pretermitted Children

Under certain circumstances, children omitted from a will or children born or adopted after will execution may be entitled to a forced share of the testator's estate. This automatic alteration of an established estate plan could have a devastating effect on the testator's dispositive desires. All wills should address the pretermitted child issue, even wills of individuals beyond child bearing years. It is becoming increasingly common for parents to adopt grandchildren and older individuals to adopt disadvantaged children—situations which increase the likelihood of triggering pretermitted child issues.

LOCATE

Does your state have a pretermitted child statute? If yes, how does it operate?

DRAFT

Draft a provision to avoid the application of your state's pretermitted child statute.

2. REVOCATION BY PHYSICAL ACT

a. Requirements

1) Revocation Intent

The testator must have the intent to revoke the will. If the testator destroys the will by mistake, i.e., without intent, the revocation is ineffective.

2) Mental Capacity

If the testator lacks mental capacity, an alleged revocation is ineffective.

3) Physical Act

State statutes indicate what physical acts are sufficient to cause a revocation, e.g., destroy, cancel, or burn. States may or may not permit revocation by proxy.

LOCATE

What types of physical acts effectively revoke a will in your state? Is a proxy revocation possible?

4) Concurrence of Intent, Mental Capacity, and Physical Act

The testator must intend to revoke the will and perform the necessary physical act while having the requisite capacity.

b. Partial Revocation by Physical Act

Many states do not permit portions of an attested will to be changed by interlineations, mark-outs, etc.

LOCATE

Assume that Testator has a valid attested will. One of its provisions leaves $20,000 to X. Evidence shows that Testator crossed out "$20,000" and wrote "$15,000" above the cross out. How much does X take under the law of your state? What if Testator wrote $100,000 instead?

3. REVOCATION BY SUBSEQUENT WRITING

Revocation by physical act is inherently ambiguous because there is no clear evidence regarding who actually did the physical destruction or why it was done. Accordingly, it is better practice to revoke a will with a subsequent writing.

a. Express Revocation

The testator may include an express statement of revocation in a will, codicil, or other writing meeting the formalities of a will. This is the preferred method and the reason most wills start with a statement that all other wills and codicils are revoked.

b. Revocation by Inconsistency

Between two conflicting will provisions, be they in the same will or in different wills, the last one controls.

QUESTIONS

1. What should each will contain to assist in determining whether one will was expressly revoked by another?

2. When a testator wants to make only a few changes to the will, is it better for the testator to execute a codicil or a new will? Why?

4. REVOCATION RELATED PROOF PROBLEMS

a. Presumption of Non–Revocation

If a will is found under normal circumstances (e.g., in a safe deposit box or with other valuable papers, and there are no suspicious circumstances), most courts will presume the will has not been revoked.

b. Presumption of Revocation

If a will was in the possession of the testator or if the testator had ready access to it when it was last seen, failure to produce the will raises, in most states, the presumption that the testator destroyed it with the intent to revoke it.

c. Lost Wills

If the original will cannot be found, the proponent has a heavy burden to overcome the revocation presumption and show that the will was inadvertently destroyed.

5. REVIVAL

Assume that Testator executes Will One and that Will One is valid. Testator then executes Will Two, which is also valid, and which expressly revokes Will One. Testator then validly revokes Will Two without executing a new will. Would Will One be effective if Testator dies without further estate planning? Jurisdictions take several approaches. Under a revival approach, a testamentary instrument has no effect until death, and thus Will One stands because Will Two containing the revocation clause never took effect because it was revoked prior to Testator's death. Under a no revival approach, the revocation clause in Will Two takes effect immediately (just like a revocation by physical act) although the dispositive provisions do not take effect until Testator's death. In an intent approach jurisdiction, the court examines the facts and permits revival if it believes that is what Testator intended.

LOCATE

Which revival approach is used in your state?

6. CONDITIONAL REVOCATION

a. Express Conditional Revocation

The testator may state in the revoking instrument that a revocation is effective upon the happening (or non-happening) of a named event. This technique is used only occasionally in estate planning to effectuate a very specialized intent of the testator.

QUESTION

When might you make a will revocation expressly conditioned on some event?

b. Implied Conditional Revocation [Dependent Relative Revocation]

Assume that Testator executes Will One and that Will One is valid. Testator then rips up Will One and executes Will Two. Will Two turns out to be invalid. If the court recognizes dependent relative revocation, it may imply a condition to the revocation, i.e., Testator intended to revoke Will One only if Will Two is effective. Thus, Will One has not been revoked because the implied condition to the revocation was not satisfied.

QUESTION

How would a comparison of the provisions of the two wills help you decide if dependent relative revocation should apply?

LOCATE

Is dependent relative revocation recognized in your state?

7. REPUBLICATION

Republication is a method of treating a prior will as if it were executed now. The testator may republish the will by signing a codicil or by re-executing the prior will. The will and codicils, if any, are now treated as one instrument speaking from the date of the codicil or the re-execution.

QUESTION

Why is republication important? How must you account for republication when you prepare an estate plan?

8. DUPLICATE ORIGINALS

The practice of executing multiple original wills should be avoided. There is generally no reason why the testator should sign more than one original will.

LOCATE

Under the law of your state, what happens if the testator dies after having destroyed some, but not all, of the originals?

PART IV. WILL INTERPRETATION AND CONSTRUCTION

1. INTRODUCTION

The purpose of will interpretation and construction is to give meaning to a will so the estate passes to the proper persons in the manner the testator outlined in the will. Although these issues may arise before the will is admitted to probate, they usually arise thereafter. Will interpretation issues are raised by (1) the personal representative who wants to do the right thing and thus avoid liability for improper administration, and (2) the beneficiaries/heirs who would take under various interpretations. Some basic maxims of will construction include:

- The fact that the testator left a will, especially if it has a residuary clause, indicates an intent not to die intestate.
- Among two or more contradictory provisions in a will, the last one prevails.
- The interpretation which results in the least unequal distribution among takers of equal relationship to the testator is preferred.
- The will is construed as a whole, not from isolated parts out of context.

2. AMBIGUITY

a. Patent Ambiguity

A patent ambiguity consists of language that is ambiguous on its face, i.e., it fails to convey a sensible meaning. Extrinsic evidence may be used to ascertain the testator's intent provided there is something to interpret. Thus, extrinsic evidence could be used to determine what the testator meant by the term "xiques" but not to fill in blank spaces.

QUESTION

How do you avoid patent ambiguities when drafting a will?

b. Latent Ambiguity

A provision is latently ambiguous if it conveys a sensible meaning on its face but cannot be carried out without further clarification. For example, (1) a will provides for a gift to, "To my sister, Pat," but the testator has a sister named Chris and a brother named Pat; or (2) the testator wrote, "I leave my car to Quan," but died owning two cars. Courts usually allow extrinsic evidence to resolve latent ambiguities.

QUESTION

How do you avoid latent ambiguity problems when you prepare a will?

c. No Apparent Ambiguity

What if the will is clear on its face and can be carried out exactly as written? May extrinsic evidence be used to show an ambiguity? The commonly applied clear meaning rule says that extrinsic evidence cannot be used to rebut the plain language of a will. This rule gives predictability to the results which flow from the use of specific language. Some courts follow a more liberal rule, however, and allow extrinsic evidence to ascertain and effectuate the testator's intent in difficult situations.

LOCATE

How does your state deal with the no apparent ambiguity situation?

QUESTION

Is there anything you can do to avoid your client's intent being circumvented by someone bringing in evidence to show an ambiguity where there is none?

3. INTEGRATION

a. External Integration

External integration is the process of establishing the testator's will by piecing together all testamentary documents (wills, codicils, etc.).

QUESTION

What steps would you take to avoid external integration problems?

b. Internal Integration

Internal integration is the continuity and relationship within the body of the instrument.

QUESTION

What steps would you take to internally integrate the will? Please review Chapter 11(B)(2).

4. INCORPORATION BY REFERENCE

Instead of writing out certain material in the will in full, the testator may incorporate an extraneous document into the will by reference. The incorporated material is then treated as if it were actually written out in the will. There are three basic elements to an incorporation by reference. (1) The testator must intend to incorporate the extraneous document. (2) The writing to be incorporated must be in existence at the time the will is executed. (3) The will must sufficiently identify the material to be incorporated so that no other document could reasonably be referred to by that description.

NOTES AND QUESTIONS

1. When would a testator intentionally use this technique?

2. It may be possible to bootstrap an invalid will (e.g., lack of formalities, capacity, etc.) with a valid codicil.

LOCATE

Does your state have any legislation dealing with the incorporation by reference of documents into a will? If yes, how does it operate?

5. FACTS OF INDEPENDENT SIGNIFICANCE

A fact of independent significance is something which has a legal purpose independent of disposing of property at death. If something has a fact of independent significance, it can control where property goes upon death without the necessity of complying with will formalities.

NOTES AND QUESTIONS

1. What are some examples of facts of independent significance?

2. A will provision reads, "I leave my free-standing Acme safe model 342X to Paula Smith." Is Paula entitled to the contents of the safe, as well as the safe itself? How will you deal with this issue when drafting a gift of an item that may contain other items?

3. Some states allow a testator to make reference in a will to a separate document which indicates the disposition of tangible personal property although such a document would not be effective under traditional incorporation by reference (document not in existence when the will is executed) or facts of independent significance (no non-testamentary purpose) theories. See U.P.C. § 2–513.

4. See Chapter 10(M) for a discussion of planning methods for clients with personal property concerns.

6. PRECATORY LANGUAGE

Instructions in a will regarding the disposition of property must be mandatory to be enforceable. Precatory language such as "I wish," "I would like," and "I recommend," is normally considered suggestive in nature and not binding on the beneficiary. Precatory language has a greater chance of being effective if it is used to instruct the personal representative.

Precatory language has no place in a will. If the testator wishes to express non-mandatory desires, a separate non-testamentary document should be used. Alternatively, a client may wish to make a videotape with precatory advice.

7. CLASS GIFTS TO CHILDREN

Many interpretation issues arise when the testator makes class gifts to children, either the testator's or another person's. Without careful planning, the identity of the actual beneficiaries may not match the testator's intent. For example, are adopted children included? What if a person is adopted with the motivation behind the adoption being to secure a share in the estate? Are non-marital children included?

NOTES AND QUESTIONS

1. What steps will you take to avoid these class gift issues?

2. In *In re Adoption of Tammy*, 416 Mass. 205, 619 N.E.2d 315 (1993), the court held that a lesbian could adopt her partner's child and that the adoption would not terminate the biological mother's legal rights with respect to the child. An incidental effect of this adoption was to make the child eligible to become a beneficiary under the adopting woman's family trust.

PART V. WILL CONTESTS

A person may want an alleged will to be invalid because that person would take more if the will failed, e.g., as an heir or as a beneficiary of a prior will. Being aware of how will contests occur makes it easier to draft wills that are not contested or which will survive a contest. Will contest avoidance techniques are covered in detail in Chapter 9(B).

If possible, it is better for a contestant to file the contest before the will is admitted to probate because the burden of proof that the will is valid is still on the proponent. Once the will is admitted to probate, the burden is on the contestant to show the will's invalidity.

1. WILL CONTEST GROUNDS

a. Failure to Meet Elements of a Valid Will

Many contests are based on allegations that the testator failed to execute a document which meets the minimum standards for a valid will, e.g., lack of legal capacity, lack of testamentary capacity, lack of testamentary intent, and lack of formalities. Review Part I of this section.

b. Insane Delusion

An insane delusion is a belief in a state of supposed facts that do not exist and which no rational person would believe. Mere illogical thought or maintenance of a false belief is insufficient. In addition, the contestant must be able to establish a connection between the insane delusion and the property disposition in the will; just because a testator had a delusion does not necessarily mean it affected the provisions of the will.

c. Undue Influence

The basic elements of undue influence are (1) the existence of an influence; (2) the subversion of the testator's mind by the influence when the testator executed the will; and (3) the execution of a will the testator would not have executed but for the undue influence.

Undue influence is usually demonstrated with extrinsic evidence because the testator is dead and the evil-doer will lie thus making direct evidence unavailable. The types of circumstantial evidence often available include: an unnatural disposition, opportunity to exert undue influence, the relationship between the parties, the testator's susceptibility and ability to resist, and a connection between will drafting and/or will execution and the beneficiary. Mere opportunity to exert undue influence, of course, is insufficient.

d. Duress

Duress is very similar to undue influence but involves the use or threat of force or violence, the withholding of food or medicine, and similar heinous activity.

e. Fraud

The basic elements of fraud are (1) a false representation is made to the testator, (2) the person who made it knew it was false, (3) the testator reasonably believed the false statement, and (4) the false statement caused the testator to execute a will the testator would not have executed but for the false statement.

There are two main types of fraud. In *fraud in the factum*, also called *fraud in the execution*, the testator is deceived as to identity or contents of the instrument, e.g., the testator does not know the testator is signing a will or, if the testator does know the testator is signing a will, the testator is unaware of its contents. In *fraud in the inducement,* the testator is deceived as to some extrinsic fact and makes the will based on that erroneous fact.

Fraud is contrasted with mistake. Unilateral mistakes cannot be fixed unless there is evil conduct or a lack of testamentary intent.

2. REMEDIES

The most common will contest remedy is for the court to refuse to admit the will to probate. In theory, it is possible to have partial invalidity but it is difficult to show that the rest of the will was unaffected. Also, most evil people seek to acquire most or all of a testator's property, not just identifiable separate items. A constructive trust remedy may also be available to prevent unjust enrichment.

C. ESTATE ADMINISTRATION

1. INTRODUCTION

ROBERT J. LYNN AND GRAYSON M.P. McCOUCH, INTRODUCTION TO ESTATE PLANNING*

§ 1.5, pages 12–15 (5th ed. 2004).

Every year people die owning property that is not subject to probate administration. This is not necessarily because decedents have skillfully arranged their affairs to "avoid probate." Rather, non-administration may reflect a lack of assets of substantial value, or absence of assets of the kind that call for administration, or willingness on the part of interested parties to settle the estate informally among themselves. If a decedent owns very little property at death, applicable state law may provide for a simplified estate settlement procedure that minimizes or eliminates the role of the probate court. If the decedent owns no land at death, no registered automobile, no registered stocks or bonds, and no bank accounts, the surviving family members might simply take over the decedent's assets, which might have substantial value; the survivors might even pay the decedent's debts voluntarily. Even if the decedent is the record owner of land at death, the family might simply continue to occupy it, and to pay the tax bills that continue to arrive in the name of the decedent, although this course of action is likely to create serious problems if the land eventually has to be sold.

In sum, court-supervised administration of a decedent's estate, as it is usually visualized, is not a process that occurs automatically on the death of a decedent. It must be started by someone. And it might not occur at all if the reasons for seeking court-supervised administration are not present in the particular case.

* Reprinted with permission of Thomson Reuters.

Keep the first sentence the same, and then change the remainder of paragraph to the following. The executor designated in the will or some other interested person might petition the probate court to admit the will to probate and grant "letters testamentary" to the executor. If the decedent died intestate, an heir or next of kin or even a creditor might petition the probate court to grant "letters of administration" to an administrator. Letters testamentary or letters of administration are the personal representative's badge of authority. Bankers, stock transfer agents, and the like, may insist on seeing them before they will turn over control of the decedent's assets to the personal representative. Notice of hearing on the petition is given to interested persons in conformity to statute. If there is a will, admitting it to probate as the last will of the decedent might not be a matter of controversy. But an heir who would benefit if the will were spurious might challenge the validity of the will. If the will is contested, its validity must be determined by the probate court in a special proceeding.

The executor or administrator is commonly called the "personal representative" of the decedent. The person representative is appointed by the probate court and remains subject to supervision by the probate court throughout the administration of the estate. Unless the will provides otherwise, an individual may be required to furnish bond in order to qualify as personal representative.

The functions of the personal representative fall into three general phases: collecting and preserving the asset of the estate; paying creditors' claims, expenses of administration, and taxes; and distributing the remaining property to the decedent's devisees and legates (to the extent that the will has dispositive effect) or to intestate successors (to the extent that the decedent died intestate).

In performing these functions, the personal representative must prepare an "inventory" (a list) of assets in the decedent's estate and obtain an "appraisal" (an estimate of their value). In conformity to statute, the personal representative gives notice to known creditors of the decedent to present their claims for payment. If the personal representative rejects a claim, the effectiveness of the claim may be determined by a lawsuit. A general creditor who fails to present a claim within the period set by statute may be forever barred from enforcing the claim.

After debts of the decedent, expenses of administration, and taxes have been paid, whatever property is left is distributable to the devisees, legatees, or intestate successors of the decedent, as the case may be. The personal representative submits a final accounting and petitions the probate court to be discharged from further liability. Upon approval by the probate court, the administration of the estate comes to an end.

LOCATE

Prepare a brief outline of the administration process under the law of your state.

2. DRAFTING CONSIDERATIONS

During the estate planning process, your client must make several decisions regarding administration. Below are some examples of the issues you must discuss with your client.

a. Selection of Personal Representative

Your client must evaluate a wide range of factors to determine the identity of the person to trust with carrying out the terms of the will. Fiduciary selection criteria are covered in detail in Chapter 8(H).

b. Designation of Alternates

Your client should designate at least one alternate personal representative in case the first named is unable or unwilling to serve.

DRAFT

Draft a will provision designating a primary and secondary executor.

c. Bond

The client must decide whether the personal representative is to serve with or without bond. Bond protects the beneficiaries against the executor's wrongful conduct but the expense reduces the amount available to the beneficiaries. See Chapter 8(H)(4)(c).

d. Fees

Is the personal representative to be compensated from the estate for work done? If yes, how will compensation be determined? See Chapter 8(H)(1)(g).

e. Type of Administration

The testator may be able to influence the type of administration by express language in the will. For example, in some states, the testator can provide for an independent, i.e., non-court supervised, administration.

LOCATE

Under the law of your state, what impact can the testator make on the type of administration? How would this be done?

f. Powers of Personal Representative

The testator may be able to control which powers the executor may exercise during the administration process. If the testator wants the executor to have more powers or fewer powers than the statutory default plan, express language in the will is necessary.

LOCATE

What powers will the personal representative automatically obtain under the law of your state? What powers may the client wish to consider adding or subtracting?

g. Waiver of Self–Dealing Prohibition

The law often prohibits a personal representative from engaging in transactions in which the person has a self-interest. For example, the personal representative may be prohibited from buying estate assets.

QUESTION

In what situations might your client wish to permit the executor to self-deal?

LOCATE

1. Locate your state's statutes that prohibit a personal representative from self-dealing.

2. Are waivers of the prohibitions allowed? If yes, how may your client waive this duty?

h. Lowering of Standard of Care

A personal representative is usually held to a high level of care when dealing with estate property. The testator may not want to subject the executor to personal liability for mere negligent conduct that causes a loss to the estate. Thus, your client may wish to include an exculpatory clause in the will.

QUESTION

Why might your client want to lower the standard of care for the executor?

LOCATE

1. What is the usual standard of care for a personal representative in your state?

2. Are exculpatory clauses enforced in your state? What are the limitations?

DRAFT

Draft the broadest exculpatory clause allowed under the law of your state.

D. TRUSTS

PART I. TRUST CREATION

1. INTRODUCTION

The owner of property may create a trust by transferring that property in a unique fashion. First, the owner must divide the title to the property into legal and equitable interests and, second, the owner must impose fiduciary duties on the holder of the legal title to deal with the property for the benefit of the holder of the equitable title.

2. SPLITTING OF OWNERSHIP

a. Legal Interest

The trustee holds legal title to the trust property. The trustee has all of the responsibilities related to property ownership but receives none of the benefits, except possibly a fee for trustee services. In carrying out ownership responsibilities, a trustee is under a duty to perform as a fiduciary, i.e., the trustee must use reasonable care when dealing with the trust property and maintain the utmost degree of loyalty. If a trustee's conduct falls beneath these standards, the trustee will be personally liable, i.e., subject to civil and perhaps even criminal liability.

b. Equitable or Beneficial Interest

The beneficiary holds the equitable interest in the trust property. The beneficiary may also be called a donee, grantee, or *cestui que trust.* The beneficiary has the right to enforce the trust. The beneficiary is entitled to the benefits of the trust property as set forth in the trust instrument but typically has little or no control over the trust or the trust property.

QUESTIONS

1. Settlor transferred both legal and equitable title to Daughter. Does a valid trust exist?

2. Settlor created a valid trust by transferring legal title to Daughter and equitable title to Son. Thereafter, Daughter transferred legal title to Son. Does a valid trust still exist?

3. THE SETTLOR

The settlor is the person who is responsible for the creation of the trust by supplying the initial trust property. The settlor may also be known as the trustor, grantor, or donor. The settlor owned both legal title and equitable title to the property prior to the creation of the trust. The settlor may choose to retain the legal title, the beneficial title, or part of each. Remember that a split of title will not exist unless at least one other person receives some interest, either legal or equitable, in the property.

4. TRUST PROPERTY

A trust is a conveyancing relationship and thus a trust must have trust property. Trust property may be referred to as the trust's principal, corpus, res, or estate. The settlor must have the power to transfer title to the property. Accordingly, if the settlor cannot transfer the settlor's interest in a particular type or item of property, that property may not be held in trust.

5. BASIC FUNCTIONING OF A TRUST

The settlor creates a trust by transferring legal title to an individual or financial institution in which the settlor has confidence and equitable title to an individual or charity deserving of a windfall. As discussed above, the settlor may retain some interest in the trust property, but a split of title must occur for a valid trust to exist.

The instructions contained in the trust instrument and state law control the actions of the trustee. The trustee must manage and invest the property in accordance with these mandates. Additionally, the payments made to or for the benefit of the beneficiary must be consistent with the instructions in the trust instrument.

A trustee's duties end when the trust terminates. Termination occurs either by the trust's own terms or upon depletion of the trust property. If property remains when the trust terminates, the legal title and equitable title are united in the remainder beneficiary.

6. PURPOSES AND USES OF TRUSTS

Trusts are one of the most powerful, useful, and advantageous tools available to the modern estate planner. This section discusses some of the reasons you may decide to recommend a trust to your clients.

a. Provides for and Protects Trust Beneficiaries

The settlor's desire to provide for and protect someone is probably the most common reason for choosing to use a trust. Although a donor could make a quick, convenient, and uncomplicated outright gift, there are many situations in which such outright gifts would not effectuate the donor's true intent.

1) Minors

Minors lack legal capacity to manage property and usually have insufficient maturity to do so as well. Thus, a trust allows a settlor to make a gift for the benefit of the minor without giving the minor control over the property. A trust is also more flexible and allows a settlor to have greater control over how the property is used when contrasted with other methods such as a transfer to a guardian or conservator of the minor's estate or to a custodian under the Uniform Transfers to Minors Act.

2) Individuals Who Lack Management Skills

A person may lack the skills necessary to properly manage the trust property. This deficiency could be the result of mental or physical incompetence or a lack of experience in the rigors of making prudent investment decisions. For example, persons who suddenly obtain a large amount of money, such as actors, professional athletes, lottery winners, or personal injury plaintiffs, tend to deplete this "windfall" rapidly because they have never learned how to manage their money wisely. By putting the money under the control of a trustee with investment experience, the settlor increases the chances that the beneficiary's interests are served for a longer period of time.

NOTE

For a discussion of how trusts are used in the settlement of large personal injury cases, see William L. Winslow, *Trusts Protect Clients with Special Needs,* TRIAL, April 1993, at 51.

3) Spendthrifts

Some individuals may be competent to manage property but are prone to use it in an excessive or frivolous manner. By using a carefully drafted trust, a settlor can protect the trust property from the beneficiary and the beneficiary's creditors.

4) Persons Susceptible to Influence

When a person suddenly acquires a significant amount of property, that person may be under pressure from family, friends, investment advisors, and many others to let them share the windfall. A trust can make it virtually impossible for the beneficiary to transfer trust property to these people.

b. Provides Flexibility of Asset Distribution

An outright gift, either inter vivos or testamentary, gives the donee total control over the way the property is used. With a trust, the settlor can restrict the beneficiary's control over the property in any manner the settlor desires so long as the restrictions are not illegal or in violation of public policy. This flexibility allows the settlor to determine how the trustee distributes trust benefits, such as by spreading the benefits over time, giving the trustee discretion as to whom receives distributions and in what amount, requiring the beneficiary to meet certain criteria to receive or continue receiving benefits, or limiting the purposes for which trust property may be used, e.g., health care or education.

c. Protects Against Settlor's Incompetence

Once a person is declared incompetent due to illness, injury, or other cause, the person cannot manage property. The court then needs to appoint a guardian of the estate or conservator to manage the property.

This process may cause the person considerable embarrassment and there is no guarantee the incompetent person will be happy with the guardian's decisions. Guardianships are also inconvenient and costly.

Trusts can be used to avoid the need for a guardian. The settlor may create a trust and maintain considerable control over the trust property by, for example, actually serving as trustee, retaining the power to revoke the trust, and even keeping a beneficial life interest. However, upon incompetency, the settlor's designated successor trustee would take over the administration of the trust property in accordance with the directions expressed by the settlor in the trust instrument.

An alternative method to protect property and avoid the need for a guardian in the event of incompetency is to have the client execute a durable power of attorney for property management. See Chapter 5(B).

d. Allows Professional Management of Property

The settlor may create a trust to obtain the services of a professional asset manager. Trustees, such as banks and trust companies, may have more expertise and experience with various types of investments than most individuals. Professional trustees also have greater investment opportunities. For example, a bank may combine funds from several trusts into one common trust fund to take advantage of opportunities that require a large investment and to diversify, thus reducing the damage to the value of a particular trust when one investment turns sour.

However, you must consider the effect of trust fees when discussing the selection of a trustee with the client. The value of the trust property and its potential for income should be high enough to insure that the benefit from professional management outweighs the cost of that management.

e. Avoids Probate

Property in an inter vivos trust is not part of the probate estate upon the settlor's death. The property remaining in the trust when the settlor dies is administered and distributed according to the terms of the trust instead of passing under a will or by intestate succession. Advantages to avoiding probate include providing for the property to reach the hands of the beneficiaries quickly, avoiding gaps in management, and evading probate publicity. These advantages, however, do not apply to testamentary trusts since they do not avoid probate. See Chapter 3(B) for a more detailed discussion of probate avoidance.

f. Provides Tax Benefits

Another popular reason for utilizing trusts is tax avoidance. Income taxes can be saved by shifting income earning property to a person in a lower tax bracket. Additionally, gift taxes may be avoided by structuring the transfers to a trust to fall within the annual exclusion from the federal gift tax. Likewise, if a trust is properly constructed, the trust property will not be treated as part of the settlor's estate and estate taxes are reduced. See Chapter 4(I) for more information on the taxation of trusts.

NOTES AND QUESTIONS

1. Despite these benefits, a trust may not be the best tool to accomplish the client's intent. For example, assume your client's main goal is to plan for disability. Although a properly drafted trust would do the job, it will entail additional time and money to establish the trust and transfer title to the property to the trust. Perhaps a durable power of attorney for property management which can be prepared quickly and economically is all the client needs. Thus, like any estate planning technique, you must evaluate the benefits and disadvantages of a trust before making your recommendation.

2. Some attorneys heavily hype inter vivos trusts as an estate planning panacea to the general public through the use of newspaper and other media advertisements and estate planning "seminars." Although a trust is an extremely useful technique, a person should not create a trust until the person carefully balances the benefits against the trust's creation, administration, and transfer costs.

3. Several states are attempting to stop the sale of living trusts by non-lawyers. Illinois' Attorney General Roland Burris stated, "Living trusts in the hands of unscrupulous con artists are one of the fastest growing areas of fraud against senior citizens." David N. Anderson, *Living Trust Fraud Bill is Approved,* ISBA BAR NEWS, June 21, 1993, at 1. How do you think purveyors of inter vivos trusts are hurting their clients?

4. To protect the public from exaggerated claims of the benefits of a living trust, some states have taken steps to regulate how attorneys advertise them. For example, in November 1997, Texas prohibited attorneys from making the following statements about trusts created during the settlor's lifetime because they are potentially misleading and may create unjustified expectations: [1]

- Living trusts will always save the client money.
- The use of a living trust in and of itself will reduce or eliminate estate taxes otherwise payable as a result of the client's death.
- Estate tax savings can be achieved only by use of a living trust.
- The use of a living trust will achieve estate tax savings that cannot be achieved using a will.
- The probate process is always lengthy and complicated.
- The probate process should always be avoided.
- The use of a living trust will reduce the total expenses incurred compared to expenses incurred using other estate planning devices intended to address the same basic function.

---

1. Interpretive Comment No. 22: Advertisement of Living Trusts, as reported in 61 TEX. B.J. 71 (1998).

- The use of a living trust avoids lengthy delays experienced in the use of other estate planning devices intended to address the same basic function.
- Lawyers use will-writing as a loss leader.

7. INTER VIVOS TRUST CREATION METHODS

A trust created during the settlor's lifetime is called an inter vivos trust. These trusts are also known as *living trusts*. The two basic methods for inter vivos trust creation are distinguished by who holds legal title.

a. Self-Declaration (of Trust)

In a self-declaration of trust, the settlor declares him-or herself to be the trustee of specific property the settlor holds for the benefit of a third person. As the trustee, the settlor retains legal title to the trust property.

b. Transfer (Conveyance) in Trust

In a conveyance in trust, the settlor transfers the legal title to another person as trustee. The settlor may retain or transfer the equitable title.

c. Relevance of Consideration

A trust is a conveyancing relationship, not a contractual relationship. Thus, consideration is generally not required for a trust to be valid.

However, two situations exist where consideration is significant in the trust context. First, consideration is required to enforce a promise to create a trust in the future. Basic contract law applies in this circumstance; all of the requirements of a valid contract must be met, including the requirement of consideration. Second, if the trust property is a promise, then that promise needs to be a valid contract to make that promise a valuable trust asset.

8. TESTAMENTARY TRUSTS

Testamentary trusts take effect upon the death of the settlor. A testamentary trust is created in the settlor's will. A precondition to the validity of a testamentary trust is for the will to be valid. After the validity of the will is determined, the trust is examined to determine its validity. If a will is invalid, any testamentary trust contained therein will also be invalid.

9. REVOCABILITY OF INTER VIVOS TRUSTS

The settlor has the power to make a trust revocable or irrevocable. Thus, revocability needs to be considered when creating an inter vivos trust. Whether to make a trust revocable or irrevocable depends on the facts of each case.

If the trust instrument contains no express language reserving to the settlor the power to revoke, most states presume that the trust is irrevocable. In a few states and under the Uniform Trust Code, however, trusts are presumed revocable absent express language to the contrary. Therefore, an estate planner should always place an express provision in the trust instrument that addresses the issue of revocability. This policy will avoid the need to resort to state law presumptions which especially cause problems when a settlor changes jurisdictions.

In creating an inter vivos trust, a settlor may retain substantial control of the trust property. In addition to retaining the power to revoke a trust, the settlor may retain a life estate, the power to change the beneficiary, the power to control the trust administration, and the power to add property to the trust. In most states, this retention of powers by the settlor will not invalidate a trust for being illusory or too testamentary in nature.

LOCATE

What is your state's presumption regarding the revocability of a trust?

QUESTION

Why might a settlor wish to make a trust revocable? Irrevocable?

DRAFT

Draft two trust provisions: one making the trust revocable and another making it irrevocable.

10. ELEMENTS OF A PRIVATE TRUST

a. Settlor Must Possess Capacity

A settlor must have the capacity to convey property. This requirement applies to both inter vivos trusts and testamentary trusts. Generally, this prerequisite does not impose any different standard on a settlor than the settlor would ordinarily face in an outright transfer of property. If a person can convey property free of trust, then the person may convey the property in trust. If a testamentary trust is involved, the settlor must have legal and testamentary capacity.

b. Trustee Appointment

A settlor may designate any person capable of taking, holding and transferring property as the trustee. However, a trust will not fail for want of a trustee. If a trustee has not been appointed in the trust instrument, or a designated trustee no longer exists, declines to take the position, or lacks capacity to serve, the court may appoint a trustee.

c. Settlor Must Have Trust Intent

For a trust to be valid, a settlor must have the present intent to create a trust. The mere use of trust language may be insufficient to demonstrate intent. Furthermore, no formal words are required to validate a trust instrument. In fact, the settlor does not have to use the word "trust." Trust intent is indicated by the presence of two elements: first, a split of legal title and equitable title, and second, the imposition of enforceable duties on the holder of legal title.

Precatory language is usually insufficient to express trust intent. For example, the words "I request," "I recommend," and "I hope" do not impose the legal obligation that is a necessary requirement of trust intent. These words, at most, create a moral obligation. In these situations, the court may examine the surrounding circumstances to determine if the settlor actually had trust intent.

d. Comply With Statute of Frauds

Trusts normally must be in writing to be enforceable. However, this writing may be less than a formal trust document. The exact formalities required to satisfy the statute of frauds vary among the states. Most states mandate that the settlor's signature appear on the trust instrument and the writing must evidence the major trust terms, e.g., identity of the beneficiaries, the property, and the trust purpose.

In some situations, a writing may not be necessary. For example, a trustee may voluntarily carry out the terms of the trust even though the statute of frauds has been violated and the trust is not legally enforceable. Also, some states allow oral trusts under certain circumstances if the trust consists of personal property.

NOTE

The settlor should have the trust instrument acknowledged by a notary, especially if the trust includes real property. In many states, acknowledgment is necessary for the trust instrument to be filed in the public record to give notice of the change in ownership.

LOCATE

1. What is your state's statute of frauds regarding trusts?

2. Are oral trusts permitted in your state? If yes, under what circumstances?

e. Trust Property Required

A trust must have property from its inception, otherwise the trust does not exist. If the settlor does not provide trust property, the court cannot attempt to fix the trust by supplying it with property. Trust property must be ascertainable with certainty.

Very few restrictions exist on the type of property that may be held in trust. Generally, any type of property which the settlor can transfer may be held in trust, e.g., present or future interests in real or personal property, tangible or intangible personal property, legal or equitable interests in property, and contract rights. For example, the contractual right to receive proceeds as a beneficiary of a life insurance policy may constitute trust property. Trust property could not include property which the settlor does not own, such as a spouse's share of community property, non-assignable contract rights, or expectancies, such as the hope of inheriting from someone who is still alive.

After a trust is properly created, it may receive additional property. However, property cannot be added to the trust if the terms of the trust prohibit additions or if the trustee finds the new property unacceptable.

Trust property must be transferred or delivered to the trustee. The trust only contains property if the property is effectively conveyed from the settlor to the trustee, in trust. Usually when real property is involved, delivery occurs when the deed is handed over to the trustee. If the settlor and the trustee are the same person, the settlor must deed the property from the settlor in a personal capacity to the settlor as a trustee. If the trust consists of personal property, the trust property should be physically delivered to the trustee. In a declaration of trust, the settlor/trustee should segregate and mark the property to indicate clearly that it is trust property. Alternatively, the settlor could execute a deed of gift, i.e., a document indicating that the settlor transferred property from the settlor as an individual to the settlor as a trustee.

LOCATE

1. What restrictions, if any, does your state impose on the type of property which may be held in trust?

2. Are any special rules applicable in your state to transfers of property into a trust?

f. Definite or Ascertainable Beneficiary

A beneficiary holds equitable title and has standing to enforce the trust. The court will not supply a private trust with a beneficiary if the settlor failed to do so. A beneficiary must have the capacity to take and hold title, but does not need to have the ability to transfer or manage the property. Remember, trusts are often established for individuals who cannot manage property themselves.

A private trust must have beneficiaries that are clearly ascertainable. Beneficiaries may be designated by class so long as class membership can be readily determined. For example, a settlor may properly designate his or her "children" as beneficiaries of a trust. Reference to a broad, indefinite class, such as "friends," is normally not a sufficiently definite class designation.

A settlor may name him- or herself as a beneficiary of a trust. A trustee may be a beneficiary provided the sole trustee is not the sole beneficiary.

Beneficiaries do not need to know they are beneficiaries of a trust. However, if a beneficiary is notified of the person's status as a beneficiary, it provides solid evidence of trust intent. Knowledge of a person's status as a beneficiary also gives the beneficiary the opportunity to enforce the trust.

LOCATE

Does your state impose any special requirements on a person to be a trust beneficiary?

g. Valid Trust Purpose

The settlor may create a trust for any purpose as long as it is not illegal or in violation of public policy. A trust cannot compel a trustee to commit acts that are criminal or tortious or acts that are contrary to public policy.

h. All Interests Must Vest Within the Rule Against Perpetuities Period

All interests in a trust must vest within the period mandated by the Rule Against Perpetuities which at common law was 21 years after some life in being at the time of the creation of the interest, plus a period of gestation. Many states have altered the Rule or provided exceptions and some states have abolished it completely.

LOCATE

1. What is the current formulation of the Rule Against Perpetuities in your state?

2. What is the effect of a Rule Against Perpetuities violation in your state?

NOTES

1. Charitable trusts are not bound by the Rule Against Perpetuities.

2. For a discussion of how preventive compliance may avoid Rule Against Perpetuities problems, see David M. Becker, *Tailoring Perpetuities Provisions to Avoid Problems*, PROB. & PROP., Mar./Apr. 1995, at 10.

3. About one-half of the states have completely abolished or substantially reformed the Rule Against Perpetuities with regard to trusts (but not necessarily with regard to other types of property interests). In these states, settlors may create *dynasty trusts* which last indefinitely and restrict benefits to remote descendants of the settlor. The decision to abolish the Rule in these

states was, at least in part, an economic decision to encourage wealthy settlors to bring their property into these states, establish trusts, employ local trustees and attorneys, and pay local taxes. See Chapter 10(E).

4. For further information, see ROBERT J. LYNN AND GRAYSON M.P. MCCOUCH, INTRODUCTION TO ESTATE PLANNING §§ 11.1–11.8 (5th ed. 2004).

DRAFT

Draft a savings provision to protect a trust from a Rule Against Perpetuities violation.

11. TRANSFERABILITY OF BENEFICIARY'S INTEREST

a. Generally

If the settlor has not placed any restrictions on the beneficiary's ability to transfer equitable title, a beneficiary can transfer the interest provided the beneficiary has legal capacity to do so. Thus, a beneficiary could sell the beneficial interest or transfer this interest by inter vivos gift, will, or intestacy. Also, if no provision in the trust instrument prevents it, creditors can attach the beneficiary's equitable interest.

Typically, the settlor's intent is frustrated if beneficiaries transfer and creditors attach. Settlors use two common methods to restrict a beneficiary's ability to transfer the equitable interest, either voluntarily or involuntarily. First, settlors give the beneficiary only life interests in trust property. A life interest gives the beneficiary nothing to transfer at death. Second, settlors insert spendthrift provisions in the trust instruments.

b. Spendthrift Clauses

Spendthrift clauses are almost always included in trust instruments, unless prohibited by state law. A typical spendthrift provision has two prongs. First, the beneficiary is prohibited from transferring his or her equitable interest in the trust. Second, the beneficiary's creditors are prevented from reaching the beneficiary's interest in the trust.

Spendthrift clauses are designed to protect a beneficiary's interest from the beneficiary's own improvidence and personal creditors. A settlor generally intends for trust property to benefit the designated beneficiary, not the beneficiary's assignees or creditors. A spendthrift clause insures that this intent is not frustrated. But, a spendthrift clause protects trust property only while it remains in the trust. Once property is distributed to a beneficiary, the protection of the spendthrift provision ends.

The settlor does not need to show that a beneficiary is incapable of managing the trust property to obtain the advantages of a spendthrift clause. Although most states enforce spendthrift provisions, some situations require that the clause be unenforceable due to public policy concerns. For example, in most states, a settlor cannot use a spendthrift clause to protect the settlor's own property. In addition, some states allow certain claims to take priority over the spendthrift clause, such as child support and claims for necessaries. Furthermore, federal tax claims will usually be able to penetrate the spendthrift shield.

NOTE

See Chapter 10(D) for additional information on the use of spendthrift provisions to provide asset protection.

LOCATE

1. Does your state permit spendthrift provisions?

2. What restrictions does your state impose on the enforceability of a spendthrift provision?

3. Does your state enforce a spendthrift clause if the settlor is a beneficiary, the so-called *self-settled spendthrift trust*?

DRAFT

Draft the broadest spendthrift limitation allowed under the law of your state.

12. DISCRETIONARY TRUSTS

Because the settlor cannot predict the needs of the beneficiary, the settlor usually does not want to provide the beneficiary with a fixed benefit. The settlor wants trust distributions to vary with the needs of the beneficiary and the trust's income. To accomplish this objective, a settlor may create a discretionary trust, also known as a *spray* or *sprinkle* trust. This type of trust gives the trustee the discretion to determine which beneficiaries to pay and how much to pay each.

The beneficiary of a discretionary trust has no right to a distribution from the trust until the trustee decides to make one. Likewise, creditors of the beneficiary cannot reach the trust property. When a distribution is made to the beneficiary, however, creditors can reach the distributed amount. As with spendthrift trusts, trust property in a discretionary trust can be reached by a creditor if the settlor and the beneficiary are the same person as well as in certain other situations where public policy requires it.

The settlor may impose restrictions on the trustee's discretion, e.g., no more than a stated amount per year per beneficiary or grant the trustee unrestricted discretion. Usually, a settlor intends for a trustee to exercise substituted judgment for the settlor, that is, a trustee is to make a decision to distribute property the same way the settlor would have made the decision.

DRAFT

The settlor decides to create a trust in favor of the settlor's three children. The settlor wants the trustee to have discretion to pay each beneficiary an amount the trustee determines is appropriate according to the trustee's opinion. The trust is to terminate on January 1, 2020. The trustee may use both income and principal, but any amount used from principal is to reduce the beneficiary's share when the trust terminates. Draft a discretionary trust provision to accomplish this settlor's intent.

13. SUPPORT TRUSTS

A trust which limits a trustee's ability to distribute to an amount necessary for the beneficiary's support is known as a support trust. This type of restriction on a trustee's ability to make distributions to a beneficiary is very common. Support typically encompasses the beneficiary's health care, education, maintenance, and support. A support trust may or may not be discretionary. To carry out the settlor's intent to provide support for the beneficiary, most courts hold that these trusts are impliedly spendthrift.

If the trust instrument is silent, the standard of support is usually deemed to be the beneficiary's accustomed standard of living prior to becoming a beneficiary of the trust. To insure that the settlor's intent is carried out, the trust instrument should define "support." The settlor needs to state whether support payments are to be used to provide a beneficiary with a lavish lifestyle or simply to serve as a safety net. In defining the appropriate standard of support, the settlor should explain whether the trustee may, must, or may not consider a beneficiary's other resources, number of dependents, or other factors.

DRAFT

Using the same facts from the discretionary trust drafting assignment, draft a support trust provision to accomplish the settlor's intent.

14. DISCLAIMERS

A beneficiary may want to disclaim the beneficiary's interest in the trust for many reasons. The burdens of property ownership, potential environmental liability, personal creditors, or tax liability may discourage a beneficiary from accepting trust benefits. A disclaimer may be complete or partial. Disclaimers are irrevocable.

To disclaim an interest in a trust effectively, a beneficiary must follow state and federal requirements which normally mandate a prompt disclaimer, usually within nine months, which complies with certain formalities. A disclaimer must occur before the property is accepted or otherwise used by the beneficiary. Because a beneficiary has no control over who benefits from the disclaimed property, the settlor should name alternate beneficiaries so that the trust does not fail.

See Chapter 4(H) for a more detailed discussion of disclaimers.

15. CHARITABLE TRUSTS

a. Liberally Construed

Because charitable trusts benefit society, courts liberally construe their terms and apply special rules in their construction. In construing a charitable trust's terms, the court looks at the purpose of the trust and construes the terms so that the charitable purpose is fulfilled.

b. Requirements

The requirements for a valid charitable trust are the same as for a private trust, except in the areas detailed below. As discussed above in relation to private trusts, charitable trusts typically require trust intent, a written trust instrument, trust property, a trustee with enforceable duties, and a settlor with capacity to convey property. The Rule Against Perpetuities does not apply to a charitable trust. If a trust fails to meet the additional requirements for a charitable trust, it may still be possible to enforce it as a private trust.

c. Indefinite Beneficiaries

Unlike private trusts, charitable trusts must be for the benefit of a sufficiently large or indefinite class of beneficiaries so the community is interested in its enforcement.

d. Trust Purpose

No bright line rule can be used to determine whether a trust purpose is charitable. Courts usually apply a "generally accepted" standard, i.e., the courts ask if the community would generally accept the trust's purpose as charitable.

The relief of poverty, advancement of education, advancement of religion, promotion of health, and governmental or municipal projects are normally considered legitimate charitable purposes. Courts tend to be more lenient in assessing a trust's purpose when it is established for a religious purpose. In this situation, a trust may be considered charitable as long as the religious purpose is not criminal or against public policy. Ordinarily, a trust established to advance a general idea or concept is considered charitable. Courts are less likely, however, to hold that a trust advancing the settlor's unusual personal views is charitable.

e. Cy Pres Doctrine

Courts may use the cy pres doctrine to preserve a charitable trust which would otherwise fail for lack of a charitable beneficiary. Generally, the need to use cy pres is triggered by a change in circumstances which makes it impossible, illegal, or impractical to carry out the original trust purpose.

Cy pres allows a court to alter the dispositive provisions of a charitable trust to fulfill the settlor's intent. The court applies this doctrine of equitable approximation so that the trust property is used for a charitable purpose similar to the original purpose specified in the trust instrument. To use cy pres, a court must find that the settlor had a general charitable intent, i.e., a charitable intent broader than the intent which cannot now be carried out. If the settlor's intent was specific, cy pres is unavailable.

QUESTION

How do you take the doctrine of cy pres into account when drafting a charitable trust or a will making a charitable gift?

f. Enforcement

The state's attorney general is usually the person charged with enforcing a charitable trust. Other individuals, such as the settlor, lack standing to enforce the trust unless they can show a special interest not shared by the general public.

PART II. TRUST ADMINISTRATION

What do you do when you discover that you or your client has been named as a trustee? This section begins by briefly outlining the steps a trustee must take in administering a trust. The sections which follow discuss areas of trust administration which are particularly important to consider when drafting a trust instrument.

1. INITIATING ADMINISTRATION

a. Decide to Accept

A person may be unwilling or unable to accept the position of trustee for many reasons. A person may want to avoid the responsibility or the potential liability of being a trustee. Lack of expertise, incompetence, or an insufficient trustee fee are other reasons to decline a trustee position. No duties are imposed and no liability attaches until a trustee accepts the position. State law provides the appropriate acceptance methods.

LOCATE

How does a trustee accept a trust under the law of your state?

b. Post Bond

Trustees are often required to post bond to protect the beneficiaries from evil trustee conduct. State law determines whether bond is presumed to be required or waived. A settlor may waive or require bond by an express provision in the trust instrument. In addition, some states exempt certain trustees from the bond requirement.

LOCATE

1. What is your state's presumption regarding bond?

2. Are any types of trustees exempted from posting bond in your state? If yes, what types?

DRAFT

Draft two trust provisions—one waiving bond and one requiring bond.

c. Register Trust

In a few states, trusts need to be registered in the public records. See U.P.C. § 7–101.

LOCATE

Does a trust need to be registered in your state? If yes, what is the procedure?

d. Obtain Control/Possession of Trust Property

1) Earmark

A trustee must obtain possession of the trust property and label the property as belonging to the trust. The marking must be clear so third parties, e.g., the trustee's personal creditors and heirs/will beneficiaries, know it is trust property and thus not subject to their claims. Holding trust assets in the name of a third party (often called a *nominee*) may be allowed with some assets such as corporate securities. Trustees are usually held liable for losses that result from a failure to earmark.

LOCATE

May the trustee hold any property in nominee form under the law of your state? If yes, is there a special procedure?

2) Avoid Commingling

A trustee must keep trust property separate from the trustee's own property and the property of other trusts. However, corporate trustees are often allowed to commingle property from several trusts in common trust funds to diversify and take advantage of greater investment opportunities.

LOCATE

Does your state have a statute authorizing corporate trustees to maintain common trust funds?

e. Ascertain Identity and Location of Beneficiaries

A trustee has a duty to locate the beneficiaries of the trust. The beneficiaries' names and addresses must be ascertained so the trustee knows who receives the trust benefits and where to send them.

f. Follow Instructions of the Trust Instrument

The trustee must follow the instructions of the trust instrument regarding trust investments, management of the trust property, and distributions to the beneficiaries.

g. Follow Requirements of Applicable Law

A trustee must also follow the requirements of state law. If the applicable state law conflicts with instructions set forth in the trust instrument, the provisions in the trust instrument usually prevail unless the trust provision is illegal, contrary to public policy, or the statute's application is mandatory.

h. Exercise Appropriate Standard of Care

A trustee must exercise the appropriate standard of care in performing all trustee duties. State law usually specifies a high standard, but the settlor can reduce or increase the standard of care with a provision in the trust instrument.

i. Exercise High Degree of Loyalty

A trustee is a fiduciary and thus must exercise a high degree of loyalty. The trustee must avoid self-dealing and conflicts of interest unless the settlor expressly permits such conduct in the trust instrument.

j. Failure to Comply Results in Personal Liability

If a trustee fails to comply with the requirements and duties of trust administration, the trustee can be held personally liable. A breach of duty may result in civil and criminal penalties.

2. STANDARD OF CARE

a. In General

A trustee must perform all duties following the required standard of care. State law usually specifies the standard of care to which a trustee must adhere, but the settlor may specify a different standard in the trust instrument. Most states use a standard which is some version of a reasonably prudent person test. This standard holds a trustee personally liable for mere negligence.

However, a trustee is not an insurer of the trust's success. Therefore, a trustee is liable for losses or depreciation of trust property only when the trustee's conduct falls beneath the required standard of care. A breach of duty must exist for personal liability to attach.

LOCATE

By what standard is a trustee's conduct judged under the law of your state?

b. Exculpatory Provisions

The settlor may not want to impose this high standard of care on a trustee, especially if the trustee is a family member. Thus, a settlor may reduce the applicable standard of care with an exculpatory clause. Jurisdictions vary as to the validity and enforceability of exculpatory provisions. Under the law of most states, the provisions will protect the trustee from liability for ordinary negligent conduct. An exculpatory provision may not excuse reckless, intentional, or bad faith conduct because the enforcement of such a provision would be against public policy.

LOCATE AND DRAFT

Are exculpatory clauses valid under the law of your state? If yes, draft the broadest exculpatory clause allowed.

3. INVESTMENTS

The Uniform Prudent Investor Act has been adopted by over forty states and provides for trust investments to be judged by the prudent investor or portfolio standard. Under this "total asset management" approach, the appropriateness of investments is based on the performance of the entire trust portfolio, instead of by examining each investment individually. A prudent investor could decide that the best investment strategy is to select some assets that appreciate and others that earn income, as well as some investments that are rock-solid balanced with some that have a reasonable degree of risk. In selecting investments, the trustee should incorporate risk and return objectives that are reasonably suited to the trust. Different trusts may call for different investment approaches depending on the trustee's abilities, the trust's purposes, the beneficiary's needs, and other circumstances. See Restatement (Third) of Trusts; Edward C. Halbach, Jr., *Trust Investment Law in the Third Restatement,* 27 REAL PROP., PROB. & TR. J. 407 (1992).

A settlor may alter the rules regarding investments in the trust instrument, either expanding or restricting the types of allowable investments.

A trustee must review investments on a periodic basis to ascertain whether they are still proper. The time period for review depends on the type of property, i.e., how rapidly does the property's value, income, and appreciation potential change. As a successor trustee, all prior investments must be reviewed. The new trustee must get out of bad investments, and if necessary, take action against a former trustee for losses resulting from breaches of duty.

LOCATE

By what standard are trust investments judged under the law of your state?

4. TRUSTEE POWERS

a. Sources of Trustee Powers

There are four main sources of trustee powers: (1) the trust instrument, (2) state statutes, (3) the common law, and (4) court orders. In the trust instrument, a settlor may expand or limit the statutory and common law powers of a trustee. The details of trustee powers statutes vary among states. Some states have extensive provisions while other states have limited codification. Approximately ten states have enacted the Uniform Trustees' Powers Act. States with few statutory provisions rely heavily on the common law powers of a trustee, also known as the implied powers. Common law gives a trustee all the necessary or appropriate powers required to carry out the trust's purpose. Court orders may also expand or restrict the powers of a trustee.

LOCATE

What is the statutory authority for trustee powers in your state?

QUESTION

What non-statutory powers might a settlor wish to grant a trustee? Why?

b. Multiple Trustees

The settlor may appoint multiple trustees for many reasons. For example, a settlor may wish to allocate duties, establish a check on each trustee's actions, take advantage of differing expertise, or ensure a split of title. When several trustees serve simultaneously, the majority usually rules. Ties in trustee voting are likely to require a court resolution. Thus, the settlor should appoint an odd number of trustees.

c. Directory Trusts

A settlor may require a trustee to follow someone else's directions such as a co-trustee or financial planner. This arrangement is known as a directory trust. A trustee is typically not liable for any loss resulting from following another individual's instructions under these circumstances.

5. PRINCIPAL AND INCOME

Settlors often grant certain beneficiaries the income benefits of trust property and other beneficiaries the principal upon trust termination. This arrangement usually creates a conflict between the income and remainder beneficiaries. Income beneficiaries want the trust property to contain high-yield items which earn high rates of return. They usually do not care about principal growth. Remainder beneficiaries, on the other hand, want the trustee to invest in high-growth items which appreciate in value. They usually do not care about income. A conflict also arises in determining how to apportion trust receipts and expenditures.

To resolve this conflict, a settlor may provide the trustee with express instructions in the trust instrument on how to invest and how to divide burdens and benefits between trust principal and income. A settlor may also leave these matters to the trustee's discretion in which case the trustee would resolve the conflict by diversifying, i.e., investing in both high-yield and high-growth investments, and allocating in a reasonable manner. If the trust instrument is silent, state statutory or common law governs the allocation scheme. Most states have enacted the 1997 version of the Uniform Principal and Income Act.

To avoid the accounting hassle of allocating receipts and expenses between the income and remainder interests, as well as to reduce the inherent conflict of interest between current and future beneficiaries, some settlors adopt a *unitrust* approach. The current beneficiary of a unitrust is entitled to receive a fixed percentage of the value of the trust property annually. The current beneficiary may or may not also be entitled to additional distributions. For example, the trust could provide: "Trustee shall distribute 5% of the value of the trust property to Current Beneficiary annually. Trustee has the discretion to make additional distributions to Current Beneficiary for Current Beneficiary's health, education, and support. Upon Current Beneficiary's death, Trustee shall deliver all remaining trust property to Remainder Beneficiary." Under a unitrust, both beneficiaries have the same goal—they want the value of the property in the trust to increase. It does not matter to them whether the increase in value is due to receipts traditionally nominated income (e.g., interest or rent) or principal (i.e., appreciation). All increases inure to the benefit of all beneficiaries. Likewise, all beneficiaries share in the expenses regardless of their usual characterization.

LOCATE

What type of statutory provisions does your state have regarding the allocation of receipts and expenditures between principal and income?

6. TRUSTEE DUTIES

a. Loyalty and Good Faith

A trustee owes the beneficiary a duty of loyalty and utmost good faith in all matters pertaining to the trust. A trustee must avoid conflicts of interest and cannot favor any beneficiary over another unless so provided in the trust instrument.

b. Avoid Self–Dealing

A trustee must avoid self-dealing. This duty prevents the trustee and individuals or entities closely connected to the trustee, such as relatives, employers, employees, and business associates, from buying trust property, selling property to the trust, and borrowing trust funds. Likewise, a trustee may not sell to another trust for which the trustee is also serving as a trustee. State statutes may provide the details of the duty not to self-deal. In some states, the instrument can vary the duties; however, it may depend on the individual or corporate nature of the trustee.

A trustee is personally liable for all profits the trustee makes because of a self-dealing transaction, even if the transaction was in good faith and for a fair consideration. This tough standard acts as a deterrent and avoids the cumbersome process of proving actual fraud or other improper conduct.

LOCATE

Locate your state's statutes detailing the trustee's duty to avoid self-dealing transactions.

c. Avoid Improper Delegation of Duties

Traditionally, a trustee could delegate ministerial duties but could not delegate discretionary acts. However, most states now follow a prudent trustee rule. The trustee may delegate any investment or management decision provided a prudent trustee of comparable skills could properly delegate under the same circumstances. The trustee must exercise reasonable care, skill, and caution in selecting the agent. The trustee must also periodically review the agent's actions. If the delegation is proper, the trustee will not be personally liable to the beneficiaries or the trust for the decisions or actions of the agent. Of course, the agent will be liable to the trust if the agent fails to exercise reasonable care in performing a delegated function.

7. DUTY TO MAKE PROPERTY PRODUCTIVE

The trustee has a duty to make trust property productive unless otherwise provided in the trust instrument. For example, this duty will not apply if the trust's purpose is to preserve certain property in its original form (e.g., the family home). A trustee has a reasonable amount of time to make trust property productive, and if the property cannot be made productive, the trustee should dispose of this property. If possible, a trustee should diversify to take advantage of various types of investments.

QUESTION

Why would a settlor want a trustee to retain unproductive property?

8. DUTY TO ACCOUNT

A trustee must keep accurate records of all trust activities and allow the beneficiaries to have reasonable access to the records. The purpose behind this duty is to allow the beneficiaries to see how the trust is being handled so that the beneficiary has the information needed to enforce the trust. A settlor cannot waive the trustee's duty to account because to do so is against public policy as it would prevent beneficiaries from enforcing trusts.

Some states mandate the trustee to render an accounting annually while other states only require accountings upon the request of a beneficiary or other interested person or upon court order. To ease the burden of rendering an accounting, trust records should be kept in a form that allows a trustee to produce an accounting quickly. A trustee may hire an accountant to assist in the preparation of the trust's financial records. Although an accounting may not be required or requested, it is a good policy to do an annual accounting to develop a relationship of trust between the trustee and the beneficiaries.

LOCATE

1. When must a trustee render an accounting under the law of your state?

2. What must a trustee's accounting contain in your state?

9. TRUSTEE'S LIABILITY TO THIRD PARTIES

a. Contract Liability

In most states, a contract plaintiff can sue the trustee in the trustee's representative capacity and recover directly against the trust property if the contract was within the trustee's authority. In addition, a contract plaintiff can hold a trustee personally liable. The trustee can avoid personal liability by including an express provision in the contract which excludes the trustee's personal liability. In some states, a trustee can raise a rebuttable presumption of an intent to exempt the trustee from personal liability by adding the phrase "as trustee" after the trustee's signature on the contract. Before signing a contract between a third party and a trustee, the trustee should usually take steps to avoid personal liability.

LOCATE

What is the law in your state regarding the liability of a trustee on contracts?

QUESTION

In what situation may a trustee not be able to avoid signing a contract which keeps the trustee's potential for liability alive?

b. Tort Liability

Depending on state law, a tort plaintiff, like a contract plaintiff, may be able to sue a trustee in the trustee's representative capacity. Of course, a tort plaintiff may also sue a trustee personally. The trustee may be responsible for the acts of agents following the state's respondeat superior laws. A trustee should obtain adequate insurance to protect against personal liability. The cost of this insurance is usually chargeable against trust property.

LOCATE

What is the law in your state regarding the liability of a trustee for torts?

10. JUDICIAL MODIFICATION OF TRUSTS

A beneficiary or trustee may petition a court to modify or terminate a trust. This process is often referred to as *deviation.* Courts use deviation in an attempt to carry out the presumed intent of the settlor. To avoid having a court guess at the settlor's intent, the settlor should plan for as many contingencies as possible in the trust instrument. If the court determines that deviation is appropriate, a court may order a variety of things, e.g., change the trustee, alter the trust terms, authorize a trustee to do acts not allowed by the trust, prohibit a trustee from doing acts allowed by the trust, or terminate the trust. Deviation is used to alter administrative provisions, not dispositive provisions.

Deviation is discretionary and a court needs a reason to deviate. For example, if the purposes of the trust are fulfilled and the trust instrument does not state what a trustee is to do next, the court may deviate. Also, deviation can occur if the purposes of the trust have become illegal or impossible to fulfill. A change in circumstances is the most common reason for deviation, i.e., because circumstances not known to or anticipated by the settlor have arisen, compliance with the terms of the trust would defeat or substantially impair the accomplishment of the purposes of the trust.

LOCATE

Under what circumstances may a court modify a trust under the law of your state?

11. TRUSTEE COMPENSATION

A trust instrument should expressly state whether a trustee is to be compensated and, if so, how compensation is to be determined. Most states presume that a trustee is entitled to reasonable compensation if the trust instrument is silent on the matter. To determine what is reasonable, a vast array of factors are considered, e.g., trust income, a trustee's experience and skill, the risk assumed, the time involved, the difficulty of the work, the custom in the community, etc. See Chapter 8(H) for a detailed discussion of fiduciary compensation.

LOCATE

What is your state's presumption regarding a trustee's compensation?

12. TRUST TERMINATION

The most common reason a trust terminates is because of the express terms of the trust. The trust instrument usually ties termination to a date or event. If a trust is revocable, termination can occur upon the settlor's revocation. A trust will also end when it runs out of property. A court may find it necessary to terminate a trust because the trust purpose has been fulfilled or has become illegal or impossible to fulfill. Termination may also occur if all legal and equitable title becomes united in one person.

Upon termination, a trustee is responsible for winding up the trust business. To accomplish this, the trustee retains the powers of a trustee for a reasonable period after trust termination. The trustee then has the duty to distribute trust property to the remainder beneficiaries.

PART III. TRUST ENFORCEMENT

When selecting a method of enforcement, the trustee's conduct, as well as the result desired by the beneficiary, must be considered.

1. REMEDIES AGAINST THE TRUSTEE

Before a breach of trust occurs, several remedies against the trustee are available. The court can issue a decree ordering the trustee to carry out the trustee's duties. Alternatively, if the trustee is threatening to commit a breach of trust, a beneficiary or co-trustee may obtain an injunction or restraining order. If the court fears that the trustee may disobey an injunction or other court order, a receiver can be appointed to take immediate charge of the property. Another possible remedy against the trustee would be to require or increase bond.

Even though the trustee has not breached a fiduciary duty, a trustee can be forced to pay to the trust any profit the trustee made as a result of the administration of the trust. For the award of any other money damages, the beneficiary or co-trustee must show that the trustee breached a duty and that this breach caused the damage. Monetary damages may be awarded for lost value of trust property, profits the trustee earned, and profits the trust failed to earn. If the breach of trust was intentional, the court may also award punitive damages.

If a trustee breaches a fiduciary duty or has become incompetent or insolvent, a beneficiary or co-trustee may seek removal of the trustee. Courts are reluctant to remove a trustee if the trustee did not have evil intent, especially if the trustee was designated by the settlor. If a trustee is not sure how to act in a certain situation, the trustee may seek the court's advice by applying for a declaratory judgment.

A successor trustee may be responsible for breaches by a predecessor trustee. For personal liability to attach, a successor trustee must have knowledge of the breach and must have acted improperly under the circumstances. Improper conduct includes allowing the bad acts of a predecessor to continue, failing to make a reasonable effort to get the property back, and failing to make a reasonable effort to compel a redress.

In many states, breaches of trust resulting from the trustee's intentional, knowing, or reckless conduct may also lead to criminal liability.

2. REMEDIES AGAINST THE BENEFICIARY

Beneficiaries are generally not liable for the trustee's breaches of trust nor for liabilities of the trust in contract or tort. However, a beneficiary is liable under limited circumstances. For example, a beneficiary who participates in or consents to a breach of trust may be held liable. Liability also attaches if the beneficiary refuses to repay an excess distribution or wrongfully uses the trust property.

3. REMEDIES INVOLVING TRUST PROPERTY

Three main remedies involving trust property exist, i.e., tracing, subrogation, and marshaling. The goal of tracing is to recover the actual trust property or the proceeds or assets acquired through the use of the trust property. Tracing is used when the trust property, or its equivalent, can be located in the trustee's hands or in the hands of a non-bona fide purchaser. Tracing gives the beneficiary a superior claim to the trust property over the trustee's other creditors. If a beneficiary recovers through tracing, a beneficiary is not also entitled to damages because this would result in a double recovery.

Subrogation may be useful if the trust property cannot be recovered through tracing. If a trustee pays a personal debt with trust funds, equity will reinstate the debt, placing the beneficiaries in the same position as the creditor who was paid. If this creditor had a special right, such as a security interest, mortgage, or bankruptcy priority, then the beneficiaries can use that right against the trustee and other creditors.

If a creditor has a right to recover out of more than one fund or asset, that creditor must first resort to the fund or asset which will not interfere with the rights of another creditor, such as a trust beneficiary, who only has recourse to one of the funds or assets. This concept is called marshaling.

4. CAUSES OF ACTION AGAINST THIRD PARTIES

In some cases, third parties are faced with liability to the trust. For example, a person who assists a trustee in breaching a trust is liable to the trust. Likewise, a third party who contracts with the trust and subsequently breaches that contract is liable. Additionally, a person is liable for torts committed against or damage caused to the trust property.

5. BARRING OF REMEDIES

A person may be barred from pursuing a trust remedy in a variety of ways. First, the beneficiaries may give prior approval to or ratify the actions of the trustee. All beneficiaries must consent to the approval or ratification if it is to give the trustee complete protection. Furthermore, since beneficiaries must have full legal capacity to consent, guardian consent is needed for beneficiaries who are minors, incompetents, or unknown.

Second, remedies against a trustee are barred if the settlor approves of the trustee's conduct in the trust instrument. Likewise, a valid exculpatory clause restricts the situations in which a trustee may be held liable.

A third bar to seeking a remedy against a trustee is a valid court decree approving the conduct. A court usually has the power to grant relief in any case it deems fit. The court may release a trustee from any liability, restriction, duty, or obligation imposed by the trust instrument, state statute, or common law.

Fourth, the running of the applicable statute of limitations may prevent a party from pursuing a remedy.

Finally, the equitable defense of laches may bar a remedy. The person raising the defense of laches must show that the other party's unreasonable delay in asserting rights caused a disadvantage to the person claiming the defense.

LOCATE

What is the statute of limitations in your state for breach of fiduciary duty?

CHAPTER 3

PROBATE AVOIDANCE TECHNIQUES

■ ■ ■

A. INTRODUCTION

Your client may wish to control the disposition of property upon death but also to avoid, at least partially, the traditional disposition at death options. That is, the prospective decedent does not want all of the person's property to pass via intestacy or be controlled by a valid will. This chapter examines why a person may want property to pass outside of the probate process and discusses some of the most commonly used probate avoidance techniques.

UNIFORM PROBATE CODE

Section 6–101. Nonprobate Transfers on Death.

(a) A provision for a nonprobate transfer on death in an insurance policy, contract of employment, bond, mortgage, promissory note, certificated or uncertificated security, account agreement, custodial agreement, deposit agreement, compensation plan, pension plan, individual retirement plan, employee benefit plan, trust, conveyance, deed of gift, marital property agreement, or other written instrument of a similar nature is nontestamentary. This subsection includes a written provision that:

(1) money or other benefits due to, controlled by, or owned by a decedent before death must be paid after the decedent's death to a person whom the decedent designates either in the instrument or in a separate writing, including a will, executed either before or at the same time as the instrument, or later;

(2) money due or to become due under the instrument ceases to be payable in the event of death of the promisee or the promisor before payment or demand; or

(3) any property controlled by or owned by the decedent before death which is the subject of the instrument passes to a person the decedent designates either in the instrument or in a separate

writing, including a will, executed either before or at the same time as the instrument, or later.

(b) This section does not limit rights of creditors under other laws of this State.

B. REASONS TO AVOID PROBATE*

In many states, probate is an expensive, cumbersome, and lengthy process. Avoiding the probate system is a key consideration when planning an estate in these jurisdictions. Even in states with inexpensive and efficient administrations, there are still compelling reasons to structure some of your client's assets so they pass via non-testamentary arrangements. This section enumerates potential benefits of using non-probate transfers. Note that no particular non-probate technique will achieve all of the potential benefits.

1. PROVIDE NON–ESTATE PLANNING BENEFITS

Every day, your clients make non-probate property transfers for a variety of reasons unrelated to estate planning. Non-probate transfers fall generally into one of two categories: non-gratuitous and gratuitous. Examples of non-gratuitous transfers include buying groceries, going out for dinner, renting videos, paying tuition, repaying loans, making rent or mortgage payments, and taking vacations. These types of non-gratuitous transfers lack significant estate planning components, other than the fact that they change the composition of the estate.

Clients make gratuitous non-probate transfers on a fairly regular basis as well. For example, your client may buy a relative or friend a birthday present, take a significant other out on a date, or make a contribution to a favorite charity. Each of these transfers has an estate planning component because, at a minimum, they lessen the value of your client's estate. Even when a client makes a non-probate transfer as part of a comprehensive estate plan, a side benefit of the transfer may be unrelated to estate planning.

2. ACCELERATE ASSET DISTRIBUTION

The probate process creates a gap between the time when your client dies and the heirs or beneficiaries physically receive your client's property. This delay may range from months, to years, and even to decades, especially if the client's will is contested. This delay is potentially damaging from three perspectives.

First, the heirs and beneficiaries are unable to use the property. During the delay period, the educational, medical, or other needs of the

* This section is adapted from GERRY W. BEYER, WILLS, TRUSTS, AND ESTATES—EXAMPLES AND EXPLANATIONS ch. 13 (5th ed. 2012).

survivors may go unmet because they cannot reach your client's property. To take an extreme example, assume that Testator left the entire estate to Pat, a friend in need of an expensive life-saving operation. Testator's family contests the will and thus Pat has no access to the funds. Before resolution of the contest, Pat dies because Pat could not afford proper medical care.

Second, your client's property may not be able to withstand a gap in management. Some types of property require constant monitoring to maintain value. Corporate securities need to be traded as the market dictates, crops need to be timely harvested and then processed or sold, and foreign investments must be evaluated in light of the constantly changing world political scene. The gap between the client's death and the beginning of an administration depends on how quickly the client's survivors take the appropriate steps to open the estate. Even if they act quickly, there is still a gap during which substantial losses may occur. Some of the non-probate techniques allow the client to appoint a property manager who will be able to take over immediately upon the client's death.

Third, your client's survivors may have to endure the emotional impact of a prolonged administration. The constant reminder of a loved one's death that results from a drawn out administration may prevent closure and keep the survivors from moving on with their lives.

3. REDUCE ESTATE PLANNING AND ADMINISTRATION EXPENSES

Estate planning and administration are relatively expensive procedures. The costs are based on a variety of factors such as the size of your client's estate and its composition. For example, planning for cash, bank deposits, and other relatively liquid assets is usually inexpensive while businesses often require more complex and sophisticated planning. Another key factor is the law of the state in which the estate is administered. Some states have expensive, cumbersome, and lengthy probate procedures while others have procedures which are relatively inexpensive and efficient. Expenses incurred in both planning and administration include attorney's fees, personal representative fees, and court costs. On the other hand, some of the non-probate transfer techniques are free or very inexpensive to use and some may even be done without legal assistance. Of course, legal counsel may be needed to maximize the benefits of a particular technique and to avoid intent-defeating traps.

4. ENHANCE CONFIDENTIALITY

Most clients like to keep their financial and family matters private. During life, it is relatively easy to keep these matters confidential, unless your client is a celebrity or politician. A client needs only to be careful with whom the client shares intimate details. However, an entirely different situation exists when your client dies. All estate proceedings are on the public record. Typical documents filed in an administration include inventories of all of the client's assets, the appraised value of each asset, and the names of the new owners, be they intestate heirs or will beneficiaries. Of course, the will itself is public record. A curious person needs no excuse to view, copy, distribute, or publish the documents. Used properly, however, many of the non-probate transfer methods can escape conspicuous notation on the public record or in other readily available sources.

5. MINIMIZE TAXES

Some non-probate transfer techniques have the potential of saving your client a considerable amount of income, gift, and estate taxes. It is important to note that many non-probate transfers may have no tax effect or an unanticipated effect and thus must be used with caution in estates large or complex enough to make tax planning an issue. You should also note that the *taxable estate*, that is, the property which is subject to federal or state death taxes, may include many assets that are not part of the client's probate estate. See Chapter 4(C).

6. RETAIN FLEXIBILITY

Intestate succession is inflexible; property passes without regard to your client's intent. A will provides many opportunities for your client to control the transfer of property, but there are limits on what a client can do in the will, either from a legal or practical perspective, and, of course, the disposition is not effective until the client dies and the will is properly probated. Many non-probate transfers, however, allow their users to exert greater control and individualization over the use and distribution of assets. In addition, non-probate transfers may be able to provide your client with immediate benefits such as tax savings and disability protection.

7. CHANGE WITH LESS DIFFICULTY

Many formalities are required to execute a valid will as well as to amend an already existing will. Changing an existing will is a hassle and may require your client to exert almost as much effort as making the will in the first place. On the other hand, your client may update and revise many of the non-probate arrangements with a minimum of effort thus avoiding extended procedures and technicalities.

8. PROTECT FROM CREDITORS

Most property that passes through your client's probate estate is subject to the claims of your client's creditors. The primary reason for having an estate administration is to make certain your client does not escape financial obligations merely by dying before paying them in full. If the property does not pass through the probate estate, however, it may escape liability for debts.

The use of some non-probate transfers to avoid creditors is very controversial. Creditors generally accept that they cannot reach certain non-probate assets such as the proceeds of a life insurance policy which is payable to a named beneficiary. This makes sense because the creditors did not have the ability to reach the proceeds while the insured was alive. At most, they may have been able to reach the policy's cash value, if any, assuming the policy was not exempt from creditors under state law. However, creditors are reluctant to agree that they cannot pursue other non-probate transfers to satisfy their claims, such as property passing via a trust which your client could have revoked while alive. The creditors do not think that the death of a debtor should protect assets that were not protected during the debtor's life. See Chapter 10(D).

9. ISOLATE FROM CONTEST

Non-probate transfers are often more resilient to contest than wills, although individuals dissatisfied with non-probate transfers may attack them on many of the same grounds which may be used to contest a will, such as the transferor's lack of mental capacity or that the transfer was the result of undue influence or fraud. Your client may make arrangements for non-probate transfers long before death. The non-probate techniques may require your client to engage in ongoing transactions with people who can testify to the client's capacity, such as bank officials, insurance agents, business associates, and trust officers. Thus, individuals who wish to sustain a non-probate transfer have a greater likelihood of locating evidence to rebut a contestant's claims.

10. INCREASE UNDERSTANDABILITY

A will may be a complex instrument, especially if your client has complicated distribution desires or a desire to minimize taxes. Some, but by no means all, of the non-probate transfer methods are effective at handling distribution wishes and tax reduction without as much confusion. Use of transfer methods which your client may more readily understand increases the likelihood that you are carrying out the client's intent.

NOTES AND QUESTIONS

1. Can you think of any other reasons your client may want to avoid probate?

2. As you study each of the non-testamentary techniques in this chapter, evaluate them in light of the reasons for avoiding probate.

C. INTER VIVOS GIFTS

ROBERT J. LYNN AND GRAYSON M.P. McCOUCH, INTRODUCTION TO ESTATE PLANNING*

§§ 1.2–1.3, pages 4–6 (5th ed. 2004).

Making inter vivos gifts is sometimes recommended as an "estate planning" device. Whether it is wise in a particular case to make lifetime gifts is a matter of informed judgment. In arriving at that judgment, both the prospective donor and the donor's lawyer should remember that in the United States the average lifespan is growing longer and the proportion of older persons in the population is increasing. In times of economic recession, early retirement of employees is often "suggested" or "encouraged" in order to reduce costs for employers. Many people depend heavily on Social Security benefits, augmented by whatever pension benefits and other savings they may have accumulated, to maintain a decent standard of living in retirement. Property is a source of consideration and respect. Many an old person who would otherwise be shunted aside gets kind treatment because it is known or suspected (perhaps erroneously) that he or she is a person of some wealth. There are exceptions, of course, but generally speaking there is much to be said for keeping property until death. Refusal to make substantial lifetime gifts may frustrate or inconvenience those who would benefit from such transfers. But a prospective donor may find it easier to put up with their suppressed resentment while they wait than to endure their open contempt after the bulk of the donor's property has been transferred to them.

An inter vivos gift of real or personal property requires a subject matter of the intended gift, an intention on the part of the transferor (the "donor") to make a gift, a "delivery" of the subject matter of the gift, and an acceptance of the intended gift by the recipient (the "donee"). Acceptance seldom causes much difficulty. Indeed, there is a "presumption" of acceptance; unless it is demonstrated that the donee does not accept the gift, the donee is deemed to have accepted it. Intention to give might alone occasionally cause legal problems, but frequently intention is in doubt because of difficulties with the abstraction called "delivery".

Suppose that A owns a ring that she is wearing. She removes the ring, hands it to B, and says, "B, I give you this ring. It is yours." B takes the ring and says, "Thank you." A has made a gift to B because the subject matter of the intended gift, intention to give, acceptance, and delivery are clear. But suppose that A, instead of removing the ring, merely twirls it on her finger, and the words of both A and B are the same as those just described. In these circumstances there is no gift because there is no delivery (relinquishment of "dominion and control") by A. Furthermore, the lack of delivery casts a gift, but arguably she does not intend to do so presently—rather, she intends to make a gift at some future time.

IN RE COHN'S WILL

Supreme Court of New York, Appellate Division, First Department, 1919.
187 App. Div. 392, 176 N.Y.S. 225.

SHEARN, J.

This appeal involves the validity of a gift of certificates of stock, effected by the execution and delivery of an instrument of gift, unaccompanied by actual delivery of the certificates. On September 20, 1911, the decedent, Leopold Cohn, a resident of the city of New York, but then temporarily residing with his family at West End, N.J., wrote out and delivered to his wife, in the presence of his entire family, on his wife's birthday, the following paper: "West End, N.J., Sept. 20, 1911. 'I give this day to my wife, Sara K. Cohn, as a present for her (46th) forty-sixth birthday (500) five hundred shares of American Sumatra Tobacco Company common stock. Leopold Cohn.' The donor died six days after the delivery of this instrument. At the time of the gift, the donor was the owner of 7,213 shares of the common stock of the American Sumatra Tobacco Company, but the stock was in the name and possession of his firm of A. Cohn & Co. and deposited in a safe deposit box in the city of New York, which was in the name of and belonged to the firm. This firm consisted of the donor, his brother, Abraham, and his nephew, Leonard A. Cohn and was dissolved by the death of Abraham Cohn on August 30, 1911. Prior to that time, the firm had 18,033 shares of the Sumatra stock, in certificates of 100 shares each, standing in the firm name. On December 20, 1910, the stock had been charged off on the books and was not an asset of the firm after that time. The testator was entitled to 40 per cent., or 7,213 shares, of the stock held in the firm name, but there had never been an actual delivery of the certificates by the firm to the donor in his lifetime. Just prior to his death the donor had agreed to enter into a new partnership, and he was to contribute some of the shares to a new firm as an asset. On September 22, 1911, two days after the delivery of the instrument of gift, the donor directed his counsel to hurry the new partnership agreement, because he wished to get the Sumatra stock belonging to him, which was to be delivered when the new partnership agreement was signed, which matter was to be closed on September 26, 1911, the day the donor died. The execution and delivery of the instrument of gift was established by the testimony of the two daughters of the donor, who were present at the time of its delivery, and their testimony is to the effect that their father handed the paper to the mother, in the presence of the whole family, and said he gave it to her as a birthday present; that he had not possession of the stock, but as soon as he got it he would give it to her.

Some stress is laid by the appellants upon the testimony that the donor 'said that he could not give her the stock, because it was in the company, but as soon as he could get it he would give it to her,' which it is claimed evidences an intent to make a gift in the future, instead of a present gift. This contention is completely overborne by the wording of the instrument itself, which reads, 'I give this day;' also by the plain intention of the donor to make a birthday gift to his wife, the birthday being the day on which the instrument of gift was executed and delivered. When the donor explained that he could not 'give' her the stock that day, 'because it was in the company,' and said that 'as soon as he could get it he would give it to her,' it is quite obvious that he meant that he could not deliver the stock that day, but would as soon as he could get it."

There being no rights of creditors involved, no suggestion of fraud, the intention to make the birthday gift being conclusively established, the gift being evidenced by an instrument of gift executed and delivered to the donee on her birthday, and ever since retained by her, and the circumstances surrounding the making of the gift affording a reasonable and satisfactory excuse for not making actual delivery of the certificates at the time the gift was made, there was in my opinion a valid and effectual gift of the certificate mentioned in the instrument of gift.

There is no doubt that it had been held in a long line of cases in this state that delivery of the thing given is, as a general rule, one of the essential elements to constitute a valid gift. Beaver v. Beaver, 117 N.Y. 421, 22 N.E. 940, 6 L.R.A. 403, 15 Am.St.Rep. 531; Young v. Young, 80 N.Y. 422, 36 Am.St.Rep. 634. But it is equally true that the rule requiring actual delivery is not inflexible. Matter of Van Alstyne, 207 N.Y. 298, 100 N.E. 802; McGavic v. Cossum, 72 App.Div. 35, 76 N.Y.Supp. 305; Matter of Mills, 172 App.Div. 530, 158 N.Y.Supp. 1100, affirmed 219 N.Y. 642, 114 N.E. 1072. In Beaver v. Beaver, supra, it was said that the delivery may be symbolical, as where the donor gives to the donee a symbol which represents possession. It was held in McGavic v. Cossum, supra, where an instrument of gift of bonds was delivered, that actual delivery of the bonds was executed where the only reason for not making delivery was the feeble condition of the donor and the fact that the bonds were in the custody of a bank in a nearby city. It was said in Matter of Van Alstyne: 'The delivery necessary to consummate a gift must be as perfect as the nature of the property and the circumstances and surroundings of the parties will reasonably permit. * * * It is true that the old rule requiring an actual delivery of the [thing] given has been very largely relaxed, but a symbolical delivery is sufficient only when the conditions are so adverse to actual delivery as to make a symbolical delivery as nearly perfect and complete as the circumstances will allow.'

As the rule requiring delivery is clearly subject to exceptions, in order to apply it correctly in varying circumstances resort should be had to the reason for the rule. Under the civil law delivery was not requisite to a valid gift, but it was made a requisite by the common law as a matter of public policy, to prevent mistake and imposition. Noble v. Smith, 2 Johns. 52, 56, 3 Am.Dec. 399; Brinckerhoff v. Lawrence, 2 Sandf. Ch. 400, 406. The necessity of delivery where gifts resting in parol are asserted against the estates of decedents is obvious; but it is equally plain that there is no such impelling necessity when the gift is established by the execution and delivery of an instrument of gift. An examination of a large number of cases in this state discloses the significant facts that (1) in every case where the gift was not sustained, the gift rested upon parol evidence; and (2) in every case of a gift evidenced by the delivery of an instrument of gift, the gift has been sustained. In the former category are included the cases of Beaver v. Beaver, supra; Matter of Van Alstyne, supra; Jackson v. Twenty-Third St.Ry. Co., 88 N.Y. 520; Young v. Young, supra; Matter of Crawford, 113 N.Y. 560, 21 N.E. 692, 5 L.R.A. 71; Curry v. Powers, 70 N.Y. 212, 26 Am.St.Rep. 577; Gannon v. McGuire, 160 N.Y. 476, 55 N.E. 7, 73 Am.St.Rep. 694; Champney v. Blanchard, 39 N.Y. 111. In the latter category are included Hunter v. Hunter, 19 Barb. 631; Matson v. Abbey, 70 Hun. 475, 24 N.Y.Supp. 284, affirmed as to the gift, 141 N.Y. 179, 36 N.E. 11; McGavic v. Cossum, supra; Matter of Mills, supra.

In Young v. Young, supra, there was a writing, but it was not an instrument of gift; it was a mere declaration of the donor that the bonds were the property of the donee and expressly reserving an interest in the donor. While the court said in Ridden v. Thrall, 125 N.Y. 572, 26 N.E. 627, 11 L.R.A. 684, 21 Am.St.Rep. 758, in sustaining a gift causa mortis, where there was both a writing and delivery, that the writing alone was not sufficient, it is to be noted that the written instrument was not delivered to the donee. It is interesting to note that in Matson v. Abbey, supra, sustaining a gift evidenced by an instrument of assignment without delivery of the property assigned, the court quotes with approval the statement of the English law in Irons v. Smallpiece, 2 Barn. & Ald. 551, 552, made by Abbott, C.J.: "I am of opinion that by the law of England, in order to transfer property by gift, there must either be a deed or instrument of gift, or there must be an actual delivery of the thing to the donee."

Based upon decisions in numerous other jurisdictions, it is stated in 20 Cyc. 1197, that: "The general rule is that a gift of property evidenced by a written instrument executed by the donor is valid without a manual delivery of the property."

I am inclined to think that this is a broader statement than the New York cases would justify, especially in view of Matter of Van Alstyne, supra, for it does not assume a delivery of the instrument of gift. But in view of the decision of this court in McGavic v. Cossum, supra, it seems to me beyond serious question that the delivery of the instrument of gift in the instant case constituted a good symbolical delivery. In the McGavic Case a woman owning bonds which had been deposited by her in a bank for safe-keeping during an illness from which she died three weeks later gave to her niece the original memorandum of the purchase of the bonds indorsed with the following statement: "Poughkeepsie, November 23, 1901. I have this day given my niece, Fannie H. McGavic, bond 2000 Reg. 4 per cent. Delia C. Robinson." Mr. Justice McLaughlin said: "We are of the opinion that the plaintiff was entitled to the bonds; that what was done constituted a good gift inter vivos. Actual delivery, by reason of the illness of the owner of the bonds and their possession at that time by the bank, was physically impossible; but there was present, as evidenced by the writing of the deceased, not only the intention to then give, but also the intention to then deliver the thing given. The owner did all she could do in this respect. It was a good constructive or symbolical delivery, and this, under the circumstances, was sufficient to vest good title in the plaintiff. 14 Am. & Eng. Ency. of Law (2d ed.) 1021, and cases cited."

In the instant case, on the day the gift was made at West End, N.J., the certificates of stock were in a safe deposit box in New York City. Furthermore, there were the complications above referred to, in the partnership relations and in the fact that the certificates were in the partnership strong box, made out in the name of the firm. These were circumstances and surroundings tending to excuse manual delivery and to make a symbolical delivery effective. In addition, as was said by Justice McLaughlin in the McGavic Case: "There was present, as evidenced by the writing of the deceased, not only the intention to then give, but also the intention to then deliver the thing given. * * * It was a good constructive or symbolical delivery."

The instrument of gift was a symbol which represented the donee's right of possession. It was no more revocable than an assignment. A gift has been judicially defined as a voluntary transfer of property by one to another, without any consideration or compensation therefor. Gray v. Barton, 55 N.Y. 68, 14 Am.Rep. 181. A voluntary transfer or assignment unaccompanied by manual delivery was upheld, as we have seen, in Matson v. Abbey, supra. It must therefore have been held irrevocable. There is no apparent reason why a gift evidenced by an instrument of gift duly delivered is any more revocable than an assignment without consideration. Both strip the donor of dominion over the subject of the gift and place in the hands of the donee evidence of right to possession.

Therefore, applying the rule of delivery in the light of the reason which gave birth to it, and finding here no possibility of fraud or imposition, and no doubt whatever concerning the intention of the donor, and finding full support in the precedent of McGavic v. Cossum, supra, it is my opinion that there was a good constructive or symbolical delivery, consisting of the delivery of the instrument of gift, and that the gift should be sustained.

The claim of the widow to the 500 shares of Sumatra stock is further resisted by the appellant on the ground that in two intermediate accountings of the widow as executrix, and with another, as trustees, under her husband's will, both of which accountings were made on applications for resignations by executors, the widow's claim was not in any way referred to, but was purposely kept out of the accounting, by advice of counsel. We are all of the opinion that these intermediate accountings and the decrees entered thereupon did not conclude the claimant from asserting her claim in this proceeding. There was a good reason for withholding the claim, and the only result of so doing has been to enhance enormously the value of the estate. The widow promptly made her claim to the other executors. Its validity could only be determined on a settlement of the accounts. The two intermediate accountings were merely for the purpose of allowing executors to resign. The question of the widow's claim was not necessary to the determination there involved. The only effect of these accountings on this claim was to set the statute of limitations running, for the executor must present his claim within six years from the first accounting. Code Civ. Proc. § 2679. While these intermediate accounts showed the entire 7,213 shares, or the proceeds thereof, as a part of the principal of the trust, the claimant was the recipient of the income therefrom, and no rights accrued to any one else, nor did any one change his position in reliance upon the statement of that fact in the accountings.

The decree of the surrogate should be affirmed, with costs and disbursements to the respondents executrix and trustees, and disbursements of the special guardian, respondent. Order filed.

CLARKE, P.J., and SMITH, J., concur.

PAGE, J. (dissenting).

In my opinion there was not a valid gift inter vivos of the 500 shares of stock of the American Sumatra Tobacco Company by the testator to Sara K. Cohn. In order to arrive at a clear understanding of the transaction, it is essential that we should bear in mind the situation of the parties, the conditions under which the stock was held, and the actions of the testator with reference thereto, before and after the delivery of the paper to his wife on September 20, 1911. A brief resume of the material facts, is as follows:

The stock stood on the books of the American Sumatra Tobacco Company in the name of the copartnership of A. Cohn & Co., and until December 28, 1910, was an asset of the corporation. On that date the stock was allotted to the copartners as their individual property; that is, the proportion to which each partner was entitled was charged against his contribution to the capital account, and proper entries made transferring the stock from the capital account of the firm to the credit of the individual members. Thus Abraham Cohn was credited with 9,466 shares, the testator with 7,213 shares, and Leonard J. Cohn with 1,352 shares. The shares were not physically delivered nor transferred on the books of the corporation, but remained in the safe deposit box in the city of New York in the firm name. Any one of the partners however, at any time, could have taken his proportion of the stock, which was in certificates of $100 each, and caused the same to be transferred to himself, individually; but by reason of the desire to control the election of directors, from which they obtained a business advantage, they allowed the stock to remain in the firm name. Abraham Cohn died in August, 1911, and the two surviving partners began liquidation of the firm's business. Negotiations were opened for the organization of a copartnership, consisting of the testator, Leonard J. Cohn, and one Lichtenstein. The testator agreed to contribute some of this stock as an asset to the new copartnership, and, as it required 7,000 shares to secure the election of a director, the testator's holdings were to be kept intact, so that the new copartnership should have the benefit thereof.

The testator died suddenly on the 26th day of September, 1911, the day upon which the articles of copartnership were to have been signed. Prior to that time the testator had been in good physical condition and was attending to the business of liquidating the affairs of the old firm and the organization of the new copartnership at his place of business in New York City. When the paper was delivered to his wife, the daughters testified that the testator said: "That he could not give her the stock because it was in the company, but as soon as he could get it he would give it to her."

From the foregoing fact, I am of opinion that the attempted gift was invalid. There was no delivery of the stock, either actual or constructive. The testator still retained dominion and control over it, for use in the business of the new copartnership.

The rules by which the validity of gifts inter vivos must be tested are thus stated in Beaver v. Beaver, 117 N.Y. 421, 428, 22 N.E. 940, 941 (6 L.R.A. 403, 15 Am.St.Rep. 531), cited with approval in Matter of Van Alstyne, 207 N.Y. 298, 306, 100 N.E. 802, 804: "The elements necessary to constitute a valid gift are well understood and are not the subject of dispute. There must be on the part of the donor an intent to give, and a delivery of the thing given, to or for the donee, in pursuance of such intent, and on the part of the donee acceptance. The subject of the gift may be chattels, choses in action, or any form of personal property, and what constitutes delivery may depend on the nature and situation of the thing given. The delivery may be symbolical or actual; that is, by actually transferring the manual custody of the chattel to the donee, or giving to him the symbol which represents possession. * * * But the delivery by the donor, either actual or constructive, operating to divest the donor of possession of and dominion over the thing, is a constant and essential factor in every transaction which takes effect as a completed gift. * * * The intention to give is often established by most satisfactory evidence, although the gift fails. Instruments may be ever so formally executed by the donor, purporting to transfer title to the donee, or there may be the most explicit declaration of intention to give, or of an actual present gift, yet unless there is delivery the intention is defeated. Several cases of this kind have been recently considered by this court. Young v. Young, 80 N.Y. 438 [36 Am.Rep. 634]; Jackson v. Twenty–Third St. Ry. Co., 88 N.Y. 520; In re Crawford, 113 N.Y. 560 [21 N.E. 692, 5 L.R.A. 71]."

In the present case, the writing, taken alone, would seem to show the intention of the donor to make an actual present gift, for he says, "I give this day to my wife." Yet the delivery of the writing was accompanied by the statement "that he could not give her the stock, because it was in the company, but as soon as he could get it he would give it." There is, therefore, a clearly expressed intention to give at a future day, and the acts of the testator showed an intention to retain the dominion and control of the stock, meanwhile, in himself.

A gift inter vivos has no reference to the future, while a gift causa mortis has reference to a condition subsequent. The latter, before the happening of the condition, is revocable, while the former is irrevocable. Some confusion has arisen in the cases from a failure to recognize this distinction between these two forms of gift. A gift is a voluntary transaction, without consideration. Until the donor has divested himself absolutely and irrevocably of the title, dominion, and control of the subject of the gift, he has the power to revoke, and a court of equity will not compel him to complete his gift. Curry v. Powers, 70 N.Y. 212, 26 Am.Rep. 577; Lehr v. Jones, 74 App.Div. 54, 77 N.Y.Supp. 213. When a chose in action has been delivered to a purchaser in good faith and for a valuable consideration, he acquires a good title in equity, although no assignment has been made, and a court of equity will compel the transfer of the legal title. There is no such right in the donee of an incomplete gift. He has paid nothing for it, and as long as the donor retains the title, dominion, or possession of the subject of the proposed gift, the donee has no standing in any court to enforce the gift. Johnson v. Spies, 5 Hun. 468.

The respondent claims, however, that the delivery of this paper writing was a constructive delivery of the stock, and argues that the above rules only apply to gifts inter vivos where the evidence of the gifts rests in parol, and that, where there is a writing which evidences the donor's intention, the courts will give effect to the delivery of the writing as a constructive delivery of the subject of the gift. This, however, in my opinion, is not the law. The writing must be such as to transfer the right of possession. There may be a symbolic delivery, or there made be a constructive delivery; but, whether it be symbolic or constructive, it must be such a delivery as divests the donor with title, dominion, and right of possession, and it must be the best delivery that can be made under the circumstances of the case, having due regard to the character of the property.

The respondent relies upon two cases decided by this court: McGavic v. Cossum, 72 App.Div. 35, 76 N.Y.Supp. 305; Matter of Mills, 172 App.Div. 530, 158 N.Y.Supp. 1100, affirmed 219 N.Y. 642, 114 N.E. 1072. In the first case the subject of the gift was two $1,000 United States government bonds known as "4 per cent. registered." These bonds were in the custody, for safe-keeping of the bank in Peekskill, N.Y., through whom she purchased them. She, being seriously ill at her residence, gave to the plaintiff the original memorandum of purchase of the bonds delivered to her by the bank, across the back of which she indorsed the following: "Poughkeepsie, November 23, 1901. I have this day given my niece, Fannie H. McGavic, bond 2000 Reg. 4 per cent."—and signed her name. The donor died shortly thereafter and it was held that: "Actual delivery, by reason of the illness of the owner of the bonds, and their possession at that time by the bank, was physically impossible; but there was present, as evidenced by the writing, not only the intention to then give, but also the intention to then deliver the thing given. The owner did all she could do in this respect. It was a good constructive or symbolical delivery, and this under the circumstances was sufficient to vest good title in the plaintiff."

In the instant case there was no physical or other impossibility to the actual delivery of the stock; it stood in the name of the company, but the stock to the extent of 7,213 shares was the property of the testator, and it had been so held merely as a matter of business convenience of the old copartnership, and at the time was so held, pending the formation of a new copartnership, when it might be desirable to hold all the certificates of the stock in solido for the same business advantages. This latter consideration, in my opinion, was the controlling cause of the failure to make an immediate delivery of the stock, and the reason why the testator retained possession, dominion, and control of the certificates. In the Matter of Mills, supra, the testator was in California, the stock was in the possession of his son in New York, and this court said the stock, which was the subject of the gift, was "in the possession of one of the donees, and no further act of Mr. Mills could make his possession more complete," and as to the daughter we held that the delivery of the stock to the son, for and on behalf of the daughter, was a good delivery.

I have been unable to find that the courts in this jurisdiction have held, heretofore, that it is only where a parol gift is sought to be established that delivery is essential, and that, where the intention to give is evidenced by a writing, delivery is not necessary. Among the cases cited in the prevailing opinion as tending to sustain the proposition that the requirement for delivery of the thing given is limited to oral gifts will be found cases where gifts evidenced by a writing have been declared invalid. It will also be found that many of those cases relate to gifts causa mortis, and not to gifts inter vivos. So far as this state is concerned, it is in my opinion settled: "Delivery by the donor, either actual or constructive, operating to divest the donor of possession of and dominion over the thing, is a constant and essential factor in every transaction which takes effect as a completed gift. Anything short of this strips it of the quality of completeness, which distinguishes an intention to give, which alone amounts to nothing, from the consummated act, which changes the title. The intention to give is often established by most satisfactory evidence, although the gift fails. Instruments may be ever so formally executed by the donor, purporting to transfer title to the donee, or there may be the most explicit declaration of an intention to give, or of an actual present gift, yet unless there is delivery the intention is defeated." Beaver v. Beaver, supra.

The writing given to Mrs. Cohn did not purport to assign, transfer, or set over to her the stock. It was not a deed or instrument of gift that divested the testator of possession over and dominion of the stock. That it was not intended that it should be so is clearly shown by the subsequent acts of the testator.

In my opinion the decree should be modified, by declaring the attempted gift void, and sustaining the objections to the account to that extent, and the executors and trustees be surcharged with the proceeds of the said 500 shares of stock, and that the same forms a part of the principal of the trust estate.

DOWLING, J., concurs.

NOTES AND QUESTIONS

1. Parents made many gifts to Child. Some of these gifts were personal items like clothes but others had significant value such as family heirlooms and an extensive coin collection. When Child went to law school, Child left many of these items at Parents' home. Parents got in financial trouble and their creditors attached Parents' property, including the heirlooms and the coin collection. Child and the creditors are now litigating the ownership of these assets. What should Child have done to have avoided this situation? Do you know anyone who could be in Child's position?

2. Same facts as in the question above but instead of Parents' creditors attaching, Parents died. The I.R.S. is claiming that the coin collection and heirlooms are part of Parents' estate for estate tax purposes. Who will prevail? See Chad A. McGowan, *Special Delivery: Does the Postman Have to Ring at All—The Current State of the Delivery Requirement for Valid Gifts*, 31 REAL PROP., PROB. & TR. J. 357 (1996).

3. Harold tells you, "I will give you $5,000 at noon tomorrow." You reply, "Thank you very much." Has a valid gift occurred? Do you have any recourse if Harold does not give you the money tomorrow at noon?

4. Assume that earlier today you gave William your watch as a gift. Can you change your mind and revoke the gift?

5. May a valid inter vivos gift of a remainder interest in personal property be made where the donor reserves a life estate and retains possession? See Gruen v. Gruen, 68 N.Y.2d 48, 505 N.Y.S.2d 849, 496 N.E.2d 869 (1986).

6. Although life estates in personal property are relatively rare, there appears to be a growing trend to use life estates in real property as an estate planning technique. The most common use is in a parent-child situation where the parent retains a life estate in the residence and transfers the remainder to the children. The children have no immediate possessory rights and will have a full interest upon the parent's death without the need for probate. Creation of the life estate may be cheaper than using a trust and may provide better creditor protection. Note that this arrangement will not remove the property from the parent's estate for federal estate tax purposes. See I.R.C. § 2036. Bryan M. Dench, *Planning With Life Estates,* PROB. & PROP., July/Aug. 1992, at 38.

7. Your client is a medical doctor who fears malpractice liability. Accordingly, he transfers a significant amount of property to others (e.g., spouse, children, grandchildren, etc.). May these gifts be set aside by patients who have already notified the doctor of their claims? By injured patients who have

not notified the doctor? By a patient who is injured by the doctor in the year 2007?

8. Inter vivos gifts are a very important tax saving tool for several reasons. First, gifts to a spouse are federal gift tax-free, regardless of amount. Second, the first $13,000[1] given per year to each donee is also tax-free, regardless of the number of donees. If the donor's spouse joins in the gift, $26,000[2] may be given each year per donee. Third, payments in any amount to an educational institution for tuition or to a health care provider for medical expenses of the donee are tax-free. Gift taxation is covered in greater detail in Chapter 4(B).

9. Under what circumstances might a court be unwilling to presume that the donee accepted the intended gift?

10. A gift causa mortis is a gift made in contemplation of death. The donor must fear a death which is impending or imminent. The donor cannot merely have a general apprehension of an upcoming death. Gifts causa mortis require donative intent, delivery, and acceptance just like outright inter vivos gifts. Unlike outright inter vivos gifts, however, a gift causa mortis is both conditional and revocable. The gift is either automatically revoked (majority view) or revocable at the donor's discretion (minority view) if the donor survives the peril that induced the donor to make the gift. The gift is also revocable by the donor at any time for any reason. Attorneys rarely, if ever, use gifts causa mortis in planning a client's estate. A client who wishes to make a revocable transfer would be better served with a trust or some other formal arrangement.

11. Review Chapter 2(D) regarding inter vivos gifts in trust.

LOCATE

1. Locate the statutes in your state which govern the formalities necessary for inter vivos gifts.

2. Locate your state's fraudulent conveyancing statute.

DRAFT

Prepare a deed of gift for the coin collection discussed in Note 1.

D. POWERS OF APPOINTMENT

A power of appointment is the right to designate the new owner of property. A property owner has this power with respect to the property the person owns because a property owner may give his or her property to another person. The power to name a new owner of your property is one of the things a person takes for granted as accompanying property ownership.

---

1. This amount is adjusted for inflation according to the scheme set forth in I.R.C. § 2503(b)(2). See Chapter 4(B)(4)(a).

2. *Id.*

The property owner may sever this power of appointment from the ownership of the property itself. When this happens, the following relationships are created. The owner of property (the person who is severing) is the donor of the power, the person with the power to appoint the property is the donee or the power holder, and the prospective new owners are the objects of the power. When the donee actually exercises the power, the new owners are called the appointees. If the donee fails to exercise the power, the property passes to the default takers. If the donor failed to name default takers, the property reverts to the donor or the donor's estate.

The donor can create a power of appointment in an inter vivos document, such as a deed or trust, or in a separate power of appointment instrument. The donor can also create a power of appointment by will.

Powers of appointment are generally categorized in one of two ways. First, the power of appointment may be general, meaning that there are no restrictions or conditions on the donee's exercise of the power. Thus, the donee could even appoint the donee's own self as the new owner. In many aspects, the donee of a general power of appointment is like the actual owner of the property. Second, the power may be specific, special, or limited, i.e., the donor may specify certain individuals or groups as the objects of the power that do not include the donee, the donee's creditors, the donee's estate, or the creditors of the donee's estate. In addition, the donor may make the donee's exercise of the power conditional on whatever factors, within legal bounds, the donor desires, for example, only for the appointees' health-related and educational expenses.

The donee of a power of appointment does not have title, either legal or equitable, to the subject property. Instead, the donee only has a power to appoint. The appointees take title from the donor, not the donee.

The donee has no duty to exercise the power of appointment in favor of the hopeful appointees. Unlike a trustee, a donee is not a fiduciary and has no duty to manage the property or to distribute the property. A power of appointment is also not an agency relationship; the donee is not the donor's agent.

The donor may dictate the method the donee must use to exercise the power of appointment. For example, the power may be an inter vivos power, indicating that the donee must exercise it while alive. Alternatively, it may be a testamentary power, which the donee may only exercise by will. The donor may also permit the donee to exercise the power in both ways.

Although the donor may create a power of appointment in anyone, powers of appointment are typically used with trusts. Trustees often have the power to decide which beneficiaries will receive distributions and in what amounts. Settlors of trusts may also give powers of appointment over trust property to the beneficiaries.

LOCATE

What legislation exists in your state regarding powers of appointment?

NOTES AND QUESTIONS

1. The National Conference of Commissioners on Uniform State Laws has appointed a drafting committee which is preparing the Powers of Appointment Act. Only a few states currently have comprehensive power of appointment legislation.

2. What is your opinion of powers of appointment? Would you recommend a power of appointment instead of a trust? If yes, under what circumstances?

3. Testator's will contains a standard residuary clause which reads, "I leave the remainder of my estate to my son, David Smith." Testator had a testamentary power of appointment over certain property. Is this will provision sufficient to exercise the power?

4. Laura had a special power permitting her to appoint property to her children by will. The instrument creating the power provides that the American Red Cross receives the property if Laura fails to exercise the power. Laura executed a valid will in 2010 which expressly exercised the power in favor of one of her children, Charles. Charles died in 2005 and Laura died in 2013 without changing her will. Charles is survived by two children. Who is entitled to the property?

5. May the creditors of a donee of a general power of appointment reach the property even if the donee has not exercised the power in the donee's favor?

DRAFT

Draft a power of appointment giving Juan Cortez the ability to appoint your automobile to one of your family members or close friends. Be sure to draft for as many contingencies as possible.

E. JOINT TENANCIES

ROBERT J. LYNN AND GRAYSON M.P. McCOUCH, INTRODUCTION TO ESTATE PLANNING*

§ 3.2, pages 49–51 (5th ed. 2004).

Not all forms of coownership have the incident of survivorship. For example, if A, owning land in fee simple absolute, grants or devises "to B and his heirs and C and his heirs," B and C are tenants in common. Each owns an undivided one-half interest in fee simple absolute in the land, and that undivided one-half interest is alienable, devisable, and descendible. If B dies survived by C, B's undivided one-half interest passes to the devisee

* Reprinted with permission of Thomson Reuters.

under B's will or, alternatively, to B's heirs under the intestacy laws. Of course, C might be the devisee of B's interest in the land under B's will or B's heir under the intestacy laws, but in either case C takes by devise or descent, not by virtue of an incident of survivorship. The incident of survivorship is not a characteristic of the tenancy in common.

The incident of survivorship was a characteristic of both the joint tenancy and the tenancy by the entirety as those tenancies existed at common law. The tenancy by the entirety existed only between husband and wife. Both the joint tenancy and the tenancy by the entirety was they existed at common law have been affected by statutory and judicial modification. Therefore, to determine both the method of creating the incident attaches, one must consult applicable state or federal law. With respect to land, savings accounts, checking accounts, certificates of deposit, stock certificates, mutual funds and safe-deposit boxes, one looks to state law. With respect to U.S. savings bonds, one looks to federal law. One should not assume that a method of creating the incident that is effective in one state will necessarily be effective in another, nor should one assume that a method effective with respect to one kind of property will necessarily be effective with respect to another. There is considerable variation in these matters (with consequential misunderstanding and frustration).

NOTES AND QUESTIONS

1. In some states, joint tenants are presumed to hold with survivorship rights while in others, the survivorship feature attaches only if the instrument specifically provides for it or if it is proven using evidence to show the owners' intent. What policies support each of these approaches?

2. Assume that Father and Son own a parcel of real property as joint tenants. Father provided all of the funds to purchase the property. During the current year, the property earns $25,000 of rental income. Who is responsible for the income tax and in what proportions?

3. Assume that Mother and Daughter own a parcel of real property as joint tenants. Mother provided all of the funds to purchase the property. Mother fails to pay the property taxes and Mrs. Palsgraf is injured because of Mother's negligent upkeep of the property. Who is responsible for the taxes and Mrs. Palsgraf's injuries and in what proportions?

4. The creation of a joint tenancy may have unintended gift and estate tax consequences. For example, a taxable gift occurs when a joint tenancy is created unless the contribution of each joint tenant is the same. Thus, if Mother changes the way she holds title to her home from herself as an individual to her and her Son as joint tenants, Mother has made a taxable gift of one-half of the home's value to Son. Gift tax matters are discussed in Chapter 4(B).

5. Father and Daughter own a parcel of property as joint tenants. Father supplied all of the funds to purchase the property. May Father undo the joint tenancy and re-vest the entire parcel of property in his name alone?

May Daughter partition the property before Father dies and then sell her share without Father's consent?

6. Grandfather and Grandson own a parcel of property as joint tenants. Grandfather supplied all of the funds to purchase the property. Grandson has incurred many debts. May Grandson's creditors reach this property even though he did not contribute to its purchase? If yes, to what extent?

7. Mother and Son own a parcel of property as joint tenants with rights of survivorship. Mother supplied all of the funds to purchase the property. When Mother died, this property was not encumbered by a mortgage or lien. Mother died insolvent. May Mother's creditors reach any of this property which is now entirely owned by Son?

8. Under what circumstances would you advise your client to create a joint tenancy?

9. Under what circumstances might you advise your client to dissolve a currently existing joint tenancy? How would this be done?

10. Unscrupulous individuals may use a non-attorney's lack of understanding about joint tenancies, especially those with survivorship rights, to obtain ownership of a person's home or other property. See JACK OLSEN, HASTENED TO THE GRAVE (1998) (reporting a devious scheme whereby the scammer befriends an elderly person, moves into the person's residence, and then has the person sign a document creating a joint tenancy with survivorship rights explaining to the elderly person that it is merely an instrument to formalize a landlord-tenant arrangement so the living arrangement appears "moral" and/or "legal" to outsiders).

11. The rules governing coownership of United States savings bonds are detailed in 31 C.F.R. Part 315. For example, § 315.37 provides that "[a] savings bond registered in coownership form will be paid to either coowner upon surrender with an appropriate request, and, upon payment * * * the other coowner will cease to have any interest in the bond."

12. For further information, see Guerino J. Turano & Philip H. Ward, *Joint Tenancy and Tenancy by the Entirety: The Pros and Cons*, 83 ILL. B.J. 309 (1995).

LOCATE

How are joint tenancies with rights of survivorship created in your state? Is any special language required?

DRAFT

1. Father would like to create a joint tenancy with survivorship rights in favor of Daughter in a parcel of real property which he is about to purchase from Friend. Prepare the documents necessary to effectuate Father's intent.

2. Father would like to create a joint tenancy with survivorship rights in favor of Daughter in a parcel of real property which he currently owns. Prepare the documents necessary to effectuate Father's intent.

3. Father and Daughter would like to create a joint tenancy with survivorship rights in a parcel of real property they currently own as tenants in common. Prepare the documents necessary to effectuate their intent.

F. MULTIPLE-PARTY ACCOUNTS

Multiple-party accounts play an important role in modern estate planning. Multiple-party accounts are relatively simple and inexpensive to obtain and thus may appear to be an unsophisticated estate planning technique. Nonetheless, prudent use of these accounts can greatly enhance estate plans, both for individuals of low or moderate means and for people with large estates.

There are four commonly recognized types of multiple-party accounts. The *joint account with rights of survivorship* which allows all parties to withdraw funds and which vests ownership of the balance in the surviving party; the *joint account without survivorship rights,* often called an *agency* or *convenience* account, in which all parties may withdraw funds but ownership remains with the contributing party; the *pay on death (P.O.D.) account* in which the pay on death payee only has rights if that payee survives all original payees; and the *trust account* in which the beneficiary only has rights if the beneficiary survives all trustees.

UNIFORM PROBATE CODE

NONPROBATE TRANSFERS ON DEATH

PART 1

PROVISIONS RELATING TO EFFECT OF DEATH

Section 6–102. Liability of Nonprobate Transferees for Creditor Claims and Statutory Allowances.

(a) In this section, "nonprobate transfer" means a valid transfer effective at death, other than a transfer of a survivorship interest in a joint tenancy of real estate, by a transferor whose last domicile was in this State to the extent that the transferor immediately before death had power, acting alone, to prevent the transfer by revocation or withdrawal and instead to use the property for the benefit of the transferor or apply it to discharge claims against the transferor's probate estate.

(b) Except as otherwise provided by statute, a transferee of a nonprobate transfer is subject to liability to any probate estate of the decedent for allowed claims against decedent's probate estate and statutory allowances to the decedent's spouse and children to the extent the estate is insufficient to satisfy those claims and allowances. The liability of a nonprobate transferee may not exceed the value of nonprobate transfers received or controlled by that transferee.

(c) Nonprobate transferees are liable for the insufficiency described in subsection (b) in the following order of priority:

(1) a transferee designated in the decedent's will or any other governing instrument, as provided in the instrument;

(2) the trustee of a trust serving as the principal nonprobate instrument in the decedent's estate plan as shown by its designation as devisee of the decedent's residuary estate or by other facts or circumstances, to the extent of the value of the nonprobate transfer received or controlled;

(3) other nonprobate transferees, in proportion to the values received.

(d) Unless otherwise provided by the trust instrument, interests of beneficiaries in all trusts incurring liabilities under this section abate as necessary to satisfy the liability, as if all of the trust instruments were a single will and the interests were devises under it.

(e) A provision made in one instrument may direct the apportionment of the liability among the nonprobate transferees taking under that or any other governing instrument. If a provision in one instrument conflicts with a provision in another, the later one prevails.

(f) Upon due notice to a nonprobate transferee, the liability imposed by this section is enforceable in proceedings in this State, whether or not the transferee is located in this State.

(g) A proceeding under this section may not be commenced unless the personal representative of the decedent's estate has received a written demand for the proceeding from the surviving spouse or a child, to the extent that statutory allowances are affected, or a creditor. If the personal representative declines or fails to commence a proceeding after demand, a person making demand may commence the proceeding in the name of the decedent's estate, at the expense of the person making the demand and not of the estate. A personal representative who declines in good faith to commence a requested proceeding incurs no personal liability for declining.

(h) A proceeding under this section must be commenced within one year after the decedent's death, but a proceeding on behalf of a creditor whose claim was allowed after proceedings challenging disallowance of the claim may be commenced within 60 days after final allowance of the claim.

(i) Unless a written notice asserting that a decedent's probate estate is nonexistent or insufficient to pay allowed claims and statutory allowances has been received from the decedent's personal representative, the following rules apply:

(1) Payment or delivery of assets by a financial institution, registrar, or other obligor, to a nonprobate transferee in accordance with the terms of the governing instrument controlling the transfer

releases the obligor from all claims for amounts paid or assets delivered.

(2) A trustee receiving or controlling a nonprobate transfer is released from liability under this section with respect to any assets distributed to the trust's beneficiaries. Each beneficiary to the extent of the distribution received becomes liable for the amount of the trustee's liability attributable to assets received by the beneficiary.

PART 2

MULTIPLE-PERSON ACCOUNTS

SUBPART 1

DEFINITIONS AND GENERAL PROVISIONS

Section 6–201. Definitions.

In this part:

(1) "Account" means a contract of deposit between a depositor and a financial institution, and includes a checking account, savings account, certificate of deposit, and share account.

(2) "Agent" means a person authorized to make account transactions for a party.

(3) "Beneficiary" means a person named as one to whom sums on deposit in an account are payable on request after death of all parties or for whom a party is named as trustee.

(4) "Financial institution" means an organization authorized to do business under state or federal laws relating to financial institutions, and includes a bank, trust company, savings bank, building and loan association, savings and loan company or association, and credit union.

(5) "Multiple-party account" means an account payable on request to one or more of two or more parties, whether or not a right of survivorship is mentioned.

(6) "Party" means a person who, by the terms of an account, has a present right, subject to request, to payment from the account other than as a beneficiary or agent.

(7) "Payment" of sums on deposit includes withdrawal, payment to a party or third person pursuant to check or other request, and a pledge of sums on deposit by a party, or a set-off, reduction, or other disposition of all or part of an account pursuant to a pledge.

(8) "POD designation" means the designation of (i) a beneficiary in an account payable on request to one party during the party's lifetime and on the party's death to one or more beneficiaries, or to one or more parties during their lifetimes and on death of all of them to one or more beneficiaries, or (ii) a beneficiary in an account in the name of one or more parties as trustee for one or more beneficiaries if the relationship is established by the terms of the account and there is no subject of the trust

other than the sums on deposit in the account, whether or not payment to the beneficiary is mentioned.

(9) "Receive," as it relates to notice to a financial institution, means receipt in the office or branch office of the financial institution in which the account is established, but if the terms of the account require notice at a particular place, in the place required.

(10) "Request" means a request for payment complying with all terms of the account, including special requirements concerning necessary signatures and regulations of the financial institution; but, for purposes of this part, if terms of the account condition payment on advance notice, a request for payment is treated as immediately effective and a notice of intent to withdraw is treated as a request for payment.

(11) "Sums on deposit" means the balance payable on an account, including interest and dividends earned, whether or not included in the current balance, and any deposit life insurance proceeds added to the account by reason of death of a party.

(12) "Terms of the account" includes the deposit agreement and other terms and conditions, including the form, of the contract of deposit.

Section 6–202. Limitation on Scope of Part.

This part does not apply to (i) an account established for a partnership, joint venture, or other organization for a business purpose, (ii) an account controlled by one or more persons as an agent or trustee for a corporation, unincorporated association, or charitable or civic organization, or (iii) a fiduciary or trust account in which the relationship is established other than by the terms of the account.

Section 6–203. Types of Account; Existing Accounts.

(a) An account may be for a single party or multiple parties. A multiple-party account may be with or without a right of survivorship between the parties. Subject to Section 6–212(c), either a single-party account or a multiple-party account may have a POD designation, an agency designation, or both.

(b) An account established before, on, or after the effective date of this part, whether in the form prescribed in Section 6–204 or in any other form, is either a single-party account or a multiple-party account, with or without right of survivorship, and with or without a POD designation or an agency designation, within the meaning of this part, and is governed by this part.

Section 6–204. Forms.

(a) A contract of deposit that contains provisions in substantially the following form establishes the type of account provided, and the account is governed by the provisions of this part applicable to an account of that type:

UNIFORM SINGLE- OR MULTIPLE-PARTY ACCOUNT FORM

PARTIES [Name One or More Parties]:

____________________ ____________________

OWNERSHIP [Select One And Initial]:

___ SINGLE–PARTY ACCOUNT

___ MULTIPLE–PARTY ACCOUNT

Parties own account in proportion to net contributions unless there is clear and convincing evidence of a different intent.

RIGHTS AT DEATH [Select One And Initial]:

___ SINGLE–PARTY ACCOUNT

At death of party, ownership passes as part of party's estate.

___ SINGLE–PARTY ACCOUNT WITH POD (PAY ON DEATH) DESIGNATION

[Name One Or More Beneficiaries]:

____________________ ____________________

At death of party, ownership passes to POD beneficiaries and is not part of party's estate.

___ MULTIPLE–PARTY ACCOUNT WITH RIGHT OF SURVIVORSHIP

At death of party, ownership passes to surviving parties.

___ MULTIPLE–PARTY ACCOUNT WITH RIGHT OF SURVIVORSHIP AND POD (PAY ON DEATH) DESIGNATION

[Name One Or More Beneficiaries]:

____________________ ____________________

At death of last surviving party, ownership passes to POD beneficiaries and is not part of last surviving party's estate.

___ MULTIPLE–PARTY ACCOUNT WITHOUT RIGHT OF SURVIVORSHIP

At death of party, deceased party's ownership passes as part of deceased party's estate.

AGENCY (POWER OF ATTORNEY) DESIGNATION [Optional]

Agents may make account transactions for parties but have no ownership or rights at death unless named as POD beneficiaries.

[To Add Agency Designation To Account, Name One Or More Agents]:

____________________ ____________________

[Select One And Initial]:

___ AGENCY DESIGNATION SURVIVES DISABILITY OR INCAPACITY OF PARTIES

____ AGENCY DESIGNATION TERMINATES ON DISABILITY OR INCAPACITY OF PARTIES

(b) A contract of deposit that does not contain provisions in substantially the form provided in subsection (a) is governed by the provisions of this part applicable to the type of account that most nearly conforms to the depositor's intent.

Section 6–205. Designation of Agent.

(a) By a writing signed by all parties, the parties may designate as agent of all parties on an account a person other than a party.

(b) Unless the terms of an agency designation provide that the authority of the agent terminates on disability or incapacity of a party, the agent's authority survives disability and incapacity. The agent may act for a disabled or incapacitated party until the authority of the agent is terminated.

(c) Death of the sole party or last surviving party terminates the authority of an agent.

Section 6–206. Applicability of Part.

The provisions of Subpart 2 concerning beneficial ownership as between parties or as between parties and beneficiaries apply only to controversies between those persons and their creditors and other successors, and do not apply to the right of those persons to payment as determined by the terms of the account. Subpart 3 governs the liability and set-off rights of financial institutions that make payments pursuant to it.

SUBPART 2

OWNERSHIP AS BETWEEN PARTIES AND OTHERS

Section 6–211. Ownership During Lifetime.

(a) In this section, "net contribution" of a party means the sum of all deposits to an account made by or for the party, less all payments from the account made to or for the party which have not been paid to or applied to the use of another party and a proportionate share of any charges deducted from the account, plus a proportionate share of any interest or dividends earned, whether or not included in the current balance. The term includes deposit life insurance proceeds added to the account by reason of death of the party whose net contribution is in question.

(b) During the lifetime of all parties, an account belongs to the parties in proportion to the net contribution of each to the sums on deposit, unless there is clear and convincing evidence of a different intent. As between parties married to each other, in the absence of proof otherwise, the net contribution of each is presumed to be an equal amount.

(c) A beneficiary in an account having a POD designation has no right to sums on deposit during the lifetime of any party.

(d) An agent in an account with an agency designation has no beneficial right to sums on deposit.

Section 6–212. Rights at Death.

(a) Except as otherwise provided in this part, on death of a party sums on deposit in a multiple-party account belong to the surviving party or parties. If two or more parties survive and one is the surviving spouse of the decedent, the amount to which the decedent, immediately before death, was beneficially entitled under Section 6–211 belongs to the surviving spouse. If two or more parties survive and none is the surviving spouse of the decedent, the amount to which the decedent, immediately before death, was beneficially entitled under Section 6–211 belongs to the surviving parties in equal shares, and augments the proportion to which each survivor, immediately before the decedent's death, was beneficially entitled under Section 6–211, and the right of survivorship continues between the surviving parties.

(b) In an account with a POD designation:

(1) On death of one of two or more parties, the rights in sums on deposit are governed by subsection (a).

(2) On death of the sole party or the last survivor of two or more parties, sums on deposit belong to the surviving beneficiary or beneficiaries. If two or more beneficiaries survive, sums on deposit belong to them in equal and undivided shares, and there is no right of survivorship in the event of death of a beneficiary thereafter. If no beneficiary survives, sums on deposit belong to the estate of the last surviving party.

(c) Sums on deposit in a single-party account without a POD designation, or in a multiple-party account that, by the terms of the account, is without right of survivorship, are not affected by death of a party, but the amount to which the decedent, immediately before death, was beneficially entitled under Section 6–211 is transferred as part of the decedent's estate. A POD designation in a multiple-party account without right of survivorship is ineffective. For purposes of this section, designation of an account as a tenancy in common establishes that the account is without right of survivorship.

(d) The ownership right of a surviving party or beneficiary, or of the decedent's estate, in sums on deposit is subject to requests for payment made by a party before the party's death, whether paid by the financial institution before or after death, or unpaid. The surviving party or beneficiary, or the decedent's estate, is liable to the payee of an unpaid request for payment. The liability is limited to a proportionate share of the amount transferred under this section, to the extent necessary to discharge the request for payment.

Comment

Subsection (b) applies to both POD and Totten trust beneficiaries. See Section 6–201(8) ("POD designation" defined). It accepts the New York view that an account opened by "A" in A's name as "trustee for B" usually is intended by A to be an informal will of any balance remaining on deposit at A's death.

Section 6–213. Alteration of Rights.

(a) Rights at death under Section 6–212 are determined by the type of account at the death of a party. The type of account may be altered by written notice given by a party to the financial institution to change the type of account or to stop or vary payment under the terms of the account. The notice must be signed by a party and received by the financial institution during the party's lifetime.

(b) A right of survivorship arising from the express terms of the account, Section 6–212, or a POD designation, may not be altered by will.

Section 6–214. Accounts and Transfers Nontestamentary.

Except as provided in Part 2 of Article II (elective share of surviving spouse) or as a consequence of, and to the extent directed by, Section 6–215, a transfer resulting from the application of Section 6–212 is effective by reason of the terms of the account involved and this part and is not testamentary or subject to Articles I through IV (estate administration).

Section 6–216. Community Property and Tenancy by the Entireties.

(a) A deposit of community property in an account does not alter the community character of the property or community rights in the property, but a right of survivorship between parties married to each other arising from the express terms of the account or Section 6–212 may not be altered by will.

(b) This part does not affect the law governing tenancy by the entireties.

SUBPART 3

PROTECTION OF FINANCIAL INSTITUTIONS

Section 6–221. Authority of Financial Institution.

A financial institution may enter into a contract of deposit for a multiple-party account to the same extent it may enter into a contract of deposit for a single-party account, and may provide for a POD designation and an agency designation in either a single-party account or a multiple-party account. A financial institution need not inquire as to the source of a deposit to an account or as to the proposed application of a payment from an account.

Section 6–222. Payment on Multiple–Party Account.

A financial institution, on request, may pay sums on deposit in a multiple-party account to:

(1) one or more of the parties, whether or not another party is disabled, incapacitated, or deceased when payment is requested and whether or not the party making the request survives another party; or

(2) the personal representative, if any, or, if there is none, the heirs or devisees of a deceased party if proof of death is presented to the financial institution showing that the deceased party was the survivor of all other persons named on the account either as a party or beneficiary, unless the account is without right of survivorship under Section 6–212.

Comment

A financial institution that makes payment on proper request under this section is protected unless the financial institution has received written notice not to.

* * *

Section 6–223. Payment on POD Designation.

A financial institution, on request, may pay sums on deposit in an account with a POD designation to:

(1) one or more of the parties, whether or not another party is disabled, incapacitated, or deceased when the payment is requested and whether or not a party survives another party;

(2) the beneficiary or beneficiaries, if proof of death is presented to the financial institution showing that the beneficiary or beneficiaries survived all persons named as parties; or

(3) the personal representative, if any, or, if there is none, the heirs or devisees of a deceased party, if proof of death is presented to the financial institution showing that the deceased party was the survivor of all other persons named on the account either as a party or beneficiary.

Section 6–224. Payment to Designated Agent.

A financial institution, on request of an agent under an agency designation for an account, may pay to the agent sums on deposit in the account, whether or not a party is disabled, incapacitated, or deceased when the request is made or received, and whether or not the authority of the agent terminates on the disability or incapacity of a party.

Section 6–225. Payment to Minor.

If a financial institution is required or permitted to make payment pursuant to this part to a minor designated as a beneficiary, payment may be made pursuant to the Uniform Transfers to Minors Act.

Section 6–226. Discharge.

(a) Payment made pursuant to this part in accordance with the type of account discharges the financial institution from all claims for amounts so paid, whether or not the payment is consistent with the beneficial ownership of the account as between parties, beneficiaries, or their successors. Payment may be made whether or not a party, beneficiary, or agent is disabled, incapacitated, or deceased when payment is requested, received, or made.

(b) Protection under this section does not extend to payments made after a financial institution has received written notice from a party, or from the personal representative, surviving spouse, or heir or devisee of a deceased party, to the effect that payments in accordance with the terms of the account, including one having an agency designation, should not be permitted, and the financial institution has had a reasonable opportunity to act on it when the payment is made. Unless the notice is withdrawn by the person giving it, the successor of any deceased party must concur in a request for payment if the financial institution is to be protected under this section. Unless a financial institution has been served with process in an action or proceeding, no other notice or other information shown to have been available to the financial institution affects its right to protection under this section.

(c) A financial institution that receives written notice pursuant to this section or otherwise has reason to believe that a dispute exists as to the rights of the parties may refuse, without liability, to make payments in accordance with the terms of the account.

(d) Protection of a financial institution under this section does not affect the rights of parties in disputes between themselves or their successors concerning the beneficial ownership of sums on deposit in accounts or payments made from accounts.

Section 6–227. Set–Off.

Without qualifying any other statutory right to set-off or lien and subject to any contractual provision, if a party is indebted to a financial institution, the financial institution has a right to set-off against the account. The amount of the account subject to set-off is the proportion to which the party is, or immediately before death was, beneficially entitled under Section 6–211 or, in the absence of proof of that proportion, an equal share with all parties.

LOCATE

Find your state's legislation governing multiple-party accounts.

NOTES AND QUESTIONS

1. What types of multiple-party accounts are recognized in your state? For each type of multiple-party account, answer the following questions:

a. What types of accounts may be held in multiple-party form?

b. In what type of financial institutions may multiple-party accounts be opened?

c. How are they created? Is any "magic language" needed? See Dominic J. Campisi, *Joint Tenancy Accounts [An Un–Uniform Law]*, 30 REAL PROP., PROB. & TR. J. 399 (1995).

d. Who has beneficial ownership during the depositors' lifetimes and in what proportions?

e. Who has withdrawal rights during the depositors' lifetimes?

f. Who has beneficial ownership after the death of a depositor? All depositors?

g. Who has withdrawal rights after the death of a depositor? All depositors?

h. What effect does the opening of the account have on the ability of a creditor of the depositor to reach funds in the account?

i. What effect does the opening of the account have on the ability of a creditor of a non-depositing party to reach funds in the account?

j. What effect does the death of a depositor have on a creditor's ability to reach the funds in the debtor's account?

k. Is a statutorily supplied disclosure statement required or recommended?

2. A and B open a joint account which unambiguously provides that upon the death of either party the entire remaining balance belongs to the survivor. After A dies, may the beneficiaries of A's will use extrinsic evidence to prove that A intended a convenience account, not a survivorship account?

3. The account contract provides that "upon the death of either of us any balance in said account or any part thereof may be withdrawn by, or upon the order of the survivor." Is this language sufficient to imbue the account with the survivorship feature in a state without a survivorship presumption? See Stauffer v. Henderson, 801 S.W.2d 858 (Tex. 1990) (no survivorship because language only authorized withdrawal, not a transfer in ownership; dissent argued that majority's approach elevated magic words over common sense reading of account).

4. Husband and Wife opened a joint account with rights of survivorship. Husband and Wife are involved in a protracted divorce proceeding. Wife dies. Is Husband still entitled to the balance of the account? What if the divorce were final before Wife died?

5. Two significant others (A and B) opened a joint account into which each deposited paychecks, interest checks, cash dividends on stock, etc. After a big fight, B closed the account and fled with all the money to Europe. Does A have a remedy against B? Against the bank?

6. Trust accounts are often referred to as *Totten* trusts after the famous New York case of In re Totten, 179 N.Y. 112, 71 N.E. 748 (1904). As these accounts gained in popularity and recognition, they lost their original connection to trust law and were governed by contract law. Because their operation

was virtually identical to P.O.D. accounts, many modern statutes have removed the distinction and now treat trust accounts as P.O.D. accounts. See U.P.C. § 6–201(8).

7. A has two bank accounts; Account One in A's name alone and Account Two that is payable on death to B. A becomes incompetent and a guardian is appointed. The guardian needs to pay A's expenses and starts spending the money in Account Two. May B complain and force the guardian to expend the funds in Account One first? See Katz v. Greeninger, 96 Cal.App.2d 245, 215 P.2d 121 (1950).

8. Individuals with large or complex estate plans may want to make minor alterations to their estate plans such as adding a small monetary gift to a relative or friend. These alterations may prove costly, time-consuming, and inconvenient if a new will, codicil, or trust amendment is necessary. Provided the proposed gift would not disturb the basic distribution scheme or tax saving strategies of the original estate plan, a P.O.D. account may be an effective method of making the gift.

9. The depositor usually does not make a taxable gift by opening a multiple-party account until a party withdraws more than that party's net contributions. A purely convenience arrangement is also not subject to gift tax. The tax ramifications of multiple-party accounts are discussed in greater detail in Chapter 4(B).

10. Multiple-party accounts are typically opened without the assistance of an attorney. The depositor simply goes to the bank and opens the account, speaking with a bank official such as a "New Accounts Officer" or "Consumer Accounts Officer." This person may explain the effect of the account, e.g., "When you die, the other person owns the money." Is this the practice of law without a license? If the bank official gives incorrect advice, may the official be sued? The bank? Who would be the proper party to sue, the depositor, the depositor's estate, or the intended recipient?

11. You should personally inspect all of your client's multiple-party account contracts to make certain they comply with applicable law and that the account will have the effect the client intends. Clients are notorious for not understanding the true effect of multiple-party accounts.

LOCATE

Visit several local banks and obtain copies of their multiple-party account contracts and signature cards. Do they clearly indicate the type and effect of the account? Do they comply with the applicable statutes? Is a non-legally trained person likely to understand the ramifications of opening an account?

G. PAY/TRANSFER ON DEATH PROPERTY

State and federal law may permit owners of certain property to designate the person who is entitled to ownership rights upon the current owner's death. For example, United States savings bonds may be registered in *beneficiary form,* i.e., the bond is payable to a named person when the current owner dies. See 31 C.F.R. § 315.7. Corporate securities such as stocks and bonds may be held in transfer on death form under the law of some states and the Uniform Transfer on Death Security Registration Act. Some states expand P.O.D. and T.O.D. designations to other tangible assets such as motor vehicles.

UNIFORM PROBATE CODE

UNIFORM TOD SECURITY REGISTRATION ACT

Section 6–301. Definitions.

In this part:

(1) "Beneficiary form" means a registration of a security which indicates the present owner of the security and the intention of the owner regarding the person who will become the owner of the security upon the death of the owner.

(2) "Register," including its derivatives, means to issue a certificate showing the ownership of a certificated security or, in the case of an uncertificated security, to initiate or transfer an account showing ownership of securities.

(3) "Registering entity" means a person who originates or transfers a security title by registration, and includes a broker maintaining security accounts for customers and a transfer agent or other person acting for or as an issuer of securities.

(4) "Security" means a share, participation, or other interest in property, in a business, or in an obligation of an enterprise or other issuer, and includes a certificated security, an uncertificated security, and a security account.

(5) "Security account" means (i) a reinvestment account associated with a security, a securities account with a broker, a cash balance in a brokerage account, cash, interest, earnings, or dividends earned or declared on a security in an account, a reinvestment account, or a brokerage account, whether or not credited to the account before the owner's death, or (ii) a cash balance or other property held for or due to the owner of a security as a replacement for or product of an account security, whether or not credited to the account before the owner's death.

Section 6–302. Registration in Beneficiary Form; Sole or Joint Tenancy Ownership.

Only individuals whose registration of a security shows sole ownership by one individual or multiple ownership by two or more with right of survivorship, rather than as tenants in common, may obtain registration in beneficiary form. Multiple owners of a security registered in beneficiary form hold as joint tenants with right of survivorship, as tenants by the entireties, or as owners of community property held in survivorship form, and not as tenants in common.

Section 6–303. Registration in Beneficiary Form; Applicable Law.

A security may be registered in beneficiary form if the form is authorized by this or a similar statute of the state of organization of the issuer or registering entity, the location of the registering entity's principal office, the office of its transfer agent or its office making the registration, or by this or a similar statute of the law of the state listed as the owner's address at the time of registration. A registration governed by the law of a jurisdiction in which this or similar legislation is not in force or was not in force when a registration in beneficiary form was made is nevertheless presumed to be valid and authorized as a matter of contract law.

Section 6–304. Origination of Registration in Beneficiary Form.

A security, whether evidenced by certificate or account, is registered in beneficiary form when the registration includes a designation of a beneficiary to take the ownership at the death of the owner or the deaths of all multiple owners.

Section 6–305. Form of Registration in Beneficiary Form.

Registration in beneficiary form may be shown by the words "transfer on death" or the abbreviation "TOD," or by the words "pay on death" or the abbreviation "POD," after the name of the registered owner and before the name of a beneficiary.

Section 6–306. Effect of Registration in Beneficiary Form.

The designation of a TOD beneficiary on a registration in beneficiary form has no effect on ownership until the owner's death. A registration of a security in beneficiary form may be canceled or changed at any time by the sole owner or all then surviving owners without the consent of the beneficiary.

Section 6–307. Ownership on Death of Owner.

On death of a sole owner or the last to die of all multiple owners, ownership of securities registered in beneficiary form passes to the beneficiary or beneficiaries who survive all owners. On proof of death of all owners and compliance with any applicable requirements of the registering entity, a security registered in beneficiary form may be reregistered in the name of the beneficiary or beneficiaries who survive the death of all owners. Until division of the security after the death of all owners, multiple beneficiaries surviving the death of all owners hold their interests as tenants in common. If no beneficiary survives the death of all owners, the security belongs to the estate of the deceased sole owner or the estate of the last to die of all multiple owners.

Section 6–308. Protection of Registering Entity.

(a) A registering entity is not required to offer or to accept a request for security registration in beneficiary form. If a registration in beneficiary form is offered by a registering entity, the owner requesting registration in beneficiary form assents to the protections given to the registering entity by this part.

(b) By accepting a request for registration of a security in beneficiary form, the registering entity agrees that the registration will be implemented on death of the deceased owner as provided in this part.

(c) A registering entity is discharged from all claims to a security by the estate, creditors, heirs, or devisees of a deceased owner if it registers a transfer of the security in accordance with Section 6–307 and does so in good faith reliance (i) on the registration, (ii) on this part, and (iii) on information provided to it by affidavit of the personal representative of the deceased owner, or by the surviving beneficiary or by the surviving beneficiary's representatives, or other information available to the registering entity. The protections of this part do not extend to a reregistration or payment made after a registering entity has received written notice from any claimant to any interest in the security objecting to implementation of a registration in beneficiary form. No other notice or other information available to the registering entity affects its right to protection under this part.

(d) The protection provided by this part to the registering entity of a security does not affect the rights of beneficiaries in disputes between themselves and other claimants to ownership of the security transferred or its value or proceeds.

Section 6–309. Nontestamentary Transfer on Death.

A transfer on death resulting from a registration in beneficiary form is effective by reason of the contract regarding the registration between the owner and the registering entity and this Act and is not testamentary.

Section 6–310. Terms, Conditions, and Forms for Registration.

(a) A registering entity offering to accept registrations in beneficiary form may establish the terms and conditions under which it will receive requests (i) for registrations in beneficiary form, and (ii) for implementation of registrations in beneficiary form, including requests for cancellation of previously registered TOD beneficiary designations and requests for reregistration to effect a change of beneficiary. The terms and conditions so established may provide for proving death, avoiding or resolving any problems concerning fractional shares, designating primary and contingent beneficiaries, and substituting a named beneficiary's descendants to take in the place of the named beneficiary in the event of the beneficiary's death. Substitution may be indicated by appending to the name of the primary beneficiary the letters LDPS, standing for "lineal descendants per stirpes." This designation substitutes a deceased beneficiary's descendants who survive the owner for a beneficiary who fails to so survive, the descendants to be identified and to share in accordance with the law of the beneficiary's domicile at the owner's death governing inheritance by descendants of an intestate. Other forms of identifying beneficiaries who are to take on one or more contingencies, and rules for providing proofs and assurances needed to satisfy reasonable concerns by registering entities regarding conditions and identities relevant to accurate implementation of registrations in beneficiary form, may be contained in a registering entity's terms and conditions.

(b) The following are illustrations of registrations in beneficiary form which a registering entity may authorize:

(1) Sole owner-sole beneficiary: John S Brown TOD (or POD) John S Brown Jr.

(2) Multiple owners-sole beneficiary: John S Brown Mary B Brown JT TEN TOD John S Brown Jr.

(3) Multiple owners-primary and secondary (substituted) beneficiaries: John S Brown Mary B Brown JT TEN TOD John S Brown Jr SUB BENE Peter Q Brown or John S Brown Mary B Brown JT TEN TOD John S Brown Jr LDPS.

Comment

Use of "and" or "or" between the names of persons registered as co-owners is unnecessary under this part and should be discouraged. If used, the two words should have the same meaning insofar as concerns a title form; *i.e.,* that of "and" to indicate that both named persons own the asset.

Descendants of a named beneficiary who take by virtue of a "LDPS" designation appended to a beneficiary's name take as TOD beneficiaries rather than as intestate successors. If no descendant of a predeceased primary beneficiary survives the owner, the security passes as a part of the owner's estate as provided in Section 6–307.

NOTE

As of September 2012, forty-eight states, the District of Columbia, and the U.S. Virgin Islands had enacted the TOD Security Registration Act. The Act was not pending in the legislatures of the two remaining states, Louisiana and Texas.

TEXAS TRANSPORTATION CODE

§ 501.031. Rights of Survivorship Agreement.

(a) The department shall include on each certificate of title a rights of survivorship agreement form. The form must:

(1) provide that if the agreement is signed by two or more eligible persons, the motor vehicle is held jointly by those persons with the interest of a person who dies to survive to the surviving person or persons; and

(2) provide blanks for the signatures of the persons.

(b) If the vehicle is registered in the name of one or more of the persons who signed the agreement, the certificate of title may contain a:

(1) rights of survivorship agreement signed by all the persons; or

(2) remark if a rights of survivorship agreement is surrendered with the application for certificate of title or otherwise on file with the department.

(c) Except as provided in Subsection (g), ownership of the vehicle may be transferred only:

(1) by all the persons acting jointly, if all the persons are alive; and

(2) on the death of one of the persons by the surviving person or persons by transferring the certificate of title, in the manner otherwise required by law for transfer of ownership of the vehicle, with a copy of the death certificate of the deceased person attached to the certificate of title application.

(d) A rights of survivorship agreement under this section may be revoked only by surrender of the certificate of title to the department and joint application by the persons who signed the agreement for a new title in the name of the person or persons designated in the application.

(e) A person is eligible to sign a rights of survivorship agreement under this section if the person:

(1) is married and the spouse of the signing person is the only other party to the agreement;

(2) is unmarried and attests to that unmarried status by affidavit; or

(3) is married and provides the department with an affidavit from the signing person's spouse that attests that the signing person's interest in the vehicle is the signing person's separate property.

(f) If the title is being issued in connection with the sale of the vehicle, the seller is not eligible to sign a rights of survivorship agreement under this section unless the seller is the child, grandchild, parent, grandparent, brother, or sister of each other person signing the agreement. A family relationship required by this subsection may be a relationship established by adoption.

(g) If an agreement, other than the agreement provided for in Subsection (a), providing for right of survivorship is signed by two or more persons, the department shall issue a new certificate of title to the surviving person or persons upon application accompanied by a copy of the death certificate of the deceased person. The department may develop for public use under this subsection an optional rights of survivorship agreement form.

LOCATE

What types of property may be held in P.O.D. form under the law of your state?

H. LIFE INSURANCE

ROBERT J. LYNN AND GRAYSON M.P. McCOUCH, INTRODUCTION TO ESTATE PLANNING*

§§ 6.2 & 6.6, pages 114–117; 124–127 (5th ed. 2004).

There are various kinds of life insurance, and innumerable life insurance "plans." Regardless, of the kind of insurance on a person's life, if the insured dies while the policy remains in force (and there is no effective "defense" available to the insurer), the proceeds are payable to the designated beneficiary. This result follows even though the proceeds payable under the policy (the "face amount") may be $100,000 and the total amount of premiums paid may be only $5,000 when death occurs. The ability to create what is sometimes called an "instant estate" through buying life insurance is of particular interest to the prospective decedent who has little or no accumulated property. Such a person might be young, never having had an opportunity to accumulate, or middle-aged and unable to accumulate much property. In either case, by maintaining an insurance policy on his or her own life, a person of modest means can provide some financial protection for dependents or other beneficiaries in the even of early death.

Even if there is no need to create an instant estate, a person might sensible consider buying life insurance to provide ready cash to meet obligations incident to death—for example, funeral costs, debts, family living expenses, and death taxes. Having cash available from insurance proceeds to meet such payments may avoid a forced sale of estate assets under unfavorable market conditions.

Because of the way payments for insurance ("premiums") are calculated and paid, life insurance other than "term" insurance includes a forced savings feature. During the early years of the contract, the premium paid if greater than the sum required to buy "pure" insurance protection, and the savings accumulate in the hands of the insurer. Consequently, the insurance policy has a "cash surrender" value. The owner of a policy (the "policyholder") who decides to terminate the insurance can surrender the policy to the issuing company (the "insurer") and receive its then cash surrender value. More importantly, because the insurance includes a savings feature, the policy can be pledged to a commercial lender or to an individual as security for a loan. The policy by its terms might enable the policyholder to pledge it to the issuing company as security for a loan from the insurance company (sometimes at a favorable rate). Although on (say) an "ordinary life" policy, premiums are payable during the lifetime of the insured, if the policyholder "drops" the insurance, that is, simply fails or refuses to pay premium, the policyholder may be able to avoid a "lapse" of the policy by using the accumulated value to convert to "paid up" life insurance with a reduced face amount. If the policyholder lives to retirement age, the policy by its terms might enable the policyholder to draw retirement benefits payable over a period of years from the accumulated savings. (While accumulating, the savings are not includible in the policyholder's gross income for federal income tax purposes.)

A prospective decedent might be a partner in a business. The partners might have an enforceable agreement providing that on the death of a partner, the surviving partners have the right to buy the deceased partner's interest for a specified price. Insurance on the life of each partner, with the other partners being designated as beneficiaries, can provide the cash required to pay for the deceased partner's interest.

Regardless of whether the prospective decedent is a person of some means, he or she might procure life insurance to serve as the principal or even sole source of funding a trust for the benefit of the decedent's family. Instead of simply directing that the life insurance proceeds be paid out to the beneficiaries immediately at the death of the insured in a "lump sum," or even paid out over time under a "settlement option," the proceeds might be paid to a trustee with discretion to make distributions from time to time to the trust beneficiaries in accordance with their respective needs and requirements.

Finally, a person may automatically receive life insurance coverage in connection with his or her employment. Many employers provide life insurance for their employees as a mandatory fringe benefit, which the employees cannot elect to forego. This protection is commonly provided through "group" life insurance, usually in the form of an annually renewable group term policy.

There are many variations in the terms and conditions that make up a life insurance plan. Below are some terms commonly employed to identify various types of life insurance.

"Whole life" insurance provides coverage during the entire lifetime of the life insured and the proceeds become payable only at death. Whole life insurance can differentiated further: In the case of "ordinary" or "straight" life insurance, premiums are payable either throughout the lifetime of the life insured or until attainment of a specified advanced age (say 100 years); in the case of "limited payment" life insurance, premiums are payable over a specified period of time (say, 20 years) or until the occurrence of a specified event (such as attaining age 60). Under a limited payment plan, the premiums are higher, and at the end of the payment period the policy is "paid up"—on the death of the life insured at any time thereafter, the face amount of the policy is payable. "Single premium" life insurance is what the words imply: Instead of paying periodic premiums over time, the purchaser pays only one premium at the outset to procure the policy. "Joint life" insurance covers more than one life (commonly, husband and wife or business partners). The face amount is payable on the death of the first of the lives insured to die. Under a policy of "survivorship" life insurance, a variation of joint life insurance, the proceeds become payable at the death of the last of lives insured to die.

"Endowment" life insurance provides for payment of a specified sum if the life insured dies within a specified endowment period (usually a fixed number of years, or the attainment of a fixed age), or for payment at the end of the endowment period if the life insured survives the endowment period.

Both whole life and endowment policies include a forced savings feature. Although the risk of death increases with the age of the life insured, the premiums remained fixed at the same amount ("level") throughout the time that they are payable. Consequently, the policyholder pays more than is required for pure insurance protection during the early years, and the excess payments generate an accumulation of cash value which is used to subsidize the increased cost of pure insurance protection during the later years.

Both "universal" and "variable" life insurance policies include a cash value component. A universal policy allows flexible premium payments, which are credited (after deductions for the cost of pure insurance protection and expenses) to a cash value account. The cash value account earns interest at a guaranteed minimum rate, plus any additional amount declared by the insurer from investment earnings. A variable policy generally requires fixed premium payments and provides a guaranteed minimum amount of insurance. The cash value of the policy is allocated to one or more mutual funds or other investment vehicles selected by the policyholder, and the performance of those investment vehicles determines the amount, if any, of additional insurance provided by the policy.

"Term" life insurance is sometimes referred to as pure insurance—it has no savings feature. If the life insured dies while the contract is in force, that is, during the term of the policy—commonly one year or five years—a stated sum is payable to designated beneficiary. Because term insurance has no savings feature, it has no cash surrender value. And once the current term expires, the insurance policy is no longer in force unless it is renewed. Nonetheless, term insurance often plays an important role in estate planning. The lack of a savings feature means that a term policy can be purchased for considerably less than a whole life policy with a comparable face amount. Term insurance is often sold as "mortgage" insurance, for the purpose of providing guaranteed source of payment for the mortgage on the family home in the event that the life insured dies while the mortgage is still outstanding. The term insurance contract might by its terms provide for optional renewal of insurance coverage for an additional term without regard to the life insured's state of health at the time of renewal. The policy might also give the policyholder the option to convert the policy from term insurance to a more permanent type of life insurance, without regard to the life insured's state of health at the time of conversion.

A life insurance policy, whether of whole life or term insurance, is said to be a "participating" policy if the policyholder is entitled to "dividends." (If the policy does not pay dividends, it is a "nonparticipating" policy.) Insurance dividends should not be confused with dividends paid to shareholders of a corporation. An insurance dividend is an annual payment made to the policyholders by the insurance company in its discretion, and represents a refund of excess premiums previously paid. Accordingly, the policyholder's actual cost for a policy in a given year is determined by subtracting the dividends received (if any) from the total premiums paid.

NOTES AND QUESTIONS

1. Professors Lynn and McCouch indicated that the insurer may be able to raise defenses to paying the beneficiary. What are some examples of these defenses?

2. Why is life insurance considered a very powerful estate planning tool?

3. A person must have an insurable interest in the life that provides the measuring event for proceeds payment. A person has an insurable interest in his or her own life. Thus, you may purchase a life insurance policy on your own life and name anyone you wish as the beneficiary. However, if you want to purchase insurance on someone else's life, you must demonstrate a sufficient relationship between you and the insured. In whom do you have an insurable interest? New Jersey Stat. Ann. 17B:24–1.1 provides:

> a. For the purpose of life insurance, health insurance or annuities:
>
> (1) An individual has an insurable interest in his own life, health and bodily safety.
>
> (2) An individual has an insurable interest in the life, health and bodily safety of another individual if he has an expectation of pecuniary advantage through the continued life, health and bodily safety of that individual and consequent loss by reason of his death or disability.
>
> (3) An individual has an insurable interest in the life, health and bodily safety of another individual to whom he is closely related by blood or by law and in whom he has a substantial interest engendered by love and affection. An individual liable for the support of a child or former wife or husband may procure a policy of insurance on that child or former wife or husband.
>
> (4) A corporation has an insurable interest: (a) in the life or physical or mental ability of any of its directors, officers, or employees, or the directors, officers, or employees of any of its subsidiaries or any other person whose death or physical or mental disability might cause financial loss to the corporation; (b) pursuant to any

contractual arrangement with any shareholder concerning the reacquisition of shares owned by him at the time of his death or disability, in the life or physical or mental ability of that shareholder for the purpose of carrying out that contractual arrangement; (c) pursuant to any contract obligating the corporation as part of compensation arrangements, in the life of the individual for whom compensation is to be provided; or (d) pursuant to a contract obligating the corporation as guarantor or surety, in the life of the principal obligor. The trustee of a trust established and fully funded by a corporation providing solely life, health, disability, retirement, or similar benefits to employees of the corporation or its affiliates and acting in a fiduciary capacity with respect to those employees, retired employees, or their dependents or beneficiaries, has an insurable interest in the lives of employees for whom such benefits are to be provided.

(5) A nonprofit or charitable entity qualified pursuant to section 501(c)(3) of the Internal Revenue Code of 1986 (26 U.S.C. § 501(c)(3)), or a government entity has an insurable interest in the life or physical or mental ability of its directors, officers, employees, supporters or their designees or others to whom it may look for counsel, guidance, fundraising or assistance in the execution of its legally established purpose, who either: (a) join with the entity in signing the application for insurance, which application names the entity as the owner and irrevocable beneficiary of the policy; or (b) after having been listed as owner, subsequently transfer ownership of the insurance to the entity and name the entity as the irrevocable beneficiary of the policy. The trustee of a trust established and fully funded by a nonprofit or charitable entity qualified pursuant to section 501(c)(3) of the Internal Revenue Code of 1986 (26 U.S.C. § 501(c)(3)), or a government entity providing solely life, health, disability, retirement, or similar benefits to employees of the entity or its affiliates and acting in a fiduciary capacity with respect to those employees, retired employees, or their dependents or beneficiaries, has an insurable interest in the lives of employees for whom such benefits are to be provided.

b. No person shall procure or cause to be procured any insurance contract upon the life, health or bodily safety of another individual unless the benefits under that contract are payable to the individual insured or his personal representative, or to a person having, at the time when that contract was made, an insurable interest in the individual insured.

c. If the beneficiary, assignee, or other payee under any contract made in violation of this section receives from the insurer any benefits thereunder accruing upon the death, disablement, or injury of the individual insured, the individual insured, or his executor or administrator, as the case may be, may maintain an action to recover those benefits from the person so receiving them.

d. An insurer shall be entitled to rely upon all statements, declarations and representations made by an applicant for insurance relating to the insurable interest of the applicant in the insured and no insurer shall incur legal liability, except as set forth in the policy, by virtue of any untrue statements, declarations or representations so relied upon in good faith by the insurer.

e. This section shall not apply to group life insurance, group health insurance, blanket insurance or group annuities.

4. What are the advantages and disadvantages of each of the following types of policies? Why would you suggest one type of policy over another?

a. Term.

b. Whole Life.

c. Universal or Variable Life.

d. Endowment.

See *Is Your Life Sufficiently Insured?*, CONSUMER REPORTS MONEY ADVISOR (Feb. 2010); *The Mysteries of Life*, CONSUMER REPORTS, July 1998, at 34; *When It's Time to Buy Life Insurance,* 58 CONSUMER REPORTS 431 (1993); *Life Insurance, Part 2,* 58 CONSUMER REPORTS 525 (1993); *Life Insurance, Part 3,* 58 CONSUMER REPORTS 595 (1993); Richard A. Schwartz, *The Scoop on Variable Life,* PROB. & PROP., Jan./Feb. 1993, at 28.

5. "Life insurance is one of the most difficult purchases people ever make. Policies are confusing, their terms opaque, their true costs often obscured. * * * The insurance industry likes people to buy on trust rather than on facts about the policies themselves." *When It's Time to Buy Life Insurance,* 58 CONSUMER REPORTS 431, 431 (1993).

6. Life insurance agents may try to encourage potential insureds to purchase policies which give the agents the best commissions. For example, term insurance is often the most economical as well as the most practical option but it is also the one that usually yields the lowest profit for the agent and the insurer.

7. How much life insurance coverage should a person have? See *The Mysteries of Life*, CONSUMER REPORTS, July 1998, at 34; *When It's Time to Buy Life Insurance,* 58 CONSUMER REPORTS 431, 431–35 (1993). The amount of coverage a person needs varies over time. "The need for insurance normally declines as children grow up and become independent and as other savings and investments gradually grow into a satisfactory estate." Id. at 435.

8. While married, Wife named Husband as the sole beneficiary of her life insurance policy. They were later divorced. Wife died without changing the beneficiary designation on the policy. Will Husband receive the proceeds?

Under traditional common law, a divorce has no effect on the life insurance beneficiary designation and thus Husband would still take the proceeds. Because of the unlikelihood of an insured intending to benefit a former spouse, several states have enacted statutes automatically revoking beneficiary designations in favor of ex-spouses. If such a law applied, the proceeds would pass to the contingent beneficiaries. However, if Wife's life insurance policy were governed by the Employee Retirement Income Security

Act of 1974 (ERISA), any state law voiding a beneficiary designation naming an ex-spouse would be preempted. Accordingly, if Wife's policy were governed by ERISA, Husband would be entitled to the proceeds regardless of any state law revoking the designation of a spouse upon divorce. See Egelhoff v. Egelhoff, 532 U.S. 141, 121 S.Ct. 1322, 149 L.Ed.2d 264 (2001).

Assuming that the policy is not governed by ERISA and that the state has an automatic voiding statute, the contingent beneficiaries would receive the proceeds. What is the impact of the contingent beneficiaries also being relatives of the former spouse? Only a few jurisdictions have statutes which also avoid beneficiary designations in favor of other ex-relatives. See U.P.C. § 2–804.

9. Insured died on July 1. Beneficiary died on July 4 from an unfortunate fireworks accident. Is Beneficiary's estate entitled to the proceeds of the policy?

10. Freddie is named as the sole beneficiary of Victoria's life insurance policy. Freddie, anxious for the money, kills Victoria. Will Freddie be able to take the proceeds?

11. The policy owner should indicate at least one contingent beneficiary in case the primary beneficiary predeceases (or is treated as predeceasing) the insured.

12. If there is no beneficiary capable of taking, the proceeds are usually paid to the owner's estate. The proceeds will also go to the estate if the estate was the named beneficiary. In most cases, the estate planner takes great care to make certain this does not happen. Why?

13. If the policy owner names multiple beneficiaries, most policies presume that each beneficiary takes an equal share. If the insured desires unequal shares, the beneficiary designation needs to contain an express provision providing for proceed allocation.

14. Insured dies owning a life insurance policy in favor of Beneficiary with a face value of $100,000. Insured's estate is too small to satisfy creditors. Who has priority over the proceeds, Beneficiary or the creditors? See William A. Brackney, *Creditors' Rights in Life Insurance,* PROB. & PROP., Mar./Apr. 1993, at 52 (includes chart citing each state's statutes and basic result in non-bankruptcy context).

15. Insurance policies usually give the insured a wide variety of options regarding how the proceeds will be paid upon the insured's death. For example, the insurer may chose a *lump-sum* payment where the beneficiary simply receives one cash payment; an *interest* or *deposit* option where the proceeds remain with the insurer who then makes periodic interest payments to the beneficiary for a fixed period of time before transferring the proceeds; and an *installment* option where a fixed amount (combined proceeds and interest) is paid periodically to the beneficiary until all proceeds are paid. How would you help your client decide which option to select?

16. Many insureds make life insurance payable to a trust, rather than to a beneficiary outright. In this manner, the insured obtains trust benefits (e.g., control of use, professional administration, etc.) for the proceeds. When is this technique appropriate? Should the trust be inter vivos or testamentary? If

inter vivos, should it be funded, i.e., contain property in addition to the contract right to receive proceeds upon the insured's death? Should it be revocable?

17. The policy owner usually retains the right to change the beneficiary designation. Care must be taken to be sure changes comply with the applicable policy (contract) provisions although courts often hold that substantial compliance with the indicated method is sufficient. See John Hancock Mutual Life Ins. Co. v. Jedynak, 250 Mich. 88, 229 N.W. 413 (1930).

18. The owner of a life insurance policy may assign the policy and all of its incidents of ownership to another person such as the beneficiary. This is a common technique if the insured wishes to keep the proceeds out of the insured's estate for tax purposes. The insured must not retain any incidents of ownership and must live at least three years after transferring the policy. Taxation of life insurance proceeds and taxation of gifts of life insurance policies are covered in Chapter 4(J).

19. *Second-to-die* or *survivorship* policies pay benefits only upon the second of two insureds to die, typically a husband and wife. What are the advantages and disadvantages of this type of arrangement?

20. *First-to-die* policies pay benefits only upon the first of two insureds to die. What are the advantages and disadvantages of this type of arrangement? See Robert W. Finnegan, *An Economical Buy–Sell Alternative: First-to-Die Life Insurance,* PROB. & PROP., Jan./Feb. 1994, at 11.

21. Who should pay the premiums on a life insurance policy—the owner, the insured, the insured's employer, or some combination thereof?

22. In *split-dollar* life insurance, the insured and the insured's employer both contribute to the premium cost. When the employee dies, the proceeds are divided between the beneficiary designated by the employee and the employer. Typically, the employer gets the amount needed to reimburse it for the premium payments it made on the employee's behalf. Why might you recommend *split-dollar* life insurance to your client? See Rev. Rul. 64–328, 1964–2 C.B. 11; Lawrence Brody & Lucinda Althauser, *An Update of Business Split–Dollar Insurance,* TR. & EST., Apr. 1994, at 10; Michael D. Weinberg, *Split-Dollar: A Dream Come True*, PROB. & PROP., May/June 1995, at 18. However, the validity of split dollar life insurance arrangements has been called into question by the passage of the Sarbanes–Oxley Corporate Responsibility Act of 2002 which bans corporate loans to employees. See also Donald O. Jansen, *Taxation of Split Dollar Life Insurance Arrangements under the Final Regulations*, 29 ACTEC J. 285 (2004).

23. Under most circumstances, the proceeds of life insurance policies are not deemed taxable income to the beneficiary. See I.R.C. § 101(a). Accelerated life insurance benefits and viatical settlements are discussed in Chapter 6(G).

24. You should personally inspect your client's life insurance policies and beneficiary designations to make sure everything is in proper order.

LOCATE

Visit with several life insurance agents and obtain information on their policies. Evaluate them and determine which policy would be best for you personally under your particular circumstances.

I. ANNUITIES

An annuity is a contract between the purchaser of the contract and an annuity provider. In exchange for a lump sum payment, the annuity provider promises to make periodic payments for the life of the *annuitant* or some other specified period of time. An annuity protects a person from exhausting the person's estate by living longer than anticipated. The purpose of an annuity is, in effect, the opposite of a life insurance policy which protects the insured's family against the risk of the insured dying earlier than anticipated and before accumulating sufficient assets to sustain the family in the manner in which its members were accustomed. Annuities may provide for payments to continue after the annuitant's death and thus annuity contracts often operate to make non-probate transfers.

Annuities are classified from several perspectives. First, they are categorized based on the type of annuity provider, that is, the entity that will make the periodic payments. A *commercial annuity* is one purchased from a company in the business of selling annuities (e.g., an insurance company). A *private annuity* is purchased from someone not in the annuity business (e.g., a family member).

Second, annuities are distinguished by the duration of the periodic payments. Under a *straight life annuity*, the provider makes payments only while the annuitant is alive. If the annuitant outlives his or her life expectancy, the provider loses money. But if the annuitant dies quickly, the provider makes a sizable profit. Straight life annuities lack a non-probate transfer component. With a *refund annuity*, the provider makes payments for the annuitant's life but if the annuitant dies before receiving at least the amount paid for the annuity, the provider pays the difference between the purchase price and the amount already distributed to the annuitant to a designated beneficiary. A *life annuity with a term certain* provides payments for the annuitant's life but if the annuitant dies before the term expires, the provider continues to make annuity payments to a designated beneficiary until the end of the term. The provider makes payments under a *joint life annuity* until the first of the annuitants dies at which time the payments cease. With a *joint and survivorship annuity*, however, the provider continues payments until both annuitants die.

Third, annuities are characterized by how the periodic payments are determined. In a *straight annuity*, each payment is of the same amount, while in a *variable annuity*, the amount of the payment changes based on the investment success of the annuity provider. Variable annuities are thus useful to offset the deflated buying power that inflation causes when all payments are of the same amount.

NOTES AND QUESTIONS

1. Why would you recommend that your client purchase an annuity rather than some other type of investment?

2. Assuming your client's estate plan would be benefited by an annuity, which type would you suggest and why? What factors would you consider in making the decision?

3. There have been many reports of annuity sellers making false representations to entice investors, especially older individuals, to place money in annuities. For example, during a recent five year period, the California Department of Insurance received approximately 2,500 complaints and inquiries pertaining to annuity products. Twenty-five percent of the complaints involved senior citizens and this percentage could even be greater because the Department does not always identify the age of the complainant and victims do not always disclose their age. California Senate Insurance Committee Hearing, Financial Planning or Fleecing of Seniors?: Insurance Products and Investments (Feb. 27, 2003).

4. For the estate tax ramifications of annuities, see Chapter 4(C)(2)(e).

LOCATE

Visit with several agents of companies that sell annuities and obtain information on their contracts. Evaluate them and determine which one would be best for you personally under your particular circumstances.

J. RETIREMENT PLANS

Your client's retirement plan may be one of your client's most valuable assets. A client may die before exhausting the property accumulated in the plan. Thus, retirement plans provide for a death benefit which is payable to the beneficiary named by the employee. Assuming the beneficiary is not the client's estate, the death benefit is not subject to probate.

If a retirement plan is carefully constructed, it will give the client tremendous benefits. For example, the amounts the client contributes to the plan are not currently subject to income tax. In addition, the income earned by the property in the plan is tax-deferred. When the client receives distributions from the plan, then the initial contributions and subsequent income are subject to income tax. Since most clients will be in a lower income tax bracket after they retire than they were when the contributions were made and the income accrued, substantial income tax savings result. The retirement plan is also beneficial for the employer because the employer can usually use its contributions as an income tax deduction.

A retirement plan that meets the requirements for this favorable income tax treatment is called a *qualified plan* and is governed by I.R.C. §§ 401–424 and the Employee Retirement Income Security Act of 1974 (ERISA). These provisions, many of which are lengthy, are extremely complicated and beyond the expertise of most estate planners. Thus, you will want to include a qualified retirement plan expert as a member of your estate planning team.

Although the details of the different types of qualified retirement plans are beyond the scope of this book, it is important for you to have a basic idea of the commonly used plans. Below is a brief explanation of the types of plans you will frequently encounter.

1. DEFINED BENEFIT PLAN

This relatively simple plan provides the employee with a determinable amount of benefits payable for a certain number of years or until the employee dies. The benefits are based on a variety of factors such as length of employment and salary.

2. DEFINED CONTRIBUTION PLAN

Under a defined contribution plan, the employer makes contributions to the plan on the employee's behalf. The contributions may be a fixed amount or they may be computed by some type of formula such as a certain percentage of the profits of the business. The amount the employee receives upon retirement is based upon the amount contributed plus the success of the plan's manager in investing the contributions.

3. CASH OR DEFERRED ARRANGEMENT

In a cash or deferred arrangement, the employee authorizes the employer to place a percentage of the employee's salary into the retirement plan. As with the defined contribution plan, the amount the employee receives upon retirement depends on the amount invested and the plan's earnings. These arrangements are also referred to as *CODAs* or *401(k) Plans.*

4. EMPLOYEE STOCK OWNERSHIP PLAN

An employee stock ownership plan or *ESOP* begins with the corporate employer creating a special type of trust. The employer then makes contributions to the trust on behalf of the employee. Upon receipt of the money, the trustee purchases the corporate employer's stock and holds the stock as the trust corpus. The amount of stock to which the employee will later be entitled depends on the plan's vesting and distribution rules.

5. KEOGH OR H.R.–10 PLANS

A major shortcoming of the qualified plans discussed above is that they require an individual to be an employee. But what if the person is self-employed? Keogh or H.R.–10 plans permit sole proprietors, partners, and other non-common law employees to create retirement plans under basically the same rules as employer plans and receive similar tax benefits.

6. INDIVIDUAL RETIREMENT ACCOUNT

Both self-employed individuals and employees may use *individual retirement accounts* or *IRAs*. The amounts which individuals may contribute are limited and the initial income tax benefit is restricted to individuals who have relatively low incomes. In the standard or *classic IRA*, the contributor does not pay income tax on qualifying contributions nor on the earnings (income and appreciation) of those contributions as they accrue but must pay tax when the contributor makes withdrawals upon retirement. If the contributor's income is too high, the contributor may not deduct the initial contributions from his or her income but the growth in the account is tax-deferred until withdrawal. When non-deductible contributions are made, the contributor needs to pay tax only on the investment income, not the original contributions. IRS Form 8608 contains a formula to determine the taxable to non-taxable ratio. I.R.C. § 408.

An opposite approach is taken by the *Roth IRA* in which the contributor must pay income tax on qualifying contributions but all distributions of both original contributions and earnings are free of income tax. I.R.C. § 408A(c).

7. SIMPLIFIED EMPLOYEE PENSION PLAN

Small businesses may not be able to afford to establish traditional qualified retirement plans because of the administrative overhead costs. Thus, the I.R.C. permits the employer to make contributions directly to the employee's IRA. This technique is called a simplified employee pension plan or *SEP* plan.

NOTES AND QUESTIONS

1. Under the Retirement Equity Act of 1984 (REA), the employee's spouse has the right to demand that the qualified plan's retirement benefit be paid as a joint and survivor annuity. Even if the employee spouse dies before retirement, the surviving spouse is entitled to a death benefit payable as an annuity. I.R.C. § 401(a)(11).

2. The married employee may regain the right to control payment of the retirement plan's death benefit by obtaining spousal consent. The spouse's waiver must meet the following requirements: (1) in writing, (2) indicate that spousal consent is needed to change the beneficiary or form of benefits at a

later time unless the spouse expressly permits re-designations without further consent, and (3) contain the spouse's acknowledgement of the effect of the waiver which is witnessed by a plan representative or a notary public. I.R.C. § 417(a)(2).

3. May a prospective spouse waive rights in a premarital agreement? See Lynn Wintriss, *Waiver of REA Rights in Premarital Agreements,* PROB. & PROP., May/June 1993, at 16 (discussing conflicting case law and regulations and suggesting solutions).

4. Who should be named as the death beneficiary of a qualified retirement plan of a single person or of a married person who was successful in obtaining the consent of the person's spouse? See William P. Kenworthy and W. Douglas Sweet, *Planning for Qualified Plan and IRA Distributions*, PROB. & PROP., Nov./Dec. 1995, at 13.

5. For a detailed discussion of the different types of IRAs, see Elizabeth R. Salasko, *Beyond Plain Vanilla: The New Flavors of IRAs,* PROB. & PROP., May/June 1998, at 23; Stephen P. Magowan, *Roth IRAs: Estate and Income Tax Planning Tool for the 21st Century*, PROB. & PROP., July/Aug. 1998, at 6; Thomas C. Foster, *Roth IRA: Final Regulations*, PROB. & PROP., May/June 1999, at 23.

6. For a discussion of the tax ramifications of retirement plans, see Chapter 4(L).

K. DEFERRED COMPENSATION CONTRACTS

Deferred compensation contracts are arrangements whereby an employee agrees to receive payment for services in a period after it has been earned. These arrangements are used to save the employee income tax by deferring income until a time when the employee is in a lower tax bracket as well as to reduce the employer's immediate cash outlay. If the employee has not received all of the deferred compensation when the employee dies, the compensation is usually payable to a designated beneficiary and thus passes outside of probate.

CHAPTER 4

TAX PLANNING

■ ■ ■

A. BACKGROUND AND HISTORY

JOHN K. McNULTY & GRAYSON M.P. McCOUCH, FEDERAL ESTATE AND GIFT TAXATION*

§§ 1–3 (7th ed. 2011).

§ 1. NATURE OF THE FEDERAL ESTATE, GIFT AND GENERATION-SKIPPING TAXES

Taxation of property transferred by an individual to others at his or her death is one of the oldest and most common forms of taxation, at least in societies where property is privately owned. Death transfer taxes often take the form of an *estate* tax, which is an excise tax levied on the privilege of transferring property at death and usually is measured by the size of the decedent's estate. Or, a death tax can be shaped as an *inheritance* tax, an excise tax levied on the privilege of receiving property from the decedent and usually measured by the amount of property received by each particular recipient, rather than by the amount of the total estate, and by the recipient's relationship to the decedent. The federal estate tax, as its name suggests, is an example of the former; many *state* death taxes are cast in the form of an inheritance tax. Both forms of tax usually, but not necessarily, employ a graduated rate scale; the larger the estate or the larger an inheritance received, the higher the *marginal* tax rates (the rates charged on the last $1 of taxable property) applied, and consequently the higher the *effective* or *average* rate of tax paid. The effective tax rate consists of the total tax paid divided by the total taxable estate or inheritance and is therefore lower than the top marginal rate.

Since a transfer tax imposed at death can so easily be avoided by lifetime gifts—"inter vivos" gifts, made between living persons—a federal transfer tax is imposed on the making of gifts during life. Several states also impose a gift tax to back-up their death transfer taxes. Gift taxes also can be progressive; the rate of tax varies with the amount of taxable transfers previously made during the donor's lifetime. Gift taxes and

* Reprinted with permission of Thomson Reuters.

death taxes in the form of estate or inheritance taxes are known as "transfer taxes." Transfer taxes can be combined or integrated so that, for example, the rate of tax on transfers made at death is affected by the aggregate amount of gift transfers made during life.

The U.S. Constitution requires that all "direct taxes" be apportioned among the several states according to their respective populations. (After the income tax was held to be a direct tax, the Sixteenth Amendment was passed to exempt the income tax from this apportionment rule.) The federal estate and gift taxes are not viewed as direct taxes. They are excise taxes, imposed on an event or a transaction (a gift or transfer of property at death), as distinguished from direct taxes, which are imposed on a person (a "poll tax") or on property itself (whether or not it has been transferred or otherwise made the subject of a transaction or an event). Consequently, the federal death and gift taxes fall outside the apportionment requirement.

§ 2. HISTORY AND EVOLUTION OF THE FEDERAL ESTATE, GIFT, AND GENERATION-SKIPPING TRANSFER TAXES

Throughout the nation's early history, federal taxes on transfers at death were imposed primarily to provide revenue in time of actual or threatened war. From 1797 to 1802 Congress levied a stamp tax on receipts of legacies and probate of wills, to finance a naval buildup in response to French attacks on American ships. An inheritance tax was enacted in 1862, during the Civil War, and repealed in 1870 after the end of the war. In 1894 Congress enacted an income tax which included gifts and inheritances in income, but this tax was struck down as unconstitutional the next year. In 1898 Congress instituted a mixed estate and inheritance tax to finance the Spanish–American War. This tax was progressive with the size of the estate and also graduated with respect to the relationship between the decedent and the recipient. It survived an attack on constitutional grounds but was repealed in 1902.

In 1916 a federal estate tax was enacted, in part out to raise revenue as the United States prepared to enter World War I, and in part to attack undue concentrations of inherited wealth. The constitutionality of this tax was upheld in New York Trust Co. v. Eisner, 256 U.S. 345 (1921); it was viewed as an *indirect tax,* an excise tax which did not have to be apportioned among the states. Meanwhile, many states had adopted estate or inheritance taxes. Some had not, however, and rates varied widely from state to state. These disparities created an inducement for wealthy people to change domicile for tax purposes. To promote greater uniformity, Congress in 1924 enacted a credit against the federal tax for state death taxes paid. As a result, states were induced to enact death transfer taxes and to bring their rates up to the maximum allowable as a credit against the federal tax. Many states enacted such "pick-up" or "sponge" taxes geared to the full amount of the credit against the federal tax.

To avoid the federal and state taxes on transmission or receipt of property at death, some property owners made large inter vivos transfers.

To counteract this technique and partly for political reasons, the federal gift tax was enacted in 1924. (It was repealed in 1926 but reinstated in 1932.) This gift tax was imposed on lifetime gifts at a rate equal to three-quarters of the estate tax rates on equivalent transfers made at death. The gift tax was, and is, progressive and cumulative over a donor's lifetime—the tax on a taxable gift of a given amount is higher if the donor has made many or large taxable gifts previously, even in prior years. Today's federal estate and gift taxes retain many of the essential features of their 1916 and 1932 forebears. In the intervening years, however, the taxes have evolved in several significant ways.

The *marital deduction* originated as an attempt to achieve roughly equal tax treatment of married couples in community property states and separate property states. Under community property law, the estate of a deceased husband (if he were the first to die) includes only one-half of the couple's community property, whereas in a separate property state the husband's estate generally includes all property titled in the decedent's name, which may well represent the bulk of the couple's wealth. To eliminate the tax advantage of automatic estate-splitting four couples in community property states, Congress amended the estate tax in 1942 to provide that the husband's estate would include almost all of the couple's community property. In 1948, Congress reversed course and reinstated the original treatment of community property while allowing a marital deduction for one-half of the value of separate property passing from the decedent to the surviving spouse. Thus, if a deceased husband left all of his property to his surviving spouse, only one-half of the value of the couple's wealth would be subject to estate tax at the husband's death, regardless of whether the couple lived in a separate property state or a community property state. Parallel treatment was afforded for lifetime gifts under the federal gift tax.

For many years, the separate lower rates on lifetimes gifts, and the fresh start up the progressive rate ladder provided by separate taxation of the estate at death, offered substantial tax benefits for wealthy families that could afford to make large inter vivos gifts. In an effort to curtail the advantages of inter vivos giving resulting from the separate gift and estate tax structures, Congress restructured the estate and gifts taxes in the Tax Reform Act of 1976, P.L. 94–455 (the "1976 Act"). Instead of two separate taxes, with two different rate schedules and a fresh start up the progressive rate later for the taxable estate at death, the 1976 Act adopted a unified tax structure, using only one rate schedule which applies to cumulative transfers made during life and at death.

The 1976 Act also adopted a *unified credit* (often referred to as an "exemption equivalent") to replace the separate gift and estate tax exemptions of prior law ($30,000 deduction for cumulative lifetime gifts, $60,000 deduction for the taxable estate). By casting the new exemption in the form of a credit rather than a deduction, Congress ensured that the dollar savings would be uniform for all taxpayers, regardless of their marginal tax brackets. As a result of subsequent legislation, the exemption equivalent has grown by leaps and bounds, reaching $1 million in 2002, $3.5 million in 2009, and $5 million in 2010. Under the unified rate schedule in I.R.C. § 2001(c), assuming a top marginal rate of 35 percent, a credit of $1,730,800 is equal to the tax that would be imposed on a transfer of $5 million and thus is equivalent to a $5 million exemption; hence the use of term "exemption equivalent" to describe the amount sheltered from tax by the unified credit. In effect, a credit of $1,730,800 produces an effective tax rate of zero on the first $5 million of cumulative taxable transfers made during life or at death.

The 1976 Act also introduced for the first time a tax on *generation-skipping transfers*, to supplement the estate and gift taxes. Under prior law it was possible for a transferor to avoid estate and gift taxes by creating trusts that spread the beneficial enjoyment of property temporally across several generations. For example, a trust to pay income to the grantor's child for life, with remainder to grandchildren, gave the child the immediate use and enjoyment of the property, but occasioned no additional estate tax on the corpus when the property passed to the grandchildren. Consequently the property, although of course taxed in the estate of the original grantor, could be passed through one (or more) succeeding generations with no further estate or gift tax liability. The only limit was imposed indirectly by applicable state law in the form of a rule against perpetuities or a similar rule, with the result that property held in trust might be sheltered from transfer taxes for 100 years or more. The generation-skipping provisions enacted in 1976 closed this avenue of tax avoidance by taxing the entire property *as though* it had passed through the estate of the skipped generation (the grantor's child, in the example above). However, those provisions were flawed by administrative complexity and other shortcomings, and they were eventually replaced in 1986 by an entirely new generation-skipping transfer (GST) tax. * * *

The 1976 Act also amended some *income tax* provisions which have great importance for estate planning and administration. The most important of these was an attempt to equalize the treatment of accrued but unrealized appreciation (or decrease) in the value of property gratuitously transferred. The old law was that the donee of an inter vivos gift took the donor's basis in the property ("carryover" basis), while the recipient of a testamentary gift took a new basis stepped up (or down) to fair market value at the date of the transferor's death ("fresh-start" basis). Under the 1976 Act, for all post–1976 transfers, both inter vivos and testamentary, the recipient was to take the transferor's basis ("carryover basis"), subject to various adjustments. However, the 1976 carryover basis provisions were postponed in 1978 and then repealed in 1980, without ever having gone into general effect. Accordingly, the "old law" rules of carryover basis for inter vivos transfers and fresh-start basis for testamentary transfers remain in effect today. See I.R.C. §§ 1014, 1015.

In the Economic Recovery Tax Act of 1981, P.L. 97–34 (the "1981 Act"), expanded the marital deduction by removing the limitations on the amount of property that can be transferred between spouses during life or at death without incurring estate or gift taxes. The 1981 Act also relaxed the restrictions on the types of transfers that qualify for the marital deduction. Broadly speaking, the adoption of an *unlimited* marital deduction has the effect of treating a married couple as a single unit for estate and gift tax purposes, thus relieving most inter-spousal transfers from transfer tax liability. See I.R.C. §§ 2056 and 2523.

The Tax Reform Act of 1986, P.L. 99–514 (the "1986 Act"), made several income tax changes which have continuing significance for estate planning. For example, the income tax rates for estates and trusts were lowered and the rate brackets were compressed, so that estates and trusts with taxable income above a rather low threshold are now subject to tax at the maximum marginal rate. See I.R.C. § 1(e). In addition, the 1986 Act also curtailed the use of so-called "*Clifford* trusts" as an income-shifting technique (see I.R.C. § 673), and introduced the "kiddie tax" of I.R.C. § 1(g), which makes the "net unearned income" over a specified amount (including trust or custodianship income) of a child under the age of 18 (or older, in some cases) taxable at the parent's marginal rate. * * *

The Economic Growth and Tax Relief Reconciliation Act of 2001, P.L. 107–16 (the "2001 Act"), as amended by the Tax Relief, Unemployment Insurance Reauthorization and Job Creation Act of 2010, P.L. 111–312 (the "2010" Act"), reduced the top marginal rate from its pre–2001 level of 55% to 45% in 2007 and then to 35% in 2010. At the same time the exemption equivalent increased dramatically reaching $1 million in 2002, $3.5 million in 2009, and $5 million in 2010.* As a result, beginning in 2011 the gift and estate taxes are imposed at a flat rate of 35% on cumulative taxable transfers above $5 million made during life or at death. * * * The exemption equivalent is indexed for inflation beginning in 2012.

In its original form, the 2001 Act called for the repeal of the estate tax (but not the gift tax) and introduced a modified carryover basis regime to replace the traditional fresh-start basis rules for testamentary transfers. Although these changes were scheduled to take effect in 2010, the 2010 amendments retroactively reinstated the estate tax (with a top marginal rate of 35% and an exemption equivalent of $5 million) along with the fresh-start basis rules and made the carryover-basis-without-estate-tax provisions optional for decedents who died in 2010. Accordingly, the executor of the decedent who died in 2010 could opt out of the estate tax and accept the carryover basis regime set forth in I.R.C. § 1022. Under that provision, property passing from the decedent generally took a basis in the recipient's hands equal to the lesser of the decedent's basis or the value of the property at death. Nevertheless, in the case of appreciated property owned by the decedent at death, the statute allowed a tax-free basis increase of up to $1.3 million, regardless of the relationship (if any) between the decedent and the recipient, as wells as separate basis increase of up to $3 million for property passing in qualifying form to the decedent's surviving spouse. For very large estates, the ability to avoid an immediate estate tax, even at the cost of foregoing a fresh-start basis, provided substantial tax savings. For most estates of small or moderate size, however, the advantages of a $5 million estate tax exemption equivalent coupled with an unlimited basis step-up for appreciated property proved irresistible. One way or another, the vast bulk of property passing from decedents in 2010 emerged undiminished by any immediate estate or income tax liability.

The 2001 Act also had a major impact on the structure of state death taxes. The federal estate tax credit for state death taxes, originally enacted in 1924, provided a powerful incentive for states to impose "pick-up" or "sponge" taxes equal to the maximum allowable credit, and by 2001 almost all of them had done so. The 2001 Act phased out the credit and replaced it with a deduction for state death taxes beginning in 2005. This change removed the underpinning for the longstanding system of pick-up taxes and forced many states to choose between reconfiguring their existing death taxes and abandoning them altogether.

The substantive changes made by the 2001 Act and the 2010 Act are not necessarily cast in stone. A special "sunset" provision ensures that those changes will automatically expire at the end of 2012, thereby reinstating prior law for 2013 and subsequent years. It seems likely that Congress will take further action before 2012, but its is not clear whether the estate, gift and GST taxes will be retained substantially in their existing form or will be subject to further tinkering. * * *

§ 3. REVENUE AND OTHER ROLES OF THE TRANSFER TAXES

The federal estate and gift taxes do not raise very large amounts of revenue now, nor have they ever done so. As of 2009, they accounted for about $24 billion annually, or about one percent of federal budget receipts, a smaller percentage by far than the corresponding figures for the individual income tax (50.1%), the corporate income tax (9.6%), the employment or payroll taxes (36.6%), or even the excise taxes (2.0%). Rates are low and exemptions are high, and, as a result, most people are not subject to federal estate or gift taxes; among those who are taxable, many pay small amounts in tax.

The transfer taxes were not enacted merely to raise revenue. In part they are designed to prevent people from accumulating large blocks of wealth and then transmitting those blocks undiminished from generation to generation. Also, these taxes make an important contribution to the progressivity of the entire tax system. Wealth and high income are closely associated, and estate and gift taxes mainly affect families with relatively high annual incomes.

For taxpayers whom the transfer taxes do affect, the impact can be great, so the prospect of these taxes looms large for such taxpayers and their lawyers. The transfer taxes, as presently structured, offer enormous opportunities for planning. Several features of the taxes can produce erratic results; often the taxes can be legally and easily avoided or drastically reduced by steps (such as regular annual gifts to children) that are perfectly acceptable on non-tax grounds. For society at large and for the finance of government, reform and revitalization of these taxes pose significant and difficult issues of redistribution of wealth, revenue potential, equity and economic effects.

NOTES AND QUESTIONS

1. The Congressional Budget Office estimated that 51,200 estates were subject to the estate tax in 2000, whereas 17,400 estates were subject to the estate tax in 2007.

2. May Congress make changes in tax laws to impose or increase a tax on a transfer which has already occurred or to disallow a deduction for a transaction already completed? See United States v. Carlton, 512 U.S. 26, 114 S.Ct. 2018, 129 L.Ed.2d 22 (1994).

3. This Chapter reviews the fundamentals of wealth transfer taxation. The material focuses on basic rules and thus there may be special rules and exceptions which are not mentioned. The discussion is designed to give you a working knowledge of the essential concepts. If you need detailed information on wealth transfer taxation, you should consult a text devoted exclusively to the subject such as REGIS W. CAMPFIELD, MARTIN B. DICKINSON, WILLIAM J. TURNIER, TAXATION OF ESTATES, GIFTS AND TRUSTS (24th ed. 2011); PAUL R. MCDANIEL, JAMES R. REPETTI, PAUL L. CARON, FEDERAL WEALTH TRANSFER TAXATION (6th ed. 2009); JOHN K. MCNULTY & GRAYSON M.P. MCCOUCH, FEDERAL ESTATE AND GIFT TAXATION (7th ed. 2011).

4. For additional background on transfer taxes, see Debra Rahmin Silberstein, *A History of the Death Tax: A Source of Revenue, or a Vehicle for Wealth Redistribution?*, PROB. & PROP., May/June 2003, at 58.

B. FEDERAL GIFT TAX—AN OVERVIEW

1. BASIC COMPUTATION

The basic computation of the federal gift tax involves the following steps.

(1) Determine All Gifts Made By Donor—The first step in computing the federal gift tax is to prepare a comprehensive list of all gifts of property the donor has made during the donor's entire lifetime. In addition to listing the transferred property, you should list the date of the gift, the identity of the donee, the relationship between the donor and the donee, and how the gift was used. These matters may be significant later in the computation process.

(2) Value Each Gift—Next, you must determine the value of each gift on the list prepared in step one. Generally, the value of a gift is its fair market value on the date the donor made the gift.

(3) Subtract Excluded Gifts—Several types of gifts are excluded from the federal gift tax and must now be removed from the list of gifts.

The two most important excluded gifts are those that qualify for the *annual exclusion* or the *educational and medical expense exclusion*.

(4) Subtract Deductions—Two other types of gifts are also subtracted from the list of gifts: gifts to a spouse, which qualify for the *marital deduction*, and gifts for the public benefit, which qualify for the *charitable deduction*.

(5) Adjust for Certain Pre–1977 Gifts—If the donor made gifts after September 8, 1976 but before January 1, 1977, an amount computed under I.R.C. § 2505(b) is subtracted.

(6) Compute Gift Tax—You may now compute the gift tax by (a) figuring the tentative tax on all taxable gifts the donor has made over the donor's entire life (prior years plus calendar year in question), (b) subtracting the tentative tax on all taxable gifts the donor has made in prior years, and (c) subtracting any unused portion of the *applicable credit amount*.

2. TRANSFERS SUBJECT TO GIFT TAX

Three basic types of transfers are subject to the federal gift tax:

- irrevocable gifts (both outright and in trust);
- transfers for less than adequate and full consideration; and
- the exercise of general power of appointment in favor of someone other than the holder or the holder's creditors.

ROBERT J. LYNN AND GRAYSON M.P. McCOUCH, INTRODUCTION TO ESTATE PLANNING*

§§ 13.4, pages 325–33 (5th ed. 2004).

Section 2501(a) of the Internal Revenue Code imposes the gift tax on the "transfer of property by gift." The statute does not offer a specific definition of what constitutes a gift for this purpose, but provides that the gift tax applies "whether the transfer is in trust or otherwise, whether the gift is direct or indirect, and whether the property is real or personal, tangible or intangible." I.R.C. § 2511(a). The Regulations state that "any transaction in which an interest in property is gratuitously passed or conferred upon another, regardless of the means or device employed, constitutes a gift subject to tax." Reg. § 25.2511–1(c)(1). Thus, a gift subject to tax may arise from "the creation of a trust, the forgiving of a debt, the assignment of a judgment, the assignment of benefits of an insurance policy, or the transfer of cash, certificates of deposit, or Federal, State or municipal bonds." Reg. § 25.2511–1(a). The tax applies only to a "transfer of a beneficial interest in property;" it does not apply to a "transfer of bare legal title to a trustee." Reg. § 25.2511–1(g)(1).

For gift tax purposes, there is no gift unless there is a transfer of property. A person named as a beneficiary of property in a will or trust or

* Reprinted with permission of Thompson Reuters.

other instrument of transfer may disclaim the property and let it pass to an alternative taker under the terms of the instrument or applicable state law. Under the federal disclaimer statute, if a person makes a "qualified" disclaimer of an interest in property, the estate, gift, and GST taxes apply as if the disclaimed interest "had never been transferred to such person." I.R.C. § 2518(a). As a result, the disclaimed interest is treated for federal tax purposes as passing directly from the original transferor to the ultimate recipient in a single transfer, without passing through the hands of the disclaimant. Note that I.R.C. § 2518 controls only the federal tax treatment of the qualified disclaimer; the devolution of the disclaimed interest is governed by state law. A qualified disclaimer must be made in writing within nine months after the date of the transfer creating the interest (or, if later, the date on which the disclaimant reaches age 21). The disclaimant must not have accepted the disclaimed interest, and as a result of the disclaimer the disclaimed interest must pass, without any direction of the part of the disclaimant, either to the original transferor's spouse or to some person other than the disclaimant. I.R.C. § 2518(b). A qualified disclaimer may be especially useful in adjusting a decedent's estate plan after death, in order to fine-tune the amount of a marital or charitable deduction. For example, if the decedent's surviving spouse disclaims a bequest, which passes instead to other beneficiaries, the disclaimed interest will not be eligible for a marital deduction. (If the disclaimed interest passes to a grandchild or more remote descendant of the original transferor, the transfer may become subject to the GST tax.)

The gift tax applies only to completed transfers of property. For gift tax purposes, a transfer generally becomes complete when the donor relinquishes dominion and control, retaining no power to revoke the transfer or change the interests of the beneficiaries in the underlying property. Reg. § 25.2511–2(b). Conversely, a transfer remains incomplete to extent that the donor retains control over the beneficial enjoyment of the transferred property. Reg. § 25.2511–2(c). If the donor retains sufficient control to prevent the transfer from becoming complete and subsequently relinquishes or terminates the power during life, the transfer will becomes complete upon the termination or relinquishment of the power; if the donor retains control until death, the transfer will generally be included in the donor's gross estate. Reg. § 25.2511–2(f). Thus, for example, the creation of an ordinary revocable trust is not a complete transfer for gift tax purposes, irrespective of whether the donor or another person serves as trustee. Less obviously, a retained power that allows the donor to name new beneficiaries or to change the interests of the original beneficiaries (but not to recover beneficial ownership) is also sufficient to prevent a completed gift. In any case, amounts of income or principal distributed to other beneficiaries while the trust remains subject to the donor's retained power constitute completed gifts at the time of distribution, and a relinquishment by the donor of the retained power during his or her life constitutes a completed gift of the remaining trust property.

If the donor's retained power is held in a fiduciary capacity and is limited by a "fixed or ascertainable standard," the power is deemed to be sufficiently circumscribed that it does not rise to the level of dominion or control and is disregarded for gift tax purposes. Reg. § 25.2511–2(c). For example, if A declares herself trustee of an irrevocable inter vivos trust for the benefits her adult children B and C, and A (in her capacity as trustee) retains a power to invade principal as needed for the "support" or "education" or "health" of the beneficiaries, the creation of the trust constitutes a completed gift. (The result would be different, however, if A retained a power to invade principal for the "welfare" or "happiness" of the beneficiaries.) The "ascertainable standard" rule is often useful to a donor who wishes to retain a restricted power without being treated as having retained dominion and control for gift (or estate) tax purposes.

Powers held solely by a person other than the donor generally do not prevent a transfer from being complete for gift tax purposes. For example, if A creates an irrevocable inter vivos trust for the benefit of B and C, and names T as trustee, with discretionary power to distribute trusts income and principal to either or both of the beneficiaries, A has made a completed gift of the entire trust property. (However, if A retained an unlimited power to remove T and substitute herself as trustee, the trustee's powers would be attributed to A and the gift would be incomplete.) Powers held jointly by the donor and another person are treated as if they were held by the donor alone, unless the other person has a "substantial adverse interest" in the underlying property. Reg. § 25.2511–2(e). The rationale for this rule is that any person selected by the donor to exercise a joint power can ordinarily be expected to be responsive to the donor's wishes, unless the other person stands to lose a substantial beneficial interest in the underlying property.

A gift may be partially complete and partially incomplete. Thus, a donor may make a completed gift of certain interests in property while retaining other interests in the same property. Reg. § 25.2511–1(e). For example, if A uses her own funds to purchase land and takes title in the names of herself and B as joint tenants with right of survivorship, A has made a completed gift of one half of the value of the property. (On the other hand, if A with her owns funds opens a joint bank account in the names of herself and B, there is no completed gift until B withdraws funds without obligation to account to A.)

If A creates an irrevocable inter vivos trust to pay income to herself for life, with remainder at her death to B, A has made a completed gift of the remainder interest. Suppose instead that A creates an irrevocable inter vivos trust to pay income to B for life, and at B's death to pay principal to A if living, or if A is not living to B's issue then living. Here there are completed gifts of a life income interest to B and a contingent remainder to B's issue. (In both cases, if the other beneficiaries are members of A's family, the transferred interest are valued under the special valuation rules of I.R.C. § 2702, resulting in a taxable gift of the entire value of the underlying property. If the special valuation rules do not apply, the transferred interests are valued under the actuarial tables promulgated pursuant to I.R.C. § 7520.) Note that the test of completion focuses on the donor's relinquishment of dominion and control; there is no requirement that the donee be identified or that their respective shares be ascertained.

Overall, the rules concerning gift completion give the donor considerable flexibility. If the donor wishes to transfer property without incurring an immediate gift tax liability, the donor can retain a power of revocation (or some other power that prevents the transfer from being complete), though of course the property will eventually be subject to gift or estate tax when the retained power expires. Alternatively, the donor may prefer to pay a gift tax at the outset in order to avoid a subsequent gift or estate tax liability. This can be accomplished if the donor is careful to tailor any retained powers in a way that will not attract an estate tax at death. It is possible for the same transfer to give rise to both gift and estate taxes, but such as overlap is almost never desirable and can usually be avoided through competent planning.

In general, a transfer of property by gift is valued at the time the gift becomes complete. The amount of the gift is equal to the value of the transferred property, reduced by any consideration "in money or money's worth" received by the donor. I.R.C. § 2512. If the donor receives "full and adequate consideration in money or money's worth," the gift tax does not apply. Reg. § 25.2511–1(g)(1). Because consideration functions as an offset in measuring the amount of the gift, it must enhance the donor's net worth in some way. It is not enough that the donee relinquishes a benefit or incurs a detriment in reliance on the donor's transfer, nor that the donee reciprocates with gratitude and affection. If A transfers $100,000 to B in exchange for B's promise to marry A or to retain from smoking and drinking, A has made a gift of $100,000. In this connection, it makes no difference that the transaction is enforceable as a contract under state law or that A lacks donative intent.

A payment made to discharge an enforcement obligation founded on a promise or agreement is ordinarily not a gift, if the obligation was "contracted bona fide and for an adequate and full consideration in money or money's worth." I.R.C. § 2053(c)(1)(A). Thus, a borrower who repays his or her own debt does not make a gift; the repayment merely discharges an existing liability and leaves the borrower's net worth unchanged. Similarly, there is no gift when a person pays money or property to satisfy his or her own legal obligation to support a spouse or a minor child; the discharge of a legal support obligation is treated as the receipt of consideration in money's worth.

The relinquishment by one spouse of the right to claim an elective share or similar "marital rights" in the other spouse's property or estate is not treated as consideration in money's worth for gift tax purposes. Reg. § 25.2512–8. Accordingly, a transfer of property in exchange for a release of marital property rights pursuant to an antenuptial or postnuptial agreement is generally subject to gift tax. For example, if A pays her husband B $100,000 for B's release of his right to claim an elective share in A's estate at her death, A has made a gift to B of $100,000; the transfer may qualify for the marital deduction, but it is a gift nonetheless. (The rule disqualifying inchoate marital property rights does not apply to a right of support or an interest in community property.)

There is a special statutory exemption for marital property settlements incident to divorce. Under I.R.C. § 2516, if one spouses transfers property to the other pursuant to a written agreement relating to their marital and property rights, and divorce occurs within two years after (or one year before) the date of the agreement, the transfer is deemed to be made for full money's-worth consideration and therefore is not subject to gift tax. Divorce settlements are commonly structured to come within the statutory exemption, in order to avoid the need to determine the values of transfers actually made or received by the respective spouses. Note that the statutory exemption applies only if divorce actually occurs within the specified time period, but § 2516 does not preclude a finding of a nongratuitous transfer in cases falling outside its terms. If a husband and wife enter into a written marital property settlement, and divorce occurs more than two years thereafter, transfers made pursuant to a decree incorporating the terms of the settlement may escape gift tax on the ground that they are involuntary. Harris v. Commissioner (1950). A separation agreement, without more, does not provide automatic protection from the gift tax, although transfers between spouses during marriage may qualify for the marital deduction.

QUESTIONS

Which of the following transfers are potentially subject to the federal gift tax? See generally Estate of Hite v. Commissioner, 49 T.C. 580, 594 (1968) (stating elements of gift for federal gift tax purposes).

1. Donor gives Donee, his child, $40,000 as a birthday present.

2. Donor gives Donee, his child, a promissory note for $40,000 signed by Donor as a birthday present.

3. Donor gives Donee, her child, a check drawn by Donor for $40,000 on December 30. Donor dies on January 1, before Donee cashes the check. See Rev. Rul. 67–396, 1967–2 C.B. 351.

4. Donor gives Donee, his child, a new automobile as a birthday present.

5. Donor transfers a certificate of deposit for $100,000 to Trustee, in trust, for Donor's child. Does it make a difference whether Donor retains the ability to revoke the trust?

6. Parent's house has a fair market value of $150,000. Parent sells the house to Child for $100,000. See I.R.C. § 2512(b).

7. To increase customer traffic, Jewelry Store conducts a big sale. Buyer purchases a wedding ring for $20,000 which has a retail value of $32,000. Would your answer change if Buyer was the store owner's son? What if the

sale was not as great as it seemed and Buyer finds out the same ring was selling for $15,000 at another store? Has Buyer made a gift to Jewelry Store?

8. Holder of a general power of appointment exercises the power to transfer $30,000 to Holder's creditor.

9. Holder of a general power of appointment exercises the power to transfer $30,000 to Child.

10. Beneficiary of a trust received all trust income and had the right to demand $15,000 per year from the trust corpus. Trust property is valued at $500,000. Beneficiary fails to exercise the invasion right this year. Would your answer change if Beneficiary had the right to demand $30,000? See I.R.C. § 2514(e) (substantially the same as § 2041(b)(2) reproduced in Chapter 4(C)(2)(d)) which authorizes the *5 or 5 power,* i.e., the lapse of a power of appointment which does not exceed the greater of either (1) $5,000 or (2) 5% of the value of the trust's corpus escapes gift taxation.

11. Beneficiary of the decedent's will disclaims $50,000 which then passes to Child. See I.R.C. § 2518 and Chapter 4(H).

12. Parent pays $50,000 of Child's student loan to Bank.

13. Parent lent Child $50,000 charging the market rate of interest. After Child made several payments on the loan, Parent tells child, "Forget the rest of the loan; you don't owe me a thing." See Treas. Reg. § 25.2511–1(a).

14. Parent lent Child $50,000 interest-free. See Dickman v. Commissioner, 465 U.S. 330, 104 S.Ct. 1086, 79 L.Ed.2d 343 (1984). See also I.R.C. § 7872.

15. Father promised Son that he would pay him $50,000 if he quits drinking and stays sober for one year. Son complies and Father pays the money.

16. Parent owns a vacation home which fronts on the ocean. When Child graduated from law school, Parent permits Child to use the home while studying for the bar. During this time, Parent could have rented the home for $200 per day.

17. Brother and Sister open a joint bank account with Brother supplying $50,000 and Sister contributing $10,000.

18. Sister purchases 100 shares of corporate stock worth $50,000 and has the shares registered in the names of both her and Brother as joint tenants.

19. Assume that you are having numerous problems with your car. Your friend, a most excellent mechanic, spends her entire weekend repairing your car with the parts that you bought at her request. Your friend does not charge you for her labor. Had you gone to the local garage, the labor would have cost you $1,500. See Commissioner v. Hogle, 165 F.2d 352 (10th Cir. 1947).

3. VALUATION OF GIFTS

INTERNAL REVENUE CODE, § 2512

VALUATION OF GIFTS

(a) If the gift is made in property, the value thereof at the date of the gift shall be considered the amount of the gift.

(b) Where property is transferred for less than an adequate and full consideration in money or money's worth, then the amount by which the value of the property exceeded the value of the consideration shall be deemed a gift, and shall be included in computing the amount of gifts made during the calendar year.

* * *

NOTES AND QUESTIONS

1. The value of the gift when the gift tax return is due or when the tax is actually paid is irrelevant.

2. "The value of property is the price at which such property would change hands between a willing buyer and a willing seller, neither being under any compulsion to buy or to sell, and both having reasonable knowledge of relevant facts." Treas. Reg. § 25.2512–1.

3. Mike bought a new car. Mike decided to give his old car to his younger brother, Tom. A car dealer would have given Mike $1,500 for his old car. Comparable old cars, however, were being sold by dealers for $3,000. What is the value of Mike's gift? See Treas. Reg. § 25.2512–1.

4. Father gave Daughter 100 shares of ABC Corporation stock for her birthday. On that day, ABC stock was traded for a high of $50 per share and a low of $36 per share. The closing price was $40 per share. What is the value of the stock for gift tax purposes? See Treas. Reg. § 25.2512–2(b)(1).

5. Mother gave Son 100 shares of XYZ Corporation stock on Thursday. No XYZ stock was traded on that day. The two closest sales dates were Monday when the mean sales price was $24 per share and Friday when the mean sales price was $20. What is the value of the stock for gift tax purposes? See Treas. Reg. § 25.2512–2(b)(1).

6. Creditor loaned Debtor $10,000 at a simple interest rate of 10% with payment of principal and interest due at the end of the year. Debtor made no payment of principal or interest. At year's end, Creditor told Debtor to keep the money and consider it a gift. What is the value of Creditor's gift? See Treas. Reg. § 25.2512–4.

7. Donor pays $2,000 in premiums to purchase a term life insurance policy on Insured's life and then immediately transfers ownership of the policy to Insured. The face value of the policy is $250,000. What is the value of Donor's gift? See Treas. Reg. § 25.2512–6(a).

8. Insured owns a paid-up life insurance policy on her life for $100,000. Insured gives the policy to her Niece as a birthday present. What is the value of Insured's gift? See Treas. Reg. § 25.2512–6(a).

9. Grandson purchased a car from Grandmother for $500. The car was only two years old and similar cars retailed for $10,000 at a local car dealer. What is the value of Grandmother's gift? See Treas. Reg. § 25.2512–8.

10. The fair market value of annuities, life estates, terms for years, remainders, and reversions is their present value based on the applicable interest rate and mortality experience. See I.R.S. Notice 89–60, 1989–1 C.B. 700; I.R.C. § 7520. This notice contains tables indicating the percentage of fair market value allocated to transferred and retained interests depending on the age of the interest holder or the number of years in a term certain. In exceptional cases, the donor's actual life expectancy may be used instead of the table period. See Estate of McLendon v. Commissioner, 135 F.3d 1017 (5th Cir. 1998); Treas. Reg. §§ 20.7520–3 & 25.7520–3.

11. The valuation of certain types of property, such as fractional interests, art work, and collectibles, is prone to controversy between the I.R.S. and the donor. See, e.g., Ralph E. Lerner, *Valuing Works of Art for Tax Purposes,* 28 REAL PROP., PROB. & TR. J. 593 (1993).

12. Mike Davidson caught St. Louis Cardinal's first baseman Mark McGwire's 61st home run ball in September 1998. Mike quickly gave the ball to McGwire. Collectors of sports memorabilia would have been willing to pay an exorbitant price for the ball, perhaps in excess of $100,000. What is the value of Mike's gift to McGwire? See IR–98–56, 1998 WL 566879.

4. EXCLUSIONS

a. Annual Exclusion

INTERNAL REVENUE CODE, § 2503

TAXABLE GIFTS

* * *

(b) Exclusion from gifts.—

(1) In general.— In the case of gifts (other than gifts of future interests in property) made to any person by the donor during the calendar year, the first $10,000 of such gifts to such person shall not, for purposes of subsection (a), be included in the total amount of gifts made during such year. Where there has been a transfer to any person of a present interest in property, the possibility that such interest may be diminished by the exercise of a power shall be disregarded in applying this subsection, if no part of such interest will at any time pass to any other person.

(2) Inflation adjustment.— In the case of gifts made in a calendar year after 1998, the $10,000 amount contained in paragraph (1) shall be increased by an amount equal to—

(A) $10,000, multiplied by

(B) the cost-of-living adjustment determined under section 1(f)(3) for such calendar year by substituting "calendar year 1997" for "calendar year 1992" in subparagraph (B) thereof.

If any amount as adjusted under the preceding sentence is not a multiple of $1,000, such amount shall be rounded to the next lowest multiple of $1,000.

(c) Transfer for the benefit of minor.— No part of a gift to an individual who has not attained the age of 21 years on the date of such transfer shall be considered a gift of a future interest in property for purposes of subsection (b) if the property and the income therefrom—

(1) may be expended by, or for the benefit of, the donee before his attaining the age of 21 years, and

(2) will to the extent not so expended—

(A) pass to the donee on his attaining the age of 21 years, and

(B) in the event the donee dies before attaining the age of 21 years, be payable to the estate of the donee or as he may appoint under a general power of appointment as defined in section 2514(c).

* * *

NOTES AND QUESTIONS

1. For gifts made from 1982 through 2001, the first $10,000 in value of present interest gifts to each donee per calendar year are not subject to federal gift tax. The annual exclusion was adjusted for inflation in December 2001 and raised to $11,000 for gifts made in 2002. The annual exclusion remained at $11,000 until January 1, 2006 when it was increased to $12,000. Most recently, on January 1, 2009 the annual exclusion was increased to $13,000. Due to low inflation, it may take several more years before the annual exclusion reaches $14,000, especially because the amount of exclusion is rounded to the closest multiple of $1,000 below the indexed amount. For example, if the indexed amount is $13,999, the annual exclusion would remain at the $13,000 level.

2. There is no limit to the number of annual exclusions a person may use each year. Thus, a donor may pass a tremendous quantity of property totally tax-free assuming the donor has many potential donees in mind, e.g., children, grandchildren, brothers, sisters, nieces, nephews, and friends. Moreover, spouses are allowed to split a gift, which means that one spouse may utilize the other spouses unused annual exclusion amount. See § B(8) of this chapter.

3. Donor gave away a total of $30,000 to four donees in one year, $15,000 to her daughter and $5,000 to each of her three grandchildren. Will the annual exclusion prevent these gifts from being taxed?

4. What is the shortest period of time that must elapse between two gifts to the same donee so the donor may obtain two annual exclusions?

5. Donor gave Donee a personal check for $13,000 on December 30. Donee did not cash the check until January 3. In which year may Donor claim

the annual exclusion for this gift? See Rev. Rul. 96–56. Would your answer change if Donor died on January 2?

6. Only gifts of *present interests* qualify for the annual exclusion. A present interest is "[a]n unrestricted right to the immediate use, possession, or enjoyment of property or the income from property (such as a life estate or term certain)." Treas. Reg. § 25.2503–3(b).

7. Gifts of *future interests* to persons 21 years of age or older will not qualify for the annual exclusion. Future interests include "reversions, remainders, and other interests or estates, whether vested or contingent, and whether or not supported by a particular interest or estate, which are limited to commence in use, possession, or enjoyment at some future date or time." Treas. Reg. § 25.2503–3(a).

8. Gifts of future interests to persons under 21 years of age will qualify for the annual exclusion if they are structured to satisfy the requirements of § 2503(c). Note that these types of transfers are often called *minor's trusts* even though the beneficiary is not necessarily a true "minor," i.e., the beneficiary could be 18, 19, or 20 years old. Basically, the trust must allow principal and income to be used by or for the benefit of the beneficiary while under age 21 and must provide for all remaining property to be paid to the beneficiary upon reaching age 21 or to the beneficiary's estate if the beneficiary dies earlier. The beneficiary does not need to be related to the settlor.

9. Settlor creates an irrevocable trust for Beneficiary by transferring stock valued at $100,000 to Trustee. The terms of the trust require Trustee to pay all income to Beneficiary at least once a year for ten years and then to pay the corpus to Beneficiary. Beneficiary's income interest is a present interest and thus may be offset by the annual exclusion. Beneficiary's remainder interest is a future interest and may not be offset with the annual exclusion. Would your analysis of this question change if Settlor retained the power to revoke?

10. Settlor created an irrevocable trust for her children, all of whom are over 21 years of age. Trustee has the discretion to distribute as much of the income and principal as is necessary for the children's health, education, and support. The entire transfer is subject to tax without reduction by the annual exclusion because the gift is of a future interest. For a clever way to circumvent this restriction, see Chapter 4(I)(2)'s discussion of the *Crummey* trust.

11. Mother creates an irrevocable trust for the benefit of her new-born child. Assuming the rest of the trust's terms comply with § 2503(c), will a limitation on Trustee's discretion to use trust income and corpus only for Child's "health, education, and support" prevent Mother from offsetting the transfer with the annual exclusion? See Treas. Reg. § 25.2503–4 & Rev. Rul. 67–270.

12. Your client is very interested in using a minor's trust but does not like the idea of the property passing into the beneficiary's estate if the beneficiary dies before reaching age 21. What technique would you recommend to your client to alleviate part of this problem? See Treas. Reg. § 25.2503–4(b)(1)(3).

13. Settlor transfers property to an irrevocable trust naming Settlor's 10 year old child as the beneficiary. The trust requires all income to be paid each year to Child. Final distribution will not occur until Child reaches age 30. Is any portion of the transfer eligible for the annual exclusion? See Treas. Reg. § 25.2503–4(c).

14. For additional advice on how to maximize your client's use of the annual exclusion, see Bradley E.S. Fogel, *Billion Dollar Babies: Annual Exclusion Gifts to Minors*, PROB. & PROP., Sept./Oct. 1998, at 6.

b. Education and Medical Expense Exclusion

INTERNAL REVENUE CODE, § 2503

TAXABLE GIFTS

* * *

(e) Exclusion for certain transfers for educational expenses or medical expenses.—

(1) In general.—Any qualified transfer shall not be treated as a transfer of property by gift for purposes of this chapter.

(2) Qualified transfer.—For purposes of this subsection, the term "qualified transfer" means any amount paid on behalf of an individual–

(A) as tuition to an educational organization described in section 170(b)(1)(A)(ii) for the education or training of such individual, or

(B) to any person who provides medical care (as defined in section 213(d)) with respect to such individual as payment for such medical care.

* * *

NOTES AND QUESTIONS

1. Assume that you are attending Big Dollar University and need $25,000 for this year's tuition payment. Your mother makes her check payable to BDU for the full amount and sends it to BDU. Has your mother made a taxable gift? Would it make a difference if a kindhearted stranger made the payment instead of your mother?

2. Now assume that your father sends you a check payable to you for the $25,000. You endorse the check over to BDU to pay your tuition. Has your father made a taxable gift?

3. You also have living expenses while attending BDU such as room, board, and books. Your uncle directly pays BDU for your dorm room and meals. In addition, he establishes a pre-paid account in your name at the bookstore. Has your uncle made taxable gifts? See Treas. Reg. § 25.2503–6(b)(2).

4. Daughter transfers $100,000 into a trust which provides that trust income and principal may be used only for the medical expenses of Parent. The trust states that all distributions must be made directly to the person who provides the medical care. Is Daughter's gift covered by the § 2503(e) exclusion? See Treas. Reg. § 25.2503–6(c).

5. Brother pays $50,000 to Hospital for the medical care of Sister. Sister submits a claim with Sister's insurance company and receives a reimbursement check for $40,000. Has Brother made a taxable gift? See Treas. Reg. § 25.2503–6(b).

6. Parent pays the premiums on adult Child's health insurance policy. Is this transfer eligible for the § 2503(e) exclusion? See Treas. Reg. § 25.2503–6(b)(3).

5. DEDUCTIONS

a. Marital Deduction

Most gifts to a donee who is, at the time of the gift, the donor's spouse are fully deductible, regardless of amount. I.R.C. § 2523(a). Note that gifts of life estates and most other terminable interests do not qualify for the deduction. In addition, special rules apply if the donor's spouse is not a United States citizen. See Chapter 4(E) for a more detailed discussion of the marital deduction.

b. Charitable Deduction

All gifts to qualifying religious, educational, governmental, or other charitable organizations are deductible, regardless of amount. I.R.C. § 2522. See Chapter 4(M) for a more detailed discussion of the charitable deduction.

6. TAX RATE SCHEDULE

INTERNAL REVENUE CODE, § 2001

IMPOSITION AND RATE OF TAX

* * *

(c) Rate schedule.—

If the amount with respect to which the tentative tax to be computed is:	**The tentative tax is:**
Not over $10,000	18 percent of such amount.
Over $10,000 but not over $20,000	$1,800, plus 20 percent of the excess of such amount over $10,000.

If the amount with respect to which the tentative tax to be computed is:	The tentative tax is:
Over $20,000 but not over $40,000	$3,800, plus 22 percent of the excess of such amount over $20,000.
Over $40,000 but not over $60,000	$8,200, plus 24 percent of the excess of such amount over $40,000.
Over $60,000 but not over $80,000	$13,000, plus 26 percent of the excess of such amount over $60,000.
Over $80,000 but not over $100,000	$18,200, plus 28 percent of the excess of such amount over $80,000.
Over $100,000 but not over $150,000	$23,800, plus 30 percent of the excess of such amount over $100,000.
Over $150,000 but not over $250,000	$38,800, plus 32 percent of the excess of such amount over $150,000.
Over $250,000 but not over $500,000	$70,800, plus 34 percent of the excess of such amount over $250,000.
Over $500,000	$155,800, plus 35 percent of the excess of such amount over $500,000.

NOTES AND QUESTIONS

1. For gifts made in 2012, the maximum rate will be 35%. See I.R.C. § 2502(a). For years 2013 and thereafter, the maximum rate will be 55% plus a 5% surcharge for gifts between $10,000,000 and $17,184,000 unless Congress enacts new legislation.

2. You have just won the lottery and are in a philanthropic mood. You make a $135,000 gift to Kristi and a $210,000 gift to Dennis. Assuming these are the only gifts greater than the annual exclusion you have ever made, what is your tentative gift tax?

3. To determine the gift tax the donor owes, you start by computing a tentative tax on all the taxable gifts which the donor has made by applying the rate schedule in I.R.C. § 2001(c) as reproduced above. You are computing a tentative tax as if all of the donor's taxable gifts (prior years and current year) were made in the current year. You then figure a tentative tax on the taxable gifts which the donor made in all prior years. In other words, you now

compute a tentative tax as if the donor made all of the donor's prior taxable gifts in the current year but did not make any of the current year's gifts. The donor's *tentative tax* for the current year is then computed by subtracting the tentative tax on all taxable gifts made in prior years from the tentative tax on all taxable gifts the donor has ever made. It is from this tentative tax that you subtract the unused applicable credit amount as discussed in the following section.

7. APPLICABLE CREDIT AMOUNT

To determine the amount of gift tax the donor owes, you subtract any portion of the donor's *applicable credit amount* that the donor has not already used to offset gift tax liability for prior years from the donor's tentative tax. In computing the applicable credit amount used on prior gifts, the gift tax rate for the year of the current gift is used, not the rate that applied when the prior gifts were made. I.R.C. §§ 2505 and 2010(c). The applicable credit amount, called the *unified credit* if the gift and estate credit amounts are the same, is a credit against the tentative tax. The table below shows the amount of the credit and the *applicable exclusion amount,* that is, the total amount of property a donor may give away without gift tax liability.

Year of Gift	Applicable Credit Amount [recalculated under 2012 rates]	Applicable Exclusion Amount
2000–2001	$217,050	$675,000
2002–2010	$330,800	$1,000,000
2011	$1,730,800	$5,000,000
2012	$1,772,800	$5,120,000
2013 and thereafter [assuming no new legislation]	$345,800	$1,000,000

QUESTION

Donor made $5,300,000 of taxable gifts in 2011. Previously, Donor had made a total of $700,000 of taxable gifts and had used $192,800 of Donor's gift tax credit to offset Donor's gift tax liability on those gifts. How much federal gift tax does Donor owe for Donor's 2011 gifts?

8. SPLIT GIFTS BETWEEN SPOUSES

INTERNAL REVENUE CODE, § 2513

GIFT BY HUSBAND OR WIFE TO THIRD PARTY

(a) Considered as made one-half by each.—

(1) In general.—A gift made by one spouse to any person other than his spouse shall, for the purposes of this chapter, be considered as made one-half by him and one-half by his spouse, but only if at the time of the gift each spouse is a citizen or resident of the United States. This paragraph shall not apply with respect to a gift by a spouse of an interest in property if he creates in his spouse a general power of appointment, as defined in section 2514(c), over such interest. For purposes of this section, an individual shall be considered as the spouse of another individual only if he is married to such individual at the time of the gift and does not remarry during the remainder of the calendar year.

(2) Consent of both spouses.—Paragraph (1) shall apply only if both spouses have signified (under the regulations provided for in subsection (b)) their consent to the application of paragraph (1) in the case of all such gifts made during the calendar year by either while married to the other.

(b) Manner and time of signifying consent.—

(1) Manner.— A consent under this section shall be signified in such manner as is provided under regulations prescribed by the Secretary.

(2) Time.—Such consent may be so signified at any time after the close of the calendar year in which the gift was made, subject to the following limitations—

(A) The consent may not be signified after the 15th day of April following the close of such year, unless before such 15th day no return has been filed for such year by either spouse, in which case the consent may not be signified after a return for such year is filed by either spouse.

(B) The consent may not be signified after a notice of deficiency with respect to the tax for such year has been sent to either spouse in accordance with section 6212(a).

(c) Revocation of consent.—Revocation of a consent previously signified shall be made in such manner as is provided under regulations prescribed by the Secretary, but the right to revoke a consent previously signified with respect to a calendar year—

(1) shall not exist after the 15th day of April following the close of such year if the consent was signified on or before such 15th day; and

(2) shall not exist if the consent was not signified until after such 15th day.

(d) Joint and several liability for tax.—If the consent required by subsection (a)(2) is signified with respect to a gift made in any calendar year, the liability with respect to the entire tax imposed by this chapter of each spouse for such year shall be joint and several.

NOTES AND QUESTIONS

1. The ability of spouses to split gifts offers the marital unit the opportunity to achieve significant tax savings. For example, two annual exclusions and two applicable credit amounts are available and the tax bracket applicable to each spouse is lowered.

2. Husband made four taxable gifts during the year, two to his children by a former spouse and two to his children by his current spouse, Wife. May Wife agree to the split gift technique with regard to Husband's gifts to her children but not to her step-children? See Treas. Reg. § 25.2513–1(b)(5).

3. Husband and Wife live in a community property state. Wife gives $22,000 in community property to Grandson. Must Husband and Wife follow the split gift procedure to prevent this from being a taxable gift?

4. The donor spouse must always file a gift tax return to use the split gift technique. The consenting spouse may also need to file a gift tax return unless certain conditions are satisfied. See page 4 of the *Instructions for Form 709* in Appendix A(2) and Treas. Reg. § 25.2513–1(c).

5. During marriage, Humble Husband agreed to split gifts with Wealthy Wife. After 20 years of marriage and enough split gifts to use up $200,000 of Husband's applicable credit amount, Husband and Wife are divorced. May Husband regain any of his applicable amount, either from the government or in an action against Wife, if he shows that all of the gifts were of Wife's property and that all gifts went to Wife's children from a prior marriage?

9. GIFT TAX RETURN

The donor must file a gift tax return by April 15 of the year following the year in which the donor made the gift. I.R.C. § 6075(b). The gift tax return is designated as *Form 709.* Study the copy of the form and its accompanying instructions found in Appendix A.

Even if the donor has no tax liability because of the gift, a gift tax return must be filed in the following circumstances, among others. See I.R.C. § 6019.

- Donor made a gift of more than $13,000 to a non-spouse donee.
- Donor transferred more than $136,000 to a non-citizen spouse.
- Donor made a gift of more than $13,000 to a charity.
- Donor made a gift of a future interest that does not qualify for the marital deduction.
- Donor and donor's spouse elect to split gifts.
- Donor desires to make a qualified terminable interest property election. See Chapter 4(E) for more information about QTIP arrangements.

Only individuals file gift tax returns. If a corporation, partnership, trust, or estate makes a gift, the stockholders, partners, or beneficiaries are considered the true donors and are responsible for the tax.

10. LIABILITY FOR PAYMENT OF GIFT TAX

The donor is responsible for paying the gift tax. I.R.C. § 2502(c). However, the donee may be responsible for the tax in two important situations.

First, the donor may fail to pay the tax. Under I.R.C. § 6324(b), the donee of any gift becomes personally liable for the tax to the extent of the value of the gift the donee received. The donee's secondary liability is for the entire gift tax the donor owes for that year, not just the unpaid gift tax on the donee's particular gift. A donee may not escape liability by demonstrating that the particular gift the donee received was exempt from gift tax because of the annual exclusion. See Baur v. Commissioner, 145 F.2d 338 (3d Cir. 1944). In addition, the gifted property is subject to a 10 year lien in favor of the federal government. I.R.C. § 6324(b).

Second, the donee may be responsible for the tax because the donee agreed to pay it as a condition of the donor's gift. This is called a *net gift*. Based on the analogous income tax case of Diedrich v. Commissioner, 457 U.S. 191, 102 S.Ct. 2414, 72 L.Ed.2d 777 (1982), a net gift is actually two transactions in one; a gift and a sale. The value of the gift is determined by subtracting the amount of the sales price (i.e., the gift tax the donee pays) from the asset's fair market value. The following formula is used to determine the amount of the tax owed on a net gift. See Rev. Rul. 75–72.

$$\frac{\text{``normal'' gift tax on asset's fair market value}}{1 + \text{marginal tax rate}} = \text{gift tax}$$

NOTES AND QUESTIONS

1. Assume that Donor makes a net gift in 2012 of property with a fair market value of $1,200,000. What is the Donor's gift tax liability assuming this is Donor's first and only taxable gift in the Donor's lifetime? What is the Donor's gift tax liability if this is the Donor's first and only taxable gift in the Donor's lifetime but it was not a net gift? Assume a flat gift tax rate of 35%.

2. Note that the formula given above would need to be altered if, after computing the tentative tax, the tax bracket on the net gift drops.

3. For income tax purposes, the net gift is treated as if the donor sold the asset for the gift tax the donee pays. Thus, the donor realizes capital gain income to the extent that the gift tax exceeds the donor's adjusted basis in the gifted property. See Diedrich v. Commissioner, 457 U.S. 191, 102 S.Ct. 2414, 72 L.Ed.2d 777 (1982); Treas. Reg. § 1.1001–1(e).

11. STATE GIFT TAX

Approximately ten states impose a gift tax on inter vivos transfers. The methods used to compute state gift taxes fall into two main categories. The first is a tax on total taxable gifts in a manner analogous to the federal gift tax. The second is a tax on each gift separately with the rate of tax being based on the relationship between the donor and the donee.

Typically, the closer that the donee is related to the donor, the lower the rate of tax and the greater the number and size of exemptions.

LOCATE

Does your state impose a gift tax? If yes, how does it operate?

12. GIFT TAX PROBLEM

Donor made the following transfers of property in 2011. All transfers are of Donor's separate property.

1. Donor gave Daughter a promissory note (Donor is the sole maker) for $100,000 on December 5, 2011 as a holiday present. The note is due on May 1, 2013.
2. Donor gave Son a collection of rare stamps on March 12, 2011. The stamps had a fair market value of $210,000 on March 12, 2011 but by the end of the year had depreciated in value to $110,000.
3. Donor sent University a check to pay for Daughter's law school tuition. The check was dated January 14, 2011 and was for $50,000, enough to cover both her current tuition and the amount she was in arrears.
4. Donor sold a ranch to Grandson for $500,000. The ranch had a fair market value of $800,000 on the date of the sale.
5. Donor opened a joint bank account with Granddaughter for $50,000 on June 17, 2011. Donor supplied all of the funds for this account. During 2011, Granddaughter withdrew $30,000.
6. Donor paid Hospital $20,000 for the medical expenses of Stranger on August 15, 2011.
7. Donor gave Spouse a gold watch on May 10, 2011. Donor paid $55,000 for the watch in 1990. The watch was valued at $175,000 on the date of the gift.
8. Donor, an attorney, performed legal serves for Client in 2011. Because Client was in financial difficulty, Donor decided on November 10, 2011 to waive the attorney fees. The reasonable value of Donor's legal services was $70,000.

What is Donor's 2011 federal gift tax liability assuming Donor had previously made a total of $800,000 of taxable gifts and had used $202,050 of Donor's gift tax credit to offset Donor's gift tax liability on those gifts?

C. FEDERAL ESTATE TAX—AN OVERVIEW

1. BASIC COMPUTATION

The basic computation of the federal estate tax involves the following steps.

(1) Determine Contents of Gross Estate—The first step in computing the federal estate tax is to determine the property in the decedent's *gross estate*. This property may include assets that are not included in the decedent's probate estate. In other words, the federal government taxes many items of property that do not pass to the decedent's heirs or will beneficiaries.

(2) Value Gross Estate—A value must then be placed on each item of property in the decedent's gross estate. Generally, this amount is the value of the property at the time of the decedent's death.

(3) Subtract Deductions—The decedent's *taxable estate* may then be determined by subtracting the marital deduction, the charitable deduction, and deductions for expenses, debts, taxes, and losses during the administration process.

(4) Determine Tax Base—All taxable gifts the decedent made after December 31, 1976 (unless they were already included as part of the gross estate in step one) are then added to the taxable estate to determine the *tax base*.

(5) Compute Estate Tax—You then compute the federal estate tax by (a) figuring the tentative tax on the decedent's tax base and (b) subtracting credits and related adjustments such as the applicable credit amount, gift tax payable on lifetime transfers, state death tax credit, and the credit for recently paid estate taxes on the same property.

(6) Determine Source of Payment—Finally, you must determine the source for the payment of the estate tax by consulting state and federal tax apportionment statutes as well as the express provisions of the decedent's will, if any. See Mark A. Segal, *Tax Apportionment: Who Picks Up the Tab?*, PROB. & PROP., July/Aug. 1994, at 33.

2. CONTENTS OF GROSS ESTATE

a. Generally

The gross estate includes "all property, real or personal, tangible or intangible, wherever situated" "to the extent of the interest therein of the decedent at the time of his death." I.R.C. §§ 2031 & 2033. As you learn about the items included in the gross estate, many of which you might not have anticipated being there, think about how your client could remove these assets from the gross estate to save taxes while simultaneously carrying out the client's non-tax objectives.

NOTES AND QUESTIONS

1. Which of the following items of property would be included in Decedent's gross estate? Assume that Decedent died domiciled in your state and was a United States citizen for tax purposes. See Treas. Reg. § 20.2033–1.

a. $47.50 in cash found in Decedent's pockets at time of death.

b. Gold wedding ring Decedent was wearing at time of death.

c. House located in your state which is protected under homestead law.

d. Ranch located in another state.

e. Vacation home in Jamaica.

f. Tax-free government bonds.

g. Promissory note signed by Decedent's child which is expressly cancelled in Decedent's will.

h. Patent on a molecular transportation device.

2. Decedent owned a life estate in property received under Grandparent's will. Is any portion of this property in Decedent's estate?

3. Decedent was named as a remainder beneficiary to take property after a life tenant's death. Decedent predeceased the life tenant. Is any portion of this property in Decedent's estate?

4. Decedent was named as the sole beneficiary of Parent's will. Decedent predeceased Parent. Is any portion of Parent's estate included in Decedent's estate?

5. One week before Decedent died, a corporation in which Decedent owned stock declared a large cash dividend for record owners as of that date. The corporation did not pay the dividend until two weeks after Decedent's death. Is any portion of the dividend part of Decedent's gross estate? Would your answer change if the dividend was declared before Decedent's death but the record date was after Decedent's death?

6. Decedent owned a certificate of deposit with a face value of $100,000 earning 5% simple interest per year. Decedent received the most recent interest payment on January 1 and died on October 31. The next payment is due January 1 of the following year. Is any portion of the interest payment part of Decedent's gross estate?

7. The term *income in respect of a decedent* (IRD) refers to income to which the decedent was entitled at the time of death but which is not reportable on the decedent's final income tax return under a properly used accounting method. Examples of this type of income may include salary, bonuses, installment sale contract receipts, partnership income, and proceeds of the sale of property where the decedent completed the sale before death but had not yet collected the proceeds. The decedent's right to this income is property and thus the proceeds received from IRD items are part of the decedent's gross estate. Depending on the circumstances, the income itself is taxed either to the estate or to the eventual recipients (i.e., heirs or beneficia-

ries). The payor of the income tax is entitled to an income tax deduction for the estate tax which the decedent's estate incurred because the gross estate included the IRD. See I.R.C. § 691.

8. "A cemetery lot owned by the decedent is part of his gross estate, but its value is limited to the salable value of that part of the lot which is not designed for the interment of the decedent and the members of his family." Treas. Reg. § 20.2033–1(b).

9. Decedent and Decedent's spouse lived in a community property state. Decedent opened a $100,000 certificate of deposit with savings solely from his salary earned during marriage. How much of the certificate of deposit will be in Decedent's gross estate?

10. "The value of the gross estate shall include the value of all property to the extent of any interest therein of the surviving spouse, existing at the time of the decedent's death as dower or curtesy, or by virtue of a statute creating an estate in lieu of dower or curtesy." I.R.C. § 2034. Does your state provide dower or curtesy rights? Note that such interests are likely to escape taxation because of the marital deduction.

11. Decedent died in an automobile accident. The driver of the other car was intoxicated and there is evidence that Saloon may have dram shop liability. Is any portion of this cause of action part of Decedent's estate?

12. Decedent was the trustee of a large trust. Are any of the trust's assets included in Decedent's estate?

b. Property Held in Joint Tenancy with Rights of Survivorship

INTERNAL REVENUE CODE, § 2040

JOINT INTERESTS

(a) General rule.—The value of the gross estate shall include the value of all property to the extent of the interest therein held as joint tenants with right of survivorship by the decedent and any other person, or as tenants by the entirety by the decedent and spouse, or deposited, with any person carrying on the banking business, in their joint names and payable to either or the survivor, except such part thereof as may be shown to have originally belonged to such other person and never to have been received or acquired by the latter from the decedent for less than an adequate and full consideration in money or money's worth: *Provided,* That where such property or any part thereof, or part of the consideration with which such property was acquired, is shown to have been at any time acquired by such other person from the decedent for less than an adequate and full consideration in money or money's worth, there shall be excepted only such part of the value of such property as is proportionate to the consideration furnished by such other person: *Provided further,* That where any property has been acquired by gift, bequest, devise, or inheritance, as a tenancy by the entirety by the decedent and spouse, then to the extent of one-half of the value thereof, or, where so acquired by the decedent and any other person as joint tenants with right of survivorship and their interests are not otherwise specified or fixed by law, then to the extent of the value of a fractional part to be determined by dividing the value of the property by the number of joint tenants with right of survivorship.

(b) Certain joint interests of husband and wife.—

(1) Interests of spouse excluded from gross estate.—Notwithstanding subsection (a), in the case of any qualified joint interest, the value included in the gross estate with respect to such interest by reason of this section is one-half of the value of such qualified joint interest.

(2) Qualified joint interest defined.—For purposes of paragraph (1), the term "qualified joint interest" means any interest in property held by the decedent and the decedent's spouse as—

(A) tenants by the entirety, or

(B) joint tenants with right of survivorship, but only if the decedent and the spouse of the decedent are the only joint tenants.

NOTES AND QUESTIONS

1. Decedent and Friend owned property as joint tenants with rights of survivorship. How much of this property is included in Decedent's gross estate?

2. Decedent and Friend purchased an asset as joint tenants with rights of survivorship. Evidence shows that Decedent paid $40,000 and Friend paid $60,000 for the asset which has appreciated to $200,000 at the time of Decedent's death. How much of this property is included in Decedent's gross estate?

3. Decedent gave Friend $13,000 in 2011 as a birthday present. In 2012, Decedent and Friend each paid $13,000 to purchase an asset which was held as joint tenants with rights of survivorship. How much of this property is included in Decedent's gross estate?

4. Decedent and Spouse owned property as joint tenants with rights of survivorship. Decedent's original contribution was 100%. How much of this property is included in Decedent's gross estate?

5. Decedent and Spouse owned property as joint tenants with rights of survivorship. Spouse's original contribution was 100%. How much of this property is included in Decedent's gross estate?

6. Decedent, Brother, and Sister inherited a valuable art collection as joint tenants from Grandparent. How much of this property is included in Decedent's gross estate?

7. If property is held as tenants in common, only the decedent's undivided interest is included in the decedent's gross estate. See Treas. Reg. § 20.2040–1(b).

c. Life Insurance Proceeds

Proceeds of life insurance policies on the decedent's life are usually part of the gross estate, regardless of whether the proceeds are payable to a named beneficiary or the decedent's estate. I.R.C. § 2042. With proper planning, however, these proceeds can be kept out of the estate if the decedent retained none of the incidents of ownership of the policy and the proceeds are not payable to the decedent's estate. See Chapter 4(J) for a more detailed discussion of the taxation of life insurance proceeds.

d. Powers of Appointment

INTERNAL REVENUE CODE, § 2041

POWERS OF APPOINTMENT

(a) In general.—The value of the gross estate shall include the value of all property.

(1) Powers of appointment created on or before October 21, 1942.

* * *

(2) Powers created after October 21, 1942.—To the extent of any property with respect to which the decedent has at the time of his death a general power of appointment created after October 21, 1942, or with respect to which the decedent has at any time exercised or released such a power of appointment by a disposition which is of such nature that if it were a transfer of property owned by the decedent, such property would be includible in the decedent's gross estate under sections 2035 to 2038, inclusive. For purposes of this paragraph (2), the power of appointment shall be considered to exist on the date of the decedent's death even though the exercise of the power is subject to a precedent giving of notice or even though the exercise of the power takes effect only on the expiration of a stated period after its exercise, whether or not on or before the date of the decedent's death notice has been given or the power has been exercised.

(3) Creation of another power in certain cases.—To the extent of any property with respect to which the decedent—

(A) by will, or

(B) by a disposition which is of such nature that if it were a transfer of property owned by the decedent such property would be includible in the decedent's gross estate under section 2035, 2036, or 2037, exercises a power of appointment created after October 21, 1942, by creating another power of appointment which under the applicable local law can be validly exercised so as to postpone the vesting of any estate or interest in such property, or suspend the absolute ownership or power of alienation of such property, for a period ascertainable without regard to the date of the creation of the first power.

(b) Definitions.—For purposes of subsection (a)—

(1) General power of appointment.—The term "general power of appointment" means a power which is exercisable in favor of the decedent, his estate, his creditors, or the creditors of his estate; except that—

(A) A power to consume, invade, or appropriate property for the benefit of the decedent which is limited by an ascertainable standard relating to the health, education, support, or maintenance of the decedent shall not be deemed a general power of appointment.

* * *

(C) In the case of a power of appointment created after October 21, 1942, which is exercisable by the decedent only in conjunction with another person—

(i) If the power is not exercisable by the decedent except in conjunction with the creator of the power—such power shall not be deemed a general power of appointment.

(ii) If the power is not exercisable by the decedent except in conjunction with a person having a substantial interest in the property, subject to the power, which is adverse to exercise of the power in favor of the decedent—such power shall not be deemed a general power of appointment. For the purposes of this clause a person who, after the death of the decedent, may be possessed of a power of appointment (with respect to the property subject to the decedent's power) which he may exercise in his own favor shall be deemed as having an interest in the property and such interest shall be deemed adverse to such exercise of the decedent's power.

(iii) If (after the application of clauses (i) and (ii)) the power is a general power of appointment and is exercisable in favor of such other person—such power shall be deemed a general power of appointment only in respect of a fractional part of the property subject to such power, such part to be determined by dividing the value of such property by the number of such persons (including the decedent) in favor of whom such power is exercisable.

For purposes of clauses (ii) and (iii), a power shall be deemed to be exercisable in favor of a person if it is exercisable in favor of such person, his estate, his creditors, or the creditors of his estate.

(2) Lapse of power.—The lapse of a power of appointment created after October 21, 1942, during the life of the individual possessing the power shall be considered a release of such power. The preceding sentence shall apply with respect to the lapse of powers during any calendar year only to the extent that the property, which could have been appointed by exercise of such lapsed powers, exceeded in value, at the time of such lapse, the greater of the following amounts:

(A) $5,000, or

(B) 5 percent of the aggregate value, at the time of such lapse, of the assets out of which, or the proceeds of which, the exercise of the lapsed powers could have been satisfied.

(3) Date of creation of power.— For purposes of this section, a power of appointment created by a will executed on or before October 21, 1942, shall be considered a power created on or before such date if the person executing such will dies before July 1, 1949, without having republished such will, by codicil or otherwise, after October 21, 1942.

NOTES AND QUESTIONS

1. Please review the powers of appointment discussion in Chapter 3(D).

2. Powers of appointment issues often arise in a trust context. A trustee of a discretionary trust has the power to appoint the property in the trust. The settlor may also have granted the beneficiary rights which may include an authorization to appoint trust property. See Treas. Reg. § 20.2041–1(b).

3. Section 2041 divides powers of appointment into two main categories: *general,* as defined in I.R.C. § 2041(b)(1) and *nongeneral,* i.e., all other powers of appointment.

4. Decedent was the holder of a general power of appointment which Decedent exercised by will. Is the appointed property part of Decedent's gross estate?

5. Decedent was the holder of a general power of appointment which Decedent failed to exercise. Under the terms of the power, X received the property as the default taker. Is the property X received included in Decedent's gross estate?

6. Decedent was the holder of a power of appointment which provided that the property could be appointed only to A, B, or C. By will, Decedent appointed all of the property to A. Is any of this property included in Decedent's gross estate?

7. Decedent was the holder of a power of appointment which provided that the Decedent could use the property but only for the Decedent's "health, education, support, and maintenance." Is any of this property included in Decedent's gross estate? Would your answer change if the power of appointment limited the property's use to the Decedent's "health, education, support, maintenance, and general happiness"? See Treas. Reg. § 20.2041–1(c)(2).

8. Parent created a trust naming Child as the income beneficiary and Grandchild as the remainder beneficiary. Child also had the right to invade

the corpus but only if Child received Grandchild's consent. Will the remaining trust property be included in Child's gross estate? Would your answer change if Child needed the approval of Parent (rather than Grandchild) to invade the corpus?

9. Decedent was the trustee of a trust. As trustee, Decedent had the authority to manage and invest the trust property as well as to allocate receipts and disbursements between income and principal. Will any of the trust's assets be included in Decedent's gross estate?

10. Decedent was a beneficiary of a trust who had a *5 or 5 power,* i.e., the right each year to demand distribution of the larger of either (1) $5,000 or (2) 5% of the value of corpus. Decedent had this power for 10 years but never exercised it. Decedent died in the middle of year 11. Assume that at all times the value of the trust property was $200,000. How much of the trust will be included in Decedent's gross estate?

e. Annuities

INTERNAL REVENUE CODE, § 2039

ANNUITIES

(a) General.—The gross estate shall include the value of an annuity or other payment receivable by any beneficiary by reason of surviving the decedent under any form of contract or agreement entered into after March 3, 1931 (other than as insurance under policies on the life of the decedent), if, under such contract or agreement, an annuity or other payment was payable to the decedent, or the decedent possessed the right to receive such annuity or payment, either alone or in conjunction with another for his life or for any period not ascertainable without reference to his death or for any period which does not in fact end before his death.

(b) Amount includible.—Subsection (a) shall apply to only such part of the value of the annuity or other payment receivable under such contract or agreement as is proportionate to that part of the purchase price therefor contributed by the decedent. For purposes of this section, any contribution by the decedent's employer or former employer to the purchase price of such contract or agreement (whether or not to an employee's trust or fund forming part of a pension, annuity, retirement, bonus or profit sharing plan) shall be considered to be contributed by the decedent if made by reason of his employment.

NOTES AND QUESTIONS

1. Please review the discussion of annuities in Chapter 3(I).

2. Decedent purchased a straight life annuity. Is any portion of the annuity included in Decedent's gross estate?

3. Decedent purchased a life annuity with a 20 year term. The annuity pays $50,000 per year. Decedent died when there was five years remaining in the term. Is any portion of the annuity included in Decedent's gross estate? If yes, how would this interest be valued?

4. If the decedent retired in 1984 or earlier, certain annuities are excludable from the decedent's gross estate. See Treas. Reg. § 20.2039–1T.

f. Certain Property Allowed Marital Deduction in Predeceased Spouse's Estate

INTERNAL REVENUE CODE, § 2044

CERTAIN PROPERTY FOR WHICH MARITAL DEDUCTION WAS PREVIOUSLY ALLOWED

(a) General rule.—The value of the gross estate shall include the value of any property to which this section applies in which the decedent had a qualifying income interest for life.

(b) Property to which this section applies.—This section applies to any property if—

(1) a deduction was allowed with respect to the transfer of such property to the decedent—

(A) under section 2056 by reason of subsection (b)(7) thereof, or

(B) under section 2523 by reason of subsection (f) thereof, and

(2) section 2519 (relating to dispositions of certain life estates) did not apply with respect to a disposition by the decedent of part or all of such property.

(c) Property treated as having passed from decedent.—For purposes of this chapter and chapter 13, property includible in the gross estate of the decedent under subsection (a) shall be treated as property passing from the decedent.

NOTES AND QUESTIONS

1. A spouse may make unlimited tax free transfers to the other spouse, both during life and at death. However, the transfers must meet the requirements of I.R.C. § 2056 (estate tax) or § 2523 (gift tax) to qualify for this favorable treatment. One of these requirements is that the surviving spouse cannot receive a terminable interest, that is, an interest that the surviving spouse could lose because of a lapse of time or the occurrence or non-occurrence of some event. Examples of terminable interests include life estates and gifts that end upon remarriage. Terminable interests do not normally qualify for the marital deduction because the property may not be in the surviving spouse's gross estate and thus the property could escape transfer taxation for a second time.

There is an extremely important exception to this rule for *qualified terminable interest property (QTIP)*. The deceased spouse can construct a trust to provide lifetime benefits for the surviving spouse, require the remaining corpus to be paid to whomever the deceased spouse desires, and still permit the deceased spouse's estate to claim the marital deduction for this property.

To prevent the property from again escaping transfer tax liability, QTIP property which remains upon the surviving spouse's death is part of the surviving spouse's gross estate despite the fact that the surviving spouse may have no control over the corpus nor any power to direct its distribution. I.R.C. § 2044. See Chapter 4(E)(1).

2. Wife's will provided that certain income producing assets valued at $800,000 were to be placed in trust with all the income payable to Husband annually. Upon Husband's death, the corpus of the trust was to be distributed to four of Wife's friends. Wife's estate elected to take the marital deduction for the entire $800,000. Husband has just died and the value of the trust property is $900,000. How much of the trust property is included in Husband's gross estate?

g. Revocable Transfers

INTERNAL REVENUE CODE, § 2038

REVOCABLE TRANSFERS

(a) In general.—The value of the gross estate shall include the value of all property—

(1) Transfers after June 22, 1936.—To the extent of any interest therein of which the decedent has at any time made a transfer (except in case of a bona fide sale for an adequate and full consideration in money or money's worth), by trust or otherwise, where the enjoyment thereof was subject at the date of his death to any change through the exercise of a power (in whatever capacity exercisable) by the decedent alone or by the decedent in conjunction with any other person (without regard to when or from what source the decedent acquired such power), to alter, amend, revoke, or terminate, or where any such power is relinquished during the 3-year period ending on the date of the decedent's death.

(2) Transfers on or before June 22, 1936.

* * *

(b) Date of existence of power.—For purposes of this section, the power to alter, amend, revoke, or terminate shall be considered to exist on the date of the decedent's death even though the exercise of the power is subject to a precedent giving of notice or even though the alteration, amendment, revocation, or termination takes effect only on the expiration of a stated period after the exercise of the power, whether or not on or before the date of the decedent's death notice has been given or the power has been exercised. In such cases proper adjustment shall be made representing the interests which would have been excluded from the power if the decedent had lived, and for such purpose, if the notice has not been given or the power has not been exercised on or before the date of his death, such notice shall be considered to have been given, or the power exercised, on the date of his death.

NOTES AND QUESTIONS

1. Settlor created a revocable trust naming Child as the life beneficiary and Grandchild as the remainder beneficiary. Is any portion of the trust included in Settlor's gross estate?

2. Settlor created a trust naming Son as the sole beneficiary but retained the right to substitute Daughter. Is any portion of the trust included in Settlor's gross estate? Would your answer change if Settlor's substitution power was restricted to an ascertainable standard (e.g., only if needed for Daughter's health, education, support, or maintenance)? See Jennings v. Smith, 161 F.2d 74 (2d Cir. 1947).

3. Settlor created a revocable trust in 2003. In 2009, Settlor validly amended the trust making it irrevocable. Settlor died in 2011. Is any portion of the trust included in Settlor's gross estate? Would your answer change if the Settlor does not die until 2013?

4. Depositor opened a pay on death account naming Friend as beneficiary. Is any portion of the account included in Depositor's gross estate? Please review Chapter 3(F).

5. Settlor created an irrevocable trust but retained the right to remove assets from the trust provided Settlor substitutes assets of equal value. Will this provision cause the trust assets to be included in Settlor's gross estate? See Estate of Jordahl v. Commissioner, 65 T.C. 92 (1975).

h. Transfers Taking Effect at Death

INTERNAL REVENUE CODE, § 2037

TRANSFERS TAKING EFFECT AT DEATH

(a) General rule.—The value of the gross estate shall include the value of all property to the extent of any interest therein of which the decedent has at any time after September 7, 1916, made a transfer (except in case of a bona fide sale for an adequate and full consideration in money or money's worth), by trust or otherwise, if—

(1) possession or enjoyment of the property can, through ownership of such interest, be obtained only by surviving the decedent, and

(2) the decedent has retained a reversionary interest in the property (but in the case of a transfer made before October 8, 1949, only if such reversionary interest arose by the express terms of the instrument of transfer), and the value of such reversionary interest immediately before the death of the decedent exceeds 5 percent of the value of such property.

(b) Special rules.—For purposes of this section, the term "reversionary interest" includes a possibility that property transferred by the decedent—

(1) may return to him or his estate, or

(2) may be subject to a power of disposition by him, but such term does not include a possibility that the income alone from such property may return to him or become subject to a power of disposition by him. The value of a reversionary interest immediately before the death of the decedent shall be determined (without regard to the fact of the decedent's death) by usual methods of valuation, including the use of tables of mortality and actuarial principles, under regulations prescribed by the Secretary. In determining the value of a possibility that property may be subject to a power of disposition by the decedent, such possibility shall be valued as if it were a possibility that such property may return to the decedent or his estate. Notwithstanding the foregoing, an interest so transferred shall not be included in the decedent's gross estate under this section if possession or enjoyment of the property could have been obtained by any beneficiary during the decedent's life through the exercise of a general power of appointment (as defined in section 2041) which in fact was exercisable immediately before the decedent's death.

NOTES AND QUESTIONS

1. Settlor established a trust with income payable to Spouse for life with the remainder to Friend, if Friend is still alive when Spouse dies. If Friend is not alive, the property reverts to Settlor or, if Settlor is deceased, to Settlor's estate. Is any portion of this trust included in Settlor's gross estate under § 2037? See Treas. Reg. § 20.2037–1(e).

2. Settlor established a trust with income payable to Spouse for life with the remainder reverting to Settlor. If Settlor predeceases Spouse, the remainder will pass to Friend. Is any portion of this trust included in Settlor's gross estate?

i. Transfers With Retained Life Interest

INTERNAL REVENUE CODE, § 2036

TRANSFERS WITH RETAINED LIFE ESTATE

(a) General rule.—The value of the gross estate shall include the value of all property to the extent of any interest therein of which the decedent has at any time made a transfer (except in case of a bona fide sale for an adequate and full consideration in money or money's worth), by trust or otherwise, under which he has retained for his life or for any period not ascertainable without reference to his death or for any period which does not in fact end before his death—

(1) the possession or enjoyment of, or the right to the income from, the property, or

(2) the right, either alone or in conjunction with any person, to designate the persons who shall possess or enjoy the property or the income therefrom.

(b) Voting rights.—

(1) In general.—For purposes of subsection (a)(1), the retention of the right to vote (directly or indirectly) shares of stock of a controlled corporation shall be considered to be a retention of the enjoyment of transferred property.

(2) Controlled corporation.—For purposes of paragraph (1), a corporation shall be treated as a controlled corporation if, at any time after the transfer of the property and during the 3–year period ending on the date of the decedent's death, the decedent owned (with the application of section 318), or had the right (either alone or in conjunction with any person) to vote, stock possessing at least 20 percent of the total combined voting power of all classes of stock.

(3) Coordination with section 2035.—For purposes of applying section 2035 with respect to paragraph (1), the relinquishment or cessation of voting rights shall be treated as a transfer of property made by the decedent.

* * *

NOTES AND QUESTIONS

1. Settlor created an irrevocable trust. Settlor was entitled to all the trust income during life with the remainder passing to Friend. Is any of the trust property included in Settlor's gross estate?

2. Parent retained a life estate in Home Place and transferred the remainder to Child. The deed was recorded in 1980 when the property was worth $50,000. Parent died in 2012. Home Place had appreciated in value to $300,000. Is Home Place included in Parent's gross estate? If yes, at what value?

3. Settlor created an irrevocable trust. Settlor was entitled to the trust income for ten years with the remainder passing to Friend. Settlor died in year six. Is any of the trust property included in Settlor's gross estate?

4. Settlor transferred property into an irrevocable trust which provides that if Settlor is alive on December 31 of each year, Settlor is entitled to all of the trust income for the prior year. Upon Settlor's death, Friend is entitled to any undistributed income and all corpus. Is any portion of the trust property included in Settlor's gross estate?

5. Parent delivered the deed to Party Place to Child while stating, "You now own the property but, of course, I retain the right to use it for entertaining my friends on special occasions." Is any portion of Party Place included in Parent's gross estate?

6. Parent creates an irrevocable trust for Parent's two children. Parent retains the right to determine how much each child receives. Is any portion of the trust included in Parent's gross estate? Would it make a difference if Parent was serving as the sole trustee?

7. Settlor creates an irrevocable trust for Child and retains the right to remove the corporate trustee, even without cause, and to substitute another corporate trustee of the Settlor's choosing, as long as the trustee is "completely independent from the Grantor." Will the trust corpus be included in Settlor's gross estate? See Estate of Wall v. Commissioner, 101 T.C. 300 (1993); Rev. Rul. 95–58 (accepting *Wall*); Martin M. Shenkman, et al., *Trustee Removal Power: How Many Strings Are Too Many*, PROB. & PROP., July/Aug. 1994, at 8.

j. Certain Transfers Made Within Three Years of Death

INTERNAL REVENUE CODE, § 2035

ADJUSTMENTS FOR CERTAIN GIFTS MADE WITHIN 3 YEARS OF DECEDENT'S DEATH

(a) Inclusion of certain property in gross estate.—If—

(1) the decedent made a transfer (by trust or otherwise) of an interest in any property, or relinquished a power with respect to any property, during the 3–year period ending on the date of the decedent's death, and

(2) the value of such property (or an interest therein) would have been included in the decedent's gross estate under section 2036, 2037, 2038, or 2042 if such transferred interest or relinquished power had been retained by the decedent on the date of his death, the value of the gross estate shall include the value of any property (or interest therein) which would have been so included.

(b) Inclusion of gift tax on gifts made during 3 years before decedent's death.—The amount of the gross estate (determined without regard to this subsection) shall be increased by the amount of any tax paid under chapter 12 by the decedent or his estate on any gift made by the decedent or his spouse during the 3–year period ending on the date of the decedent's death.

(c) Other rules relating to transfers within 3 years of death.—

(1) In general.—For purposes of—

(A) section 303(b) (relating to distributions in redemption of stock to pay death taxes),

(B) section 2032A (relating to special valuation of certain farms, etc., real property), and

(C) subchapter C of chapter 64 (relating to lien for taxes), the value of the gross estate shall include the value of all property to the extent of any interest therein of which the decedent has at any time made a transfer, by trust or otherwise, during the 3–year period ending on the date of the decedent's death.

(2) Coordination with section 6166.— An estate shall be treated as meeting the 35 percent of adjusted gross estate requirement of section 6166(a)(1) only if the estate meets such requirement both with and without the application of subsection (a).

(3) Marital and small transfers.—Paragraph (1) shall not apply to any transfer (other than a transfer with respect to a life insurance policy) made during a calendar year to any donee if the decedent was not required by section 6019 (other than by reason of section 6019(2)) to file any gift tax return for such year with respect to transfers to such donee.

(d) Exception.— Subsection (a) and paragraph (1) of subsection (c) shall not apply to any bona fide sale for an adequate and full consideration in money or money's worth.

(e) Treatment of certain transfers from revocable trusts.—For purposes of this section and section 2038, any transfer from any portion of a trust during any period that such portion was treated under section 676 as owned by the decedent by reason of a power in the grantor (determined without regard to section 672(e)) shall be treated as a transfer made directly by the decedent.

NOTES AND QUESTIONS

1. Donor gave Child $50,000. One year later, Donor died. Is this gift included in Donor's gross estate?

2. Donor gave Child a life insurance policy on Donor's life with a face value of $50,000. Donor died one year later. Is any portion of the proceeds included in Donor's estate? Would your answer change if the face value was only $7,500?

3. Donor made a large gift to Friend and timely paid a gift tax of $45,000. Donor died two years later. Is any portion of this $45,000 included in Donor's estate? If yes, what policy supports the inclusion?

4. Settlor created a trust for Children and retained the right to determine how much each child receives. Settlor amended the trust to eliminate this right after realizing that the trust property would be included in Settlor's gross estate under § 2036. Settlor died two years after making the amendment. Is any portion of the trust included in Settlor's gross estate?

k. Qualified Family–Owned Business Exclusion

A portion of the value of certain family-owned businesses may be excludable from the decedent's gross estate if the decedent died before January 1, 2004. See I.R.C. § 2057. The requirements to qualify for this exclusion were exceedingly complex. For example, the business must pass to specified close family members, the value of the business interest had to exceed fifty percent of the decedent's adjusted gross estate, and the decedent or members of the decedent's family must have materially participated in the business for at least five of the eight years before the decedent's death. If the heirs fail to materially participate for a sufficiently long enough period of time following the decedent's death, the heirs are subject to a recapture tax. Despite the complexity, the exclusion could have saved the estate over $100,000 in estate taxes. The EGTRRA repealed this exclusion for the estates of decedents who die after December 31, 2003.

l. Qualified Conservation Easement Exclusion

The personal representative may elect to exclude from the gross estate a portion of the value of real property in the decedent's estate which is subject to a qualified conservation easement. See I.R.C. § 2031(c).

3. VALUATION OF GROSS ESTATE

a. General Rule

INTERNAL REVENUE CODE, § 2031

DEFINITION OF GROSS ESTATE

(a) General.—The value of the gross estate of the decedent shall be determined by including to the extent provided for in this part, the value at the time of his death of all property, real or personal, tangible or intangible, wherever situated.

(b) Valuation of unlisted stock and securities.—In the case of stock and securities of a corporation the value of which, by reason of their not being listed on an exchange and by reason of the absence of sales thereof, cannot be determined with reference to bid and asked prices or with reference to sales prices, the value thereof shall be determined by taking into consideration, in addition to all other factors, the value of stock or securities of corporations engaged in the same or a similar line of business which are listed on an exchange.

* * *

NOTES AND QUESTIONS

1. An asset is valued at its fair market value at date of the decedent's death. The value of the asset when the estate tax return is due, when the tax is actually paid, or when the property is distributed to the beneficiaries or heirs is irrelevant.

2. "The fair market value is the price at which the property would change hands between a willing buyer and a willing seller, neither being under any compulsion to buy or to sell and both having reasonable knowledge of relevant facts." Treas. Reg. § 20.2031–1(b).

3. Please review questions 3–5 and 9–10 in Chapter 4(B)(3). The rules for valuing assets in the gross estate are basically the same as for valuing gifts. See Treas. Reg. § 20.2031–1 (general rules), § 20.2031–2 (stocks and bonds), § 20.2031–3 (business interests), § 20.2031–4 (notes), § 20.2031–5 (cash), § 20.2031–6 (household and personal effects), § 20.2031–7 (annuities,

life estates, terms for years, remainders, and reversions), and § 20.2031–8 (life insurance and annuity contracts, and shares in an open-end investment company).

4. Assume you are preparing an inventory of the items in Decedent's gross estate. Must you list every item individually along with its value? Just think how tedious it would be to list every shirt, paper clip, pen, dish, fork, book, etc.

"A room by room itemization of household and personal effects is desirable. All the articles should be named specifically, except that a number of articles contained in the same room, none of which has a value in excess of $100, may be grouped. * * * In lieu of an itemized list, the executor may furnish a written statement, containing a declaration that it is made under penalties of perjury, setting forth the aggregate value as appraised by a competent appraiser or appraiser of recognized standing and ability, or by a dealer or dealers in the class of personalty involved." Treas. Reg. § 20.2031–6(a).

The appraisal of an expert under oath is required if there are household or personal effects having an artistic or intrinsic value exceeding $3,000 such as "jewelry, furs, silverware, paintings, etchings, engravings, antiques, books, statuary, vases, oriental rugs, [or] coin or stamp collections." Treas. Reg. § 20.2031–6(b).

5. Decedent owned an undivided one-half interest in a parcel of real property that had a fair market value of $100,000. Is Decedent's interest simply worth $50,000 or are there reasons to justify a *fractional interest discount*?

6. Decedent owned an asset valued at $100,000. Because of the specialized nature of the property, very few people would be willing to purchase the asset. The search for a buyer could be time-consuming and costly. May the asset's value be reduced by a *marketability discount?* See Jung v. Commissioner, 101 T.C. 412 (1993).

7. Decedent died owning a large block of stock. May the executor take a *blockage discount* in valuing the stock because liquidating the stock within a reasonable time would depress the stock's market price? See Gillespie v. United States, 23 F.3d 36 (2d Cir. 1994).

b. Alternate Valuation Date

INTERNAL REVENUE CODE, § 2032

ALTERNATE VALUATION

(a) General.—The value of the gross estate may be determined, if the executor so elects, by valuing all the property included in the gross estate as follows:

(1) In the case of property distributed, sold, exchanged, or otherwise disposed of, within 6 months after the decedent's death such property shall be valued as of the date of distribution, sale, exchange, or other disposition.

(2) In the case of property not distributed, sold, exchanged, or otherwise disposed of, within 6 months after the decedent's death such property shall be valued as of the date 6 months after the decedent's death.

(3) Any interest or estate which is affected by mere lapse of time shall be included at its value as of the time of death (instead of the later date) with adjustment for any difference in its value as of the later date not due to mere lapse of time.

(b) Special rules.—No deduction under this chapter of any item shall be allowed if allowance for such item is in effect given by the alternate valuation provided by this section. Wherever in any other subsection or section of this chapter reference is made to the value of property at the time of the decedent's death, such reference shall be deemed to refer to the value of such property used in determining the value of the gross estate. In case of an election made by the executor under this section, then—

(1) for purposes of the charitable deduction under section 2055 or 2106(a)(2), any bequest, legacy, devise, or transfer enumerated therein, and

(2) for the purpose of the marital deduction under section 2056, any interest in property passing to the surviving spouse,

shall be valued as of the date of the decedent's death with adjustment for any difference in value (not due to mere lapse of time or the occurrence or nonoccurrence of a contingency) of the property as of the date 6 months after the decedent's death (substituting, in the case of property distributed by the executor or trustee, or sold, exchanged, or otherwise disposed of, during such 6–month period, the date thereof).

(c) Election must decrease gross estate and estate tax.—No election may be made under this section with respect to an estate unless such election will decrease—

(1) the value of the gross estate, and

(2) the sum of the tax imposed by this chapter and the tax imposed by chapter 13 with respect to property includible in the decedent's gross estate (reduced by credits allowable against such taxes).

(d) Election.—

(1) In general.—The election provided for in this section shall be made by the executor on the return of the tax imposed by this chapter. Such election, once made, shall be irrevocable.

(2) Exception.—No election may be made under this section if such return is filed more than 1 year after the time prescribed by law (including extensions) for filing such return.

NOTES AND QUESTIONS

1. The executor may elect to value property as of the date six months after the decedent's death only if the election reduces both (1) the value of the gross estate and (2) the estate tax due. This dual requirement prevents the executor from increasing the income tax basis of appreciating assets, and thus reducing the amount of capital gains tax imposed when the asset is sold, in cases where there is no estate tax liability (e.g., no tax is owed because of the marital deduction or the applicable credit amount). See Chapter 4(D).

2. The personal representative must study the overall tax ramifications of making an alternate valuation date election. From an estate tax perspective, lower values are favored because a lower value leads to a lower estate tax. However, from an income tax viewpoint, higher values are preferred because a higher value means a higher carry over basis and thus less capital gains tax when the asset is sold. See Chapter 4(D). Because income tax rates are generally lower than the estate tax rates, an alternate valuation date election is usually recommended if it would reduce the estate tax.

3. The personal representative wants assets valued as low as possible to reduce estate tax liability. May the executor look at each asset individually and elect to value the asset either at the date of decedent's death or the date which is six months later?

4. Assume that Executor elected the alternate valuation date. When Decedent died, an asset was worth $100,000. Executor sold the asset four months after Decedent's death for $80,000, its fair market value at that time. The asset was worth $120,000 on the alternate valuation date. How is this asset valued for estate tax purposes?

5. May the personal representative return to the normal date of death valuation method after electing to use the alternate valuation date?

6. See Treas. Reg. § 20.2031–1.

c. Special Use Valuation

QUESTION

Grandparent owned and operated a farm which had been in the family for several generations. Grandparent died and the will left the entire estate to Grandchild. Grandparent's estate consisted of the farm and $50,000 in savings. Grandchild plans to continue operating the farm. Because the farm is situated near a major metropolitan area, the fair market value of the land is $2,000,000. As a farm, however, the land has a value of only $500,000. What is the value of the farm for estate tax purposes? Must the farm be sold to pay the estate taxes?

JOHN K. McNULTY & GRAYSON M.P. McCOUCH, FEDERAL ESTATE AND GIFT TAXATION*

§ 50 (7th ed. 2011).

There is one exception to the general rule that the value of the gross estate shall be determined by including property at its fair market value. Section 2032A, added to the Code in 1976 and significantly liberalized by subsequent amendments, authorizes the decedent's executor to elect "special use valuation" for estate tax purposes. This election, if available, allows qualifying real property used in a farm or other business to be valued at less than its fair market value. See Reg. §§ 20.2032A-l through–8.

This special relief was needed because the normal concept of fair market value presupposes that property will be valued at its potential "highest and best use." Therefore the fair market value of a particular piece of property, a farm for example, may well greatly exceed its income potential as a farm, because of the possibilities of developing the land for other, more lucrative uses. In other words, what might be called "speculative value" is reflected in fair market value. If the decedent's heirs wish to keep the property in use as a farm, an estate tax liability based on fair market value may cause severe liquidity problems. Special use valuation serves to ameliorate these liquidity problems and thus to encourage the continued existence of family-owned farms and businesses, by relieving the need to sell the property in order to pay the estate tax.

To qualify for the election, the real property itself must have been owned and used by the decedent or a family member for farming or other business purposes, both prior to and at the time of the decedent's death. The property must pass from the decedent to a "qualified heir," that is, to a member of the decedent's family. In addition, the property must constitute a substantial portion of the gross estate. If all of the statutory conditions are met, the property may be included in the gross estate at its special use valuation rather than at its fair market value; however, the resulting reduction in the includable amount cannot exceed $750,000 (indexed for inflation, $1,020,000 in 2011). One of two separate valuation methods may be elected to determine the special use valuation. There are also recapture provisions, which will impose an "additional estate tax" on the property in the event that the qualified heir transfers the property (other than to a family member) or ceases to use the property for its qualifying use. The additional estate tax is the personal liability of the qualified heir, and the recapture period lasts for ten years after the decedent's death or until the death of the qualified heir, whichever is earlier.

The provisions of § 2032A are labyrinthine. In addition to the internal complexity of the provision, there are several unresolved questions relating to its interaction with other aspects of the transfer tax system, for example, the marital deduction. Other trouble spots involve its application in a corporate or partnership context, and the transfer tax and income tax consequences in cases of a subsequent transfer within the recapture period. In appropriate circumstances, special use valuation can produce substantial estate tax savings that outweigh the concomitant increase in administrative costs.

d. Valuation Penalties

As you have now realized, a personal representative may have several incentives for intentionally misstating the value of estate property. For example, to save estate tax, it is advantageous to have assets valued as low as possible. To save income tax, high asset values are beneficial. To dissuade both under and over valuation, I.R.C. § 6662 imposes significant penalties for valuation misstatements.

4. DEDUCTIONS

a. Marital Deduction

Most interests passing to a beneficiary or heir who is the decedent's spouse at the time of the decedent's death are deductible regardless of the amount. I.R.C. § 2056(a). Note that gifts of life estates and most other terminable interests do not qualify for the deduction. In addition, special rules apply if the surviving spouse is not a United States citizen. See Chapter 4(E) for a more detailed discussion of the marital deduction.

b. Charitable Deduction

All transfers to qualifying religious, educational, governmental, or other charitable organizations are deductible, regardless of the amount. I.R.C. § 2055. See Chapter 4(M) for a more detailed discussion of the charitable deduction.

c. Deduction for Expenses, Debts, and Taxes

INTERNAL REVENUE CODE, § 2053

EXPENSES, INDEBTEDNESS, AND TAXES

(a) General rule.—For purposes of the tax imposed by section 2001, the value of the taxable estate shall be determined by deducting from the value of the gross estate such amounts—

(1) for funeral expenses,

(2) for administration expenses,

(3) for claims against the estate, and

(4) for unpaid mortgages on, or any indebtedness in respect of, property where the value of the decedent's interest therein, undiminished by such mortgage or indebtedness, is included in the value of the gross estate,

as are allowable by the laws of the jurisdiction, whether within or without the United States, under which the estate is being administered.

* * *

NOTES AND QUESTIONS

1. "A reasonable expenditure for a tombstone, monument, or mausoleum, or for a burial lot, either for the decedent or his family, including a reasonable expenditure for its future care, may be deducted * * * provided such an expenditure is allowable by the local law. Included in funeral expenses is the cost of transportation of the person bringing the body to the place of burial." Treas. Reg. § 20.2053–2. How do you use your knowledge of the extent of this deduction in planning an estate and advising survivors?

2. Which of the following expenses are deductible as administration expenses? See Treas. Reg. § 20.2053–3.

a. Personal representative's compensation.

b. Decedent required Executor to serve without compensation but did leave Executor a sizable gift under the will instead.

c. Your compensation for serving as the personal representative's attorney.

d. Court costs.

e. Accountant's fees.

f. Appraiser's fees.

g. Expenses incurred storing the decedent's property prior to distribution to the beneficiaries.

h. Expenses incurred making additions and improvements to the decedent's property prior to distribution to the beneficiaries.

i. Expenses incurred in selling estate property to pay debts and taxes.

j. Expenses to ship a bequeathed item to the beneficiary.

3. Instead of deducting administration expenses from the decedent's gross estate, the expenses may be deducted on the decedent's estate income tax return. Deducting the same expenses on both returns is generally not allowed. See I.R.C. § 642(g). Thus, the personal representative needs to evaluate which use of the deduction will yield the better result. See Chapter 4(N) for a discussion of post-mortem tax planning issues.

4. Which of the following expenses are deductible as claims against the estate? See Treas. Reg. §§ 20.2053–4, 20.2053–5, & 20.2053–6.

a. Utility bills (e.g., electric, telephone, gas, water, cable, etc.).

b. Principal due on credit cards.

c. Interest due on credit cards.

d. Balance due on a pledge to a local public television station.

e. Property taxes.

f. Federal estate tax.

g. State estate or inheritance tax.

h. Federal gift tax owed on the decedent's pre-death gifts which was not paid as of the decedent's death.

i. Federal income tax owed on the decedent's pre-death income which was not paid as of the decedent's death.

5. Principal and interest due on the decedent's collateralized transactions (e.g., mortgages on real property, Article 9 security interests on personal property) are deductible. The deduction is for the full unpaid balance plus interest accrued as of the date of the decedent's death "provided the value of the property, undiminished by the amount of the mortgage or indebtedness, is included in the value of the gross estate." Treas. Reg. § 20.2053–7.

d. Deduction for Losses

INTERNAL REVENUE CODE, § 2054

LOSSES

For purposes of the tax imposed by section 2001, the value of the taxable estate shall be determined by deducting from the value of the gross estate losses incurred during the settlement of estates arising from fires, storms, shipwrecks, or other casualties, or from theft, when such losses are not compensated for by insurance or otherwise.

NOTES AND QUESTIONS

1. To save estate expenses, Executor did not insure a house which was included in Decedent's gross estate. The house, valued at $500,000, was destroyed by fire. May Executor deduct this loss? Does Executor have anything else to worry about?

2. Executor insured a house included in Decedent's gross estate for $400,000. The house, valued at $500,000, was destroyed by a tornado. May Executor deduct any portion of this loss? See Treas. Reg. § 20.2054–1.

3. Decedent died owning, among other things, a Picasso painting worth $250,000. Beneficiary took possession of the painting three months after Decedent died. Shortly thereafter, Thief stole the painting. The painting was uninsured and has not been recovered. May Executor deduct any portion of this loss? See Treas. Reg. § 20.2054–1.

4. Decedent died owning an investment with a market value of $300,000. Because of market conditions, the property dropped in value to $100,000. May Executor deduct any portion of this loss?

5. Instead of deducting losses from the decedent's gross estate, losses may be deducted on the estate's income tax return. Deducting the same loss on both returns is generally not allowed. See I.R.C. § 642(g). Thus, the

personal representative needs to evaluate which use of the losses will yield the better result. See Chapter 4(N) for a discussion of post-mortem tax planning issues.

e. Deduction for State Death Taxes

INTERNAL REVENUE CODE, § 2058

STATE DEATH TAXES

(a) Allowance of deduction.–For purposes of the tax imposed by section 2001, the value of the taxable estate shall be determined by deducting from the value of the gross estate the amount of any estate, inheritance, legacy, or succession taxes actually paid to any State or the District of Columbia, in respect of any property included in the gross estate (not including any such taxes paid with respect to the estate of a person other than the decedent).

(b) Period of limitations.– The deduction allowed by this section shall include only such taxes as were actually paid and deduction therefor claimed before the later of—

(1) 4 years after the filing of the return required by section 6018, or

(2) if–

(A) a petition for redetermination of a deficiency has been filed with the Tax Court within the time prescribed in section 6213(a), the expiration of 60 days after the decision of the Tax Court becomes final,

(B) an extension of time has been granted under section 6161 or 6166 for payment of the tax shown on the return, or of a deficiency, the date of the expiration of the period of the extension, or

(C) a claim for refund or credit of an overpayment of tax imposed by this chapter has been filed within the time prescribed in section 6511, the latest of the expiration of–

(i) 60 days from the date of mailing by certified mail or registered mail by the Secretary to the taxpayer of a notice of the disallowance of any part of such claim,

(ii) 60 days after a decision by any court of competent jurisdiction becomes final with respect to a timely suit instituted upon such claim, or

(iii) 2 years after a notice of the waiver of disallowance is filed under section 6532(a)(3).

Notwithstanding sections 6511 and 6512, refund based on the deduction may be made if the claim for refund is filed within the period provided in the preceding sentence. Any such refund shall be made without interest.

NOTE

Under the EGTRRA and subsequent legislation, state death taxes on property included in the decedent's gross estate are deductible from the gross estate provided the decedent dies in 2005 or thereafter (but before 2013). If the decedent dies before January 1, 2005 or after December 31, 2012, a credit for state death taxes may be available as discussed in § C(9), below.

5. COMPUTATION OF TENTATIVE TAX

The computation of the federal estate tax begins by determining the *taxable estate*. The taxable estate is the value of the gross estate reduced by the estate tax deductions.

You next determine the *tax base* by adding to the taxable estate all taxable gifts (except those already in the gross estate) which the decedent made on or after January 1, 1977 at their date of gift values. Only taxable gifts are included in the tax base so gifts covered by the annual exclusion, medical and educational expense exclusion, marital deduction, and charitable deduction are not thrown back into the tax base. The reason the decedent's inter vivos gifts are added to the tax base is to determine the total amount of taxable gratuitous transfers the decedent has ever made. In effect, the gift tax is nothing more than "estimated payments" on the estate tax.

The next step is to compute a *tentative tax* on the tax base by using the rate schedule in I.R.C. § 2001(c) with two important differences. First, if the decedent died in 2010, there was no federal estate tax owed regardless of the size of the estate. Second, if the decedent dies in 2013 or thereafter, a different rate chart applies, that is, the one that was in effect before the enactment of EGTRRA and subsequent legislation. Review Chapter 4(B)(6).

6. ESTATE TAX CREDITS AND RELATED ADJUSTMENTS

From the tentative tax, you now subtract various estate tax credits and related adjustments as delineated in this section. The sum remaining is the amount of federal estate tax due to the government.

a. Adjustment for Gift Taxes

The gift tax payable on the decedent's inter vivos taxable gifts made after December 31, 1976 is subtracted from the tentative tax. I.R.C. § 2001(b)(2). This amount is *not* necessarily the actual amount of gift tax which the decedent paid on the inter vivos gifts. Instead, it is the amount of tax that the decedent would have paid if the tax were computed by using the rate schedule in effect at the time of the decedent's death, rather than when the gift was made. In doing this calculation, the amount subtracted as the unused applicable credit amount is, however, still based on the credit which was in effect for the year in which the gift was made. Consequently, you must do "mini" gift tax calculations for each year in which the decedent made taxable gifts and then add the results together to determine the total transfer taxes payable. This amount is then subtracted from the tentative tax.

If the decedent made taxable gifts before January 1, 1977, the estate receives a credit for any gift tax which the decedent actually paid on those gifts if the gifted property is included in the decedent's gross estate. I.R.C. § 2012.

QUESTION

Only taxable gifts made on or after January 1, 1977 are added to the taxable estate in determining the tax base. Please review Chapter 4(C)(1). How could a pre–1977 gift be included in the gross estate?

b. Applicable Credit Amount

The tentative tax is reduced by the *applicable credit amount*. I.R.C. § 2010(c). The applicable credit amount, called the *unified credit* if the gift and estate credits are the same, is a credit against the tentative tax. The table below shows the amount of the credit and the applicable exclusion amount, that is, the total amount of property that an individual may pass upon death without estate tax liability. This estate tax credit is available even if the decedent exhausted the gift tax applicable credit amount with lifetime transfers because those transfers were added back to the gross estate to ascertain the tax base. Of course, the effect of returning the gifts to the estate is to have the decedent's at-death transfers taxed at a higher marginal rate.

Year of Death	Applicable Credit Amount [recalculated under 2012 rates]	Applicable Exclusion Amount
2002–2010	$330,800	$1,000,000
2011	$1,730,800	$5,000,000
2012	$1,772,800	$5,120,000
2013 and thereafter [assuming no new legislation]		$1,000,000

c. State Death Tax

INTERNAL REVENUE CODE, § 2011

CREDIT FOR STATE DEATH TAXES

(a) In general.—The tax imposed by section 2001 shall be credited with the amount of any estate, inheritance, legacy, or succession taxes actually paid to any State or the District of Columbia, in respect of any property included in the gross estate (not including any such taxes paid with respect to the estate of a person other than the decedent).

(b) Amount of credit.

(1) In general—Except as provided in paragraph (2), the credit allowed by this section shall not exceed the appropriate amount stated in the following table:

If the adjusted taxable estate is:	The maximum tax credit shall be:
Over $90,000 but not over $140,000	$400 plus 1.6% of the excess over $90,000.
Over $140,000 but not over $240,000	$1,200 plus 2.4% of the excess over $140,000.
Over $240,000 but not over $440,000	$3,600 plus 3.2% of the excess over $240,000.
Over $440,000 but not over $640,000	$10,000 plus 4% of the excess over $440,000.
Over $640,000 but not over $840,000	$18,000 plus 4.8% of the excess over $640,000.
Over $840,000 but not over $1,040,000	$27,600 plus 5.6% of the excess over $840,000.
Over $1,040,000 but not over $1,540,000	$38,800 plus 6.4% of the excess over $1,040,000.
Over $1,540,000 but not over $2,040,000	$70,800 plus 7.2% of the excess over $1,540,000.
Over $2,040,000 but not over $2,540,000	$106,800 plus 8% of the excess over $2,040,000.
Over $2,540,000 but not over $3,040,000	$146,800 plus 8.8% of the excess over $2,540,000.
Over $3,040,000 but not over $3,540,000	$190,800 plus 9.6% of the excess over $3,040,000.
Over $3,540,000 but not over $4,040,000	$238,800 plus 10.4% of the excess over $3,540,000.
Over $4,040,000 but not over $5,040,000	$290,800 plus 11.2% of the excess over $4,040,000.
Over $5,040,000 but not over $6,040,000	$402,800 plus 12% of the excess over $5,040,000.

If the adjusted taxable estate is:	The maximum tax credit shall be:
Over $6,040,000 but not over $7,040,000	$522,800 plus 12.8% of the excess over $6,040,000.
Over $7,040,000 but not over $8,040,000	$650,800 plus 13.6% of the excess over $7,040,000.
Over $8,040,000 but not over $9,040,000	$786,800 plus 14.4% of the excess over $8,040,000.
Over $9,040,000 but not over $10,040,000	$930,800 plus 15.2% of the excess over $9,040,000.
Over $10,040,000	$1,082,800 plus 16% of the excess over $10,040,000.

(2) Reduction of maximum credit.–

(A) In general.— In the case of estates of decedents dying after December 31, 2001, the credit allowed by this section shall not exceed the applicable percentage of the credit otherwise determined under paragraph (1).

(B) Applicable percentage.—

In the case of estates of decedents dying during:	The applicable percentage is:
2002	75 percent
2003	50 percent
2004	25 percent.

(3) Adjusted taxable estate.– For purposes of this section, the term "adjusted taxable estate" means the taxable estate reduced by $60,000.

* * *

(f) Termination.–This section shall not apply to the estates of decedents dying after December 31, 2004.

NOTES AND QUESTIONS

1. If the decedent dies in 2005 or before January 1, 2013, there is no credit for state tax taxes. Instead, there is a deduction for state death taxes under I.R.C. § 2058 as discussed in § C(4)(e), above. In 2010, there was no federal estate tax. Unless EGTRRA or subsequent legislation is enacted, 100% of the credit will be available for decedents who die in 2013 or thereafter.

2. Decedent died in 2004 leaving a taxable estate of $1,000,000. Decedent's estate paid $10,000 in state death taxes. What is the maximum credit Decedent's estate may claim? Would your answer change if Decedent's estate paid only $5,000 in state death taxes?

3. See § C(9), below, for a discussion of state death taxes.

d. Previously Taxed Property Credit

I.R.C. § 2013 provides a credit if property which is taxed in the decedent's estate has recently been taxed in another decedent's estate. For example, assume that in January, Parent died leaving Parent's entire estate to Child. Child died in April leaving all of Child's property (which now includes all of Parent's property) to Friend. Child's estate will be entitled to a credit for the estate tax Parent's estate recently paid.

Computation of the credit is complex. The explanation which follows summarizes the two-step process. First, you must determine the maximum allowable credit. This amount is the smaller of (1) the amount of estate tax that was attributable to the property because the property was included in the first-to-die's estate (Parent), and (2) the amount of estate tax that would be attributable to the property because the property is included in the decedent's estate (Child). Second, you ascertain what percentage of the maximum allowable credit is available to the decedent's estate based on how long the decedent (Child) survived the first-to-die (Parent). The entire amount is usable as a credit in the first two years. The credit decreases by 20% over each subsequent two year period. Thus, once 10 years elapse, the credit is no longer available.

e. Other Credits

Credits are also allowed for certain foreign death taxes under I.R.C. § 2014 and certain death taxes on remainders under I.R.C. § 2015.

7. ESTATE TAX RETURN

An estate tax return is usually not required if the decedent's gross estate combined with inter vivos taxable gifts does not exceed the applicable exclusion amount. If the estate is large enough, then the return, designated as *Form 706,* and the tax itself are due nine months from the decedent's death. The I.R.S. may grant a six month extension for filing the return for reasonable cause. In addition, the Service may grant extensions for up to ten years for the payment of the estate tax. However, the estate must pay interest on any unpaid tax liability during the extension periods. I.R.C. §§ 6081 & 6161(a). Deferral of estate tax may be possible if (1) the estate consists largely of an interest in a closely held business under I.R.C. § 6166 or (2) the estate contains a reversionary or remainder interest in property under I.R.C. § 6163.

Study the copy of Form 706 and its accompanying instructions found in Appendix B.

8. LIABILITY FOR PAYMENT OF ESTATE TAX

The personal representative of the decedent's estate is obligated to pay the federal estate tax. I.R.C. § 2002. If the court has not appointed a personal representative, "any person in actual or constructive possession of any property of the decedent is required to pay the entire tax to the extent of the value of the property in [the person's] possession." Treas. Reg. § 20.2002–1.

9. STATE DEATH TAX

Many states impose a tax on at-death transfers. These taxes fall into three main categories. Traditionally, the most common type of death tax is the *pick-up* tax, also called the *sponge, sop,* or *soak-up* tax. Under this type of tax, the state estate tax is set at the maximum amount of credit which the decedent's estate could claim for paying state death taxes. See § C(6)(c), above. A pick-up tax is a cost-free tax. The amount of the state death tax is the same as the amount of the federal credit; if the state did not impose the tax, the decedent's estate would owe more tax to the federal government. The decedent's personal representative simply sends two checks, one to the I.R.S. and one to the state government, totaling the same amount that would be owed to the I.R.S. alone if the state did not have an estate tax.

The amount of the federal state death tax credit is decreasing rapidly and it will no longer exist as of 2005 (instead, there will be a deduction for state death taxes as discussed in § C(4)(e), above). The reduction and elimination of the credit will cause a decrease in revenue for pick-up tax states. Because the impact of this loss of revenue may be significant, state legislatures are taking steps to offset the impact of the phase out of the credit. For example, some states have "decoupled," that is, enacted a stand-alone estate tax or have imposed a state estate tax equal to the amount of the credit as it existed prior to the enactment of EGTRRA. States could also replace the lost revenue by increasing other taxes such as the sales tax or the income tax. See Jeffrey A. Cooper, et al., *State Estate Taxes After EGTRRA: A Long Day's Journey Into Night*, 17 QUINNIPIAC PROB. L.J. 317 (2004).

States impose two other types of taxes on at death transfers which may be in place of or in addition to the pick-up tax. The first of these is an estate tax imposed on the privilege of transferring property at death. State estate taxes operate in a similar fashion to the federal estate tax although the property included in the gross estate and the types and amounts of deductions and credits may differ significantly. The second type is an inheritance tax imposed on the heir's or beneficiary's privilege of receiving property. Typically, the closer that the heir or beneficiary is related to the decedent, the lower the rate of tax and the greater the number and size of exemptions.

LOCATE

Does your state impose a death tax? If yes, what type is it and how does it operate?

QUESTION

How might the type of death tax imposed by your state influence some of the advice you give to your clients?

10. ESTATE TAX PROBLEM

Compute the amount of federal and state estate tax owed under the following facts. As you do so, think about what steps you would have taken to reduce Decedent's estate tax liability had you planned the estate.

Decedent died on September 1, 2012 with a valid will leaving Decedent's entire estate to Child. Personal Representative (PR) is properly appointed as the executor of Decedent's will. PR discovers the following information while administering the estate.

1. Decedent had made only one taxable gift during Decedent's life. Decedent made this gift in 2001 when the property was valued at $400,000. Decedent paid no gift taxes. This property is now worth $100,000.
2. Decedent purchased a house in 1998 for $500,000. The house was worth $1,000,000 on September 1, 2012. Decedent still owed $50,000 on the house.
3. Decedent and Grandchild were named on a bank account as joint tenants with rights of survivorship. The account contained $100,000 at the date of Decedent's death. Decedent's records can prove that Grandchild contributed all of the funds to the account.
4. Decedent created a revocable trust for the benefit of Child in 2002 with property then valued at $400,000. The property in this trust was worth $200,000 at the date of Decedent's death.
5. Decedent was the insured under a life insurance policy. Decedent paid a total of $4,000 in premiums on this policy before giving the entire policy and all rights thereunder to Parent on July 1, 2010. Parent has paid all premiums since receiving the policy. The proceeds of $500,000 were paid directly to Parent.
6. Decedent's Grandparent named Decedent as the life tenant of a cabin in a rural area. The cabin and associated property had a fair market value of $175,000 on September 1, 2012. Child was the sole remainder beneficiary.
7. PR incurred reasonable administrative expenses of $50,000.
8. Decedent's estate paid $80,000 in state estate taxes.

D. FEDERAL INCOME TAX—BASIS OF TRANSFERRED PROPERTY

JOHN K. McNULTY & GRAYSON M.P. McCOUCH, FEDERAL ESTATE AND GIFT TAXATION*

§ 80 (7th ed. 2011).

In planning transfers to effect the wishes of a donor and to minimize the transfer tax consequences, it should never be forgotten that various dispositions may have significant income tax consequences as well. To take a simple example, an outright, no-strings inter vivos gift of corporate stock will not only remove that stock from the donor's gross estate, but will also cause any future dividends from it to be taxable to the donee for income tax purposes, and not to the donor. The interrelations between the gift, estate and income taxes are many and complicated * * *.

First, it must be remembered that a person who receives property by gift or bequest is not subject to income tax on the receipt of the property. I.R.C. § 102 excludes the transferred property from the recipient's gross income at the time of the transfer. Nevertheless, the recipient may have occasion to report income as a result of a subsequent sale of the property. For as a price of tax-free receipt, the donee of an inter vivos gift must take over the donor's basis as his own basis in the gift property for purposes of determining gain on a sale of that property (with an adjustment for any gift tax attributable to net appreciation in the value of the property). See I.R.C. § 1015(a) and (d). Consequently, if A owns Blackacre for which he paid $10,000 (his cost basis) and gives it to B when Blackacre is worth $15,000, and if B later sells Blackacre for $17,000, B will have taxable gain of $7,000. If Blackacre had been worth just $8,000 when A gave it to B, B would still have $7,000 gain when he sold it for $17,000 later. This is an entirely lawful and proper way to shift taxation of the gain in appreciated property to a donee.

Deductible loss, however, cannot be shifted in this way. For purposes of determining loss on a subsequent sale, the donee must take as his basis the lesser of (1) the donor's own basis or (2) the fair market value (FMV) of the property at the time of the gift. Consequently, if A had a basis of $10,000 and Blackacre was worth $8,000 at the time of the gift, and B later sold Blackacre for $7,000, B would realize a loss of only $1,000; A's loss of $2,000 will never be recognized by A or B. If, perchance, B sold Blackacre for $9,000 (an amount in between A's basis of $10,000 and the FMV of $8,000 at the time of the gift), B would realize neither gain nor loss, a strange result that follows from selling the property in the "gray" area between the two basis rules of I.R.C. § 1015(a). (The rule for computing gain is irrelevant because the sale price is less than the basis of the property in the donor's hands; the rule for determining loss is also inapplicable because the sale price is higher than FMV at the time of the gift.)

The potential loss deduction will have disappeared; no deduction will be available to anyone. Perhaps the policy justification for allowing gain and tax burden to be shifted is that the donee will be in a more liquid position than the donor when the gain is realized by sale; such policy, however, does not support shifting losses between taxpayers.

Very different rules apply to property passing from a decedent which is includable in the decedent's gross estate. The recipient's basis is the fair market value of the property at the date of death (or the alternate valuation date, if applicable). I.R.C. § 1014(a). Thus if A devises Blackacre, which he originally purchased for $10,000, to B, and if Blackacre is worth $12,000 at A's death, B's basis in Blackacre will be $12,000. If the value at death were $9,000, B's basis would be $9,000. Thus, in the gift situation, the donor's gain is later taxed to the donee, if the donee sells the property and realizes a price in excess of the donor's basis, but in the case of a transfer at death the decedent's gain (or loss) goes unrealized and the recipient begins with a fresh basis equal to the value of the property in the decedent's gross estate.

In the case of property acquired from a decedent, gain accrued before death often goes untaxed. Predeath loss in property cannot be shifted, just as in the case of an inter vivos gift, because the recipient of property passing from the decedent takes a basis equal to value at death for purposes of computing gain or loss on a subsequent sale. Again, the reason for not taxing gain at death may be a concern over lack of liquidity. And the decedent's old basis is not carried over after death because of the heavy administrative burdens involved in tracing the decedent's basis. So potentially taxable gain escapes tax altogether, and potentially deductible loss disappears without a deduction.

Under these rules for transfers at death, an elderly taxpayer has a strong income tax incentive to sell property that has decreased in value below his basis, in order to realize and deduct the loss, and to retain property that has risen in value in order to avoid realizing the gain and to pass the property on to his heirs with a stepped-up basis—equal to fair market value—at death. Gift property with built-in appreciation can often be donated to a low-bracket (or tax-exempt) person and the gain shifted to that person; loss property is better sold, if the loss is deductible by the high-bracket original owner.

Although § 1014(a) generally allows a fresh-start basis for property passing from a decedent, the general rule does not apply to appreciated property that was given to the decedent within one year of death and was then reacquired from the decedent by the original owner (or his spouse). In this instance, the basis of the reacquired property in the hands of the original owner will be the same as the decedent's basis immediately before death. I.R.C. § 1014(e). For example, suppose that A owns appreciated property which she cannot sell without realizing a large capital gain. A is the sole beneficiary under the will of her parent B, who is terminally ill. But for the special rule of § 1014(e), A might give the property to B with the expectation of getting it back with a stepped-up basis after it passed through B's estate. It is not clear that this sort of "basis laundering" was ever widely used, since it might well give rise to gift or estate tax liability exceeding the income tax saved, but § 1014(e) clearly requires that A take a carryover basis in the property. A similar rule also covers the case where the property is sold by B's estate and A is entitled to receive the proceeds. Note the possibility that this rule may easily be avoided if B leaves the property not to A or her spouse, but to another family member (e.g., A's child).

Over the years, the fresh-start basis rule of § 1014 has come under heavy criticism, largely on the grounds that it violates principles of horizontal and vertical equity and undermines economic efficiency. Allowing a permanent exemption from income taxation for built-in gain in property transferred at death is thought to be unacceptable as a matter of tax equity, both because it favors taxpayers who hold appreciated property at death over those who realize gain during life (a horizontal inequity) and because it favors wealthy taxpayers who can afford to retain appreciated property over long periods of time (a vertical inequity). Moreover, the resulting incentive to retain appreciated property until death (and to sell loss property in order to realize the tax deduction before death) is believed to create a "lock-in" effect with undesirable effects on investment behavior. To be sure, the estate tax already reaches the fair market value of property transferred at death, but that does not justify an income tax preference for unrealized appreciation. The main advantage of the fresh-start basis rule is that it avoids the difficulty of ascertaining the decedent's basis in property owned at death. Ascertaining the fair market value of property owned at death is relatively easy, especially if that value must be determined in any event for estate tax purposes.

It would be possible to maintain the fresh-start basis rule while closing the escape route for unrealized appreciation if death were to be treated as a realization event for income tax purposes. Constructive realization, however, raises potential liquidity problems; assets might have to be sold to pay income tax at a time when there was no voluntary disposition, such as a sale or exchange, to justify imposing a tax. This problem could be especially severe for small businesses, farms and estates consisting mainly of a family residence or other illiquid assets.

In 1976 Congress repealed the longstanding fresh-start basis rule for property transferred at death and attempted to bring unrealized appreciation within reach of the income tax. The solution adopted, however, did not take the form of a constructive realization rule. Instead, Congress opted for a carryover basis rule somewhat similar to the existing rule for inter vivos gifts. In general, the recipient's basis in property acquired from a decedent was to be the same as the decedent's basis immediately before death, with an adjustment for transfer taxes paid. See former I.R.C. § 1023. The new rule gave rise to a host of problems involving administration and compliance. How is the decedent's basis to be determined after death, on an asset acquired years earlier, with adjustments for depreciation or capital improvements? And how is an executor to treat beneficiaries fairly and impartially in distributing assets that have bases different from their respective fair market values, especially if there are material differences in the tax brackets and other tax characteristics of the various recipients? A piece of property worth $100,000 with a basis of $90,000 might well be worth more than another asset with the same fair market value but a lower basis. And the basis differential would matter more to a high-bracket recipient than to a low bracket one, or to someone planning to sell the asset soon or to use it in a trade or business where depreciation deductions would be a factor, than to someone planning to retain the asset for personal use.

The carryover basis rule enacted in 1976 became the focus of much comment and criticism, both because of basic policy concerns and also as a consequence of the greatly increased burdens on fiduciaries administering decedents' estates. Opponents of the carryover basis rule persuaded Congress first to postpone its effective date and ultimately to repeal the rule in 1980 before it ever became generally effective.

Undaunted by the failure of the 1976 experiment, Congress in 2001 enacted a modified carryover basis rule to replace the longstanding fresh-start basis rule for property acquired from a decedent. The carryover basis rule, set forth in former § I.R.C. 1022, eventually took effect in 2010, in conjunction with repeal of the estate tax, but only on an optional basis for estates of decedents who died during that year. Nevertheless, the carryover basis rule was subject to two important exceptions which allowed a basis increase of up to $1,300,000 for appreciated property "owned" by the decedent at death (including revocable trust property) and a separate, additional basis increase of up to $3 million for appreciated property passing to a surviving spouse (either outright or in the form of qualified terminable interest property). The opportunity to opt out of the estate tax, even at the cost of foregoing a fresh-start basis for appreciated property, provided substantial tax savings, especially to very large estates, but that option is no longer available for estates of decedents dying after 2010.

NOTES AND QUESTIONS

1. The maximum capital gains rate for most assets held at least one year is 15%. See I.R.C. § 1(h) (rates may range from 0–28% depending on the type of asset and income level of the taxpayer). This is substantially less than the estate tax marginal rates which can reach as high as 60% depending on the year of death.

2. Deceased Spouse left the entire estate to Surviving Spouse. Does Surviving Spouse receive a step-up in basis for the estate assets even though no estate tax is due on Deceased Spouse's estate because of the marital deduction? What if the couple lived in a community property state so that Surviving Spouse already owned one-half of the assets? See I.R.C. § 1014(b)(6).

3. Income in respect of a decedent does not receive a step-up in basis. See Chapter 4(C)(2)(a), note #7; I.R.C. § 1014(c).

4. The basis of an asset acquired by gift is increased by the amount of the federal gift tax paid on the gain portion of the transfer. Note that the basis increase is not for all of the gift tax paid but merely for the proportional amount of gift tax paid on the amount of the gift that, if it had been sold on the date of the gift, would have been a gain. See I.R.C. § 1015(d). Assume that Donor transfers an asset with a basis of $50,000 and a fair market value of $100,000. Donor paid $23,800 in gift taxes. What is Donee's basis?

E. MARITAL DEDUCTION

1. DOMESTIC SPOUSE

ESTATE OF CLAYTON v. COMMISSIONER

United States Court of Appeals, Fifth Circuit, 1992.
976 F.2d 1486.

WIENER, CIRCUIT JUDGE.

This federal estate tax case concerns the eligibility, for purposes of the estate tax Marital Deduction (Marital Deduction), of that portion of a legacy in trust for the benefit of the surviving spouse for which a timely Qualified Terminable Interest Property (QTIP) election was made by the surviving spouse in her capacity as Independent Executrix. On appeal Petitioners–Appellants, Mary Magdalene Clayton (Surviving Spouse) and The First National Bank of Lamesa (the Bank), as Independent Co–Executors of the Estate of Arthur M. Clayton, Jr. (Testator), seek reversal of the Tax Court's holding that the portion of the residue of Testator's estate passing to a trust created in the testament for the benefit of Surviving Spouse (Trust B) is not eligible for a marital deduction because a provision in the testament specifies that any portion of the residue for which a timely QTIP election is not made will pass to and constitute a part of the corpus of another trust created in the testament (Trust A).

The Co–Executors contend that the Tax Court's holding, sustaining the position of Respondent–Appellee, the Commissioner of Internal Revenue (the Commissioner), that the subject testamentary provision is "tantamount" to a proscribed power of appointment, cannot be squared with the plain language of the QTIP provision of the United States Internal Revenue Code of 1954, as amended (the Code), which was added to the Code by the Economic Recovery Act of 1981 (ERTA). Considering the same uncontested, straightforward facts upon which the Tax Court made its legal determination, we reach precisely the opposite conclusion. For the reasons set forth below, we reverse the Tax Court's judgment and hold that the portion of the residue of Testator's estate for which the timely QTIP election was made and which passes to and constitutes the corpus of Trust B is eligible for the marital deduction. We therefore remand this case to the Tax Court to redetermine the estate tax deficiency, if any, after allowing the marital deduction consistent herewith, and to calculate the net amount of estate tax and interest, if any, that is due and owing to the Commissioner from the estate of the Testator—or vice versa—after thus redetermining the deficiency.

I.

FACTS AND PROCEEDINGS

The facts found by the Tax Court, largely on the basis of stipulations, reflect that Testator, a Texas domiciliary, died there on December 22, 1987, survived by Surviving Spouse (his second wife) and his four children from his first marriage. Testator had executed a Last Will and Testament (the Will) on April 8, 1982, and a First Codicil (the Codicil) to the Will on June 23, 1982. In the Will, Testator created several trusts, two of which are for the benefit of Surviving Spouse during her lifetime: The first, Trust A, is a "Credit Shelter Trust" to be funded with properties or interests in properties from the Testator's estate equal in value to the amount exempt from federal estate tax by virtue of the Unified Credit.

The second trust, Trust B, is a "Marital Deduction Trust" or "QTIP Trust" to be funded with that portion of the residue of Testator's estate for which a timely QTIP election is made. Trust B is created for the benefit of Surviving Spouse "for and during the rest of her life." Upon her death, the remainder of Trust B is to "be added to and become part of the corpus of Trust 'A,' for the use and benefit of [Testator's] then living children." It is undisputed that Trust A is ineligible for the Marital Deduction.

Central to the instant case is Article THIRD, paragraph D of the Will:

> In the event my executors fail or refuse to make the election under Section 2056(b)(7)(B)(II)(v) of the Internal Revenue Code of 1954, as amended [QTIP election], with respect to my Trust "B" property on the return of tax imposed by Section 2001 of the Internal Revenue Code of 1954, as amended, then the property with respect to which such election was not made shall pass to and become a part of the corpus of Trust "A" for the benefit of my Trust "A" beneficiaries.

Also central to the instant case is the mandate in Article SIXTH, paragraph A of the Will, regarding current income of Trust B:

> [I]n no event shall the amount distributable by my trustees from Trust "B" to [Surviving Spouse] during any year be less than the current net income, to include all taxable net income under the [Code] as then existing, of Trust "B" during that year.

[In the Will, Testator also (1) leaves lesser assets to Surviving Spouse outright; (2) specifies that if Surviving Spouse should make a "qualified disclaimer" of any portion of the Trust B assets such portion would pass to and form part of the corpus of yet a third trust, for the benefit of Testator's children; and (3) gives Surviving Spouse the power to appoint assets of various trusts in favor of Testator's children, both by deed during her lifetime or by her Last Will, but specifies that the power of appointment by deed during her lifetime could not be exercised with respect to assets of Trust "B"; neither could those powers of appointment be exercised in favor of Surviving Spouse, her estate, her creditors, or the creditors of the estate.]

In paragraph V of Article EIGHTH of the Will, Testator spells out his intentions concerning QTIP treatment of Trust B property:

> It is my intention that the assets of the Trust "B" be eligible to be treated, for federal estate tax purposes, as a [sic] "qualified terminable interest property" within the meaning of Section 2056 of the Internal Revenue Code, as amended. In no event shall my Trust "B" trustees be deemed to have any authority or power over Trust "B" assets which would prevent Trust "B" assets from being eligible to be treated as qualified terminable trust [sic] properties, if my executors make the timely election to have such properties treated as such.

The Will nominates Surviving Spouse and the Bank to serve as co-trustees of all trusts created therein and as Independent Co-Executors. In both instances the Will specifies that if Surviving Spouse does not or cannot serve, the Bank is to serve alone. The Co-Executors are granted the same powers, duties, privileges, authorities, and responsibilities as those granted to the co-trustees under the terms of the Will.

In due course following the death of Testator, an Application for Probate of a Written Will and for Letters Testamentary (the application) was filed in the proper court. In an apparent effort to comply with the position of the Internal Revenue Service (IRS) announced in a 1986 Technical Advice Memorandum, the application requested:

> That the qualification of the [Bank] as an Independent Co-Executor be deferred until it makes and files its oath as required by law after the estate's Federal Estate Tax Return has been filed, and the time for timely filing of the return has expired.... The request is made that Letters Testamentary issue first to [Surviving Spouse] as sole independent executrix of the estate upon her making and filing her oath, and that when the [Bank] as Independent Co-Executor shall qualify by filing its oath, new Letters Testamentary shall issue to [Surviving Spouse and the Bank] as Independent Co-Executors of the estate.

The Will was admitted to probate and issuance of Letters Testamentary was authorized by an order which states that Surviving Spouse and the Bank are qualified to act as Independent Co-Executors and to receive Letters Testamentary. In conformity with the application, however, that order directed that initially Letters Testamentary issue only to Surviving Spouse as sole Independent Executrix until such time as the Bank should execute and file its oath as required by law, following the filing of the estate's Federal Estate Return, Form 706, at which time new Letters Testamentary would be issued to Surviving Spouse and the Bank as Independent Co-Executors. When new Letters Testamentary were eventually issued jointly to Surviving Spouse and the Bank as Co-Executors, the

Form 706 had already been prepared, signed by Surviving Spouse as sole Independent Executrix, and mailed to the appropriate office of the IRS together with payment of the estate taxes as calculated on the Form 706.

When Surviving Spouse executed the Form 706 as sole Independent Executrix, she checked the appropriate box on Schedule M, "Bequests, etc. to Surviving Spouse," required to elect "to claim a marital deduction for Qualified Terminable Interest Property (QTIP) under Section 2056(b)(7)." The total value of deductible property interests left outright to Surviving Spouse (for which a QTIP election was neither required nor appropriate) was $78,950; the total value of terminable interest property for which the QTIP election was made was $1,077,635, being the value of an undivided .563731 interest in specified bonds, notes and cash listed on Schedules B and C of the Form 706 (the securities). Thus, the total amount claimed as the marital deduction was $1,156,585.

The Commissioner's decision to disallow the Marital Deduction to the extent claimed by the estate for the undivided .563731 interest in the securities—for which the QTIP election was timely made—is reflected in a statement contained in the Notice of Deficiency issued by the IRS to Surviving Spouse and the Bank as Independent Co–Executors: "the marital deduction is $78,950.00 rather than $1,156,585.00 as reported on the Estate Tax Return. Accordingly, the reported taxable estate is increased $1,077,635.00." In response to the Commissioner's Notice of Deficiency, the Co–Executors filed a timely petition for redetermination in the Tax Court, the proper court to hear such cases. That court's opinion was filed on September 16, 1991, and its decision was entered on December 18, 1991, finally disposing of the lone contested issue of the case. The Co–Executors, on behalf of the estate, timely filed a Notice of Appeal to this court, which has jurisdiction to review such cases.

II

ANALYSIS

A. *Standard of Review*

"Our standard of review for appeals from the United States Tax Court is the same as for appeals from the district court: We review findings of fact for clear error and legal conclusions *de novo.*" As the facts of the instant case are largely stipulated and totally undisputed, our standard of review of the facts thus found is not a matter of concern. The issue we here review is a purely legal one.

B. *Issue*

Like the uncontested facts of this case, the sole legal issue before us is a straightforward one. As posed by the Tax Court, "[t]he issue in this case is whether an estate tax marital deduction should be allowed for the property in Trust B for which a timely election was made pursuant to Section 2056(b)(7)." Thus stated, the issue is concise but only skeletal; the true substance of that issue is encapsulated entirely in the previously quoted provision from Article THIRD, paragraph D, of the Will, which specifies that any portion of the residue of the estate for which the executor does not elect QTIP shall pass to and become a part of the corpus of Trust A, a trust concededly not eligible for QTIP treatment. Posed even more precisely, the question we must answer is "Does the effect of that testamentary provision, causing the undivided interest in the securities for which the QTIP election is not made to be excluded from the corpus of Trust B (the QTIP Trust) when it is funded, so taint the entire residuary bequest that the value of the undivided interest in those assets for which the QTIP election is made and which will form the corpus of Trust B when funded cannot be eligible for the marital deduction?"

C. Estate Tax Marital Deduction: A Historical Perspective

This case is ultimately decided on the legal meaning of the plain and unambiguous words of the Will and Code § 2056. This is a true "eight-corners" case, determinable within the four corners of the Will and the four corners of the statute. Nevertheless, Code § 2056 as the sole statutory well-spring of the estate tax Marital Deduction—as well as both the general exception thereto (the terminable interest) and the one among the several exceptions to that general exception for terminable interests with which we are here concerned (QTIP)—can be completely understood and appreciated only when viewed in the perspective of their collective historical development.

From 1916 to 1942, the federal estate tax law took into account the differences between community property states and common-law states. Abiding by state law, however, produced a disparity between community property states and common-law states. The first effort of Congress to eliminate that disparity was included in the 1942 amendments to the Internal Revenue Code of 1939. As a result of the 1942 enactment, however, the value of the entire community property was taxed in full in the estate of the first spouse to die. Rather than creating equality, the 1942 enactment put married couples residing in community property states at a distinct disadvantage.

> Despite this new geographical disparity [between community property and common-law states], the Supreme Court upheld the constitutionality of the 1942 Economic Source Rule in Fernandez v. Weiner, [sic] decided in 1945.[1]

In the first major tax bill after World War II, Congress undid the result of *Wiener,* which had been so unpalatable to community property

1. [5 Boris I. Bitker, Federal Taxation of Income, Estates and Gifts] 129–5 [1984]. Some have suggested that this treatment in the Revenue Act of 1942 and its approbation by the Supreme Court in Fernandez v. Wiener can be understood only in the context of the extreme fixation of Congress on raising revenue to finance the war effort for World War II, and the equally pervasive patriotism of those times, which even seeped uphill to the Supreme Court. How else, they ask rhetorically, could one explain that the majority opinion in Korematsu v. United States, 323 U.S. 214, 65 S.Ct. 193, 89 L.Ed. 194 (1944), the landmark case condoning internment of Americans of Japanese ancestry, was written by Associate Justice Hugo Black, one of the most ardent and active advocates of the Bill of Rights and individual freedoms ever to sit on the Court.

states, enacting for the first time the "new concept of 'estate-splitting' as a corollary to 'income-splitting' between husband and wife." The vehicle employed for so doing was the Marital Deduction.

The original Marital Deduction was quite obviously a device designed to allow estate "equalization," i.e., to recognize the 50–50 situation in community property jurisdictions while allowing common-law couples to equalize, through the Marital Deduction, their combined estate irrespective of which spouse was actually the wealthier. An essential feature of the Marital Deduction from its very beginning, however, was that any property of the first spouse to die that passed untaxed to the surviving spouse should be taxed in the estate of the surviving spouse. This concept persists to the present time; and it is an indispensable ingredient of the result we reach today.

A corollary of taxability in the estate of the surviving spouse was and remains the exclusion of "terminable interests" from the category of properties for which the Marital Deduction is available. An interest that terminates does not form part of the death estate of the surviving spouse, so if a terminable interest in property were deductible in the first estate, such property would escape tax in the estates of *both* spouses. Thus, in 1948 and today, "[t]o qualify for the Marital Deduction, an interest in property must ... avoid being disqualified by a complex set of rules relating to 'terminable interests.' " As shall be shown, however, a number of exceptions to the terminable interest exception are recognized.

In 1976 Congress liberalized the Marital Deduction significantly by establishing dual yardsticks for measuring the maximum estate tax Marital Deduction. For decedents dying after December 31, 1976, the maximum Marital Deduction was *the greater of* $250,000 or one-half of the adjusted gross estate. Nevertheless, many other features of Code § 2056, including the unavailability of the Marital Deduction for terminable interest property, remained essentially unaffected by the TRA of 1976.

D. Backdrop for QTIP

During the five years following 1976 no statutory changes of particular significance to the Marital Deduction occurred. The stage was set, however, for the most dramatic and expansive liberalization of the Marital Deduction in history. Not surprisingly, the overarching consideration of the sweeping Marital Deduction changes of 1981 was the resurgence of the decades-old concept of marital property as the unitary estate of both spouses, and 1948's "new concept" for "estate-splitting" as a corollary to "income-splitting" between husband and wife.

Leading to the 1981 enactment of ERTA was the burgeoning realization that an ever-increasing number of testators were encountering a serious dilemma: They could not provide maximum lifetime benefits to their surviving spouses and, at the same time, control who would be the ultimate recipients of the property after the death of the surviving spouse. Congress recognized that the ranks of such testators included a growing number of those who expect to be survived by children of a first marriage and by a spouse of a subsequent marriage. Under pre–1982 Marital Deduction rules, particularly the one prohibiting the deduction of terminable interests, such a testator faced a classic Catch–22 decision: He or she could either 1) provide maximum financial benefits and security for the surviving spouse but only at the risk that the survivor might waste the property or appoint it to successors other than the children of the testator's first marriage; or 2) ensure that the property would devolve to his or her children of a prior marriage (or other objects of his or her bounty) but at the cost of losing the Marital Deduction and risking underendowment of the surviving spouse. Even the pre–1982 vehicle of the power-of-appointment marital trust would not allow such a testator to ensure ultimate inheritance by children of his or her first marriage.

The strong sense of Congress was that if the concept of the marital property regime as a single unit, preservable intact until the death of the second spouse, was to realize its full potential, something truly new and innovative would be required. None can quarrel with that description of the fundamental change in the Marital Deduction wrought by ERTA: the unlimited Marital Deduction. "Congress flew into the wild blue yonder in 1981 by exempting all transfers between husband and wife ... subject [only] to rules ... to insure that the exempted property will be taxed if and when the surviving spouse disposes of it by gratuitous transfer, whether inter vivos or at death."

Thus, to retain the "article of faith" that property which is untaxed in the estate of the first spouse to die must be taxable in the estate of the surviving spouse, Code § 2056's general denial of marital deduction treatment for terminable interests was preserved as an exception to the new general rule of unlimited deductibility of interspousal transfers. Even so, Congress realized that, without something else, the aforesaid dilemma would persist for many testators. The well-verbalized realization by Congress that married testators—particularly those with children of a former marriage—would be left with a Hobson's Choice as long as terminable interest property was ineligible for the Marital Deduction, prompted genuine creativity. Out of thin air and from whole cloth, Congress invented a brand new, theretofore unseen concept: Qualified Terminable Interest Property. If "unlimiting" the Marital Deduction was a flight into the wild blue yonder, Congress truly "slipped the surly bonds of earth" with the advent of QTIP.

E. Qualified Terminable Interest Property

In the perspective of the long history of continual expansion and liberalization of the Marital Deduction during the decades since its introduction in 1948, and against the backdrop of the adoption in 1981 of the unlimited marital deduction, the intent, function and purpose of QTIP is not difficult to discern. Unmistakably, the Marital Deduction is the embodiment of a strong public policy. By itself, ERTA's removal of the dollar and percentage limitations on the Marital Deduction to make it "unlimited" was purely quantitative. Although transfers to the surviving spouse in outright ownership or fee simple title were freed of all quantitative limits, other categories of property—principally terminable interests—would remain totally excluded from deductibility unless something qualitative were done. QTIP was invented to produce the desired qualitative expansion of the classes of property eligible for the Marital Deduction, i.e., to extend, for the first time ever, the availability of the Marital Deduction to those types of terminable interests in property that Congress deigned to "qualify." Hence the moniker "qualified terminable interest property" and the acronym "QTIP."

As thus created by Congress, QTIP is an exception-to-the-exception for non-deductibility of terminable interests in general. And, as is universally recognized and applauded, Congress accomplished this revolutionary change using uncommonly clear and cohesive language, particularly for tax provisions, with the insertion of subsection (b)(7) in Code § 2056.

1. Statutory Scheme

Subsection (a) of Code § 2056 states the broad, general grant of a deduction from the estate of the first spouse to die. The amount of the deduction is the value of any interest in property that passes or has passed from the decedent to the surviving spouse, to the extent that such interest is included in determining the value of the decedent's gross estate.

Subsection (b) of Code § 2056 expresses the general, terminable interest exception to subsection (a)'s general grant of the deduction. As it has the effect of limiting a public policy matter, this exception to the unlimited Marital Deduction must be construed narrowly. By its title, the exception applies to a "Life Estate or Other Terminable Interest." Code § 2056(b)(1) defines "terminable interest" and states generally that a deduction will not be allowed for such an interest.

There then follow, however, a number of particular exceptions to that general terminable interest exception. Particular types of terminable interests that are in fact deductible by virtue of being exceptions-to-the-exception include 1) a legacy conditioned on survivorship for a limited period, 2) a life estate with power of appointment in the surviving spouse, 3) life insurance or annuity payments with power of appointment in the surviving spouse, and 4) a charitable remainder trust. QTIP is another specific "counter-exception" to the general exception of Code § 2056(b)'s denial of a marital deduction for terminable interest property. The entire statutory concept of QTIP is contained in Code § 2056(b)(7) * * *.

2. Important QTIP Features

A. Election. Gifts or bequests of terminable interests that appear to be eligible for the Marital Deduction are nonetheless not automatically deductible. An irrevocable, affirmative election must be made on the estate tax return by the executor before an apparently deductible terminable interest meets the definition of QTIP.

It is axiomatic that any estate tax election which is not made inter vivos by the testator can only be made (a) by someone else (b) after the death of the decedent. And we are aware of no post-mortem estate tax election that is required to be made earlier than the time for filing the Form 706. In keeping with the congressional purposes of 1) eliminating the need for testators to risk predicting the future, and 2) providing both flexibility and the opportunity for post-mortem estate planning either to minimize or "optimize" the estate tax impact on the combined marital property of the spouses, the QTIP election can be made at any time before such filing date. Still, like other estate tax elections (and other exceptions to the terminable interest rules), the *effect* of the QTIP election is retroactive to the instant of death, irrespective of when it is actually made. Significantly, the party statutorily vested with the exclusive right to make the post-mortem QTIP election is *not* the surviving spouse, as one might expect, but the executor. Congress obviously did this as an extension of the testator's volition but with all of the guesswork removed.

Congress also recognized the need for post-mortem flexibility when it vested the executor with the additional option of making a *partial* QTIP election. The election need not be "all or nothing"; rather, the executor may choose QTIP treatment for any percentage or share of the property interest, from zero to 100%.

B. Property. A limitation which was clear prior to ERTA was that, "[i]n applying the terminable interest rules, it [was] essential to honor the statutory distinction between an 'interest' in property and the underlying property itself." In ERTA, Congress recognized that if this distinction were made applicable to QTIP, it could prove unduly restrictive of the kinds of property interest (other than perfect ownership or fee simple title) that would be eligible for the deduction. Such a potential restriction was eliminated by the inclusion of a new definition of *property.* "The term 'property' includes an interest in property." This feature dovetails with the partial QTIP election.

C. Separate Shares. The QTIP portion of Code § 2056 which follows on the heels of the definition of property mandates that "[a] specific portion of property shall be treated as separate property." Like the partial election and the definition of property to include an "interest in property," the "separate share" concept enhances post-mortem flexibility and planning. "[T]he Treasury construes the 'specific portion' rule to permit the executor to elect Q–TIP treatment for a fraction or percentage of an otherwise qualifying trust." Of interest in the instant case is the position announced by the Treasury, in proposed regulations, that would permit separate trusts to be created by a partial election:

> [T]he trust may be divided into separate trusts to reflect a partial election that *has been made* or is to be made.

"[A]s ... the statute provides that 'a specific portion of property shall be treated as separate property,' the executor can elect only for a portion of corpus. This greatly extends the usefulness of this provision." "In case of a qualified terminable interest property trust, 'property' includes an interest in property, and a 'specific portion' of property is treated as separate property. Thus it is possible to obtain the Marital Deduction for a specific portion of the corpus of the trust for which the spouse is entitled to the income interest."

D. Property Passing to the Surviving Spouse. Entitlement to the Marital Deduction for any property, including QTIP, requires that the property pass to a person who as a matter of law is the "surviving spouse" of the testator. That requirement is not an issue in the instant case.

E. Property Passing From the Decedent. Another requirement of the Marital Deduction is that property for which the deduction is claimed in fact be an "interest in property which passes or has passed from the decedent." That the decimal interest in the securities "passes from the decedent" within the meaning of Code § 2056 is not in dispute here.

F. Property Included in Determining the Value of the Gross Estate. Also uncontested in the instant case is that the value of the undivided interest in the securities was included in determining the value of the testator's gross estate, as is required for any legacy to be eligible for the Marital Deduction.

3. Definition as Substance

The position of the Commissioner and the judgment of the Tax Court rises or falls on the definition of QTIP. The same is true for the opposite position of the Co–Executors and for the holding we make today.

The Code contains a three-pronged functional definition of QTIP, which is followed immediately by specific definitions of terms used in that tripartite definition. As the definition of QTIP begins with the statement that " 'qualified terminable interest property' means property," the first step is to identify the "property" to be tested under the elements of the definition. Relying on two specifically defined terms—that "property" includes an *interest in* property; and that a "specific portion" of property is to be treated as *separate* property—the Co–Executors argue that the "property" under examination here is the separate, undivided .563731 interest in the securities that was identified on the Form 706 as the property to which the QTIP election applies. Relying on nothing that has either been cited to us or that our independent research has produced, the Commissioner and the Tax Court insist that the "property" here under examination is the entire residue of testator's estate, being the maximum amount of property and interests in property with which Trust B could be funded were a total QTIP election to be made. For reasons explained in more detail below, we agree with the position of the Co–Executors and reject the position of the Commissioner and the Tax Court.

The second step is to see if the identified "separate interest in property" (the undivided interest in the securities for which the QTIP election was made) meets the Code's definition of QTIP. That is done by testing it for compliance with each of the three prongs of that statutory definition.

All agree that one of those prongs, i.e., that the separate interest in property "passes from the decedent," is met. We conclude that a second prong is met, i.e., that the property be an interest "to which an election under this paragraph applies." We reach that conclusion by observing that election is a defined term: "An election under this paragraph in respect to any property shall be made by the executor on the return ... [and] ... shall be irrevocable." Here, Surviving Spouse as Independent Executrix duly and timely completed the Form 706, checked the appropriate box on Schedule M, and identified the property "in respect to" which that election is made, i.e., the undivided .563731 interest in the securities listed on Schedules B and C. Thus, the property being tested for eligibility is the same property to which the election made by the Independent Executrix applies.

The third prong requires that the separate interest in property be one "in which the surviving spouse has a *qualifying income interest for life.*" This phrase too is a defined term of art: Such an interest is one in which "the surviving spouse is entitled to all the income ... payable annually or at more frequent intervals ... [and of which] no person has a power to appoint any part of the property to any person other than surviving spouse."

Under the terms of the Will, Surviving Spouse is expressly given the right for life to receive all income from Trust B, the corpus of which is the separate property interest in question. The executors and trustees are directed to pay such income to her no less frequently than annually. Even so, "[t]he statute does not require that each day income accumulates that the income be paid immediately to the spouse." In fact, "[n]o provision need be made for paying income before the executor distributes the property to the trustee." Clearly, the annual-income-for-life element is met even if the income is not disbursed until a year after the trust is funded—an event that can only occur during or at the end of the orderly administration of the estate. Obviously funding of every testamentary trust occurs after the death of the testator; the executor cannot possibly ascertain on "day one" the amount of the income. Just as obviously, then, the beneficiary must wait a reasonable time before the income is actually received. But receipt and entitlement are not congruent. The requirement of life income interest is met as long as the eventual disbursements include all income accruing from and after the moment of the testator's death.

The other definitional element of "qualifying income interest for life" is that no one may have a power to appoint any of the property to anyone other than the surviving spouse. We have already determined that the "property" being considered is the undivided interest in the securities for which the executor made a timely QTIP election. No reasonable reading or construction of the Will or the statute can validate the position of the

Commissioner, as endorsed by the Tax Court, that the Independent Executrix's QTIP election itself is "tantamount" to a power of appointment to the testator's children. Clearly, the estate's entitlement to a QTIP deduction is not meant to be abrogated simply because making a partial election for a separate interest in the property, i.e., not making a full election as to all interest in the property, results in a portion of the estate's residue—one that would have passed to Trust B under a full election—passing to Trust A. To embrace the Commissioner's flawed logic and deliberate disregard of the plain wording of the pertinent part of Code § 2056 would be to engage in pure sophistry.

Besides being unable to direct our attention to anything that might support their interpretation, the Commissioner and the Tax Court cannot escape the effects of their own interpretative pronouncements on the election prong of the QTIP definition. As shall be seen, such pronouncements implicitly acknowledge that the election element of the definition is viewed in the past tense, i.e., that although the *effect* of the election is tested as of the instant of the testator's death, the definitional *eligibility* of the separate terminable interest under examination is tested as though QTIP election had already been made.

In the Treasury's own proposed regulation interpreting the *definition* of QTIP, cited to us by the Commissioner in the appendix to her brief, the Department identifies the "property" as that "which the executor elected to treat as qualified terminable interest property." Likewise, the Tax Court, in citing its decision in the instant case to support its judgment in *Estate of Willard E. Robertson v. Commissioner,* refers to the election element of the definition pertaining to property "for which an election *has been* made."

4. Additional Flaws in the Commissioner's Position

The Commissioner misses the mark by insisting that the QTIP provision should be construed narrowly because it is an exception to the prohibition of deducting terminable interest under the Marital Deduction. As we have noted, however, it is Code § 2056(b)'s general prohibition of deducting terminable interests that is the exception. It is an exception to the broad rule of deductibility of interspousal transfers which in turn implements the clear will of Congress favoring, as a matter of public policy, deferral of estate tax until the death of the second spouse—to the extent such deferral is desired by the parties. It is that general terminable interest exception that must be narrowly construed. As QTIP is an exception to that exception, however, QTIP enjoys the same favored position and liberal construction as is properly afforded to the Marital Deduction itself.

More importantly, there is nothing in the plain wording of the entire QTIP subsection which, when viewed in light of the definition of terms therein provided, even remotely supports the position of the Commissioner that if anything occurs *after* the death of the testator—such as the QTIP election—to prevent even a modicum of property which under the testament would have passed from the decedent to the surviving spouse, the deduction is unavailable for all otherwise eligible property. To reach that strained result, the Commissioner would have us ignore the overarching truism that many acts must be done and many facts must be determined after the death of the testator in order to determine the taxable estate. The question is not *when* those determinations are made or *when* those acts are performed but whether their *effects* relate back, *ab initio,* to the moment of death. For example, a qualified disclaimer by the Surviving Spouse has precisely the effect of the QTIP election here: Both are volitional acts; both can be made only after the death of the testator; both relate back, *ab initio,* to the date of death of the testator; and both have the effect of causing estate property which would otherwise pass to the Surviving Spouse to pass instead directly to or for the benefit of other parties. Likewise, while seldom volitional, the death of the Surviving Spouse within six months following the death of the testator who conditions the legacy on survivorship would have the same effect, but again retroactive to the moment of the testator's death.

Curiously, the Commissioner and the Tax Court appear to view QTIP legislation as some sort of congressional paternalism aimed at ensuring the financial stability of the surviving spouse. Clearly such protectionism played no part in it. If the intention had been to dangle the carrot of deductibility in front of testators to induce them to ensure the financial well-being of the surviving spouse, Congress would surely have given the power to make the QTIP election to the surviving spouse, not the executor. The point we here emphasize is that for tax purposes Congress was and is interested only in that portion of terminable interest property for which the QTIP election is made; it has no interest whatsoever in the portion of any terminable interest property for which the election is *not* made. Being ineligible for the Marital Deduction, that property is taxed right where the Commissioner and Congress want it taxed—in the estate of the first spouse to die. Congress could not care less whether the portion of the terminable interest property for which the QTIP election is *not* made goes to the surviving spouse, to the children, or to a stranger. Obviously, that is why Congress placed the election *in the definition* of QTIP property. If Congress had intended the result advocated by the Commissioner, it could have 1) defined the property without reference to the election, 2) specified a subsequent election, or 3) provided separately for the election to apply to all property meeting the definition, thereby separating the election from the definition. Facially, the statute eschews any such separation.

From whence it came we know not, but the Tax Court here made the pronouncement that the QTIP election gave the executor "control over trust assets [that] is tantamount to a power to appoint property that was subject to the qualifying income interest." That unsubstantiated, conclusionary statement can only be the product of a circular argument—one that we reject. First, the QTIP election cannot vest the executor with control over "trust assets" before they become trust assets! The undivided interests in the securities for which the election is made are *estate* assets but they do not become *trust* assets until the trust is funded, even though the economic effect of funding is retroactive to the instant of death. Assets used to fund each testamentary trust get there by virtue of the provisions of the Will and the administration of the estate. The same analysis is applicable to that portion of the quotation from the Tax Court's opinion that refers to *property that was subject to the qualifying income interest.* No income interest is qualifying until it meets the full definition for QTIP, including the election prong. As we have just noted, one of the three essential elements in the definition of such property interest is that it be property for which—in the Tax Court's own words—"an election has *been* made."

Additionally, the Commissioner appears to have seized on a gratuitous statement from the Tax Court opinion in the instant case to bootstrap an even more adventuresome government position, i.e., that "any QTIP trust that pours nonelected property over is flawed, apparently even if the bypass trust is QTIPable in its own right." Such an arbitrary and unsupported misconstruction of the statute cannot be justified by any reasonable reading. It can only be explained as overzealousness in revenue collection, deliberate disregard for the clear purpose, intent and policy behind the statute, and a historic aversion to the Marital Deduction which is well documented in the Tax Court Reports, the Federal Reporter System, Treasury Regulations, Revenue Rulings, Technical Advice Memoranda, Private Letter Rulings, and the like.

"Loophole" is a term frequently used as a pejorative in the context of taxation. Although it is usually reserved for taxpayers and their professional advisors, in truth the Commissioner and the Service are no less active in probing tax statutes for loopholes. Historically, that has been part of the game, leaving to Congress the damage control of plugging loopholes through technical amendments. The position taken by the IRS and advocated by the Commissioner in the instant case, however, goes beyond mere probing for loopholes overlooked by Congress. Rather, it reflects an effort to batter such a hole in the statutory wall where none exists. We will not approbate such overreaching. From every standpoint—history, expressed intent, logic, reading *in pari materiae* with other post-mortem provisions, and—above all—the plain language of the statute—the position of the Co–Executors meets muster while the Commissioner's fails.

5. The End Result

Having thoroughly parsed the statute, examined the terms as therein defined, and eliminated the flawed construction of the Commissioner, we now reassemble Humpty Dumpty by reconstituting the statutory definition of QTIP by replacing all terms of art with their statutory, jurisprudential, or regulatory definitions:

> Qualified Terminable Interest Property means a separate interest in property, which was included in determining the value of the gross estate, and (1) which passes from the decedent, (2) from which the

surviving spouse is entitled to all income for life, payable no less frequently than annually, no part of which can be appointed by any person (including the surviving spouse) to any person other than the surviving spouse, and (3) which the executor elected to treat as Qualified Terminable Interest Property.

When all definitions are thus factored into the applicable Code section's tripartite definition of QTIP, it is clear beyond cavil that the election given to the executor by Congress is *not* "tantamount" to a power of appointment, and does not divest the surviving spouse of anything about which Congress was or is concerned. The provisions of the Will that effect the funding of Trust B with a terminable interest in that separate decimal fraction of the estate's residual assets for which the election is made, and which effect the funding of Trust A with that portion of the residue for which the election is not made (including the "other" separate interest in the securities) are indisputably effective as of the moment of death, albeit retroactively from the time the election is made. Such retroactivity is an expected and indispensable characteristic of all estate tax elections, not to mention many non-tax aspects of will implementation. Even though Trust B is not funded until after the QTIP election is made, the Surviving Spouse as QTIP beneficiary of that trust is entitled to and assured of receiving every dollar of net income generated by such corpus from and after the instant of the testator's death. Neither the corpus of that trust nor the income thereof can be appointed by any person to any person other than the Surviving Spouse.

Congress clearly could not care less about the post-mortem disposition of that portion of the residue of the testator's estate for which the QTIP election was not made, *because* every dollar's worth of that property was taxed currently in the estate of the Testator as the first spouse to die. That is the very reason for allowing a *partial* election and for treating specific portions of interests in property separately. As such the Will and the administration of the Testator's estate, including the partial QTIP election, met the only conditions that Congress has placed on the ability to defer estate tax on a terminable interest via the Marital Deduction, i.e., that the specific portion of the terminable interest property for which the election is made be taxed in the estate of the surviving spouse, and that all other property and interests in property—terminable or not—be taxed in the estate of the first spouse to die.

III

CONCLUSION

The Marital Deduction of Code § 2056 excludes from taxability in the estate of the first spouse to die those properties or interests in property used in calculating the gross estate that pass from the decedent to the Surviving Spouse. For decedents dying after December 31, 1981, the Marital Deduction is unlimited in both quantum and share. Although the Marital Deduction is not generally available for interspousal transfers of terminable interests in property, Code § 2056 contains express exceptions.

One such exception exists for terminable interest property that meets the Code's definition of "qualified terminable interest property." That exception is set forth in full in Code § 2056(b)(7), and the particular type of terminable interest for which the exception is available—"qualified terminable interest property"—is defined in sub-subsection (B) thereof.

As sub-subsection (B)(iii) defines the term "property" to include an "interest in property"; and as sub-subsection (B)(iv) mandates that a "specific portion" of property be treated as a "separate property," any testing of terminable interest "property" which is the object of an inter-spousal transfer must treat such interest as a specific portion of the property, separate and apart from the underlying property. Conducting such a test to determine eligibility for the Marital Deduction by virtue of being qualified terminable interest property must begin with the statutory definition.

That definition, found in sub-subsection (B)(i), opens with the statement that the term "qualified terminable interest property" means "property." Focusing on the separate interest in property being tested in the instant case—an undivided .563731 interest in the securities listed on the Form 706—we conclude that it meets each of the three prongs of the definition. First, it is a separate interest in property to which the QTIP election applies. To borrow the words of the Tax Court and the Treasury respectively, it is property "for which an election has been made" or "which the executor elected to treat as qualified terminable interest property." The separate interest in property here under examination meets the "election" prong of the definition as set forth in sub-subsection (B)(i)(III).

That the separate interest in property meets a second prong, the one set forth in sub-section (B)(i)(I)—a separate interest in property "which passes from the decedent,"—is not in dispute.

The remaining prong, set forth in sub-subsection (B)(i)(II)—a separate interest in property in which the surviving spouse has a qualifying income interest for life—is met by virtue of the unambiguous language of the Will. The trustees of Trust B are commanded to pay all net income generated by the corpus of that trust—beginning with the death of the testator—to the Surviving Spouse at least annually for the remainder of her life. Under equally unambiguous language of the Will, the corpus of Trust B will consist of any portion of the residue of testator's estate which the Independent Executor elected to treat as QTIP, here the undivided .563731 interest in the subject securities. Because the election and income provisions under the trust are retroactively effective, *ab initio,* to the moment of the testator's death, the income interest of the Surviving Spouse covers the period that begins with the testator's death and ends with the Surviving Spouse's death.

Moreover, by the express language of the Will, no party—including Surviving Spouse—has the power or authority to appoint any part of the separate interest in property, which passes from the decedent, as to which

QTIP election was made, and in which the Surviving Spouse has an annually payable income interest for life. The Will contains no express power of appointment of the interest for which the election is made; in fact, the Will expressly negates such possibility. And we reject out of hand the strained construction of the partial election and its effect on the funding of the several residuary trusts as being "tantamount" to a power of appointment.

Therefore we hold that the terminable interest in property for which the Marital Deduction was taken on Testator's Form 706 by virtue of the QTIP election is eligible for that deduction. To disallow it for the circular reasoning advanced by the Commissioner would defy logic, common sense, and the purpose for which QTIP was designed and implemented.

We perceive no appropriate basis for the Commissioner's concern with separate interests in property for which no election was made and for which no deduction was taken, i.e., the balance of the residue of testator's estate, including the remaining undivided .436269 interest in the subject securities. No QTIP election was made for it; no deduction was claimed for it; and federal estate taxes were timely paid on it. Neither do we perceive a reason for the Commissioner's concern that such other separate interests in property could have passed to Trust B and formed a part of the corpus thereof if the QTIP election had been made for it. By definition, the Commissioner need only be concerned with separate interests in property for which the QTIP election is made, not that for which no election is made—except to see that tax is paid on it in the estate of the first spouse to die. And the Independent Co–Executrix did that in a complete and timely manner.

Finally, as we hold that the subject clause in the Will does not make the QTIP election here "tantamount" to a power of appointment for purposes of Code § 2056(b)(7)(B)(ii)(II), the identity of the party or parties serving in such capacity is of no consequence. It is irrelevant that under the Will a party other than Surviving Spouse might have served with her as Independent Co–Executor or in her stead as sole Independent Executor.

For the foregoing reasons, the judgment of the Tax Court is reversed and the case remanded to that court for redetermination of the estate tax deficiency in the estate of the Testator, allowing the Marital Deduction for the qualified terminable interest property for which the Surviving Spouse, in her capacity as Independent Executrix, duly made the QTIP election on the Form 706. Such redetermination shall include consideration of any other applicable adjustments not at issue in this appeal, as well as interest.

REVERSED AND REMANDED.

INTERNAL REVENUE CODE, § 2056

BEQUESTS, ETC., TO SURVIVING SPOUSE

(a) Allowance of marital deduction.—For purposes of the tax imposed by section 2001, the value of the taxable estate shall, except as limited by subsection (b), be determined by deducting from the value of the gross estate an amount equal to the value of any interest in property which passes or has passed from the decedent to his surviving spouse, but only to the extent that such interest is included in determining the value of the gross estate.

(b) Limitation in the case of life estate or other terminable interest.—

(1) General rule. Where, on the lapse of time, on the occurrence of an event or contingency, or on the failure of an event or contingency to occur, an interest passing to the surviving spouse will terminate or fail, no deduction shall be allowed under this section with respect to such interest—

(A) if an interest in such property passes or has passed (for less than an adequate and full consideration in money or money's worth) from the decedent to any person other than such surviving spouse (or the estate of such spouse); and

(B) if by reason of such passing such person (or his heirs or assigns) may possess or enjoy any part of such property after such termination or failure of the interest so passing to the surviving spouse;

and no deduction shall be allowed with respect to such interest (even if such deduction is not disallowed under subparagraphs (A) and (B))—

(C) if such interest is to be acquired for the surviving spouse, pursuant to directions of the decedent, by his executor or by the trustee of a trust.

For purposes of this paragraph, an interest shall not be considered as an interest which will terminate or fail merely because it is the ownership of a bond, note, or similar contractual obligation, the discharge of which would not have the effect of an annuity for life or for a term.

(2) Interest in unidentified assets.—Where the assets (included in the decedent's gross estate) out of which, or the proceeds of which, an interest passing to the surviving spouse may be satisfied include a particular asset or assets with respect to which no deduction would be allowed if such asset or assets passed from the decedent to such spouse, then the value of such interest passing to such spouse shall, for purposes of subsection (a), be reduced by the aggregate value of such particular assets.

(3) Interest of spouse conditional on survival for limited period.—For purposes of this subsection, an interest passing to the surviving spouse shall not be considered as an interest which will terminate or fail on the death of such spouse if—

(A) such death will cause a termination or failure of such interest only if it occurs within a period not exceeding 6 months after the decedent's death, or only if it occurs as a result of a common disaster resulting in the death of the decedent and the surviving spouse, or only if it occurs in the case of either such event; and

(B) such termination or failure does not in fact occur.

(4) Valuation of interest passing to surviving spouse.—In determining for purposes of subsection (a) the value of any interest in property passing to the surviving spouse for which a deduction is allowed by this section—

(A) there shall be taken into account the effect which the tax imposed by section 2001, or any estate, succession, legacy, or inheritance tax, has on the net value to the surviving spouse of such interest; and

(B) where such interest or property is encumbered in any manner, or where the surviving spouse incurs any obligation imposed by the decedent with respect to the passing of such interest, such encumbrance or obligation shall be taken into account in the same manner as if the amount of a gift to such spouse of such interest were being determined.

(5) Life estate with power of appointment in surviving spouse.—In the case of an interest in property passing from the decedent, if his surviving spouse is entitled for life to all the income from the entire interest, or all the income from a specific portion thereof, payable annually or at more frequent intervals, with power in the surviving spouse to appoint the entire interest, or such specific portion (exercisable in favor of such surviving spouse, or of the estate of such surviving spouse, or in favor of either, whether or not in each case the power is exercisable in favor of others), and with no power in any other person to appoint any part of the interest, or such specific portion, to any person other than the surviving spouse—

(A) the interest or such portion thereof so passing shall, for purposes of subsection (a), be considered as passing to the surviving spouse, and

(B) no part of the interest so passing shall, for purposes of paragraph (1)(A), be considered as passing to any person other than the surviving spouse.

This paragraph shall apply only if such power in the surviving spouse to appoint the entire interest, or such specific portion thereof, whether exercisable by will or during life, is exercisable by such spouse alone and in all events.

(6) Life insurance or annuity payments with power of appointment in surviving spouse.—In the case of an interest in property passing from the decedent consisting of proceeds under a life insurance, endowment, or annuity contract, if under the terms of the contract such proceeds are payable in installments or are held by the insurer subject to an agreement to pay interest thereon (whether the proceeds, on the termination of any interest payments, are payable in a lump sum or in annual or more frequent installments), and such installment or interest payments are payable annually or at more frequent intervals, commencing not later than 13 months after the decedent's death, and all amounts, or a specific portion of all such amounts, payable during the life of the surviving spouse are payable only to such spouse, and such spouse has the power to appoint all amounts, or such specific portion, payable under such contract (exercisable in favor of such surviving spouse, or of the estate of such surviving spouse, or in favor of either, whether or not in each case the power is exercisable in favor of others), with no power in any other person to appoint such amounts to any person other than the surviving spouse—

(A) such amounts shall, for purposes of subsection (a), be considered as passing to the surviving spouse, and

(B) no part of such amounts shall, for purposes of paragraph (1)(A), be considered as passing to any person other than the surviving spouse.

This paragraph shall apply only if, under the terms of the contract, such power in the surviving spouse to appoint such amounts, whether exercisable by will or during life, is exercisable by such spouse alone and in all events.

(7) Election with respect to life estate for surviving spouse.—

(A) In general.—In the case of qualified terminable interest property—

(i) for purposes of subsection (a), such property shall be treated as passing to the surviving spouse, and

(ii) for purposes of paragraph (1)(A), no part of such property shall be treated as passing to any person other than the surviving spouse.

(B) Qualified terminable interest property defined.—For purposes of this paragraph—

(i) In general.—The term "qualified terminable interest property" means property—

(I) which passes from the decedent,

(II) in which the surviving spouse has a qualifying income interest for life, and

(III) to which an election under this paragraph applies.

(ii) Qualifying income interest for life.—The surviving spouse has a qualifying income interest for life if—

(I) the surviving spouse is entitled to all the income from the property, payable annually or at more frequent intervals, or has a usufruct interest for life in the property, and

(II) no person has a power to appoint any part of the property to any person other than the surviving spouse.

Subclause (II) shall not apply to a power exercisable only at or after the death of the surviving spouse. To the extent provided in regulations, an annuity shall be treated in a manner similar to an income interest in property (regardless of whether the property from which the annuity is payable can be separately identified).

(iii) Property includes interest therein.—The term "property" includes an interest in property.

(iv) Specific portion treated as separate property.—A specific portion of property shall be treated as separate property.

(v) Election.—An election under this paragraph with respect to any property shall be made by the executor on the return of tax imposed by section 2001. Such an election, once made, shall be irrevocable.

(C) Treatment of survivor annuities.—In the case of an annuity included in the gross estate of the decedent under section 2039 (or, in the case of an interest in an annuity arising under the community property laws of a State, included in the gross estate of the decedent under section 2033) where only the surviving spouse has the right to receive payments before the death of such surviving spouse—

(i) the interest of such surviving spouse shall be treated as a qualifying income interest for life, and

(ii) the executor shall be treated as having made an election under this subsection with respect to such annuity unless the executor otherwise elects on the return of tax imposed by section 2001.

An election under clause (ii), once made, shall be irrevocable.

(8) Special rule for charitable remainder trusts.—

(A) In general.—If the surviving spouse of the decedent is the only beneficiary of a qualified charitable remainder trust who is not a charitable beneficiary nor an ESOP beneficiary, paragraph (1) shall not apply to any interest in such trust which passes or has passed from the decedent to such surviving spouse.

(B) Definitions.—For purposes of subparagraph (A)—

(i) Charitable beneficiary.—The term "charitable beneficiary" means any beneficiary which is an organization described in section 170(c).

(ii) ESOP beneficiary.—The term "ESOP beneficiary" means any beneficiary which is an employee stock ownership plan (as defined in section 4975(e)(7)) that holds a remainder interest in qualified employer securities (as defined in section 664(g)(4)) to be transferred to such plan in a qualified gratuitous transfer (as defined in section 664(g)(1)).

(iii) Qualified charitable remainder trust.—The term "qualified charitable remainder trust" means a charitable remainder annuity trust or a charitable remainder unitrust (described in section 664).

(9) Denial of double deduction.—Nothing in this section or any other provision of this chapter shall allow the value of any interest in property to be deducted under this chapter more than once with respect to the same decedent.

(10) Specific Portion.—For purposes of paragraphs (5), (6), and (7)(B)(iv), the term "specific portion" only includes a portion determined on a fractional or percentage basis.

(c) Definition.—For purposes of this section, an interest in property shall be considered as passing from the decedent to any person if and only if—

(1) such interest is bequeathed or devised to such person by the decedent;

(2) such interest is inherited by such person from the decedent;

(3) such interest is the dower or curtesy interest (or statutory interest in lieu thereof) of such person as surviving spouse of the decedent;

(4) such interest has been transferred to such person by the decedent at any time;

(5) such interest was, at the time of the decedent's death, held by such person and the decedent (or by them and any other person) in joint ownership with right of survivorship;

(6) the decedent had a power (either alone or in conjunction with any person) to appoint such interest and if he appoints or has appointed such interest to such person, or if such person takes such interest in default on the release or nonexercise of such power; or

(7) such interest consists of proceeds of insurance on the life of the decedent receivable by such person.

Except as provided in paragraph (5) or (6) of subsection (b), where at the time of the decedent's death it is not possible to ascertain the particular person or persons to whom an interest in property may pass from the decedent, such interest shall, for purposes of subparagraphs (A) and (B) of subsection (b)(1), be considered as passing from the decedent to a person other than the surviving spouse.

* * *

In addition to QTIP transfers, the following types of transfers qualify for the marital deduction.

Outright Unconditional Gift: The most common and straightforward technique to qualify a gift to a spouse for the marital deduction is the basic outright gift. An outright gift is easy for you to draft and simple for your clients to understand. The surviving spouse has maximum flexibility because there are no restrictions on the use of the transferred property. A spouse, however, may want to impose restrictions on how the surviving spouse uses the property or the surviving spouse may lack the skills necessary to prudently manage the property. Accordingly, a spouse may want to consider other types of marital gifts which qualify for the deduction.

Outright Gift Conditioned on Survival by Six Months or Less: A gift to a surviving spouse conditioned on the surviving spouse outliving the deceased spouse for six months or less qualifies for the marital deduction. A period longer than six months violates the terminable interest rule. See I.R.C. § 2056(b)(3).

Power of Appointment Trust: The deceased spouse may establish a power of appointment trust granting the surviving spouse the power to appoint trust property which will qualify for the marital deduction. I.R.C. § 2056(b)(5). Prior to the advent of the QTIP trust in 1981, this technique was commonly used by spouses who did not want to make an outright gift to the surviving spouse but did want to take advantage of the marital deduction. A power of appointment trust will qualify for the marital deduction only if the following requirements are satisfied. Note that many of these requirements are the same as for a QTIP trust.

1. The surviving spouse must be entitled to all income from the property.
2. The surviving spouse's income interest must last for the surviving spouse's life.
3. The surviving spouse must be entitled to receive the income at least once per year.
4. The surviving spouse must have a general power of appointment over the trust corpus. The deceased spouse cannot place any restrictions or limitations on this power of appointment. Consequently, the surviving spouse could elect to appoint all of the property directly to the surviving spouse (assuming the power may be exercised inter vivos). However, the deceased spouse may indicate the beneficiary of the remaining trust property if the

surviving spouse dies without exercising the power of appointment.

5. The surviving spouse must have the right to exercise the power of appointment without the consent or permission of any other person. The deceased spouse may, however, give the surviving spouse only a testamentary power of appointment. The trust will still qualify for the marital deduction even though the surviving spouse cannot exercise the power of appointment while alive.

6. The surviving spouse's interest cannot be subject to a power in anyone else, such as a trustee, to appoint the property to someone other than the surviving spouse.

Life Estate Coupled With General Power of Appointment: Instead of placing the property in trust and giving the surviving spouse the general power of appointment, the deceased spouse could skip the middleperson (i.e., the trustee) and simply give the surviving spouse a life estate in the property along with a general power of appointment over the property. See I.R.C. § 2056(b)(5).

Estate Trust: The *estate trust* is a relatively inflexible technique which is rarely used to qualify a gift for the marital deduction. Instead of leaving the property to the surviving spouse outright, the deceased spouse leaves the property to a trust in which the surviving spouse is named as the exclusive beneficiary. The surviving spouse has the entire beneficial interest during the surviving spouse's lifetime and, upon death, all remaining principal and income is paid to the surviving spouse's estate. However, annual distributions of income to the surviving spouse are not necessary. I.R.C. § 2056(b)(1). The estate trust becomes advantageous where property comprising the trust corpus is primarily unproductive, such as raw land being held for appreciation or closely held corporate stock which does not pay dividends. Under both a QTIP trust and a power of appointment trust, the surviving spouse would need to have the power to force the trustee to convert the unproductive property into income producing assets or to invade the principal to make up for the lost income. The deceased spouse can avoid this problem with an estate trust because there is no requirement that the surviving spouse receive annual income payments. The downside is, of course, that the estate trust gives the deceased spouse absolutely no control over where the property goes upon the surviving spouse's death.

NOTES AND QUESTIONS

1. What are the significant factors that would cause a spouse to opt for each of the possible methods of obtaining the marital deduction?

2. Partner One and Partner Two lived together for 20 years but were never married. Partner One died with a will leaving $5,000,000 to Partner Two. Is the marital deduction available to Partner One's estate? Would it make a difference if the partners were of the same or opposite sexes?

3. Wife and Husband were severely injured in a parachuting accident. Wife died immediately and Husband died 45 days later. Wife's will left $5,000,000 to Husband. Assume that state law imposes a 120 hour survival requirement. Is the marital deduction available to Wife's estate? Would your answer change if Wife's will contained a 60 day survival requirement?

4. Husband died leaving all of his property to a trust. The trustee has the discretion to distribute income to Wife or to accumulate it in the trust. Upon Wife's death, undistributed trust income and principal are to be paid to Wife's estate and then pass under her will. Does this transfer qualify for the marital deduction? Would your answer change if the trustee also had the discretion to distribute to Grandchild?

5. Husband and Wife lived in a community property state and acquired Ranch with community funds. When Husband died, Ranch had a fair market value of $400,000. Husband's will left all of his property to Wife. What is the maximum marital deduction which may be claimed for Ranch?

6. Husband bequeathed a patent to Wife and Son as tenants in common. The patent expires in 5 years. Is this a terminable interest and thus nondeductible by Husband's estate? See Treas. Reg. § 20.2056(b)(1).

7. Wife bequeathed $500,000 to Trustee. Trustee must pay all of the trust income to Husband on April 15 of each year but is not authorized to invade principal regardless of Husband's needs. Husband was given the right to appoint all remaining trust property in his will. If Husband fails to make the appointment, all of the property passes to Friend. What is the maximum allowable marital deduction which Wife's estate may claim? If Husband fails to exercise the power of appointment, is the property included in Husband's gross estate?

8. The trustee of a power of appointment trust may carry out normal administrative matters such as allocating receipts and expenses between income and principal without jeopardizing the marital deduction. However, the power to retain non-income producing property or to accumulate income may cause disqualification unless the surviving spouse has a superior right to demand reinvestment or income.

9. Husband owned a personal residence valued at $250,000 for estate tax purposes. Husband died leaving Wife the exclusive and unrestricted right to use the residence for the rest of her life. Upon her death, the residence will pass to Husband's children from a former marriage. What is the maximum allowable marital deduction?

10. Will a homestead right under state law which provides the surviving spouse with the ability to remain in the family home until the surviving spouse dies or abandons it qualify for QTIP treatment?

11. Wife's will established a trust providing that all of the trust income is payable every six months to Husband. Upon Husband's remarriage or death, the trust terminates with the remaining property payable to Brother. May Wife's estate claim a marital deduction for any portion of this property assuming that Husband is alive and has not remarried?

12. Gifts of QTIP qualify for the marital deduction only if the deceased spouse's executor makes an irrevocable election on the estate tax return. Why might an executor choose *not* to make this election?

13. Deceased Spouse created a testamentary trust which provided for all income to be paid to Surviving Spouse every six months. The most recent payment was made on January 1 and Surviving Spouse died on April 15. The trust does not require this "stub income" to be paid to Surviving Spouse's estate. Will the trust qualify for QTIP treatment? See Treas. Reg. § 20.2056(b)–7(d)(4).

14. Remaining terminable interest property is taxed in the estate of the surviving spouse even though none of this property may be in the surviving spouse's probate estate. To remedy the unfairness to the surviving spouse's beneficiaries or heirs who would actually bear the burden of tax to the exclusion of the actual recipients, I.R.C. § 2207A(a) authorizes the executor to recover any tax owed because the QTIP was included in the surviving spouse's estate. The recovery is at the highest marginal rate applicable to the surviving spouse's estate. Of course, the surviving spouse's wishes as contained in the surviving spouse's will have priority, i.e., the will could expressly direct that taxes on QTIP be paid from the surviving spouse's estate. Under what circumstances would a surviving spouse decide to do this?

2. NON-DOMESTIC SPOUSE

INTERNAL REVENUE CODE, § 2056

BEQUESTS, ETC., TO SURVIVING SPOUSE

* * *

(d) Disallowance of marital deduction where surviving spouse not United States citizen.—

(1) In general.— Except as provided in paragraph (2), if the surviving spouse of the decedent is not a citizen of the United States—

(A) no deduction shall be allowed under subsection (a), and

(B) section 2040(b) shall not apply.

(2) Marital deduction allowed for certain transfers in trust.—

(A) In general.— Paragraph (1) shall not apply to any property passing to the surviving spouse in a qualified domestic trust.

(B) Special rule.—If any property passes from the decedent to the surviving spouse of the decedent, for purposes of subparagraph (A), such property shall be treated as passing to such spouse in a qualified domestic trust if—

(i) such property is transferred to such a trust before the date on which the return of the tax imposed by this chapter is made, or

(ii) such property is irrevocably assigned to such a trust under an irrevocable assignment made on or before such date which is enforceable under local law.

(3) Allowance of credit to certain spouses.— If—

(A) property passes to the surviving spouse of the decedent (hereinafter in this paragraph referred to as the "first decedent"),

(B) without regard to this subsection, a deduction would be allowable under subsection (a) with respect to such property, and

(C) such surviving spouse dies and the estate of such surviving spouse is subject to the tax imposed by this chapter,

the Federal estate tax paid (or treated as paid under section 2056A(b)(7)) by the first decedent with respect to such property shall be allowed as a credit under section 2013 to the estate of such surviving spouse and the amount of such credit shall be determined under such section without regard to when the first decedent died and without regard to subsection (d)(3) of such section.

(4) Special rule where resident spouse becomes citizen.— Paragraph (1) shall not apply if—

(A) the surviving spouse of the decedent becomes a citizen of the United States before the day on which the return of the tax imposed by this chapter is made, and

(B) such spouse was a resident of the United States at all times after the date of the death of the decedent and before becoming a citizen of the United States.

(5) Reformations permitted.

(A) In general.— In the case of any property with respect to which a deduction would be allowable under subsection (a) but for this subsection, the determination of whether a trust is a qualified domestic trust shall be made—

(i) as of the date on which the return of the tax imposed by this chapter is made, or

(ii) if a judicial proceeding is commenced on or before the due date (determined with regard to extensions) for filing such return to change such trust into a trust which is a qualified domestic trust, as of the time when the changes pursuant to such proceeding are made.

(B) Statute of limitations.—If a judicial proceeding described in subparagraph (A)(ii) is commenced with respect to any trust, the period for assessing any deficiency of tax attributable to any failure of such trust to be a qualified domestic trust shall not expire before the date 1 year after the date on which the Secretary is notified that the trust has been changed pursuant to such judicial proceeding or that such proceeding has been terminated.

JOHN PARKER HUGGARD, QUALIFIED DOMESTIC TRUST*

N.C. Estate Settlement Practice Guide § 30:6 (2012).

Property passing from a deceased spouse to a surviving spouse who is not a U.S. citizen is not eligible for the unlimited marital deduction unless the property is placed in a Qualified Domestic Trust (QDOT). A QDOT requires that at least one trustee be a U.S. citizen or domestic corporation with the power to withhold U.S. estate taxes if a distribution or corpus is made. The QDOT must be set up before death by the decedent or after death by the decedent's personal representative. The personal representative must make an irrevocable QDOT election on the federal estate tax return. The election must be made no later than one year after the federal death tax return is due, including all extensions.

Example: Larry recently died and left a two million dollar estate to his wife, Mary, who is a Canadian citizen living in North Carolina. Mary is the executor of Larry's will. Because Mary is not a U.S. citizen, Larry's estate cannot take advantage of the unlimited marital deduction. The tax on Larry's estate will be in excess of $550,000. Larry's executor (his surviving spouse) can elect to create a QDOT. This allows the unlimited marital deduction to apply to property passing via the QDOT to the non-citizen wife. The creation and election to use this trust will result in an estate tax savings of more than $550,000. A non-citizen spouse is always free to obtain U.S. citizenship before or after a spouse's death and thereby eliminate the need to a QDOT and be treated as any other surviving citizen spouse. This option may not be possible after the death of a spouse occurs because of the time needed to qualify for U.S. citizenship, which would have to be obtained before the due date of the QDOT.

NOTES AND QUESTIONS

1. The EGTRRA and subsequent legislation provides that if the citizen spouse dies before January 1, 2012, (a) there will continue to be a tax on principal distributions made before January 1, 2021, and (b) there will be no estate tax on the balance of the trust if the non-citizen spouse dies after December 31, 2011. Of course, like the rest of the EGTRRA and subsequent legislation, these changes cease to be effective on January 1, 2013 unless reenacted by Congress.

2. Many countries, with Germany being in the forefront, have expressed their displeasure with how the United States has handled the marital deduction for non-domestic spouses. How do you think this impacts on fiscal negotiations, treaties, and trade agreements with other nations?

3. See Treas. Regs. §§ 20.2056A & 25.2523(i) for extensive treatment of QDTs.

---

* Reprinted with permission of Thomson Reuters.

F. BYPASS PLANNING

A married person may pass the entire estate to the surviving spouse totally tax free by using transfers which qualify for the marital deduction. This simple strategy to avoid estate tax in the estate of the first spouse to die may be short-sighted because the surviving spouse's estate is now larger. This property will be taxed upon the surviving spouse's death unless the surviving spouse spends the property, leaves it to a new spouse, or otherwise disposes of it in a tax-free manner. The government's granting of the unlimited marital deduction is viewed by some people as a subterfuge to lure people into leaving property to their surviving spouses so that the government can tax the property at higher rates when the surviving spouses die. In effect, the government "invests" in each surviving spouse because the government obtains greater revenue by collecting more tax on one large estate than two taxes on two smaller estates.

As an estate planner wise to this ploy, you must advise your client not to waste the client's ability to leave property valued at the applicable exclusion amount to individuals other than the surviving spouse without incurring federal estate tax liability. Failure to do so wastes a spouse's applicable exclusion amount and is costly. The amount that could have been transferred to a non-spouse tax-free may be subject to tax in the surviving spouse's estate at high rates. If the surviving spouse died in the year 2005, for example, the extra tax burden could be as much as $705,000.

The simplest way to use the applicable exclusion amount is to leave property, either outright or in trust, equal in value to the exclusion amount to individuals other than the surviving spouse such as children and grandchildren. This technique works very well if the deceased spouse wants to prefer certain beneficiaries over the surviving spouse, such as children from a prior partner, or if the surviving spouse is so wealthy that the surviving spouse will not need the money.

When Congress extended the EGTRRA from December 2010 to December 2012, Congress also provided a $5 million federal estate tax exemption and a maximum federal estate tax rate of 35%. Such significant tax measures must be taken into consideration when planning a large estate. Further, you must take extreme care in drafting bypass provision which base the size of the bypass gift on the largest non-spousal gift which results in the decedent's estate incurring no estate tax liability (often called formula clauses). The amount left for the surviving spouse may end up being considerably smaller than the decedent intended and, if the estate tax does not exist in the year of the decedent's death, could result in the entire estate passing into the bypass arrangement with nothing left for the surviving spouse. Prudent planning may require you to draft a will with alternate disposition plans based on the year of the decedent's death to account for the high exclusion from now through December 31, 2012, the possible return to pre-EGTRRA law in 2013, and the possible abolition of the estate tax in the future.

In many situations, the deceased spouse actually wants to leave everything to the surviving spouse but does not like the prospect of a high tax in the surviving spouse's estate. This additional tax reduces the amount available for the surviving spouse's beneficiaries who are often their children and grandchildren. Accordingly, the deceased spouse wants to give the surviving spouse as many rights in the property as possible without causing the property to qualify for the marital deduction. This arrangement is called a *bypass trust*, *credit shelter trust*, or *B trust* (as contrasted with an *A trust* which qualifies for marital deduction treatment).

The deceased spouse can grant the surviving spouse many rights in the bypass trust. As long as the surviving spouse does not have a general power of appointment over the property, the property will not qualify for the marital deduction and thus will be subject to tax in the deceased spouse's estate. Of course, no tax should actually be payable in the deceased spouse's estate because the value of property going into the bypass trust would be the same as the applicable exclusion amount.

Below is a list of rights which the deceased spouse may give the surviving spouse in a bypass trust. If the surviving spouse has all of these rights, the trust is often called a *maximum benefit bypass trust*. Remember that this is a list of maximums; the deceased spouse does not need to give the surviving spouse any of these rights.

- **All trust income.**
- **Power to invade principal under an ascertainable standard.** The surviving spouse's invasion power must be limited by a standard relating to the surviving spouse's support, maintenance, health, or education. A vague standard such as "happiness and comfort" is insufficient. [A third party may have the power to make discretionary distributions to the surviving spouse which are not limited by an ascertainable standard.]
- **Serve as sole trustee.** The surviving spouse may act as the sole trustee if the surviving spouse's power to invade principal is limited to an ascertainable standard.
- **Five and five power.** The surviving spouse may withdraw the greater of $5,000 or 5% of the principal one time each calendar year for any purpose.
- **Special power of appointment to third parties.** The surviving spouse may have the right during life or upon death to appoint any or all of the trust property to anyone the deceased spouse indicated as long as the surviving spouse cannot appoint to the surviving spouse, the surviving spouse's estate, or the surviving spouse's creditors.

Diagram

Study the following diagram which shows the interrelationship between marital deduction and bypass planning.

Perhaps the most important provision of the 2010 Tax Relief Act is the creation of *portability* which allows the executor of a deceased spouse's estate to transfer any unused estate tax applicable exclusion amount of the deceased spouse to the surviving spouse. Portability eliminates the need for the spouses to retitle property and create by-pass trusts if the only reason for taking such action is to take full advantage of each spouse's exclusion amount. Portability became effective for deaths on or after January 1, 2010 and is set to expire at the end of 2012 unless extended by Congress.

For an illustration, imagine if Husband and Wife were married for 35 years and had only one relative, the Wife's sister, between the two of them. Additionally, Husband and Wife played the lottery on a weekly basis as a hobby. In February of 2012, Husband died unexpectedly, leaving everything to Wife. Wife continued to play the lottery and soon became the lucky lottery winner of $12,000,000 in September of 2012. If Wife were to die in December of 2012 with a will leaving all of her assets to her sister, how much would Wife be able to pass to her sister without incurring estate tax consequences?

For a deaths in 2012, each person has a $5,120,000 exclusion. Thus, Wife may be able to pass as much as $10,240,000 to her sister without triggering any estate tax consequences. Married couples may use any amount of the $5,120,000 exclusion unused by a deceased spouse. Because Husband left everything to his Wife avoiding estate tax with the marital deduction, Wife may use Husband's unused $5,120,000 exclusion amount assuming that the executor of his estate filed an estate tax return and made the proper election. In addition, Wife may use her full $5,120,000 estate tax exclusion, thus sheltering a combined total $10,240,000.

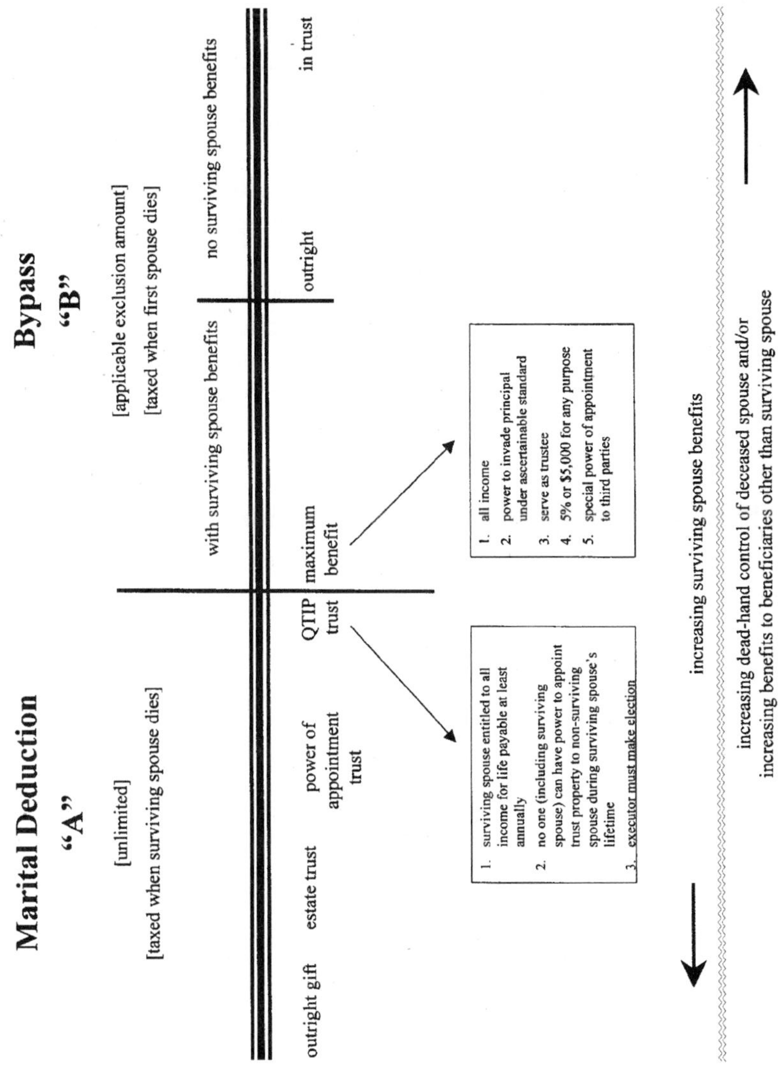

NOTES AND QUESTIONS

1. Your client's primary motivation for using a bypass arrangement may not be to provide the surviving spouse with maximum benefits. Instead, your client may want to preserve as much of the property as possible for non-spouse beneficiaries (e.g., children from a prior marriage) while keeping the property available to the surviving spouse in case of emergency. Thus, it is extremely important to determine your client's purpose before deciding what type of bypass planning is appropriate.

2. Bypass planning is typically used in a spousal context. Can you think of any other scenario where bypass planning would be appropriate?

3. Debate exists over the wisdom of granting the surviving spouse the power to use property in a bypass trust for individuals the surviving spouse

has a legal duty to support, i.e., minor children. The authority to do so could make the power general and thus part of the surviving spouse's estate. Despite arguments to the contrary, many commentators and practitioners recommend that the surviving spouse not be given a power to invade the trust for the support of the surviving spouse's dependents. See HAROLD WEINSTOCK, PLANNING AN ESTATE—A GUIDEBOOK OF PRINCIPLES AND TECHNIQUES § 5.5, at 93 (3d ed. 1988). In addition, any distributions from trust income for the support of the surviving spouse's dependents may be deemed income of the surviving spouse. See I.R.C. § 662.

4. If the surviving spouse serves as the trustee, the spouse's ability to invade principal must be limited by an ascertainable standard. However, if someone else serves as the trustee, the distributions to the surviving spouse do not need to be based on a standard but may be discretionary or limited by a standard too vague to be deemed ascertainable (e.g., the surviving spouse's "happiness"). Remember that if the surviving spouse has the ability to invade the corpus, that power must be limited to an ascertainable standard regardless of who is serving as the trustee.

5. Surviving Spouse is serving as the trustee of a trust. The trust grants the trustee the discretion to allocate receipts and expenditures between principal and income. Will this power cause the trust to be included in Surviving Spouse's estate?

6. It is important to select carefully the assets used to fund a bypass trust. See Anne K. Hilker & Steven A. Ruben, *Planning and Drafting Bypass Trusts [with Form],* PRAC. TAX LAW., Fall 1993, at 43.

DRAFT

Draft a maximum benefit bypass trust.

G. GENERATION-SKIPPING TRANSFER TAX

ROBERT L. MOSHMAN, AVOIDING A GSTT ASTEROID: REVISITING A DANGEROUS ADVERSARY: THE GENERATION SKIPPING TRANSFER TAX*

Estate Analyst (Sept. 2011).

"It hit with the force of 10,000 nuclear weapons. A trillion tons of dirt and rock hurtled into the atmosphere, creating a suffocating blanket of dust the sun was powerless to penetrate for a thousand years. It happened before. It will happen again. It's just a question of when."

From Armageddon *(1998), a motion picture starring Bruce Willis, in which an asteroid heads toward planet Earth.*

The odds that an estate will run afoul of the generation skipping transfer tax (GSTT) may be rather slim nowadays, but estate planners must never let down their guard against this virulent adversary.

---

* © R. Moshman 2011. Reprinted with permission. *Avoiding a GSTT Asteroid* was originally published as the August 1998 issue of The Estate Analyst. About one-third of that issue consisted

The GSTT sneaks up without warning and packs a powerful punch. Just the convoluted process of calculating this tax can send an estate planning professional into a black hole of despair.

Let us review GSTT rules and strategies. But first, to set the GSTT in proper context, we must travel back through the time-space continuum to a more innocent time, before the GSTT existed, when the estate tax was the primary opponent for estate planning.

The Kennedy Fortune

Joseph P. Kennedy (1888–1969) was the president of a bank at age 25. He boldly invested during the Roaring Twenties and was a master of stock market manipulation and insider trading before such practices were regulated. He became a millionaire by age 30 and had the instinct to sell his stocks before the Great Crash of 1929. He then used short sales to make huge profits during the Great Depression. Ironically, Kennedy later became the first Chairman of the Securities and Exchange Commission.

Other fortunes were made in Hollywood and in real estate. There are rumors that Kennedy had a bootlegging operation, but this may be exaggerated considering Kennedy's foresight in cornering the market on importing legitimate pre-Prohibition alcohol.

The net result was one of America's great fortunes. By 1935, he had amassed $180 million, the equivalent of $2.8 billion today.

Pre-GSTT Planning

During the years of Joseph Kennedy's peak wealth until his death in 1969, the estate tax had a top rate of 70% or 77%. It was a harsh gatekeeper that applied to every generation. From 1941 on, the 77% top rate applied to assets exceeding $10 million. If taxed at that rate at Joseph Kennedy's death, and then again only one generation later, the Kennedy fortune would have been erased.

Kennedy saw the wisdom of avoiding a 77% tax. By passing wealth directly to his grandchildren, he skipped an entire layer of estate taxation.

For example, trusts that Joseph Kennedy established for John F. Kennedy provided JFK with income for life, as well as the right to withdraw up to 5% of principal in any year. During the Kennedy administration, the President's trust funds were said to be paying him $500,000 in annual income. Because Joseph Kennedy gave only a life estate to his son, the assets were not subject to estate tax at JFK's death. Thus, the government taxed the assets only once, in Joseph P. Kennedy's estate, before those assets reached Joseph's grandchildren, John F. Kennedy, Jr., and Caroline Kennedy Schlossberg.

The Kennedy estate plan shows that when assets are unencumbered by transfer taxes or the need to benefit one particular generation, the

of footnotes due to the author's youthful infatuation with trivia. This article was then rewritten and published in the March/April 1999 issue of the ABA's Property & Probate journal. This new version is produced with updates for inclusion in this book.

family can productively invest those assets in long-term pursuits. The Kennedy trusts held assets ranging from businesses to real estate. The family holding company, Joseph P. Kennedy Enterprises, contained the Merchandise Mart in Chicago, which Joseph Kennedy purchased in 1945 for $13 million and which was eventually sold for $625 million.

The Next Generation: Camelot

At the time of his assassination in 1963, President John F. Kennedy left a 1954 will that made no provision for his children. Had he lived, he might have adopted a multigenerational trust approach in the same manner as his father.

For the same reasons, it made sense for the President's widow, Jacqueline Kennedy Onassis, to direct her wealth to her grandchildren. She coordinated her GSTT strategy with a charitable lead trust (CLT) that would have reduced taxes and maintained privacy.

Ironically, the public identified the Onassis estate with the use of CLTs, even though the estate's executors ultimately decided not to fund the trusts, demonstrating the flexibility of the Onassis estate plan. One reason for the change may have been the size of the estate, which fell short of the $100–$200 million amounts noted in the press, even with $34.4 million from a 1996 Sotheby's auction of the Kennedy family's personal property. On the other hand, the acclaimed CLT/GSTT arrangement may have resulted in too much GSTT after all.

Deep Impact: The First GSTT

An entire generation of estate planners has never known a time when the GSTT did not exist. Travel back 35 years to a pre-GSTT age of innocence when Congress first began to sow the seeds of change.

The summer of 1976 was a bicentennial time of tall ships and fireworks. In North Carolina, 5′8″ Larry Jordan was beating his little brother Michael in one-on-one in the backyard. On Wall Street, the formation of Kohlberg Kravis Roberts and Drexel Burnham Lambert presaged a future era of hostile takeovers and junk bond deals. Silicon Valley did not yet exist. Steve Jobs, a 21–year-old college dropout, had just started Apple Computers in a garage, one year after 19–year-old college dropout Bill Gates founded Microsoft.

A typical estate planning lawyer might have spent the summer of 1976 musing over the latest Clifford trust techniques and pecking out letters on an IBM Selectric typewriter.

Suddenly, a screaming comes across the sky. It is October, and the Tax Reform Act of 1976 has reached President Gerald Ford's desk. A meteor shower of tax changes unifies estate and gift taxes, increases the marital deduction, provides throwback rules for accumulation distributions from trusts, and makes other profound changes in the transfer tax system including the birth of a new tax, the first GSTT.

A Fallible Authority

Congress makes mistakes. Tax experiments go awry. Lawyers take for granted the stepped-up basis for assets held at death under Code § 1014. Nevertheless, in 1976, Congress attempted to impose carryover basis at death, only to postpone it and ultimately retroactively repeal it (and with quite a low profile) in the Crude Oil Windfall Profit Tax Act of 1980. It was as if the whole messy chapter was just erased, like the 1985 bad-dream season of Dallas. Forgetting this lesson, Congress dabbled with the carryover basis in 2010 and once again cleaned up the mess with a retroactive wipe down of its fingerprints.

Likewise, problems soon became apparent with the first GSTT. For example, instead of a flat tax rate of 55%, Congress imposed the tax at the tax rate of the deemed transferor—the grantor's child or some other member of the generation that was skipped. To calculate the tax rate, the tax return preparer needed to know the size of the deemed transferor's taxable estate, including prior adjusted taxable gifts. This proved to be highly infeasible.

Due to this and numerous other problems, Congress first postponed the 1976 GSTT, amended it three times, and ultimately repealed it retroactively 10 years after the fact. In 1986, Congress provided an entirely new GSTT law. Codes §§ 2601–2663 comprise the 1986 GSTT. Here are five key points about that version of the GSTT.

1. The GSTT did not have a progressive rate schedule. Rather, Congress imposed the tax on nonexempt property at a flat 55% rate.
2. Each person had a GSTT exemption of $1 million, subject to adjustment for inflation.
3. A gift or bequest skips a generation when assets pass to an individual who is two or more generations below the transferor.
4. In the case of unrelated individuals, a transfer generation skips under Code § 2651(d)(2) if assets pass to an individual who is more than 37.5 years younger than the transferor.
5. Each generation is considered to be 25 years.

The current version of the GSTT is similar but has an exemption of $5 million and a tax rate of 35%. If only it were this simple.

The X Files

Just to keep things interesting, there are several distinct types of generation-skipping transfers subject to the GSTT, each with its own horrendous and paranormal tax implications. A transfer in trust may not result in immediate GSTT. As circumstances unfold, however, a taxable termination or distribution in the future may involve skip persons and may trigger GSTT without triggering additional gift or estate taxes. By comparison, direct skips arise in a more straightforward fashion, i.e., when a direct transfer to a skip person triggers gift or estate taxes, as well as GSTT.

- **Taxable terminations.** Assume that a testamentary trust provides a life interest for Son with the remainder to Grandchild. At Son's death, his intervening trust interest ends and the only remaining trust beneficiary is a skip person, Grandchild. This results in GSTT liability to be paid by the trustee out of the transferred assets. See Code § 2612(a)(1) and Code § 2603(a)(2). Considering the 35% estate tax that Grandparent's estate paid, the additional GSTT on the remaining assets brings the effective tax rate on the gift to Grandchild up to about 58%.
- **Taxable distributions.** A testamentary trustee's discretionary distribution from a spray trust to a skip person results in GSTT liability to be paid by the skip person and effectively reduces the transferred amount. Code § 2603(a)(1). Treas. Reg. § 26.2612–1(C)(1) treats the trustee's payment of GSTT as a taxable transfer subject to additional GSTT. What happens if the transferor pays that tax as well? Will there be a gift tax on a GSTT tax after an initial estate tax? With higher rates in the past, this resulted in confiscatory tax rates exceeding 100%. Nowadays, with lower rates, the impact is merely brutal, exceeding 75%.
- **Direct skips with tax payment.** Grandma makes a direct transfer to Grandson. It is a taxable gift with no exclusions. Grandma pays the gift tax. Grandma also pays the GSTT. Grandma's payment of the GSTT is treated as an additional taxable gift. One transfer, three tax hits.
- **Adding to GSTT-exempt trusts.** Never, never do this. A trust that is otherwise exempt from GSTT consequences can become exposed to GSTT consequences if it receives a generation skipping transfer. Separating trusts into GSTT-exempt and non-exempt is an effective strategy, however.

GSTT Strategies

Reverse QTIPs. Clients and their lawyers should not overlook the grantor's GSTT exemption by transferring all assets to a surviving spouse. If a "reverse" QTIP election is made under Code § 2652, those assets will remain in the deceased spouse's estate for purposes of claiming the $5 million GSTT exemption. Because that election applies to an entire QTIP, a client should use two separate QTIP trusts to make the reverse QTIP election for one of the trusts and use the grantor's GSTT exemption, while the other QTIP remains in the surviving spouse's estate for GSTT purposes. That way, the surviving spouse's GSTT exemption can also be used. The resulting alignment of three trusts looks like this:

Trust #1: A credit shelter trust to which the grantor's executor allocates GSTT exemption.

Trust #2: A separate QTIP trust to which the grantor's executor allocates the grantor's GSTT exemption remaining after allocation of the exemption to the credit shelter trust and with respect to which the executor makes a reverse QTIP election.

Trust #3: Remaining assets in a standard QTIP trust to which the surviving spouse's GSTT exemption will be allocated at his or her death.

Anti–GSTT approaches. A client should use intervening generations when appropriate. If the client exhausts his or her GSTT exemption and plans to skip a generation by leaving assets to a grandchild, this will actually produce a higher tax. The client should consider the alternative of not skipping a generation and leaving assets to a child, in whose hands the assets will be taxed. This may result in a lower overall transfer tax rate. For future flexibility, clients should consider a power of appointment that will allow the child to treat a transfer to a skip person as a taxable gift rather than a distribution subject to the GSTT.

Leveraging. The most effective estate planning is implemented long before death. This is especially true of multigenerational living trusts. A client can apply his or her $5–million GSTT exemption to assets that appreciate by 100% by the time of death, thereby being as valuable as two exemptions. When a client pursues a lifetime generation-skipping gift, he or she should use assets that are most likely to appreciate rapidly.

Disclaimer trusts. When a client plans outright gifts to his or her children, the client can establish unfunded multigenerational trusts that will be activated only if the children, seeing an opportunity to take advantage of unused GSTT exemption, disclaim inherited assets or powers of appointment and thereby fund the trusts.

Let's All Skip

As long as a client skips one generation, why not skip more for the price of one? Taking Kennedy's estate plan concept to its logical conclusion, a client could create a trust that is a perpetual source of revenue that would avoid transfer taxes forever and would serve as a family bank to finance his or her descendants.

Although the common law rule against perpetuities imposes a time limit—a life in being plus 21 years can reach about 100 to 120 years—true dynasty trusts can be established, with various limitations, in a growing number of perpetuity havens: Delaware, Idaho, Ohio, New Hampshire, South Dakota, and Wisconsin now permit perpetual trusts, while Alaska, Colorado, Utah and Wyoming provide for 1,000–year trusts. Nevada and Florida also provide trusts lasting 365 years and 360 years, respectively.[1]

1. Any arrangements like these can skip a lot of generational transfer taxation. Arizona, Illinois, Maine, New Jersey, Rhode Island, and Virginia have also abrogated their perpetuity rules. Most of these states joined the trend in or after 1994. Other states have also included modifications by adopting the Uniform Statutory Rule Against Perpetuities. This approach extends the waiting period to 90 years after creation of the interest. There is some uncertainty, however, about how the GSTT would apply to statutory perpetuity periods that have simply been

Skipping additional generations does not add to the GSTT bill for direct skips—that is, outright transfers—but see Code § 2653 for multiple skips held in trust.

The GSTT's Third Incarnation

With its fate tied to the Federal estate tax, the GSTT had a $3.5 million exemption and a 45% top rate in 2009. It was then terminated in 2010 but was then reinstated retroactively for 2010 with a zero tax rate and a $5–million exemption. Why an exemption for a zero tax rate? Avoiding a paradox in the event of chronosynclastic infundibular time travel has not yet been confirmed as the intent of Congress, but the truth is out there.

For the moment, the GSTT will have a 35% top rate and a $5–million exemption for 2011 and 2012 and will likely ride along with the reunited estate and gift tax when it is revised in the next major wave of tax reforms.

No GSTT Portability: It should be noted that the new estate tax exclusion's portability rule for married couples does not apply to the GSTT. Example: Rocky leaves his $10 million estate to his wife, Ramona, and Rocky's timely estate tax return elects to transfer his unused estate tax exclusion to Ramona. At Ramona's death, she has her full $5 million exclusion available, as well as the $5 million from Rocky. Ramona leaves $10 million to her grandson. Her $10 million exclusion shields her estate from estate tax on that transfer, but only $5 million of the transfer is exempt for generation skipping transfer tax purposes.

Conclusion

GSTT isn't quite the nightmare it once was with combined taxes exceeding 100%. But even with $5 million in exclusions and a 35% tax rate, the combined impact is still a force to be reckoned with that will rock an estate backwards. With care and planning, a lawyer can avoid a GSTT asteroid. Keep watching the night skies, and may the force be with you.

NOTES AND QUESTIONS

1. Which of the following transfers are subject to the GST tax? Please assume that Donor's GST exemption has already been exhausted and that Donor is 60 years old.

   a. Donor gives $13,000 to Grandson.
   b. Donor pays Grandson's law school tuition of $25,000.
   c. Donor gives $25,000 to Spouse. Spouse is 55 years old.
   d. Donor gives $25,000 to Spouse. Spouse is 20 years old.
   e. Donor gives $25,000 to Grandchild. Grandchild's parent, i.e., Donor's child, is alive.

---

extended, as opposed to those in jurisdictions in which the rule has simply been abrogated or where exceptions are created for certain types of trusts.

f. Donor gives $25,000 to Grandchild. Grandchild's parent, i.e., Donor's child, is deceased.

g. Donor gives $25,000 to Grandnephew. Grandnephew's parent, i.e., Donor's nephew, is alive.

h. Donor gives $25,000 to Grandnephew. Grandnephew's parent, i.e., Donor's nephew, is deceased.

i. Donor gives $25,000 to Friend. Friend is 20 years old.

2. Donor transfers $3,000,000 into an irrevocable trust with income to Grandchild and remainder to Grandchild when Grandchild reaches age 30. Is GST tax imposed when Donor creates the trust? Gift tax?

3. Donor's will leaves $3,000,000 to Grandchild. Is GST tax imposed on this transfer? Estate tax?

4. Donor transfers $3,000,000 into an irrevocable trust with income to Child and remainder upon Child's death to Grandchild. Is GST tax imposed when Donor creates the trust? Gift tax? Is GST tax imposed when the trustee makes distributions to Child? When Child dies, does Child's gross estate include the corpus of the trust? Is GST tax imposed when the trustee turns over the remainder to Grandchild?

5. Donor transfers $3,000,000 into an irrevocable trust with income payable to Child and Grandchild at the trustee's discretion. Is GST tax imposed when Donor creates the trust? Gift tax? Is GST tax imposed when the trustee pays income to Child? To Grandchild?

6. A married couple has the potential of leaving two GSTT exemption amounts to skip persons without triggering the GST tax. What steps would you take to be sure they do not inadvertently waste their exemptions?

7. Who is responsible for paying the GST tax on the following types of transfers?

a. Direct skip.

b. Taxable termination.

c. Taxable distribution.

8. Donor's goal is to give $100,000 to Donor's Grandchild outright in the year 2012. Donor has already exhausted all applicable exclusions and deductions. Assuming that this gift would be subject to gift tax at a 35 percent rate and that Grandchild's parent (Donor's child) is still alive, how much money does Donor need to make the desired transfer?

9. There is no separate GST tax return. Instead, GSTs are reported on the appropriate gift (if inter vivos) or estate (if at death) return. Study the copies of Forms 709 and 706, and their accompanying instructions, found in Appendices A and B.

H. DISCLAIMERS

No one can force another to accept free property. Thus, a beneficiary of a will, trust, or insurance policy, as well as a taker under intestacy, may decide to forgo the offered bounty. Why would anyone refuse to accept property as a gift? It is possible that the property carries with it an onerous burden, such as the responsibility of cleaning up a hazardous waste site, or is of such little value that ownership is undesirable. Additionally, a person may believe that it is wrong to benefit from the demise of another and refuse the property on moral or religious grounds. A person may also disclaim to prevent the property from being subject to the disclaimant's creditors.

Another significant reason a person may decide to disclaim property is to avoid taxes. If a disclaimer is properly made, the person disclaiming is considered as never owning the property. Instead, the property is treated as passing directly from the transferor to the person entitled to the property because of the disclaimer. Thus, the disclaimant does not make a gift when the property passes to another person and the property is not part of the disclaimant's estate.

For example, assume that Father dies leaving $1,000,000 to Daughter. Daughter is very wealthy on her own and does not need the money but the contingent beneficiary is Grandson, a recent medical school graduate, who is in need of capital to open his own office. If Daughter were to accept the legacy and then give the money to Grandson, Daughter may be subject to gift tax. If Daughter were to accept the legacy and die before making the gift, Daughter's estate may incur estate tax liability on the money. If Daughter were to accept the gift and distribute it to Grandson as needed, Daughter may be subject to tax on both the interest the retained money earned as well as on the gifted amounts. However, if Daughter properly disclaims the legacy, she will be treated as never owning the property and will successfully avoid these adverse tax consequences.

Consider this situation. Husband and Wife would like to leave their entire estates to each other outright but are hesitant to do so because of the adverse tax consequences of wasting the applicable exclusion amount. However, they are not extremely wealthy so they are reluctant to make outright bypass gifts or create bypass trusts because the surviving spouse may prefer to have full control over all the property and assume the responsibility of planning to reduce estate taxes upon the surviving spouse's death. In addition, they recognize that the applicable exclusion amount is increasing and that they could die in a year during which there is no estate tax.

It is often difficult to decide how to plan for married individuals who have estates with uncertain estate tax consequences or who have estates large enough to incur tax liability, but not so large that the surviving spouse is comfortable with sacrificing the opportunity to have all of the deceased spouse's property outright. A common solution is to create a *bypass disclaimer trust*. The will first makes an outright gift of all the desired property to the surviving spouse followed by an express provision that any property which the surviving spouse disclaims, passes into a bypass trust for the surviving spouse's benefit. Thus, the surviving spouse can examine the actual situation at the time of the deceased spouse's death and make the best decision.

INTERNAL REVENUE CODE, § 2518

DISCLAIMERS

(a) General rule.—For purposes of this subtitle, if a person makes a qualified disclaimer with respect to any interest in property, this subtitle shall apply with respect to such interest as if the interest had never been transferred to such person.

(b) Qualified disclaimer defined.—For purposes of subsection (a), the term "qualified disclaimer" means an irrevocable and unqualified refusal by a person to accept an interest in property but only if—

(1) such refusal is in writing,

(2) such writing is received by the transferor of the interest, his legal representative, or the holder of the legal title to the property to which the interest relates not later than the date which is 9 months after the later of—

(A) the day on which the transfer creating the interest in such person is made, or

(B) the day on which such person attains age 21,

(3) such person has not accepted the interest or any of its benefits, and

(4) as a result of such refusal, the interest passes without any direction on the part of the person making the disclaimer and passes either—

(A) to the spouse of the decedent, or

(B) to a person other than the person making the disclaimer.

(c) Other rules.—For purposes of subsection (a)—

(1) Disclaimer of undivided portion of interest.—A disclaimer with respect to an undivided portion of an interest which meets the requirements of the preceding sentence shall be treated as a qualified disclaimer of such portion of the interest.

(2) Powers.—A power with respect to property shall be treated as an interest in such property.

(3) Certain transfers treated as disclaimers.—A written transfer of the transferor's entire interest in the property—

(A) which meets requirements similar to the requirements of paragraphs (2) and (3) of subsection (b), and

(B) which is to a person or persons who would have received the property had the transferor made a qualified disclaimer (within the meaning of subsection (b)), shall be treated as a qualified disclaimer.

NOTES AND QUESTIONS

1. Disclaimers may be made by the intended recipient or the person's legal representative such as an executor or administrator. Why would a personal representative disclaim property on behalf of a decedent?

2. Testator's will provides, "I leave my coin collection to Barbara. If Barbara predeceases me, I leave the coin collection to Lisa." Barbara tells Lisa that she will disclaim if Lisa pays her $20,000. If Lisa agrees, will this be considered a qualified disclaimer?

3. Testator died on January 1 with a valid will leaving $100,000 to Brother, but if Brother predeceased Testator, to Sister. Brother did not find Testator's will until November 15. May Brother now make a qualified disclaimer?

4. Testator died on January 1, 2013 with a valid will which established a trust providing income to Troy for Troy's life with remainder to Bruce. Troy died three months ago. May Bruce now make a qualified disclaimer assuming Bruce has not accepted any benefits of the property?

5. "A beneficiary who is under 21 years of age has until 9 months after his twenty-first birthday in which to make a qualified disclaimer of his interest in property. Any actions taken with regard to an interest in property by a beneficiary or a custodian prior to the beneficiary's twenty-first birthday will not be an acceptance by the beneficiary of the interest." Treas. Reg. § 25.2518–2(d)(3).

6. If the last day of the nine month period falls on a Saturday, Sunday, or a legal holiday, then delivery is still timely if made on the first succeeding day which is not a Saturday, Sunday, or legal holiday.

7. The regulations adopt the mailbox rule with respect to the delivery of disclaimers. Thus, a timely and proper mailing of a disclaimer will be treated as a timely delivery. See Treas. Reg. § 25.2518–2(c)(2).

8. If the disclaimant has accepted the interest or any of its benefits, expressly or impliedly, it is too late to make a qualified disclaimer. Acceptance is manifested by an affirmative act which is consistent with ownership of the interest in the property, e.g., using the property or the interest in the property; accepting dividends, interest, or rents from the property; directing others to act with respect to the property; exercising a power of appointment to any extent; and accepting any consideration in return for making the disclaimer. Acts which will not, by themselves, constitute acceptance include taking delivery of an instrument of title, obtaining title because under local law title to the property vested immediately in the disclaimant upon the decedent's death, paying property taxes with personal funds, accepting one interest will not constitute an acceptance of any other separate interests created by the transferor and held by the disclaimant in the same property, and residing on residential property held in joint tenancy prior to making the disclaimer. See Treas. Reg. § 25.2518–2(d)(1).

9. Special care needs to be taken if the disclaimant is also a fiduciary with respect to the property. Normally, actions taken by a person in the

exercise of fiduciary powers to preserve or maintain the disclaimed property will not be treated as an acceptance of the property. Thus, an executor who is also a beneficiary may direct the harvesting of a crop or the general maintenance of a home. However, a fiduciary may not retain a wholly discretionary power to direct the enjoyment of the disclaimed interest. See Treas. Reg. § 25.2518–2(d)(2).

10. Many states have disclaimer statutes that contain provisions similar to I.R.C. § 2518. See U.P.C. § 2–801. However, there are often significant differences between state and federal law. A disclaimer effective under one law may not necessarily be effective under the other. See Treas. Reg. § 25.2518–2(c)(3).

11. The disclaimed interest must pass without any direction on the part of the disclaiming party. The disclaimant may not, either alone or in conjunction with another, direct the redistribution of the disclaimed property to another nor may there be an express or implied agreement that the disclaimed property is to be given inter vivos or at death to a person specified by the disclaimant. Precatory language in a disclaimer naming takers of disclaimed property will not be considered as directing the redistribution of the property to such persons as long as local law does not give the precatory language legal effect. See Treas. Reg. § 25.2518–2(e)(4).

12. Normally, the disclaimed property must pass to a person other than the disclaimant. The fact that the disclaimant may still have a fiduciary power to distribute to designated beneficiaries after making the disclaimer does not prevent the disclaimer from being qualified as long as the power to distribute is subject to an ascertainable standard. However, if a disclaimer is not effective to pass the entire interest to another person because the disclaimant also has a right to receive the property as an heir, residuary beneficiary, etc. and the disclaimant does not effectively disclaim these rights as well, the disclaimer will not be a qualified disclaimer with respect to the portion of the disclaimed property which the disclaimant has a right to receive.

The exception to the general rule that the disclaimed property must pass to someone other than the disclaimant is where the disclaimant is the decedent's spouse. In this case, the disclaimed property may pass to the disclaimant and still meet the requirements of a qualified disclaimer.

13. Parent's will contained the following dispositive clause, "I leave Homeplace to Child. If Child predeceases me, I leave Homeplace to Grandchild." Child executes a qualified disclaimer of Homeplace which is valued at $1,500,000. Is Parent's estate now subject to GST tax? Does it matter that Child is treated as predeceasing Parent under state law, i.e., will the predeceased child exception prevent Grandchild from being a skip person?

14. A disclaimer of an interest created prior to the enactment of the gift tax is subject to the same qualification rules as any other interest. See United States v. Irvine, 511 U.S. 224, 114 S.Ct. 1473, 128 L.Ed.2d 168 (1994).

15. For further information, see Kristi N. Elsom, *The Yin and Yang of Disclaimers*, PROB. & PROP., May/June 2002, at 54.

LOCATE

Locate the disclaimer statutes of your state. You may find several (e.g., for testamentary interests, for inter vivos trusts interests, for survivorship interests, etc.). How similar are your state requirements to the federal requirements?

DRAFT

Draft a disclaimer form that would be effective under both state and federal law.

I. INTER VIVOS TRUSTS

1. GENERAL PRINCIPALS

a. Income Tax

A revocable trust has no income tax consequence; all income from trust property is still taxed to the donor. See I.R.C. § 676. When the donor is responsible for the tax, the trust is often called a *grantor trust.*

Four entities are potentially responsible for the tax on income earned by an irrevocable trust: the donor, the beneficiary, the trust itself, or a third party. The donor is responsible for the income tax if the donor, the donor's spouse, or any nonadverse party has one or more prohibited powers. These powers include the ability to revoke the trust, to control the beneficial enjoyment of the trust, to exercise certain administrative powers, and to regain trust income for the donor or the donor's spouse. See I.R.C. §§ 671–679.

If the donor is not liable for the income tax, the trust itself is responsible for the tax on the amount of net trust income which is neither currently distributed nor required to be currently distributed to the beneficiary, i.e., the income which is properly retained by the trust. See I.R.C. § 641. The tax on the rest of the income is borne by the beneficiary. See I.R.C. § 662.

A third party may be responsible for the tax if the third party has the power to withdraw income (1) for the third party's use or (2) for the use of a person the third party has a legal duty to support (e.g., a minor child). The third party is usually taxed on the income even if the third party does not exercise the withdrawal right. See I.R.C. § 678. A third party is also taxed if the trust income is used to satisfy a legal obligation of the third party, even if the third party has no control over the distribution decision (e.g., is not a trustee). See I.R.C. § 662.

b. Gift Tax

A transfer to a revocable trust has no gift tax ramifications. A gift to an irrevocable trust may be a gift for tax purposes and, if properly constructed, also qualify for the annual exclusion. See the discussion of *Crummey* trusts in § (I)(2), below.

c. Estate Tax

Property transferred into a revocable trust is included in the estate of the donor because the donor retained the right to revest the property in the donor. Transfers to an irrevocable trust may escape taxation in the donor's estate provided the donor did not retain a beneficial interest in the transferred property (e.g., life estate or power to revoke) and did not retain the power to control the beneficial interests (e.g., change the beneficiary or exercise an unlimited discretionary power to determine the amount the beneficiary receives). See I.R.C. §§ 2036–2038. Please review § (C)(2)(g)–(i), above.

2. CRUMMEY TRUSTS

CRUMMEY v. COMMISSIONER

United States Court of Appeals Ninth Circuit, 1968.
397 F.2d 82.

BYRNE, DISTRICT JUDGE:

* * * On February 12, 1962, the petitioners executed, as grantors, an irrevocable living trust for the benefit of their four children. The beneficiaries and their ages at relevant times are as follows:

	Age 12/31/62	12/31/63
John Knowles Crummey	22	23
Janet Sheldon Crummey	20	21
David Clarke Crummey	15	16
Mark Clifford Crummey	11	12

Originally the sum of $50 was contributed to the trust. Thereafter, additional contributions were made by each of the petitioners in the following amounts and on the following dates:

$ 4,267.77	6/20/62
49,550.00	12/15/62
12,797.81	12/19/63

The dispute revolves around the tax years of 1962 and 1963. Each of the petitioners filed a gift tax return for each year. Each petitioner claimed a $3,000 per beneficiary tax exclusion under the provisions of 26 U.S.C. 2503(b). The total claimed exclusions were as follows:

D.C. Crummey 1962—$12,000 1963—$12,000

E.E. Crummey 1962—$12,000 1963—$12,000

The Commissioner of Internal Revenue determined that each of the petitioners was entitled to only one $3,000 exclusion for each year. This determination was based upon the Commissioner's belief that the portion of the gifts in trust for the children under the age of 21 were "future interests" which are disallowed under 2503(b). The taxpayers contested the determination of a deficiency in the Tax Court. The Commissioner conceded by stipulation in that proceeding that each petitioner was entitled to an additional $3,000 exclusion for the year 1963 by reason of Janet Crummey having reached the age of 21.

The Tax Court followed the Commissioner's interpretation as to gifts in trust to David and Mark, but determined that the 1962 gift in trust to Janet qualified as a gift of a present interest because of certain additional rights accorded to persons 18 and over by California law. Thus, the Tax Court held that each petitioner was entitled to an additional $3,000 exclusion for the year 1962.

The key provision of the trust agreement is the "demand" provision which states:

"THREE. Additions. The Trustee may receive any other real or personal property from the Trustors (or either of them) or from any other person or persons, by lifetime gift, under a Will or Trust or from any other source. Such property will be held by the Trustee subject to the terms of this Agreement. A donor may designate or allocate all of his gift to one or more Trusts, or in stated amounts to different Trusts. If the donor does not specifically designate what amount of his gift is to augment each Trust, the Trustee shall divide such gift equally between the Trusts then existing, established by this Agreement. The Trustee agrees, if he accepts such additions, to hold and manage such additions in trust for the uses and in the manner set forth herein. With respect to such additions, each child of the Trustors may demand at any time (up to and including December 31 of the year in which a transfer to his or her Trust has been made) the sum of Four Thousand Dollars ($4,000.00) or the amount of the transfer from each donor, whichever is less, payable in cash immediately upon receipt by the Trustee of the demand in writing and in any event, not later than December 31 in the year in which such transfer was made. Such payment shall be made from the gift of that donor for that year. If a child is a minor at the time of such gift of that donor for that year, or fails in legal capacity for any reason, the child's guardian may make such demand on behalf of the child. The property received pursuant to the demand shall be held by the guardian for the benefit and use of the child."

The whole question on this appeal is whether or not a present interest was given by the petitioners to their minor children so as to qualify as an exclusion under 2503(b). The petitioners on appeal contend that each minor beneficiary has the right under California law to demand partial distribution from the Trustee. In the alternative they urge that a parent as natural guardian of the person of his minor children could make such a demand. As a third alternative, they assert that under California law a minor over the age of 14 has the right to have a legal guardian appointed who can make the necessary demand. The Commissioner, as cross petitioner, alleges as error the Tax Court's ruling that the 1962 gifts in trust to Janet (then age 20) were present interests.

It was stipulated before the Tax Court in regard to the trust and the parties thereto that at all times relevant all the minor children lived with the petitioners and no legal guardian had been appointed for them. In addition, it was agreed that all the children were supported by petitioners and none of them had made a demand against the trust funds or received any distribution from them.

The tax regulations define a "future interest" for the purposes of 2503(b) as follows:

> " 'Future interests' is a legal term, and includes reversions, remainder, and other interests or estates, whether vested or contingent, and whether or not supported by a particular interest or estate, which are limited to commence in use, possession or enjoyment at some future date or time." Treasury Regulations of Gift Tax, 25.2503–3.

This definition has been adopted by the Supreme Court. Fondren v. Commissioner of Internal Revenue, 324 U.S. 18, 65 S.Ct. 499, 89 L.Ed. 668 (1945); Commissioner of Internal Revenue v. Disston, 325 U.S. 442, 65 S.Ct. 1328, 89 L.Ed. 1720 (1945). In Fondren the court stated that the important question is when enjoyment begins. There the court held that gifts to an irrevocable trust for the grantor's minor grandchildren were "future interests" where income was to be accumulated and the corpus and the accumulations were not to be paid until designated times commencing with each grandchild's 25th birthday. The trustee was authorized to spend the income or invade the corpus during the minority of the beneficiaries only if need were shown. The facts demonstrated that need had not occurred and was not likely to occur.

Neither of the parties nor the Tax Court has any disagreement with the above summarization of the basic tests. The dispute comes in attempting to narrow the definition of a future interest down to a more specific and useful form.

The Commissioner and the Tax Court both placed primary reliance on the case of Stifel v. Commissioner of Internal Revenue, 197 F.2d 107 (2d Cir.1952). In that case an irrevocable trust was involved which provided that the beneficiary, a minor, could demand any part of the funds not expended by the Trustee and, subject to such demand, the Trustee was to accumulate. The trust also provided that it could be terminated by the beneficiary or by her guardian during minority. The court held that gifts to this trust were gifts of "future interests." They relied upon Fondren for the proposition that they could look at circumstances as well as the trust agreement and under such circumstances it was clear that the minor could not make the demand and that no guardian had ever been appointed who could make such a demand.

The leading case relied upon by the petitioners is Kieckhefer v. Commissioner of Internal Revenue, 189 F.2d 118 (7th Cir.1951). In that case the donor set up a trust with his newly born grandson as the beneficiary. The trustee was to hold the funds unless the beneficiary or his legally appointed guardian demanded that the trust be terminated. The Commissioner urged that the grandson could not effectively make such a demand and that no guardian had been appointed. The court disregarded these factors and held that where any restrictions on use were caused by disabilities of a minor rather than by the terms of the trust, the gift was a "present interest." The court further stated that the important thing was the right to enjoy rather than the actual enjoyment of the property.

The Kieckhefer case had been followed in several decisions. In Gilmore v. Commissioner of Internal Revenue, 213 F.2d 520 (6th Cir.1954) there was an irrevocable trust for minors. It provided that all principal and accumulated income would be paid on demand of the beneficiary. The trust was to terminate on the beneficiary's death. Anything remaining in the trust at the time of death would go to the beneficiary's estate.

The Tax Court stated that the demand provision would have made the advancements "present interests" but for spendthrift provisions and the authority of the Trustee to invest in non-income producing properties. The Circuit agreed that the demand provision made the advancements "present interests" and further held that the other provisions did not change that character. Reliance was placed on the "right to enjoy" language of Kieckhefer.

In United States v. Baker, 236 F.2d 317 (4th Cir.1956) the court followed the Kieckhefer case in holding that advances were "present interests" where:

> "The trust agreements with which we are concerned here created no barriers to the present enjoyment by the infants of the trust property beyond those which are established by the laws of North Carolina."

That case involved a trust for minors where income and principal were to be used for the support, education and benefit of the beneficiaries according to the discretion of the trustee who was to act as if he were a guardian. What was not expended went to the beneficiary on his 21st birthday.

A final case of interest is Trust No. 3 v. Commissioner, 285 F.2d 102 (7th Cir.1960). This involved the question of whether certain income was taxable to a trust or to the beneficiaries. The court held the income was taxable to the beneficiaries where they had the right to terminate the trust or take any part of it on demand. The beneficiaries were minors, and no guardian had been appointed. The Commissioner urged that no one was ever qualified to make the demand and thus that the beneficiaries could not have taken any property from the trust in the tax year. The court relying on Kieckhefer said:

> "This distinction is unconvincing in view of the fact that the appointment of a guardian for a minor under a state law is a matter of routine in which the federal government has no concern."

Although there are certainly factual distinctions between the Stifel and Kieckhefer cases, it seems clear that the two courts took opposing positions on the way the problem of defining "future interests" should be resolved. As we read the Stifel case, it says that the court should look at the trust instrument, the law as to minors, and the financial and other circumstances of the parties. From this examination it is up to the court to determine whether it is likely that the minor beneficiary is to receive any present enjoyment of the property. If it is not likely, then the gift is a "future interest." At the other extreme is the holding in Kieckhefer which says that a gift to a minor is not a "future interest" if the only reason for a delay in enjoyment is the minority status of the donee and his consequent disabilities. The Kieckhefer court noted that under the terms there present, a gift to an adult would have qualified for the exclusion and they refused to discriminate against a minor. The court equated a present interest with a present right to possess, use or enjoy. The facts of the case and the court's reasoning, however, indicate that it was really equating a present interest with a present right to possess, use or enjoy except for the fact that the beneficiary was a minor. In between these two positions there is a third possibility. That possibility is that the court should determine whether the donee is legally and technically capable of immediately enjoying the property. Basically this is the test relied on by the petitioners. Under this theory, the question would be whether the donee could possibly gain immediate enjoyment and the emphasis would be on the trust instrument and the laws of the jurisdiction as to minors. It was primarily on this basis that the Tax Court decided the present case, although some examination of surrounding circumstances was apparently made. This theory appears to be the basis of the decision in George W. Perkins, 27 T.C. 601 (1956). There the Tax Court stated that where the parents were capable of making the demand and there was no showing that the demand could be resisted, the gift was of a present interest. This approach also seems to be the basis of the "right to enjoy" language in both Kieckhefer and Gilmore.

Under the provisions of this trust the income is to be accumulated and added to the corpus until each minor reaches the age of 21, unless the trustee feels in his discretion that distributions should be made to a needy beneficiary. From 21 to 35 all income is distributed to the beneficiary. After 35 the trustee again has discretion as to both income and corpus, and may distribute whatever is necessary up to the whole thereof. Aside from the actions of the trustee, the only way any beneficiary may get at the property is through the "demand" provision, quoted above.

One question raised in these proceedings is whether or not the trust prohibits a minor child from making a demand on the yearly additions to the trust. The key language from paragraph three is as follows:

> "If a child is a minor at the time of such gift of that donor for that year, or fails in legal capacity for any reason, the child's guardian may make such demand on behalf of the child."

The Tax Court interpreted this provision in favor of the taxpayers by saying that "may" is permissive and thus that the minor child can make the demand if allowed by law, or, if not permitted by law, the guardian may do it. Although, as the Commissioner suggests, this strains the language somewhat, it does seem consistent with the obvious intent in drafting this provision. Surely, this provision was intended to give the minor beneficiary the broadest demand power available so that the gift tax exclusion would be applicable.

There is very little dispute between the parties as to the rights and disabilities of a minor accorded by the California statutes and cases. The problem comes in attempting to ascertain from these rights and disabilities the answer to the question of whether a minor may make a demand upon the trustee for a portion of the trust as provided in the trust instrument.

It is agreed that a minor in California may own property. Estate of Yano, 188 Cal. 645, 206 P. 995 (1922). He may receive a gift. DeLevillain v. Evans, 39 Cal. 120. A minor may demand his own funds from a bank (Cal.Fin.Code, 850 & 853), a savings institution (Cal.Fin.Code, 7600 & 7606), or a corporation (Cal.Corp.Code, 2221 & 2413). A minor of the age of 14 or over has the right to secure the appointment of a guardian and one will be appointed if the court finds it "necessary or convenient." Cal.Prob.Code, 1406; Guardianship of Kentera, 41 Cal.2d 639, 262 P.2d 317 (1953).

It is further agreed that a minor cannot sue in his own name (Cal.Civ.Code, 42) and cannot appoint an agent. (Cal.Civ.Code, 33). With certain exceptions a minor can disaffirm contracts made by him during his minority. Cal.Civ.Code, 35. A minor under the age of 18 cannot make contracts relating to real property or personal property not in his possession or control. Cal.Civ.Code, 33.

The parent of a child may be its natural guardian, but such a guardianship is of the person of the child and not of his estate. Kendall v. Miller, 9 Cal. 591; Cal.Civ.Code, 202.

After examining the same rights and disabilities, the petitioners, the Commissioner, and the Tax Court each arrived at a different solution to our problem. The Tax Court concentrated on the disabilities and concluded that David and Mark could not make an effective demand because they could not sue in their own name, nor appoint an agent and could disaffirm contracts. The court, however, concluded that Janet could make an effective demand because Cal.Civ.Code, 33 indirectly states that she could make contracts with regard to real and personal property.

The Commissioner concentrated on the inability to sue or appoint an agent and concluded that none of the minors had anything more than paper rights because he or she lacked the capacity to enforce the demand.

The petitioners urge that the right to acquire and hold property is the key. In the alternative they argue that the parent as a natural guardian could make the demand although it would be necessary to appoint a legal guardian to receive the property. Finally, they urge that all the minors over 14 could make a demand since they could request the appointment of a legal guardian.

The position taken by the Tax Court seems clearly untenable. The distinction drawn between David and Mark on the one hand, and Janet on the other, makes no sense. The mere fact that Janet can make certain additional contracts does not have any relevance to the question of whether she is capable of making an effective demand upon the trustee. We cannot agree with the position of the Commissioner because we do not feel that a lawsuit or the appointment of an agent is a necessary prelude to the making of a demand upon the trustee. As we visualize the hypothetical situation, the child would inform the trustee that he demanded his share of the additions up to $4,000. The trustee would petition the court for the appointment of a legal guardian and then turn the funds over to the guardian. It would also seem possible for the parent to make the demand as natural guardian. This would involve the acquisition of property for the child rather than the management of the property. It would then be necessary for a legal guardian to be appointed to take charge of the funds. The only time when the disability to sue would come into play, would be if the trustee disregarded the demand and committed a breach of trust. That would not, however, vitiate the demand.

All this is admittedly speculative since it is highly unlikely that a demand will ever be made or that if one is made, it would be made in this fashion. However, as a technical matter, we think a minor could make the demand.

Given the trust, the California law, and the circumstances in our case, it can be seen that very different results may well be achieved, depending upon the test used. Under a strict interpretation of the Stifel test of examining everything and determining whether there is any likelihood of present enjoyment, the gifts to minors in our case would seem to be "future interests." Although under our interpretation neither the trust nor the law technically forbid a demand by the minor, the practical difficulties of a child going through the procedures seem substantial. In addition, the surrounding facts indicate the children were well cared for and the obvious intention of the trustors was to create a long term trust. No guardian had been appointed and, except for the tax difficulties, probably never would be appointed. As a practical matter, it is likely that some, if not all, of the beneficiaries did not even know that they had any right to demand funds from the trust. They probably did not know when contributions were made to the trust or in what amounts. Even had they known, the substantial contributions were made toward the end of the year so that the time to make a demand was severely limited. Nobody had made a demand under the provision, and no distributions had been made. We think it unlikely that any demand ever would have been made.

All exclusions should be allowed under the Perkins test or the "right to enjoy" test in Gilmore. Under Perkins, all that is necessary is to find that the demand could not be resisted. We interpret that to mean legally resisted and, going on that basis, we do not think the trustee would have any choice but to have a guardian appointed to take the property demanded.

Under the general language of Kieckhefer which talked of the "right to enjoy," all exclusions in our case would seem to be allowable. The broader Kieckhefer rule which we have discussed is inapplicable on the facts of this case. That rule, as we interpret it, is that postponed enjoyment is not equivalent to a "future interest" if the postponement is solely caused by the minority of the beneficiary. In Kieckhefer, the income was accumulated and added to the corpus until the beneficiary reached the age of 21. At that time everything was to be turned over to him. This is all that happened unless a demand was made. In our case, on the contrary, if no demand is made in any particular year, the additions are forever removed from the uncontrolled reach of the beneficiary since, with the exception of the yearly demand provision, the only way the corpus can ever be tapped by a beneficiary, is through a distribution at the discretion of the trustee.

We decline to follow a strict reading of the Stifel case in our situation because we feel that the solution suggested by that case is inconsistent and unfair. It becomes arbitrary for the I.R.S. to step in and decide who is likely to make an effective demand. Under the circumstances suggested in our case, it is doubtful that any demands will be made against the trust—yet the Commissioner always allowed the exclusion as to adult beneficiaries. There is nothing to indicate that it is any more likely that John will demand funds than that any other beneficiary will do so. The only distinction is that it might be easier for him to make such a demand. Since we conclude that the demand can be made by the others, it follows that the exclusion should also apply to them. In another case we might follow the broader Kieckhefer rule, since it seems least arbitrary and establishes a clear standard. However, if the minors have no way of making the demand in our case, then there is more than just a postponement involved, since John could demand his share of yearly additions while the others would never have the opportunity at their shares of those additions but would be limited to taking part of any additions added subsequent to their 21st birthdays.

We conclude that the result under the Perkins or "right to enjoy" tests is preferable in our case. The petitioners should be allowed all of the exclusions claimed for the two year period.

The decision of the Tax Court denying the taxpayers' exclusions on the gifts to David and Mark Crummey is reversed. The decision of the Tax Court allowing the taxpayers' exclusions on the 1962 gift to Janet Crummey is affirmed.

NOTES AND QUESTIONS

1. Below is a sample *Crummey* provision adapted from Priv. Ltr. Rul. 8004172.

> **Withdrawal Rights.** Within seven (7) days of receipt of any and all property placed in this trust as a gift, the Trustee shall notify each of the living children of the Settlor's son, * * * (hereinafter referred to as the "Settlor's grandchildren"), of the nature and value of the property received. From the time of the transfer to the trust, each such grandchild shall have the unrestricted right until thirty (30) days after the date of notification to demand and immediately receive from the trust a share of the additional contribution equal to one (1) divided by the number of such grandchildren living at the time of the transfer to the trust. The maximum value of property that may be received by a grandchild at any time shall be an amount which when added to all other amounts received by such grandchild during the calendar year pursuant to this provision shall not exceed the greater of Five Thousand Dollars ($5,000.00) or five percent (5%) of the value of the additional contribution. Should any of the Settlor's grandchildren be a minor, this power of withdrawal may be exercised by his or her natural or legal guardian.

2. It is essential for the beneficiary to have a realistic opportunity to exercise the withdrawal power. For example, the IRS determined that the annual exclusion was not available because the beneficiary was not told of the withdrawal right and, even if the beneficiary had been notified, had only two days in which to make the withdrawal. Rev. Rul. 81–7. How long would you advise your client to allow beneficiaries to exercise the withdrawal power?

3. In addition to the withdrawal right, does the beneficiary need to have a present interest or a vested remainder? Is a contingent remainder sufficient? See Estate of Cristofani v. Commissioner, 97 T.C. 74 (1991); Kohlsaat v. Commissioner, 73 T.C.M. 2732 (1997).

4. Clever taxpayers may attempt to expand the number of annual exclusions they claim by creating *naked withdrawal powers*. In other words, the only interest the beneficiary has in the trust is the right to make the withdrawal; the beneficiary is not otherwise entitled to the trust property such as by being a remainder beneficiary. As is usually the case with *Crummey* provisions, the settlor anticipates that the beneficiary will not exercise the withdrawal right. Will this technique work? See Bradley E.S. Fogel, *The Emperor Does Not Need Clothes—The Expanding Use of "Naked" Crummey Withdrawal Powers to Obtain Federal Gift Tax Annual Exclusions*, 73 TUL. L. REV. 555 (1998).

5. Additional information about *Crummey* powers is contained in the article on life insurance trusts in § J, below.

6. For a comprehensive review of how to use the *Crummey* technique successfully, see David Pratt & Elaine M. Bucher, *Updated Practical Planning With Crummey Powers*, 29 Est. Plan. 73 (2002).

3. GRANTOR RETAINED INTEREST TRUSTS

A. SILVANA GINER, GRITS, GRATS, AND GRUTS*

Drafting Irrevocable Trusts in Massachusetts, Ch. 9, 2005, 1st Supp. 2009.

I. History

Prior to the enactment of Section 2702 of the Internal Revenue Code in 1990, taxpayers wishing to transfer appreciating assets at reduced transfer tax costs often utilized grantor-retained income trusts (GRITs). A taxpayer would transfer property to an irrevocable trust, retaining an income interest for a certain specified term with the remainder passing to the remainder beneficiaries at the termination of the trust.

The value of the retained income interest was determined based on set assumptions established by the IRS regarding the rate of return on the underlying property. The taxpayer's gift for gift tax purposes was the value of the remainder interest passing at the end of the specified term, which was derived by subtracting the retained interest from the value of the property transferred. If the income produced by the trust during the term of the GRIT trailed the assumed interest rate and the taxpayer survived the term of the GRIT, the taxpayer would succeed in removing some postgift appreciation from his or her estate at a reduced transfer tax cost. The strategy was especially successful where trust property appreciated greatly in value after transfer.

Predictably, taxpayers began to take advantage of what had become a significant loophole in the Internal Revenue Code. By transferring property that generated little or no income (such as growth stocks which paid no dividends), a taxpayer could effectively defeat the relevant interest rate assumptions, leaving the trust property with the best opportunity for growth outside the taxpayer's estate.

Congressional Response to Estate Freeze Techniques: I.R.C. § 2702

Congress recognized that GRITs provided taxpayers with a significant estate freeze technique. According to a 1990 senate report on proposed revisions to the Internal Revenue Code, "because [a] taxpayer decides what property to give, when to give it, and often controls the return on the property, use of Treasury tables undervalues the transferred interests in the aggregate, more often than not." 136 Cong. Rec. 30, 538–39 (S15,679–15,683 (Oct. 18, 1990).

In response to this estate freeze technique, Congress enacted the Revenue Reconciliation Act of 1990, which added a new chapter, Chapter 14, to the Internal Revenue Code. Chapter 14 includes I.R.C. § 2702, which sets forth certain rules for transfers to trusts where the transferor retains an interest. Under I.R.C. § 2702, an interest retained either by the transferor or a member of the transferor's family, other than a "qualified interest," is valued at zero where the transferor makes a transfer in trust to (or for the benefit of) a member of the transferor's family. I.R.C. § 2702(a). A member of the transferor's family is defined for these purposes as the transferor's spouse, an ancestor or lineal descendant of the transferor or the transferor's spouse (and the spouse of any such ancestor or lineal descendant), and any sibling of the transferor and any spouse of such sibling. I.R.C. § 2704(c)(2).

Because I.R.C. § 2702 values the transferor's retained interest at zero, the value of a transferor's gift where the remainder interest passes to (or for the benefit of) a member of the family will equal the value of the property transferred, with no reduction for the retained income interest. This result makes the GRIT a useless estate planning strategy where any member of the transferor's family, as defined above, is a remainder beneficiary of the GRIT.

However, Congress also sanctioned under I.R.C. § 2702 certain strategies in which the retained interest could be reasonably valued. So long as the retained interest is a "qualified interest," such interest will be valued using the interest rates applicable under I.R.C. § 7520 for the month of transfer and will therefore be subtracted for gift tax purposes from the value of the property transferred. A qualified interest is defined in Section 2702 to include:

(1) Any interest which consists of the right to receive fixed amounts payable not less frequently than annually,

(2) Any interest which consists of the right to receive amounts which are payable not less frequently than annually and are a fixed percentage of the fair market value of the property in the trust (determined annually), and

(3) Any noncontingent remainder interest if all of the other interests in the trust consist of interests described in [sub]paragraph (1) or (2), above.

II. Choosing a GRIT, GRAT, or GRUT

* * *

(a) Basic Differences

As a result of the addition of Chapter 14 to the Code, GRITs are now useful only in very limited circumstances. Specifically, a GRIT may provide transfer tax benefits where the remainder interest passes to (or is held in trust for) the benefit of someone other than a member of the transferor's family (as defined above). Nevertheless, even those who wish to benefit nonfamily members might find a zeroed-out GRAT-which the transferor funds without making any taxable gift-to be a preferable alternative. Given these circumstances, GRITs are of minimal utility under current tax laws.

Of the remaining options, GRATs are almost always preferable to GRUTs. GRUTs provide the transferor with a retained interest equal to a fixed percentage of the fair market value of the trust, determined annually. The fixed percentage may increase by as much as, but not more than, 20 percent from one year to the next (so long as the increase is mandatory under the terms of the governing instrument). Any appreciation in the assets transferred to a GRUT will increase the transferor's retained interest, thereby increasing the size of the transferor's estate and partially defeating the transferor's intention of gifting maximum asset appreciation at minimal gift tax cost.

A GRAT, on the other hand, allows the transferor to retain an interest that will not mirror the fluctuation in value of the assets transferred. The retained GRAT interest is expressed either as a set dollar amount or as a fixed percentage of the initial fair market value of the assets at the time of transfer, although the fixed percentage may increase by as much as 20 percent from one year to the next (so long as the increase is mandatory under the terms of the governing instrument). The retained annuity payment is therefore a predetermined amount for each year of the GRAT, and any subsequent increase (or decrease) in the value of the transferred assets will have no effect on the value of the annual annuity payment.

*** * *(b) Additional Planning Considerations**

Some taxpayers may prefer an annuity stream that fluctuates according to the appreciation (or depreciation) of the assets transferred to the trust. The GRUT may appear to be an appropriate estate planning strategy, given that the taxpayer has the opportunity to share in any appreciation in the transferred assets. This is an understandable motive, but it should be emphasized that the GRUT strategy is at least partly inconsistent with the goal of removing appreciation from the estate of the taxpayer making the transfer. By retaining an interest in the appreciation itself, the taxpayer reduces the value passing to the remainder beneficiaries at the end of the term. If the goal in utilizing a GRUT or a GRAT is to maximize the value that can be transferred at a minimum transfer tax cost by "defeating" the interest rate assumptions of the I.R.C. § 7520 rate, the GRUT is an inferior strategy.

Moreover, a GRUT is somewhat more burdensome to administer, as it requires annual revaluation of all trust assets. The GRAT does not require such revaluation, except to the extent that the assets used to fund the annuity payments do not have a readily ascertainable value. If the GRAT holds sufficient cash to fund the annuity payment in any given year (because the trustees sold a portion of the assets in the trust, for example), no revaluation would be required.

III. GRATS

GRATs provide a useful estate planning strategy where assets are expected to appreciate at a higher rate than the I.R.C. § 7520 rate and the transferor has a high probability of surviving the selected term.

A GRAT could "implode" if the assets do not appreciate as expected. Implosion occurs where the taxpayer receives the entire trust property back in the form of the required annuity payments, leaving nothing for the remainder beneficiaries. Although implosion is an undesirable result, the taxpayer utilizing a zeroed-out GRAT (described below) is essentially in the same position as if he or she had not established the GRAT, save for the legal and administrative expense involved in setting up and administering the GRAT. Moreover, as described in more detail below, the taxpayer could then gift the assets into a new GRAT if the assets were still expected to appreciate.

Once the GRAT is established, the assets in the GRAT should be actively managed by a sophisticated investment advisor. The investment advisor must be aware of the underlying GRAT strategy, and should seek to implement a plan for asset management to obtain the best result. Specifically, the investment advisor should recognize that properly timed sales of appreciated GRAT assets will provide the transferor with the greatest opportunity for success.

(a) "Zeroed–Out" GRATs

According to regulations in effect prior to July 26, 2004, a retained annuity interest was valued based on the shorter of the term of the trust or the life expectancy of the transferor. Former Reg. § 25.2702–3(e) ex. 5. Under this valuation methodology, a gift to the GRAT could never be reduced to zero because the interest passing to the transferor's estate if the transferor did not survive the term of the GRAT was deemed a contingent interest and therefore not a qualified interest under I.R.C. § 2702. The IRS took the position that a zeroed-out GRAT was not possible.

The Tax Court disagreed with the IRS, holding unanimously in the case of Walton v. Commissioner, 115 T.C. 589, 604 (2000), that Example 5 of Treas. Reg. § 25.2702–3(e) was "an unreasonable interpretation and an invalid extension of IRC § 2702." 115 T.C. 589, 604 (2000). According to the court, the contingent annuity interest passing to the transferor's estate if the transferor did not survive the term should be valued as part of the transferor's retained interest and not disregarded. The IRS acquiesced to the Tax Court's decision in Walton in 2003. IRS Notice 2003–72. In 2005, the IRS revised Treas. Reg. § 25.2702–3(e) to conform with Walton in this regard. T.D. 9181 (February 24, 2005) (publishing revised regulations, effective as of July 26, 2004).

The concept of a zeroed-out GRAT is quite simple. The transferor merely retains an annuity interest whose present value is equivalent to the value of the property transferred. The resulting gift has no gift tax consequences, since no value is passed to the remainder beneficiaries at the time the trust is funded. Nevertheless, the transferor should file a gift tax return when funding the trust so that the statute of limitations begins to run with respect to the value of the transfer. If the transferor does not file a gift tax return, the IRS retains the right to challenge the initial valuation at any time.

(b) Structuring the GRAT

A client interested in funding a GRAT must make a number of initial decisions regarding the form of the GRAT. In particular, the client must consider the appropriate term for the GRAT, the assets that should be transferred to the GRAT, and how the remainder interest should be structured.

(c) GRAT Term

If the transferor dies before the expiration of the GRAT term, some or all of the GRAT property will be included in the transferor's estate for estate tax purposes (see § 9.2.2(b), below). It is important that the transferor establish the GRAT with a term that the transferor is likely to survive. With a shorter GRAT term, however, a larger annuity payment will be required in order to minimize (or zero out) the taxable gift made at funding.

It appears that the shortest allowable term for a GRAT is two years. I.R.C. § 2702(b)(1) (referring to qualified annuity interests as "amounts [plural] payable not less frequently than annually"); but see Kerr v. Commissioner, 113 T.C. 449 (1999), aff'd 292 F.3d 490 (5th Cir. 2002) (IRS contested valuation of property contributed to 367–day GRATs with annuity payments to the respective transferors on days two and 367, but not the validity of the GRATs themselves). The Walton case involved two-year GRATs, the validity of which the Tax Court approved. However, the IRS has indicated that it is wary of both zeroed-out GRATs and short-term GRATs. See, e.g., Rev. Proc. 2008–3(51) (IRS will not issue rulings on whether a retained interest is a qualified annuity interest under Section 2702 where the amount of the annuity payable annually is more than 50 percent of the initial net fair market value of the property transferred to the trust, or if the value of the remainder interest is less than 10 percent of the initial net fair market value of the property transferred to the trust). Such GRATs may be subject to closer scrutiny.

Regardless, a short term will generally be preferable even though larger annuity payments are required. The transferor may employ a "cascading GRAT" strategy by simply gifting the annuity payments from the existing GRAT to new GRATs as the annuities are received; the transferor may continue to re-GRAT such assets if they remain likely to appreciate. The short term of each GRAT provides the grantor with the greatest likelihood of surviving the term and removing at least some asset appreciation from his or her estate. A short term also allows the grantor to mitigate the effect of timing (for example, to make adjustments if the assets perform poorly for certain periods during the term of the GRAT).

Practice Note

In most cases, a three-year GRAT would be appropriate, but the practitioner must consider various growth and interest-rate assumptions before selecting an appropriate strategy.

Of course, other factors may influence the transferor's determination of the appropriate length of the GRAT term. For example, if the I.R.C. § 7520 rate is low but is expected to rise in the near future, the transferor may decide to utilize a longer GRAT to take advantage of the low-interest-rate assumptions rather than attempting to re-GRAT assets at two-year intervals, when interest rates may have risen. The transferor may also view as unappealing the additional administrative and legal costs of establishing multiple short-term GRATs. Finally, the transferor's age and health also will be relevant factors in selecting an appropriate GRAT term, as will the nature of the assets transferred.

The transferor must also select how frequently the annuity payments will be made (annually, quarterly, or monthly, for example). In most cases, the transferor will select an annual payment period to allow the assets the greatest opportunity to appreciate before each annuity payment must be made. Further, annual annuity payments may actually be made as many as 105 days after the payment date (or by April 15 of the following year if the payment date is December 31). Treas. Reg. § 25.2702–3(b)(4).

Assets for Transfer

The transferor may fund a GRAT with assets of any kind, although the GRAT strategy is most useful where assets have significant volatility (and a high likelihood for appreciation). Assets whose values may be reduced because of lack-of-control and lack-of-marketability discounts are also useful if those assets are sold before the first annuity payment (when no discount need be taken in valuing the property used to pay the annuity amount).

The transferor may receive annuity payments either in cash or in kind, depending upon the assets available to make the payments. However, the trustees may not issue a note, other debt instrument, option, or other similar financial arrangement in satisfaction of the annuity obligation. Treas. Reg. § 25.2702–3(d)(5). Also, the trust itself must expressly prohibit the trustees from issuing such instruments in payment of the annuity amount.

When transferring assets to a GRAT, the transferor must also comply with any relevant corporate law issues. For example, Section 16(b) of the Securities Exchange Act of 1934 provides that any officers, directors, or major shareholders (i.e., those owning more than a 10 percent interest in the company) must file with the Securities and Exchange Commission (SEC) when they purchase and sell company securities, and they must disgorge any profits received in a "short-swing" period (when securities are both purchased and sold within a six-month period).

Under a no-action letter, the SEC held that a transferor would not run afoul of Section 16(b) merely by transferring shares to a GRAT and receiving the regular annuity payments during the term of the GRAT. Peter J. Kight, SEC No–Action Letter, Fed. Sec. L. Rep. (CCH) P 77,403 (Oct. 16, 1997). The SEC determined that the arrangement would effect a change in the form of beneficial ownership, but not a change in the transferor's pecuniary interest.

However, the court in Morales v. Quintiles Transnational Corp., 25 F. Supp. 2d 369 (S.D.N.Y. 1998) found that Section 16(b) will apply where the transferor exercises a power to substitute property held in a GRAT for property of equal value (discussed in Exhibit 9A, below). The court reasoned that because the substitution of property is akin to a sale of the property at fair market value, Section 16(b) applies and any subsequent sales by the transferor within six months after the substitution will lead to a disgorgement of profits.

The transferor should also be aware of any other securities law issues and insider trading rules that may be implicated by the creation and administration of a GRAT.

In addition, the transferor should analyze the provisions of I.R.C. § 2036(b). If the transferor serves as trustee with the right to vote the stock of the GRAT but also owns at least 20 percent of the voting stock with respect to any stock transferred to the trust, the transferor will be deemed to have retained an interest in the property for estate tax purposes until three years after the GRAT terminates. I.R.C. § 2036(b)(2). This provision represents a significant trap for the unwary corporate insider.

Finally, the transferor should confirm that assets used to fund the GRAT are not prohibited from being transferred and that the provisions of the trust are consistent with any restrictions on the transfer of the asset. For example, a restrictive stock agreement for the closely held stock of a private company may limit the permissible class of transferees to spouse and children.

(d) Disposition of the Remainder

The transferor must decide to whom trust property will pass at the expiration of the trust term. The property may either pass outright or be held in trust for the benefit of the remainder beneficiaries. Although the GRAT instrument itself may include the further trust provisions, in most cases the transferor will prefer to have property pass to an altogether separate trust (or outright to designated persons) so that no argument can be made that the transferor has retained some interest in the remainder that would cause inclusion in the transferor's gross estate. The transferor should be certain to hold no powers over the separate trust that would cause the property to be included in his or her gross estate.

As described in more detail in § 9.2.2(b) below, a generation-skipping transfer (GST) tax may be imposed if the GRAT property passes at the end of the annuity term to or for the benefit of the transferor's grandchildren or more remote descendants (or to or for the benefit of any unrelated individuals who are 37.5 years or more younger than the transferor and are therefore deemed to be two generations below the transferor under I.R.C. § 2651(d)). Although the transferor has the ability to allocate GST exemption at the end of the term, the property may have appreciated to such an extent that the fair market value exceeds the available exemption. The transferor should be aware of this possibility when structuring a GRAT whose remainder interest passes to any such beneficiaries.

IV. Tax Issues

(a) Income Tax

The transferor will likely prefer that both the income portion and the corpus portion of the trust be subject to grantor-trust treatment. If the transferor is treated as the owner of both portions, all income, deductions, and credits against the taxes of the trust will be attributable to the transferor in computing the transferor's taxable income and tax credits. I.R.C. § 671. One significant benefit of this treatment is that any in-kind payment of the transferor's annuity interest will not be a recognition transaction for income tax purposes. Priv. Ltr. Rul. 9519029 (May 12, 1995).

Under I.R.C. § 673, a transferor will be treated as the owner of any portion of a trust in which the transferor has a reversionary interest in either the corpus or the income therefrom if, at the inception of that portion of the trust, the value of such interest exceeds 5 percent of the value of such portion. In most cases, this statute alone should ensure that both portions of the trust will be subject to grantor-trust treatment.

Where the transferor retains an annuity interest that will be satisfied first out of income and then out of principal, and the trust provides that any property included in the grantor's estate if the transferor dies during the annuity term will be paid to the grantor's estate, the reversionary interest in both portions should exceed 5 percent. Nevertheless, the transferor may wish to include additional provisions in the trust as evidence for grantor trust treatment for income tax purposes. As indicated in the form GRAT set forth in Exhibit 9A, the transferor may retain the power to reacquire trust property corpus by substituting other property of an equivalent value. I.R.C. § 675(4)(C).

(b) Transfer Taxes

Estate Tax

Some or all of the GRAT property will be included in the transferor's gross estate for estate tax purposes under I.R.C. § 2036 if the transferor does not survive the term of the GRAT. According to regulations issued on July 11, 2008, the portion included is the lesser of:

* that portion of the trust corpus necessary to provide the decedent's retained use or retained annuity interest without reducing or invading principal and

* the fair market value of all of the GRAT property.

Treas. Reg. § 20.2036–1(c)(2)(i). This amount may be determined by the following formula:

Annual annuity / Section 7520 rate (date of death or alternate valuation date) = Amount included

Treas. Reg. § 20.2036–1(c)(2)(iii), ex. 2. If GRAT payments are made more frequently than annually (for example, quarterly or monthly), the "annual annuity" figure must be adjusted as provided in Treas. Reg. §§ 20.2031–7 or 20.2031–7A (as applicable). Treas. Reg. § 20.2036–1(c)(2)(i).

The IRS has provided an example of a GRAT with an initial value of $100,000 and a retained annuity of $12,000 (payable monthly) for a period of ten years, or until the transferor's earlier death. Treas. Reg. § 20.2036–1(c)(2)(iii), ex. 2. The transferor dies before the end of the GRAT term, when the value of the trust property is $300,000 and the I.R.C. § 7520 rate is 6 percent. Because payments are made monthly in this example, the annual annuity must be adjusted by a factor of 1.0272 (determined according to Table K of Treas. Reg. § 20.2031–7). The amount included in the transferor's gross estate for estate tax purposes is as follows:

($12,000 x 1.0272) / 6% = $205,400

Therefore, $205,400 is included in the transferor's gross estate for estate tax purposes, and $94,600 is not.

Note that it does not matter how many annuity payments actually remain to be paid at the time of the transferor's death, or when during the term the transferor dies. The amount included under I.R.C. § 2036 is the amount necessary to generate annual growth equal to the annuity payment indefinitely without reducing principal (assuming growth at the applicable I.R.C. § 7520 rate). For this reason, the above calculation applies equally to a GRAT that continues after the transferor's death (such as a zeroed-out GRAT) and to a GRAT that terminates upon the death of the transferor. See, e.g., Treas. Reg. § 20.2036–1(c)(2)(iii), ex. 1(ii) (the amount of a GRAT included in the transferor's gross estate is the same regardless of whether the transferor retained an interest in the GRAT for his or her lifetime or retained an interest for a term of years and died during the term).

(c) Gift Tax

Given that zeroed-out GRATs have been authorized by court authority, there is little reason to establish a GRAT in which any taxable gift is made upon funding. Moreover, in an environment where the estate tax could be permanently repealed, it is especially difficult to find merit in the payment of any gift tax at funding.

(d) GST Tax

As noted in § 9.2.1(b) above, a GRAT is not an effective tool for leveraging the taxpayer's exemption against the GST tax. The term of the GRAT is considered an estate tax inclusion period (ETIP), and GST exemption cannot be allocated until after the end of the ETIP. I.R.C. § 2642(f)(3). At the end of the ETIP, the property may have appreciated to such a level that the taxpayer would need to allocate a large portion, or all, of his or her exemption against the GST tax.

Practice Note

A taxpayer who values the ability to leverage GST exemption over the ability to reduce transfer tax costs when a trust is funded might prefer some other estate planning strategy, such as funding a standard irrevocable trust with assets that are expected to appreciate and allocating GST exemption at the funding date. A GRAT is not an effective tool for leveraging GST exemption.

V. GRITs

The Internal Revenue Code does not set forth sample provisions for the common law GRIT. Nevertheless, the GRIT instrument may include the same form provisions regarding trustees and administrative powers as the GRAT.

The GRIT differs in a few significant ways from the GRAT. As the name implies, a GRIT involves a retained income interest, rather than a retained annuity interest. Therefore, the section of the trust describing retained powers should provide that the trustee will distribute to the transferor during the trust term all net income of the trust no less frequently than annually.

Unlike the GRAT, the GRIT may authorize additional contributions (although such contributions will be valued at the time of transfer according to the remaining trust term). The GRIT need not include the provisions required under Treas. Reg. § 25.2702–3(b) and Treas. Reg. § 25.2702–3(d); these requirements do not apply to GRITs. The "saving clause" that references these sections should therefore be revised.

The GRIT need not specify the character of annuity payments, because the design of the instrument requires that the trustees simply distribute all net income to the transferor. For the same reason, the GRIT need not include a provision regarding the redetermination of the retained interest if assets are ever incorrectly valued, nor must the GRIT provide for pro rata distributions in a short taxable year.

The GRIT should, however, provide that only the transferor will receive distributions during the term of the GRIT.

Finally, under the 2008 Regulations regarding I.R.C. § 2036, a percentage of the GRIT corpus equal to that percentage of the GRIT income retained by the transferor is included in the transferor's estate for estate tax purposes under Section 2036 if the transferor dies during the term of the GRIT. Treas. Reg. § 20.2036–1(c)(2)(iii), ex. 4. The transferor should provide in the GRIT instrument that the portion included in his or her gross estate for estate tax purposes will revert to his or her estate. There is no tax benefit in continuing the income interest payments to the transferor's estate for the balance of a specified number of years if the transferor does not survive the term.

VI. GRUTs

The GRUT instrument may include the same form provisions regarding trustees and administrative powers as the GRAT.

The most obvious substantive difference with a GRUT is that the retained interest is expressed as a unitrust that fluctuates with the appreciation or depreciation of the trust property. The GRUT should provide that the trustees will pay to the transferor a percentage of the trust assets as determined annually on the first day of each taxable year. As with a GRAT, the percentage payable each year need not be level, so long as the payment in any year does not exceed 120 percent of the payment in a prior year. Treas. Reg. § 25.2702–3(c)(1)(ii).

The GRUT need not prohibit additional contributions. Otherwise, the provisions of the GRUT are generally identical to the provisions of the standard GRAT, except that the "saving clause" should refer specifically to Treas. Reg. § 25.2702–3(c) and Treas. Reg. § 25.2702–3(d).

J. LIFE INSURANCE

INTERNAL REVENUE CODE, § 2042

PROCEEDS OF LIFE INSURANCE

The value of the gross estate shall include the value of all property—

(1) Receivable by the executor.—To the extent of the amount receivable by the executor as insurance under policies on the life of the decedent.

(2) Receivable by other beneficiaries.—To the extent of the amount receivable by all other beneficiaries as insurance under policies on the life of the decedent with respect to which the decedent possessed at his death any of the incidents of ownership, exercisable either alone or in conjunction with any other person. For purposes of the preceding sentence, the term "incident of ownership" includes a reversionary interest (whether arising by the express terms of the policy or other instrument or by operation of law) only if the value of such reversionary interest exceeded 5 percent of the value of the policy immediately before the death of the decedent. As used in this paragraph, the term "reversionary interest" includes a possibility that the policy, or the proceeds of the policy, may return to the decedent or his estate, or may be subject to a power of disposition by him. The value of a reversionary interest at any time shall be determined (without regard to the fact of the decedent's death) by usual methods of valuation, including the use of tables of mortality and actuarial principles, pursuant to regulations prescribed by the Secretary. In determining the value of a possibility that the policy or proceeds thereof may be subject to a power of disposition by the decedent, such possibility shall be valued as if it were a possibility that such policy or proceeds may return to the decedent or his estate.

SEBASTIAN V. GRASSI, JR., KEY ISSUES TO CONSIDER WHEN DRAFTING LIFE INSURANCE TRUSTS*

31 EST. PLAN. 390 (2004).

Four unique elements of life insurance, in the context of estate planning, make it an appealing investment for an irrevocable life insurance trust (ILIT). The spread between the lifetime and death values of life insurance makes it an attractive candidate for transfer to an ILIT. Life insurance blooms when the insured dies; dollars of 'seed' premium blossom into thousands of dollars of death benefits. Life insurance premiums generally represent a fraction of the death benefit value, and if the life insurance policy is held in an ILIT, the grantor's annual gift tax exclusion, gift tax applicable exclusion amount, and generation-skipping transfer (GST) tax exemption can be significantly leveraged. An ILIT also permits multiple beneficiaries to have any interest in the death benefits, with management and control of the policy and death benefits being handled by a trustee. These characteristics make an ILIT a formidable estate planning vehicle.

The need for ILITs has not been diminished by the Economic Growth and Tax Relief Reconciliation Act of 2001 (EGTRRA), due to states decoupling from the federal estate tax applicable exclusion amount, and the uncertainty surrounding the permanency of the repeal of the federal estate tax and GST tax. (EGTRRA's sunset provisions, which take effect 1/1/11, reinstate the pre-EGTRRA transfer tax regime.) This legislative uncertainty underscores the need for clients with estates greater than $1 million to consider using an ILIT to hold life insurance and remove it from their gross estate. Of course, there is a corresponding need to draft ILITs with sufficient flexibility to deal with the possibility of a permanent increase in the applicable exclusion amount (in lieu of permanent estate and GST tax repeal) or the possibility of a permanent repeal of the estate and GST taxes.

BENEFITS OF AN ILIT

With proper planning, an ILIT offers the following potential benefits.

Avoid inclusion of life insurance proceeds in insured's estate. The primary benefit and goal of an ILIT is the removal of the life insurance proceeds from the insured-grantor's estate. Therefore, when

* "Key Issues to Consider When Drafting Life Insurance Trusts" by Sebastian V. Grassi Jr., published in Estate Planning, Volume 31, 2004. © 2004 by Thomson Reuters/WG&L. Reprinted with permission.

drafting the ILIT, be sure that the insured does not hold or retain any incidents of ownership over the insurance policies or possess any powers over the ILIT or its trustee that would cause the ILIT or the insurance proceeds to be included in the insured-grantor's gross estate for estate tax purposes.

Minimize the adverse tax consequences of the three-year rule of Section 2035. Although the three-year rule has generally been eliminated with respect to most gifts, life insurance transferred within three years of the grantor-insured's death for less than full and adequate consideration is includable in the grantor-insured's estate under Section 2035. If an insurance policy that a married grantor transfers to the ILIT is included in the grantor's estate because the grantor dies within three years of the transfer, the ILIT can, under certain circumstances, minimize or eliminate the payment of federal estate taxes. The ILIT trustee could pay or hold the life insurance proceeds in a manner that qualifies for the estate tax marital deduction (or the estate tax charitable deduction). If both spouses die within three years of transferring the policy to the ILIT, absent a bequest of the policy proceeds that qualifies for the estate tax charitable deduction (with a corresponding waiver in the spouses' will of the apportionment provisions of Section 2206), the proceeds will be includable in the gross estate of the surviving spouse.

If the proceeds do not qualify for a marital or charitable deduction, consider who should be responsible for the payment of the estate tax attributable to the proceeds that are held by the ILIT. Under Section 2206, the executor of a decedent's estate is entitled to recover federal estate taxes paid by the estate that are attributable to life insurance proceeds included in the gross estate. The executor's right of apportionment/recovery is on a pro rata basis. A decedent can opt out of the recovery/apportionment provisions of Section 2206 by so stating in his or her will. A general provision in the decedent's will directing that all taxes be paid from the residue is sufficient to opt out of the Code's apportionment/recovery scheme.

The three-year recapture rule of Section 2035 can be avoided completely if the life insurance policy is initially acquired directly by the ILIT, without any incidents of ownership in the grantor-insured. In this situation, the proceeds will not be included in the grantor-insured's estate, even if the insured pays all the premiums (through the use of Crummey withdrawal gifts to the ILIT) and dies within three years of the ILIT's acquisition of the policy.

Insulate trust corpus from successive taxation at multiple generations. With proper planning, life insurance proceeds can benefit successive generations without being included in the estates of the spouse and other beneficiaries. Be careful that the spouse and other beneficiaries are not deemed to hold a retained interest (due to a taxable release of a Crummey withdrawal right). Also be careful when drafting the ILIT that the spouse and beneficiaries do not hold any general powers of appointment over the trust assets, either as a beneficiary or as a trustee.

If a spouse or beneficiary serves as a trustee or co-trustee, that person's powers (as trustee) must be limited to non-discretionary standards that are ascertainable, such as distributions pertaining to a beneficiary's 'health, education, support and maintenance,' as permitted under Regs. § 25.2511–1(g)(2), 20.2514–1(c)(2), and 20.2041–1(c)(2). The beneficiary-trustee's exercise or non-exercise of powers and discretions must not be in that person's 'uncontrolled discretion' or be 'conclusive;' otherwise, the ascertainable standard will be rendered unascertainable and will constitute a general power of appointment. Furthermore, the beneficiary-trustee must be prohibited from using the trust property to discharge his or her legal obligations; otherwise, the ability to do so will constitute a general power of appointment. An ascertainable standard does not protect the beneficiary-trustee in this instance.

Care must also be taken to make sure that the grantor's spouse or a beneficiary does not hold any powers as a beneficiary that constitute a general power of appointment, such as the beneficiary's unrestricted right to remove and replace a trustee with a related or subordinate party (as defined in Section 672(c)). If a beneficiary can appoint him or herself as trustee or as a co-trustee (unless the other co-trustee has a substantially adverse interest in the trust), the beneficiary will be treated as possessing the powers of the trustee, which may result in the beneficiary holding a general power of appointment.

Do not give the spouse or other beneficiaries a withdrawal right in excess of the greater of $5,000 or 5% of the trust corpus (a five-or-five power). (Or, if a hanging power is granted to a beneficiary other than the grantor's spouse, make sure the hanging power is limited to the annual gift tax exclusion amount and lapses each calendar year within the five-or-five safe harbor rules.) Otherwise, the lapse in excess of the five-or-five amount, in conjunction with an income/principal interest in the trust, will constitute a retained interest in the spouse's (or other beneficiaries') share of the excess property, which will be included in the spouse's (or other beneficiaries') estate as a retained interest (following the release of a general power of appointment).

Also be careful about the powers and rights the beneficiaries may have over any policies of insurance on their lives held by the ILIT trustee. An insured beneficiary should: (1) not be permitted to serve as trustee of a trust that holds the insurance on his or her life, (2) not hold any incidents of ownership over the life insurance policy, and (3) not hold a power of appointment over the policy.

Leverage the grantor's GST exemption. Use of an ILIT as a generation-skipping trust, or so-called dynasty trust, is an extremely efficient technique to leverage the transferor's GST exemption and applicable exclusion amount. The dynasty trust can be established with no withdrawal rights being granted. In that case, the grantor's transfer of property to the ILIT will be a transfer of a future interest and so will not qualify for the gift tax annual exclusion; the grantor will have to allocate his or her gift tax applicable exclusion amount and GST exemption to the transfer. Nevertheless, the result will be a guaranteed insulation of the transfer and subsequent proceeds from successive generational tax.

If the grantor does grant Crummey withdrawal rights over the premium contributions to the dynasty trust, the grantor could end up wasting some of his or her GST exemption that has been allocated to the trust. This could happen if a beneficiary holding a Crummey right dies before the withdrawal right lapses.

In such instance, the amount of the unlapsed withdrawal right will be included in the deceased beneficiary's estate under Section 2041. The deceased beneficiary will become the 'new' transferor for GST tax purposes with regard to the unlapsed Crummey withdrawal amount, thus losing and wasting the grantor's previously allocated GST exemption. To maintain the dynasty trust's GST tax-exempt status, the deceased beneficiary's executor will have to allocate GST exemption for the amount of the Crummey withdrawal right included in the beneficiary's estate. The possibility of a beneficiary dying while a Crummey right remains outstanding (i.e., unlapsed) may be outweighed by the grantor's desire to make gifts to the dynasty trust that qualify for the gift tax annual exclusion.

Incur little or no gift tax upon creation of the trust and payment of subsequent premiums. A Crummey withdrawal right granted to each beneficiary, when used in conjunction with the gift tax annual exclusion under Section 2503(b) and gift-splitting under Section 2513 (if applicable), allows the grantor's payment of premiums to be gift tax-free.

Create liquidity for the grantor's estate. If the insurance proceeds are needed to provide liquidity to the grantor's estate, the trustee can be specifically authorized to buy assets from the grantor's estate or loan funds to the estate. Similarly, the trustee can also have this authority with regard to the grantor's spouse and descendants. The trustee must not be required to purchase assets or loan monies; otherwise, such requirements may be tantamount to 'insurance proceeds being receivable by an executor.'

Provide professional management of the insurance proceeds. An ILIT provides a vehicle for the management of the grantor's life insurance policy and subsequent proceeds. The ILIT protects beneficiaries who are inexperienced in managing and investing money. If a beneficiary is a minor or under some other disability that prevents the beneficiary from properly managing and investing the proceeds, the ILIT protects that beneficiary. In these situations, the ILIT can provide for proper management, investment, and conservation of the life insurance proceeds for the continued benefit of the beneficiaries.

Provide creditor and divorce protection to the beneficiaries. An ILIT can also ensure that the grantor's beneficiaries are protected from their inabilities, disabilities, predators, creditors, in-laws and outlaws, including potential ex-spouses (in some instances). An outright transfer of an insurance policy to beneficiaries cannot provide such protection nor provide the control that the grantor may desire. Maximum flexibility and creditor protection can be achieved through the use of a disinterested or independent trustee with broad discretionary powers over the trust, a spendthrift provision, and the grantor's surviving spouse having a testamentary limited power of appointment over the trust (after the death of the grantor-insured).

DRAFTING CHECKLIST

Avoid ETIPs and taxable releases—Limit the spouse's Crummey withdrawal right to five-or-five and 60 days after the contribution. If the grantor is going to allocate GST exemption to the ILIT, the spouse's withdrawal right should: (1) be limited to the greater of $5,000 or 5% of the trust corpus, and (2) lapse 60 days after the date of the contribution (not 60 days after the Crummey notice). This will avoid the estate tax inclusion period (ETIP) issue for the spouse under the GST tax rules. Furthermore, the spouse should not be given a hanging power of withdrawal because it does not come within the ETIP safe harbor rules set forth in Reg. § 26.2632–1(c)(2)(ii).

Avoid naked Crummey withdrawal rights. The IRS frowns on discretionary or contingent remainder beneficiaries who have Crummey withdrawal rights. Therefore, if possible, draft the ILIT so that there are multiple present interest beneficiaries, who hold either a current income interest or a vested remainder interest.

Fortunately, the Tax Court disagrees with the IRS concerning contingent remainder beneficiaries who hold Crummey withdrawal rights, and has permitted contingent remainder beneficiaries (grandchildren, who would take only if their parents (the current income beneficiaries) predeceased them) to be recognized as valid Crummey beneficiaries for whom the gift tax annual exclusion was available to the grantor. The IRS has also stated that it will not recognize Crummey withdrawal rights granted to persons whose only interest in the ILIT is the Crummey power itself.

Use tiered Crummey withdrawal rights. Consider providing for tiered withdrawal rights by which the spouse may withdraw the gift contribution first, and the children withdraw second. Tiered withdrawal rights make Crummey notices easier, particularly if the annual gift contributions to the ILIT are limited in amount.

Crummey withdrawal rights must be ascertainable. Ensure that the amount subject to the Crummey withdrawal right is ascertainable. If there are multiple beneficiaries holding a Crummey power over the same gift amount, make sure that each donee's right of withdrawal over the gift amount is pro rata. For example, assume that a tiered Crummey right permits the grantor's spouse to withdraw the first $5,000 of annual gift contribution, and the grantor's children can withdraw any amount above $5,000. In this case, the amount withdrawable by the children must be the pro rata amount in excess of the first $5,000 of annual gift contribution.

Do not condition the amount of the withdrawal on whether a split-gift election is to be made under Section 2513. The IRS has ruled that this constitutes a condition subsequent to the gift and makes the gift amount (i.e., the withdrawal amount) unascertainable until the condition subsequent occurs. Instead, limit the withdrawal right to a single present interest annual exclusion amount or provide that if a donor is married at the time of the contribution, the amount subject to withdrawal is the amount otherwise available under gift-splitting, irrespective of whether the gift-splitting election is, in fact, made. Condition any distribution of principal, trust termination, trustee discretion, or exercise of any lifetime power of appointment over the ILIT property, so that such distributions, terminations, discretions, or exercises will not thwart or otherwise defeat an existing Crummey withdrawal right that is unexercised and has not yet lapsed.

Provide beneficiaries with sufficient time to exercise their Crummey powers. A beneficiary must have a reasonable amount of time to exercise his or her Crummey withdrawal right before it lapses. Consequently, provide for a minimum Crummey withdrawal period of 15 days, although 30 days is preferable. For ETIP purposes, the grantor's spouse's withdrawal right must be limited to no more than 60 days from the date of the contribution to the ILIT.

Give the trustee broad powers to satisfy any Crummey withdrawal right. Make sure that any Crummey withdrawal right may be satisfied not only by the contribution but also by other trust property, including any insurance policy or fractional interests in the insurance policy. This will provide substance to a Crummey withdrawal right, especially in the case of any split-dollar or group term policies held by the trust. Fortunately, the IRS has sanctioned the ILIT trustee's ability to distribute fractional interests in the insurance policies as sufficient to satisfy a Crummey withdrawal right.

Permit the trustee to appoint a guardian for minor Crummey beneficiaries. Because a minor beneficiary is legally incapable of exercising a Crummey withdrawal right, a guardian or next friend needs to be able to exercise the right on behalf of the minor beneficiary. A court-appointed guardian is not required if there is a natural guardian, such as a parent (other than the grantor, or the grantor's spouse in the case of a second-to-die policy), who can exercise the right of withdrawal on behalf of the minor. If there is no natural guardian and there is no impediment under the trust or local law to the appointment of a guardian for a minor, the minor's Crummey withdrawal right still qualifies the contribution to the trust as a gift of a present interest under Section 2503(b).

Prohibit the grantor from possessing or exercising any powers over the ILIT. To avoid any potential issues under Section 2036 and Section 2038, prohibit the grantor from retaining any interests in the property transferred by the grantor to the ILIT. In addition, prohibit the grantor (and the grantor's spouse in the case of a second-to-die policy) from exercising Crummey withdrawal rights on behalf of the beneficiaries (including the ability to exercise the Crummey power pursuant to a power of attorney or as a natural or legal guardian of the beneficiary).

Prohibit the grantor (and an insured spouse) from becoming a trustee of the ILIT. This is a required provision of the ILIT. If the grantor serves as a trustee of the ILIT, the insurance on the grantor's life will be included in his or her gross estate for estate tax purposes because of the grantor's incidents of ownership in the policy (since the trustee is the owner of the life insurance policy). Similarly, neither spouse should serve as trustee of an ILIT that holds a second-to-die policy insuring both spouses' lives.

Vest ownership of the life insurance exclusively in the ILIT trustee. The ILIT should provide that the grantor has relinquished all rights over transferred policies, and that any life insurance policies purchased by the ILIT on the grantor's life are owned exclusively by the trustee.

Grant the ILIT trustee broad powers to deal with life insurance matters. In addition to the usual trustee powers, the ILIT trustee should be granted broad powers to deal with life insurance. Such powers will serve as a road map for the trustee concerning various matters pertaining to the life insurance policy, especially the payment of premiums. These powers include: (1) the acquisition and retention of life insurance, (2) the ability to request indemnification from a trust beneficiary before making a distribution of the insurance proceeds to that beneficiary, (3) the vesting of all incidents of ownership in the trustee, (4) how the trustee is to pay premiums due on the policies insuring the grantor's life and the options available to the trustee if the grantor stops making gifts to the ILIT, (5) the ability to compromise and settle with the life ***396** insurance companies, and (6) the ability of the trustee to undertake litigation to collect the insurance proceeds and request indemnification from the trust beneficiaries.

Appoint a special powerholder. Although not mandatory, appointing a special powerholder with a limited power to appoint the ILIT property (including life insurance policies) will provide significant flexibility to both the trustee and the grantor in the event of changed circumstances. For example, the special powerholder could exercise its power in 2010, when there is no GST tax, to distribute assets to skip persons. If the trust is not GST tax-exempt (i.e., the trust has an inclusion ratio greater than zero), the special powerholder could appoint trust assets to skip persons. Such an appointment would be a direct skip, and if the assets were appointed to a dynasty trust in which all the beneficiaries were skip persons, the trust would be a skip person. Arguably, no post–2010 distributions to skip persons from the dynasty trust should attract GST tax because the distributions will not be taxable terminations or taxable distributions. However, this point is not exactly clear, and the safer approach may be to make outright distributions to skip beneficiaries in year 2010.

Make sure the special powerholder's limited power of appointment cannot be exercised so as to defeat a Crummey withdrawal right which has not been exercised and has not yet lapsed. The special powerholder should not be the insured, the grantor, a beneficiary of the ILIT, or a permissible recipient of the appointed trust property. Be aware of the potential gift tax consequences if the special powerholder is also a beneficiary of the ILIT. The lifetime exercise of a special power of appointment over trust corpus by the trust's income beneficiary is a gift equal to the present value of the beneficiary's income interest. The beneficiary's exercise of the power over the corpus does not terminate the income interest. Instead, when trust corpus is transferred, the income generated by the transferred corpus is also (gratuitously) transferred to the transferee of the corpus, thus resulting in a gift of the beneficiary's transferred income interest.

Permit grantor to vary annual Crummey withdrawal rights. Another method of providing flexibility to the grantor (although this provision is not required) is to allow the grantor to vary the Crummey rights of withdrawal before each year's contribution to the ILIT. The grantor cannot change the beneficiaries of the ILIT without running afoul of Section 2036, but can change (on an annual basis) which beneficiaries are to be granted Crummey withdrawal rights. The grantor should exercise great care in using this power, since the constant toggling of Crummey withdrawal rights among beneficiaries may raise the ire of the ILIT trustee. An example where a grantor might want to vary the rights of withdrawal involves a beneficiary who subsequently experiences creditor problems, is going through a divorce, or has previously exercised his or her withdrawal right.

Permit trustee to terminate the ILIT. If the estate tax is repealed permanently or the applicable exclusion amount is increased substantially (in lieu of repeal), trusts that were originally designed to minimize estate tax may no longer be necessary. If the non-estate tax reasons for an ILIT no longer justify its existence, consideration should be given to allowing an independent trustee to terminate the trust. Such a power will provide great flexibility to both the grantor and the trustee in the event of changed or unforeseen circumstances.

The power of a beneficiary-trustee to terminate a trust in his or her sole discretion or as a co-trustee with another trustee who does not have a substantial and adverse interest in the trust may be a power to affect the beneficial enjoyment of the trust property or its income, and could constitute a general power of appointment for estate and gift tax purposes. Accordingly, the power to terminate a trust should be held by an independent trustee.

Under common law, a spendthrift clause prevents a trust from being terminated. Hence, the trust's spendthrift clause should include language that permits the trust's early termination. If the trust contains Crummey withdrawal rights (as most ILITs do), be sure to include in the trust termination clause a prohibition of termination while a withdrawal right remains outstanding and has not lapsed. Otherwise, the IRS may argue that the withdrawal right can be unilaterally cut off by the trustee, and therefore is illusory (i.e., the withdrawal right does not enable the contribution to the trust to qualify as a present interest gift).

If the ILIT contains a marital deduction trust or a charitable remainder trust, the trustee should be prohibited from exercising its termination power in a manner that would impair the marital or charitable deduction. To induce the trustee to exercise its discretion, the trust should provide that the trustee is entitled to be held harmless and be indemnified by the trust and by the beneficiaries who benefit from the termination of the trust. Such language might read: "Prior to terminating a trust hereunder, trustee may request and shall be entitled to be held harmless and receive appropriate indemnification from the trust and the beneficiaries who are going to receive a terminating distribution."

Give the spouse and children testamentary limited powers of appointment. Although not mandatory, a testamentary limited power of appointment provides tremendous postmortem flexibility upon the death of the surviving spouse, and the subsequent deaths of the children. Because the donee of the power must be prohibited from appointing the trust property to himself or herself, his or her estate or the creditors of either, the donee's possession of the power will not, in and of itself, result in the power's inclusion in the donee's gross estate.

Coordinate ILIT with grantor's durable power of attorney. The grantor's durable power of attorney should contain gift-giving provisions and should permit the attorney-in-fact to make irrevocable gifts and transfers directly to beneficiaries and to any irrevocable trust that has been established by the grantor. This ensures that in the event of the grantor's incapacity, the trust can continue to be funded, and thus a potential lapse of the insurance policies can be avoided. Absent the agent's express authority to make gifts under the durable power of attorney (or applicable state law), the gifts to the ILIT will be challenged by the IRS as being revocable by the grantor, and subject to inclusion in the grantor's gross estate.

Coordinate ILIT's dispositive provisions with dispositive provisions of grantor's other documents. The dispositive provisions of the grantor's base estate plan—typically the grantor's revocable living trust—should be coordinated with the dispositive provisions of the ILIT. This will permit the two trusts to be merged at a later date. It is particularly important that the trustee have the authority not only to merge the trusts but also to keep separate any shares that may have different GST tax inclusion ratios or that have different starting times with respect to the application of the rule against perpetuities. The rule against perpetuities starts at the date that an irrevocable trust is established, whereas the rule against perpetuities for a revocable living trust generally starts at the time of the grantor's death.

NOTES AND QUESTIONS

1. Historically, it was a simple matter to find a bank or trust company willing to serve as the trustee of an unfunded life insurance trust. Because the trustee had little, if anything, to do while the insured was alive, the trustee's fee was nominal until the insured died. Trustees are now beginning to realize that their exposure to potential liability for managing life insurance trusts may be significantly higher than originally anticipated. Trustees may have the duty to review the status of the insurance company on a regular basis. In addition, if the policy has a high cash value, the trustee may have the duty to cash it in and invest the proceeds in a more productive manner. Accordingly, trustees may decline to serve, demand higher fees, or insist on exculpatory or indemnification provisions in the trust. See Jon J. Gallo, *Life Insurance Due Diligence for Dummies: What the Attorney Preparing a Life Insurance Trust Ought to Know*, PRAC. LAW., Sept. 1998, at 75; Agnes C. Powell, *The Need for Increased Life Insurance Due Diligence,* TR. & EST., May 1992, at 39.

2. See Stephan R. Leimberg & Thomas P. Langdon, *Insurance Planning: Who Should Be the Beneficiary and Owner?*, PROB. & PROP., July/Aug. 1996, at 19.

K. BUSINESS INTERESTS

1. CLOSELY HELD BUSINESSES—GENERALLY

Many problems arise when the owner of a closely held business interest dies. For example, the interest may be difficult to value, the family may need ready cash instead of an interest in a business, or the business may fail if the deceased was instrumental to its success. In addition, the business owner may want to reduce the estate tax liability which will result when the business interest is included in the gross estate. The business owner may use several techniques to remedy these problems.

One of the most common solutions is to use a buy-sell agreement so the deceased's interest is automatically purchased by the other business owners or the business itself. The estate then has cash rather than an unmarketable business interest. In addition, the business continues smoothly without the surviving business owners dealing with the deceased owner's estate and relatives.

Other methods the business owner may wish to consider include an I.R.C. § 303 redemption (allows a limited amount of corporate distributions to escape taxation as a dividend), a recapitalization of stock under I.R.C. § 2701 (an *estate freeze*), and deferred compensation contracts to replace the salary of the deceased business owner. In addition, the executor may elect to pay some of the federal taxes in deferred installments under I.R.C. § 6166.

NOTES AND QUESTIONS

1. How could you assure that money will be available for the surviving business owners to purchase the deceased owner's share under a buy-sell agreement?

2. For a detailed analysis of buy-sell agreements, see HOWARD M. ZARITSKY, STRUCTURING BUY-SELL AGREEMENTS: ANALYSIS WITH FORMS (1993).

3. The basics of an estate freeze have been explained as follows:

> [P]arents split the interests [of a family-owned asset such as a closely-held corporation] into an interest that will not appreciate and an interest that will. They keep the split interest that will not appreciate and transfer to their children the split interest that will. The appreciating asset thereafter will gain value in the hands of their children, free of wealth transfer taxation.

Hamlin C. King, *A Primer to the New Estate Freeze Rules,* OHIO LAW., Jan./Feb. 1991, at 20. Typically, the parents would retain control of the business with non-appreciating preferred stock while the children would receive common stock with the potential of significant appreciation. Any appreciation may then escape inclusion in the parents' estates. To accomplish an effective estate freeze, the business owner must comply with the highly technical provisions of I.R.C. §§ 2701–2704.

4. The business owner may elect to sell the business prior to death. This alleviates the estate's liquidity and valuation problems. However, the business owner may incur unanticipated income tax liability.

2. FAMILY LIMITED PARTNERSHIPS AND LIMITED LIABILITY COMPANIES

ROBERT L. MOSHMAN, COMPARING FLPS AND LLCS*

Adapted from *FLP vs. LLC & Sam Walton's FLP Estate,* The Estate Analyst, Jun. 2008.

There have been "bull markets" and "recessions" for the FLP (at least in the professional literature covering the progression of cases on point). Indeed, there has been a succession of cases honing the rules on particular nuances of FLPs every few months. Meanwhile, the LLC has evolved from "novel" to being accepted and "fundamental."

So where does that leave the estate-planning professional? Is the old faithful FLP still the arrangement of choice? Or has the family LLC taken over that role? Let's compare.

For practical purposes an estate with various real estate investments and other assets may bridge the generational gap from parents to children by establishing one of several alternatives. How does the family limited partnership (FLP) stack up against the family limited liability company (FLLC)?

---

* Reprinted with permission of Robert L. Moshman.

The FLP Revolution

The ability to a) create an FLP quickly and b) qualify a deceased partner's FLP shares for a minority discount prompted a number of practitioners to establish FLPs that truly maximized discounts despite the fact that FLPs were established only weeks prior to death. Taxable estates could be transformed overnight.

FLPs have many estate planning advantages, including:

- Simple to set up and maintain.
- Owner can remain in control as general partner.
- Ability to apportion revenues among partners in different proportion from control or percentage of ownership.
- Tried and true technique with a long history.
- At death, a partner's shares are typically entitled to minority and/or marketability discounts.

One downside is that the general partner ends up exposed to liability for the entity. To contend with this factor, the general partner can be set up as a corporation so that any liability to the general partner is trapped inside that corporation. However, that means the simplicity of the arrangement for tax purposes has been offset by all of the tax compliance attendant upon a corporation.

Sam Walton's FLP Estate

It is a classic rags-to-riches American success story. Sam Walton was 27 years old and just out of the service when he borrowed $20,000 to open a variety store. It was a Ben Franklin franchise in an Arkansas town with a population of 7,000. The year was 1945.

Flash forward 17 years to 1962. Sam and his brother had opened numerous stores and their discounting approach would change the landscape of American merchandising. Now they opened their first Wal–Mart. By the time Sam Walton died in 1992, the family business was worth billions.

In 1985, Forbes magazine estimated the Walton fortune at $20 to $25 billion. By 1998, the estimate was $48 billion. By 2006, estimates of the estate had reached $80 billion.

The families of the four Walton children each have their own fortunes totaling, collectively, in excess of $81 billion as of March, 2008 (up from $69 billion in September, 2007. (Source: *Forbes*.)

What's remarkable about this $80 billion juggernaut of wealth? It might not be nearly as large but for excellent use of a family limited partnership (FLP).

With a top estate tax rate of 55%, The Sam Walton estate could potentially have been hit with a $13.75 billion federal estate tax. How did the Walton estate avoid paying any transfer tax whatsoever?

The main reason dates back to 1953, when the business was going well, but had not yet burgeoned into the largest retailing empire in American. Sam Walton took that opportunity to create a family limited partnership that included his wife and his four children.

Walton Enterprises acquired real estate, banks, a newspaper, and various other businesses, but all of the assets were included in the partnership. Eventually, the partnership financed a variety of businesses that Sam's children wanted to develop. At his death, Sam Walton only owned 10% of the partnership. That $2.5 billion went to a marital trust for his wife, Helen. This move deferred tax since interests transferred between spouses are not subject to estate or gift tax.

Helen Walton, the widow of Sam Walton, became the world's wealthiest woman at some point. She died on April 19, 2007 and her estate of $16.4 billion will go to family-run charities over the next several years.

Although Sam and Helen Walton's estate plan took advantage of the charitable estate tax deduction, if was drafted so that all voting shares remain within the family's control. The plan balanced transfer taxation, charitable giving, business control, and the inter-generational transfer of wealth.

Obviously, it helps to have the foresight to set up a family limited partnership half a century ahead of time and have the world's biggest retail chain grow at a phenomenal rate. Once the FLP was established, the appreciation of assets took place outside of Sam Walton's estate.

Yet family businesses have benefited from family limited partnerships that were established only a short time before the principal owner's death, taking advantage of minority and marketability discounts.

The LLC Alternative

Over the past decade, however, even while significant cases were affirming the miraculous use of the FLP to provide last-minute valuation discounts to estates as a viable alternative to long-term planning, there were other cases in which FLPs were challenged.

As a result of these negative cases, some practitioners began to question whether the FLP was still a concept worth investing in, or whether the "modern" estate plan had moved on.

One widely used alternative to FLPs are LLCs. Had LLCs existed in 1953, it is possible the Walton estate might have employed them in lieu of the FLP. In a broad array of respects, the LLC or FLLC resemble the FLP:

- It is a "pass through entity" for tax purposes, just like an FLP.
- Distinct classes or tiers of ownership can be established with a management class and a non-management class.
- The transferability of assets can be limited to family members but assignability of assets can be provided for in the operating agreement.

- A creditor's sole remedy is a charging order against the entity, not the owners.
- For transfer tax purposes, an FLLC is entitled to the same minority interest and marketability discounts that apply to FLPs.

However, the LLC has several additional distinctions, some of them preferable to the FLP:

- The benefit of an LLC is revealed right in its name. It limits liability. That essential attribute places the LLC nearly on a par with a C corporation. And because the LLC addresses liability, the personal assets of all the owners of the LLC are protected from business liability. This is particularly useful where real estate assets are involved.
- An LLC does not require a general partner, so setting up a Corporation or LLC to be the general partner of the FLP is not necessary.
- Limited partners cannot participate in management. Members of an LLC are able to fully participate in management without sacrificing liability protection.
- Partnership losses such as the rental real estate loss allowance under IRC section 469 cannot be passed through to the limited partners due to the passive activity loss rules. By comparison, loss in an LLC can be passed through to members who meet the IRS definition of "active participant." Someone devoting more than 500 hours annually would qualify as an active participant.

Organizing Chaos

Both the family limited partnership and the family limited liability corporation can provide the organization of assets and asset protection that can serve as the foundation for the family's long-term financial stability and prosperity.

As with any complex plans, there are specific state rules to observe and unique family circumstances to incorporate into the plan. As opposed to selecting one or the other, it is the fine tuning of either an FLP or an FLLC that is the key to success.

Post Script

The use of an FLP or LLC for estate planning purposes must be considered a multi-dimensional and dynamic exercise.

The taxation of estates and capital gains has undergone dramatic shifts since 2008 and has not settled into a long-term pattern of rules for which taxpayers can rely on with any long-term certainty.

In addition, the creation of minority discounts for valuation purposes, whether in an FLP or LLC, can always attract scrutiny and cause new laws and regulations to correct any strategies that are too good to be true.

However, the concept of dividing up shares of a growing business among family members continues to have resilience and relevance. Modest consequences for current transfers to family members help remove assets as well as future appreciation from estates.

LOCATE

Does your state have specific legislation authorizing limited liability companies?

L. EMPLOYEE BENEFITS

NOTE

Please review Chapter 3(J).

ROBERT J. LYNN AND GRAYSON M.P. MCCOUCH, INTRODUCTION TO ESTATE PLANNING*

§§ 7.5, 7.8–7.9, pages 150–153, 156–160 (5th ed. 2004).

§ 7.5 Other Government and Private Pension Plans

Even before the Social Security Act was enacted in 1935, federal, state, and local governments as well as many businesses had already established pension plans for their employees. During World War II, creation of new "private" pension plans (plans sponsored by private corporations, or labor unions, or corporations and labor union together) was stimulated by the permissibility of extending "fringe" benefits to employees in the form of pension benefits at a time when wages were fixed or "frozen" by law.

A substantial portion of all full-time nongovernmental employees in the United States are covered by private pension plans. Many persons employed by federal and state governments are covered by government pension plans (often referred to as "civil service" pension plans). The accumulated funds of pension plans are enormous. Indeed, at times there seems to be greater public concern with the behavior and impact of pension plans as "institutional investors" in the capital markets than with their ostensible purpose of providing a reliable source of income for retired employees.

Some of the language that has become a part of the standard working vocabulary with respect to pension plans should be noted. In a traditional "defined benefit" plan, the level of pension benefits payable to retired employee is determined under a formula. For example, under a typical formula, an employee might be entitled upon retirement to receive monthly pension benefits equal to a fixed percentage of his or her average salary multiplied by the number of years of service. An important feature of a defined benefit plan is that the promised pension benefits represent an

* Reprinted with permission of Thomson Reuters.

obligation of the employer. If the amounts contributed to the plan, with any net investment gains, are insufficient to pay the promised pension benefits, the employer is liable to make up the difference. In contrast, a "defined contribution" plan does not specify any level of promised pension benefits. Instead, the plan maintains an individual account for each employee, and amounts contributed by the employer are allocated to the employees' accounts. The amount of an employee benefits depends on the balance in his or her account at retirement, including any investment gains or losses. Accordingly, a defined contribution plan places the risk of investment gain or loss squarely on the individual employee.

A "qualified" plan is one which qualifies for favorable tax treatment under the Internal Revenue Code. As an example of favorable tax treatment, contributions made by the employer on behalf of a covered employee, but neither the contributions nor the income thereon are taxable to the employee until he or she actually receives distributions from the plan. The tax incentives provided by the Internal Revenue Code for qualified plans are intended to encourage persons through so-called "Koegh" plans (named after the Congressman who sponsored the legislation).

A qualified plan generally takes the form of a trust fund which is held and administered by a trustee for the benefit of covered employees. The trustee is subject to fiduciary duties based on the traditional law of trusts, and is responsible for receiving contributions, investing the assets held in trust, and making distributions according to the terms of the plan.

There is a great variation in the employee benefit plans sponsored by federal, state, and local governments, by employers, by unions, and by employers and unions working in concert, but even so, "health" and "welfare" benefits, in addition to pension benefits, are a characteristic feature of many such plans. And so one frequently encounters the expression "pension and welfare" plans. (In this connection, it should be noted that "welfare" does not carry its common connotation of need-based public assistance. Rather, the expression "health and welfare" benefits under a private employee benefit plan usually refers to benefits other than retirement income benefits.)

§ 7.8 Distributions From Qualified Plans

The Internal Revenue Code offers substantial tax benefits for retirement savings through qualified plans. An employer who makes contributions to a qualified plan on behalf of a covered employee is entitled to an immediate income tax deduction, but the employee is not taxable on any of the plan's assets or income until he or she actually receives distributions from the plan. A qualified pension trust is exempt from tax, with the result that contributions to the trust fund and investment earnings thereon are sheltered from income tax until they are distributed from the plan.

To ensure that qualified plans fulfill their intended purpose of providing retirement benefits, the statute imposes restrictions (backed up by a

10% penalty tax) on distributions made to an employee before age 59 ½. Moreover, to prevent a defined contribution plan from serving as an open-ended tax shelter, the employee is generally required to receive at least a specified amount (the "minimum distribution") from the plan each year upon reaching age 70 ½. (In some cases, the required minimum distributions may be deferred until the employee actually retires.) Any balance remaining in the employee's account at death must be distributed to the employee's designated beneficiary or to the employee's estate within a limited period of time. I.R.C. § 401(a)(9). The minimum distribution rules do not prohibit larger or earlier distributions, if permitted by the terms of the plan; their purpose is merely to ensure that the employee's entire interest in the plan will be distributed during the employee's lifetime or within a limited period of time after death.

Under ERISA, a qualified pension plan must prohibit employees from assigning or alienating their benefits under the plan. I.R.C. § 401(a)(13). According, subject to limited exceptions, an employee's interest in a qualified plan is protected from the claims of creditors in much the same way as the interest of a beneficiary of a traditional "spendthrift" trust.

In general, an employee is free to designate a beneficiary to receive any pension benefits payable at or after the employee's death under a qualified plan and select a method of payment in accordance with the terms of the plan. As a matter of federal law, however, the options available to a married employee are constrained. Under amendments to ERISA enacted in 1984, pension benefits must generally be paid to the employee and his or her spouse in the form of a "qualified joint and survivor annuity" if the employee reaches retirement age. (If the employee dies before retirement age, survived by a spouse, the spouse is entitled to receive the pension benefits in the form of a "qualified preretirement survivor annuity.") In some cases, the surviving spouse may be entitled to receive the entire remaining benefit at the employee's death. I.R.C. § 417. The employee may designate a beneficiary other than the spouse, but only with the spouse's written consent. In effect, the surviving spouse's rights are functionally equivalent to a special elective share in the deceased employee's pension benefits. Note that the spouse must survive the statute. If the spouse dies first, the employee is free to dispose of the post-death pension benefits in any manner permitted by the terms of the plan. Moreover, the Supreme Court has held that the federal statute preempts state community property law, with the result that if the spouse dies before the employee, the spouse has no right to dispose of any interest in undistributed pension benefits. Boggs v. Boggs (1997).

§ 7.9 Individual Retirement Accounts

An individual retirement account ("IRA"), as authorized by ERISA, commonly takes the form of a savings account administered by a qualified "custodian" who invests the IRA funds in any of a board range of permissible investments selected by the owner. (An IRA can also be established in the form of an annuity administered through an insurance company). A person who has earned income and meets additional eligibility requirements can make limited annual tax-deductible contributions to an IRA. (Non-deductible contributions are also possible, but the tax benefits are correspondingly reduced.) The investment earnings on funds in an IRA accumulate free of federal income tax until they are withdrawn, resulting in tax benefits comparable to those available under qualified pension plans. The owner of an IRA can withdraw funds without penalty upon reaching age 59 ½. Upon reaching age 70 ½, he or she must begin to make annual withdrawals at least equal to the required "minimum distributions" specified by statute. Amounts withdrawn from an IRA (other than non-deductible contributions, if any) are taxed as ordinary income for federal income tax purposes. Any amount remaining in the IRA at the owner's death becomes payable to the owner's designated beneficiary, if any, or to the owner's estate. If the owner's surviving spouse is the designated beneficiary, the spouse may "roll over" funds from the decedent's IRA into the spouse's own IRA free of income tax. Any other designated beneficiary must continue to make annual withdrawals at least equal to the required minimum distributions. The minimum distribution rules establish an outer limit on the tax benefit of income deferral. The federal income tax treatment of IRAs is governed by § 408 of the Internal Revenue Code and the Regulations thereunder.

In 1997 Congress amended the Internal Revenue Code to authorize the creation of anew type of individual retirement account, known as the "Roth IRA" (after the name of the Senator who sponsored the legislation). Unlike a traditional IRA, a Roth IRA is funded with "after-tax" contributions–that is, no federal income tax deduction is allowed for contributions when they are made. However, the investment earnings on those contributions accumulate tax-free, and "qualified distributions" are completely exempt from federal income tax. Moreover, although there are restrictions on early withdrawals, the statute does not require any minimum distributions during the owner's life or after death. As a result, once contributions have been made, the Roth IRA provides potentially unlimited income tax exemption for investment earnings prior to distribution. The federal income tax treatment of Roth IRAs is governed by § 408A of the Internal Revenue Code, which sets forth detailed requirements and restrictions concerning eligibility, contributions, and distributions.

M. CHARITABLE GIFTS

TOBY EISENBERG, CHARITABLE TOOL BOX*

SAN ANTONIO ESTATE PLANNERS COUNCIL'S DOCKET CALL IN PROBATE COURT (2011).

A. INTRODUCTION

The purpose of this article is to provide an overview of many of the charitable techniques available to practitioners who encounter charitably minded clients. As such, a full discussion of each of the techniques mentioned is beyond the scope of this article. Instead, the author has attempted to provide enough detail for the practitioner to make an informed decision about which techniques might be worth exploring in more detail for any given client as well as enough of a warning about treading too deeply into unfamiliar waters. Accordingly, the practitioner would be well advised to conduct further research before seeking to implement any of the techniques described in this article.

B. BASIC CONSIDERATIONS

1. Federal Income Tax Deduction

The rules described in this article are for charitable gifts made by individuals; different rules apply for charitable gifts made by corporations or other entities.

The rules for the income tax charitable deduction are described under I.R.C. § 170.

a. Gifts of Cash

1) 50% AGI Limitation

A gift of cash to a public charity is deductible up to 50% of the donor's adjusted gross income.

2) 30% AGI Limitation

A gift of cash to a private foundation is deductible up to 30% of the donor's adjusted gross income. Likewise, the 30% limitation applies to all gifts "for the use of" any charity (i.e. required to be used by the charity in the pursuit of its charitable activities). Gifts subject to this 30% limitation are also limited to the excess of (i) 50% of adjusted gross income over (ii) total contributions to public charities subject to the 50% limitation.

b. Gifts of Property

In general, the amount deductible for property contributions to charity is the fair market value of such property, subject to the AGI limitations described below. However, deductions for gifts of appreciated property (other than "qualified appreciated stock" as defined in I.R.C. § 170(e)(5)) to private foundations and for gifts of certain types of property (e.g. inventory property, short-term capital gain property) are limited to the donor's basis in such property, subject further to the AGI limitations described below.

A gift of "qualified appreciated stock" (e.g. publicly traded securities) to a private foundation is deductible up to the fair market value of such stock.

1) 30% AGI Limitation

A gift of appreciated property to a public charity is deductible up to 30% of the donor's adjusted gross income.

2) 20% AGI Limitation

A gift of appreciated property to a private foundation or "for the use of" any charity is deductible up to 20% of the donor's AGI. Gifts subject to this 20% limitation are also limited to the excess of (i) 30% of adjusted gross income over (ii) total contributions to public charities subject to the 30% limitation.

c. Five–Year Carryforward

Excess charitable deductions (i.e. that portion of a gift to charity that exceed the AGI limitation for a particular year) may be carried forward and deducted in the succeeding five years, subject to AGI limitations for each of those years.

2. Federal Gift Tax Deduction

I.R.C. § 2522(a) allows a gift tax charitable deduction for gifts made to qualifying charities. The entire gift is deductible since there are no percentage limitations as with the income tax charitable deduction.

Generally, the gift tax charitable deduction is available only for outright gifts of cash or property, whether such gifts are made during lifetime or at death. Split-interest gifts do not qualify for the deductions unless a specific exception is made in the Internal Revenue Code, which currently authorizes the following techniques: charitable gift annuities, gifts of fractional interests in artwork or jewelry, gifts of remainder interests in real property, conservation easements, charitable gift annuities, pooled income funds, charitable remainder trusts, and charitable lead trusts.

3. Federal Estate Tax Deduction

I.R.C. § 2055 allows an estate tax charitable deduction for gifts made to qualifying charities. As with the gift tax charitable deduction, there are no percentage limitations for deductibility, so the entire gift is deductible.

Split-interest gifts do not qualify for the estate tax charitable deduction unless in one of the forms listed above under "Federal Gift Tax Deduction."

The estate tax charitable deduction is reduced by the amount of tax or expenses allocated against the gift by will or under local law.

C. CHARITABLE ENTITIES

In order to understand the variety of charitable techniques available, the practitioner must first understand the range of charitable entities to which tax deductible charitable gifts may be made. Even if never asked to establish any of these entities, the practitioner should have at least some familiarity with them in order to provide sound advice.

At the risk of oversimplification, the various rules governing different charitable entities can be said to revolve around two central issues: (1) how much control do the founders of the organization retain over the assets they contribute to the organization, and (2) whether the organization conducts charitable activities or merely accumulates assets for later distribution to organizations that conduct charitable activities. The centrality of these issues can be seen in the following descriptions of the various charitable entities.

1. Public Charities

Public charities are those organizations that are responsive to the general needs of the public and/or are dependent upon public support for their operations. Public charities are those entities meeting the requirements of I.R.C. § 501(c)(3) and the requirements described in the provisions of I.R.C. § 170(b)(1)(A)(i-iv) or 509(a)(2–4), including churches, universities, hospitals, medical research organizations, and governmental units. Public charities conduct charitable activities, accept contributions from a wide range of donors, and are governed by directors whose contributions to the organization (if any) are a miniscule portion of the overall assets of the organization. As such, public charities are not subject to the excise taxes and self-dealing prohibitions applicable to private foundations (see below). Furthermore, contributions to public charities are subject to the higher AGI limitations (described above).

2. Private Foundations

Private foundations are those organizations that meet the requirements of I.R.C. § 501(c)(3) but do not meet the other requirements of a public charity. See I.R.C. § 509(a). Private foundations are typically set up by a donor who wants to receive current charitable deductions, build a legacy, accumulate assets for future significant gifts to other charities, while also maintaining control over such assets within the family. The cost of retained control over the assets contributed by the donor is a set of restrictions (e.g. excise taxes and self-dealing prohibitions) applicable to private foundations but not public charities. The effect of these restrictions is to limit the founders' flexibility with respect to certain assets and/or estate planning techniques that may be used in tandem with the private foundation.

Donors who establish private foundations may chose to utilize either charitable trusts or nonprofit corporations. This choice is primarily a matter of state law rather than federal tax law, since both entities receive the same tax-favored status offered to all private foundations. Most donors find that the added flexibility of nonprofit corporations under state law, combined with lower fiduciary standards, make them the more favorable choice. However, charitable trusts are difficult to change without judicial approval, an advantage some clients find appealing if they do not want their family to be able to modify the charitable goals of the private foundation.

a. Operating Foundations

Operating foundations are private foundations that conduct one or more charitable activities (as does a public charity) rather than simply making grants to other charitable organizations. Operating foundations are treated as public charities for purposes of the income tax charitable deduction (e.g. the higher AGI limitations). However, because the founders are permitted to retain management flexibility over contributed assets, operating foundations remain subject to the excise taxes and self-dealing prohibitions applicable to all private foundations.

b. Nonoperating Foundations

Nonoperating foundations are private foundations that do not conduct any charitable activities and exist merely to accumulate assets for the future benefit of other organizations that do conduct charitable activities. Nonoperating foundations are subject to the lower AGI limitations as well as the excise taxes and self-dealing prohibitions applicable to all private foundations.

3. Communities Foundations

Communities foundations offer many advantages for donors who are charitably minded, do not have particular charities they want to benefit, and are willing to give up control over contributed assets. Because communities foundations are funded by various donors, each of whom gives up significant (if not complete) control, gifts are treated as made to a public charity and the excise taxes and self-dealing prohibitions do not apply.

Communities foundations provide several useful services and forms of giving that are typically under-appreciated by donors and practitioners. Among other benefits, the donor need not worry with the administration of the ongoing funds maintained at the community foundation (e.g. tax compliance, corporate records, minimum distributions, etc.), a luxury not available to founders of private foundations unless they hire officers or employees. Some of the forms of giving offered by communities foundations are described below, all of which qualify as gifts to a public charity.

a. Donor Advised Funds

The donor creates a fund within the community foundation and makes non-binding recommendations as to how the fund assets are granted to other charities.

b. Endowed Funds

If the donor has a particular charity it wants to benefit but has concerns about how it might manage or conserve its assets, the donor can create an endowed fund for the exclusive benefit that charity. The community foundation manages the fund and can divert the fund assets to a different charity if the original charity closes its doors.

c. Field of Interest Funds

The donor specifies a particular area of concern, such as the arts, education, social services, or health. The field of interest can be narrow (e.g. childhood leukemia research) or broad (e.g. cancer research in general), and the practitioner or community foundation helps the donor to define an appropriate scope. The fund managers at the community foundation will select the most appropriate grant recipients within the field of interest, based upon the strongest grant applications received by the managers.

d. Scholarship Funds

The donor makes contributions to a scholarship fund and works with the community foundation to design the scholarship criteria and application process as well as to select an advisory committee (which may include the donor).

e. Unrestricted Funds

The donor makes a contribution to the community foundation and leaves total discretion to the foundation's management to direct funds to meet the most pressing needs and problems of the local community. Donors who feel a particular debt of gratitude to the community in which they made their fortune often find these funds appealing.

4. Supporting Organizations

Supporting organizations must be organized for the exclusive benefit of one or more public charities. Furthermore, the entity must require the participation of its public charity in the management of the supporting organization and may not be controlled by the donor or other disqualified persons. Gifts to supporting organizations are treated as gifts to a public charity, and the excise taxes and self-dealing rules applicable to private foundations do not apply.

5. Pooled Income Funds

A pooled income fund is a trust that is maintained by a public charity with the income interest distributed to the various donors who have contributed property to the trust. The charity hires a money manager to manage and maintain the fund. The various donors divide the income earned by the fund proportionately.

The donor receives income and gift tax charitable deductions equal to the fair market value of the property transferred to the fund less the present value of the income interest retained by the donor. As with outright gifts of appreciated property to a public charity, the donor does not recognize any capital gain upon contribution, nor does the charity recognize gain because of its tax-exempt status. The donor must recognize all income payments from the trust as taxable income in the year such payments are received. Accordingly, a pooled income fund functions very much like a charitable remainder trust (described below) but without the range of options available for the charitable remainder trust or the costs of establishing and maintaining it.

Although the pooled income fund could be considered a charitable technique as much as it is considered an entity, it is listed here as an organization since most practitioners and donors think of the pooled income fund as an existing entity to which a donor may make contributions. Charitable lead trusts and charitable remainder trusts are likewise often thought of in terms of both techniques and entities; however, because the practitioner will be responsible for creating such arrangements, they have been included in this article as techniques and discussed at more length below.

D. OVERVIEW OF BASIC TECHNIQUES

1. Outright Gifts

a. Lifetime

A donor may give cash or property to a qualified charity during the donor's lifetime. Such gifts are eligible for the income tax and gift tax charitable deductions and remove the property permanently from the donor's estate.

b. Testamentary

A donor may give cash or property to a qualified charity at the donor's death (e.g. by will or living trust). Such gifts are eligible for the estate tax charitable deduction only–neither the donor nor the donor's estate receives an income tax deduction for the gift. However, all items of gross income of an estate paid to or permanently set aside for a charity in accordance with the terms of the decedent's will are allowed as a deduction in the year such income is recognized by the estate (see I.R.C. § 642(c)).

c. Pledges

If a donor makes a pledge to a charity during lifetime and such pledge is not satisfied prior to the donor's death, the pledge does not qualify for the income, gift, or estate tax charitable deduction. However, if enforceable under local law, the pledge is deductible under I.R.C. § 2053 as claim against the donor's estate.

2. Charitable Gift Annuities

Like the pooled income fund, a charitable gift annuity provides the same general economic and tax benefits as a charitable remainder trust. The charitable gift annuity is a contract between the donor and a charity whereby the donor contributes cash or property to the charity (usually appreciated property) in exchange for guaranteed annuity payments to the donor or other annuitant for the remainder of such annuitant's lifetime. Because the donor exchanges the cash or property for a less valuable annuity interest (i.e. for less than adequate consideration), the contract is considered a bargain sale and thus characterized as a part-gift, part sale transaction.

The donor receives income and gift tax charitable deductions equal to the value of the gift component of the transaction–the excess of the value of the property contributed over the present value of the annuity retained (or given to another annuitant). Additionally, because the contract is a bargain sale, the donor must recognize capital gain on part of the transaction. The donor must allocate basis between the gift component and the sale component, meaning that the donor may not use the donor's entire basis in the property against the sales proceeds. However, a part of each annuity payment received by the annuitant in future years will be free from income tax until the annuitant's original life expectancy is reached.

If the annuity payments are to be made to someone other than the donor, the present value of such annuity payments will be a taxable gift and must be reported on the donor's gift tax return. If such beneficiary is the donor's spouse, the annuity should qualify for the marital deduction.

3. Gift of Fractional Interest in Artwork and Jewelry

A contribution of an undivided fractional interest in the donor's entire interest in personal property is eligible for the income, gift, and estate tax deductions. The gift must consist of a fraction or percentage of each and every substantial right the donor has in the property and must extend over the entire term of the donor's interest in the property. The charity becomes a tenant in common with the donor with respect to such property and therefore has all of the rights and responsibilities associated with such status, including possession, dominion, control, and duty to contribute towards maintenance expenses.

Technically, any personal property may be used in this technique, though the most common property acceptable to both the donor and a charity is artwork and/or jewelry that would be of interest to a viewing public.

The right to possession of the property must be allocated on a pro-rata basis, usually based on time, or else the IRS may disallow the deduction (even retroactively). If the IRS believes there is an implied agreement between the charity and the donor that the charity will not use the property during the donor's lifetime, the IRS will recharacterize the transaction as a gift of a remainder interest in personal property, which does not qualify for any charitable deduction.

4. Gift of Remainder Interest In Real Property

A contribution of a remainder interest in a personal residence or farm is eligible for income, gift, and estate tax charitable deductions. The residence need not be a principal residence; it can be a condominium, cooperative apartment, farm, mountain home, beach house, or other residential property.

The donor retains the current use and enjoyment of the property during the donor's lifetime (or for a term of years) while also obtaining a current income tax charitable deduction for the present value of the remainder interest passing to charity. The donor will also be entitled to additional charitable deductions if the donor makes capital improvements to the property (such as add-ons, new heating system, new barn, etc.).

This technique is also a way to avoid ancillary probate of real property located in a foreign jurisdiction. Since the property passes to charity immediately upon the death of the donor by operation of law, such property is not part of the donor's probate estate.

5. Conservation Easements

Qualified conservation contributions are eligible for the income, gift, and estate tax charitable deductions. I.R.C. § 170(h) defines a qualified conservation contribution as a contribution of a qualified real property interest to a qualified organization exclusively for conservation purposes, though I.R.C. §§ 2055 and 2522 do not require such transfers to be exclusively for conservation purposes. This technique is not a traditional easement but rather a permanent restriction on the use of the subject property. Examples of such easements include the preservation of an historical building, precluding the development of farmland while permitting continued farming, or protecting forest land. This technique is useful when the donor wants to restrict future usage of the property while retaining the current use and enjoyment of the property.

The amount of the charitable deduction for income, gift, and estate tax purposes is based upon a "before and after" test since there is no "market" for property restrictions. Thus, the value of the deduction is equal to the decrease in value of the real property by the placement of the restriction on the property. Rev. Rul. 73–339 (1973–2 C.B. 68).

6. Tax–Free Distributions From IRA's to Qualified Charities

Under current law, individuals age 70½ or older can direct that distributions up to $100,000 be made in 2011 to one or more qualified charities from their IRAs. Such distributions are not included in the individual's taxable income, though they do count towards the satisfaction of any required minimum distributions for the year. This means that an individual who does not itemize deductions or who has excess charitable contribution carryovers can greatly benefit by taking such distributions since doing so effectively excludes income that would otherwise be includible had the individual taken the $100,000 as a minimum distribution.

These tax-free distributions can be made from traditional IRAs (including "inherited IRAs") and from Roth IRAs, though they really only make sense from traditional IRAs.

Not all charities are considered "qualified charities" for purposes of the rule. Specifically, an entity is eligible only if it is described in IRC § 170(b)(1)(A) and is not a donor advised fund or a supporting organization. Thus, for example, private foundations, charitable remainder trusts, and charitable lead trusts are not "qualified charities."

The current rule is an extension of a prior law (IRC § 408(d)(8)) that expired at the end of 2009 but was extended for the 2010 and 2011 tax years. The extension is set to expire at the end of 2011 unless Congress acts to extend it further.

7. Beneficiary Designations

a. Life Insurance Beneficiary Designation

An overinsured donor with charitable intentions may designate a charity as the beneficiary of a life insurance policy. Such life insurance proceeds will still be includible in a decedent's estate unless someone else (e.g. a properly drafted life insurance trust) owns the incidents of ownership. However, the donor may claim an estate tax charitable deduction for the full amount passing to charity pursuant to the beneficiary designation.

Alternatively, if the policy has a significant cash value (e.g. a whole life policy in effect for many years), the donor could assign the policy during the donor's lifetime so that the charity will own the incidents of ownership. The charity can then decide whether to surrender the policy and take the cash surrender value or continue to pay premiums in order to receive the death benefit upon the donor's death. In either case, the donor may claim an income tax charitable deduction equal to the present value of the policy (approximately equal to the cash surrender value).

b. IRA, 401(k), and Other Retirement Plan Benefits

401(k)'s and traditional IRAs, among other retirement plan benefits with tax deferral mechanisms, are subject both to income tax and estate tax upon the owner's death. Even though the income tax on such assets may not be immediately due upon the owner's death because the minimum distribution rules allow for continued deferral, such assets will ultimately be subject to income tax. Simply put, given the choice between cashing out a $1 million brokerage account (which gets a step-up in basis at death) and cashing out a $1 million traditional IRA (which will be subject to income tax), a non-charity beneficiary would obviously chose the brokerage account. However, a charity would not have any preference between the two accounts since no income tax will be due from either account if left to a charity at the owner's death.

By designating a charity as the beneficiary of a 401(k) or other similar account, the donor will avoid both estate and income tax on the account. Assuming a 48% estate tax and a 35% income tax, the taxes on the 401(k) could be enormous (upwards of $700,000). Of course this assumes the IRA is cashed out and income tax is triggered immediately (rather than deferred over the lifetime(s) of the non-charity beneficiaries according to the minimum distribution rules).

It is worth mentioning that a better plan in some cases would be to leave the $1 million 401(k) to children, $1 million brokerage account to charity, and pay estate taxes on the 401(k) from other assets in the donor's estate. The estate tax charitable deduction would be the same whether the 401(k) or the brokerage account is left to charity (i.e. $1 million), thus resulting in the same estate taxes under either plan. Assuming the estate taxes are paid out of other assets in either plan, the children would either receive $1 million in a tax deferred account or $1 million in a standard brokerage account (perhaps held in trust). If the children are likely to take large distributions and spend their inheritance, they would be better off with the brokerage account. However, if the children are likely to continue deferring the income tax over their lifetime (particularly if they are younger children), the 401(k) account may ultimately produce more tax savings.

If the donor wishes to replace the wealth for the donor's descendants (who would otherwise receive the assets if not passed to charity), the donor could purchase a life insurance policy through an irrevocable life insurance trust. The taxes that will be saved by leaving the 401(k) to charity can be used to pay the premiums on the policy. However, see "Life Insurance As Wealth Replacement" under the discussion about CRT's below.

The donor should be careful not to use a 401(k) or similar account either (1) to satisfy a charitable pledge made during lifetime or (2) to fund a charitable pecuniary gift made at death under the donor's will or living trust. In either situation, the pledge or the pecuniary gift would be treated as an enforceable claim against the donor's estate. The satisfaction of such a claim with a 401(k) or similar asset (i.e. assets with untaxed income, known as "income in respect of a decedent") would arguably trigger deemed taxable income to the estate.

E. CHARITABLE REMAINDER TRUSTS (CRT's)

A charitable remainder trust (CRT) is a split-interest trust in which one or more non-charity beneficiaries receive a lead interest in the form of annuity or unitrust payments (described below) for the donor's lifetime or a term of years, with any remaining property passing to one or more charities at the end of the trust term. The donor establishes the trust by transferring cash or other property to the trust and establishing its terms, including naming the trustee and specifying the beneficiaries.

If the donor retains the lead interest, no taxable gift is made at the time the CRT is established. However, if the lead interest is transferred to one or more of the donor's family members, the present value of the lead interest is a taxable gift made by the donor at the time the trust is established. CRT's are particularly attractive when interest rates are high because of the mechanics of how the present value of the lead interest is calculated. The present value of the remainder interest essentially reflects growth of the trust assets at the assumed interest rate under I.R.C. § 7520. The value of the lead interest is essentially what is left after subtracting the value of the remainder interest from the total value of the assets transferred to the trust. Thus, if the assumed rate is high, the present value of the remainder interest will also be high and thus the value of the lead interest will be low.

The lead interest payable to charity must be in the form of annuity or unitrust payments and may not simply be an income interest. If the lead interest were structured so that a non-charity beneficiary would receive all the income of the trust, the trustee would be able to manage the assets so as to maximize income (for the donor's family) and minimize the long-term growth of the assets ultimately passing to the charity. While the trustee has fiduciary duties to both the lead and remainder beneficiaries, a wide degree of discretion would be permissible. The end result would be a technique susceptible to abuse, with very little correlation between the amount of the charitable deduction and the amount actually passing to charity. By requiring an annuity or unitrust interest, Congress has ensured that donors would only receive charitable deductions for amounts very likely passing to charity.

1. CRAT's

A charitable remainder annuity trust (CRAT) is a CRT in which the annual payments to the non-charitable beneficiary are in the form of a fixed annuity. The annuity is expressed in terms of a fixed dollar amount or a fixed percentage of the fair market value of the assets on the date the trust is established. Thus, regardless of how the trust assets appreciate or depreciate, the amount passing to the non-charity beneficiary is fixed. In other words, the charity alone, as the remainderman, participates in the appreciation or depreciation of the trust assets. If the trust assets grow faster than the I.R.C. § 7520 rate, more wealth passes to the charity than what was calculated at the time the trust was created. Of course, if the assets depreciate significantly, the charity may not receive anything at all.

2. CRUT's

A charitable remainder unitrust (CRUT) is a CRT in which the annual payments to the non-charity beneficiary are in the form of a fixed unitrust. The unitrust is expressed in terms of a fixed percentage of the fair market value of the assets revalued on the same day each year of the trust term. Thus, the amount paid to charity each year increases or decreases as the assets appreciate or depreciate each year. In other words, both the non-charity beneficiary and the charity participate in the appreciation or depreciation of the trust assets.

3. NIOCRUT's

A net income only charitable remainder unitrust (NIOCRUT) is a CRT in which the annual payments are in the form of the lesser of (1) a fixed unitrust or (2) the net income for the year. Even though the annual payments could essentially amount to an income interest (which is not a qualified form of payment), the NIOCRUT still qualifies for the income, gift, and estate tax charitable deductions since there is no potential for abuse. The danger associated with an income interest–that the trustee will invest trust assets to produce maximum income to the detriment of long-term growth for the charitable remainderman–simply is not present in the NIOCRUT. Instead, only the charity (and not the non-charity beneficiary) stands to gain since small annual payments to the non-charity beneficiary mean more assets accumulating for the charitable remainderman. However, the donor gets the same charitable deduction with a NIOCRUT that the donor would get for a CRUT with the same unitrust percentage. Thus, while the charitable remainderman of a NIOCRUT may get even more wealth at the end of the trust term than it would with a CRUT, the donor is not able to claim a higher deduction.

This form of CRT is virtually never used because it does not provide any additional benefit to the donor or the donor's heirs, and if the donor wishes to provide additional benefits to charity, the donor simply raises the unitrust percentage so that the donor can claim a higher charitable deduction. Thus, while the practitioner may never utilize the NIOCRUT, it is described in this outline in order to set the stage for a much more commonly used technique–the NIMCRUT (described below).

4. NIMCRUT's

A net income make-up charitable remainder unitrust (NIMCRUT) is a NIOCRUT (described above) in which any excess income in a particular year may be used to make-up for years in which the income was less than the unitrust amount. Thus, if in year 1 the unitrust amount is $100,000 but the net income is only $30,000, the non-charity beneficiary would receive only $30,000 (a difference of $70,000). Then, if in year 2, the unitrust amount is $110,000 but the net income is $140,000, the non-charity beneficiary will receive $140,000, calculated as follows: the NIO-CRUT amount of $110,000 (since the unitrust was the less than the net income), plus a $30,000 "make-up" for the $70,000 deficit in year 1 (since the total payout cannot be more than the amount of net income in the current year). Likewise, if in year 3 the unitrust amount is $120,000 but the net income is $200,000, the non-charity beneficiary will receive $160,000, calculated as follows: the NIOCRUT amount of $120,000 (since the unitrust was the less than the net income), plus a "make-up" amount equal to the remaining $40,000 of the $70,000 deficit in year 1.

The economics of the NIMCRUT can be very powerful if the trust assets are managed appropriately, thereby giving the non-charity beneficiary a mechanism for deferring income tax. In the early years, the trust assets are invested in long-term growth assets and thus produce little or no income. The non-charity beneficiary receives little or no annual payments but accrues a large "make up" amount for future distributions. Then, in the later years of the trust term, the trust assets are invested in high-yield assets, producing income well in excess of the unitrust amount. The non-charity beneficiary cashes in on the "make up" accruals and receives large distributions from the trust. In the early years, little or no income tax will be due even though the non-charity beneficiary essentially "accrues" income to be distributed to such beneficiary in later years (if the trust yield is high enough in those later years). The receipt of actual distributions in later years (e.g. during retirement) triggers income tax to the non-charity beneficiary.

As with the NIOCRUT, the NIMCRUT entitles the donor to the same income, gift, and estate tax charitable deductions as the donor would receive for a CRUT with the same unitrust percentage.

5. Income Tax Considerations

a. Sizable Deduction in 1st Year

If the CRT is established during the donor's lifetime, the donor will receive a sizeable income tax charitable deduction in the year the CRT is established. The deduction will be based upon the present value of the remainder interest passing to charity, as determined by a complex calculation taking into account the I.R.C. § 7520 rate (i.e. assumed rate of growth) and the annuity or unitrust percentage.

However, neither the donor nor the donor's estate will receive an income tax deduction if the CRT is created as a testamentary gift.

b. Tax–Exempt Status

CRT's are tax-exempt entities for federal income tax purposes (assuming no unrelated business taxable income), one of the primary advantages of CRT's. Thus, a donor may transfer appreciated stock to a CRT, which then sells the stock without triggering capital gain for either the donor or the CRT.

c. Annuity Payments Taxable to Grantor

The sizeable income tax deduction in the first year plus the ability to sell appreciated stock without recognizing capital gain provides the donor with a "double" deduction for income tax purposes. However, all payments received by the donor (or other non-charity beneficiary) are taxable to the donor (or other non-charity beneficiary) in the year received. Essentially, then, only the non-recognition of capital gain is a permanent tax benefit. The deduction in the first year serves as an upfront deduction, allowing the donor to defer income recognition until annual payments are actually received. Of course, the deduction can only be used to offset income in the year the CRT is created and during the following five-year carryforward period. Thus, if a NIMCRUT is used and little or no income is generated by the trust in the early years of the trust term, the donor's upfront deduction will be wasted, unless of course the donor has other income (e.g. compensation such as a large bonus).

6. Marital Deduction Considerations

If the donor wishes to establish a trust with the donor's spouse as the lead beneficiary and a charity as the remainderman, the practitioner must take great care to ensure the lead interest (i.e. the spouse's interest) qualifies for the marital deduction. The practitioner may make the trust a QTIP trust (i.e. all income to the spouse for the spouse's lifetime with no other beneficiaries during the spouse's lifetime) with the remainder interest passing to charity. However, a QTIP trust will not qualify as a CRT, and thus none of the income tax benefits of a CRT will apply. The QTIP trust will be includible in the spouse's estate but will be offset by an estate tax charitable deduction since the property will pass to charity. Additionally, principal may be invaded for the benefit of the spouse.

Alternatively, the donor could establish a qualified CRT in which (1) the spouse is the only non-charity beneficiary and (2) the trust meets the requirements for a CRT. As a CRT, all of the income tax benefits described above will apply. However, the spouse may not receive any distributions other than the annuity or unitrust payments according to the CRT terms. Thus, the principal of the trust may not be invaded for the benefit of the spouse. Finally, the private foundation restrictions (including self-dealing prohibitions) will apply to the CRT, though they would not apply to a QTIP with the remainder passing to charity.

7. Life Insurance As Wealth Replacement

If the donor desires to take advantage of the tax benefits of a CRT but does not wish to deplete assets ultimately passing to descendants, the donor could create an irrevocable life insurance trust, using the tax savings from the CRT to pay all or part of the premiums on the life insurance policy. The insurance trust, if properly designed and drafted, would pass wealth to the donor's descendants free of estate or gift taxes.

Many donors and practitioners find the combination of a CRT and an insurance trust to be a practical way to benefit charity without taking too much wealth away from the donor's descendants. However, if the donor outlives the donor's life expectancy, the funds used to purchase the insurance policy would likely have yielded a better result if invested in a mutual fund (for example) or used to fund a different estate planning technique (such as a grantor retained annuity trust or a simple gift trust). In other words, there is no greater reason to invest in a life insurance policy because a CRT is established than if one were not established—the benefits of life insurance are the same with or without the creation of the CRT.

What is appealing about combining an insurance trust with a CRT is the fact that the donor can point to the insurance trust as a tangible step taken to ensure that the CRT does not deplete the inheritance of the donor's descendants. Even if the donor's descendants may ultimately be better off if the insurance trust were not used, the mere fact that the donor can "see" the donor's descendants' inheritance remaining roughly unchanged can be of great comfort. Of course, the goal of the practitioner should not be to sell one technique (i.e. a CRT) by enhancing its appeal with another (i.e. an insurance trust). However, making sophisticated techniques easily understandable for clients who stand to benefit greatly from them ultimately serves the client's interests best and can separate good estate planners from great ones.

F. CHARITABLE LEAD TRUSTS (CLT's)

A charitable lead trust (CLT) is a split-interest trust in which one or more charities receive a lead interest in the form of annuity or unitrust payments (described below) for the donor's lifetime or a term of years, with any remaining property passing to one or more non-charity beneficiaries at the end of the trust term. The donor establishes the trust by transferring cash or other property to the trust and establishing its terms, including naming the trustee and specifying the beneficiaries.

The CLT is basically a mirror image of the CRT–the essential difference between the two is whether the charity is the lead beneficiary (CLT) or the remainder beneficiary (CRT). The economics and tax consequences of the two techniques are thus based on very similar principles.

The present value of the remainder interest passing to non-charitable beneficiaries is a taxable gift made by the donor at the time the trust is established. CLT's are particularly attractive when interest rates are low because the present value of the remainder interest essentially reflects growth of the trust assets at the I.R.C. § 7520. Thus, if the assumed rate is low, the present value of the remainder interest will also be low.

The lead interest payable to charity must be in the form of annuity or unitrust payments and may not simply be an income interest. As with the CRT, if the lead interest were structured so that a charity would receive all the income of the trust, the trustee would have wide discretion to manage the assets in favor of the donor's family and to the detriment of income passing to the charity. Accordingly, Congress saw fit to curb such potential abuse by disallowing the use of an income interest as the lead interest.

1. CLAT's

A charitable lead annuity trust (CLAT) is a CLT in which the annual payments to charity are in the form of a fixed annuity. The annuity is expressed in terms of a fixed dollar amount or a fixed percentage of the fair market value of the assets on the date the trust is established. Thus, regardless of how the trust assets appreciate or depreciate, the amount passing to charity is fixed. In other words, the remaindermen alone participate in the appreciation or depreciation of the trust assets. If the trust assets grow faster than the I.R.C. § 7520 rate, more wealth passes to the remaindermen (usually the donor's family) than what was calculated at the time the trust was created. Of course, if the assets depreciate significantly, the remaindermen may not receive anything at all. The CLAT technique therefore allows the donor the opportunity to leverage the donor's gift tax or estate tax exemption to transfer more wealth to the donor's descendants than could be transferred by outright gift. If the trustee hits a "home run" with the trust assets, the remaindermen stand to benefit greatly.

2. CLUT's

A charitable lead unitrust (CLUT) is a CLT in which the annual payments to charity are in the form of a fixed unitrust. The unitrust is expressed in terms of a fixed percentage of the fair market value of the assets revalued on the same day each year of the trust term. Thus, the amount paid to charity each year increases or decreases as the assets appreciate or depreciate each year. In other words, both the charity and the remaindermen participate in the appreciation or depreciation of the trust assets. As with a CLAT, if the trust assets grow faster than the I.R.C. § 7520 rate, more wealth passes to the remaindermen (usually the donor's family) than what was calculated at the time the trust was created. However, not all of the appreciation accrues to the benefit of the remaindermen since it will also increase the annual payments made to charity. If the assets depreciate, even if they depreciation dramatically, the remaindermen will almost certainly still receive something from the trust since the annual payments to charity in the later years would also decrease dramatically. The CLUT technique therefore allows the donor some opportunity to leverage the donor's gift tax or estate tax exemption, though the lever is smaller than that for the CLAT technique.

3. Income Tax Considerations

CLT's may be structured either as grantor trusts or nongrantor trusts, with very different income tax results that dramatically affect how the CLT is utilized.

a. Taxation as Grantor Trust

If the CLT is structured as a grantor trust, the donor will be entitled to an upfront income tax charitable deduction equal to the present value of the charitable lead interest. The donor will then be required to include the income and capital gains generated by the trust assets on the donor's individual income tax return. Of course, because the donor has already received an upfront charitable deduction, the donor will not receive annual deductions for amounts actually paid to charity. If the donor has sufficient income in the year of the gift and the five subsequent years that the excess charitable deduction may be used and/or carried forward, the deduction will be useful to shield income from taxation.

b. Taxation as Non–Grantor Trust

If the CLT is structured as a nongrantor trust, the donor will not receive any income tax charitable deduction in the first year or any subsequent year. However, by transferring assets to the CLT, the donor effectively shifts income to the CLT which is able to claim a charitable deduction for the full amount paid to charity each year. The CLT is not subject to any AGI limitations. For the donor who is concerned about maximizing the donor's income tax charitable deduction (i.e. concerned with AGI limitations), shifting income off of the donor's individual tax return to a nongrantor CLT effectively allows the donor a 100% income tax deduction for amounts paid to charity by the CLT.

c. Upfront Deduction vs. Annual Deductions

Unless the donor has an unusually large amount of income in the year the CLT is established, taking an upfront deduction will likely result in a charitable deduction that may not be entirely utilized the year of the gift or the following 5 years that the excess deduction may be carried forward. Most donors find that a nongrantor CLT provides the best income tax results, allowing them in effect to assign income to a trust that may take a dollar for dollar charitable deduction (i.e. not subject to AGI limitations).

4. Zero–Gift CLAT's

A zero-gift CLAT maximizes the leveraging of the donor's gift tax exemption. The donor sets the annuity payments to charity high enough so that the present value of the charitable lead interest is equal to (or almost equal to) the full value of the assets contributed to the trust. The value of the gift passing to the remaindermen for gift tax purposes is thus zero (or nearly zero), meaning none (or very little) of the donor's gift tax exemption is utilized. The trust assets need only appreciate slightly faster than the I.R.C. § 7520 rate for the remaindermen to receive assets at the end of the trust term. If I.R.C. § 7520 rate is low (e.g. 3.8% in March 2004) and the trust assets appreciate rapidly, the effect will be a substantial gift to the donor's family free of any transfer tax costs (i.e. payment of gift tax or use of gift tax exemption). Combining this technique with discounted assets (such as a limited partnership interest) will increase the likelihood that the trust assets will outperform the I.R.C. § 7520 rate.

5. Zero–Gift CLUT's?

It should be noted that a zero-gift CLUT (or near zero gift CLUT) is technically possible but requires a much higher payout rate than does a zero-gift CLAT. The chances that any assets would be remaining at the end of the trust term are thus much lower than they would be for a zero-gift CLAT. However, if the donor is willing to use some of the donor's gift tax or estate tax exemption to fund the CLT, the CLUT payout rate necessary to produce a $1 million taxable gift (i.e. the gift tax exemption amount) is not much higher than the CLAT payout rate to produce a $1 million taxable gift. While the zero-gift CLAT usually makes more sense for lifetime gifts because of the up-side potential to "hit a home run," a CLUT with a small taxable gift usually makes more sense for testamentary gifts where the goal is to minimize or even eliminate estate taxes while passing wealth both to charity and family (as discussed below at "Lifetime vs. Testamentary CLT's").

6. Generation–Skipping Transfer Tax Considerations

A less beneficial rule applies to the allocation of the donor's generation-skipping transfer (GST) tax exemption to CLAT's than the rule applied to CLUT's, making CLAT's less favorable for transferring wealth to grandchildren or other skip persons. Essentially, the donor may allocate GST exemption to a CLUT based upon the present value of the remainder interest at the time the trust is established. By contrast, the allocation of GST exemption to a CLAT is not effective until the end of the trust term (i.e. after appreciation of assets has already occurred), meaning that the CLAT may not be used to leverage the GST exemption.

Because of the dramatic upside potential of CLAT's for gift and estate tax purposes, it appears Congress has determined that allowing leverage of the GST exemption would simply be too big of a carrot to fit the policy of encouraging charitable giving.

7. Use of Family Limited Partnership Interests

a. Discounts Available

Family limited partnerships have been used in estate planning as a vehicle for pooling family assets, as well as transferring wealth to younger generations while retaining centralized control, usually at the older generation. Because of the control and transfer restrictions typically placed on limited partnership interests, such interests usually receive significant valuation discounts (e.g. between 25% and 40%, depending on several factors). The effect of such discounts on CLT's is to increase the chances that the trust assets will not be depleted at the end of the trust term, thereby passing wealth to the donor's family.

Assuming a donor creates a zero-gift CLAT with a 25% limited partnership interest in a partnership holding $4 million in assets, the donor will thus transfer $1 million of wealth to the CLAT (i.e. 25% x $4 million = $1 million). However, assuming the control and transfer restrictions in the partnership agreement result in a 30% discount, the fair market value of the 25% limited partnership interest will be only $700,000. If the I.R.C. § 7520 rate is 3.8% and the trust term is twenty years, the annuity amount necessary to "zero-out" the gift will be 7.23% of the initial fair market value of the trust assets or $50,610 per year (7.23% x $700,000 = $50,610). But, the assets held in the partnership need only grow at 5.061% in order to meet the annuity requirement (5.061% x $1,000,000 = $50,610). To put it another way, the CLT need only beat 70% of the I.R.C. § 7520 rate or 2.66% (3.8% x 70% = 2.66%) in order to ensure assets will remain in the trust at the end of the trust term.

b. Separate CLT's For Each Beneficiary

By establishing a single CLT for each child, the donor may utilize a single family limited partnership to manage assets and fund the CLT's. Transferring a 75% (or even 99%) limited partnership interest to a single CLT will likely enable the trustee of the CLT to determine who the general partner of the partnership will be and thus indirectly control the assets of the partnership. This is because most partnership agreements rightly allow a super-majority of limited partners (e.g. 70%) to remove and replace a general partner (to do otherwise is potentially too aggressive for valuation discount purposes). The enhanced control resulting from the right to remove the general partner most certainly would reduce the valuation discount applicable to the limited partnership interest. If the donor has at least two children, establishing two or more CLT's will entail that no CLT will own a 50% or more limited partnership interest, thereby maximizing the lack of control discount applicable to each interest.

c. Separate Partnership for CLT's

The family limited partnership used to establish the CLT's should be a separate partnership so that it can have its own investment goals. The investment philosophy appropriate for the CLT's will likely not be compatible with the donor's other investment goals. A partnership dedicated to the investment goals of the CLT's would not effectively advance the investment goals of non-CLT partners, and vice versa. Accordingly, a separate partnership should be established for the CLT's.

8. Lifetime vs. Testamentary CLT's

CLT's may be established during the donor's lifetime or at the donor's death. Charitably minded donors with large estates who want to retain the use of their assets during their lifetimes may use testamentary CLT's to minimize estate taxes while ultimately providing substantial assets for their descendants. CLUT's are best suited for testamentary CLT's since they are least affected by fluctuations in the I.R.C. § 7520 rate, which may fluctuate dramatically between the date the donor's will or living trust is signed and the date of the donor's death. Since the goal of testamentary CLT is not to "hit a home run" but rather to reduce estate taxes while providing for both charity and family, most donors find the CLUT to be a better testamentary technique than the CLAT. For similar reasons, zero-gift CLAT's should only be established during the donor's lifetime since they are highly sensitive to fluctuations in the I.R.C. § 7520 rate.

a. Ladder CLT's

One effective technique for balancing the donor's desire to benefit charity with the desire not to delay the transfer of wealth to the donor's descendants is to set up a series of CLT's with varying trust terms. For example, the donor may create four CLT's with terms lasting five, ten, fifteen, and twenty years, respectively. Every five years, the donor's descendants would acquire wealth, with assets in the remaining CLT's continuing to appreciate for their benefit.

This technique is most frequently utilized with testamentary CLUT's. The donor uses the CLUT rather than the CLAT in order to minimize the risks of a fluctuating I.R.C. § 7520 rate (see "Lifetime vs. Testamentary CLT's" above). The payout rates for each of the testamentary CLUT's are sufficiently high to ensure that the taxable gifts do not exceed the donor's remaining estate tax exemption but not so high as to deplete the amount of wealth ultimately passing to the donor's heirs. The twenty year CLUT is most heavily funded and is designed to shoulder most of the burden of minimizing estate taxes (i.e. with the highest payout rate) since the assets in that trust will have the longest investment horizon and thus the greatest opportunity to beat the I.R.C. § 7520 rate. The five year CLUT has the lowest payout rate and is designed to pass wealth more quickly to the donor's descendants than utilizing a single twenty year CLUT would allow. Without exceeding the donor's remaining estate tax exemption, the donor can combine this technique with certain outright gifts to the donor's descendants so that they need not wait even five years before receiving some wealth.

G. OTHER CONSIDERATIONS

What have been described in this article are the basic and somewhat sophisticated charitable techniques with which a practitioner should be familiar. To be sure, there are other charitable techniques that could be suggested to one's clients. However, the techniques described herein are the standard "workhorses" of charitable planning and will achieve the goals of the vast majority of clients, particularly if tailored to fit their particular facts and circumstances.

1. Cutting Edge Techniques

Nonetheless, there some professionals who dedicate their careers to the development of more powerful, and usually more sophisticated, techniques. Many of these "cutting edge" techniques push the envelope too far, some are worth further investigation, and still fewer will prove to be viable after all the dust settles. Such techniques should not be ignored, but neither should they be implemented, without more reflection, on the advice of those who promote them.

The professionals who seek to develop cutting edge techniques provide an invaluable service to the rest of the planning community, since it is they who develop the "workhorses" of tomorrow. Until their proposed techniques are scrubbed by the rest of the planning community, however, the practitioner who recommends, and the donor who implements, such techniques must be willing to stomach the risks associated with trailblazing. The wise practitioner will know when to explore further, when to seek the help of charitable planning experts, and when to discard the proposed technique.

2. Ethical and Malpractice Considerations

a. If It Looks Too Good To Be True, It Probably Is.

Many of the techniques described in this article will provide significant tax breaks to those who employ them. However, a donor who does not possess charitable intentions will likely be hard pressed to find an overall benefit to any such technique. Seeking to stretch the benefits of the charitable deduction beyond the congressional purpose of encouraging gifts to charity will leave the donor and practitioner alike in murky water, and possibly facing penalties, interest, or other sanctions. If a technique promises charitable deductions without any real benefit passing to charity, the technique will likely not hold up to scrutiny. "If it looks too good to be true, it probably is."

b. Know When to Get a Specialist

There are many professionals who specialize in charitable planning, whether attorneys, CPA's, financial planners, or other advisors. Practitioners without such specialized knowledge should consult with such advisors on the more complex techniques, and even consider referring their clients directly to such specialists. Additionally, many community foundations, supporting organizations, and public charities have invaluable resources for practitioners and donors alike, including, in many cases, full-time charitable advisors, model forms, illustrations, and personalized advice and planning.

At the end of the day, if the level of required planning is beyond the practitioner's charitable expertise, giving up the fees that would come with developing or implementing a charitable plan for a client will pay off in the long run. Being able to make referrals to other professionals usually results in reciprocal referrals, when appropriate. Likewise, clients appreciate and respect practitioners who know their limits and know the right people to get the job done; they will trust such practitioners and will return to them for other work. Finally, nothing can hurt a practitioner's career more than an ethical violation or malpractice suit for rendering improper or deficient services.

NOTES AND QUESTIONS

1. What type of client do you think is most likely to make a charitable gift—married or single, male or female? See Barry W. Johnson & Jeffrey P. Rosenfeld, *Examining the Factors That Affect Charitable Giving,* TR. & EST., Aug. 1991, at 29, 30.

2. To which of the following entities may you make a gift which would qualify for the charitable deduction?

a. Your law school.

b. University of Scotland.

c. The Royal Order of the Reindeer, a fraternal society.

d. Democratic or Republican Party.

e. Your state government.

3. Charitable organizations often publish booklets for both attorneys and potential contributors. These materials may contain extensive discussions of the benefits of charitable giving as well as trust forms which have been approved by the I.R.S. Major charities frequently conduct seminars for estate planners and prospective donors.

4. At least one survey revealed that tax savings is not a significant reason why your client wants to make a charitable gift. See Independent Sector, *Giving and Volunteering in the United States* (1990). Should Congress repeal the charitable deduction so that your clients who do not make charitable gifts would no longer subsidize the tax obligations of individuals who do?

5. For additional information, see Christopher P. Cline, *On the Flip Side: A New Spin on Charitable Remainder Trusts*, PROB. & PROP., Nov./Dec. 1997, at 7; Stephen P. Magowan, *Doing Right by Doing Good: Giving IRAs to Charity*, PROB. & PROP., Sept./Oct. 1997, at 17; Gail K. Neuharth, *A Primer on Private Foundations*, PROB. & PROP., Nov./Dec. 1998, at 33.

N. POST-MORTEM TAX PLANNING

KAREN S. COHEN, THE 10 MOST POWERFUL POSTMORTEM PLANNING POINTERS FOR TRUSTS AND ESTATES*

Journal of Accountancy, May 2012.

After a client passes away, there is much more to do than just prepare a final Form 1040, U.S. Individual Income Tax Return. Taking control of the postmortem planning process can be a powerful way to save tax dollars for the decedent's estate and family. Postmortem planning also

* Reproduced with permission of the Journal of Accountancy.

applies to Form 706, United States Estate (and Generation–Skipping Transfer) Tax Return; state death tax returns, if needed; and income tax returns for the estate and any revocable trusts set up during life.

Although many accountants routinely handle the preparation of the final personal return, fewer accountants acting as fiduciaries are as adept at taking advantage of the alternatives available to them when preparing Form 1041, U.S. Income Tax Return for Estates and Trusts. What follows are the most important tips for doing so:

1. Select a Fiscal Year End for the Estate

The assets that earned income during a client's lifetime will continue to do so after his or her death. Until the estate distributes those assets to beneficiaries, an estate income tax return will need to be filed each year, generating a Schedule K–1 to each residual beneficiary to the extent distributions are made. Using a fiscal year end can be a powerful tool to defer tax on that income and allow beneficiaries time to plan for its inclusion in their personal returns. Any of the 12 month-end dates that follow the decedent's death can be the fiscal year-end date, but the year cannot exceed 12 months.

For example, the maximum fiscal year for a decedent dying Oct. 5 is through Sept. 30 of the following year. The year can be shorter than 12 months, an effective choice if a large, income-producing transaction will occur in the months after the selected year end. Choose wisely for maximum income deferral. Estates do not have to make federal quarterly estimated tax payments for the first two years after the decedent's death.

2. Elect to Include Income Earned in the Decedent's Trust on the Estate's Income Tax Return

Trusts are required to use a calendar year end. However, a tax adviser can elect to include the income from a decedent's qualified revocable trust on the estate income tax return. Doing that provides an array of benefits not normally available to trusts, the most significant of which may be the ability to use the estate's fiscal year end for trust income. This election lasts two years beyond the decedent's date of death (longer if a Form 706 is required to be filed; consult the instructions to Form 8855, Election to Treat a Qualified Revocable Trust as Part of an Estate), which is normally plenty of time to deal with closing out a trust. Known as a Sec. 645 election, it is made by filing Form 8855 with the Form 1041. This election can be made even if there are no income-producing probate assets in the estate.

3. Manage Distributions to Minimize Overall Tax

Estate and trust income taxes reach the highest tax bracket of 35% at $11,650 of taxable income for 2012. If residual beneficiaries are in lower brackets, it will save tax for the family overall to distribute income out of the estate to them in a timely fashion. The fiduciary has until 65 days after the end of the tax year to make distributions for that tax year.

Capital gains stay at the Form 1041 level and are taxed there, except on a final return.

4. Prepare Form 1041 on the Accrual Basis

Excess deductions over income on an estate Form 1041 do not carry over to the next year and therefore are wasted (except on a final return; see below). If the fiduciary finds that the estate has paid large expenses without much income during the first year or, as is more often the case, the estate has ample income but will not pay related legal and administrative expenses until later, the fiduciary can prepare Form 1041 on the accrual basis and accrue the income or expenses into the current year.

5. Prepare a "First and Final" Return When Possible

Smaller estates often can be settled within a year plus 65 days. Then the fiduciary can file only one estate Form 1041 that is both an initial and a final return, saving the family money. Where possible, the fiduciary can make that happen by ensuring that timely distributions are made to beneficiaries and that any remaining assets are unlikely to generate the more than $600 of taxable gross receipts that would trigger an additional return filing requirement (by putting the remaining cash in a non–interest-bearing account, for example).

6. Update Basis of Assets

Capital gains are relatively rare on an estate Form 1041 because assets generally get a step-up in basis to date-of-death values. (However, executors of estates of 2010 decedents had until Jan. 17, 2012, to elect a modified carryover basis and holding period.) If the estate sells those assets quickly, there usually is not a lot of time for them to appreciate in value. Any asset acquired from a decedent generates long-term capital gain when it is sold, no matter how long the asset was held before or after the decedent's death. Stockbrokers often fail to adjust cost basis to date-of-death values before disposing of assets in an estate. It usually falls to the accountant to follow up on this issue and report the correct basis and long-term holding period for the sale and to provide brokers with a list of date-of-death values to update their basis for the remaining assets.

When an unmarried decedent owns a home at death and the estate sells it, there is no available exclusion from gain; however, because the basis in the residence will typically be the date-of-death value, the sale of the home will often generate a loss resulting from selling expenses, commissions, and repairs. Unlike a loss on a home sale during life, this loss is deductible.

7. Claim an Estate Tax Deduction for IRD

Not all assets get a step-up in basis. A category of assets known as income in respect of a decedent (IRD) does not. The beneficiary of such an asset or its income will "step into the shoes" of the decedent and report the income in the same way the decedent would have if he or she had lived to collect it. Common examples include wages earned but not yet paid when death occurs, installment notes receivable, dividends declared before death but paid later, traditional IRA accounts, and investments in annuities. Because the value of these assets is included on the decedent's balance sheet and is taxed for federal estate tax purposes, these assets are in essence double taxed when the money is collected and reported for income tax. If federal estate tax is paid on these assets, the entity that later reports the items for income tax is entitled to a deduction for the estate tax paid, known as the estate tax deduction for IRD. This may somewhat mitigate the double-taxation effect (Regs. Sec. 1.691(c)–2(a)(1)).

8. Claim DRD on Estate Tax Returns

Just as IRD is taxed twice, deductions in respect of a decedent (DRD) can be deducted twice: once for federal estate tax and once for income tax (Sec. 642(g)). Such items include business expenses, interest expense, taxes, expenses for production of income, depletion, and the foreign tax credit. Taxes are perhaps the most common, including state income taxes and real estate taxes. State death taxes, however, are not deductible anywhere except on Form 706.

9. Set Aside Income From Charitable Assets

If a decedent's estate will ultimately go to charity after all debts and expenses are paid, income earned while the estate is being settled need not be subject to income tax. An estate is allowed to set aside income from assets destined for charity (Sec. 642(c)). The mechanism to keep that income from being taxed on an estate Form 1041 is Form 1041–A, U.S. Information Return, Trust Accumulation of Charitable Amounts, a separate return filed to set aside this income. If a decedent's trust will ultimately go to charity, there is no set-aside for the income earned in the trust. However, a trust can take a charitable contribution deduction for its income. As long as that income actually is paid to the charity by the end of the following year, there will be no income tax on it. An election statement must be filed with the Form 1041 when this mechanism is used. The details of what should be included in this election statement can be found in the 2011 Form 1041 instructions at page 25.

10. Allocate Estimated Taxes From the Final Return

In a final return, all income tax liability, even on capital gains, rests with the beneficiaries of the estate. The final Schedules K–1 will carry out all the income. For this reason, there is no need to make any estimated tax payments if the fiduciary knows that the year or partial year will be the final time Form 1041 will be needed. If estimated tax payments are required or inadvertently made, they can be allocated to the beneficiaries for use on their personal returns by filing Form 1041–T, Allocation of Estimated Tax Payments to Beneficiaries, within 65 days of the end of the estate's tax year. Deductions in excess of income in the final year are also allocated on Schedule K–1 and are available to beneficiaries as a miscellaneous itemized deduction on their personal returns. Any capital loss carryovers not used by the estate are also passed through to the beneficiaries.

NOTE

For a comprehensive treatment of this subject, see FRANCIS J. ANTONUCCI & ROBERT WHITMAN, AFTER DEATH TAX PLANNING: MINIMIZING TAX LIABILITIES (3d ed. 2004).

CHAPTER 5

DISABILITY PLANNING—PROPERTY MANAGEMENT

■ ■ ■

A. INTRODUCTION

For centuries, the primary goal of estate planning was to carry out the client's intent regarding the disposition of the client's property at death, that is, to make sure the specified beneficiaries received the property with the smallest diminution by taxes as possible. A significant shift in focus was triggered in 1954 when Virginia became the first state to authorize a durable power of attorney for property management. The importance of including comprehensive disability arrangements in every estate plan has increased in importance since that time, with dramatic acceleration in recent years. Approximately one-half of the population will be disabled for at least ninety days. In addition, persons under the age of 60 are significantly more likely to become disabled sometime during the next year than to die.[1] "[P]erhaps the most tragic matter that probate courts must deal with is that of a physically, mentally or emotionally disabled person"[2] who has not made adequate provisions for disability.

Despite the advantages of disability planning, "[a]ttorneys and clients have long failed to pay adequate attention to the possibility that a client may incur a serious mental or physical disability and the problems that such a disability can create."[3] Why is this the case? First, estate planners may not realize the significance of this "non-traditional" area of estate planning. Second, clients may find it difficult to face the potential of future incapacity; many people delude themselves with the belief that such things only happen to others.

---

1. A male age 35 is 3.71 times more likely to become disabled than die in the next year while a female of the same age is 14.90 times more likely to become disabled than die. For a chart detailing these differences, see Pamela Yip, *Accident or Illness Could Take a Greater Financial Toll on Your Family Than Your Death,* HOUSTON CHRON., June 3, 1996, at 1B (reproducing chart supplied by Society of Actuaries).

2. Albert C. Koontz, *Planning for Disability: A Neglected Area of the Estate Planning Process,* 72 ILL. B.J. 366, 366 (1984).

3. John E. Bos, *The Durable Power of Attorney,* 64 MICH. B.J. 690, 690 (1985).

Perhaps the best way of recognizing the tremendous benefits of disability planning is to consider the alternative. When no planning is done, the disabled person flounders in society without protection until a family member, friend, or other individual petitions the court for the appointment of a guardian. The court then conducts proceedings to determine if the person is indeed incapable of managing personal or business matters. The person does not always need to be present at these hearings. Thus, the person may lack the opportunity to rebut the allegations of incapacity or express preferences regarding choice of guardian. The embarrassment to the person, not to mention the cost and time-consuming nature of the process, are legendary. If the court determines that the person is unable to manage the person's own affairs, a guardian of the person and/or a guardian of the estate will be appointed.

Once a person is deemed mentally incompetent, unpleasant ramifications from that finding impact that person's right of self-determination; important decisions regarding personal and business matters are now made by a guardian who may well be someone the disabled person never intended to have any power over personal or financial decisions. Every aspect of the person's existence is subject to the control and direction of others; where to live, what to eat, what to wear, what to watch on television, what medical treatment to have, and when and how to die.

Few, if any, clients would voluntarily subject themselves to this torment. Thus, you have a duty to include comprehensive arrangements for disability in estate plans. These plans should be structured to achieve at least three goals: (1) to provide a knowledgeable manager for the person's property; (2) to furnish a trusted proxy to make health care decisions; and (3) to prevent loss of the person's estate due to medical expenses. This chapter focuses on disability planning for property management and Chapter 6 concentrates on disability planning for health care decisions.

NOTE

For a general overview of disability planning, see Stephanie L. Schneider, *Planning Options for the Elderly and Disabled*, PROB. & PROP., May/June 1996, at 8.

B. DURABLE POWER OF ATTORNEY

GERRY W. BEYER, STATUTORILY ENACTED ESTATE PLANNING FORMS: DEVELOPMENT, EXPLANATION, ANALYSIS, STUDIES, COMMENTARY, AND RECOMMENDATIONS

Part I, pages 238–40 (1990).

Durable powers of attorney are of very recent origin compared to wills which began to evolve several millennia ago and trusts which started developing shortly after the Norman Conquest. The belief was firmly entrenched in Anglo–American law that an agent's authority terminated upon the principal's incapacity. It was not until the middle of the twentieth century that this traditional viewpoint was seriously questioned. Estate planners began to realize the utility of a power of attorney that would permit the agent to handle the principal's affairs during incompetency, the time when the principal most needs the agent's assistance. This need ultimately led to the durable power of attorney, a power which authorizes the agent to act until the principal's death notwithstanding the principal's incompetency.

This shift in attitude was, to a small extent, reflected by the *Restatements of Agency* that admitted some exception to the strict common law rule. A comment to the 1933 *Restatement* stated that a power of attorney would be terminated by the principal's mental incompetency if the incompetency created a legal incapacity but if the incapacity were only temporary, the agent's authority would merely be suspended. The comment explained that the agent retained the authority to act during very short periods of incompetency, such as when the principal had "a delirium accompanying a fever." In 1957, the *Second Restatement* added a caveat stating that no opinion was being given "as to the effect of the principal's temporary incapacity due to a mental disease." Although the new commentary echoed the traditional rule that "a declaration by a court having jurisdiction that the principal is insane or otherwise incompetent to act in his own affairs terminates or suspends the authority of his agent," the rule was partially eroded providing that "[v]ery brief periods of insanity caused by the temporary mental or physical illness of the principal do not destroy the power of a previously appointed agent to act in his behalf." The *Second Restatement* opened the door to durable powers but it stopped short of approving them and left the issue unsettled declaring that the matter was "too amorphous for a statement of a definite rule." In a similar fashion, courts were reluctant to alter the well-established rule.

In 1954, Virginia enacted pioneering legislation that authorized the creation of durable powers of attorney by the principal including language demonstrating "the intent of the principal that such power or authority shall not terminate upon his disability." If the power evidenced this intent, the agent's authority to act would continue "notwithstanding any subsequent disability, incompetence, or incapacity of the principal." Virginia's progressive approach to durable powers did not gain appreciable acceptance until over a decade later when durable powers were integrated into the original version of the Uniform Probate Code promulgated in 1969.

Even though jurisdictions were slow to adopt the entire Uniform Probate Code, durable powers of attorney started to enjoy enthusiastic popularity as states began to enact enabling legislation. To make powers of attorney more useful and to encourage adoption of durable power legislation, the National Conference of Commissioners on Uniform State Laws designed a free-standing Uniform Durable Power of Attorney Act.

The Act's provisions were identical to the corresponding provisions of the 1979 amendments to the Uniform Probate Code.[4] All fifty states and the District of Columbia now have legislation of a similar nature sanctioning durable powers of attorney.

The first durable power of attorney statutes did not contain fill-in forms but rather recommended certain phraseology to annex durability to a normal power of attorney. In the 1980's, however, comprehensive fill-in forms were enacted by a substantial number of states. * * * In 1988, the Uniform Statutory Form Power of Attorney Act, which includes a fill-in form, was approved and recommended for adoption in all states by the National Conference of Commissioners on Uniform State Laws at its annual meeting.

UNIFORM PROBATE CODE

1998 Revision

DURABLE POWER OF ATTORNEY

Section 5–501. [Definition.]

A durable power of attorney is a power of attorney by which a principal designates another his attorney in fact in writing and the writing contains the words "This power of attorney shall not be affected by subsequent disability or incapacity of the principal, or lapse of time," or "This power of attorney shall become effective upon the disability or incapacity of the principal," or similar words showing the intent of the principal that the authority conferred shall be exercisable notwithstanding the principal's subsequent disability or incapacity, and unless it states a time of termination, notwithstanding the lapse of time since the execution of the instrument.

Section 5–502. [Durable Power of Attorney Not Affected by Lapse of Time, Disability or Incapacity.]

All acts done by an attorney in fact pursuant to a durable power of attorney during any period of disability or incapacity of the principal have the same effect and inure to the benefit of and bind the principal and his successors in interest as if the principal were competent and not disabled. Unless the instrument states a time of termination, the power is exercisable notwithstanding the lapse of time since the execution of the instrument.

Section 5–503. [Relation of Attorney in Fact to Court–Appointed Fiduciary.]

(a) If, following execution of a durable power of attorney, a court of the principal's domicile appoints a conservator, guardian of the estate, or other fiduciary charged with the management of all of the principal's

4. Unif. Durable Power of Attorney Act, Prefatory Note (1979); UNIF. PROB. CODE §§ 5–501 to 5–505 (1979).

property or all of his property except specified exclusions, the attorney in fact is accountable to the fiduciary as well as to the principal. The fiduciary has the same power to revoke or amend the power of attorney that the principal would have had if he were not disabled or incapacitated.

(b) A principal may nominate, by a durable power of attorney, the conservator, guardian of his estate, or guardian of his person for consideration by the court if protective proceedings for the principal's person or estate are thereafter commenced. The court shall make its appointment in accordance with the principal's most recent nomination in a durable power of attorney except for good cause or disqualification.

Section 5–504. [Power of Attorney Not Revoked Until Notice.]

(a) The death of a principal who has executed a written power of attorney, durable or otherwise, does not revoke or terminate the agency as to the attorney in fact or other person, who, without actual knowledge of the death of the principal, acts in good faith under the power. Any action so taken, unless otherwise invalid or unenforceable, binds successors in interest of the principal.

(b) The disability or incapacity of a principal who has previously executed a written power of attorney that is not a durable power does not revoke or terminate the agency as to the attorney in fact or other person, who, without actual knowledge of the disability or incapacity of the principal, acts in good faith under the power. Any action so taken, unless otherwise invalid or unenforceable, binds the principal and his successors in interest.

Section 5–505. [Proof of Continuance of Durable and Other Powers of Attorney by Affidavit.]

As to acts undertaken in good faith reliance thereon, an affidavit executed by the attorney in fact under a power of attorney, durable or otherwise, stating that he did not have at the time of exercise of the power actual knowledge of the termination of the power by revocation or of the principal's death, disability, or incapacity is conclusive proof of the nonrevocation or nontermination of the power at that time. If the exercise of the power of attorney requires execution and delivery of any instrument that is recordable, the affidavit when authenticated for record is likewise recordable. This section does not affect any provision in a power of attorney for its termination by expiration of time or occurrence of an event other than express revocation or a change in the principal's capacity.

UNIFORM POWER OF ATTORNEY ACT

2006 Act.

Prefatory Note

The catalyst for the Uniform Power of Attorney Act (the "Act") was a national review of state power of attorney legislation. The review revealed growing divergence among states' statutory treatment of powers of attorney. The original Uniform Durable Power of Attorney Act ("Original Act"), last amended in 1987, was at one time followed by all but a few jurisdictions. Despite initial uniformity, the review found that a majority of states had enacted non-uniform provisions to deal with specific matters upon which the Original Act is silent. The topics about which there was increasing divergence included: 1) the authority of multiple agents; 2) the authority of a later-appointed fiduciary or guardian; 3) the impact of dissolution or annulment of the principal's marriage to the agent; 4) activation of contingent powers; 5) the authority to make gifts; and 6) standards for agent conduct and liability. Other topics about which states had legislated, although not necessarily in a divergent manner, included: successor agents, execution requirements, portability, sanctions for dishonor of a power of attorney, and restrictions on authority that has the potential to dissipate a principal's property or alter a principal's estate plan.

A national survey was then conducted by the Joint Editorial Board for Uniform Trust and Estate Acts (JEB) to ascertain whether there was actual divergence of opinion about default rules for powers of attorney or only the lack of a detailed uniform model. . . . Forty-four jurisdictions were represented in the 371 surveys returned.

The survey responses demonstrated a consensus of opinion in excess of seventy percent that a power of attorney statute should:

(1) provide for confirmation that contingent powers are activated;

(2) revoke a spouse-agent's authority upon the dissolution or annulment of the marriage to the principal;

(3) include a portability provision;

(4) require gift making authority to be expressly stated in the grant of authority;

(5) provide a default standard for fiduciary duties;

(6) permit the principal to alter the default fiduciary standard;

(7) require notice by an agent when the agent is no longer willing or able to act;

(8) include safeguards against abuse by the agent;

(9) include remedies and sanctions for abuse by the agent;

(10) protect the reliance of other persons on a power of attorney; and

(11) include remedies and sanctions for refusal of other persons to honor a power of attorney.

Informed by the review and the survey results, the Conference's drafting process also incorporated input from the American College of Trust and Estate Counsel, the ABA Section of Real Property, Probate and Trust Law, the ABA Commission on Law and Aging, the Joint Editorial Board for Uniform Trust and Estate Acts, the National Conference of

Lawyers and Corporate Fiduciaries, the American Bankers Association, AARP, other professional groups, as well as numerous individual lawyers and corporate counsel. As a result of this process, the Act codifies both state legislative trends and collective best practices, and strikes a balance between the need for flexibility and acceptance of an agent's authority and the need to prevent and redress financial abuse. * * *

SECTION 101. SHORT TITLE. This [act] may be cited as the Uniform Power of Attorney Act.

SECTION 102. DEFINITIONS. In this [act]:

(1) "Agent" means a person granted authority to act for a principal under a power of attorney, whether denominated an agent, attorney-in-fact, or otherwise. The term includes an original agent, coagent, successor agent, and a person to which an agent's authority is delegated.

(2) "Durable," with respect to a power of attorney, means not terminated by the principal's incapacity.

(3) "Electronic" means relating to technology having electrical, digital, magnetic, wireless, optical, electromagnetic, or similar capabilities.

(4) "Good faith" means honesty in fact.

(5) "Incapacity" means inability of an individual to manage property or business affairs because the individual:

(A) has an impairment in the ability to receive and evaluate information or make or communicate decisions even with the use of technological assistance; or

(B) is:

(i) missing;

(ii) detained, including incarcerated in a penal system; or

(iii) outside the United States and unable to return.

(6) "Person" means an individual, corporation, business trust, estate, trust, partnership, limited liability company, association, joint venture, public corporation, government or governmental subdivision, agency, or instrumentality, or any other legal or commercial entity.

(7) "Power of attorney" means a writing or other record that grants authority to an agent to act in the place of the principal, whether or not the term power of attorney is used.

(8) "Presently exercisable general power of appointment," with respect to property or a property interest subject to a power of appointment, means power exercisable at the time in question to vest absolute ownership in the principal individually, the principal's estate, the principal's creditors, or the creditors of the principal's estate. The term includes a power of appointment not exercisable until the occurrence of a specified event, the satisfaction of an ascertainable standard, or the passage of a specified period only after the occurrence of the specified event, the satisfaction of the ascertainable standard, or the passage of the specified

period. The term does not include a power exercisable in a fiduciary capacity or only by will.

(9) "Principal" means an individual who grants authority to an agent in a power of attorney.

(10) "Property" means anything that may be the subject of ownership, whether real or personal, or legal or equitable, or any interest or right therein.

(11) "Record" means information that is inscribed on a tangible medium or that is stored in an electronic or other medium and is retrievable in perceivable form.

(12) "Sign" means, with present intent to authenticate or adopt a record:

(A) to execute or adopt a tangible symbol; or

(B) to attach to or logically associate with the record an electronic sound, symbol, or process.

(13) "State" means a state of the United States, the District of Columbia, Puerto Rico, the United States Virgin Islands, or any territory or insular possession subject to the jurisdiction of the United States.

(14) "Stocks and bonds" means stocks, bonds, mutual funds, and all other types of securities and financial instruments, whether held directly, indirectly, or in any other manner. The term does not include commodity futures contracts and call or put options on stocks or stock indexes.

SECTION 103. APPLICABILITY. This [act] applies to all powers of attorney except:

(1) a power to the extent it is coupled with an interest in the subject of the power, including a power given to or for the benefit of a creditor in connection with a credit transaction;

(2) a power to make health-care decisions;

(3) a proxy or other delegation to exercise voting rights or management rights with respect to an entity; and

(4) a power created on a form prescribed by a government or governmental subdivision, agency, or instrumentality for a governmental purpose.

SECTION 104. POWER OF ATTORNEY IS DURABLE. A power of attorney created under this [act] is durable unless it expressly provides that it is terminated by the incapacity of the principal.

SECTION 105. EXECUTION OF POWER OF ATTORNEY. A power of attorney must be signed by the principal or in the principal's conscious presence by another individual directed by the principal to sign the principal's name on the power of attorney. A signature on a power of attorney is presumed to be genuine if the principal acknowledges the signature before a notary public or other individual authorized by law to take acknowledgments.

SECTION 106. VALIDITY OF POWER OF ATTORNEY.

(a) A power of attorney executed in this state on or after [the effective date of this [act]] is valid if its execution complies with Section 105.

(b) A power of attorney executed in this state before [the effective date of this [act]] is valid if its execution complied with the law of this state as it existed at the time of execution.

(c) A power of attorney executed other than in this state is valid in this state if, when the power of attorney was executed, the execution complied with:

(1) the law of the jurisdiction that determines the meaning and effect of the power of attorney pursuant to Section 107; or

(2) the requirements for a military power of attorney pursuant to 10 U.S.C. Section 1044b [, as amended].

(d) Except as otherwise provided by statute other than this [act], a photocopy or electronically transmitted copy of an original power of attorney has the same effect as the original.

SECTION 107. MEANING AND EFFECT OF POWER OF ATTORNEY. The meaning and effect of a power of attorney is determined by the law of the jurisdiction indicated in the power of attorney and, in the absence of an indication of jurisdiction, by the law of the jurisdiction in which the power of attorney was executed.

SECTION 108. NOMINATION OF [CONSERVATOR OR GUARDIAN]; RELATION OF AGENT TO COURT-APPOINTED FIDUCIARY.

(a) In a power of attorney, a principal may nominate a [conservator or guardian] of the principal's estate or [guardian] of the principal's person for consideration by the court if protective proceedings for the principal's estate or person are begun after the principal executes the power of attorney. [Except for good cause shown or disqualification, the court shall make its appointment in accordance with the principal's most recent nomination.]

(b) If, after a principal executes a power of attorney, a court appoints a [conservator or guardian] of the principal's estate or other fiduciary charged with the management of some or all of the principal's property, the agent is accountable to the fiduciary as well as to the principal. [The power of attorney is not terminated and the agent's authority continues unless limited, suspended, or terminated by the court.]

SECTION 109. WHEN POWER OF ATTORNEY EFFECTIVE.

(a) A power of attorney is effective when executed unless the principal provides in the power of attorney that it becomes effective at a future date or upon the occurrence of a future event or contingency.

(b) If a power of attorney becomes effective upon the occurrence of a future event or contingency, the principal, in the power of attorney, may authorize one or more persons to determine in a writing or other record that the event or contingency has occurred.

(c) If a power of attorney becomes effective upon the principal's incapacity and the principal has not authorized a person to determine whether the principal is incapacitated, or the person authorized is unable or unwilling to make the determination, the power of attorney becomes effective upon a determination in a writing or other record by:

(1) a physician [or licensed psychologist] that the principal is incapacitated within the meaning of Section 102(5)(A); or

(2) an attorney at law, a judge, or an appropriate governmental official that the principal is incapacitated within the meaning of Section 102(5)(B).

(d) A person authorized by the principal in the power of attorney to determine that the principal is incapacitated may act as the principal's personal representative pursuant to the Health Insurance Portability and Accountability Act, Sections 1171 through 1179 of the Social Security Act, 42 U.S.C. Section 1320d, [as amended,] and applicable regulations, to obtain access to the principal's health-care information and communicate with the principal's health-care provider.

SECTION 110. TERMINATION OF POWER OF ATTORNEY OR AGENT'S AUTHORITY.

(a) A power of attorney terminates when:

(1) the principal dies;

(2) the principal becomes incapacitated, if the power of attorney is not durable;

(3) the principal revokes the power of attorney;

(4) the power of attorney provides that it terminates;

(5) the purpose of the power of attorney is accomplished; or

(6) the principal revokes the agent's authority or the agent dies, becomes incapacitated, or resigns, and the power of attorney does not provide for another agent to act under the power of attorney.

(b) An agent's authority terminates when:

(1) the principal revokes the authority;

(2) the agent dies, becomes incapacitated, or resigns;

(3) an action is filed for the [dissolution] or annulment of the agent's marriage to the principal or their legal separation, unless the power of attorney otherwise provides; or

(4) the power of attorney terminates.

(c) Unless the power of attorney otherwise provides, an agent's authority is exercisable until the authority terminates under subsection (b), notwithstanding a lapse of time since the execution of the power of attorney.

(d) Termination of an agent's authority or of a power of attorney is not effective as to the agent or another person that, without actual knowledge of the termination, acts in good faith under the power of attorney. An act so performed, unless otherwise invalid or unenforceable, binds the principal and the principal's successors in interest.

(e) Incapacity of the principal of a power of attorney that is not durable does not revoke or terminate the power of attorney as to an agent or other person that, without actual knowledge of the incapacity, acts in good faith under the power of attorney. An act so performed, unless otherwise invalid or unenforceable, binds the principal and the principal's successors in interest.

(f) The execution of a power of attorney does not revoke a power of attorney previously executed by the principal unless the subsequent power of attorney provides that the previous power of attorney is revoked or that all other powers of attorney are revoked.

SECTION 111. COAGENTS AND SUCCESSOR AGENTS.

(a) A principal may designate two or more persons to act as coagents. Unless the power of attorney otherwise provides, each coagent may exercise its authority independently.

(b) A principal may designate one or more successor agents to act if an agent resigns, dies, becomes incapacitated, is not qualified to serve, or declines to serve. A principal may grant authority to designate one or more successor agents to an agent or other person designated by name, office, or function. Unless the power of attorney otherwise provides, a successor agent:

(1) has the same authority as that granted to the original agent; and

(2) may not act until all predecessor agents have resigned, died, become incapacitated, are no longer qualified to serve, or have declined to serve.

(c) Except as otherwise provided in the power of attorney and subsection (d), an agent that does not participate in or conceal a breach of fiduciary duty committed by another agent, including a predecessor agent, is not liable for the actions of the other agent.

(d) An agent that has actual knowledge of a breach or imminent breach of fiduciary duty by another agent shall notify the principal and, if the principal is incapacitated, take any action reasonably appropriate in the circumstances to safeguard the principal's best interest. An agent that fails to notify the principal or take action as required by this subsection is liable for the reasonably foreseeable damages that could have been avoided if the agent had notified the principal or taken such action.

SECTION 112. REIMBURSEMENT AND COMPENSATION OF AGENT. Unless the power of attorney otherwise provides, an agent is entitled to reimbursement of expenses reasonably incurred on behalf of the principal and to compensation that is reasonable under the circumstances.

SECTION 113. AGENT'S ACCEPTANCE. Except as otherwise provided in the power of attorney, a person accepts appointment as an agent under a power of attorney by exercising authority or performing duties as an agent or by any other assertion or conduct indicating acceptance.

SECTION 114. AGENT'S DUTIES.

(a) Notwithstanding provisions in the power of attorney, an agent that has accepted appointment shall:

(1) act in accordance with the principal's reasonable expectations to the extent actually known by the agent and, otherwise, in the principal's best interest;

(2) act in good faith; and

(3) act only within the scope of authority granted in the power of attorney.

(b) Except as otherwise provided in the power of attorney, an agent that has accepted appointment shall:

(1) act loyally for the principal's benefit;

(2) act so as not to create a conflict of interest that impairs the agent's ability to act impartially in the principal's best interest;

(3) act with the care, competence, and diligence ordinarily exercised by agents in similar circumstances;

(4) keep a record of all receipts, disbursements, and transactions made on behalf of the principal;

(5) cooperate with a person that has authority to make health-care decisions for the principal to carry out the principal's reasonable expectations to the extent actually known by the agent and, otherwise, act in the principal's best interest; and

(6) attempt to preserve the principal's estate plan, to the extent actually known by the agent, if preserving the plan is consistent with the principal's best interest based on all relevant factors, including:

(A) the value and nature of the principal's property;

(B) the principal's foreseeable obligations and need for maintenance;

(C) minimization of taxes, including income, estate, inheritance, generation-skipping transfer, and gift taxes; and

(D) eligibility for a benefit, a program, or assistance under a statute or regulation.

(c) An agent that acts in good faith is not liable to any beneficiary of the principal's estate plan for failure to preserve the plan.

(d) An agent that acts with care, competence, and diligence for the best interest of the principal is not liable solely because the agent also benefits from the act or has an individual or conflicting interest in relation to the property or affairs of the principal.

(e) If an agent is selected by the principal because of special skills or expertise possessed by the agent or in reliance on the agent's representation that the agent has special skills or expertise, the special skills or expertise must be considered in determining whether the agent has acted with care, competence, and diligence under the circumstances.

(f) Absent a breach of duty to the principal, an agent is not liable if the value of the principal's property declines.

(g) An agent that exercises authority to delegate to another person the authority granted by the principal or that engages another person on behalf of the principal is not liable for an act, error of judgment, or default of that person if the agent exercises care, competence, and diligence in selecting and monitoring the person.

(h) Except as otherwise provided in the power of attorney, an agent is not required to disclose receipts, disbursements, or transactions conducted on behalf of the principal unless ordered by a court or requested by the principal, a guardian, a conservator, another fiduciary acting for the principal, a governmental agency having authority to protect the welfare of the principal, or, upon the death of the principal, by the personal representative or successor in interest of the principal's estate. If so requested, within 30 days the agent shall comply with the request or provide a writing or other record substantiating why additional time is needed and shall comply with the request within an additional 30 days.

SECTION 115. EXONERATION OF AGENT. A provision in a power of attorney relieving an agent of liability for breach of duty is binding on the principal and the principal's successors in interest except to the extent the provision:

(1) relieves the agent of liability for breach of duty committed dishonestly, with an improper motive, or with reckless indifference to the purposes of the power of attorney or the best interest of the principal; or

(2) was inserted as a result of an abuse of a confidential or fiduciary relationship with the principal.

SECTION 116. JUDICIAL RELIEF.

(a) The following persons may petition a court to construe a power of attorney or review the agent's conduct, and grant appropriate relief:

(1) the principal or the agent;

(2) a guardian, conservator, or other fiduciary acting for the principal;

(3) a person authorized to make health-care decisions for the principal;

(4) the principal's spouse, parent, or descendant;

(5) an individual who would qualify as a presumptive heir of the principal;

(6) a person named as a beneficiary to receive any property, benefit, or contractual right on the principal's death or as a beneficiary of a trust created by or for the principal that has a financial interest in the principal's estate;

(7) a governmental agency having regulatory authority to protect the welfare of the principal;

(8) the principal's caregiver or another person that demonstrates sufficient interest in the principal's welfare; and

(9) a person asked to accept the power of attorney.

(b) Upon motion by the principal, the court shall dismiss a petition filed under this section, unless the court finds that the principal lacks capacity to revoke the agent's authority or the power of attorney.

SECTION 117. AGENT'S LIABILITY. An agent that violates this [act] is liable to the principal or the principal's successors in interest for the amount required to:

(1) restore the value of the principal's property to what it would have been had the violation not occurred; and

(2) reimburse the principal or the principal's successors in interest for the attorney's fees and costs paid on the agent's behalf.

SECTION 118. AGENT'S RESIGNATION; NOTICE. Unless the power of attorney provides a different method for an agent's resignation, an agent may resign by giving notice to the principal and, if the principal is incapacitated:

(1) to the [conservator or guardian], if one has been appointed for the principal, and a coagent or successor agent; or

(2) if there is no person described in paragraph (1), to:

(A) the principal's caregiver;

(B) another person reasonably believed by the agent to have sufficient interest in the principal's welfare; or

(C) a governmental agency having authority to protect the welfare of the principal.

SECTION 119. ACCEPTANCE OF AND RELIANCE UPON ACKNOWLEDGED POWER OF ATTORNEY.

(a) For purposes of this section and Section 120, "acknowledged" means purportedly verified before a notary public or other individual authorized to take acknowledgements.

(b) A person that in good faith accepts an acknowledged power of attorney without actual knowledge that the signature is not genuine may rely upon the presumption under Section 105 that the signature is genuine.

(c) A person that in good faith accepts an acknowledged power of attorney without actual knowledge that the power of attorney is void, invalid, or terminated, that the purported agent's authority is void, invalid, or terminated, or that the agent is exceeding or improperly exercising the agent's authority may rely upon the power of attorney as if the power of attorney were genuine, valid and still in effect, the agent's authority were genuine, valid and still in effect, and the agent had not exceeded and had properly exercised the authority.

(d) A person that is asked to accept an acknowledged power of attorney may request, and rely upon, without further investigation:

(1) an agent's certification under penalty of perjury of any factual matter concerning the principal, agent, or power of attorney;

(2) an English translation of the power of attorney if the power of attorney contains, in whole or in part, language other than English; and

(3) an opinion of counsel as to any matter of law concerning the power of attorney if the person making the request provides in a writing or other record the reason for the request.

(e) An English translation or an opinion of counsel requested under this section must be provided at the principal's expense unless the request is made more than seven business days after the power of attorney is presented for acceptance.

(f) For purposes of this section and Section 120, a person that conducts activities through employees is without actual knowledge of a fact relating to a power of attorney, a principal, or an agent if the employee conducting the transaction involving the power of attorney is without actual knowledge of the fact.

Alternative A

SECTION 120. LIABILITY FOR REFUSAL TO ACCEPT ACKNOWLEDGED POWER OF ATTORNEY.

(a) Except as otherwise provided in subsection (b):

(1) a person shall either accept an acknowledged power of attorney or request a certification, a translation, or an opinion of counsel under Section 119(d) no later than seven business days after presentation of the power of attorney for acceptance;

(2) if a person requests a certification, a translation, or an opinion of counsel under Section 119(d), the person shall accept the power of attorney no later than five business days after receipt of the certification, translation, or opinion of counsel; and

(3) a person may not require an additional or different form of power of attorney for authority granted in the power of attorney presented.

(b) A person is not required to accept an acknowledged power of attorney if:

(1) the person is not otherwise required to engage in a transaction with the principal in the same circumstances;

(2) engaging in a transaction with the agent or the principal in the same circumstances would be inconsistent with federal law;

(3) the person has actual knowledge of the termination of the agent's authority or of the power of attorney before exercise of the power;

(4) a request for a certification, a translation, or an opinion of counsel under Section 119(d) is refused;

(5) the person in good faith believes that the power is not valid or that the agent does not have the authority to perform the act requested, whether or not a certification, a translation, or an opinion of counsel under Section 119(d) has been requested or provided; or

(6) the person makes, or has actual knowledge that another person has made, a report to the [local adult protective services office] stating a good faith belief that the principal may be subject to physical or financial abuse, neglect, exploitation, or abandonment by the agent or a person acting for or with the agent.

(c) A person that refuses in violation of this section to accept an acknowledged power of attorney is subject to:

(1) a court order mandating acceptance of the power of attorney; and

(2) liability for reasonable attorney's fees and costs incurred in any action or proceeding that confirms the validity of the power of attorney or mandates acceptance of the power of attorney.

Alternative B

SECTION 120. LIABILITY FOR REFUSAL TO ACCEPT ACKNOWLEDGED STATUTORY FORM POWER OF ATTORNEY.

(a) In this section, "statutory form power of attorney" means a power of attorney substantially in the form provided in Section 301 or that meets the requirements for a military power of attorney pursuant to 10 U.S.C. Section 1044b [, as amended].

(b) Except as otherwise provided in subsection (c):

(1) a person shall either accept an acknowledged statutory form power of attorney or request a certification, a translation, or an opinion of counsel under Section 119(d) no later than seven business days after presentation of the power of attorney for acceptance;

(2) if a person requests a certification, a translation, or an opinion of counsel under Section 119(d), the person shall accept the statutory form power of attorney no later than five business days after receipt of the certification, translation, or opinion of counsel; and

(3) a person may not require an additional or different form of power of attorney for authority granted in the statutory form power of attorney presented.

(c) A person is not required to accept an acknowledged statutory form power of attorney if:

(1) the person is not otherwise required to engage in a transaction with the principal in the same circumstances;

(2) engaging in a transaction with the agent or the principal in the same circumstances would be inconsistent with federal law;

(3) the person has actual knowledge of the termination of the agent's authority or of the power of attorney before exercise of the power;

(4) a request for a certification, a translation, or an opinion of counsel under Section 119(d) is refused;

(5) the person in good faith believes that the power is not valid or that the agent does not have the authority to perform the act requested, whether or not a certification, a translation, or an opinion of counsel under Section 119(d) has been requested or provided; or

(6) the person makes, or has actual knowledge that another person has made, a report to the [local adult protective services office] stating a good faith belief that the principal may be subject to physical or financial abuse, neglect, exploitation, or abandonment by the agent or a person acting for or with the agent.

(d) A person that refuses in violation of this section to accept an acknowledged statutory form power of attorney is subject to:

(1) a court order mandating acceptance of the power of attorney; and

(2) liability for reasonable attorney's fees and costs incurred in any action or proceeding that confirms the validity of the power of attorney or mandates acceptance of the power of attorney.

SECTION 121. PRINCIPLES OF LAW AND EQUITY. Unless displaced by a provision of this [act], the principles of law and equity supplement this [act].

SECTION 122. LAWS APPLICABLE TO FINANCIAL INSTITUTIONS AND ENTITIES. This [act] does not supersede any other law applicable to financial institutions or other entities, and the other law controls if inconsistent with this [act].

SECTION 123. REMEDIES UNDER OTHER LAW. The remedies under this [act] are not exclusive and do not abrogate any right or remedy under the law of this state other than this [act].

SECTION 201. AUTHORITY THAT REQUIRES SPECIFIC GRANT; GRANT OF GENERAL AUTHORITY.

(a) An agent under a power of attorney may do the following on behalf of the principal or with the principal's property only if the power of attorney expressly grants the agent the authority and exercise of the authority is not otherwise prohibited by another agreement or instrument to which the authority or property is subject:

(1) create, amend, revoke, or terminate an inter vivos trust;

(2) make a gift;

(3) create or change rights of survivorship;

(4) create or change a beneficiary designation;

(5) delegate authority granted under the power of attorney;

(6) waive the principal's right to be a beneficiary of a joint and survivor annuity, including a survivor benefit under a retirement plan; [or]

(7) exercise fiduciary powers that the principal has authority to delegate[; or

(8) disclaim property, including a power of appointment].

(b) Notwithstanding a grant of authority to do an act described in subsection (a), unless the power of attorney otherwise provides, an agent that is not an ancestor, spouse, or descendant of the principal, may not exercise authority under a power of attorney to create in the agent, or in an individual to whom the agent owes a legal obligation of support, an interest in the principal's property, whether by gift, right of survivorship, beneficiary designation, disclaimer, or otherwise.

(c) Subject to subsections (a), (b), (d), and (e), if a power of attorney grants to an agent authority to do all acts that a principal could do, the agent has the general authority described in Sections 204 through 216.

(d) Unless the power of attorney otherwise provides, a grant of authority to make a gift is subject to Section 217.

(e) Subject to subsections (a), (b), and (d), if the subjects over which authority is granted in a power of attorney are similar or overlap, the broadest authority controls.

(f) Authority granted in a power of attorney is exercisable with respect to property that the principal has when the power of attorney is executed or acquires later, whether or not the property is located in this state and whether or not the authority is exercised or the power of attorney is executed in this state.

(g) An act performed by an agent pursuant to a power of attorney has the same effect and inures to the benefit of and binds the principal and the principal's successors in interest as if the principal had performed the act.

SECTION 202. INCORPORATION OF AUTHORITY.

(a) An agent has authority described in this [article] if the power of attorney refers to general authority with respect to the descriptive term for the subjects stated in Sections 204 through 217 or cites the section in which the authority is described.

(b) A reference in a power of attorney to general authority with respect to the descriptive term for a subject in Sections 204 through 217 or a citation to a section of Sections 204 through 217 incorporates the entire section as if it were set out in full in the power of attorney.

(c) A principal may modify authority incorporated by reference.

SECTION 203. CONSTRUCTION OF AUTHORITY GENERALLY. Except as otherwise provided in the power of attorney, by executing a power of attorney that incorporates by reference a subject described in Sections 204 through 217 or that grants to an agent authority to do all acts that a principal could do pursuant to Section 201(c), a principal authorizes the agent, with respect to that subject, to:

(1) demand, receive, and obtain by litigation or otherwise, money or another thing of value to which the principal is, may become, or claims to be entitled, and conserve, invest, disburse, or use anything so received or obtained for the purposes intended;

(2) contract in any manner with any person, on terms agreeable to the agent, to accomplish a purpose of a transaction and perform, rescind, cancel, terminate, reform, restate, release, or modify the contract or another contract made by or on behalf of the principal;

(3) execute, acknowledge, seal, deliver, file, or record any instrument or communication the agent considers desirable to accomplish a purpose of a transaction, including creating at any time a schedule listing some or all of the principal's property and attaching it to the power of attorney;

(4) initiate, participate in, submit to alternative dispute resolution, settle, oppose, or propose or accept a compromise with respect to a claim existing in favor of or against the principal or intervene in litigation relating to the claim;

(5) seek on the principal's behalf the assistance of a court or other governmental agency to carry out an act authorized in the power of attorney;

(6) engage, compensate, and discharge an attorney, accountant, discretionary investment manager, expert witness, or other advisor;

(7) prepare, execute, and file a record, report, or other document to safeguard or promote the principal's interest under a statute or regulation;

(8) communicate with any representative or employee of a government or governmental subdivision, agency, or instrumentality, on behalf of the principal;

(9) access communications intended for, and communicate on behalf of the principal, whether by mail, electronic transmission, telephone, or other means; and

(10) do any lawful act with respect to the subject and all property related to the subject.

SECTION 204. REAL PROPERTY. Unless the power of attorney otherwise provides, language in a power of attorney granting general authority with respect to real property authorizes the agent to:

(1) demand, buy, lease, receive, accept as a gift or as security for an extension of credit, or otherwise acquire or reject an interest in real property or a right incident to real property;

(2) sell; exchange; convey with or without covenants, representations, or warranties; quitclaim; release; surrender; retain title for security; encumber; partition; consent to partitioning; subject to an easement or covenant; subdivide; apply for zoning or other governmental permits; plat or consent to platting; develop; grant an option concerning; lease; sub-lease; contribute to an entity in exchange for an interest in that entity; or otherwise grant or dispose of an interest in real property or a right incident to real property;

(3) pledge or mortgage an interest in real property or right incident to real property as security to borrow money or pay, renew, or extend the time of payment of a debt of the principal or a debt guaranteed by the principal;

(4) release, assign, satisfy, or enforce by litigation or otherwise a mortgage, deed of trust, conditional sale contract, encumbrance, lien, or other claim to real property which exists or is asserted;

(5) manage or conserve an interest in real property or a right incident to real property owned or claimed to be owned by the principal, including:

(A) insuring against liability or casualty or other loss;

(B) obtaining or regaining possession of or protecting the interest or right by litigation or otherwise;

(C) paying, assessing, compromising, or contesting taxes or assessments or applying for and receiving refunds in connection with them; and

(D) purchasing supplies, hiring assistance or labor, and making repairs or alterations to the real property;

(6) use, develop, alter, replace, remove, erect, or install structures or other improvements upon real property in or incident to which the principal has, or claims to have, an interest or right;

(7) participate in a reorganization with respect to real property or an entity that owns an interest in or right incident to real property and receive, and hold, and act with respect to stocks and bonds or other property received in a plan of reorganization, including:

(A) selling or otherwise disposing of them;

(B) exercising or selling an option, right of conversion, or similar right with respect to them; and

(C) exercising any voting rights in person or by proxy;

(8) change the form of title of an interest in or right incident to real property; and

(9) dedicate to public use, with or without consideration, easements or other real property in which the principal has, or claims to have, an interest.

SECTION 205. TANGIBLE PERSONAL PROPERTY. Unless the power of attorney otherwise provides, language in a power of attorney granting general authority with respect to tangible personal property authorizes the agent to:

(1) demand, buy, receive, accept as a gift or as security for an extension of credit, or otherwise acquire or reject ownership or possession of tangible personal property or an interest in tangible personal property;

(2) sell; exchange; convey with or without covenants, representations, or warranties; quitclaim; release; surrender; create a security interest in; grant options concerning; lease; sublease; or, otherwise dispose of tangible personal property or an interest in tangible personal property;

(3) grant a security interest in tangible personal property or an interest in tangible personal property as security to borrow money or pay, renew, or extend the time of payment of a debt of the principal or a debt guaranteed by the principal;

(4) release, assign, satisfy, or enforce by litigation or otherwise, a security interest, lien, or other claim on behalf of the principal, with respect to tangible personal property or an interest in tangible personal property;

(5) manage or conserve tangible personal property or an interest in tangible personal property on behalf of the principal, including:

(A) insuring against liability or casualty or other loss;

(B) obtaining or regaining possession of or protecting the property or interest, by litigation or otherwise;

(C) paying, assessing, compromising, or contesting taxes or assessments or applying for and receiving refunds in connection with taxes or assessments;

(D) moving the property from place to place;

(E) storing the property for hire or on a gratuitous bailment; and

(F) using and making repairs, alterations, or improvements to the property; and

(6) change the form of title of an interest in tangible personal property.

SECTION 206. STOCKS AND BONDS. Unless the power of attorney otherwise provides, language in a power of attorney granting general authority with respect to stocks and bonds authorizes the agent to:

(1) buy, sell, and exchange stocks and bonds;

(2) establish, continue, modify, or terminate an account with respect to stocks and bonds;

(3) pledge stocks and bonds as security to borrow, pay, renew, or extend the time of payment of a debt of the principal;

(4) receive certificates and other evidences of ownership with respect to stocks and bonds; and

(5) exercise voting rights with respect to stocks and bonds in person or by proxy, enter into voting trusts, and consent to limitations on the right to vote.

SECTION 207. COMMODITIES AND OPTIONS. Unless the power of attorney otherwise provides, language in a power of attorney granting general authority with respect to commodities and options authorizes the agent to:

(1) buy, sell, exchange, assign, settle, and exercise commodity futures contracts and call or put options on stocks or stock indexes traded on a regulated option exchange; and

(2) establish, continue, modify, and terminate option accounts.

SECTION 208. BANKS AND OTHER FINANCIAL INSTITUTIONS. Unless the power of attorney otherwise provides, language in a power of attorney granting general authority with respect to banks and other financial institutions authorizes the agent to:

(1) continue, modify, and terminate an account or other banking arrangement made by or on behalf of the principal;

(2) establish, modify, and terminate an account or other banking arrangement with a bank, trust company, savings and loan association, credit union, thrift company, brokerage firm, or other financial institution selected by the agent;

(3) contract for services available from a financial institution, including renting a safe deposit box or space in a vault;

(4) withdraw, by check, order, electronic funds transfer, or otherwise, money or property of the principal deposited with or left in the custody of a financial institution;

(5) receive statements of account, vouchers, notices, and similar documents from a financial institution and act with respect to them;

(6) enter a safe deposit box or vault and withdraw or add to the contents;

(7) borrow money and pledge as security personal property of the principal necessary to borrow money or pay, renew, or extend the time of payment of a debt of the principal or a debt guaranteed by the principal;

(8) make, assign, draw, endorse, discount, guarantee, and negotiate promissory notes, checks, drafts, and other negotiable or nonnegotiable paper of the principal or payable to the principal or the principal's order,

transfer money, receive the cash or other proceeds of those transactions, and accept a draft drawn by a person upon the principal and pay it when due;

(9) receive for the principal and act upon a sight draft, warehouse receipt, or other document of title whether tangible or electronic, or other negotiable or nonnegotiable instrument;

(10) apply for, receive, and use letters of credit, credit and debit cards, electronic transaction authorizations, and traveler's checks from a financial institution and give an indemnity or other agreement in connection with letters of credit; and

(11) consent to an extension of the time of payment with respect to commercial paper or a financial transaction with a financial institution.

SECTION 209. OPERATION OF ENTITY OR BUSINESS. Subject to the terms of a document or an agreement governing an entity or an entity ownership interest, and unless the power of attorney otherwise provides, language in a power of attorney granting general authority with respect to operation of an entity or business authorizes the agent to:

(1) operate, buy, sell, enlarge, reduce, or terminate an ownership interest;

(2) perform a duty or discharge a liability and exercise in person or by proxy a right, power, privilege, or option that the principal has, may have, or claims to have;

(3) enforce the terms of an ownership agreement;

(4) initiate, participate in, submit to alternative dispute resolution, settle, oppose, or propose or accept a compromise with respect to litigation to which the principal is a party because of an ownership interest;

(5) exercise in person or by proxy, or enforce by litigation or otherwise, a right, power, privilege, or option the principal has or claims to have as the holder of stocks and bonds;

(6) initiate, participate in, submit to alternative dispute resolution, settle, oppose, or propose or accept a compromise with respect to litigation to which the principal is a party concerning stocks and bonds;

(7) with respect to an entity or business owned solely by the principal:

(A) continue, modify, renegotiate, extend, and terminate a contract made by or on behalf of the principal with respect to the entity or business before execution of the power of attorney;

(B) determine:

(i) the location of its operation;

(ii) the nature and extent of its business;

(iii) the methods of manufacturing, selling, merchandising, financing, accounting, and advertising employed in its operation;

(iv) the amount and types of insurance carried; and

(v) the mode of engaging, compensating, and dealing with its employees and accountants, attorneys, or other advisors;

(C) change the name or form of organization under which the entity or business is operated and enter into an ownership agreement with other persons to take over all or part of the operation of the entity or business; and

(D) demand and receive money due or claimed by the principal or on the principal's behalf in the operation of the entity or business and control and disburse the money in the operation of the entity or business;

(8) put additional capital into an entity or business in which the principal has an interest;

(9) join in a plan of reorganization, consolidation, conversion, domestication, or merger of the entity or business;

(10) sell or liquidate all or part of an entity or business;

(11) establish the value of an entity or business under a buy-out agreement to which the principal is a party;

(12) prepare, sign, file, and deliver reports, compilations of information, returns, or other papers with respect to an entity or business and make related payments; and

(13) pay, compromise, or contest taxes, assessments, fines, or penalties and perform any other act to protect the principal from illegal or unnecessary taxation, assessments, fines, or penalties, with respect to an entity or business, including attempts to recover, in any manner permitted by law, money paid before or after the execution of the power of attorney.

SECTION 210. INSURANCE AND ANNUITIES. Unless the power of attorney otherwise provides, language in a power of attorney granting general authority with respect to insurance and annuities authorizes the agent to:

(1) continue, pay the premium or make a contribution on, modify, exchange, rescind, release, or terminate a contract procured by or on behalf of the principal which insures or provides an annuity to either the principal or another person, whether or not the principal is a beneficiary under the contract;

(2) procure new, different, and additional contracts of insurance and annuities for the principal and the principal's spouse, children, and other dependents, and select the amount, type of insurance or annuity, and mode of payment;

(3) pay the premium or make a contribution on, modify, exchange, rescind, release, or terminate a contract of insurance or annuity procured by the agent;

(4) apply for and receive a loan secured by a contract of insurance or annuity;

(5) surrender and receive the cash surrender value on a contract of insurance or annuity;

(6) exercise an election;

(7) exercise investment powers available under a contract of insurance or annuity;

(8) change the manner of paying premiums on a contract of insurance or annuity;

(9) change or convert the type of insurance or annuity with respect to which the principal has or claims to have authority described in this section;

(10) apply for and procure a benefit or assistance under a statute or regulation to guarantee or pay premiums of a contract of insurance on the life of the principal;

(11) collect, sell, assign, hypothecate, borrow against, or pledge the interest of the principal in a contract of insurance or annuity;

(12) select the form and timing of the payment of proceeds from a contract of insurance or annuity; and

(13) pay, from proceeds or otherwise, compromise or contest, and apply for refunds in connection with, a tax or assessment levied by a taxing authority with respect to a contract of insurance or annuity or its proceeds or liability accruing by reason of the tax or assessment.

SECTION 211. ESTATES, TRUSTS, AND OTHER BENEFICIAL INTERESTS.

(a) In this section, "estate, trust, or other beneficial interest" means a trust, probate estate, guardianship, conservatorship, escrow, or custodianship or a fund from which the principal is, may become, or claims to be, entitled to a share or payment.

(b) Unless the power of attorney otherwise provides, language in a power of attorney granting general authority with respect to estates, trusts, and other beneficial interests authorizes the agent to:

(1) accept, receive, receipt for, sell, assign, pledge, or exchange a share in or payment from an estate, trust, or other beneficial interest;

(2) demand or obtain money or another thing of value to which the principal is, may become, or claims to be, entitled by reason of an estate, trust, or other beneficial interest, by litigation or otherwise;

(3) exercise for the benefit of the principal a presently exercisable general power of appointment held by the principal;

(4) initiate, participate in, submit to alternative dispute resolution, settle, oppose, or propose or accept a compromise with respect to litigation to ascertain the meaning, validity, or effect of a deed, will,

declaration of trust, or other instrument or transaction affecting the interest of the principal;

(5) initiate, participate in, submit to alternative dispute resolution, settle, oppose, or propose or accept a compromise with respect to litigation to remove, substitute, or surcharge a fiduciary;

(6) conserve, invest, disburse, or use anything received for an authorized purpose; [and]

(7) transfer an interest of the principal in real property, stocks and bonds, accounts with financial institutions or securities intermediaries, insurance, annuities, and other property to the trustee of a revocable trust created by the principal as settlor [; and

(8) reject, renounce, disclaim, release, or consent to a reduction in or modification of a share in or payment from an estate, trust, or other beneficial interest].

SECTION 212. CLAIMS AND LITIGATION. Unless the power of attorney otherwise provides, language in a power of attorney granting general authority with respect to claims and litigation authorizes the agent to:

(1) assert and maintain before a court or administrative agency a claim, claim for relief, cause of action, counterclaim, offset, recoupment, or defense, including an action to recover property or other thing of value, recover damages sustained by the principal, eliminate or modify tax liability, or seek an injunction, specific performance, or other relief;

(2) bring an action to determine adverse claims or intervene or otherwise participate in litigation;

(3) seek an attachment, garnishment, order of arrest, or other preliminary, provisional, or intermediate relief and use an available procedure to effect or satisfy a judgment, order, or decree;

(4) make or accept a tender, offer of judgment, or admission of facts, submit a controversy on an agreed statement of facts, consent to examination, and bind the principal in litigation;

(5) submit to alternative dispute resolution, settle, and propose or accept a compromise;

(6) waive the issuance and service of process upon the principal, accept service of process, appear for the principal, designate persons upon which process directed to the principal may be served, execute and file or deliver stipulations on the principal's behalf, verify pleadings, seek appellate review, procure and give surety and indemnity bonds, contract and pay for the preparation and printing of records and briefs, receive, execute, and file or deliver a consent, waiver, release, confession of judgment, satisfaction of judgment, notice, agreement, or other instrument in connection with the prosecution, settlement, or defense of a claim or litigation;

(7) act for the principal with respect to bankruptcy or insolvency, whether voluntary or involuntary, concerning the principal or some other person, or with respect to a reorganization, receivership, or application for the appointment of a receiver or trustee which affects an interest of the principal in property or other thing of value;

(8) pay a judgment, award, or order against the principal or a settlement made in connection with a claim or litigation; and

(9) receive money or other thing of value paid in settlement of or as proceeds of a claim or litigation.

SECTION 213. PERSONAL AND FAMILY MAINTENANCE.

(a) Unless the power of attorney otherwise provides, language in a power of attorney granting general authority with respect to personal and family maintenance authorizes the agent to:

(1) perform the acts necessary to maintain the customary standard of living of the principal, the principal's spouse, and the following individuals, whether living when the power of attorney is executed or later born:

(A) the principal's children;

(B) other individuals legally entitled to be supported by the principal; and

(C) the individuals whom the principal has customarily supported or indicated the intent to support;

(2) make periodic payments of child support and other family maintenance required by a court or governmental agency or an agreement to which the principal is a party;

(3) provide living quarters for the individuals described in paragraph (1) by:

(A) purchase, lease, or other contract; or

(B) paying the operating costs, including interest, amortization payments, repairs, improvements, and taxes, for premises owned by the principal or occupied by those individuals;

(4) provide normal domestic help, usual vacations and travel expenses, and funds for shelter, clothing, food, appropriate education, including postsecondary and vocational education, and other current living costs for the individuals described in paragraph (1);

(5) pay expenses for necessary health care and custodial care on behalf of the individuals described in paragraph (1);

(6) act as the principal's personal representative pursuant to the Health Insurance Portability and Accountability Act, Sections 1171 through 1179 of the Social Security Act, 42 U.S.C. Section 1320d, [as amended,] and applicable regulations, in making decisions related to the past, present, or future payment for the provision of health care consented to by the principal or anyone authorized under the law of this state to consent to health care on behalf of the principal;

(7) continue any provision made by the principal for automobiles or other means of transportation, including registering, licensing, insuring, and replacing them, for the individuals described in paragraph (1);

(8) maintain credit and debit accounts for the convenience of the individuals described in paragraph (1) and open new accounts; and

(9) continue payments incidental to the membership or affiliation of the principal in a religious institution, club, society, order, or other organization or to continue contributions to those organizations.

(b) Authority with respect to personal and family maintenance is neither dependent upon, nor limited by, authority that an agent may or may not have with respect to gifts under this [act].

SECTION 214. BENEFITS FROM GOVERNMENTAL PROGRAMS OR CIVIL OR MILITARY SERVICE.

(a) In this section, "benefits from governmental programs or civil or military service" means any benefit, program or assistance provided under a statute or regulation including Social Security, Medicare, and Medicaid.

(b) Unless the power of attorney otherwise provides, language in a power of attorney granting general authority with respect to benefits from governmental programs or civil or military service authorizes the agent to:

(1) execute vouchers in the name of the principal for allowances and reimbursements payable by the United States or a foreign government or by a state or subdivision of a state to the principal, including allowances and reimbursements for transportation of the individuals described in Section 213(a)(1), and for shipment of their household effects;

(2) take possession and order the removal and shipment of property of the principal from a post, warehouse, depot, dock, or other place of storage or safekeeping, either governmental or private, and execute and deliver a release, voucher, receipt, bill of lading, shipping ticket, certificate, or other instrument for that purpose;

(3) enroll in, apply for, select, reject, change, amend, or discontinue, on the principal's behalf, a benefit or program;

(4) prepare, file, and maintain a claim of the principal for a benefit or assistance, financial or otherwise, to which the principal may be entitled under a statute or regulation;

(5) initiate, participate in, submit to alternative dispute resolution, settle, oppose, or propose or accept a compromise with respect to litigation concerning any benefit or assistance the principal may be entitled to receive under a statute or regulation; and

(6) receive the financial proceeds of a claim described in paragraph (4) and conserve, invest, disburse, or use for a lawful purpose anything so received.

SECTION 215. RETIREMENT PLANS.

(a) In this section, "retirement plan" means a plan or account created by an employer, the principal, or another individual to provide retirement benefits or deferred compensation of which the principal is a participant, beneficiary, or owner, including a plan or account under the following sections of the Internal Revenue Code:

(1) an individual retirement account under Internal Revenue Code Section 408, 26 U.S.C. Section 408 [, as amended];

(2) a Roth individual retirement account under Internal Revenue Code Section 408A, 26 U.S.C. Section 408A [, as amended];

(3) a deemed individual retirement account under Internal Revenue Code Section 408(q), 26 U.S.C. Section 408(q) [, as amended];

(4) an annuity or mutual fund custodial account under Internal Revenue Code Section 403(b), 26 U.S.C. Section 403(b) [, as amended];

(5) a pension, profit-sharing, stock bonus, or other retirement plan qualified under Internal Revenue Code Section 401(a), 26 U.S.C. Section 401(a) [, as amended];

(6) a plan under Internal Revenue Code Section 457(b), 26 U.S.C. Section 457(b) [, as amended]; and

(7) a nonqualified deferred compensation plan under Internal Revenue Code Section 409A, 26 U.S.C. Section 409A [, as amended].

(b) Unless the power of attorney otherwise provides, language in a power of attorney granting general authority with respect to retirement plans authorizes the agent to:

(1) select the form and timing of payments under a retirement plan and withdraw benefits from a plan;

(2) make a rollover, including a direct trustee-to-trustee rollover, of benefits from one retirement plan to another;

(3) establish a retirement plan in the principal's name;

(4) make contributions to a retirement plan;

(5) exercise investment powers available under a retirement plan; and

(6) borrow from, sell assets to, or purchase assets from a retirement plan.

SECTION 216. TAXES. Unless the power of attorney otherwise provides, language in a power of attorney granting general authority with respect to taxes authorizes the agent to:

(1) prepare, sign, and file federal, state, local, and foreign income, gift, payroll, property, Federal Insurance Contributions Act, and other tax returns, claims for refunds, requests for extension of time, petitions regarding tax matters, and any other tax-related documents, including receipts, offers, waivers, consents, including consents and agreements under Internal Revenue Code Section 2032A, 26 U.S.C. Section 2032A, [as

amended,] closing agreements, and any power of attorney required by the Internal Revenue Service or other taxing authority with respect to a tax year upon which the statute of limitations has not run and the following 25 tax years;

(2) pay taxes due, collect refunds, post bonds, receive confidential information, and contest deficiencies determined by the Internal Revenue Service or other taxing authority;

(3) exercise any election available to the principal under federal, state, local, or foreign tax law; and

(4) act for the principal in all tax matters for all periods before the Internal Revenue Service, or other taxing authority.

SECTION 217. GIFTS.

(a) In this section, a gift "for the benefit of" a person includes a gift to a trust, an account under the Uniform Transfers to Minors Act, and a tuition savings account or prepaid tuition plan as defined under Internal Revenue Code Section 529, 26 U.S.C. Section 529 [, as amended].

(b) Unless the power of attorney otherwise provides, language in a power of attorney granting general authority with respect to gifts authorizes the agent only to:

(1) make outright to, or for the benefit of, a person, a gift of any of the principal's property, including by the exercise of a presently exercisable general power of appointment held by the principal, in an amount per donee not to exceed the annual dollar limits of the federal gift tax exclusion under Internal Revenue Code Section 2503(b), 26 U.S.C. Section 2503(b), [as amended,] without regard to whether the federal gift tax exclusion applies to the gift, or if the principal's spouse agrees to consent to a split gift pursuant to Internal Revenue Code Section 2513, 26 U.S.C. 2513, [as amended,] in an amount per donee not to exceed twice the annual federal gift tax exclusion limit; and

(2) consent, pursuant to Internal Revenue Code Section 2513, 26 U.S.C. Section 2513, [as amended,] to the splitting of a gift made by the principal's spouse in an amount per donee not to exceed the aggregate annual gift tax exclusions for both spouses.

(c) An agent may make a gift of the principal's property only as the agent determines is consistent with the principal's objectives if actually known by the agent and, if unknown, as the agent determines is consistent with the principal's best interest based on all relevant factors, including:

(1) the value and nature of the principal's property;

(2) the principal's foreseeable obligations and need for maintenance;

(3) minimization of taxes, including income, estate, inheritance, generation-skipping transfer, and gift taxes;

(4) eligibility for a benefit, a program, or assistance under a statute or regulation; and

(5) the principal's personal history of making or joining in making gifts.

SECTION 301. STATUTORY FORM POWER OF ATTORNEY. A document substantially in the following form may be used to create a statutory form power of attorney that has the meaning and effect prescribed by this [act].

[INSERT NAME OF JURISDICTION] STATUTORY FORM POWER OF ATTORNEY

IMPORTANT INFORMATION

This power of attorney authorizes another person (your agent) to make decisions concerning your property for you (the principal). Your agent will be able to make decisions and act with respect to your property (including your money) whether or not you are able to act for yourself. The meaning of authority over subjects listed on this form is explained in the Uniform Power of Attorney Act [insert citation].

This power of attorney does not authorize the agent to make health-care decisions for you.

You should select someone you trust to serve as your agent. Unless you specify otherwise, generally the agent's authority will continue until you die or revoke the power of attorney or the agent resigns or is unable to act for you.

Your agent is entitled to reasonable compensation unless you state otherwise in the Special Instructions.

This form provides for designation of one agent. If you wish to name more than one agent you may name a coagent in the Special Instructions. Coagents are not required to act together unless you include that requirement in the Special Instructions.

If your agent is unable or unwilling to act for you, your power of attorney will end unless you have named a successor agent. You may also name a second successor agent.

This power of attorney becomes effective immediately unless you state otherwise in the Special Instructions.

If you have questions about the power of attorney or the authority you are granting to your agent, you should seek legal advice before signing this form.

DESIGNATION OF AGENT

I ____ name the following

(Name of Principal)

person as my agent:

Name of Agent: ______________________________

Agent's Address: ______________________________

Agent's Telephone Number: ______________________________

DESIGNATION OF SUCCESSOR AGENT(S) (OPTIONAL)

If my agent is unable or unwilling to act for me, I name as my successor agent:

Name of Successor Agent: ______________________________

Successor Agent's Address: ______________________________

Successor Agent's Telephone Number: ______________________________

If my successor agent is unable or unwilling to act for me, I name as my second successor agent:

Name of Second Successor Agent: ______________________________

Second Successor Agent's Address: ______________________________

Second Successor Agent's Telephone Number: ______________________________

GRANT OF GENERAL AUTHORITY

I grant my agent and any successor agent general authority to act for me with respect to the following subjects as defined in the Uniform Power of Attorney Act [insert citation]:

(INITIAL each subject you want to include in the agent's general authority. If you wish to grant general authority over all of the subjects you may initial "All Preceding Subjects" instead of initialing each subject.)

(______) Real Property

(______) Tangible Personal Property

(______) Stocks and Bonds

(______) Commodities and Options

(______) Banks and Other Financial Institutions

(______) Operation of Entity or Business

(______) Insurance and Annuities

(______) Estates, Trusts, and Other Beneficial Interests

(______) Claims and Litigation

(_____) Personal and Family Maintenance

(_____) Benefits from Governmental Programs or Civil or Military Service

(_____) Retirement Plans

(_____) Taxes

(_____) All Preceding Subjects

GRANT OF SPECIFIC AUTHORITY (OPTIONAL)

My agent MAY NOT do any of the following specific acts for me UNLESS I have INITIALED the specific authority listed below:

(CAUTION: Granting any of the following will give your agent the authority to take actions that could significantly reduce your property or change how your property is distributed at your death. INITIAL ONLY the specific authority you WANT to give your agent.)

(_____) Create, amend, revoke, or terminate an inter vivos trust

(_____) Make a gift, subject to the limitations of the Uniform Power of Attorney Act [insert citation to Section 217 of the act] and any special instructions in this power of attorney

(_____) Create or change rights of survivorship

(_____) Create or change a beneficiary designation

(_____) Authorize another person to exercise the authority granted under this power of attorney

(_____) Waive the principal's right to be a beneficiary of a joint and survivor annuity, including a survivor benefit under a retirement plan

(_____) Exercise fiduciary powers that the principal has authority to delegate

[(_____) Disclaim or refuse an interest in property, including a power of appointment]

LIMITATION ON AGENT'S AUTHORITY

An agent that is not my ancestor, spouse, or descendant MAY NOT use my property to benefit the agent or a person to whom the agent owes an obligation of support unless I have included that authority in the Special Instructions.

SPECIAL INSTRUCTIONS (OPTIONAL)

You may give special instructions on the following lines:

____
____
____
____
____
____

EFFECTIVE DATE

This power of attorney is effective immediately unless I have stated otherwise in the Special Instructions.

NOMINATION OF [CONSERVATOR OR GUARDIAN] (OPTIONAL)

If it becomes necessary for a court to appoint a [conservator or guardian] of my estate or [guardian] of my person, I nominate the following person(s) for appointment:

Name of Nominee for [conservator or guardian] of my estate:

____

Nominee's Address: ______________________________

Nominee's Telephone Number:______________________

Name of Nominee for [guardian] of my person: ______________

Nominee's Address: ______________________________

Nominee's Telephone Number: ______________________

RELIANCE ON THIS POWER OF ATTORNEY

Any person, including my agent, may rely upon the validity of this power of attorney or a copy of it unless that person knows it has terminated or is invalid.

SIGNATURE AND ACKNOWLEDGMENT

______________________________ __________

Your Signature Date

____

Your Name Printed

____

____

Your Address

____

Your Telephone Number

State of ______________________________

[County] of ______________________________

This document was acknowledged before me on ____________________,
(Date)

by ______________________________.
(Name of Principal)

______________________________ (Seal, if any)
Signature of Notary

My commission expires: ____________________

[This document prepared by:

____

____]

IMPORTANT INFORMATION FOR AGENT

Agent's Duties

When you accept the authority granted under this power of attorney, a special legal relationship is created between you and the principal. This relationship imposes upon you legal duties that continue until you resign or the power of attorney is terminated or revoked. You must:

(1) do what you know the principal reasonably expects you to do with the principal's property or, if you do not know the principal's expectations, act in the principal's best interest;
(2) act in good faith;
(3) do nothing beyond the authority granted in this power of attorney; and
(4) disclose your identity as an agent whenever you act for the principal by writing or printing the name of the principal and signing your own name as "agent" in the following manner:
(Principal's Name) by (Your Signature) as Agent

Unless the Special Instructions in this power of attorney state otherwise, you must also:

(1) act loyally for the principal's benefit;
(2) avoid conflicts that would impair your ability to act in the principal's best interest;
(3) act with care, competence, and diligence;
(4) keep a record of all receipts, disbursements, and transactions made on behalf of the principal;
(5) cooperate with any person that has authority to make health-care decisions for the principal to do what you know the principal reasonably expects or, if you do not know the principal's expectations, to act in the principal's best interest; and

(6) attempt to preserve the principal's estate plan if you know the plan and preserving the plan is consistent with the principal's best interest.

Termination of Agent's Authority

You must stop acting on behalf of the principal if you learn of any event that terminates this power of attorney or your authority under this power of attorney. Events that terminate a power of attorney or your authority to act under a power of attorney include:

(1) death of the principal;
(2) the principal's revocation of the power of attorney or your authority;
(3) the occurrence of a termination event stated in the power of attorney;
(4) the purpose of the power of attorney is fully accomplished; or
(5) if you are married to the principal, a legal action is filed with a court to end your marriage, or for your legal separation, unless the Special Instructions in this power of attorney state that such an action will not terminate your authority.

Liability of Agent

The meaning of the authority granted to you is defined in the Uniform Power of Attorney Act [insert citation]. If you violate the Uniform Power of Attorney Act [insert citation] or act outside the authority granted, you may be liable for any damages caused by your violation.

If there is anything about this document or your duties that you do not understand, you should seek legal advice.

SECTION 302. AGENT'S CERTIFICATION. The following optional form may be used by an agent to certify facts concerning a power of attorney.

AGENT'S CERTIFICATION AS TO THE VALIDITY OF POWER OF ATTORNEY AND AGENT'S AUTHORITY

State of ____________________

[County] of ________________]

I, ______________________________ (Name of Agent), [certify] under penalty of perjury that ______________________________(Name of Principal) granted me authority as an agent or successor agent in a power of attorney dated ______________.

I further [certify] that to my knowledge:

(1) the Principal is alive and has not revoked the Power of Attorney or my authority to act under the Power of Attorney and the Power of Attorney and my authority to act under the Power of Attorney have not terminated;

(2) if the Power of Attorney was drafted to become effective upon the happening of an event or contingency, the event or contingency has occurred;

(3) if I was named as a successor agent, the prior agent is no longer able or willing to serve; and

(4) ____

____

____

____

(Insert other relevant statements)

SIGNATURE AND ACKNOWLEDGMENT

______________________________ ________

Agent's Signature Date

____

Agent's Name Printed

____

____

Agent's Address

____

Agent's Telephone Number

This document was acknowledged before me on ____________________,
(Date)

by ____________________________.
(Name of Agent)

______________________________ (Seal, if any)

Signature of Notary

My commission expires: ____________________

[This document prepared by:

____]

SECTION 401. UNIFORMITY OF APPLICATION AND CONSTRUCTION. In applying and construing this uniform act, consideration must be given to the need to promote uniformity of the law with respect to its subject matter among the states that enact it.

SECTION 402. RELATION TO ELECTRONIC SIGNATURES IN GLOBAL AND NATIONAL COMMERCE ACT. This [act] modifies, limits, and supersedes the federal Electronic Signatures in Global and National Commerce Act,15 U.S.C. Section 7001 et seq., but does not modify, limit, or supersede Section 101(c) of that act, 15 U.S.C. Section 7001(c), or authorize electronic delivery of any of the notices described in Section 103(b) of that act, 15 U.S.C. Section 7003(b).

SECTION 403. EFFECT ON EXISTING POWERS OF ATTORNEY. Except as otherwise provided in this [act], on [the effective date of this [act]]:

(1) this [act] applies to a power of attorney created before, on, or after [the effective date of this [act]];

(2) this [act] applies to a judicial proceeding concerning a power of attorney commenced on or after [the effective date of this [act]];

(3) this [act] applies to a judicial proceeding concerning a power of attorney commenced before [the effective date of this [act]] unless the court finds that application of a provision of this [act] would substantially interfere with the effective conduct of the judicial proceeding or prejudice the rights of a party, in which case that provision does not apply and the superseded law applies; and

(4) an act done before [the effective date of this [act]] is not affected by this [act].

SECTION 404. REPEAL. The following are repealed:

(1) [Uniform Durable Power of Attorney Act]

(2) [Uniform Statutory Form Power of Attorney Act]

(3) [Article 5, Part 5 of the Uniform Probate Code]

SECTION 405. EFFECTIVE DATE. This [act] takes effect ______.

LOCATE

Locate the legislation in your state that authorizes durable powers of attorney for property management. Study it carefully and then work through the following questions.

NOTES AND QUESTIONS

1. What capacity (age and mental state) must a person possess to execute a durable power of attorney?

2. Will an oral agency appointment be effective?

3. Must the principal sign the durable power of attorney? Is a proxy signature sufficient?

4. Is any "magic language" needed to attach the durability feature to the power of attorney?

5. Does the durable power of attorney need to be acknowledged? Even if acknowledging is not necessary, is there a reason you might want to have it acknowledged anyway?

6. Must the durable power of attorney be witnessed?

7. Is recording of the durable power of attorney a condition precedent to validity?

8. See Linda S. Whitton, *Everything You Needed to Know About Good Lawyering, You Can Learn from Elder Law*, 40 Stetson L. Rev. 73, 82–87 (Fall 2010) (analyzing the problem of determining whether an elderly client seeking to revoke a power of attorney has the requisite capacity to do so).

9. Will a mere lapse of time automatically revoke the power of attorney?

10. What is the effect on the agent's authority if the court appoints a guardian for the principal? Note that the effect may be different depending on the type of guardian appointed, i.e., of the person or of the estate (conservator). What can the principal do to reduce the impact of having a guardian appointed?

11. What characteristics should you look for in an agent? Would you consider appointing a family member? See also Chapter 8(H).

12. What powers, if any, does an agent receive automatically?

13. The principal needs to make sure the power of attorney gives the agent all necessary powers but none which the principal does not wish to delegate. What powers might the principal like to delegate that are not covered by normal boiler plate language? See Linda S. Whitton, *Durable Powers as an Alternative to Guardianship: Lessons We Have Learned*, 37 Stetson L. Rev. 7, 35–36 (Fall 2007) (discussing how "courts have implied gift-making authority . . . when the IRS has claimed that the value of gifts made by the agent should be included in the decedent's estate because the power of attorney did not expressly authorize gift-making authority"). What powers might the principal wish to withhold from the agent? Are there any powers which the principal may not delegate? *Id.* at 14–15 (explaining how omitting the power to make gifts can reduce the potential for abuse, but can also "work to the client's detriment").

14. If the principal elects to use a springing power, how should disability or incapacity be determined?

15. Should the principal provide for the agent to receive compensation? If yes, how should compensation be computed?

16. What potential problem arises if the principal's spouse is named as the agent? How could you try to prevent it?

17. Principal executed a valid durable power of attorney on January 10 and Agent assumed her duties immediately. On February 14, Principal followed the appropriate state law procedure to revoke the power of attorney. On February 15, Agent sold an item of Principal's property to Barbara. This sale was permitted under the terms of the durable power. Neither Agent nor Barbara knew of Principal's revocation one day earlier. May Principal undo the sale? If Principal had died on February 14 instead, may the personal representative of Principal's estate undo the sale?

18. Agent is serving under a valid power of attorney. Agent goes into Bank and wants to close Principal's bank account. The power of attorney expressly allows Agent to take this action. Bank, however, refuses to comply with Agent's request. What recourse, if any, does Agent have to force Bank to

accept Agent's authority? What steps can a principal take to avoid this problem? Note that some banks include a term in their deposit agreements stating that they are not obligated to accept or honor an agent's request to withdraw funds. See 2 Vicki L. Shemin, *Advanced Medical Directive: Living Wills, Durable Powers of Attorney, and Health–Care Proxies,* A PRACTICAL GUIDE TO ESTATE PLANNING IN MASSACHUSETTS § 8 (3d ed. 2011) (explaining that [a]n inherit problem that frequently arises in connection with DPOA is that some third parties (i.e., banks and transfer agents) have an ingrained hostility to honor these documents); Daniel A. Wentworth, *Durable Powers of Attorney: Considering the Financial Institution's Perspective,* PROB. & PROP., Nov./Dec. 2003, at 37 (providing suggestions for estate planners to increase the likelihood of acceptance).

19. May an agent gain access to the principal's will? For example, an agent may want to determine which asset to sell based on who would receive it upon death.

20. See Jennifer L. Rhein, *No One in Charge: Durable Powers of Attorney and the Failure to Protect Incapacitated Principals*, 17 ELDER L.J. 165, at 174 (2009) (explaining that some states have imposed penalties for abuse of durable powers of attorney and have created oversight mechanisms to help prevent abuse); Russell E. Haddleton, *The Durable Power of Attorney is on the Way*, PROB. & PROP., May/June 2010 at 51–52 (suggesting that requiring registration of the power of attorney with a government agent and an accounting by the agent could help solve the problem of misuse and abuse).

21. Who should retain the original power of attorney document? See Glen A. Yale, *It's Right to Be Left, Holding the Power of Attorney*, PROB. & PROP., Jan./Feb. 2003, at 54.

DRAFT

Draft a durable power of attorney which will permit the agent to continue all of the principal's financial and business affairs, including the ability to continue a program of making tax-motivated gifts each year to children, grandchildren, and charities. See Kathleen Ford Bay, *Repercussions of Gifts Under Powers of Attorney—The Ripple Effect,* PROB. & PROP., Nov./Dec. 1989, at 6.

C. SELF-DESIGNATION OF GUARDIAN OF ESTATE OR CONSERVATOR

GERRY W. BEYER, ENHANCING SELF–DETERMINATION THROUGH GUARDIAN SELF–DECLARATION*

23 IND. L. REV. 71, 72–87 (1990).

The early history of recorded law provided evidence of the existence of legal protection for adults lacking the capacity necessary to act for themselves. The Roman Law of the Twelve Tables in 449 B.C. contained a type of guardianship for mentally disabled persons who were thought to be capable of having lucid intervals. The Praetors later extended similar protection to all adults suffering from mental incapacity, even if the incapacity was permanent.

Early English law also contains references to the special protections extended to incompetent individuals. A distinction was made between the guardianship of two categories of disabled adults: "idiots" or "born fools," and "lunatics." "Idiots" were individuals so mentally disabled that they were unlikely to regain sufficient mental capacity to act on their own at any time. On the other hand, "lunatics" had the potential of regaining their mental faculties at a future date. Under the early common law, lords were entitled to become the guardians of the land and person of incompetents. The lord could actually seize the land of an incurable idiot but he could only administer the real property of a lunatic because the land would have to be restored to the lunatic should he recover.

In approximately 1216, near the end of the reign of King Henry III, the crown acquired the right of guardianship over incompetent persons, to the exclusion of lords, by virtue of a statute or ordinance. The crown's right was documented in the statute *de Praerogativa regis* which has been traced to the early years of King Edward I. The king was granted custody of idiots' lands and the right to take the profits produced from the lands without waste and had the reciprocal duty of providing for the idiots' necessaries. Upon the death of an idiot, the lands were returned to the idiot's rightful heirs. In a similar manner, the king managed the lunatic's lands and tenements and maintained the lunatic and his household with the profits. If the lunatic regained competency, the residue of the lunatic's estate would then be returned to him; the king was not permitted to claim anything for his own use.

Originally, jurisdiction over persons of unsound mind was regarded as a valuable right and was therefore vested in the Court of Exchequer. As time passed, the management of incompetents and their estates became viewed as a duty. By 1660, jurisdiction was almost always delegated to the Chancellor. The Chancellor would typically appoint a committee to oversee the affairs of the incompetent person and to carefully administer his property.

In the United States, jurisdiction over incompetent persons was originally exercised by equity or law courts under specific statutory authority. As the law developed, most, if not all, matters that involved the guardianship of incompetent persons became highly regulated by statute. Upon a proper petition and a finding that the person was incompetent, a guardian or committee was appointed by the court to care for the person and his estate. State statutes typically prioritize the persons who may be appointed as guardian of the ward's person and estate. The incompetent's spouse and adult children are favored in these statutory preferences as evidenced by their placement at or near the top of the list. These statutes codify the public's belief that close relatives are the most likely individuals to be solicitous of the ward's personal and financial welfare.

The central issue for consideration * * * is the extent to which an incompetent person may influence or control the court's selection of the person who will be charged with the management of his person and his estate. Once a person is deemed incompetent by the court, unpleasant ramifications from that finding impact the incompetent's right of self-determination; important decisions regarding personal and business matters once made by the incompetent are now made by the guardian. Despite the withdrawal of the legal power to make decisions even as mundane as which washing machine to purchase, most state statutes that originally guided the court in the appointment of a guardian did not require the court to consider the desires or preferences of the incompetent as to whom the guardian should be. Although an incompetent individual may lack the legal capacity to contract, he certainly retains his emotional and psychological sense of self-worth. Thus, the appointment of a person with statutory priority, such as a spouse or adult child, may not be in the best interest of the incompetent due to conflicting interests or personal grudges against the incompetent that do not typically surface during the appointment process. Even if it is assumed that the person with priority would be adequate as a guardian of the person, the incompetent may prefer a different person as guardian of his estate, especially if the estate consists of assets requiring special management skills.

The case law which developed in the United States in the nineteenth and early twentieth centuries was inconclusive as to the ability of an incompetent to influence the court's decision regarding the person to be appointed as his guardian. Most courts held that they were not required to give weight to the incompetent's preferences. Nonetheless, other courts gave serious consideration to the incompetent's recommendation believing that the incompetent's best interests were often served by the appointment of a self-preferred guardian. For example, the Massachusetts Supreme Court stated:

> A man may be insane so as to be a fit subject for guardianship, and yet have a sensible opinion and strong feeling upon the question who that guardian shall be. And that opinion and feeling it would be the duty as well as the pleasure of the court anxiously to consult, as the happiness of the ward and his restoration to health might depend upon it.[2]

The right of an incompetent to determine his fate to the greatest extent possible is increasingly recognized in the law. For example, the Utah Supreme Court recently stated that "a court in appointing a guardian must consider the interest of the ward in retaining as broad a power of self-determination as is consistent with the reason for appointing a guardian...."[3] Likewise, one Illinois court emphasized that "[g]uardian-

2. Allis v. Morton, 70 Mass. 63, 64 (1855).

3. In re Boyer, 636 P.2d 1085 (Utah 1981). Cf. In re Reed's Guardianship, 173 Wis. 628, 182 N.W. 329 (1921) (in determining whether it was proper to appoint a guardian for a spendthrift,

ship is to be used to encourage self-reliance and independence."[4]

In an effort to provide the incompetent person with greater input into the court's decision-making process, most states have enacted statutes which grant the incompetent the right to express a non-binding preference regarding the person to be appointed as his guardian. Despite the incompetent's right to have his desires considered, one study has concluded that "in a majority of guardianship proceedings, little or no thought is given to whether the *particular* guardian to be named is one who would be personally acceptable to the ward."[5]

In more recent years, commentators have urged and legislatures have recognized that during the selection of a guardian, attention should focus on preferences expressed by the incompetent while the individual was competent, rather than on nominations made while incompetent. Nevertheless, it must also be recognized that an incompetent person's expression of preference is inherently suspect; a person lacking the capacity to handle personal and property matters may also lack the capacity to select a proper guardian. Likewise, an incompetent person is more susceptible to influence from those who wish to be appointed as guardian but who do not actually have the person's best interests in mind.

[There is a] growing trend in the United States to permit competent individuals to select their guardians before the onset of incompetency * * *.

METHODS TO SELF-DESIGNATE GUARDIANS PRIOR TO INCOMPETENCY

This section discusses and analyzes the six different methods which legislatures have developed to enable a person to nominate guardians prior to incompetency or disability. The methods vary considerably and some jurisdictions authorize several disparate techniques.

A. Appointment of a Guardian While Competent

At least one state permits individuals to secure a court appointed guardian prior to incompetency. In Vermont, a competent adult may petition the court for the appointment of a guardian. * * *

This procedure provides an individual with tremendous flexibility: a person may secure the appointment of a guardian without being required to demonstrate an inability to care for himself or his property; the guardianship may be revoked without proving a just cause; and the guardian receives only those powers requested by the petitioner. This technique provides the petitioner with a degree of certainty because the individual dictates the person who is originally appointed as guardian * * *. However, a person may be reluctant to submit to this procedure

court stated that "liberty of the person and the right to the control of one's own property are very sacred rights which should not be taken away or withheld except for very urgent reasons").

4. In re Estate of Bennett, 122 Ill. App. 3d 756, 78 Ill. Dec. 83, 461 N.E.2d 667 (1984) * * *.

5. [R. ALLEN, E. FERSTER & H. WEIHOFEN, MENTAL IMPAIRMENT AND LEGAL INCOMPETENCY 90] (emphasis in original).

while competent; he may not wish to relinquish control over his property or person or may be unwilling to incur the court costs and guardian fees which may accompany the voluntary guardianship. This type of statute is akin to a durable power of attorney. It was probably designed to allow a person to obtain immediate assistance with some aspect of his personal or business affairs without a complicated or embarrassing guardianship proceeding rather than as a method to obtain the appointment of a guardian who is to stand in the wings until actually needed.

B. Standby Guardianship/Conservatorship

A somewhat recent approach adopted by several states authorizes a competent person to prepare and file a petition for the appointment of a guardian of his person or conservator of his estate before the need arises but delays court action on the petition until the occurrence of a specified triggering event.[6] * * *

C. Nomination by Durable Power of Attorney

The most common method adopted by state legislatures to permit individuals to select their own guardians is by an express nomination in a durable power of attorney. This technique permits the principal to nominate both a guardian of his person and a guardian of his estate (conservator).

Many of these state statutes are based on * * * the Uniform Probate Code * * * which permit[s] the principal to include fiduciary nominations in a durable power of attorney. * * * The drafters opined that the best reason for making a guardian self-designation was that such action would warrant the authority granted to the agent against future challenges by "arranging matters so that the likely appointee in any future protective proceedings will be the [agent] or another equally congenial to the principal and his plans."[7]

D. Nomination in Living Will

[pertains only to health care agents] * * *

E. Nomination in Will-like Document

The second most common method by which a state grants a person the ability to designate his own guardian is through a document which must be executed with many, if not all, of the formalities of a valid will. Some states refer directly to their will statutes and incorporate those requirements while others list requirements akin to those for a will. In addition to nominating guardians, some states permit the self-declaration to control other aspects of the guardianship; for example, waiver of bond, designation of successors, grant of guardianship powers, and disqualification of named individuals. The enabling legislation may also govern other

---

6. See IOWA CODE ANN. §§ 633.560, 633.591–633.597 (West 1964); WYO. STAT. §§ 3–3–301 to 3–3–302 (1985).

7. UNIF. PROB. CODE § 5–503 comment, 8 U.L.A. 515–16 (1987) * * *.

aspects of the self-designation process such as the method of resolving a conflicting designation in a durable power of attorney, evidentiary presumptions, revocation methods, the effect of the declarant's divorce from a designated guardian, and the recommendation of the format of the self-designation document.

States that employ will-like documents provide an easy method for a person to designate a guardian before the need arises, as do jurisdictions that provide for nomination in a durable power of attorney. However, the will-like document technique may have difficulties because of the rigid formalities associated with their execution. To be valid, will-like documents must comply with the technical requirements for wills or with similar formalities such as attestation, and are thus susceptible to invalidation for minor errors in their execution, e.g., one witness signing rather than the required two witnesses, witness attesting out of the declarant's sight, witness signing the self-proving affidavit rather than declaration. No case was located where a formality problem led to an ineffective designation of guardian, but cases are legion where a technical error has caused an otherwise valid will to fail.

In contrast to this formal will-like procedure which is wrought with hazards, durable powers of attorney have few formal requirements; a writing signed by the principal and properly notarized is often sufficient. This method may thus be more effective in carrying out the desires of the declarant because of its ease of execution and the decreased chance of inadvertently failing to fulfill all of the necessary formalities.

F. Other Written Designations

Rather than impose a formalistic set of requirements for a valid self-declaration of a guardian, several jurisdictions permit competent adults to nominate a guardian in a simple written document. The technical requirements of these written designations vary: some must be signed, some must be acknowledged, while others merely need to be written. The statutes authorizing these written designations also vary with respect to the time at which the declarant may make the designation: some must be made while the declarant is still competent, while others may be made after the person becomes incompetent provided he had sufficient mental capacity to make an intelligent selection at the time the designation was executed. In addition, some statutes expressly permit the nomination of alternate guardians and provide rules of interpretation for use if the same person has executed multiple self-declarations.

These written designations are straightforward and relatively simple to use. They avoid many of the problems which accompany the will-like designations because technical formalities are eliminated or are considerably reduced. However, the lack of formalities may make these designations easier to forge or alter and may increase the chance of undetected undue influence, duress, or fraud. Thus, jurisdictions considering the two approaches may conclude that the protective aspect of the formalities outweighs the potential frustration of intent that may occur if a self-declaration is executed with proper intent but fails to comport with the required formalities. On the other hand, if forgery, undue influence, or other evil conduct is involved, there will usually be a person contesting the designation and the contest will often expose this improper behavior. * * *

ANALYSIS

* * *

A. Increased Chance of Desired Person Serving as Guardian

Perhaps the most important reason a person would elect to use a self-declaration of guardian is to increase the likelihood that a specific person will be appointed as guardian in the event of later incompetency or incapacity. Without such a designation, there is no assurance that a court-appointed guardian will be the person the disabled individual would have desired to control his person or estate. To the contrary, the person the court appoints could be someone the incompetent person would never have wanted to serve as his guardian.

The psychological benefits of self-selection are considerable, both before and after the declarant needs a guardian. After designating a guardian, a person may be more secure about the future, knowing that should anything happen to him, his personal affairs and business concerns would be handled by a trusted family member, friend, or financial institution. Just as a will may relieve some of the fears that accompany the anticipation of death, a self-declaration of guardian may alleviate the stress associated with accepting the prospect of becoming unexpectedly disabled or that a current disease or injury will worsen, leading to incapacity. Likewise, a disabled person will gain strength from knowing that he is still having an effect on his situation by seeing a guardian appointed in accordance with his wishes. The self-selected guardian may have more detailed knowledge of the ward's desires and may thus be able to provide a more supportive environment as well as one more conducive to comfort and perhaps even recovery.

B. Reduced Chance of Undesired Person Serving as Guardian

If a valid self-declaration of guardian exists, the chance of a person being appointed as guardian who is unsuitable to the ward is greatly reduced. Presumably, the declarant would give careful thought to the nomination so that undesirable family members, friends, and institutions are not listed. If the court believes it to be in the ward's best interests, however, others may be appointed in contradiction to the ward's intent, albeit unexpressed.

Accordingly, the best method to prevent a particular person from serving as guardian is for the declarant to include a statement in the designating document which indicates that person's unsuitability without requiring the declarant to detail the reasons behind his decision to exclude that person. Inclusion of such information would open the door to the court making an evaluation of the declarant's reasoning. This evaluation would be unproductive because the only issue in disqualification situations is whether the declarant had sufficient mental capacity when he excluded the named person; it is irrelevant whether the court agrees with the wisdom of the declarant's decision.

The effect of a non-nomination is questionable in most jurisdictions because most statutes and accompanying fill-in forms fail to address the issue; only the Texas form provides for express disqualification. The inclusion of an express disqualification provision is especially important in cases where the ward is so disabled that he is unable to express his displeasure with a particular guardian.

C. *Conservation of Resources*

Self-declarations of guardians may also conserve valuable resources. When a guardian is pre-selected, the court's expenditure of time to ascertain the identity of a proper guardian is reduced. Unless the appointment of the nominee is contested for cause, the court will be able to handle guardian appointments quickly and effectively. Should reasons for the preferred guardian's disqualification be discovered from evidence presented in court, that same evidence is likely to indicate the reasons the court should appoint the designated alternate, again conserving the court's resources. Because less court time will be required, fewer assets of the declarant's estate will be dissipated for court costs and attorney's fees. The accelerated appointment procedure will also place the ward's person and estate into competent hands more rapidly, perhaps before serious personal or business problems arise.

D. *Potential for Abuse*

Perhaps the greatest concern with the enactment of self-declaration of guardian fill-in forms is the potential for abuse. If a self-designation document is obtained through fraud, duress, or other coercion, the negative ramifications to the ward are particularly harmful because the designated guardian could abuse his power causing the declarant tremendous financial and psychological hardship, physical pain, and even a premature death. Likewise, a document executed by a declarant who does not fully understand the legal significance of what is being done may result in designations that do not actually reflect the declarant's intent.

LOCATE

How may a person in your state designate a guardian before the need arises? Remember that there may be more than one method. Study your state's legislation and answer the questions below.

QUESTIONS

1. What formalities must be satisfied for a valid self-designation of guardian?

2. What considerations should be taken into account when determining whom to nominate? See also Chapter 8(H).

3. May certain people be specifically excluded from possible appointment?

4. What effect does the nominated guardian's divorce from the ward have on the designation?

5. How are conflicting designations in multiple documents handled?

6. May statutory guardian powers be expanded or limited by the self-designation document?

DRAFT

Prepare a guardian self-declaration document nominating the client's spouse and, alternately the client's daughter, as guardian of the person and expressly disqualifying the client's son.

D. CUSTODIAL TRUSTS

UNIFORM CUSTODIAL TRUST ACT

1987 Act.

PREFATORY NOTE

This Uniform Act provides for the creation of a statutory custodial trust for adults to be governed by the provisions of the Act whenever property is delivered to another "as custodial trustee under the (Enacting state) Uniform Custodial Trust Act." The provisions of this Act are based on trust analogies to concepts developed and used in establishing custodianships for minors under the Uniform Transfers to Minors Act (UTMA). The Custodial Trust Act is designed to provide a statutory standby inter vivos trust for individuals who typically are not very affluent or sophisticated, and possibly represented by attorneys engaged in general rather than specialized estate practice. The most frequent use of this trust would be in response to the commonly occurring need of elderly individuals to provide for the future management of assets in the event of incapacity. The statute will also be available for accomplishing distribution of funds by judgment debtors and others to incapacitated persons for whom a conservator has not been appointed. Since this Act allows any person, competent to transfer property, to create custodial trusts for the benefit of themselves or others, with the beneficial interest in custodial trust property in the beneficiary and not in the custodial trustee, its potential for use is extensive. Although the most frequent use probably will be by elderly persons, it is also available for a parent to establish a custodial trust for an adult child who may be incapacitated; for adult persons in the military, or those leaving the country temporarily, to place their property with another for management without relinquishing beneficial ownership of their property; or for young people who have received property under the Uniform Transfers to Minors Act to continue a custodial trust as adults in order to obtain the benefit and convenience of management services performed by the custodial trustee.

This Act follows the approach taken by the Uniform Transfers to Minors Act and allows any kind of property, real or personal, tangible or intangible, to be made the subject of a transfer to a custodial trustee for the benefit of a beneficiary. However, the most typical transaction envisioned would involve a person who would transfer intangible property, such as securities or bank accounts, to a custodial trustee but with retention by the transferor of direction over the property. Later, this direction could be relinquished, or it could be lost upon incapacity. The objective of the statute is to provide a simple trust that is uncomplicated in its creation, administration, and termination. The potential for tax problems is minimized by permitting the beneficiary in most instances to retain control while the beneficiary has capacity to manage the assets effectively. The statute contains an asset specific transfer provision that it is believed will be simple to use and will gain the acceptance of the securities and financial industry. A simple transfer document, examples of which are set forth in the Act, and a receipt from the custodian, also in the Act, would provide for identification of beneficiaries or distributees upon death of the beneficiary. Protection is extended to third parties dealing with the custodian. Although the Act is patterned on the Uniform Transfers to Minors Act and meshes into the Uniform Probate Code, it is appropriate for enactment as well in states which have not adopted either UTMA or the UPC.

An adult beneficiary, who is not incapacitated, may: (1) terminate the custodial trust on demand (Section 2(e)); (2) receive so much of the income or custodial property as he or she may request from time to time (Section 9(a)); and (3) give the custodial trustee binding instructions for investment or management (Section 7(b)). In the absence of direction by the beneficiary, who is not incapacitated, the custodial trustee manages the property subject to the standard of care that would be observed by a prudent person dealing with the property of another and is not limited by other statutory restrictions on investments by fiduciaries (Section 7).

A principal feature of the Custodial Trust under this Act is designed to protect the beneficiary and his or her dependents against the perils of the beneficiary's possible future incapacity without the necessity of a conservatorship. Under Section 10, the incapacity of the beneficiary does not terminate (1) the custodial trust, (2) the designation of a successor custodial trustee, (3) any power or authority of the custodial trustee, or (4) the immunities of third persons relying on actions of the custodial trustee. The custodial trustee continues to manage the property as a discretionary trust under the prudent person standard for the benefit of the incapacitated beneficiary.

Means of monitoring and enforcing the custodial trust include provisions requiring the custodial trustee to keep the beneficiary informed, requiring accounting by the custodial trustee (Section 15), providing for removal of the custodial trustee (Section 13), and the distribution of the assets on termination of the custodial trust (Section 17). The custodial trustee is protected in Section 16 by the statutes of limitation on proceedings against the custodial trustee.

Transactions with the custodial trustee should be executed readily and quickly by third parties because their rights and protections are determined by the Act and a third party acting in good faith has no need to determine the custodial trustee's authority to bind the beneficiary with respect to property and investment matters (Section 11). The Act generally limits the claims of third parties to recourse against the custodial property, with the beneficiary insulated against personal liability unless he or she is personally at fault and the custodial trustee is similarly insulated unless the custodial trustee is personally at fault or failed to disclose the custodial capacity when entering into a contract (Section 12).

As a consequence of the mobility of our population, particularly the mature persons who are most likely to utilize this Act, uniformity of the laws governing custodial trusts is highly desirable, and the Act is designed to avoid conflict of laws problems. A custodial trust created under this Act remains subject to this Act despite a subsequent change in the residence of the transferor, the beneficiary, or the custodial trustee or the removal of the custodial trust property from the state of original location (Section 19).

Section 1. Definitions

As used in this [Act]:

(1) "Adult" means an individual who is at least 18 years of age.

(2) "Beneficiary" means an individual for whom property has been transferred to or held under a declaration of trust by a custodial trustee for the individual's use and benefit under this [Act].

(3) "Conservator" means a person appointed or qualified by a court to manage the estate of an individual or a person legally authorized to perform substantially the same functions.

(4) "Court" means the [________] court of this State.

(5) "Custodial trust property" means an interest in property transferred to or held under a declaration of trust by a custodial trustee under this [Act] and the income from and proceeds of that interest.

(6) "Custodial trustee" means a person designated as trustee of a custodial trust under this [Act] or a substitute or successor to the person designated.

(7) "Guardian" means a person appointed or qualified by a court as a guardian of an individual, including a limited guardian, but not a person who is only a guardian ad litem.

(8) "Incapacitated" means lacking the ability to manage property and business affairs effectively by reason of mental illness, mental deficiency,

physical illness or disability, chronic use of drugs, chronic intoxication, confinement, detention by a foreign power, disappearance, minority, or other disabling cause.

(9) "Legal representative" means a personal representative or conservator.

(10) "Member of the beneficiary's family" means a beneficiary's spouse, descendant, stepchild, parent, stepparent, grandparent, brother, sister, uncle, or aunt, whether of the whole or half blood or by adoption.

(11) "Person" means an individual, corporation, business trust, estate, trust, partnership, joint venture, association, or any other legal or commercial entity.

(12) "Personal representative" means an executor, administrator, or special administrator of a decedent's estate, a person legally authorized to perform substantially the same functions, or a successor to any of them.

(13) "State" means a state, territory, or possession of the United States, the District of Columbia, or the Commonwealth of Puerto Rico.

(14) "Transferor" means a person who creates a custodial trust by transfer or declaration.

(15) "Trust company" means a financial institution, corporation, or other legal entity, authorized to exercise general trust powers.

Section 2. Custodial Trust; General

(a) A person may create a custodial trust of property by a written transfer of the property to another person, evidenced by registration or by other instrument of transfer, executed in any lawful manner, naming as beneficiary, an individual who may be the transferor, in which the transferee is designated, in substance, as custodial trustee under the [Enacting state] Uniform Custodial Trust Act.

(b) A person may create a custodial trust of property by a written declaration, evidenced by registration of the property or by other instrument of declaration executed in any lawful manner, describing the property and naming as beneficiary an individual other than the declarant, in which the declarant as titleholder is designated, in substance, as custodial trustee under the [Enacting state] Uniform Custodial Trust Act. A registration or other declaration of trust for the sole benefit of the declarant is not a custodial trust under this [Act].

(c) Title to custodial trust property is in the custodial trustee and the beneficial interest is in the beneficiary.

(d) Except as provided in subsection (e), a transferor may not terminate a custodial trust.

(e) The beneficiary, if not incapacitated, or the conservator of an incapacitated beneficiary, may terminate a custodial trust by delivering to the custodial trustee a writing signed by the beneficiary or conservator declaring the termination. If not previously terminated, the custodial trust terminates on the death of the beneficiary.

(f) Any person may augment existing custodial trust property by the addition of other property pursuant to this [Act].

(g) The transferor may designate, or authorize the designation of, a successor custodial trustee in the trust instrument.

(h) This [Act] does not displace or restrict other means of creating trusts. A trust whose terms do not conform to this [Act] may be enforceable according to its terms under other law.

Section 3. Custodial Trustee for Future Payment or Transfer

(a) A person having the right to designate the recipient of property payable or transferable upon a future event may create a custodial trust upon the occurrence of the future event by designating in writing the recipient, followed in substance by: "as custodial trustee for ______ (name of beneficiary) under the [Enacting state] Uniform Custodial Trust Act."

(b) Persons may be designated as substitute or successor custodial trustees to whom the property must be paid or transferred in the order named if the first designated custodial trustee is unable or unwilling to serve.

(c) A designation under this section may be made in a will, a trust, a deed, a multiple-party account, an insurance policy, an instrument exercising a power of appointment, or a writing designating a beneficiary of contractual rights. Otherwise, to be effective, the designation must be registered with or delivered to the fiduciary, payor, issuer, or obligor of the future right.

Section 4. Form and Effect of Receipt and Acceptance by Custodial Trustee, Jurisdiction

(a) Obligations of a custodial trustee, including the obligation to follow directions of the beneficiary, arise under this [Act] upon the custodial trustee's acceptance, express or implied, of the custodial trust property.

(b) The custodial trustee's acceptance may be evidenced by a writing stating in substance:

CUSTODIAL TRUSTEE'S RECEIPT AND ACCEPTANCE

I, ______ (name of custodial trustee) acknowledge receipt of the custodial trust property described below or in the attached instrument and accept the custodial trust as custodial trustee for ______ (name of beneficiary) under the [Enacting state] Uniform Custodial Trust Act. I undertake to administer and distribute the custodial trust property pursuant to the [Enacting state] Uniform Custodial Trust Act. My obligations as custodial trustee are subject to the directions of the beneficiary unless the beneficiary is designated as, is, or becomes incapacitated. The custodial trust property consists of ________________________________.

Dated: ______

____

(Signature of Custodial Trustee)

(c) Upon accepting custodial trust property, a person designated as custodial trustee under this [Act] is subject to personal jurisdiction of the court with respect to any matter relating to the custodial trust.

Section 5. Transfer to Custodial Trustee by Fiduciary or Obligor; Facility of Payment

(a) Unless otherwise directed by an instrument designating a custodial trustee pursuant to Section 3, a person, including a fiduciary other than a custodial trustee, who holds property of or owes a debt to an incapacitated individual not having a conservator may make a transfer to an adult member of the beneficiary's family or to a trust company as custodial trustee for the use and benefit of the incapacitated individual. If the value of the property or the debt exceeds [$20,000], the transfer is not effective unless authorized by the court.

(b) A written acknowledgment of delivery, signed by a custodial trustee, is a sufficient receipt and discharge for property transferred to the custodial trustee pursuant to this section.

Section 6. Multiple Beneficiaries; Separate Custodial Trusts; Survivorship

(a) Beneficial interests in a custodial trust created for multiple beneficiaries are deemed to be separate custodial trusts of equal undivided interests for each beneficiary. Except in a transfer or declaration for use and benefit of husband and wife, for whom survivorship is presumed, a right of survivorship does not exist unless the instrument creating the custodial trust specifically provides for survivorship [or survivorship is required as to community or marital property].

(b) Custodial trust property held under this [Act] by the same custodial trustee for the use and benefit of the same beneficiary may be administered as a single custodial trust.

(c) A custodial trustee of custodial trust property held for more than one beneficiary shall separately account to each beneficiary pursuant to Sections 7 and 15 for the administration of the custodial trust.

Section 7. General Duties of Custodial Trustee

(a) If appropriate, a custodial trustee shall register or record the instrument vesting title to custodial trust property.

(b) If the beneficiary is not incapacitated, a custodial trustee shall follow the directions of the beneficiary in the management, control, investment, or retention of the custodial trust property. In the absence of effective contrary direction by the beneficiary while not incapacitated, the custodial trustee shall observe the standard of care that would be observed by a prudent person dealing with property of another and is not limited by any other law restricting investments by fiduciaries. However, a custodial trustee, in the custodial trustee's discretion, may retain any custodial trust property received from the transferor. If a custodial trustee has a special skill or expertise or is named custodial trustee on the basis of representation of a special skill or expertise, the custodial trustee shall use that skill or expertise.

(c) Subject to subsection (b), a custodial trustee shall take control of and collect, hold, manage, invest, and reinvest custodial trust property.

(d) A custodial trustee at all times shall keep custodial trust property of which the custodial trustee has control, separate from all other property in a manner sufficient to identify it clearly as custodial trust property of the beneficiary. Custodial trust property, the title to which is subject to recordation, is so identified if an appropriate instrument so identifying the property is recorded, and custodial trust property subject to registration is so identified if it is registered, or held in an account in the name of the custodial trustee, designated in substance: "as custodial trustee for _______ (name of beneficiary) under the [Enacting state] Uniform Custodial Trust Act."

(e) A custodial trustee shall keep records of all transactions with respect to custodial trust property, including information necessary for the preparation of tax returns, and shall make the records and information available at reasonable times to the beneficiary or legal representative of the beneficiary.

(f) The exercise of a durable power of attorney for an incapacitated beneficiary is not effective to terminate or direct the administration or distribution of a custodial trust.

Section 8. General Powers of Custodial Trustee

(a) A custodial trustee, acting in a fiduciary capacity, has all the rights and powers over custodial trust property which an unmarried adult owner has over individually owned property, but a custodial trustee may exercise those rights and powers in a fiduciary capacity only.

(b) This section does not relieve a custodial trustee from liability for a violation of Section 7.

Section 9. Use of Custodial Trust Property

(a) A custodial trustee shall pay to the beneficiary or expend for the beneficiary's use and benefit so much or all of the custodial trust property as the beneficiary while not incapacitated may direct from time to time.

(b) If the beneficiary is incapacitated, the custodial trustee shall expend so much or all of the custodial trust property as the custodial trustee considers advisable for the use and benefit of the beneficiary and individuals who were supported by the beneficiary when the beneficiary became incapacitated, or who are legally entitled to support by the beneficiary. Expenditures may be made in the manner, when, and to the extent that the custodial trustee determines suitable and proper, without court order and without regard to other support, income, or property of the beneficiary.

(c) A custodial trustee may establish checking, savings, or other similar accounts of reasonable amounts under which either the custodial trustee or the beneficiary may withdraw funds from, or draw checks against, the accounts. Funds withdrawn from, or checks written against, the account by the beneficiary are distributions of custodial trust property by the custodial trustee to the beneficiary.

Section 10. Determination of Incapacity; Effect

(a) The custodial trustee shall administer the custodial trust as for an incapacitated beneficiary if (i) the custodial trust was created under Section 5, (ii) the transferor has so directed in the instrument creating the custodial trust, or (iii) the custodial trustee has determined that the beneficiary is incapacitated.

(b) A custodial trustee may determine that the beneficiary is incapacitated in reliance upon (i) previous direction or authority given by the beneficiary while not incapacitated, including direction or authority pursuant to a durable power of attorney, (ii) the certificate of the beneficiary's physician, or (iii) other persuasive evidence.

(c) If a custodial trustee for an incapacitated beneficiary reasonably concludes that the beneficiary's incapacity has ceased, or that circumstances concerning the beneficiary's ability to manage property and business affairs have changed since the creation of a custodial trust directing administration as for an incapacitated beneficiary, the custodial trustee may administer the trust as for a beneficiary who is not incapacitated.

(d) On petition of the beneficiary, the custodial trustee, or other person interested in the custodial trust property or the welfare of the beneficiary, the court shall determine whether the beneficiary is incapacitated.

(e) Absent determination of incapacity of the beneficiary under subsection (b) or (d), a custodial trustee who has reason to believe that the beneficiary is incapacitated shall administer the custodial trust in accordance with the provisions of this [Act] applicable to an incapacitated beneficiary.

(f) Incapacity of a beneficiary does not terminate (i) the custodial trust, (ii) any designation of a successor custodial trustee, (iii) rights or powers of the custodial trustee, or (iv) any immunities of third persons acting on instructions of the custodial trustee.

Section 11. Exemption of Third Person From Liability

A third person in good faith and without a court order may act on instructions of, or otherwise deal with, a person purporting to make a transfer as, or purporting to act in the capacity of, a custodial trustee. In the absence of knowledge to the contrary, the third person is not responsible for determining:

(1) the validity of the purported custodial trustee's designation;

(2) the propriety of, or the authority under this [Act] for, any action of the purported custodial trustee;

(3) the validity or propriety of an instrument executed or instruction given pursuant to this [Act] either by the person purporting to make a transfer or declaration or by the purported custodial trustee; or

(4) the propriety of the application of property vested in the purported custodial trustee.

Section 12. Liability to Third Person

(a) A claim based on a contract entered into by a custodial trustee acting in a fiduciary capacity, an obligation arising from the ownership or control of custodial trust property, or a tort committed in the course of administering the custodial trust, may be asserted by a third person against the custodial trust property by proceeding against the custodial trustee in a fiduciary capacity, whether or not the custodial trustee or the beneficiary is personally liable.

(b) A custodial trustee is not personally liable to a third person:

(1) on a contract properly entered into in a fiduciary capacity unless the custodial trustee fails to reveal that capacity or to identify the custodial trust in the contract; or

(2) for an obligation arising from control of custodial trust property or for a tort committed in the course of the administration of the custodial trust unless the custodial trustee is personally at fault.

(c) A beneficiary is not personally liable to a third person for an obligation arising from beneficial ownership of custodial trust property or for a tort committed in the course of administration of the custodial trust unless the beneficiary is personally in possession of the custodial trust property giving rise to the liability or is personally at fault.

(d) Subsections (b) and (c) do not preclude actions or proceedings to establish liability of the custodial trustee or beneficiary to the extent the person sued is protected as the insured by liability insurance.

Section 13. Declination, Resignation, Incapacity, Death, or Removal of Custodial Trustee, Designation of Successor Custodial Trustee

(a) Before accepting the custodial trust property, a person designated as custodial trustee may decline to serve by notifying the person who made the designation, the transferor, or the transferor's legal representative. If an event giving rise to a transfer has not occurred, the substitute custodial trustee designated under Section 3 becomes the custodial trustee, or, if a substitute custodial trustee has not been designated, the person who made the designation may designate a substitute custodial trustee pursuant to Section 3. In other cases, the transferor or the transferor's legal representative may designate a substitute custodial trustee.

(b) A custodial trustee who has accepted the custodial trust property may resign by (i) delivering written notice to a successor custodial trustee, if any, the beneficiary and, if the beneficiary is incapacitated, to the beneficiary's conservator, if any, and (ii) transferring or registering, or recording an appropriate instrument relating to, the custodial trust property, in the name of, and delivering the records to, the successor custodial trustee identified under subsection (c).

(c) If a custodial trustee or successor custodial trustee is ineligible, resigns, dies, or becomes incapacitated, the successor designated under Section 2(g) or 3 becomes custodial trustee. If there is no effective provision for a successor, the beneficiary, if not incapacitated, may designate a successor custodial trustee. If the beneficiary is incapacitated, or fails to act within 90 days after the ineligibility, resignation, death, or incapacity of the custodial trustee, the beneficiary's conservator becomes successor custodial trustee. If the beneficiary does not have a conservator or the conservator fails to act, the resigning custodial trustee may designate a successor custodial trustee.

(d) If a successor custodial trustee is not designated pursuant to subsection (c), the transferor, the legal representative of the transferor or of the custodial trustee, an adult member of the beneficiary's family, the guardian of the beneficiary, a person interested in the custodial trust property, or a person interested in the welfare of the beneficiary, may petition the court to designate a successor custodial trustee.

(e) A custodial trustee who declines to serve or resigns, or the legal representative of a deceased or incapacitated custodial trustee, as soon as practicable, shall put the custodial trust property and records in the possession and control of the successor custodial trustee. The successor custodial trustee may enforce the obligation to deliver custodial trust property and records and becomes responsible for each item as received.

(f) A beneficiary, the beneficiary's conservator, an adult member of the beneficiary's family, a guardian of the person of the beneficiary, a person interested in the custodial trust property, or a person interested in the welfare of the beneficiary, may petition the court to remove the custodial trustee for cause and designate a successor custodial trustee, to require the custodial trustee to furnish a bond or other security for the faithful performance of fiduciary duties, or for other appropriate relief.

Section 14. Expenses, Compensation, and Bond of Custodial Trustee

Except as otherwise provided in the instrument creating the custodial trust, in an agreement with the beneficiary, or by court order, a custodial trustee:

(1) is entitled to reimbursement from custodial trust property for reasonable expenses incurred in the performance of fiduciary services;

(2) has a noncumulative election, to be made no later than six months after the end of each calendar year, to charge a reasonable compensation for fiduciary services performed during that year; and

(3) need not furnish a bond or other security for the faithful performance of fiduciary duties.

Section 15. Reporting and Accounting by Custodial Trustee; Determination of Liability of Custodial Trustee

(a) Upon the acceptance of custodial trust property, the custodial trustee shall provide a written statement describing the custodial trust property and shall thereafter provide a written statement of the administration of the custodial trust property (i) once each year, (ii) upon request at reasonable times by the beneficiary or the beneficiary's legal representative, (iii) upon resignation or removal of the custodial trustee, and (iv) upon termination of the custodial trust. The statements must be provided to the beneficiary or to the beneficiary's legal representative, if any. Upon termination of the beneficiary's interest, the custodial trustee shall furnish a current statement to the person to whom the custodial trust property is to be delivered.

(b) A beneficiary, the beneficiary's legal representative, an adult member of the beneficiary's family, a person interested in the custodial trust property, or a person interested in the welfare of the beneficiary may petition the court for an accounting by the custodial trustee or the custodial trustee's legal representative.

(c) A successor custodial trustee may petition the court for an accounting by a predecessor custodial trustee.

(d) In an action or proceeding under this [Act] or in any other proceeding, the court may require or permit the custodial trustee or the custodial trustee's legal representative to account. The custodial trustee or the custodial trustee's legal representative may petition the court for approval of final accounts.

(e) If a custodial trustee is removed, the court shall require an accounting and order delivery of the custodial trust property and records to the successor custodial trustee and the execution of all instruments required for transfer of the custodial trust property.

(f) On petition of the custodial trustee or any person who could petition for an accounting, the court, after notice to interested persons, may issue instructions to the custodial trustee or review the propriety of the acts of a custodial trustee or the reasonableness of compensation determined by the custodial trustee for the services of the custodial trustee or others.

Section 16. Limitations of Action Against Custodial Trustee

(a) Except as provided in subsection (c), unless previously barred by adjudication, consent, or limitation, a claim for relief against a custodial trustee for accounting or breach of duty is barred as to a beneficiary, a person to whom custodial trust property is to be paid or delivered, or the legal representative of an incapacitated or deceased beneficiary or payee:

(1) who has received a final account or statement fully disclosing the matter unless an action or proceeding to assert the claim is commenced within two years after receipt of the final account or statement; or

(2) who has not received a final account or statement fully disclosing the matter unless an action or proceeding to assert the claim is commenced within three years after the termination of the custodial trust.

(b) Except as provided in subsection (c), a claim for relief to recover from a custodial trustee for fraud, misrepresentation, or concealment related to the final settlement of the custodial trust or concealment of the existence of the custodial trust, is barred unless an action or proceeding to assert the claim is commenced within five years after the termination of the custodial trust.

(c) A claim for relief is not barred by this section if the claimant:

(1) is a minor, until the earlier of two years after the claimant becomes an adult or dies;

(2) is an incapacitated adult, until the earliest of two years after (i) the appointment of a conservator, (ii) the removal of the incapacity, or (iii) the death of the claimant; or

(3) was an adult, now deceased, who was not incapacitated, until two years after the claimant's death.

Section 17. Distribution on Termination

(a) Upon termination of a custodial trust, the custodial trustee shall transfer the unexpended custodial trust property:

(1) to the beneficiary, if not incapacitated or deceased;

(2) to the conservator or other recipient designated by the court for an incapacitated beneficiary; or

(3) upon the beneficiary's death, in the following order:

(i) as last directed in a writing signed by the deceased beneficiary while not incapacitated and received by the custodial trustee during the life of the deceased beneficiary;

(ii) to the survivor of multiple beneficiaries if survivorship is provided for pursuant to Section 6;

(iii) as designated in the instrument creating the custodial trust; or

(iv) to the estate of the deceased beneficiary.

(b) If, when the custodial trust would otherwise terminate, the distributee is incapacitated, the custodial trust continues for the use and benefit of the distributee as beneficiary until the incapacity is removed or the custodial trust is otherwise terminated.

(c) Death of a beneficiary does not terminate the power of the custodial trustee to discharge obligations of the custodial trustee or beneficiary incurred before the termination of the custodial trust.

Section 18. Methods and Forms for Creating Custodial Trusts

(a) If a transaction, including a declaration with respect to or a transfer of specific property, otherwise satisfies applicable law, the criteria of Section 2 are satisfied by:

(1) the execution and either delivery to the custodial trustee or recording of an instrument in substantially the following form:

TRANSFER UNDER THE [ENACTING STATE] UNIFORM CUSTODIAL TRUST ACT

I, _______ (name of transferor or name and representative capacity if a fiduciary), transfer to _______ (name of trustee other than transferor), as custodial trustee for _______ (name of beneficiary) as beneficiary and _______ as distributee on termination of the trust in absence of direction by the beneficiary under the [Enacting state] Uniform Custodial Trust Act, the following: (insert a description of the custodial trust property legally sufficient to identify and transfer each item of property).

Dated: _______

____

(Signature)

or

(2) the execution and the recording or giving notice of its execution to the beneficiary of an instrument in substantially the following form:

DECLARATION OF TRUST UNDER THE [ENACTING STATE] UNIFORM CUSTODIAL TRUST ACT

I, _______ (name of owner of property), declare that henceforth I hold as custodial trustee for _______ (name of beneficiary other than transferor) as beneficiary and ______ as distributee on termination of the trust in absence of direction by the beneficiary under the [Enacting state] Uniform Custodial Trust Act, the following: (Insert a description of the custodial trust property legally sufficient to identify and transfer each item of property).

Dated: ______

____

(Signature)

(b) Customary methods of transferring or evidencing ownership of property may be used to create a custodial trust, including any of the following:

(1) registration of a security in the name of a trust company, an adult other than the transferor, or the transferor if the beneficiary is other than the transferor, designated in substance "as custodial trustee for ______ (name of beneficiary) under the [Enacting state] Uniform Custodial Trust Act";

(2) delivery of a certificated security, or a document necessary for the transfer of an uncertificated security, together with any necessary endorsement, to an adult other than the transferor or to a trust company as custodial trustee, accompanied by an instrument in substantially the form prescribed in subsection (a)(1);

(3) payment of money or transfer of a security held in the name of a broker or a financial institution or its nominee to a broker or financial institution for credit to an account in the name of a trust company, an adult other than the transferor, or the transferor if the beneficiary is other than the transferor, designated in substance: "as custodial trustee for ______ (name of beneficiary) under the [Enacting state] Uniform Custodial Trust Act";

(4) registration of ownership of a life or endowment insurance policy or annuity contract with the issuer in the name of a trust company, an adult other than the transferor, or the transferor if the beneficiary is other than the transferor, designated in substance: "as custodial trustee for ______ (name of beneficiary) under the [Enacting state] Uniform Custodial Trust Act";

(5) delivery of a written assignment to an adult other than the transferor or to a trust company whose name in the assignment is designated in substance by the words: "as custodial trustee for ______ (name of beneficiary) under the [Enacting state] Uniform Custodial Trust Act";

(6) irrevocable exercise of a power of appointment, pursuant to its terms, in favor of a trust company, an adult other than the donee of the power, or the donee who holds the power if the beneficiary is other than the donee, whose name in the appointment is designated

in substance: "as custodial trustee for ______ (name of beneficiary) under the [Enacting state] Uniform Custodial Trust Act";

(7) delivery of a written notification or assignment of a right to future payment under a contract to an obligor which transfers the right under the contract to a trust company, an adult other than the transferor, or the transferor if the beneficiary is other than the transferor, whose name in the notification or assignment is designated in substance: "as custodial trustee for ______ (name of beneficiary) under the [Enacting state] Uniform Custodial Trust Act";

(8) execution, delivery, and recordation of a conveyance of an interest in real property in the name of a trust company, an adult other than the transferor, or the transferor if the beneficiary is other than the transferor, designated in substance: "as custodial trustee for ______ (name of beneficiary) under the [Enacting state] Uniform Custodial Trust Act";

(9) issuance of a certificate of title by an agency of a state or of the United States which evidences title to tangible personal property:

(i) issued in the name of a trust company, an adult other than the transferor, or the transferor if the beneficiary is other than the transferor, designated in substance: "as custodial trustee for ______ (name of beneficiary) under the [Enacting state] Uniform Custodial Trust Act"; or

(ii) delivered to a trust company or an adult other than the transferor or endorsed by the transferor to that person, designated in substance: "as custodial trustee for ______ (name of beneficiary) under the [Enacting state] Uniform Custodial Trust Act"; or

(10) execution and delivery of an instrument of gift to a trust company or an adult other than the transferor, designated in substance: "as custodial trustee for ______ (name of beneficiary) under the [Enacting state] Uniform Custodial Trust Act."

Section 19. Applicable Law

(a) This [Act] applies to a transfer or declaration creating a custodial trust that refers to this [Act] if, at the time of the transfer or declaration, the transferor, beneficiary, or custodial trustee is a resident of or has its principal place of business in this State or custodial trust property is located in this State. The custodial trust remains subject to this [Act] despite a later change in residence or principal place of business of the transferor, beneficiary, or custodial trustee, or removal of the custodial trust property from this State.

(b) A transfer made pursuant to an act of another state substantially similar to this [Act] is governed by the law of that state and may be enforced in this State.

Section 20. Uniformity of Application and Construction

This [Act] shall be applied and construed to effectuate its general purpose to make uniform the law with respect to the subject of this [Act] among states enacting it.

Section 21. Short Title

This [Act] may be cited as the "[Name of Enacting State] Uniform Custodial Trust Act."

LOCATE

Has your state enacted the U.C.T.A. or a similar type of statute? If yes, what changes did your state legislature make to the uniform text?

NOTES AND QUESTIONS

1. At least eighteen jurisdictions have enacted the U.C.T.A. including Alaska, Arizona, Arkansas, Colorado, District of Columbia, Hawaii, Idaho, Indiana, Louisiana, Massachusetts, Minnesota, Missouri, Nebraska, New Mexico, North Carolina, Rhode Island, Virginia, and Wisconsin.

2. Under what circumstances would a custodial trust be an appropriate part of an estate plan?

3. What type of property may be placed into a custodial trust?

4. Custodial trusts may be created by (1) a transfer in trust, (2) a self-declaration of trust, (3) a designation to take effect upon a future event, and (4) a delivery of property or payment of a debt of an incapacitated person who does not have a conservator. How is a custodial trust created under each of these circumstances?

5. What is the significance of the trustee accepting the property? How should acceptance be documented?

6. May other people augment the corpus of a custodial trust? Is this a good idea?

7. May a custodial trust be established for multiple beneficiaries? If yes, how are the interests of each beneficiary treated?

8. Does the U.C.T.A. permit successive beneficiaries, e.g., may the trust continue after the current beneficiary dies for the benefit of a different beneficiary?

9. What authority does the beneficiary have over custodial trust property?

10. What are the duties of a custodial trustee and how do they compare to the duties of a trustee of a traditional trust?

11. What powers may a custodial trustee exercise?

12. What is the trustee's liability when dealing with third parties on behalf of the trust? What steps can the trustee take to reduce the likelihood of personal liability?

13. What protection does the U.C.T.A. provide to persons who deal in good faith with a custodial trustee?

14. Is the trustee entitled to expense reimbursement? Compensation?

15. When must the trustee provide accountings? To whom are they delivered? What should they contain?

16. How may a beneficiary's claim against a custodial trustee be barred?

17. What happens if the trustee resigns or is removed by the court for cause? How is a successor trustee selected?

18. How is custodial trust property distributed while the beneficiary is not incapacitated?

19. When does the trust convert from one that is revocable by the beneficiary to a discretionary trust?

20. Who determines whether the beneficiary is incapacitated? What standard is used to ascertain incapacity?

21. How is custodial trust property distributed during the beneficiary's incapacity?

22. How may a custodial trust be terminated?

23. Assume that the beneficiary is incapacitated and the beneficiary's agent under a durable power of attorney wants to terminate the custodial trust. Will the agent succeed?

24. How is the remaining trust property distributed when a custodial trust terminates?

25. The U.C.T.A. is designed to function without court supervision or interference. Under what circumstances may the court's jurisdiction be invoked?

26. How does a custodial trust carry out the following purposes of a traditional inter vivos trust?

a. Providing for and protecting the trust beneficiary.

b. Flexibility and control of asset distribution and administration.

c. Protection against the settlor's incompetence.

d. Professional management of property.

e. Probate avoidance.

f. Tax benefits.

See Gerry W. Beyer, *Simplification of Inter Vivos Trust Instruments—From Incorporation by Reference to the Uniform Custodial Trust Act and Beyond,* 32 S. TEX. L. REV. 203, 239–45 (1991).

DRAFT

Prepare the documents necessary to transfer your client's home, 25 shares of Mega Enterprises stock, and a coin collection to a custodial trust. Remember that the statutory transfer form in § 18 is a bare-bones form; there are many other issues which should be addressed in the instrument creating the trust.

E. DISABILITY INCOME INSURANCE

When disability occurs, a person's expenses usually increase and the ability to earn money decreases. Disability income insurance provides regular payments to substitute for the income a person cannot earn because of a disability.

If a person does not have disability insurance, the person will be stuck with receiving only Social Security benefits. Reliance on Social Security is a bad option for several reasons. First, it is often harder for a person to be considered disabled under Social Security law than under insurance policies. Under Social Security, the person must be unable to "engage in any substantial gainful activity"[1] while insurance definitions of disability are often more liberal such as being unable to perform the job, or a reasonable equivalent thereof, which the person was performing prior to becoming disabled. Second, Social Security pays relatively low benefits compared to disability insurance. This difference is especially important for people who are highly compensated.

There are three main sources of disability income insurance. First, many employers make this type of insurance available to employees at very favorable rates. Second, professional and social organizations often contract with insurance companies to offer disability insurance to its members at competitive rates. Third, and usually the most expensive option, insurance agents sell this type of policy to their customers. An insured should expect the policy to pay between 60–80% of the insured's current income—the policies will not pay 100% of current income because a person would lack a financial incentive to recover and return to work. Of course, an insured should look for the lowest premiums consistent with maximum benefits. Policies will differ regarding the degree of disability the insured must have to collect benefits, how long insured must wait from the onset of disability to collect benefits (the longer the waiting period, the more economical the premiums), whether the insurer will adjust benefits for inflation, the reliability of the insurer, the requirements to renew, and whether the policy will cover preexisting conditions. In most cases, the insured (rather than insured's employer as a fringe benefit) should pay all the premiums so that the proceeds will not be subject to income tax.

NOTES AND QUESTIONS

1. According to the Life Insurance Marketing and Research Association, "[a]mong households with children under 18, 4 in 10 say they would immediately have trouble meeting everyday living expenses if a primary wage-earner died today . . . [a]nother 3 in 10 would have trouble keeping up with expenses after several months. *Facts from LIMRA*, Life Insurance Awareness Month, September 2010 at 1 (indicating that many Americans are underinsured, and might difficulty supporting a family because many Americans lack an appropriate amount of insurance.)

---

1. 42 U.S.C. § 416(i)(1).

2. See *Do You Need Disability Insurance?*, ConsumerReports.org, Aug. 2010.

3. As mentioned above, it is poor planning to rely on Social Security disability benefits because of low payments and the difficulty in satisfying disability requirements. To find out what your client's potential Social Security benefits would be, you may complete an application for a statement of estimated benefits and submit it to the Social Security Administration.

4. In addition to Social Security and disability income insurance, a disabled person may have other resources such as (1) sick pay, (2) workers compensation, and (3) military or veterans benefits.

LOCATE

Contact several agents who sell disability income insurance and obtain information about their policies. Compare the costs and features of the policies and decide which ones you would recommend to your clients.

CHAPTER 6

DISABILITY PLANNING—HEALTH CARE

■ ■ ■

A. INTRODUCTION

In Chapter 5, we learned the techniques for protecting your client's property during periods of disability. In this chapter, we examine how a person may make arrangements to provide for health care decisions and to finance such care. Health care matters are of equal, if not greater, importance because of their intensely personal nature and the tremendous ramifications they may have on the quality of your client's life. "Perhaps the single worst thing a client can do to his or her family is fail to provide for death or incapacity."[1] If no planning is done, the burden of health care decisions will fall on a statutorily authorized surrogate or the court. These entities may then make decisions without your client's guidance. In addition, without proper planning, the client's own resources will be depleted to pay health care expenses during periods of disability.

NOTE

For a comprehensive treatment of disability planning, see CAROL KROHM & SCOTT SUMMERS, ADVANCE HEALTH CARE DIRECTIVES: A HANDBOOK FOR PROFESSIONALS (2002).

B. STATUTORY SURROGATES

ARDATH A. HAMANN, FAMILY SURROGATE LAWS: A NECESSARY SUPPLEMENT TO LIVING WILLS AND DURABLE POWERS OF ATTORNEY*

38 VILL. L. REV. 103, 103–06, 130–32, 134–37, 160, 162–76 (1993).

Advances in medical technology are usually heralded as miraculous. In recent years, however, there has been a growing recognition that there are problems associated with these advances. With the development of

1. John J. Scroggin, *Protecting and Preserving the Family: The True Goal of Estate Planning, Part II–Some of the Tools*, PROB. & PROP., July/Aug. 2002, at 34, 35.

medical technology such as respirators and artificial feeding techniques, physicians are now able to sustain the bodily functions of the irreversibly comatose and those in persistent vegetative states. During the 1970s, state legislatures began to deal with this issue by enacting "living will" statutes. Today, only three states do not have some form of living will statute. A more recent development is the durable power of attorney for health care. Although the durable power of attorney is considerably more flexible than a living will, both documents have a major defect: they only apply to individuals who have the foresight to execute them.

Despite the development of these self-determination tools, studies suggest that as few as nine percent of the population have executed living wills. Reasons for such a limited response vary from ignorance to procrastination. Even increased education, however, is unlikely to significantly change these figures. For example, in the analogous area of wills, only thirty percent of the population die with a valid will. All states have intestacy laws to provide for the distribution of the decedent's property without a will. A comparable alternative is needed to provide for those individuals who fail to execute a living will or a durable power of attorney.

The thesis of this Article is that decisions about medical treatment for an incompetent person should be made within the family. Judges, hospital ethics committees and other strangers to the family unit should not interfere in these very personal decisions. It is the family that knows the person's preferences about medical care. It is the family that has to live with the results of the decisions about medical care. Therefore, it should be the family that makes the decisions about medical care. * * *

States have begun to recognize the deficiencies in living wills and durable powers of attorney for health care. Sixteen states and the District of Columbia now provide for family decisionmaking even in the absence of these two documents. Generally, these statutes provide that if a person who is incapable of making medical decisions has not named an agent to make health care decisions, a family member may make such decisions on the person's behalf. Each statute includes a list of family members who may consent, sometimes in order of priority. Some statutes give a court-appointed guardian priority in making medical decisions and others only allow the guardian to make medical decisions if no family member is available. Some extend to all relatives, even distant ones, others allow friends to make decisions if no family member is available, and two allow a religious superior to make the decision for a member of a religious order.

As is true of both living wills and durable powers of attorney, there are many variations among the statutes. The two most troublesome variations center around the issue of consensus. Illinois and Utah require that at least one physician agree with the named family member before life-sustaining treatment can be terminated. Consequently, the family can make the decision only if the medical establishment approves.

The other variation is that some states require unanimity or majority agreement among family members who are in the same class of priority, e.g. the person's adult children. If there are a substantial number of class members, the objection of one could frustrate the intent of the person. One particularly egregious example is New Mexico which requires the agreement of the spouse and adult children, thus preventing the spouse from acting alone. This may be a significant barrier when the spouse is from a second marriage and the children are from a first marriage. * * *

Judicial involvement in medical decisionmaking is a relatively recent phenomenon. Until the late 1950s and early 1960s, medical decisionmaking was exercised almost exclusively by the patient's personal physician. Not only were judges and hospital ethics committees not part of the decisionmaking process, but frequently, not even the patient and his family were consulted. By the mid–1970s, however, the entire decisionmaking process had changed. Physicians, patients, family members, hospital ethics committees and the judiciary were all involved.

Several events were critical in causing these changes. First, public concern was aroused about abuses in human experimentation. In the notorious Tuskegee study, men with syphilis were left untreated in order to study the effects of the disease. Such abuses led to increasing public distrust in allowing physicians to exercise full control in health care decisionmaking. The second lightning rod was the 1969 death of a Down's syndrome baby born with a digestive abnormality. The child died fifteen days after birth because surgery was not performed. At the same time, the abortion issue was becoming heated, culminating with the decision in Roe v. Wade. Thus, public distrust expanded to include parents who were believed to be colluding with the physicians.

The final event which galvanized this area was the case of Karen Ann Quinlan. Karen entered a persistent vegetative state in 1975 from an unknown cause and required mechanical ventilation to sustain her respiratory function. Karen's father requested the removal of the respirator, but the doctors refused. Because the medical profession would not comply with his request, Joseph Quinlan turned to the legal profession. Thus began the involvement of the judiciary in medical decisionmaking.

In general, society has benefited from the public attention to medical decisionmaking. People have been forced to grapple with major medical, ethical and religious issues. Families are now involved in decisions affecting their lives rather than leaving these personal decisions to the unsupervised control of individual physicians. The pendulum, however, has swung past the middle to the opposite extreme. The government, through the courts, has merely replaced the physicians as the decisionmaker.

Before the Quinlan case, physicians, outside of the glare of the public spotlight, discontinued treatment "when they believed that a patient's death was imminent and irreversible," and hospitals allowed the physicians to make those decisions without the interference of regulations and committees. Even today, it is acknowledged that many physicians continue to quietly turn off machines when further treatment is futile. Not all hospitals, however, will allow this informal decisionmaking. Moreover, some physicians are unwilling to take this responsibility. The result is that a patient's rights depend on the personal views of his physician and the policies of the hospital he has selected. * * *

The issue of termination of medical treatment does not belong in court. Judges have no special expertise that allows them to make the decision to terminate medical treatment. Many courts recognize that decisions made by courts concerning withdrawal of medical treatment are not inherently better than decisions made by doctors or families. * * *

ADVANTAGES OF FAMILY DECISIONMAKING

Life and death decisions about medical care are family decisions that should be made without the expensive and time consuming interference of the courts. * * * [P]eople generally do not want life-sustaining medical treatment if they have no chance for recovery. Thus, the basic goal of the proposal is to put the decisionmaking power back with the family where it belongs. Treatment should not be imposed when it is not wanted, and it should not be denied when it is desired. Family members who know the person's desires and who care about him should make the decision.

1. No One Cares More About the Person Than Family

Medical decisionmaking for an incompetent person should rest with the person's family because no one loves the person more than his own family. Traditionally, certain decisions were made solely within the confines of the family. Society respected the family's decisions in these areas and did not even attempt to determine whether the decision made was the best decision. * * *

There are four basic reasons that families are inherently better decisionmakers than strangers.

First, families generally exhibit more concern about the welfare of the person than anyone else. Families spend time with the person at the hospital and assist the medical personnel in caring for and in comforting him. Family members often advise and counsel the person faced with treatment decisions. One study noted that families ask the medical staff more questions about the individual's condition and prognosis than even the competent person does. As a result, family members often become advocates for persons who, although competent, find it difficult to assert themselves in their weakened condition.

Second, and even more importantly, it is the family that has to live with the decision. Much discussion has focused on the argument that families may wish to terminate treatment in order to relieve themselves of the emotional and financial burdens associated with caring for the person. That argument neglects the fact that guilt and the fear of making the wrong decision for a loved one may actually cause the family to continue treatment even if it is contrary to the person's best interests.

Third, contrary to common belief, physicians are not impartial observers. They also may face conflicts of interest. For example, when infants are involved, they are frequently transferred to hospitals with neonatal intensive care units. The resident physicians may have a vested interest in aggressively treating a dying child. Physicians' interests in advancing their own training or advancing the state of research in the field may conflict with the interest of individual infants and their families.

Finally, a person's family is adversely affected by his incapacitation. When the family considers the adverse impact of the person's illness on the family unit, it is considering exactly what the person himself would consider. Most persons do not want to become a burden to their families. Few want the fruits of their life's labors decimated by a futile attempt to treat the last stages of a painful terminal illness, or worse, to be kept alive in a coma for years. * * *

2. *No One Knows the Person's Religious Beliefs and Personal Values Better Than Family*

Knowledge of a person's wishes is critical to any decision about life-sustaining treatment, and no one knows the person's wishes better than close family or friends. Courts developed the theory of substituted judgment in an attempt to reach a result consistent with the person's desires. The problem with the substituted judgment test is that the person often has not expressed his desires in language that satisfies evidentiary standards. However, what is unclear to the judge, who is a stranger, may be obvious to a family member who understands the person's attitudes towards medical care and general view of life and the world. * * *

3. *Strangers With Political Agenda Should Not Be Allowed to Intervene*

In recent years, there has been a proliferation of "right to life" groups. These groups no longer focus solely on abortion; they are also active in opposing the termination of medical treatment. For example, these groups were instrumental in convincing the Reagan Administration to issue regulations preventing the termination of treatment for neonates. Today they invariably appear as amicus against a family that seeks to have life support equipment or feeding tubes removed from a dying family member. These groups do not see the patient as a person but as a symbol of a cause. * * *

Judges are so accustomed to the adversary nature of most legal proceedings that they sometimes search to find a party with a contrary view even when that party is a stranger to the litigation and is using the litigation to forward its own agenda. Intervention of such lobbying groups does not benefit the person and should not be allowed to continue. By changing the legal presumption to favor family decisionmaking, political groups will be prevented from turning private tragedies into political soapboxes.

4. *Judicial Intervention in Medical Decisionmaking Is Costly and Unnecessarily Intrusive*

Family decisionmaking also allows families to avoid the burdens of litigation. Litigation is expensive. Many, perhaps most, families facing high medical expenses do not also have the resources to pay an attorney. Hospitals and nursing homes, on the other hand, typically have substantial resources. Thus, if a hospital wishes to oppose the family's petition, it has the financial ability to fight a long court battle, including any lengthy appeals process. * * *

DISADVANTAGES OF FAMILY DECISIONMAKING

The proposed surrogate decisionmaking statute will simplify most medical treatment decision situations. There are five situations, however, where this proposal may not be as effective. Four of these potential problem areas already exist under the current systems. When a family is dysfunctional, when there is conflict among family members, when a person has no close family members or when the family is unwilling or unable to make the decisions, judicial intervention may still be necessary to determine whether to continue medical treatment for an incompetent person. The problem unique to this proposal is determining what mechanism should be used when outsiders believe the family's decision is unreasonable. The final topic in this area, titled the right of conscience, addresses the problem of medical personnel who refuse to defer to the wishes of the person's family.

1. The Dysfunctional Family

One disadvantage with giving families exclusive authority to make a person's medical treatment decisions is that some families are dysfunctional. The experience of the past fifteen years, however, indicates that a dysfunctional family is unlikely to be involved in this type of case. In fact, in none of the cases from Quinlan to Cruzan have the family members been anything less than loving and devoted to the individual. * * *

In the final analysis there will always be problems when the person's family is dysfunctional or when the person was involved in a nontraditional relationship. These problems will be no greater when the presumption is in favor of family decisionmaking than under the current system. Consequently, the existence of dysfunctional families is no real disadvantage to the proposal.

2. Conflict Among Family Members

A second disadvantage with giving families authority to make decisions regarding a person's medical treatment is that family members may disagree about the treatment that should be provided to the person. The most obvious situation occurs when the person is an unmarried child and the statutory surrogate decisionmakers are the person's divorced parents who are unable to agree. Similarly the person may be an elderly individual whose statutory surrogate decisionmakers are his adult children who are unable to agree. In these cases, the courts will probably be forced to make the decision whether to terminate or to continue treatment. * * *

3. *No Close Family*

A third disadvantage with giving families exclusive authority to decide on a person's medical treatment is that some individuals do not have close family members. Many of these individuals are elderly and live in nursing homes where the average age is eighty-two. Furthermore, among nursing home residents, more than half have no living descendants. Consequently, it is unrealistic to expect caring family members to be involved in decisionmaking in every situation.

When a person has no close family member, however, it still may be possible to resolve the dilemma without court intervention. For example, a close friend could act as the surrogate decisionmaker. Admittedly, even today, close friends can seek court appointment as a guardian, although, with the cost and difficulty of these proceedings, few are willing to commit to this undertaking. The proposed priority of decisionmakers should include a final category of close friends. Then, so long as the physician knows that the person has no close family members and the physician knows that this person was a close friend of the person, the physician should follow the direction of the friend acting as a surrogate decisionmaker.

4. *Family Uncomfortable Making the Decision*

Another problem present under the current systems that will still be present under the proposal is that some family members may feel uncomfortable, or may be unwilling to make surrogate medical decisions for a family member. As discussed previously, polls indicate that some people are more willing to make such decisions for themselves than for other family members. In addition, research studies reveal that family members are not always able to accurately predict the resuscitation and medical care decision preferences of other family members.

Frequently, such reluctance on the part of family members arises from a lack of knowledge regarding the medical care preferences of their loved ones. The best way to eliminate such reluctance is the encouragement of communication between families on the topic of medical decisionmaking. The legal and medical communities can assist in this task by providing educational and support services to accomplish this goal. * * *

The ultimate success of legislative enactments, such as existing living will and durable power of attorney statutes, lies in the development of mechanisms to educate the public regarding this right of self-determination.

In the situation where the family is uncomfortable making medical care decisions, as in the previous three problem areas discussed, the concerns with the proposed family decisionmaking statute are really no greater than under the current system. Moreover, the proposed statute has the advantage of allowing decisions to be made free from judicial intervention in some circumstances when court intervention would be necessary in most jurisdictions today.

5. *The Unreasonable Decision*

Perhaps the most difficult problem posed by the proposal is when a decision by the surrogate appears to be unreasonable, favoring either continuation or discontinuation of treatment. In a diverse society, a wide range of alternative decisions regarding medical treatment should be acceptable. Sometimes these choices are made based on personal views and at other times based on religious beliefs. For example, Jehovah's Witnesses refuse to submit to blood transfusions. Some legislatures have recognized this diversity of choice in statutes that authorize durable powers of attorney for health care. For example, under the Illinois statute, an individual can direct his agent to refuse amputations or blood transfusions on his behalf. Although most of society probably views refusal of a blood transfusion as an unacceptable decision, this refusal should be within the range of acceptable decisions.

There may be instances, however, when a decision is so unreasonable that it should not be enforced. In response to this problem, the standard that the court should use in reviewing a statutory surrogate's decision should be a higher barrier than merely "best interests." This deference to the decisionmaker is certainly not unique to this proposal. Appellate courts routinely defer to trial court's factual determinations. Courts also defer to administrative agencies in their factual determinations. These examples of deference are based on the fact that the record often does not convey the subtle nuances of testimony on which fact finders judge credibility. Similarly, courts should defer to family decisions in the area of medical care because family impressions of a person's desires often are not easily translated into testimony.

A significant problem arises if hospitals are allowed to take the lead in objecting to termination of treatment. Because an institution's resources are significant, it can challenge decisions with which the administration does not agree. The doctor or hospital administrator should be required to convince a prosecuting attorney that the family's decision constitutes abuse before the case can be litigated. A hospital or doctor should also be required to transfer the patient if they do not agree with the surrogate decisionmaker's treatment choice. If another doctor or hospital will comply, then prima facie the treatment choice is not unreasonable.

6. *Right of Conscience*

The final problem with this proposal to allow family decisionmaking is called, for lack of a better term, the right of conscience. The right of conscience first arose in the area of abortion. Both federal and state statutes exist that allow medical personnel to refuse to perform or to assist in performing abortions if doing so is contrary to their religious or moral beliefs. Some courts have created a similar right of conscience in the right to die area. For example, in *Brophy,* the Massachusetts court ruled that while the patient had the right to have the gastrostomy tube removed, the hospital and its agents were not required to remove it. The hospital only had to transfer the patient pursuant to the family's request. * * *

It is a doctor's duty to provide the necessary medical facts, and it is the person's right to make the treatment decision based on his interpretation of those facts. A person's right to choose should not be frustrated simply because the doctor or hospital disagrees with the choice. To allow a doctor to continue to provide certain treatment in the face of the person's objection merely because the doctor believes it should be done would render the concept of informed consent meaningless.

NOTES AND QUESTIONS

1. Professor Hamann's article also discusses how judges operate under allegedly erroneous assumptions when deciding to continue treatment. These assumptions include (1) it is better to err in favor of preserving life; (2) the state has an interest in preserving life; (3) most people want to be kept alive by machines; (4) there is no harm in postponing the decision; (5) youth withdraw medical treatment from the elderly; (6) the family will terminate medical treatment for financial reasons; (7) removal of life-sustaining treatment is a step toward euthanasia; and (8) religions oppose termination of life-sustaining treatment. See Hamann, at 138–58. Do you agree with the author that these assumptions are erroneous?

2. For a sample surrogacy statute, see § 5 of the 1993 Uniform Health Care Decisions Act reproduced in the next section.

3. Do you approve of statutes providing for surrogates to make decisions when a person has not made other arrangements? Or, do you believe that court authorization should be required to protect an individual from family members who are more concerned with their own needs than those of the disabled person?

4. Would you want a statutory surrogate making decisions for you or would you prefer to exercise greater self-determination with a durable power of attorney for health care or a living will? See Dinah Wisenberg, *Loved Ones Often Make Wrong Medical Prediction*, SAN ANTONIO EXPRESS-NEWS, Apr. 15, 1998, at 10B (reporting study which revealed that close relatives accurately predict treatment only about two-thirds of the time and noting that relatives generally erred on the side of authorizing additional treatment rather than withholding it).

5. How will you use this knowledge about surrogate legislation to advise your clients?

6. A battle of potential surrogates lasted from 1998 to 2005 in the case of Terri Schiavo. At issue was whether her husband had the right to terminate her life support because she was diagnosed by doctors as being in a persistent vegetative state. The highly publicized and prolonged series of legal challenges presented by her parents and by state and federal legislative intervention effected a seven-year delay before life support finally was terminated.

Terri collapsed in her St. Petersburg, Florida, home in full cardiac arrest on February 25, 1990. She suffered massive brain damage due to lack of oxygen and, after two and a half months in a coma, her diagnosis was changed to vegetative state. For the next few years, doctors attempted speech and physical therapy and other experimental therapy, hoping to return her to a state of awareness. In 1998 Terri's husband, Michael, petitioned the Sixth Circuit Court of Florida (Pinellas County), to remove her feeding tube pursuant to Florida Statutes § 765.401(3). He was opposed by Terri's parents, Robert and Mary Schindler, who argued that she was conscious. The court determined that she would not wish to continue life-prolonging measures, and on April 24, 2001, her feeding tube was removed for the first time, only to be reinserted several days later. On February 25, 2005, a Pinellas County judge ordered the removal of Terri's feeding tube. Several appeals and federal government intervention followed, which included President George W. Bush returning to Washington D.C. to sign legislation designed to keep her alive. After all attempts at appeals through the federal court system upheld the original decision to remove the feeding tube, staff at the Pinellas Park hospice facility where Terri was being cared for disconnected the feeding tube on March 18, 2005, and she died on March 31, 2005.

In all, the Schiavo case involved 14 appeals and numerous motions, petitions, and hearings in the Florida courts; five suits in federal district court; Florida legislation struck down by the Supreme Court of Florida; federal legislation (the Palm Sunday Compromise); and four denials of certiorari from the Supreme Court of the United States.

For a detailed discussion of this case from which this note is adapted, see http://en.wikipedia.org/wiki/Terri_Schiavo_case.

LOCATE

Does your state have surrogate legislation? If yes, how does your statute operate?

C. MEDICAL POWER OF ATTORNEY

Traditionally, a person could not use a power of attorney to delegate the authority to make health care decisions. These decisions were considered too personal to delegate. In addition, the existence of the patient's informed consent to any medical treatment was problematic because the agent, not the patient, would make the decision. However, there are persuasive arguments in favor of this type of delegation. Medical decisions could then be made by a person the patient actually specified. This person is likely to have a better understanding of how the patient would like to be treated than a guardian, doctor, or family member.

The first significant attempt to settle this debate was the National Conference of Commissioners on Uniform State Laws' approval of the Model Health–Care Consent Act in 1982. Motivated by a concern for personal autonomy and recognizing that a competent person may want to delegate health-care decision authority to a relative or friend, the Commissioners included a provision permitting a person to transfer this power to a "health-care representative." The next year, California became the first state to address this issue when it enacted legislation approving a durable power of attorney for health care accompanied by a statutory fill-in-the-blank form. Almost all states have followed California's lead.

UNIFORM HEALTH CARE DECISIONS ACT

1993 Act.

PREFATORY NOTE

Since the Supreme Court's decision in *Cruzan v. Commissioner, Missouri Department of Health*, 497 U.S. 261 (1990), significant change has occurred in state legislation on health-care decision making. Every state now has legislation authorizing the use of some sort of advance health-care directive. All but a few states authorize what is typically known as a living will. Nearly all states have statutes authorizing the use of powers of attorney for health care. In addition, a majority of states have statutes allowing family members, and in some cases close friends, to make health-care decisions for adult individuals who lack capacity.

This state legislation, however, has developed in fits and starts, resulting in an often fragmented, incomplete, and sometimes inconsistent set of rules. Statutes enacted within a state often conflict and conflicts between statutes of different states are common. In an increasingly mobile society where an advance health-care directive given in one state must frequently be implemented in another, there is a need for greater uniformity.

The Health–Care Decisions Act was drafted with this confused situation in mind. The Act is built around the following concepts. *First*, the Act acknowledges the right of a competent individual to decide all aspects of his or her own health care in all circumstances, including the right to decline health care or to direct that health care be discontinued, even if death ensues. An individual's instructions may extend to any and all health-care decisions that might arise and, unless limited by the principal, an agent has authority to make all health-care decisions which the individual could have made. The Act recognizes and validates an individual's authority to define the scope of an instruction or agency as broadly or as narrowly as the individual chooses.

Second, the Act is comprehensive and will enable an enacting jurisdiction to replace its existing legislation on the subject with a single statute. The Act authorizes health-care decisions to be made by an agent who is designated to decide when an individual cannot or does not wish to; by a designated surrogate, family member, or close friend when an individual is unable to act and no guardian or agent has been appointed or is reasonably available; or by a court having jurisdiction as decision maker of last resort.

Third, the Act is designed to simplify and facilitate the making of advance health-care directives. An instruction may be either written or oral. A power of attorney for health care, while it must be in writing, need not be witnessed or acknowledged. In addition, an optional form for the making of a directive is provided.

Fourth, the Act seeks to ensure to the extent possible that decisions about an individual's health care will be governed by the individual's own desires concerning the issues to be resolved. The Act requires an agent or surrogate authorized to make health-care decisions for an individual to make those decisions in accordance with the instructions and other wishes of the individual to the extent known. Otherwise, the agent or surrogate must make those decisions in accordance with the best interest of the individual but in light of the individual's personal values known to the agent or surrogate. Furthermore, the Act requires a guardian to comply with a ward's previously given instructions and prohibits a guardian from revoking the ward's advance health-care directive without express court approval.

Fifth, the Act addresses compliance by health-care providers and institutions. A health-care provider or institution must comply with an instruction of the patient and with a reasonable interpretation of that instruction or other health-care decision made by a person then authorized to make health-care decisions for the patient. The obligation to comply is not absolute, however. A health-care provider or institution may decline to honor an instruction or decision for reasons of conscience or if the instruction or decision requires the provision of medically ineffective care or care contrary to applicable health-care standards.

Sixth, the Act provides a procedure for the resolution of disputes. While the Act is in general to be effectuated without litigation, situations will arise where resort to the courts may be necessary. For that reason, the Act authorizes the court to enjoin or direct a health-care decision or order other equitable relief and specifies who is entitled to bring a petition.

The Health–Care Decisions Act supersedes the Commissioners' Model Health–Care Consent Act (1982), the Uniform Rights of the Terminally Ill Act (1985), and the Uniform Rights of the Terminally Ill Act (1989). A state enacting the Health–Care Decisions Act which has one of these other acts in force should repeal it upon enactment.

Section 1. Definitions.

In this [Act]:

(1) "Advance health-care directive" means an individual instruction or a power of attorney for health care.

(2) "Agent" means an individual designated in a power of attorney for health care to make a health-care decision for the individual granting the power.

(3) "Capacity" means an individual's ability to understand the significant benefits, risks, and alternatives to proposed health care and to make and communicate a health-care decision.

(4) "Guardian" means a judicially appointed guardian or conservator having authority to make a health-care decision for an individual.

(5) "Health care" means any care, treatment, service, or procedure to maintain, diagnose, or otherwise affect an individual's physical or mental condition.

(6) "Health-care decision" means a decision made by an individual or the individual's agent, guardian, or surrogate, regarding the individual's health care, including:

(i) selection and discharge of health-care providers and institutions;

(ii) approval or disapproval of diagnostic tests, surgical procedures, programs of medication, and orders not to resuscitate; and

(iii) directions to provide, withhold, or withdraw artificial nutrition and hydration and all other forms of health care.

(7) "Health-care institution" means an institution, facility, or agency licensed, certified, or otherwise authorized or permitted by law to provide health care in the ordinary course of business.

(8) "Health-care provider" means an individual licensed, certified, or otherwise authorized or permitted by law to provide health care in the ordinary course of business or practice of a profession.

(9) "Individual instruction" means an individual's direction concerning a health-care decision for the individual.

(10) "Person" means an individual, corporation, business trust, estate, trust, partnership, association, joint venture, government, governmental subdivision, agency, or instrumentality, or any other legal or commercial entity.

(11) "Physician" means an individual authorized to practice medicine [or osteopathy] under [appropriate statute].

(12) "Power of attorney for health care" means the designation of an agent to make health-care decisions for the individual granting the power.

(13) "Primary physician" means a physician designated by an individual or the individual's agent, guardian, or surrogate, to have primary responsibility for the individual's health care or, in the absence of a designation or if the designated physician is not reasonably available, a physician who undertakes the responsibility.

(14) "Reasonably available" means readily able to be contacted without undue effort and willing and able to act in a timely manner considering the urgency of the patient's health-care needs.

(15) "State" means a State of the United States, the District of Columbia, the Commonwealth of Puerto Rico, or a territory or insular possession subject to the jurisdiction of the United States.

(16) "Supervising health-care provider" means the primary physician or, if there is no primary physician or the primary physician is not reasonably available, the health-care provider who has undertaken primary responsibility for an individual's health care.

(17) "Surrogate" means an individual, other than a patient's agent or guardian, authorized under this [Act] to make a health-care decision for the patient.

Section 2. Advance Health–Care Directives.

(a) An adult or emancipated minor may give an individual instruction. The instruction may be oral or written. The instruction may be limited to take effect only if a specified condition arises.

(b) An adult or emancipated minor may execute a power of attorney for health care, which may authorize the agent to make any health-care decision the principal could have made while having capacity. The power must be in writing and signed by the principal. The power remains in effect notwithstanding the principal's later incapacity and may include individual instructions. Unless related to the principal by blood, marriage, or adoption, an agent may not be an owner, operator, or employee of [a residential long-term health-care institution] at which the principal is receiving care.

(c) Unless otherwise specified in a power of attorney for health care, the authority of an agent becomes effective only upon a determination that the principal lacks capacity, and ceases to be effective upon a determination that the principal has recovered capacity.

(d) Unless otherwise specified in a written advance health-care directive, a determination that an individual lacks or has recovered capacity, or that another condition exists that affects an individual instruction or the authority of an agent, must be made by the primary physician.

(e) An agent shall make a health-care decision in accordance with the principal's individual instructions, if any, and other wishes to the extent known to the agent. Otherwise, the agent shall make the decision in accordance with the agent's determination of the principal's best interest. In determining the principal's best interest, the agent shall consider the principal's personal values to the extent known to the agent.

(f) A health-care decision made by an agent for a principal is effective without judicial approval.

(g) A written advance health-care directive may include the individual's nomination of a guardian of the person.

(h) An advance health-care directive is valid for purposes of this [Act] if it complies with this [Act], regardless of when or where executed or communicated.

Comment

The individual instruction authorized in subsection (a) may but need not be limited to take effect in specified circumstances, such as if the individual is dying. An individual instruction may be either written or oral.

Subsection (b) authorizes a power of attorney for health care to include instructions regarding the principal's health care. This provision has been included in order to validate the practice of designating an agent and giving individual instructions in one document instead of two. The authority of an agent falls within the discretion of the principal as expressed in the instrument creating the power and may extend to any health-care decision the principal could have made while having capacity.

Subsection (b) excludes the oral designation of an agent. Section 5(b) authorizes an individual to orally designate a surrogate by personally informing the supervising health-care provider. A power of attorney for health care, however, must be in writing and signed by the principal, although it need not be witnessed or acknowledged.

Subsection (b) also limits those who may serve as agents to make health-care decisions for another. The subsection addresses the special vulnerability of individuals in residential long-term health-care institutions by protecting a principal against those who may have interests that conflict with the duty to follow the principal's expressed wishes or to determine the principal's best interest. Specifically, the owners, operators or employees of a residential long-term health-care institution at which the principal is receiving care may not act as agents. An exception is made for those related to the principal by blood, marriage or adoption, relationships which are assumed to neutralize any consequence of a conflict of interest adverse to the principal. The phrase 'a residential long-term health-care institution' is placed in brackets to indicate to the legislature of an enacting jurisdiction that it should substitute the appropriate terminology used under local law.

Subsection (c) provides that the authority of the agent to make health-care decisions ordinarily does not become effective until the principal is determined to lack capacity and ceases to be effective should the principal recover capacity. A principal may provide, however, that the authority of the agent becomes effective immediately or upon the happening of some event other than the loss of capacity but may do so only by an express provision in the power of attorney. For example, a mother who does not want to make her own health-care decisions but prefers that her daughter make them for her may specify that the daughter as agent is to have authority to make health-care decisions immediately. The mother in that circumstance retains the right to later revoke the power of attorney as provided in Section 3.

Subsection (d) provides that unless otherwise specified in a written advance health-care directive, a determination that a principal has lost or recovered capacity to make health-care decisions must be made by the primary physician. For example, a principal might specify that the determination of capacity is to be made by the agent in consultation with the primary physician. Or a principal, such as a member of the Christian Science faith who relies on a religious method of healing and who has no primary physician, might specify that capacity be determined by other means. In the event that multiple decision makers are specified and they cannot agree, it may be necessary to seek court instruction as authorized by Section 14.

Subsection (d) also provides that unless otherwise specified in a written advance health-care directive, the existence of other conditions which affect an individual instruction or the authority of an agent must be determined by the primary physician. For example, an individual might specify that an agent may withdraw or withhold treatment that keeps the individual alive only if the individual has an incurable and irreversible condition that will result in the individual's death within a relatively short time. In that event, unless otherwise specified in the advance health-care directive, the determination that the individual has that condition must be made by the primary physician.

Subsection (e) requires the agent to follow the principal's individual instructions and other expressed wishes to the extent known to the agent. To the extent such instructions or other wishes are unknown, the agent must act in the principal's best interest. In determining the principal's best interest, the agent is to consider the principal's personal values to the extent known to the agent. The Act does not prescribe a detailed list of factors for determining the principal's best interest but instead grants the agent discretion to ascertain and weigh the factors likely to be of importance to the principal. The legislature of an enacting jurisdiction that wishes to add such a list may want to consult the Maryland Health–Care Decision Act, Md. Health–Gen. Code Ann. § 5–601.

Subsection (f) provides that a health-care decision made by an agent is effective without judicial approval. A similar provision applies to health-care decisions made by surrogates (Section 5(g)) or guardians (Section 6(c)).

Subsection (g) provides that a written advance health-care directive may include the individual's nomination of a guardian of the person. A nomination cannot guarantee that the nominee will be appointed but in the absence of cause to appoint another the court would likely select the nominee. Moreover, the mere nomination of the agent will reduce the likelihood that a guardianship could be used to thwart the agent's authority.

Subsection (h) validates advance health-care directives which conform to the Act, regardless of when or where executed or communicated. This includes an advance health-care directive which would be valid under the Act but which was made prior to the date of its enactment and failed to comply with the execution requirements then in effect. It also includes an advance health-care directive which was made in another jurisdiction but which does not comply with that jurisdiction's execution or other requirements.

Section 3. Revocation of Advance Health–Care Directive.

(a) An individual may revoke the designation of an agent only by a signed writing or by personally informing the supervising health-care provider.

(b) An individual may revoke all or part of an advance health-care directive, other than the designation of an agent, at any time and in any manner that communicates an intent to revoke.

(c) A health-care provider, agent, guardian, or surrogate who is informed of a revocation shall promptly communicate the fact of the revocation to the supervising health-care provider and to any health-care institution at which the patient is receiving care.

(d) A decree of annulment, divorce, dissolution of marriage, or legal separation revokes a previous designation of a spouse as agent unless otherwise specified in the decree or in a power of attorney for health care.

(e) An advance health-care directive that conflicts with an earlier advance health-care directive revokes the earlier directive to the extent of the conflict.

Comment

Subsection (b) provides that an individual may revoke any portion of an advance health-care directive at any time and in any manner that communicates an intent to revoke. However, a more restrictive standard applies to the revocation of the portion of a power of attorney for health care relating to the designation of an agent. Subsection (a) provides that an individual may revoke the designation of an agent only by a signed writing or by personally informing the supervising health-care provider. This higher standard is justified by the risk of a false revocation of an agent's designation or of a misinterpretation or miscommunication of a principal's statement communicated through a third party. For example, without this higher standard, an individual motivated by a desire to gain control over a patient might be able to assume authority to act as agent by falsely informing a health-care provider that the principal no longer wishes the previously designated agent to act but instead wishes to appoint the individual.

* * *

The section does not specifically address amendment of an advance health-care directive because such reference is not necessary. Subsection (b) specifically authorizes partial revocation, and subsection (e) recognizes that an advance health-care directive may be modified by a later directive.

Section 4. Optional Form.

The following form may, but need not, be used to create an advance health-care directive. The other sections of this [Act] govern the effect of this or any other writing used to create an advance health-care directive. An individual may complete or modify all or any part of the following form:

ADVANCE HEALTH-CARE DIRECTIVE

Explanation

You have the right to give instructions about your own health care. You also have the right to name someone else to make health-care decisions for you. This form lets you do either or both of these things. It also lets you express your wishes regarding donation of organs and the designation of your primary physician. If you use this form, you may complete or modify all or any part of it. You are free to use a different form.

Part 1 of this form is a power of attorney for health care. Part 1 lets you name another individual as agent to make health-care decisions for you if you become incapable of making your own decisions or if you want someone else to make those decisions for you now even though you are still capable. You may also name an alternate agent to act for you if your first choice is not willing, able, or reasonably available to make decisions for you. Unless related to you, your agent may not be an owner, operator, or employee of [a residential long-term health-care institution] at which you are receiving care.

Unless the form you sign limits the authority of your agent, your agent may make all health-care decisions for you. This form has a place for you to limit the authority of your agent. You need not limit the authority of your agent if you wish to rely on your agent for all health-care decisions that may have to be made. If you choose not to limit the authority of your agent, your agent will have the right to:

(a) consent or refuse consent to any care, treatment, service, or procedure to maintain, diagnose, or otherwise affect a physical or mental condition;

(b) select or discharge health-care providers and institutions;

(c) approve or disapprove diagnostic tests, surgical procedures, programs of medication, and orders not to resuscitate; and

(d) direct the provision, withholding, or withdrawal of artificial nutrition and hydration and all other forms of health care.

Part 2 of this form lets you give specific instructions about any aspect of your health care. Choices are provided for you to express your wishes regarding the provision, withholding, or withdrawal of treatment to keep you alive, including the provision of artificial nutrition and hydration, as well as the provision of pain relief. Space is also provided for you to add to the choices you have made or for you to write out any additional wishes.

Part 3 of this form lets you express an intention to donate your bodily organs and tissues following your death.

Part 4 of this form lets you designate a physician to have primary responsibility for your health care.

After completing this form, sign and date the form at the end. It is recommended but not required that you request two other individuals to sign as witnesses. Give a copy of the signed and completed form to your physician, to any other health-care providers you may have, to any health-care institution at which you are receiving care, and to any health-care agents you have named. You should talk to the person you have named as agent to make sure that he or she understands your wishes and is willing to take the responsibility.

You have the right to revoke this advance health-care directive or replace this form at any time.

* * * * * * * * * * * * * * *

PART 1

POWER OF ATTORNEY FOR HEALTH CARE

(1) DESIGNATION OF AGENT: I designate the following individual as my agent to make health-care decisions for me:

____
(name of individual you choose as agent)

______________________ ______________________
(address) (city)

__________ __________
(state) (zip code)

______________________ ______________________
(home phone) (work phone)

OPTIONAL: If I revoke my agent's authority or if my agent is not willing, able, or reasonably available to make a health-care decision for me, I designate as my first alternate agent:

____
(name of individual you choose as first alternate agent)

______________________ ______________________
(address) (city)

__________ __________
(state) (zip code)

______________________ ______________________
(home phone) (work phone)

OPTIONAL: If I revoke the authority of my agent and first alternate agent or if neither is willing, able, or reasonably available to make a health-care decision for me, I designate as my second alternate agent:

____
(name of individual you choose as second alternate agent)

______________________ ______________________

(address) (city)

__________ __________

(state) (zip code)

______________________ ______________________

(home phone) (work phone)

(2) AGENT'S AUTHORITY: My agent is authorized to make all health-care decisions for me, including decisions to provide, withhold, or withdraw artificial nutrition and hydration and all other forms of health care to keep me alive, except as I state here:

____

____

____

(Add additional sheets if needed.)

(3) WHEN AGENT'S AUTHORITY BECOMES EFFECTIVE: My agent's authority becomes effective when my primary physician determines that I am unable to make my own health-care decisions unless I mark the following box. If I mark this box [ ], my agent's authority to make health-care decisions for me takes effect immediately.

(4) AGENT'S OBLIGATION: My agent shall make health-care decisions for me in accordance with this power of attorney for health care, any instructions I give in Part 2 of this form, and my other wishes to the extent known to my agent. To the extent my wishes are unknown, my agent shall make health-care decisions for me in accordance with what my agent determines to be in my best interest. In determining my best interest, my agent shall consider my personal values to the extent known to my agent.

(5) NOMINATION OF GUARDIAN: If a guardian of my person needs to be appointed for me by a court, I nominate the agent designated in this form. If that agent is not willing, able, or reasonably available to act as guardian, I nominate the alternate agents whom I have named, in the order designated.

PART 2

INSTRUCTIONS FOR HEALTH CARE

If you are satisfied to allow your agent to determine what is best for you in making end-of-life decisions, you need not fill out this part of the form. If you do fill out this part of the form, you may strike any wording you do not want.

(6) END–OF–LIFE DECISIONS: I direct that my health-care providers and others involved in my care provide, withhold, or withdraw treatment in accordance with the choice I have marked below:

[ ] (a) Choice Not To Prolong Life

I do not want my life to be prolonged if (i) I have an incurable and irreversible condition that will result in my death within a relatively short time, (ii) I become unconscious and, to a reasonable degree of medical certainty, I will not regain consciousness, or (iii) the likely risks and burdens of treatment would outweigh the expected benefits, OR

[ ] (b) Choice To Prolong Life

I want my life to be prolonged as long as possible within the limits of generally accepted health-care standards.

(7) ARTIFICIAL NUTRITION AND HYDRATION: Artificial nutrition and hydration must be provided, withheld, or withdrawn in accordance with the choice I have made in paragraph (6) unless I mark the following box. If I mark this box [ ], artificial nutrition and hydration must be provided regardless of my condition and regardless of the choice I have made in paragraph (6).

(8) RELIEF FROM PAIN: Except as I state in the following space, I direct that treatment for alleviation of pain or discomfort be provided at all times, even if it hastens my death:

____

____

____

(9) OTHER WISHES: (If you do not agree with any of the optional choices above and wish to write your own, or if you wish to add to the instructions you have given above, you may do so here.) I direct that:

____

____

____

(Add additional sheets if needed.)

PART 3

DONATION OF ORGANS AT DEATH

(OPTIONAL)

(10) Upon my death (mark applicable box)

[ ] (a) I give any needed organs, tissues, or parts, OR

[ ] (b) I give the following organs, tissues, or parts only

____

____

(c) My gift is for the following purposes (strike any of the following you do not want)

(i) Transplant

(ii) Therapy

(iii) Research

(iv) Education

PART 4

PRIMARY PHYSICIAN

(OPTIONAL)

(11) I designate the following physician as my primary physician:

____
(name of physician)

______________________________ _____________________
(address) (city)

_________ _________
(state) (zip code)

____
(phone)

OPTIONAL: If the physician I have designated above is not willing, able, or reasonably available to act as my primary physician, I designate the following physician as my primary physician:

____
(name of physician)

______________________________ _____________________
(address) (city)

_________ _________
(state) (zip code)

____
(phone)

* * * * * * * * * * * * * * * * * * * *

(12) EFFECT OF COPY: A copy of this form has the same effect as the original.

(13) SIGNATURES: Sign and date the form here:

_____________________ ______________________________
(date) (sign your name)

______________________ ______________________

(address) (print your name)

______________________ ______________________

(city) (state)

(Optional) SIGNATURES OF WITNESSES:

First witness	Second witness
______________________	______________________
(print name)	(print name)
______________________	______________________
(address)	(address)
______________________	______________________
(city) (state)	(city) (state)
______________________	______________________
(signature of witness)	(signature of witness)
______________________	______________________
(date)	(date)

Section 5. Decisions by Surrogate.

(a) A surrogate may make a health-care decision for a patient who is an adult or emancipated minor if the patient has been determined by the primary physician to lack capacity and no agent or guardian has been appointed or the agent or guardian is not reasonably available.

(b) An adult or emancipated minor may designate any individual to act as surrogate by personally informing the supervising health-care provider. In the absence of a designation, or if the designee is not reasonably available, any member of the following classes of the patient's family who is reasonably available, in descending order of priority, may act as surrogate:

(1) the spouse, unless legally separated;

(2) an adult child;

(3) a parent; or

(4) an adult brother or sister.

(c) If none of the individuals eligible to act as surrogate under subsection (b) is reasonably available, an adult who has exhibited special care and concern for the patient, who is familiar with the patient's personal values, and who is reasonably available may act as surrogate.

(d) A surrogate shall communicate his or her assumption of authority as promptly as practicable to the members of the patient's family specified in subsection (b) who can be readily contacted.

(e) If more than one member of a class assumes authority to act as surrogate, and they do not agree on a health-care decision and the supervising health-care provider is so informed, the supervising health-care provider shall comply with the decision of a majority of the members of that class who have communicated their views to the provider. If the class is evenly divided concerning the health-care decision and the supervising health-care provider is so informed, that class and all individuals having lower priority are disqualified from making the decision.

(f) A surrogate shall make a health-care decision in accordance with the patient's individual instructions, if any, and other wishes to the extent known to the surrogate. Otherwise, the surrogate shall make the decision in accordance with the surrogate's determination of the patient's best interest. In determining the patient's best interest, the surrogate shall consider the patient's personal values to the extent known to the surrogate.

(g) A health-care decision made by a surrogate for a patient is effective without judicial approval.

(h) An individual at any time may disqualify another, including a member of the individual's family, from acting as the individual's surrogate by a signed writing or by personally informing the supervising health-care provider of the disqualification.

(i) Unless related to the patient by blood, marriage, or adoption, a surrogate may not be an owner, operator, or employee of [a residential long-term health-care institution] at which the patient is receiving care.

(j) A supervising health-care provider may require an individual claiming the right to act as surrogate for a patient to provide a written declaration under penalty of perjury stating facts and circumstances reasonably sufficient to establish the claimed authority.

Comment

Subsection (a) authorizes a surrogate to make a health-care decision for a patient who is an adult or emancipated minor if the patient lacks capacity to make health-care decisions and if no agent or guardian has been appointed or the agent or guardian is not reasonably available. Health-care decision making for unemancipated minors is not covered by this section. The subject of consent for treatment of minors is a complex one which in many states is covered by a variety of statutes and is therefore left to other state law.

While a designation of an agent in a written power of attorney for health care is preferred, situations may arise where an individual will not be in a position to execute a power of attorney for health care. In that event, subsection (b) affirms the principle of patient autonomy by allowing an individual to designate a surrogate by personally informing the supervising health-care provider. The supervising health-care provider would then, in accordance with Section 7(b), be obligated to promptly record the designation in the individual's health-care record. An oral designation of a surrogate made by a patient directly to the supervising health-care provider revokes a previous designation of an agent. See Section 3(a).

If an individual does not designate a surrogate or if the designee is not reasonably available, subsection (b) applies a default rule for selecting a family member to act as surrogate. Like all default rules, it is not tailored to every situation, but incorporates the presumed desires of a majority of those who find themselves so situated. The relationships specified in subsection (b) include those of the half-blood and by adoption, in addition to those of the whole blood.

Subsection (c) permits a health-care decision to be made by a more distant relative or unrelated adult with whom the individual enjoys a close relationship but only if all family members specified in subsection (b) decline to act or are otherwise not reasonably available. Consequently, those in non-traditional relationships who want to make certain that health-care decisions are made by their companions should execute powers of attorney for health care designating them as agents or, if that has not been done, should designate them as surrogates.

Subsections (b) and (c) permit any member of a class authorized to serve as surrogate to assume authority to act even though there are other members in the class.

Subsection (d) requires a surrogate who assumes authority to act to immediately so notify the members of the patient's family who in given circumstances would be eligible to act as surrogate. Notice to the specified family members will enable them to follow health-care developments with respect to their now incapacitated relative. It will also alert them to take appropriate action, including the appointment of a guardian or the commencement of judicial proceedings under Section 14, should the need arise.

Subsection (e) addresses the situation where more than one member of the same class has assumed authority to act as surrogate and a disagreement over a health-care decision arises of which the supervising health-care provider is informed. Should that occur, the supervising health-care provider must comply with the decision of a majority of the members of that class who have communicated their views to the provider. If the members of the class who have communicated their views to the provider are evenly divided concerning the health-care decision, however, then the entire class is disqualified from making the decision and no individual having lower priority may act as surrogate. When such a deadlock arises, it may be necessary to seek court determination of the issue as authorized by Section 14.

Subsection (f) imposes on surrogates the same standard for health-care decision making as is prescribed for agents in Section 2(e). The surrogate must follow the patient's individual instructions and other expressed wishes to the extent known to the surrogate. To the extent such instructions or other wishes are unknown, the surrogate must act in the patient's best interest. In determining the patient's best interest, the surrogate is to consider the patient's personal values to the extent known to the surrogate.

Subsection (g) provides that a health-care decision made by a surrogate is effective without judicial approval. A similar provision applies to health-care decisions made by agents (Section 2(f)) or guardians (Section 6(c)).

Subsection (h) permits an individual to disqualify any family member or other individual from acting as the individual's surrogate, including disqualification of a surrogate who was orally designated.

Subsection (i) disqualifies an owner, operator, or employee of a residential long-term health-care institution at which a patient is receiving care from acting as the patient's surrogate unless related to the patient by blood, marriage, or adoption. This disqualification is similar to that for appointed agents. See Section 2(b) and Comment.

Subsection (j) permits a supervising health-care provider to require an individual claiming the right to act as surrogate to provide a written declaration under penalty of perjury stating facts and circumstances reasonably sufficient to establish the claimed relationship. The authority to request a declaration is included to permit the provider to obtain evidence of claimed authority. A supervising health-care provider, however, does not have a duty to investigate the qualifications of an individual claiming authority to act as surrogate, and Section 9(a) protects a health-care provider or institution from liability for complying with the decision of such an individual, absent knowledge that the individual does not in fact have such authority.

Section 6. Decisions by Guardian.

(a) A guardian shall comply with the ward's individual instructions and may not revoke the ward's advance health-care directive unless the appointing court expressly so authorizes.

(b) Absent a court order to the contrary, a health-care decision of an agent takes precedence over that of a guardian.

(c) A health-care decision made by a guardian for the ward is effective without judicial approval.

Comment

The Act affirms that health-care decisions should whenever possible be made by a person whom the individual selects to do so. For this reason, subsection (b) provides that a health-care decision of an agent takes precedence over that of a guardian absent a court order to the contrary, and subsection (a) provides that a guardian may not revoke the ward's power of attorney for health care unless the appointing court expressly so authorizes. Without these subsections, a guardian would in many states have authority to revoke the ward's power of attorney for health care even though the court appointing the guardian might not be aware that the principal had made such alternate arrangement.

The Act expresses a strong preference for honoring an individual instruction. Under the Act, an individual instruction must be honored by an agent, by a surrogate, and, subject to exceptions specified in Section 7(e)-(f), by an individual's health-care providers. Subsection (a) extends this principle to guardians by requiring that a guardian effectuate the ward's individual instructions. A guardian may revoke the ward's individual instructions only if the appointing court expressly so authorizes.

Courts have no particular expertise with respect to health-care decision making. Moreover, the delay attendant upon seeking court approval may undermine the effectiveness of the decision ultimately made, particularly but not only when the patient's condition is life-threatening and immediate decisions concerning treatment need to be made. Decisions should whenever possible be made by a patient, or the patient's guardian, agent, or surrogate in consultation with the patient's health-care providers without outside interference. For this reason, subsection (c) provides that a health-care decision made by a guardian for the ward is effective without judicial approval, and the Act includes similar provisions for health-care decisions made by agents (Section 2(f)) or surrogates (Section 5(g)).

Section 7. Obligations of Health–Care Provider.

(a) Before implementing a health-care decision made for a patient, a supervising health-care provider, if possible, shall promptly communicate to the patient the decision made and the identity of the person making the decision.

(b) A supervising health-care provider who knows of the existence of an advance health-care directive, a revocation of an advance health-care directive, or a designation or disqualification of a surrogate, shall promptly record its existence in the patient's health-care record and, if it is in writing, shall request a copy and if one is furnished shall arrange for its maintenance in the health-care record.

(c) A primary physician who makes or is informed of a determination that a patient lacks or has recovered capacity, or that another condition exists which affects an individual instruction or the authority of an agent, guardian, or surrogate, shall promptly record the determination in the patient's health-care record and communicate the determination to the patient, if possible, and to any person then authorized to make health-care decisions for the patient.

(d) Except as provided in subsections (e) and (f), a health-care provider or institution providing care to a patient shall:

(1) comply with an individual instruction of the patient and with a reasonable interpretation of that instruction made by a person then authorized to make health-care decisions for the patient; and

(2) comply with a health-care decision for the patient made by a person then authorized to make health-care decisions for the patient to the same extent as if the decision had been made by the patient while having capacity.

(e) A health-care provider may decline to comply with an individual instruction or health-care decision for reasons of conscience. A health-care institution may decline to comply with an individual instruction or health-care decision if the instruction or decision is contrary to a policy of the institution which is expressly based on reasons of conscience and if the policy was timely communicated to the patient or to a person then authorized to make health-care decisions for the patient.

(f) A health-care provider or institution may decline to comply with an individual instruction or health-care decision that requires medically ineffective health care or health care contrary to generally accepted health-care standards applicable to the health-care provider or institution.

(g) A health-care provider or institution that declines to comply with an individual instruction or health-care decision shall:

(1) promptly so inform the patient, if possible, and any person then authorized to make health-care decisions for the patient;

(2) provide continuing care to the patient until a transfer can be effected; and

(3) unless the patient or person then authorized to make health-care decisions for the patient refuses assistance, immediately make all reasonable efforts to assist in the transfer of the patient to another health-care provider or institution that is willing to comply with the instruction or decision.

(h) A health-care provider or institution may not require or prohibit the execution or revocation of an advance health-care directive as a condition for providing health care.

Section 8. Health–Care Information.

Unless otherwise specified in an advance health-care directive, a person then authorized to make health-care decisions for a patient has the same rights as the patient to request, receive, examine, copy, and consent to the disclosure of medical or any other health-care information.

Section 9. Immunities.

(a) A health-care provider or institution acting in good faith and in accordance with generally accepted health-care standards applicable to the health-care provider or institution is not subject to civil or criminal liability or to discipline for unprofessional conduct for:

(1) complying with a health-care decision of a person apparently having authority to make a health-care decision for a patient, including a decision to withhold or withdraw health care;

(2) declining to comply with a health-care decision of a person based on a belief that the person then lacked authority; or

(3) complying with an advance health-care directive and assuming that the directive was valid when made and has not been revoked or terminated.

(b) An individual acting as agent or surrogate under this [Act] is not subject to civil or criminal liability or to discipline for unprofessional conduct for health-care decisions made in good faith.

Section 10. Statutory Damages.

(a) A health-care provider or institution that intentionally violates this [Act] is subject to liability to the aggrieved individual for damages of $[500] or actual damages resulting from the violation, whichever is greater, plus reasonable attorney's fees.

(b) A person who intentionally falsifies, forges, conceals, defaces, or obliterates an individual's advance health-care directive or a revocation of an advance health-care directive without the individual's consent, or who coerces or fraudulently induces an individual to give, revoke, or not to give an advance health-care directive, is subject to liability to that individual for damages of $[2,500] or actual damages resulting from the action, whichever is greater, plus reasonable attorney's fees.

Section 11. Capacity.

(a) This [Act] does not affect the right of an individual to make health-care decisions while having capacity to do so.

(b) An individual is presumed to have capacity to make a health-care decision, to give or revoke an advance health-care directive, and to designate or disqualify a surrogate.

Section 12. Effect of Copy.

A copy of a written advance health-care directive, revocation of an advance health-care directive, or designation or disqualification of a surrogate has the same effect as the original.

Comment

The need to rely on an advance health-care directive may arise at times when the original is inaccessible. For example, an individual may be receiving care from several health-care providers or may be receiving care at a location distant from that where the original is kept. To facilitate prompt and informed decision making, this section provides that a copy of a valid written advance health-care directive, revocation of an advance health-care directive, or designation or disqualification of a surrogate has the same effect as the original.

Section 13. Effect of [Act].

(a) This [Act] does not create a presumption concerning the intention of an individual who has not made or who has revoked an advance health-care directive.

(b) Death resulting from the withholding or withdrawal of health care in accordance with this [Act] does not for any purpose constitute a suicide or homicide or legally impair or invalidate a policy of insurance or an annuity providing a death benefit, notwithstanding any term of the policy or annuity to the contrary.

(c) This [Act] does not authorize mercy killing, assisted suicide, euthanasia, or the provision, withholding, or withdrawal of health care, to the extent prohibited by other statutes of this State.

(d) This [Act] does not authorize or require a health-care provider or institution to provide health care contrary to generally accepted health-care standards applicable to the health-care provider or institution.

[(e) This [Act] does not authorize an agent or surrogate to consent to the admission of an individual to a mental health-care institution unless the individual's written advance health-care directive expressly so provides.]

[(f) This [Act] does not affect other statutes of this State governing treatment for mental illness of an individual involuntarily committed to a [mental health-care institution under appropriate statute].]

Section 14. Judicial Relief.

On petition of a patient, the patient's agent, guardian, or surrogate, a health-care provider or institution involved with the patient's care, or an individual described in Section 5(b) or (c), the [appropriate] court may enjoin or direct a health-care decision or order other equitable relief. A proceeding under this section is governed by [here insert appropriate reference to the rules of procedure or statutory provisions governing expedited proceedings and proceedings affecting incapacitated persons].

Comment

While the provisions of the Act are in general to be effectuated without litigation, situations will arise where judicial proceedings may be appropriate. For example, the members of a class of surrogates authorized to act under Section 5 may be evenly divided with respect to the advisability of a particular health-care decision. In that circumstance, authorization to proceed may have to be obtained from a court. Examples of other legitimate issues that may from time to time arise include whether an agent or surrogate has authority to act and whether an agent or surrogate has complied with the standard of care imposed by Sections 2(e) and 5(f).

This section has a limited scope. The court under this section may grant only equitable relief. Other adequate avenues exist for those who wish to pursue money damages. The class of potential petitioners is also limited to those with a direct interest in a patient's health care.

The final portion of this section has been placed in brackets in recognition of the fact that states vary widely in the extent to which they codify procedural matters in a substantive act. The legislature of an enacting jurisdiction is encouraged, however, to cross-reference to its rules on expedited proceedings or rules on proceedings affecting incapacitated persons. The legislature of an enacting jurisdiction which wishes to include a detailed procedural provision in its adoption of the Act may want to consult Guidelines for State Court Decision Making in Life–Sustaining Medical Treatment Cases (2d ed. 1992), published by the National Center for State Courts.

Section 15. Uniformity of Application and Construction.

This [Act] shall be applied and construed to effectuate its general purpose to make uniform the law with respect to the subject matter of this [Act] among States enacting it.

Section 16. Short Title.

This [Act] may be cited as the Uniform Health–Care Decisions Act.

Section 17. Severability Clause.

If any provision of this [Act] or its application to any person or circumstance is held invalid, the invalidity does not affect other provisions or applications of this [Act] which can be given effect without the invalid provision or application, and to this end the provisions of this [Act] are severable.

Section 18. Effective Date.

This [Act] takes effect on ______.

Section 19. Repeal.

The following acts and parts of acts are repealed:

LOCATE

Does your state have specific authority for a durable power of attorney for health care (DPAHC)? If yes, study the statute carefully and then answer the following questions.

NOTES AND QUESTIONS

1. What characteristics would you look for in a health care agent? Are they different from the features you would look for in an agent for property matters? Would you name the same person as your health care agent that you named as your property management agent? See ABA COMMISSION ON LEGAL PROBLEMS OF THE ELDERLY, LAWYER'S TOOL KIT FOR HEALTH CARE ADVANCE PLANNING (2000). See also Chapter 8(H).

2. The principal should name alternates in case the first-named agent refuses or is unable to serve.

3. Assume your client has two trusted children and wants to name them as co-agents. Is this a good idea? Why or why not?

4. What capacity (age and mental state) must a person possess to execute a DPAHC?

5. Will an oral agency appointment be effective?

6. Must the principal sign the DPAHC? Will a proxy signature be sufficient?

7. Does the DPAHC need to be witnessed?

8. Does the DPAHC need to be acknowledged?

9. Is a disclosure statement required? If yes, does the statute provide the actual form or merely indicate what the statement must contain?

10. Does the statute contain a form to use for a DPAHC? If yes, may the principal make changes or must it be used substantially as provided?

11. How may the principal revoke the DPAHC? Does a mere lapse of time work to revoke the DPAHC automatically?

12. When does the agent's authority begin? See HIPAA discussion, below.

13. What is the effect on the agent's authority if a court appoints a guardian of the person for the principal?

14. Should the principal provide for the agent to receive compensation? If yes, how should compensation be determined?

15. Does a health care provider have any obligation to follow the agent's directions? What should the health care provider do if the provider believes the agent is misusing the authority?

16. Mary completed a valid DPAHC naming Daughter as her agent. When Mary became seriously ill with no realistic chance of recovery, Daughter asked Mary's doctors to remove life support equipment. One of Mary's sons disagreed; he thought Mary should be given more time on the machines before giving up on recovery hopes. A lengthy legal battle ensued and before it was resolved, Mary died. See Doloros Kong, *Patient Proxy Laws Face Hitches,* BOSTON GLOBE, Dec. 3, 1992, at 29. What steps can you take to avoid this problem?

17. For further information, see Kristen Lewis Grice, *Advance Health Care Planning: Filling the Void,* PROB. & PROP., July/Aug. 1990, at 40.

HEALTH INSURANCE PORTABILITY AND ACCOUNTABILITY ACT PRIVACY RULES

The agent named in a springing power may have difficulty obtaining the medical information necessary for a determination of incapacity because of the privacy requirements of the Health Insurance Portability and Accountability Act (HIPAA). HIPAA authorizes the release of medical information to a patient's "personal representative." This term is defined in such a way as to include a health care agent. However, the named agent has no authority until the patient is declared incompetent but the named agent cannot obtain the medical information necessary for a determination of incompetence until the agent has authority. Some experts believe that the only way out of this Catch–22 situation is to have the client sign a separate authorization permitting medical information to be released to the agent regardless of the patient's condition. Other experts, on the other hand, are convinced that the HIPAA regulations are broad enough to permit the named agent to obtain the information necessary to determine if the agent's authority is triggered. If you elect to prepare a separate release for the principal to sign, you must make certain it complies with HIPAA and that it is in a separate document; HIPAA prohibits the authorization from being included in another document such as a medical power of attorney. See Daniel B. Evans, *What Estate Lawyers Need to Know About HIPAA and "Protected Health Information,"* PROB. & PROP., July/Aug. 2004, at 20; Helen W. Gunnarsson, *Are Statutory Health Care POAs HIPAA–Compliant?*, 92 ILL. B.J. 302 (2004).

AUTHORIZATION TO RELEASE MEDICAL INFORMATION[1]

(HIPAA Authorization Under 45 C.F.R. § 164.508)

A) Statement of Intent

It is my understanding that Congress passed a law entitled the Health Insurance Portability and Accountability Act of 1996 ("HIPAA"), that there are federal regulations that interpret and implement that law, and that HIPAA limits disclosure of my "Individually Identifiable Health Information" to certain of my family and friends, regardless of my state of health. I am signing this authorization so my Health Care Providers can disclose my health care information to the persons listed below, and openly discuss that information with them.

B) Authorization

I, [client], hereby authorize my physicians, nurses, hospitals and other Health Care Providers to fully disclose my Individually Identifiable Health Information to any or all of the following authorized persons (my "Personal Representatives"):

Name: ______________________________

Address: ______________________________

____

Phone: ______________________________

Name: ______________________________

Address: ______________________________

____

Phone: ______________________________

Further, if I have executed and have not revoked a Medical Power of Attorney and/or a Durable Power of Attorney naming other agents to make health care decisions and/or business and personal decisions on my

1. Adapted from Georgia Akers, *HIPAA Law and Practice*, in STATE BAR OF TEXAS, 28TH ANNUAL ADVANCED ESTATE PLANNING AND PROBATE COURSE ch. 2, at 31–33 (2004).

behalf, then said agents shall be deemed automatically added to the above list of persons to have access to my personal medical records.

The fact that I may have named more than one party to have access to my protected medical records shall not be interpreted as requiring all of their joint consent or signatures. Each person I designated shall have the authority to act individually and without notice to any other designated person.

C) Authority to Discuss and Answer Questions

My Health Care Providers are expressly authorized to answer questions posed by the Personal Representatives listed above and openly discuss with them my condition, treatment, test results, prognosis, and all other information pertinent to my health care, even if I am fully competent to ask questions and discuss my medical condition. This document constitutes a full authorization to disclose any Individually Identifiable Health Information to the Personal Representatives named in this Authorization.

D) Waiver and Release

I hereby release any Health Care Provider who acts in reliance on this Authorization from any liability that may accrue from releasing my Individually Identifiable Health Information and for any actions taken by my Personal Representatives.

E) Termination

This Authorization is effective as of the date shown as the date of its signing and shall not be affected by my subsequent disability or incapacity. This authorization shall terminate on this first to occur of: (1) two years following my death or (2) upon my written revocation actually received by the Health Care Provider. Proof of receipt of my written revocation may be by certified mail, registered mail, facsimile, or any other receipt evidencing actual receipt by the Health Care Provider.

F) Re-disclosure

By signing this Authorization, I readily acknowledge that the information used or disclosed pursuant to this Authorization may be subject to re-disclosure by the Personal Representatives named in this Authorization and no longer by protected by the HIPAA rules. I realize that such re-disclosure might be improper, cause me embarrassment, cause family strife, be misinterpreted by non-health care professionals, and otherwise cause me and my family various forms of injury. I fully indemnify my Health Care Providers for all consequences which may occur as a result of their good faith reliance and compliance with this Authorization. No Health Care Provider shall require my Personal Representatives to indemnify the Health Care Provider or agree to perform any act in order for the Health Care Provider to comply with this Authorization.

G) Enforcement

My Personal Representatives shall have the right to bring a legal action in any applicable forums against any Health Care Provider who refuses to recognize and accept this Authorization. Additionally, my Personal Representatives are authorized to sign any documents that my Personal Representatives deem necessary or appropriate to obtain my Individually Identifiable Health Information.

H) Conflicts With Other Authorizations

This Authorization is in addition to other medical release authorizations I may have granted in the past or future; it does not replace them. This Authorization may be relied upon by my Health Care Providers regardless of any real or perceived conflict with any Medical Power of Attorney signed by me, whether prior to or subsequent to the date of this Authorization. I recognize and intend that this may result in multiple persons having the authority to obtain my protected Individually Identifiable Health Information. This Authorization is not intended to replace a Medical Power of Attorney, nor to grant any person the authority to make health care decisions, but merely to obtain information and explanations.

I) Copies

A copy or facsimile of this original Authorization may be accepted and relied upon as though it was an original document.

J) Definitions

1) Individually Identifiable Health Information

The term "Individually Identifiable Health Information" includes (but is not limited to) the following:

All health care information, reports and/or records concerning my medical history, condition, diagnosis, testing, prognosis, treatment, billing information, the identity of health care providers and insurers, whether past, present or future, and any other medical information which is in any way related to my health care. In this Authorization, the term also includes the term "Protected Medical Information" as sometimes used in HIPAA.

2) Health Care Providers

The term "Health Care Providers" includes (but is not limited to) the following:

Doctors (including, but not limited to, physicians, podiatrists, chiropractors, or osteopaths), psychiatrists, psychologists, dentists, therapists, nurses, hospitals, clinics, pharmacies, laboratories, ambulance services, assisted living facilities, residential care facilities, bed and board facilities, nursing homes, medical insurance companies, and any other medical providers or affiliates. In this Authorization, the term also includes the term "Covered Entity" as sometimes used in HIPAA.

Signed this ______ day of ______, 200__.

____

[client]

State of ______
County of ______________________

This document was acknowledged before me on [date] by [client].

____

(signature of notarial officer)

(Seal, if any, of notary)

____

(printed name)

My commission expires: ______

DRAFT

Prepare a DPAHC. Be sure to dodge as many potential problems as you can.

D. SELF-DESIGNATION OF GUARDIAN OF THE PERSON

Please review Chapter 5(C) discussing self-designation of guardians of the estate.

LOCATE

Does your state permit self-designation of guardians of the person? If yes, is the procedure different from the one used for designating an estate guardian?

NOTES AND QUESTIONS

1. Work through the notes for Chapter 5(C) again and answer based on a self-designation of a personal guardian.

2. Would you want the same person to serve as both types of guardians? Why or why not?

3. For continuity, you should name the same person as guardian of the person as you named as your health care agent. The Uniform Health Care Decisions Act reflects this approach. Review section 5 of the form found in § 4 of the Act as reproduced in Chapter 6(C).

DRAFT

Prepare a guardian self-designation document for yourself. Be sure to follow the statutory requirements, name alternates, and provide appropriate individualization as needed.

E. LONG-TERM CARE INSURANCE

SAM E. BELLER, HOW TO COMPARE LONG-TERM CARE INSURANCE POLICIES*

26 EST. PLAN. 296 (1999).

Insurance is sometimes confusing to people. The more intricate the policy, the more difficult it is to understand. Health insurance—with its exclusions and limitations—is perhaps more intimidating than life insurance. Long-term care (LTC) insurance has created more misunderstanding because of the nature of the population it is directed toward (over age 50), and the number of variables available to choose from.

This is not a criticism of the insurance industry, nor of any of the companies that sell this coverage. Rather, the complexity results simply from the nature of the LTC insurance contract. If anything, the industry has reacted to the needs of the public in this area very vigorously, adding benefits to contracts when necessary. Most states have also adopted very specific laws concerning the provisions of LTC insurance policies, and the National Association of Insurance Commissioners (NAIC) has drafted a model bill for the guidance of any state that wishes to enact such legislation.

No one LTC insurance plan is correct for everyone. No one company has the best plan all the time. This is a changing environment. New provisions, new laws, and new policies will come into existence in the future. For the present, however, the guidelines presented here will give you a better understanding of LTC insurance and will enable you to evaluate the policies in a more knowledgeable and professional manner.

BACKGROUND

One out of every three people age 65 or over will spend 90 days or longer in a health-related facility before he or she dies, and one in four will spend more than one year. These statistics are extremely discomforting, but the one that is possibly the most unnerving is found in a March 1996 report of the Life Insurance Agency Management & Research Association (LIMRA), which said that 50% of those people whose lives end in a nursing home die destitute.

---

* "How to Compare Long-Term Care Insurance Policies," by Sam E. Beller, published in Estate Planning, Volume 26, 1999. ©1999 by Thomson Reuters/WG&L. Reprinted with permission.

The chances of needing home health care are considerably greater than the likelihood of needing nursing home care. Although statistics are not a readily available, the number of disabled senior citizens living with family or living alone is overwhelmingly larger than the number in health-related facilities.

Not everyone needs LTC insurance. A person in the upper economic bracket probably doesn't need the insurance protection. If an individual is indigent (with little or no assets or income), government programs will pay the costs associated with nursing home and/or home health care. For many of us, though, the need for LTC insurance may no longer be a question. The question now is:

- What kind of policy do I need?
- Can I afford the premiums now and in the future?
- What are the terms of the various contracts that are available to me?

LTC policies offer a wide range of benefits. Some policies cover nursing home care alone, some cover only home health care, and some cover nursing home care and/or home health care. The cost of these plans varies, depending on such factors as age, current physical condition, how long benefits will be paid, how much will be paid, when benefits will commence, and what services are covered. The terms of the contracts available to an individual differ by company and by state of domicile.

POLICY DEFINITIONS

Before comparing policy features, it may be useful to review certain definitions relating to LTC insurance.

Activities of daily living (ADLs). There are generally six ADLs used as the determination for receiving LTC insurance benefits. These ADLs are: (1) bathing, (2) eating, (3) toileting, (4) dressing, (5) continence, and (6) transferring.

Quality policies typically use the inability to perform two of the six ADLs as the "trigger" for availability of benefits. Some policies list only five ADLs. Some contracts require the inability to perform three of the five or six ADLs to be eligible for benefits.

Cognitive disorders or mental incompetency. Under many policies, benefits are automatically triggered in the event of a "cognitive impairment," such as Alzheimer's disease. Most states prohibit policies from containing exclusions for Alzheimer's disease.

Elimination period. Benefits commence after a specific number of days of disability, usually anywhere from 0 to 365 days. Different elimination periods may apply for home health care and for nursing home care.

Benefit period. How long will benefits be paid? This could range from one year to life. Benefit periods may differ for home health care and for nursing home care.

Inflation protection. Will benefits increase automatically with an increase in the cost of living? In many policies, this adjustment for inflation is automatic. In others, it is an option that may be purchased at additional cost. In still other contracts, the insured has the option to buy the added COLI (cost of living increase) coverage annually.

Nursing home. This term is defined as a facility certified by the state to provide nursing home care. All LTC insurance policies cover 100% of the daily benefit up to the limits of the policy.

Assisted living facility. This is a facility that is certified by the state and is engaged primarily in providing ongoing care and related services to support needs resulting from the inability to perform two of the ADLs. Some plans cover 100% of the daily benefit, while others cover 80%, in an assisted living facility.

Adult day care center. This term refers to a facility certified by the state to provide community-based group programs in the areas of health, social, and related support services in the facility. Adult day care is not 24–hour care.

Hospice. A hospice is an institution specifically for planned programs of care relating to a terminally ill individual.

Home health care. This refers to care received at home, under a written plan of care, from one or more of the following licensed home care providers: (1) licensed nurse (RN or LPN), (2) occupational therapist, (3) speech therapist, (4) physical therapist, (5) respiratory therapist, and/or (6) dietician.

Some policies cover home health aides who provide assistance with the ADLs and perform such tasks as cooking and cleaning. Some plans cover 100% of the daily nursing home benefits, while others cover 80%, for home health aides.

Licensed health care practitioner. Many policies cover the services of a licensed health care practitioner. This health care professional assesses the patient's condition, helps evaluate care options, and develops an individualized plan of care. Generally, the cost of this service is paid under the LTC insurance policy in addition to the regular daily benefit. If the policy covers this service, there is usually no elimination period and payment is made up to a specific multiple of the daily benefit (e.g., 20 times the daily benefit).

Most institutions providing long-term care have licensed personnel who work with the patient, his or her physician, and the institution to create a plan of care for the patient. The additional cost for this service, if any, is covered by this policy provision. This policy feature also covers the cost of the health care practitioner if no inpatient care is required, up to the limit described.

Renewability option. Most policies are guaranteed renewable. This means that the company must renew the policy each year if the premiums are paid as billed. The premium is not guaranteed but can be changed only by "class." An insured's premium cannot be increased individually.

If there is an existing policy in force, check for the renewability option to make sure the policy is guaranteed renewable. Most new policies are guaranteed renewable; however, some of the older policies are not, and may not be renewed by the insurance company for any reason.

Waiver of premium. If an insured is disabled, premiums coming due during disability need not be paid (i.e., payment of premiums is "waived"). Under some policies, the waiver of premium is active only during a compensable claim. Other policies provide for the return of any premiums paid during the waiting or elimination period.

Bed reservation. This feature reserves a bed in a health-related facility for a number of days while the insured is hospitalized.

Spousal reduction in premium. Many companies will reduce the premiums on the LTC insurance policies if both the husband and wife are insured for LTC with the company. This reduction could be substantial—for example, 10% or 20%. Therefore, if this situation is applicable, be sure the reduction is given. Some companies offer this reduction in premiums even to unmarried people living together for a number of years.

Notification option. This clause specifies that if the insured names a third party (e.g., son, daughter, or friend), that person will be notified before the insured's policy lapses for non-payment of premium. This is an extremely important clause: Should the insured be disabled and unable to pay the premium, the person notified may make sure the policy stays in force, and a claim, if any, can be paid without any difficulties.

Respite care. This benefit gives temporary relief to a spouse or other family member who is providing care to the patient. The costs of temporary professional care in the home or in a health-related facility (a nursing home or an assisted living facility) are covered, if the primary caregiver needs some time off.

Covered expenses are generally payable up to a multiple of the daily benefit (e.g., 20 times the daily benefit) in a calendar year. Usually, no elimination period needs to be met.

PRACTICE NOTES

Review LTC insurance policies offered by several companies. Don't hesitate to ask questions. Compare benefits and costs of policies. Find out the 'rating' of LTC insurance companies.

Purchasing a policy

It is a good idea to review LTC insurance policies offered by several companies. Don't hesitate to ask questions. Policies that seem identical might not be. * * * Find out the "rating" of the companies; insurers are rated by Best's, Duff & Phelps, Moody's, and Standard & Poor's, among others. These ratings address in large measure an insurance company's ability to pay claims and the company's stability—major issues in LTC.

The insurance agent can be one of the most important resources in the purchase of an LTC policy. You may wish to speak with more than one agent. Have each of them give you proposals from more than one company. Check the credentials of the agent. Is he or she a CLU (Chartered Life Underwriter), a ChFC (Chartered Financial Consultant), a CFP (Certified Financial Planner), or does the agent have some other professional designation? Most agents selling LTC insurance are honest, hardworking individuals who care about their clients. There are a few, however, who prey on older people in this marketplace. Buy the policy from an agent who knows the field or is willing to do the research to get the answers.

Neither Medicare nor any federal agency sells or endorses LTC insurance policies. Medicare covers only acute or rehabilitative care in a nursing home. It does not cover long-term care in a health-related facility. Don't buy multiple policies to get enough coverage. One good policy is sufficient.

Keep in mind that the application for an LTC policy is submitted to an insurance company that will check the medical history supplied by the applicant on the application form. It is important to be truthful on the application so as to avoid problems that may arise later if a claim is submitted. After the application is completed, review it for accuracy.

When an LTC insurance policy is received, compare it to the proposal. In most states, the agent is required to review the policy with the insured upon delivery. Even after the agent leaves, and the premium has been paid, there is still a "free-look" period (usually 30 days), during which time the policy can be returned for a full refund if the purchaser is not satisfied.

Policy Cost

LTC insurance is very important. It is also not inexpensive. Both the need for protection and the individual's pocketbook should be viewed together. The cost of care in a health-related facility is increasing. Be especially mindful of this in purchasing LTC insurance coverage. Premiums can range from about $1,000 per year to $15,000 per year or more, depending on coverage, age, and health at the time the policy is issued.

The cost of long-term care varies substantially throughout the U.S. The average cost of a nursing home in most large urban areas (e.g., New York, Chicago, Los Angeles, and Boston) is over $200 per day. In the midwest and far west (e.g., Indiana, Arizona, Colorado), the cost about $175 per day, and in the South (e.g., Mississippi, Alabama, Tennessee), the daily cost is approximately $150.

Premiums for LTC insurance policies vary by region. A policy purchased in New York may cost more than a similar policy purchased in Oklahoma. The premium for an LTC insurance policy is calculated based on the following criteria:

1. Benefit periods (e.g., three years, five years, lifetime);

2. Elimination period (e.g., 20 days, 60 days, 100 days);

3. Amount of benefit (e.g., $150/day, $200/day, $250/day);

4. Riders added (e.g., automatic cost of living index increase, non-forfeiture option); and

5. Coverage (e.g., nursing home only, home health care only, both nursing home and home health care).

The condition of an applicant's health also may affect the cost and benefits of the policy. The insurance companies know that the average person purchasing this coverage is over 60 years of age; consequently, the underwriters give some leeway for minor health conditions, such as slightly elevated blood pressure. Any major health problem, however, may require that the condition be excluded from coverage, or—as more often occurs—all conditions are covered, but either a higher premium is charged or the benefits are reduced, or both. These "rated policies," as they are called, can have premiums that increase the cost of the policy from as little as 10% to as much as 100%. As noted earlier, be truthful on the application; it may save you a lot of trouble later on.

* * *

Additional Considerations

In many estate planning situations, the transfer of assets to qualify for Medicaid has long been an issue. To alleviate the problems and pitfalls associated with this divestiture of assets, some states have enacted so-called state partnership laws with respect to LTC insurance. Generally, under these state partnership programs, a person buys an LTC insurance policy that meets certain requirements. When the benefits under the policy have been exhausted, the individual becomes eligible for Medicaid without being forced to "spend down" his assets to the level normally required for Medicaid eligibility.

Because state partnership programs may differ, it is wise to check the specifics of the program, if any, in the state of domicile of the individual. If an individual changes domicile (e.g., he moves from New York to Florida), the original "qualified" LTC insurance policy may no longer afford him the same protection against being forced to "spend down" his assets.

For income tax purposes, part or all of the premiums for LTC insurance policies may be deductible as medical expenses. However, policies must meet certain federal standards before the premiums are deductible. Under Code Section 213, all of an individual's medical expenses, including LTC insurance premiums, must exceed 7.5% of adjusted gross income (AGI) in order to qualify for the deduction.

These tax-qualified LTC contracts also generally enable benefits to be tax-free. Benefits received from a non-qualified LTC policy may be taxable income to the insured. Most LTC policies issued after 1996 are tax-qualified. Many insurers have added riders to existing policies to make them tax-qualified. Clearly, tax qualification can mean savings of thousands of dollars to the insured.

There are some LTC insurance policies that use an "indemnity" approach to claims payments. Once the insured meets the qualification to receive claim payments, the full daily room and board rate is paid regardless of the actual cost to the insured. Technically, any amount received over the actual cost of care is taxable income. Most current policies will pay the actual cost of care up to the limits of the policy under the reimbursement approach.

New benefits in LTC insurance are arising continuously. Most companies, when changing or adding new enhancements to their contracts, will offer these to existing policyholders—frequently at no cost or with no additional underwriting requirements.

A brief note for the "Sandwich Generation": Many younger people are purchasing LTC insurance policies for their parents. The rationale behind this is that should an elderly parent need nursing home or home health care, the children would pay the bill. The children are therefore buying the LTC insurance to protect their own assets from depletion.

CONCLUSION

While it is important for an individual to review the available options, procrastination can be expensive. A person's health may be fine today but may deteriorate relatively quickly. Not making a decision about an LTC insurance policy may be worse than making a wrong decision. * * * [C]ompare policies, make the analysis, and determine whether LTC insurance makes sense. If it does, buy the policy. It is a purchase that creates peace of mind at an extremely vulnerable time in a person's life.

NOTES AND QUESTIONS

1. At this point in time, do you think you need long-term care insurance? Why or why not? Do you foresee ever being in a different situation so that your answer would change?

2. "This year, about nine million men and women over the age of 65 will need long-term care. By 2020, 12 million older Americans will need long-term care. Most will be cared for at home; family and friends are the sole caregivers for 70 percent of the elderly. A study by the U.S. Department of Health and Human Services says that people who reach age 65 will likely have a 40 percent chance of entering a nursing home. About 10 percent of the people who enter a nursing home will stay there five years or more." *What is Long–Term Care?*, MEDICARE.GOV, http://www.medicare.gov/longtermcare/static/home.asp (last updated Mar. 25, 2009).

A study by the American Association for Long–Term Care Insurance recently revealed that an increasing number of claimants are young, that is, in their 20s. The study "dispels the misperception that long term care insurance is purchased by and benefits only older individuals who need care as a result of conditions typically associated with aging." See *Younger Long Term Care Insurance Claimants Examined*, PRN NEWSWIRE, Sept. 5, 2012.

3. When is long-term care insurance financially feasible? See *Ask Our Experts*, CONSUMER REPORTS, Aug. 2012, at 5 ("Financial planners have told us that people with a net worth of less than $200,000 to $300,000 (excluding a house and depending on the regional cost of care) could probably not afford a policy and should plan to rely on family or government programs for help. Those with assets of $2 million or more should be able to pay for care. People in between are the most likely candidates for coverage.").

4. If your client is eligible for Medicare (e.g., 65 years old or, in some cases, disabled even though under age 65), you may need to assist your client in locating the appropriate insurance to cover the gaps in Medicare coverage. See Christopher J. Gearon, *The ABCs of Filing Medicare Gaps*, KIPLINGER'S RETIREMENT REPORT, Sept. 9, 2008.

5. For further information, see Moriah Adamo, Randy Breidbart, Charon Kovacs, Gruer, Felicia Pasculli, John Lensky Robert, and Fred S. Sganga, *Paying for Long–Term Care,* 83 N.Y. ST. B.J. 66 (July/Aug. 2011).

LOCATE

Visit with several health insurance agents and obtain information about various long-term care plans. Compare features and decide which policy you would recommend to a client who needs long-term care insurance.

F. ACCELERATED LIFE INSURANCE PAYMENTS AND VIATICAL SETTLEMENTS*

This section discusses two innovative uses of life insurance to provide valuable benefits to an insured while the insured is still alive but facing a rapidly approaching death. One technique involves a life insurance policy that requires the insurer to prepay all or a portion of the death benefit to the insured when the insured has a disabling or life threatening condition which doctors predict will cause death within a relatively short period of time. Life insurance companies and insurance regulations may use several terms to refer to this type of provision such as *accelerated death benefit*, *living needs benefit*, *acceleration-of-life-insurance benefit*, and *living payout option*. These payments allow "seriously ill people and their families to keep their homes, to receive quality care, and otherwise live their lives with a measure of independence, security, and peace." 137 CONG. REC. S1294–02 (Jan. 30, 1991) (statement of Sen. Lieberman). Depending on the debilitating extent of the illness, the extra money could allow the insured to enjoy the remainder of his or her life to its fullest such as by taking a vacation before the insured becomes too ill to do so. Some policies will also provide benefits to pay for a life-saving organ transplant.

---

* Portions of this section are adapted from Gerry W. Beyer, *Accelerated Life Insurance Payments and Viatical Settlements*, EST. PLAN. STUD. (April 1998).

The other technique provides basically the same result but through a different means. In a *viatical settlement*, a third party purchases the life insurance policy of an insured (the *viator*) who has a life-threatening disease or illness. The term viatical settlement has an interesting history. It "originated from the Latin word 'viaticum,' which means 'provision for a journey.' In ancient Rome, viatica were the supplies soldiers were given in preparation for their journey into battle, a journey from which they might not return." Michael Todd Scott, *An Illinois Lawyer's Guide to Viatical Settlements*, 85 ILL. B.J. 276, 276 (1997).

An insured who elects to enter into a viatical settlement receives either (a) a one-time payment which usually ranges from fifty to eighty percent of the policy's face value, or (b) periodic payments. Most purchasers require the insured to have two years or less to live. The shorter the insured's life expectancy, the greater the purchase price will be. In 2001, The Life Insurance and Annuities Committee adopted a Model Act aimed at regulating the purchase of insurance policies by viatical settlement companies. The Model Act has subsequently been adopted by several states. The Model Act sets forth standards that may be used to determine a reasonable or fair purchase price. The reasonableness of a settlement price depends heavily on the life expectancy of the viator. A reasonable purchase price for a $100,000 policy when the viator has a life expectancy of less than six months is $80,000 or 80%. For more information about these standards visit the National Association of Insurance Commissioners at; http://www.naic.org.

The purchaser becomes the owner of the policy and typically names itself as the beneficiary. The purchaser continues to pay any required premiums and receives the policy's entire face value when the insured dies.

1. Historical Background

Before life insurance companies offered accelerated benefits, entrepreneurs formed viatical settlement companies to provide accelerated payments to insureds. These businesses purchased life insurance policies of terminally ill individuals and others who had a relatively short life expectancy. As the desire for accelerated benefits increased, particularly from AIDS and cancer patients, the life insurance industry quickly reacted to meet the growing demand.

Although accelerated benefits had been available from some insurers in the United States as early as 1965, the first large insurance company to enter the accelerated benefits arena was the Prudential Insurance Company which introduced the "living needs benefits" rider as an option to its life insurance policies in 1990. Connecticut Mutual Life Insurance Company entered the field shortly thereafter. Today, hundreds of insurance companies offer living benefits riders in a variety of formats.

State governments have been quick to authorize insurance companies to offer policies that contain accelerated benefits. By the end of 1991, the insurance commissions of all states had authorized accelerated benefits. In addition, many states have extensive provisions regulating viatical settlements.

2. Evaluating the Accelerated Benefits/Viatical Settlement Option

a. Financial Strength of Insurer

"Life insurance continues to be the central source of financial security for most families in this country." *Association Leaders Speak Out; Life Insurance History*, BEST'S REV.: LIFE/HEALTH, June 1990, at 76. Because so many people place their trust and financial future in the hands of insurance companies, it is crucial that consumers ascertain the financial stability of a particular insurance company prior to purchasing any insurance policy, especially one that provides a living needs benefit.

An estate planner who wants to recommend that a client obtain a policy providing for accelerated benefits should first investigate prospective insurers. Information about insurance policies and insurers can be gathered from organizations such as the Health Insurance Association of America, the American Council on Life Insurance, National Council on the Aging, and individual state insurance boards. It is important to deal with a company with an established track record so that the chances are good that the company will still be in existence to pay the accelerated benefits if the time comes.

Several sources are available to ascertain insurer solvency. The National Association of Insurance Commissioners (NAIC) developed a solvency policing agenda to improve the ability of state regulators to monitor and regulate industry solvency. Alternatively, A.M. Best Company, Standard & Poor's Corporation (S & P), Moody's, and Duff and Phelps publish ratings of insurance companies. For example, S & P has developed a system of "qualified solvency ratings." The basis of these ratings is information obtained from the NAIC database and special requests from specific insurance companies.

b. Eligibility Requirements

Eligibility requirements for accelerated benefits vary among insurance companies. While some companies include a living needs benefits rider in both their new and existing life insurance policies, other companies add the rider only to new policies. The purchaser should inquire as to cost, if any, for an accelerated benefit provision. In many instances, there is no additional cost for including such a rider; however, the purchaser may be required to buy a designated minimum amount of coverage. In addition, most insurance companies restrict the use of living needs benefits riders to permanent and universal life insurance policies.

Every insurance company requires that the purchaser generally be in good health and pass a physical at the time the policy is paid for. An accelerated benefit policy is not available to a buyer diagnosed as terminally ill prior to the purchase. In addition, no two life benefits riders will be identical. It is wise to shop around for policies because insurance companies can set their own requirements regarding many aspects of these plans.

In a similar manner, viatical settlement companies may apply different criteria in deciding whether to purchase a policy as well as the percentage of the face value they are willing to pay.

c. *Effect on Policy's Death Benefit*

The insured should determine how the accelerated payments or viatical settlement will affect the policy's overall death benefit. For instance, will the accelerated payments reduce or eliminate the death benefit? If the death benefit is reduced, is the reduction based upon the amount paid to the insured or is there an additional processing fee or other penalty which will be deducted from the death benefit? With most viatical settlements, the insured has no control over the death benefit because the policy belongs to the viatical settlement company.

d. *Restrictions on Payment of Accelerated Benefit*

1) Designated Diseases

Insurance companies vary as to the illnesses which can trigger the payment of accelerated benefits under their living benefits rider. While some companies include any type of terminal illness for which the insured has only a short time to live, other companies restrict coverage to specified diseases. Generally, the following medical conditions are covered under all insurance plans: AIDS, heart attack, stroke, Alzheimer's disease, renal failure or liver transplant, life threatening cancer, and coronary artery bypass. Most insurance companies further restrict availability of this benefit to persons with twelve months or less to live.

2) Amount of Accelerated Payment

The amount payable to the insured under a life benefits rider varies between 2 to 95 percent of the death benefit depending upon the insurer.

3) Form of Accelerated Payment

Generally, the insured may receive the accelerated benefits in one of three ways: one lump sum payment, regular installments, or installments based on the insured's expenses. If the installment option is selected, the insured should inquire as to whether accelerated payments can be canceled once the benefits start. It is important to remember that a benefit received during life reduces the amount payable to the beneficiary. Under certain circumstances, the insured may wish to cancel accelerated payments and retain the remaining value of the life insurance proceeds for the beneficiary. Another concern with installment payments is what happens if the benefits cease before the insured dies. If the accelerated payments are likely to be depleted prior to death, the insured should consider seeking alternative methods of financing medical and personal expenses.

4) Restrictions on Use of Funds

Insurance companies may also vary on the restrictive uses of benefits received by the insured. Some companies may require that the funds be used strictly for medical care while others may have no limitation on the expenditure of the funds. Though some policyholders may view accelerated benefits as a means of "making dreams come true," these riders are generally designed for health care and medical expenses.

e. Death Before Completion of Payments

If an installment payout option is available, the insured should ascertain what will happen to the remaining payments if the insured dies prior to completion of accelerated benefits. Some possible consequences may be: (1) the remaining payments are forfeited; (2) the beneficiary receives the remaining payments in installments; or (3) the beneficiary receives a death benefit after adjustment for the accelerated payments.

f. Deciding Between Accelerated Benefits or a Viatical Settlement

An insured may have a choice between electing to take accelerated payments from the insurance company or to enter into a viatical settlement with a third party. The insured must carefully make this decision. The insured should "take advantage of competitive forces and the free market to obtain the highest payment for the life insurance contract." Gary J. Gasper, *Viatical Settlements—Cashing Out Life Insurance*, PROB. & PROP., March/April 1997, at 20. "As a general rule, accelerated death benefits will provide * * * a higher payout, but are usually more restrictive regarding medical condition than viatical settlements." Julia K. Brazelton & Rebecca Kaenzig, *Accelerated Death Benefits Finally Afforded Exclusion*, TAXES, Jan. 1997, at 57, 63.

The American Council of Life Insurance has a helpful set of frequently asked questions and answers designed to aid an insured in deciding whether to elect accelerated life insurance benefits. The questions and answers are available on the American Council of Life Insurance website at http://www.acli.org. In a similar fashion, the Viatical and Life Settlement Association of America, which can be reached at http://www.viatical.org, has prepared helpful information about viatical settlements along with a list of companies that purchase life insurance policies which is available at http://www.viatical.org/providers.htm.

3. Potential Drawbacks

a. Decreased Beneficiary Protection

Accepting accelerated benefits reduces the face amount of the insured's policy thereby reducing or eliminating death benefits payable to the beneficiary when the insured dies. An insured may not wish to sacrifice the financial security of a spouse or children in exchange for accelerated benefits. Accordingly, the type of individual who would most benefit from taking an accelerated benefit or a viatical settlement is a person "who has no spouse (or a spouse who can be financially independent), has no dependents, has no long-term care or disability insurance, is unable to work, and is financially independent." Julia K. Brazelton & Rebecca Kaenzig, *Accelerated Death Benefits Finally Afforded Exclusion*, TAXES, Jan. 1997, at 57, 63.

b. Eligibility for Governmental Assistance Programs

If the insured's contract is designed with a voluntary election provision, it is uncertain whether a local, state, or federal government agency could force the insured to take accelerated benefits, i.e., is the availability of the benefit deemed property of or potential income to the insured when computing eligibility for benefits. Several of the bills introduced into Congress over the past years have expressly dealt with this issue. For example, the Living Benefits Act of 1991 was drafted with the assumption that it "would not be fair to force the terminally ill to choose between their own welfare and the future welfare of their survivors." 137 CONG. REC. S1294–02 (Jan. 30, 1991) (S. 284). The bill would have amended "the Social Security Act to ensure that policyholders are not compelled to elect prepayment of death benefits in order to become eligible or remain eligible for Federal means-tested programs such as Medicaid." *Id.*

c. Proceeds May be Subject to Creditors' Claims

When life insurance proceeds are paid to the designated beneficiary, most states exempt them from the claims of the insured/deceased's creditors. Once those proceeds are paid to a living insured, however, the insured's creditors may be able to reach them unless state law has extended creditor protection to accelerated benefits and viatical settlements.

A problem may arise even if the insured does not claim the proceeds but merely has the ability to demand the benefits. Would the benefits be within the reach of the insured's creditors? Could the creditors force the insured to accept benefits so that they could then attach them? These issues have not been resolved in many jurisdictions.

d. Continued Need for Health Insurance

A life insurance policy containing accelerated benefits should not be considered as a replacement for comprehensive health insurance or long-term care insurance. In fact, the regulations of many states prohibit insurers and insurance agents from mentioning, illustrating, or referring to the accelerated benefit provision as an alternative or substitute for catastrophic major medical health insurance. Insureds must be strongly advised to obtain appropriate health and long-term care insurance because these policies only benefit individuals who have terminal illnesses and short times to live.

e. Financial Vulnerability After Receiving Proceeds

"Some critics caution that an unscrupulous con artist could easily take advantage of the seriously ill, who receive large sums of money while under stress." Miller, *Getting Paid Before the Funeral*, ORANGE COUNTY BUS. J., April 9, 1990, at 19. An insured may be vulnerable to charlatans claiming that they can cure the insured's ailment or by scam artists who claim they can earn large returns on the insured's newly gained wealth. See also Anna D. Halechko, *Viatical Settlements: The Need for Regulation to Preserve the Benefits While Protecting the Ill and the Elderly from Fraud*. 42 DUQ. L. REV. 803 (2004).

4. Tax Consequences

a. Federal Income Tax

As a general rule, proceeds of a life insurance policy are excluded from the recipient's gross income under IRC § 101(a)(1). To secure this exclusion, the proceeds must be payable "by reason of the death of the insured." Accelerated benefits are not payable by reason of the insured's death (the insured is still alive) and thus it appeared likely that the proceeds would be subject to income tax.

The same was true for viatical settlements. In Priv. Ltr. Rul. 94–43–020, the Service indicated that the amount received by the insured under a viatical settlement, to the extent that the amount exceeded the insured's adjusted basis in the life insurance contract, was includable in the insured's gross income.

Numerous bills were introduced into Congress to exclude accelerated benefits and viatical settlements from the insured's income. At the same time Congress was debating these bills, the Treasury proposed regulations in December of 1992 which would allow certain accelerated benefits to be considered as being paid by reason of the insured's death so they would escape taxation. Despite predictions that these regulations would be approved as early as 1993, they were not. The taxability of the payments continued to be the subject of rulings and litigation with mixed results.

The issue was finally resolved in August 1996 when President Clinton signed the Health Insurance Portability and Accountability Act of 1996, Pub. L. No. 104–191, 110 Stat. 1936, which included an express provision excluding most accelerated payments, as well as viatical settlements, from gross income by deeming them to be "paid by reason of the death" of the insured. The payments must meet the following requirements to escape taxation.

1) Medical Status of Insured

The insured must either be a *terminally ill individual* or a *chronically ill individual*. Under IRC § 101(g)(4)(A), a terminally ill individual is one "who has been certified by a physician as having an illness or physical condition which can reasonably be expected to result in death in 24 months or less after the date of the certification." Once the insured obtains this certification based upon the doctor's reasonable medical opinion, the reality of what later happens does not matter. In other words, the statute does not contain a "look-back" rule. If the insured actually lives months, years, or decades longer than expected, the accelerated benefits or viatical settlement continues to be excluded from income. The statute does not place an upper limit on the amount of proceeds which a terminally ill insured may exclude from income.

A chronically ill individual is defined as a person "who has been certified by a licensed health care practitioner as (i) being unable to perform (without substantial assistance from another individual) at least 2 activities of daily living [i.e., eating, toileting, transferring, bathing, dressing, and continence] for a period of at least 90 days due to a loss of functional capacity, (ii) having a level of disability similar (as determined under regulations prescribed by the Secretary in consultation with the Secretary of Health and Human Services) to the level of disability described in clause (i), or (iii) requiring substantial supervision to protect such individual from threats to health and safety due to severe cognitive impairment. Such term shall not include any individual otherwise meeting the requirements of the preceding sentence unless within the preceding 12–month period a licensed health care practitioner has certified that such individual meets such requirements." IRC §§ 101(g)(4)(B) & 7702B(c)(2). The legislative history for this provision reflects an intent to include individuals who have Alzheimer's disease, Parkinson's disease, and AIDS. See H.R. Conf. Rep. No. 104–350 (1995).

Note that a person cannot be both terminally ill and chronically ill. Under § 101(b)(4)(B), a person cannot qualify as chronically ill if the person can be classified as terminally ill.

2) Type of Life Insurance Policy

Not all life insurance policies will qualify for preferred treatment of their accelerated benefits. Under IRC § 7702, the contract must meet either a cash value accumulation test or a two-prong test consisting of guideline premium requirements coupled with a cash value corridor requirement. The purpose of limiting the tax-favorable status of accelerated benefits to distributions from these types of policies is to make certain the contracts are true life insurance rather than some type of investment-oriented product which the insured is attempting to use to shelter income.

3) Personal Nature of Policy

Payments made to someone other than the taxpayer under key person and other business policies are not protected by the new legislation. "Any amount paid to any taxpayer other than the insured [is not treated as being paid by reason of the death of an insured] if such taxpayer has an insurable interest with respect to the life of the insured by reason of the insured being a director, officer, or employee of the taxpayer or by reason of the insured being financially interested in any trade or business carried on by the taxpayer." IRC § 101(g)(5).

4) Limitations On Payments to Chronically Ill Individuals

The payments to chronically ill individuals must be reimbursements for the costs of *qualified long-term care services* provided for the insured which are not compensated for by insurance or otherwise. § 101(g)(3)(A)(i). These services include "necessary diagnostic, preventive, therapeutic, curing, treating, mitigating, and rehabilitative services, and maintenance or personal care services, which (A) are required by a chronically ill individual, and (B) are provided pursuant to a plan of care prescribed by a licensed health care practitioner." §§ 101(g)(4)(C) & 7702B(c)(1). In other words, unlike terminally ill insureds, chronically ill individuals do not have the discretion to use accelerated benefits or viatical settlements in whatever manner they so desire. Despite the limitation to long-term care costs, § 101(g)(3)(C) protects periodic payments by providing that "[a] payment shall not fail [to qualify] by reason of being made on a per diem or other periodic basis without regard to the expenses incurred during the period to which the payment relates." These payments, however, "will be subject to the cap on excludable benefits that applies for amounts that are excludable under per diem type long-term care insurance contracts." Julia K. Brazelton & Rebecca Kaenzig, *Accelerated Death Benefits Finally Afforded Exclusion*, TAXES, Jan. 1997, at 57, 61.

The statute also provides that to qualify for the favorable tax treatment, the life insurance or viatical settlement contract may not "pay or reimburse expenses incurred for services or items to the extent that such expenses are reimbursable under title XVIII of the Social Security Act [Medicare] or would be so reimbursable but for the application of a deductible or coinsurance amount." §§ 101(g)(3)(A)(ii)(I) & 7702B(b)(1)(B).

In addition to the limitations on the use of the proceeds, the terms of the contract giving rise to the payments to the chronically ill individual must meet specified requirements designed to protect consumers from seeking accelerated payments or viatical settlements without first having the information necessary to make an informed decision and preserving the insured's right to rescind the arrangement within thirty days. Some of these detailed requirements are in § 101 while others are incorporated from various provisions of the Code as well as standards adopted by the National Association of Insurance Commissioners which apply to chronically ill individuals. §§ 101(g)(3)(A)(ii)(II), (g)(3)(B) & 7702B(g).

Section 101(g)(3)(D) limits the exclusion for certain periodic payments that are made to chronically ill individuals. The method for computing this limitation is explained in § 7702B(d). This section provides for a maximum of $175 per day which works out to $63,875 per year. These amounts began to be indexed for inflation beginning in 1998.

5) Additional Rules For Viatical Settlements

Viatical settlements must comply with additional requirements for the proceeds of the sale or assignment to be excluded from income tax. First, the payments must be made by a *viatical settlement provider*. To qualify as a viatical settlement provider, the purchaser must be "regularly engaged in the trade or business of purchasing, or taking assignments of, life insurance contracts on the lives of insureds" who are terminally ill or chronically ill. § 101(g)(2)(B)(i).

Second, the provider must either be licensed to provided viatical settlements under the laws of the state in which the insured resides or, if the insured's state does not require licensing of viatical settlement providers, the provider meets the requirements specified in § 101(g)(2)(B). With regard to terminally ill individuals, the viatical settlement provider must meet the requirements of (1) §§ 8 & 9 of the Viatical Settlements Model Act prepared by the National Association of Insurance Commissioners and (2) the Model Regulations of the National Association of Insurance Commissioners relating to standards for evaluation of reasonable payments in determining amounts paid by the viatical settlement provider in connection with the purchase or assignment of life insurance contracts. § 101(g)(2)(B)(ii). With respect to chronically ill insureds, the provider must meet requirements similar to those contained in §§ 8 & 9 of the Viatical Settlements Model Act along with the standards of the National Association of Insurance Commissioners, if any exist at the time of the settlement, for evaluating the reasonableness of the amounts paid by the provider in connection with viatical settlements for chronically ill individuals. § 101(g)(2)(B)(iii).

6) Unanswered Questions

Although the new legislation addresses many issues that were previously unresolved, unanswered questions still remain. Here are some examples. How will payments made to an insured who is chronically ill be treated if that person becomes terminally ill in a subsequent year? If excess payments are made to a chronically ill insured, will those payments be treated as ordinary income or as capital gains?

b. Federal Estate and Gift Tax

As a general rule, the proceeds of a life insurance policy an insured owns at the time of the insured's death are included as part of the insured's gross estate under § 2042. However, these proceeds are not taxed as income when the beneficiary receives them under § 101(a). Consequently, if the insured's policy has a face value of $100,000 and the insured is in the 45% estate tax bracket, only $55,000 will actually pass to the beneficiary.

On the other hand, if the insured opts for accelerated benefits or enters into a viatical settlement, the insured will immediately receive a discounted amount of the face value and will not have to pay income tax on that amount. Using the same example of an insured with a policy having a face value of $100,000 and assuming a discount of 25%, the insured would receive $75,000 income tax free. The insured could then use this money either to pay expenses or to make gifts to beneficiaries. If the insured elected to make gifts with the money, they could easily be structured to avoid transfer taxation such as by keeping them within the annual exclusion or by using them for the donee's medical expenses or tuition. In this case, an extra $20,000 (20%) of the original face value can be transferred. The savings would even be greater for lower discount rates. Accordingly, the potential tax savings of accelerating benefits or selling the policy for insureds with estates large enough to trigger transfer taxes are significant. A terminally ill or chronically ill insured should seriously consider electing accelerated benefits, or making a viatical settlement, even if the insured does not need the money for expenses simply to achieve the substantial tax savings.

c. *State and Local Taxes*

State law may treat accelerated benefits and viatical settlements differently than federal law. Thus, a payment may be excluded from income tax on the federal level but still subject to tax on the state and local levels.

5. CONCLUSION

Accelerated life insurance benefits and viatical settlements may provide much needed assistance for terminally ill persons during the last years of life and for chronically ill individuals. Under recently enacted IRC § 101(g), these payments will usually be excluded from the insured's income. In addition, assuming the payments are spent or gifted using tax-free transfers, the insured's gift and estate tax burden can be greatly reduced. Estate planners need to cautiously select insurers and settlement providers to maximize both the non-tax and tax benefits of accelerated benefits and viatical settlements for their clients.

NOTES AND QUESTIONS

1. Your client has just been diagnosed with a condition that will result in your client's death within one year. Your client needs ready cash and wants to use the client's life insurance as the source of the money. Which option do you think would be better for your client, accelerated payments or a viatical settlement? Why?

2. Your client is in excellent health and needs a significant amount of cash, for example, to build a house, start a new business, pay tuition for children, or go on vacation. Do you recommend that your client sell his or her life insurance policy? Why or why not? If the client sells the policy, will the proceeds be taxed as income? See Joseph B. Treaster, *Cash Before Death a Growing Trend in Life Insurance*, SAN ANTONIO EXPRESS-NEWS, Oct. 4, 1998, at 1L.

LOCATE

Visit with several life insurance agents and obtain information about policies that include the option of accelerated payments. Be sure to get price information. Compare features and decide which policy you would recommend to your clients.

G. HOME CARE CONTRACTS

DONNA S. HARKNESS, LIFE CARE AGREEMENTS: A CONTRACTUAL JEKYLL AND HYDE?*

5 Marq. Elder's Advisor 39 (Fall 2003).

With every day, and from both sides of my intelligence, the moral and the intellectual, I thus drew steadily nearer to that truth by whose partial discovery I have been doomed to such a dreadful shipwreck: that man is not truly one, but truly two.[1]

Ms. Oldaker is eighty years old, alone and in despair, and has come to see an attorney hoping for a miracle. Approximately ten years ago, knowing that she was getting older and fearing that she would face declining health, she spoke with her favorite niece, a much younger woman in her late thirties, about coming to live with her to take care of her. The niece did not agree to live with Ms. Oldaker all the time, but did agree to provide any personal care she might need in return for receiving outright ownership of Ms. Oldaker's home, valued at $250,000. So, to consummate the deal, Ms. Oldaker executed a simple quitclaim deed, transferring her home to her niece, and the deed was duly recorded. The recitation in the deed describing the consideration states merely that the property was exchanged for a token ten dollars. There is no other writing memorializing the agreement between Ms. Oldaker and her niece.

For several years thereafter, the niece behaved as she always had, calling frequently to check up on her aunt and visiting her in person at least once a week. Ms. Oldaker became ill in 2003 and the niece came and stayed with her for several weeks until she recovered. During that stay, the niece provided personal care services in the form of housecleaning, laundry services, grocery shopping, food preparation, and assisting Ms. Oldaker with bathing. * * *

In July 2011, Ms. Oldaker was advised that she needed inpatient surgery, which would require not only a brief hospitalization, but also a significant nursing home stay for rehabilitation services. The discharge planner at the hospital told Ms. Oldaker that the rehabilitation services could be provided by a home health agency in her home rather than the nursing home IF she could find someone to stay with her. Not wanting to go to the nursing home, Ms. Oldaker immediately called her niece for help. To her dismay, the phone number she had for her niece had been disconnected with no forwarding number. Left with no other choice, Ms. Oldaker was forced to enter the nursing home. After she had recuperated and returned home, Ms. Oldaker was finally able to contact her niece. She told her niece she believed the arrangement was not working and that the niece should deed the house back to her. The niece's response was to

---

* Reprinted with permission of Donna S. Harkness.

1. Robert Louis Stevenson, *The Strange Case of Dr. Jekyll and Mr. Hyde* 48–49? (Wordsworth Editions Ltd. 1993) (1886).

laugh and hang up the phone. Ms. Oldaker now lives in fear that the niece will sell the house and evict her. All of a sudden, Ms. Oldaker has realized that the promised assurance of personalized, loving care that she contracted for has transformed into a hideous Mr. Hyde threatening to devour her and leave her destitute and homeless.

I. Life Care or Independent Care Agreements

Ms. Oldaker's unfortunate circumstances are the result of her informal and unsophisticated attempt to fashion an individual "life care" or "independent care" agreement to provide her with personal care services in her home for the duration of her life, if circumstances so required. * * * For many seniors, the home is the major asset, both in terms of economic and psychological value. Thus, a contract that enables senior citizens to use the value of their homes to secure personal care services that will allow them to remain living at home is exceedingly attractive. Because the elderly person is dealing with friends and family members, the agreement itself is almost always vague, informal and unwritten. * * *

A. *Duration of services*

The first major issue that needs to be addressed in the fashioning of a life care agreement is the length of time during which the caregiver is expected to render services. As the name implies, the expectation is generally that the elderly person will be served "for life," whether that means six months or the next sixteen years. It is important that both the elderly client and the caregiver be realistic in deciding whether the agreement should be so open-ended. * * *

B. *Type of services*

The next issue to be determined is the type of services the caregiver is expected to render. Assuming that the elderly person is in fairly good health and still able to live independently at the outset of the agreement, both parties to the contract may have widely divergent concepts of what services are to be expected, and both sets of expectations may differ drastically from the level of services that actually prove to be required. * * *

C. *Nature of payment*

As with any other contract, payment for life care contract services may be lump sum, either at the outset of the contract or at the end, or in installments as the services are rendered. Where real property is transferred immediately as consideration for the services, the contract can be likened to an annuity. * * *

D. *Quality of care*

As already noted above, emotional expectations and needs already present in the relationship between the client and caregiver add an additional dimension of difficulty and again give rise to neglect and psychological, if not outright physical, abuse. And this may represent the best possible scenario—at the other end of the spectrum, the quality of care may deteriorate to the point where the elder's very life is endangered:

> "The 91 year old widow was found comatose and all alone on a sweltering day ... because she had trusted a home care worker with her life ... this self-assured patrician, who grew up on Fifth Avenue in New York City, wound up a penniless prisoner in her Lincoln home ... a cleaning woman found her alone and crying because she had not been cared for all day and had soiled her bedclothes ... like many other widows in similar predicaments, she lost control of her beloved home through a desperate attempt to stay there forever. She gave it away to a health aide worker in exchange for daily care that she could no longer afford from a full-time nursing service costing $72,000 a year ... Specialists in elder care say that it is an increasingly common sign of the times, especially in suburban settings: infirm widows with mortgage-free houses and dwindling funds trade their homes for care and wind up with neither."[2]

II. Addressing the Problems of Life Care Contracts

A. Assessing the situation

If anything is clear from the foregoing discussion, it is that individual life care contracts are plagued by a lack of critical examination and consensus as to the terms of the agreement and by unrealistic thinking with respect to performance of those terms. The first step in addressing the host of problems outlined above is by meeting with the client to determine exactly what the needs are and how they can best be met in the client's situation. This will involve a frank and honest assessment of the client's circumstances with respect to current and projected health, life expectancy, familial and social support systems, assets and income, as well as the client's wishes concerning how he or she will live out his or her life, and how these wishes can best be achieved. Therefore, the first advice that elderly clients should receive from an attorney concerning life care agreements is that some sort of familial or social counseling will be a necessary prerequisite to consideration of any such agreement.* * * In preparation for the counseling the client should provide a comprehensive listing and valuation of all assets, identification of all close relatives (or persons who would be expected to be close relatives, such as spouse, children, parents, siblings, nieces and nephews), friends and any existing caregivers, and the results of a current health examination that addresses cognitive functioning as well as physical condition. With this information as a foundation, the attorney can begin to explore with the client whether or not a life care contract is appropriate at all.

---

2. Gerard O'Neil, *Elderly Face Peril in Trading Homes for Care*, BOSTON GLOBE, May 17, 1992 * * *.

B. Assessing the caregiver

If the client determines that a life care contract is appropriate, the next step will be to ascertain the fitness of the proposed caregiver. How well does the client actually know this person? The question is obvious if the proposed caregiver is someone who the client only recently became acquainted with, but if the proposed caregiver is an adult child or long time friend, the client may dismiss such an inquiry as absurd. Yet, the fact is that there is a wealth of information many parents don't have about their adult children, let alone their friends. Has the child ever been convicted of a crime? Any drug problems? * * * Honest examination of these things at the outset can eliminate much heartache later. If the attorney feels the client is downplaying any frictions in recounting the relationship, then a request to the client for names of persons who have observed how good the adult child is in responding to the parent's needs is in order. Letters of reference, a credit check and an adult abuse background check are imperative if the client is contemplating a life care contract with a non-relative.

C. Crafting the agreement defining reasonable services

If it is determined that the caregiver is suitable and willing to serve, then the task of crafting the agreement begins. The nature, type and duration of services needs to be defined with enough specificity to make enforcement of the contract meaningful and yet with enough adaptability to preserve the unique flexibility afforded by the life care concept? * * * For such contracts to be reasonable, the definition of services must exclude the sorts of services that rise to the level of "long term," or nursing home, care. To expect one unskilled caregiver to provide long-term care services around-the-clock for a lifetime is at best unreasonable and at worst dangerous. Counsel should emphasize this point with both client and caregiver that unless the caregiver happens to be a health care professional, it is simply not realistic to assume that he or she can provide adequate nursing services to some one in need of long term-care. In addition, unless there is more than one caregiver involved, the provision of such services on a twenty-four hour basis is clearly impossible. So, if the client wants to avoid institutional nursing home care altogether, he or she would have to contract with at least two licensed caregivers, because one person is simply not equal to the task. If the client's home represents the only source of compensation, dividing it between two caregivers may not be attractive to them at all unless they are closely related to each other, such as a husband and wife. The bottom line is that a client with moderate income and assets generally cannot afford the luxury of around-the-clock in-home nursing care unless the client has close relatives willing and able to provide it without payment, because even the value of the client's home will usually not be sufficient to provide adequate compensation for such care.

So the client MUST be advised that the life care contract is NOT a guarantee that he or she will never be placed in a nursing home. If and when long-term care is necessary, personal services under the contract should either cease or, if they continue, be defined as only those that are supplementary to the long-term care services provided either by a long-term care facility or under a program of community based long-term care. * * * If the agreement specifies that the services are not sufficient to rise to the level of long-term care, this should serve to preserve eligibility for Medicaid as well. The need for long-term care is established by reference to whether one meets the criteria of a "chronically ill individual" as defined by federal law. The life care contract should incorporate this definition as a trigger for temporary cessation of the contract or as a limiting factor delineating the boundaries of personal services, which the caregiver is obligated to perform. Otherwise, since Medicaid is payor of last resort, the contractual obligation of the caregiver to provide services may be deemed a third party payment source, which would obviate any entitlement by the client to Medicaid payment for the services, despite the fact that it is manifestly unrealistic to expect that an unskilled caregiver will actually be able to perform these services. Because the house itself is an exempt resource for purposes of Medicaid eligibility, transfer of the house and creation of the life care agreement without a definitional limit excluding long-term care could leave the client without a source of adequate care in the event that long-term care is needed. Thus, rather than have the contract terminate at the point where the client is deemed to be in need of long-term care, it may be preferable to have the services be modified when that point is reached so as to differentiate them from the kind of nursing services that must be provided in nursing homes. * * * In addition to stating whether or not the services will still be expected and on what basis in the event the client requires nursing home care, the duration of the contract should also be correlated with the client's life expectancy.

Within these parameters, definition of the personal services to be provided should be as flexible as possible and generally should be on an "as needed" basis. Personal services can include personal assistance in accomplishing whatever tasks the elder client may choose to delegate, such as setting doctor's or hairdresser's appointments, providing transportation, grocery shopping, preparing meals, housekeeping, etc. The contract should enumerate the specific categories of services that are expected. For example, "personal errands," "housekeeping," "advocacy," "health care oversight and management," etc., so that the parties will be aware of expectations and can better substantiate the fair market value of the services by reference to actual providers in the community. The contract should specify whether or not the caregiver will have any responsibility for financial management, and if so, whether such responsibility extends beyond simple collection of information and preparation of paperwork for the client to sign to actual authority to act on the client's behalf. If the latter arrangement is desired, a power of attorney should be drafted as well to delineate the caregiver's additional fiduciary relationship to the client. * * *

NOTES AND QUESTIONS

1. How prevalent do you think "latent and insidious abuse" of elderly individuals occurs? Are the despicable situations described in Mr. Kruse's article relatively rare or are they commonplace?

2. Should state legislatures act to regulate home care contracts to reduce the abuse potential? If yes, what specifically should the statutes address and what remedies would be appropriate?

3. Do you think most people who enter into home care arrangements consult first with an attorney?

4. Assume your client is considering entering into a contract to execute a will in favor of a relative, friend, or stranger in exchange for home health care. What precautions should you take to protect your client's interests?

H. MEDICAID PLANNING

Medicaid is a jointly funded effort of the federal government and the states to provide medical assistance and institutional care for elderly or disabled individuals who have limited assets. Congress enacted Medicaid in 1965 as a companion to Medicare, the federal health insurance program for citizens age 65 and over. Medicaid is administered by state agencies. Payments are made directly to the health care provider, not the patient.

Medicaid eligibility is based on a variety of factors. Both the person's income and assets must be below specified amounts which vary among the states. In addition, voluntary transfers by the person or the person's spouse within the *look-back period* of 36 months are treated as if the person still owned them. If the transfer was to an irrevocable trust under which the trustee cannot make a principal distribution to the person, the look-back period is extended to 60 months. The person is then disqualified from receiving Medicaid for the period of time those assets could have paid for the person's care.

Because Medicaid is need based, some individuals plan to be poor so they will qualify for Medicaid benefits. These people wonder why they should save money and hold on to their assets only to pay their own medical costs until they exhaust their funds and become eligible for Medicaid. Why not just start off on the Medicaid dole? Of course, people do not like to give up total control of their assets and the federal government is wise to the "let's look poor" ploy and thus great care must be used in sheltering a person's assets to give the client the greatest amount of control over the property but yet prevent it from being considered for Medicaid eligibility. Hence, certain types of trust arrangements have grown in popularity. Money can also be strategically invested in property that is not counted toward Medicaid eligibility such as a car, jewelry, and in some cases, a home.

Is it morally right for a person to do this type of planning which may prevent funds from reaching the truly needy as well as increasing taxes for everyone? Medicaid was designed for people without other options—not for middle class individuals who want to save money for their heirs and beneficiaries. "The surge of 'middle class' Medicaid patients terrifies state budget directors struggling to hold down Medicaid costs." Melinda Beck, et al., *Planning to Be Poor: With a Little Help, the Nursing Home Won't Get Your Savings—Your Kids Will,* NEWSWEEK, Nov. 30, 1992, at 66. On the other hand, what is wrong with exploiting loopholes in the rules to save money just like a person may use the annual gift tax exclusion, the unlimited marital deduction, and income tax itemized deductions?

As you read the articles below, keep in mind that the precise figures used are based on the law in effect at the time the articles were written. You need to update the figures to comport with current federal and state law.

CHADWICK BOTHE, THE STIGMA OF SURVIVAL: MEDICAID ESTATE PLANNING*

51 S. Tex. L. Rev. 815 (2010).

I. Introduction

Many commentators, as well as taxpayers generally, have criticized the practice of "Medicaid estate planning, [when] individuals shelter or divest their assets to qualify for Medicaid without first depleting their life savings." At first blush, it may appear that sheltering or divesting one's assets to qualify for Medicaid is immoral, and several authors seem to share this sentiment. However, Medicaid estate planning is not only rational, but it is also consistent with notions of morality and fairness. Akin to tax planning, Medicaid estate planning is as justifiable as any other legal advice an attorney may give to a client to obtain favorable governmental treatment, despite recent measures taken by Congress that might suggest otherwise. The public perception seems to be that tax planning is perfectly acceptable, whereas Medicaid estate planning is morally questionable * * * Ultimately, this Comment proposes solutions to reduce the costs of long-term health care for an aging population. Ethical considerations suggest, if anything, that punishing the elderly for seeking medical care and criminalizing legal advice are real social concerns today—not Medicaid estate planning. * * *

II. Historical Underpinnings

In 1965, Congress enacted Medicaid as a cooperative federal-state program for the purpose of providing health care to individuals. States that elect to participate in the Medicaid program are required to implement a plan that conforms to the requirements of 42 U.S.C. § 1396. In turn, the federal government provides funding to those states that reimburse certain costs of qualified citizens' medical treatment.

---

* Reprinted with permission of Chadwick Bothe.

Since the inception of the Medicaid program, Congress has often succumbed to political pressure from various interest groups and has repeatedly passed complicated piecemeal legislation to discourage the practice of Medicaid estate planning. Congress has imposed penalties that require the elderly to wait to receive Medicaid benefits—regardless of the severity of their condition—when the applicant divested himself or herself of "assets for less than fair market value." Each time an individual applies for Medicaid, a state Medicaid agency reviews, or "looks back at" transfers of the individual's assets within the past three years, or within the past five years for transfers to or from certain trusts. If the individual or the individual's spouse made a transfer within the look-back period and no exception applies, then a "transfer penalty period," or a "period of [Medicaid] ineligibility," is imposed from the beginning of the month immediately following the transfer. For example, in Florida when one transfers assets for less than fair market value within three years of his or her Medicaid application, payments for long-term care services are withheld for the duration of the transfer penalty period. The transfer penalty period "is calculated by dividing the dollar amount of the transfer by the average monthly cost of nursing home care in the state or community." For example, if an individual were to transfer $10,000 during the look-back period, without an applicable exception, then the individual would be denied Medicaid benefits for ten months in a state with an average monthly cost of nursing home care of $1,000. Under 42 U.S.C. § 1320(a)–7(b), the imposition of such a transfer penalty period triggers criminal liability for Medicaid applicants as well as their attorneys. Thus, not only is one denied Medicaid benefits for a protracted penalty period, but one is also subject to criminal fines and imprisonment for following their lawyer's advice!

One specific piece of the piecemeal federal legislation is the Omnibus Budget Reconciliation Act (OBRA). The Act "identified 'trusts' as the single most offensive Medicaid estate planning vehicle and tried, in almost every manner short of criminalization, to inhibit their use." OBRA expanded the class of assets that are attributable to trust beneficiaries. Thus, Medicaid applicants that are trust beneficiaries must include "[a]ny payments from the trust that are not specifically covered by the statute," because those payments are deemed to be "assets transferred by the individual." Accordingly, OBRA has resulted in the imposition of a greater number of transfer penalty periods, since the duration of Medicaid ineligibility is determined by the amount of assets transferred by the Medicaid applicant within the look-back period.

Three trusts were excepted from OBRA's rules: supplemental needs trusts, Miller trusts, and pooled trusts. These exceptions highlight the conflicting congressional approach to Medicaid estate planning, which ultimately undermines opponents of Medicaid estate planning who rely on the congressional record to support their view. Each exception is discussed below.

Supplemental needs trusts, which are also commonly referred to as payback trusts or special needs trusts, are trusts containing assets of disabled individuals who are under the age of sixty-five. These trusts may be established by a parent, grand-parent, legal guardian, or a court for the benefit of the Medicaid applicant. Supplemental needs trusts are exempted from 42 U.S.C. § 1396p(d)(3)'s unsympathetic treatment if the trust is structured so that all residuary amounts in the trust go to the state upon the applicant's death, to the extent necessary to reimburse the state for medical expenses paid on the individual's behalf.

Dissimilar to supplemental needs trusts, Miller trusts have no disability requirement to be exempted from § 1396p(d)(3), but these trusts may only consist of pension, Social Security, and other income to the individual. As long as the state is reimbursed upon the individual's death for medical expenses paid on behalf of the individual, Miller trusts will not count towards the individual's income for Medicaid eligibility purposes.

Pooled trusts, unlike supplemental needs trusts, have no age requirement. For a pooled trust to be exempted from § 1396p(d)(3), Congress requires that: (1) the individual be disabled; (2) "the trust is established and managed by a non-profit association"; (3) the trust pools the individual accounts that are maintained for each beneficiary for purposes of management and investment; (4) each individual account is established by the individual, the individual's parent, grandparent, legal guardian, or a court solely for the benefit of individuals; and (5) "[t]o the extent that amounts remaining in the beneficiary's account upon the death of the beneficiary are not retained by the trust, the trust pays to the [s]tate from such remaining amounts in the account an amount equal to the total amount of medical assistance paid on behalf of the beneficiary by the [s]tate."

The common thread running through each of the trust exceptions is that the state must be reimbursed for benefits paid to individuals upon their death. In other words, these exceptions allow individuals to have the benefit of their assets during their lifetime while nonetheless qualifying for Medicaid. A cynic might point out that Congress's exceptions reach precisely the same result as Medicaid estate planning, allowing individuals to qualify for Medicaid without first depleting their life savings—the only difference being that under Congress's exceptions, future generations foot the bill by receiving less from the decedent's estate. By engaging in Medicaid estate planning, as opposed to using these exceptions, one can at least provide for their friends or family now instead of providing for Big Brother later. * * *

III. Medicaid Estate Planning is Necessary

A. The Costs of Long-term Care

The skyrocketing costs of elder care are crippling millions of Americans each year. The average annual costs of one per-son's room and board in a nursing home are $52,195 in Houston, Texas; $100,010 in New York,

New York; and $120,815 in Anchorage, Alaska. The figures are often even higher for home health care. Although assisted living is less expensive than a nursing home or home health care, the cost of assisted living programs may be prohibitive for many members of the middle class. Moreover, medical expenses must also be accounted for in determining the costs of long-term elder care.

What is Congress's solution to this health care pandemic? Section 1320a–7b of the United States Code. Originally a part of the Health Insurance Portability and Accountability Act of 1996 (HIPAA), § 1320a–7b labels Medicaid estate planning as a crime. In particular, the statute provides that:

> Whoever . . . for a fee knowingly and willfully disposes of assets (including any transfer in trust) in order for an individual to become eligible for medical assistance under a [s]tate plan under Title XIX, if disposing of the assets results in the imposition of a period of ineligibility for such assistance . . . shall (i) in the case of such a statement, representation, concealment, failure, or conversion by any person in connection with the furnishing (by that person) of items or services for which payment is or may be made under the program, be guilty of a felony and upon conviction thereof fined not more than $25,000 or imprisoned for not more than five years or both, or (ii) in the case of such a statement, representation, concealment, failure, or conversion by any other person, be guilty of a misdemeanor and upon conviction thereof fined not more than $10,000 or imprisoned for not more than one year, or both.

This statute has caused some attorneys and their clients' anxiety, although these fears may be unfounded according to one federal district court case. Nonetheless, Congress's reasoning may be summarized as follows: (1) the vast majority of elderly citizens cannot afford the stifling costs of elder care, whether it be in the form of nursing homes or assisted living; (2) Medicaid is a program capable of meeting the needs of the elderly; and (3) therefore we, as the representative body elected to speak for the people, must penalize any citizens who engage in Medicaid estate planning to survive and imprison lawyers who advise their clients of how they might qualify for a government program. If this line of reasoning appears baffling, then you are thinking clearly. The approach taken by Congress to the unaffordable elder care epidemic is a nonsequitur; it does not follow from the recognition that many elderly Americans, or their children for that matter, cannot afford elder care, that we should criminalize perhaps the only viable option for these citizens and their families. Put simply, the only thing more astounding than the stifling costs of long-term health care is our government's treatment of citizens attempting to deal with these costs.

B. Actuarial Data: Compounding Costs

Medicaid cannot support the needs of an estimated thirty-four million Americans—a number that will undoubtedly increase with the advent of better medical practices and longer life expectancies. A report from USAToday.com states that life expectancies in the United States are likely shorter than some countries. The report points out that lifestyle factors, such as tobacco use and overeating, may be the primary cause for shorter life expectancies. However, shorter life expectancies do not necessarily reduce the costs of long-term care, since the costs of medications in addition to medical care resulting from poor lifestyle habits must also be considered in computing the costs of elder care. At any rate, Americans are living 77.9 years on average—despite the Marlboros and McDonald's. Considering that the costs of nursing homes or home health care may run into the six-figure range annually, elder care, needless to say, is simply unaffordable for many Americans. * * *

IV. Medicaid Estate Planning is Moral

It is apparent that Medicaid estate planning is not necessarily immoral if one allows for the possibility that some individuals will leave a significant part of their estate to charities. It is unlikely that most people would consider a charitable disposition upon death an act of moral turpitude. * * * Medicaid estate planning is consistent with traditional notions of morality because it benefits: (1) society, when individuals infuse capital into the economy by spending down their assets, and (2) individuals, not only where the attorney-client relationship remains candid and frank because lawyers are unconcerned about criminal sanctions for legal advice, but also where Medicaid applicants give money or assets to family, friends, or charities to spend down their estates. In short, Medicaid estate planning is moral since it is beneficial for the public generally as well as citizens on an individual level. * * *

The definition of Medicaid estate planning is slightly misleading. To reiterate, Medicaid estate planning is where "individuals shelter or divest their assets to qualify for Medicaid without first depleting their life savings." This emphasis implies that the elderly are able "to have their cake and eat it too" by simultaneously qualifying for Medicaid assistance and retaining their life savings to draw upon for other expenses. However, an analogy to property law illustrates why individuals are indeed forced to deplete their life savings when they transfer title to their assets to a third party.

In property law, there is a fundamental difference between an interest in land that is an estate and an interest in land that is an easement. A person owning an estate in land is free to sell or allow others to use the land without consulting the previous owner of the land. In contrast, a person owning an easement on a parcel of land is limited in what she is able to do on or with the land depending upon the scope of the easement. For instance, the scope of the easement may limit the easement holder's use of the land to railroad purposes and preclude the easement owner from selling or otherwise profiting from the land. Thus, it matters whether a conveyance of land is a conveyance of an estate or of an easement, because it determines who has the final say over the use and disposition of the property.

Some commentators have argued that the practice of transferring assets to a relative or friend so that one becomes eligible for Medicaid is deleterious to society. The thrust of the criticism is that "transferring" assets to family or friends is a guise to trick the government into dispensing Medicaid benefits to people who are not truly in need. However, if a person in need of elder care were to transfer their assets to a friend or relative so that they would be eligible for Medicaid, then that third party (the friend or relative) would have legal control over the use and disposition of the assets, much like an owner of an estate in land. Those who claim that a transfer of assets to a friend or relative is really no transfer at all, fail to grasp the legal ramifications of transferring assets to a third party, even if it is a friend or relative. While it is true that the third party may allow the elderly person seeking Medicaid to control the disposition of the assets, nothing, legally speaking, compels them to do so, as is the case with an owner of an estate in land as opposed to a holder of an easement.

In short, the counterargument that divesting assets to receive government assistance is a sham because elders never actually relinquish control of their property is founded upon an incorrect legal assumption; namely, that anyone other than the holder of the title to the property has legal control over its disposition. This is even more apparent in context of giving to a charity. There are undoubtedly few commentators willing to argue that once an elder has donated property to a charity that he or she retains control over its subsequent disposition.

Since Medicaid estate planning often involves transferring assets to family, friends, or charities, it seems to be moral because it encourages generosity on an individual level. Removing the illegality, and thus the stigma, of Medicaid estate planning will strengthen the attorney-client relationship. Society also benefits from individuals engaging in Medicaid estate planning when the elderly stimulate the economy by infusing capital into local businesses in an effort to spend down assets. If minimizing tax liability is morally justified, then it is difficult to maintain that Medicaid estate planning is immoral, particularly when evaluating its attendant societal and individual benefits.

QUESTIONS

1. Do the Medicaid requirements of your state make it easier or harder for a person to qualify for benefits?

2. Would you ever recommend that a client change his or her state of domicile to take advantage of easier to meet Medicaid requirements?

3. For additional information, see Kristen Lewis Denzinger, *Special Needs Trusts*, PROB. & PROP., May/June 2003, at 11.

NEW YORK STATE BAR ASSOC. v. RENO

United States District Court, N.D. New York, 1998.
999 F.Supp. 710.

MCAVOY, CHIEF JUDGE.

Plaintiff, the New York State Bar Association ("NYSBA"), seeks to enjoin the Attorney General of the United States from enforcing section 4734 of the Balanced Budget Act of 1997, which was incorporated into section 217 of the Health Insurance Portability and Accountability Act of 1996, 42 U.S.C. § 1320a–7b(a). Plaintiff asserts that section 4734 violates the First and Fifth Amendments to the United States Constitution.

I. BACKGROUND

A. *Statutory Background*

Before Congress enacted section 217 of the Health Insurance Portability and Accountability Act of 1996, certain transfers of assets up to 36 months prior to an application for Medicaid benefits and certain transfers to trusts up to 60 months prior to application, could result in a period of ineligibility for Medicaid benefits. 42 U.S.C. § 1396p(c). In enacting section 217, Congress left the ineligibility period intact, but added certain criminal penalties. Essentially, section 217 made it a crime to dispose of assets in order to become eligible for Medicaid benefits if the disposition of assets "resulted in the imposition of a period of ineligibility." § 1320a–7b(a)(6) (sometimes referred to as the "Granny Goes to Jail Act"). Violators were subject to fines of up to $25,000 or imprisonment for up to 5 years, or both. Id.

A number of organizations lobbied for the repeal of section 217, including the NYSBA. Rather than repeal the Granny Goes to Jail Act, Congress amended section 217 by enacting section 4734 of the Balanced Budget Act of 1997. Section 4734, which became effective August 5, 1997, struck the former language and added a provision making it illegal to counsel or assist an individual to dispose of certain assets to qualify for Medicaid:

> "Criminal penalties for acts involving Federal health care programs (a) Making or causing to be made false statements or representations"
>
> Whoever—
>
> * * *
>
> (6) for a fee knowingly and willfully counsels or assists an individual to dispose of assets (including by any transfer in trust) in order for the individual to become eligible for medical assistance under a State plan under subchapter XIX of this chapter, if disposing of the assets results in the imposition of a period of ineligibility for such assistance under section 1396p(c) of this title, shall ... (ii) in the case

of such a statement, representation, concealment, failure, conversion, or provision of counsel or assistance by any other person, be guilty of a misdemeanor and upon conviction thereof fined not more than $10,000 or imprisoned for not more than one year, or both.

42 U.S.C. § 1320a–7b(a).

While section 4734 was in conference, the Congressional Research Service ("CRS") prepared a memorandum, dated July 11, 1997, analyzing the legal and constitutional issues raised by the proposed language of section 4734. CRS expressed concern that the language would infringe the First Amendment, noting: "To the extent that the provision would prohibit counseling about legal activities, a court would seem likely to declare it unconstitutional." (Witmer Aff., Ex. F at 2).

Congress nevertheless passed the provision without modification, and the President signed section 4734 into law.

B. Procedural Background

Plaintiff filed the instant motion for a preliminary injunction on January 27, 1998. After a number of extensions and adjournments, Defendant now states that it will neither defend the constitutionality of 42 U.S.C. section 1320a–7b(a)(6) nor enforce its criminal provisions. On March 11, 1998, Attorney General Janet Reno notified the United States House of Representatives and the United States Senate that the Department of Justice would not enforce the aforementioned criminal provisions. Not surprisingly, Defendant now argues that a preliminary injunction is no longer needed.

In response, NYSBA filed opposition arguing that its members' free speech rights are still being chilled. Essentially, NYSBA argues that section 4734 is unconstitutional for the following reasons: (1) it violates the First Amendment because it unconstitutionally restricts free speech; (2) it violates the First Amendment because it is overly broad; and (3) it violates the Fifth Amendment because it is vague.

II. DISCUSSION

A. Standing

Initially, the court confronts the issue of the NYSBA'S standing to bring this action. * * *

The modern version of [the organizational standing] doctrine provides that an organization has standing to sue on behalf of its members if: "(a) its members would otherwise have standing to sue in their own right; (b) the interests it seeks to protect are germane to the organization's purpose; and (c) neither the claim asserted nor the relief requested requires the participation of the individual members in the lawsuit." Sun City Taxpayers' Ass'n v. Citizens Utilities Co., 45 F.3d 58, 61 (2d Cir.1995) (quoting Hunt v. Washington State Apple Advertising Comm'n, 432 U.S. 333, 97 S.Ct. 2434, 2441, 53 L.Ed.2d 383 (1977)) * * *.

It is clear that under the associational standing test, the New York State Bar Association may bring the instant constitutional claims. First, the affidavits of attorney Witmer, a current member and past president of the NYSBA, and attorney Reixach, a current member of the Elder Law Section of the NYSBA, demonstrate that NYSBA members would otherwise have standing to sue in their own right. * * * Second, the interests the NYSBA seeks to protect are germane to the organization's purpose as stated in Article II of its Bylaws. * * * Third, neither the constitutional claims asserted nor the relief requested requires the participation of the individual members in the lawsuit.

Consequently, the NYSBA has standing to bring the instant claims.

B. Preliminary Injunction

In this circuit the standard for obtaining a preliminary injunction is well established. In order to obtain a preliminary injunction the movant must make an affirmative showing of: (1) irreparable harm; and either (2) likelihood of success on the merits; or (3) sufficiently serious questions going to the merits to make them a fair ground for litigation and a balance of hardships tipping decidedly in favor of the movant. * * * However,

> [W]here the moving party seeks to stay governmental action taken in the public interest pursuant to a statutory or regulatory scheme, the district court ... should not grant the injunction unless the moving party establishes, along with irreparable injury, a likelihood that he will succeed on the merits of his claim.

Plaza Health Laboratories, Inc. v. Perales, 878 F.2d 577, 580 (2d Cir.1989) * * *.

i. Irreparable Harm

As this Court recently noted, "[c]ourts in this circuit have repeatedly stated that '[p]erhaps the single most important prerequisite for the issuance of a preliminary injunction is a demonstration that if it is not granted the applicant is likely to suffer irreparable harm before a decision on the merits can be rendered.'" Nakatomi Investments v. City of Schenectady, 949 F.Supp. 988, 990 (N.D.N.Y.1997) (quoting Borey v. National Union Fire Ins. Co., 934 F.2d 30, 34 (2d Cir.1991)). Irreparable injury, moreover, means injury for which a monetary award cannot be adequate compensation. * * *

Turning to the first prong of this test, if the government's enforcement of section 4734 will deprive Plaintiff of its First Amendment rights, this constitutes per se irreparable injury to Plaintiff. See Elrod v. Burns, 427 U.S. 347, 96 S.Ct. 2673, 49 L.Ed.2d 547 (1976). In Elrod v. Burns, the Supreme Court instructed that "[t]he loss of First Amendment freedoms, for even minimal periods of time, unquestionably constitutes irreparable injury." 427 U.S. at 373 * * *

Here, the Attorney General states that the Department of Justice will not enforce section 1320a–7b(a)(6)'s criminal provisions. The Attorney

General argues that NYSBA members face no threat of criminal sanction. As a result, Plaintiff will not suffer any irreparable harm, thus obviating Plaintiff's need for injunctive relief. Defendant's argument, however, misses the point.

Although Defendant does not attack Plaintiff's case on ripeness grounds, the question of irreparable harm in this context is inextricably intertwined with the issue of ripeness. Ripeness is "peculiarly a question of timing," Regional Rail Reorganization Act Cases, 419 U.S. 102, 95 S.Ct. 335, 357, 42 L.Ed.2d 320 (1974), intended "to prevent the courts, through avoidance of premature adjudication, from entangling themselves in abstract disagreements." Abbott Labs. v. Gardner, 387 U.S. 136, 87 S.Ct. 1507, 1515, 18 L.Ed.2d 681 (1967). In determining whether a matter is ripe, courts use a two-pronged test: (1) whether the issue is fit for review, and (2) whether injury or hardship will result if judicial consideration is withheld. AMSAT Cable v. Cablevision of Conn., 6 F.3d 867, 872 (2d Cir.1993) * * *.

Among the factors affecting whether a matter is fit for judicial decision is "whether the issue is purely legal or whether 'consideration of the underlying legal issues would necessarily be facilitated if they were raised in the context of a specific attempt to enforce the regulations.' " In re Combustion Equip. Assoc., Inc., 838 F.2d 35, 38–39 (2d Cir.1988) (quoting Gardner v. Toilet Goods Association, 387 U.S. 167, 87 S.Ct. 1526, 1528, 18 L.Ed.2d 704 (1967)). Here, the matter is fit for judicial review because the issue is purely legal; the First Amendment challenge will not be significantly clarified by further factual development. * * *

Turning to the question of whether injury or hardship will result if judicial consideration is withheld, this is where the question of ripeness and the injunctive requirement of irreparable harm converge. In assessing the hardship to the parties of withholding judicial resolution, the question is whether the challenged action creates a direct and immediate dilemma for the parties. * * * Hence, when relief against the enforcement of a criminal statute is sought, a plaintiff generally must show either actual prosecution under the statute or that a sufficiently real and immediate threat of prosecution exists. * * *

The customary ripeness analysis is, however, relaxed somewhat in circumstances involving a facial challenge implicating the First Amendment. * * * Thus, while "the mere existence of a statute . . . is ordinarily not enough to sustain a judicial challenge," National Student Ass'n v. Hershey, 412 F.2d 1103, 1110 (D.C.Cir.1969), in contesting the constitutionality of a criminal statute, "it is not necessary that [a plaintiff] first expose himself to actual arrest or prosecution to be entitled to challenge [the] statute that he claims deters the exercise of his constitutional rights." Babbitt v. United Farm Workers Nat'l Union, 442 U.S. 289, 99 S.Ct. 2301, 2309, 60 L.Ed.2d 895 (1979) (quoting Steffel v. Thompson, 415 U.S. 452, 94 S.Ct. 1209, 1215–16, 39 L.Ed.2d 505 (1974)) * * *.

Here, the parties have staked out starkly opposing positions on the issue of whether a threat of enforcement presently exists. The Attorney General assures the Court that she will not enforce section 4734. Plaintiff responds that the Attorney General's statements do not eliminate the threat of future enforcement, and, in fact, may not represent the position of the President of the United States—who has been silent regarding his intentions concerning enforcement.

Fortunately, the Court need not resolve this issue definitively because the Court finds that Plaintiff will suffer injury irrespective of the imminent enforcement of section 4734.

Governmental infringement of the First Amendment does not exist merely in the imposition of criminal sanctions. As the Supreme Court noted in Elrod, the First Amendment is implicated whenever free speech is "either threatened or in fact being impaired at the time the relief [is] sought." Elrod, 96 S.Ct. at 2689. "These freedoms are delicate and vulnerable, as well as supremely precious in our society. The threat of sanctions may deter their exercise almost as potently as the actual application of sanctions." National Ass'n for Advancement of Colored People v. Button, 371 U.S. 415, 83 S.Ct. 328, 338, 9 L.Ed.2d 405 (1963) * * *.

Even in the absence of hardship from imminent prosecution or threat of prosecution, however, a "claim might still be ripe under First Amendment jurisprudence if . . . First Amendment rights have been restricted or 'chilled.' " Sanger, 966 F.Supp. at 162 * * *. "First Amendment interests are fragile interests, and a person who contemplates protected activity might be discouraged by the in terrorem effect of the statute." Bates v. State Bar of Arizona, 433 U.S. 350, 97 S.Ct. 2691, 2707, 53 L.Ed.2d 810 (1977) (citing NAACP v. Button, 83 S.Ct. at 337–38).

The reasons for relaxing the ripeness analysis in this context is the chilling effect that unconstitutional burdens on free speech may occasion:

> First Amendment rights of free expression and association are particularly apt to be found ripe for immediate protection, because of the fear of irretrievable loss. In a wide variety of settings, courts have found First Amendment claims ripe, often commenting directly on the special need to protect against any inhibiting chill.

13A Charles A. Wright, Arthur R. Miller & Edward H. Cooper, Federal Practice and Procedure § 3532.3, at 159.

The irreparable harm that exists here is the potential for self-censorship among NYSBA members. NYSBA members have an ethical obligation as attorneys to respect and uphold the law. In fact, Plaintiff's affidavits state that section 4734 actually has resulted in NYSBA members refraining from providing certain counsel and assistance to clients. * * * Furthermore, Defendant provides no assurance that NYSBA members will not be prosecuted on some future date or that state Medicaid fraud units will also not enforce section 4734.

Accordingly, inasmuch as section 4734 remains part of the laws of the United States, which NYSBA members are ethically bound to uphold, the limitation on free speech found in section 4734 constitutes irreparable injury to Plaintiff. Thus, Plaintiff has satisfied the first of the two elements required for a preliminary injunction.

ii. Likelihood of Success

The second element requires the Court to determine whether Plaintiff is likely to succeed on the merits of its constitutional challenge. As this Court stated in Nakatomi Investments, "it has long been axiomatic that once a party shows that a regulation deprives them of a protected First Amendment interest, the burden shifts to the Government to justify the infringement." 949 F.Supp. at 990 * * *.

At this time, however, it does not appear that the government contests the unconstitutionality of section 4734. Therefore, the Court must find that Plaintiff will likely succeed on the merits of its claims.

III. CONCLUSION

For the foregoing reasons, Plaintiff's Motion for a Preliminary Injunction is GRANTED. It is hereby ORDERED that pending final judgment, the United States, its agents, servants, employees, attorneys, and all persons in active concert and participation with Defendant are enjoined from commencing, maintaining, or otherwise taking action to enforce 42 U.S.C. § 1320a–7b(a)(6).

IT IS SO ORDERED.

NOTES AND QUESTIONS

1. Why might a client decide to forego Medicaid planning, other than for monetary, moral, or ethical reasons?

2. You may wish to consider including a clause to protect a Medicaid trust from future challenges.

> "A court * * * shall have the continuing jurisdiction to modify any provision of this trust to the extent necessary to maintain the eligibility of the individual beneficiary for medical assistance or other public benefits under applicable law, taking into consideration the effective date of any such law and the date of the establishment of this trust."

James D. Palmer, Jr., *Medicaid Eligibility—OBRA Raises the Hurdles,* PROB. & PROP., Sept./Oct. 1994, at 44.

3. For additional information, see Cynthia L. Barrett, *Advising the Elder Client: Trusts and Medicaid Eligibility*, PRAC. LAW., Oct. 1997, at 57; A. Margot Gordon and Howard S. Berk, *Medicaid Planning for the Disabled: The Use of OBRA '93 Pay-Back Trusts*, 86 ILL. B.J. 16 (1998).

WESLEY E. WRIGHT, MEDICAID ESTATE RECOVERY: WHEN THE GOVERNMENT WANTS YOUR HOMESTEAD*

TEXAS STATE BAR COLLEGE, SUMMER SCHOOL, ch. 12 (2004, revised 2012).

Since the Medicaid program began in 1965, federal allowed, but did not require, states to file claims against the estate of Medicaid recipients aged 65 or older. Under this first estate recovery program, recovery was only allowed if the Medicaid recipient did not have a spouse, minor or disabled child. Lifetime liens against property were prohibited, except in instances where benefits were incorrectly paid through fraud. In 1993, 28 states operated estate recovery programs and these programs collected approximately $63 million in 1992. * * *

Two separate statutes provide authority for Medicaid estate recovery. The Tax Equity and Fiscal Responsibility Act (TEFRA), enacted in 1982, provides for the implementation of liens against the real property of Medicaid recipients whom the state has determined to be permanently institutionalized. The second statute, which requires mandatory estate recovery provisions, is the Omnibus Reconciliation Act of 1993 (OBRA 1993).

TEFRA provisions provide the states may impose a pre-death lien against the real property of a permanently institutionalized Medicaid beneficiary. TEFRA applies to a Medicaid beneficiary of any age who resides in a nursing home, intermediate care facility-mental retardation (ICF–MR facility) or medical institution if the state has made a reasonable determination after notice and opportunity for fair hearing that the individual is permanently institutionalized and will not return home. If the Medicaid assistance is improperly paid due to fraud, then the state may impose a lien against both the real and personal property of the Medicaid recipient through a court judgment that the Medicaid benefits were improperly paid.

Any pre-death TEFRA lien placed against the real property of a Medicaid recipient who is permanently institutionalized dissolves should that individual, in fact, return home. Recovery is made under a TEFRA lien when the single individual dies or when the property is sold. Also, under the TEFRA provisions, the state may elect to recover for the costs of institutional services for the costs of all medical assistance, whether or not the other medical assistance was provided in connection with institutionalized.

TEFRA provides that a lien will not be placed against the real property of a Medicaid recipient if the Medicaid recipient's spouse, children under the age of 21 or children who are blind or disabled (pursuant to Social Security Administration provisions) who are lawfully residing in the Medicaid recipient's home. Moreover, a sibling of the Medicaid recipients who has lived in the one at least one year immediately prior to the Medicaid recipient's institutionalization and who owns an equity interest in the home, is protected against the placement of a TEFRA lien. Also, any sibling who has lived with the Medicaid recipient for at least one year, and any child of the Medicaid recipient who has lived with the recipient for two years, prior to the institutionalization of the Medicaid recipient, and who provided care which delayed institutionalization, are protected from the enforcement of the TEFRA lien, but are not protected from the placement of such lien.

LOCATE

How does estate recovery operate in your state?

CHAPTER 7

PLANNING FOR THE PHYSICAL ASPECTS OF DEATH

■ ■ ■

A. INTRODUCTION

"It hath often been said that it is not death but dying that is terrible."[1] As an estate planner, you have the opportunity to make the inevitable dying process more palatable. Many aspects of this process are subject to your client's control; whether to use heroic means to sustain life (living wills), whether to allow others to benefit from the death by donating various organs or the entire body (anatomical gifts), and the method of disposing of the remains (body disposition directives).

Although discussing death may be difficult for your client, it is interesting to note that a survey of fears revealed that the apprehension of dying ranked only seventh.[2] What do you think is most feared? Hint: think about your first day of law school.

CRUZAN v. DIRECTOR, MISSOURI DEPARTMENT OF HEALTH

Supreme Court of the United States, 1990.
497 U.S. 261, 110 S.Ct. 2841, 111 L.Ed.2d 224.

CHIEF JUSTICE REHNQUIST delivered the opinion of the Court.

Petitioner Nancy Beth Cruzan was rendered incompetent as a result of severe injuries sustained during an automobile accident. Copetitioners Lester and Joyce Cruzan, Nancy's parents and coguardians, sought a court order directing the withdrawal of their daughter's artificial feeding and hydration equipment after it became apparent that she had virtually no chance of recovering her cognitive faculties. The Supreme Court of Missouri held that because there was no clear and convincing evidence of Nancy's desire to have life-sustaining treatment withdrawn under such circumstances, her parents lacked authority to effectuate such a request. We granted certiorari * * * and now affirm.

---

1. HENRY FIELDING, AMELIA 108 (Dutton 1962) (1752).

2. See Madeline Drexler, *Center Stage,* THE BOSTON GLOBE MAG., Nov. 8, 1992, at 8.

On the night of January 11, 1983, Nancy Cruzan lost control of her car as she traveled down Elm Road in Jasper County, Missouri. The vehicle overturned, and Cruzan was discovered lying face down in a ditch without detectable respiratory or cardiac function. Paramedics were able to restore her breathing and heartbeat at the accident site, and she was transported to a hospital in an unconscious state. An attending neurosurgeon diagnosed her as having sustained probable cerebral contusions compounded by significant anoxia (lack of oxygen). The Missouri trial court in this case found that permanent brain damage generally results after 6 minutes in an anoxic state; it was estimated that Cruzan was deprived of oxygen from 12 to 14 minutes. She remained in a coma for approximately three weeks and then progressed to an unconscious state in which she was able to orally ingest some nutrition. In order to ease feeding and further the recovery, surgeons implanted a gastrostomy feeding and hydration tube in Cruzan with the consent of her then husband. Subsequent rehabilitative efforts proved unavailing. She now lies in a Missouri state hospital in what is commonly referred to as a persistent vegetative state: generally, a condition in which a person exhibits motor reflexes but evinces no indications of significant cognitive function.[3] The State of Missouri is bearing the cost of her care.

After it had become apparent that Nancy Cruzan had virtually no chance of regaining her mental faculties, her parents asked hospital

3. The State Supreme Court, adopting much of the trial court's findings, described Nancy Cruzan's medical condition as follows: " . . . (1) [H]er respiration and circulation are not artificially maintained and are within the normal limits of a thirty-year-old female; (2) she is oblivious to her environment except for reflexive responses to sound and perhaps painful stimuli; (3) she suffered anoxia of the brain resulting in a massive enlargement of the ventricles filling with cerebrospinal fluid in the area where the brain has degenerated and [her] cerebral cortical atrophy is irreversible, permanent, progressive and ongoing; (4) her highest cognitive brain function is exhibited by her grimacing perhaps in recognition of ordinarily painful stimuli, indicating the experience of pain and apparent response to sound; (5) she is a spastic quadriplegic; (6) her four extremities are contracted with irreversible muscular and tendon damage to all extremities; (7) she has no cognitive or reflexive ability to swallow food or water to maintain her daily essential needs and . . . she will never recover her ability to swallow sufficient [sic] to satisfy her needs. In sum, Nancy is diagnosed as in a persistent vegetative state. She is not dead. She is not terminally ill. Medical experts testified that she could live another thirty years." Cruzan v. Harmon, 760 S.W.2d 408, 411 (Mo.1988) (en banc) (quotations omitted; footnote omitted). In observing that Cruzan was not dead, the court referred to the following Missouri statute: "For all legal purposes, the occurrence of human death shall be determined in accordance with the usual and customary standards of medical practice, provided that death shall not be determined to have occurred unless the following minimal conditions have been met: (1) When respiration and circulation are not artificially maintained, there is an irreversible cessation of spontaneous respiration and circulation; or (2) When respiration and circulation are artificially maintained, and there is total and irreversible cessation of all brain function, including the brain stem and that such determination is made by a licensed physician." Mo.Rev.Stat. § 194.005 (1986). Since Cruzan's respiration and circulation were not being artificially maintained, she obviously fit within the first proviso of the statute. Dr. Fred Plum, the creator of the term "persistent vegetative state" and a renowned expert on the subject, has described the "vegetative state" in the following terms: " 'Vegetative state describes a body which is functioning entirely in terms of its internal controls. It maintains temperature. It maintains heart beat and pulmonary ventilation. It maintains digestive activity. It maintains reflex activity of muscles and nerves for low level conditioned responses. But there is no behavioral evidence of either self-awareness or awareness of the surroundings in a learned manner.' " In re Jobes, 108 N.J. 394, 403, 529 A.2d 434, 438 (1987). See also Brief for American Medical Association et al. as Amici Curiae 6 ("The persistent vegetative state can best be understood as one of the conditions in which patients have suffered a loss of consciousness").

employees to terminate the artificial nutrition and hydration procedures. All agree that such a removal would cause her death. The employees refused to honor the request without court approval. The parents then sought and received authorization from the state trial court for termination. The court found that a person in Nancy's condition had a fundamental right under the State and Federal Constitutions to refuse or direct the withdrawal of "death prolonging procedures." App. to Pet. for Cert. A99. The court also found that Nancy's "expressed thoughts at age twenty-five in somewhat serious conversation with a housemate friend that if sick or injured she would not wish to continue her life unless she could live at least halfway normally suggests that given her present condition she would not wish to continue on with her nutrition and hydration." Id., at A97–A98.

The Supreme Court of Missouri reversed by a divided vote. The court recognized a right to refuse treatment embodied in the common-law doctrine of informed consent, but expressed skepticism about the application of that doctrine in the circumstances of this case. Cruzan v. Harmon, 760 S.W.2d 408, 416–417 (1988) (en banc). The court also declined to read a broad right of privacy into the State Constitution which would "support the right of a person to refuse medical treatment in every circumstance," and expressed doubt as to whether such a right existed under the United States Constitution. Id., at 417–418. It then decided that the Missouri Living Will statute, Mo.Rev.Stat. § 459.010 et seq. (1986), embodied a state policy strongly favoring the preservation of life. 760 S.W.2d, at 419–420. The court found that Cruzan's statements to her roommate regarding her desire to live or die under certain conditions were "unreliable for the purpose of determining her intent," id., at 424, "and thus insufficient to support the co-guardians['] claim to exercise substituted judgment on Nancy's behalf." Id., at 426. It rejected the argument that Cruzan's parents were entitled to order the termination of her medical treatment, concluding that "no person can assume that choice for an incompetent in the absence of the formalities required under Missouri's Living Will statutes or the clear and convincing, inherently reliable evidence absent here." Id., at 425. The court also expressed its view that "[b]road policy questions bearing on life and death are more properly addressed by representative assemblies" than judicial bodies. Id., at 426.

We granted certiorari to consider the question whether Cruzan has a right under the United States Constitution which would require the hospital to withdraw life-sustaining treatment from her under these circumstances.

At common law, even the touching of one person by another without consent and without legal justification was a battery. * * * Before the turn of the century, this Court observed that "[n]o right is held more sacred, or is more carefully guarded, by the common law, than the right of every individual to the possession and control of his own person, free from all restraint or interference of others, unless by clear and unquestionable authority of law." Union Pacific R. Co. v. Botsford, 141 U.S. 250, 251, 11

S.Ct. 1000, 1001, 35 L.Ed. 734 (1891). This notion of bodily integrity has been embodied in the requirement that informed consent is generally required for medical treatment. Justice Cardozo, while on the Court of Appeals of New York, aptly described this doctrine: "Every human being of adult years and sound mind has a right to determine what shall be done with his own body; and a surgeon who performs an operation without his patient's consent commits an assault, for which he is liable in damages." Schloendorff v. Society of New York Hospital, 211 N.Y. 125, 129–130, 105 N.E. 92, 93 (1914). The informed consent doctrine has become firmly entrenched in American tort law. * * *

The logical corollary of the doctrine of informed consent is that the patient generally possesses the right not to consent, that is, to refuse treatment. Until about 15 years ago and the seminal decision in In re Quinlan, 70 N.J. 10, 355 A.2d 647, cert. denied sub nom. Garger v. New Jersey, 429 U.S. 922, 97 S.Ct. 319, 50 L.Ed.2d 289 (1976), the number of right-to-refuse-treatment decisions was relatively few. Most of the earlier cases involved patients who refused medical treatment forbidden by their religious beliefs, thus implicating First Amendment rights as well as common-law rights of self-determination. More recently, however, with the advance of medical technology capable of sustaining life well past the point where natural forces would have brought certain death in earlier times, cases involving the right to refuse life-sustaining treatment have burgeoned. See 760 S.W.2d, at 412, n. 4 (collecting 54 reported decisions from 1976 through 1988).

In the Quinlan case, young Karen Quinlan suffered severe brain damage as the result of anoxia and entered a persistent vegetative state. Karen's father sought judicial approval to disconnect his daughter's respirator. The New Jersey Supreme Court granted the relief, holding that Karen had a right of privacy grounded in the Federal Constitution to terminate treatment. In re Quinlan, 70 N.J., at 38–42, 355 A.2d, at 662–664. Recognizing that this right was not absolute, however, the court balanced it against asserted state interests. Noting that the State's interest "weakens and the individual's right to privacy grows as the degree of bodily invasion increases and the prognosis dims," the court concluded that the state interests had to give way in that case. Id., at 41, 355 A.2d, at 664. The court also concluded that the "only practical way" to prevent the loss of Karen's privacy right due to her incompetence was to allow her guardian and family to decide "whether she would exercise it in these circumstances." Ibid.

After Quinlan, however, most courts have based a right to refuse treatment either solely on the common-law right to informed consent or on both the common-law right and a constitutional privacy right. * * * In Superintendent of Belchertown State School v. Saikewicz, 373 Mass. 728, 370 N.E.2d 417 (1977), the Supreme Judicial Court of Massachusetts relied on both the right of privacy and the right of informed consent to permit the withholding of chemotherapy from a profoundly retarded 67–year-old man suffering from leukemia. Id., at 737–738, 370 N.E.2d, at 424.

Reasoning that an incompetent person retains the same rights as a competent individual "because the value of human dignity extends to both," the court adopted a "substituted judgment" standard whereby courts were to determine what an incompetent individual's decision would have been under the circumstances. Id., at 745, 752–753, 757–758, 370 N.E.2d, at 427, 431, 434. Distilling certain state interests from prior case law—the preservation of life, the protection of the interests of innocent third parties, the prevention of suicide, and the maintenance of the ethical integrity of the medical profession—the court recognized the first interest as paramount and noted it was greatest when an affliction was curable, "as opposed to the State interest where, as here, the issue is not whether, but when, for how long, and at what cost to the individual [a] life may be briefly extended." Id., at 742, 370 N.E.2d, at 426.

In In re Storar, 52 N.Y.2d 363, 438 N.Y.S.2d 266, 420 N.E.2d 64, cert. denied, 454 U.S. 858, 102 S.Ct. 309, 70 L.Ed.2d 153 (1981), the New York Court of Appeals declined to base a right to refuse treatment on a constitutional privacy right. Instead, it found such a right "adequately supported" by the informed consent doctrine. Id., at 376–377, 438 N.Y.S.2d, at 272, 420 N.E.2d, at 70. In In re Eichner (decided with In re Storar, supra), an 83–year-old man who had suffered brain damage from anoxia entered a vegetative state and was thus incompetent to consent to the removal of his respirator. The court, however, found it unnecessary to reach the question whether his rights could be exercised by others since it found the evidence clear and convincing from statements made by the patient when competent that he "did not want to be maintained in a vegetative coma by use of a respirator." Id., at 380, 438 N.Y.S.2d, at 274, 420 N.E.2d, at 72. In the companion Storar case, a 52–year-old man suffering from bladder cancer had been profoundly retarded during most of his life. Implicitly rejecting the approach taken in Saikewicz, supra, the court reasoned that due to such life-long incompetency, "it is unrealistic to attempt to determine whether he would want to continue potentially life prolonging treatment if he were competent." 52 N.Y.2d, at 380, 438 N.Y.S.2d, at 275, 420 N.E.2d, at 72. As the evidence showed that the patient's required blood transfusions did not involve excessive pain and without them his mental and physical abilities would deteriorate, the court concluded that it should not "allow an incompetent patient to bleed to death because someone, even someone as close as a parent or sibling, feels that this is best for one with an incurable disease." Id., at 382, 438 N.Y.S.2d, at 275, 420 N.E.2d, at 73.

Many of the later cases build on the principles established in Quinlan, Saikewicz, and Storar/Eichner. For instance, in In re Conroy, 98 N.J. 321, 486 A.2d 1209 (1985), the same court that decided Quinlan considered whether a nasogastric feeding tube could be removed from an 84–year-old incompetent nursing-home resident suffering irreversible mental and physical ailments. While recognizing that a federal right of privacy might apply in the case, the court, contrary to its approach in Quinlan, decided to base its decision on the common-law right to self-determination and informed consent. 98 N.J., at 348, 486 A.2d, at 1223. "On balance, the right to self-determination ordinarily outweighs any countervailing state interests, and competent persons generally are permitted to refuse medical treatment, even at the risk of death. Most of the cases that have held otherwise, unless they involved the interest in protecting innocent third parties, have concerned the patient's competency to make a rational and considered choice." Id., at 353–354, 486 A.2d, at 1225.

Reasoning that the right of self-determination should not be lost merely because an individual is unable to sense a violation of it, the court held that incompetent individuals retain a right to refuse treatment. It also held that such a right could be exercised by a surrogate decisionmaker using a "subjective" standard when there was clear evidence that the incompetent person would have exercised it. Where such evidence was lacking, the court held that an individual's right could still be invoked in certain circumstances under objective "best interest" standards. Id., at 361–368, 486 A.2d, at 1229–1233. Thus, if some trustworthy evidence existed that the individual would have wanted to terminate treatment, but not enough to clearly establish a person's wishes for purposes of the subjective standard, and the burden of a prolonged life from the experience of pain and suffering markedly outweighed its satisfactions, treatment could be terminated under a "limited-objective" standard. Where no trustworthy evidence existed, and a person's suffering would make the administration of life-sustaining treatment inhumane, a "pure-objective" standard could be used to terminate treatment. If none of these conditions obtained, the court held it was best to err in favor of preserving life. Id., at 364–368, 486 A.2d, at 1231–1233.

The court also rejected certain categorical distinctions that had been drawn in prior refusal-of-treatment cases as lacking substance for decision purposes: the distinction between actively hastening death by terminating treatment and passively allowing a person to die of a disease; between treating individuals as an initial matter versus withdrawing treatment afterwards; between ordinary versus extraordinary treatment; and between treatment by artificial feeding versus other forms of life-sustaining medical procedures. Id., at 369–374, 486 A.2d, at 1233–1237. As to the last item, the court acknowledged the "emotional significance" of food, but noted that feeding by implanted tubes is a "medical procedur[e] with inherent risks and possible side effects, instituted by skilled health-care providers to compensate for impaired physical functioning" which analytically was equivalent to artificial breathing using a respirator. Id., at 373, 486 A.2d, at 1236.[4]

4. In a later trilogy of cases, the New Jersey Supreme Court stressed that the analytic framework adopted in Conroy was limited to elderly, incompetent patients with shortened life expectancies, and established alternative approaches to deal with a different set of situations. See In re Farrell, 108 N.J. 335, 529 A.2d 404 (1987) (37-year-old competent mother with terminal illness had right to removal of respirator based on common law and constitutional principles which overrode competing state interests); In re Peter, 108 N.J. 365, 529 A.2d 419 (1987) (65-year-old woman in persistent vegetative state had right to removal of nasogastric feeding tube—under Conroy subjective test, power of attorney and hearsay testimony constituted clear and

In contrast to Conroy, the Court of Appeals of New York recently refused to accept less than the clearly expressed wishes of a patient before permitting the exercise of her right to refuse treatment by a surrogate decisionmaker. In re Westchester County Medical Center on behalf of O'Connor, 72 N.Y.2d 517, 534 N.Y.S.2d 886, 531 N.E.2d 607 (1988) (O'Connor). There, the court, over the objection of the patient's family members, granted an order to insert a feeding tube into a 77–year-old woman rendered incompetent as a result of several strokes. While continuing to recognize a common-law right to refuse treatment, the court rejected the substituted judgment approach for asserting it "because it is inconsistent with our fundamental commitment to the notion that no person or court should substitute its judgment as to what would be an acceptable quality of life for another. Consequently, we adhere to the view that, despite its pitfalls and inevitable uncertainties, the inquiry must always be narrowed to the patient's expressed intent, with every effort made to minimize the opportunity for error." Id., at 530, 534 N.Y.S.2d, at 892, 531 N.E.2d, at 613 (citation omitted). The court held that the record lacked the requisite clear and convincing evidence of the patient's expressed intent to withhold life-sustaining treatment. Id., at 531–534, 534 N.Y.S.2d, at 892–894, 531 N.E.2d, at 613–615.

Other courts have found state statutory law relevant to the resolution of these issues. In Conservatorship of Drabick, 200 Cal.App.3d 185, 245 Cal.Rptr. 840, cert. denied, 488 U.S. 958, 109 S.Ct. 399, 102 L.Ed.2d 387 (1988), the California Court of Appeal authorized the removal of a nasogastric feeding tube from a 44–year-old man who was in a persistent vegetative state as a result of an auto accident. Noting that the right to refuse treatment was grounded in both the common law and a constitutional right of privacy, the court held that a state probate statute authorized the patient's conservator to order the withdrawal of life-sustaining treatment when such a decision was made in good faith based on medical advice and the conservatee's best interests. While acknowledging that "to claim that [a patient's] 'right to choose' survives incompetence is a legal fiction at best," the court reasoned that the respect society accords to persons as individuals is not lost upon incompetence and is best preserved by allowing others "to make a decision that reflects [a patient's] interests more closely than would a purely technological decision to do whatever is possible." Id., 200 Cal.App.3d, at 208, 245 Cal.Rptr., at 854–855. See also In re Conservatorship of Torres, 357 N.W.2d 332 (Minn.1984) (Minnesota court had constitutional and statutory authority to authorize a conservator to order the removal of an incompetent individual's respirator since in patient's best interests).

In In re Estate of Longeway, 133 Ill.2d 33, 139 Ill.Dec. 780, 549 N.E.2d 292 (1989), the Supreme Court of Illinois considered whether a 76–

convincing proof of patient's intent to have treatment withdrawn); In re Jobes, 108 N.J. 394, 529 A.2d 434 (1987) (31–year-old woman in persistent vegetative state entitled to removal of jejunostomy feeding tube—even though hearsay testimony regarding patient's intent insufficient to meet clear and convincing standard of proof, under Quinlan, family or close friends entitled to make a substituted judgment for patient).

year-old woman rendered incompetent from a series of strokes had a right to the discontinuance of artificial nutrition and hydration. Noting that the boundaries of a federal right of privacy were uncertain, the court found a right to refuse treatment in the doctrine of informed consent. Id., at 43–45, 139 Ill.Dec. at 784–785, 549 N.E.2d, at 296–297. The court further held that the State Probate Act impliedly authorized a guardian to exercise a ward's right to refuse artificial sustenance in the event that the ward was terminally ill and irreversibly comatose. Id., at 45–47, 139 Ill.Dec., at 786, 549 N.E.2d, at 298. Declining to adopt a best interests standard for deciding when it would be appropriate to exercise a ward's right because it "lets another make a determination of a patient's quality of life," the court opted instead for a substituted judgment standard. Id., at 49, 139 Ill.Dec., at 787, 549 N.E.2d, at 299. Finding the "expressed intent" standard utilized in O'Connor, supra, too rigid, the court noted that other clear and convincing evidence of the patient's intent could be considered. 133 Ill.2d, at 50–51, 139 Ill.Dec., at 787, 549 N.E.2d, at 300. The court also adopted the "consensus opinion [that] treats artificial nutrition and hydration as medical treatment." Id., at 42, 139 Ill.Dec., at 784, 549 N.E.2d, at 296. Cf. McConnell v. Beverly Enterprises–Connecticut, Inc., 209 Conn. 692, 705, 553 A.2d 596, 603 (1989) (right to withdraw artificial nutrition and hydration found in the Connecticut Removal of Life Support Systems Act, which "provid[es] functional guidelines for the exercise of the common law and constitutional rights of self-determination"; attending physician authorized to remove treatment after finding that patient is in a terminal condition, obtaining consent of family, and considering expressed wishes of patient).

As these cases demonstrate, the common-law doctrine of informed consent is viewed as generally encompassing the right of a competent individual to refuse medical treatment. Beyond that, these cases demonstrate both similarity and diversity in their approaches to decision of what all agree is a perplexing question with unusually strong moral and ethical overtones. State courts have available to them for decision a number of sources—state constitutions, statutes, and common law—which are not available to us. In this Court, the question is simply and starkly whether the United States Constitution prohibits Missouri from choosing the rule of decision which it did. This is the first case in which we have been squarely presented with the issue whether the United States Constitution grants what is in common parlance referred to as a "right to die." We follow the judicious counsel of our decision in Twin City Bank v. Nebeker, 167 U.S. 196, 202, 17 S.Ct. 766, 769, 42 L.Ed. 134 (1897), where we said that in deciding "a question of such magnitude and importance ... it is the [better] part of wisdom not to attempt, by any general statement, to cover every possible phase of the subject."

The Fourteenth Amendment provides that no State shall "deprive any person of life, liberty, or property, without due process of law." The principle that a competent person has a constitutionally protected liberty interest in refusing unwanted medical treatment may be inferred from our prior decisions. In Jacobson v. Massachusetts, 197 U.S. 11, 24–30, 25 S.Ct. 358, 360–361, 49 L.Ed. 643 (1905), for instance, the Court balanced an individual's liberty interest in declining an unwanted smallpox vaccine against the State's interest in preventing disease. Decisions prior to the incorporation of the Fourth Amendment into the Fourteenth Amendment analyzed searches and seizures involving the body under the Due Process Clause and were thought to implicate substantial liberty interests. See, e.g., Breithaupt v. Abram, 352 U.S. 432, 439, 77 S.Ct. 408, 412, 1 L.Ed.2d 448 (1957) ("As against the right of an individual that his person be held inviolable ... must be set the interests of society ... ").

Just this Term, in the course of holding that a State's procedures for administering antipsychotic medication to prisoners were sufficient to satisfy due process concerns, we recognized that prisoners possess "a significant liberty interest in avoiding the unwanted administration of antipsychotic drugs under the Due Process Clause of the Fourteenth Amendment." Washington v. Harper, 494 U.S. 210, 221–222, 110 S.Ct. 1028, 1036, 108 L.Ed.2d 178 (1990); see also id., at 229, 110 S.Ct., at 1041 ("The forcible injection of medication into a nonconsenting person's body represents a substantial interference with that person's liberty"). Still other cases support the recognition of a general liberty interest in refusing medical treatment. Vitek v. Jones, 445 U.S. 480, 494, 100 S.Ct. 1254, 1264, 63 L.Ed.2d 552 (1980) (transfer to mental hospital coupled with mandatory behavior modification treatment implicated liberty interests); Parham v. J.R., 442 U.S. 584, 600, 99 S.Ct. 2493, 2503, 61 L.Ed.2d 101 (1979) ("[A] child, in common with adults, has a substantial liberty interest in not being confined unnecessarily for medical treatment").

But determining that a person has a "liberty interest" under the Due Process Clause does not end the inquiry;[5] "whether respondent's constitutional rights have been violated must be determined by balancing his liberty interests against the relevant state interests." Youngberg v. Romeo, 457 U.S. 307, 321, 102 S.Ct. 2452, 2461, 73 L.Ed.2d 28 (1982). See also Mills v. Rogers, 457 U.S. 291, 299, 102 S.Ct. 2442, 2448, 73 L.Ed.2d 16 (1982).

Petitioners insist that under the general holdings of our cases, the forced administration of life-sustaining medical treatment, and even of artificially delivered food and water essential to life, would implicate a competent person's liberty interest. Although we think the logic of the cases discussed above would embrace such a liberty interest, the dramatic consequences involved in refusal of such treatment would inform the inquiry as to whether the deprivation of that interest is constitutionally permissible. But for purposes of this case, we assume that the United States Constitution would grant a competent person a constitutionally protected right to refuse lifesaving hydration and nutrition.

5. Although many state courts have held that a right to refuse treatment is encompassed by a generalized constitutional right of privacy, we have never so held. We believe this issue is more properly analyzed in terms of a Fourteenth Amendment liberty interest. See Bowers v. Hardwick, 478 U.S. 186, 194–195, 106 S.Ct. 2841, 2846, 92 L.Ed.2d 140 (1986).

Petitioners go on to assert that an incompetent person should possess the same right in this respect as is possessed by a competent person. They rely primarily on our decisions in Parham v. J.R., supra, and Youngberg v. Romeo, supra, 102 S.Ct. 2452, 73 L.Ed.2d 28 (1982). In Parham, we held that a mentally disturbed minor child had a liberty interest in "not being confined unnecessarily for medical treatment," 442 U.S., at 600, 99 S.Ct., at 2503, but we certainly did not intimate that such a minor child, after commitment, would have a liberty interest in refusing treatment. In Youngberg, we held that a seriously retarded adult had a liberty interest in safety and freedom from bodily restraint, 457 U.S., at 320, 102 S.Ct., at 2460. Youngberg, however, did not deal with decisions to administer or withhold medical treatment.

The difficulty with petitioners' claim is that in a sense it begs the question: An incompetent person is not able to make an informed and voluntary choice to exercise a hypothetical right to refuse treatment or any other right. Such a "right" must be exercised for her, if at all, by some sort of surrogate. Here, Missouri has in effect recognized that under certain circumstances a surrogate may act for the patient in electing to have hydration and nutrition withdrawn in such a way as to cause death, but it has established a procedural safeguard to assure that the action of the surrogate conforms as best it may to the wishes expressed by the patient while competent. Missouri requires that evidence of the incompetent's wishes as to the withdrawal of treatment be proved by clear and convincing evidence. The question, then, is whether the United States Constitution forbids the establishment of this procedural requirement by the State. We hold that it does not.

Whether or not Missouri's clear and convincing evidence requirement comports with the United States Constitution depends in part on what interests the State may properly seek to protect in this situation. Missouri relies on its interest in the protection and preservation of human life, and there can be no gainsaying this interest. As a general matter, the States—indeed, all civilized nations—demonstrate their commitment to life by treating homicide as a serious crime. Moreover, the majority of States in this country have laws imposing criminal penalties on one who assists another to commit suicide. We do not think a State is required to remain neutral in the face of an informed and voluntary decision by a physically able adult to starve to death.

But in the context presented here, a State has more particular interests at stake. The choice between life and death is a deeply personal decision of obvious and overwhelming finality. We believe Missouri may legitimately seek to safeguard the personal element of this choice through the imposition of heightened evidentiary requirements. It cannot be disputed that the Due Process Clause protects an interest in life as well as an interest in refusing life-sustaining medical treatment. Not all incompetent patients will have loved ones available to serve as surrogate decisionmakers. And even where family members are present, "[t]here will, of course, be some unfortunate situations in which family members will not act to protect a patient." In re Jobes, 108 N.J. 394, 419, 529 A.2d 434, 447 (1987). A State is entitled to guard against potential abuses in such situations. Similarly, a State is entitled to consider that a judicial proceeding to make a determination regarding an incompetent's wishes may very well not be an adversarial one, with the added guarantee of accurate factfinding that the adversary process brings with it.[6] See Ohio v. Akron Center for Reproductive Health, 497 U.S. 502, 515–516, 110 S.Ct. 2972, 2981–2982, 111 L.Ed.2d 405 (1990). Finally, we think a State may properly decline to make judgments about the "quality" of life that a particular individual may enjoy, and simply assert an unqualified interest in the preservation of human life to be weighed against the constitutionally protected interests of the individual.

In our view, Missouri has permissibly sought to advance these interests through the adoption of a "clear and convincing" standard of proof to govern such proceedings. "The function of a standard of proof, as that concept is embodied in the Due Process Clause and in the realm of factfinding, is to 'instruct the factfinder concerning the degree of confidence our society thinks he should have in the correctness of factual conclusions for a particular type of adjudication.'" Addington v. Texas, 441 U.S. 418, 423, 99 S.Ct. 1804, 1808, 60 L.Ed.2d 323 (1979) (quoting In re Winship, 397 U.S. 358, 370, 90 S.Ct. 1068, 1076, 25 L.Ed.2d 368 (1970) (Harlan, J., concurring)). "This Court has mandated an intermediate standard of proof—'clear and convincing evidence'—when the individual interests at stake in a state proceeding are both 'particularly important' and 'more substantial than mere loss of money.'" Santosky v. Kramer, 455 U.S. 745, 756, 102 S.Ct. 1388, 1397, 71 L.Ed.2d 599 (1982) (quoting Addington, supra, at 424, 99 S.Ct., at 1808). Thus, such a standard has been required in deportation proceedings, Woodby v. INS, 385 U.S. 276, 87 S.Ct. 483, 17 L.Ed.2d 362 (1966), in denaturalization proceedings, Schneiderman v. United States, 320 U.S. 118, 63 S.Ct. 1333, 87 L.Ed. 1796 (1943), in civil commitment proceedings, Addington, supra, and in proceedings for the termination of parental rights, Santosky, supra.[7] Further,

6. Since Cruzan was a patient at a state hospital when this litigation commenced, the State has been involved as an adversary from the beginning. However, it can be expected that many disputes of this type will arise in private institutions, where a guardian ad litem or similar party will have been appointed as the sole representative of the incompetent individual in the litigation. In such cases, a guardian may act in entire good faith, and yet not maintain a position truly adversarial to that of the family. Indeed, as noted by the court below, "[t]he guardian ad litem [in this case] finds himself in the predicament of believing that it is in Nancy's 'best interest to have the tube feeding discontinued,' but 'feeling that an appeal should be made because our responsibility to her as attorneys and guardians ad litem was to pursue this matter to the highest court in the state in view of the fact that this is a case of first impression in the State of Missouri.'" 760 S.W.2d, at 410, n. 1. Cruzan's guardian ad litem has also filed a brief in this Court urging reversal of the Missouri Supreme Court's decision. None of this is intended to suggest that the guardian acted the least bit improperly in this proceeding. It is only meant to illustrate the limits which may obtain on the adversarial nature of this type of litigation.

7. We recognize that these cases involved instances where the government sought to take action against an individual. See Price Waterhouse v. Hopkins, 490 U.S. 228, 253, 109 S.Ct. 1775, 1792, 104 L.Ed.2d 268 (1989) (plurality opinion). Here, by contrast, the government seeks to protect the interests of an individual, as well as its own institutional interests, in life. We do not see any reason why important individual interests should be afforded less protection simply because the government finds itself in the position of defending them. "[W]e find it significant

this level of proof, "or an even higher one, has traditionally been imposed in cases involving allegations of civil fraud, and in a variety of other kinds of civil cases involving such issues as ... lost wills, oral contracts to make bequests, and the like." Woodby, supra, 385 U.S., at 285, n. 18, 87 S.Ct., at 488, n. 18.

We think it self-evident that the interests at stake in the instant proceedings are more substantial, both on an individual and societal level, than those involved in a run-of-the-mine civil dispute. But not only does the standard of proof reflect the importance of a particular adjudication, it also serves as "a societal judgment about how the risk of error should be distributed between the litigants." Santosky, supra, 455 U.S. at 755, 102 S.Ct., at 1395; Addington, supra, 441 U.S., at 423, 99 S.Ct., at 1807–1808. The more stringent the burden of proof a party must bear, the more that party bears the risk of an erroneous decision. We believe that Missouri may permissibly place an increased risk of an erroneous decision on those seeking to terminate an incompetent individual's life-sustaining treatment. An erroneous decision not to terminate results in a maintenance of the status quo; the possibility of subsequent developments such as advancements in medical science, the discovery of new evidence regarding the patient's intent, changes in the law, or simply the unexpected death of the patient despite the administration of life-sustaining treatment at least create the potential that a wrong decision will eventually be corrected or its impact mitigated. An erroneous decision to withdraw life-sustaining treatment, however, is not susceptible of correction. In Santosky, one of the factors which led the Court to require proof by clear and convincing evidence in a proceeding to terminate parental rights was that a decision in such a case was final and irrevocable. Santosky, supra, 445 U.S., at 759, 102 S.Ct., at 1397–1398. The same must surely be said of the decision to discontinue hydration and nutrition of a patient such as Nancy Cruzan, which all agree will result in her death.

It is also worth noting that most, if not all, States simply forbid oral testimony entirely in determining the wishes of parties in transactions which, while important, simply do not have the consequences that a decision to terminate a person's life does. At common law and by statute in most States, the parol evidence rule prevents the variations of the terms of a written contract by oral testimony. The statute of frauds makes unenforceable oral contracts to leave property by will, and statutes regulating the making of wills universally require that those instruments be in writing. See 2 A. Corbin, Contracts § 398, pp. 360–361 (1950); 2 W. Page, Law of Wills §§ 19.3–19.5, pp. 61–71 (1960). There is no doubt that statutes requiring wills to be in writing, and statutes of frauds which require that a contract to make a will be in writing, on occasion frustrate the effectuation of the intent of a particular decedent, just as Missouri's

that ... the defendant rather than the plaintiff" seeks the clear and convincing standard of proof—"suggesting that this standard ordinarily serves as a shield rather than ... a sword." Id., at 253, 109 S.Ct., at 1792. That it is the government that has picked up the shield should be of no moment.

requirement of proof in this case may have frustrated the effectuation of the not-fully-expressed desires of Nancy Cruzan. But the Constitution does not require general rules to work faultlessly; no general rule can.

In sum, we conclude that a State may apply a clear and convincing evidence standard in proceedings where a guardian seeks to discontinue nutrition and hydration of a person diagnosed to be in a persistent vegetative state. We note that many courts which have adopted some sort of substituted judgment procedure in situations like this, whether they limit consideration of evidence to the prior expressed wishes of the incompetent individual, or whether they allow more general proof of what the individual's decision would have been, require a clear and convincing standard of proof for such evidence. * * *

The Supreme Court of Missouri held that in this case the testimony adduced at trial did not amount to clear and convincing proof of the patient's desire to have hydration and nutrition withdrawn. In so doing, it reversed a decision of the Missouri trial court which had found that the evidence "suggest[ed]" Nancy Cruzan would not have desired to continue such measures, App. to Pet. for Cert. A98, but which had not adopted the standard of "clear and convincing evidence" enunciated by the Supreme Court. The testimony adduced at trial consisted primarily of Nancy Cruzan's statements made to a housemate about a year before her accident that she would not want to live should she face life as a "vegetable," and other observations to the same effect. The observations did not deal in terms with withdrawal of medical treatment or of hydration and nutrition. We cannot say that the Supreme Court of Missouri committed constitutional error in reaching the conclusion that it did.

Petitioners alternatively contend that Missouri must accept the "substituted judgment" of close family members even in the absence of substantial proof that their views reflect the views of the patient. They rely primarily upon our decisions in Michael H. v. Gerald D., 491 U.S. 110, 109 S.Ct. 2333, 105 L.Ed.2d 91 (1989), and Parham v. J.R., 442 U.S. 584, 99 S.Ct. 2493, 61 L.Ed.2d 101 (1979). But we do not think these cases support their claim. In Michael H., we upheld the constitutionality of California's favored treatment of traditional family relationships; such a holding may not be turned around into a constitutional requirement that a State must recognize the primacy of those relationships in a situation like this. And in Parham, where the patient was a minor, we also upheld the constitutionality of a state scheme in which parents made certain decisions for mentally ill minors. Here again petitioners would seek to turn a decision which allowed a State to rely on family decisionmaking into a constitutional requirement that the State recognize such decisionmaking. But constitutional law does not work that way.

No doubt is engendered by anything in this record but that Nancy Cruzan's mother and father are loving and caring parents. If the State were required by the United States Constitution to repose a right of "substituted judgment" with anyone, the Cruzans would surely qualify.

But we do not think the Due Process Clause requires the State to repose judgment on these matters with anyone but the patient herself. Close family members may have a strong feeling—a feeling not at all ignoble or unworthy, but not entirely disinterested, either—that they do not wish to witness the continuation of the life of a loved one which they regard as hopeless, meaningless, and even degrading. But there is no automatic assurance that the view of close family members will necessarily be the same as the patient's would have been had she been confronted with the prospect of her situation while competent. All of the reasons previously discussed for allowing Missouri to require clear and convincing evidence of the patient's wishes lead us to conclude that the State may choose to defer only to those wishes, rather than confide the decision to close family members.[8]

The judgment of the Supreme Court of Missouri is

Affirmed.

B. LIVING WILLS

A competent individual has the right to refuse medical treatment for any reason even if that refusal will lead to an otherwise preventable death. What happens, though, if the person is in a coma, brain damaged, or for some other reason cannot communicate the person's wishes? Perhaps the person designated an agent in a durable power of attorney for health care. This agent would now have the authority to make medical decisions, including a refusal of treatment. See Chapter 6(C). Alternatively, the person may have signed a *living will*, also called a *directive to physicians*, *natural death statement*, *declaration*, or *advance directive*, expressing the person's desire not to be kept alive through the use of medical technology when the person is in a terminal condition and unable to communicate the person's wishes to decline further treatment.

California was the first state to statutorily authorize a person to make an advance statement regarding the use of life-sustaining procedures when its legislature enacted living will legislation in 1976. Other states quickly followed suit so that practically all states now have enabling statutes, most of which contain fill-in-the blank forms. The scope of these statutes and the accompanying forms, however, varies tremendously. Some permit a person to make only basic statements regarding the

8. We are not faced in this case with the question whether a State might be required to defer to the decision of a surrogate if competent and probative evidence established that the patient herself had expressed a desire that the decision to terminate life-sustaining treatment be made for her by that individual. Petitioners also adumbrate in their brief a claim based on the Equal Protection Clause of the Fourteenth Amendment to the effect that Missouri has impermissibly treated incompetent patients differently from competent ones, citing the statement in Cleburne v. Cleburne Living Center, Inc., 473 U.S. 432, 439, 105 S.Ct. 3249, 3254, 87 L.Ed.2d 313 (1985), that the clause is "essentially a direction that all persons similarly situated should be treated alike." The differences between the choice made by a competent person to refuse medical treatment, and the choice made for an incompetent person by someone else to refuse medical treatment, are so obviously different that the State is warranted in establishing rigorous procedures for the latter class of cases which do not apply to the former class.

person's intent while others ask for the person's opinion on a variety of issues (e.g., whether nutrition and hydration are included within the scope of life-sustaining procedures) or provide extensive opportunities for the person to indicate the type of treatment and the length of its application under a number of circumstances. Likewise, the formal requirements (e.g., whether the documents must be witnessed or notarized) are not uniform among the states.

UNIFORM HEALTH CARE DECISIONS ACT

1993 Act

[See Chapter 6(C).]

LOCATE

Locate your state's living will statute. Study it carefully and then answer the questions in the Notes and Questions based on your state's law. Are there significant differences between the answers under your state's law and the Uniform Health Care Decisions Act?

NOTES AND QUESTIONS

1. In the absence of a living will, durable power of attorney for health care, or statutory surrogate, courts must still decide life-sustaining medical treatment issues as in *Cruzan*. See COORDINATING COUNCIL ON LIFE-SUSTAINING MEDICAL TREATMENT DECISION MAKING BY THE COURTS, GUIDELINES FOR STATE COURT DECISION MAKING IN LIFE-SUSTAINING MEDICAL TREATMENT CASES (rev. 2d ed. 1993) (extensive analysis of cases and commentary, specific guidelines for judges, and thorough bibliography). These guidelines will be very useful to courts especially in light of the fact that only about twenty percent of Americans have executed a living will or a durable power of attorney for health care. See Madeline Drexler, *Mortal Thoughts,* BOSTON GLOBE MAG., Feb. 7, 1993, at 8.

2. The term "living will" is, of course, a misnomer. A living will concerns dying, not living, and it does not control the disposition of property upon death.

3. What are the requirements for a valid living will? Are witnesses needed? Must the document be notarized? Must the document be given immediately to the declarant's doctor?

4. Is a statutory living will form provided? If yes, is it a suggested form which the declarant may alter or must it be used essentially as written?

5. If your state has a form, does it provide sufficient opportunity for the declarant to state the declarant's specific desires, i.e., does the form provide adequate provisions for individualization? At least one study has revealed that "[m]ost such documents are far too vague to guide decision making in the midst of a life-threatening illness." *Living Wills: Tackle the Hard Stuff,* HEALTH, July/Aug. 1997, at 20. The form suggested by the American Medical Association provides four sample medical conditions (e.g., brain damaged but not terminal, in a coma with no hope of regaining awareness) and a long list

of potential treatments (e.g., mechanical breathing, artificial nutrition and hydration, minor surgery, antibiotics, pain medications). The user then checks boxes (48 possible) to show intent to (1) have treatment, (2) try treatment but stop if no clear improvement, (3) not have treatment, or (4) be undecided. See L.L. Emanuel & E.J. Emanuel, *The Medical Directive: A New Comprehensive Advance Care Document,* 261 J. AM. MED. ASS'N 3288–93 (1989). The Minnesota form also provides extensive opportunity for the declarant to state intent. See MINN. STAT. ANN. § 145B.04. For another detailed living will form claimed to be valid in 42 states, see Aging with Dignity, *Five Wishes* (2012).

6. May a patient control the treatment decision in any non-written manner, either orally or by gestures such as blinking or thumbs down?

7. If your state has a living will form, may the declarant use it to designate an agent to make the decision to withhold or withdraw life-sustaining procedures?

8. Under what circumstances may interested persons, such as family members, heirs, and beneficiaries, make treatment decisions for a terminally ill patient? See also the discussion of surrogates in Chapter 6(B).

9. What level of mental capacity must a declarant possess to be competent to make a directive?

10. May a minor execute a directive? If not, what can a minor do to express the person's intent?

11. How may a directive be revoked? Does the declarant need capacity to revoke?

12. Does the living will need to be reaffirmed on a regular basis for continued validity?

13. "Few people ever revoke living wills after they have taken the time to think through their own mortality. Nevertheless, many states provide revocation procedures which are so broad that any family member who desires care to be continued against the desires of the declarant can do so by claiming they heard the declarant revoke the directive before losing competency." Alan D. Lieberson, *Natural Death Act Directives, in* 16 WEST'S LEGAL FORMS 99–100 (Supp. 1992). Do you think this is a realistic fear?

14. What effect does executing a living will have on the declarant's ability to obtain life and health insurance?

15. How does the declarant's doctor learn that the declarant has a living will? Several businesses have been formed to act as living will depositories. The declarant carries a credit-card sized document which indicates that the person has a living will and contains instructions on how to contact the company for a copy. For a more extreme method, see *Indiana Nurse Tattoos Living Will on Stomach*, PALM BEACH POST, Jan. 22, 1995, at 14A ("The red and black tattoo features a red heart slashed with the universal 'no' sign with the words 'No Code.' ").

16. In what condition must the declarant be before a physician removes or withholds life-sustaining procedures?

17. Does the declarant's doctor need approval before removing or withholding life-sustaining procedures from either another doctor or a committee

of doctors who agree that the declarant is incompetent and suffering from a terminal condition?

18. May nutrition and hydration be withheld under a living will?

19. What is a physician's liability for following a living will?

20. What is a physician's liability for failing to follow a living will? Can the surviving patient sue the doctor for "wrongful life"? See Anderson v. St. Francis–St. George Hospital, Inc., 77 Ohio St.3d 82, 671 N.E.2d 225 (1996). See generally M. Rose Gasner, *Financial Penalties For Failing to Honor Patient Wishes to Refuse Treatment,* 11 ST. LOUIS U. PUB. L. REV. 499 (1992).

21. What is a person's liability for tampering with or hiding a living will?

22. What is a person's liability for forging a living will which is then acted upon to accelerate the alleged declarant's death?

23. Assume that your client wants to implement all life-prolonging procedures. What should you do? Is there an "anti-directive" or "life-prolonging procedures directive?" See *Doctors Fighting to End a Life,* PITTSBURGH PRESS, May 29, 1991, at A9 (husband asserted wife would have wanted life-prolonging procedures used but wife's doctors sought appointment of independent conservator who would allow the doctors to remove respirator and feeding tube).

24. Might there be reasons to delay carrying out a valid living will? See Robert Jorrie & Mason Standley, *The Tax Advantages of Lingering Death,* 48 TEX. B.J. 1070 (1985); A.L. Moses, *Determining That Death Has Occurred,* PROB. & PROP., July/Aug. 1987, at 59.

25. A 1994 study revealed that patients without living wills pay over 300% more for their final hospital stay than do patients with living wills. See *Patients with Living Wills Have Lower Hospital Costs,* SAN ANTONIO EXPRESS-NEWS, March 4, 1994, at 2A. On average, a person with an advance directive saves more than $60,000 in health care costs. Bill Staton, *Writing a living will can give you control of your life later*, SAN ANTONIO BUS. J., Oct. 1994. In addition, half of all money used for health care is spent in the last five days of life. See Section of Real Property, Probate, and Trust Law, *Leadership Letter,* June 1994, at 1. This has lead some estate planners to believe that a living will is the best asset protection technique available. Do you think the reduction of medical care costs is a valid reason for your client to consider executing a living will?

26. The "effectiveness of written advance directives is limited by inattention to them and by decisions to place priority on considerations other than the patient's autonomy." Marion Danis, et al., *A Prospective Study of Advance Directives for Life–Sustaining Care,* 324 NEW ENG. J. MED. 882, 882 (1991). "If terminally ill patients have a living will * * * chances are the doctor and hospital will ignore [them]. Whether motivated by fear of liability, desire for financial gain, or sheer mismanagement, the result is the same: The patient continues to suffer. * * * 80 percent of doctors either misunderstood or ignored their patients' dying requests." Donald C. Dilworth, *Dying Wishes Are Ignored by Hospitals, Doctors*, TRIAL, Feb. 1996, at 79. How do you compensate for this when planning for health care decisions?

27. In 1994, former President Richard Nixon and former first-lady Jacqueline Kennedy Onassis used living wills to reject potentially life-prolonging treatment. What effect do you think this notoriety had on the use and effectiveness of living wills?

28. "There is a growing body of evidence that living wills are being misapplied so as to deny care to people with treatable medical conditions." Wesley J. Smith, *The Living Will's Fatal Flaw,* WALL ST. J., May 4, 1994, at A14. Mr. Smith indicates that living wills cause patients to give up the traditional protection of requiring a doctor to obtain the patient's informed consent before performing or withholding treatment. He fears doctors view living wills as a request for no treatment for an emergency medical situation even if the person is not in a terminal condition and could fully recover. Do you think his fears are justified? What do you think he recommends to solve this problem? See also Clifton B. Kruse, Jr., *A Call for New Perspectives for Living Wills (You Might Like it Here),* 37 REAL PROP., PROB. & TR. J. 545 (2002) (cautioning estate planners to be careful when advising clients about living wills because changes in circumstances and enhanced medical technology may previous medical decisions no longer desirable); Louis J. Sirico, Jr., *Life and Death: Stories of a Heart Transplant Patient,* 37 REAL PROP., PROB. & TR. J. 553 (2002) (first-hand account of a law professor's experience with a heart transplant and how actually being in a critical stage may change a person's desires).

29. Should all states have the same law regarding living wills? What problems are caused by the lack of uniformity? See Harold C. Warnock, *Living Wills—The Need for Uniform State Laws,* PROB. & PROP., May/June 1991, at 52.

30. Your client's religious beliefs may significantly impact the client's decision whether to sign a living will. For a comprehensive bibliography of sources of information for most major religions, see Michael S. Arlein, *Religious Guidance on End-of-Life Decisions*, ELDER L. REP., Jan. 1999, at 4.

31. Living wills need to be contrasted with *orders not to resuscitate* often abbreviated DNR for "do not resuscitate." Unlike a living will, "the execution of an order not to attempt to resuscitate patients if they experience a cardiac or pulmonary arrest is almost always initiated by the attending physician, frequently as part of protocols or guidelines developed by the individual health care facility. Such protocols or guidelines vary greatly between facilities, but invariably require the physician to obtain the approval of the patient or a surrogate decision maker before it is initiated." Alan D. Lieberson, *Overview of Orders Not to Resuscitate, in* 16 WEST'S LEGAL FORMS 133 (Supp. 1992). State legislatures are beginning to codify DNR regulations. See New York–McKinney's Public Health Law §§ 2960–79.

32. Shirley shot Georgette, her daughter, when she learned that Georgette wanted to place her in a nursing home. Georgette wants to have life-sustaining equipment, such as a ventilator, removed. If Georgette dies as a result of the removal, will Shirley be criminally liable for murder? See Rick Bragg, *Daughter Implicates Mom, Now Will Die*, SAN JOSE MERCURY NEWS, May 19, 1999, at 1A.

DRAFT

Prepare the instruments necessary to document your intent with regard to the use of artificial life support equipment.

A. KIMBERLEY DAYTON, TIMOTHY H. GUARE, AND MOLLY M. WOOD, ADVISING THE ELDERLY CLIENT*

§ 33:10, Patient Self–Determination Act (2011).

A year after *Cruzan* was decided, Congress enacted the Patient Self–Determination Act (PSDA) of 1991. The PSDA is a federal mandate to educate the public regarding their legal rights in medical situations similar to those faced by Nancy Cruzan and her family. The PSDA requires all Medicare and Medicaid provider entities, such as hospitals and long-term care facilities, to furnish each patient, at the time of admission to the facility, written information concerning her legal rights respecting informed consent and health care decision-making. This written information—which usually takes the form of a "patients' bill of rights" or other educational brochure—must discuss the patient's options regarding decisions about medical care, including the right to accept or refuse medical treatment, as well as the right to make advance directives. Providers are mandated to document on the patient's chart whether the patient has an advance directive. In addition to these responsibilities to the individual patients, the provider organizations are also required to maintain written policies and procedures about advance directives and to educate staff and the community about end-of-life healthcare decision-making.

The PSDA prohibits discrimination against a patient based on whether or not she has an advance directive. Specifically, it provides that Medicare and Medicaid facilities cannot "condition the provision of care or otherwise discriminate against an individual based on whether or not the individual has executed an advance directive." To further the Act's goal of information dissemination, the PSDA the directs the states to develop a written description of state law concerning advance directives as a condition of receiving federal Medicare and Medicaid funding. The United States Department of Health and Human Services is required to assist states in developing state-specific documents and educational materials. Regulations over the years have supplemented the PSDA to give guidance to states and health care providers regarding their obligation to educate patients about advance directives. For example, the Centers for Medicare and Medicaid (formerly known as the Health Care Financing Administration) have issued guidelines for hospitals and other Medicare and Medicaid providers emphasizing that patients' rights brochures or materials should be available in multiple languages to accommodate the needs of patients who do not speak English.

Although the PSDA's mandates have been in place for more than a decade, its overall effectiveness in motivating individuals to execute advance directive is unclear. There is no question that the Act has generated increased attention to the interest of individuals in controlling their own medical destinies. But the vast majority of Americans do not have a written advance directive—it is likely that no more than 2–15% have actually executed any kind of medical directive. Some advocacy organizations are convinced that many Medicare and Medicaid participating facilities fail consistently to comply with the terms of the PSDA. Moreover, there is disturbing evidence that in many cases, advance directives are not honored, either because medical professionals are unaware of their existence, because family members or other persons close to the incapacitated patient choose not to direct treatment as the patient would have wanted, or for other reasons.

There are, as well, questions about the substantive aspects of the PSDA. One wonders whether a discussion about advance directives at the time of admission, with an admissions receptionist or a clerk, is appropriate, particularly if the patient is extremely ill or under the stress associated with an unplanned hospital admission. Using the admissions process as a point of entry for the critical discussion over end-of-life health care in the event of incapacity is convenient from an administrative perspective, but probably not conducive to a patient's understanding, much less her confidence in the medical treatment she is about to receive. This is yet another reason that elder law attorneys have an obligation to engage their own clients in discussions about end-of-life decision-making *before* serious illness or incapacity strikes. In addition, one of the most useful *pro bono* services the an elder law attorney can perform in his community is volunteering to educate hospital admissions staff, other attorneys and advocates for the aging, and the lay public, about state and federal law regarding advance directives.

NOTE

For further information, see ALAN D. LIEBERSON, ADVANCE MEDICAL DIRECTIVES (1992 & most recent Supp.); Claire C. Obade, *Advance Healthcare Planning Under the New Federal Patient Self–Determination Act,* 38 PRAC. LAW. 83 (1992).

C. PHYSICIAN ORDERS FOR LIFE–SUSTAINING TREATMENT

MARILYN J. MAAG, THE DEVELOPMENT OF POLST TO HONOR MEDICAL TREATMENT GOALS AT END–OF–LIFE*

ACTEC Summer Meeting, June 2012.

I. Definition of POLST (Physician Orders for Life–Sustaining Treatment)

POLST is a program, developing nationwide, to elicit and to honor the medical treatment goals of persons with advanced progressive illness or frailty. POLST involves:

1. Conversation. First and foremost, POLST requires a conversation, or a series of conversations, between health care professionals and the patient or the patient's authorized surrogate. The purpose of the conversations is to clarify the patient's goals and treatment decisions in light of the patient's current condition. The quality of the conversation is key to the success of POLST.

2. Medical Orders. The conversation results in medical orders that are recorded in a standardized form, which is kept in the front of the patient's medical records or with the patient in the patient's home. The orders generally address end-of-life health care issues, such as cardiopulmonary resuscitation, the level of medical intervention desired in an emergency, the use of artificially supplied nutrition and hydration, the use of antibiotics, and the use of ventilation.

3. Continuity of Care. Ideally, POLST forms should be available wherever the patient goes, so that care is provided in a consistent fashion and so that the patient's end-of-life health care decisions can be reevaluated and updated as needed.

4. A Process. The POLST paradigm is most accurately viewed as a process, not a form. The form is only one part of the process.

POLST is not an advance directive. While all adults are encouraged to think about and sign advance directives, POLST forms are presented to patients in approximately the final year of their lives. POLST forms include medical orders addressing the patient's current situation, not a possible future scenario. Advance directives are signed at home, in law offices, at hospitals, or wherever convenient. POLST forms are signed in medical settings and result in medical orders. The Table below clearly shows the differences between these documents:

* Reprinted with permission of Marilyn J. Maag (Porter Wright Morris & Arthur LLP).

Differences between POLST and Advance Directives[3]

Characteristics	POLST Paradigm	Advance Directive
Population	Advanced progressive chronic conditions	All adults
Timeframe	Current care	Future care
Where completed	In medical setting	In any setting
Resulting Product	Medical orders (POLST)	Advance directive
Surrogate role	Can do if patient lacks capacity	Cannot do
Portability	Provider responsibility	Patient/family responsibility
Periodic review	Provider responsibility	Patient/family responsibility

The actual forms used vary from state to state.

II. History of POLST

A. Oregon. POLST started in the State of Oregon in 1991 as the result of the observation of clinical ethics leaders that patients' preferences regarding life sustaining treatment frequently were not found or not transferable and, therefore, not honored. The decision was made to implement a system to honor patients' values and wishes regarding their end-of-life medical treatment.

The POLST form was developed, revised, pilot-tested, and ultimately released for use throughout the State of Oregon. In 1999, the administrative rules in Oregon were changed to provide that First Responders or EMTs would respect patients' wishes, including choices regarding life-sustaining treatments. Over time, the administrative rules were modified further to allow minors with terminal illness to participate in the POLST program, and to allow nurse practitioners and physicians' assistants to sign POLST medical orders. In 2008, the Oregon POLST form was modified to include a section for the special concerns of persons with disabilities.

In 2009, legislation was passed creating a statewide registry of POLST forms in Oregon, permitting access to the forms as needed, including by providers of emergency medical care. There are now over one million forms distributed in Oregon, and the use of POLST is the accepted medical standard of care. The Oregon POLST form is used by almost all hospices and nursing homes in the state.

B. LaCrosse, Wisconsin. At around the same time that the POLST paradigm was emerging in Oregon, the leaders of the two major health organizations in LaCrosse, Wisconsin decided to focus on end-of-life planning and decision-making. Like the state of Oregon, the community of LaCrosse, Wisconsin has taken on a leadership role in effectively using both advance directives and POLST forms.

In 1991, the LaCrosse health organizations launched a unique program to increase the use and effectiveness of advance directives. They

3. Sabatino & Karp, Improving Advanced Illness Care: The Evolution of State POLST Programs, AARP Public Policy Institute (2011) 4.

used printed materials and videos to educate the community and they trained the staff of their organizations as well.

The community of LaCrosse decided to establish the use of advance directives as a routine standard of care. The goal of their program was to create consistent practices throughout their community. Community leaders and health care leaders supported the program.

A study completed in 1995/1996 found that advance directives were written by 85% of persons who died in LaCrosse. The study also found that 96% of those advance directives actually were found in the medical records and typically were followed by family members and physicians.

The community of LaCrosse started using POLST forms in 1997, although there is no legislation in Wisconsin authorizing the use of the forms. In a follow-up study of the LaCrosse community, researchers reviewed medical record and death certificate data of persons who died in 2007 /2008. The researchers concluded that "POLST can be a highly effective program to ensure that patient preferences are known and honored in all settings. [Powers of Attorney for Health Care] are valuable because they identify appropriate surrogates when patients are incapacitated."

The leaders of the LaCrosse end-of-life health care projects developed a curriculum known as *Respecting Choices.* Their work in this area over the past 20 years has lead them to the conclusion that a staged approach to choices about end-of-life health care is most effective. First Step: Adult signs Living Will Declaration and Durable Power of Attorney for Health Care. Next Step: As adult ages, agent and family members become more involved and are prepared to act. (iii) Last Step: POLST paradigm implemented.

C. A Nationwide Movement. There is now a nationwide movement focusing on improving the end-of-life health care process. Approximately one quarter of the states have implemented POLST and most, if not all, of the other states are considering it. The forms used in the states are known by various names, including MOST (Medical Orders for Scope of Treatment) or MOLST (Medical Orders for Life–Sustaining Treatment) or POST (Physician Orders for Scope of Treatment).

D. The National POLST Paradigm Task Force. This Task Force has been created to provide information and guidance to the organizations that are pursuing the process of implementing POLST in their various states. The Task Force was convened by the Center for Ethics in Health Care at Oregon Health & Science University. Each state with an *endorsed* program provides one member to serve on the Board of Directors. The Task Force includes committees that consist of members from both endorsed and developing POLST programs.

III. State Statutes

A. Approaches to Authorization. Generally speaking, the states that are using POLST to date have used many different approaches to introduce POLST into their end-of-life health care framework. In some states, such as Oregon, there is no legislation adopting POLST. Rather, it has been adopted by clinical consensus and/or administrative regulation. In other states, some form of legislation has been passed. The legislation varies from authorizing the health department to establish the procedures for implementing POLST in the state to more detailed legislation that creates uniform procedures, and includes patient protections and provider immunity.

B. Required Signatures on Form. Because a POLST form is a medical order, it requires a clinician's signature. Some states have decided that only a physician may sign the form, while others permit nurse practitioners and physician assistants to sign. All states except three (Minnesota, New York, Oregon) require the patient's signature on the form.

C. Surrogate Decision–Making. All the states that are using POLST allow a surrogate decision-maker to sign a POLST form on behalf of a patient if the patient is no longer able to make his or her own health care decisions. Surrogate decision-making is not governed by POLST legislation in particular; it is governed by the broader body of state statutes and common law that addresses health care decision-making.

D. Immunity and Enforceability. The states with POLST generally offer immunity to institutions and clinicians for complying with POLST orders and procedures. They do not mandate completion of POLST forms by patients. In most cases, health care providers are required to comply with a POLST form if a patient has decided to sign one.

IV. Opposition to POLST

A. Opening the Door to Euthanasia. Some opponents state that POLST authorizes euthanasia.

B. Protection of Persons with Disabilities. Opponents have argued that third parties may use the POLST paradigm to euthanize vulnerable individuals. Disability advocacy groups are very concerned about this issue. Thus, protections are needed to ensure appropriate decision-making by surrogates. The State of New York, for example, has a checklist for completion on behalf of patients with developmental disabilities, minors, and patients in mental health facilities.

C. Confusion about POLST and Advance Directives. Education of physicians, patients and the general public is needed because the differences between POLST and advance directives are not clearly understood.

D. Resistance to New Standard of Care. Institutional protocols are very difficult to change; there tends to be resistance to any change in the standard of care.

E. Difficulty in Changing Medical Orders. Opponents have argued that people do not fully understand that a POLST form is an actionable medical order and that it is not easy to change such an order.

F. Fear. Some opponents are afraid of POLST simply because of who supports it. For example, it has been referred to as the document of choice of The Hemlock Society.

G. Non-Physician Involvement. Some object to the fact that a nurse, physician's assistant, or trained facilitator is the person who actually has the conversation with the patient about end-of-life health care, with the result that a physician could sign a POLST form without actually talking with the patient about it. Others are grateful that trained facilitators are actually talking about end-of-life with patients, because they argue that physicians historically have not devoted enough time and effort to these discussions.

H. Confusion About Whose Orders Hospital Must Implement. Much debate has occurred over the issue of whether a hospital physician is bound by a POLST form that is signed by a physician who is not credentialed by the hospital. Some opponents state that persons who sign POLST forms are pressured to refuse treatment; other people argue that most of the pressure is coming from the opposite direction, *i.e.,* that the default position is that treatment will be given. A patient must take action to opt out.

J. Debate in Catholic Literature. POLST is being used in some Catholic health care facilities. Nonetheless, there is a debate occurring among some Catholic leaders in the health care industry about POLST's appropriateness. The primary arguments against POLST are that (i) a patient does not have to be in a terminal condition for life-sustaining treatment to be withdrawn and, therefore, without actually using the term "euthanasia," POLST authorizes euthanasia; (ii) too many forms are not properly signed (in some instances, no patient signature is required on the forms and in some instances the signature of the physician who is actually treating the patient when POLST is implemented is not required); (iii) trained non-physician facilitators are implementing POLST and they do not have the expertise and personal knowledge of physicians; and (iv) POLST's check-the-box format is not appropriate for complex decision-making. The arguments by Catholic health care leaders in support of POLST are that (i) Catholic tradition and teaching requires a person to use ordinary means to sustain his or her life, but not extraordinary means, and this is true regardless of whether the person is terminally ill; (ii) objections to POLST tend to ignore the fact that the actual POLST form is the end-point in a process that involves ongoing discussions with a patient, and it's the *discussions* that are critical from a Catholic moral perspective; and (iii) there is nothing in the POLST paradigm itself that is contrary to church teaching; rather, how POLST is handled with a particular patient could be problematic, but that is true of every patient decision and every medical order.

LOCATE

Find the statutory authority, if any, in your state for POLST. How does the statute operate? Is there a statutory form? If not, locate a form which is generally used in your state.

NOTES & QUESTIONS

1. What is your opinion of POLST? Do you think these orders are an effective way to carry out your client's intent or is it just a step toward legalized euthanasia?

2. For more information on POLST, see http://www.ohsu.edu/polst/index.htm.

D. ASSISTED SUICIDE

Assisted suicide arises when the person committing suicide needs help in procuring the means to commit the act such as a weapon, drugs, or Dr. Jack Kevorkian's "suicide machine." The person, however, self-administers the lethal agent by pulling the trigger, swallowing the pills, turning on the gas, or the like. If a doctor assists the person in procuring the fatal drugs, the term *physician assisted suicide* is often used. Assisted suicide in general is sometimes called *passive euthanasia* because the euthanatizer merely supplies the means of death rather than directly causing the death. Assisted suicide can be contrasted with *voluntary euthanasia* in which the euthanatizer actually kills the person at that person's request. The term *involuntary euthanasia* is reserved for cases where the euthanatizer kills a person out of reasons of mercy but where the person did not specifically request to be killed.

THE OREGON DEATH WITH DIGNITY ACT

§ 127.800. § 1.01. Definitions.

The following words and phrases, whenever used in ORS 127.800 to 127.897, shall have the following meanings:

(1) "Adult" means an individual who is 18 years of age or older.

(2) "Attending physician" means the physician who has primary responsibility for the care of the patient and treatment of the patient's terminal disease.

(3) "Capable" means that in the opinion of a court or in the opinion of the patient's attending physician or consulting physician, psychiatrist or psychologist, a patient has the ability to make and communicate health care decisions to health care providers, including communication through persons familiar with the patient's manner of communicating if those persons are available.

(4) "Consulting physician" means a physician who is qualified by specialty or experience to make a professional diagnosis and prognosis regarding the patient's disease.

(5) "Counseling" means one or more consultations as necessary between a state licensed psychiatrist or psychologist and a patient for the purpose of determining that the patient is capable and not suffering from a psychiatric or psychological disorder or depression causing impaired judgment.

(6) "Health care provider" means a person licensed, certified, or otherwise authorized or permitted by the law of this State to administer health care in the ordinary course of business or practice of a profession, and includes a health care facility.

(7) "Informed decision" means a decision by a qualified patient, to request and obtain a prescription to end his or her life in a humane and dignified manner, that is based on an appreciation of the relevant facts and after being fully informed by the attending physician of:

(a) His or her medical diagnosis;

(b) His or her prognosis;

(c) The potential risks associated with taking the medication to be prescribed;

(d) The probable result of taking the medication to be prescribed;

(e) The feasible alternatives, including, but not limited to, comfort care, hospice care and pain control.

(8) "Medically confirmed" means the medical opinion of the attending physician has been confirmed by a consulting physician who has examined the patient and the patient's relevant medical records.

(9) "Patient" means a person who is under the care of a physician.

(10) "Physician" means a doctor of medicine or osteopathy licensed to practice medicine by the Board of Medical Examiners for the State of Oregon.

(11) "Qualified patient" means a capable adult who is a resident of Oregon and has satisfied the requirements of ORS 127.800 to 127.897 in order to obtain a prescription for medication to end his or her life in a humane and dignified manner.

(12) "Terminal disease" means an incurable and irreversible disease that has been medically confirmed and will, within reasonable medical judgment, produce death within six (6) months.

§ 127.805. § 2.01. Who may initiate a written request for medication.

(1) An adult who is capable, is a resident of Oregon, and has been determined by the attending physician and consulting physician to be suffering from a terminal disease, and who has voluntarily expressed his

or her wish to die, may make a written request for medication for the purpose of ending his or her life in a humane and dignified manner in accordance with ORS 127.800 to 127.897.

(2) No person shall qualify under the provisions of ORS 127.800 to 127.897 solely because of age or disability.

§ 127.810. § 2.02. Form of the written request.

(1) A valid request for medication under ORS 127.800 to 127.897 shall be in substantially the form described in ORS 127.897, signed and dated by the patient and witnessed by at least two individuals who, in the presence of the patient, attest that to the best of their knowledge and belief the patient is capable, acting voluntarily, and is not being coerced to sign the request.

(2) One of the witnesses shall be a person who is not:

(a) A relative of the patient by blood, marriage or adoption;

(b) A person who at the time the request is signed would be entitled to any portion of the estate of the qualified patient upon death under any will or by operation of law; or

(c) An owner, operator or employee of a health care facility where the qualified patient is receiving medical treatment or is a resident.

(3) The patient's attending physician at the time the request is signed shall not be a witness.

(4) If the patient is a patient in a long term care facility at the time the written request is made, one of the witnesses shall be an individual designated by the facility and having the qualifications specified by the Department of Human Resources by rule.

§ 127.815. § 3.01. Responsibilities of the attending physician.

(1) The attending physician shall:

(a) Make the initial determination of whether a patient has a terminal disease, is capable, and has made the request voluntarily;

(b) Request that the patient demonstrate Oregon residency pursuant to ORS 127.860;

(c) To ensure that the patient is making an informed decision, inform the patient of:

(A) His or her medical diagnosis;

(B) His or her prognosis;

(C) The potential risks associated with taking the medication to be prescribed;

(D) The probable result of taking the medication to be prescribed; and

(E) The feasible alternatives, including, but not limited to, comfort care, hospice care and pain control;

(d) Refer the patient to a consulting physician for medical confirmation of the diagnosis, and for a determination that the patient is capable and acting voluntarily;

(e) Refer the patient for counseling if appropriate pursuant to ORS 127.825;

(f) Recommend that the patient notify next of kin;

(g) Counsel the patient about the importance of having another person present when the patient takes the medication prescribed pursuant to ORS 127.800 to 127.897 and of not taking the medication in a public place;

(h) Inform the patient that he or she has an opportunity to rescind the request at any time and in any manner, and offer the patient an opportunity to rescind at the end of the 15 day waiting period pursuant to ORS 127.840;

(i) Verify, immediately prior to writing the prescription for medication under ORS 127.800 to 127.897, that the patient is making an informed decision;

(j) Fulfill the medical record documentation requirements of ORS 127.855;

(k) Ensure that all appropriate steps are carried out in accordance with ORS 127.800 to 127.897 prior to writing a prescription for medication to enable a qualified patient to end his or her life in a humane and dignified manner; and

(*l*)(A) Dispense medications directly, including ancillary medications intended to facilitate the desired effect to minimize the patient's discomfort, provided the attending physician is registered as a dispensing physician with the Board of Medical Examiners, has a current Drug Enforcement Administration certificate and complies with any applicable administrative rule; or

(B) With the patient's written consent:

(i) Contact a pharmacist and inform the pharmacist of the prescription; and

(ii) Deliver the written prescription personally or by mail to the pharmacist, who will dispense the medications to either the patient, the attending physician or an expressly identified agent of the patient.

(2) Notwithstanding any other provision of law, the attending physician may sign the patient's death certificate.

§ 127.820. § 3.02. Consulting physician confirmation.

Before a patient is qualified under ORS 127.800 to 127.897, a consulting physician shall examine the patient and his or her relevant medical records and confirm, in writing, the attending physician's diagnosis that the patient is suffering from a terminal disease, and verify that the patient is capable, is acting voluntarily and has made an informed decision.

§ 127.825. § 3.03. Counseling referral.

If in the opinion of the attending physician or the consulting physician a patient may be suffering from a psychiatric or psychological disorder or depression causing impaired judgment, either physician shall refer the patient for counseling. No medication to end a patient's life in a humane and dignified manner shall be prescribed until the person performing the counseling determines that the patient is not suffering from a psychiatric or psychological disorder or depression causing impaired judgment.

§ 127.830. § 3.04. Informed decision.

No person shall receive a prescription for medication to end his or her life in a humane and dignified manner unless he or she has made an informed decision as defined in ORS 127.800 (7). Immediately prior to writing a prescription for medication under ORS 127.800 to 127.897, the attending physician shall verify that the patient is making an informed decision.

§ 127.835. § 3.05. Family notification.

The attending physician shall recommend that the patient notify the next of kin of his or her request for medication pursuant to ORS 127.800 to 127.897. A patient who declines or is unable to notify next of kin shall not have his or her request denied for that reason.

§ 127.840. § 3.06. Written and oral requests.

In order to receive a prescription for medication to end his or her life in a humane and dignified manner, a qualified patient shall have made an oral request and a written request, and reiterate the oral request to his or her attending physician no less than fifteen (15) days after making the initial oral request. At the time the qualified patient makes his or her second oral request, the attending physician shall offer the patient an opportunity to rescind the request.

§ 127.845. § 3.07. Right to rescind request.

A patient may rescind his or her request at any time and in any manner without regard to his or her mental state. No prescription for medication under ORS 127.800 to 127.897 may be written without the attending physician offering the qualified patient an opportunity to rescind the request.

§ 127.850. § 3.08. Waiting periods.

No less than fifteen (15) days shall elapse between the patient's initial oral request and the writing of a prescription under ORS 127.800 to

127.897. No less than 48 hours shall elapse between the patient's written request and the writing of a prescription under ORS 127.800 to 127.897.

§ 127.855. § 3.09. Medical record documentation requirements.

The following shall be documented or filed in the patient's medical record:

(1) All oral requests by a patient for medication to end his or her life in a humane and dignified manner;

(2) All written requests by a patient for medication to end his or her life in a humane and dignified manner;

(3) The attending physician's diagnosis and prognosis, determination that the patient is capable, acting voluntarily and has made an informed decision;

(4) The consulting physician's diagnosis and prognosis, and verification that the patient is capable, acting voluntarily and has made an informed decision;

(5) A report of the outcome and determinations made during counseling, if performed;

(6) The attending physician's offer to the patient to rescind his or her request at the time of the patient's second oral request pursuant to ORS 127.840; and

(7) A note by the attending physician indicating that all requirements under ORS 127.800 to 127.897 have been met and indicating the steps taken to carry out the request, including a notation of the medication prescribed.

§ 127.860. § 3.10. Residency requirement.

Only requests made by Oregon residents under ORS 127.800 to 127.897 shall be granted. Factors demonstrating Oregon residency include but are not limited to:

(1) Possession of an Oregon driver license;

(2) Registration to vote in Oregon;

(3) Evidence that the person owns or leases property in Oregon; or

(4) Filing of an Oregon tax return for the most recent tax year.

§ 127.865. § 3.11. Reporting requirements.

(1)(a) The Oregon Health Authority shall annually review a sample of records maintained pursuant to ORS 127.800 to 127.897.

(b) The authority shall require any health care provider upon dispensing medication pursuant to ORS 127.800 to 127.897 to file a copy of the dispensing record with the authority.

(2) The authority shall make rules to facilitate the collection of information regarding compliance with ORS 127.800 to 127.897. Except as

otherwise required by law, the information collected shall not be a public record and may not be made available for inspection by the public.

(3) The authority shall generate and make available to the public an annual statistical report of information collected under subsection (2) of this section.

§ 127.870. § 3.12. Effect on construction of wills, contracts and statutes.

(1) No provision in a contract, will or other agreement, whether written or oral, to the extent the provision would affect whether a person may make or rescind a request for medication to end his or her life in a humane and dignified manner, shall be valid.

(2) No obligation owing under any currently existing contract shall be conditioned or affected by the making or rescinding of a request, by a person, for medication to end his or her life in a humane and dignified manner.

§ 127.875. § 3.13. Insurance or annuity policies.

The sale, procurement, or issuance of any life, health, or accident insurance or annuity policy or the rate charged for any policy shall not be conditioned upon or affected by the making or rescinding of a request, by a person, for medication to end his or her life in a humane and dignified manner. Neither shall a qualified patient's act of ingesting medication to end his or her life in a humane and dignified manner have an effect upon a life, health, or accident insurance or annuity policy.

§ 127.880. § 3.14. Construction of Act.

Nothing in ORS 127.800 to 127.897 shall be construed to authorize a physician or any other person to end a patient's life by lethal injection, mercy killing or active euthanasia. Actions taken in accordance with ORS 127.800 to 127.897 shall not, for any purpose, constitute suicide, assisted suicide, mercy killing or homicide, under the law.

§ 127.885. § 4.01. Immunities in general.

Except as provided in ORS 127.890:

(1) No person shall be subject to civil or criminal liability or professional disciplinary action for participating in good faith compliance with ORS 127.800 to 127.897. This includes being present when a qualified patient takes the prescribed medication to end his or her life in a humane and dignified manner.

(2) No professional organization or association, or health care provider, may subject a person to censure, discipline, suspension, loss of license, loss of privileges, loss of membership or other penalty for participating or refusing to participate in good faith compliance with ORS 127.800 to 127.897.

(3) No request by a patient for or provision by an attending physician of medication in good faith compliance with the provisions of ORS 127.800 to 127.897 shall constitute neglect for any purpose of law or provide the sole basis for the appointment of a guardian or conservator.

(4) No health care provider shall be under any duty, whether by contract, by statute or by any other legal requirement to participate in the provision to a qualified patient of medication to end his or her life in a humane and dignified manner. If a health care provider is unable or unwilling to carry out a patient's request under ORS 127.800 to 127.897, and the patient transfers his or her care to a new health care provider, the prior health care provider shall transfer, upon request, a copy of the patient's relevant medical records to the new health care provider.

(5)(a) Notwithstanding any other provision of law, a health care provider may prohibit another health care provider from participating in ORS 127.800 to 127.897 on the premises of the prohibiting provider if the prohibiting provider has notified the health care provider of the prohibiting provider's policy regarding participating in ORS 127.800 to 127.897. Nothing in this paragraph prevents a health care provider from providing health care services to a patient that do not constitute participation in ORS 127.800 to 127.897.

(b) Notwithstanding the provisions of subsections (1) to (4) of this section, a health care provider may subject another health care provider to the sanctions stated in this paragraph if the sanctioning health care provider has notified the sanctioned provider prior to participation in ORS 127.800 to 127.897 that it prohibits participation in ORS 127.800 to 127.897:

(A) Loss of privileges, loss of membership or other sanction provided pursuant to the medical staff bylaws, policies and procedures of the sanctioning health care provider if the sanctioned provider is a member of the sanctioning provider's medical staff and participates in ORS 127.800 to 127.897 while on the health care facility premises, as defined in ORS 442.015, of the sanctioning health care provider, but not including the private medical office of a physician or other provider;

(B) Termination of lease or other property contract or other nonmonetary remedies provided by lease contract, not including loss or restriction of medical staff privileges or exclusion from a provider panel, if the sanctioned provider participates in ORS 127.800 to 127.897 while on the premises of the sanctioning health care provider or on property that is owned by or under the direct control of the sanctioning health care provider; or

(C) Termination of contract or other nonmonetary remedies provided by contract if the sanctioned provider participates in ORS 127.800 to 127.897 while acting in the course and scope of the sanctioned provider's capacity as an employee or independent contractor of the sanctioning health care provider. Nothing in this subparagraph shall be construed to prevent:

(i) A health care provider from participating in ORS 127.800 to 127.897 while acting outside the course and scope of the provider's capacity as an employee or independent contractor; or

(ii) A patient from contracting with his or her attending physician and consulting physician to act outside the course and scope of the provider's capacity as an employee or independent contractor of the sanctioning health care provider.

(c) A health care provider that imposes sanctions pursuant to paragraph (b) of this subsection must follow all due process and other procedures the sanctioning health care provider may have that are related to the imposition of sanctions on another health care provider.

(d) For purposes of this subsection:

(A) "Notify" means a separate statement in writing to the health care provider specifically informing the health care provider prior to the provider's participation in ORS 127.800 to 127.897 of the sanctioning health care provider's policy about participation in activities covered by ORS 127.800 to 127.897.

(B) "Participate in ORS 127.800 to 127.897" means to perform the duties of an attending physician pursuant to ORS 127.815, the consulting physician function pursuant to ORS 127.820 or the counseling function pursuant to ORS 127.825. "Participate in ORS 127.800 to 127.897" does not include:

(i) Making an initial determination that a patient has a terminal disease and informing the patient of the medical prognosis;

(ii) Providing information about the Oregon Death with Dignity Act to a patient upon the request of the patient;

(iii) Providing a patient, upon the request of the patient, with a referral to another physician; or

(iv) A patient contracting with his or her attending physician and consulting physician to act outside of the course and scope of the provider's capacity as an employee or independent contractor of the sanctioning health care provider.

(6) Suspension or termination of staff membership or privileges under subsection (5) of this section is not reportable under ORS 441.820. Action taken pursuant to ORS 127.810, 127.815, 127.820 or 127.825 shall

not be the sole basis for a report of unprofessional or dishonorable conduct under ORS 677.415 (3), (4), (5) or (6).

(7) No provision of ORS 127.800 to 127.897 shall be construed to allow a lower standard of care for patients in the community where the patient is treated or a similar community.

§ 127.890. § 4.02. Liabilities.

(1) A person who without authorization of the patient willfully alters or forges a request for medication or conceals or destroys a rescission of that request with the intent or effect of causing the patient's death shall be guilty of a Class A felony.

(2) A person who coerces or exerts undue influence on a patient to request medication for the purpose of ending the patient's life, or to destroy a rescission of such a request, shall be guilty of a Class A felony.

(3) Nothing in ORS 127.800 to 127.897 limits further liability for civil damages resulting from other negligent conduct or intentional misconduct by any person.

(4) The penalties in ORS 127.800 to 127.897 do not preclude criminal penalties applicable under other law for conduct which is inconsistent with the provisions of ORS 127.800 to 127.897.

§ 127.892. Claims by governmental entity for costs incurred.

Any governmental entity that incurs costs resulting from a person terminating his or her life pursuant to the provisions of ORS 127.800 to 127.897 in a public place shall have a claim against the estate of the person to recover such costs and reasonable attorney fees related to enforcing the claim.

§ 127.895. § 5.01. Severability.

Any section of ORS 127.800 to 127.897 being held invalid as to any person or circumstance shall not affect the application of any other section of ORS 127.800 to 127.897 which can be given full effect without the invalid section or application.

§ 127.897. § 6.01. Form of the request.

A request for a medication as authorized by ORS 127.800 to 127.897 shall be in substantially the following form:

REQUEST FOR MEDICATION TO END MY LIFE IN A HUMANE AND DIGNIFIED MANNER

I, _______, am an adult of sound mind.

I am suffering from _______, which my attending physician has determined is a terminal disease and which has been medically confirmed by a consulting physician.

I have been fully informed of my diagnosis, prognosis, the nature of medication to be prescribed and potential associated risks, the expected result, and the feasible alternatives including comfort care, hospice care and pain control.

I request that my attending physician prescribe medication that will end my life in a humane and dignified manner.

Initial One:

___ I have informed my family of my decision and taken their opinions into consideration.

___ I have decided not to inform my family of my decision.

___ I have no family to inform of my decision.

I understand that I have the right to rescind this request at any time.

I understand the full import of this request and I expect to die when I take the medication to be prescribed. I further understand that although most deaths occur within three hours, my death may take longer and my physician has counseled me about this possibility.

I make this request voluntarily and without reservation, and I accept full moral responsibility for my actions.

Signed: ______________________________

Dated: ______________________________

DECLARATION OF WITNESSES

We declare that the person signing this request:

(a) Is personally known to us or has provided proof of identity;

(b) Signed this request in our presence;

(c) Appears to be of sound mind and not under duress, fraud or undue influence;

(d) Is not a patient for whom either of us is attending physician.

______________ Witness 1/Date

______________ Witness 2/Date

NOTE: One witness shall not be a relative (by blood, marriage or adoption) of the person signing this request, shall not be entitled to any portion of the person's estate upon death and shall not own, operate or be employed at a health care facility where the person is a patient or resident. If the patient is an inpatient at a health care facility, one of the witnesses shall be an individual designated by the facility.

THANE JOSEF MESSINGER, A GENTLE AND EASY DEATH: FROM ANCIENT GREECE TO BEYOND CRUZAN TOWARD A REASONED LEGAL RESPONSE TO THE SOCIETAL DILEMMA OF EUTHANASIA*

71 DENV. U. L. REV. 175, 175–78 (1993).

* * * The subject of euthanasia has presented societies throughout history with a deeply troubling dilemma of defining the meaning of death—and the value of life. Advocates on both sides are pointed in their criticisms, with little common ground for compromise. The law often skirts the issues involved, primarily because society is unable to deal with the explosive problems associated with euthanasia. Euthanasia, however, should not be viewed through the narrow lens of our own society or time. It is important to understand the historical and philosophical developments surrounding euthanasia if we are to strive to devise an acceptable legal structure to resolve these difficult problems.

Those opposed reject euthanasia on the ground that it places in jeopardy a fundamental inviolability of human life. From Biblical proscriptions to "natural" law, human life is considered sacrosanct, and efforts to destroy even a fraction of our time on earth are a direct violation of God's will. Suffering is itself seen as a positive influence. The objection has two levels: first, rejecting the possibility that life can have negative value, and second, rejecting the power of man to choose for himself to end his own life. Further, opponents point to a parade of horribles, which they fear will inexorably follow any loosening of proscriptions against killing. One example often cited is the Nazi German debacle, during which millions died—hundreds of thousands under the auspices of "euthanasia" programs. Opponents further argue that any legitimization of euthanasia will erode medical and societal values and will deprive the individual of the will to live.

Against these contentions, proponents of euthanasia cite examples of human suffering that have become increasingly frequent as medical technologies improve. Medicine can now save many who, arguably, should not be saved; some, in essence, outlive their own deaths. The noble goal of medicine has proved a double-edged sword: in the race to preserve life, suffering is sometimes prolonged instead. Those in favor of euthanasia must necessarily reject—or ignore—the theological arguments regarding the sanctity of life. Sanctity itself is, by definition, absolute. This is an uncomfortable position for many, but an unavoidable one when faced with the very real problems of miserable deaths.

As with other issues that are inextricably linked to disparate moral, medical, philosophical, theological, and legal considerations, euthanasia

* Reprinted with permission of the Denver University Law Review.

provides little room for agreement. Each side in the debate enters the arena with incompatible presuppositions; either one accepts theological precepts—and all that that implies—or one does not. Progress in the form of reasoned, balanced public debate and policies are unlikely. In this version of the zero sum game, one side will be the loser. Unfortunately, in this debate the loser won't be able to easily live—or die—with the loss.

NOTES AND QUESTIONS

1. At least three states have legalized physician assisted suicides; Oregon with the Oregon Death with Dignity Act, Washington with the 2009 Washington Death with Dignity Act, and Montana through case law. See *Baxter v. Montana*, 224 P.3d 1211 (Mont. 2009).

2. Do you think the Oregon statute contains sufficient safeguards? Assorted physicians, patients, and residential care facilities challenged the law on the grounds that it violated the Religious Freedom Act, the Americans with Disabilities Act, due process, and equal protection. The district court began by issuing a preliminary injunction preventing the Act from taking effect. Lee v. State of Oregon, 869 F.Supp. 1491 (D. Or. 1994). The next year, the court granted summary judgment on the equal protection claim and issued a permanent injunction against the Act's enforcement. Lee v. State of Oregon, 891 F.Supp. 1439 (D. Or. 1995) (declaratory judgment and permanent injunction); Lee v. State of Oregon, 891 F.Supp. 1429 (D. Or. 1995) (equal protection opinion). "Essentially, the district court found that the Act violated the Equal Protection Clause because it provided insufficient safeguards to prevent against an incompetent (i.e., depressed) terminally-ill adult from committing suicide, thereby irrationally depriving terminally-ill adults of safeguards against suicide provided to adults who are not terminally ill."[9]

On appeal, however, the court held that the federal courts did not have jurisdiction to entertain the plaintiffs' claims. Accordingly, the district court's decision was vacated and the case remanded with instructions to dismiss plaintiffs' complaint. Lee v. Oregon, 107 F.3d 1382 (9th Cir. 1997).

3. In 2001, United States Attorney General John Ashcroft determined that assisted suicide was not a legitimate medical practice and thus doctors who prescribe the deadly drugs would be in violation of the Controlled Substances Act (CSA). In Oregon v. Ashcroft, 368 F.3d 1118 (9th Cir. 2004), the court held that this attempt to hold physicians criminally responsible if they help terminally ill patients commit suicide exceeded Ashcroft's authority under the Controlled Substances Act (CSA). The court stated, "To be perfectly clear, we take no position on the merits or morality of physician assisted suicide. We express no opinion on whether the practice is inconsistent with the public interest or constitutes illegitimate medical care. This case is simply about who gets to decide. All parties agree that the question before us is whether Congress authorized the Attorney General to determine that physician assisted suicide violates the CSA. We hold that the Attorney General lacked Congress' requisite authorization. The Ashcroft Directive violates the 'clear statement' rule, contradicts the plain language of the CSA, and contra-

9. Lee v. Oregon, 107 F.3d 1382, 1386 (9th Cir. 1997).

venes the express intent of Congress." Id. at 1123. The Supreme Court of the United States affirmed the Ninth Circuit's holding in *Gonzales v. Oregon,* 546 U.S. 243, 126 S.Ct. 904, 163 L.Ed.2d 748 (2006).

4. The first incident of a person using the Oregon statute was documented in March 1998 with fifteen additional people following suit by the end of the year. The statistics for subsequent years are as follows:

Year	Deaths by Assisted Suicide in Oregon
1999	27
2000	27
2001	21
2002	38
2003	42
2004	37
2005	38
2006	46
2007	49
2008	60
2009	59
2010	65 (plus up to 15 more who were unaccounted for as of January 2011).

5. What is your opinion regarding physician-assisted suicide? Do you think the option should be available? Or do you agree with Dr. Gardner who says, "If you, as a terminally ill patient, wish to commit suicide, please have the courage and decency to do so by yourself. Why expose your treating physician to felony indictments in this world and to perdition's flames in the next." J. Francis Gardner, *Assisted Suicide Not So Dignified*, SAN ANTONIO EXPRESS-NEWS, Nov. 24, 2001.

6. All states except Oregon, Washington, and Montana have statutes that prohibit assisted suicide. Oregon makes it a crime for a person to provide another with a substance or object for the purpose of assisting in a suicide unless the person is assisting in a physician assisted suicide. See 2011 Ore. Laws. Ch. 552. In states that have statutes prohibiting assisted suicide, a person who successfully assists a suicide may be criminally liable for murder, manslaughter, or the specific crime of aiding a suicide. Are these statutes constitutional?

WASHINGTON v. GLUCKSBERG

Supreme Court of the United States, 1997.
521 U.S. 702, 117 S.Ct. 2258, 138 L.Ed.2d 772.

CHIEF JUSTICE REHNQUIST delivered the opinion of the Court.

The question presented in this case is whether Washington's prohibition against "caus[ing]" or "aid[ing]" a suicide offends the Fourteenth Amendment to the United States Constitution. We hold that it does not.

It has always been a crime to assist a suicide in the State of Washington. In 1854, Washington's first Territorial Legislature outlawed "assisting another in the commission of self-murder." Today, Washington law provides: "A person is guilty of promoting a suicide attempt when he knowingly causes or aids another person to attempt suicide." Wash. Rev.Code 9A.36.060(1) (1994). "Promoting a suicide attempt" is a felony, punishable by up to five years' imprisonment and up to a $10,000 fine. §§ 9A.36.060(2) and 9A.20.021(1)(c). At the same time, Washington's Natural Death Act, enacted in 1979, states that the "withholding or withdrawal of life-sustaining treatment" at a patient's direction "shall not, for any purpose, constitute a suicide." Wash. Rev.Code § 70.122.070(1).

Petitioners in this case are the State of Washington and its Attorney General. Respondents Harold Glucksberg, M. D., Abigail Halperin, M. D., Thomas A. Preston, M. D., and Peter Shalit, M. D., are physicians who practice in Washington. These doctors occasionally treat terminally ill, suffering patients, and declare that they would assist these patients in ending their lives if not for Washington's assisted-suicide ban. In January 1994, respondents, along with three gravely ill, pseudonymous plaintiffs who have since died and Compassion in Dying, a nonprofit organization that counsels people considering physician-assisted suicide, sued in the United States District Court, seeking a declaration that Wash Rev.Code 9A.36.060(1) (1994) is, on its face, unconstitutional. Compassion in Dying v. Washington, 850 F.Supp. 1454, 1459 (W.D.Wash.1994).

The plaintiffs asserted "the existence of a liberty interest protected by the Fourteenth Amendment which extends to a personal choice by a mentally competent, terminally ill adult to commit physician-assisted suicide." Id., at 1459. Relying primarily on Planned Parenthood v. Casey, 505 U.S. 833, 112 S.Ct. 2791, 120 L.Ed.2d 674 (1992), and Cruzan v. Director, Missouri Dept. of Health, 497 U.S. 261, 110 S.Ct. 2841, 111 L.Ed.2d 224 (1990), the District Court agreed, 850 F.Supp., at 1459–1462, and concluded that Washington's assisted-suicide ban is unconstitutional because it "places an undue burden on the exercise of [that] constitutionally protected liberty interest." Id., at 1465. The District Court also decided that the Washington statute violated the Equal Protection Clause's requirement that " 'all persons similarly situated ... be treated alike.' " Id., at 1466 (quoting Cleburne v. Cleburne Living Center, Inc., 473 U.S. 432, 439, 105 S.Ct. 3249, 3253–3254, 87 L.Ed.2d 313 (1985)).

A panel of the Court of Appeals for the Ninth Circuit reversed, emphasizing that "[i]n the two hundred and five years of our existence no constitutional right to aid in killing oneself has ever been asserted and upheld by a court of final jurisdiction." Compassion in Dying v. Washington, 49 F.3d 586, 591 (1995). The Ninth Circuit reheard the case en banc, reversed the panel's decision, and affirmed the District Court. Compassion in Dying v. Washington, 79 F.3d 790, 798 (1996). Like the District Court, the en banc Court of Appeals emphasized our Casey and Cruzan decisions. 79 F.3d, at 813–816. The court also discussed what it described as "historical" and "current societal attitudes" toward suicide and assisted suicide, id., at 806–812, and concluded that "the Constitution encompasses a due process liberty interest in controlling the time and manner of one's death—that there is, in short, a constitutionally-recognized 'right to die.' " Id., at 816. After "[w]eighing and then balancing" this interest against Washington's various interests, the court held that the State's assisted-suicide ban was unconstitutional "as applied to terminally ill competent adults who wish to hasten their deaths with medication prescribed by their physicians." Id., at 836, 837. The court did not reach the District Court's equal-protection holding. Id., at 838. We granted certiorari, 519 U.S. ___, 117 S.Ct. 37, 135 L.Ed.2d 1128 (1996), and now reverse.

I

We begin, as we do in all due-process cases, by examining our Nation's history, legal traditions, and practices. * * * In almost every State—indeed, in almost every western democracy—it is a crime to assist a suicide. The States' assisted-suicide bans are not innovations. Rather, they are longstanding expressions of the States' commitment to the protection and preservation of all human life. Cruzan, 497 U.S., at 280, 110 S.Ct., at 2852 ("[T]he States—indeed, all civilized nations—demonstrate their commitment to life by treating homicide as a serious crime. Moreover, the majority of States in this country have laws imposing criminal penalties on one who assists another to commit suicide"); see Stanford v. Kentucky, 492 U.S. 361, 373, 109 S.Ct. 2969, 2977, 106 L.Ed.2d 306 (1989) ("[T]he primary and most reliable indication of [a national] consensus is ... the pattern of enacted laws"). Indeed, opposition to and condemnation of suicide—and, therefore, of assisting suicide—are consistent and enduring themes of our philosophical, legal, and cultural heritages. See generally, Marzen, O'Dowd, Crone & Balch, Suicide: A Constitutional Right?, 24 Duquesne L.Rev. 1, 17–56 (1985) (hereinafter Marzen); New York State Task Force on Life and the Law, When Death is Sought: Assisted Suicide and Euthanasia in the Medical Context 77–82 (May 1994) (hereinafter New York Task Force).

More specifically, for over 700 years, the Anglo–American common-law tradition has punished or otherwise disapproved of both suicide and assisting suicide. Cruzan, 497 U.S., at 294–295, 110 S.Ct., at 2859–2860 (SCALIA, J., concurring). In the 13th century, Henry de Bracton, one of the first legal-treatise writers, observed that "[j]ust as a man may commit felony by slaying another so may he do so by slaying himself." 2 Bracton on Laws and Customs of England 423 (f.150) (G. Woodbine ed., S. Thorne transl., 1968). The real and personal property of one who killed himself to avoid conviction and punishment for a crime were forfeit to the king; however, thought Bracton, "if a man slays himself in weariness of life or because he is unwilling to endure further bodily pain ... [only] his movable goods [were] confiscated." Id., at 423–424 (f.150). Thus, "[t]he principle that suicide of a sane person, for whatever reason, was a punishable felony was ... introduced into English common law." Centuries later, Sir William Blackstone, whose Commentaries on the Laws of England not only provided a definitive summary of the common law but was also a primary legal authority for 18th and 19th century American lawyers, referred to suicide as "self-murder" and "the pretended heroism, but real cowardice, of the Stoic philosophers, who destroyed themselves to avoid those ills which they had not the fortitude to endure.... " 4 W. Blackstone, Commentaries *189. Blackstone emphasized that "the law has ... ranked [suicide] among the highest crimes," ibid, although, anticipating later developments, he conceded that the harsh and shameful punishments imposed for suicide "borde[r] a little upon severity." Id., at *190.

For the most part, the early American colonies adopted the common-law approach. For example, the legislators of the Providence Plantations, which would later become Rhode Island, declared, in 1647, that "[s]elf-murder is by all agreed to be the most unnatural, and it is by this present Assembly declared, to be that, wherein he that doth it, kills himself out of a premeditated hatred against his own life or other humor: ... his goods and chattels are the king's custom, but not his debts nor lands; but in case he be an infant, a lunatic, mad or distracted man, he forfeits nothing." The Earliest Acts and Laws of the Colony of Rhode Island and Providence Plantations 1647–1719, p. 19 (J. Cushing ed.1977). Virginia also required ignominious burial for suicides, and their estates were forfeit to the crown. A. Scott, Criminal Law in Colonial Virginia 108, and n. 93, 198, and n. 15 (1930).

Over time, however, the American colonies abolished these harsh common-law penalties. William Penn abandoned the criminal-forfeiture sanction in Pennsylvania in 1701, and the other colonies (and later, the other States) eventually followed this example. * * * Zephaniah Swift, who would later become Chief Justice of Connecticut, wrote in 1796 that

> "[t]here can be no act more contemptible, than to attempt to punish an offender for a crime, by exercising a mean act of revenge upon lifeless clay, that is insensible of the punishment. There can be no greater cruelty, than the inflicting [of] a punishment, as the forfeiture of goods, which must fall solely on the innocent offspring of the offender.... [Suicide] is so abhorrent to the feelings of mankind, and that strong love of life which is implanted in the human heart, that it cannot be so frequently committed, as to become dangerous to society. There can of course be no necessity of any punishment." 2 Z. Swift, A System of the Laws of the State of Connecticut 304 (1796).

This statement makes it clear, however, that the movement away from the common law's harsh sanctions did not represent an acceptance of suicide; rather, as Chief Justice Swift observed, this change reflected the growing consensus that it was unfair to punish the suicide's family for his wrongdoing. Cruzan, supra, at 294, 110 S.Ct., at 2859 (SCALIA, J., concurring). Nonetheless, although States moved away from Blackstone's treatment of suicide, courts continued to condemn it as a grave public wrong. * * *

That suicide remained a grievous, though nonfelonious, wrong is confirmed by the fact that colonial and early state legislatures and courts did not retreat from prohibiting assisting suicide. Swift, in his early 19th century treatise on the laws of Connecticut, stated that "[i]f one counsels another to commit suicide, and the other by reason of the advice kills himself, the advisor is guilty of murder as principal." 2 Z. Swift, A Digest of the Laws of the State of Connecticut 270 (1823). * * * And the prohibitions against assisting suicide never contained exceptions for those who were near death. Rather, "[t]he life of those to whom life ha[d] become a burden—of those who [were] hopelessly diseased or fatally wounded—nay, even the lives of criminals condemned to death, [were] under the protection of law, equally as the lives of those who [were] in the full tide of life's enjoyment, and anxious to continue to live." Blackburn v. State, 23 Ohio St. 146, 163 (1872); see Bowen, supra, at 360 (prisoner who persuaded another to commit suicide could be tried for murder, even though victim was scheduled shortly to be executed).

The earliest American statute explicitly to outlaw assisting suicide was enacted in New York in 1828, Act of Dec. 10, 1828, ch. 20, § 4, 1828 N.Y. Laws 19 (codified at 2 N.Y.Rev.Stat. pt. 4, ch. 1, tit. 2, art. 1, § 7, p. 661 (1829)), and many of the new States and Territories followed New York's example. Marzen 73–74. Between 1857 and 1865, a New York commission led by Dudley Field drafted a criminal code that prohibited "aiding" a suicide and, specifically, "furnish[ing] another person with any deadly weapon or poisonous drug, knowing that such person intends to use such weapon or drug in taking his own life." Id., at 76–77. By the time the Fourteenth Amendment was ratified, it was a crime in most States to assist a suicide. See Cruzan, supra, at 294–295, 110 S.Ct., at 2859–2860 (SCALIA, J., concurring). The Field Penal Code was adopted in the Dakota Territory in 1877, in New York in 1881, and its language served as a model for several other western States' statutes in the late 19th and early 20th centuries. Marzen 76–77, 205–206, 212–213. California, for example, codified its assisted-suicide prohibition in 1874, using language similar to the Field Code's. In this century, the Model Penal Code also prohibited "aiding" suicide, prompting many States to enact or revise their assisted-suicide bans. The Code's drafters observed that "the interests in the sanctity of life that are represented by the criminal homicide laws are threatened by one who expresses a willingness to participate in taking the life of another, even though the act may be accomplished with the consent, or at the request, of the suicide victim." American Law Institute, Model Penal Code § 210.5, Comment 5, p. 100 (Official Draft and Revised Comments 1980).

Though deeply rooted, the States' assisted-suicide bans have in recent years been reexamined and, generally, reaffirmed. Because of advances in medicine and technology, Americans today are increasingly likely to die in institutions, from chronic illnesses. President's Comm'n for the Study of Ethical Problems in Medicine and Biomedical and Behavioral Research, Deciding to Forego Life–Sustaining Treatment 16–18 (1983). Public concern and democratic action are therefore sharply focused on how best to protect dignity and independence at the end of life, with the result that there have been many significant changes in state laws and in the attitudes these laws reflect. Many States, for example, now permit "living wills," surrogate health-care decisionmaking, and the withdrawal or refusal of life-sustaining medical treatment. * * * At the same time, however, voters and legislators continue for the most part to reaffirm their States' prohibitions on assisting suicide.

The Washington statute at issue in this case, Wash. Rev.Code § 9A.36.060 (1994), was enacted in 1975 as part of a revision of that State's criminal code. Four years later, Washington passed its Natural Death Act, which specifically stated that the "withholding or withdrawal of life-sustaining treatment ... shall not, for any purpose, constitute a suicide" and that "[n]othing in this chapter shall be construed to condone, authorize, or approve mercy killing.... " Natural Death Act, 1979 Wash. Laws, ch. 112, §§ 8(1), p. 11 (codified at Wash. Rev.Code §§ 70.122.070(1), 70.122.100 (1994)). In 1991, Washington voters rejected a ballot initiative which, had it passed, would have permitted a form of physician-assisted suicide. Washington then added a provision to the Natural Death Act expressly excluding physician-assisted suicide. 1992 Wash. Laws, ch. 98, § 10; Wash. Rev.Code § 70.122.100 (1994).

California voters rejected an assisted-suicide initiative similar to Washington's in 1993. On the other hand, in 1994, voters in Oregon enacted, also through ballot initiative, that State's "Death With Dignity Act," which legalized physician-assisted suicide for competent, terminally ill adults. Since the Oregon vote, many proposals to legalize assisted-suicide have been and continue to be introduced in the States' legislatures, but none has been enacted. And just last year, Iowa and Rhode Island joined the overwhelming majority of States explicitly prohibiting assisted suicide. See Iowa Code Ann. §§ 707A.2, 707A.3 (Supp.1997); R.I. Gen. Laws §§ 11–60–1, 11–60–3 (Supp.1996). Also, on April 30, 1997, President Clinton signed the Federal Assisted Suicide Funding Restriction Act of 1997, which prohibits the use of federal funds in support of physician-assisted suicide. Pub.L. 105–12, 111 Stat. 23 (codified at 42 U.S.C. § 14401 et seq.).

Thus, the States are currently engaged in serious, thoughtful examinations of physician-assisted suicide and other similar issues. For example, New York State's Task Force on Life and the Law—an ongoing, blue-ribbon commission composed of doctors, ethicists, lawyers, religious leaders, and interested laymen—was convened in 1984 and commissioned with "a broad mandate to recommend public policy on issues raised by medical advances." New York Task Force vii. Over the past decade, the Task Force has recommended laws relating to end-of-life decisions, surrogate pregnancy, and organ donation. Id., at 118–119. After studying physician-assisted suicide, however, the Task Force unanimously concluded that "[l]egalizing assisted suicide and euthanasia would pose profound risks to many individuals who are ill and vulnerable.... [T]he potential dangers of this dramatic change in public policy would outweigh any benefit that might be achieved." Id., at 120.

Attitudes toward suicide itself have changed since Bracton, but our laws have consistently condemned, and continue to prohibit, assisting suicide. Despite changes in medical technology and notwithstanding an increased emphasis on the importance of end-of-life decisionmaking, we have not retreated from this prohibition. Against this backdrop of history, tradition, and practice, we now turn to respondents' constitutional claim.

II

The Due Process Clause guarantees more than fair process, and the "liberty" it protects includes more than the absence of physical restraint. * * * The Clause also provides heightened protection against government interference with certain fundamental rights and liberty interests. * * * In a long line of cases, we have held that, in addition to the specific freedoms protected by the Bill of Rights, the "liberty" specially protected by the Due Process Clause includes the rights to marry, Loving v. Virginia, 388 U.S. 1, 87 S.Ct. 1817, 18 L.Ed.2d 1010 (1967); to have children, Skinner v. Oklahoma ex rel. Williamson, 316 U.S. 535, 62 S.Ct. 1110, 86 L.Ed. 1655 (1942); to direct the education and upbringing of one's children, Meyer v. Nebraska, 262 U.S. 390, 43 S.Ct. 625, 67 L.Ed. 1042 (1923); Pierce v. Society of Sisters, 268 U.S. 510, 45 S.Ct. 571, 69 L.Ed. 1070 (1925); to marital privacy, Griswold v. Connecticut, 381 U.S. 479, 85 S.Ct. 1678, 14 L.Ed.2d 510 (1965); to use contraception, ibid; Eisenstadt v. Baird, 405 U.S. 438, 92 S.Ct. 1029, 31 L.Ed.2d 349 (1972); to bodily integrity, Rochin v. California, 342 U.S. 165, 72 S.Ct. 205, 96 L.Ed. 183 (1952), and to abortion, Casey, supra. We have also assumed, and strongly suggested, that the Due Process Clause protects the traditional right to refuse unwanted lifesaving medical treatment. Cruzan, 497 U.S., at 278–279, 110 S.Ct., at 2851–2852.

But we "ha[ve] always been reluctant to expand the concept of substantive due process because guideposts for responsible decisionmaking in this unchartered area are scarce and open-ended." Collins, 503 U.S., at 125, 112 S.Ct., at 1068. By extending constitutional protection to an asserted right or liberty interest, we, to a great extent, place the matter outside the arena of public debate and legislative action. We must therefore "exercise the utmost care whenever we are asked to break new ground in this field," ibid, lest the liberty protected by the Due Process Clause be subtly transformed into the policy preferences of the members of this Court, Moore, 431 U.S., at 502, 97 S.Ct., at 1937 (plurality opinion).

Our established method of substantive-due-process analysis has two primary features: First, we have regularly observed that the Due Process Clause specially protects those fundamental rights and liberties which are, objectively, "deeply rooted in this Nation's history and tradition," * * * and "implicit in the concept of ordered liberty," such that "neither liberty nor justice would exist if they were sacrificed" * * *. Second, we have required in substantive-due-process cases a "careful description" of the asserted fundamental liberty interest. * * * Our Nation's history, legal traditions, and practices thus provide the crucial "guideposts for responsible decisionmaking," Collins, supra, at 125, 112 S.Ct., at 1068, that direct and restrain our exposition of the Due Process Clause. As we stated recently in Flores, the Fourteenth Amendment "forbids the government to infringe ... 'fundamental' liberty interests at all, no matter what process is provided, unless the infringement is narrowly tailored to serve a compelling state interest." 507 U.S., at 302, 113 S.Ct., at 1447.

Justice Souter, relying on Justice Harlan's dissenting opinion in Poe v. Ullman, would largely abandon this restrained methodology, and instead ask "whether [Washington's] statute sets up one of those 'arbitrary impositions' or 'purposeless restraints' at odds with the Due Process Clause of the Fourteenth Amendment," post, at 2275 (quoting Poe, 367 U.S. 497, 543, 81 S.Ct. 1752, 1776–1777, 6 L.Ed.2d 989 (1961) (Harlan, J., dissenting)). In our view, however, the development of this Court's substantive-due-process jurisprudence, described briefly above, supra, at 2267, has been a process whereby the outlines of the "liberty" specially protected by the Fourteenth Amendment—never fully clarified, to be sure, and perhaps not capable of being fully clarified—have at least been carefully refined by concrete examples involving fundamental rights found to be deeply rooted in our legal tradition. This approach tends to rein in the subjective elements that are necessarily present in due-process judicial review. In addition, by establishing a threshold requirement—that a challenged state action implicate a fundamental right—before requiring more than a reasonable relation to a legitimate state interest to justify the action, it avoids the need for complex balancing of competing interests in every case.

Turning to the claim at issue here, the Court of Appeals stated that "[p]roperly analyzed, the first issue to be resolved is whether there is a liberty interest in determining the time and manner of one's death," 79 F.3d, at 801, or, in other words, "[i]s there a right to die?," id., at 799. Similarly, respondents assert a "liberty to choose how to die" and a right to "control of one's final days," Brief for Respondents 7, and describe the asserted liberty as "the right to choose a humane, dignified death," id., at 15, and "the liberty to shape death," id., at 18. As noted above, we have a tradition of carefully formulating the interest at stake in substantive-due-process cases. For example, although Cruzan is often described as a "right to die" case, * * *, we were, in fact, more precise: we assumed that the Constitution granted competent persons a "constitutionally protected right to refuse lifesaving hydration and nutrition." * * * The Washington statute at issue in this case prohibits "aid[ing] another person to attempt suicide," Wash. Rev.Code § 9A.36.060(1) (1994), and, thus, the question before us is whether the "liberty" specially protected by the Due Process Clause includes a right to commit suicide which itself includes a right to assistance in doing so.

We now inquire whether this asserted right has any place in our Nation's traditions. Here, as discussed above, supra, at 2262–2267, we are confronted with a consistent and almost universal tradition that has long rejected the asserted right, and continues explicitly to reject it today, even for terminally ill, mentally competent adults. To hold for respondents, we would have to reverse centuries of legal doctrine and practice, and strike down the considered policy choice of almost every State. * * *

Respondents contend, however, that the liberty interest they assert is consistent with this Court's substantive-due-process line of cases, if not with this Nation's history and practice. Pointing to Casey and Cruzan, respondents read our jurisprudence in this area as reflecting a general tradition of "self-sovereignty," Brief of Respondents 12, and as teaching that the "liberty" protected by the Due Process Clause includes "basic and intimate exercises of personal autonomy" * * *. According to respondents, our liberty jurisprudence, and the broad, individualistic principles it reflects, protects the "liberty of competent, terminally ill adults to make end-of-life decisions free of undue government interference." Brief for Respondents 10. The question presented in this case, however, is whether the protections of the Due Process Clause include a right to commit suicide with another's assistance. With this "careful description" of respondents' claim in mind, we turn to Casey and Cruzan.

In Cruzan, we considered whether Nancy Beth Cruzan, who had been severely injured in an automobile accident and was in a persistive vegetative state, "ha[d] a right under the United States Constitution which would require the hospital to withdraw life-sustaining treatment" at her parents' request. Cruzan, 497 U.S., at 269, 110 S.Ct., at 2846–2847. We began with the observation that "[a]t common law, even the touching of one person by another without consent and without legal justification was a battery." Ibid. We then discussed the related rule that "informed consent is generally required for medical treatment." Ibid. After reviewing a long line of relevant state cases, we concluded that "the common-law doctrine of informed consent is viewed as generally encompassing the right of a competent individual to refuse medical treatment." Id., at 277, 110 S.Ct., at 2851. Next, we reviewed our own cases on the subject, and stated that "[t]he principle that a competent person has a constitutionally protected liberty interest in refusing unwanted medical treatment may be inferred from our prior decisions." Id., at 278, 110 S.Ct., at 2851. Therefore, "for purposes of [that] case, we assume [d] that the United States Constitution would grant a competent person a constitutionally protected right to refuse lifesaving hydration and nutrition." Id., at 279, 110 S.Ct., at 2852; see id., at 287, 110 S.Ct., at 2856 (O'Connor, J., concurring). We concluded that, notwithstanding this right, the Constitution permitted Missouri to require clear and convincing evidence of an incompetent patient's wishes concerning the withdrawal of life-sustaining treatment. Id., at 280–281, 110 S.Ct., at 2852–2853.

Respondents contend that in Cruzan we "acknowledged that competent, dying persons have the right to direct the removal of life-sustaining medical treatment and thus hasten death," Brief for Respondents 23, and that "the constitutional principle behind recognizing the patient's liberty to direct the withdrawal of artificial life support applies at least as strongly to the choice to hasten impending death by consuming lethal medication," id., at 26. Similarly, the Court of Appeals concluded that "Cruzan, by recognizing a liberty interest that includes the refusal of artificial provision of life-sustaining food and water, necessarily recognize[d] a liberty interest in hastening one's own death." 79 F.3d, at 816.

The right assumed in Cruzan, however, was not simply deduced from abstract concepts of personal autonomy. Given the common-law rule that forced medication was a battery, and the long legal tradition protecting the decision to refuse unwanted medical treatment, our assumption was entirely consistent with this Nation's history and constitutional traditions. The decision to commit suicide with the assistance of another may be just as personal and profound as the decision to refuse unwanted medical treatment, but it has never enjoyed similar legal protection. Indeed, the two acts are widely and reasonably regarded as quite distinct. * * * In Cruzan itself, we recognized that most States outlawed assisted suicide—and even more do today—and we certainly gave no intimation that the right to refuse unwanted medical treatment could be somehow transmuted into a right to assistance in committing suicide. 497 U.S., at 280, 110 S.Ct., at 2852.

Respondents also rely on Casey. There, the Court's opinion concluded that "the essential holding of Roe v. Wade should be retained and once again reaffirmed." Casey, 505 U.S., at 846, 112 S.Ct., at 2804. We held, first, that a woman has a right, before her fetus is viable, to an abortion "without undue interference from the State"; second, that States may restrict post-viability abortions, so long as exceptions are made to protect a woman's life and health; and third, that the State has legitimate interests throughout a pregnancy in protecting the health of the woman and the life of the unborn child. Ibid. In reaching this conclusion, the opinion discussed in some detail this Court's substantive-due-process tradition of interpreting the Due Process Clause to protect certain fundamental rights and "personal decisions relating to marriage, procreation, contraception, family relationships, child rearing, and education," and noted that many of those rights and liberties "involv[e] the most intimate and personal choices a person may make in a lifetime." Id., at 851, 112 S.Ct., at 2807.

The Court of Appeals, like the District Court, found Casey " 'highly instructive' "and " 'almost prescriptive' "for determining " 'what liberty interest may inhere in a terminally ill person's choice to commit suicide' ":

> "Like the decision of whether or not to have an abortion, the decision how and when to die is one of 'the most intimate and personal choices a person may make in a lifetime,' a choice 'central to personal dignity and autonomy.' " 79 F.3d, at 813–814.

Similarly, respondents emphasize the statement in Casey that:

> "At the heart of liberty is the right to define one's own concept of existence, of meaning, of the universe, and of the mystery of human

> life. Beliefs about these matters could not define the attributes of personhood were they formed under compulsion of the State." Casey, 505 U.S., at 851, 112 S.Ct., at 2807.

Brief for Respondents 12. By choosing this language, the Court's opinion in Casey described, in a general way and in light of our prior cases, those personal activities and decisions that this Court has identified as so deeply rooted in our history and traditions, or so fundamental to our concept of constitutionally ordered liberty, that they are protected by the Fourteenth Amendment. The opinion moved from the recognition that liberty necessarily includes freedom of conscience and belief about ultimate considerations to the observation that "though the abortion decision may originate within the zone of conscience and belief, it is more than a philosophic exercise." Casey, 505 U.S., at 852, 112 S.Ct., at 2807 (emphasis added). That many of the rights and liberties protected by the Due Process Clause sound in personal autonomy does not warrant the sweeping conclusion that any and all important, intimate, and personal decisions are so protected, San Antonio Independent School Dist. v. Rodriguez, 411 U.S. 1, 33–35, 93 S.Ct. 1278, 1296–1298, 36 L.Ed.2d 16 (1973), and Casey did not suggest otherwise.

The history of the law's treatment of assisted suicide in this country has been and continues to be one of the rejection of nearly all efforts to permit it. That being the case, our decisions lead us to conclude that the asserted "right" to assistance in committing suicide is not a fundamental liberty interest protected by the Due Process Clause. The Constitution also requires, however, that Washington's assisted-suicide ban be rationally related to legitimate government interests. * * * This requirement is unquestionably met here. As the court below recognized, 79 F.3d, at 816–817, Washington's assisted-suicide ban implicates a number of state interests. * * *

First, Washington has an "unqualified interest in the preservation of human life." Cruzan, 497 U.S., at 282, 110 S.Ct., at 2853. The State's prohibition on assisted suicide, like all homicide laws, both reflects and advances its commitment to this interest. * * * This interest is symbolic and aspirational as well as practical:

> "While suicide is no longer prohibited or penalized, the ban against assisted suicide and euthanasia shores up the notion of limits in human relationships. It reflects the gravity with which we view the decision to take one's own life or the life of another, and our reluctance to encourage or promote these decisions." New York Task Force 131–132.

Respondents admit that "[t]he State has a real interest in preserving the lives of those who can still contribute to society and enjoy life." Brief for Respondents 35, n. 23. The Court of Appeals also recognized Washington's interest in protecting life, but held that the "weight" of this interest depends on the "medical condition and the wishes of the person whose life is at stake." 79 F.3d, at 817. Washington, however, has rejected this sliding-scale approach and, through its assisted-suicide ban, insists that all persons' lives, from beginning to end, regardless of physical or mental condition, are under the full protection of the law. * * * As we have previously affirmed, the States "may properly decline to make judgments about the 'quality' of life that a particular individual may enjoy," Cruzan, 497 U.S., at 282, 110 S.Ct., at 2853. This remains true, as Cruzan makes clear, even for those who are near death.

Relatedly, all admit that suicide is a serious public-health problem, especially among persons in otherwise vulnerable groups. * * * The State has an interest in preventing suicide, and in studying, identifying, and treating its causes. * * *

Those who attempt suicide—terminally ill or not—often suffer from depression or other mental disorders. * * * Research indicates, however, that many people who request physician-assisted suicide withdraw that request if their depression and pain are treated. * * * The New York Task Force, however, expressed its concern that, because depression is difficult to diagnose, physicians and medical professionals often fail to respond adequately to seriously ill patients' needs. * * * Thus, legal physician-assisted suicide could make it more difficult for the State to protect depressed or mentally ill persons, or those who are suffering from untreated pain, from suicidal impulses.

The State also has an interest in protecting the integrity and ethics of the medical profession. In contrast to the Court of Appeals' conclusion that "the integrity of the medical profession would [not] be threatened in any way by [physician-assisted suicide]," 79 F.3d, at 827, the American Medical Association, like many other medical and physicians' groups, has concluded that "[p]hysician-assisted suicide is fundamentally incompatible with the physician's role as healer." American Medical Association, Code of Ethics § 2.211 (1994); see Council on Ethical and Judicial Affairs, Decisions Near the End of Life, 267 JAMA 2229, 2233 (1992) ("[T]he societal risks of involving physicians in medical interventions to cause patients' deaths is too great"); New York Task Force 103–109 (discussing physicians' views). And physician-assisted suicide could, it is argued, undermine the trust that is essential to the doctor-patient relationship by blurring the time-honored line between healing and harming. * * *

Next, the State has an interest in protecting vulnerable groups—including the poor, the elderly, and disabled persons—from abuse, neglect, and mistakes. The Court of Appeals dismissed the State's concern that disadvantaged persons might be pressured into physician-assisted suicide as "ludicrous on its face." 79 F.3d, at 825. We have recognized, however, the real risk of subtle coercion and undue influence in end-of-life situations. Cruzan, 497 U.S., at 281, 110 S.Ct., at 2852. Similarly, the New York Task Force warned that "[l]egalizing physician-assisted suicide would pose profound risks to many individuals who are ill and vulnerable.... The risk of harm is greatest for the many individuals in our society whose autonomy and well-being are already compromised by poverty, lack of access to good medical care, advanced age, or membership in a stigmatized social group." New York Task Force 120; * * *. If physician-assisted suicide were permitted, many might resort to it to spare their families the substantial financial burden of end-of-life health-care costs.

The State's interest here goes beyond protecting the vulnerable from coercion; it extends to protecting disabled and terminally ill people from prejudice, negative and inaccurate stereotypes, and "societal indifference." 49 F.3d, at 592. The State's assisted-suicide ban reflects and reinforces its policy that the lives of terminally ill, disabled, and elderly people must be no less valued than the lives of the young and healthy, and that a seriously disabled person's suicidal impulses should be interpreted and treated the same way as anyone else's. * * *

Finally, the State may fear that permitting assisted suicide will start it down the path to voluntary and perhaps even involuntary euthanasia. The Court of Appeals struck down Washington's assisted-suicide ban only "as applied to competent, terminally ill adults who wish to hasten their deaths by obtaining medication prescribed by their doctors." 79 F.3d, at 838. Washington insists, however, that the impact of the court's decision will not and cannot be so limited. Brief for Petitioners 44–47. If suicide is protected as a matter of constitutional right, it is argued, "every man and woman in the United States must enjoy it." * * * The Court of Appeals' decision, and its expansive reasoning, provide ample support for the State's concerns. The court noted, for example, that the "decision of a duly appointed surrogate decision maker is for all legal purposes the decision of the patient himself," 79 F.3d, at 832, n. 120; that "in some instances, the patient may be unable to self-administer the drugs and ... administration by the physician ... may be the only way the patient may be able to receive them," id., at 831; and that not only physicians, but also family members and loved ones, will inevitably participate in assisting suicide. Id., at 838, n. 140. Thus, it turns out that what is couched as a limited right to "physician-assisted suicide" is likely, in effect, a much broader license, which could prove extremely difficult to police and contain. Washington's ban on assisting suicide prevents such erosion.

This concern is further supported by evidence about the practice of euthanasia in the Netherlands. The Dutch government's own study revealed that in 1990, there were 2,300 cases of voluntary euthanasia (defined as "the deliberate termination of another's life at his request"), 400 cases of assisted suicide, and more than 1,000 cases of euthanasia without an explicit request. In addition to these latter 1,000 cases, the study found an additional 4,941 cases where physicians administered lethal morphine overdoses without the patients' explicit consent. Physician–Assisted Suicide and Euthanasia in the Netherlands: A Report of Chairman Charles T. Canady, at 12–13 (citing Dutch study). This study suggests that, despite the existence of various reporting procedures, euthanasia in the Netherlands has not been limited to competent, terminally ill adults who are enduring physical suffering, and that regulation of the practice may not have prevented abuses in cases involving vulnerable persons, including severely disabled neonates and elderly persons suffering from dementia. * * * The New York Task Force, citing the Dutch experience, observed that "assisted suicide and euthanasia are closely linked," New York Task Force 145, and concluded that the "risk of ... abuse is neither speculative nor distant," id., at 134. Washington, like most other States, reasonably ensures against this risk by banning, rather than regulating, assisting suicide. * * *

We need not weigh exactingly the relative strengths of these various interests. They are unquestionably important and legitimate, and Washington's ban on assisted suicide is at least reasonably related to their promotion and protection. We therefore hold that Wash. Rev.Code § 9A.36.060(1) (1994) does not violate the Fourteenth Amendment, either on its face or "as applied to competent, terminally ill adults who wish to hasten their deaths by obtaining medication prescribed by their doctors." 79 F.3d, at 838. * * *

Throughout the Nation, Americans are engaged in an earnest and profound debate about the morality, legality, and practicality of physician-assisted suicide. Our holding permits this debate to continue, as it should in a democratic society. The decision of the en banc Court of Appeals is reversed, and the case is remanded for further proceedings consistent with this opinion.

It is so ordered.

VACCO v. QUILL

Supreme Court of the United States, 1997.
521 U.S. 793, 117 S.Ct. 2293, 138 L.Ed.2d 834.

CHIEF JUSTICE REHNQUIST delivered the opinion of the Court.

In New York, as in most States, it is a crime to aid another to commit or attempt suicide, but patients may refuse even lifesaving medical treatment. The question presented by this case is whether New York's prohibition on assisting suicide therefore violates the Equal Protection Clause of the Fourteenth Amendment. We hold that it does not.

Petitioners are various New York public officials. Respondents Timothy E. Quill, Samuel C. Klagsbrun, and Howard A. Grossman are physicians who practice in New York. They assert that although it would be "consistent with the standards of [their] medical practice[s]" to prescribe lethal medication for "mentally competent, terminally ill patients" who are suffering great pain and desire a doctor's help in taking their own lives, they are deterred from doing so by New York's ban on assisting suicide. App. 25–26. Respondents, and three gravely ill patients who have since died, sued the State's Attorney General in the United States District Court. They urged that because New York permits a competent person to refuse life-sustaining medical treatment, and because the refusal of such treatment is "essentially the same thing" as physician-assisted suicide,

New York's assisted-suicide ban violates the Equal Protection Clause. * * *

The District Court disagreed: "[I]t is hardly unreasonable or irrational for the State to recognize a difference between allowing nature to take its course, even in the most severe situations, and intentionally using an artificial death-producing device." Id., at 84. The court noted New York's "obvious legitimate interests in preserving life, and in protecting vulnerable persons," and concluded that "[u]nder the United States Constitution and the federal system it establishes, the resolution of this issue is left to the normal democratic processes within the State." Id., at 84–85.

The Court of Appeals for the Second Circuit reversed. 80 F.3d 716 (1996). The court determined that, despite the assisted-suicide ban's apparent general applicability, "New York law does not treat equally all competent persons who are in the final stages of fatal illness and wish to hasten their deaths," because "those in the final stages of terminal illness who are on life-support systems are allowed to hasten their deaths by directing the removal of such systems; but those who are similarly situated, except for the previous attachment of life-sustaining equipment, are not allowed to hasten death by self-administering prescribed drugs." Id., at 727, 729. In the court's view, "[t]he ending of life by [the withdrawal of life-support systems] is nothing more nor less than assisted suicide." Id., at 729 (emphasis added) (citation omitted). The Court of Appeals then examined whether this supposed unequal treatment was rationally related to any legitimate state interests, and concluded that "to the extent that [New York's statutes] prohibit a physician from prescribing medications to be self-administered by a mentally competent, terminally-ill person in the final stages of his terminal illness, they are not rationally related to any legitimate state interest." Id., at 731. We granted certiorari, 519 U.S. ___, 117 S.Ct. 36, 135 L.Ed.2d 1127 (1996), and now reverse.

The Equal Protection Clause commands that no State shall "deny to any person within its jurisdiction the equal protection of the laws." This provision creates no substantive rights. * * * Instead, it embodies a general rule that States must treat like cases alike but may treat unlike cases accordingly. * * * If a legislative classification or distinction "neither burdens a fundamental right nor targets a suspect class, we will uphold [it] so long as it bears a rational relation to some legitimate end." Romer v. Evans, 517 U.S. 620, ___, 116 S.Ct. 1620, 1627, 134 L.Ed.2d 855 (1996).

New York's statutes outlawing assisting suicide affect and address matters of profound significance to all New Yorkers alike. They neither infringe fundamental rights nor involve suspect classifications. * * * These laws are therefore entitled to a "strong presumption of validity." * * *

On their faces, neither New York's ban on assisting suicide nor its statutes permitting patients to refuse medical treatment treat anyone differently than anyone else or draw any distinctions between persons. Everyone, regardless of physical condition, is entitled, if competent, to refuse unwanted lifesaving medical treatment; no one is permitted to assist a suicide. Generally speaking, laws that apply evenhandedly to all "unquestionably comply" with the Equal Protection Clause. * * *

The Court of Appeals, however, concluded that some terminally ill people—those who are on life-support systems—are treated differently than those who are not, in that the former may "hasten death" by ending treatment, but the latter may not "hasten death" through physician-assisted suicide. 80 F.3d, at 729. This conclusion depends on the submission that ending or refusing lifesaving medical treatment "is nothing more nor less than assisted suicide." Ibid. Unlike the Court of Appeals, we think the distinction between assisting suicide and withdrawing life-sustaining treatment, a distinction widely recognized and endorsed in the medical profession and in our legal traditions, is both important and logical; it is certainly rational. * * *

The distinction comports with fundamental legal principles of causation and intent. First, when a patient refuses life-sustaining medical treatment, he dies from an underlying fatal disease or pathology; but if a patient ingests lethal medication prescribed by a physician, he is killed by that medication. * * *

Furthermore, a physician who withdraws, or honors a patient's refusal to begin, life-sustaining medical treatment purposefully intends, or may so intend, only to respect his patient's wishes and "to cease doing useless and futile or degrading things to the patient when [the patient] no longer stands to benefit from them." Assisted Suicide in the United States, Hearing before the Subcommittee on the Constitution of the House Committee on the Judiciary, 104th Cong., 2d Sess., 368 (1996) (testimony of Dr. Leon R. Kass). The same is true when a doctor provides aggressive palliative care; in some cases, painkilling drugs may hasten a patient's death, but the physician's purpose and intent is, or may be, only to ease his patient's pain. A doctor who assists a suicide, however, "must, necessarily and indubitably, intend primarily that the patient be made dead." Id., at 367. Similarly, a patient who commits suicide with a doctor's aid necessarily has the specific intent to end his or her own life, while a patient who refuses or discontinues treatment might not. * * *

The law has long used actors' intent or purpose to distinguish between two acts that may have the same result. * * * Put differently, the law distinguishes actions taken "because of" a given end from actions taken "in spite of" their unintended but foreseen consequences. * * *

Given these general principles, it is not surprising that many courts, including New York courts, have carefully distinguished refusing life-sustaining treatment from suicide. * * * In fact, the first state-court decision explicitly to authorize withdrawing lifesaving treatment noted the "real distinction between the self-infliction of deadly harm and a self-determination against artificial life support." * * * And recently, the

Michigan Supreme Court also rejected the argument that the distinction "between acts that artificially sustain life and acts that artificially curtail life" is merely a "distinction without constitutional significance—a meaningless exercise in semantic gymnastics," insisting that "the Cruzan majority disagreed and so do we." Kevorkian, 447 Mich., at 471, 527 N.W.2d, at 728.

Similarly, the overwhelming majority of state legislatures have drawn a clear line between assisting suicide and withdrawing or permitting the refusal of unwanted lifesaving medical treatment by prohibiting the former and permitting the latter. Glucksberg, at ___–___, ___–___, 117 S.Ct., at 2262–2263, 2265–2267. And "nearly all states expressly disapprove of suicide and assisted suicide either in statutes dealing with durable powers of attorney in health-care situations, or in 'living will' statutes." * * * Thus, even as the States move to protect and promote patients' dignity at the end of life, they remain opposed to physician-assisted suicide.

New York is a case in point. The State enacted its current assisted-suicide statutes in 1965. Since then, New York has acted several times to protect patients' common-law right to refuse treatment. * * * In so doing, however, the State has neither endorsed a general right to "hasten death" nor approved physician-assisted suicide. Quite the opposite: The State has reaffirmed the line between "killing" and "letting die." * * * More recently, the New York State Task Force on Life and the Law studied assisted suicide and euthanasia and, in 1994, unanimously recommended against legalization. * * * In the Task Force's view, "allowing decisions to forego life-sustaining treatment and allowing assisted suicide or euthanasia have radically different consequences and meanings for public policy." * * *

This Court has also recognized, at least implicitly, the distinction between letting a patient die and making that patient die. In Cruzan, * * * we concluded that "[t]he principle that a competent person has a constitutionally protected liberty interest in refusing unwanted medical treatment may be inferred from our prior decisions," and we assumed the existence of such a right for purposes of that case * * * But our assumption of a right to refuse treatment was grounded not, as the Court of Appeals supposed, on the proposition that patients have a general and abstract "right to hasten death," 80 F.3d, at 727–728, but on well established, traditional rights to bodily integrity and freedom from unwanted touching * * *. In fact, we observed that "the majority of States in this country have laws imposing criminal penalties on one who assists another to commit suicide." * * * Cruzan therefore provides no support for the notion that refusing life-sustaining medical treatment is "nothing more nor less than suicide."

For all these reasons, we disagree with respondents' claim that the distinction between refusing lifesaving medical treatment and assisted suicide is "arbitrary" and "irrational." * * * Granted, in some cases, the line between the two may not be clear, but certainty is not required, even were it possible. Logic and contemporary practice support New York's judgment that the two acts are different, and New York may therefore, consistent with the Constitution, treat them differently. By permitting everyone to refuse unwanted medical treatment while prohibiting anyone from assisting a suicide, New York law follows a longstanding and rational distinction.

New York's reasons for recognizing and acting on this distinction—including prohibiting intentional killing and preserving life; preventing suicide; maintaining physicians' role as their patients' healers; protecting vulnerable people from indifference, prejudice, and psychological and financial pressure to end their lives; and avoiding a possible slide towards euthanasia—are discussed in greater detail in our opinion in Glucksberg, ante. These valid and important public interests easily satisfy the constitutional requirement that a legislative classification bear a rational relation to some legitimate end.

The judgment of the Court of Appeals is reversed.

It is so ordered.

NOTES AND QUESTIONS

1. For detailed discussions of the *Vacco* and *Washington* cases, see, e.g., Alexandra Dylan Lowe, *Facing the Final Exit*, A.B.A. J., Sept. 1997, at 48; Erwin Chemerinsky, *A Right to Physician–Assisted Suicide?*, TRIAL, Sept. 1997, at 68; Gina Patterson, *The Supreme Court Passes the Torch on Physician–Assisted Suicide: Washington v. Glucksberg and Vacco v. Quill*, 35 HOUS. L. REV. 851 (1998); *Symposium—Physician–Assisted Suicide: Legal Rights in Life and Death*, 12 ST. JOHN'S J. LEGAL COMMENT. (1997); Kelly Lyn Mitchell, *Physician-Assisted Suicide: A Survey of the Issues Surrounding Legalization*, 74 N.D. L. REV 341 (1998); Craig Peyton Gaumer & Paul R. Griffith, *Whose Life Is It Anyway? An Analysis and Commentary on the Emerging Law of Physician–Assisted Suicide*, 42 S.D. L. REV. 357 (1996–1997); Larry J. Pittman, *Physician-Assisted Suicide in the Dark Ward: The Intersection of the Thirteenth Amendment and Health Care Treatments Having Disproportionate Impacts on Disfavored Groups*, 28 SETON HALL L. REV. 774 (1998).

2. For a comprehensive examination of the positions of over twenty-five of the world's major religions on assisted suicide, see GERALD A. LARVE, EUTHANASIA AND RELIGION (1985).

3. By a margin of almost 2 to 1, attorneys support the legalization of voluntary active euthanasia. See Paul Reidinger, *Lawpoll: Should Active Euthanasia be Legal?*, A.B.A. J., June 1988, at 20 (Gallup survey in March 1988 with 5% margin of error).

4. Is there a difference morally and should there be a difference legally between assisted suicide (i.e., where the soon-to-be decedent self-administers the killing agent that was procured by another) and voluntary active euthanasia (i.e., where someone else administers the killing agent upon the request of the soon-to-be decedent)? See Yale Kamisar, *Who Should Live—or Die? Who Should Decide?*, TRIAL, Dec. 1991, at 20.

5. In 2001, The Netherlands became the first nation to legalize not only assisted suicide but also euthanasia. "The law * * * allows patients to leave a written request for euthanasia, giving doctors the right to use their own discretion when patients become too physically or mentally ill to decide for themselves." *Netherlands Passes Euthanasia Option*, USA TODAY, Apr. 12, 2001. Belgium followed suit in 2002 with a broader law which even allows non-terminally ill individuals to request euthanasia under certain circumstances. *Belgium Passes Death Law*, RADIO NETHERLANDS WERELDOMROEP, May 16, 2002 available at http://www.rnw.nl/hotspots/html/bel020516.html.

6. "Deep within the fabric of established medicine, assisted suicide and outright euthanasia are increasingly common considerations, driven by changing morals, the ferocity of terminal illnesses, patient fears about misuses of high-tech medicine and physician views that are in dramatic flux." Dick Lehr, *Death and the Doctor's Hand,* BOSTON GLOBE, April 25, 1993, at 1, 24. "One in five US physicians say they have deliberately taken action to cause a patient's death, according to a survey conducted by the American Society of Internal Medicine." Richard A. Knox, *1 in 5 Doctors Say They Assisted a Patient's Death, Survey Finds,* BOSTON GLOBE, Feb. 28, 1992, at 5. Should doctors who assist suicide be vigorously prosecuted for breaking the law or should prosecutors avert their eyes?

7. In March 1999, Dr. Jack Kevorkian was convicted of second degree murder for his role in assisting in a man's suicide. Dr. Kevorkian had videotaped the event and portions aired on the *60 Minutes* television program. Dr. Kevorkian allegedly helped about 130 individuals to commit suicide since 1990. Justin Hyde, *Kevorkian verdict creates void*, SAN JOSE MERCURY NEWS, Mar. 28, 1999, at 7A. He was released from prison for good behavior on June 1, 2007 and died on June 3, 2011.

8. How would you advise a client who asks you for help in arranging an assisted suicide or active euthanasia?

9. The National Association of Social Workers' ethics code allows its members to attend assisted suicides provided they do not provide the agent or device that causes death. See *Psychotherapists Adopt Policy on Witnessing Assisted Suicides,* PLAIN DEALER, Aug. 25, 1993, at 5C.

10. The general trend in society of recognizing living wills, the right to die, and assisted suicide is often called the "happy-death" movement. See JAMES M. HOEFLER, DEATHRIGHT: CULTURE, MEDICINE, POLITICS, AND THE RIGHT TO DIE 125–166 (1994).

11. For an extensive collection of articles, commentaries, and essays by noted legal and ethical scholars, see *The Seventeenth Annual Law Review Symposium—"The Right to Die,"* OHIO N.U.L. REV. 559 (1993).

12. There are several how-to manuals on the market including DEREK HUMPHRY, FINAL EXIT: THE PRACTICALITIES OF SELF-DELIVERANCE AND ASSISTED SUICIDE FOR THE DYING (1991) which was number one on the *New York Times'* best seller list for eighteen weeks.

E. ANATOMICAL GIFTS

REVISED UNIFORM ANATOMICAL GIFT ACT

2006 Act as amended in 2009.

Prefatory Note

As of January, 2006 there were over 92,000 individuals on the waiting list for organ transplantation, and the list keeps growing. It is estimated that approximately 5,000 individuals join the waiting list each year. *See* "Organ Donation: Opportunities for Action," Institute of Medicine of the National Academies (2006) www.nap.edu. Every hour another person in the United States dies because of the lack of an organ to provide a life saving organ transplant.

The lack of organs results from the lack of organ donors. For example, according to the Scientific Registry of Transplant Recipients in 2005 when there were about 90,000 people on the organ transplant waiting list, there were 13,091 individuals who died under the age of 70 using cardiac and brain death criteria and who were eligible to be organ donors. Of these, only 58% or 7,593 were actual donors who provided just over 23,000 organs. Living donors, primarily of kidneys, contributed about 6,800 more organs. Between them about 28,000 organs were transplanted into patients on the waiting list in 2005. (See www.optn.org).

The 2005 data on cadaveric organ donors suggests there were 5,498 individuals who died that year that could have been donors who weren't and that had they been organ donors there would have been approximately 17,000 additional organs potentially available for transplantation. (*See generally*, www.unos.org and www.ustransplant.org). However, these numbers to some extent are only estimates. First, they exclude individuals dying over the age of 70. Second, the data are self reported for eligible donors. Indicative of the absence of precision in this area is the report from the Institute of Medicine. According to the IOM, it has been estimated that donor-eligible deaths range between 10,500 and 16,800 per year. *See* Organ Donation: Opportunities for Action," Institute of Medicine of the National Academies (2006) at page 27. www.nap.edu Using the 2005 figures for deceased organ donors, this would suggest that between approximately 3,000 and 9,000 decedents could have been donors but weren't. Further, if one assumes an average of three solid organs recovered from each of them, there could be between 9,000 and 27,000 more organs that might have been available to transplant into individuals on the waiting list.

The data for eye and tissue is, however, more encouraging. On an annual basis there are approximately 50,000 eye donors and tissue donors and over 1,000,000 ocular and tissue transplants.

This Revised Uniform Anatomical Gift Act ("UAGA") is promulgated by the National Conference of Commissioners on Uniform State Laws

("NCCUSL") to address in part the critical organ shortage by providing additional ways for making organ, eye, and tissue donations. The original UAGA was promulgated by NCCUSL in 1968 and promptly enacted by all states. In 1987, the UAGA was revised and updated, but only 26 states adopted that version. Since 1987, many states have adopted non-uniform amendments to their anatomical gift acts. The law among the various states is no longer uniform and harmonious, and the diversity of law is an impediment to transplantation. Furthermore the federal government has been increasingly active in the organ transplant process.

Since 1987, there also have been substantial improvements in the technology and practice of organ, eye, and tissue transplantation and therapy. And, the need for organs, eyes, and tissue for research and education has increased to assure more successful transplantations and therapies. The improvements in technology and the growing needs of the research community have correspondingly increased the need for more donors. * * *

This [act] adheres to the significant policy determinations reflected in existing anatomical gift acts. First, the [act] is designed to encourage the making of anatomical gifts. Second, the [act] is designed to honor and respect the autonomy interest of individuals to make or not to make an anatomical gift of their body or parts. Third, the [act] preserves the current anatomical gift system founded upon altruism by requiring a positive affirmation of an intent to make a gift and prohibiting the sale and purchase of organs. This [act] includes a number of provisions, discussed below, that enhance these policies.

History of 1968 and 1987 Acts

The first reported medical transplant occurred in the third century. However, medical miracles flowing from transplants are truly a modern story beginning in the first decade of the twentieth century with the first successful transplant of a cornea. But, not until three events occurred in the twentieth century, in addition to the development of surgical techniques to effectuate a transplant, could transplants become a viable option to save and meaningfully extend lives.

The first event was the development in the late 1960s of the first set of neurological criteria for determining death. These criteria allowed persons to be declared dead upon the cessation of all brain activity. Ultimately these criteria, together with the historic measure of determining death by cessation of circulation and respiration, were incorporated into Section 1 of the Uniform Determination of Death Act providing that: "An individual who has sustained either (1) irreversible cessation of circulatory and respiratory function, or (2) irreversible cessation of all functions of the entire brain, including the brain stem, is dead."

The second event, following shortly after Dr. Christian Barnard's successful transplant of a heart in November, 1967, was this Conference's adoption of the first Uniform Anatomical Gift Act. In short order, every jurisdiction uniformly adopted the 1968 Act. The most significant contribution of the 1968 Act was to create a right to donate organs, eyes, and tissue. This right was not clearly recognized at common law. By creating this right, individuals became empowered to donate their parts or their loved one's parts to save or improve the lives of others.

The last event was the development of immunosuppressive drugs that prevented organ recipients from rejecting transplanted organs. This permitted many more successful organ transplants, thus contributing to the rapid growth in the demand for organs and the need for changes in the law to facilitate the making of anatomical gifts.

In 1987, a revised Uniform Anatomical Gift Act was promulgated to address changes in circumstances and in practice. Only 26 jurisdictions enacted the 1987 revision. Consequently, there is significant non-uniformity between states with the 1968 Act and those with the 1987 revisions. Neither of those acts comports with changes in federal law adopted subsequent to the 1987 Act relating to the role of hospitals and procurement organization in securing organs, eyes, and tissues for transplantation. And, both of them have impediments that are inconsistent with a policy to encourage donation.

The two previous anatomical gift acts, as well as this [act], adhere to an "opt in" principle as its default rule. Thus, an individual becomes a donor only if the donor or someone acting on the donor's behalf affirmatively makes an anatomical gift. The system universally adopted in this country is contrary to the system adopted in some countries, primarily in Europe, where an individual is deemed to be a donor unless the individual or another person acting on the individual's behalf "opts out." This other system is known as "presumed consent." While there are proponents of presumed consent who believe the concept of presumed consent could receive in the future a favorable reception in this country, the professional consensus appears to be not to replace the present opt-in principle at this time. *See* "Organ Donation: Opportunities in Action," Institute of Medicine of the National Academies (2006) at page 12.

Scope of the 2006 Revised Act

This [act] is limited in scope to donations from deceased donors as a result of gifts made before or after their deaths. Although recently there has been a significant increase in so-called "living donations," where a living donor immediately donates an organ (typically a kidney or a section of a liver) to a recipient, donations by living donors are not covered in this [act] because they raise distinct and difficult legal issues that are more appropriate for a separate act.

A majority of donors or prospective donors are candidates for donation of eyes or tissue, but only a small percentage of individuals die under circumstances that permit an anatomical gift of an organ. To procure an anatomical gift for transplantation, therapy, research, or education, a donor or prospective donor must be declared dead (*see* Uniform Determination of Death Act). In cases of potential organ donation, measures necessary to ensure the medical suitability of an organ for transplantation or therapy are administered to a patient who is dead or near death to determine if the patient could be a prospective donor.

Pursuant to federal law, when a donor or a patient who could be a prospective donor is dead or near death, a procurement organization, or a designee, must be notified. The organization begins to develop a medical and social history to determine whether the dying or deceased individual's body might be medically suitable for donation. If the body of a dying or deceased person might be medically suitable for donation, the procurement organization checks for evidence of a donation, if not otherwise known, and seeks consent to donation from authorized persons, if necessary. In the case of an organ, the organ procurement organization obtains from the Organ Procurement and Transplantation Network ("OPTN") a prioritized list of potential recipients from the national organ waiting list and takes the necessary steps to see that the organ finds its way to the appropriate recipient. If eye or tissue is donated, the appropriate procurement organization procures the eye or tissue and takes the necessary steps to screen, test, process, store, or distribute them as required for transplantation, therapy, research, or education. All must be done expeditiously.

Recent technological innovations have increased the types of organs that can be transplanted, the demand for organs, and the range of individuals who can donate or receive an organ, thereby increasing the number of organs available each year and the number of transplantations that occur each year. Nonetheless, the number of deaths for lack of available organs also has increased. While the Commissioners are under no illusion that any anatomical gift act can fully satisfy the need for organs, any change that could increase the supply of organs and thus save lies is an improvement.

Transplantation occurs across state boundaries and requires speed and efficiency if the organ is to be successfully transplanted into a recipient. There simply is no time for researching and conforming to variations of the laws among the states. Thus, uniformity of state law is highly desirable. Furthermore, the decision to be a donor is a highly personal decision of great generosity and deserves the highest respect from the law. Because current state anatomical gift laws are out of harmony with both federal procurement and allocation policies and do not fully respect the autonomy interests of donors, there is a need to harmonize state law with federal policy as well as to improve the manner in which anatomical gifts can be made and respected.

Summary of the Changes in the Revised Act

This revision retains the basic policy of the 1968 and 1987 anatomical gift acts by retaining and strengthening the "opt-in" system that honors the free choice of an individual to donate the individual's organ (a process known in the organ transplant community as "first person consent" or "donor designation"). This revision also preserves the right of other persons to make an anatomical gift of a decedent's organs if the decedent had not made a gift during life. And, it strengthens the right of an individual not to donate the individual's organs by signing a refusal that also bars others from making a gift of the individual's organs after the individual's death. This revision:

1. Honors the choice of an individual to be or not to be a donor and strengthens the language barring others from overriding a donor's decision to make an anatomical gift (Section 8);
2. Facilitates donations by expanding the list of those who may make an anatomical gift for another individual during that individual's lifetime to include health-care agents and, under certain circumstances, parents or guardians (Section 4);
3. Empowers a minor eligible under other law to apply for a driver's license to be a donor (Section 4);
4. Facilitates donations from a deceased individual who made no lifetime choice by adding to the list of persons who can make a gift of the deceased individual's body or parts the following persons: the person who was acting as the decedent's agent under a power of attorney for health care at the time of the decedent's death, the decedent's adult grandchildren, and an adult who exhibited special care and concern for the decedent (Section 9) and defines the meaning of "reasonably available" which is relevant to who can make an anatomical gift of a decedent's body or parts (Section 2(23));
5. Permits an anatomical gift by any member of a class where there is more than one person in the class so long as no objections by other class members are known and, if an objection is known, permits a majority of the members of the class who are reasonably available to make the gift without having to take account of a known objection by any class member who is not reasonably available (Section 9);
6. Creates numerous default rules for the interpretation of a document of gift that lacks specificity regarding either the persons to receive the gift or the purposes of the gift or both (Section 11);
7. Encourages and establishes standards for donor registries (Section 20);
8. Enables procurement organizations to gain access to documents of gifts in donor registries, medical records, and the records of a state motor vehicle department (Sections 14 and 20);
9. Resolves the tension between a health-care directive requesting the withholding or withdrawal of life support systems and anatomical gifts by permitting measures necessary to ensure the medical suitability of organs for intended transplantation or therapy to be administered (Sections 14 and 21);

10. Clarifies and expands the rules relating to cooperation and coordination between procurement organizations and coroners or medical examiners (Sections 22 and 23);
11. Recognizes anatomical gifts made under the laws of other jurisdictions (Section 19); and
12. Updates the [act] to allow for electronic records and signatures (Section 25).

In addition, Section 2 provides a number of new definitions that are used in the substantive provisions of the [act] to clarify and expand the opportunities for anatomical gifts. These include: adult, agent, custodian, disinterested witness, donee, donor registry, driver's license, eye bank, guardian, know, license, minor, organ procurement organization, parent, prospective donor, reasonably available, recipient, record, sign, tissue, tissue bank, and transplant hospital.

Section 4 authorizes individuals to make anatomical gifts of their bodies or parts. It also permits certain persons, other than donors, to make an anatomical gift on behalf of a donor during the donor's lifetime. The expanded list includes agents acting under a health-care power of attorney or other record, parents of unemancipated minors, and guardians. The section also recognizes that it is appropriate that minors who can apply for a driver's license be empowered to make anatomical gifts, but, under Section 8(g), either parent can revoke the gift if the minor dies under the age of 18.

Section 5 recognizes that, since the adoption of the previous versions of this [act], some states and many private organizations have created donor registries for the purpose of making anatomical gifts. Thus, in addition to evidencing a gift on a donor card or driver's license, this [act] allows for the making of anatomical gifts on donor registries. It also permits gifts to be made on state-issued identification cards and, under limited circumstances, to be made orally. Except for oral gifts, there is no witnessing requirement to make an anatomical gift.

Section 6 permits anatomical gifts to be amended or revoked by the execution of a later-executed record or by inconsistent documents of gifts. It also permits revocation by destruction of a document of gift and, under limited circumstances, permits oral revocations.

Section 7 permits an individual to sign a refusal that bars all other persons from making an anatomical gift of the individual's body or parts. A refusal generally can be made by a signed record, a will, or, under limited circumstances, orally. By permitting refusals, this [act] recognizes the autonomy interest of an individual either to be or not to be a donor. The section also recognizes that a refusal can be revoked.

Section 8 substantially strengthens the respect due a decision to make an anatomical gift. While the 1987 Act provided that a donor's anatomical gift was irrevocable (except by the donor), until quite recently it had been a common practice for procurement organizations to seek affirmation of the gift from the donor's family. This could result in unnecessary delays in the recovery of organs as well as a reversal of a donor's donation decision. Section 8 intentionally disempowers families from making or revoking anatomical gifts in contravention of a donor's wishes. Thus, under the strengthened language of this [act], if a donor had made an anatomical gift, there is no reason to seek consent from the donor's family as they have no right to give it legally. *See* Section 8(a). Of course, that would not bar, nor should it bar, a procurement organization from advising the donor's family of the donor's express wishes, but that conversation should focus more on what procedures will be followed to carry out the donor's wishes and on answering a family's questions about the process rather than on seeking approval of the donation. A limited exception applies if the donor is a minor at the time of death. In this case, either parent may amend or revoke the donor's anatomical gift. *See* Section 8(g).

Section 8 also recognizes that some decisions of a donor are inherently ambiguous, making it appropriate to adopt rules that favor the making of anatomical gifts. For example, a donor's revocation of a gift of a part is not to be construed as a refusal for others to make gifts of other parts. Likewise, a donor's gift of one part is not to be construed as a refusal that would bar others from making gifts of other parts absent an express, contrary intent.

Section 9 sets forth a prioritized list of classes of persons who can make an anatomical gift of a decedent's body or part if the decedent was neither a donor nor had signed a refusal. The list is more expansive than under previous versions of this [act]. It includes persons acting as agents at the decedent's death, adult grandchildren, and close friends.

Section 10 deals with the manner of making, amending, or revoking an anatomical gift following the decedent's death.

Section 11 deals with the passing of parts to named persons and more generally to eye banks, tissue banks, and organ procurement organizations. In part, the section is designed to harmonize this [act] with federal law, particularly with respect to organs donated for transplantation or therapy. The National Organ Transplant Act created the Organ Procurement and Transplantation Network ("OPTN") to facilitate the nationwide, equitable distribution of organs. Currently, United Network Organ Sharing ("UNOS") operates the OPTN under contract with the U.S. Department of Health and Human Services. When an organ donor dies, the donor's organs, barring the rare instance of a donation to a named individual, are recovered by the organ procurement organization for the service area in which the donor dies, as custodian of the organs, to be allocated by it either locally, regionally, or nationally in accordance with allocation policies established by the OPTN.

Section 11 includes two important improvements to previous versions of this [act]. First, it creates a priority for transplantation or therapy over research or education when an anatomical gift is made for all four purposes in a document of gift that fails to establish a priority.

Second, it specifies the person to whom a part passes when the document of gift merely expresses a "general intent" to be an "organ donor." This type of general designation is common on a driver's license. Under Section 11(f) a general statement of intent to be a donor results only in an anatomical gift of the donor's eyes, tissues, and organs (not the whole body) for transplantation or therapy. Since a general statement of intent to be an organ donor does not result in the making of an anatomical gift of the whole body, or any part, for research or education, more specific language is required to make such a gift.

Section 11(b) provides that, if an anatomical gift of the decedent's body or parts does not pass to a named person designated in a document of gift, it passes to a procurement organization typically for transplantation or therapy and possibly for research or education. Custody of a body or part that is the subject of an anatomical gift that cannot be used for any intended purpose passes to the "person under obligation to dispose of the body or parts." *See* Section 11(i).

Section 11(j) prohibits a person from accepting an anatomical gift if the person knows that the gift was not validly made. For this purpose, if a person knows that an anatomical gift was made on a document of gift, the person is deemed to know of a refusal to make a gift if the refusal is on the same document of gift.

Lastly, Section 11(k) clarifies that nothing in this [act] affects the allocation of organs for transplantation or therapy except to the extent there has been a gift to a named recipient. *See* Section 11(a)(2). The allocation of organs is administered exclusively under policies of the Organ Procurement and Transplantation Network.

In part, Section 14 has been redrafted to accord with controlling federal law when applicable. The federal rules require hospitals to notify an organ procurement organization or third party designated by the organ procurement organization of an individual whose death is imminent or who has died in the hospital to increase donation opportunity, and thus, transplantation. *See* 42 CFR § 482.45 (Medicare and Medicaid Programs: Conditions of Participation: Identification of Potential Organ, Tissue, and Eye Donors and Transplant Hospitals' Provision of Transplant–Related Data). The right of the procurement organization to inspect a patient's medical records in Section 14(e) does not violate HIPAA. *See* 45 CFR § 164.512(h) ("A covered entity may use or disclose protected health information to organ procurement organizations or other entities engaged in the procurement, banking, or transplantation of cadaveric organs, eyes, or tissue for the purpose of facilitating organ, eye, or tissue donation and transplantation"). Section 14(c) permits measures necessary to ensure the medical suitability of parts to be administered to a patient who is being evaluated to determine whether the patient has organs that are medically suitable for transplantation.

Section 17 and Section 18 deal with liability and immunity, respectively. (Section 16, dealing with the sale of parts, also provides for potential liabilities but is essentially the same as prior law). Section 17 includes a new provision establishing criminal sanctions for falsifying the making, amending, or revoking of an anatomical gift. Section 18, in substance, is the same as the 1987 Act providing immunity for "good faith" efforts to comply with this [act]. However, while the [act] contains no provisions relating to bad faith it is important to note that other laws of the state and federal governments may provide for further remedies and sanctions for bad faith, including those under regulatory rules, licensing requirements, Unfair and Deceptive Practices acts, and the common law.

Section 18(c) provides that in determining whether an individual has a right to make an anatomical gift under Section 9, a person, such as an organ procurement organization, may rely on the individual's representation regarding the individual's relationship to the donor or prospective donor.

Section 19 sets forth rules relating to the validity of documents of gift executed outside of the state while providing that any document of gift shall be interpreted in accordance with the laws of the state.

Section 20 authorizes an appropriate state agency to establish or contract for the establishment of a donor registry. It also provides that a registry can be established without a state contract. While this [act] does not specify in great detail what could or should be on a donor registry, it does mandate minimum requirements for all registries. First, the registry must provide a database that allows a donor or other person authorized to make an anatomical gift to include in the registry a statement or symbol that the donor has made a gift. Second, at or near the death of a donor or prospective donor, the registry must be accessible to all procurement organizations to obtain information relevant to determine whether the donor or prospective donor has made, amended, or revoked an anatomical gift. Lastly, the registry must be accessible on a twenty four hour, seven day a week basis.

Section 21 creates a default rule to adjust the tension that might exist between preserving organs to assure their medical suitability for transplantation or therapy and the expression of intent by a prospective donor in either a declaration or advance health-care directive not to have life prolonged by use of life support systems. The default rule under this [act] is that measures necessary to ensure the medical suitability of an organ for transplantation or therapy may not be withheld or withdrawn from the prospective donor. A prospective donor could expressly provide otherwise in the declaration or advance health-care directive.

Sections 22 and 23 represent a complete revision of the relationship of the [coroner] [medical examiner] to the anatomical gift process. Previous versions of this [act] permitted the [coroner] [medical examiner], under limited circumstances, to make anatomical gifts of the eyes of a decedent in the [coroner's] [medical examiner's] possession. In light of a series of Section 1983 lawsuits in which the [coroner's] [medical examiner's] actions were held to violate the property rights of surviving family members, *see, e.g.*, Brotherton v. Cleveland, 923 F.2d 477 (6th Cir. 1991), the authority of the [coroner] [medical examiner] to make anatomical gifts was deleted from this [act]. Parts, with the rare exception discussed in the comments to Section 9, can be recovered for the purpose of transplantation, therapy, research, or education from a decedent whose body is under the jurisdiction of the [coroner] [medical examiner] only if there was an anatomical gift of those parts under Section 5 or Section 10 of this [act].

This [act] includes a series of new provisions in Sections 22 and 23 relating to the relationship between the [coroner] [medical examiner] and procurement organizations. These provisions should encourage meaningful cooperation between these groups in hopes of increasing the number of anatomical gifts. Importantly, the section does not permit a [coroner] [medical examiner] to make an anatomical gift.

SECTION 1. SHORT TITLE.

This [act] may be cited as the Revised Uniform Anatomical Gift Act.

SECTION 2. DEFINITIONS.

In this [act]:

(1) "Adult" means an individual who is at least [18] years of age.

(2) "Agent" means an individual:

(A) authorized to make health-care decisions on the principal's behalf by a power of attorney for health care; or

(B) expressly authorized to make an anatomical gift on the principal's behalf by any other record signed by the principal.

(3) "Anatomical gift" means a donation of all or part of a human body to take effect after the donor's death for the purpose of transplantation, therapy, research, or education.

(4) "Decedent" means a deceased individual whose body or part is or may be the source of an anatomical gift. The term includes a stillborn infant and, subject to restrictions imposed by law other than this [act], a fetus.

(5) "Disinterested witness" means a witness other than the spouse, child, parent, sibling, grandchild, grandparent, or guardian of the individual who makes, amends, revokes, or refuses to make an anatomical gift, or another adult who exhibited special care and concern for the individual. The term does not include a person to which an anatomical gift could pass under Section 11.

(6) "Document of gift" means a donor card or other record used to make an anatomical gift. The term includes a statement or symbol on a driver's license, identification card, or donor registry.

(7) "Donor" means an individual whose body or part is the subject of an anatomical gift.

(8) "Donor registry" means a database that contains records of anatomical gifts and amendments to or revocations of anatomical gifts.

(9) "Driver's license" means a license or permit issued by the [state department of motor vehicles] to operate a vehicle, whether or not conditions are attached to the license or permit.

(10) "Eye bank" means a person that is licensed, accredited, or regulated under federal or state law to engage in the recovery, screening, testing, processing, storage, or distribution of human eyes or portions of human eyes.

(11) "Guardian" means a person appointed by a court to make decisions regarding the support, care, education, health, or welfare of an individual. The term does not include a guardian ad litem.

(12) "Hospital" means a facility licensed as a hospital under the law of any state or a facility operated as a hospital by the United States, a state, or a subdivision of a state.

(13) "Identification card" means an identification card issued by the [state department of motor vehicles].

(14) "Know" means to have actual knowledge.

(15) "Minor" means an individual who is under [18] years of age.

(16) "Organ procurement organization" means a person designated by the Secretary of the United States Department of Health and Human Services as an organ procurement organization.

(17) "Parent" means a parent whose parental rights have not been terminated.

(18) "Part" means an organ, an eye, or tissue of a human being. The term does not include the whole body.

(19) "Person" means an individual, corporation, business trust, estate, trust, partnership, limited liability company, association, joint venture, public corporation, government or governmental subdivision, agency, or instrumentality, or any other legal or commercial entity.

(20) "Physician" means an individual authorized to practice medicine or osteopathy under the law of any state.

(21) "Procurement organization" means an eye bank, organ procurement organization, or tissue bank.

(22) "Prospective donor" means an individual who is dead or near death and has been determined by a procurement organization to have a part that could be medically suitable for transplantation, therapy, research, or education. The term does not include an individual who has made a refusal.

(23) "Reasonably available" means able to be contacted by a procurement organization without undue effort and willing and able to act in a timely manner consistent with existing medical criteria necessary for the making of an anatomical gift.

(24) "Recipient" means an individual into whose body a decedent's part has been or is intended to be transplanted.

(25) "Record" means information that is inscribed on a tangible medium or that is stored in an electronic or other medium and is retrievable in perceivable form.

(26) "Refusal" means a record created under Section 7 that expressly states an intent to bar other persons from making an anatomical gift of an individual's body or part.

(27) "Sign" means, with the present intent to authenticate or adopt a record:

(A) to execute or adopt a tangible symbol; or

(B) to attach to or logically associate with the record an electronic symbol, sound, or process.

(28) "State" means a state of the United States, the District of Columbia, Puerto Rico, the United States Virgin Islands, or any territory or insular possession subject to the jurisdiction of the United States.

(29) "Technician" means an individual determined to be qualified to remove or process parts by an appropriate organization that is licensed, accredited, or regulated under federal or state law. The term includes an enucleator.

(30) "Tissue" means a portion of the human body other than an organ or an eye. The term does not include blood unless the blood is donated for the purpose of research or education.

(31) "Tissue bank" means a person that is licensed, accredited, or regulated under federal or state law to engage in the recovery, screening, testing, processing, storage, or distribution of tissue.

(32) "Transplant hospital" means a hospital that furnishes organ transplants and other medical and surgical specialty services required for the care of transplant patients.

Legislative note: If this state does not license "hospitals", the definition of "hospital" should include a reference to the facility or facilities with equivalent functions by an additional sentence such as the following: "The term includes an acute care facility."

SECTION 3. APPLICABILITY.

This [act] applies to an anatomical gift or amendment to, revocation of, or refusal to make an anatomical gift, whenever made.

SECTION 4. WHO MAY MAKE ANATOMICAL GIFT BEFORE DONOR'S DEATH.

Subject to Section 8, an anatomical gift of a donor's body or part may be made during the life of the donor for the purpose of transplantation, therapy, research, or education in the manner provided in Section 5 by:

(1) the donor, if the donor is an adult or if the donor is a minor and is:

(A) emancipated; or

(B) authorized under state law to apply for a driver's license because the donor is at least [insert the youngest age at which an individual may apply for any type of driver's license] years of age;

(2) an agent of the donor, unless the power of attorney for health care or other record prohibits the agent from making an anatomical gift;

(3) a parent of the donor, if the donor is an unemancipated minor; or

(4) the donor's guardian.

SECTION 5. MANNER OF MAKING ANATOMICAL GIFT BEFORE DONOR'S DEATH.

(a) A donor may make an anatomical gift:

(1) by authorizing a statement or symbol indicating that the donor has made an anatomical gift to be imprinted on the donor's driver's license or identification card;

(2) in a will;

(3) during a terminal illness or injury of the donor, by any form of communication addressed to at least two adults, at least one of whom is a disinterested witness; or

(4) as provided in subsection (b).

(b) A donor or other person authorized to make an anatomical gift under Section 4 may make a gift by a donor card or other record signed by the donor or other person making the gift or by authorizing that a statement or symbol indicating that the donor has made an anatomical gift be included on a donor registry. If the donor or other person is physically unable to sign a record, the record may be signed by another individual at the direction of the donor or other person and must:

(1) be witnessed by at least two adults, at least one of whom is a disinterested witness, who have signed at the request of the donor or the other person; and

(2) state that it has been signed and witnessed as provided in paragraph (1).

(c) Revocation, suspension, expiration, or cancellation of a driver's license or identification card upon which an anatomical gift is indicated does not invalidate the gift.

(d) An anatomical gift made by will takes effect upon the donor's death whether or not the will is probated. Invalidation of the will after the donor's death does not invalidate the gift.

COMMENT

The execution formalities associated with the making of an anatomical gift generally remain the same as under the 1987 Act. However, in addition to the making of an anatomical gift by a donor card, will, or state-issued driver's license, an anatomical gift can also be made on a state-issued identification card or a donor registry.

* * *

A decision was made in drafting this [act] not to include a specific form in the statute for the making of an anatomical gift. Rather, the drafting committee concluded that suggested forms consistent with this [act] be included in these comments. Three such forms follow:

DONOR CARD

I wish to donate my organs, eyes, and tissue. I give:

Any needed organs, eyes, and tissue ONLY the following organs, eyes, and tissue:

____

Date: ____________________ Donor's Signature ______________

Subject of Gift:			**Purpose of Gift:**		
			Transplantation or therapy	**Research or Education**	**Both**
Section A	**Yes**	**No**			
ALL of my organs, eyes, and tissue					
Section B					
My Organs					
My Eyes					
My Tissue					
Section C					

Special Instructions (If none of the above apply), I wish to give ONLY:

____

Date: ____________________ Donor's Signature: ______________

DONOR CARD

I give, upon my death, the following gifts for the purpose of (*choose whichever applies*): [ ] only transplantation and therapy, [ ] only research and education, [ ] transplantation, therapy, research, or education

For the purposes specified above, I give:

[ ] ALL needed organs, tissues, and eyes; or

(If you checked the box immediately above, you should not check specific boxes below).

[ ] Organs [ ] Tissues [ ] Eyes

If none of the above applies, I wish to give ONLY:

The following organs and tissues:______________________________

Date: ________________________ Donor's Signature ______________

SECTION 6. AMENDING OR REVOKING ANATOMICAL GIFT BEFORE DONOR'S DEATH.

(a) Subject to Section 8, a donor or other person authorized to make an anatomical gift under Section 4 may amend or revoke an anatomical gift by:

(1) a record signed by:

(A) the donor;

(B) the other person; or

(C) subject to subsection (b), another individual acting at the direction of the donor or the other person if the donor or other person is physically unable to sign; or

(2) a later-executed document of gift that amends or revokes a previous anatomical gift or portion of an anatomical gift, either expressly or by inconsistency.

(b) A record signed pursuant to subsection (a)(1)(C) must:

(1) be witnessed by at least two adults, at least one of whom is a disinterested witness, who have signed at the request of the donor or the other person; and

(2) state that it has been signed and witnessed as provided in paragraph (1).

(c) Subject to Section 8, a donor or other person authorized to make an anatomical gift under Section 4 may revoke an anatomical gift by the destruction or cancellation of the document of gift, or the portion of the document of gift used to make the gift, with the intent to revoke the gift.

(d) A donor may amend or revoke an anatomical gift that was not made in a will by any form of communication during a terminal illness or injury addressed to at least two adults, at least one of whom is a disinterested witness.

(e) A donor who makes an anatomical gift in a will may amend or revoke the gift in the manner provided for amendment or revocation of wills or as provided in subsection (a).

SECTION 7. REFUSAL TO MAKE ANATOMICAL GIFT; EFFECT OF REFUSAL.

(a) An individual may refuse to make an anatomical gift of the individual's body or part by:

(1) a record signed by:

(A) the individual; or

(B) subject to subsection (b), another individual acting at the direction of the individual if the individual is physically unable to sign;

(2) the individual's will, whether or not the will is admitted to probate or invalidated after the individual's death; or

(3) any form of communication made by the individual during the individual's terminal illness or injury addressed to at least two adults, at least one of whom is a disinterested witness.

(b) A record signed pursuant to subsection (a)(1)(B) must:

(1) be witnessed by at least two adults, at least one of whom is a disinterested witness, who have signed at the request of the individual; and

(2) state that it has been signed and witnessed as provided in paragraph (1).

(c) An individual who has made a refusal may amend or revoke the refusal:

(1) in the manner provided in subsection (a) for making a refusal;

(2) by subsequently making an anatomical gift pursuant to Section 5 that is inconsistent with the refusal; or

(3) by destroying or canceling the record evidencing the refusal, or the portion of the record used to make the refusal, with the intent to revoke the refusal.

(d) Except as otherwise provided in Section 8(h), in the absence of an express, contrary indication by the individual set forth in the refusal, an individual's unrevoked refusal to make an anatomical gift of the individual's body or part bars all other persons from making an anatomical gift of the individual's body or part.

SECTION 8. PRECLUSIVE EFFECT OF ANATOMICAL GIFT, AMENDMENT, OR REVOCATION.

(a) Except as otherwise provided in subsection (g) and subject to subsection (f), in the absence of an express, contrary indication by the donor, a person other than the donor is barred from making, amending, or revoking an anatomical gift of a donor's body or part if the donor made an anatomical gift of the donor's body or part under Section 5 or an amendment to an anatomical gift of the donor's body or part under Section 6.

(b) A donor's revocation of an anatomical gift of the donor's body or part under Section 6 is not a refusal and does not bar another person specified in Section 4 or 9 from making an anatomical gift of the donor's body or part under Section 5 or 10.

(c) If a person other than the donor makes an unrevoked anatomical gift of the donor's body or part under Section 5 or an amendment to an anatomical gift of the donor's body or part under Section 6, another person may not make, amend, or revoke the gift of the donor's body or part under Section 10.

(d) A revocation of an anatomical gift of a donor's body or part under Section 6 by a person other than the donor does not bar another person from making an anatomical gift of the body or part under Section 5 or 10.

(e) In the absence of an express, contrary indication by the donor or other person authorized to make an anatomical gift under Section 4, an anatomical gift of a part is neither a refusal to give another part nor a limitation on the making of an anatomical gift of another part at a later time by the donor or another person.

(f) In the absence of an express, contrary indication by the donor or other person authorized to make an anatomical gift under Section 4, an anatomical gift of a part for one or more of the purposes set forth in Section 4 is not a limitation on the making of an anatomical gift of the part for any of the other purposes by the donor or any other person under Section 5 or 10.

(g) If a donor who is an unemancipated minor dies, a parent of the donor who is reasonably available may revoke or amend an anatomical gift of the donor's body or part.

(h) If an unemancipated minor who signed a refusal dies, a parent of the minor who is reasonably available may revoke the minor's refusal.

SECTION 9. WHO MAY MAKE ANATOMICAL GIFT OF DECEDENT'S BODY OR PART.

(a) Subject to subsections (b) and (c) and unless barred by Section 7 or 8, an anatomical gift of a decedent's body or part for purpose of transplantation, therapy, research, or education may be made by any member of the following classes of persons who is reasonably available, in the order of priority listed:

(1) an agent of the decedent at the time of death who could have made an anatomical gift under Section 4(2) immediately before the decedent's death;

(2) the spouse of the decedent;

(3) adult children of the decedent;

(4) parents of the decedent;

(5) adult siblings of the decedent;

(6) adult grandchildren of the decedent;

(7) grandparents of the decedent;

(8) an adult who exhibited special care and concern for the decedent;

(9) the persons who were acting as the [guardians] of the person of the decedent at the time of death; and

(10) any other person having the authority to dispose of the decedent's body.

(b) If there is more than one member of a class listed in subsection (a)(1), (3), (4), (5), (6), (7), or (9) entitled to make an anatomical gift, an anatomical gift may be made by a member of the class unless that member or a person to which the gift may pass under Section 11 knows of an objection by another member of the class. If an objection is known, the gift may be made only by a majority of the members of the class who are reasonably available.

(c) A person may not make an anatomical gift if, at the time of the decedent's death, a person in a prior class under subsection (a) is reasonably available to make or to object to the making of an anatomical gift.

SECTION 10. MANNER OF MAKING, AMENDING, OR REVOKING ANATOMICAL GIFT OF DECEDENT'S BODY OR PART.

(a) A person authorized to make an anatomical gift under Section 9 may make an anatomical gift by a document of gift signed by the person making the gift or by that person's oral communication that is electronically recorded or is contemporaneously reduced to a record and signed by the individual receiving the oral communication.

(b) Subject to subsection (c), an anatomical gift by a person authorized under Section 9 may be amended or revoked orally or in a record by any member of a prior class who is reasonably available. If more than one member of the prior class is reasonably available, the gift made by a person authorized under Section 9 may be:

(1) amended only if a majority of the reasonably available members agree to the amending of the gift; or

(2) revoked only if a majority of the reasonably available members agree to the revoking of the gift or if they are equally divided as to whether to revoke the gift.

(c) A revocation under subsection (b) is effective only if, before an incision has been made to remove a part from the donor's body or before invasive procedures have begun to prepare the recipient, the procurement organization, transplant hospital, or physician or technician knows of the revocation.

SECTION 11. PERSONS THAT MAY RECEIVE ANATOMICAL GIFT; PURPOSE OF ANATOMICAL GIFT.

(a) An anatomical gift may be made to the following persons named in the document of gift:

(1) a hospital; accredited medical school, dental school, college, or university; organ procurement organization; or other appropriate person, for research or education;

(2) subject to subsection (b), an individual designated by the person making the anatomical gift if the individual is the recipient of the part;

(3) an eye bank or tissue bank.

(b) If an anatomical gift to an individual under subsection (a)(2) cannot be transplanted into the individual, the part passes in accordance with subsection (g) in the absence of an express, contrary indication by the person making the anatomical gift.

(c) If an anatomical gift of one or more specific parts or of all parts is made in a document of gift that does not name a person described in subsection (a) but identifies the purpose for which an anatomical gift may be used, the following rules apply:

(1) If the part is an eye and the gift is for the purpose of transplantation or therapy, the gift passes to the appropriate eye bank.

(2) If the part is tissue and the gift is for the purpose of transplantation or therapy, the gift passes to the appropriate tissue bank.

(3) If the part is an organ and the gift is for the purpose of transplantation or therapy, the gift passes to the appropriate organ procurement organization as custodian of the organ.

(4) If the part is an organ, an eye, or tissue and the gift is for the purpose of research or education, the gift passes to the appropriate procurement organization.

(d) For the purpose of subsection (c), if there is more than one purpose of an anatomical gift set forth in the document of gift but the purposes are not set forth in any priority, the gift must be used for transplantation or therapy, if suitable. If the gift cannot be used for transplantation or therapy, the gift may be used for research or education.

(e) If an anatomical gift of one or more specific parts is made in a document of gift that does not name a person described in subsection (a) and does not identify the purpose of the gift, the gift may be used only for transplantation or therapy, and the gift passes in accordance with subsection (g).

(f) If a document of gift specifies only a general intent to make an anatomical gift by words such as "donor", "organ donor", or "body donor", or by a symbol or statement of similar import, the gift may be used only for transplantation or therapy, and the gift passes in accordance with subsection (g).

(g) For purposes of subsections (b), (e), and (f) the following rules apply:

(1) If the part is an eye, the gift passes to the appropriate eye bank.

(2) If the part is tissue, the gift passes to the appropriate tissue bank.

(3) If the part is an organ, the gift passes to the appropriate organ procurement organization as custodian of the organ.

(h) An anatomical gift of an organ for transplantation or therapy, other than an anatomical gift under subsection (a)(2), passes to the organ procurement organization as custodian of the organ.

(i) If an anatomical gift does not pass pursuant to subsections (a) through (h) or the decedent's body or part is not used for transplantation, therapy, research, or education, custody of the body or part passes to the person under obligation to dispose of the body or part.

(j) A person may not accept an anatomical gift if the person knows that the gift was not effectively made under Section 5 or 10 or if the person knows that the decedent made a refusal under Section 7 that was not revoked. For purposes of the subsection, if a person knows that an anatomical gift was made on a document of gift, the person is deemed to know of any amendment or revocation of the gift or any refusal to make an anatomical gift on the same document of gift.

(k) Except as otherwise provided in subsection (a)(2), nothing in this [act] affects the allocation of organs for transplantation or therapy.

SECTION 12. SEARCH AND NOTIFICATION.

(a) The following persons shall make a reasonable search of an individual who the person reasonably believes is dead or near death for a document of gift or other information identifying the individual as a donor or as an individual who made a refusal:

(1) a law enforcement officer, firefighter, paramedic, or other emergency rescuer finding the individual; and

(2) if no other source of the information is immediately available, a hospital, as soon as practical after the individual's arrival at the hospital.

(b) If a document of gift or a refusal to make an anatomical gift is located by the search required by subsection (a)(1) and the individual or deceased individual to whom it relates is taken to a hospital, the person responsible for conducting the search shall send the document of gift or refusal to the hospital.

(c) A person is not subject to criminal or civil liability for failing to discharge the duties imposed by this section but may be subject to administrative sanctions.

SECTION 13. DELIVERY OF DOCUMENT OF GIFT NOT REQUIRED; RIGHT TO EXAMINE.

(a) A document of gift need not be delivered during the donor's lifetime to be effective.

(b) Upon or after an individual's death, a person in possession of a document of gift or a refusal to make an anatomical gift with respect to the individual shall allow examination and copying of the document of gift or refusal by a person authorized to make or object to the making of an anatomical gift with respect to the individual or by a person to which the gift could pass under Section 11.

SECTION 14. RIGHTS AND DUTIES OF PROCUREMENT ORGANIZATION AND OTHERS.

(a) When a hospital refers an individual at or near death to a procurement organization, the organization shall make a reasonable search of the records of the [state department of motor vehicles] and any donor registry that it knows exists for the geographical area in which the individual resides to ascertain whether the individual has made an anatomical gift.

(b) A procurement organization must be allowed reasonable access to information in the records of the [state department of motor vehicles] to ascertain whether an individual at or near death is a donor.

(c) When a hospital refers an individual at or near death to a procurement organization, the organization may conduct any reasonable examination necessary to ensure the medical suitability of a part that is or could be the subject of an anatomical gift for transplantation, therapy, research, or education from a donor or a prospective donor. During the examination period, measures necessary to ensure the medical suitability of the part may not be withdrawn unless the hospital or procurement organization knows that the individual expressed a contrary intent.

(d) Unless prohibited by law other than this [act], at any time after a donor's death, the person to which a part passes under Section 11 may conduct any reasonable examination necessary to ensure the medical suitability of the body or part for its intended purpose.

(e) Unless prohibited by law other than this [act], an examination under subsection (c) or (d) may include an examination of all medical and dental records of the donor or prospective donor.

(f) Upon the death of a minor who was a donor or had signed a refusal, unless a procurement organization knows the minor is emancipated, the procurement organization shall conduct a reasonable search for the parents of the minor and provide the parents with an opportunity to revoke or amend the anatomical gift or revoke the refusal.

(g) Upon referral by a hospital under subsection (a), a procurement organization shall make a reasonable search for any person listed in Section 9 having priority to make an anatomical gift on behalf of a prospective donor. If a procurement organization receives information that an anatomical gift to any other person was made, amended, or revoked, it shall promptly advise the other person of all relevant information.

(h) Subject to Sections 11(i) and 23, the rights of the person to which a part passes under Section 11 are superior to the rights of all others with respect to the part. The person may accept or reject an anatomical gift in whole or in part. Subject to the terms of the document of gift and this [act], a person that accepts an anatomical gift of an entire body may allow embalming, burial or cremation, and use of remains in a funeral service. If the gift is of a part, the person to which the part passes under Section 11, upon the death of the donor and before embalming, burial, or cremation, shall cause the part to be removed without unnecessary mutilation.

(i) Neither the physician who attends the decedent at death nor the physician who determines the time of the decedent's death may participate in the procedures for removing or transplanting a part from the decedent.

(j) A physician or technician may remove a donated part from the body of a donor that the physician or technician is qualified to remove.

SECTION 15. COORDINATION OF PROCUREMENT AND USE.

Each hospital in this state shall enter into agreements or affiliations with procurement organizations for coordination of procurement and use of anatomical gifts.

SECTION 16. SALE OR PURCHASE OF PARTS PROHIBITED.

(a) Except as otherwise provided in subsection (b), a person that for valuable consideration, knowingly purchases or sells a part for transplantation or therapy if removal of a part from an individual is intended to occur after the individual's death commits a [[felony] and upon conviction is subject to a fine not exceeding [$50,000] or imprisonment not exceeding [five] years, or both][class[ ] felony].

(b) A person may charge a reasonable amount for the removal, processing, preservation, quality control, storage, transportation, implantation, or disposal of a part.

SECTION 17. OTHER PROHIBITED ACTS.

A person that, in order to obtain a financial gain, intentionally falsifies, forges, conceals, defaces, or obliterates a document of gift, an amendment or revocation of a document of gift, or a refusal commits a [[felony] and upon conviction is subject to a fine not exceeding [$50,000] or imprisonment not exceeding [five] years, or both] [class[ ] felony].

SECTION 18. IMMUNITY.

(a) A person that acts in accordance with this [act] or with the applicable anatomical gift law of another state, or attempts in good faith to do so, is not liable for the act in a civil action, criminal prosecution, or administrative proceeding.

(b) Neither the person making an anatomical gift nor the donor's estate is liable for any injury or damage that results from the making or use of the gift.

(c) In determining whether an anatomical gift has been made, amended, or revoked under this [act], a person may rely upon representations of an individual listed in Section 9(a)(2), (3), (4), (5), (6), (7), or (8) relating to the individual's relationship to the donor or prospective donor unless the person knows that the representation is untrue.

SECTION 19. LAW GOVERNING VALIDITY; CHOICE OF LAW AS TO EXECUTION OF DOCUMENT OF GIFT; PRESUMPTION OF VALIDITY.

(a) A document of gift is valid if executed in accordance with:

(1) this [act];

(2) the laws of the state or country where it was executed; or

(3) the laws of the state or country where the person making the anatomical gift was domiciled, has a place of residence, or was a national at the time the document of gift was executed.

(b) If a document of gift is valid under this section, the law of this state governs the interpretation of the document of gift.

(c) A person may presume that a document of gift or amendment of an anatomical gift is valid unless that person knows that it was not validly executed or was revoked.

SECTION 20. DONOR REGISTRY.

(a) The [insert name of appropriate state agency] may establish or contract for the establishment of a donor registry.

(b) The [state department of motor vehicles] shall cooperate with a person that administers any donor registry that this state establishes, contracts for, or recognizes for the purpose of transferring to the donor registry all relevant information regarding a donor's making, amendment to, or revocation of an anatomical gift.

(c) A donor registry must:

(1) allow a donor or other person authorized under Section 4 to include on the donor registry a statement or symbol that the donor has made, amended, or revoked an anatomical gift;

(2) be accessible to a procurement organization to allow it to obtain relevant information on the donor registry to determine, at or near death of the donor or a prospective donor, whether the donor or prospective donor has made, amended, or revoked an anatomical gift; and

(3) be accessible for purposes of paragraphs (1) and (2) seven days a week on a 24–hour basis.

(d) Personally identifiable information on a donor registry about a donor or prospective donor may not be used or disclosed without the express consent of the donor, prospective donor, or person that made the anatomical gift for any purpose other than to determine, at or near death of the donor or prospective donor, whether the donor or prospective donor has made, amended, or revoked an anatomical gift.

(e) This section does not prohibit any person from creating or maintaining a donor registry that is not established by or under contract with the state. Any such registry must comply with subsections (c) and (d).

Legislative Note: If the state has an existing donor registry statute, it should consider whether this section is necessary. It should also consider whether subsections (c) and (d), and Section 14(g)(last sentence), should be incorporated into its existing statute. Subsection (b) may be deleted if the state department of motor vehicles is the agency specified in subsection (a).

SECTION 21. EFFECT OF ANATOMICAL GIFT ON ADVANCE HEALTH–CARE DIRECTIVE.

(a) In this section:

(1) "Advance health-care directive" means a power of attorney for health care or a record signed or authorized by a prospective donor containing the prospective donor's direction concerning a health-care decision for the prospective donor.

(2) "Declaration" means a record signed by a prospective donor specifying the circumstances under which a life support system may be withheld or withdrawn from the prospective donor.

(3) "Health-care decision" means any decision regarding the health care of the prospective donor.

(b) If a prospective donor has a declaration or advance health-care directive and the terms of the declaration or directive and the express or implied terms of a potential anatomical gift are in conflict with regard to the administration of measures necessary to ensure the medical suitability of a part for transplantation or therapy, the prospective donor's attending physician and prospective donor shall confer to resolve the conflict. If the prospective donor is incapable of resolving the conflict, an agent acting under the prospective donor's declaration or directive, or, if none or the agent is not reasonably available, another person authorized by law other than this [act] to make health-care decisions on behalf of the prospective donor, shall act for the donor to resolve the conflict. The conflict must be resolved as expeditiously as possible. Information relevant to the resolution of the conflict may be obtained from the appropriate procurement organization and any other person authorized to make an anatomical gift for the prospective donor under Section 9. Before resolution of the conflict, measures necessary to ensure the medical suitability of the part may not be withheld or withdrawn from the prospective donor if withholding or withdrawing the measures is not contraindicated by appropriate end-of-life care.

SECTION 22. COOPERATION BETWEEN [CORONER] [MEDICAL EXAMINER] AND PROCUREMENT ORGANIZATION.

(a) A [coroner] [medical examiner] shall cooperate with procurement organizations to maximize the opportunity to recover anatomical gifts for the purpose of transplantation, therapy, research, or education.

(b) If a [coroner] [medical examiner] receives notice from a procurement organization that an anatomical gift might be available or was made with respect to a decedent whose body is under the jurisdiction of the [coroner] [medical examiner] and a post-mortem examination is going to be performed, unless the [coroner] [medical examiner] denies recovery in accordance with Section 23, the [coroner] [medical examiner] or designee shall conduct a post-mortem examination of the body or the part in a manner and within a period compatible with its preservation for the purposes of the gift.

(c) A part may not be removed from the body of a decedent under the jurisdiction of a [coroner] [medical examiner] for transplantation, therapy, research, or education unless the part is the subject of an anatomical gift. The body of a decedent under the jurisdiction of the [coroner] [medical examiner] may not be delivered to a person for research or education unless the body is the subject of an anatomical gift. This subsection does not preclude a [coroner] [medical examiner] from performing the medicolegal investigation upon the body or parts of a decedent under the jurisdiction of the [coroner] [medical examiner].

SECTION 23. FACILITATION OF ANATOMICAL GIFT FROM DECEDENT WHOSE BODY IS UNDER JURISDICTION OF [CORONER] [MEDICAL EXAMINER].

(a) Upon request of a procurement organization, a [coroner] [medical examiner] shall release to the procurement organization the name, contact information, and available medical and social history of a decedent whose body is under the jurisdiction of the [coroner] [medical examiner]. If the decedent's body or part is medically suitable for transplantation, therapy, research, or education, the [coroner] [medical examiner] shall release post-mortem examination results to the procurement organization. The procurement organization may make a subsequent disclosure of the post-mortem examination results or other information received from the [coroner] [medical examiner] only if relevant to transplantation or therapy.

(b) The [coroner] [medical examiner] may conduct a medicolegal examination by reviewing all medical records, laboratory test results, x-rays, other diagnostic results, and other information that any person possesses about a donor or prospective donor whose body is under the jurisdiction of the [coroner] [medical examiner] which the [coroner] [medical examiner] determines may be relevant to the investigation.

(c) A person that has any information requested by a [coroner] [medical examiner] pursuant to subsection (b) shall provide that information as expeditiously as possible to allow the [coroner] [medical examiner] to conduct the medicolegal investigation within a period compatible with the preservation of parts for the purpose of transplantation, therapy, research, or education.

(d) If an anatomical gift has been or might be made of a part of a decedent whose body is under the jurisdiction of the [coroner] [medical examiner] and a post-mortem examination is not required, or the [coroner] [medical examiner] determines that a post-mortem examination is required but that the recovery of the part that is the subject of an anatomical gift will not interfere with the examination, the [coroner] [medical examiner] and procurement organization shall cooperate in the timely removal of the part from the decedent for the purpose of transplantation, therapy, research, or education.

(e) If an anatomical gift of a part from the decedent under the jurisdiction of the [coroner] [medical examiner] has been or might be made, but the [coroner] [medical examiner] initially believes that the recovery of the part could interfere with the post-mortem investigation into the decedent's cause or manner of death, the [coroner] [medical examiner] shall consult with the procurement organization or physician or technician designated by the procurement organization about the proposed recovery. After consultation, the [coroner] [medical examiner] may allow the recovery.

(f) Following the consultation under subsection (e), in the absence of mutually agreed-upon protocols to resolve conflict between the [coroner] [medical examiner] and the procurement organization, if the [coroner] [medical examiner] intends to deny recovery, the [coroner] [medical examiner] or designee, at the request of the procurement organization, shall attend the removal procedure for the part before making a final determination not to allow the procurement organization to recover the part. During the removal procedure, the [coroner] [medical examiner] or designee may allow recovery by the procurement organization to proceed, or, if the [coroner] [medical examiner] or designee reasonably believes that the part may be involved in determining the decedent's cause or manner of death, deny recovery by the procurement organization.

(g) If the [coroner] [medical examiner] or designee denies recovery under subsection (f), the [coroner] [medical examiner] or designee shall:

(1) explain in a record the specific reasons for not allowing recovery of the part;

(2) include the specific reasons in the records of the [coroner] [medical examiner]; and

(3) provide a record with the specific reasons to the procurement organization.

(h) If the [coroner] [medical examiner] or designee allows recovery of a part under subsection (d), (e), or (f), the procurement organization, upon request, shall cause the physician or technician who removes the part to provide the [coroner] [medical examiner] with a record describing the condition of the part, a biopsy, a photograph, and any other information and observations that would assist in the post-mortem examination.

(i) If a [coroner] [medical examiner] or designee is required to be present at a removal procedure under subsection (f), upon request the procurement organization requesting the recovery of the part shall reimburse the [coroner] [medical examiner] or designee for the additional costs incurred in complying with subsection (f).

Legislative Note: Section 23 could be incorporated into the provisions of the state's code where the provisions relating to a coroner or medical examiner are codified rather than included in this act. If codified in that manner, the definitions in Section 2 of "anatomical gift", "donor", "eye bank", "organ procurement organization", "part", "procurement organization", "prospective donor" (first sentence only), "tissue", and "tissue bank" also should be included.

SECTION 24. UNIFORMITY OF APPLICATION AND CONSTRUCTION.

In applying and construing this uniform act, consideration must be given to the need to promote uniformity of the law with respect to its subject matter among states that enact it.

SECTION 25. RELATION TO ELECTRONIC SIGNATURES IN GLOBAL AND NATIONAL COMMERCE ACT.

This act modifies, limits, and supersedes the Electronic Signatures in Global and National Commerce Act, 15 U.S.C. Section 7001 et seq., but does not modify, limit or supersede Section 101(a) of that act, 15 U.S.C. Section 7001, or authorize electronic delivery of any of the notices described in Section 103(b) of that act, 15 U.S.C. Section 7003(b).

SECTION 26. REPEALS.

The following acts and parts of acts are repealed:

(1) [Uniform Anatomical Gift Act];

(2)

(3)

SECTION 27. EFFECTIVE DATE.

This [act] takes effect ____.

LOCATE

1. Which version of the Uniform Anatomical Gift Act does your state have, the 2006 Act, which you have just read, or the 1987 or 1968 Acts? What changes has your state made to the uniform text?

2. Does your state allow a person to indicate donor status on the person's driver's license?

NOTES AND QUESTIONS

1. The official United States government website for organ donation is located at http://www.organdonor.gov/ and contains a wealth of information including downloadable donor cards.

2. The American Bar Association's Section of Real Property, Probate and Trust Law Council approved a resolution in October 1991 urging "all attorneys to raise with their clients, when appropriate, the topic of organ and tissue donations." *Organ Donor Resolution,* PROB. & PROP., Jan./Feb. 1992, at 6. See also David M. English, *Gift of Life: The Lawyer's Role in Organ and Tissue Donation,* PROB. & PROP., March/April 1994, at 10. The ABA publishes a booklet you may purchase for distribution to your clients entitled *A Legacy for Life—Becoming an Organ or Tissue Donor.*

3. One of the most often cited reasons a person does not want to make anatomical gifts is a fear that a doctor may accelerate death to obtain needed organs. Is this fear justified? See *'Drowned' Tottler Alive, Improving,* SAN ANTONIO EXPRESS-NEWS, May 31, 2004, at 14A (child was "declared dead an hour before a nurse preparing his body for a funeral noticed his chest was moving slightly" and his condition was upgraded from dead to fair); *'Dead' Man's Foot Twitch Stops Removal of Organs,* PITTSBURGH PRESS, Sept. 29, 1990, at A2 (man pronounced brain dead, family agreed to donate organs, body transported 150 miles, then transplant doctors noticed life signs and changed condition from dead to critical); *Checking for Pulse Misses Some Who Are Still Alive,* BOSTON GLOBE, Feb. 3, 1992, at 27 (12% of people pronounced dead by physicians had beating hearts and thus were technically alive); *Man Cheats Death, Loses His Fiancée,* NEW ORLEANS TIMES PICAYUNE, Mar. 22, 1993, at E15 (man declared dead after a traffic accident and taken to mortuary, woke up 48 hours later and was spurned by his fiancée who believed he was a zombie); *'Dead' N.Y. Woman on Road to Recovery,* SAN FRANCISCO CHRONICLE, June 17, 1993, at A18 (investigator was beginning medical examination to determine cause of death when he heard gurgling sound alerting him to fact woman still alive); *Brain–Dead Teen Fights Back, Writes Mom,* SAN ANTONIO EXPRESS-NEWS, Oct. 20, 1989, at 10–J (days after doctor asked parents to donate daughter's organs, daughter upgraded from brain-dead to stable condition).

4. Some individuals are opposed to organ donation on religious grounds. See *Organ Gift a Blessing,* PHILADELPHIA DAILY NEWS, June 8, 1989, at 53 (letter to "Dear Abby" from T.G. Hayes stating, "I consider my body as the temple that God built to house my soul. It was not meant to be cut to pieces at death

as if it were an old radio or some other non-living structure."). Pope John Paul II has spoken in favor of organ donation. See Pope John Paul II, *Blood and Organ Donors,* 30 THE POPE SPEAKS 1–2 (1985) (donation is "laudable in that you are motivated, not by a desire for earthly gain or ends, but by a generous impulse of the heart, by human and Christian solidarity—the love of neighbor, which forms the inspiring motive of the Gospel message, and which has been defined, indeed, as the *new commandment.*"). However, Hispanic Americans, who are predominantly Catholic, still oppose organ donation for religious reasons. See Jim Forsyth, *Many Hispanics Hesitant About Organ Donation*, REUTERS, Mar. 28, 2011. Most religious groups support organ donation. See *Religious Views on Organ/Tissue Donation,* in AMERICAN BAR ASSOCIATION, ORGAN DONATION AND TRANSPLANTATION C9–11 (1992).

5. Some people believe that the need for organs prolongs intra-minority violence because the resulting deaths provide young, healthy organs for whites. Do you think this analysis is sound? See *Farrakhan: Whites Want Internal Organs,* PHOENIX GAZETTE, July 2, 1994, at A4. But see Claire Bourne, *Group is On a Mission to Sign Up More Black Organ Donors*, USA TODAY, Aug. 4, 2003, at 6D ("Of the 16 people who die waiting for organ transplants each day in the USA, half of them are ethnic minorities, and a quarter of them are black.").

6. Reluctant donors may fear that donation will disfigure the body making it unsuitable for viewing at the funeral service. Is this fear justified?

7. Who may make an anatomical gift? May a minor make an anatomical gift? May an anatomical gift be made by an individual other than the donor? If so, under what conditions? Psychologists argue that parents of children who die prematurely sometimes donate the organs and tissues of their children to give meaning to their child's life. See Rita Rubin, *Transplants Offer Solace in Time of Heartache*, USA TODAY, Jan. 23, 2011.

8. Who are the proper recipients of anatomical gifts? Must a specific donee be named by the donor?

9. What are the requirements for a valid donor card?

10. The donor may make an anatomical gift by will or by a donor card. Which method would you recommend and why?

11. An anatomical gift is not effective until the donor's death. Prior to death, how may the donor revoke the gift?

12. After the donor's death, may the donor's spouse or children *legally* prevent the gift from taking effect? In reality? See *Would-be Donors' Kin Sometimes Refuse Vital Organ Donations*, SAN ANTONIO EXPRESS-NEWS, Aug. 28, 1995, at 14A. Who, if anyone, has rights superior to those of the donee?

13. Must a donee accept an anatomical gift?

14. Assume that an anatomical gift is made by will and the will is declared invalid or is not probated. Is the donee or transplanting professionals liable for any type of damages?

15. If your client does not want to become a donor, is it sufficient merely to do nothing? Should any special steps be taken to make certain the client's intent is carried out? What would you suggest?

16. What responsibilities regarding anatomical gifts does a hospital have when deaths occur in the hospital?

17. State law often permits the justice of the peace or a medical examiner to permit an anatomical gift to take place even without the consent of the donor or the donor's family. For a discussion of the constitutionality of this type of statute, see Georgia Lions Eye Bank, Inc. v. Lavant, 255 Ga. 60, 335 S.E.2d 127 (1985), cert. denied, 475 U.S. 1084, 106 S.Ct. 1464, 89 L.Ed.2d 721 (1986). See also Erik S. Jaffe, Note, *"She's Got Bette Davis['s] Eyes": Assessing the Nonconsensual Removal of Cadaver Organs Under the Takings and Due Process Clauses,* 90 COLUM. L. REV. 528 (1990). A growing trend in other nations is to presume that all citizens consent to organ donation unless they have formalized their objection. Diana Jean Schemo, *Brazilians Half-Heartedly Support Organ Donor Law*, SAN ANTONIO EXPRESS-NEWS, Jan. 18, 1998, at 5B (reporting that support for organ donation has dropped since enactment of the new law and discussing similar legislation in European countries such as Spain).

18. May or should a brain-dead donor be kept "alive" (as a *biomort*) so that research may be performed while the body is, to some extent, still functioning on its own? See Susan R. Martyn, *Using the Brain Dead for Medical Research,* 1986 UTAH L. REV. 1.

19. Should a donor be able to sell "extra" organs such as a kidney while alive?

20. Underground organ markets exist in some foreign countries, especially for kidneys, skin, and corneas. Some individuals sell organs for money and other people are abducted and later found dead with missing organs or alive with scars of unknown origin.

21. Should a donor be able to sell a future interest to his or her organs which would entitle the purchaser to the organs upon the donor's death? See Lloyd Cohen, *Increasing the Supply of Transplant Organs: The Virtues of a Futures Market,* 58 GEO. WASH. L. REV. 1 (1989); Gregory S. Crespi, *Overcoming the Legal Obstacles to the Creation of a Futures Market in Bodily Organs,* 55 OHIO ST. L.J. 1 (1994). J. Randall Boyer, *Gifts of the Heart ... And Other Tissues: Legalizing The Sale of Human Organs and Tissues*, 2012 BYU L. REV. 313 (2012).

22. In summer 2001, President George Bush signed Executive Order 13435 which limited federal funding for stem cell research to a limited number of existing embryonic stem cell lines. After the death of President Ronald Reagan from Alzheimer's in 2004, there was a growing movement to relax these restrictions. In 2009, President Barack Obama issued Executive Order 13505 which removed the limitations on federal funding for embryonic stem cell research.

23. Should a legal property right in human bodies be legislatively created? See Michelle Bourianoff Bray, Note, *Personalizing Personalty: Toward a Property Right in Human Bodies,* 69 TEX. L. REV. 209 (1990).

24. There is a scarcity of organs available for transplant. How should recipients be chosen? Youngest? Oldest? Most likely to die first? Highest bidder? On waiting list the longest? Best prognosis? Person located in closest

proximity to the donor? Person who contributed or will contribute more to society than other potential donees? See 42 C.F.R. § 121.8.

25. Should a person who has never received a transplant have priority over someone who has received a transplant but needs another? See *Scarce Organs Fuel Controversy Over Repeat Transplants,* SAN ANTONIO EXPRESS-NEWS, Dec. 3, 1993, at 8A (stating that one in five livers and one in ten hearts goes to a donee who has a failed transplant).

26. Donated organs, such as livers, are sometimes cut into pieces so that one donated organ can be used in several donees. See Clinton Colmenares, *The Paradox of Transplants*, SAN ANTONIO EXPRESS-NEWS, Mar. 16, 1998, at 1F.

27. Organs are sometimes recycled. After the donee dies, the donated organ is removed and transplanted into a second donee. See *Man's Transplanted Heart on its Third Time Around,* WICHITA EAGLE, June 27, 1993, at 3A.

28. Should death row inmates be allowed to donate organs during the execution process? Donny J. Perales, *Rethinking the Prohibition of Death Row Prisoners as Organ Donors: A Possible Lifeline to Those on Organ Donor Waiting Lists*, 34 ST. MARY'S L.J. 687 (2003) (concluding that "the benefits of saving lives considerably outweigh the competing concerns that condemned prisoners should not be organ donors"); Theresa Humphrey, *Killer Offers Mom Gift of Life*, ALBUQUERQUE J., Mar. 9, 1995, at C16 (condemned killer sought stay of execution so he could donate a kidney to his mother); Mark Curriden, *Inmate's Last Wish is to Donate Kidney*, A.B.A. J., June 1996, at 26. Is it proper for potential donees, their families, or the government to offer financial incentives to the inmate's family to encourage the inmate to consent to the donation? See *Chinese Harvesting Inmates' Organs,* BALTIMORE MORNING SUN, Aug. 29, 1994, at 1A (Human Rights Watch/Asia alleges executions are intentionally botched to allow doctors to harvest organs from living donors; families of inmates threatened with financial obligation for prisoner's expenses as well as execution expenses if they withhold consent for organ donations). Should death row inmates have the opportunity to donate organs in exchange for having their sentences reduced to life in prison without parole? Is this a good idea? Why or why not? See also Anna Stolley Persky, *Life from Death Row*, ABA J., April 2012, at 16.

29. Assume that it can be proven that a donor's organs caused cancer or AIDS in a donee. May the donee recover damages from the professionals involved in the transplant process or from the donor's estate?

30. Scientists are genetically engineering pigs so that their hearts, lungs, kidneys, and other organs may be transplanted into humans without triggering rejection responses. See *Experiment in Organ Farming Going on With Help of Pigs,* SAN ANTONIO EXPRESS-NEWS, Dec. 5, 1993, at 13D. In addition, researchers are attempting to grow tissue and organs by using healthy cells from the patient. Charles Hirshberg, *The Body Shop*, LIFE, Fall 1998, at 50. What impact will these experiments have on organ donation if they are successful?

31. Who is responsible for the costs of removing the donor's organs, the donor's estate or the donee?

32. Should a patient be compensated when unwanted tissue is removed and then used to create profitable products? See Moore v. Regents of the University of California, 51 Cal.3d 120, 271 Cal.Rptr. 146, 793 P.2d 479 (1990), cert. denied, 499 U.S. 936, 111 S.Ct. 1388, 113 L.Ed.2d 444 (1991) (doctor removed spleen of patient with hairy-cell leukemia and used blood to create profitable cell line; court held no cause of action for conversion but potential liability for removal without informed consent and breach of fiduciary duty); John J. O'Connor, Note, *The Commercialization of Human Tissue—The Source of Legal, Ethical and Social Problems: An Area Better Suited to Legislative Resolution,* 24 LOY. L.A .L. REV. 115 (1990) (proposing a Uniform Tissue Source Compensation Act to resolve problems arising when tissue of a living person is used for commercial purposes).

33. What if the organ or tissue is removed after the person's death without proper authority and sold for a profit? For example, the German government revealed in May 1994 that workers at 90 hospitals were removing brain membranes from corpses and selling them for $18 each. See *Sales of Brain Membranes by Hospital Aides Reported,* BUFFALO NEWS, May 21, 1994, at A3.

34. In January 2004, "Wisconsin became the first state * * * to offer [living donors] a tax deduction for expenses incurred in donating an organ. People who donate a liver, lung, pancreas, kidney, intestines or bone marrow can deduct up to $10,000 in expenses for such things as travel and lost wages." *Wisconsin Gives Tax Break to Organ Donors*, USA TODAY, Feb. 2, 2004, at 6D. Do you think this is a wise idea?

35. To encourage people to sign donor cards, should only individuals who have agreed to donate organs be eligible to receive donated organs? See *Joe Bob's America*, SAN ANTONIO CURRENT, Aug. 10, 1995, at 31; Lawrence W. Reed, *Encourage Organ Donors With a Little Quid Pro Quo*, USA TODAY, July 24, 2003, at 13A.

DRAFT

1. Draft the proper documents to reflect a client's intent to donate all needed organs.

2. Draft the documents necessary to restrict an anatomical gift to the donor's heart.

3. Draft the documents necessary to carry out your client's intent that no organ donation is to occur under any circumstance.

IN RE T.A.C.P.

Supreme Court of Florida, 1992.
609 So.2d 588.

KOGAN, JUSTICE.

We have for review an order of the trial court certified by the Fourth District Court of Appeal as touching on a matter of great public importance requiring immediate resolution by this Court. We frame the issue as follows: Is an anencephalic newborn considered "dead" for purposes of organ donation solely by reason of its congenital deformity? We have jurisdiction. * * *

I. FACTS

At or about the eighth month of pregnancy, the parents of the child T.A.C.P. were informed that she would be born with anencephaly. This is a birth defect invariably fatal, in which the child typically is born with only a "brain stem" but otherwise lacks a human brain. In T.A.C.P.'s case, the back of the skull was entirely missing and the brain stem was exposed to the air, except for medical bandaging. The risk of infection to the brain stem was considered very high. Anencephalic infants sometimes can survive several days after birth because the brain stem has a limited capacity to maintain autonomic bodily functions such as breathing and heartbeat. This ability soon ceases, however, in the absence of regulation from the missing brain.

In this case, T.A.C.P. actually survived only a few days after birth. The medical evidence in the record shows that the child T.A.C.P. was incapable of developing any sort of cognitive process, may have been unable to feel pain or experience sensation due to the absence of the upper brain, and at least for part of the time was placed on a mechanical ventilator to assist her breathing. At the time of the hearing below, however, the child was breathing unaided, although she died soon thereafter.

On the advice of physicians, the parents continued the pregnancy to term and agreed that the mother would undergo caesarian section during birth. The parents agreed to the caesarian procedure with the express hope that the infant's organs would be less damaged and could be used for transplant in other sick children. Although T.A.C.P. had no hope of life herself, the parents both testified in court that they wanted to use this opportunity to give life to others. However, when the parents requested that T.A.C.P. be declared legally dead for this purpose, her health care providers refused out of concern that they thereby might incur civil or criminal liability.

The parents then filed a petition in the circuit court asking for a judicial determination. After hearing testimony and argument, the trial court denied the request on grounds that section 382.009(1), Florida Statutes (1991), would not permit a determination of legal death so long as the child's brain stem continued to function. On appeal, the Fourth District summarily affirmed but then certified the trial court's order to this Court for immediate resolution of the issue. We have accepted jurisdiction to resolve this case of first impression.

II. THE MEDICAL NATURE OF ANENCEPHALY

Although appellate courts appear never to have confronted the issue, there already is an impressive body of published medical scholarship on anencephaly. From our review of this material, we find that anencephaly is a variable but fairly well defined medical condition. Experts in the field have written that anencephaly is the most common severe birth defect of the central nervous system seen in the United States, although it apparently has existed throughout human history.

A statement by the Medical Task Force on Anencephaly ("Task Force") printed in the New England Journal of Medicine generally described "anencephaly" as "a congenital absence of major portions of the brain, skull, and scalp, with its genesis in the first month of gestation." David A. Stumpf et al., The Infant with Anencephaly, 322 New Eng. J.Med. 669, 669 (1990). The large opening in the skull accompanied by the absence or severe congenital disruption of the cerebral hemispheres is the characteristic feature of the condition. Id.

The Task Force defined anencephaly as diagnosable only when all of the following four criteria are present: (1) A large portion of the skull is absent. (2) The scalp, which extends to the margin of the bone, is absent over the skull defect. (3) Hemorrhagic, fibrotic tissue is exposed because of defects in the skull and scalp. (4) Recognizable cerebral hemispheres are absent. Id. at 670. Anencephaly is often, though not always, accompanied by defects in various other body organs and systems, some of which may render the child unsuitable for organ transplantation. Id.

Thus, it is clear that anencephaly is distinguishable from some other congenital conditions because its extremity renders it uniformly lethal. Id. Less severe conditions are not "anencephaly." There has been a tendency by some parties and amici to confuse lethal anencephaly with these less serious conditions, even to the point of describing children as "anencephalic" who have abnormal but otherwise intact skulls and who are several years of age. We emphasize that the child T.A.C.P. clearly met the four criteria described above. The present opinion does not apply to children with less serious conditions; they are not anencephalic because they do not have large openings in their skulls accompanied by the complete or near total absence of normal cerebral hemispheres, which defines "anencephaly." See id.

The Task Force stated that most reported anencephalic children die within the first few days after birth, with survival any longer being rare. After reviewing all available medical literature, the Task Force found no study in which survival beyond a week exceeded nine percent of children meeting the four criteria. Id. at 671. Two months was the longest confirmed survival of an anencephalic, although there are unconfirmed reports of one surviving three months and another surviving fourteen months. The Task Force reported, however, that these survival rates are confounded somewhat by the variable degrees of medical care afforded to anencephalics. Id. Some such infants may be given considerable life support while others may be given much less care. See id.

The Task Force reported that the medical consequences of anencephaly can be established with some certainty. All anencephalics by definition are permanently unconscious because they lack the cerebral cortex necessary for conscious thought. Their condition thus is quite similar to that of persons in a persistent vegetative state. Where the brain stem is functioning, as it was here, spontaneous breathing and heartbeat can occur. In addition, such infants may show spontaneous movements of the extremities, "startle" reflexes, and pupils that respond to light. Some may show feeding reflexes, may cough, hiccup, or exhibit eye movements, and may produce facial expressions. Id. at 671–72.

The question of whether such infants actually suffer from pain is somewhat more complex. It involves a distinction between "pain" and "suffering." The Task Force indicated that anencephaly in some ways is analogous to persons with cerebral brain lesions. Such lesions may not actually eliminate the reflexive response to a painful condition, but they can eliminate any capacity to "suffer" as a result of the condition. Likewise, anencephalic infants may reflexively avoid painful stimuli where the brain stem is functioning and thus is able to command an innate, unconscious withdrawal response; but the infants presumably lack the capacity to suffer. Id. 672. It is clear, however, that this incapacity to suffer has not been established beyond all doubt. See id.

After the advent of new transplant methods in the past few decades, anencephalic infants have successfully been used as a source of organs for donation. However, the Task Force was able to identify only twelve successful transplants using anencephalic organs by 1990. Transplants were most successful when the anencephalic immediately was placed on life support and its organs used as soon as possible, without regard to the existence of brain-stem activity. However, this only accounted for a total of four reported transplants. Id. at 672–73.

There appears to be general agreement that anencephalics usually have ceased to be suitable organ donors by the time they meet all the criteria for "whole brain death," i.e., the complete absence of brain-stem function. Stephen Ashwal et al., Anencephaly: Clinical Determination of Brain Death and Neuropathologic Studies, 6 Pediatric Neurology 233, 239 (1990). There also is no doubt that a need exists for infant organs for transplantation. Nationally, between thirty and fifty percent of children under two years of age who need transplants die while waiting for organs to become available. Joyce L. Peabody et al., Experience with Anencephalic Infants as Prospective Organ Donors, 321 New Eng.J.Med. 344, 344 (1989).

III. LEGAL DEFINITIONS OF "DEATH" & "LIFE"

As the parties and amici have argued, the common law in some American jurisdictions recognized a cardiopulmonary definition of "death": A human being was not considered dead until breathing and heartbeat had stopped entirely, without possibility of resuscitation. * * *

However, there is some doubt about the exact method by which this definition was imported into the law of some states. Apparently the definition was taken from earlier editions of Black's Law Dictionary, which itself did not cite to an original source. * * * The definition thus may only have been the opinion of Black's earlier editors.

We have found no authority showing that Florida ever recognized the original Black's Law Dictionary definition or any other definition of "death" as a matter of our own common law. Even if we had adopted such a standard, however, it is equally clear that modern medical technology has rendered the earlier Black's definition of "death" seriously inadequate. With the invention of life-support devices and procedures, human bodies can be made to breathe and blood to circulate even in the utter absence of brain function.

As a result, the ability to withhold or discontinue such life support created distinct legal problems in light of the "cardiopulmonary" definition of death originally used by Black's Dictionary. For example, health care providers might be civilly or criminally liable for removing transplantable organs from a person sustained by life support, or defendants charged with homicide might argue that their victim's death actually was caused when life support was discontinued. Andrea K. Scott, Death Unto Life: Anencephalic Infants as Organ Donors, 74 Va.L.Rev. 1527, 1538–41 (1988) (citing actual cases).

In light of the inadequacies of a cardiopulmonary definition of "death," a number of jurisdictions began altering their laws in an attempt to address the medical community's changing conceptions of the point in time at which life ceases. An effort was made to synthesize many of the new concerns into a Uniform Determination of Death Act issued by the National Conference of Commissioners on Uniform State Laws.[10] The uniform statute states: An individual who has sustained either (1) irreversible cessation of circulatory and respiratory functions, or (2) irreversible cessation of all functions of the entire brain, including the brain stem, is dead. A determination of death must be made in accordance with accepted medical standards. Unif. Determination of Death Act § 1, 12 U.L.A. 340 (Supp.1991). Thus, the uniform act both codified the earlier common law standard and extended it to deal with the specific problem of "whole brain death." While some American jurisdictions appear to have adopted substantially the same language, Florida is not among these. * * *

Indeed, Florida appears to have struck out on its own. The statute cited as controlling by the trial court does not actually address itself to the problem of anencephalic infants, nor indeed to any situation other than patients actually being sustained by artificial life support. The statute provides: For legal and medical purposes, where respiratory and circulatory functions are maintained by artificial means of support so as to preclude a determination that these functions have ceased, the occurrence of death may be determined where there is the irreversible cessation of

10. Author's note: At least thirty-six states as well as the District of Columbia and the U.S. Virgin Islands have adopted the Uniform Determination of Death Act.

the functioning of the entire brain, including the brain stem, determined in accordance with this section. § 382.009(1), Fla.Stat. (1991) * * *. A later subsection goes on to declare: Except for a diagnosis of brain death, the standard set forth in this section is not the exclusive standard for determining death or for the withdrawal of life-support systems. § 382.009(4), Fla.Stat. (1991). This language is highly significant for two reasons.

First, the statute does not purport to codify the common law standard applied in some other jurisdictions, as does the uniform act. The use of the permissive word "may" in the statute in tandem with the savings clause of section 382.009(4) buttresses the conclusion that the legislature envisioned other ways of defining "death." Second, the statutory framers clearly did not intend to apply the statute's language to the anencephalic infant not being kept alive by life support. To the contrary, the framers expressly limited the statute to that situation in which "respiratory and circulatory functions are maintained by artificial means of support."

There are a few Florida authorities that have addressed the definitions of "life" and "death" in somewhat analogous though factually distinguishable contexts. Florida's Vital Statistics Act, for example, defines "live birth" as the complete expulsion or extraction of a product of human conception from its mother, irrespective of the duration of pregnancy, which, after such expulsion, breathes or shows any other evidence of life such as beating of the heart, pulsation of the umbilical cord, and definite movement of the voluntary muscles, whether or not the umbilical cord has been cut or the placenta is attached. § 382.002(10), Fla.Stat. (1991). Conversely, "fetal death" is defined as death prior to the complete expulsion or extraction of a product of human conception from its mother if the 20th week of gestation has been reached and the death is indicated by the fact that after such expulsion or extraction the fetus does not breathe or show any other evidence of life such as beating of the heart, pulsation of the umbilical cord, or definite movement of voluntary muscles. § 382.002(7), Fla.Stat. (1991). From these definitions, it is clear that T.A.C.P. was a "live birth" and not a "fetal death," at least for purposes of the collection of vital statistics in Florida. These definitions obviously are inapplicable to the issues at hand today, but they do shed some light on the Florida legislature's thoughts regarding a definition of "life" and "death."

Similarly, an analogous (if distinguishable) problem has arisen in Florida tort law. In cases alleging wrongful death, our courts have held that fetuses are not "persons" and are not "born alive" until they acquire an existence separate and independent from the mother. * * * We believe the weight of the evidence supports the conclusion that T.A.C.P. was "alive" in this sense because she was separated from the womb, and was capable of breathing and maintaining a heartbeat independently of her mother's body for some duration of time thereafter. Once again, however, this conclusion arises from law that is only analogous and is not dispositive of the issue at hand.

We also note that the 1988 Florida Legislature considered a bill that would have defined "death" to include anencephaly. * * * The bill died in committee. While the failure of legislation in committee does not establish legislative intent, it nevertheless supports the conclusion that as recently as 1988 no consensus existed among Florida's lawmakers regarding the issue we confront today.

The parties have cited to no authorities directly dealing with the question of whether anencephalics are "alive" or "dead." Our own research has disclosed no other federal or Florida law or precedent arguably on point or applicable by analogy. We thus are led to the conclusion that no legal authority binding upon this Court has decided whether an anencephalic child is alive for purposes of organ donation. In the absence of applicable legal authority, this Court must weigh and consider the public policy considerations at stake here.

IV. COMMON LAW & POLICY

Initially, we must start by recognizing that section 382.009, Florida Statutes (1991), provides a method for determining death in those cases in which a person's respiratory and circulatory functions are maintained artificially. § 382.009(4), Fla.Stat. (1991). Likewise, we agree that a cardiopulmonary definition of death must be accepted in Florida as a matter of our common law, applicable whenever section 382.009 does not govern. Thus, if cardiopulmonary function is not being maintained artificially as stated in section 382.009, a person is dead who has sustained irreversible cessation of circulatory and respiratory functions as determined in accordance with accepted medical standards. We have found no credible authority arguing that this definition is inconsistent with the existence of death, and we therefore need not labor the point further.

The question remaining is whether there is good reason in public policy for this Court to create an additional common law standard applicable to anencephalics. Alterations of the common law, while rarely entertained or allowed, are within this Court's prerogative. * * * However, the rule we follow is that the common law will not be altered or expanded unless demanded by public necessity, * * *, or where required to vindicate fundamental rights. * * * We believe, for example, that our adoption of the cardiopulmonary definition of death today is required by public necessity and, in any event, merely formalizes what has been the common practice in this state for well over a century.

Such is not the case with petitioners' request. Our review of the medical, ethical, and legal literature on anencephaly discloses absolutely no consensus that public necessity or fundamental rights will be better served by granting this request.

We are not persuaded that a public necessity exists to justify this action, in light of the other factors in this case—although we acknowledge much ambivalence about this particular question. We have been deeply touched by the altruism and unquestioned motives of the parents of

T.A.C.P. The parents have shown great humanity, compassion, and concern for others. The problem we as a Court must face, however, is that the medical literature shows unresolved controversy over the extent to which anencephalic organs can or should be used in transplants.

There is an unquestioned need for transplantable infant organs. * * * Yet some medical commentators suggest that the organs of anencephalics are seldom usable, for a variety of reasons, and that so few organ transplants will be possible from anencephalics as to render the enterprise questionable in light of the ethical problems at stake—even if legal restrictions were lifted. * * *

Others note that prenatal screening now is substantially reducing the number of anencephalics born each year in the United States and that, consequently, anencephalics are unlikely to be a significant source of organs as time passes. * * * And still others have frankly acknowledged that there is no consensus and that redefinition of death in this context should await the emergence of a consensus. * * *

A presidential commission in 1981 urged strict adherence to the Uniform Determination of Death Act's definition, which would preclude equating anencephaly with death. * * * Several sections of the American Bar Association have reached much the same conclusion. * * *

Some legal commentators have argued that treating anencephalics as dead equates them with "nonpersons," presenting a "slippery slope" problem with regard to all other persons who lack cognition for whatever reason. * * * Others have quoted physicians involved in infant-organ transplants as stating, "[T]he slippery slope is real," because some physicians have proposed transplants from infants with defects less severe than anencephaly. Beth Brandon, Anencephalic Infants as Organ Donors: A Question of Life or Death, 40 Case Western L.Rev. 781, 802 (1989–90).

We express no opinion today about who is right and who is wrong on these issues—if any "right" or "wrong" can be found here. The salient point is that no consensus exists as to: (a) the utility of organ transplants of the type at issue here; (b) the ethical issues involved; or (c) the legal and constitutional problems implicated.

V. CONCLUSION

Accordingly, we find no basis to expand the common law to equate anencephaly with death. We acknowledge the possibility that some infants' lives might be saved by using organs from anencephalics who do not meet the traditional definition of "death" we reaffirm today. But weighed against this is the utter lack of consensus, and the questions about the overall utility of such organ donations. The scales clearly tip in favor of not extending the common law in this instance.

To summarize: We hold that Florida common law recognizes the cardiopulmonary definition of death as stated above; and Florida statutes create a "whole-brain death" exception applicable whenever cardiopulmonary function is being maintained artificially. There are no other legal standards for determining death under present Florida law.

Because no Florida statute applies to the present case, the determination of death in this instance must be judged against the common law cardiopulmonary standard. The evidence shows that T.A.C.P.'s heart was beating and she was breathing at the times in question. Accordingly, she was not dead under Florida law, and no donation of her organs would have been legal. § 732.912, Fla.Stat. (1991). The trial court reached the correct result, although we do not agree with its determination that section 382.009 applied here. We answer the question posed by this case in the negative and approve the result reached below.

It is so ordered.

QUESTIONS

1. Do you agree with the result in this case? Why or why not?

2. Assume that your client is in the same predicament as T.A.C.P.'s mother. How would you proceed to best carry out her intent that the baby's organs be available for transplantation?

F. DISPOSITION OF BODY

IN RE SCHECK'S ESTATE

New York Surrogate's Court, Kings County, 1939.
172 Misc. 236, 14 N.Y.S.2d 946.

WINGATE, SURROGATE.

This proceeding presents an apparently unprecedented situation, to the legal complications of which, the parties appear oblivious. The decedent died in 1936, leaving a will and two codicils which were admitted to probate in this court, and which, in addition to directing the manner of disposal of her possessions and the administration of her estate, provided that her body should be transported to Palestine and there buried. Her instructions in this regard were quite circumstantial and explicit, and provided for the expenditure of $1,200 for the purpose.

In ignorance of these directions, the children of the decedent had her remains interred in a cemetery in this State, and according to the present account, expended a total of $189.33 in the process.

The distributees are unanimous in their wish that the remains of the decedent be left undisturbed, and have tendered four affidavits, two of which, executed by Rabbis, while in certain respects somewhat equivocal, may be taken to assert that the disinterment and removal to Palestine of the body of the deceased, would be contrary to Jewish Tenets and to Hebrew Laws.

The remaining affidavits are made by a son of the deceased and his wife, and recite that at the time of the execution of the codicils in which the questioned directions were included, the decedent was living with her second husband in Palestine and was making payments on a burial plot in that country; that she later became estranged from him, returned here, discontinued the payments and thereafter made regular payments in respect of the burial plot in which her remains have actually been interred. These affidavits further recite that during this latter period, and up to the time of her death, the decedent frequently expressed a wish to be buried in the latter plot.

For the purpose of discussion, the statements of all of these affidavits will be accepted as true, and it will be assumed that the disinterment and removal of the body of the deceased, and its re-interment in Palestine, as directed in the codicils, would be contrary to Hebrew Laws and that the final, verbally expressed, wish of the testatrix was that her remains should be buried where this has taken place.

The relevancy and materiality of the statements that a compliance with the written wishes of the testatrix respecting the disposal of her remains, would be in contravention of Jewish Tenets and Hebrew Law, is capable of ready decision. Every faith, when honestly entertained and practiced, is entitled to respect and, as far as is compatible with local law, to recognition. The laws of this state, however, have never countenanced the possibility of imperium in imperio. Insofar, therefore, as the customs, beliefs or individual practices of any particular race or group contravene the established law of the state, they are nugatory and incapable of effectuation. * * *

The observations of the court in the last cited authority are strikingly apposite to the present situation. It said: "* * * we have persistently, constantly, and successfully thus far resisted all attempts on the part of ecclesiastical authorities or churches to usurp or control the powers and rights of the legislative or judicial departments of this country. * * * When an ecclesiastical body assumes jurisdiction and control over a corpse its acts are of a temporal and jurisdical character, and not in any sense spiritual; and, under our laws and institutions, when it attempts so to do it is acting outside of its proper jurisdiction and domain."

The law of the State of New York on the subject of the right of a person to dispose of his own body has been clearly and unequivocally stated by the legislature: "A person has the right to direct the manner in which his body shall be disposed of after his death * * *." Penal Law, § 2210. The courts have repeatedly, either expressly or by implication, recognized and effectuated this right. * * *

A majority of the last group of citations related primarily to litigations concerning the respective rights of surviving relatives to custody of the body of a deceased person and the customary language in these pronouncements is that such relatives have a preferred right "in the absence of any testamentary disposition" of his body by the decedent himself.

Two questions naturally suggest themselves as a result of this frequently reiterated statement, namely, first, whether the authority of a person to dispose of his body is exercisable only by will; and secondly, whether if a will, as in the present case, actually makes directions in this regard, they are properly construable as an integral part of the testamentary document.

The implications arising from an affirmative answer to the second question are far reaching. If a direction for the disposal of the body of the testator is essentially testamentary and dispositive in character and its insertion in a will effects its integration into the composite directions of the instrument, it would apparently follow as a logical matter that, like any other testamentary direction, it would be capable of revocation only in the manner expressly specified in section 34 of the Decedent Estate Law, with the result that, when once inserted, it could be nullified only either by a total destruction of the document or by the execution of a new instrument authenticated with the formalities specified in section 21 of the Decedent Estate Law.

In evaluating this possibility, two principles appear worthy of recollection. The first is that there is no right of property in a dead body in any commercial sense * * * but merely a personal right * * *, primarily of the decedent himself, but if not exercised by him pursuant to the authorization of section 2210 of the Penal Law, then of his surviving spouse or nearest relative.

It is well established that mere personal rights are not deemed property, and are ordinarily not subject to delegation, devolutionary direction or intestate succession. * * * The personal right or privilege here in question presents no characteristics sufficient to take it out of the general rule.

It would follow as a logical conclusion that a direction in a will respecting disposal of the body of the testator is not testamentary in character to a degree which would require revocation of the direction to be accomplished in the manner prescribed in section 34 of the Decedent Estate Law. As noted, a dead body is not properly viewable as property or assets, and since time immemorial, it has been the settled law in all common law jurisdictions that a will is "the affirmative expression of intent of the testator respecting the administration and disposition of his material possessions upon his death." 5 Bacon Abr. tit. Of Wills and Testaments (A) p. 497; * * *.

The correctness of this conclusion is additionally evident from the fact that whereas the requirement of section 21 of the Decedent Estate Law that a will must be subscribed at its end has always received strict enforcement with the result that an additional at a subsequent point, if material, has been held to void the instrument, the test of materiality, as uniformly applied, has been as to whether the writing following the subscription bore any direct relation to the disposition of the property of the testator or to the administration of his estate. If it did, the entire instrument was voided, if not, it was admissible to probate. * * *

It follows from this rule that if the direction for disposal of the remains of the testator followed the subscription, the document would still be admissible to probate since it "neither affects the disposition of the estate nor appoints executor or guardian." Matter of Gibson's Will, 128 App.Div. 769, 773, 113 N.Y.S. 266, 269. In other words it is not testamentary in character and is not in any particular, either as to initial insertion, or subsequent revocation, to be governed by the ordinary rules relating to strictly testamentary directions.

The court is accordingly in complete agreement with the dictum of Surrogate Delehanty in his scholarly review of the history of the right of a testator to dispose of his own body on death (Matter of Johnson's Estate, 169 Misc. 215, 217, 7 N.Y.S.2d 81, 83) that the text of section 2210 of the Penal Law according the right in this regard "imports no special formality in the directions to be given. It would seem that whether directions pursuant to this statute had been given would be a question of fact to be determined under the ordinary rules of evidence and that parol or nonformal dispositions, if proved, would be equally valid under this section as directions given by formal instruments."

An inevitable sequence of this conception is the right of a particular decedent, from time to time in his discretion, to vary the directions respecting disposal of his remains, with the result that the inquiry of the court must be directed to the ascertainment of the latest expression of wish by the testator on the subject.

Whereas, however, the question is merely one of proof, a demonstration, as in the present case, that a formal and deliberate expression has been made, raises an inference of a continuance of the indicated desire which may not lightly be overcome. Especially is this true in a situation such as is here disclosed, in which a disregard of the formally expressed wish would result in a material increase in the distributable assets of the estate with consequent financial advantage to those seeking its nullification. In the present instance this would amount to more than $1,000, since the testatrix devoted $1,200 to the effectuation of her mortuary wishes and the amount actually expended on the disposal of her remains was but $189.33.

That the primary obligation of Surrogates' Courts is to effectuate the expressed wishes of a testator insofar as this process involves no infringement of positive rules of law, is axiomatic. For this purpose, the Surrogate is a virtual added party to all proceedings relating to the disposal of a decedent's assets. * * * It follows, in the present situation, that reversal of the formally expressed wishes of this decedent respecting disposal of her remains is permissible only upon a clear and convincing demonstration by competent and credible testimony, that such was in fact her desire.

The testimony of the son and daughter-in-law is asserted to be competent since it is alleged that neither would receive any part of the sum which would be saved by leaving the remains of the decedent in their present place of interment. Whether or not the court would deem their statements credible to the extent necessary in the present situation, is incapable of decision until they have appeared in person and have testified before it, since such questions are incapable of evaluation on affidavits alone.

It follows that the issue must be set down for hearing before the court, at which time a determination will be possible as to whether the testimony of the witnesses possesses cogency and persuasiveness adequate for a rebuttal of the wish indicated by the will.

Proceed in conformity herewith.

Perhaps the most difficult thought to ponder is one's own mortality. Most of us avoid confronting the grim reality that we and our loved ones will someday die. Estate planners constantly urge their clients to face the inevitability of death to insure well-reasoned dispositions of property. Many clients are also concerned with how their bodies will be disposed of upon their death. For example, some people want to be buried while others would rather be cremated.

You need to take steps to help insure that your client's body will be handled after death in accordance with the client's wishes. You must also work to reduce the chances of those wishes being frustrated either by lack of information regarding disposition desires or by survivors who are unhappy with the deceased's disposition requests.

1. WHAT HAPPENS UPON DEATH

It is important to understand what happens when someone dies. Unless a close family member or friend has died, many of us may not really know the chain of events that occur after death. A practical examination of what to expect when death occurs may lessen its mystique and prepare us to advise our clients.

When death initially occurs, a coroner or medical examiner must officially pronounce the person's death. If a person dies at home, the police should be contacted and they will report the death to the appropriate authorities. If a person has an uncertain cause of death, dies in jail, commits suicide, or if suspicious circumstances surround the death, an inquest or autopsy may be required.

If the deceased made any anatomical gifts, the proper authorities should be informed immediately for optimal organ usefulness.

The person authorized to make disposition arrangements, generally the spouse or next of kin, should contact relatives, locate the deceased's instructions regarding disposition of the body (if any), and then contact the desired funeral home. The funeral director will arrange to have the body transferred from the place of death or autopsy to the funeral home.

As soon as possible, the funeral home may need to secure written or oral permission to embalm the body because embalming is not required under the law of many states. Historically, embalming was performed to make sure the person was actually dead. Now, embalming preserves the body for open casket viewing and/or for transportation to distant locations. The sooner permission is obtained to embalm, the more lifelike the deceased will appear for viewing purposes.

The spouse or next of kin now decides whether to (a) have a traditional funeral with burial, (b) cremate the body with or without traditional burial services, or (c) bury the body themselves. If the family desires to bury its own dead without the assistance of a licensed funeral director, they must obtain a statement of death, a death certificate and a burial-transit permit. Most local city ordinances, however, prohibit do-it-yourself burials.

Formal services are usually desired. The spouse or next of kin meets with the funeral director to complete necessary paper work and make decisions regarding the funeral. The funeral home usually prepares the death certificate and any desired obituary notice for the newspaper. In discussing funeral arrangements, the funeral director must fully disclose various funeral-related costs (e.g., transportation of the body, embalming, use of facilities for viewing and ceremonies, renting hearses and limousines, caskets, burial vaults) so that informed choices can be made. See 16 C.F.R. §§ 453.1–453.10.

Interment is generally more costly than cremation because a more decorative casket is usually selected and a burial vault is normally used. Note that a casket is typically not mandated by law for a burial, but some type of container is usually required by cemeteries. Likewise, state law may not require a burial vault, but local law or cemeteries often require a durable container to prevent cave-ins.

An alternative to interment is cremation. A casket is not required, but crematoriums often require some type of container to avoid direct handling of the remains. If a viewing and/or a religious service is planned, the funeral home may have rental caskets available at significantly lower prices than if they were purchased. After cremation, the resulting ashes may be privately scattered, placed in an urn and buried, placed in a niche in a columbarium, or kept at home by a family member or friend.

2. DECEASED'S INSTRUCTIONS

The general common law rule is that the deceased person's burial instructions are precatory, not mandatory. However, many states have changed this rule giving priority to the deceased's instructions provided they are expressed as required by statute.

If a person can obtain the spouse's or other closest relative's agreement to the proposed disposition plan, the chances are quite good that the person's instructions will be followed. Even if state law gives priority to the deceased's wishes, it may be difficult to have the instructions enforced over the contrary wishes of a surviving spouse or the next of kin.

a. Inter Vivos Document

A person with strong feelings regarding disposal of the remains should clearly state those desires in writing to the persons who will be involved with the events surrounding death, e.g., family members, attorney, family doctor, spiritual adviser, funeral director, close friends. This is important because it is essential that those individuals who must make the initial decisions about a person's dead body know the person's wishes. Otherwise, the decedent's wishes may be inadvertently frustrated. For example, the deceased may express the desire to be buried by express language in the will, but if cremation takes place before the deceased's will is read, it is too late. Similarly, if the decedent is buried before the desire to be cremated is made known, some courts will not permit an exhumation for the purpose of having the body cremated. "Except in cases of necessity or for laudable purposes the policy of the law is that the sanctity of the grave should be maintained, and that a body suitably buried should remain undisturbed." Fowlkes v. Fowlkes, 133 S.W.2d 241, 242–43 (Tex. Civ. App. 1939).

The deceased's letter of directions should cover the following concerns:

- Name of desired funeral home.
- Preferred location of services.
- Preferred spiritual adviser to conduct the services.
- Whether burial or cremation is desired.
- Location of burial plot (if any) or desired cemetery.
- Whether an obituary is desired (warning: burglars read obituaries and funeral notices so they can break into the deceased's home while the family is gone).
- Type of headstone and information desired thereon.
- Whether ceremony is to be open or closed casket.
- Desired burial clothes and jewelry.
- Type of coffin and vault desired.
- Any other directions or preferences may also be included such as types of flowers, music selections, prayers, etc.

b. Will

Although a testator's instructions as to the final disposition of the body are not testamentary in nature, it may be advisable to confirm them in a testamentary document. Many jurisdictions permit the instructions to be acted upon without the necessity of probate. The use of will provisions alone to give disposition instructions is not recommended, however, because the will may not be found and/or read until after the funeral.

A testator may want to make gifts to the surviving spouse or other next of kin responsible for disposition of the body conditioned upon following the directions set forth in the will or inter vivos document. The fear of losing a sizable bequest may encourage individuals hostile to the testator's plans to carry them out or, at least, not object.

c. Preplanning

A person may want to purchase a burial plot and/or plan ahead for the funeral with the desired funeral home. This will help insure particular instructions are followed and will relieve the survivors of the heavy burden of making funeral arrangements. Funeral homes are very willing to make such arrangements and will permit funeral costs to be prepaid. Depending upon one's age, health, reliability of the funeral home, etc., prearrangement coupled with prepayment may also be financially beneficial to the deceased's estate and family.

d. Special Agent

Some states allow a person to designate an agent to make decisions regarding the disposition of the body after the person dies. This is truly a "durable" power since the agent's authority continues even after the principal's death. State law may provide a statutory form for the agency designation. See, e.g., TEXAS HEALTH & SAFETY CODE § 711.002(b).

LOCATE

1. How may a person control the disposition of remains in your state?

2. If a person does not leave instructions, who makes disposition decisions in your state?

3. Visit several local funeral homes and obtain information about their services. Be sure to get price information as well financing options. Which funeral home would you select and why?

4. Check Internet sites such as http://www.plan4ever.com/ for methods of planning a funeral on-line.

NOTES AND QUESTIONS

1. According to the National Funeral Directors Association, as of 2010 the cremation rate in the U.S. was 40.62%, up from 26.17% in 2000. Nevada had the highest cremation rate at 73.46%, Washington had 70.96%, and Oregon had 69.40%. The lowest cremation rates are Mississippi (13.84%), Alabama (17.18%), and Kentucky (19.24%).

2. In 1997, an American Pegasus rocket was launched into earth orbit from Grand Canary Island containing the ashes of 24 people. A small quantity of each person's remains was placed in aluminum capsules and labeled with the person's name and a commemorative phrase. People whose remains were launched included Gene Roddenberry of *Star Trek* fame and Timothy Leary. *Heavenly Bodies*, DALLAS MORNING NEWS, Apr. 22, 1997, at 1A.

3. Another business will preserve a person's DNA and store it in an engraved case. Richard Liebmann–Smith, *Checkups*, AMER. HEALTH, July/Aug. 1995, at 13.

4. The southern California firm Celebrate Life! takes cremated human remains and includes them with gunpowder and other materials in fireworks rockets. The funeral party sets sail around sunset for a three mile offshore trip where they anchor. After the appropriate funeral ceremony, a choreographed fireworks show begins set to music. Managing director Dick Hassenger reported that the pieces such as *Stairway to Heaven* and *The Marine Hymn* are popular selections. Michael Precker, *Fireworks Company Will Help You Go Out In a Blaze of Glory*, SAN ANTONIO EXPRESS-NEWS, Nov. 27, 1998, at 10F.

5. The ashes of comic-book creator Mark Gruenwald were mixed with ink and used to print comic books which were then sold in bookstores across the country. *Comic-book Creator's Ashes Mixed in Ink to Create Body of Work,* DALLAS MORNING NEWS, Aug. 28,1997, at 9A.

6. Students of an embalming school observed or participated in the embalming procedures performed on several decedents without the permission of the decedents' relatives. Is the school liable for damages to the estates or families of these decedents? See Pierce Mortuary Colleges, Inc. v. Bjerke, 841 S.W.2d 878 (Tex. App. 1992).

7. For a discussion of the historical background of bodily disposition, see James R. Marshall, *Testamentary Rights of Bodily Disposition,* LAW NOTES, Spring 1982, at 31.

8. To fund a prearranged funeral, your client could earmark a certain bank account, pay the bottom-line cost to the funeral home, or purchase a life insurance policy payable to the funeral home with a face value equal to the funeral cost. Which method would you recommend and why?

9. The average funeral costs between $7,000 and $10,000. How will the decedent's family pay for the funeral if no prearrangement was made?

10. There is a distinction between prepaying for the funeral service and purchasing a burial plot. Your client may wish to consider these separately. Why might your client wish to prepay for a burial plot but not the funeral or visa-versa? What happens if your client has already paid for a funeral in Chicago and then moves to San Francisco and wishes to be buried there?

11. May a funeral home charge extra for handling a person with a contagious disease? "Funeral-industry experts and federal health officials agree that there is no medical rationale for handling people who die from AIDS complications any differently from other corpses. The disinfectants and protective gloves, goggles, and suits that some funeral directors cite as reasons for the surcharges are universal precautions already required for all morticians by the federal Occupational Safety and Health Administration. The reason is simple: funeral directors, like ambulance EMTs and emergency-room doctors, cannot tell if a person in a car accident has a contagious disease—be it hepatitis, AIDS, or tuberculosis—so the same protective measures are used for all people." Tim Sandler, *Grave Robbers,* THE BOSTON PHOENIX, Mar. 12, 1993, at 32.

12. A and B entered into a contract with a crematorium that provided that when A died, A would be cremated and the ashes turned over to B. When A died, the crematorium scattered the ashes at sea instead. May B recover from the crematorium? On what theory? See Saari v. Jongordon Corp., 5 Cal.App.4th 797, 7 Cal.Rptr.2d 82 (1992).

13. For a review of prearrangement issues written for the non-attorney, see American Association of Retired Persons, *Pre-Paying Your Funeral?* (Aug. 1992).

14. Should your travels ever take you to Houston, Texas, you may visit the Funeral Service Museum which is dedicated to the history of funeral services in the United States. Displays include an all-glass coffin and a casket designed for three people.

15. Some people are preparing video recordings to be shown at the funeral which memorialize their lives with pictures, mood music, narration, etc. Survivors appear to receive comfort from viewing these tapes. See Mark Muro, *This Was Your Life,* BOSTON GLOBE, Sept. 16, 1992, at 69.

16. Tombstones may now include a small computer with an LCD screen like those used in notebook computers. Visitors to the cemetery can trigger the display of textual, audio, and video messages which the deceased or the deceased's family and friends left behind.

In a similar fashion, some tombstones now include QR codes which visitors can scan with their smartphones or tablets to access information about the decedent. See Jeff Seidel, *A New Way to Remember Loved Ones: QR Code Tombstone*, USA Today, June 8, 2012.

17. Some casket suppliers are now marketing caskets on which mourners can write final messages or draw pictures expressive of their feelings. Michelle Koidin, *Casket Company Gets Last Word In*, DALLAS MORNING NEWS, Jan. 19, 1997, at 27A.

18. There are occasional reports of individuals having unique burials such as George Swanson who was buried in his Corvette in Hempfield Township, Pennsylvania in 1994. However, there are also reports where the decedent's wishes were not carried out such as Donal Russell's request to have his skin removed and tanned for use in binding a volume of his poetry. How would you proceed if your client had an unusual burial request?

19. Transportation of the body from the place of the person's death to the place of final distribution is a very competitive business. Family members need to be aware that funeral directors may have selfish interests in recommending one transportation method over another. For example, some airlines give funeral directors free tickets for booking a certain number of corpses.

20. Does a person have a right to be frozen while still alive and then thawed out at a later time (e.g., when a cure for the person's ailment is discovered or at a set date so the person can experience the future)? See Velly B. Polycarpe, *Examining the Right to Premortem Cryopreservation,* 21 HOFSTRA L. REV. 1385 (1993).

21. The increasing girth of the average American is impacting the funeral industry. The standard casket is 24 inches wide. "In the past five

years [a Columbus, Ohio funeral director] has seen the need for plus-size caskets in two of every five funerals." Pamela J. Willits, *Worth the Weighty?*, OHIO STATE, Jan./Feb. 2004, at 19, 21.

22. There is a growing movement to skip the embalming of the body and to bury the body in a biodegradable container to conserve land. Beginning as a humble idea in the backwoods of South Carolina, this method is now being used in "trendy" areas such as California's wealthy Marin County. See Barbara Basler, *Green Graveyards—A Natural Way to Go*, AARP BULL., July/Aug. 2004, at 3.

23. Some companies will take the decedent's cremains and place them inside of standard ammunition such as shotgun shells. Advocates of this disposition method claim it is the "perfect way for avid hunters to honor their loved ones for eternity." See Marty Roney, *Company Will Load Loved Ones' Ashes Into Ammunition*, USA Today, Sept. 30, 2011.

DRAFT

Prepare the appropriate documents reflecting your body disposition desires.

PART 2

THE PRACTICE

■ ■ ■

CHAPTER 8

CLIENT CONTACT

■ ■ ■

A. INTRODUCTION

The excerpts from the following article by Professor Shaffer provide valuable insight into the mindset of clients as they approach estate planning. Note that the article is over three decades old and thus contains some dated terminology which is reflective of the writing style of the period.

THOMAS L. SHAFFER, THE "ESTATE PLANNING" COUNSELOR AND VALUES DESTROYED BY DEATH*

55 IOWA L. REV. 376, 376–86, 388, 393–95, 407–09 (1969).

Lawyers who advise clients and draft documents in the "estate planning" practice are counselors in more than the traditional legal sense. They are also counselors in the therapeutic or developmental sense. They live with their clients an experience which results in change and in choice. They are companions in another man's world. They ought to be among those professionals addressed by Dr. Rogers, and by another teacher of counselors:

> The counselor who grounds his efforts in a developmental theory of human possibilities can approach any of the tasks that may confront him with a feeling that he knows what it is that he is trying to accomplish. He can deal with clients who have problems and those who do not, clients who are anxious and those who appear serene and confident. He can formulate a reasonable objective for counseling in the case of a person of limited intelligence . . . or for a person of many gifts and unlimited opportunities. He is equally comfortable with the counseling that is "therapy" and the counseling that is not.[1]

Lawyers show little concern about the therapeutic counseling that goes on in an "estate planning" client's experience. Counseling literature

* Thomas S. Shaffer, *The Estate Planning Counselor and Values Destroyed by Death*, 55 IOWA L. REV. 376 (1969) (reprinted with permission).

1. L. Tyler, The Work of the Counselor 32 (3D ED. 1969).

which is available for the legal profession is not focused on the psychology of testation. The legal-counseling or "human relations" literature is helpful because it gives lawyers some understanding of the way people react to law and to law offices, but it falls short of information or guidance, or inspiration, on the narrower and more specific aspects of planning for one's death with property.

Clients in "estate planning" are invited into a relation with property which is probably new to them and which may be unsettling. Death is a part of this confrontation, and death is an unpleasant fact to modern man. With death as his focus, the client experiences property as a part of his person which is immortal. Confrontation with property as immortal is carried out in a context of giving in the client's life, maybe even giving of his life, because property is a personal part of his life. Death in this atmosphere is no less inevitable than it is anywhere else; it is here being planned for, however, which is both encouraging and traumatic. Planning for death is encouraging because modern man is attracted to the idea of plans which will organize his future life for him, but traumatic because it involves planning for death and personal death is a thought modern man will do almost anything to avoid. The evidence for these generalizations is developed below.

The testamentary experience is death-confronting, novel, and taboo-defying. For that reason it is probably much more vivid in the mind and heart of the client than lawyers who go through the experience every day suppose it to be. Taboo-defying experiences usually tend to be vivid. People going through them tend to be upset. People who are able to go through their upsetting experiences in the company of a competent, comfortable, accepting professional, however, come out more aware of their lives, more reconciled to what is real in their lives, and better able to make choices and to develop. The question here is not whether the lawyer is a counselor in this relationship—he cannot avoid being a counselor. The question is whether the lawyer realizes what he is doing, is able to accept what it involves for himself and for his client, and has the wisdom and courage to be a helpful companion.

I believe that the client who receives the professional legal service he seeks in this "estate planning" relationship will leave the law office having faced death realistically, and having faced his property and his loved ones in the context of his own death. It seems to me that the "estate planning" experience is one way the client can be helped in his personal reconciliation to death, a reconciliation which comes about partly because he is encouraged to be realistic about death, and partly because he reflects on the fact that his property gives him a limited, temporary immortality. "You can't take it with you," is a maxim of the law of property as well as a *memento mori*. The maxim has in it a consoling corollary, a promise of influence after death, which is the psychological center of "estate planning."

Most lawyers would like to know more about how clients feel in law-office encounters with death, property, and giving. The immediate source of experience and information should be psychology—research psychology as well as therapeutic psychology. However, psychology has not concerned itself with the substance of the law; what is usually called "law and psychology" as an interdisciplinary area of study is confined to border areas—insanity as a criminal defense, testamentary capacity, civil commitment to mental institutions. The task of developing psychological models which reach the substance of law itself, and the dynamics of lawyer-client relationships, is one psychologists have not taken up. It is left to reflective lawyers and law professors to find psychological models and apply them to our professional lives. I attempt to do this, on the question of "estate planning" clients and their attitudes toward death, in this article.

There has been a substantial amount of recent psychological scholarship on attitudes toward death; it is a new area in that science, but an area which has taken on remarkable impetus in the last decade. None of this research has examined the psychology of will preparation, which I call the psychology of testation, but some of the data is closely enough related to testation to justify a bold layman's attempt to relate it to the law office. * * *

I. THE DIGGORY-ROTHMAN MODEL

In 1961, James C. Diggory and Doreen Z. Rothman, a teaching psychologist and a clinical psychologist, published the results of a study applying a simple death-attitude, sentence-completion test to 563 casually-selected respondents. My present venture is an attempt to compare the Diggory–Rothman test and its results with some of the factors that are involved in the death-property-giving relationship and with my own empirical test. The purpose of this effort is to determine whether death attitudes in testation have characteristics of their own.

Diggory and Rothman asked several hundred people the following question:

> Here are seven consequences of death. Would you please indicate the one that seems to you worst, or most distasteful.
>
> A. I could no longer have any experiences.
>
> B. I am uncertain as to what might happen to me if there is a life after death.
>
> C. I am afraid of what might happen to my body after death.
>
> D. I could no longer care for my dependents.
>
> E. My death would cause grief to my relatives and friends.
>
> F. All my plans and projects would come to an end.
>
> G. The process of dying might be painful.

These seven possibilities, labeled "values destroyed by death" in their project, may not exhaust all of the reasons for death anxiety, but they are at least a respectable attempt in that direction. My present interest is to inquire how each of these values relates to the feelings of a client preparing for the post-mortem disposition of his property-personality. * * *

II. APPLICATION OF THE DIGGORY-ROTHMAN MODEL TO WILLS CLIENTS

A. *Cessation of Experience*

The first question is whether wills clients are likely to be concerned about the fact that death will end their experiences. In the Diggory–Rothman results, a significant number of respondents chose this "A" answer. Their response in this first category was higher than their "E" (grief), "F" (projects), and "G" (fear of pain) answers, and was especially high among single-divorced persons. It tended to be higher in the highest of three economic sub-groups than in the two lower sub-groups. Protestants responded to "A" more than Catholics did, and Jews more than Protestants. It was the first choice among persons who listed their religion as "other" or "none."

My impression is that this level of response to death as the cessation of experience would not be maintained where the subject speaks in reference to the preparation of wills. Wills clients would probably tend to focus more on care for dependents, or on cessation of projects, or even on bodily deterioration, than they would on cessation of experience. Diggory and Rothman suggest this when they analyze "A" (experience) and "F" (project) as concomitant.

The testamentary device would perhaps appear to clients as a method to *prolong experience* through continuation of projects, provision of support, or maintenance of a bodily surrogate in the form of a monument or perpetually-cared-for gravesite. The wills client, because his confrontation with death involves also a consideration of his property, may tend to regard his property as representing and, in effect, immortalizing him. "The possessed object as possessed is a continuous creation.... If I turn away from it, it does not thereby cease to exist; if I go away, it *represents* me in my desk, in my room, in *this* place, in the world. That thought may not occur as readily to a person who is unexpectedly asked what he dislikes about death. My test of this hypothesis indicates virtually no response to the 'A' answer, in comparison with a heavy response to the 'D', 'F', and 'G' answers."

Some reports on infantile formation of death attitudes suggest that the survival of environment—including property—is one of the ways in which the idea of personal termination becomes bearable. * * *

One of the things a wills client learns is that death will not rob him of power. In death, he may possess "powers, qualities, and advantages not possessed in the living state." In the realm of power, therefore, death may be a "last step forward." For this reason, psychologists who conclude that preparation of wills increases fear of death may be wrong. Data obtained from my will-interview study indicates that will-preparation actually reduces fear of death and has a constructive or even therapeutic effect on death anxiety. * * *

Thus, psychological evidence, some research, and some speculation combine to suggest that the testamentary experience is a relatively hopeful confrontation with death. Property is part of personality, and personality is involved with property in the life of a wills client. His seeing death in relation to property and the survival of property-personality robs death of some of its stark power.

B. Life After Death

Diggory and Rothman found that very few respondents related their death to a fear about eternity. Their level of "B" responses (the worst or most distasteful consequence of death is that I am uncertain as to what might happen to me if there is a life after death) fell between "4" and "5" on a scale ranging from "1" (very high response) to "7" (lowest response). The only subgroup in their study which chose "B" at a significantly higher level were Roman Catholics, whom they found to rate at about "3." * * *

C. Dissolution of Body

Diggory and Rothman report the "C" response (the worst or most distasteful consequence of death is that I am afraid of what might happen to my body after death) as the least significant "value destroyed by death." This low level of response was uniformly maintained among their sub-groups and is in accordance with the results of my test of their conclusions on will subjects. Most of us appear to be relatively unconcerned about what will happen to our bodies after death, even though we usually are concerned about what happens to our property. Perhaps the reason for this is that our property continues to live while our bodies do not. * * *

D. Dependents

My general impression is that wills clients find the "D" answer (the worst or most distasteful consequence of death is that I could no longer care for my dependents) more compelling than any other. This comes from empirical analysis of will interviews, and from my observation that clients show greatest concern about death when it is focused on the members of their families. Property and considerations of support give death a special focus in the client's mind. I would therefore, expect wills clients to respond more heavily to "D" than the Diggory–Rothman respondents did. This impression was confirmed in my test of wills clients. I found 46 percent of them chose the "D" answer (33 percent of the men and 56 percent of the women; with somewhat higher choices of "D" among younger subjects). The Diggory–Rothman scale put the "D" response at "4"—which is in the middle of the scale ranging from "1" to "7." They found this response higher in sub-groups under age 39 and highest in age groups between 40 and 55. It ranked especially high among men, Protestants, lower income groups, and among married and single-divorced respondents. * * *

E. *Grief to Others*

The concern wills clients show for dependent support may be misleading. It may suggest that the testamentary context creates concern about loved ones. I doubt that the experience creates anxiety, but it may be that the property relationship involved in testamentary planning shifts existing anxiety toward concern for support rather than toward concern at causing grief. The Diggory–Rothman response to "E" (the worse or more distasteful consequence of death is that my death would cause grief to my relatives and friends) was the highest in their survey. The "E" response was highest in all age groups under 40, women, Protestants, Catholics, upper and middle economic sub-groups and single (not divorced or widowed) persons. My test of the Diggory–Rothman results on wills clients, however, indicates a much lower level of response on "E" and a much higher response on "D." * * *

F. *End to Projects*

Wills clients are more concerned about providing support than they are at causing grief. This is true even though their emphasis might be reversed if they were asked about death in the absence of a testamentary environment. One might expect a similar reversal of emphasis when concern at causing grief is compared with concern at having to leave work undone. This does not appear to be the case, however, in the Diggory–Rothman study. Their respondents chose the "F" answer (the worst or most distasteful consequence of my death is that all my plans and projects would come to an end) more often than any other except the "E" (causing grief) answer. Their response to "F" was notably high among sub-groups of teenagers, people between the ages of 25 and 39, people expressing no religious belief, and people in the middle economic class. It was the highest from single-widowed respondents. My results with wills clients were similar, although the overall choice of "F" by my audience was lower than theirs. * * *

G. *Fear of Pain*

Do people as wills clients express more or less fear of pain in death than people outside the testamentary context? Diggory and Rothman reported a relatively high incidence of "G" answers (the worst or most distasteful consequence of death is that the process of dying might be painful). They rated this response at "3" on their "1" to "7" scale, and noted that the "G" response was especially high in the 20–24 age subgroup, among women, among Catholics and Jews, among the upper and lower wealth levels (but not the middle level), and among unmarried-engaged people. My test of their results on wills clients yielded a much lower response to "G." * * *

V. CONCLUSION

There are two ways in which consideration of the preceding discussion should be helpful to the practicing attorney. One is that behavioral information should help lawyers to realize how their clients feel, especially about death and the values that death will destroy. Psychology presents a significant amount of information on the subject and promises to develop more as the decade-old effort to explore death as psychologically significant continues in the hospitals and laboratories commanded by that science. The other source of value, less tangible than the first, is a matter of a counseling attitude, an openness, which is more affective than systematic.

Although most lawyers do not realize the influence they exert on clients, the realities and values of the client's situation are heavily influenced by the verbal and non-verbal reactions of the lawyer to what the client says. "The selection of value and facts should then largely dictate the conceptual and idea framework that helps to set the direction for both problem and solution," according to Dr. Redmount. "The counselor needs logical skills and he needs to develop an experimental mode of inquiry if he is to perceive and organize the realities and possibilities in a party's situation most effectively."

This suggests a number of attitudes in testamentary counseling. One is an "experimental mode of inquiry," which is a search for feelings and attitudes as well as for information. It cannot be fulfilled with a fill-in-the-blanks system of will interviews, and lawyers who insist on operating their wills practice as if they were taking driver-license applications should get into another line of work.

The "experimental mode of inquiry" also excludes narrow value systems which reflect what the lawyer thinks the client should do with his property. At the very least, an openness to the client's own feelings and values about property and family requires that the lawyer realize that he communicates his values and attitudes to the client, whether he wants to or not. It may be that a life-estate trust for the client's wife is, in the lawyer's opinion, a poor idea. But the value of the idea should be tested against the way the client feels about his wife, about—for instance—her remarriage after his death, and about her ability to plan for and support their children. It should not be based on a moral absolute which represents the lawyer's own feelings and values:[2]

> Poor legal counseling, with the adumbrated view of facts and highly parochial, legalistic conceptions of experience, may be particularly ill-suited to preventive means of dealing with experience. Failures of perception and a restricted range of information and understanding may make the prediction of other than very narrow issues quite hazardous and unreliable. The lawyer who is not "counseling-oriented" has the opportunity and perhaps the disposition to be more effective in highly identified matters that require correction. He is

2. [Redmount, *Humanistic Law Through Legal Counseling,* 2 CONN.L.REV. 98,] 112 (1969).

less likely to handle well somewhat unidentified matters that require future planning.

Affectively significant counseling equipment is not altogether the result of attitudes, nor is it altogether the result of study and preparation. Both sensitivity and information seem to be required, and, although this is not the place for a comprehensive discussion of the process of making counselors from lawyers, it may be helpful to suggest two avenues to more skillful counseling.

One is study. The literature of counseling, suggested in the introduction of this article, and in Professor Freeman's excellent case-book, is readily available to lawyers. Other "helping professions" (medicine, nursing, social work) have been aware of it, and have been systematically developing their own versions for decades. The legal profession has, meanwhile, neglected its ancient claim to the title "counselor." That neglect should be redressed in law-school curricula and in the professional reading of those in the practicing profession.

The other avenue is an effective openness, a candor, that is probably inconsistent with the image of lawyers as tough-minded, relevance-centered, masters of order. If, for example, the "estate planning" lawyer thinks it a poor idea to set up support trusts for wives, and an even poorer idea to attempt to restrict a widow's ability to remarry, rapport would probably be advanced by his candid admission of his feelings and some expression of an honest interest in his client's reaction to them.

> I find that the best interpretations come out of what is actually transpiring in the relationship, where both are in the grip of the same complex, which seems to travel back and forth. The implication of the foregoing is that the relationship itself is central and that the desired objectivity, individuality and understanding come out of the actual experience, rather than out of some presumed knowledge or objectivity (intellectual or feeling) in the analyst.[3]

If the lawyer expresses his negative feelings obliquely (by, say, making faces or shaking his head), the client perceives an obstacle between him and his counselor that he cannot deal with. Candor, and sympathetic interest, are what Rogers was talking about when his ideal counselor said

---

3. Spiegelman, *Some Implications of the Transference,* in FESTCHRIFT FON C.A. MEIER 5 (R. Verlac ed. 1965). Dr. Spiegelman's personal experience with candor in analysis is analogically helpful:

> I somewhere decided to abandon myself to this process of openness and follow the flow of talk, imagery, impulse going on in myself as well as the patient. I found it necessary to acknowledge my personal involvement and to speak out of what came to me . . . I found . . . that I had to go farther in even coming out with my reactions when they seemed to be immoral, unaesthetic, inopportune, untherapeutic (from any rational standpoint), indeed, at times all wrong. I expected this, after all, from my patient. How often my reactions matched what was going on in the patient was startlingly high and this encouraged me to proceed in this manner. When there was a matching experience, one could interpret (and thus raise into consciousness) what the actual transference situation was at the moment. Even when I was alone in my reaction, I found that there was no great loss, but that I, too, was shown to be human, limited, have complexes, and not be responding to the patient or the collective unconscious, but to my own complexes. * * *

to the client that he wanted "to enter into your world of perception as completely as I am able ... become in a sense, another self for you ... an alter ego of your own attitudes and feelings.... " That is a sound and lofty aspiration for the "counselor at law."

NOTES AND QUESTIONS

1. Which of the Diggory–Rothman consequences of death do you find most distasteful? Why?

2. You will be unable to resolve some of the consequences of death. For example, you lack the ability to give your client earthly experiences after death and details of afterlife are fuzzy. But see BETTY J. EADIE, EMBRACED BY THE LIGHT (1993). You may, however, take concrete steps to assist clients with many of their post-death concerns. What techniques would you use to address the remaining five Diggory–Rothman consequences?

3. Your client's view of death may have a direct impact on how you develop the estate plan. As Professor Shaffer explained, you cannot obtain this type of information from a client with the normal "fill-in-the-blanks system of will interviews" which are discussed later in this chapter. How do you acquire this information from your client? Could expanding an interview to uncover this information make the estate planning process too expensive for some clients? How do you resolve this problem?

B. SECURING EMPLOYMENT IN THE ESTATE PLANNING FIELD

As an estate planner, you have the ability to provide valuable and essential legal services to every person. Your potential client base includes all competent adults living in the state in which you are licensed. There are a wide variety of ways in which you can use your estate planning expertise in the practice of law. Below is a non-exclusive list of type of positions which you might want to pursue.

- *Sole practitioner in general practice.* Regardless of why a client originally seeks your advice, any client would benefit from estate planning as well.
- *Sole practitioner specializing in estate planning.*
- *Associate or partner at a firm in general practice.* As with the sole practitioner, the firm's clients for other matters may also need estate planning services.
- *Associate or partner at a firm working in an estate planning section.* Many large firms have a section devoted to estate planning.
- *Associate or partner at a "boutique" firm which specializes in estate planning.* There are a growing number of firms which limit their practice to estate planning concerns.
- *Associate or partner at a firm specializing in elder law.* Although elder law encompasses a wide range of topics, estate planning is a significant portion of an elder law practice.

- *Legal clinics*. Low income individuals often lack the foresight or finances to obtain estate planning advice. Even though these individuals lack significant assets, they need estate planning for matters such as designating the guardians of their minor children and planning for disability and death just as much as the most wealthy individuals.
- *Court attorney*. Many courts with specialized probate jurisdiction, especially in populous areas, employ attorneys to assist in the court and the judge. These individuals, who are referred to by a variety of titles such as "court coordinator," "staff attorney," or "probate assistant," work with attorneys to make certain the docket runs smoothly. These positions are usually held by recent law school graduates for one to three years.
- *Judge*. Many large cities and counties have special courts dealing with probate matters. These specialized courts are referred to by a variety of names such as "probate courts," "orphans' courts," or "surrogate's courts." After gaining practical estate planning experience, you may wish to consider seeking election or appointment to the bench of one of these courts.
- *Professional fiduciary*. Financial institutions and independent trust companies hire estate planning attorneys for a variety of functions. The types of duties that you might perform include reviewing documents prior to the company's decision to accept the position as executor or trustee, administering the estate of a decedent, serving as the trustee of a trust and making decisions regarding trust investments or distributions, and cultivating new business by meeting with prospective users of the company's fiduciary services.
- *Internal Revenue Service*. The IRS employs many attorneys with expertise in estate planning matters, especially (obviously) wealth transfer taxation. As an IRS employee, your duties could range from reviewing gift and estate tax returns and conducting audits to litigating disputed issues in the courts.
- *Planned giving office of an educational institution or a charity.*

NOTES AND QUESTIONS

1. Can you think of other legal positions where an expertise in estate planning would be a significant asset?

2. Thomas J. Stanley and William D. Danko, authors of the best-selling book THE MILLIONAIRE NEXT DOOR—THE SURPRISING SECRETS OF AMERICA'S WEALTHY, predict that the demand for estate attorneys will be strongest in the states of California, Florida, New York, Illinois, Texas, and Pennsylvania. *Id.* at 216. They also believe that "estate attorneys will likely generate more than $25 billion in revenue from servicing estates in the $1 million or more range during the 1996–2005 period. This figure is greater than the net income generated by all law partnerships for all services in 1994!" *Id.* at 215.

C. OBTAINING CLIENTS*

A practicing attorney may obtain clients in several different manners. A client might contact an attorney if the client is (1) an existing client, (2) a new client referred to the attorney by an existing client, or (3) is a new client looking for advice.

A client might contact an attorney for estate planning services if the client has already contacted the attorney for legal advice in a different area of law. In other words, Client A might contact Attorney B to discuss a matter such as impending litigation. A might want to have B examine his or her estate planning documents following the conclusion of the litigation to ensure that the estate plan was not affected by the outcome of the litigation. This applies to several areas of the law. The most prominent are, of course, divorce actions, tax disputes, and real estate work.

This type of attorney client relationship may prove to be beneficial to the client. Because the attorney helped the client in a different matter, that same attorney might be able to use his or her knowledge of the case to help give advice on estate planning matters to the client. With this concept in mind, it is also important to remember that estate planning attorneys often do not work alone and refer clients to other professionals, such as certified public accountants, in conducting their practice and providing assistance to the client.

Sometimes clients seek the advice of certain attorneys because other people referred them to the attorney. Usually the person making the referral is an existing client who was pleased with the attorney's work. The importance of an attorney performing well for his or her clients is obvious. As mentioned earlier, estate planning attorneys often work with other professionals. These other professionals often play a role in providing referrals on behalf of attorneys. In this type of case, a professional, such as a certified public accountant, might refer his client to an attorney if the client needs legal services. These types of professionals are often a good source of business for an attorney; therefore, it is important for an attorney to maintain a good relationship with these other professionals. However, this is often balanced with an attorney's duty to provide clients with independent advice. This obligation might not always prove to be what is best for the referring professional. An attorney should develop relationships with professionals who understand this aspect of an attorney's job.

An attorney may also receive referrals from other attorneys. This has become a more popular practice with the reduction or elimination of estate planning attorneys from some larger law firms. These firms often refer their clients to estate planning lawyers to take of their client's needs.

How does attorney obtain referrals from other professionals such as attorneys and accountants? The answer in short is networking. An attor-

* The author acknowledges the assistance of Justin M. Lopez in the preparation of this section.

ney might want to attend conferences where accountants, insurance agents, and brokers meet to make contact with these professionals. An estate planning attorney might also want to join the local, state, and national bar associations and become an active participant in bar activities and make contacts with other attorneys. An attorney might also want to improve his or her reputation among fellow attorneys by speaking and writing on estate planning topics. These contacts could provide attorneys who specialize in one particular area of the law the opportunity to create mutual referral relationships with other attorneys who specialize in different areas of law.

An estate planning also can bring in new clients to their practice through advertising and other forms of marketing.

NOTE

For a comprehensive discussion, see DANIEL B. EVANS, HOW TO BUILD AND MANAGE AN ESTATES PRACTICE (1999) (Stephan R. Leimberg says, "Trust me—the chapter on 'Finding Clients' alone is worth the price of the book."). See also Peter P.J. Ng, *Building a Successful Practice at a Small Firm*, TR. & EST., Sept. 1993, at 22.

D. CLIENT INTERVIEW

1. PRELIMINARY MATTERS

BRIAN L. DOBBEN, ESTATE PLANNING: THE INITIAL CLIENT INTERVIEW*

81 ILL. B.J. 261, 261 (1993).

Your first contact with an estate planning client is usually over the telephone. In this initial conversation you should (1) collect basic personal information such as names, addresses, and telephone numbers; (2) inquire generally into the family circumstances (whether the client has a spouse, children, etc.); (3) roughly determine the overall size of the estate; and (4) make an appointment to meet the client. Frequently one spouse will contact you on behalf of a couple. Although discussion of this issue is outside of the scope of this article, be aware of the growing body of literature addressing potential conflicts of interest in representing both spouses.

This first telephone conversation usually includes little detail about tax implications or dispositive schemes. However, you should inform the client that at the meeting you will explore in detail the nature, value, and ownership designation of the client's assets. Also tell your client to start considering possible executors, trustees, and guardians for minor children.

After the telephone contact, many lawyers send a questionnaire to the client asking about his or her assets. Other practitioners simply inform clients to review their personal asset situations before the initial meeting.

The advantage of the questionnaire is that it imposes some structure on the asset analysis and prods the client into bringing an accurate list of assets to the meeting. The disadvantage is that clients may delay or even cancel the initial meeting if they have not completed the form. Almost everyone procrastinates about estate planning, and a questionnaire, especially one that appears complex, can cause further delay. Whether you use a questionnaire or wait until the initial meeting, you should fully discuss all the assets.

CONFIDENTIAL ESTATE PLANNING QUESTIONNAIRE*

PLEASE FILL OUT THIS FORM AS COMPLETELY AS POSSIBLE

Date: ____________

Full Name____________	Name of Spouse____________
Birth Date________ Age:____	Birth Date________ Age:____
United States Citizen? Yes____ No___	United States Citizen? Yes____ No___
If no, where? ____________	*If no, where?* ____________
Social Security Number________	Social Security Number________
Employer____________	Employer____________
Business Address____________	Business Address____________
____________	____________
Business Telephone________	Business Telephone________
Business Fax Number________	Business Fax Number________
Occupation____________	Occupation____________

Home Address (Number and Street)____________

County______ City______ State______ Zip______ Home Phone________

A. MARRIAGE INFORMATION

Date of Marriage__________ Place of Marriage____________

Previously Married? Yes______ No______

If yes, list to whom, for how long, and date of divorce on the back of this page.

How long have you resided in [state]? You______ Your Spouse______

Please list the states in which you have lived, or if you have not lived in another state but own property there, please indicate that state.

____

____

B. CHILDREN

Name: ____________	Name: ____________
Date of Birth: ____________	Date of Birth: ____________
Place of Birth: ____________	Place of Birth: ____________
Social Security Number: ________	Social Security Number: ________
Citizenship: ____________	Citizenship: ____________
Is This Child Adopted? ________	Is This Child Adopted? ________
Special Needs: ____________	Special Needs: ____________
____________	____________

Name: ____________	Name: ____________
Date of Birth: ____________	Date of Birth: ____________
Place of Birth: ____________	Place of Birth: ____________

* The author gratefully acknowledges the excellent assistance of Michael French and Gilbert Loredo in the preparation of this form.

Social Security Number: ____________ Social Security Number: ____________
Citizenship: ____________ Citizenship: ____________
Is This Child Adopted? ____________ Is This Child Adopted? ____________
Special Needs: ____________ Special Needs: ____________
____________ ____________

Do any of your children have significant assets of their own? Yes____ No____
Do you have any children that are deceased? Yes____ No____
If you have deceased children, did any die leaving surviving descendants? Yes____ No____
Are any of your children disabled or in poor health? Yes____ No____
Explain each yes answer on the back of this page.
Do you have any children born out of wedlock? Yes____ No____
Explain each "yes" answer on the back of this page.
Is there a physical possibility of more children? Yes____ No____

C. MILITARY SERVICE

Have you or your spouse ever served in the military? Yes____ No____
If yes, give branch of service and rank.____________

D. MISCELLANEOUS INFORMATION

Do you have a will? Yes______ No______ Date______
Location____________
Do you or anyone you intend to include in your Will have any unusual health problems?
Yes____ No____ *If yes, please explain on the back of this form.*
Do you have a safe deposit box? Yes____ No____ Location____________
Do you and your spouse have a pre-nuptial or nuptial agreement? Yes____ No____
Please describe any significant health problems you may have.
____
____

If you have minor children living when you die, who do you want to raise them and be their guardian?
Primary Guardian (Name and Address): ____________
Alternate Guardian (Name and Address): ____________
Alternate Guardian (Name and Address): ____________

Should you become physically incapacitated, do you have any special wishes or instructions for your physician (i.e., refusing life support or certain procedures)?
Yes____ No____ *If yes, explain on back.*

Who do you want to appoint as Executor to manage your estate upon your death? This person will be responsible for gathering your assets, paying any debts, taxes and expenses, liquidating assets as may be required, distributing money and assets as you direct, and selling your estate. Please list the person's name, address, and relationship to you.
Primary Executor:____________
____
Alternate Executor:____________
____
Alternate Executor:____________
____

Who do you wish to appoint as guardian of your estate? This person will handle the affairs of your estate while you are unable to do so. Your inability to do so may be due to incapacity or your being unavailable. Please list the person's name, address, and relationship to you.
Primary Guardian of Your Estate: ____________
____
Alternate Guardian of Your Estate: ____________
____

Alternate Guardian of Your Estate: ______________________________
____

Who do you wish to appoint as guardian of your person? This person will make decisions for you, concerning your person, should you be medically incapacitated. Please list the person's name, address, and relationship to you.
Primary Guardian of Your Person: ______________________________
____

Alternate Guardian of Your Person: ______________________________
____

Alternate Guardian of Your Person: ______________________________
____

Do you wish to have a Mental Health Treatment Declaration which states specifically what type of treatment you will receive in the event that you become mentally ill? You may choose to create a Mental Health Treatment Declaration or you may leave this decision to the Guardian of your person.
Yes, I would like to specify the type of treatment.______ No, I will let my Guardian decide.______
Who referred you to this office? ______________________________

E. INVENTORY OF ASSETS

1. REAL ESTATE

Do you own any real estate? Yes_____ No_____ *If yes, list below.*

	RESIDENCE	**OTHER PROPERTY**
Address	______________	______________
Date Acquired	______________	______________
Title / Owner(s)	______________	______________
Mortgage Balance	$______ Lender______	$______ Lender______
	______________	______________
Approximate Value	$______________	$______________

If you own additional property, check here ______, and continue on the back of this page.

2. BANK ACCOUNTS / CHECKING ACCOUNTS / CDs, ETC.

Name of Institution	Type of Account	Name of Account Owner	Approximate Balance

If you have additional accounts, check here ______, and list them on the reverse side.

3. STOCKS, BONDS, AND OTHER SECURITIES

Do you own any stocks, bonds, mutual funds, or other securities? Yes______ No______
Amount in your name only $________ In spouse's sole name $____________
Amount joint with spouse $________ Joint with others $____________
Please list your holdings on the reverse side

4. RETIREMENT BENEFITS

Describe your company plan, type, amount of benefits, and present beneficiary designation:
____
____
____

5. BUSINESS ASSETS

Do you own an interest in a business? Yes______ No______
Name of Business ______________________________
Address of Business ______________________________
Describe your business, ownership, percentage of each owner's share, approximate value, and buy-sell agreement. ______________________________
____

Continue on reverse side.

6. NOTES, LOANS, OR ANY OTHER AMOUNTS OWED TO YOU

Does anyone owe you money? Yes______ No______ *If yes, explain the circumstances:*
____
____
____
______________________________ Total $______________

7. LIFE INSURANCE

Insurance Company	Policy Number	Type of Policy	Face Amount	Owner	Beneficiary

8. OTHER—PERSONAL PROPERTY, ETC.

What is the approximate value of your general household property? $______
What is the approximate value of your special items (jewelry, furs, collections, etc.)? $______
What is the approximate current value of your automobiles? $______
Please briefly describe each of your automobiles on the back of this page. Total $______

F. TRUSTS AND INHERITANCES

Are you the beneficiary of any trust? Yes______ No______ *If yes, give details.*
____
____
____

Do you or any immediate family member expect to inherit significant assets in the foreseeable future?

Yes ______ No ______ *If yes, to the best of your ability, estimate amount(s), source(s), and other pertinent information.* ______________________________
____
____

G. LIABILITIES

Do you currently owe money on any loan including car loans, mortgages, bank loans, and student loans? Yes______ No______ *If yes, please list:*

Type of Loan	Amount	Holder of the Loan

Do you have any credit card debt? Yes______ No______ *If yes, please list.*

Type of Account	Amount Owed

____
____
____

Do you owe any debt that is not listed above? Yes ______ No ______ *If yes, please list.*

____
____

H. DISTRIBUTIONS TO BENEFICIARIES AFTER YOUR DEATH

As to any inheritance you may choose your children to receive, do you want them to receive their inheritance in a lump sum at a particular age, or in installments at specified ages? Please indicate your preference, if any.

____
____
____

If one of your children should die before you, how would you want any inheritance that child was to receive to be distributed?

____
____

Do you wish to make any special gifts of property or cash to any individual?

____
____

Do you wish to make any gifts to a charitable organization? If so, please indicate specifically the name and address of the organization.

____
____

Is there any relative whom you specifically do not want to receive anything from your estate?

____

Are there any debts that you wish to forgive?

____
____

After all special gifts have been distributed, who do you want to receive the rest of your estate (this may be one or more persons)?

____
____

Do you have any miscellaneous bequests or special instructions regarding the disposition of your property?

____
____

Do you wish to make an anatomical gift (organ, tissue, or body donation) upon your death?
Yes ______ No ______ *If yes, explain on back.*

Please list any special instructions you may have regarding your funeral service on the back of this form. Include your preferences as to burial or cremation, religious service, length of service, expense, etc.

NOTES AND QUESTIONS

1. Before scheduling the interview, you must check to be certain you have no conflicts of interest with the prospective client. How will you do this?

2. What is your opinion about the pre interview questionnaire—will you use one? Do you think you will have a standard policy or will it depend on the particular circumstances of the client?

3. Will you use the same questionnaire for all clients? What reasons might you have for giving different versions of your questionnaire to different types of clients?

4. Evaluate the sample questionnaire. Is it sufficiently comprehensive or is it too detailed? What questions would you add or delete? How could you improve its format so that your client would have an easier time understanding and completing it?

5. For additional sample questionnaires, see 1 FREDERICK K. HOOPS, FREDERICK H. HOOPS, III, DANIEL S. HOOPS, FAMILY ESTATE PLANNING GUIDE, Ch. 3 (4th ed. 1997); Frederick R. Keydel, *Forms Can Streamline Your Estate Planning Practice*, PROB. & PROP., May/June 1988, at 56, 57–61; Kenneth M. Rudisill, Jr., *Information to Be Considered in Preparing an Estate Plan (Efficiency = Inexpensive)*, LAW NOTES, Spring 1984, 31, 34–38; Edward S. Schlesinger, *Getting Your Clients to Think About Healthcare Directives*, PRAC. LAW., Jan. 1993, at 75, 76–84; Lynn Wintriss & Cristin P. Carnell, *A Checklist of Predeath Planning for the Dying Client*, PROB. & PROP., July/Aug. 1987, at 9.

6. Your first contact with a new client will typically be by telephone when the client calls to inquire about fees and your availability. Some attorneys will visit briefly with the prospective client about the client's situation while other attorneys prefer to have their secretary simply schedule an appointment. Clients who have the opportunity to speak with you even before coming to the office may be impressed and reassured by the personal touch. However, locating and interrupting you each time a new client calls may be too great of an inconvenience. If you elect to have office staff schedule appointments, it is important that they be carefully trained.

7. You must give consideration to the length of time to allot to the initial interview. Even in relatively simple situations, a comprehensive estate planning interview may take several hours. On the other hand, long interviews increase the cost of estate planning.

8. Where should the interview be held—your office, a conference room, or the client's home?

> Normally the interview will be held in your office. There may be exceptions when the client is ill or very feeble so that it becomes necessary to go to his or her home, a nursing home or a hospital. You should be very willing to meet the needs of the client in this respect * * *.
>
> In a desire to serve your older clients well, you may think it advisable to hold most of your meetings with them in their homes. That is not to be encouraged, unless necessary, for several reasons. Elderly people may be largely confined to their homes and welcome an excuse to get out. Going to the lawyer's office is a good excuse, even though it is rather difficult for them, unless they are just too feeble to get around. Don't deprive them of that opportunity.
>
> You can work much better in your office. Your secretary and your files, as well as the dictating and copy machines [are there]. But there is another reason that is a little more subtle. There is always a need to establish clearly, although very inconspicuously, that you are in charge of

the meeting. A person rarely respects a professional person who is not in charge. When it is held in their homes, clients often fail to develop the proper relationship with the lawyer. Therefore, meetings should never be held in their homes unless necessary.

1 ROBERT S. HUNTER, HOW TO BUILD A SUCCESSFUL ESTATE PRACTICE § 12.2, at 151 (1984). Do you agree with Judge Hunter's recommendations? Why or why not?

9. Your client is likely to arrive at your office early and thus will spend some time in your reception area. This area should be dignified and comfortable, i.e., it "should give the impression of quality, though it need not be lavishly furnished. * * * [T]he seating should be comfortable. The decor should be dignified, and soothing, too. * * * [R]eading material should be selected to appeal to the clients' interests, not yours. * * * [N]o ashtrays should be available, and a discreet 'Thank you for not smoking' sign should be perched on the table. * * * [I]f the seating is such that the receptionist's back is turned toward the clients when typing or answering the phone, the client may feel ignored. Make sure the receptionist asks no questions concerning the nature of the client's business; many consider the mere fact that they are meeting with an attorney to be privileged information. And ask the receptionist to offer clients coffee or a soft drink as they wait; studies * * * have shown that strong psychological bonds form when people associate food and drink with meetings. * * * [Receptionists] should have more personality than the rest of the firm put together." Daniel B. Kennedy, *Designing a Client–Friendly Office*, 82 ILL. B.J. 443, 443–44 (1994). Other useful waiting room amenities include accessible restroom facilities and a telephone for free local calls. Should background music be playing? Should a television be available? Should there be a special area for young children? What other features would you include (or exclude) from your waiting room?

10. Should the client be allowed to bring a guest to the interview such as a spouse, child, parent, or friend? How might the presence of these people interfere with the interview?

11. See Larry E. Lauterjung, *Compassionate Consultations: Winning Over Prospective Clients*, 100 ILL. B.J. 364 (2012).

DRAFT

1. Prepare a pre-interview questionnaire for a client who does not need tax planning.

2. Prepare a pre-interview questionnaire for a client who needs tax planning.

3. Prepare cover letters to accompany these questionnaires.

2. INTRODUCTION

The first few minutes of the interview set the tone for the entire session. Consider incorporating the following features into this important time.

- Greet the client in the reception area or at your office door.
- Introduce yourself and shake hands with the client.
- Ascertain how the client would like to be addressed, e.g., Mr., Mrs., Ms., Dr., first name, nickname, etc.
- Offer refreshments, e.g., coffee, soda, water.
- Small talk, if appropriate, to "break the ice," e.g., weather, finding office, validating parking ticket, recent news or sports event, etc.
- Offer paper and pen for the client to take notes, if desired.
- Determine if the client has ever been to an attorney before; the client may be especially apprehensive if this is a first visit.
- Assure the client that as far as you now know, you have no conflicts of interest with another client.
- Speak in plain language and avoid inappropriate "tones of voice" such as those that are condescending, sarcastic, or elitist.

3. DISCUSS FEES

You or your secretary should already have informed the client of the fee for the initial interview. Restate this fee and indicate that you cannot state a fee for further work until you determine what is involved. See Chapter 8(G).

4. EXPLAIN ATTORNEY–CLIENT PRIVILEGE

Explain the attorney-client privilege and use an example which is relevant to estate planning. The client must understand that you can prepare a good estate plan only if the client is candid, honest, and provides full disclosure. For example, you need to know about children born out of wedlock, marital problems, illegally held assets, etc. Assure your client that you will tell no one about the contents of your discussions without your client's permission.

5. ALLOW CLIENT TO EXPLAIN BASIC WISHES

In an unstructured format, allow the client to explain in narrative form what the client is seeking. Guide the client with basic questions if necessary but resist the urge to control or use cross-examination type tactics. Let the client tell his or her "story"; it is something the client has probably been rehearsing and wants to get out and it gives you a good perspective on what the client initially feels is most important.

6. EXPLORE FACTS

BRIAN L. DOBBEN, ESTATE PLANNING: THE INITIAL CLIENT INTERVIEW*

81 ILL. B.J. 261, 261–62 (1993).

Begin your meeting by gathering the following necessary information: Client's (1) full name, (2) birthdate, and (3) home address; (4) spouse's name and (5) birthdate; (6) telephone numbers (home and work); (7) employer's name and client's position; (8) full name and ages of children; (9) whether client and spouse are U.S. citizens, (10) filed a gift tax return, (11) lived in any community property states, and (12) have any wills, trust agreements, premarital, or postmarital agreements; (13) whether any of the children are adopted or (14) developmentally disabled; and (15) whether the client has a safety deposit box.

After obtaining this routine information, begin discussing the client's assets. For each asset, determine who owns it, whether it should be owned in that manner, how much it is worth, and whether some specific planning suggestion should be made with respect to the asset. These suggestions will fall into three general categories: (1) Can the asset be eliminated from the gross estate for tax purposes? (2) Can the asset be valued in a manner beneficial to the client? (3) Can the asset be used to equalize the estates of married couples?

If you do not use a questionnaire to collect asset data, adopt a consistent style for gathering information during the meeting. One approach is to create in your notes a grid with the names of the husband, wife, and "joint" across the top. Write the various categories of assets you will discuss down the left hand side of the grid. Then place the net value of each asset in the appropriate spot on the grid. When completed, the grid permits you to determine at a glance the size of the estate and how much is in each spouse's name (or held jointly).

CATEGORIES OF ASSETS

Your discussion (and your grid) should cover the following categories of assets.

Real estate. Ask not only about the personal residence but also about investment real estate, oil and gas interests, summer homes, co-ops, and condominiums. For each real estate interest, get an estimate of the current market value and the mortgage balance. If the real estate is investment grade, ask for the net annual revenue. Real estate ownership is often used to equalize estates. Also consider whether any out-of-state real estate should be placed in a trust to avoid ancillary probate.

Cash and cash equivalents. Determine the current balances in any checking, savings, money market, and certificate of deposit accounts.

* Reprinted with permission of the *Illinois Bar Journal*, Vol. 81 #5, May 1993. Copyright by the Illinois State Bar Association. www.isba.org

Remember that cash and cash equivalents make for the easiest "gifting" programs and can also be used to equalize assets between spouses.

Stocks and bonds. Review the client's publicly traded stocks and bonds. It is generally best to list tax-exempt and taxable bonds separately.

Insurance. Be careful to ask about all varieties of insurance. Clients occasionally overlook employer-purchased group life benefits. For each policy, determine the insured, the owner, the beneficiary, and the cash value. From a planning perspective, you can often remove insurance from large estates by placing it into an irrevocable life insurance trust.

Tax-sheltered benefit plans. This category covers a wide variety of areas. Obtain information on the client's pension, retirement, profit sharing, thrift, ESOP, Keogh and individual retirement accounts. For each account, determine the owner and beneficiary designation. From a planning perspective, you might explore whether to fund any planned charitable gifts from these assets to eliminate the tax on IRD items.

Business assets. Devote a great deal of time to discussing any business interest owned by the client. Inquire into the form of business ownership (i.e. partnership, proprietorship, C or S corporation) and the percentage of ownership. Valuation of the closely held business assets is very difficult. Perhaps the best starting point is simply to ask the client how much he or she would demand before selling the business to a third party. The value of business interests can be affected by buy/sell arrangements; if the business is subject to such an agreement, ask for a copy.

The many planning possibilities for a closely held business are far beyond the scope of this article. However, you should discuss how the client wishes to transfer the business to the next generation, whether he or she wants to "gift" interests in the business, and whether he or she should freeze the value of the business.

Inheritance potential. While this is an easy area to overlook, possible inheritances can have a substantial impact on planning decisions. If the client expects a large inheritance, it may influence your decision about whether generation skipping is appropriate. The client often does not have a clear idea of the expectancies. Unless you represent the entire family, it may be impossible to obtain all the information you would like.

Tangible personal property. While tangible personal property is rarely important from a tax perspective, the presence of valuable collections, automobiles, and boats in the estate may have an impact on tax planning. Even if it lacks significant monetary value, tangible personal property may have great sentimental value and should be handled circumspectly.

Other property. You should ask an open-ended question about any assets that may not have been covered (i.e. copyrights, patents, etc.).

Liabilities. Generally, you will discuss liabilities in connection with the asset that secures the debt. For example, in discussing the value of the personal residence you usually ask about the mortgage. To be certain you have a handle on all the liabilities, ask if any other liabilities exist that were not discussed.

NOTES AND QUESTIONS

1. You should review a detailed checklist to be sure you obtain all relevant information. See SANFORD J. SCHLESINGER, ESTATE PLANNING FOR THE ELDERLY CLIENT § 1.10, at 8–16 (1984); HAROLD WEINSTOCK & MARTIN NEUMANN, PLANNING AN ESTATE: A GUIDEBOOK OF PRINCIPLES AND TECHNIQUES § 1.11 (4th ed. 2002).

2. You "should not overlook the possibility that a client may have overlooked some of his or her own property. This overlooked property can take many forms: dormant savings accounts; uncashed dividend checks and the underlying stock certificates on which the dividends were issued; life insurance policies; and more unusual items such as gift certificates, utility deposits and wage or salary checks." J. Brooke Spotswood, *Laying Claim to Decedent's Unclaimed Property,* PROB. & PROP., Jan./Feb. 1993, at 46. Can you think of other types of "forgotten" property?

DRAFT

Prepare a checklist to gather facts during the initial interview. You may need to prepare several, depending on the type of client.

7. DISCUSS CLIENT'S DESIRES

After you have acquired all the relevant facts, you should then concentrate on what the client actually wants to do. You need to focus on the following concerns:

- *Recipients of Property*—Whom does the client wish to benefit from the client's property, e.g., spouse, children, parents, other relatives, friends, or charities?
- *Timing of Benefits*—When does the client want the donees to enjoy the property, e.g., immediately, upon the occurrence of a specific event, when a condition is satisfied, upon the client's death, or at some other time? Do any recipients have special needs which must be met immediately while other recipients can benefit by receiving the property later in life?
- *Uses of Property*—How does the client want the donees to be able to use the property, e.g., an unrestricted outright gift or a gift in trust with limitations or conditions on use?
- *Administration Matters*—Whom does the client want to manage the property now and in the future, e.g., donee, trustee, executor, or agent? Should the manager be compensated and should bond be waived?
- *Tax Concerns*—Is the client's estate large enough, either now or anticipated to be so by the time of the client's death, to necessitate

tax planning? If yes, is the client willing to take steps to save taxes even though such steps remove property from the client's control or otherwise disrupt the client's power to deal with the property without restriction?

- *Disability Matters*—What plans does the client wish to make for potential disability regarding property management and health care, e.g., durable powers of attorney, self-designation of guardians, insurance, etc.?
- *Death Planning*—How does the client want matters relating to the physical aspects of death handled, e.g., use of heroic medical techniques, implementation of anatomical gifts, and the final disposition of the body?

8. EMPLOYMENT DISCUSSION—WRITTEN FEE AGREEMENT

You now need to determine if the client wants to hire you to prepare the estate plan. Do not make the assumption that you have been hired; you must ask directly. You should first outline the services you would provide as well as how your fee would be determined. If the client hires you, be sure to have the client read and sign a written employment contract. See Chapter 8(G) for a discussion of fee setting methods.

9. CONCLUDE INTERVIEW

End the interview by reviewing a plan of action, that is, who is going to do what by when. You may need to do research and prepare documents; the client may need to ponder and gather documents or information. Schedule the client's next appointment, tell the client you are looking forward to working together, and walk the client to the door.

10. POST-INTERVIEW MATTERS

a. Letter to Client

As soon as practical, you should prepare a letter to the client confirming the plan of action agreed to during the interview. Many estate planners also send a memorandum which restates the basic elements of an estate plan and the applicable law. Estate planning issues are unfamiliar to most clients; they will welcome a plain language document they can review at home. See Theodore M. David, *Guiding Your Client Through the Estate Planning Process*, PRAC. LAW., Dec. 1992, at 13 for a list of elements that should be contained in a client memorandum for estate planning.

If the interviewee did not hire you or if you turned down the job, it is important to send a declination letter. This letter should cover at least the following matters: (1) confirm that you will not be performing any estate planning services for the interviewee; (2) indicate that you will not advise the interviewee of changes in the law that may effect the interviewee; (3) warn that a statute of limitations or other relevant time period may expire shortly; and (4) state the confidential nature of the information revealed during the interview and that you will not accept conflicting employment. A prudent attorney may want to get the interviewee to sign and return a copy of this letter.

There has been considerable debate whether attorneys who practice in the estate planning or tax fields are required to comply with the privacy requirements of the Gramm–Leach–Bliley Act (GLB), 15 U.S.C. §§ 6801–09, such as by providing notices of privacy policies and practices when the attorney-client relationship is established and thereafter on an annual basis. The Federal Trade Commission ruled that attorneys were within the scope of GLB. But, in *New York State Bar Ass'n v. F.T.C.*, No. Civ. A. 02–810 (RBW) & Civ. A. 02–1883 (RBW), 2004 WL 964173 (D. D.C. 2004), the court held that the F.T.C.'s decision that attorneys are covered by GLB and its disclosure requirements was an arbitrary and capricious agency action. Subsequently, the General Counsel of the F.T.C. stated that "unless and until the district court's April 30, 2004 order or any judgment embodying that order is reversed, [the F.T.C.] will not bring any enforcement actions or conduct any investigations against practicing lawyers under [GLB] for any action, inaction, or failure to comply by them during the period preceding reversal." Letter from William E. Kovacic to David L. Roll & Steven C. Krane (May 7, 2004).

b. Post-Interview Checklist

Prudent estate planners will also complete a concise checklist after the client leaves to be sure all important matters were covered. See Francis J. Collin, Jr., *A Post–Interview Estate Planning Checklist*, PROB. & PROP., Mar./April 1988, at 58, 59–60.

c. Memorandum to File

If your interview notes are incomplete, you should prepare a file memorandum detailing the facts and plan of action.

d. Tickler File Entry

Determine when you should contact the client if you have no further communications with the client, e.g., the client fails to schedule another interview as promised. You or your secretary should enter this date into your tickler system, be it a simple paper calendar or a sophisticated computer program.

DRAFT

1. Prepare a basic letter to send to a client after the estate planning interview.

2. Prepare a client memorandum based on the law of your state.

3. Prepare a post-interview checklist.

E. INFORMATION AND DOCUMENT COLLECTION

The client is unlikely to supply all the information and documents necessary to prepare the estate plan during the initial interview. In addition, it is risky to rely on the client to remember accurately important dates, values of assets and debts, methods of holding title, etc.

Below is a list of documents you should examine. What other documents should be added to the list?

- Prior wills and other estate planning documents (trusts, powers of attorney, living wills, etc.).
- Birth certificates—client and children.
- Adoption records—client and children.
- Marriage certificates.
- Divorce decrees and property settlements.
- Military records.
- Deeds.
- Stock certificates.
- Insurance policies.
- Retirement plans.
- Annuity contracts.
- Signature cards for accounts at financial institutions.
- Signature cards for safe deposit boxes.
- Business documents, e.g., articles of incorporation, partnership agreements, buy-sell agreements, etc.
- Evidences of debt, e.g., mortgages, security agreements, notes, contracts, etc.
- Old gift and income tax returns.

Who should actually gather the documents? You have basically three choices. First, the client could obtain the documents. This saves the client money and the client often has easy access to the documents. On the other hand, the client may lack the knowledge of how to acquire the documents, especially if they must be obtained from the public records in distant locations. Second, you or your staff could search for the documents. This is a more costly option but your office personnel are more likely to know how to get the documents in a timely fashion. Third, you could hire an outside person or firm to track down the documents. The pros and cons of this method are basically the same as for performing the search yourself except for the greater chance of confidentiality breaches because more people are involved in the process.

NOTE

Your client should collect and organize important documents and information so that this material is readily accessible to the appropriate person(s) after your client dies. See LYNN MCPHELIMY, IN THE CHECKLIST OF LIFE: A WORKING BOOK TO HELP YOU LIVE AND LEAVE THIS LIFE! (2d ed. 1997) which includes a list of items such as:

- Social security number;
- Medical history;
- Financial information describing bank accounts, credit cards, investments, insurance, and related matters;
- Maintenance tips for the house, yard, and vehicles;
- Interesting stories accompanying items of personal property;
- Hiding places of property and documents;
- Personal material such as family history, names of special friends, photographs, audio and video recordings, and similar material;
- Letters to children and other loved ones; and
- Estate planning information such as the will, living will, and body disposition desires.

See also DAVID S. MAGEE, EVERYTHING YOUR HEIRS NEED TO KNOW—YOUR ASSETS, FAMILY HISTORY AND FINAL WISHES (1991) (providing forms for recording information and pockets for the user to insert relevant documents); John J. Scroggin, *The Family Love Letter*, PRAC. TAX LAW., Winter 1999, at 5 (form for client to complete to supply "basic information which will be needed upon the client's incapacity or death").

F. ATTORNEY-CLIENT RELATIONSHIP

PERSONAL FINANCIAL PLANNING HANDBOOK: WITH FORMS & CHECKLISTS*

Second Edition (2011).

¶ 14.06 Planner–Client Communications

Effective planner-client communications are necessary to keep clients informed and interested and to attract prospective clients. Clients should feel that the planner is always thinking about how to improve their finances. Nothing will go further in accomplishing this aim than a planner's good faith effort to contact clients on a regular basis. Well-established lines of communication are key to developing the sort of long-term planner-client relationships that are at the core of every successful financial planning practice. Planners may find the following ways of communicating effective in maintaining and attracting clients.

---

* Chapter 14 "Practice Management and Development," published in Personal Financial Planning Handbook: With Forms & Checklists, Second Edition, by Jonathan Pond. © 2011 by Thomson Reuters/WG&L. Reprinted with permission. All rights reserved. This information or any portion thereof may not be copied or disseminated in any form or by any means or stored in an electronic database or retrieval system without the express written consent of Thomson Reuters/WG&L.

¶ 14.06[1] Newsletters

Publishing a periodic newsletter is a particularly effective means of keeping clients informed and thinking about financial planning. A good newsletter gives the planner a forum in which to showcase his or her financial expertise, thereby enhancing the attitude of the client or prospect toward the planner. In addition, the planner can use back issues as an effective marketing tool, especially when including them in information kits sent to prospective clients. The planner can provide copies to the local media in the hope that they may be noted as a source in a story, thereby improving recognition.

Now that nearly every office is equipped with a personal computer and laser printer, planners have the ability to produce attractive newsletters at low cost. Alternatively, a number of services offer prepackaged client newsletters. Clearly, the home-grown variety of newsletter, if professional in design and content, is most effective. But these require a larger investment of time—time that many planners cannot spare.

Some companies offering prepackaged newsletters have proposed an alternative solution, providing space in each issue for a planner to submit one or more articles. Some also offer specialized newsletters on such topics as estate planning, financial planning, and accounting. At least one publisher allows a planner to select from a story list the articles that will appear in the next issue. Companies generally offer prepackaged newsletters on a monthly, bi-monthly, or quarterly basis.

Planners may want to include a short cover letter with whatever type of newsletter they select, explaining what the client or prospect will find in the newsletter and encouraging them to call with questions or for further information. Letters sent to prospects to introduce the newsletter can include more information about the firm. * * *

Planners may want to consider producing a newsletter in league with another planner or other planners, thereby sharing the workload and tapping a greater breadth of knowledge. Most importantly, each planner can make his or her own imprint on the publication. However, unless participating planners clearly define responsibilities and out-line procedures, they will find that group publications can ultimately require more time than individually produced newsletters.

Planners should also consider the use of e-mail as an effective and efficient means of communicating with clients. With minimal hard cost, e-mailed newsletters allow planners to keep lines of communication open and to solicit responses and retrieve information easily.

¶ 14.06[2] Correspondence

Although a newsletter is an excellent way to keep general information flowing to clients, written communication between planner and client is also an essential way to maintain client contact as well as to document important client matters. Some planners maintain a program of regular written communications to clients in lieu of or in addition to a periodic newsletter. Others correspond with clients if and when they feel that they should inform the client about a timely matter—e.g., about a change in a tax regulation or in a letter accompanying a newspaper or magazine article that will be of interest to the client. Some planners find that periodically telephoning the client to impart timely information can accomplish the same ends at a lower cost than drafting a letter. E-mail can be an even more efficient way to communicate with clients.

¶ 14.06[3] Meetings and Telephone Contact

Planners should not overlook the importance of face-to-face meetings and occasional planner-initiated telephone calls in maintaining strong client relationships. One common lament of financial planning clients is that they do not meet or hear from their advisers on a regular basis.

NOTES AND QUESTIONS

1. For additional information on the attorney-client relationship, see Maureen B. Collins, *Communicating with Your Client*, 83 ILL. B.J. 653 (1995) (proposing a six step approach to effective client communications: (1) listen to your client, (2) be simple and direct, (3) respond early and often, (4) keep the client up to speed, (5) communicate "just because," and (6) come up with a plan); Christina Pesoli, *Best Kept Secrets to Keeping Your Clients Happy*, 61 TEX. B.J. 1002 (1998) (recommending a five step approach: (1) treat every client like a big fish, (2) act like a professional attorney, (3) treat your word as your bond, (4) round down, not up when billing, and (5) nurture the relationship between you and the client). See also Bill Jones, *Practice Building & Client Development*, 60 TEX. B.J. 1161 (1997); Bradford W. Hildebrandt & Blane R. Prescott, *9 Ways to be a Lawyer Clients Love*, 59 TEX. B.J. 66 (1996).

2. Some attorneys provide their clients with client-relation questionnaires. For a sample questionnaire, see Anne E. Thar, *What Do Clients Really Want? It's Time You Found Out*, 87 ILL. B.J. 331 (1999).

3. Can you think of additional ways to enhance your relationship with your client?

G. FEES

RONALD R. CRESSWELL & LENDY LEGGETT, SETTING AND COLLECTING FEES*

STATE BAR OF TEXAS, FIFTEENTH ANNUAL ADVANCED ESTATE PLANNING AND PROBATE COURSE, Chapter O (1991).

I. INTRODUCTION

As client loyalty to individual attorneys and law firms dwindles and competition among the ever increasing number of attorneys skyrockets, the legal environment today mandates a careful reevaluation of billing practices and procedures. Such examination requires an analysis of fee setting as well as fee collecting and should include an honest evaluation of the methodology incorporated in conducting the entire billing practice and

* Reprinted with permission.

procedure. Such examination should determine whether the same systematic method of billing is incorporated into every bill sent to *and* collected from estate planning and probate clients and that such procedures are efficient and cost effective.

II. FEE SETTING

The first step in an attorney's or law firm's billing practice involves formulation of the best method for calculating the proper fee to charge for a particular type of project, and making certain that the fee charged is reasonable.

A. Ethical Considerations

The American Bar Association Model Rules of Professional Conduct (the "Model Rules") do not give specific guidelines for setting attorney fees but instead generally provide that "a lawyer's fee shall be reasonable." Model Rules of Professional Conduct Rule 1.5 (1983). Model Rule 1.5(a) explains that:

> The factors to be considered in determining the reasonableness of a fee include the following:
>
> (1) The time and labor required, the novelty and difficulty of the questions involved, and the skill requisite to perform the legal service properly;
>
> (2) The likelihood, if apparent to the client, that the acceptance of the particular employment will preclude other employment by the lawyer;
>
> (3) The fee customarily charged in the locality for similar legal services;
>
> (4) The amount involved and the results obtained;
>
> (5) The time limitations imposed by the client or by the circumstances;
>
> (6) The nature and length of the professional relationship with the client;
>
> (7) The experience, reputation, and ability of the lawyer or lawyers performing the services;
>
> (8) Whether the fee is fixed or contingent....

Therefore, in developing a formula for fee setting in the estate and probate area, the attorney must be mindful of the guidance, limited as it may be, provided in the Model Rules.

B. Factors for Analysis

There are numerous other factors, in addition to those presented in Model Rule 1.5, that should be included in the fee setting formula. One systematic approach to follow in the practical implementation is a cost method of accounting. By using the cost method as a model, an attorney will consider the various expenses incurred in providing legal services to all clients in determining the fee to charge each individual client. At a minimum, the fees charged must cover the cost of labor, direct materials, and overhead.

1. *Labor.* The cost of labor is probably the most easily adjusted factor in the cost equation used for setting fees, as long as there are other associates or paralegals available to work and familiar with the estate and probate practice. In the cost accounting formula, labor costs include the cost of all labor directly required to produce the end result, whether an estate plan or the completion of a probate matter. Many of the routine steps involved in drafting an estate plan or preparing probate documents could be handled by a paralegal, whose hourly billing rate might be one-third of a partner's hourly rate. With price competition so prevalent today as clients shop for less expensive legal services, attorneys will want to consider using associate attorneys or paralegals with lower billing rates whenever possible in providing client services. * * *

2. *Direct Materials.* The cost of direct materials is more frequently charged directly to the client today than has been the case in the past. For instance, attorneys and law firms are now passing on directly to the client the cost of photocopying, long distance phone calls, postage and even clerical work as specified charges instead of assuming that those costs would be covered by the hourly rate charged to the clients today. Many attorneys and law firms now prepare bills with a separate section for disbursements which breaks out the cost of specific expenditures made in completing the clients' work.

3. *Overhead.* The cost of overhead is likely the most rapidly increasing element of the cost accounting system in the estate planning and probate practice. With the development of computer programs to draft documents less attorney time is necessary to draft documents, however, the considerable cost of this capital investment must be passed on to the client. Price, *Contemporary Estate Planning,* (1983) p. 34. Additionally, overhead costs include clerical and secretarial salaries, equipment, depreciation, office supplies, electricity, and numerous other necessary expenses not directly attributable to any individual project or client.

C. Possible Methods for Setting Fees

Considering the very general ethical standard of "reasonable fees" and the varied factors which contribute to costs, each attorney or firm can establish a formula for setting fees which is appropriate for their practice, with some limitations. Such fee formulas could involve a fee based entirely on hours worked at an hourly rate, a fixed fee for given estate planning documents or probate services, a fee based on the percentage of the estate or amount of money the attorney saves for the client, or a combination of the above. This outline does not attempt to provide an in-depth analysis of each possible fee setting formula. However, for a more thorough analysis, see Jerold I. Horn's outline "Setting and Deducting Fees in an Estates Practice," ABA 1991 Mid-Winter Tax Section Meeting. Whichever the appropriate method, the attorney or law firm should determine which method is best suited to their specific estate and probate practice and apply that formula consistently to ensure that all costs including labor, materials, and overhead, and the desired profit are included.

1. *Hourly Rate.* Simply, this method involves multiplying the number of hours worked by the attorney's hourly rate. With the technological advances in computer-aided drafting, this figure may not generate sufficient fees to cover the cost of technology since less time is required for drafting. Therefore, some additional elements should be added to this fee formula or the hourly rate adjusted to ensure that all costs are covered. The formula could be modified to include an additional factor for overhead factored into the equation to allocate, to each clients' bill, the costs of technology, the cost of attorney time spent on revising and updating forms, and the cost of attorney time spent personalizing and developing a computer program to conform the attorney's forms to the client. Under this approach, each client would contribute to the overall costs incurred in the capital expenditure necessary to provide a timely and quality product.

2. *Fixed Fee.* A fixed fee involves charging a client a pre-set price for a particular estate planning document or set of estate planning documents (i.e., a simple will, directive to physicians and durable power of attorney for one set price). Prior to utilizing this system, careful examination of overhead and costs is necessary to ensure that all costs, including salary, direct materials and overhead are covered based on the number of clients the lawyer anticipates, realistically to serve. If the estate and probate lawyer is charging a flat fee, that lawyer should continue to track the time spent on each estate plan or probate matter because a client might not hesitate to call or repeatedly modify documents realizing that the fee is fixed regardless of attorney time expended. Considering that possibility, the attorney might want to mix two methods together. For instance, as suggested in Jerold I. Horn's outline "Setting and Deducting Fees in an Estates Practice," presented at the ABA 1991 Mid–Winter Tax Section Meeting p. 168, the fixed fee might include a specified maximum amount of attorney time, and if the time expended by the attorney is greater than that maximum, an hourly rate element would be factored into the fee, as well.

3. *Percentage Fees.* A percentage fee includes the value of the estate assets as a factor in determining the fee charged. The percentage charged to the client may be arbitrarily set, set by the market, or set by a court. According to Jerold I. Horn's outline "Setting and Deducting Fees in an Estates Practice," the number of dollars included in the equation may include not only the fair market value of all probate assets, but also a percentage of the non probate assets as well, which are included on tax returns. *Id.* at p. 168.

4. *Combinations of Fee Methods.* A variety of combinations of the above-referenced methods for setting fees could be incorporated into an established fee setting procedure. Jerold I. Horn's outline provides numer-

ous "hybrid" possibilities including: (i) product-oriented and time-oriented fees for estate planning where more than a set maximum number of attorney hours is expended; (ii) percentage-oriented fees and time-oriented fees for an estate administration in which time expended exceeds a "normal" amount; (iii) product-oriented and percentage-oriented fees for a set product and to compensate the attorney for any value which he created or preserved; or (iv) a combination of all three methods which additionally compensates the attorney based on the time spent.

5. *Which Method to Use.* Evaluate your practice and choose a system best suited to your practice, or create a system that works well in your particular circumstances. While evaluating possible methods, remember that a purely time-oriented system may encourage inefficiency. * * * Additionally, the system incorporated into your practice should not be so complicated that billing consumes large amounts of valuable attorney time. Whichever method is used, the fee charged should reflect the costs incurred in preparing the client's estate planning documents or in completing the probate procedures. These costs include the cost of research, and revisions of will forms, the cost of computer and computer programs utilized in document preparation and other overhead expenses. * * * Attorneys and law firms need to be in touch with the market for legal services in the estate planning area so that they are not left behind, with their clients looking elsewhere for legal services. An attorney should periodically reevaluate the fee-setting system in existence to ensure that it is functioning properly and that all costs are covered and the desired profit is achieved.

III. FEE COLLECTING

Although a consistent method of billing is achieved, if the bill is not collected, the attorney or law firm will be unable to cover all expenses and will be forced out of business. Therefore, collection procedures must be in place. Many attorneys feel that the only chore permeating the legal profession which is worse than billing the client is having to follow-up and attempt to collect fees from a client unwilling, unable or reluctant to pay for the lawyer's services. Therefore, the best approach to take in the area of collecting fees is a proactive one. In a proactive system of collection, fee collection begins when an attorney decides whether to represent a client. Even when planning ahead, however, there will always be instances where follow-up must be pursued in order to keep the lights turned on and the electric company at bay. Remember, your job for a client as an attorney is not complete until your fee is collected.

A. Choosing Your Clients Carefully

Although your selection of who your clients will be may not appear to be important to collecting your fee, it is definitely a factor. The groundwork for collection of fees begins at the outset of the estate planning or probate process, even before you have accepted a potential client's work.

1. *Ability to Pay.* After meeting the client, ask yourself whether that potential client will be able to pay your fees. If you have a substantial doubt, chances are your instinct is correct and you can avoid the hassles of fee collection difficulties by deciding not to represent such person at the outset. If you do represent the person, you may not only spend your time preparing documents for which you will not be compensated, you will also expend time and energy in attempting to collect your fees.

2. *Get It in Writing.* Model Rule 1.5(b) provides that "[w]hen the lawyer has not regularly represented the client, the basis or rate of the fee shall be communicated to the client, preferably in writing, before or within a reasonable time after commencing the representation." In addition to the direction given in Model Rule 1.5, there are several advantages to entering into a fee arrangement or having your client sign an engagement letter prior to performing services for the client. First, it forces the attorney and client to openly and fully discuss fees prior to providing services for the client. Also, the letter may state explicitly what the attorney's responsibilities and limits are in the representation. Misunderstandings often arise between clients and attorneys concerning fees. These misunderstandings possibly arise from an attorney's reluctance to discuss fees at the beginning of the representation and from the misunderstanding that often arises in oral communication. ABA/BNA Lawyers' Manual on Professional Conduct 41:502. A written letter specifically addressing fees helps avoid future conflicts and reduce disputes concerning fees since the parties, both attorney and client, were well informed at the outset. *Id.* In drafting fee agreements, the attorney should clearly specify the terms since, if contested, any ambiguity in the fee agreement will be construed against the lawyer. * * *

B. Bill Promptly and Completely

As important as any other step in the fee setting and collecting process is billing the client promptly. Billing promptly is not only important to assure cash flow but also because clients are often less reluctant to pay their bill when the work is ongoing or recently completed, and the services you provided are present on their mind. "Economics and Ethics," Robert M. Bandy, ABA 1991 Mid–Winter Tax Section Meeting. The longer the period of time that elapses from the date of completion of the work to the date of billing, the more reluctant the client may be to pay the bill and the more likely he is to contest the amount of the fee. Similarly, when the bill is sent, if the attorney does not conduct interim billing, the attorney should be certain that all fees are included on the bill when mailed to the client or notify the client that one more bill will be sent to cover any additional time and disbursements. By informing the client that another bill is forthcoming, the attorney might avoid the clients' irritation of receiving an additional bill after believing that the bill was paid in full. If the attorney wants to send one bill after the services are completed, the attorney should calculate, at the time of billing the client, any additional expenses for photocopies, postage, delivery or filing fees, and attorney time and add those to the bill so that the client does not receive one bill, thinking the total fees and expenses have been entirely paid, and thirty days later receives a second bill for additional fees and expenses.

David P. Hassler expresses an additional reason to bill promptly in "The Economics of Estate Planning: Finding the Clients, Doing Their Work and Getting Paid for It" concerning a client's general tendency to delay or "put-off" completing their estate planning work. One suggestion that article provides to motivate clients to complete their estate planning work is to conduct interim billing, even if the work is not complete. Upon receiving an interim bill, the client is generally more readily inclined to review the drafts of the documents and call the attorney to execute the documents.

C. *Follow–Up—"The Gorilla Approach"*

1. *Reminders.* A law firm or a lawyer should maintain an organized and systematic follow-up mechanism to collect late fees. For instance, a planned bill collection system might include reminder letters sent for bills outstanding 30, 60, 90 and 120 days. Bandy, "Economics and Ethics," 14th Annual Advanced Estate Planning and Probate Course (1990) p. 7. Such reminders should be prepared regularly and sent directly to the client.

2. *Other Alternatives.* Some other alternatives for collection of fees are available in certain jurisdictions. For instance, in California, before an action may be instituted in any court for the collection of fees, the parties must comply with mandatory arbitration procedures. Rules of Procedure of the State Bar of California, rules 690–733. Several states have voluntary fee arbitration plans including Georgia and Connecticut. ABA/BNA Lawyers' Manual on Professional Conduct 41:2003. Some states also allow lawyers to utilize commercial collection agencies or other laws to recover unpaid fees. *Id.*

3. *Lawsuit and Ethical Considerations.* After a client has failed to pay an outstanding bill and the follow-up procedures for fee collection have been exhausted, a lawyer must take into account the fact that a lawsuit to recover unpaid fees is often an invitation for a malpractice counterclaim by the client. ABA/BNA Lawyers Manual on Professional Conduct § 301:1010. In the estate and probate arena, the fees are often not substantial when compared to fees charged by other departments of the law firm. Thus, the estate and probate section of the firm is often supported by volume of work rather than individual fees. Therefore, an attorney should weigh the amount of fee owed against the cost of the lawsuit, especially if a malpractice counterclaim might possibly be filed. *Id.* A possible guideline to follow is that an attorney should only pursue an action to recover fees if a written fee agreement was utilized and another independent lawyer examines the file finding no cause for complaint. Blumberg, "Risk Management: Preventing Malpractice Claims" 13 Legal Economics 52, 54 (Sept. 1987). The attorney should be mindful, however, of the Comment to the Model Rule 1.5 which suggests that fee disputes be

settled out of court. This Comment provides that "[i]f a procedure has been established for resolution of fee disputes, such as an arbitration or mediation procedure established by the bar, the lawyer should conscientiously consider submitting to it. Law may prescribe a procedure for determining a lawyer's fee, for example, in representation of an executor or administrator, a class or a person entitled to a reasonable fee as part of the measure of damages. The lawyer entitled to such a fee and a lawyer entitled representing another party concerned with the fee should comply with the prescribed procedure."

D. Summary

Remember that collecting fees begins at the time you first encounter your potential client. And, your services as an attorney are not complete until you have collected a reasonable fee for your services. There are several alternative means for collecting fees that might be utilized, however, be certain to evaluate the total fee unpaid compared with the amount expended in collection procedures to determine whether such attempts are cost effective. Also, be realistic when a considerable length of time has expired without collection and write off those accounts receivable.

IV. CONCLUSION

Fee setting and fee collecting involve numerous considerations. Considering the many factors to remember in creating a fee setting formula, including ethical rules, overhead expenses, the cost of attorney time, and the benefits conferred to the client, fee setting is an essential and often difficult responsibility of the attorney in the estate planning and probate area. The estate planners job is not complete until all fees are collected from the client, which may involve follow-up after the initial billing has taken place and should include a signed fee agreement at the outset to avoid later conflict between the attorney and client concerning fees. To survive in the economic climate prevailing in the legal profession today, attorneys must spend time establishing set procedures for setting fees and for collecting fees. And, the attorney must make certain that these policies and procedures are followed.

NOTES AND QUESTIONS

1. Another fee-setting arrangement gaining in popularity is the *reverse contingent fee*. Under this method, the fee for the estate plan is a percentage of the tax liability saved because of the plan. What do you think of this arrangement? See ABA Formal Opinion 93–373.

2. What method of fee determination will you use? Might you use different methods for different situations?

3. What portion of your estate planning fees may your client claim on the client's income tax return as a miscellaneous itemized deduction? See I.R.C. § 212(3) (deduction for expenses "in connection with the determination, collection, or refund of any tax"). How can you help your client secure

this deduction? See Louis S. Harrison & John M. Janiga, *Deductibility of Estate Planning Fees: An Old Strategy Revisited,* PROB. & PROP., Sept./Oct. 1994, at 32.

4. For a discussion of attorney fees in general, see Darlene Ricker, *The Vanishing Hourly Fee,* A.B.A. J., Mar. 1994, at 66.

DRAFT

Prepare a fee agreement.

H. FIDUCIARY SELECTION

Your client must exercise great care in selecting fiduciaries, e.g., executors, trustees, guardians, and agents. These decisions will affect the client and the client's family members for many years. The decision regarding the appropriate person to select is, naturally, for the client to make. However, you have a duty to explain to the client the factors which should be considered before making a designation. In this section, we will focus on the criteria for executors and trustees. Many of these considerations are also important in selecting other fiduciaries. Please review Chapter 5(B) (property management agent), Chapter 6(C) (health care agent), and Chapters 5(C) and 6(D) (self-designation of guardian). Guardians for minors are discussed in Chapter 10(A).

NOTES

1. A person considering accepting a fiduciary position must think carefully about whether to accept the job and its accompanying burdens. For assistance in explaining the duties and responsibilities to your client, see Stephan R. Leimberg & Charles K. Plotnick, *A Sample Letter to Clients on Their Duties as Executors and Trustees*, PRAC. LAW., Sept. 1986, at 23.

2. For general information, see Steve R. Akers, *Twenty–Five Things You* Have *to Know About Appointing Trustees*, PROB. & PROP., July/Aug. 2003, at 36; Kimbrough Street, *Practical Guidelines for Selecting an Individual Trustee,* 20 EST. PLAN. 268 (1993).

1. BASIC CRITERIA

a. Legal

Individuals and corporations must have the legal capacity under local law to serve as fiduciaries. You need to verify that your client's executor and trustee selections meet the applicable legal criteria.

Although these criteria vary among the states, the basic requirements are relatively uniform. For example, an individual fiduciary must typically be (1) an adult (usually at least eighteen years of age unless the court has removed a younger person's disabilities of minority or the person is married), (2) not incompetent or incapacitated, (3) not a convicted felon, and (4) not found to be otherwise unsuitable by the court. In some states, a non-resident may not serve as a fiduciary unless the non-resident takes special steps such as appointing a resident agent to accept service of process.

A corporate fiduciary must comply with state law to be authorized to act as a fiduciary. States may impose relatively few requirements on a bank or savings and loan (e.g., merely having a corporate charter authorizing the corporation to act as a fiduciary may be sufficient) while imposing additional requirements on (1) other types of corporations (e.g., the state will grant a trust company a charter only if the corporation satisfies certain requirements), and (2) non-domestic corporations (e.g., foreign corporations have authority to act locally as fiduciaries only if the foreign state permits local corporations to act in the foreign state).

LOCATE

1. What are the requirements to serve as an executor in your state?
2. What are the requirements to serve as a trustee in your state?

b. Honesty

The fiduciary must be someone in whom your client has complete trust. If the client has any doubt, the client should select a different person.

QUESTION

How could you help your client determine if a prospective fiduciary is honest and trustworthy?

c. Common Sense and Good Judgment

The fiduciary must make many discretionary decisions. Accordingly, it is important for the fiduciary to have a good measure of common sense; the fiduciary must act prudently and reasonably at all times.

QUESTION

How would you assist your client in determining whether a prospective fiduciary is capable of exercising common sense and good judgment?

d. Financial Responsibility

Individuals and corporations who have experienced success in their own financial matters are more likely to be able to do the same for assets managed in a fiduciary capacity. In addition, financially stable individuals are usually not as motivated to embezzle estate property as are persons who continuously experience financial difficulties. Your client should seek fiduciaries who are financially solid and not involved in litigation which could lead to the individual's or corporation's bankruptcy.

QUESTION

What steps would you advise your client to take to determine the financial status of a prospective fiduciary?

e. Experience and Skill

The level of experience, skill, and knowledge needed to serve as an executor or trustee depends on the type, amount, and value of property that the fiduciary will manage. Vastly different expertise is needed to manage diverse investments such as high-rise apartment buildings in a large city, farms, portfolios of stocks, bonds, commodity futures, derivatives, and other securities, retail businesses, and oil and gas properties.

QUESTION

How would you suggest that your client investigate the skill and experience of a prospective fiduciary?

f. Awareness of Legal Issues

Closely connected with the importance of the fiduciary possessing skill and experience in asset management, is an inquiry into whether the fiduciary has a solid grasp of the legal issues that may arise during the administration. Although a fiduciary need not be an attorney, the fiduciary must be aware of potential legal issues or at least know that consultation with an attorney or other expert is essential.

g. Impartiality

The fiduciary, especially a trustee of a discretionary trust, may be called upon to decide which beneficiary is to receive distributions and the timing and size of the payments. This requires the fiduciary to be fair and evenhanded to all potential distributees as well as to resist the persistent claims of greedy beneficiaries who want larger payouts.

QUESTION

How can your client anticipate the reaction of a prospective fiduciary to pressure from the beneficiaries who may even threaten to sue if they do not get their way?

h. Fiduciary "Personality"

An individual needs to possess a special type of personality to successfully serve as a fiduciary. "A calm demeanor and a tolerant and understanding frame of mind will encourage beneficiaries to feel that their requests and points of view will be given a fair hearing. A willingness to spend time doing the job, an abundance of patience, and an objective outlook will gain the respect of those whose interests are at stake." JEROME A. MANNING, ESTATE PLANNING 509–10 (3d ed. 1988).

i. Longevity

An executor may need to serve for several years while a trustee may need to serve for many decades. Thus, the age and health of an individual fiduciary are often important considerations. The prospect of a corporate fiduciary being in business in the future must also be taken into account.

j. Proximity

The fiduciary should be someone who would be geographically available to serve. For example, it is difficult for an executor living in Alaska or a trustee from Hawaii to handle fiduciary matters in Maine.

k. Lack of Distractions

Just like people who sit in airplane exit rows, a fiduciary must be able to perform the required duties without being occupied by other concerns. If the client selects an individual, the individual (or a close member of the individual's family) should not be "experiencing any major personal problems, a divorce, change or loss of job, or illness" which could prevent the person from giving the trust or estate the attention it requires. Kimbrough Street, *Practical Guidelines for Selecting an Individual Trustee*, 20 EST. PLAN. 268, 268, 270 (1993). In a corporate setting, the client should avoid fiduciaries in the midst of mergers, takeovers, bankruptcy proceedings, or significant litigation.

l. Prior Approval

Before naming any fiduciary, the fiduciary should be shown a copy of the will or trust and asked if the fiduciary would be willing to serve. It is costly, both in terms of time and money, if the named fiduciary refuses to accept the position. Note that a fiduciary, especially a corporate one, may indicate a willingness to accept the position provided your client makes certain changes to the document. These changes frequently relate to (1) clarifying investment and distribution duties, and (2) including language which exculpates the fiduciary for breaches of duty which are not a result of the fiduciary's bad faith or gross negligence.

m. Tax Issues

"Trustee selection involves important wealth transfer tax considerations. If a beneficiary is a trustee, there are also important income tax considerations. Careless drafting could cause an irrevocable trust to be included unnecessarily in the estate of a settlor or a beneficiary, or make the trust a grantor trust for income tax purposes." Kathryn A. Johnson & Adam J. Wiensch, *Trustee Selection for Successful Trust Administration*, PROB. & PROP., May/June 1994, at 38, 41.

2. INDIVIDUAL OR CORPORATE FIDUCIARY

Whether to select an individual or a corporate fiduciary is one of the most important decisions your clients must make when designating executors and trustees. The decision involves a careful consideration of a variety of factors.

a. Individual Fiduciary

Some clients may be motivated to select an individual trustee, such as a family member or friend, believing that they are bestowing some sort of honor or privilege. This is not the case. As one commentator has colorfully explained,

> "From the trustee's point of view, entering into a trust relationship has some disturbing parallels to acquiring a puppy: initial enthusiasm, followed first by acute awareness that the owner's life is going to be disrupted not only for two weeks of housebreaking but for the foreseeable future, and then by the recognition that the puppy soon will have large teeth and a voracious appetite for everything."

Kimbrough Street, *Practical Guidelines for Selecting an Individual Trustee*, 20 EST. PLAN. 268, 268 (1993).

Fiduciary positions are tough and demanding jobs filled with potentially overwhelming responsibilities, duties, and exposure to personal liability. The appointment of fiduciaries is a business decision, not an emotional one. An individual should be named as a fiduciary only if that person is well-suited to administering the estate or trust. This section examines the wisdom of your client selecting an individual fiduciary.

1) Potential Benefits

Your client may obtain some important benefits by selecting an individual fiduciary. One of the most significant advantages is the individual's willingness to serve without charge. In many cases, individual fiduciaries are close family members or friends who accept the position out of love and affection rather than to make a profit. Professional trustees such as attorneys, accountants, financial planners, and brokers typically charge a fee on an hourly basis unlike corporate trustees who usually base their fee on a percentage of the value of estate or trust assets. Depending on the circumstances, the professional fiduciary's hourly fee may be more cost effective than the corporate fiduciary's percentage fee.

Because most individual fiduciaries are well-acquainted with the testator or settlor (e.g., a surviving spouse or child), they have knowledge of the family situation, the testator's or settlor's goals, and the needs and personalities of the beneficiaries. Accordingly, they are in a good position to exercise the "substituted judgment" which the testator or settlor intended.

The individual fiduciary may have an appreciation for certain types of estate property which the testator or settlor would like to see preserved and kept in the family such as heirlooms and collectable items. Likewise, an individual may have familiarity with the operation of family and closely-held businesses.

Even if the testator or settlor selects a corporate trustee, consideration should be given to naming an individual, often a beneficiary, as well. As one authority has written, "A spouse or a child should be given every consideration as a cotrustee of his [or her] own trust. In that way, the beneficiary will gain a sense of participation in the handling of his [or her] finances. The presence of at least one experienced cotrustee should be enough to preclude the beneficiary from decisions that might be destructive." JEROME A. MANNING, ESTATE PLANNING 522–23 (3d ed. 1988). If a beneficiary is excluded from serving, the client may soften the effect with a separate letter tactfully explaining the reasons behind the decision.

2) Potential Disadvantages

Your client must also evaluate the potential problems which may flow from appointing an individual trustee. Most non-professionals who serve as executors or trustees have not done so in the past. Thus, they are unfamiliar with carrying out fiduciary obligations and performing the required duties such as submitting accountings and making allocations between principal and income. Clients "tend to gloss over the gritty details and think in terms of such broad generalizations as 'manage my estate' and 'take care of my kids.' " J.E. Harker, *Choosing a Trustee: The Case for the Corporate Fiduciary*, PROB. & PROP., May/June 1994, at 44, 44. A client's failure to examine the actual function of a fiduciary may lead to several undesired results. First, the fiduciary may simply not perform the fiduciary duties adequately resulting in loss to the estate or beneficiaries. Second, the individual fiduciary may hire professional assistance, such as accountants and attorneys, thereby increasing expenses to the detriment of the estate or beneficiaries.

In a similar manner, the individual fiduciary's lack of experience may also impact the type, quality, and management of investments. A non-professional trustee may lack experience in making prudent investment decisions and in managing estate assets. Third parties, such as stock transfer agents and insurance companies, may require additional documentation from an individual trustee which slows down the asset transfer process as well as increasing the cost.

An individual fiduciary is less likely to be financially solvent than a corporate fiduciary. Thus, the individual may lack significant assets which the beneficiaries could reach to remedy a breach of fiduciary duty.

If the individual fiduciary is a family member, there may be increased family strife and conflict of interest concerns. "The family relative who serves as trustee could see his [or her] family relationship destroyed because of arguments over favoritism." Sheldon G. Gilman, *Trustee Selec-*

tion: Corporate vs. Individual, TR. & EST., June 1984, at 29, 30. The client may not want to place a surviving spouse in the position of playing favorites among the children or force a child to make decisions regarding the child's siblings. Likewise, "naming children from an earlier marriage as trustees of a QTIP marital trust for a surviving spouse may invite trouble." Kathryn A. Johnson & Adam J. Wiensch, *Trustee Selection for Successful Trust Administration*, PROB. & PROP., May/June 1994, at 38, 41. This situation is acerbated if the spouse or child serving as a fiduciary is also a beneficiary.

Similar problems may arise even if the fiduciary is not a family member. Due to the individual fiduciary's close contact with the beneficiaries, many of whom may have conflicting desires and goals (e.g., income vs. remainder beneficiary), the fiduciary could "become a hapless umpire for disputes among disgruntled and unreasonable parties—a thankless job compensated primarily by sleepless nights and heartburn." Kimbrough Street, *Practical Guidelines for Selecting an Individual Trustee*, 20 EST. PLAN. 268, 268 (1993).

b. Corporate Fiduciary

Naming a corporate fiduciary, such as a bank or trust company, is your client's main alternative to designating an individual. This section discusses the benefits of a corporate fiduciary as well as the potential difficulties which may arise.

1) Potential Benefits

There are many potential benefits of having a corporate entity serve as an executor or trustee. Probably the foremost of these advantages is the skill and experience the corporate fiduciary brings to the job. The corporate fiduciary handles fiduciary matters on a regular basis and is usually well-equipped to handle the day-to-day affairs of an estate or trust (e.g., accounting services, record keeping, allocation of receipts and expenditures between principal and income, determining the tax basis of property, filing tax returns, etc.). In addition, the corporate fiduciary has the ability to provide certain services without additional cost to the estate, e.g., protecting valuables in the bank's vault, providing routine administration services, rendering advice on investment and tax matters, etc.

Likewise, the corporate fiduciary usually has vast experience with making prudent investments and will have investment opportunities available to it that individual fiduciaries do not. For example, state law often permits corporate fiduciaries to create common trust funds to achieve diversification and risk-spreading for estates and trusts with relatively small values. Large corporate fiduciaries employ experts in a variety of areas and have separate departments to deal with different types of investments such as securities, real property, farms and ranches, closely-held businesses, mineral properties, and perhaps even collectibles. The staff of a corporate fiduciary will have far more experience collectively than any individual fiduciary.

Investments held by corporate fiduciaries are likely to be more closely monitored than they could be by an individual. This constant watch permits the fiduciary to respond rapidly as the market or other circumstances require and to adjust investment strategies accordingly. Likewise, the corporate fiduciary has an enhanced opportunity to spot good investment opportunities and to take advantage of them.

Another significant advantage is the corporate fiduciary's continuous existence. Corporate fiduciaries do not get sick, take vacations, have family emergencies, or die.

Unlike individual fiduciaries, corporate fiduciaries are typically regulated by state and federal laws and are subject to inspections by state or federal examiners. This regulation increases accountability and results in the beneficiaries having greater security.

If a fiduciary breaches its fiduciary duties, the aggrieved beneficiaries often have a greater chance of recovery against a corporate fiduciary than against an individual. Most individuals lack sufficient non-exempt property to permit a full recovery while corporate fiduciaries typically have significant assets against which the beneficiaries may proceed. In addition, corporate fiduciaries are more likely to settle disputes rather than litigate them.

2) *Potential Disadvantages*

Your client must also consider several reasons why the selection of a corporate fiduciary may not be the better choice. One reason that often comes to mind is that corporate fiduciaries impose fees for providing fiduciary services, unlike most individual trustees who are typically family members or friends. However, the fee is often a small price to pay for the expertise the corporate fiduciary brings to the job. Of course, if the value of the estate or trust is relatively low, the fee may be prohibitive. Nonetheless, even in some low value estate situations, the extra expense may be worth the benefits of professional management.

Corporate fiduciaries are often viewed as impersonal because they lack the rich history with the client, the client's property, and the beneficiaries which a family member or friend could bring to the job. Accordingly, corporate fiduciaries may lack the insight necessary to give adequate attention to the specific facts of each estate or trust. The corporate fiduciary may not be able to exercise as accurate of a substituted judgment for the testator or settlor as could an individual trustee. Clients may also fear a lack of accountability in one specific individual. These concerns may be overcome by the client establishing a long-term relationship with the particular individuals who administer estates and trusts. Although it is true that these individuals may be reassigned, quit, or die, and the corporation may be the subject of a merger or reorganization, similar risks exist for individual fiduciaries. Your client may wish to prepare a detailed memorandum providing background information about the client's assets and family situation which the corporate fiduciary could use as a reference. "[F]or every 'horror story' about big, impersonal trust departments, there is a corresponding anecdote about a trust officer who has taken a more caring, personal approach toward a client than the client's own family members." J.E. Harker, *Choosing a Trustee: The Case for the Corporate Fiduciary,* PROB. & PROP., May/June 1994, at 44, 46.

On the other hand, your client may be seeking an impersonal approach. A corporate fiduciary is able to make unbiased decisions when beneficiaries of a discretionary trust make demands for distributions. They are unencumbered by the emotions and feelings of family loyalty and sympathy which could prevent a family member trustee from making an objective decision.

Another often cited reason to be leery of corporate fiduciaries is that they make overly conservative investments which do not keep up with inflation. This concern has less merit today than it had in the past. Many states have enacted the Uniform Prudent Investor Rule (or a similar statute) based on the Restatement (Third) of Trusts which liberalizes the standard of care applicable to trust investment and management. Under this Rule, fiduciaries are bound to consider the purposes, terms, distribution requirements, and other circumstances of the trust. The fiduciary's decisions regarding individual assets are no longer evaluated in isolation, one investment at a time, but rather are examined in the context of the trust portfolio as a whole and as a part of an overall investment strategy which has risks and return objectives that are reasonably suited to the particular trust. The fiduciary is authorized to consider a wide range of factors including (1) general economic conditions, (2) potential inflation and deflation, (3) tax consequences, (4) the ramifications of each investment on the entire portfolio, (5) anticipated income and appreciation, (6) the beneficiaries' other resources, (7) the need for liquidity, income, or appreciation, and (8) any special relationship that an asset has to the purposes of the trust or to a beneficiary (e.g., real estate that has been in the family for generations or family heirlooms). If the state has not enacted this type of rule or if your client wishes to authorize investments that would not satisfy the prudent investor standard, the client may provide specific instructions in the trust.

3. MULTIPLE FIDUCIARIES

Your client may appoint as many individuals or corporations as your client desires to serve as executors or trustees. Of course, "[a] plethora of fiduciaries [is] a mistake, for too many will clutter up the administration of the estate or trust." JEROME A. MANNING, ESTATE PLANNING 521 (3d ed. 1988). This section reviews the reasons why your client may or may not wish to appoint co-fiduciaries.

a. Potential Benefits

When more than one fiduciary is currently serving, the trust or estate benefits from the experience and expertise of several persons. Better decisions may result because of the deliberation which occurs when the co-fiduciaries present and discuss multiple viewpoints.

Multiple fiduciaries also give the client a greater chance of achieving continuity in management. This is an extremely important consideration if the trust is expected to last for a long time such as a dynasty trust or a charitable trust. The settlor can provide in the trust instrument that when any trustee no longer is serving for whatever reason, the remaining trustees are authorized to select a replacement. This self-perpetuation is likely to result in replacement trustees who share the settlor's philosophy, understand the settlor's goals, and have the appropriate experience and expertise.

Multiple fiduciaries also provide greater protection to the estate and beneficiaries. There are built-in checks and balances because each fiduciary should evaluate the conduct of the other fiduciaries. An evil fiduciary will have a harder time carrying out any untoward schemes when there are other fiduciaries looking over his or her shoulder.

Appointing multiple fiduciaries is one way of resolving the debate between appointing a corporate or an individual trustee. The client can obtain the benefits of both individual and corporate fiduciaries by naming one of each. "[T]he individual would supply the personal touch and insight that the corporate trustee might lack, and the corporate institution could provide the fiduciary expertise." Sheldon G. Gilman, *Trustee Selection: Corporate vs. Individual*, TR. & EST., June 1984, at 29, 35. This approach, however, must be used with care. "An individual co-trustee can make the operation of the trust more inefficient if both trustees must agree before many actions can be taken. Often the individual co-trustee's consent is hard to obtain, because the individual is unavailable, is ill, or simply is unresponsive." J.E. Harker, *Choosing a Trustee: The Case for the Corporate Fiduciary,* PROB. & PROP., May/June 1994, at 44, 46.

The client's appointment of multiple fiduciaries may increase the likelihood that the designated persons will agree to serve. The duties and responsibilities of administration are spread among several persons, thus reducing the burden on any one fiduciary.

The appointment of multiple trustees may be a good technique to save expenses in life insurance trust situations. Corporate trustees are beginning to realize that their exposure to potential liability for managing life insurance trusts may be significantly higher than they originally anticipated. They may have a duty to monitor the financial condition of the insurer and take appropriate steps at the first sign of trouble. Likewise, the trustee may have a duty to redeem a high cash value policy and make more aggressive investments. Thus, corporate trustees are less willing to serve as trustees of life insurance trusts and those that do serve are more likely to charge a fee. This problem may be solved by the settlor selecting an individual trustee to serve without compensation during the settlor's life with a corporate fiduciary taking over upon the settlor's death. The corporate trustee thus avoids potential liability during the settlor's life but yet is available to manage the proceeds when the settlor dies.

b. Potential Disadvantages

Before appointing multiple fiduciaries, the client must consider the problems that may result. For example, there is the potential of a deadlock and paralysis upon a tie vote if an even number of fiduciaries are serving.[4] A costly judicial resolution of this standstill would then be needed. This problem can be avoided if the client either (1) appoints an odd number of fiduciaries, or (2) provides a method for resolving tie votes.

The requirement of obtaining a majority vote may cause an additional problem. If a decision regarding management or investment needs to be made quickly, such as is often the case with securities and foreign investments, it may be difficult to obtain the consent of a majority of the fiduciaries in time to take the appropriate action.

If the client appoints multiple fiduciaries, you need to advise the client of the likelihood of additional expenses. For example, if professional fiduciaries are employed, there will be multiple fiduciary fees. In most cases, there will be additional administrative fees as well because of the extra conferences, telephone calls, and paperwork that is required. Some corporate fiduciaries may charge a higher fee if a co-fiduciary is an individual because of the additional time it usually takes to deal with an individual.

An individual or corporation may be reluctant to serve with other fiduciaries for fear of personal liability for the acts of the other fiduciaries. Normally, each co-trustee is jointly and severally liable for the acts of all trustees.

c. "Special" Fiduciary or Committee

Instead of appointing multiple fiduciaries, the client could name a "special" fiduciary or advisory committee who would have responsibility for only a limited portion of estate or trust business. "The special trustee is most often used to run a closely held business, for example, in cases where the client would prefer to have his partner run the business, be in full control, and operate it in the same way that it has been operated during the client's lifetime." Sheldon G. Gilman, *Trustee Selection: Corporate vs. Individual*, TR. & EST., June 1984, at 29, 36. Of course, the client must adjust other portions of the estate or trust to reflect the use of a special fiduciary, e.g., the normal fiduciary's fee may be reduced because management of certain assets is being handled by the special fiduciary.

---

4. In the past, decisions required the consent of all co-fiduciaries. Many states have now adopted a majority rules approach.

4. EXPENSES

a. Fiduciary Fees

Individuals such as family members and close friends may perform fiduciary services without charge. Professional trustees and corporate trustees, on the other hand, expect compensation. You should help your client comparison shop for the best fees for comparable services. Within a city, you may find a wide range of fees for essentially the same services. You may even discover that different fiduciaries have the best price depending on the size of the estate or trust.

QUESTION

What factors would you have your client consider in deciding whether it is advisable to name a person who must be paid for fiduciary services rather than an individual willing to do the work for free?

LOCATE

1. How are fiduciary fees determined in your state? Are they statutorily based?

2. Visit with several professional trustees and obtain their fee schedules to get an idea of customary fees.

b. Bond

Some states have statutes requiring bond for all fiduciaries unless the will or trust provides otherwise, while other states require fiduciaries to post bond only if the instrument or a court requires it. In addition, some states exempt corporate fiduciaries from the bonding requirement.

Your client must make the decision whether or not to waive bond during the drafting stage of the will or trust. Bond provides the beneficiaries with protection from evil fiduciaries. However, bond is expensive and its cost, as well as the expenses of the court hearings to set the amount of bond, are proper estate or trust expenses. Thus, requiring bond to protect the beneficiaries actually ends up reducing the amount of property the beneficiaries eventually receive.

QUESTIONS

1. What factors should the client consider in deciding whether or not to waive bond?

2. Might the client decide to waive bond for some fiduciaries but not others? In what situation would this be a good technique?

LOCATE

What is the presumption regarding bond in your state? Are certain fiduciaries exempt from the bond requirement?

DRAFT

Draft a will provision that waives bond for a named fiduciary.

5. ALTERNATES

Your client should always name alternate fiduciaries in case the first choice is unable or unwilling to serve. The client may also specify a method for selecting a successor fiduciary. If there are no alternates and no selection method, court action will be necessary to fill the vacancy. The client may wish to include a provision specifying under what circumstances a fiduciary may be removed from office. This type of provision may eliminate or reduce court costs if a currently serving trustee is no longer in office due to illness, incompetency, or dishonesty.

NOTES AND QUESTIONS

1. Why might your client not want the court to fill vacancies?

2. In some states, a successor corporate fiduciary is automatically substituted when the named corporation is sold, merged, or divided. Would this be acceptable to your client or do you need to plan around it?

I. PROFESSIONAL RESPONSIBILITY

1. INTRODUCTION

JENNIFER HASLEY, AVOIDING RISK FACTORS AND UNDERSTANDING THE ATTORNEY GRIEVANCE PROCESS*

Revised June 2012.

For those individuals who dream of joining the noble legal profession and becoming an attorney, it is almost unimaginable to consider that at some point after completing four years of college, three years of law school, taking and passing a bar examination, and actually representing clients, there could be an allegation of professional misconduct–or worse, a finding of professional misconduct. While certain risk factors may increase the likelihood of an attorney being the subject of a grievance (e.g., working in the criminal, family, or personal injury field), these are not necessarily synonymous with the type of conduct that results in the imposition of a disciplinary sanction.

I. OVERVIEW OF THE TEXAS ATTORNEY DISCIPLINARY SYSTEM

[Although this section reviews the Texas disciplinary system, most states have a similar process.]

* Reprinted with permission of Jennifer Hasley.

[Texas is the only state that allows for a jury trial.]

The conduct of attorneys practicing law in the state of Texas is governed by the Texas Disciplinary Rules of Professional Conduct (TDRPC). With authority from the Supreme Court of Texas and the Texas Legislature, the State Bar of Texas Office of the Chief Disciplinary Counsel (CDC) administers a disciplinary system for those whose conduct does not comply with the TDRPC. The Texas Rules of Disciplinary Procedure (TRDP) establish the procedures to be used in the attorney disciplinary and disability system. The disciplinary system is a complaint driven process. Any person or entity including, for example, a current or former client, employee, spouse, witness, opposing counsel, judge, etc., may file a grievance against an attorney.

Within thirty days after a grievance has been filed, the CDC makes an initial classification decision. The CDC will either dismiss the grievance as an "inquiry" subject to approval by a summary disposition panel, or upgrade the grievance to a "complaint" which requires a formal written response from the attorney who is identified as the "Respondent." For complaints, the CDC is obligated to investigate the allegation(s) and make a "just cause" determination within sixty days. If the CDC determines that "just cause" exists to proceed forward, the Respondent is given the opportunity to elect a proceeding before an Evidentiary Panel or a trial in district court.

Evidentiary Panels are composed of volunteer attorneys and public members. The proceedings are generally confidential until a public sanction is imposed, and provide for the *possibility* of a private reprimand as a potential disciplinary sanction. Evidentiary proceedings are less formal than traditional court trials and may not comply with the rules of procedure or evidence. Evidentiary judgments may be appealed to the Board of Disciplinary Appeals, a 12–attorney tribunal, appointed by the Supreme Court of Texas.

District Court actions require the appointment by the Supreme Court of Texas of an active district judge who does not reside in the same Administrative Judicial District as the Respondent. The district court action offers the option of either a bench or jury trial and adheres to traditional rules of procedure and evidence. Generally, a private reprimand is not an available disciplinary sanction. A district court judgment may be appealed to the state appellate court.

Upon the finding of just cause and the filing of the Evidentiary or District Court petition, the CDC represents the Commission for Lawyer Discipline (CFLD), referred to as the "Petitioner." The CFLD is a standing committee of the State Bar of Texas composed of twelve volunteer, non-paid members (six attorneys appointed by the President of the State Bar of Texas and six non-attorney members appointed by the Supreme Court of Texas). The CFLD has the burden of proving a Respondent's violation of the disciplinary rule(s) at issue by a preponderance of the evidence. If no professional misconduct is found, the case is dismissed. If there is a finding of professional misconduct, disciplinary sanctions that may be imposed range from a private reprimand, public reprimand, fully probated suspension, partially probated suspension, active suspension, to disbarment. The CDC, as the prevailing party, routinely seeks attorney's fees and costs; however, these are discretionary to the panel or court.

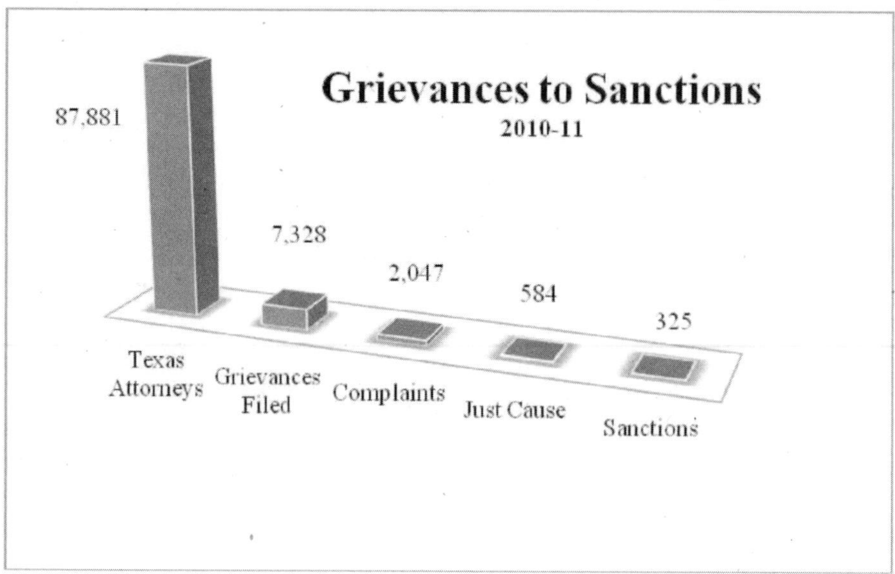

II. AVOIDING THE TOP ALLEGED DISCIPLINARY RULE VIOLATIONS

The ten most frequently cited rule violations alleged against Texas attorneys involve (1) failure to communicate, (2) neglect, (3) circumstances surrounding the termination of representation, (4) integrity issues, (5) failure to safeguard client funds and property, (6) reasonableness and division of fees including the failure to enter into a written contingent fee agreement, (7) non-client relationships, (8) boundaries of advocacy and candor toward the tribunal, (9) conflicts of interest, and (10) confidentiality.

Over the last five years, these rule violations have consistently made the top ten list. In 2010–11, communication passed neglect for the first time since 2005–06. Declining or terminating representation and integrity have traded places, but always hold the third and fourth positions. Safekeeping property and fees have steadily remained at number five and six, respectively. The top five alleged violations account for 86.5 percent of the total cited rule violations and, therefore, are discussed at length below. Slight variations as to the remaining alleged violations can create some shifting in position. For example, advertising and solicitation has twice in the last five years bumped confidentiality out of the top ten.

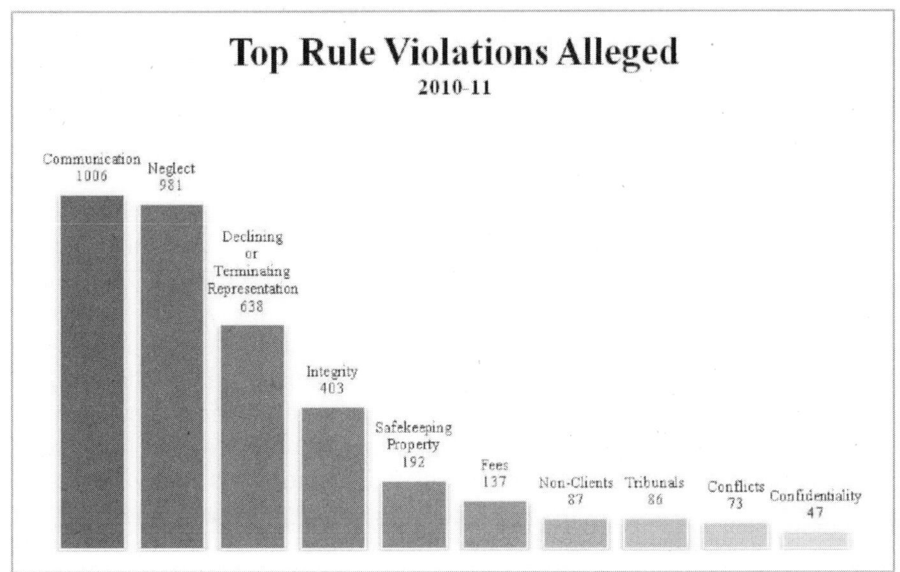

Communication

Good client relationships begin with good communication. Attorneys' failure to communicate is the most frequently cited disciplinary rule violation in complaints (27 percent). According to TDRPC 1.03:

(a) A lawyer shall keep a client reasonably informed about the status of a matter and promptly comply with reasonable requests for information.

(b) A lawyer shall explain a matter to the extent reasonably necessary to permit the client to make informed decisions regarding the representation.

Client complaints that fall into this category focus on a complete lack of or lapses in communication, inadequate information, dissatisfaction with the representation, and/or a disappointing case outcome.

Communication is the cornerstone for being an effective advocate for the client. At the inception of the attorney-client relationship, it is important for the attorney to establish a clear and mutual understanding of the level of communication that is expected and will be maintained throughout the representation.

It is often insufficient to rely solely on oral communications with a client. Documenting the conversation in a follow-up letter or email not only gives the client a chance to review and reflect upon the information conveyed, but also establishes a solid record of compliance with the attorney's obligations under TDRPC 1.03.

Lack of adequate communication often stems from several root causes: (1) inattentiveness to cases perceived by the attorney as less important; (2) difficult or demanding clients; and (3) deficient office policies and staff training. Before undertaking the representation, a critical assessment of both the prospective client and the legal issues can help identify and circumvent potential problems. Clients will generally be at their best during the initial meeting. If presented with a difficult or needy client, the attorney should consider either passing on the representation or establishing clear boundaries and reasonable expectations. Clients who demand the most time from their attorneys are often the first to file grievances when they do not receive the attention they feel they deserve. Similarly, if a legal matter is not going to generate the fees to warrant the attorney's full interest and commitment, the attorney should not accept the representation. Disciplinary cases citing failure to communicate frequently result from undertaking a case at a discounted rate or as a "favor" to a friend, family member or colleague. Under these circumstances, an attorney may not follow customary formalities, feel less obliged to the client, and be less attentive, all of which may lead to the filing of a grievance.

Good office policies and procedures can reduce the likelihood that a client will complain about lack of communication. Written communications do not always have to include a substantive analysis or be a time consuming event. For example, forwarding pleadings or relevant documents, sending regular and detailed billing statements, and simple scheduling reminders, all build a record of the requisite level of communication. Once these basic practices are integrated into the office procedures they can be maintained with minimal effort.

Neglect

Neglect by attorneys is the second most frequently alleged disciplinary rule violation cited in 26 percent of all complaints. According to TDRPC 1.01(b):

In representing a client, a lawyer shall not:

(1) neglect a legal matter entrusted to the lawyer; or

(2) frequently fail to carry out completely the obligations that the lawyer owes to a client or clients.

Neglect is further defined as "inattentiveness involving a conscious disregard for the responsibilities owed to a client or clients."

From a client's perspective, "neglect" may be something very different from the standard set forth by the TDRPC. Any perceived inattentiveness by the attorney may be viewed as neglect. Regardless of whether the impression is justified, the following actions, or inactions, by the attorney may lead to client dissatisfaction:

- Unavailability and unresponsiveness to client-initiated communications.
- Late arrival to appointments and court appearances.
- Perceived lack of case-specific knowledge or limited expertise.
- Apparent lack of commitment.

- Failure to listen carefully and explain clearly.
- Inattentiveness during client meetings.
- Procrastination.

An attorney can be proactive in warding off unnecessary grievances by:

- Regularly communicating with clients by promptly returning phone calls, responding to emails, providing status reports, sending detailed bills, etc.
- Using and maintaining a reliable calendaring and docketing system.
- Keeping detailed records of time spent on a case (regardless of whether it is an hourly, flat, or contingency fee case).
- During periods of inactivity, maintaining contact with clients and explaining how the inactivity benefits their case.
- Training attorneys and staff on professionalism, ethics, organization, and confidentiality.

Declining or Terminating Representation

Declining or terminating representation is cited in slightly more than 17 percent of all complaints. TDRPC 1.15 sets forth the requirements for declining representation, or when representation has commenced, the circumstances under which withdrawal may or may not be accomplished. The part of the rule that is most often cited in grievances is the failure, or perceived failure on the part of a disgruntled former client, of the attorney to refund an unearned fee or to return the client file.

More often than not, if the circumstances giving rise to termination of representation predate the conclusion of the case, the client feels as if he/she did not receive the full benefit of the bargain and wants a refund. Attorneys should objectively evaluate each case upon conclusion of the representation to determine if any refund is due to the client. That evaluation should include a reasoned business decision about potential alternatives. For example, while the attorney may think no refund is due the client, the attorney should weigh against that the potential cost of defending a grievance. An untold number of attorneys have been introduced to the wrong side of the grievance process simply for being unwilling to part with a few hundred dollars–an amount much less than that required for presenting a grievance defense.

After-the-fact created time sheets or billing records are rarely considered persuasive evidence for proving that the fee was fully earned. An attorney should make every effort to promptly respond to a request for the return of the client file.

Integrity

Integrity is at the very heart of our legal system as it is the foundation upon which trust depends. It is disconcerting that allegations of dishonesty, fraud, deceit, and misrepresentation, are the basis for almost 11 percent of all complaints. Integrity is governed by TDRPC Part VIII and encompasses a broad range of conduct that extends beyond the attorney-client relationship including, specifically, compliance with regulatory requirements (e.g., application for admission, responding to disciplinary matters, reporting professional misconduct, etc.).

Some attorneys, unfortunately, simply lack the integrity to practice law. They may excel in school, but are missing core values in their moral compass. These attorneys will generally find their way into the disciplinary system.

Oftentimes, a violation of an integrity provision starts with a simple, inadvertent mistake. A pattern then may begin to emerge with a not-so-innocuous "white lie" to explain away the mistake, followed by carefully crafted statements or silent omissions, and then the blockbuster—a misguided attempt to "fix" the mistake that started the cycle. At that point, a multitude of disciplinary infractions overwhelm any notion of common sense and the acts that follow lead the attorney down the road to disbarment.

The scenario seems almost unimaginable to most attorneys; but it is the precipitating event, the inadvertent mistake, that may occur at some point in any busy legal practitioner's career. Generally speaking, remedies exist to address the most common mistakes (e.g., missing a deadline, failing to respond to a discovery request, inadvertent disclosure of confidential information, etc.). Acknowledging the mistake is crucial to avoiding integrity violations. It is the cover up–not the mistake–that violates the TDRPC. Candor is an essential part of explaining the circumstances to a client and the courts. Even if the client has a potential civil claim, there is no reason to fight the battle on two fronts by creating a separate claim for professional misconduct. Any attempt to conceal these facts from a client, to mislead a court, or to alter or destroy documents, will guarantee a significant disciplinary sanction and, more likely, the loss of the right to practice law. Inevitably, the truth will be revealed. Seeking advice from a mentor, partner, or trusted colleague, might often be the best first step when discovering a mistake has been made. An objective third party can help to dismiss any temptation to avoid the disclosure obligation.

Safekeeping Property

Failure to safeguard property is asserted in 5 percent of all complaints. TDRPC 1.14 prohibits commingling of attorney and client funds, prescribes the use of trust accounts, mandates prompt notification and delivery of funds to clients and third persons, requires attorneys to account for all funds received on behalf of clients and third persons, and imposes an obligation on the attorney to safeguard disputed funds.

This rule aims to protect the fundamental notion—lawyers do not steal or borrow their client's money. Violations of the safekeeping rule generally result in some of the harshest sanctions that the disciplinary system can assess. Unfortunately, the purpose of this rule has been diluted by the prosecution of attorneys for accounting errors, fee disputes which are non-disciplinary in nature, and third party collection claims.

Rules governing how to handle trust accounts sometimes can be tedious, requiring multiple transactions, additional trips to the bank, etc. For an attorney who is unable to balance a personal checkbook, balancing a trust account ledger can be a daunting task. Extra special care must be taken to comply with the rules. Employment of a bookkeeper or trained staff member may be a necessity. Trust account violations are among the easiest violations to prove. The bank records do not lie and must be in order. Even an unsupported allegation of a safekeeping violation may result in multiple rule violations once the CDC obtains trust account records that show any irregularities.

III. CONCLUSION

The TDRPC provide the minimum standards of conduct expected for attorneys practicing in Texas. Failure to abide by these rules may be a result of intentional misconduct, lack of supervision, poor office procedures, or a host of other reasons. Physical or mental illness, emotional distress, substance abuse, and financial difficulties can be distracting and influence any attorney's ability to focus on client needs, running a law practice, and other professional obligations.

Whether an attorney grievance is based upon a genuine concern for the integrity of the profession, a valid complaint about legal services rendered, a fee dispute, or an attempt to gain an advantage in a civil or other claim, it must always be taken seriously. In each stage of the grievance process, there must be a clear and objective examination of the facts, circumstances, and mitigation involved; however, a failure to respond at any point in the proceedings will undermine the attorney's credibility and guarantee that the matter will proceed to the next level.

2. DRAFTING ATTORNEY AS BENEFICIARY

MAHONING COUNTY BAR ASSOCIATION v. THEOFILOS

Supreme Court of Ohio, 1988.
36 Ohio St.3d 43, 521 N.E.2d 797.

On September 8, 1986, relator, Mahoning County Bar Association, filed a complaint against respondent, Gus K. Theofilos, alleging a single count of misconduct. This complaint was amended on November 24, 1986 to identify the Disciplinary Rules allegedly violated. Respondent answered the amended complaint on January 20, 1987. A hearing was held before a panel of the Board of Commissioners on Grievances and Discipline of the Bar on April 8, 1987.

The complaint as amended alleged that respondent was retained by Philomena G. Dailey in September 1984 to probate the will of her sister, Elizabeth Dailey. Philomena had initially appeared in respondent's office without an appointment. Respondent thereafter performed the services necessary to probate Elizabeth Dailey's will. Elizabeth's estate, to which Philomena had been named executor, was opened on October 4, 1984 and closed on February 4, 1985.

Philomena was born on April 18, 1903. She was a school teacher for much of her life and had lived with her sister at the time of Elizabeth's death. Neither she nor Elizabeth had ever married.

Both Elizabeth and Philomena had executed identical wills which left their assets to each other. During the period in which respondent handled Elizabeth's estate, respondent and Philomena discussed the effect of Elizabeth's demise on the terms of Philomena's will. Respondent was of the opinion that since Elizabeth had predeceased Philomena, Philomena's will would be ineffectual, such that Philomena's estate would pass to her next of kin. According to respondent, Philomena responded to this information by saying that she did not want her estate to be distributed in such a way. She added that "we'll tend to * * * [the matter] when Elizabeth's estate is wrapped up."

Philomena apparently visited respondent's office regularly during the last three months of 1984. She would often have respondent look over a bill for which she had already drawn a check and balanced her checkbook, just to see if it was "okay." Their discussions turned to the subject of respondent's son, Ian, who was going to nursery school at the time. Respondent testified at the hearing that Philomena had indicated interest in Ian's education.

Philomena did not again refer to her desire to have a new will prepared until January 1985. About the time Elizabeth's estate was to be closed, Philomena told respondent, "When we do my new will, I'm going to want to leave my savings bonds to your son Ian for his education." These savings bonds had a value of approximately $6,600. Respondent attested to having thanked Philomena and having said: "I'm sure when Ian is of age, he'll appreciate this and thank you too, but, if that's the case, then you should consider having another attorney involved with the drawing up of this will." Philomena supposedly replied to this suggestion, "Well, I don't think I want to go to any other attorney."

A week or so later, Philomena came to respondent's office and told him that she had decided what to do with her estate. Respondent testified that Philomena then explained how she wanted her funeral arranged and that she wanted flowers placed on her family's plot on Memorial Day for a number of years to come. She also indicated her desire to insert some derogatory language in her will about several living members of her family and that she wanted a no-contest clause. According to respondent, Philomena then stated:

"I don't know what I would have done without you, I think the world of you. * * * I think God must have led me to you and after my bills are paid, I want to leave the rest of my estate to you."

Respondent apparently realized the ethical difficulties associated with his preparing a will in which he and his son were to be designated heirs. He was also concerned about the problems that Philomena's relatives, a group she collectively referred to as "the cousins," might create. While he suggested on several occasions that Philomena secure the services of another attorney to draft her will, respondent did prepare Philomena's last will and testament in which he and his son were named sole beneficiaries. Respondent was also named executor of the estate. On February 8, 1985, the will was executed in the presence of three witnesses.

Philomena died on June 18, 1985. Respondent filed tax release forms with the Mahoning County Probate Court on June 21, 1985. The entire estate did not pass through probate, however, because Philomena had previously authorized respondent to establish joint and survivorship bank accounts in both their names. These accounts totaled approximately $206,000. Thus, respondent and his son stood to receive over $200,000 from respondent's relationship with Philomena.

Relator charged that respondent's actions in the foregoing matter violated DR 1–102(A)(4) (engaging in conduct involving dishonesty, fraud, deceit, or misrepresentation) and DR 5–101(A) (accepting employment where the exercise of professional judgment on behalf of a client will or reasonably may be affected by one's own financial or personal interest and where the client's consent after full disclosure was not secured). Relator additionally charged that respondent's conduct violated EC 5–5 (other than in exceptional circumstances, a lawyer should insist that an instrument in which his client desires to name him beneficially be prepared by another lawyer selected by the client) and EC 5–6 (a lawyer should not consciously influence a client to name him as executor, trustee, or lawyer in an instrument and, in those cases where a client wishes to name his lawyer as such, care should be taken by the lawyer to avoid even the appearance of impropriety).

The board found that respondent failed to observe the standards delineated in EC 5–5, inasmuch as he did not "insist" that Philomena consult other independent counsel before agreeing to prepare her will. Rather, respondent merely suggested that Philomena "consider" seeing another attorney. In making this finding, the board took note of the facts that: (1) respondent had known Philomena only from her office visits over a four-month period before he prepared the instruments from which he and his son would receive substantial sums of money, and (2) no documentary or testimonial evidence corroborated respondent's version of his professional relationship with Philomena or offset respondent's particular susceptibility to charges of undue influence. Given these circumstances, the board concluded that respondent's conduct violated DR "1–104(A)(6) [sic, 1–102(A)(6)]" (engaging in conduct which adversely reflects on one's fitness to practice law) and recommended that respondent be suspended from the practice of law in Ohio for six months.

* * *

PER CURIAM.

This court finds that respondent violated the aforementioned Disciplinary Rule. While we adopt the board's findings, we find that respondent's conduct requires a more severe sanction than that recommended by the board. Accordingly, respondent is hereby ordered suspended from the practice of law in Ohio for one year. Costs taxed to respondent.

Judgment accordingly.

* * *

HOLMES, JUSTICE, dissenting.

I must dissent insofar as I would require as condition of reinstatement that the monies and assets received from this estate be returned to those who would otherwise have inherited such assets.

Model Rules of Professional Conduct

Rule 1.8(c).

A lawyer shall not solicit any substantial gift from a client, including a testamentary gift, or prepare on behalf of a client an instrument giving the lawyer or a person related to the lawyer any substantial gift unless the lawyer or other recipient of the gift is related to the client. For purposes of this paragraph, related persons include a spouse, child, grandchild, parent, grandparent or other relative or individual with whom the lawyer or the client maintains a close, familial relationship.

ACTEC Commentary on MRPC 1.8*

ACTEC COMMENTARIES ON MODEL RULES OF PROFESSIONAL CONDUCT, page 112 (4th ed. 2006).

Gifts to Lawyer. MRPC 1.8 generally prohibits a lawyer from soliciting a substantial gift from a client, including a testamentary gift, or preparing for a client an instrument that gives the lawyer or a person related to the lawyer a substantial gift. A lawyer may properly prepare a will or other document that includes a substantial benefit for the lawyer or a person related to the lawyer if the lawyer or other recipient is related to the client. The term "related person" is defined in MRPC 1.8(c) and may include a person who is not related by blood or marriage but has a close familial relationship. However, the lawyer should exercise special care if the proposed gift to the lawyer or a related person is disproportionately large in relation to the gift the client proposes to make to others who are equally related. Neither the lawyer nor a person associated with the lawyer can assist an unrelated client in making a substantial gift to the lawyer or to a person related to the lawyer. See MRPC 1.8(k) (Conflict of Interest: Current Clients: Specific Rules).

For the purposes of this Commentary, the substantiality of a gift is determined by reference both to the size of the client's estate and to the

* Reprinted with permission of the American College of Trust and Estate Counsel.

size of the estate of the designated recipient. The provisions of this rule extend to all methods by which gratuitous transfers might be made by a client including life insurance, joint tenancy with right of survivorship, and pay-on-death and trust accounts. As noted in ABA Formal Opinion 02–426 (2002), the client's appointment of the lawyer as a fiduciary is not a gift to the lawyer and is not a business transaction that would subject the appointment to MRPC 1.8. Nevertheless, such an appointment is subject to the general conflict of interest provisions of MRPC 1.7 (Conflict of Interest: Current Clients).

NOTES AND QUESTIONS

1. One of your parents wants to leave you the parent's entire estate to the exclusion of your siblings. Could you ethically draft this will? Would you?

2. Does Rule 1.8(c) permit an attorney to prepare a client's will which leaves a substantial gift to the attorney's grandchild? Cousin? Mother-in-law? Assume that the client is not related to these potential donees.

3. How is the substantialness of a gift determined?

4. For further information, see William M. McGovern, Jr., *Undue Influence and Professional Responsibility,* 28 REAL PROP., PROB. & TR. J. 643 (1994).

CALIFORNIA PROBATE CODE

LIMITATIONS ON TRANSFERS TO DRAFTERS AND OTHERS.

§ 21350. Prohibited transferees; definitions

(a) Except as provided in Section 21351, no provision, or provisions, of any instrument shall be valid to make any donative transfer to any of the following:

(1) The person who drafted the instrument.

(2) A person who is related by blood or marriage to, is a domestic partner of, is a cohabitant with, or is an employee of, the person who drafted the instrument.

(3) Any partner or shareholder of any law partnership or law corporation in which the person described in paragraph (1) has an ownership interest, and any employee of that law partnership or law corporation.

(4) Any person who has a fiduciary relationship with the transferor, including, but not limited to, a conservator or trustee, who transcribes the instrument or causes it to be transcribed.

(5) A person who is related by blood or marriage to, is a domestic partner of, is a cohabitant with, or is an employee of a person who is described in paragraph (4).

(6) A care custodian of a dependent adult who is the transferor.

(7) A person who is related by blood or marriage to, is a domestic partner of, is a cohabitant with, or is an employee of, a person who is described in paragraph (6).

(b) For purposes of this section, "a person who is related by blood or marriage" to a person means all of the following:

(1) The person's spouse or predeceased spouse.

(2) Relatives within the third degree of the person and of the person's spouse.

(3) The spouse of any person described in paragraph (2).

In determining any relationship under this subdivision, Sections 6406, 6407, and Chapter 2 (commencing with Section 6450) of Part 2 of Division 6 shall be applicable.

(c) For purposes of this section, the term "dependent adult" has the meaning as set forth in Section 15610.23 of the Welfare and Institutions Code and also includes those persons who (1) are older than age 64 and (2) would be dependent adults, within the meaning of Section 15610.23, if they were between the ages of 18 and 64. The term "care custodian" has the meaning as set forth in Section 15610.17 of the Welfare and Institutions Code.

(d) For purposes of this section, "domestic partner" means a domestic partner as defined under Section 297 of the Family Code.

§ 21350.5. Disqualified person

For purposes of this part, "disqualified person" means a person specified in subdivision (a) of Section 21350, but only in cases where Section 21351 does not apply.

§ 21351. Exceptions to § 21350; conditions

Section 21350 does not apply if any of the following conditions are met:

(a) The transferor is related by blood or marriage to, is a cohabitant with, or is the registered domestic partner, pursuant to Division 2.5 (commencing with Section 297) of the Family Code, of the transferee or the person who drafted the instrument. For purposes of this section, "cohabitant" has the meaning set forth in Section 13700 of the Penal Code. This subdivision shall retroactively apply to an instrument that becomes irrevocable on or after July 1, 1993.

(b) The instrument is reviewed by an independent attorney who (1) counsels the client (transferor) about the nature and consequences of the intended transfer, (2) attempts to determine if the intended consequence is the result of fraud, menace, duress, or undue influence, and (3) signs and delivers to the transferor an original certificate in substantially the following form, with a copy delivered to the drafter:

"CERTIFICATE OF INDEPENDENT REVIEW

I, (attorney's name), have reviewed (name of instrument) and counseled my client, (name of client), on the nature and consequences of the transfer, or transfers, of property to (name of potentially disqualified person) contained in the instrument. I am so disassociated from the interest of the transferee as to be in a position to advise my client independently, impartially, and confidentially as to the consequences of the transfer. On the basis of this counsel, I conclude that the transfer, or transfers, in the instrument that otherwise might be invalid under Section 21350 of the Probate Code are valid because the transfer, or transfers, are not the product of fraud, menace, duress, or undue influence.

__________________________ __________________________

(Name of Attorney) (Date)"

Any attorney whose written engagement signed by the client is expressly limited solely to the preparation of a certificate under this subdivision, including the prior counseling, shall not be considered to otherwise represent the client.

(c) After full disclosure of the relationships of the persons involved, the instrument is approved pursuant to an order under Article 10 (commencing with Section 2580) of Chapter 6 of Part 4 of Division 4.

(d) The court determines, upon clear and convincing evidence, but not based solely upon the testimony of any person described in subdivision (a) of Section 21350, that the transfer was not the product of fraud, menace, duress, or undue influence. If the court finds that the transfer was the product of fraud, menace, duress, or undue influence, the disqualified person shall bear all costs of the proceeding, including reasonable attorney's fees.

(e) Subdivision (d) shall apply only to the following instruments:

(1) Any instrument other than one making a transfer to a person described in paragraph (1) of subdivision (a) of Section 21350.

(2) Any instrument executed on or before July 1, 1993, by a person who was a resident of this state at the time the instrument was executed.

(3) Any instrument executed by a resident of California who was not a resident at the time the instrument was executed.

(f) The transferee is a federal, state, or local public entity, an entity that qualifies for an exemption from taxation under Section 501(c)(3) or 501(c)(19) of the Internal Revenue Code, or a trust holding an interest for this entity, but only to the extent of the interest of the entity, or the trustee of this trust. This subdivision shall retroactively apply to an instrument that becomes irrevocable on or after July 1, 1993.

(g) For purposes of this section, "related by blood or marriage" shall include persons within the fifth degree or heirs of the transferor.

(h) The transfer does not exceed the sum of three thousand dollars ($3,000). This subdivision shall not apply if the total value of the property in the estate of the transferor does not exceed the amount prescribed in Section 13100.

(i) The transfer is made by an instrument executed by a nonresident of California who was not a resident at the time the instrument was executed, and that was not signed within California.

§ 21352. Liability for prohibited transfers; actual notice of possible invalidity

No person shall be liable for making any transfer pursuant to an instrument that is prohibited by this part unless that person has received actual notice of the possible invalidity of the transfer to the disqualified person under Section 21350 prior to making the transfer. A person who receives actual notice of the possible invalidity of a transfer prior to the transfer shall not be held liable for failing to make the transfer unless the validity of the transfer has been conclusively determined by a court.

§ 21353. Failed transfers; effect on instrument

If a transfer fails under this part, the transfer shall be made as if the disqualified person predeceased the transferor without spouse or issue, but only to the extent that the value of the transfer exceeds the intestate interest of the disqualified person.

§ 21354. Contrary provisions in instrument

This part applies notwithstanding a contrary provision in the instrument.

§ 21355. Application of part

(a) This part shall apply to instruments that become irrevocable on or after September 1, 1993, and before January 1, 2011. For the purposes of this section, an instrument that is otherwise revocable or amendable shall be deemed to be irrevocable if on or after September 1, 1993, the transferor by reason of incapacity was unable to change the disposition of his or her property and did not regain capacity before the date of his or her death.

(b) This part shall remain in effect only until January 1, 2014, and as of that date is repealed, unless a later enacted statute, that is enacted before January 1, 2014, deletes or extends that date.

§ 21356. Commencement of action; time limitation

An action to establish the invalidity of any transfer described in Section 21350 can only be commenced within the periods prescribed in this section as follows:

(a) In case of a transfer by will, at any time after letters are first issued to a general representative and before an order for final distribution is made.

(b) In case of any transfer other than by will, within the later of three years after the transfer becomes irrevocable or three years from the date the person bringing the action discovers, or reasonably should have discovered, the facts material to the transfer.

3. DRAFTING ATTORNEY AS FIDUCIARY

STATE v. GULBANKIAN

Supreme Court of Wisconsin, 1972.
54 Wis.2d 605, 196 N.W.2d 733.

PER CURIAM.

Gulbank K. (George) Gulbankian was admitted to practice law in Wisconsin in 1926 and practiced alone in Racine until his sister Miss Vartak Gulbankian was admitted to practice law in 1935. They shared offices until 1955 when they commenced to practice law as partners and have so practiced until the present time. The complaint alleges the Gulbankians have solicited the probate of estates by inserting in the wills which they draft a provision that they should be the attorney for the executor and in some wills the executor or executrix. The answer denies any solicitation and alleges their designation as attorneys or executor in the wills was at the request of the respective clients.

From January 1, 1955, through January 23, 1971, the Gulbankians filed for probate in the county court of Racine county 147 wills, of which 135 were drafted by them. Of these 135 wills, 71 directed the employment of one or the other of the Gulbankians for the purpose of probating the estate. Twenty-six of the wills directed the employment of Gulbank K. Gulbankian and four directed the appointment of Vartak Gulbankian; in 41 wills Akabe Gulbankian, a sister of the attorneys, was appointed either executrix or co-executrix; and in three wills Vartak Gulbankian was named executrix. Prior to 1957 about 50 percent of the wills drawn contained a provision for the employment of either Gulbank or Vartak Gulbankian, but since that time in about 94 percent of the wills the executor was instructed to retain either G.K. Gulbankian or Vartak Gulbankian as attorney. Only one will drafted after 1957 failed to name a member of the Gulbankian family to some fiduciary capacity. On the basis of this record it is argued that because such a large percentage of wills drawn by the Gulbankians contain a direction to the executor to retain them as attorneys, an inference must of necessity be drawn that the Gulbankians at the time the wills were drafted suggested to or solicited the testators to provide for their employment to probate the estates. Such conduct it is argued amounts to unprofessional conduct.

It is, of course, unprofessional to solicit professional employment, not only by advertisement, touters or runners, but also by personal communication or interviews. Canon 27, Canons of Ethics of the American Bar Association. The new Code of Professional Responsibility, Disciplinary Rules DR 2–103, provides in paragraph (A) that a lawyer shall not recommend employment of himself or his partner or associate to a nonlawyer who has not sought his advice regarding the employment of a lawyer. The object of these canons is to prevent lawyers from engaging in competitive advertising and from attempting to explain to the public why they could serve better or accomplish more than other lawyers could. Such advertising is the lifeline of business, but it has traditionally been prohibited in the professions. While solicitation of cases may not involve the high degree of moral turpitude which fraud does, nevertheless solicitation is considered inimical to the good reputation of the legal profession and likely to bring the profession into disrepute.

The narrow question in this case is whether this court should draw an inference of solicitation on the record. This matter was referred to and heard by the Honorable John K. Callahan, a reserve judge, as referee. We have great respect for his judgment. He does not find actual solicitation but he does think that lay people might infer solicitation if they were not cognizant of the facts.

The Gulbankians claim they did not suggest the inclusion of such a clause but rather their clients spontaneously directed that they put in the will the requirement that they be retained to take care of the probate or that they act as executor. They point out many of their clients are of Armenian descent and have difficulty conversing in English; and because of the common ethnic background, there is a closer relationship between the Gulbankians and their clients than ordinarily exists between other attorneys and clients.

The Gulbankian family were Armenian immigrants to America, coming here to escape the massacre by the Turks in the early part of the 20th Century. Their family presently consists of two attorneys (the defendants), a sister Akabe who is engaged as a real estate saleswoman and does income tax work, and a sister Rose who for the most part is the housekeeper for the family. There was also a brother Harry who was the first of the family to come to this country but who is now deceased. The Gulbankians arrived in this country as penniless immigrants and settled in Racine county, where there is now a large population of Armenians, Slovaks, Greeks, and southern Europeans. Apparently the Gulbankians have helped the Armenian community, gained the confidence of a large segment of the foreign-speaking people in the area, and for many years were the only Armenian attorneys in Racine. The defense produced several clients who have had their wills prepared by the Gulbankians and who testified they wanted the Gulbankians to probate their estates as well.

We are asked to consider that the clients of the Gulbankians' firm are different than the average law client in that they place unusually great trust in their attorneys and look to them for counsel and advice in many areas, some of which do not involve legal matters. This confidence is based not only on the fact the Gulbankians are professional people but also on language and ethnic affinity. The record shows the Gulbankians have a substantial probate practice in the county of Racine and are well respected and regarded by the community. The referee was impressed with these features of the case.

As a part of their defense, the Gulbankians claim there is a custom in Racine county for attorneys to name themselves attorneys for the estate in some form of language. The defendants' exhibits show that 23 to 71 percent of the wills drafted by other law firms in the Racine area contain a provision for employment to probate the estate. There is oral testimony tending to prove a practice in Racine county of attorneys putting in a clause directing he be retained to probate the estate in 5 to 50 percent of the wills. There was other testimony that one attorney seldom put the clause in a will and never without a voluntary direction by the client. Of course, the extensiveness of a practice does not mean the practice is legitimate if in fact the practice amounts to solicitation of business. It is most difficult to determine from statistics whether the recurrence of such clauses is the result of voluntary and unsuggested directions from the testator or whether such recurrence reflects the effectiveness of subtle suggestions.

It is clear an attorney cannot solicit either directly or by any indirect means a request or direction of a testator that he or a member of his firm be named executor or be employed as an attorney to probate the estate. In those fairly rare cases where a client, because of the unusual familiarity of the attorney with the testator's business or family problems or because of a relationship which transcends the ordinary client-attorney relationship, asks his attorney to act as executor or to provide for his employment to probate the estate, there is no solicitation. A gray area, however, exists when an attorney explains the duties of an executor and the question is reached concerning probate. In preparing a will the attorney must know the identity of the executor. In many cases the testator is unfamiliar with the duties of an executor. It is the lawyer's right and duty to advise the testator what the duties of the executor are, to explain that the executor may hire an attorney to help him probate the estate, and that in the case of a corporate executor that sec. 856.31 (effective April 1, 1971), Stats., may apply. When the section is applicable, the person receiving the largest interest may name the attorney unless good cause is shown otherwise. Whether the naming of the attorney by the testator constitutes such good cause has raised problems but so have directions to a noncorporate executor to hire a designated attorney. * * *

This problem must be discussed by the attorney and his client objectively and uninfluenced by any desire of the attorney to eventually probate the estate. An attorney should not use a will form which provides for a designation of an attorney for the probate of the estate or executor for submission to the testator on the theory it is properly a part of a standard form of a will; no such form of suggestion may be used. An attorney, merely because he drafts a will, has no preferential claim to probate it. Estate of Ainsworth (1971), 52 Wis.2d 152, 187 N.W.2d 828. Nor do we approve of attorneys' "safekeeping" wills. In the old days this may have been explained on the ground many people did not have a safe place to keep their valuable papers, but there is little justification today because most people do have safekeeping boxes, and if not, sec. 853.09, Stats., provides for the deposit of a will with the register in probate for safekeeping during the lifetime of the testator. The correct practice is that the original will should be delivered to the testator and should only be kept by the attorney upon specific unsolicited request of the client.

We emphasize that while an attorney is discussing the identity and the duties of an executor, he must especially be careful that his conversation does not intimate or suggest or solicit, directly or indirectly, his employment as the possible attorney to assist the executor in the probate of the estate or his appointment as executor. We realize this is an area in which it is difficult to police professional standards, but circumstantial evidence as well as direct testimony may be relied upon to prove that solicitation has occurred.

Upon this record this court is constrained not to draw an inference the Gulbankians solicited the probate of estates by drafting wills designating themselves as executors or to be retained as attorneys by the executor. We are concerned, however, that the high percentage of such provisions in the wills drafted by the Gulbankians and by other attorneys in Racine county might well lead lay people and the public generally to conclude there has been solicitation. A lawyer must not only avoid solicitation but also the appearance of solicitation so as not to damage the confidence the public has in the legal profession. We do not hold that a lawyer may not draft a will in which he is designated as executor or contains a direction to the executor to employ him in suggestive or even the mandatory language required by the Estate of Sieben, supra, if in fact that is the unprompted intent of his client; but the number of times this will occur will be few and the percentage in total of such wills drawn low.

Because this is the first disciplinary case which raises this important issue, we have spent some time giving guidelines for the future. This may not be the total answer to the problem and improvements may be worked out on a case-to-case basis in the future.

Therefore, it is ordered and adjudged that the complaint herein be, and it is hereby, dismissed.

McKINNEY'S CONSOLIDATED LAWS OF NEW YORK SURROGATE'S COURT PROCEDURE ACT CHAPTER 59–A OF THE CONSOLIDATED LAWS ARTICLE 23—COSTS, ALLOWANCES AND COMMISSIONS

§ 2307–a Commissions of attorney-executor

1. Disclosure. When an attorney prepares a will to be proved in the courts of this state and such attorney, a then affiliated attorney, or an employee of such attorney or a then affiliated attorney is therein an executor-designee, the testator shall be informed prior to the execution of the will that:

(a) subject to limited statutory exceptions, any person, including the testator's spouse, child, friend or associate, or an attorney, is eligible to serve as an executor;

(b) absent an agreement to the contrary, any person, including an attorney, who serves as an executor is entitled to receive an executor's statutory commissions;

(c) absent execution of a disclosure acknowledgment, the attorney who prepared the will, a then affiliated attorney, or an employee of such attorney or a then affiliated attorney, who serves as an executor shall be entitled to one-half the commissions he or she would otherwise be entitled to receive; and

(d) if such attorney or an affiliated attorney renders legal services in connection with the executor's official duties, such attorney or a then affiliated attorney is entitled to receive just and reasonable compensation for such legal services, in addition to the executor's statutory commissions.

2. Testator's written acknowledgment of disclosure. An acknowledgment by the testator of the disclosure required by subdivision one of this section must be set forth in a writing executed by the testator in the presence of at least one witness other than the executor-designee. Such writing, which must be separate from the will, but which may be annexed to the will, and which may be executed prior to, concurrently with or subsequently to a will in which an attorney, a then affiliated attorney, or an employee of such attorney or a then affiliated attorney is an executor-designee and must be filed in the proceeding for the issuance of letters testamentary to the executor-designee.

3. Models of acknowledgment of disclosure. The following are models of the testator's written acknowledgment of disclosure:

(a) When set forth in a writing executed prior to or concurrently with a will:

Prior to signing my will, I was informed that:

(i) subject to limited statutory exceptions, any person, including my spouse, my child, a friend or associate, or an attorney, is eligible to serve as my executor;

(ii) absent an agreement to the contrary, any person, including an attorney, who serves as an executor for me is entitled to receive statutory commissions for executorial services rendered to my estate;

(iii) absent execution of this disclosure acknowledgment, the attorney who prepared the will, a then affiliated attorney, or an employee of such attorney or a then affiliated attorney, who serves as an executor shall be entitled to one-half the commissions he or she would otherwise be entitled to receive; and

(iv) if such attorney serves as my executor, and he or she or another attorney affiliated with such attorney renders legal services in connection with the executor's official duties, he or she is entitled to receive just and reasonable compensation for those legal services, in addition to the commissions to which an executor is entitled.

______________________	______________________
(Witness)	(Testator)
Dated:______________	Dated:______________

(b) When set forth in a writing executed subsequently to the will:

I, ______________, have designated [my attorney], __________, [an attorney affiliated with my attorney] [an employee of my attorney or an affiliated attorney,] [a] [an] [executor] [alternate executor] [co-executor] (delete what is inapplicable) in my will dated __________.

Prior to signing my will, I was informed that:

(i) subject to limited statutory exceptions, any person, including my spouse, my child, a friend or associate, or an attorney, is eligible to serve as my executor;

(ii) absent an agreement to the contrary, any person, including an attorney, who serves as an executor for me is entitled to receive statutory commissions for executorial services rendered to my estate;

(iii) absent execution of this disclosure acknowledgment, the attorney who prepared my will, a then affiliated attorney, or an employee of such attorney or a then affiliated attorney, who serves as an executor shall be entitled to one-half the commissions he or she would otherwise be entitled to receive; and

(iv) if such attorney serves as my executor, and he or she or another attorney affiliated with such attorney renders legal services in connection with the executor's official duties, he or she is entitled to receive just and reasonable compensation for those legal services, in addition to the commissions to which an executor is entitled.

______________________	______________________
(Witness)	(Testator)
Dated:______________	Dated:______________

4. Compliance.

(a) The testator's written acknowledgment of disclosure that conforms or substantially conforms to either model in subdivision 3 of this section shall be deemed compliance with subdivision 2 of this section.

(b) An attorney's compliance with subdivision 2 of this section creates neither the presumption nor the inference:

(i) that the testator's designation of such attorney, a then affiliated attorney, or an employee of such attorney or a then affiliated attorney, as executor, is proper;

(ii) that such attorney has complied with the disciplinary rules of the code of professional responsibility.

5. Effect of absence of acknowledgment. Absent compliance with the requirements of subdivision 2 of this section, the commissions of an attorney, or an employee of the attorney who prepared the will or a then affiliated attorney, who serves as an executor shall be one-half the statutory commissions to which such person as executor would otherwise be entitled pursuant to sections 2307 and 2313 of this article.

6. Rents. Notwithstanding the provisions of subdivision 5 of this section, the additional commissions to which an attorney, or an employee of the attorney who prepared the will or a then affiliated attorney, who serves as an executor may be entitled pursuant to subdivision 6 of section 2307 shall not be diminished.

7. Time of determination of compliance. A determination of compliance with the requirements of subdivisions 1 and 2 of this section shall be made in a proceeding for the issuance of letters testamentary to an executor-designee to whom subdivision 1 of this section applies.

8. Definitions. For purposes of this section, the words or phrases hereafter shall be construed as follows:

(a) *Affiliated attorney*. An attorney who, by reason of partnership, share holding, association or other relationship, express or implied, could participate directly or indirectly, with the attorney who prepared the will in fees for legal services rendered.

(b) *Executor-designee*. A person named in a will or codicil, separately or jointly with one or more persons, as a primary, successor, ancillary, or preliminary executor.

(c) *Employee*. A person who was employed by the attorney who prepared the will or an affiliated attorney when the will was executed.

ACTEC COMMENTARY ON MRPC 1.7*

ACTEC COMMENTARIES ON MODEL RULES OF PROFESSIONAL CONDUCT, page 95 (4th ed. 2006).

Appointment of Scrivener as Fiduciary. An individual is generally free to select and appoint whomever he or she wishes to a fiduciary office (e.g., trustee, executor, attorney-in-fact). None of the provisions of the MRPC deals explicitly with the propriety of a lawyer preparing for a client a will or other document that appoints the lawyer to a fiduciary office. As a general proposition lawyers should be permitted to assist adequately informed clients who wish to appoint their lawyers as fiduciaries. Accordingly, a lawyer should be free to prepare a document that appoints the lawyer to a fiduciary office so long as the client is properly informed, the appointment does not violate the conflict of interest rules of MRPC 1.7 (Conflict of Interest: General Rule), and the appointment is not the product of undue influence or improper solicitation by the lawyer.

* Reprinted with permission of the American College of Trust and Estate Counsel.

The designation of the lawyer as fiduciary will implicate the conflict of interest provisions of MRPC 1.7 when there is a significant risk that the lawyer's interests in obtaining the appointment will materially limit the lawyer's independent professional judgment in advising the client concerning the choice of an executor or other fiduciary. See ACTEC Commentary to MRPC 1.8. (addressing transactions entered into by lawyers with clients).

For the purposes of this Commentary a client is properly informed if the client is provided with information regarding the role and duties of the fiduciary, the ability of a lay person to serve as fiduciary with legal and other professional assistance, and the comparative costs of appointing the lawyer or another person or institution as fiduciary. The client should also be informed of any significant lawyer-client relationship that exists between the lawyer or the lawyer's firm and a corporate fiduciary under consideration for appointment.

NOTES AND QUESTIONS

1. May the drafting attorney also include an exculpatory clause relieving the attorney, when serving as an executor or trustee, from liability for negligent conduct? How does Model Rule 1.8's limitation on making prospective agreements to limit the lawyer's liability to a client for malpractice come into play?

2. The rules governing attorney advertising have been considerably liberalized since the *Gulbankian* decision. Do you think this trend would change the court's analysis if this case were decided today? If yes, how?

4. DRAFTING ATTORNEY AS FIDUCIARY'S ATTORNEY

ACTEC COMMENTARY ON MRPC 1.7*

ACTEC COMMENTARIES ON MODEL RULES OF PROFESSIONAL CONDUCT, pages 95–96 (4th ed. 2006).

Designation of Scrivener as Attorney for Fiduciary. The ethical propriety of a lawyer drawing a document that directs a fiduciary to retain the lawyer as his or her counsel involves essentially the same issues as does the appointment of the scrivener as fiduciary. However, although the appointment of a named fiduciary is generally necessary and desirable, it is usually unnecessary to designate any particular lawyer to serve as counsel to the fiduciary or to direct the fiduciary to retain a particular lawyer. Before drawing a document in which a fiduciary is directed to retain the scrivener or a member of his firm [see MRPC 1.8(k) (Conflict of Interest: Current Clients: Specific Rules)] as counsel, the scrivener should advise the client that it is neither necessary nor customary to include such a direction in a will or trust. A client who wishes to include such a

* Reprinted with permission of the American College of Trust and Estate Counsel.

direction in a document should be advised as to whether or not such a direction is binding on the fiduciary under the governing law. In most states such a direction is usually not binding on a fiduciary, who is generally free to select and retain counsel of his or her own choice without regard to such a direction.

5. RETENTION OF ORIGINAL ESTATE PLANNING DOCUMENTS

STATE v. GULBANKIAN

Supreme Court of Wisconsin, 1972.
54 Wis.2d 605, 196 N.W.2d 733.

[see Chapter 8(I)(3)]

ACTEC COMMENTARY ON MRPC 1.8*

ACTEC COMMENTARIES ON MODEL RULES OF PROFESSIONAL CONDUCT, pages 113–14 (4th ed. 2006).

Retention of Original Documents. A lawyer who has drawn a will or other estate planning documents for a client may offer to retain the executed originals of the documents subject to the client's order. However, a lawyer who retains a client's documents for safekeeping should provide the client with a written receipt, which may be in the form of a letter, acknowledging that the documents are held subject to the client's order. The receipt may, but need not, also indicate that the fiduciary designated in the documents is not required to retain as counsel the lawyer with whom the documents were left for safekeeping. The documents should be held by the lawyer in a manner consistent with the requirements of MRPC 1.15 (Safekeeping Property) regarding the duties of a lawyer who receives and holds property on behalf of a client. In particular, the documents should be properly identified and appropriately safeguarded. Subject to otherwise applicable laws, the lawyer should comply with the client's written directions regarding disposition of the documents.

The retention of the client's original estate planning documents does not itself make the client an "active" client or impose any obligation on the lawyer to take steps to keep informed regarding the client's management of property and family status. Similarly, sending a client periodic letters encouraging the client to review the sufficiency of the client's estate plan or calling the client's attention to subsequent legal developments do not increase the lawyer's obligations to the client. See ACTEC Commentary on MRPC 1.4 (Communication) for a discussion of the concept of dormant representation.

---

* Reprinted with permission of the American College of Trust and Estate Counsel.

6. FIDUCIARY HIRING SELF AS ATTORNEY FOR ESTATE OR TRUST

NORRIS v. BISHOP

Court of Appeals of Kentucky, 1925.
207 Ky. 621, 269 S.W. 751.

CLAY, J. In 1912, T.P. Norris conveyed a tract of land in Carlisle county to certain named trustees and their successors to be held and used as a public burying ground. Later on, he placed $5,000 with the Bardwell Deposit Bank, and $5,000 with the First National Bank, to be used in improving and maintaining the property as a cemetery. At the same time the president of the Bardwell Deposit Bank, the president of the First National Bank, and the county judge and their successors were appointed to manage the fund for the purposes mentioned in the deed. About 10 years later, the settlor brought this suit against the trustees to recover the trust property, on the ground that the public had never made any use of the cemetery, and the object of the charity had wholly failed. Conceiving it to be their duty to defend the trust, John E. Kane, one of the trustees, and a lawyer of high standing, was employed for that purpose, and conducted the defense. On final hearing the chancellor adjudged Norris the relief prayed, and the judgment was affirmed. Carlisle County et al. v. Norris, 200 Ky. 338, 254 S.W. 1044. In settling the accounts of the trustees on the return of the case the chancellor allowed John E. Kane an attorney's fee of $750, to be taxed as costs and paid out of the trust fund. From that order this appeal is prosecuted.

The reasonableness of the fee is not attacked, but it is insisted that no allowance whatever should have been made to the trustee for the services that he performed as attorney. Many of the courts take the position that an executor, administrator, or trustee, who is also an attorney, is not entitled to extra compensation for the services which he renders as an attorney in the administration of the estate. * * *

The reason for the rule is that a trustee cannot be expected to exercise the same prudence and foresight in employing himself that he would exercise in the employment of another, and he should not be subjected to the temptation of being ignorant as trustee in order that he may consult himself as attorney and profit by his wisdom in that capacity. On the other hand, many of the courts hold that, where a trustee renders professional services for the benefit of the estate, he is entitled to compensation therefor. In such a case, the rule is not to allow him the usual professional charges for such services, but a compensation fixed and determined according to what is fair and reasonable in view of all the circumstances.

* * *

These cases do not recognize any right to compensation based on the contract of employment, or agreement as to the amount of the fee, but proceed on the theory that the question of compensation is solely for the courts, and may be made in cases where legal proceedings necessary for the protection of the estate, and such as a prudent man would institute in a matter affecting his individual interests, are undertaken and conducted in good faith.

In England, where ordinarily the trustee is not allowed compensation for any service, the rule is that, when a trustee is a solicitor, and employs himself in matters relating to the trust, he is only entitled to be paid his disbursements, or money out of pocket, and is entitled to nothing for his time or professional trouble. * * * But an exception has been made in the case of two or more trustees where one of them, being a solicitor, acts for himself and his co-trustees in a suit. * * * Though the exception does not extend to a case where a trustee acts for himself and his cotrustees in the administration of the trust estate out of court. * * *

In the case at bar, there were three trustees who served without compensation, and no allowance was asked or granted for professional services rendered in the administration of the trust estate out of court. The compensation was allowed solely for services rendered in defending the suit to set aside the trust. The trustees would have been recreant to their duty if they had permitted judgment to go by default. In making defense the trustees had no personal interests to subserve. The professional services were rendered, not in behalf of the trustees, but in behalf of the beneficiaries of the trust, and between them and the trustees there was no conflict of interests. As the defense was undertaken and conducted in good faith, and the whole matter of compensation is one for the court, it seems to us that the case falls within the exception, and that there is no rule of public policy that forbids a reasonable allowance for the professional services rendered.

Judgment affirmed.

ACTEC COMMENTARY ON MRPC 1.2*

ACTEC COMMENTARIES ON MODEL RULES OF PROFESSIONAL CONDUCT, pages 36–37 (4th ed. 2006).

Lawyer Serving as Fiduciary and Counsel to Fiduciary. Some states permit a lawyer who serves as a fiduciary to serve also as lawyer for the fiduciary. Such dual service may be appropriate where the lawyer previously represented the decedent or is a primary beneficiary of the fiduciary estate. It may also be appropriate where there has been a long-standing relationship between the lawyer and the client. Generally, a lawyer should serve in both capacities only if the client insists and is aware of the alternatives, and the lawyer is competent to do so. A lawyer who is asked to serve in both capacities should inform the client regarding the costs of such dual service and the alternatives to it. A lawyer undertaking to serve in both capacities should attempt to ameliorate any disadvantages that may come from dual service, including the potential loss of the benefits that are obtained by having a separate fiduciary and lawyer, such as the

* Reprinted with permission of the American College of Trust and Estate Counsel.

checks and balances that a separate fiduciary might provide upon the amount of fees sought by the lawyer and vice versa.

7. REPRESENTATION OF BOTH SPOUSES

Today you are meeting with a new estate planning client. During the initial telephone contact, the client indicated a need for a simple plan, "nothing too complex" were the exact words. As you enter your reception area to greet the client, you are surprised to see *two* people waiting—the client and the client's spouse. The client explains that the client wants you to prepare estate plans for both of them. Your mind immediately becomes flooded with thoughts of the potential horrors of representing both husband and wife. You remember stories from colleagues about their married clients who placed them in an awkward position when one spouse confided sensitive information that would be relevant to the estate plan with the admonition to "not tell my spouse." You also recall the professional ethics rules which prohibit representing clients with conflicting interests. What do you do? What is the best way to protect the interests and desires of the client and the client's spouse and still avoid ethical questions as well as potential liability?

This scenario is replayed many times each day in law offices across the United States. The joint representation of a husband and wife in drafting wills and establishing a coordinated estate plan can have considerable benefits for all of the participants involved. However, depending on the circumstances, joint representation may result in substantial disadvantages to one or both spouses and may subject the drafting attorney to liability.

a. Potential Dangers of Joint Representation

1) Conflicts of Interest

A conflict of interest between the spouses or between the spouses and their attorney can arise for many reasons. These conflicts often do not become apparent until well into the representation. If the attorney is skillful (or lucky), the conflict can be resolved and the joint representation continued. In other cases, however, the conflict may force the attorney to withdraw from representing one or both of the spouses.

(A) Family Structure

With the frequency of remarriage and blended families in today's society, it is not surprising that non-traditional families are a ripe source of conflict. A step-parent spouse may not feel the need or desire to provide for children that biologically are not his or her own. This fact can come into direct conflict with the expectations of the parent spouse who may feel that the children are entitled to such support and that the step-parent spouse is just being selfish. Alternatively, the spouses may be in conflict over how the estate plan should provide for "our" children, "your" children, and "my" children, and whether any of these classifications should receive preferential treatment.

(B) Past Relationship Of One Spouse With Attorney

Where one of the spouses has a prior relationship with the drafting attorney, regardless of whether that relationship is personal or professional, there is a potential for conflict. The longer, closer, and more financially rewarding the relationship between one of the spouses and the attorney, the less likely the attorney will be free from that spouse's influence.[6] Because the spouses rely on the attorney's independent judgment to assist them in effectuating their testamentary wishes, it is important that neither of the parties has any actual or perceived disproportionate influence over the attorney.

(C) Differing Testamentary Goals

Spouses may also have different ideas and expectations regarding the forms and limitations of support provided by their estate plan to the survivor of them, their children, grandchildren, and so forth. By including need-based or other restrictions on property, one spouse may believe that the other spouse will be "protected" while that spouse may view the limitations as unjustifiable, punitive, or manipulative. If one spouse has children from a prior relationship, that spouse may wish to restrict the interest of the non-parent spouse via a QTIP trust or other arrangement to the great dismay of the other spouse who would prefer to be the recipient of an outright bequest. No one distribution plan may be able to satisfy the desires of both spouses.

(D) Power Difference Between Spouses

One spouse may dominate the client side of the attorney-client relationship. If one spouse is unfamiliar or uncomfortable with the prospect of working with an attorney or if one spouse is emotionally unable to make his or her desires known to the drafting attorney and instead simply defers to the other spouse, it will be difficult for the attorney to fairly represent both parties.

(E) Stability Of The Marriage

If the attorney seriously questions the stability of the marriage, it will be practically impossible to create an estate plan which contemplates the couple being separated only by death. As one commentator explained, "[N]o court would permit a lawyer to go forward when such a situation involves partners in a partnership or the principals in a close corporation, or a trustee and beneficiary of a trust, or a corporation and its officers. The courts will not take a different view when the clients are husband and wife."[7]

---

6. *See* James R. Wade, *When Can A Lawyer Represent Both Husband and Wife in Estate Planning?*, PROB. & PROP., Mar./Apr. 1987, at 13.

7. Geoffrey C. Hazard, Jr., *Conflict of Interest in Estate Planning for Husband and Wife*, 20 PROB. LAW. 1, 14 (1994).

(F) Characterization Of Property And Relative Size Of Separate Estates

Significant conflict may arise if one spouse has a separate estate that is of substantially greater value than that of the other spouse, especially if the wealthier spouse wants to make a distribution which differs from the traditional plan where each spouse leaves everything to the survivor and upon the survivor's death to their descendants. The attorney may generate a great deal of conflict among all of the parties if, to act in the best interest of the not-so-wealthy spouse, the attorney provides information regarding that spouse's financial standing under the contemplated distribution, if the wealthy spouse were to die first.

Conflict may also exist in situations where one spouse wants to make a gift of property which the other spouse believes is that spouse's property and therefore not an item which the first spouse is entitled to give. The potential for this type of conflict is especially great where the spouses have extensively commingled their property.

2) Release of Confidentiality and Evidentiary Privileges

Joint representation may force spouses to forego their normal confidentiality and evidentiary privileges. Disclosure of all relevant information is the only way to work toward the common goal of developing an effective estate plan. In subsequent litigation between the spouses regarding the estate plan, none of the material provided to the attorney may be protected. Release of these privileges protects the attorney by eliminating the potential conflict between the attorney's duty to inform and the duty to keep confidences.

3) Discourages Revelation of Pertinent Information

The fact that there is no confidentiality between the spouses in joint representation situations may not be a problem if the spouses have nothing to hide and have common estate planning goals. On the other hand, joint representation can place one or both of the spouses in the compromising position of having to reveal long held secrets in the presence of his or her spouse, e.g., the existence of a child born out-of-wedlock. Even worse is the scenario where the spouse withholds the information leaving the other spouse vulnerable and unprotected from the undisclosed information which, if known, may have resulted in a significantly different estate plan.

4) Withdrawing From Representation

A potential conflict which becomes an actual conflict during the course of representation may not prevent the attorney from continuing the representation if the spouses previously gave their informed consent. However, if the conflict materially and substantially affects the interests of one or both of the spouses, the attorney must carefully consider the negative impact that the conflict will have on the results of the representation and on the attorney's independent judgment. The prudent action may be withdrawal. A midstream withdrawal can be very disruptive to the estate planning process and result in a substantial loss of time (and money) to both the spouses and the attorney.

5) Difficulty Determining When Representation Completed

There is some question as to whether a spouse who sought joint representation in the creation of his or her estate plan can, at a later date, return to the same attorney for representation as an individual. The determination as to when the joint representation ends is quite settled with respect to subsequent attempts to unilaterally revise the estate plan—it does not end. Any subsequent representation of either spouse which relates to estate planning matters would constitute information that the attorney would be obligated to share with the other spouse/client. Regarding other legal matters, representation "should be undertaken by separate agreement, maintaining a clear line between those matters that are joint and those matters that are individual to each client."[8]

b. Models of Representation for Married Couples

When a married couple comes to an attorney's office for estate planning advice, the chances are that they are unaware of the different forms of representation which are available or the specific factors they must consider to determine which form of representation is appropriate. The attorney has the burden to use his or her skills of observation and information gathering and apply the relevant professional conduct rules to help the couple to make a choice that best fits their situation.

1) Family Representation

Under the concept of family representation, the attorney represents the family as an entity rather than its individual members. This approach attempts to achieve a common good for all of the participants and thus the attorney's duty is to the family interest, rather than the desires of one or both of the spouses. However, representation of the family does not end the potential for conflict between the spouses, instead it broadens the potential basis of conflict by adding other family members to the equation. Further, even where there is no conflict of purposes between the spouses, the attorney may feel an obligation to the family to discourage or even prevent the spouses from effectuating their common desires where those desires do not benefit the family as a whole (e.g., where the spouses choose not to take advantage of tax saving tools, such as annual exclusion gifts, in favor of retaining the assets to benefit themselves). This type of representation, at least for spousal estate planning purposes, is unnecessarily complicated and may even frustrate the common desires of the spouses. In addition, this model of representation has not been clearly recognized by the courts.

8. Teresa Stanton Collett, *And the Two Shall Become One . . . Until the Lawyers Are Done*, 7 NOTRE DAME J.L. ETHICS & PUB. POL'Y 101, 141 (1993).

2) *Joint Representation*

Joint representation is probably the most common form of representation estate planners use to develop a coordinated estate plan for spouses. Joint representation is based on the presumption that the husband, wife, and attorney will work together to achieve a coordinated estate plan. In situations where the attorney does not discuss the specific representative capacity in which he or she will serve, joint representation serves as the "default" categorization. Despite its widespread acceptance, however, joint representation has its pitfalls.

A critical issue faced by an attorney who represents multiple parties is the attorney's obligation to make sure that the representation complies with the applicable rules of professional conduct. Most relevant in the joint representation of husband and wife is Model Rule of Professional Conduct 1.6 which prohibits representation where it "involves a substantially related matter in which that person's interests are materially and directly adverse to the interests of another client of the lawyer.... " Additionally, the Rule provides that if in the course of multiple representation such a conflict becomes evident, the lawyer must withdraw from representing one or both of the parties.

The rule does, however, contain a savings clause which permits the attorney to accept or continue a representation where a conflict of interest exists if (1) the attorney believes that the representation will not be materially affected, and (2) both of the parties consent to the representation after full disclosure of all of the potential disadvantages and advantages involved. Many attorneys, regardless of whether potential conflicts are apparent, take advantage of this part of the rule and routinely disclose all advantages and disadvantages and then obtain oral and/or written consent to the representation. This approach exceeds the minimum requirements of the rule and helps protect all participants from unanticipated results. Of course, there are still situations which cannot be overcome by disclosure and consent, such as where the attorney gained relevant, but confidential, information during the course of a previous representation of one of the parties. In this type of situation, the attorney has no choice but to withdraw from the joint representation and recommend separate counsel for each spouse.

As noted previously, there is no confidentiality or evidentiary privilege afforded the married couple as to anything said or any materials produced in the course of planning the estate and for as long as the couple may be considered a client of the attorney. In situations where the attorney fails to adequately explain this fact, the attorney may, months or even years later, be presented by one of the spouses with confidential information which affects the estate plan. This leaves the attorney in the unenviable position of having to explain to the revealing spouse that the information cannot be held in confidence because (1) it affects the estate plan, and (2) the other spouse remains a client as to that estate plan. The attorney must then attempt to convince the revealing spouse to disclose the information to the other spouse. If the revealing spouse refuses, the attorney is forced to decide between making the disclosure him-or herself or withdrawing from the representation (which, of course, will make the other spouse wonder what triggered the withdrawal).

3) Separate Concurrent Representation of Both Spouses

The theory of separate concurrent representation in a spousal estate planning context is that a single attorney will undertake the representation of both the husband and the wife, but as separate clients. All information revealed by either of the parties to the attorney is fully protected by confidentiality and evidentiary privileges, regardless of the information's pertinence to establishing a workable estate plan. Thus, one spouse may provide the attorney with confidential information that undoubtedly would be important for the other spouse to have in establishing the estate plan, but the attorney would not be able to share the information because the duty of confidentiality would be superior to the duty to act in the other spouse's best interest. Proponents of this approach claim that informed consent given by the parties legitimizes this form of representation. However, due to the confusion it creates for the attorney regarding to whom the duty of loyalty is owed and whose best interest is to be served, it is hard to understand why any truly informed person would consent. The dual personality that this form of representation requires of the attorney has resulted in it being dubbed a "legal and ethical oxymoron."[9]

4) Separate Representation

A final option for the attorney and the married clients is for each of the spouses to seek his or her own separate counsel. This approach is embraced by many estate planning attorneys as the best way to protect a client's confidences and ensure that the client's interests are not being compromised or influenced by another. By seeking independent representation, spouses forego the efficiency, in terms of money and time spent, that joint representation offers, but they gain confidence that their counsel will protect their individual priorities rather than be diluted by the priorities of the spouse. Additionally, separate representation substantially decreases the potential that the attorney will be trapped in an ethical morass because of unanticipated conflicts or unwanted confidences.

c. Recommendations

Decisions regarding the form of representation most appropriate for a husband and wife seeking estate planning assistance could be made by the attorney alone, based on his or her past experiences, independent judgment, and skills of observation regarding the potential for conflict between the spouses. The better course of action is for the attorney to explain the choices available to the spouse along with the related advantages and disadvantages and then permit the spouses to decide how they would like

---

9. *See* Hazard, *supra* note 7, at 11.

to proceed. The two viable options are joint representation and representation of only one spouse.[10] As previously mentioned, representation of the family as an entity and separate concurrent representation by one attorney are appropriate forms of representation for a husband and wife only in extremely rare cases.

1) Representation of Only One Spouse

This form of representation allows each of the spouses to be fully autonomous in dealing with their attorney. Only the information the client spouse is comfortable with sharing is revealed to the other spouse. As one commentator explained, "it [separate representation for each spouse] is consistent with the present dominant cultural view of marriage as a consensual arrangement and is most consistent with the assumptions about the attorney-client relationship."[11]

Where it is obvious to the attorney that the couple would be best served by this style of representation, it is the attorney's responsibility to convince the couple of this fact. Examples of facts that alert the attorney that separate representation is probably the best choice include situations where the marriage was not the first for either or both of the parties, where there are children from previous relationships, where one party has substantially more assets than the other, where one spouse is a former client or friend of the consulted attorney and where one spouse is obviously dominant over the other spouse.

When recommending separate representation, the attorney should take care to point out that this suggestion is not an inference that their relationship is unstable or that one or both parties may have something to hide. Instead, it is merely a reflection that each spouse has his or her own responsibilities, concerns, and priorities which may or may not be exactly aligned with those of the other spouse. Even if they appear to be the same at the present, they could change in the future. Accordingly, and the best way to achieve a win-win result and reduce present and future family conflict is for each spouse to retain separate counsel.

2) Joint Representation of Both Spouses

Despite the potential dangers to clients and attorneys alike, joint representation is the most common form of representation of husband and wife for estate planning matters. With appropriate and routine use of waiver and consent agreements, the attorney may undertake this type of representation with a minimum of risk to the attorney and a maximum of efficiency for the clients. Unfortunately, however, use of disclosure and consent agreements is far from a standard procedure. One survey revealed that over forty percent of the estate planning attorneys questioned do not, as a matter of practice, explain to the couple the potential for conflict that exists in such a representation, much less put such an explanation in

---

10. *See* Malcolm A. Moore, *Representing Both Husband and Wife Ethically,* ALI-ABA EST. PLAN. COURSE MAT. J., April 1996, at 5, 7.

11. *See* Collett, *supra* note 8, at 128.

writing. One attorney stated that he only felt it was necessary to discuss potential conflicts where the representation involved multiple marriages, and that he only put it in writing if he felt a real problem was indicated in the first meeting. Another respondent failed to disclose the potential for conflict because he was afraid it would appear as if he were issuing a disclaimer for any mistakes he might make. Finally, it seems that denial of the existence of potential conflicts occurs on the part of the attorney as well as the spouses, as evidenced by one practitioner's statement, "I have a hard time believing that I should tell clients who have been married for a long time and who come in together to see me that there may be problems if they get a divorce."[12]

The recommended practice is to provide parties with (1) full disclosure and (2) obtain their informed consent, regardless of the perceived potential for conflict. These steps are detailed below.

Informed consent is not possible without full disclosure. Because estate planning attorneys often meet one or both of the spouses for the first time the day of the initial appointment, it is not possible for the attorney to know more about the couple than what he or she sees and hears during the interview. Because there is no way to be sure which specific issues are relevant to the spouses, it is extremely important for the attorney to discuss as many different potential conflicts as are reasonably possible. Even if the attorney has some familiarity with the couple, it is better to cover too many possibilities than too few.

The amount of disclosure that must be provided for consent to be considered "informed" is different for each client. The attorney has the responsibility to seek information from the parties to be sure that all relevant potential conflicts are addressed as well as the effects of certain other incidents, such as divorce or death of one of the spouses. It is also a good idea to include a discussion of the basic ground rules of the representation detailing exactly what is and is not confidential, rights of all parties to withdraw, and other procedural matters such as attendance at attorney-client meetings and responsibility for payment of fees.

An oral discussion of potential conflicts which exist or which may arise between the couple will allow the attorney to gather information about the clients while disseminating information for them to use in making their decisions. Oral disclosure also permits a dialogue to begin which may encourage the clients to ask questions and thereby create a more expansive description of the advantages and disadvantages of joint representation as they apply to the couple.

Though there is no rule or standard which requires that disclosure or the clients' consent be evidenced by a written document, the seriousness and legitimacy that go along with a signed agreement serve as additional protection for all participants. By documenting the disclosure statement and each client's individual consent to the joint representation, the couple

---

12. Francis J. Collin, Jr., et al., *A Report on the Results of a Survey About Everyday Ethical Concerns in the Trust and Estate Practice,* 20 ACTEC NOTES 201 (1994).

may be forced to reconsider the advantages and disadvantages of joint representation and may feel more committed to the agreement. Additionally, if there are any issues which they do not feel were addressed in the document, they may be more likely to express them so that the issue can also be included in the agreement. Finally, reducing the agreement to written form helps protect the attorney should any future dispute arise regarding the propriety or parameters of the representation.

A. v. B.

Supreme Court of New Jersey, 1999.
158 N.J. 51, 726 A.2d 924.

POLLOCK, J.

This appeal presents the issue whether a law firm may disclose confidential information of one co-client to another co-client. Specifically, in this paternity action, the mother's former law firm, which contemporaneously represented the father and his wife in planning their estates, seeks to disclose the existence of the father's illegitimate child to the wife.

A law firm, Hill Wallack, (described variously as "the law firm" or "the firm") jointly represented the husband and wife in drafting wills in which they devised their respective estates to each other. The devises created the possibility that the other spouse's issue, whether legitimate or illegitimate, ultimately would acquire the decedent's property.

Unbeknown to Hill Wallack and the wife, the husband recently had fathered an illegitimate child. Before the execution of the wills, the child's mother retained Hill Wallack to institute this paternity action against the husband. Because of a clerical error, the firm's computer check did not reveal the conflict of interest inherent in its representation of the mother against the husband. On learning of the conflict, the firm withdrew from representation of the mother in the paternity action. Now, the firm wishes to disclose to the wife the fact that the husband has an illegitimate child. To prevent Hill Wallack from making that disclosure, the husband joined the firm as a third-party defendant in the paternity action.

In the Family Part, the husband, represented by new counsel, Fox, Rothschild, O'Brien & Frankel ("Fox Rothschild"), requested restraints against Hill Wallack to prevent the firm from disclosing to his wife the existence of the child. The Family Part denied the requested restraints. The Appellate Division reversed and remanded "for the entry of an order imposing preliminary restraints and for further consideration."

Hill Wallack then filed motions in this Court seeking leave to appeal, to present oral argument, and to accelerate the appeal. Pursuant to Rule 2:8–3(a), we grant the motion for leave to appeal, accelerate the appeal, and reverse the judgment of the Appellate Division and remand the matter to the Family Part. Hill Wallack's motion for oral argument is denied.

I.

Although the record is both informal and attenuated, the parties agree substantially on the relevant facts. Because the Family Part has sealed the record, we refer to the parties without identifying them by their proper names. So viewed, the record supports the following factual statement.

In October 1997, the husband and wife retained Hill Wallack, a firm of approximately sixty lawyers, to assist them with planning their estates. On the commencement of the joint representation, the husband and wife each signed a letter captioned "Waiver of Conflict of Interest." In explaining the possible conflicts of interest, the letter recited that the effect of a testamentary transfer by one spouse to the other would permit the transferee to dispose of the property as he or she desired. The firm's letter also explained that information provided by one spouse could become available to the other. Although the letter did not contain an express waiver of the confidentiality of any such information, each spouse consented to and waived any conflicts arising from the firm's joint representation.

Unfortunately, the clerk who opened the firm's estate planning file misspelled the clients' surname. The misspelled name was entered in the computer program that the firm uses to discover possible conflicts of interest. The firm then prepared reciprocal wills and related documents with the names of the husband and wife correctly spelled.

In January 1998, before the husband and wife executed the estate planning documents, the mother coincidentally retained Hill Wallack to pursue a paternity claim against the husband. This time, when making its computer search for conflicts of interest, Hill Wallack spelled the husband's name correctly. Accordingly, the computer search did not reveal the existence of the firm's joint representation of the husband and wife. As a result, the estate planning department did not know that the family law department had instituted a paternity action for the mother. Similarly, the family law department did not know that the estate planning department was preparing estate plans for the husband and wife.

A lawyer from the firm's family law department wrote to the husband about the mother's paternity claim. The husband neither objected to the firm's representation of the mother nor alerted the firm to the conflict of interest. Instead, he retained Fox Rothschild to represent him in the paternity action. After initially denying paternity, he agreed to voluntary DNA testing, which revealed that he is the father. Negotiations over child support failed, and the mother instituted the present action.

After the mother filed the paternity action, the husband and wife executed their wills at the Hill Wallack office. The parties agree that in their wills, the husband and wife leave their respective residuary estates to each other. If the other spouse does not survive, the contingent beneficiaries are the testator's issue. The wife's will leaves her residuary estate to her husband, creating the possibility that her property ultimately may pass to his issue. Under N.J.S.A. 3C:1–2, :2–48, the term "issue" includes both legitimate and illegitimate children. When the wife executed her will, therefore, she did not know that the husband's illegitimate child ultimately may inherit her property.

The conflict of interest surfaced when Fox Rothschild, in response to Hill Wallack's request for disclosure of the husband's assets, informed the firm that it already possessed the requested information. Hill Wallack promptly informed the mother that it unknowingly was representing both the husband and the wife in an unrelated matter.

Hill Wallack immediately withdrew from representing the mother in the paternity action. It also instructed the estate planning department not to disclose any information about the husband's assets to the member of the firm who had been representing the mother. The firm then wrote to the husband stating that it believed it had an ethical obligation to disclose to the wife the existence, but not the identity, of his illegitimate child. Additionally, the firm stated that it was obligated to inform the wife "that her current estate plan may devise a portion of her assets through her spouse to that child." The firm suggested that the husband so inform his wife and stated that if he did not do so, it would. Because of the restraints imposed by the Appellate Division, however, the firm has not disclosed the information to the wife.

II.

This appeal concerns the conflict between two fundamental obligations of lawyers: the duty of confidentiality, Rules of Professional Conduct (RPC) 1.6(a), and the duty to inform clients of material facts, RPC 1.4(b). The conflict arises from a law firm's joint representation of two clients whose interests initially were compatible, but now conflict.

Crucial to the attorney-client relationship is the attorney's obligation not to reveal confidential information learned in the course of representation. Thus, RPC 1.6(a) states that "[a] lawyer shall not reveal information relating to representation of a client unless the client consents after consultation, except for disclosures that are impliedly authorized in order to carry out the representation." Generally, "the principle of attorney-client confidentiality imposes a sacred trust on the attorney not to disclose the client's confidential communication." State v. Land, 73 N.J. 24, 30, 372 A.2d 297 (1977).

A lawyer's obligation to communicate to one client all information needed to make an informed decision qualifies the firm's duty to maintain the confidentiality of a co-client's information. RPC 1.4(b), which reflects a lawyer's duty to keep clients informed, requires that "[a] lawyer shall explain a matter to the extent reasonably necessary to permit the client to make informed decisions regarding the representation." * * * In limited situations, moreover, an attorney is permitted or required to disclose confidential information. Hill Wallack argues that RPC 1.6 mandates, or at least permits, the firm to disclose to the wife the existence of the husband's illegitimate child. RPC 1.6(b) requires that a lawyer disclose "information relating to representation of a client" to the proper authorities if the lawyer "reasonably believes" that such disclosure is necessary to prevent the client "from committing a criminal, illegal or fraudulent act that the lawyer reasonably believes is likely to result in death or substantial bodily harm or substantial injury to the financial interest or property of another.... " RPC 1.6(b)(1). Despite Hill Wallack's claim that RPC 1.6(b) applies, the facts do not justify mandatory disclosure. The possible inheritance of the wife's estate by the husband's illegitimate child is too remote to constitute "substantial injury to the financial interest or property of another" within the meaning of RPC 1.6(b).

By comparison, in limited circumstances RPC 1.6(c) permits a lawyer to disclose a confidential communication. RPC 1.6(c) permits, but does not require, a lawyer to reveal confidential information to the extent the lawyer reasonably believes necessary "to rectify the consequences of a client's criminal, illegal or fraudulent act in furtherance of which the lawyer's services had been used." RPC 1.6(c)(1). Although RPC 1.6(c) does not define a "fraudulent act," the term takes on meaning from our construction of the word "fraud," found in the analogous "crime or fraud" exception to the attorney-client privilege. N.J.R.E. 504(2)(a) (excepting from attorney-client privilege "a communication in the course of legal service sought or obtained in the aid of the commission of a crime or fraud") * * *. When construing the "crime or fraud" exception to the attorney-client privilege, "our courts have generally given the term 'fraud' an expansive reading." Fellerman v. Bradley, 99 N.J. 493, 503–04, 493 A.2d 1239 (1985).

We likewise construe broadly the term "fraudulent act" within the meaning of RPC 1.6(c). So construed, the husband's deliberate omission of the existence of his illegitimate child constitutes a fraud on his wife. When discussing their respective estates with the firm, the husband and wife reasonably could expect that each would disclose information material to the distribution of their estates, including the existence of children who are contingent residuary beneficiaries. The husband breached that duty. Under the reciprocal wills, the existence of the husband's illegitimate child could affect the distribution of the wife's estate, if she predeceased him. Additionally, the husband's child support payments and other financial responsibilities owed to the illegitimate child could deplete that part of his estate that otherwise would pass to his wife.

From another perspective, it would be "fundamentally unfair" for the husband to reap the "joint planning advantages of access to information and certainty of outcome," while denying those same advantages to his wife. Teresa S. Collett, Disclosure, Discretion, or Deception: The Estate Planner's Ethical Dilemma from a Unilateral Confidence, 28 Real Prop. Prob. Tr. J. 683, 743 (1994). In effect, the husband has used the law firm's services to defraud his wife in the preparation of her estate. The New Jersey RPCs are based substantially on the American Bar Association Model Rules of Professional Conduct ("the Model Rules"). RPC 1.6, however, exceeds the Model Rules in authorizing the disclosure of confidential information. A brief review of the history of the Model Rules and of RPC 1.6 confirms New Jersey's more expansive commitment to the disclosure of confidential client information.

In 1977, the American Bar Association appointed a Commission on Evaluation of Professional Standards, chaired by the late Robert J. Kutak. The Commission, generally known as the "Kutak Commission," originally proposed a rule that permitted a lawyer to disclose confidential information in circumstances comparable to those permitted by RPC 1.6. The House of Delegates of the American Bar Association, however, rejected the Kutak Commission's recommendation. As adopted by the American Bar Association, Model Rule 1.6(b) permits a lawyer to reveal confidential information only "to the extent the lawyer reasonably believes necessary to prevent the client from committing a criminal act that the lawyer believes is likely to result in imminent death or substantial bodily harm." Unlike RPC 1.6, Model Rule 1.6 does not except information relating to the commission of a fraudulent act or that relating to a client's act that is likely to result in substantial financial injury. In no situation, moreover, does Model Rule 1.6 require disclosure. Thus, the Model Rules provide for narrower disclosure than that authorized by RPC 1.6.

In 1982, this Court appointed a committee to consider the Model Rules. The committee, chaired by the Honorable Dickinson R. Debevoise, became known as the "Debevoise Committee." It determined that the original provisions proposed by the Kutak Commission more closely reflected the existing ethics rules in New Jersey. Thus, the Committee concluded that Model Rule 1.6 would "narrow radically the circumstances in which New Jersey attorneys either may or must disclose the information of their clients' criminal or fraudulent behavior." Report of the New Jersey Supreme Court Committee on the Model Rules of Professional Conduct (1983), reprinted in Michels, supra, Appendix D at 1043. When adopting the RPCs, this Court substantially followed the recommendation of the Debevoise Committee. Described as an "openly-radical experiment," Geoffrey C. Hazard, Jr. & W. William Hodes, 2 The Law of Lawyering § AP4:104 (1998), RPC 1.6 "contained the most far-reaching disclosure requirements of any attorney code of conduct in the country," Leslie C. Levin, Testing the Radical Experiment: A Study of Lawyer Response to Clients Who Intend to Harm Others, 47 Rutgers L. Rev. 81, 92 (1994).

Under RPC 1.6, the facts support disclosure to the wife. The law firm did not learn of the husband's illegitimate child in a confidential communication from him. Indeed, he concealed that information from both his wife and the firm. The law firm learned about the husband's child through its representation of the mother in her paternity action against the husband. Accordingly, the husband's expectation of nondisclosure of the information may be less than if he had communicated the information to the firm in confidence.

In addition, the husband and wife signed letters captioned "Waiver of Conflict of Interest." These letters acknowledge that information provided by one client could become available to the other. The letters, however, stop short of explicitly authorizing the firm to disclose one spouse's confidential information to the other. Even in the absence of any such explicit authorization, the spirit of the letters supports the firm's decision to disclose to the wife the existence of the husband's illegitimate child.

Neither our research nor that of counsel has revealed a dispositive judicial decision from this or any other jurisdiction on the issue of disclosure of confidential information about one client to a co-client. Persuasive secondary authority, however, supports the conclusion that the firm may disclose to the wife the existence of the husband's child.

The forthcoming Restatement of The Law Governing Lawyers § 112 comment l (Proposed Final Draft No. 1, 1996) ("the Restatement") suggests, for example, that if the attorney and the co-clients have reached a prior, explicit agreement concerning the sharing of confidential information, that agreement controls whether the attorney should disclose the confidential information of one co-client to another. Ibid. ("Co-clients ... may explicitly agree to share information" and "can also explicitly agree that the lawyer is not to share certain information ... with one or more other co-clients. A lawyer must honor such agreements."); see also Report of the ABA Special Study Committee on Professional Responsibility: Comments and Recommendations on the Lawyer's Duties in Representing Husband and Wife, 28 Real Prop. Prob. Tr. J. 765, 787 (1994) ("Although legally and ethically there is no need for a prior discussion and agreement with the couple about the mode of representation, discussion and agreement are the better practice. The agreement may cover ... the duty to keep or disclose confidences."); American College of Trust and Estate Counsel, ACTEC Commentaries on the Model Rules of Professional Conduct 65–66 (2d ed. 1995) ("When the lawyer is first consulted by the multiple potential clients the lawyer should review with them the terms upon which the lawyer will undertake the representation, including the extent to which information will be shared among them.").

As the preceding authorities suggest, an attorney, on commencing joint representation of co-clients, should agree explicitly with the clients on the sharing of confidential information. In such a "disclosure agreement," the co-clients can agree that any confidential information concerning one co-client, whether obtained from a co-client himself or herself or from another source, will be shared with the other co-client. Similarly, the co-clients can agree that unilateral confidences or other confidential information will be kept confidential by the attorney. Such a prior agreement will clarify the expectations of the clients and the lawyer and diminish the need for future litigation.

In the absence of an agreement to share confidential information with co-clients, the Restatement reposes the resolution of the lawyer's competing duties within the lawyer's discretion: The lawyer, after consideration of all relevant circumstances, has the ... discretion to inform the affected co-client of the specific communication if, in the lawyer's reasonable judgment, the immediacy and magnitude of the risk to the affected co-client outweigh the interest of the communicating client in continued secrecy. [Restatement (Third) of The Law Governing Lawyers, supra, § 112 comment l.]

Additionally, the Restatement advises that the lawyer, when withdrawing from representation of the co-clients, may inform the affected co-client that the attorney has learned of information adversely affecting that client's interests that the communicating co-client refuses to permit the lawyer to disclose. Ibid.

In the context of estate planning, the Restatement also suggests that a lawyer's disclosure of confidential information communicated by one spouse is appropriate only if the other spouse's failure to learn of the information would be materially detrimental to that other spouse or frustrate the spouse's intended testamentary arrangement. Id. § 112 comment l, illustrations 2, 3. The Restatement provides two analogous illustrations in which a lawyer has been jointly retained by a husband and wife to prepare reciprocal wills.

The first illustration states:

> Lawyer has been retained by Husband and Wife to prepare wills pursuant to an arrangement under which each spouse agrees to leave most of their property to the other (compare § 211, Comment c, Illustrations 1–3). Shortly after the wills are executed, Husband (unknown to Wife) asks Lawyer to prepare an inter vivos trust for an illegitimate child whose existence Husband has kept secret from Wife for many years and about whom Husband had not previously informed Lawyer. Husband states that Wife would be distraught at learning of Husband's infidelity and of Husband's years of silence and that disclosure of the information could destroy their marriage. Husband directs Lawyer not to inform Wife. The inter vivos trust that Husband proposes to create would not materially affect Wife's own estate plan or her expected receipt of property under Husband's will, because Husband proposes to use property designated in Husband's will for a personally favored charity. In view of the lack of material effect on Wife, Lawyer may assist Husband to establish and fund the inter vivos trust and refrain from disclosing Husband's information to Wife. [Id. § 112 comment l, illustration 2.]

In authorizing non-disclosure, the Restatement explains that an attorney should refrain from disclosing the existence of the illegitimate child to the wife because the trust "would not materially affect Wife's own estate plan or her expected receipt of property under Husband's will." Ibid.

The other illustration states:

> Same facts as [the prior Illustration], except that Husband's proposed inter vivos trust would significantly deplete Husband's estate, to Wife's material detriment and in frustration of the Spouses' intended testamentary arrangements. If Husband will neither inform Wife nor

permit Lawyer to do so, Lawyer must withdraw from representing both Husband and Wife. In the light of all relevant circumstances, Lawyer may exercise discretion whether to inform Wife either that circumstances, which Lawyer has been asked not to reveal, indicate that she should revoke her recent will or to inform Wife of some or all the details of the information that Husband has recently provided so that Wife may protect her interests. Alternatively, Lawyer may inform Wife only that Lawyer is withdrawing because Husband will not permit disclosure of information that Lawyer has learned from Husband. [Id. § 112 comment l, illustration 3.] Because the money placed in the trust would be deducted from the portion of the husband's estate left to his wife, the Restatement concludes that the lawyer may exercise discretion to inform the wife of the husband's plans. Ibid.

An earlier draft of the Restatement described the attorney's obligation to disclose the confidential information to the co-client as mandatory. Id. (Council Draft No. 11, 1995); cf. Collett, supra, at 743 (arguing that nature of joint representation of husband and wife supports mandatory disclosure rule). When reviewing the draft, however, the governing body of the American Law Institute, the Council, modified the obligation to leave disclosure within the attorney's discretion.

Similarly, the American College of Trust and Estate Counsel (ACTEC) also favors a discretionary rule. It recommends that the "lawyer should have a reasonable degree of discretion in determining how to respond to any particular case." American College of Trust and Estate Counsel, supra, at 68. The ACTEC suggests that the lawyer first attempt to convince the client to inform the co-client. Ibid. When urging the client to disclose the information, the lawyer should remind the client of the implicit understanding that all information will be shared by both clients. The lawyer also should explain to the client the potential legal consequences of non-disclosure, including invalidation of the wills. Ibid. Furthermore, the lawyer may mention that failure to communicate the information could subject the lawyer to a malpractice claim or disciplinary action. Ibid. The ACTEC reasons that if unsuccessful in persuading the client to disclose the information, the lawyer should consider several factors in deciding whether to reveal the confidential information to the co-client, including: (1) duties of impartiality and loyalty to the clients; (2) any express or implied agreement among the lawyer and the joint clients that information communicated by either client to the lawyer regarding the subject of the representation would be shared with the other client; (3) the reasonable expectations of the clients; and (4) the nature of the confidence and the harm that may result if the confidence is, or is not, disclosed. Id. at 68–69.

The Section of Real Property, Probate and Trust Law of the American Bar Association, in a report prepared by its Special Study Committee on Professional Responsibility, reached a similar conclusion: Faced with any adverse confidence, the lawyer must act as a fiduciary toward joint clients. The lawyer must balance the potential for material harm to the confiding spouse caused by disclosure against the potential for material harm to the other spouse caused by a failure to disclose. [Report of the Special Study Committee on Professional Responsibility: Comments and Recommendations on the Lawyer's Duties in Representing Husband and Wife, supra, 28 Real Prop. Prob. Tr. J. at 787.]

The report stresses that the resolution of the balancing test should center on the expectations of the clients. Id. at 784. In general, "the available ruling authority ... points toward the conclusion that a lawyer is not required to disclose an adverse confidence to the other spouse." Id. at 788. At the same time, the report acknowledges, as did the Restatement, that the available ruling authority is "scant and offers little analytical guidance." Id. at 788 n.27.

The Professional Ethics Committees of New York and Florida, however, have concluded that disclosure to a co-client is prohibited. New York State Bar Ass'n Comm. on Professional Ethics, Op. 555 (1984); Florida State Bar Ass'n Comm. on Professional Ethics, Op. 95–4 (1997).

The New York opinion addressed the following situation:

> A and B formed a partnership and employed Lawyer L to represent them in connection with the partnership affairs. Subsequently, B, in a conversation with Lawyer L, advised Lawyer L that he was actively breaching the partnership agreement. B preceded this statement to Lawyer L with the statement that he proposed to tell Lawyer L something "in confidence." Lawyer L did not respond to that statement and did not understand that B intended to make a statement that would be of importance to A but that was to be kept confidential from A. Lawyer L had not, prior thereto, advised A or B that he could not receive from one communications regarding the subject of the joint representation that would be confidential from the other. B has subsequently declined to tell A what he has told Lawyer L. [New York State Bar Ass'n Comm. On Professional Ethics, Op. 555, supra.]

In that situation, the New York Ethics Committee concluded that the lawyer may not disclose to the co-client the communicating client's statement. The Committee based its conclusion on the absence of prior consent by the clients to the sharing of all confidential communications and the fact that the client "specifically in advance designated his communication as confidential, and the lawyer did not demur." Ibid.

The Florida Ethics Committee addressed a similar situation:

> Lawyer has represented Husband and Wife for many years in a range of personal matters, including estate planning. Husband and Wife have substantial individual assets, and they also own substantial jointly-held property. Recently, Lawyer prepared new updated wills that Husband and Wife signed. Like their previous wills, their new wills primarily benefit the survivor of them for his or her life, with beneficial disposition at the death of the survivor being made equally to their children. Several months after the execution of the new wills,

> Husband confers separately with Lawyer. Husband reveals to Lawyer that he has just executed a codicil (prepared by another law firm) that makes substantial beneficial disposition to a woman with whom Husband has been having an extra-marital relationship. [Florida State Bar Ass'n Comm. On Professional Ethics, Op. 95–4, supra.]

Reasoning that the lawyer's duty of confidentiality takes precedence over the duty to communicate all relevant information to a client, the Florida Ethics Committee concluded that the lawyer did not have discretion to reveal the information. In support of that conclusion, the Florida committee reasoned that joint clients do not necessarily expect that everything relating to the joint representation communicated by one co-client will be shared with the other co-client.

In several material respects, however, the present appeal differs from the hypothetical cases considered by the New York and Florida committees. Most significantly, the New York and Florida disciplinary rules, unlike RPC 1.6, do not except disclosure needed "to rectify the consequences of a client's ... fraudulent act in the furtherance of which the lawyer's services had been used." RPC 1.6(c). But see New York Code of Professional Responsibility DR 4–101; Florida Rules of Professional Conduct 4–1.6. Second, Hill Wallack learned of the husband's paternity from a third party, not from the husband himself. Thus, the husband did not communicate anything to the law firm with the expectation that the communication would be kept confidential. Finally, the husband and wife, unlike the co-clients considered by the New York and Florida Committees, signed an agreement suggesting their intent to share all information with each other.

Because Hill Wallack wishes to make the disclosure, we need not reach the issue whether the lawyer's obligation to disclose is discretionary or mandatory. In conclusion, Hill Wallack may inform the wife of the existence of the husband's illegitimate child.

Finally, authorizing the disclosure of the existence, but not the identity, of the child will not contravene N.J.S.A. 9:17–42, which provides:

> All papers and records and any information pertaining to an action or proceeding held under [the New Jersey Parentage Act] which may reveal the identity of any party in an action, other than the final judgment or the birth certificate, whether part of the permanent record of the court or of a file with the State registrar of vital statistics or elsewhere, are confidential and are subject to inspection only upon consent of the court and all parties to the action who are still living, or in exceptional cases only upon an order of the court for compelling reason clearly and convincingly shown.

The law firm learned of the husband's paternity of the child through the mother's disclosure before the institution of the paternity suit. It does not seek to disclose the identity of the mother or the child. Given the wife's need for the information and the law firm's right to disclose it, the disclosure of the child's existence to the wife constitutes an exceptional case "for compelling reason clearly and convincingly shown."

The judgment of the Appellate Division is reversed and the matter is remanded to the Family Part.

NOTES AND QUESTIONS

1. One commentator has suggested a five-step approach to representing spouses.

   a. Determine if "both spouses are genuinely autonomous in their situation, and whether either may have a tendency to fabricate or fantasize."

   b. Conduct separate interviews with each spouse.

   c. Feel comfortable revealing what each spouse says and desires to the other.

   d. Obtain simple written consent letters.

   e. Document actions with letters to the clients and memorandums to the file.

Geoffrey C. Hazard, Jr., *Conflict of Interest in Estate Planning for Husband and Wife,* 20 PROB. LAW 1, 23 (1994).

2. For further information, see Teresa Stanton Collett, *Disclosure, Discretion, or Deception: The Estate Planner's Ethical Dilemma From a Unilateral Confidence,* 28 REAL PROP., PROB. & TR. J. 683 (1994), and Malcolm A. Moore & Anne K. Hilker, *Representing Both Spouses: The New Section Recommendations,* PROB. & PROP., July/Aug. 1993, at 26.

8. REPRESENTATION OF NON-SPOUSAL RELATIVES

Clients pleased with your legal work are likely to refer family members to you. These referrals raise many ethical concerns. As you prepare an estate plan for a client, you gain access to many details regarding the client's personal and financial matters. Thus, representation of more than one family member raises various ethical concerns such as avoiding conflicts, maintaining confidences, and preserving independent professional judgment.

NOTES AND QUESTIONS

1. If you are confronted with an intra-family estate planning situation (e.g., parent and child), what will you do? Consider the pros and cons of each of the following options:

   a. Decline to represent any member of the client's family.

   b. Act as an intermediary between the family members.

   c. Jointly represent the family members.

2. Some commentators suggest that estate planners be allowed to represent the family as an entity. Do you think this is a good idea? Why or why not?

3. Of what importance, if any, would the following factors have on your deliberations in deciding whether to accept employment by a client's family member?

a. Closeness of family relationship, e.g., child or other descendant, parent or other ancestor, sibling, niece/nephew, aunt/uncle, cousin, etc.

b. Current family harmony and future potential for disharmony.

c. Existence of a family-owned business or other joint investment.

4. For a comprehensive examination of estate planning for non-spousal relatives of a client, see Teresa Stanton Collett, *The Ethics of Intergenerational Representation,* 62 FORDHAM L. REV. 1453 (1994).

9. PREPARING ESTATE PLAN FOR ANOTHER UPON CLIENT'S REQUEST

ACTEC COMMENTARY ON MRPC 1.8*

ACTEC COMMENTARIES ON MODEL RULES OF PROFESSIONAL CONDUCT, page 92 (4th ed. 2006).

Existing Client Asks Lawyer to Prepare Will or Trust for Another Person. A lawyer should exercise particular care if an existing client asks the lawyer to prepare for another person a will or trust that will benefit the existing client, particularly if the existing client will pay the cost of providing the estate planning services to the other person. If the representation of both the existing client and the new client would create a significant risk that the representation of one or both clients would be materially limited, the representation can only be undertaken as permitted by MRPC 1.7(b). In any case, the lawyer must comply with MRPC 1.8(f) (Conflict of Interest: Current Clients: Specific Rules) and should consider cautioning both clients of the possibility that the existing client may be presumed to have exerted undue influence on the other client because the existing client was involved in the procurement of the document.

10. CAPACITY OF REPRESENTATION

Assume that you are hired by the executor of an estate or the trustee of a trust to serve as the fiduciary's attorney. To whom do you owe your duties, the fiduciary personally, the estate, the estate's creditors, or the beneficiaries? This determination is significant if the client breaches a fiduciary duty, i.e., whose interests do you represent? Compare Steinway v. Bolden, 185 Mich. App. 234, 238, 460 N.W.2d 306, 307 (1990) ("the attorney's client is the estate rather than the personal representative")

* Reprinted with permission of the American College of Trust and Estate Counsel.

with OR. ETHICS OP. 1991–62 ("an attorney for a personal representative represents the personal representative and not the estate or the beneficiaries as such") and Spinner v. Nutt, 417 Mass. 549, 631 N.E.2d 542, 544–45 (1994) (court unwilling to impose duty on trustee's attorney in favor of beneficiary because "conflicting loyalties could impermissibly interfere with the attorney's task of advising the trustee"). See Alan D. Wingfield, *Fiduciary Attorney–Client Communications: An Illusory Privilege?*, PROB. & PROP., July/Aug. 1994, at 60.

QUESTION

May an attorney represent a client as both a fiduciary and a beneficiary?

ACTEC COMMENTARY ON MRPC 1.2*

ACTEC COMMENTARIES ON MODEL RULES OF PROFESSIONAL CONDUCT, pages 33, 35 (4th ed. 2006).

Representation of Fiduciary in Representative and Individual Capacities. The lawyer may represent the fiduciary in a representative capacity and as a beneficiary, except as otherwise proscribed, as it may be in some cases by MRPC 1.7 (Conflict of Interest: Current Clients).

> Example 1.2–1. Lawyer (L) drew a will for X in which X left her entire estate in equal shares to A and Band appointed A as executor. X died, survived by A and B. A asked L to represent her both as executor and as beneficiary. L explained to A the duties A would have as personal representative, including the duty of impartiality toward the beneficiaries. L also described to A the implications of the common representation, to which A consented. L may properly represent A in both capacities. However, L should inform B of the dual representation and indicate that B may, at his or her own expense, retain independent counsel. In addition, L should maintain separate records with respect to the individual representation of A, who should be charged a separate fee (payable by A individually) for that representation. L may properly counsel A with respect to her interests as beneficiary. However, L may not assert A's individual rights on A's behalf in a way that conflicts with A's duties as personal representative. If a conflict develops that materially limits L's ability to function as A's lawyer in both capacities, L should withdraw from representing A in one or both capacities. See MRPC 1.7 (Conflict of Interest: Current Clients) and MRPC 1.16 (Declining or Terminating Representation).

* * *

Representation of Fiduciary in Representative, Not Individual, Capacity. If a lawyer is retained to represent a fiduciary generally with respect to the fiduciary estate, the lawyer represents the fiduciary in a representa-

* Reprinted with permission of the American College of Trust and Estate Counsel.

tive and not an individual capacity—the ultimate objective of which is to administer the fiduciary estate for the benefit of the beneficiaries. Giving recognition to the representative capacity in which the lawyer represents the fiduciary is appropriate because in such cases the lawyer is retained to perform services that benefit the fiduciary estate and, derivatively, the beneficiaries—not to perform services that benefit the fiduciary individually. The nature of the relationship is also suggested by the fact that the fiduciary and the lawyer for the fiduciary are both compensated from the fiduciary estate. Under some circumstances it is appropriate for the lawyer also to represent one or more of the beneficiaries of the fiduciary estate. See ACTEC Commentary on MRPC 1.7 (Conflict of Interest: Current Clients) and Example 1.7–2.

General and Individual Representation Distinguished. A lawyer represents the fiduciary generally (i.e., in a representative capacity) when the lawyer is retained to advise the fiduciary regarding the administration of the fiduciary estate or matters affecting the estate. On the other hand, a lawyer represents a fiduciary individually when the lawyer is retained for the limited purpose of advancing the interests of the fiduciary and not necessarily the interests of the fiduciary estate or the persons beneficially interested in the estate. For example, a lawyer represents a fiduciary individually when the lawyer, who may or may not have previously represented the fiduciary generally with respect to the fiduciary estate, is retained to negotiate with the beneficiaries regarding the compensation of the fiduciary or to defend the fiduciary against charges or threatened charges of maladministration of the fiduciary estate. A lawyer who represents a fiduciary generally may normally also undertake to represent the fiduciary individually. If the lawyer has previously represented the fiduciary generally and is now representing the fiduciary individually, the lawyer should advise the beneficiaries of this fact.

11. TRANSACTIONS WITH BENEFICIARY OR FIDUCIARY

"A lawyer generally should not enter into purchase or sale transactions with a client or with the beneficiaries of a fiduciary estate if the lawyer is serving as fiduciary or as counsel to the fiduciary. Similarly, a lawyer generally should neither borrow from, nor lend to, a client or beneficiary." ACTEC COMMENTARIES ON MODEL RULES OF PROFESSIONAL CONDUCT, MRPC 1.8 (4th ed. 2006).

J. MALPRACTICE

The potential malpractice liability of an attorney for negligently preparing an estate plan is great because estate planning requires an especially high degree of competence. The attorney must have a thorough knowledge of many areas of the law including wills, probate, trusts, taxation, insurance, property, government benefits, business associations, and domestic relations. Surprisingly, however, the most common errors do not involve complicated or sophisticated matters. Instead, problems usually arise because of clerical errors in the preparation of wills and the attorney's failure to understand the effect of the language used in dispositive provisions which results in beneficiaries not receiving what the testator or settlor intended.

When a defect in an estate plan is discovered during the client's lifetime, the client's only loss may be the cost of having the errors corrected, for example, the expense of having a new will prepared and executed. This is not the type of situation where malpractice liability is likely to be litigated. The attorney may be able to avoid becoming a defendant by simply correcting the errors without cost to the client and offering appropriate apologies for the inconvenience. Of course, if the attorney's negligence caused tax or other benefits to be permanently lost, the attorney's potential liability would be much greater.

Errors often do not manifest themselves until after the client has died. At that time, the decedent's estate may be able to sue the negligent attorney. The damages would probably consist only of the fees paid for drafting the estate plan because no other diminution of the decedent's property would have resulted from the error. Consequently, if there is a flaw in the estate plan which renders it invalid or ineffective and that flaw can be traced to the negligent conduct of the attorney in charge, it is the intended beneficiaries who now find themselves short-changed who are likely to bring the malpractice action.

BIAKANJA v. IRVING

Supreme Court of California, 1958.
49 Cal.2d 647, 320 P.2d 16.

GIBSON, CHIEF JUSTICE.

Plaintiff's brother, John Maroevich, died, leaving a will which devised and bequeathed all of his property to plaintiff. The will, which was prepared by defendant, a notary public, was denied probate for lack of sufficient attestation. Plaintiff, by intestate succession, received only one-eighth of the estate, and she recovered a judgment against defendant for the difference between the amount which she would have received had the will been valid and the amount distributed to her.

Defendant, who is not an attorney, had for several years written letters and prepared income tax returns for Maroevich. The will was typed in defendant's office and "subscribed and sworn to" by Maroevich in the presence of defendant, who affixed his signature and notarial seal to the instrument. Sometime later Maroevich obtained the signatures of two witnesses to the will neither of whom was present when Maroevich signed it. These witnesses did not sign in the presence of each other, and Maroevich did not acknowledge his signature in their presence.

An attorney who represented Maroevich's stepson in the probate proceedings testified that he had a telephone conversation with defendant shortly after Maroevich's death, in which defendant said he prepared the will and notarized it. According to the attorney, defendant, in discussing how the will was witnessed, "admonished me to the effect that I was a young lawyer, I'd better go back and study my law books some more, that anybody knew a will which bore a notarial seal was a valid will, didn't have to be witnessed by any witnesses."

The court found that defendant agreed and undertook to prepare a valid will and that it was invalid because defendant negligently failed to have it properly attested. The findings are supported by the evidence.

(1) The principal question is whether defendant was under a duty to exercise due care to protect plaintiff from injury and was liable for damage caused plaintiff by his negligence even though they were not in privity of contract. In Buckley v. Gray, 1895, 110 Cal. 339, 42 P. 900, 31 L.R.A. 862, it was held that a person who was named as a beneficiary under a will could not recover damages from an attorney who negligently drafted and directed the execution of the will with the result that the intended beneficiary was deprived of substantial benefits. The court based its decision on the ground that the attorney owed no duty to the beneficiary because there was no privity of contract between them. Mickel v. Murphy, 147 Cal.App.2d 718, 305 P.2d 993, relying on Buckley v. Gray, supra, held that a notary public who prepared a will was not liable to the beneficiary for failing to have it properly executed. When Buckley v. Gray, supra, was decided in 1895, it was generally accepted that, with the few exceptions noted in the opinion in that case, there was no liability for negligence committed in the performance of a contract in the absence of privity. Since that time the rule has been greatly liberalized, and the courts have permitted a plaintiff not in privity to recover damages in many situations for the negligent performance of a contract.

Liability has been imposed, in the absence of privity, upon suppliers of goods and services which, if negligently made or rendered, are "reasonably certain to place life and limb in peril." See Kalash v. Los Angeles Ladder Co., 1 Cal.2d 229, 231, 34 P.2d 481 (manufacturer of ladders); Hale v. Depaoli, 33 Cal.2d 228, 231, 201 P.2d 1, 13 A.L.R.2d 183 (building contractor); Dahms v. General Elevator Co., 214 Cal. 733, 738–742, 7 P.2d 1013 (elevator maintenance company); MacPherson v. Buick Motor Co., 217 N.Y. 382, 111 N.E. 1050, L.R.A. 1916F, 696 (automobile manufacturer); Prosser, Torts (2d ed. 1955), §§ 84–85, p. 497 et seq. There is also authority for the imposition of liability where there is no privity and where the only foreseeable risk is of damage to tangible property. * * *

Recovery has been allowed in some cases to a third party not in privity where the only risk of harm created by the negligent performance of a contract was to an intangible interest. For example, in the leading case of Glanzer v. Shepard, 233 N.Y. 236, 135 N.E. 275, 23 A.L.R. 1425, a purchaser of beans overpaid the vendor in reliance on an erroneous certificate negligently furnished by a public weigher employed by the vendor. In holding the weigher liable to the purchaser, the court stated, in an opinion by Justice Cardozo, that the purchaser's use of the certificate was, to the weigher's knowledge, the "end and aim" of the transaction. * * * In another group of cases the addressee of a telegram has been allowed to recover from the telegraph company for loss of the opportunity of a job because of the company's failure to deliver a message. * * *

Imposition of liability for injuries to intangible interests has been refused, however, in the absence of privity where any potential advantage to the plaintiff from the performance of the contract was only a collateral consideration of the transaction or where the injury to the particular person bringing suit was not foreseeable. * * *

(2) The determination whether in a specific case the defendant will be held liable to a third person not in privity is a matter of policy and involves the balancing of various factors, among which are the extent to which the transaction was intended to affect the plaintiff, the foreseeability of harm to him, the degree of certainty that the plaintiff suffered injury, the closeness of the connection between the defendant's conduct and the injury suffered, the moral blame attached to the defendant's conduct, and the policy of preventing future harm. * * * Here, the "end and aim" of the transaction was to provide for the passing of Maroevich's estate to plaintiff. See Glanzer v. Shepard, 233 N.Y. 236, 135 N.E. 275, 23 A.L.R. 1425. Defendant must have been aware from the terms of the will itself that, if faulty solemnization caused the will to be invalid, plaintiff would suffer the very loss which occurred. As Maroevich died without revoking his will, plaintiff, but for defendant's negligence, would have received all of the Maroevich estate, and the fact that she received only one-eighth of the estate was directly caused by defendant's conduct.

Defendant undertook to provide for the formal disposition of Maroevich's estate by drafting and supervising the execution of a will. This was an important transaction requiring specialized skill, and defendant clearly was not qualified to undertake it. His conduct was not only negligent but was also highly improper. He engaged in the unauthorized practice of the law (Bus. & Prof.Code, § 6125), * * * which is a misdemeanor in violation of section 6126 of the Business and Professions Code. Such conduct should be discouraged and not protected by immunity from civil liability, as would be the case if plaintiff, the only person who suffered a loss, were denied a right of action.

We have concluded that plaintiff should be allowed recovery despite the absence of privity, and the cases of Buckley v. Gray, 110 Cal. 339, 42 P. 900, 31 L.R.A. 862, and Mickel v. Murphy, 147 Cal.App.2d 718, 305 P.2d 993, are disapproved insofar as they are in conflict with this decision.

The judgment is affirmed.

BARCELO v. ELLIOTT

Supreme Court of Texas, 1996.
923 S.W.2d 575.

PHILLIPS, CHIEF JUSTICE, delivered the opinion of the Court.

The issue presented is whether an attorney who negligently drafts a will or trust agreement owes a duty of care to persons intended to benefit under the will or trust, even though the attorney never represented the intended beneficiaries. The court of appeals held that the attorney owed no duty to the beneficiaries, affirming the trial court's summary judgment for the defendant-attorney. * * * Because the attorney did not represent the beneficiaries, we likewise conclude that he owed no professional duty to them. We accordingly affirm the judgment of the court of appeals.

I

After Frances Barcelo retained attorney David Elliott to assist her with estate planning, Elliott drafted a will and inter vivos trust agreement for her. The will provided for specific bequests to Barcelo's children, devising the residuary of her estate to the inter vivos trust. Under the trust agreement, trust income was to be distributed to Barcelo during her lifetime. Upon her death, the trust was to terminate, assets were to be distributed in specific amounts to Barcelo's children and siblings, and the remainder was to pass to Barcelo's six grandchildren. The trust agreement contemplated that the trust would be funded by cash and shares of stock during Barcelo's lifetime, although the grandchildren contend that this never occurred. Barcelo signed the will and trust agreement in September 1990.

Barcelo died on January 22, 1991. After two of her children contested the validity of the trust, the probate court, for reasons not disclosed on the record before us, declared the trust to be invalid and unenforceable. Barcelo's grandchildren—the intended remainder beneficiaries under the trust—subsequently agreed to settle for what they contend was a substantially smaller share of the estate than what they would have received pursuant to a valid trust.

Barcelo's grandchildren then filed the present malpractice action against Elliott and his law firm (collectively "Elliott"). Plaintiffs allege that Elliott's negligence caused the trust to be invalid, resulting in foreseeable injury to the plaintiffs.[13] Elliott moved for summary judgment

---

13. The plaintiffs alleged that Elliott acted negligently when he:

A. provided in the trust agreement that it would not be effective until signed by the trustee, designated to be First City Bank of Houston, and then failed to obtain the execution of the trust document by the trustee;

B. drafted Mrs. Barcelo's will so as to provide that the residuary of her estate would pass into the trust he sought to create for Mrs. Barcelo, and then provided in the trust agreement that the trust would terminate upon Mrs. Barcelo's death, leaving her residuary to pass by intestacy to her children instead of her six grandchildren, including Plaintiffs, as provided in the trust agreement; and

on the sole ground that he owed no professional duty to the grandchildren because he had never represented them. The trial court granted Elliott's motion for summary judgment.

The court of appeals affirmed, concluding that under Texas law an attorney preparing estate planning documents owes a duty only to his or her client—the testator or trust settlor—not to third parties intended to benefit under the estate plan. * * *

II

The sole issue presented is whether Elliott owes a duty to the grandchildren that could give rise to malpractice liability even though he represented only Frances Barcelo, not the grandchildren, in preparing and implementing the estate plan.

A

At common law, an attorney owes a duty of care only to his or her client, not to third parties who may have been damaged by the attorney's negligent representation of the client. * * * Without this "privity barrier," the rationale goes, clients would lose control over the attorney-client relationship, and attorneys would be subject to almost unlimited liability. * * * Texas courts of appeals have uniformly applied the privity barrier in the estate planning context. * * *

Plaintiffs argue, however, that recognizing a limited exception to the privity barrier as to lawyers who negligently draft a will or trust would not thwart the rule's underlying rationales. They contend that the attorney should owe a duty of care to persons who were specific, intended beneficiaries of the estate plan. We disagree.

B

The majority of other states addressing this issue have relaxed the privity barrier in the estate planning context. * * *

While some of these states have allowed a broad cause of action by those claiming to be intended beneficiaries, * * * others have limited the class of plaintiffs to beneficiaries specifically identified in an invalid will or trust. * * * The Supreme Court of Iowa, for example, held that a cause of action ordinarily will arise only when as a direct result of the lawyer's professional negligence the testator's intent as expressed in the testamentary instruments is frustrated in whole or in part and the beneficiary's interest in the estate is either lost, diminished, or unrealized. Schreiner v. Scoville, 410 N.W.2d 679, 683 (Iowa 1987).

C

We agree with those courts that have rejected a broad cause of action in favor of beneficiaries. These courts have recognized the inevitable

C. failed to take the necessary steps on behalf of Mrs. Barcelo to fund the trust with the shares of stock....

problems with disappointed heirs attempting to prove that the defendant-attorney failed to implement the deceased testator's intentions. Certainly allowing extrinsic evidence would create a host of difficulties. In DeMaris v. Asti, 426 So.2d 1153, 1154 (Fla.Dist.Ct.App.1983), for example, the court concluded that "[t]here is no authority—the reasons being obvious—for the proposition that a disappointed beneficiary may prove, by evidence totally extrinsic to the will, the testator's testamentary intent was other than as expressed in his solemn and properly executed will." Such a cause of action would subject attorneys to suits by heirs who simply did not receive what they believed to be their due share under the will or trust. This potential tort liability to third parties would create a conflict during the estate planning process, dividing the attorney's loyalty between his or her client and the third-party beneficiaries.

Moreover, we believe that the more limited cause of action recognized by several jurisdictions also undermines the policy rationales supporting the privity rule. These courts have limited the cause of action to beneficiaries specifically identified in an invalid will or trust. Under these circumstances, courts have reasoned, the interests of the client and the beneficiaries are necessarily aligned, negating any conflict, as the attorney owes a duty only to those parties which the testator clearly intended to benefit. * * *

In most cases where a defect renders a will or trust invalid, however, there are concomitant questions as to the true intentions of the testator. Suppose, for example, that a properly drafted will is simply not executed at the time of the testator's death. The document may express the testator's true intentions, lacking signatures solely because of the attorney's negligent delay. On the other hand, the testator may have postponed execution because of second thoughts regarding the distribution scheme. In the latter situation, the attorney's representation of the testator will likely be affected if he or she knows that the existence of an unexecuted will may create malpractice liability if the testator unexpectedly dies.

The present case is indicative of the conflicts that could arise. Plaintiffs contend in part that Elliott was negligent in failing to fund the trust during Barcelo's lifetime, and in failing to obtain a signature from the trustee. These alleged deficiencies, however, could have existed pursuant to Barcelo's instructions, which may have been based on advice from her attorneys attempting to represent her best interests. An attorney's ability to render such advice would be severely compromised if the advice could be second-guessed by persons named as beneficiaries under the unconsummated trust.

In sum, we are unable to craft a bright-line rule that allows a lawsuit to proceed where alleged malpractice causes a will or trust to fail in a manner that casts no real doubt on the testator's intentions, while prohibiting actions in other situations. We believe the greater good is served by preserving a bright-line privity rule which denies a cause of action to all beneficiaries whom the attorney did not represent. This will ensure that attorneys may in all cases zealously represent their clients without the threat of suit from third parties compromising that representation.

We therefore hold that an attorney retained by a testator or settlor to draft a will or trust owes no professional duty of care to persons named as beneficiaries under the will or trust.[14]

D

Plaintiffs also contend that, even if there is no tort duty extending to beneficiaries of an estate plan, they may recover under a third-party-beneficiary contract theory. While the majority of jurisdictions that have recognized a cause of action in favor of will or trust beneficiaries have done so under negligence principles, some have allowed recovery in contract.

In Texas, however, a legal malpractice action sounds in tort and is governed by negligence principles. * * * Even assuming that a client who retains a lawyer to draft an estate plan intends for the lawyer's work to benefit the will or trust beneficiaries, the ultimate question is whether, considering the competing policy implications, the lawyer's professional duty should extend to persons whom the lawyer never represented. For the reasons previously discussed, we conclude that the answer is no.

For the foregoing reasons, we affirm the judgment of the court of appeals.

OWEN, J., did not participate in the decision.

CORNYN, JUSTICE, joined by ABBOTT, JUSTICE, dissenting.

With an obscure reference to "the greater good," * * * the Court unjustifiably insulates an entire class of negligent lawyers from the consequences of their wrongdoing, and unjustly denies legal recourse to the grandchildren for whose benefit Ms. Barcelo hired a lawyer in the first place. I dissent.

By refusing to recognize a lawyer's duty to beneficiaries of a will, the Court embraces a rule recognized in only four states, while simultaneously rejecting the rule in an overwhelming majority of jurisdictions. Notwithstanding the fact that in recent years the Court has sought to align itself with the mainstream of American jurisprudence, the Court inexplicably balks in this case.

The threshold question in a negligence action, including a legal malpractice suit, is duty. * * * Whether a defendant owes a duty to the plaintiff depends on several factors, including risk, foreseeability, and likelihood of injury weighed against the social utility of the actor's

14. We express no opinion as to whether the beneficiary of a trust has standing to sue an attorney representing the trustee for malpractice. Cf. Thompson v. Vinson & Elkins, 859 S.W.2d 617, 621–23 (Tex.App.—Houston [1st Dist.] 1993, writ denied) (holding that beneficiary lacked standing to sue trustee's attorney).

conduct, the magnitude of the burden of guarding against injury, and the consequences of placing the burden on the defendant. * * *

The foreseeability of harm in this case is not open to serious question. Because Ms. Barcelo hired Mr. Elliott to accomplish the transfer of her estate to her grandchildren upon her death, the potential harm to the beneficiaries if the testamentary documents were incorrectly drafted was plainly foreseeable. * * * Foreseeability of harm weighs heavily in favor of recognizing a duty to intended beneficiaries.

Additionally, the Court's decision means that, as a practical matter, no one has the right to sue for the lawyer's negligent frustration of the testator's intent. A flaw in a will or other testamentary document is not likely be discovered until the client's death. And, generally, the estate suffers no harm from a negligently drafted testamentary document. * * * Allowing beneficiaries to sue would provide accountability and thus an incentive for lawyers to use greater care in estate planning. * * * Instead, the Court decides that an innocent party must bear the burden of the lawyer's error. The Court also gives no consideration to the fair adjustment of the loss between the parties, one of the traditional objectives of tort law. * * * These grounds for the imposition of a legal duty in tort law generally, which apply to lawyers in every other context, are no less important in estate planning.

Nor do the reasons the Court gives for refusing to impose a duty under these circumstances withstand scrutiny. Contrary to the Court's view, recognizing an action by the intended beneficiaries would not extend a lawyer's duty to the general public, but only to a limited, foreseeable class. Because estate planning attorneys generally do not face any liability in this context, potential liability to the intended beneficiaries would not place them in a worse position than attorneys in any other setting.

The Court also hypothesizes that liability to estate beneficiaries may conflict with the attorney's duty to the client. Before the beneficiaries could prevail in a suit against the attorney, however, they would necessarily have to show that the attorney breached a duty to the decedent. This is because the lawyer's duty to the client is to see that the client's intentions are realized by the very documents the client has hired the lawyer to draft. No conflicting duty to the beneficiaries is imposed.

Searching for other hypothetical problems that might arise if a cause of action for the beneficiaries is recognized, the Court observes that a will not executed at the testator's death could in fact express the testator's true intentions. * * * Granted, such a scenario may be the result of either the testator's indecision or the attorney's negligence. Similarly, a family member might be intentionally omitted from a will at the testator's direction, or negligently omitted because of the drafting lawyer's mistake. In other words, what appears to be attorney negligence may actually reflect the testator's wishes.

But surely these are matters subject to proof, as in all other cases. Nothing distinguishes this class of cases from many others in this respect.

The Court fails to consider that the beneficiaries will in each case bear the burden of establishing that the attorney breached a duty to the testator, which resulted in damages to the beneficiaries. Lawyers, wishing to protect themselves from liability, may document the testator's intentions.

In addition, Elliott suggests that allowing beneficiaries to sue the testator's attorney would interfere with the attorney-client privilege, by either encouraging attorneys to violate clients' confidences or by hindering attorneys' ability to defend their actions. This concern, too, is unfounded. Under Texas law, the attorney-client privilege does not survive the testator. * * * This is because the lawyer-client privilege applies only to confidential communications, which are "not intended to be disclosed to third persons." Tex.R.Civ.Evid. 503(a)(5). And, as Professor Wigmore has explained, "[a]s to the tenor and execution of the will, it seems hardly open to dispute that they are the very facts which the testator expected and intended to be disclosed after his death." Wigmore § 2314, at 613 (emphasis in original).

In sum, I would hold that the intended beneficiary of a will or testamentary trust may bring a cause of action against an attorney whose negligence caused the beneficiary to lose a legacy in whole or in part. Accordingly, I would reverse the judgment of the court of appeals and remand this case to the trial court.

SPECTOR, JUSTICE, dissenting.

The issue in this case is whether the attorney, David Elliott, owed a duty to Frances Barcelo's intended beneficiaries. The majority holds that he did not. The other dissenting justices would recognize a broad cause of action in favor of any person claiming to be an intended beneficiary, regardless of whether the plaintiff is identified in the will or trust instrument. Because I would recognize only a limited cause of action for the intended beneficiaries of wills and trusts, I write separately to dissent.

At common law, an attorney owes no duty to third parties who may have been damaged by the attorney's negligent representation of the attorney's client. * * * As the majority notes, although Texas courts of appeals have consistently accepted this restriction in the estate planning context, most other states addressing this issue have lowered the privity barrier in this area. * * *

I believe that recognizing such a cause of action would further public policy by requiring attorneys to exercise due care in implementing a testator's estate plan. Under current law, only the attorney's client has standing to sue for negligent preparation of the will or trust. Although the testator's personal representative would succeed to this cause of action upon the testator's death, the estate itself may suffer no damage from an invalid will or trust that frustrates the testator's intentions. * * * Consequently, an attorney who negligently drafts a will or trust that is discovered to be invalid after the testator's death is accountable to no one.

I would not go so far as to hold that attorneys who draft wills and trusts have a duty to persons who are not beneficiaries named in the will or trust. Recognizing such a broad cause of action is as likely to frustrate the testator's intent as it is to carry it out. I would, however, allow beneficiaries who are specifically identified on the face of an invalid will or trust to assert a claim.

Recognizing a limited cause of action would subject attorneys who prepare wills and trusts documents to the same standard of care governing attorneys generally. Because I believe that this is sound public policy, I dissent.

NOTES AND QUESTIONS

1. When a personal representative brings an action against the drafting attorney for malpractice, however, the privity shield is of no defensive value because the client was in privity with the attorney and the personal representative is merely stepping into the client's position. A leading case demonstrating this principle is *Belt v. Oppenheimer, Blend, Harrison & Tate, Inc.*, 192 S.W.3d 780 (Tex. 2006), in which the executors sued the attorneys who prepared the testator's will asserting that the attorneys provided negligent advice and drafting services. The executors believed that the testator's estate incurred over $1.5 million in unnecessary federal estate taxes because of the malpractice. The briefs reveal that the main problem was that the testator did not form a family limited partnership or take other steps which could have led to a lowering of the estate's value.

Both the trial and appellate courts agreed that the executors had no standing to pursue the claim because of lack of privity. *Belt v. Oppenheimer, Blend, Harrison & Tate, Inc.*, 141 S.W.3d 706 (Tex. App.—San Antonio 2004). The appellate court explained that privity was mandated by *Barcelo* and thus the court had no choice but to affirm the trial court's grant of a summary judgment in favor of the attorneys.

The Supreme Court of Texas reversed and held that "there is no legal bar preventing an estate's personal representative from maintaining a legal malpractice claim on behalf of the estate against the decedent's estate planners." The court did not express an opinion as to whether the attorneys' conduct actually amounted to malpractice.

2. Which approach to privity do you think would be preferred by each of the following individuals and why?

a. Potential client.

b. Testator.

c. Intended beneficiary.

d. Attorney who prepared the estate plan.

e. You.

3. To avoid the privity bar, creative intended beneficiaries may seek other remedies against the negligent attorney. For example, some states do not require privity for a person to sue under deceptive trade practices acts,

e.g., the attorney represented to the testator that the will had a characteristic (i.e., validity) which it actually did not.

4. According to one study, estate planning and probate is the third most popular legal field in which malpractice claims are made. See Stephanie B. Casteel, Letitia A. McDonald, Jennifer D. Odom, Nicole J. Wade, *The Modern Estate Planning Lawyer: Avoiding the Maelstrom of Malpractice Claims,* PROB. & PROP., Dec. 2008, at 46 (noting most malpractice claims in estate planning fall under the tort of negligence and include behavior such as "error in execution, failure to adhere to testator's goals..., error of law, failure to update the estate plan with new laws or facts, failure to investigate heirs and assets..."). Further, estate planning malpractice claims often fall under the following general areas: (1) undue influence alleged by a disinherited family member; (2) scope of retainer issues in failing to adequately represent a client's intentions; (3) proofreading errors leading to contradictory terms as well as failure to supervise non-lawyers in drafting estate documents; and (4) pressure from beneficiaries to wind up the estate quickly. See Thomas J. Watson, *Estate Planning Work—Not for the Timid*, WIS. LAW., Dec. 2011, at 30.

5. Attorney drafted Client's will but Client died without executing the will. A disappointed beneficiary of the unexecuted will sued Attorney for malpractice. What result is appropriate in a state which has removed the privity bar? See Radovich v. Locke–Paddon, 35 Cal.App.4th 946, 41 Cal. Rptr.2d 573 (1995).

6. Studies performed in California and Illinois have shown that approximately 20% of attorneys forego attorney malpractice insurance. See Ed Poll, *A Bigger Burden: Mandatory Malpractice Insurance Disclosure: Who Benefits?,* 25 No. 7 Legal Mgmt. 24 (Nov./Dec. 2006). Further, one study determined that 40% of solo practitioners do not hold malpractice insurance compared to the overall 20% of uninsured attorneys. Id. Similarly, the State Bar of Texas found that approximately 36.2% of attorneys do not carry malpractice insurance. See Jeffrey D. Watters, *What They Don't Know Can Hurt Them: Why Clients Should Know if Their Attorney Does Not Carry Malpractice Insurance,* 62 Baylor L. Rev. 245 (2010). In 2003, approximately 10% of malpractice claims involved estate, trust, and probate work, which demonstrates the likely need for estate planning attorneys to carry malpractice insurance. See *Legal-Malpractice-Lawyers-Attorneys.com*, Legal Malpractice Statistics (2002–2004).

7. One out of ten legal malpractice claims is caused by the attorney's failure to know the law or apply it properly. Anne E. Thar, *Do You Know Your Limits?*, 86 ILL. B.J. 227 (1998) (noting that most claims are made against attorneys who have been practicing for over ten years).

8. Regular use of engagement letters is one of the best protections against malpractice claims. See Anne E. Thar, *Engagement Letters Can Reduce Malpractice Claims*, 84 ILL. B. J. 99 (Feb. 1996). See Chapter 8(D)(8).

9. For additional information, see Martin D. Begleiter, *The Gambler Breaks Even: Legal Malpractice in Complicated Estate Planning Cases*, 20 GA. ST. UNIV. L. REV. 277 (2003) (arguing that a beneficiary should be required to present written evidence such as letters, unexecuted wills, or notes from the testator's attorney to prove that the will did not accomplish the testator's objectives); Martin D. Begleiter, *Attorney Malpractice in Estate Planning—*

You've Got to Know When to Hold Up, Know When to Fold Up, 38 U. KAN. L. REV. 193 (1990); Bradley E.S. Fogel, *Attorney v. Client—Privity, Malpractice, and the Lack of Respect for the Primacy of the Attorney–Client Relationship in Estate Planning,* 68 TENN. L. REV. 261 (2001); Anne E. Thar, *Nightmare on Main Street: Estate Planning and Probate Pitfalls,* 85 ILL. B.J. 497 (1997).

LOCATE

Is privity required under the law of your state? Will the answer to this question affect how you conduct your estate planning practice? Your malpractice premiums?

K. ROLE OF LEGAL ASSISTANTS

GERRY W. BEYER & KERRI M. GRIFFIN, THE ROLE OF LEGAL ASSISTANTS IN THE ESTATE PLANNING PRACTICE

EST. PLAN. DEVEL. FOR TEX. PROF., Jan. 2012, at 1, 1–4.

A. INTRODUCTION

The employment of legal assistants, paralegals, and similar personnel by the legal community has rapidly gained momentum since the 1960s. The legal community promptly recognized the benefits of paralegals and began to define and organize the emerging profession. * * * The paralegal profession was first defined in 1986 when the American Bar Association adopted the definition of the term "legal assistant," and the legal community began to use the term interchangeably with "paralegal" soon thereafter. * * * In 2005, the State Bar of Texas Board of Directors, the Paralegal Division of the State Bar of Texas, and the State Bar of Texas Standing Committee on Paralegals adopted a new definition for the term "paralegal":

> A paralegal is a person, qualified through various combinations of education, training, or work experience, who is employed or engaged by a lawyer, law office, governmental agency, or other entity in a capacity or function which involves the performance, under the ultimate direction and supervision of a licensed attorney, of specifically delegated substantive legal work, which work, for the most part, requires a sufficient knowledge of legal principles and procedures that, absent such person, an attorney would be required to perform the task.

* * * The explosion of the profession of paralegals is a result of attorneys in general, as well as those who specialize in estate planning, realizing the tremendous cost effectiveness and efficiency that may result from the prudent use of legal assistants. Despite the valuable services which may be rendered by legal assistants, however, attorneys must exercise caution in their employment, supervision, and education.

B. REASONS TO USE PARALEGALS IN THE ESTATE PLANNING PROCESS

The use of a paralegal allows an estate planning attorney to provide economical services, increase efficiency, improve the quality of the work product, provide the client with an additional contact person, and promote good client relations and retention.

1. Provide Economical Services

Many of the tasks in the estate planning process are time-consuming and tedious, e.g., proofreading lengthy documents; gathering family, financial, and other information; obtaining copies of important documents from courthouses, insurance companies, and other sources; making telephone calls and spending considerable time on "ignore," etc. In *Missouri v. Jenkins*, 491 U.S. 274, 288 n.10 (1989), the United States Supreme Court noted that the lower courts frequently recognize that "paralegals are capable of carrying out many tasks, under the supervision of an attorney, that might otherwise be performed by a lawyer and billed at a higher rate." A legal assistant can competently complete these tasks and thus permit the attorney to charge less for estate planning services because the hourly rate of a legal assistant is considerably less than that of an attorney. Beltrán at 1.

2. Increase Efficiency of Attorney

The delegation of time-consuming tasks to legal assistants may directly result in an increase in the attorney's efficiency. Estate plans may be prepared in a more timely fashion much to the delight of the client. As a result, the attorney will have more time to devote to complex issues or in obtaining new clients. Ultimately, this may lead to a more profitable practice.

3. Improve Quality of Work Product

A knowledgeable and thorough legal assistant may also improve the quality of an attorney's work product. Instead of having only the attorney reviewing an estate plan, there are now two trained individuals with a working knowledge of the facts and the law overseeing the project. Accordingly, errors, both major and minor, are more likely to be detected. In addition, the attorney may concentrate on difficult aspects of the estate plan because the legal assistant has relieved the attorney of many routine tasks.

4. Provide Client With Additional Contact Person

A legal assistant may be more accessible to the client than the lawyer. If the client understands that the legal assistant's time is billed at a lower rate than the lawyer's time, the client may call the legal assistant directly. If the legal assistant can answer the client's questions without rendering legal advice, the legal assistant should be able to handle the call. If the lawyer is unavailable when the client wishes to speak to him, the call can be directed to the legal assistant. A client often feels more comfortable leaving a message with someone who knows the facts of his or her case.

5. Promote Good Client Relations and Retention

In today's fast-paced legal environment, it is common for an estate planner to have very little contact with the client. After the initial interview, the lawyer and the client may communicate only via e-mail or telephone and not meet again until the execution ceremony. Under these circumstances, it is difficult for a lawyer to maintain a relationship with each client. A legal assistant may form a relationship with these clients by spending time speaking with the client throughout the drafting process and focusing on the "small talk." The legal assistant can keep the attorney abreast of the major events in the client's life. A legal assistant may also help the attorney retain clients by keeping in touch with the client after the legal relationship has ended, for example, by sending birthday or holiday cards each year. * * *

C. IMPROPER USE OF LEGAL ASSISTANTS

1. Appearing in Court on Behalf of a Client

Section 81.101 of the Texas Government Code includes in its definition of "practice of law" the "preparation of a pleading or other document incident to an action or special proceeding or the management of the action or proceeding on behalf of a client before a judge in court." Thus, a paralegal who works for an estate planning attorney may not appear in court to probate a will, conduct an heirship proceeding, or raise any objections to the administration of an estate. A paralegal also cannot sign pleadings, motions, or other formal documents.

2. Giving Legal Advice to Clients

Section 81.101 of the Texas Government Code further defines the "practice of law" to include "the giving of advice or the rendering of any service requiring the use of legal skill or knowledge." A legal assistant may have frequent contact with the client, especially in gathering the facts, documents, and other materials necessary to prepare the estate plan. The legal assistant needs to be aware of how easy it is to cross the line between mere conversation to the giving of legal advice. For example, a client may ask what would happen if various contingencies were to occur (e.g., a child being born or predeceasing, a divorce or marriage, or a specific gift not being in the estate.). The fact that the legal assistant has acquired a specialized area of competence and knows the answer does not warrant the legal assistant to engage in the business of offering legal advice based on his or her knowledge of the subject. *See In re Roel*, 144 N.E.2d 24, 28 (N.Y. 1957). The legal assistant must be instructed not to answer any of these types of questions, and the attorney has a duty to ensure that the legal assistant does not give legal advice to the client during the estate planning process or at any other time.

3. Supervising the Will Execution Ceremony

In *Palmer v. Unauthorized Practice Comm. of State Bar of Tex.*, 438 S.W.2d 374 (Tex. Civ. App.—Houston [14th Dist.] 1969, no writ), the court was confronted with an individual who was offering for sale to the general public will forms containing blanks to be filled in by the non-attorney user. In holding that such conduct constituted the unlicensed practice of law, the court stated that "supervising the execution of wills is [the] practice of law" and that such "duties cannot be performed by an unlicensed person, not an attorney." Cases in other jurisdictions have reached a similar result. In *In re Flynn's Estate,* 253 N.Y.S. 638, 639 (N.Y. Sur.1931), the New York Surrogate's Court condemned the supervision of a will execution ceremony by a notary public and denied probate of the will because the execution ceremony lacked substantial compliance with statutory requirements.

In addition to amounting to the unauthorized practice of law, the supervision of the will execution ceremony needs to be performed by the attorney to prevent future litigation surrounding the will. A New York ethical opinion stated that the will execution ceremony was "tantamount to counseling a client about law matters and [therewith] permitting a paralegal to engage in the practice of law. Not only is strict compliance with a statute required, but the presence of the attorney provides added assurance that the Will was properly executed by a competent testator." Opinion No. 343, 46 N.Y. St. B.J. 462 (1974). The requirements for a valid will include many elements which cannot be detected from a mere examination of the executed documents, e.g., the testator's capacity and formalities such as the witnesses attesting in the testator's presence. Attorneys are more likely to know these will execution requirements, so there is an inference that if an attorney supervised the execution, the execution was made in accordance with statutory requirements, and future will contests are less likely. C. Raymond Radigan & Frank J. Gobes, *Additional Means to Avoid Contested Probate*, N.Y. L.J., July 29, 2005.

Although allowing a legal assistant to conduct the will execution ceremony amounts to the unauthorized practice of law and could potentially lead to future litigation, a legal assistant may nonetheless participate in and assist the attorney during the will execution ceremony. The legal assistant can help make certain all formalities are satisfied. If the legal assistant is also a notary, he or she can notarize the self-proving affidavit.

4. Making Discretionary Decisions

The attorney may not delegate discretionary decisions to the legal assistant. Assembling an estate plan requires an understanding of trusts, fiduciary duties and powers, legal and equitable estates, taxation laws, business entity succession, and many other complex concepts. The decisions regarding which estate planning tools should be utilized in a particular client's situation necessarily involves the practice of law and can only be performed by licensed attorneys. See *Fadia v. Unauthorized Practice of Law Comm.*, 830 S.W.2d 162, 164 (Tex. App.—Dallas 1992, writ denied).

The legal assistant's role is to provide help with time-consuming tasks that are necessary in many aspects of the estate planning process. However, discretionary decisions, such as the type of marital deduction provision to include in a will, must be made by the attorney. Although the legal assistant may make suggestions, the attorney needs to be the final arbiter of such decisions.

5. Accepting or Rejecting Clients; Setting Fees for Legal Services

Independent of the lawyer's instruction, a legal assistant may not engage, accept, or reject a client, or set the fee for the legal services to be performed. Beltrán at 2. Fee setting is a core function of a lawyer, and legal assistants would be engaging in the unauthorized practice of law if they did it. Even if the attorney typically charges one amount for the drafting of a will, the attorney should review each case and personally discuss the fees with the client. Each client is different, and the time expended on each project will vary. The decision whether to engage in the attorney-client relationship, as well as the determination of fees, may only be made by the attorney.

6. Negotiating Settlement Agreements

A paralegal is prohibited from negotiating settlement agreements. Texas Paralegal Standards, § C(2). The client is entitled to an attorney's judgment regarding the sufficiency of offers and counter-offers. *See* Frequently Asked Questions, State Bar of Texas Paralegal Division. Thus, if an attorney is working with battling beneficiaries of an estate or trust, the paralegal may not step in and negotiate a settlement agreement among the beneficiaries. Only the attorney may perform this task.

D. PROPER USE OF LEGAL ASSISTANTS

This section reviews some of the tasks for which legal assistants are best suited. This discussion is not intended to provide an exclusive list but rather to demonstrate the wide range of responsibilities which a legal assistant may assume.

1. Gather Information

It is nearly impossible for the attorney to acquire all necessary information at an initial client interview. Kay Redburn, *The Ethical and Effective Use of Paralegals in the Practice of Law* 1, 7, State Bar of Texas (December 5, 2007) [hereinafter Redburn]. The development of facts and client history will continue throughout the duration of each individual case. One of the chief functions of a legal assistant is to gather and organize the information that the attorney needs to prepare estate plans and administer estates. If the attorney explains to the client that dealing with the paralegal will be faster and more economical, the client will work with the paralegal willingly. The legal assistant can obtain information from the client through interviews, telephone calls, faxes, letters, or e-mails. Likewise, the legal assistant can track down important data and documents from other sources such as family members, courthouses, insurance companies, financial advisors, and banks. The attorney should periodically review the information the paralegal acquired and note any gaps that need to be filled in with additional information.

2. File Organization

The paralegal may be given control over the organization of files. Correspondence, document production, exhibits, and everything else related to a particular client should pass through the paralegal so that at least one person in the office can locate every item in a particular file. To keep the attorney abreast of new facts and developments, the paralegal should draft a memo to the file to record the substance of each client interaction. Redburn at 8.

3. Draft and Proofread Documents

Another primary function of a legal assistant is to draft and proofread documents. The legal assistant may prepare initial drafts of many types of documents, such as client letters, wills, trusts, tax returns, and pleadings. If the attorney has an established set of forms and accompanying instructions, the legal assistant can prepare documents for the attorney's review that are practically in final form. Prior to the execution of any document, the legal assistant's careful proofreading is likely to detect mistakes, both typographical and substantive, which have not yet been noticed.

4. Legal Research

A properly trained legal assistant will be able to perform legal research. The legal assistant can locate relevant cases, statutes, and rulings and IRS forms using the internet and legal databases to which the attorney subscribes such as the State Bar of Texas online CLE library, Casemaker, BNA, RIA Checkpoint, Westlaw, and Lexis Nexis. The legal assistant may also perform traditional research at the local law school or county law library.

E. RECOMMENDATIONS

To maximize the benefits of the services provided by legal assistants, the attorney must give consideration to the role they are to play in the estate planning process. Obviously, the legal assistant needs to avoid the conduct previously discussed in this article. In addition, the attorney should take the following steps to obtain further protection from claims of improperly using the services of legal assistants.

1. Select Legal Assistants With Care

Selecting the individual to work as a legal assistant is not a decision to be made quickly, casually, or without careful deliberation. An attorney should begin by considering the desired education, experience, personality, and work characteristics of the paralegal. Some key skills for paralegals include meticulous attention to detail, excellent written and oral communications, organization, an even disposition in dealing with difficult clients, and the ability to assess a situation and summarize key concepts for the attorney. Beltrán at 1. Attorneys should be careful not to limit their options based on certain qualifications. For example, there are highly qualified paralegals who have only received on-the-job training rather than a paralegal education who would be excellent additions to a law practice. Redburn at 9.

In addition, the legal assistant should be someone who will display loyalty to the attorney and the law firm. Six months or more will usually be needed to familiarize a new legal assistant with an attorney's practice and to learn the basics of estate planning and probate. If this newly trained person were to quit and go work for another firm, re-locate, return to school, etc., a tremendous investment of time, effort, and money would be lost.

It is also important for attorneys to consider conflicts of interest when selecting paralegals. In *Phoenix Founders, Inc. v. Marshall*, 887 S.W.2d 831 (Tex. 1994), the Texas Supreme Court addressed standards with regard to disqualifying paralegals from working on a particular case. The court determined that there is a conclusive presumption that a paralegal obtained confidential information while working on the case at the first firm and a rebuttable presumption that the paralegal shared confidential information with the new firm. If an attorney wants to hire a paralegal who has previously worked at another estate planning firm, the attorney needs to determine if there are any conflicts. If there are, the attorney must ensure the paralegal does no work in connection with matters on which the paralegal previously worked. Beltrán at 3.

Finally, if the legal assistant is inept, the employment should be terminated; incompetent legal assistants can cause more problems than they solve, including dissatisfied clients who may bring legal action against the attorney.

2. Consider Hiring Board Certified Paralegal

Since 1994, the Texas Board of Legal Specialization has administered a voluntary certification program for paralegals through which they can become Board Certified Paralegals in a specialty area of law. Kline at 2. To become Board Certified in a specialty area, a paralegal must: (1) have five years of paralegal experience (three years in Texas); (2) currently work under the supervision of a licensed attorney practicing in Texas; (3) concentrate at least 50% of paralegal duties in the specialty area; (4) attend continuing education seminars regularly; (5) successfully complete one of several educational programs; (6) have been evaluated by judges, lawyers, and other professionals associated with the specialty area; and (7) pass a four-hour written exam. The Texas Board of Legal Specialization currently certifies paralegals in six specialty areas of law, including one for Estate Planning and Probate Law. Of the over 300 board certified paralegals in Texas, less than 20 are certified in Estate Planning and Probate Law. Board certified paralegals are extremely rare, but attorneys can locate them on the Texas Board of Legal Specialization's website on the "Search" page.

There are also national certification options for paralegals, including becoming a Certified Legal Assistant (CLA) or a Certified Paralegal (CP) through the National Association of Legal Assistants or becoming a PACE

Registered Paralegal by taking the Paralegal Advanced Competency Exam through the National Federation of Paralegal Associations.

3. Comprehensive Instruction

It is essential that the legal assistant receive comprehensive instruction before working on any case. The legal assistant must have a firm grasp of the basics of estate planning and the type of duties which he or she will be performing. The attorney should, as much as possible, teach the legal assistant the proverbial ropes so that the legal assistant does not flounder on his or her first assignments. It will often be helpful for the legal assistant to read articles and books relating to estate planning (especially, at first, those written for non-legally trained persons), to enroll in appropriate courses at local colleges or paralegal schools, and to attend relevant seminars. A.B.A. Special Comm. on Legal Assistants, *New Careers in Law II* 45–72 (1972).

In addition, it is equally or even more important for the instruction to include comprehensive coverage of the rules set forth in the Texas Disciplinary Rules of Professional Conduct. The attorney should attempt to instill in the legal assistant a strong sense of responsibility to the client, the law firm, and the legal profession. For example, the legal assistant must fully comprehend the extreme importance of keeping all client matters confidential. The legal assistant needs to realize that estate planning often requires the client to reveal personal or embarrassing information (e.g., financial status, health conditions, marital discord, and children born out of wedlock) and that this information, which would make good material for gossip with co-workers, families, and friends, must be kept in the strictest confidence. Additionally, even the fact of representation, unless it is a matter of public record, must also be kept confidential.

As discussed * * * above, the legal assistant must also understand which actions constitute giving legal advice and be firmly warned to avoid any conduct which may be interpreted as the unlicensed practice of law.

4. Careful Supervision

Perhaps the most important recommendation is to monitor constantly the conduct and work product of the legal assistant. Not only will this better protect the client's interests, but it will protect the attorney as the attorney is ultimately responsible for all acts of the legal assistant. In a busy practice, an attorney may become lax and fail to review periodically the legal assistant's work. The attorney must carefully guard against relinquishing control of the client's case to the legal assistant.

The attorney should not be reluctant to offer constructive criticism of the legal assistant's work. Only through an honest evaluation of their performance will legal assistants be able to improve their work so it will conform to the required standards. Conversely, the attorney should have realistic expectations of what legal assistants can do; attorneys must remember that their assistants do not have law school educations.

5. Inform Client of Legal Assistant's Status

"An attorney should instruct the legal assistant to disclose at the commencement of communications with any other entity that he or she is not an attorney." *General Guidelines for the Utilization of the Services of Legal Assistants by Attorneys*, Commentary to Guideline IV, Board of Directors of State Bar of Texas (May 1993). Early disclosure of the paralegal's status is necessary to prevent misunderstandings regarding the responsibilities and the role the paralegal will play in the estate planning process. If at any time the paralegal or the attorney becomes aware that the client mistakenly believes the paralegal is an attorney, it should be made clear that the paralegal is not an attorney.

LOCATE

1. What duties may a paralegal perform in your state to help an attorney provide estate planning services?
2. Does your state license or certify paralegals?

QUESTIONS

1. How would you use a legal assistant in your estate planning practice?
2. Do you think state legislatures should expand the role of paralegals in estate planning to reduce cost and thus make estate planning available to a greater segment of the population?

L. SELF-HELP TECHNIQUES USED BY NON-ATTORNEYS

A solid understanding of self-help techniques is vital to all estate planners because many clients will be familiar with these alternatives and may have already used them. For you to evaluate the wisdom of the client's use of these techniques and to give knowledgeable advice, you need to know why the client chose a particular technique and its potential benefits and dangers. In addition, you may wish to study some of the available descriptive material so you can make specific recommendations to clients who would like to do background reading. Clients may be able to play a more active part in the estate planning process if they have done some reading prior to coming to your office.

Entrepreneurs, desiring to profit from the public's need for estate planning and recognizing the public's reluctance to incur legal fees to obtain it, have authored a variety of self-help publications targeted at the non-attorney audience. These products are sold by aggressive marketing strategies designed to increase the likelihood that people from different social and economic levels will be exposed to the alleged virtues of the particular package being offered. Some self-help products are sold in typical shopping mall bookstores next to other popular legal books, while others are advertised through slick commercials on late-night television, complete with toll-free telephone numbers for ordering with major credit cards. Orders for some estate planning kits are solicited through bulk-mail letters which extol the evils of probate with language such as, "All across the nation, greedy lawyers in league with conniving judges and bureaucrats plunder huge chunks—and sometimes all—of an estate." Letter LPK–3 from Homestead Publishing Company to Friend (undated), at 1. Still other self-help estate planning tools are sold with a high-tech approach; they are marketed as computer software programs that enable a minimally computer literate person to obtain a will by simply answering questions in response to questions generated by the software. Wills and other estate planning documents may also be created by using interactive websites such as http://www.legalzoom.com/wills.

State legislatures have entered the self-help arena. In recent years, several fill-in-the-blank forms have been included in estate planning legislation. Some of these forms were drafted primarily for attorney use while others include instructions and warnings so they can be readily completed by non-attorneys.

1. FILL-IN-THE-BLANK FORMS

The most primitive self-help drafting technique is the fill-in-the-blank form. The user need only purchase the form, usually for a nominal price, and insert the appropriate information in the blanks. These forms often cannot be customized to the user's specific situation and carry a high risk of improper completion and execution.

a. Commercially Prepared

Many companies publish fill-in-the-blank forms for wills, inter vivos trusts, living wills, durable powers of attorney, and other estate planning documents. These forms are sold at a variety of locations, especially office supply stores and bookstores. The purchaser may be able to buy a single form but often will need to buy a package containing many copies of the same form. Some of the forms will be drafted with local state law in mind while others are generic, often containing a guarantee that they are valid in all states. *See generally* Cameron Harvey, *Stationers' Will Forms: Re Philip and Other Cases,* 10 MANITOBA L.J. 481 (1980) (discussing problems with improperly completed commercial will forms).

b. Legislatively Enacted

State statutes may provide forms for a variety of estate planning documents including wills, self-proving affidavits, durable powers of attorney (property management and health care), guardian self-designations, living wills, anatomical gifts, and disposition of remains. See Chapter 11(C)(1)(e).

2. KITS

Rather than selling just forms, many businesses have elected to market kits—packages containing instruction manuals along with the forms. These kits range in quality from those that provide only a brief and often inaccurate explanation of the law to those supplying fairly sophisticated and accurate guidance. Some of the kits also include worksheets, envelopes for document storage, checklists, and other informal estate related forms such as a listing of where important documents are located or who should be notified upon death. Kits are available for a wide range of documents such as wills, inter vivos trusts, durable powers of attorney for property management and health care, and living wills. Kits are usually priced between $10 and $50.

Businesses promote kit sales using a variety of marketing techniques. Kits may often be found in the popular law section of bookstores and in office supply stores. Radio and television advertisements are extensively used by some kit manufacturers. This technique usually stresses the benefits of a kit over going to an attorney, rather than claiming one kit is better than another. The listener or viewer is urged to make a telephone call, usually toll-free, to place an order. Other manufacturers promote their kits via direct mail solicitation. In addition, other vendors place ads in newspapers to solicit orders.

3. ARTICLES

The popular media frequently reports on self-help estate planning methods. Be it an item in a newspaper advice column, an attorney's advertisement, a review in a computer magazine, or an article in a news magazine, people are subjected to a wide variety of opinions on self-help techniques. All of this information will influence how an individual views estate planning and what steps are finally taken, especially if the article recommends or criticizes self-help techniques.

4. PAMPHLETS

Various organizations prepare and distribute pamphlets relating to estate planning. These booklets are widely distributed and are usually free.

a. Bar Associations

Pamphlets prepared by legal associations typically explain the benefits of estate planning, the problems that can arise if proper planning does not take place, and the wisdom of seeking legal assistance. These materials do not usually contain forms. The Real Property, Probate and Trust Law Section of the American Bar Association publishes six client-friendly brochures: *Estate Planning: Getting Started—Wills and Other Techniques; Revocable Living Trusts; You Are the Fiduciary: A Handbook for Individu-*

als Named as Executor or Trustee; *Planning with Retirement Benefits: General Information for Plan Participants*; *Power of Attorney*; and *Living Wills, Health Care Proxies, and Advance Health Care Directives*.

b. Estate Planning Businesses

Businesses that specialize in estate planning matters, such as trust companies, bank trust departments, and financial planning firms, also produce pamphlets to encourage readers to plan their estates and to seriously consider allowing the distributing business to play a part in the planning process. Many of these recommend that an attorney be consulted as well.

c. Other Organizations

Non-profit or special interest organizations may also supply estate planning information and forms to its members or the public as part of their normal activities.

5. BOOKS

The law sections of most bookstores are brimming with self-help legal books, especially books focusing on estate planning. Some of the books are authored by attorneys or even bar associations while others reflect the author's personal disgust with the legal profession. *Compare* AMERICAN BAR ASSOCIATION, GUIDE TO WILLS & ESTATES (1995) *with* NORMAN DACEY, HOW TO AVOID PROBATE II (1983) (anti-legal profession tone). Prices for these books typically range from $10 to $35.

The number of generic self-help estate planning books appears to grow with each visit the author makes to the bookstore. These books range in size from paperbacks of less than 100 pages to hardcover books reminiscent of college textbooks. The quality of these books ranges from the dangerous to the very helpful. You should visit local bookstores and evaluate the books that are available. This will be especially helpful if your client is interested in doing some independent reading.

6. COMPUTER PROGRAMS

Computer software and on-line (Internet) programs are rapidly becoming the most popular of the self-help document drafting techniques. Although the programs vary significantly in features and quality, they all operate in basically the same way. The program asks the user a series of questions and based on the user's answers, the program fills in blanks in boilerplate text and prints out the resulting document. More sophisticated programs ask the user a greater number of questions, plan for additional contingencies, prepare different types of estate planning documents, and provide greater opportunity for individualization. The programs typically range in cost from $10 to $100 and can be found on-line and practically anywhere computer programs are sold.

Several of these programs were reviewed in *Write Your Own Will?* which appeared in the July 2011 issue of the Consumer Reports Money Advisor newsletter. The report concluded, "All three are better than nothing if you have no will. But unless your needs are very simple-say, you want to leave everything to your spouse with no other provisions, none of them is likely to meet your needs." The types of problems included (1) outdated information, (2) insufficient customization, (3) too little flexibility, (4) too much flexibility, (5) incompleteness, and (6) no way to handle some tax issues.

UNAUTHORIZED PRACTICE OF LAW COMMITTEE v. PARSONS TECHNOLOGY, INC. D/B/A QUICKEN FAMILY LAWYER.

United States District Court, Northern District of Texas, 1999.
1999 WL 47235.

SANDERS, SENIOR J.

* * * Having considered the motions, briefs, and arguments of both parties, and for the reasons set forth below, the Court concludes that there are no genuine issues of material fact and that Plaintiff Unauthorized Practice of Law Committee is entitled to judgment as a matter of law. Therefore, Plaintiff's Motion for Summary Judgment is granted and Defendant's Motion for Summary Judgment is denied.

I. BACKGROUND

The Plaintiff, the Unauthorized Practice of Law Committee ("the UPLC"), is comprised of six Texas lawyers and three lay citizens appointed by the Supreme Court of Texas. The UPLC is responsible for enforcing Texas' unauthorized practice of law statute, Tex. Gov't Code §§ 81.101–.106 (Vernon's 1998) ("the Statute").[15]

The Defendant, Parsons Technology, Inc., ("Parsons") is a California corporation, whose principal place of business is Iowa, and is engaged in the business of developing, publishing and marketing software products, such as Quicken Financial Software, Turbo Tax, and Webster's Talking Dictionary. Parsons has published and offered for sale through retailers in Texas a computer software program entitled Quicken Family Lawyer, version 8.0, and its updated version Quicken Family Lawyer '99 ("QFL").[16]

---

15. Tex. Gov't Code § 81.101 defines the practice of law, as follows:

(a) In this chapter the "practice of law" means the preparation of a pleading or other document incident to an action or special proceeding or the management of the action or proceeding on behalf of a client before a judge in court as well as a service rendered out of court, including the giving of advice or the rendering of any service requiring the use of legal skill or knowledge, such as preparing a will, contract, or other instrument, the legal effect of which under the facts and conclusions involved must be carefully determined.

(b) The definition in this section is not exclusive and does not deprive the judicial branch of the power and authority under both this chapter and the adjudicated cases to determine whether other services and acts not enumerated may constitute the practice of law.

16. * * * QFL is the product at the center of this controversy. In its most recent version, QFL offers over 100 different legal forms (such as employment agreements, real estate leases,

The first time a user accesses QFL after installing it on her computer the following disclaimer appears as the initial screen:

> This program provides forms and information about the law. We cannot and do not provide specific information for your exact situation.
>
> For example, we can provide a form for a lease, along with information on state law and issues frequently addressed in leases. But we cannot decide that our program's lease is appropriate for you.
>
> Because we cannot decide which forms are best for your individual situation, you must use your own judgment and, to the extent you believe appropriate, the assistance of a lawyer.

This disclaimer does not appear anywhere on QFL's packaging. Additionally, it does not appear on subsequent uses of the program unless the user actively accesses the "Help" pull-down menu at the top of the screen and then selects "Disclaimer."

On the initial use of QFL, or anytime a new user name is created, QFL asks for the user's name and state of residence. It then inquires whether the user would like QFL to suggest documents to the user. If the user answers "Yes," QFL's "Document Advisor" asks the user a few short questions concerning the user's marital status, number of children, and familiarity with living trusts. QFL then displays the entire list of available documents, but marks a few of them as especially appropriate for the user based on her responses.

When the user accesses a document, QFL asks a series of questions relevant to filling in the legal form. With certain questions, a separate text box explaining the relevant legal considerations the user may want to take into account in filling out the form also appears on the screen. As the user proceeds through the questions relevant to the specific form, QFL either fills in the appropriate blanks or adds or deletes entire clauses from the form. For example, in the "Real Estate Lease—Residential" form, depending on how the user answers the question regarding subleasing the apartment, a clause permitting subleasing with the consent of the landlord is either included or excluded from the form.

If a user selects a "health care document" (i.e., a living will, an advance health care directive, or a health care power of attorney) the following screen appears:

> Health Care laws vary from state to state. Your state may not offer every type of health care document.

---

premarital agreements, and seven different will forms) along with instructions on how to fill out these forms. QFL's packaging represents that the product is "valid in 49 states including the District of Columbia;" is "developed and reviewed by expert attorneys;" and is "updated to reflect recent legislative formats." * * * The packaging also indicates that QFL will have the user "answer a few questions to determine which estate planning and health care documents best meet [the user's] needs;" * * *, and that QFL will "interview you in a logical order, tailoring documents to your situation." * * * Finally, the packaging reassures the user that "[h]andy hints and comprehensive legal help topics are always available." * * *

> Family Lawyer assumes that you wish to have a health care document based on the laws of your state.
>
> When you select a living will, health care power of attorney, or advance health care directive, Family Lawyer will open the appropriate document based on your state.

When a Texas user selects a health care document a form entitled "Directive to Physicians and Durable Power of Attorney for Health Care" appears.

In addition to the separate text boxes providing question and form specific information, at any time throughout the program, the user may access various other help features which provide additional legal information. One such feature is "Ask Arthur Miller," where the user selects a general topic and then a specific question,[17] after which either a text-based answer is provided or, if the user's computer has a CD-ROM player, a sound card and a video card, a sound and video image of Arthur Miller answering the question appears.

The UPLC filed this action in state court alleging that the selling of QFL violates Texas' unauthorized practice of law statute * * * and seeking, among other things, to enjoin the sale of QFL in Texas. Parsons subsequently removed this case to this Court. Both parties now seek summary judgment. The UPLC argues that Parsons has violated the Statute as a matter of law. Parsons responds that the mere selling of books or software cannot violate the statute because some form of personal contact beyond publisher-consumer is required by a plain reading of the Statute. Alternatively, if the statute is not construed to require some form of personal relationship, Parsons argues that the application of the Statute to the mere sale and distribution of QFL would infringe upon Parsons' speech rights under the United States and Texas Constitutions. Parsons also argues that the Statute, if utilized to prevent the sale and distribution of QFL, should be void for vagueness.

II. RELEVANT STANDARD

Summary judgment is appropriate where the facts and law as represented in the pleadings, affidavits and other summary judgment evidence show that no reasonable trier of fact could possibly find for the nonmoving party as to any material fact. * * * "The moving party bears the initial burden of identifying those portions of the pleadings and discovery in the record that it believes demonstrate the absence of a genuine issue of material fact, but is not required to negate elements of the nonmoving party's case." Lynch Properties, Inc. v. Potomac Ins. Co. of Ill., 140 F.3d

17. The "Ask Arthur Miller" feature answers a number of predetermined frequently asked legal questions in the general topics of estate planning, family and personal, powers of attorney, health and medical, real estate, employment, financial, corporate, consumer and credit, and common questions. Some of the specific questions contained within these general topics are "What if I have a dispute, but don't want to go to the expense and delay of bringing a law suit?", "Why should I go to the trouble of writing a will?", "What is probate?", and "Doesn't a Premarital agreement take the romance out of marriage?" After the user clicks on the general question, a general response to the question appears. * * *

622, 625 (5th Cir.1998) (citing Celotex, 477 U.S. at 322–25). If the movant fails to meet its initial burden, the motion must be denied, regardless of the nonmovant's response. Little v. Liquid Air Corp., 37 F.3d 1069, 1075 (5th Cir.1994).

If the movant does meet its burden, the nonmovant must go beyond the pleadings and designate specific facts showing that a genuine issue of material fact exists for trial. * * * A party opposing summary judgment may not rest on mere conclusory allegations or denials in its pleadings unsupported by specific facts presented in affidavits opposing the motion for summary judgment. * * *

In determining whether genuine issues of fact exist, "[f]actual controversies are construed in the light most favorable to the nonmovant, but only if both parties have introduced evidence showing that a controversy exists." Lynch, 140 F.3d at 625 * * *. However, in the absence of any proof, the Court will not assume that the nonmoving party could or would prove the necessary facts. * * * A party must do more than simply show some "metaphysical doubt as to the material facts." * * * "If the record, taken as a whole, could not lead a rational trier of fact to find for the non-moving party, there is no genuine issue for trial." Friou v. Phillips Petroleum Co., 948 F.2d 972, 974 (5th Cir.1991).

With these summary judgment standards in mind, the Court turns to the cross-motions for summary judgment.

III. ANALYSIS

A. Determination of This Suit on Summary Judgment.

Under both Texas substantive law and the Federal Rules of Civil Procedure, it is appropriate for this Court to decide this case on summary judgment at this time. Under Texas law, a court may determine whether the undisputed acts of a defendant fall within the statutory definition of the unauthorized practice of law. Unauthorized Practice of Law Committee v. Cortez, 692 S.W.2d 47, 51 (Tex.1985). While the right to trial by jury exists where the alleged acts purportedly constituting the unauthorized practice of law are disputed, the "courts ultimately decide whether certain undisputed activities constitute the unauthorized practice of law." Id. Therefore, if there are no disputed facts, it is appropriate for this Court to decide the issue of whether the undisputed acts fit within the definition of the unauthorized practice of law.

In this case, there are no genuine issues of material fact or disputed acts. Parsons' act of publishing QFL is undisputed. The contents of QFL are undisputed. All that remains to be determined is the legal consequences, if any, of these undisputed acts, and according to Cortez, the power to make this determination ultimately resides with the Court. Therefore, under both Texas law and the traditional federal summary judgment standards, this case is ripe for decision on summary judgment.

B. The Violation of the Texas Unauthorized Practice of Law Statute.

The UPLC moves for summary judgment because it claims, as a matter of law, the sale and distribution of QFL violates the Statute. The UPLC argues that QFL gives advice concerning legal documents and selects legal documents for users, both of which involve the use of legal skill and knowledge, and this constitutes the practice of law. Additionally, the UPLC argues that the Defendant's forms are misleading and incorrect. * * * In sum, the UPLC alleges that QFL acts as a "high tech lawyer by interacting with its 'client' while preparing legal instruments, giving legal advice, and suggesting legal instruments that should be employed by the user." * * * In other words, QFL is a "cyber-lawyer."

No one disputes that the practice of law encompasses more than the mere conduct of cases in the courts. See In re Duncan, 65 S.E. 210 (S.C.1909) (finding that the practice of law includes "the preparation of legal instruments of all kinds, and, in general, all advice to clients, and all action taken for them in matters connected with the law."). However, a comprehensive definition of just what qualifies as the practice of law is "impossible," and "each case must be decided upon its own particular facts." Palmer v. Unauthorized Practice of Law Committee, 438 S.W.2d 374, 376 (Tex. App.—Houston 1969, no writ) * * *.

The UPLC, in arguing that the publication and sale of QFL constitutes the unauthorized practice of law, relies on two Texas Court of Appeals cases, Palmer v. Unauthorized Practice of Law Committee, 438 S.W.2d 374 (Tex. App.—Houston 1969, no writ), and Fadia v. Unauthorized Practice of Law Committee, 830 S.W.2d 162 (Tex. App.—Dallas 1992, writ denied).

Palmer held that the sale of will forms containing blanks to be filled in by the user, along with instructions, constituted the unauthorized practice of law. The Palmer court observed that the form sold by Mr. Palmer was "almost a will itself" and that the form purported to make specific testamentary bequests. The court feared that the unsuspecting layman "by reading defendants' advertisements, by reading the will form, and by reading the definitions that are attached, ... [would be] led to believe that defendants' will 'form' is in fact only a form and that all testamentary dispositions may be thus standardized." Id. at 376. The Palmer court held that the preparation of legal instruments of all kinds involves the practice of law. * * * The Palmer court further held that the exercise of judgment in the proper drafting of legal instruments, or even the selecting of the proper form of instrument, necessarily affects important legal rights, and thus, is the practice of law. * * *

In Fadia, the pro se defendant sold and distributed a manual entitled "You and Your Will: A Do–It–Yourself Manual." The defendant in Fadia attempted to get around Palmer's conclusion that the selling of a will manual constitutes the unauthorized practice of law, by arguing that the court should reject Palmer in light of recent state court decisions requiring some form of personal contact or relationship between the alleged unauthorized lawyer and the putative client in order to violate the unauthorized practice of law statute. The court rejected the defendant's argument, stating that it would not overrule Palmer and if there were to be a pre-requisite of personal contact between the parties, such a change to the Statute would have to come from the legislature and not the courts. * * * The Fadia court went on to hold that because a will secures legal rights and its drafting involves the giving of advice requiring the use of legal skill or knowledge, the preparation of a will involves the practice of law. * * * Since the selection of the proper legal form also affects important legal rights, the court reasoned that it too constituted the practice of law. * * * Therefore, since the will manual both purported to advise a layman on how to draft a will and selected a specific form for the layman to use, the court determined that the Defendant's selling of a will manual qualified as the unauthorized practice of law. * * *

As already mentioned, the Palmer court found that the preparation of legal instruments of all kinds involves the practice of law. * * * The Texas Supreme Court has since held that the mere advising of a person as to whether or not to file a form requires legal skill and knowledge, and therefore, would be the practice of law. Unauthorized Practice of Law Committee v. Cortez, 692 S.W.2d 47, 50 (Tex.1985).

Based on the interpretations of the Statute by the Texas courts, QFL falls within the range of conduct that Texas courts have determined to be the unauthorized practice of law. For instance, QFL purports to select the appropriate health care document for an individual based upon the state in which she lives. QFL customizes the documents, by adding or removing entire clauses, depending upon the particular responses given by the user to a set of questions posed by the program. The packaging of QFL represents that QFL will "interview you in a logical order, tailoring documents to your situation." Additionally, the packaging tells the user that the forms are valid in 49 states and that they have been updated by legal experts. This creates an air of reliability about the documents, which increases the likelihood that an individual user will be misled into relying on them. This false impression is not diminished by QFL's disclaimer. The disclaimer only actively appears the first-time the program is used after it is installed, and there is no guarantee that the person who initially uses the program is the same person who will later use and rely upon the program.

QFL goes beyond merely instructing someone how to fill in a blank form. While no single one of QFL's acts, in and of itself, may constitute the practice of law, taken as a whole Parsons, through QFL, has gone beyond publishing a sample form book with instructions, and has ventured into the unauthorized practice of law.

Parsons attempts to avoid the conclusion that it is guilty of the unauthorized practice of law by arguing that the Statute requires personal contact or a lawyer-client relationship. Parsons bases its argument first on the language of the Statute, which it contends requires that the prohibited services must be provided "on behalf of a client" in order to be the practice of law.

Even assuming that Parsons is correct that paragraph (a) of the Statute requires the prohibited services to be completed "on behalf of" a client, paragraph (a) of the Statute is not an exclusive definition of the unauthorized practice of law. Paragraph (b) of the Statute gives the Court the authority to determine that other acts constitute the unauthorized practice of law. Therefore, a judge could legitimately determine, under the authority granted in paragraph (b), that services provided to the public as a whole, as opposed to a singular client, qualify as the practice of law.

Next, Parsons argues that this Court should require a personal relationship between the party charged with the unauthorized practice of law and the party who benefits from the "advice" since this is the logic of almost every other court to consider the issue. * * * However, as noted above, the pro se defendant in Fadia made this exact argument and the Texas Court of Appeals rejected it. * * *

Nonetheless, Parsons contends that if the Texas Supreme Court were to consider the issue it would follow the lead of the other states. Although this Court is not Erie bound to follow the Fadia decision, it believes the Texas Supreme Court would find the Fadia decision a persuasive precedent. * * * For this Court to be the first to impose a new interpretation of a state statute which has been on the books in its current form since 1987, and some form since 1939, would fly in the face of generally accepted notions of federal-state comity. If Parsons believes such a personal contact requirement should be included in the Statute, it should address these concerns to the Texas legislature. It is not appropriate for this Court to be the first to read such a requirement into the Statute.

Parsons' arguments to the contrary notwithstanding, QFL is far more than a static form with instructions on how to fill in the blanks. For instance, QFL adapts the content of the form to the responses given by the user. QFL purports to select the appropriate health care document for an individual based upon the state in which she lives. The packaging of QFL makes various representations as to the accuracy and specificity of the forms. In sum, Parsons has violated the unauthorized practice of law statute.

C. Does the Statute Withstand Scrutiny Under the United States Constitution?

Having determined that the publication of QFL violates the Texas unauthorized practice of law statute, the Court must now examine whether applying the Statute in such a manner infringes upon the rights guaranteed by the First Amendment of the United States Constitution. The First Amendment is plainly implicated by the UPLC's desire to halt the sale of QFL in the state of Texas. While there is no right of unlicensed laymen to represent another under the First Amendment's guarantees of freedom of association and freedom to petition one's government, * * *

Parsons' rights under the First Amendment's protections of a free press still apply.

1. Determining the Appropriate Level of Scrutiny: Content–Neutral v. Content–Based

The Court's initial First Amendment inquiry is to determine whether the Statute is a content-neutral or content-based restriction of speech because this answer will determine the level of scrutiny to which the Statute and its application will be subjected. If the Statute is determined to prevent speech based on its content, it is subject to strict scrutiny. If the Statute is merely a content-neutral restriction on speech, it is subject only to intermediate scrutiny.

The principal inquiry in determining content neutrality in speech cases is whether the government has adopted a regulation of speech because of disagreement with the message it conveys. * * * If the answer is "no," then the statute is content-neutral and subject only to intermediate scrutiny. The government's purpose is the controlling consideration in this inquiry. A regulation that serves purposes unrelated to the content of the expression is deemed neutral, even if it has an incidental effect on some speakers or messages but not others. * * *

Parsons vehemently asserts that the Statute's prohibition is a content-based restriction on speech. It bases this assertion, not on the general purpose of the Statute, but on the deposition testimony of the UPLC's designated representative that the UPLC would not prosecute Parsons for the publication of its non-legal software titles. * * * Thus, according to Parsons, since only its legal titles are subject to restriction, the Statute is based on the content of the software title, and therefore, the Statute is subject to strict scrutiny.

However, it is not what specific speech (or conduct) the Statute prohibits, but whether the government is evidencing a disagreement with the speaker's message, as well as the underlying purpose behind the statute, which determines content-neutrality. The mere fact that the Statute sanctions speech-based conduct does not make the Statute content-based. * * *

The Statute at issue is aimed at eradicating the unauthorized practice of law. The Statute's purpose has nothing to do with suppressing speech. The UPLC's decision to challenge some of Parsons' software titles but not others has less to do with their content than with the likelihood that the title has possibly violated the unauthorized practice of law statute. Of course, the UPLC would not subject Parson's non-legal titles to scrutiny under the Statute, it is unlikely that the Life Application Bible engages in the prohibited conduct of practicing law without a license. Such discrimination between products does not evidence a disagreement with the message of Parsons' software.

There being no other arguments that the Statute is anything but content-neutral, the Court finds that the Statute is aimed at the noncommunicative impact of Parsons' speech, and therefore, is a content-neutral regulation which only incidentally affects speech and therefore is subject only to intermediate scrutiny.

2. *Determining Whether a Content–Neutral Statute Overburdens Protected Speech Rights*

Having determined that the Statute is content-neutral, the Court must still decide whether the Statute nonetheless overburdens protected speech. To make this determination, the Court subjects the Statute to intermediate scrutiny and the four part test of United States v. O'Brien, 391 U.S. 367 (1968). Under O'Brien, the UPLC must establish that:

1) The regulation is within the constitutional power of the state;
2) It furthers an important or substantial government interest;
3) The government interest is unrelated to the suppression of free expression; and
4) The incidental restriction of speech is no greater than is essential to the furtherance of that interest.

The Court will examine each of the O'Brien factors in turn.

a. Is the Statute Within the Constitutional Power of the State?

The first prong of O'Brien requires that the government have the constitutional power to enact the regulation in question. * * * Parsons does not dispute that the state of Texas has the power to prohibit the unauthorized practice of law. Therefore, the first prong of O'Brien is satisfied.

b. Does the Statute Further an Important Government Interest?

The State has a significant interest in regulating the practice of law and protecting its citizens from being mislead. The Supreme Court has said that states have a "substantial interest in regulating the practice of law within the State." Sperry v. Florida, 373 U.S. 379, 383 (1963). Therefore, the second prong of O'Brien is satisfied.

c. Is the government interest unrelated to the suppression of free expression?

A regulation satisfies O'Brien's third criterion if it can be justified without reference to the content of the regulated speech. J & B Entertainment v. City of Jackson, 152 F.3d 362, 376 (5th Cir.1998). This criterion is essentially no different than the initial test to establish if the regulation was content-neutral. Since the Statute can be justified on the need to prevent people who are not lawyers from giving legal advice and harming the citizens of Texas, the Statute satisfies the third prong of O'Brien.

d. Is the incidental restriction of speech no greater than is essential to the furtherance of the governmental interest?

A regulation satisfies the final prong, often referred to as "the narrow tailoring requirement," "so long as the . . . regulation promotes a substantial government interest that would be achieved less effectively absent the regulation." United States v. Albertini, 472 U.S. 675, 689 (1985). The regulation must also "not burden substantially more speech than is necessary to further the government's legitimate interest." Ward, 491 U.S. at 799.

The version of the narrow tailoring requirement for intermediate scrutiny does not require the government to chose the "least-restrictive alternative" in achieving its interests. * * * Furthermore, a court should not invalidate the government's preferred remedial scheme because some alternative solution is marginally less intrusive on a speaker's First Amendment interests. * * * A statute should be struck down under intermediate scrutiny only when a "substantial portion of the burden on speech does not serve to advance [the State's content-neutral goals]." Simon & Schuster v. New York Crime Victims Bd., 502 U.S. at 122 n.* (quoting Ward, 491 U.S. at 799).

While the Court recognizes that the issue is close, it is of the opinion that the Statute does not "substantially burden" more speech than necessary, and that the government's interest would be achieved less effectively absent the regulation. Absent the regulation, as it is being applied in this case, the State's ability to combat the unauthorized practice of law in the computer age would be hindered. The State possesses an interest in protecting the uninformed and unwary from overly-simplistic legal advice. The UPLC does not seek to prevent the simple provision of information concerning legal rights; rather, it seeks to prevent the citizens of Texas from being lulled into a false sense of security that if they use QFL they will have a "legally valid" document that's "tailored to [their] situation" and "best meets their needs." If the UPLC is prevented from prosecuting Parsons, the State's interests in preventing those who are not authorized to practice law from giving legal advice would be less effectively achieved. Additionally, while the Statute burdens some speech, that burden does not rise to the level of a substantial burden. Moreover, the burden which the Statute does place on speech is necessary to serve the State's legitimate content-neutral interests. Thus, the Statute satisfies the fourth prong of O'Brien.

Since the Statute meets all four of O'Brien' s requirements, it survives review under intermediate scrutiny. The Statute does not violate the First Amendment to the United States Constitution.

D. Speech Rights Under the Texas Constitution

Parsons also alleges that the UPLC's actions in enforcing the Statute against it violates Parsons' rights to free speech under Article I, Section 8 of the Texas Constitution. It does not. Granted, Davenport v. Garcia, 834 S.W.2d 4 (Tex.1992), requires a showing of immediate and irreparable harm before issuing an injunction. This test is more stringent than the test under federal law. However, the cases since Davenport have limited this higher standard under the Texas Constitution to cases which "have involved prior restraints in the form of court orders prohibiting or restricting speech." Commission for Lawyer Discipline v. Benton, 980 S.W.2d 425, 434 (Tex.1998). Furthermore, the Fifth Circuit has refused to expand the Davenport' s heightened standard outside of the narrow areas specifically addressed by the Texas Supreme Court, Woodall v. City of El Paso, 49 F.3d 1120 (5th Cir.1995), and the Court will not do so here. Furthermore, the UPLC has made a sufficient showing of immediate and irreparable harm to the citizens of Texas from the sale and publication of QFL that the heightened standard of Davenport has been satisfied.

Since the injunction this Court will issue will be limited to only Quicken Family Lawyer, version 8.0, and Quicken Family Lawyer § 99, which have already been published, the injunction is not a "prior restraint," and the heightened standards of Davenport should not apply. "Not all injunctions that may incidentally affect expression are 'prior restraints.' " Madsen v. Women's Health Center, Inc., 512 U.S. 753, 763 n. 2 (1994). When an injunction issues "not because of the content of petitioners' expression ... but because of their prior unlawful conduct," it is not a prior restraint. Id. * * * The injunction that will issue in accordance with this Memorandum Opinion and Order will not be the broad relief sought by the UPLC. Rather, this Court will limit relief to enjoining the sale and distribution of Quicken Family Lawyer, version 8.0, and Quicken Family Lawyer § 99 within the state of Texas.

Thus, enforcement of the Statute here does not violate the Texas Constitution.

E. Is the Statute Unconstitutionally Vague as Applied to Parsons?

Finally, Parsons challenges the Statute as being impermissibly vague as it is being applied to them. This challenge also fails.

Vagueness is a constitutional infirmity rooted in due process. "An enactment is void for vagueness if its prohibitions are not clearly defined." J & B Entertainment, 152 F.3d at 367 (quoting Grayned v. City of Rockford, 408 U.S. 104, 109 (1972)) * * *. Vague laws are prohibited because they do not give citizens fair warning that their conduct is illegal. In determining whether a statute is vague, we view the law from the standpoint of a person of ordinary intelligence. * * *

This Statute was challenged for vagueness in Drew v. Unauthorized Practice of Law Comm., 970 S.W.2d 152 (Tex. App.—Austin 1998, writ denied). Mr. Drew, a non-lawyer, had filed habeas corpus petitions on behalf of people who believed they had been denied their rights. An order was entered enjoining Mr. Drew from practicing law. On appeal, he challenged the Statute as being void for vagueness. The Court of Appeals concluded that "the statute is sufficiently specific as concerns the actions the court enjoined, including preparation of pleadings, giving legal advice, preparing legal documents, and attempting to appear before a judge on behalf of another." Id. at 155. This holding is consistent with every other court which has considered a vagueness challenge to a state's unauthorized practice law. * * *

While the Statute is not a model of clarity, "condemned to the use of words, we can never expect mathematical certainty from our language." Grayned, 408 U.S. at 110. The Statute and the surrounding case law set forth a core of prohibited conduct with sufficient definiteness to guide those who must interpret it. The Statute speaks of the preparation of a will or contract or other legal instrument as being potentially prohibited conduct. This should have put Parsons or anyone else who assists others in the preparation of a legal document on notice that they may run afoul of the unauthorized practice of law statute. Moreover, while Parsons may believe it to be wrongly decided, Fadia v. Unauthorized Practice of Law Comm., 830 S.W.2d 162 (Tex. App.—Dallas 1992, writ denied), should have also placed Parsons on notice that in Texas the selling of forms, without more, may be considered the unauthorized practice of law. The acts prohibited by the Statute were sufficiently defined that Parsons had fair warning that the publication and sale of QFL was potentially illegal in Texas. Consequently, Parsons' claim that the Statute is unconstitutionally vague as applied fails.

IV. CONCLUSION

Plaintiff's Motion for Summary Judgment is GRANTED. Defendant's Motion for Summary Judgment is DENIED.

Plaintiff will submit a proposed judgment conforming with this order.

SO ORDERED.

NOTES AND QUESTIONS

1. Within a few months of the *Parsons* decision, the 1999 Texas Legislature effectively overruled the case by amending its definition of the practice of law. The key text of the amendment to § 81.101 of the Texas Government Code is as follows:

> (c) In this chapter, the "practice of law" does not include the design, creation, publication, distribution, display, or sale, including publication, distribution, display, or sale by means of an Internet web site, of written materials, books, forms, computer software, or similar products if the products clearly and conspicuously state that the products are not a substitute for the advice of an attorney. * * *

2. Do you agree with Judge Sanders or with the response of the Texas Legislature? Why? See Marie A. Vida, *Legality of Will–Creating Software: Is the Sale of Computer Software to Assist in Drafting Will Documents Considered the Unauthorized Practice of Law?*, 41 SANTA CLARA L. REV. 231 (2000) (arguing that Judge Sanders was correct; "Although the need for low cost legal advice is great, society should not lower its standards to fulfill that need. * * * If courts and the legislature truly want to protect lay individuals from those inexperienced to practice law, then they must prevent the use of will creating software.").

3. See Brent L. Barringer, *When Cyberlawyering Fails: What Remedies Are Or Should Be Available To Those Harmed From Relying On Self–Help*

Legal Software?, 2005 U. Ill. J.L. Tech. & Pol'y 171 (concluding that "[w]hen these cyberlawyering products fail to meet consumer expectations, the publishers should be held liable only in limited circumstances. Remedies should be available to the users of deficient software only when the software publisher has acted fraudulently.").

7. INTERNET

The Internet is brimming with sites devoted to supplying non-attorneys with estate planning information. Some of these sites are coupled with promotional materials for computer software or for law firms while others are designed to supply public service information. As mentioned earlier, some of these websites are interactive and allow the user to complete estate planning forms on-line.

LOCATE

Visit local bookstores, office supply stores, and public libraries to determine what type of self-help materials are available in your community. Surf the Internet to look for on-line resources. What is your impression of what you found?

M. ENHANCING PROFESSIONAL STATUS

If you decide to pursue estate planning as a significant portion of your practice, there are a variety of steps you can take to enhance your professional status. Below is a non-exclusive list of some of the things you may want to consider.

- *Earn LL.M. Degree.* Many law schools offer LL.M. degrees in estate planning or in taxation. An LL.M. degree often provides a competitive edge in securing employment.
- *Obtain Certification.* Many states permit an attorney to obtain a special certification in estate planning. Typically, you must demonstrate that you have practiced heavily in the area and pass a rigorous written examination. This credential may be helpful in obtaining clients.
- *Attend Continuing Legal Education Programs.* Estate planning is one of the most common topics for continuing legal education programs. Sponsors of these seminars include state, local, and national bar associations, estate planning organizations, law schools, and private businesses.
- *Join Estate Planning Organizations.* There are many organizations which emphasize the estate planning practice. Many local and state bar associations, as well as the American Bar Association, have sections devoted to wills, trusts, and related matters. These sections are generally open to any attorney willing to pay the nominal dues. In fact, as a law student, you may be able to join at reduced rates.

You may also seek membership in estate planning organizations whose membership is not restricted to attorneys, but which bring together professionals from a variety of interrelated fields such as accounting, banking, insurance, and financial planning. As you gain expertise in the field and after a minimum of ten years of practice, you may be nominated for membership in the American College of Trust and Estate Counsel, the premier estate planning organization in the United States.

CHAPTER 9

WILL CONTEST AVOIDANCE

■ ■ ■

A. ANTICIPATING WILL CONTESTS*

You must always be on guard when preparing an estate plan which may supply an incentive for someone to contest a will. Anytime an individual would take more through intestacy or under a prior will, the potential for a will contest exists, especially if the estate is large. Although will contests are relatively rare, you must recognize situations which are likely to inspire a will contest and take steps during the drafting stage to reduce the probability of a will contest being brought and, if it is filed, the chances of its success.

1. EXCLUSION OF NATURAL OBJECTS OF BOUNTY

A will leaving nothing or only nominal gifts to close family members, such as a spouse of many years or children, is ripe for a contest action, especially if the beneficiaries are distant relatives, friends, or charities. Juries are prone in close cases to invalidate a will which disinherits the surviving spouse and children, although "[i]t is not for courts, juries, relatives, or friends to say how property should be passed by will, or to rewrite a will for a testator because they do not believe he made a wise or fair distribution of his property." Stephen v. Coleman, 533 S.W.2d 444, 445 (Tex. Civ. App. 1976) (quoting Farmer v. Dodson, 326 S.W.2d 57, 61 (Tex. Civ. App. 1959)).

Will contests based on property passing outside of the traditional family are likely to increase because of various societal changes. Many older individuals have greater involvement with people outside of the family in retirement communities and senior citizen organizations. The lifestyles of younger people include more divorces, childless marriages, and cohabitation. As a result, estate plans of these individuals are more likely

---

* This section is adapted from Gerry W. Beyer, *Drafting in Contemplation of Will Contests,* in AMERICAN BAR ASSOCIATION, ESTATE AND TRUST LITIGATION: DRAFTING IN CONTEMPLATION OF CONTESTS; THE TRIAL; AND THE JUDICIAL PERSPECTIVE—A VIEW FROM THE BENCH (1991).

to include gifts to non-family members and thus increase the likelihood of contests. One insightful commentator has noted:

> Inheritance has traditionally been an occasion when families reconfirm the importance of kinship ties. The scant evidence from research on will contests shows more than property is at stake when families go to court. Usually there is concern that a traditional aspect of the family—a role, relationship or the balance of power—has been violated by the terms of the trust or estate plan. Bequests outside the family—to friends, lovers, step-heirs and so forth—may never become socially acceptable, even if they are increasingly common. These unconventional estate plans mean that family members will be more prone to litigate instead of accepting a decedent's estate plan * * * [M]ost families are unable—and unwilling—to inherit less so that friends, organizations or lovers can inherit more.

Jeffrey P. Rosenfeld, *To Heir is Human,* PROB. & PROP., July/Aug. 1990, at 21, 25.

2. UNEQUAL TREATMENT OF CHILDREN

A will which treats children unequally, especially if the children receiving disproportionately large amounts have no special needs, is likely to encourage spurned siblings to contest the will. The contestant's appeal to the inherent fairness of all children sharing equally may sway a wavering jury.

3. SUDDEN OR SIGNIFICANT CHANGE IN DISPOSITION PLAN

When a testator makes a sudden or significant change to the will's dispositive scheme, the beneficiaries of the prior will who take less under the new will may be motivated to contest the new will. These beneficiaries will strive to show that the testator lacked capacity to change the will or that the testator was unduly influenced to make the alterations. See Matter of Estate of Seegers, 733 P.2d 418, 423 (Okla. Ct. App. 1986)

4. IMPOSITION OF EXCESSIVE RESTRICTIONS ON GIFTED PROPERTY

A testator may impose restrictions on gifts to heirs. For example, the will may create a testamentary trust for the children with expenditures limited to certain items (e.g., health care, room and board, or education) or with lump-sum distributions authorized only upon the beneficiary's fulfilling certain criteria (e.g., graduating from college or reaching a certain age). Although the trust may treat all of the testator's children equally, the imposition of restrictions may give the beneficiaries reason to contest the will and, if successful, immediately obtain the property free from limitations and conditions.

5. ELDERLY OR DISABLED TESTATOR

The age, health, mental condition, or physical capacity of a testator may provide contestants with a basis to claim lack of testamentary capacity or undue influence. Although the mere fact of advanced age, debilitating illness, or severe handicap does not necessarily diminish capacity, these circumstances can play an important role in supporting a will contest.

6. UNUSUAL BEHAVIOR OF TESTATOR

A peculiar acting testator is apt to give dissatisfied heirs a basis for contesting the will either on the ground that the testator lacked capacity or was suffering from an insane delusion. Despite judicial statements such as, "A man may believe himself to be the supreme ruler of the universe and nevertheless make a perfectly sensible disposition of his property, and the courts will sustain it when it appears that his mania did not dictate its provisions," a will executed by a person with behavior or beliefs out of the mainstream of society's definition of "normal" is apt to trigger a contest action. Fraser v. Jennison, 42 Mich. 206, 3 N.W. 882, 900 (1879). For example, a famous musician consulted a psychic who revealed the identity of the person in whom he would be reincarnated and then executed a will leaving a sizable bequest to this person. Looks ripe for a contest, don't you think? See Janet Charlton, *Star People,* THE SAN ANTONIO STAR, July 21, 1991, at 2.

NOTES AND QUESTIONS

1. What other facts would alert you to the greater than normal likelihood of your client's will being contested? See John L. Carroll & Brian K. Carroll, *Avoiding the Will Contest,* PROB. & PROP., May/June 1994, at 61.

2. For a treatise devoted exclusively to will contests, see EUNICE L. ROSS & THOMAS J. REED, WILL CONTESTS (2d ed. 1999 & most recent Supp.).

B. PREVENTING WILL CONTESTS*

This section discusses a wide range of techniques which you may find helpful in preventing a contest of your client's will. These techniques vary widely in both cost and predictability of results. There is no uniform approach to use for all clients. You need to examine each case on its own merits before deciding which, if any, of the techniques to use. In addition, you must study state law to determine the validity and effectiveness of each technique.

* This section is adapted from Gerry W. Beyer, *Drafting in Contemplation of Will Contests,* in AMERICAN BAR ASSOCIATION, ESTATE AND TRUST LITIGATION: DRAFTING IN CONTEMPLATION OF CONTESTS; THE TRIAL; AND THE JUDICIAL PERSPECTIVE—A VIEW FROM THE BENCH (1991).

1. INCLUDE IN TERROREM PROVISION

An *in terrorem* provision, also called a *no-contest* or *forfeiture* clause, provides that a beneficiary who contests the will loses all or most of the benefits given under the will. *In terrorem* provisions are one of the most frequently used contest prevention techniques. This widespread use is probably due to the technique's low cost (a few extra lines in the will), low risk (no penalty incurred if clause declared unenforceable), and potential for effectuating the testator's intent (property passing via the will rather than through intestacy or under a prior will).

a. Validity and Enforceability

People have used *in terrorem* clauses since the earliest recorded history to control the conduct of others. Often the clauses would threaten physical violence, monetary penalties, or banishment from the household. After the birth of Christ, the drafters of *in terrorem* clauses focused on society's biggest apprehension at the time, the fear of God and eternal damnation. Influenced by the "enlightened" thinking of the Renaissance, testators began to realize that their heirs were more concerned with the present than with any potential after life, be it a reward or a punishment. Thus, as society became more materialistic, *in terrorem* clauses shifted from appealing to the beneficiary's intangible fear of future unending suffering to immediate threats of losing a valuable devise or bequest.

The earliest reported case involving a forfeiture provision drafted after the English Parliament enacted Statute of Wills was decided in 1674. In Anonymous, 2 Mod. 7, 7, 86 Eng. Rep. 910, 910 (1674), the court held that a forfeiture provision was valid. Cooke v. Turner, 15 M. & W. 727, 153 Eng. Rep. 1044 (Ex. 1846), decided in 1846 by the English High Court of Chancery, is the most notable early decision declaring a forfeiture based upon a beneficiary's post-testamentary conduct. The court stated, "There appears to be no more reason why a person may not be restrained by a condition from disputing sanity, than from disputing any other doubtful question whether of fact or of law, on which the title to a devise or grant may depend."

In 1869, an American court for the first time directly ruled on the validity of an *in terrorem* clause and upheld the provision in the process. Bradford v. Bradford, 19 Ohio St. 546 (1869). Subsequently, the United States Supreme Court examined the validity of an *in terrorem* provision in 1898. The Court reviewed the authorities which indicated that *in terrorem* provisions were valid and decided that this view was consistent with good law and morals. Smithsonian Institution v. Meech, 169 U.S. 398, 415, 18 S.Ct. 396, 403, 42 L.Ed. 793 (1898).

Although usually deemed valid and enforceable, no-contest provisions are unpopular with the courts and are strictly construed. Forfeiture will "be avoided if possible; only where the act of a party comes strictly within the clause may a breach thereof be declared." In re Estate of Newbill, 781

S.W.2d 727, 728 (Tex. App. 1989). Courts frequently treat the beneficiary's suit as one to construe the will, rather than as one to contest the will, to avoid triggering a forfeiture.

Some jurisdictions have cases or statutes limiting the scope of *in terrorem* provisions so that forfeiture is avoided if the beneficiary contests the will in good faith and with probable cause. Courts support the good faith/probable cause distinction on several grounds. First, the testator would not have intended to preclude a contest under such circumstances; and second, enforcing the clause would be contrary to public policy. Nonetheless, other courts hold that a general condition against contest is enforceable regardless of the contestant's good faith or the existence of probable cause.

In terrorem provisions are often justified on the basis that "they allow the intent of the testator to be given full effect and avoid vexatious litigation, often among members of the same family. Such contests often result in considerable waste of the estate and hard feelings that can never be repaired." Gunter v. Pogue, 672 S.W.2d 840, 842–43 (Tex. App. 1984). On the other hand, the enforcement of a no-contest provision under certain circumstances may be against public policy. For example, an *in terrorem* provision would be a powerful tool in the hands of a person who fraudulently or through undue influence procured the execution of a will. The clause may give the evil-doer an increased chance of success by terrorizing potential contestants who are given substantial benefits under the will.

b. Drafting Guidelines

There are no formal requirements for *in terrorem* provisions. Memorializing the testator's intent with clear and unambiguous language is your foremost consideration.

1) Create Substantial Risk

For an *in terrorem* provision to deter a will contest effectively, it must be carefully drafted to place the disgruntled beneficiary at significant risk. The clause should make the beneficiary think, "Do I keep quiet and get a sure thing (although less than I would get by intestacy or a prior will), or do I contest the will and risk receiving nothing?" In other words, the testator hopes that the beneficiary will follow the "one in the hand is worth two in the bush" philosophy. The clause must place the beneficiary in this dilemma and thus it is vital that the potential contestant's gift be large enough to elicit a genuine fear of contesting the will.

For example, assume that X, an unmarried person with three children (A, B, and C), anticipates a distributable estate of $300,000. Under the applicable intestacy statute, each child would receive $100,000 if X dies without a valid will. X's wishes are, however, considerably different; X desires to leave the bulk of the estate to A and B. If X leaves nothing to C, or only a nominal amount, e.g., $5,000, an *in terrorem* provision will have little impact on C because C gains tremendously if the will is invalid and loses little if the will and accompanying *in terrorem* provision are upheld. However, if X leaves C a substantial sum, e.g., $50,000, C will hesitate to forfeit a guaranteed $50,000, and incur court costs and legal fees, for fear of taking nothing if the will is upheld, even though C would receive a $100,000 intestate share if the contest succeeds. (Note that the intestate share could be considerably reduced by the contingent fee of the contestant's attorney, court costs, and other expenses.)

2) Describe Triggering Conduct

The *in terrorem* clause should indicate the conduct triggering forfeiture. Does the testator wish to prevent only a will contest or is the testator's intent to prohibit a broader range of conduct? Does forfeiture occur upon the filing of a contest action or must actual judicial proceedings first occur? Is an indirect attack (e.g., where a beneficiary assists another person's contest) punishable the same as a direct attack? Will a contest by one beneficiary cause other beneficiaries to forfeit their gifts (e.g., five beneficiary/heirs are left a significant sum but less than intestacy, one of them agrees to take the risk of contest because the other four secretly agree to make up the loss if the contest fails)? Will a beneficiary's challenge to the appointment of the designated executor trigger forfeiture?

3) Indicate Beneficiary of Forfeited Property

The testator should name the recipient of the property that is subject to forfeiture under an *in terrorem* provision. This provides someone with a strong interest in upholding the will and the forfeiture provision. This contingent beneficiary, especially if it is a large charity able to elicit the support of the state's attorney general, may be able to place significant resources into fighting the contest. In addition, the law of some states requires a gift over for an enforceable no-contest provision.

4) Indicate Whether a Good Faith/Probable Cause Contest Triggers Forfeiture

Although the enforceability of an *in terrorem* provision which provides that it operates despite the contestant's good faith and probable cause may be uncertain under local law, the clause should contain an express statement of the testator's intent in this regard. The beneficiaries and the court will then have better evidence of the testator's intent, and the court can focus on the clause's legal effect rather than on a determination of the testator's wishes.

LOCATE

1. Are *in terrorem* provisions valid in your state? If yes, are there any conditions such as an express gift over?

2. Is the contestant's good faith in bringing a will contest upon probable cause a defense to forfeiture?

NOTES AND QUESTIONS

1. *In terrorem* clauses are occasionally discussed when they appear in the wills of famous people who die. For example, a no-contest clause in Frank Sinatra's will is credited as preventing his will from being contested. See *Sinatra's Will Goes Unchallenged by Heirs*, SAN ANTONIO EXPRESS-NEWS, June 19, 1998, at 2A.

2. For a detailed discussion of no-contest clauses, see Gerry W. Beyer, et al., *The Fine Art of Intimidating Disgruntled Beneficiaries with In Terrorem Clauses*, 51 SMU L. REV. 225 (1998).

DRAFT

Prepare the broadest *in terrorem* clause allowed under the law of your state.

2. EXPLAIN REASONS FOR DISPOSITION

An explanation in the will of the reasons motivating particular dispositions may reduce will contests. For example, a parent could indicate that a larger portion of the estate is being left to a certain child because that child is mentally challenged, requires expensive medical care, supports many children, or is still in school. If the testator makes a large charitable donation, the reasons for benefiting that particular charity may be set forth along with an explanation that family members have sufficient assets of their own. The effectiveness of this technique is based on the assumption that disgruntled heirs are less likely to contest if they realize the reasons for receiving less than their fair (intestate) share.

It is possible, however, for this technique to backfire. The explanation may upset some heirs, especially if they disagree with the facts or reasons given, and thus spur them to contest the will. Likewise, the explanation may provide the heirs with material to bolster claims of lack of capacity or undue influence. For example, assume that the testator's will states that one child is receiving a greater share of the estate because that child frequently visited the aging parent. Another child may use this statement as evidence that the visiting child unduly influenced the parent. If the explanation is factually incorrect, the heirs may contest on grounds ranging from insane delusion to mistake or assert that the will was conditioned on the truth of the stated facts.

If you decide to use this technique, you must carefully draft the language used to explain reasons for a disposition to avoid encouraging a will contest or creating testamentary libel. An alternative approach is to provide explanations in a separate document which could be produced in court if needed to defend a will contest, but which would not otherwise be made public.

3. AVOID BITTER OR HATEFUL LANGUAGE

a. Encourages Will Contests

If you decide it is advisable to explain the reasons for a particular dispositive scheme in a way which requires you to present a negative image of an heir, you must exercise care to ensure that this language does not provoke a contest. Any explanation of gifts or descriptions of heirs should be even-handed, free of bitterness or spite, and factually correct. An heir who feels slighted both emotionally and monetarily may be more likely to contest than one who is hurt only financially.

b. Potential for Testamentary Libel

Testamentary libel may become an issue when a will containing defamatory statements is probated and thereby published in the public records. Typically, such situations arise when a testator explains the reasons for making, or not making, particular gifts. For example, "To my grandson * * * I give and bequeath the sum of ten Dollars ($10.00). I have already given my said grandson the sum of One Thousand Dollars ($1,000.00) which he squandered. This provision is no different than that I have made for my said grandson in preceding wills over a number of years and expresses the regard in which I hold my said grandson, who deserted his mother and myself by taking sides against me in a lawsuit, and because he is a slacker, having shirked his duty in World War II." Kleinschmidt v. Matthieu, 201 Or. 406, 266 P.2d 686, 687 (1954). The courts are then presented with the question of whether the defamed individual is entitled to recover from the testator's estate or the executor.

Courts addressing the issue of testamentary libel have reached varying conclusions. Some courts simply delete the offensive material from the probated will, while others hold the estate liable for the damages caused by the libelous material. Other courts, however, rule that there is no cause of action for testamentary libel because statements relating to judicial proceedings are privileged or because actions for personal injuries against the testator died along with the testator. See generally Paul T. Whitcombe, *Defamation by Will: Theories and Liabilities,* 27 J. MARSHALL L. REV. 749 (1994); L.M. Hudak, *The Sleeping Tort: Testamentary Libel,* 12 CAL. W. L. REV. 491 (1976).

4. USE HOLOGRAPHIC WILL

Wills entirely in the testator's own handwriting appear to have an aura of validity because they show that the testator was sufficiently competent to choose the testator's own words and to write them down without outside assistance. You may use the courts' somewhat liberal attitude toward holographic wills to good advantage if you anticipate a will contest. Before executing a detailed attested will, the testator could hand write a will which, although not as comprehensive as the formal will, contains a disposition plan preferred to intestacy. If the attested will is invalidated, the holographic will could serve as an unrevoked prior will.

5. OBTAIN AFFIDAVITS FROM INDIVIDUALS FAMILIAR WITH TESTATOR

One of the most convincing types of evidence of a testator's capacity is testimony from individuals who observed the testator at and around the time the will was executed. Frequently, however, this testimony is unavailable at the time of the will contest action; the witnesses to the will may be dead, difficult to locate, or lack a good recollection of the testator. The same may be true of other individuals who had personal, business, or professional contacts with the testator. One way of preserving this valuable evidence is to obtain affidavits from these people detailing the testator's conduct, physical and mental condition, and related matters. Affidavits of attesting witnesses, individuals who spoke with the testator on a regular basis, or health care providers (doctors, psychiatrists, nurses) who examined the testator close to the time of will execution, will protect this potentially valuable testimony for use should a will contest arise.

6. DOCUMENT TRANSACTIONS WITH TESTATOR VERIFYING INTENT

Under normal circumstances, the testator orally explains the desired disposition plan and the reasons therefor, you explain the testator's options, and then you prepare a draft of the will. After reviewing the will, the testator makes oral corrections, and you prepare the final version. This procedure supplies little in the way of documentation which can be admitted into evidence in a will contest action. If a contest is anticipated, all of these steps should be documented in writing, on videotape, or both. For example, the testator could write you a letter explaining the disposition scheme and motivating factors behind it. Your written reply would warn that a contest may occur because of the disinheritance of prospective heirs, unequal treatment of children, excessive restrictions on gifts, etc. The testator would respond in writing that the testator has considered these factors but prefers to have property pass as originally indicated. You would then carefully preserve these documents for use should a contest arise.

The testator may wish to prepare a videotape explaining the testator's intent. For example, Henry Ford II prepared a 15 minute tape in which he explained his estate plan and the reasons for it. Excerpts from the tape are reproduced in Joe Swickard, *Henry Ford's Video Asks No Fuss Over Will,* DETROIT FREE PRESS, Sept. 24, 1988, at 1A.

7. OBTAIN OTHER EVIDENCE TO DOCUMENT TESTATOR'S ACTIONS

Gathering evidence to rebut a will contest is always easier while the testator is alive. In addition to obtaining affidavits from individuals familiar with the testator and documenting the testator's intent, you may want to acquire other evidence as well. For example, the testator may have letters from a child showing family discord supporting the testator's reasons for disinheriting the child. You may also wish to collect the testator's medical records and may easily do so by having the testator sign a release.

8. PRESERVE PRIOR WILL

When a testator executes a new will, it is common practice to physically destroy prior wills. If the testator's capacity is in doubt, however, and the testator indicates a preference for the prior will compared to intestacy, it is a good idea to retain the prior will. If a court holds that the new will is invalid, you may offer the old will for probate much to the chagrin of the contestant.

9. REEXECUTE SAME WILL ON REGULAR BASIS

If a will contest is successful, the estate passes under a prior will, or if none, via intestacy. You may want to preserve a prior will if the testator prefers its dispositive scheme to intestacy. Of course, the testator clearly prefers the new will to both the old will and intestacy. Thus, you could have the testator reexecute the same will on a regular basis, for example, once every six months. At the time of the testator's death, the most recent will would be offered for probate. If a contest is successful, then the will executed six months prior would be introduced. If that one is likewise set aside, the will executed one year prior would be introduced, and so on until all wills are exhausted. A potential contestant might forego a contest when the contestant realizes that sufficient reasons for contest would have to be proved for many different points in time.

QUESTION

How could you combine this technique with *in terrorem* provisions to create a *will wall?*

10. SUGGEST THAT THE TESTATOR CONSIDER MAKING A MORE TRADITIONAL DISPOSITION

Unusual dispositions, such as those disinheriting close family members, treating like-situated children differently, and imposing excessive restrictions on gifts, are apt to trigger contests. Therefore, you may wish to suggest that the testator consider toning down the disposition plan to bring it closer to conforming to a traditional arrangement. Of course, the client may balk at this recommendation. You should explain that although this may cause the testator to deal with property in an undesired way, it may reduce the motives for a contest and thus increase the chances of the will being uncontested. (Or stated another way, half a loaf is better than no loaf at all.) Alternatively, other estate planning techniques may be used to make unconventional dispositions.

11. MAKE SIGNIFICANT INTER VIVOS GIFT TO DISINHERITED HEIR APPARENT AT TIME OF WILL EXECUTION

The testator may wish to make an inter vivos gift, either outright or in trust, to a disinherited heir apparent at the same time the will is executed (i.e., minutes after will execution). This gift should be substantial but, of course, far less than the amount the heir apparent would take via intestacy. After the testator's death, the heir is less likely to contest the will on the basis of lack of testamentary capacity. If the contestant asserted lack of capacity, the contestant would be forced to concede that the contestant accepted property from a person who lacked the capacity to make a gift or establish a trust. In addition, should the contest succeed, the heir would be required to return any property already received to the estate or use it to offset the intestate share.

12. CONTRACT NOT TO CONTEST

The testator and the potential contestant may enter into a contract in which the contestant contractually relinquishes all rights to contest, take under a will, take under intestacy, claim homestead or other exempt property, etc. Assuming the contract is supported by sufficient consideration, it should be effective to prevent the potential contestant from interfering with the probate of the will or the administration of the estate.

13. TORT SUIT FOR INTENTIONAL INTERFERENCE WITH THE RIGHT TO INHERIT

Some jurisdictions permit a tort action for interference with inheritance rights. In some states, this tort action may be brought while the person is still alive, even though the property is merely an expectancy interest which does not vest until death. See Carlton v. Carlton, 575 So.2d 239 (Fla. App.1991); Harmon v. Harmon, 404 A.2d 1020 (Me. 1979). The analysis of one commentator is especially useful.

> Thus, a plaintiff may maintain a cause of action during a testator's lifetime for interference with an intended legacy, for instance, due to revocation or execution of a will as a result of undue influence or fraud. In this situation, the tort action is something of a "living" will contest in that it may resolve conclusively many of the issues that ordinarily would be considered only after a decedent's death ... preventing relitigation of those issues after death.

M. Read Moore, *At the Frontier of Probate Litigation: Intentional Interference With the Right to Inherit*, Prob. & Prop., Nov./Dec. 1993, at 6, 7.

NOTE

For additional information, see Steven K. Mignogna, *On the Brink of Tortious Interference With Inheritance*, PROB. & PROP., Mar./Apr. 2002, at 45; Nita Ledford, *Note—Intentional Interference With Inheritance*, 30 REAL PROP., PROB. & TR. J. 325 (1995); Marilyn Marmai, *Tortious Interference With Inheritance: Primary Remedy or Last Recourse,* 5 CONN. PROB. L.J. 295 (1991).

14. SUGGEST USE OF OTHER ESTATE PLANNING TECHNIQUES

Whenever you anticipate a will contest, you should consider using other estate planning techniques to supplement the will. Inter vivos gifts, either outright or in trust, multiple-party accounts, and life insurance, annuities, and other death benefit plans are just some of the alternative techniques available. Although these arrangements may be set aside on grounds similar to those for contesting a will, such as lack of capacity or undue influence, they may be more difficult for a contestant to undo. More people may be involved with the creation or administration of these non-probate arrangements thereby providing a greater number of individuals competent to testify about the client's mental condition. In addition, the contestant may be estopped from contesting certain arrangements if the contestant has already accepted benefits as, for example, a beneficiary of a trust. Furthermore, many of these techniques may be used to secure other benefits such as tax reduction, reduced need for guardianship, probate avoidance, and increased flexibility.

NOTES AND QUESTIONS

1. Several other methods to prevent will contests are discussed elsewhere in this book. Ante-mortem probate is covered in the next section of this chapter, selection of witnesses in Chapter 11(E), enhancing the will execution ceremony in Chapter 11(F), videotaping the will execution ceremony in Chapter 11(G), and internal integration in Chapter 11(B)(2).

2. What will prevention techniques do you like the best? Least? Why?

3. What other methods would you consider using to reduce the likelihood of a will contest?

C. ANTE-MORTEM PROBATE

GERRY W. BEYER, PRE-MORTEM PROBATE*

PROB. & PROP., July/Aug. 1993, at 6, 7–9.

"[T]he post mortem squabblings and contests on mental condition ... have made a will the least secure of all human dealings."—*Lloyd v. Wayne Circuit Judge,* 23 N.W. 28, 30 (Mich. 1885).

The post-mortem probate model prevalent in the United States contains a glaring deficiency. The key witness—the testator—is deceased and for this reason the courts are limited to indirect evidence concerning the testator's capacity, intent and freedom from undue influence. Post-mortem probate provides a feeding ground for spurious will contests that eat away at the corpus of an estate no longer protected by the evidentiary power that lies buried with the testator. This unacceptable result can be avoided if procedures exist for validating the will while the testator is still alive, i.e., a pre-mortem or "living" probate.

AN EXAMPLE

Assume that your client asks you to draw a new will. The client is divorced and has two children. The original will, drafted 10 years earlier, divided the client's estate equally between the two children. The client was diagnosed as HIV positive about four years ago and now has AIDS. The client's son lives nearby and has been a constant companion, even reducing a busy work schedule to provide care and support. The client's daughter, a very successful and wealthy business owner, makes only brief and infrequent visits. For these reasons, your client wants the new will to leave the son 75% of the estate with the remaining passing to a local hospital that conducts extensive AIDS research.

This situation is ripe for a will contest. The daughter is likely to challenge the will, claiming that illness stripped away her parent's testamentary capacity and that her brother exerted undue influence over their parent. What should the client do? Outright gifts to the son and the hospital are not feasible because the client has extensive and unpredictable medical expenses that require financial liquidity. A trust would provide some solace but is open to attacks based on lack of capacity or undue influence. A videotape of the will execution ceremony may help but could backfire if the illness has caused physical deterioration that would give the daughter ammunition to challenge the will, even though the client's mental capabilities are not impaired. How will the estate planner solve this seemingly intractable problem?

If the client is fortunate enough to live in a state authorizing pre-mortem probate, the answer is easy: follow the statutory procedure to obtain a judgment declaring the will to be valid. This judgment would then prevent the will from being successfully contested after the client's death.

DEVELOPMENT AND MODELS

Although pre-mortem probate may seem to be a modern and progressive concept, its roots can be traced to ancient laws and customs recorded in the Old Testament. Underpinnings of pre-mortem probate can also be found in both English common law and European civil law.

The modern lineage of ante-mortem probate in the United States stems from a statute passed by the Michigan legislature in 1883. Although this statute was declared unconstitutional by the Michigan Supreme Court in 1885, recognition of judicial authority to render declaratory judgments led to a rebirth of the concept. Arkansas, North Dakota and Ohio enacted ante-mortem statutes in the waning years of the 1970s. See Ark. Code Ann. §§ 28–40–201 to–203 (Michie 1987); N.D. Cent. Code §§ 30.1–08.1–01 to–04 (Supp. 1991); Ohio Rev. Code Ann. §§ 2107.081–.085 (Baldwin 1987). [In 2010, Alaska reignited the interest in ante-mortem probate when it enacted the first ante-mortem probate legislation since the Arkansas statute. Alaska Stat. § 13.12.530–.590 (2010) (also providing for the validation of a trust during the settlor's lifetime). Nevada considered ante-mortem legislation in 2011 but it failed to pass.]

All states that authorize ante-mortem probate have statutes based on the adversarial contest model. Under this method of ante-mortem probate, the testator executes a will in the normal manner and then asks the court for a declaratory judgment ruling the will valid, e.g., that all technical formalities were satisfied, and the testator had the required testamentary capacity to execute a will and was not under undue influence. The beneficiaries of the will and the heirs apparent are given notice so they may contest the probate of the will. If the court finds that the will is valid, it is effective to dispose of the testator's property at death unless the testator makes a new will or otherwise revokes the one proven via the pre-mortem procedure.

Two additional ante-mortem probate models have received extensive discussion but neither has been adopted. The conservatorship model, like the contest model, is adversarial and based on a declaratory judgment action, but a court-appointed guardian ad litem represents the heirs apparent rather than the heirs apparent representing themselves. The administrative model provides for the court to make an ex parte determination of the will's validity, based on the report of a guardian ad litem.

The National Conference of Commissioners on Uniform State Laws gave serious consideration to a Uniform Ante-mortem Probate of Wills Act. Because of disagreement on whether a contest or administrative format should be followed, the project was abandoned in the early 1980s.

BENEFITS

Many of the problems arising under post-mortem probate are caused by the testator's absence. Ante-mortem probate eradicates this inherent difficulty and provides at least three significant benefits: it discourages spurious will contests, alleviates evidentiary problems and helps effectuate the testator's intent. Subsumed within these benefits are welcome side effects such as the preservation of court time and estate resources that otherwise would be wasted by disputes based on artificial grounds.

Spurious Will Contests Discouraged

One of the major policies underlying a post-mortem will contest is to ensure that deserving heirs do not lose a portion of the decedent's estate as a result of fraud, undue influence or insufficient capacity that may have affected the decedent at the time of will execution. In many cases, however, the will contest is wielded by greedy and unscrupulous disinherited heirs attempting to bludgeon an estate into a settlement to avoid depletion of assets during a lengthy court battle.

Pre-mortem probate serves as a barrier to unfounded challenges to the testator's will. The presence of the testator will dissuade many unhappy heirs from bringing a spurious contest. It is certainly easier to testify about a person's lack of capacity when the person is not looking you straight in the eye. In addition, formal validation of the will before the testator's death will speed the process of distributing the estate to the designated beneficiaries once the testator dies. Hence, the additional costs a testator incurs while alive to secure an ante-mortem probate may prevent the even greater expense of defending a baseless suit.

Evidentiary Problems Alleviated

A recurring problem with post-mortem probate is that the trier of fact must determine the capacity and intent of a person who is unable to testify or be observed. Even when everyone involved acts with the utmost propriety, this procedure often slips into an exercise of pure speculation. The quality of evidence presented may be very poor, having inevitably deteriorated with the passage of time. Even worse, disinherited heirs may deliberately misrepresent past events in hopes of having the will declared invalid. The lack of direct evidence becomes particularly troublesome when a jury views the distribution as unwise or unfair. Sympathetic juries are prone to invalidate a will that fails to provide for a surviving spouse or child, even though it is clearly not their role to rewrite a valid will because of personal objections.

Ante-mortem probate permits a court to evaluate testamentary capacity at the most logical time: when the testator is alive to present evidence. Instead of inferences drawn from testimony about the testator's past conduct, direct observation and cross-examination of the testator are possible. Because the burden of proving testamentary capacity is on the proponent of a will, living probate appeals to a basic consideration of fairness to the testator. Undoubtedly, most people would prefer to defend personally against assaults on their integrity or mental states.

Frustration of Testator's Intent Prevented

The ability to transfer one's property by will is taken for granted by property owners. Testators expect their wishes to be carried out after their deaths. But no matter how sane or lucid a testator is at the time of will execution, the will contest and evidentiary problems discussed above prevent the post-mortem probate system from reasonably guaranteeing that this property right is protected. Even simple "technical" errors can lead to the invalidity of a will.

By validating the will during the testator's lifetime, ante-mortem probate can protect a person's basic property right to dispose of property at death. Problems with the will may be detected while the testator is still alive and capable of remedying the situation. In addition, many property transfers that are accepted and even applauded when made inter vivos, such as large donations to reputable charities, serve as the basis for contest when included in a will. These attacks may succeed when a fact finder evaluates the testator's actions based on preconceived notions of a "normal" estate distribution. Ante-mortem probate helps ameliorate this paradox between inter vivos and testamentary property transfers by allowing the testator to explain personally the reasons behind the gift. Accordingly, the likelihood that the testator's intent will be carried out is dramatically increased.

DEFICIENCIES

Ante-mortem probate is not a panacea. There are problems associated with the technique that will make it impractical or unsuitable for many testators. There is no doubt that post-mortem probate will retain its status as the procedure of choice for many, if not most, testators. However, in appropriate situations, the availability of ante-mortem probate provides a welcome alternative to anxious testators despite the up-front cost.

Many of the problems with ante-mortem probate stem from its potential psychological effects on the testator and the testator's family. The testator may not wish to disclose the contents of the will or face the embarrassment that may occur if the testator's testamentary capacity is litigated. Presumptive heirs who genuinely believe that the testator lacks capacity or is being unduly influenced may be reluctant to bring a contest while the testator lives.

From a legal standpoint, questions may be raised concerning the binding effect of the court's declaration that the testator's will is valid. The traditional maxim that "the living have no heirs" still retains validity, despite the seeming applicability of declaratory judgment principles to living probate. Another potential problem involves a posthumous challenge on the ground that undue influence was exerted over the testator after the ante-mortem probate judgment was rendered, and that this influence prevented the testator from revoking the will. In addition, ante-mortem probate may raise due process issues if notice requirements are not carefully drafted and followed.

Although this discussion of potential problems with pre-mortem probate is not exhaustive, it is apparent that this procedure is not a substitute for post-mortem probate. Instead, ante-mortem probate provides a valuable alternative.

CONCLUSION

Pre-mortem probate has the potential of greatly improving the legal system's ability effectively to transmit an individual's wealth by fortifying the testator's distribution desires. This process places the most important source of evidence, the testator, directly before the court and thus ameliorates many of the inherit difficulties of post-mortem probate that encourage the filing of spurious will contests. Besides the psychological and financial benefits that would accrue to the testator and the intended beneficiaries, ante-mortem probate may lead to a more efficient use of judicial resources.

When a will contest seems all but inevitable, such as in the example at the beginning of this article, the estate planner might consider advising the testator to establish a domicile in one of the [four] ([Alaska,] Arkansas, North Dakota, and Ohio) that currently has an ante-mortem procedure. Naturally, not all clients will be willing and able to make such a change. Instead, these clients are relegated to other estate planning techniques that may not achieve the desired level of protection. The ability to dispose of property is a prized property right that may be thwarted by the traditional post-mortem procedure. The bench, bar and legislators of states without ante-mortem procedures should consider offering the benefits of this technique to their citizens.

OHIO ANTE-MORTEM STATUTES

DECLARATION OF VALIDITY OF WILL

§ 2107.081 Petition by testator for declaration of validity of will; failure to file not evidence

(A) A person who executes a will allegedly in conformity with the laws of this state may petition the probate court of the county in which he is domiciled, if he is domiciled in this state, or the probate court of the county in which any of his real property is located, if he is not domiciled in this state, for a judgment declaring the validity of the will.

The petition may be filed in the form determined by the probate court of the county in which it is filed.

The petition shall name as parties defendant all persons named in the will as beneficiaries, and all of the persons who would be entitled to inherit from the testator under Chapter 2105 of the Revised Code had the testator died intestate on the date the petition was filed.

For the purposes of this section, "domicile" shall be determined at the time of filing the petition with the probate court.

(B) The failure of a testator to file a petition for a judgment declaring the validity of a will he has executed shall not be construed as evidence or an admission that the will was not properly executed pursuant to section 2107.03 of the Revised Code or any prior law of this state in effect at the time of execution or as evidence or an admission that the testator did not have the requisite testamentary capacity and freedom from undue influence under section 2107.02 of the Revised Code.

§ 2107.082 Service of process

Service of process in an action authorized by section 2107.081 of the Revised Code shall be made on every party defendant named in that action by the following methods:

(A) By certified mail, or any other valid personal service permitted by the Rules of Civil Procedure, if the party is an inhabitant of this state or is found within this state;

(B) By certified mail, with a copy of the summons and petition, to the party at his last known address or any other valid personal service permitted by the Rules of Civil Procedure, if the party is not an inhabitant of this state or is not found within this state;

(C) By publication, according to Civil Rule 4.4, in a newspaper of general circulation published in the county where the petition was filed, for three consecutive weeks, if the address of the party is unknown, if all methods of personal service permitted under division (B) of this section were attempted without success, or if the interest of the party under the will or in the estate of the testator should the will be declared invalid is unascertainable at that time.

§ 2107.083 Validity of will, hearing

When a petition is filed pursuant to section 2107.081 of the Revised Code, the probate court shall conduct a hearing on the validity of the will. The hearing shall be adversary in nature and shall be conducted pursuant to section 2721.10 of the Revised Code, except as otherwise provided in sections 2107.081 to 2107.085 of the Revised Code.

§ 2107.084 Declaration of validity; effects; disposition; revocation or modification of will after declaration

(A) The probate court shall declare the will valid if, after conducting a proper hearing pursuant to section 2107.083 of the Revised Code, it finds that the will was properly executed pursuant to section 2107.03 of the Revised Code or under any prior law of this state that was in effect at the time of execution and that the testator had the requisite testamentary capacity and freedom from undue influence pursuant to section 2107.02 of the Revised Code.

Any such judgment declaring a will valid is binding in this state as to the validity of the will on all facts found, unless provided otherwise in this section, section 2107.33, or division (B) of section 2107.71 of the Revised Code, and, if the will remains valid, shall give the will full legal effect as the instrument of disposition of the testator's estate, unless the will has been modified or revoked according to law.

(B) Any declaration of validity issued as a judgment pursuant to this section shall be sealed in an envelope along with the will to which it pertains, and filed by the probate judge or his designated officer in the offices of that probate court. The filed will shall be available during the testator's lifetime only to the testator. If the testator removes a filed will from the possession of the probate judge, the declaration of validity rendered under division (A) of this section no longer has any effect.

(C) A testator may revoke or modify a will declared valid and filed with a probate court pursuant to this section by petitioning the probate court in possession of the will and asking that the will be revoked or modified. The petition shall include a document executed pursuant to sections 2107.02 and 2107.03 of the Revised Code, and shall name as parties defendant those persons who were parties defendant in any previous action declaring the will valid, those persons who are named in any modification as beneficiaries, and those persons who would be entitled because of the revocation or modification, to inherit from the testator under Chapter 2105 of the Revised Code had the testator died intestate on the date the petition was filed. Service of the petition and process shall be made on these parties by the methods authorized in section 2107.082 of the Revised Code.

Unless waived by all parties, the court shall conduct a hearing on the validity of the revocation or modification requested under this division in the same manner as it would on any initial petition for a judgment declaring a will to be valid under this section. If the court finds that the revocation or modification is valid, as defined in division (A) of this section, the revocation or modification shall take full effect and be binding, and revoke the will or modify it to the extent of the valid modification. The revocation or modification, the judgment declaring it valid, and the will itself shall be sealed in an envelope and filed with the probate court, and shall be available during the testator's lifetime only to the testator.

(D) A testator may also modify a will by any later will or codicil executed according to the laws of this state or any other state and may revoke a will by any method permitted under section 2107.33 of the Revised Code.

(E) A declaration of validity of a will, or of a revocation or modification of a will previously determined to be valid, given under division (C) of this section, is not subject to collateral attack, except by a person and in the manner specified in division (B) of section 2107.71 of the Revised Code, but is appealable subject to the terms of Chapter 2721 of the Revised Code.

§ 2107.085 Effects in relation to other matters

The finding of facts by a probate court in a proceeding brought under sections 2107.081 to 2107.085 of the Revised Code is not admissible as evidence in any proceeding other than one brought to determine the validity of a will.

The determination or judgment rendered in a proceeding under these sections is not binding upon the parties to such a proceeding in any action not brought to determine the validity of a will.

The failure of a testator to file a petition for a judgment declaring the validity of a will he has executed is not admissible as evidence in any proceeding to determine the validity of that will or any other will executed by the testator.

LOCATE

Does your state authorize ante-mortem probate? If not, could it arguably fit under your state's declaratory judgment statutes?

NOTES AND QUESTIONS

1. Are ante-mortem statutes constitutional? See Cooper v. Woodard, 1983 WL 6566 (Ohio App.).

2. In what situations do you think ante-mortem probate is most often used by estate planners in the states that have ante-mortem legislation? See Horst v. First Nat'l Bank in Massillon, 1990 WL 94654 (Ohio App.).

3. The impetus for the *contest model* used by Arkansas, North Dakota, and Ohio was Howard P. Fink, *Ante-Mortem Probate Revisited: Can An Idea Have a Life After Death?,* 37 OHIO ST. L.J. 264 (1976).

4. The *conservatorship model* is, like the contest model, built on a declaratory judgment base. The testator would petition the court for a declaration that the will is valid, and notice would be given to all the beneficiaries and heirs apparent. In addition, a guardian ad litem would be appointed to represent these interested parties as well as unborn and unascertained beneficiaries and heirs. Thus, an heir apparent or beneficiary would not need to contest the ante-mortem probate; the guardian ad litem would represent these individuals. The judge would evaluate the results of a medical examination of the testator and other relevant evidence before determining whether the testator had the required mental capacity to make a will. See John H. Langbein, *Living Probate: The Conservatorship Model,* 77 MICH. L. REV. 63 (1978).

5. Departing from both the contest and conservatorship models, the *administrative model* is based on an ex parte proceeding rather than on an adversarial action. The ante-mortem probate would begin in the same manner

as the other two models, i.e., the testator would petition the court for a declaration that the will complies with all necessary formalities and that the testator had the requisite capacity and was not being unduly influenced. The court would then appoint a guardian ad litem. However, unlike proceedings under the conservatorship model, the guardian would be acting for the court to determine facts, rather than representing the individual interests of the heirs apparent or beneficiaries. The guardian would interview the testator and others to ascertain the testator's capacity and freedom from undue influence. Notice to the heirs apparent or to others would not be required; the court would examine the evidence brought forth by the guardian ad litem in deciding whether the will is entitled to ante-mortem probate. See Gregory S. Alexander & Albert M. Pearson, *Alternative Models of Ante–Mortem Probate and Procedural Due Process Limitations on Succession,* 78 MICH. L. REV. 89 (1980).

6. Would you support the enactment of ante-mortem legislation in your state? Why or why not? What model would you recommend?

7. For an article critical of ante-mortem probate, see Mary Louise Fellows, *The Case Against Living Probate,* 78 MICH. L. REV. 1066 (1980).

8. For further information on ante-mortem probate, see Aloysius Leopold & Gerry Beyer, *Ante-Mortem Probate: A Viable Alternative,* 43 ARK. L. REV. 131 (1990); Forrest J. Heyman, *A Patchwork Quilt: The Case for Collage Contest Model Ante–Mortem Probate in Light of Alaska's Recent Ante Mortem Legislation*, 19 ELDER L.J. 385 (2012); and Joe R. Savoie, *The Commissioners' Model of Ante–Mortem Probate*, 37 ACTEC L.J. ___ (2012).

D. ALTERNATIVE DISPUTE RESOLUTION

1. MEDIATION—WHILE CLIENT IS ALIVE

DAVID GAGE & JOHN GROMALA, MEDIATION IN ESTATE PLANNING: A STRATEGY FOR EVERYONE'S BENEFIT*

4 MARQ. ELDER'S ADVISOR, Fall 2002, at 23.

How much better would this world be if we all believed that most disputes could be avoided? Mediation is offered as a tool to reach agreement, but the hard work of mediating a dispute requires a knowledgeable, experienced professional. These authors offer observations and strategies based on their expertise and successes in the field.

With a few modifications, the estate-planning process could be less prone to conflicts, and a more rewarding and rich experience for everyone involved. Estate planning is a process by which one generation passes wealth to others, usually their adult children. It has become a highly complex and specialized field in which tax and financial experts fine-tune

* Reprinted with the permission of Marquette University Law School Elder's Advisor. Originally published in 4 MARQ. ELDER'S ADVISOR, Fall 2002, at 23. Also see *Business Mediation & Collaboration Services*, http://www.bmcassociates.com/index.htm and http://www.mediate.com/articles/gromala7.cfm.

plans to minimize taxes and maximize economic gain. The essence of what is transpiring within the family, however, often gets lost in the process. That essence is a gift from parents to children, or to their children's children, to charities, and others. Parents who have worked hard and accumulated some measure of wealth are deciding to make their final gift to their children. It is the last note of a family-long song. It is something that could be celebrated but rarely is. It is something that begs to be discussed openly but rarely is.

We will discuss why the human side of this extremely important family transition has been so muted that it is barely audible, and how some changes in the estate-planning process could restore it.

Lack of Communication: A Big Part of the Problem

The problems with the existing methods of estate planning are more serious than just short-circuiting an important family transition. Even though parents spend hours upon hours and thousands of dollars conferring with attorneys and advisors to draw up carefully crafted estate plans, some of these plans simply go awry. Families are torn asunder by allegations, claims, and counterclaims. Litigation drags on for years. Attorneys and other advisors are sued for malpractice. What should be positive family experiences devolve into family horror stories. The horror stories have made many parents afraid of the process.

Having worked in this area, and mediated trust and will contests for some years, we have concluded that the nexus of these problems stems from the lack of communication and miscommunication among family members, and between family members and their advisors. Changing the patterns of communication that typically occur during the estate-planning process can make a huge difference in the family's experience and the advisors' experience.

Parents need encouragement to have serious conversations between themselves and with their adult children about setting estates, dividing property, and their own dying. Most families are going to experience a significant challenge when they try to have these conversations. Many families face a challenge even in their regular, day-to-day communications.

People do not typically explain their thinking or describe their feelings particularly well, thereby creating vast room for misperceptions to flourish. People also have trouble listening to one another and make assumptions about what they are hearing. So having serious, open communication about estate matters is usually going to be extremely challenging. Nevertheless, that does not mean these conversations should be avoided.

Avoiding the conversations can lead to a host of other problems. For example, in one family we are aware of, a bachelor uncle and an unmarried aunt died within a year of each other, and each left a sizable estate to their nieces and nephews. Neither of them had whispered a word of it to any of their nieces or nephews before they passed away.

Months after the aunt and uncle died, all the nieces and nephews received generous checks along with the completed relevant tax forms. Although they were happy to receive their windfall shares in the two estates, most of them reported having an empty feeling as well. The personal element, the "contact" was missing. They wished that they could have thanked their aunt and uncle in person, before they died. They explained that it would have been a very different and much "richer" experience for them than simply receiving the check and tax forms in the mail months later.

The conversation that begins, "I want you to know that I'm going to leave some money for you when I die..." is a difficult one for many reasons. It references one's own death and it raises the subject of money. For many people, these are two taboo subjects. But the responsibility for why these conversations fail to occur rests in part with the culture of estate planning.

In this culture, an underlying assumption seems to be that people are better off not discussing their intentions with family members; that doing so might only stir things up, exacerbate problems, or diminish the benefactor's prerogative to do whatever he or she wishes. Furthermore, if avoiding issues causes problems to arise later among coinheritors, the benefactor will not be bothered with it—now being permanently removed!

Most situations in life are not like estate planning in this regard. During our lifetime, we might choose short-term benefits, but there is always the distinct possibility that we will still be around when the longterm consequences come home to roost. When it comes to wills and trusts, people will not be around to face the fallout. The culture of estate planning seems to have taken the fact that benefactors won't be around and concluded that what happens after their deaths is not their concern.

Conflicting Needs and Conflicts of Interest

In the best of all worlds, when couples with adult children hire estate planners, they enter the process with a solid, healthy marital relationship. Ideally, they both have access to the same financial information. They have spoken to their adult children, listened to them, and understand their needs and interests. They have communicated to their children what they are generally thinking with regard to their estate. The children accept and can live with their parents' wishes.

When the parents have gathered all this information, had the conversations, and rehashed it all, the two of them are still in sync about what they would generally like to accomplish. That is when they hire their estate planner. The estate planner is then in a perfect position to collect all the relevant information from the couple and go to work. That is the best of all possible worlds. Unfortunately, such a couple is a rarity.

The fact that most families are much more complicated than this ideal was less of a problem years ago. Prior to the era of specialization and stringent conflict rules, attorneys who knew their clients and families well created their wills and estate plans. Like family doctors, those attorneys knew all the children and were aware of the families' trials, tribulations, successes, and failures. In that climate, it was common for attorneys to counsel spouses without discussing the possibility of a conflict of interest. Today, that deep level of familiarity is rare. The legal climate is one in which conflict-of-interest concerns are always a part of the attorneys' thinking, and family dynamics are typically more complex than in years past.

Estate planners, at times, advise couples who do not have solid, healthy relationships. The husbands and wives may not have access to the same financial information, and it is doubtful that they share the same level of understanding about their situation—especially if they are wealthy. It is unlikely they have had open, candid conversations with each other or with their adult children about their own or their children's needs and interests. The likelihood that such couples are truly in sync with one another is slim.

Couples who are not in sync about how they should handle the transfer of their assets if one or both of them dies pose a potentially serious problem for estate planners. Smoothing over, minimizing, denying, or failing to explore possible differences can have disastrous consequences for couples, their families, and their advisors. When couples are only seen together by their planners, they may never express their real thoughts, feelings, wishes, or apprehensions because their only opportunity to speak is in front of their spouses.

Estate planning attorneys are not really free to have separate conversations or interviews when they represent couples because of the likelihood of a conflict of interest. In separate sessions they would be more likely to hear divergent views, differences of opinion, and conflicting needs and interests. However, to avoid the potential for a conflict of interest, the attorney would need to advise the clients that the substance of any discussions with either spouse would be shared with the other. This would probably negate the benefit of a separate conference.

Suggesting to couples that they both should have their own counsel can actually create problems between spouses where none may have existed. Because these situations inherently have the potential to become adversarial, when spouses obtain separate representation it increases the probability that they will, in fact, become adversaries. If the suggestion is made for separate counsel and the couple declines, they may be asked to sign a "consent to joint representation." While this may satisfy ethical requirements, it too can foster feelings of being adversaries, stir up suspicions, and even cause one or the other spouse to put off or abort the estate-planning process.

In summary, the steps commonly used by estate planners to remedy their concerns regarding conflicts of interest can limit their malpractice exposure, but are unlikely to open up communication or lead to plans that satisfy the needs of spouses and work for all their children as well.

Introducing the process of mediation into the estate-planning process gives estate planners a way to handle ethical concerns without sacrificing the clarity that is achieved when one person has separate discussions with each interested party. It also gives estate planners a way to feel confident that the information developed through mediation represents their clients' real wishes.

The Role of Mediators

In the estate-planning process, mediators are uniquely positioned to help planners with the preparatory work of clarifying the real needs and interests of the spouses and adult children, thereby increasing the likelihood that everyone will be comfortable and satisfied with the plan that is developed. The expertise of mediators is in fostering an open, constructive dialogue of difficult subjects, building a collaborative spirit (especially when people feel at odds with one another), and helping people arrive at mutual understandings and consensual agreements.

The mediation process is designed to achieve successful resolution of highly emotional and contentious conflicts. It does so in the following way: The mediators are neutral and work for the common good of all the people involved. They may work for the entire family even while recognizing the different roles, authority, and positions of the various family members. In estate planning, this means that they recognize that it is the parents' prerogative to do whatever they wish with their assets.

Mediators also recognize that parents want all their family members to feel as good as possible about their decisions and not feel angry, cheated, or resentful over the final plan. In consultation with parents and their estate planners, mediators decide whom to include in the process. Mediators may bring all the involved adult parties into the process in order to achieve the best possible result, with the greatest buy-in and the least chance of having the final plan contested for any reason. When all the participants are agreed upon, the mediators meet with everyone involved—together and separately—in order to ensure that everyone's concerns are known and dealt with, that hidden agendas see the light of day, and that the process moves along as swiftly as possible.

Mediation is an informal, flexible process that mediators actively direct and guide. The discussions range from emotional, interpersonal dynamics to hard, cold dollars and cents. Mediators do not give advice. While they never tell people what they should do, they do encourage, coax, and motivate people to create consensual agreements that have the greatest potential for working in the long term for everyone involved.

It is helpful for mediators to be familiar with the basic principles and terminology of estate planning. They will not give advice about strategies, though. Mediators are likely to consult with the estate planners, but the expert role and all advice given is clearly reserved for the planner. It is also important for mediators to understand family systems. Being skilled at working with individual personalities, personal values, family history, and interpersonal dynamics can help keep sensitive discussions constructive. In many of these situations it is helpful to have two mediators working together, one experienced in estate planning and the other experienced in family systems.

Confidentiality Fosters Candor

The fact that what transpires in mediation cannot be used later if there are adversarial proceedings is a real advantage of mediation. Oral and written communications, admissions, offers, notes, etc., made during mediation cannot be used in later litigation or arbitration, so it is not risky for the parties to be completely open. Most mediators describe the bounds of confidentiality in a mediation agreement, and most jurisdictions provide broad protection to mediation proceedings, including prohibiting the mediator from testifying if there is subsequent litigation.

The result is that people involved in mediation tend to be open and candid with the mediators. This is especially true in separate caucus sessions during which they can verbalize their worst fears and suspicions, their angriest feelings, and their wildest ideas about possible resolutions to the problems. People understand that it is part of the mediators' job to help them sort through what is real and what's not, and what is productive and what's not.

When Mediation Is Needed

Mediation is advisable whenever an estate is very large, whenever a potential conflict of interest becomes apparent during the estate-planning process, or whenever family circumstances are particularly complex. In large estates, the potential for conflict is high because of human nature and the pervasiveness of misunderstanding and greed. It is easier to uncover the existence of a family member's secret plans, desires, and hidden agendas and resolve them before conflicts erupt than it is to get people to sit at the same table and negotiate after an eruption has occurred.

If there are no ticking bombs—something that may take a family systems specialist to discern quickly—then the mediation goes very rapidly and the family and the estate planner can proceed with confidence that the plan the advisor designs will truly meet the desires of all the people involved. After mediation, the estate planner also has a record that his or her advice and plan documents correctly address clients' desires.

There are many family circumstances that have the ability to complicate estate planning. Among them are the following:

- A mentally or physically challenged child
- Economic or educational disparity among heirs
- Divorce and multiple marriages
- Different ideas and desires related to charitable endeavors
- Inherited or other separate property
- Verbal promises that certain possessions will go to certain people

- A child who is caring for a parent
- A testator who is either very indecisive or dogmatic
- A closely held business as a family asset

None of these issues is straightforward. For example, a child who provides years of care for a sick parent may expect a larger share of the estate. A parent may look upon the years of help and see it as balancing the years of special attention that child received earlier in life. A sister may look at the help and see it as precisely what she would have done had her circumstances allowed her to help. The nature of family relations in these types of situations can foster suppressed emotions and many hidden agendas.

Poor communication and misconceptions may cause people who love one another to become antagonists.

Whenever any of these types of complications exist, it behooves families to have mediators assist them with the discussions. Mediators can help family members and their advisors to find and resolve the hidden issues. This can eliminate the tendency for procrastination or avoidance on the part of one person or another. In this way mediation can expedite the estate-planning process, even as it appears to add another step. We have been discussing the need for mediation in the estate-planning process but it has actually been used more frequently to resolve problems after death during probate and trust administration. Relations between executors or trustees and beneficiaries can turn sour because of divergent priorities, differences on matters of substance, perceptions, or perspectives on family history. Often differences are in perception rather than substance. Mediators help the parties clear up areas of ambiguity and aid them in developing a plan of interaction that promotes all their interests. As a result, executors and trustees no longer dread the beneficiaries' phone calls, and beneficiaries may feel less need to call the fiduciaries.

In situations that involve estate contests or disputes over the administration of wills and trusts, the courts are not charged with working out the best possible solution. Judges are forced to listen to scripted testimony and render decisions, typically for one party and against the other. Their judgments may be cumbersome, with little actual relief to either party. If the goal is a genuine solution rather than a finding of fault, then mediation is a far better approach because achieving a genuine solution requires far more flexible communication and discussion of needs and interests than formal court procedures will allow.

Mediation is also desirable in these types of situations for other reasons. First and foremost for many people is that it keeps family matters private. Disputes can be resolved without court involvement and public scrutiny. Because mediated solutions are usually achieved in much less time than those that result from arbitration or litigation, the cost of mediation is typically much less. Because the mediation process is essentially a collaborative one, it is far easier on the relationships among the people involved than adversarial proceedings. In fact, it often has a healing effect on the relationships and individuals. Since all the outcomes from mediation are consensual, family members never have the feeling that an outsider is telling them what to do; they are the ones deciding what is best for them.

Case Studies

The following case studies are either situations we know about personally or have worked on. The first two of the four cases illustrate the problems that arise in estate-planning situations when there is insufficient communication among the parents and their adult children. The first one was not a large or complicated estate, but the fallout created a most regrettable family rift. The second case revolves around just one asset and thus, on the surface, looks deceptively simple. The second two cases show how mediation can very meaningfully alter the typical communication patterns.

Case Study #1—Secrecy Leads to Alienation Of Brother and Sister

A widowed mother decided to leave all of her estate to her daughter because of a wide disparity in the net worths of her son and daughter. She told neither one of them for fear that the son would be angry. She was right.

The son was speechlessly angry when the will was read. He claimed that his anger was a result of the way his mother and sister plotted behind his back. He assumed that his sister talked his mother into the plan. He says that the money was insignificant to him and that he would have been happy for his sister to have their mother's money if he had just been consulted.

Now, years later, he still does not talk to his sister and his memories of his mother remain clouded—tainted by what he discovered after she died. What made the secrecy doubly hard for the son, he says, was that his mother seemed to trust and respect him. She had solicited and received his help with many of her financial decisions in the years prior to her death.

It seems apparent that even had the brother not liked his mother's idea of leaving her money to his sister, or had the mother been encouraged—and perhaps assisted—to converse about her intentions when she drafted her will, the family's experience would likely have been far healthier than the way it turned out. What was a potential conflict between the mother and son was transposed into an actual conflict between the brother and sister, one that so far has been intractable.

Case Study #2—Secrecy Scuttles an Estate Plan

A husband and wife who owned a hundred-year-old mansion on the Atlantic coast had every good intention to leave the house to all five of their children so that their children could enjoy it with their own children, just as they had done. Their estate plan included mechanisms for transferring the property in the most tax-advantaged way.

One day, the father absent-mindedly leaked their secret to one of their sons who then told a sister. The sister blew up at the mother, telling her in no uncertain terms that she wanted no part in such a housesharing arrangement with her siblings. The parents are currently in the process of considering using mediation to facilitate a more open dialog with their five children and respective spouses so the second plan will have a better chance of working for everyone than the first one did.

In this case, a couple did not talk with their adult children in advance of planning their estate, but had their eyes opened accidentally after their plan had been drawn up. Parental decisions about giving their possessions to their children are among the most difficult decisions they have to make, whether it involves dividing up various possessions or not dividing something and having the children share it. Knowing who has emotional attachments to what possessions is extremely difficult. Having conversations about giving property or other objects of worth to various children is not easy, but avoiding the conversations is often a greater problem.

Case Study #3—Mediation Dispels Misconceptions Among Family

The parents in this case—Richard and Judy—had had grown children and wisely recognized that it could be in everyone's interests to talk together about what they were planning to do with their estate. Because of the conflict-of-interest concerns, their estate attorney recommended that each child have his or her own counsel.

For the most part, everybody conferred with his or her own attorneys, accountants, and financial advisors. The experts corresponded among themselves and their proposals were circulated among the family. Everyone understood the concepts being presented. Each attorney spent much time with her or his client, and family members had many conferences—yet the family was not communicating effectively.

During the family meetings, Richard and Judy were basically on their own with their children and children's spouses. Each meeting would begin cordially, but before long someone was yelling. Others would refuse to talk. Weeks and sometimes months would go by before they would attempt another meeting. Some people talked between meetings but rather than help, it only raised the suspicions of others who were not privy to those conversations. As the relationships became increasingly strained, family members suspected one another of conniving to gain advantage. The suspicions grew both within and between generations. It was adversely affecting Richard and Judy's relationship. It also was causing, or worsening, rifts in two of their children's marriages.

The proposed plans that were circulating had great technical merit with respect to tax minimization, but the lines of communication between and among attorneys and clients (dictated by conflict-of-interest rules) did not provide a vehicle for the family members' real interests to become known to one another and their advisors. Consequently, each professional was working with only a few pieces of a much larger puzzle. They were unable to put the pieces together since each had a different concept of what the final picture should look like. Spouses and siblings had nonmonetary needs that were either obfuscated or couched in terms of dollars.

Hours upon hours were spent by different experts trying to shape a plan that would satisfy various family members' dollar demands. One person or another continually vetoed or sabotaged the plans, causing everyone to view everyone else as irrational. Richard and Judy wanted to give up and threatened to not give anything to their kids. An attorney for one of the children suggested that the family engage a lawyer and psychologist mediator team. After clarifying exactly what their role would be vis à vis all the other professionals, the mediators set up a two-and-a-half-day retreat for the entire family, including spouses and the one fiancé.

During the first afternoon and evening, the mediators met with Richard and Judy together and separately, and likewise with their children and spouses. The next morning they started by meeting with the entire family together. At that meeting, the mediators' role was discussed and the family agreed on ground rules for the retreat. Each person had an opportunity to speak without interruption about what he or she hoped could be achieved and his or her own vision for how it could happen. A master list of all the issues was started on flipcharts. Subsequently, there were individual and subgroup meetings as well as more meetings with everyone. The list of issues grew at the same time issues were being negotiated. There were numerous issues that were total surprises to some of the family members.

One of the hidden agendas unearthed involved the family business run by Richard with considerable help from his youngest son, Bob. Richard wanted to recognize Bob's contribution by giving the enterprise to him. What he never knew was that Bob hated the business and wanted no part of it. Bob was afraid to tell his father because of the great sentimental value he perceived that his father attached to it. The business was taking too much of Bob's time, to the detriment of his own business and his relations with his wife and children. What Richard told the mediators in a separate session was that he was continuing the business only because he believed Bob loved it and would want to inherit it. He had lost his emotional ties to the business. The dynamics of the family were such that this one issue seemed to touch all of them in an inexplicable way. When the mediators brought everyone together and facilitated a discussion of the business between Richard and Bob, everyone first held their breaths, and then released a sigh of relief.

Some of the other issues that were negotiated included: What would happen to a summer cottage that some of the children were extremely attached to and others felt no attachment to? How would Richard and Judy deal with certain valuable items that one or the other of them had promised to certain children? and How they would account for considerable money that had been given or loaned to some of the children over the years?

The number of family members and advisors in this case created a complex situation—however, any estate with a closely owned business poses a significant challenge to the planner. Such cases always involve tough decisions on many people's parts about their lives, their careers, and whether or not they see themselves staying with the business for years to come. It is critical in these situations to explore the expectations of various family members. It is also important to explore the expectations of spouses. (There are instances when children's spouses have even higher expectations than the children themselves do.) Control and succession in a family business are issues waiting to explode if not properly addressed early on. As this case illustrates, until these issues become transparent, they can derail estate planning.

This family was wealthier than most, but they were similar to other families in an important way. Although reluctant to admit it, most families have secrets, some emotionally charged bits of information that not everyone is privy to or even aware of. It is that nature of the secrets and histories that make families unique. A major advantage of mediation and the skill of experienced mediators is uncovering critical secrets in families.

Case Study #4—Open Communication Produces Harmony

Mike and Nancy had been telling their adult children for some time that they were going to be planning their estate. The estate's major asset was a 150–employee mechanical contracting company that they had founded in Connecticut forty years earlier. The eldest son, John, who was president of the company, suggested to them that he and the four other children who were actively involved in the business should work together to devise a plan for how they would divide ownership of the company and run the business. Mike and Nancy agreed to put their estate planning on hold until they had a chance to talk with their two children who were not part of the business, and the five of them who were in the business had had an opportunity to formulate a plan. The parents conferred numerous times with their other two children to ensure that there was no possibility that either of them had any interest in being part of the business. They made it clear to them that they would inherit other assets if they elected not to be part of the business.

The children in the business hired a lawyer and psychologist mediator team to lead a two-and-a-half-day retreat in which they created a Family Business Charter, a twenty-five-page document that spelled out in detail all aspects of how they would own and run the company together. Over the course of the retreat, they discussed their personal values, their very different personal styles, and the implications that their different values and styles had for working effectively together.

They looked at the management of the company and how they would each have very different roles to play. They talked about the fact that John was president and doing a good job, but that they would create a board to evaluate his performance and replace him if his performance did not meet certain specified standards. They made tough decisions about ownership, not only for their generation but also for the generation after them. They examined their expectations of themselves and one another, and engaged in scenario planning.

All of these things, as well as others, went into the Charter, which then went to Mike and Nancy. When they approved it, the Charter was sent to their estate-planning attorney, who relied on the document to help draft the larger plan for the parents' entire estate.

In many families with businesses, the most significant asset is the business. Advising parents to divide that asset equally among the children and give it to them over a period of years may create serious problems for siblings long after the parents have died. When parents look at their adult children and see them getting along, it rarely occurs to them that they are the cement that holds their children together. Time and again, when one or both parents die, the cement weakens and differences that were latent for decades begin rising to the surface. The consequences are frequently siblings who co-own businesses but rarely talk, siblings who supposedly work together but in reality work in parallel, and siblings who end up fighting over who will buy out whom and for what price.

Now two years after the five children completed their retreat, the five children who own the company continue to rely on the agreements they documented in the Charter to guide them through the challenges they face as a result of inheriting their parents' business. Nancy recently said, "Because they have the Charter, it's probably the salvation of the whole deal."

Using mediation in this preventative manner to negotiate issues that are as complex as owning and managing a business was a bold and creative step for them. Rather than Mike and Nancy deciding on their own what their children were and were not capable of, they put the matter squarely in the hands of the children, where it belonged. After all, it was their children who would eventually have to prove to the world—not just to them—that they could do it.

Engaging Adult Children in the Process

Engaging adult children in the estate-planning process has real advantages, whether it is done informally with private discussions or with the assistance of mediators. First, talking about this family transition openly with adult children is a respectful thing to do. When children are very little there are no expectations about consulting with them or keeping them informed about major decisions, even those that directly affect them. But as children grow, parents slowly and gradually bring their children into the loop of family decision-making.

Teenagers often struggle with parents because they want to be consulted on everything and make all the decisions as well. Parents are wise to keep teenagers informed, consult with them as the situation and their maturity permit, but retain decisionmaking authority as they see fit. When children truly reach adulthood (i.e., not a chronological set point but a stage determined by their level of maturity), they are ready for—and genuinely desire—a new type of relationship with their parents. They wish to be loved, trusted, and respected. Parents can, and often do, demonstrate their respect for them by consulting with them and keeping them informed about decisions and choices in their lives. When parents engage their adult children in discussions about how they are contemplating passing their assets on to their children (and to their children's children), it creates an environment of respect.

Second, because the decisions that parents make about their estates affect their children so directly, it is very helpful for adult children to know what they might expect. Estate planning is often looked at as something that parents should do on their own, but it is really a family transition and one that affects children in many ways.

There are many things that parents do in their lives that primarily affect themselves, and have little direct effect on their children. Estate planning is interesting and unique because it is the opposite of that. In many ways it is one of the few things parents do that actually affects their children more than themselves.

It is important to recognize that involving adult children in some way in the estate planning process does not imply that the parents are turning over the process to the children; they are simply bringing them into it. Turning over the process, or surrendering control of the outcome, would be as large a mistake as keeping it a secret. Neither extreme is helpful to adult children. Exactly how they are brought in depends on many factors, including the assets, the children, and the expected longevity of the parents.

Talking openly with adult children about estate planning greatly lessens the probability of conflicts developing among the children after the parents have died. It accomplishes this in various ways. First, it establishes a precedent of coming together and talking. With this precedent set, people are more likely to talk if they have a problem rather than hire an advocate to talk for them. Also, when people are brought into the process, they have a better understanding of how decisions are being made. Finally, people have a tendency to go along with decisions when they have been involved in the process—even when they do not particularly like the outcome. Adult children appreciate being included, and that can go a long way toward assuaging hurt feelings.

Bringing adult children into the planning process can actually bring about pleasant surprises. The mother in Case #1 might have heard her son concur with her wish that her daughter should receive her money. She then could have discarded her wellgrounded fear that her son would be angry with her and his sister.

Parents who operate in secret often feel compelled to divide their estate equally, believing that it is the only equitable path. Equal is not always what is truly equitable, but this can be hard for parents to realize—especially parents who have a tendency to deny or minimize individual differences and "treat everyone the same." Adult children are much better than their parents at recognizing and accepting the differences among themselves.

When adult children with disparate economic resources learn of their parents' estate decisions after the fact, they sometimes wish it had been done differently—that their parents had done more to recognize the differences among them. Once estates are divided, however, things rarely change voluntarily. Talking openly during the planning process can produce pleasant surprises, such as parents and siblings acknowledging and addressing these differences in constructive and creative ways.

Conclusion

Estate planning is part of a very important, and often emotionally charged, transition in the life of a family—the death of one generation and the transfer of one generation's accumulated wealth to others. A great deal is often at stake—emotionally as well as financially.

Mediation can be a useful adjunct in the estate planning process. Because so much is potentially at risk, and because the problems that develop are so frequently related to communication (misperceptions, hidden agendas, etc.), it makes sense to have mediators help parents explore their intentions and the potential consequences of their intentions before the actual planning work begins. Sometimes mediators engage adult children directly in the mediation process with the parents.

Attorneys whose clients have the benefit of mediation will have more confidence that their clients are truly of one mind about their intentions. The nature of the mediation process helps ensure that the result will be equitable, realistic, and acceptable to the key parties. Consequently, the planner's risk of malpractice claims will be reduced.

The practice of using mediation to resolve will and trust disputes is in its adolescence. The practice of using mediation during estate planning—before any disputes arise—is in its infancy. During the past decade trial lawyers have come to recognize how mediation can provide a better outcome for their clients. Now estate, business, and tax planners can also utilize professional mediators to enhance the scope and quality of their services and their relationships with their clients. Estate planners have an opportunity to help estate-planning mediation develop in a manner that is most useful to clients and professionals. Dialogue between estate planners and mediators, as well as continuing education seminars focusing on mediation in estate planning, should be a high priority. Of course, mediation is a useful vehicle for resolving will and trust contests and disputes among heirs and between heirs and personal representatives. But it is much better to nip these problems in the bud—during the planning stage—before they have the chance to damage important relationships.

2. MEDIATION—AFTER CLIENT'S DEATH

JAMES CRIST, MEDIATING PROBATE DISPUTES*

HENNEPIN LAW., Oct. 22, 2008.

In recent years, probate court disputes have increased in number and legal expense. Probate disputes can be factually intensive cases. They can involve numerous witnesses and multiple parties, and present several issues for determination. The amount of money at issue can often exceed the verdict sought in personal injury or commercial litigation proceedings. A contested will can take a week or more of the court's time. While mediation is not required by District Court Rules in probate matters, it should be considered by parties and encouraged by judges in larger cases. This article provides an overview of probate mediation.

An Increase in Probate Litigation

There may be several reasons the number of contested probate cases has increased. Assets left by frugal post-depression era parents can be significant. They saved their money and saw their homes skyrocket in value. As a result, the estate "pie" is bigger and their children want full slices.

In addition, family dynamics have changed. Families are no longer as close as they used to be. Siblings move out of their neighborhoods, across town or even out of state. It is easier to fight with a family member they have not seen in years. Similarly, more people are willing to do battle with a deceased parent's surviving second spouse or second set of children.

Lastly, for too many people, an inheritance has become the cornerstone of their retirement plan. They need it, count on it, and will fight for it.

Probate Contests

While some contested probate matters can be heard and determined within an hour of the court's time, others require days of testimony. Parties seek to declare a will or trust void under a variety of theories including undue influence, lack of capacity, or a technical flaw in its execution. Other contests involve ambiguities in the will or trust, a dispute as to valuation of assets, or even whether an asset should be included in the estate. As most of these questions turn on the facts, summary judgment is rarely sought or granted.

The Mediation Process

By now, most attorneys are familiar with the mechanics of a mediation. Consequently, this will not be reviewed here in detail. However, most

* Reprinted with permission of James Crist, Partner, Steinhagen & Crist.

probate mediation participants expect the process to be completed in a day or less. As time is of the essence, this author favors short written submissions of party positions before the day of mediation, staggered arrival time for participants, the elimination of joint sessions/opening statements, segregation of parties, and breakout meetings with lawyers. Many parties prefer not to interact with other participants.

Benefits of Probate Mediation

1. Early Resolution

Probate matters are now litigated like most other civil matters. There are pretrial conferences, scheduling orders, protracted discovery (usually followed by a request for additional time to complete discovery), expert witnesses, and numerous trial exhibits. While most probate court proceedings are jury free, they have still become bloated and time consuming.

For many participants, probate disputes are their first and only exposure to the legal system. They are not used to day-to-day contact with lawyers. They do not realize their case will be a part-time job assisting the lawyer in answering discovery or preparing for trial. Mediation offers an opportunity for an early resolution of an otherwise life-disrupting process.

2. Avoids Expensive Trial

Probate litigation is as expensive as any other type of civil litigation. A probate attorney who litigates infrequently may even surprise himself or herself with the time spent preparing for trial and the fees that are generated. The cases are factually intensive and require significant client and witness preparation. Often, the cases require a thorough review of financial records and medical records. The clients, in such personal matters, can be high maintenance. One-day mediation, if successful, can avoid a hundred hours of trial and trial preparation.

3. Potential for Creative Solutions

Mediation opens the door to creative solutions not available to the court. A will contest may result in an all-or-nothing determination by the court. A mediation can result in a division of assets without rigid adherence to the terms of the prevailing will or the laws of intestacy. Assets in dispute can be diverted to a charity favored by both litigants, or other family members not provided for in the will. Real estate can be divided in ways not previously contemplated by the parties. Tax issues may be considered. Mediation can craft clever resolutions participants will accept.

4. Family Harmony

For many families, trial is the point of no return. Fighting with your brother in court is different than fighting with your brother in the backyard or over the kitchen table. Trials often make a family disagreement a permanent dispute, in part because somebody wins and somebody loses. Somebody was right and somebody was wrong. Mediation allows litigants to privately save face, to pretend the dispute never happened, or to rationalize in their own minds that they won and the other guy lost.

Mediations are by their nature agreements to disagree. They leave open the possibility of reconciliation and future family harmony.

5. Privacy

Almost all probate proceedings are in open court. Mediation, if successful, can avoid a public record of family discord or embarrassment.

6. Benefits to Attorneys

Probate disputes are unique in that they often begin as routine probate proceedings. Then, sometimes without warning, an objection is filed and an estate administration turns into ugly estate litigation. Even if the probate attorney has the appetite for the litigation, it can be terribly disruptive to his or her practice. Mediation allows the probate attorney who typically does not litigate to participate in the resolution of a dispute on behalf of his or her client.

Even assuming the matter is not resolved before litigation, mediation provides value to the attorney. It is essentially free discovery. The trading of offers in mediation is usually accompanied by an opponent's rationale for why he or she is right and you are wrong. That rationale becomes more defined throughout the day and by the end of the day, both parties have essentially disclosed their theory of the case. The information obtained is generally superior to information contained in formal discovery responses. In addition, a participant's case theory undergoes an attack from the opposing counsel, and in most cases, a thoughtful and objective review by the mediator. Weaknesses exposed in mediation provide a valuable insight into trial preparation, even if the mediation is unsuccessful.

Special Benefits of Mediation to the Probate Court

A Hennepin County Probate Court judge or referee can hear 15 to 20 routine probate matters on a single day. A contested matter concerning a single family can take several days of the court's time. Some disputes go on for weeks or even months, as the court is forced to schedule prolonged trials around its routine, uncontested probate court proceedings. Mediation has the potential to save hours of court time as well as taxpayer money. Moreover, it sometimes seems like the judicial officer is not enjoying his or her job by day two of the contested probate case requiring protracted testimony over ownership or division of personal property. Perhaps a mediator could more efficiently assist the parties in dividing old tools, knick knacks, and jewelry. The court would still have plenty of other business.

What Is Important to Participants?

1. Being Heard

Most participants want to convince the mediator of the merits of their case. The discussion may expose frustration or hurt feelings. As probate matters are personal in nature, there can be crying and even fist pounding. Topics often include who (1) did more for a parent, (2) disappointed a parent, or (3) was loved more by a parent. While much of what was said would not be relevant at trial, such conversations (venting) can be critical to a participant's willingness to settle the dispute. If a participant feels as if he or she has been heard and understood, mediations can often be a satisfactory substitute for a party's "day in court."

2. Understanding the Weaknesses of Their Case

Participants may have to be convinced as to why they should compromise and settle. The same facts often suggest different conclusions. For example, the child cut out of the will may argue that the favored child spent hours unduly influencing the parent. The child favored in the will claims she was rewarded for hours she spent cleaning the parents' home, making them dinner, buying them groceries, or taking them to the doctor's office. An evaluative approach to mediation seems more likely to result in a resolution. A credible evaluation of a participant's case requires that the mediator have knowledge of the law, probate trial experience, and an understanding of how a judge will likely view the situation. There are almost always risks and the participants generally embrace compromise once they see their case is not perfect or there are other compelling reasons to settle.

3. Finality and Understanding the Agreement

Most participants want to be sure that a mediation agreement is a "done deal." They want to be assured of what they are going to get, when they are going to get it, and what happens if the other side attempts to not honor the deal. Settlement is often sold by the participants' attorneys as a way for them to get on with their lives and to resolve all disputes. If family members are involved, there is the fear a grudge will persist leading to another court battle. Consequently, finality represents an important benefit of the bargain.

Moreover, participants must understand their rights and obligations under the mediated settlement. If they do not, arguably there has been no agreement. Mediated probate settlements can be simple or complex. They often address real estate, cash, and personal property. An ambiguous agreement is worse than no agreement at all.

Special Challenges in Probate Mediation

1. Decedent Cannot Participate

Wouldn't it be nice if the mediator could check the voracity of the participant's story with the decedent. As this is not possible, the mediator hears from one participant that Dad promised to split his estate five ways, and hears from another participant that Dad gave him a bigger piece of the pie because he mowed Dad's lawn. Some participants can be more convincing telling a lie than others are at telling the truth. Without the decedent's participation, the truth is sometimes impossible to determine.

2. Emotional Participants

Most estate disputes occur while participants are still grieving the loss of a family member or friend. Many disputes involve a disproportionate division of assets among family members. While mediators are not psychologists, it may seem like the participants are equating their share of the estate with their share of Mom's or Dad's love. Other participants use an estate dispute as a new reason to fight old fights.

3. Multiple Parties

Probate disputes can involve multiple parties. A mediator must know enough about the case prior to the mediation to ensure all of the parties necessary for an agreement will be present or available by telephone. Multiple parties make settlement difficult because a serious, thoughtful proposal can be effectively vetoed by one unreasonable party. In fact, it is not unusual for the "difficult" participant to carve out a larger share of an estate, simply because he or she is willing to block a multiparty deal.

4. Lack of Information

Ideally, mediation would resolve a dispute prior to the completion of an expensive course of discovery. However, the mediation process can stall when important information has not been provided or cannot be documented as of the date of the mediation. It is important for the mediator to encourage the parties to exchange whatever information they believe they may need to make an informed decision regarding settlement. It is the responsibility of the participants' attorneys to identify such information prior to the mediation and make an informal request if discovery has not been completed. It is astounding how often the assets of the estate have not been fully determined by the parties as of the date of the mediation.

5. Tax Considerations

A mediated settlement can have tax consequences. Few mediators would offer themselves as experts on the tax ramifications of a settlement. Most mediators defer to the participants' tax experts. Many probate attorneys do not possess the tax knowledge and experience necessary to advise their clients at a mediation. If they do not, they should meet with a qualified accountant prior to the mediation and warn the accountant that he or she may receive a call during the mediation.

6. In–Laws

At the beginning of the mediation process, participants will often say that their spouse is present to provide "support." Too often, the spouse is there to project a total unwillingness to compromise, make outrageous allegations, or second-guess the participant's difficult decision to reach settlement. A probate mediator must be firm when dealing with the "In-law."

7. Lack of Preparation

Probate mediation can address a variety of issues. The participants should prepare for the mediation by identifying the issues they want to be governed by a mediation agreement. Some issues may not be part of the pending court proceedings, but are related to nonprobate assets or personal property. Regardless, each party should identify the important issues and have an opening position for negotiations at the beginning of the session.

Summary

Probate case mediation can offer great benefit to prepared participants, their attorneys, and the court if handled thoughtfully by mediators with experience in contested probate proceedings. Attorneys should consider mediating every contested probate case.

NOTE

See generally, Charles B. Craver, *Mediation: A Trial Lawyer's Guide*, TRIAL, June 1999, at 37.

3. FAMILY SETTLEMENT AGREEMENTS

IN RE MORRIS

Court of Civil Appeals of Texas, Amarillo, 1979.
577 S.W.2d 748.

REYNOLDS, JUSTICE.

The probate of an earlier will was set aside upon proof of a later, valid will made more than two years afterwards and against the contention that the application to probate the last will is a will contest barred by the two-year statute of limitations, but probate of the last will was denied after the jury found an agreement between the principal beneficiaries not to offer the last will for probate. Absent a concurrent agreement for a division of the estate, the agreement not to offer the last will for probate is ineffective to prevent its probate. Affirmed in part; reversed and remanded in part.

Margaret Jane Morris died 1 April 1975. She had executed a 19 November 1965 will leaving her property to her surviving husband, Henry M. Morris, the named independent executor, who offered the will for probate. A 29 April 1975 order entered in Cause No. 13,132 on the docket of the County Court of Potter County admitted the will to probate and decreed that Henry M. Morris receive letters testamentary.

Two years and five months later on 16 September 1977, Becky Jean Woodward Whitaker, the daughter of Mr. and Mrs. Morris, filed an application for probate of a will not produced in court, seeking the probate of a 22 March 1968 will of Margaret Jane Morris and the issuance to her of letters testamentary. By the provisions of the 1968 document, all previous wills were revoked; Henry M. Morris was bequeathed one dollar and the remainder of the decedent's estate was devised and bequeathed to her two surviving children, Henry Lee Morris and Becky Jean Woodward, share and share alike; and Becky Jean Woodward was appointed independent executor without bond. In her application, Becky Jean alleged that the 22 March 1968 will was destroyed after the decedent's funeral by Henry Lee, who stated that the will would upset their father. She further alleged that the 1968 will specifically revoked the 1965 will, the probate of which should be set aside and held for naught.

Henry M. Morris opposed the probate of the 1968 will. He alleged, inter alia, that Becky Jean is foreclosed from making the present application by the Tex. Prob. Code Ann. § 93 (Vernon 1956) two year limitation period for the contest of the probated 1965 will, is estopped by her knowledge and actions from asserting the 1965 will is not the last will and from offering the 1968 will for probate, and is bound by an agreement with her brother, to which Henry M. Morris is a third party beneficiary, to destroy the 1968 will.

Following a jury trial, the court submitted a charge to which no objection was made. Responsive to the special issues submitted, the jury found that Becky Jean and Henry Lee agreed not to offer for probate the 1968 will, and that the agreement was made for the benefit of their father, Henry M. Morris. The jury failed to find that Becky Jean knew her father was relying on the belief that the 1965 will was the last will of the decedent, or that Becky Jean unreasonably delayed in offering the 1968 will for probate or that Becky Jean waived her right to probate the 1968 will. Accepting the verdict, the trial court found that, as a matter of law, the 1968 will has been proved in a manner required by the Probate Court, and that it revoked all prior wills.

The court then rendered judgment setting aside the probate of the 1965 will, denying the probate of the 1968 will and the grant of letters testamentary to Becky Jean, and decreeing that the estate of Margaret Jane Morris, deceased, pass according to the laws of intestate succession. Both Henry M. Morris and Becky Jean have appealed. * * *

Because a testatrix has the legal right to devise her property as she sees fit and to prescribe terms upon which her bounty should be enjoyed, * * * the intent of the Probate Code is more accurately reflected by a determination, and we hold, that a timely application for probate of the testator's will is neither a contest of the validity nor barred by the probate of an earlier will. If the probate of the last will is to be defeated, it must be for some other reason. * * *

More than eighty years ago it was determined that the beneficiaries of a will may agree among themselves as to the distribution of the property devised and bequeathed to them, and the agreement may be effected by an agreement not to probate the will. Stringfellow v. Early, 15 Tex. Civ. App. 597, 40 S.W. 871, 874 (1897, no writ). This is the family settlement doctrine, supported by the general principle that the property belongs to the beneficiaries under the will and since they may, by transfers made immediately after the distribution, divide the property as they wish, there is no reason why they may not divide it by agreement before they receive it in the regular course of judicial administration of the estate. * * * For this reason and because such agreements tend to put an end to family controversies by way of compromise, family settlement agreements are favored in law. * * * And it remains our law that a family settlement in which all of the heirs and beneficiaries agree that a purported will shall not be probated is valid and enforceable. Salmon v. Salmon, 395 S.W.2d 29, 32 (Tex. 1965).

Those cases, and their progeny, were concerned with an agreement not to probate a will coupled with an express agreement for the disposition of the estate. Here, however, there was no agreement for any disposition of the estate. Becky Jean denied any agreement at all; and Henry Lee testified, "We did not agree as to where the estate was going. We agreed as to what to do with the will." The destruction of the will, Henry Lee stated, was to prevent "shock" to and the "upsetting" of their father.

None of the cases cited by the parties or discovered in our independent research speak only to an agreement not to probate a will. The initial inquiry, then, is whether the agreement not to offer the 1968 will for probate, standing alone, is effective to bar probate.

Every person who meets the requirements prescribed in Section 57 of the Probate Code "shall have the right and power to make a last will and testament, under the rules and limitations prescribed by law." When one meets the legal requirements, properly executes a will and provides for a disposition of his property not violative of public policy, his testamentary disposition should be respected. * * * The right of testamentary disposition conferred by statute is as absolute as the right to convey property during life. * * * Because one has the legal right to devise his property as he sees fit, * * * neither courts, juries, relatives nor friends of a testator may say how property should be passed by a will or rewrite a will because they do not like the distribution of the property. * * * Indeed, it has been held that any contract which would modify established law or deprive the courts of their power to protect private rights and liabilities is contrary to public policy and void. * * * It logically follows that an agreement not to probate a will unaccompanied by any agreement for distribution of the property would, if upheld, destroy the statutory right of testamentary disposition and the right of the courts to enforce that right.

Moreover, an agreement merely not to probate a will fails to invoke the principle which imparts vitality to the family settlement doctrine. The principle is that all of the decedent's heirs and beneficiaries have the right to contract with reference to the property in lieu of probating the will, * * * i.e., the right to make a family settlement. * * * Consequently, the agreement found to exist here is ineffective to deny probate of the 1968 will unless it can be said, as Henry M. Morris argues, that there was an implied agreement for distribution of the estate.

The argument for an implied agreement is premised on the fact that Becky Jean and Henry Lee had knowledge of an alternative vehicle—the 1965 will—for disposing of the property, and the conclusion that, even though they might not have known of the prior will's contents, they knew the property would pass under it if the 1968 will was destroyed. Yet, courts cannot make contracts for the parties; and, under the general law of contracts, before an implied agreement for disposition of the estate can be said to exist in the agreement not to offer the 1968 will for probate, it must appear that an agreement for the disposition of the property was so clearly within the contemplation of Becky Jean and Henry Lee that they deemed it unnecessary to express it and, therefore, omitted to do so, or that it is necessary to imply the agreement to effectuate the purpose of the agreement made. * * * But, here, the undisputed evidence is that there was no agreement at all for the disposition of the estate, and that the destruction of the will was not for the purpose of making some other particular disposition of the estate. Under these circumstances, we are not authorized to write a contract for the parties contrary to their expressed intentions.

The validity of the 1968 will, which revoked all prior wills, having been established and no legal reason being shown why its admission to probate should be denied, the probate of the 1965 will must be set aside and the 1968 will admitted to probate. The 1968 will appoints Becky Jean the independent executrix without bond. She sought letters testamentary, but the court, pursuant to its judgment, did not determine her entitlement to letters; however, because the 1968 will is entitled to probate, the court must, under the provisions of Sections 78 and 88(c), determine whether she is entitled to receive letters testamentary. * * * To this extent indicated, the points of error presented by the parties are granted; otherwise, the points and the crosspoints are overruled.

Accordingly, the portion of the trial court's judgment setting aside the probate of the 1965 will is affirmed, and the remaining portions of the court's judgment are reversed. The cause is remanded to the trial court for the entry of judgment admitting the 22 March 1968 will of Margaret Jane Morris to probate and providing for, after a hearing to determine, a representative of the estate.

UNIFORM PROBATE CODE

1993 Text.

PART 11

COMPROMISE OF CONTROVERSIES

Section 3–1101. [Effect of Approval of Agreements Involving Trusts, Inalienable Interests, or Interests of Third Persons.]

A compromise of any controversy as to admission to probate of any instrument offered for formal probate as the will of a decedent, the construction, validity, or effect of any governing instrument, the rights or interests in the estate of the decedent, of any successor, or the administration of the estate, if approved in a formal proceeding in the Court for that purpose, is binding on all the parties thereto including those unborn, unascertained or who could not be located. An approved compromise is binding even though it may affect a trust or an inalienable interest. A compromise does not impair the rights of creditors or of taxing authorities who are not parties to it.

Section 3–1102. [Procedure for Securing Court Approval of Compromise.]

The procedure for securing court approval of a compromise is as follows:

(1) The terms of the compromise shall be set forth in an agreement in writing which shall be executed by all competent persons and parents acting for any minor child having beneficial interests or having claims which will or may be affected by the compromise. Execution is not required by any person whose identity cannot be ascertained or whose whereabouts is unknown and cannot reasonably be ascertained.

(2) Any interested person, including the personal representative, if any, or a trustee, then may submit the agreement to the Court for its approval and for execution by the personal representative, the trustee of every affected testamentary trust, and other fiduciaries and representatives.

(3) After notice to all interested persons or their representatives, including the personal representative of any estate and all affected trustees of trusts, the Court, if it finds that the contest or controversy is in good faith and that the effect of the agreement upon the interests of persons represented by fiduciaries or other representatives is just and reasonable, shall make an order approving the agreement and directing all fiduciaries subject to its jurisdiction to execute the agreement. Minor children represented only by their parents may be bound only if their parents join with other competent persons in execution of the compromise. Upon the making of the order and the execution of the agreement, all further disposition of the estate is in accordance with the terms of the agreement.

Comment

This section and the one preceding it outline a procedure which may be initiated by competent parties having beneficial interests in a decedent's estate as a means of resolving controversy concerning the estate. If all competent persons with beneficial interests or claims which might be affected by the proposal and parents *properly* representing interests of their children concur, a settlement scheme differing from that otherwise governing the devolution may be substituted. The procedure for securing representation of minors and unknown or missing persons with interests must be followed. See Section 1–403. The ultimate control of the question of whether the substitute proposal shall be accepted is with the court which must find: "that the contest or controversy is in good faith and that the effect of the agreement upon the interests of parties represented by fiduciaries is just and reasonable."

The thrust of the procedure is to put the authority for initiating settlement proposals with the persons who have beneficial interests in the estate, and to prevent executors and testamentary trustees from vetoing any such proposal. The only reason for approving a scheme of devolution which differs from that framed by the testator or the statutes governing intestacy is to prevent dissipation of the estate in wasteful litigation. Because executors and trustees may have an interest in fees and commissions which they might earn through efforts to carry out testator's intention, the judgment of the court is substituted for that of such fiduciaries in appropriate cases. A controversy which the court may find to be in good faith, as well as concurrence of all beneficially interested and competent persons and parent-representatives provide prerequisites which should prevent the procedure from being abused. Thus, the procedure does not threaten the planning of a testator who plans and drafts with sufficient clarity and completeness to eliminate the possibility of good faith controversy concerning the meaning and legality of his plan. * * *

LOCATE

Does your state have a formal method of obtaining court approval of a family settlement? If yes, how does this procedure operate?

NOTES AND QUESTIONS

1. What policies favor the enforceability of family settlement agreements?

2. Would a family settlement be enforceable even if the distribution of property agreed to by the heirs and beneficiaries was tremendously different from how the property would be distributed under the will?

3. Can the will forbid or preclude a family settlement?

4. Must the executor named in the will join in the agreement? If the executor does not join, may the executor probate the will? See Biddy v. Jones, 475 S.W.2d 321 (Tex. Civ. App. 1971).

5. May a binding settlement agreement be reached even if some beneficiaries are minors, unborn, or unascertainable?

6. Must a family settlement agreement be approved by the court?

7. Will an amount passing to a surviving spouse under a settlement agreement qualify for the marital deduction? See Treas. Reg. § 20.2056(e)–2(d).

8. Is a payment to settle a will contest deductible as a claim against the estate? See L.B. Howard Estate, 2 T.C.M. 1075 (1943).

9. Is the portion of the estate received by the settling heir or beneficiary excluded from income tax? See Lyeth v. Hoey, 305 U.S. 188, 59 S.Ct. 155, 83 L.Ed. 119 (1938).

10. Under his father's will, Sam was entitled to the entire estate. Sam settled with Kendall, his contesting sister, for $100,000. Has Sam made a

taxable gift to Kendall? See Irma Lampert v. Commissioner, 15 T.C.M. 1184 (1956).

11. What items would you include in a settlement agreement?

4. ARBITRATION

AMERICAN ARBITRATION ASSOCIATION, ARBITRATION RULES FOR WILLS AND TRUSTS*

Pages 1–2 (2009).

INTRODUCTION

Every year billions of dollars are administered by executors and trustees. Occasionally disputes arise about whether those funds are being properly administered and whether the governing will or trust is being interpreted correctly by the fiduciary. Many of these disputes can be resolved by the use of arbitration, the voluntary submission of a dispute to a disinterested lawyer or lawyers with substantial experience in the area of trusts and estates for final and binding, determination. Arbitration is an effective way to resolve these disputes privately, promptly, and economically.

The American Arbitration Association (AAA) is a public-service, not-for-profit organization offering a broad range of dispute resolution services to business executives, attorneys individuals, trade associations, unions, management, consumers, families, communities, and all levels of government. Services are available through AAA headquarters in New York city and through offices located in major cities throughout the United States. Hearings may be held at locations convenient for the parties and are not limited to cities with AAA offices. In addition, the AAA serves as a center for education and training, issues specialized publications, and conducts research on all forms of out-of-court dispute settlement.

Executors and trustees, and beneficiaries of estates and trusts, can voluntarily agree to arbitrate an existing dispute under these rules. However, they should review state law to determine whether a guardian *ad litem* is necessary to represent any minor, incapacitated, or unborn beneficiary. Testators or settlers can require that future disputes be arbitrated by inserting the following clause into their wills and trusts.

Standard Arbitration Clause

In order to save the cost of court proceedings and promote the prompt and final resolution of any dispute regarding the interpretation of my will (or my trust) or the administration of my estate or any trust under my will (or my trust), I direct that any such dispute shall be settled by arbitration administered by the American Arbitration Association under its arbitration Rules for Wills and Trusts then in

> effect. Nevertheless the following matters shall not be arbitrable—questions regarding my competency, attempts to remove a fiduciary, or questions concerning the amount of bond of a fiduciary. In addition, arbitration may be waived by all *sui juri* parties in interest.
>
> The arbitrator(s) shall be a practicing lawyer licensed to practice law in the state my will (or my trust) and whose practice has been devoted primarily to will and trusts for at least ten years. The arbitrator(s) shall apply the substantive law (and the law of remedies, if applicable) of the state whose laws govern my will (or my trust). The arbitrator's decision shall not be appealable to any court, but shall be final and binding on any and all persons who have or may have an interest in my estate or any trust under my will (or my trust), including unborn or incapacitated persons, such as minors or incompetents. Judgment on the arbitrator's award may be entered in any court having jurisdiction thereof.

ADMINISTRATIVE FEES

The AAA's administrative fees are based on service charges. The fees cover AAA administrative services; they do not cover arbitrator compensation or expenses, if any, reporting services or any postaward charges incurred by the parties in enforcing the award.

There is no additional administrative fee where parties to a pending arbitration attempt to mediate their dispute under the AAA's auspices.

MEDIATION

The parties might wish to submit their dispute to mediation prior to arbitration. In mediation, the neutral mediator assists the parties in reaching a settlement but does not have the authority to make a binding decision or award. Mediation is administered by the AAA in accordance with its Commercial Mediation Rules.

If the parties want to use a mediator to resolve an existing dispute, they can enter into the following submission.

> The parties hereby submit the following dispute to mediation administered by the American Arbitration Association under its Commercial Mediation Rules. (The clause may also provide for the qualifications of the mediator(s), the method of payment, locale of meetings, and any other item of concern to the parties.)

The services of the AAA are generally concluded with the transmittal of the award. Although there is voluntary compliance with the majority of awards, judgment on the award can be entered in a court having appropriate jurisdiction if necessary.

NOTE

Will a court enforce a provision in a will or trust which mandates arbitration of disputes? In *Rachal v. Reitz*, 347 S.W.3d 305 (Tex. App.—Dallas 2011, pet. filed), a settlor included a provision in his trust requiring the beneficiaries to arbitrate any dispute with the trustees. Both the trial and appellate courts held that this provision was unenforceable. A person cannot be compelled to arbitrate a dispute if the person did not agree to relinquish the person's ordinary right to litigate. The beneficiary is merely a recipient of equitable title to property and not a party to the trust instrument. A trust is a conveyance of property coupled with a split of legal and equitable title and the imposition of fiduciary duties on the trustee. A trust is not an agreement or contract.

However, a four judge dissent argued that the settlor's intent for disputes to be arbitrated should prevail and that the beneficiaries were benefiting from the trust and thus "agreed" to the trust even though the trust is not a contract.

At least one state (Arizona) authorizes settlors to mandate arbitration or other alternative dispute resolution methods as long as the method is reasonable. See ARIZ. REV. STAT. § 14–10205.

CHAPTER 10

CLIENTS WITH SPECIAL CIRCUMSTANCES

■ ■ ■

A. CLIENT WITH MINOR CHILD OR MINOR BENEFICIARY

1. GUARDIANS

A client must plan for the management of a child's personal and financial needs should the client die during the child's minority. Failure to plan may result in the court appointing people to control the child's life and property who may be individuals neither the child nor the parent would have desired. Many of your clients will find the nomination of a guardian to be the most important part of their estate plan; even people who care little about estate planning in general (usually because they have no estate) are extremely concerned about who will rear their children. Note, however, that reports reveal that 75% of Americans have not formally designated guardians for their minor children. *Choosing a Guardian Helps Secure Your Children's Future*, SAN ANTONIO EXPRESS-NEWS, Apr. 1, 1994, at 22A.

a. Guardian of the Person

The surviving parent may nominate a guardian of the person's child. Although the parent's preference is not binding on the court, it is highly persuasive. The nomination is typically done in a will but many states also authorize a nomination in a separate document. State law may give older minors significant input into the appointment process.

Your client needs to consider a variety of factors in selecting the appropriate person to nominate as guardian of the minor's person.

- The prospective guardian should have (or be able to develop) a close emotional relationship with the child. Is the client satisfied with the guardian's views toward education, medical care, lifestyle, religion, etc.?
- If the client has many children, thought must be given to whether the client wants the children to be kept together as a family unit. If one person is named as guardian of several minors, the client must

make certain the guardian has the ability (emotional stability, space, and financial resources) to handle a big influx of new family members. Although the guardian is entitled to expense reimbursement from the minor's estate, the estate may be inadequate to cover the cost. If so, how will the guardian's children and spouse react to a lower standard of living? Will they resent the new additions?

- The client must evaluate the prospective guardian's age and health. For example, grandparents may not want or be physically able to handle the responsibilities of rearing children.
- The client must also consider whether the children will be comfortable in the prospective guardian's environment. Does the child like the guardian, the guardian's spouse and their children (if any), and the home (size of room, yard, amenities, etc.)? What is the proximity of same-aged children for potential friendships?

LOCATE

Find the statutory authority in your state which allows a surviving parent to nominate a guardian of the person of a minor child. How does the statute operate?

DRAFT

Draft the appropriate document or will provision to designate a guardian of a person for a minor child.

NOTES AND QUESTIONS

1. May your client waive bond for a guardian of the person? If yes, when would a waiver be appropriate?

2. For an article directed to non-attorneys recommending key factors in selecting the proper guardian of the person, see Louise Tutelian, *How to Choose a Guardian for Your Child*, GOOD HOUSEKEEPING, April 1998, at 156.

3. Please review Chapter 8(H) regarding general concerns when selecting a fiduciary.

b. Guardian of the Estate

The surviving parent may also nominate a guardian of the estate (conservator) for a minor child via a will or other document. This guardian is in charge of managing the child's property which includes (1) property which the child receives from the deceased parent under the will, through intestacy, or because of a non-probate transfer as well as (2) property which the child has already acquired or will acquire through gift, inheritance, employment, etc. prior to becoming an adult.

LOCATE

Find the statutory authority in your state which allows a surviving parent to nominate a guardian of the estate of a minor child. How does the statute operate?

NOTES AND QUESTIONS

1. Is there a significant difference between the judicial procedures for the two types of guardians?

2. What factors would you consider in selecting an estate guardian and how are they different from the factors you would use in naming a guardian of the person?

3. Should the guardian of the estate be the same individual as the guardian of the person? Why or why not?

4. May your client waive bond for a guardian of the person? If yes, when would a waiver be appropriate?

5. Please review Chapter 8(H) regarding general concerns when selecting a fiduciary.

DRAFT

Draft the appropriate documents to designate a guardian of the estate for a minor child.

2. PROPERTY TRANSFERS

Clients who wish to make gifts to their young children, grandchildren, or other minors are faced with some important decisions. In addition to choosing the appropriate property to transfer and deciding to whom it should be given, the client must carefully select the method used to make the transfer. The appropriate method depends on the client's individual goals and motivation for making the transfer. The size of the gift, the needs and maturity of the recipient, the client's desire to control the use of the donated property, and the potential tax consequences of the gift are all relevant factors in making this decision.

Reasons a client may wish to transfer property to a minor include the following:

Provides Emotional Rewards for Client. Clients often receive emotional satisfaction when they make a gift to a minor, especially when the minor is a close relative such as a child or grandchild. Clients may have feelings of peace and pride for ensuring the physical, educational, or financial independence of a young person. These benefits attach to all gifts to minors, but especially to gifts made outright, as the client has the immediate opportunity to witness the minor benefiting from and enjoying the gift. On the other hand, a client making a gift through a trust may be comforted by the knowledge that the property is available to the beneficiary but yet protected from the beneficiary's unsupervised and uncontrolled use.

Assures Support and Education for Minor. Many clients make gifts to minors to provide for the donee's health, education, maintenance, and support. This is particularly the case where the minor has special medical needs or specific talents best developed by specialized educational facilities.

Avoids Guardianship Proceedings. Although minors may own property, they lack the legal capacity to manage it. This problem is typically solved by having the appropriate court appoint a guardian of the estate or conservator who, as a fiduciary representing the minor, is granted the authority to manage the minor's property. This is not an optimal solution because guardianships are often costly, time-consuming, and inconvenient. Gifts in trust and those made through a custodianship, however, avoid the expense and aggravation often linked with guardianships that are necessitated by outright gifts.

Creates Tax Savings for Client. Gifts to minors may be structured to take advantage of the (1) annual exclusion or (2) the medical and educational expense exclusion, and thus achieve significant transfer tax savings. See Chapter 4(B)(4)(a) & (b).

Avoids Claims By Donor's Creditors. Property gifted to a minor is not susceptible to the claims of the client's creditors because the donor no longer has any interest in the property. Thus, the client may provide for the educational or personal needs of his or her children by making transfers to a trust for their benefit and be confident that the client's future financial status will not impact the trust's ability to meet the children's needs. This result, of course, assumes that the client did not make the transfers in violation of the applicable fraudulent conveyancing statutes.

There are several ways for a client to make a transfer to a minor, each with its own set of benefits and drawbacks.

a. Outright Gift

1) Benefits

Gift Tax Savings. Because an outright gift is a gift of a present interest, it easily qualifies for the annual exclusion.

Simplicity. Outright gifts to a minor are by far the easiest type of transfer for the client to make. For relatively de minimus transfers, such as holiday gifts and pocket money, the simplicity of outright gifts makes it the technique of choice. However, as discussed below, if the gift is substantial, there are many drawbacks to outright gifts.

2) Drawbacks

Appointment of Guardian Required. As previously discussed, minors can generally own property, but without a guardian, they cannot effectively deal with it. The necessity of a guardian and the related inconvenience and court costs are serious limitations to making outright gifts to a minor. Court permission is often required before a guardian may act. The delay is not only inconvenient but could cause financial loss if, for example, the guardian needs to sell one of the ward's assets quickly due to market conditions. Many states require annual accountings which are both time consuming and costly. The guardian must keep each child's property separate and thus cannot use property from one child's share to assist another child who has special needs.

Mandatory Distribution Upon Majority. Once a minor reaches majority, which in most states is on his or her eighteenth birthday, the guardian must turn over all property to the new adult who may now do with the property as he or she desires. Thus, outright transfers have no safeguards to protect the property from the potential whims of its new managing owner who is scarcely out of high school.

Possible Immaturity of Beneficiary. Many donees, having just turned eighteen and gained control of their estates, lack sufficient maturity, wisdom, and experience to properly manage their own finances or property. As one commentator remarked, "[T]he prospect of the minor dissipating the property is a disquieting one;" and may significantly decrease the desirability of making an outright gift.[1]

Property Reacquisition if Minor Dies Prior to Reaching Majority. Most states do not permit a minor to make a will. Thus, if the minor donee dies before reaching majority and executing a will, the property often returns to the minor's parents through intestacy. If the parents were the original donors, their intent to save transfer taxes is likely to be defeated.

b. Custodianship

The Uniform Transfers to Minors Act (UTMA) allows a client to make a gift to a minor by transferring the property to a custodian for the minor. The UTMA, or some modified form thereof, has been enacted in almost all states and in most cases replaced the outdated Uniform Gifts to Minors Act (UGMA).

UNIFORM TRANSFERS TO MINORS ACT

1983 Act.

§ 1. Definitions

In this [Act]:

(1) "Adult" means an individual who has attained the age of 21 years.

(2) "Benefit plan" means an employer's plan for the benefit of an employee or partner.

1. Richard Atkinson, *Gifts to Minors: A Roadmap,* 42 ARK. L. REV. 567, 577 (1989).

(3) "Broker" means a person lawfully engaged in the business of effecting transactions in securities or commodities for the person's own account or for the account of others.

(4) "Conservator" means a person appointed or qualified by a court to act as general, limited, or temporary guardian of a minor's property or a person legally authorized to perform substantially the same functions.

(5) "Court" means [______ court].

(6) "Custodial property" means (i) any interest in property transferred to a custodian under this [Act] and (ii) the income from and proceeds of that interest in property.

(7) "Custodian" means a person so designated under Section 9 or a successor or substitute custodian designated under Section 18.

(8) "Financial institution" means a bank, trust company, savings institution, or credit union, chartered and supervised under state or federal law.

(9) "Legal representative" means an individual's personal representative or conservator.

(10) "Member of the minor's family" means the minor's parent, stepparent, spouse, grandparent, brother, sister, uncle, or aunt, whether of the whole or half blood or by adoption.

(11) "Minor" means an individual who has not attained the age of 21 years.

(12) "Person" means an individual, corporation, organization, or other legal entity.

(13) "Personal representative" means an executor, administrator, successor personal representative, or special administrator of a decedent's estate or a person legally authorized to perform substantially the same functions.

(14) "State" includes any state of the United States, the District of Columbia, the Commonwealth of Puerto Rico, and any territory or possession subject to the legislative authority of the United States.

(15) "Transfer" means a transaction that creates custodial property under Section 9.

(16) "Transferor" means a person who makes a transfer under this [Act].

(17) "Trust company" means a financial institution, corporation, or other legal entity, authorized to exercise general trust powers.

§ 2. Scope and Jurisdiction

(a) This [Act] applies to a transfer that refers to this [Act] in the designation under Section 9(a) by which the transfer is made if at the time of the transfer, the transferor, the minor, or the custodian is a resident of this State or the custodial property is located in this State. The custodianship so created remains subject to this [Act] despite a subsequent change in residence of a transferor, the minor, or the custodian, or the removal of custodial property from this State.

(b) A person designated as custodian under this [Act] is subject to personal jurisdiction in this State with respect to any matter relating to the custodianship.

(c) A transfer that purports to be made and which is valid under the Uniform Transfers to Minors Act, the Uniform Gifts to Minors Act, or a substantially similar act, of another state is governed by the law of the designated state and may be executed and is enforceable in this State if at the time of the transfer, the transferor, the minor, or the custodian is a resident of the designated state or the custodial property is located in the designated state.

§ 3. Nomination of Custodian

(a) A person having the right to designate the recipient of property transferable upon the occurrence of a future event may revocably nominate a custodian to receive the property for a minor beneficiary upon the occurrence of the event by naming the custodian followed in substance by the words: "as custodian for ______ (name of minor) under the [name of Enacting State] Uniform Transfers to Minors Act." The nomination may name one or more persons as substitute custodians to whom the property must be transferred, in the order named, if the first nominated custodian dies before the transfer or is unable, declines, or is ineligible to serve. The nomination may be made in a will, a trust, a deed, an instrument exercising a power of appointment, or in a writing designating a beneficiary of contractual rights which is registered with or delivered to the payor, issuer, or other obligor of the contractual rights.

(b) A custodian nominated under this section must be a person to whom a transfer of property of that kind may be made under Section 9(a).

(c) The nomination of a custodian under this section does not create custodial property until the nominating instrument becomes irrevocable or a transfer to the nominated custodian is completed under Section 9. Unless the nomination of a custodian has been revoked, upon the occurrence of the future event the custodianship becomes effective and the custodian shall enforce a transfer of the custodial property pursuant to Section 9.

§ 4. Transfer by Gift or Exercise of Power of Appointment

A person may make a transfer by irrevocable gift to, or the irrevocable exercise of a power of appointment in favor of, a custodian for the benefit of a minor pursuant to Section 9.

§ 5. Transfer Authorized by Will or Trust

(a) A personal representative or trustee may make an irrevocable transfer pursuant to Section 9 to a custodian for the benefit of a minor as authorized in the governing will or trust.

(b) If the testator or settlor has nominated a custodian under Section 3 to receive the custodial property, the transfer must be made to that person.

(c) If the testator or settlor has not nominated a custodian under Section 3, or all persons so nominated as custodian die before the transfer or are unable, decline, or are ineligible to serve, the personal representative or the trustee, as the case may be, shall designate the custodian from among those eligible to serve as custodian for property of that kind under Section 9(a).

§ 6. Other Transfer by Fiduciary

(a) Subject to subsection (c), a personal representative or trustee may make an irrevocable transfer to another adult or trust company as custodian for the benefit of a minor pursuant to Section 9, in the absence of a will or under a will or trust that does not contain an authorization to do so.

(b) Subject to subsection (c), a conservator may make an irrevocable transfer to another adult or trust company as custodian for the benefit of the minor pursuant to Section 9.

(c) A transfer under subsection (a) or (b) may be made only if (i) the personal representative, trustee, or conservator considers the transfer to be in the best interest of the minor, (ii) the transfer is not prohibited by or inconsistent with provisions of the applicable will, trust agreement, or other governing instrument, and (iii) the transfer is authorized by the court if it exceeds [$10,000] in value.

§ 7. Transfer by Obligor

(a) Subject to subsections (b) and (c), a person not subject to Section 5 or 6 who holds property of or owes a liquidated debt to a minor not having a conservator may make an irrevocable transfer to a custodian for the benefit of the minor pursuant to Section 9.

(b) If a person having the right to do so under Section 3 has nominated a custodian under that section to receive the custodial property, the transfer must be made to that person.

(c) If no custodian has been nominated under Section 3, or all persons so nominated as custodian die before the transfer or are unable, decline, or are ineligible to serve, a transfer under this section may be made to an adult member of the minor's family or to a trust company unless the property exceeds [$10,000] in value.

§ 8. Receipt for Custodial Property

A written acknowledgment of delivery by a custodian constitutes a sufficient receipt and discharge for custodial property transferred to the custodian pursuant to this [Act].

§ 9. Manner of Creating Custodial Property and Effecting Transfer; Designation of Initial Custodian; Control

(a) Custodial property is created and a transfer is made whenever:

(1) an uncertificated security or a certificated security in registered form is either:

(i) registered in the name of the transferor, an adult other than the transferor, or a trust company, followed in substance by the words: "as custodian for ______ (name of minor) under the [Name of Enacting State] Uniform Transfers to Minors Act"; or

(ii) delivered if in certificated form, or any document necessary for the transfer of an uncertificated security is delivered, together with any necessary endorsement to an adult other than the transferor or to a trust company as custodian, accompanied by an instrument in substantially the form set forth in subsection (b);

(2) money is paid or delivered, or a security held in the name of a broker, financial institution, or its nominee is transferred, to a broker or financial institution for credit to an account in the name of the transferor, an adult other than the transferor, or a trust company, followed in substance by the words: "as custodian for ______ (name of minor) under the [Name of Enacting State] Uniform Transfers to Minors Act";

(3) the ownership of a life or endowment insurance policy or annuity contract is either:

(i) registered with the issuer in the name of the transferor, an adult other than the transferor, or a trust company, followed in substance by the words: "as custodian for ______ (name of minor) under the [Name of Enacting State] Uniform Transfers to Minors Act"; or

(ii) assigned in a writing delivered to an adult other than the transferor or to a trust company whose name in the assignment is followed in substance by the words: "as custodian for ______ (name of minor) under the [Name of Enacting State] Uniform Transfers to Minors Act";

(4) an irrevocable exercise of a power of appointment or an irrevocable present right to future payment under a contract is the subject of a written notification delivered to the payor, issuer, or other obligor that the right is transferred to the transferor, an adult other than the transferor, or a trust company, whose name in the notification is followed in substance by the words: "as custodian for ______ (name of minor) under the [Name of Enacting State] Uniform Transfers to Minors Act";

(5) an interest in real property is recorded in the name of the transferor, an adult other than the transferor, or a trust company,

followed in substance by the words: "as custodian for _______ (name of minor) under the [Name of Enacting State] Uniform Transfers to Minors Act";

(6) a certificate of title issued by a department or agency of a state or of the United States which evidences title to tangible personal property is either:

(i) issued in the name of the transferor, an adult other than the transferor, or a trust company, followed in substance by the words: "as custodian for _______ (name of minor) under the [Name of Enacting State] Uniform Transfers to Minors Act"; or

(ii) delivered to an adult other than the transferor or to a trust company, endorsed to that person followed in substance by the words: "as custodian for _______ (name of minor) under the [Name of Enacting State] Uniform Transfers to Minors Act"; or

(7) an interest in any property not described in paragraphs (1) through (6) is transferred to an adult other than the transferor or to a trust company by a written instrument in substantially the form set forth in subsection (b).

(b) An instrument in the following form satisfies the requirements of paragraphs (1)(ii) and (7) of subsection (a):

"TRANSFER UNDER THE [NAME OF ENACTING STATE] UNIFORM TRANSFER TO MINORS ACT"

I, _______ (name of transferor or name and representative capacity if a fiduciary) hereby transfer to _______ (name of custodian), as custodian for _______ (name of minor) under the [Name of Enacting State] Uniform Transfers to Minors Act, the following: (insert a description of the custodial property sufficient to identify it).

Dated: _______

____

(Signature)

_______ (name of custodian) acknowledges receipt of the property described above as custodian for the minor named above under the [Name of Enacting State] Uniform Transfers to Minors Act.

Dated: _______

________________________________"

(Signature of Custodian)

(c) A transferor shall place the custodian in control of the custodial property as soon as practicable.

§ 10. Single Custodianship

A transfer may be made only for one minor, and only one person may be the custodian. All custodial property held under this [Act] by the same custodian for the benefit of the same minor constitutes a single custodianship.

§ 11. Validity and Effect of Transfer

(a) The validity of a transfer made in a manner prescribed in this [Act] is not affected by:

(1) failure of the transferor to comply with Section 9(c) concerning possession and control;

(2) designation of an ineligible custodian, except designation of the transferor in the case of property for which the transferor is ineligible to serve as custodian under Section 9(a); or

(3) death or incapacity of a person nominated under Section 3 or designated under Section 9 as custodian or the disclaimer of the office by that person.

(b) A transfer made pursuant to Section 9 is irrevocable, and the custodial property is indefeasibly vested in the minor, but the custodian has all the rights, powers, duties, and authority provided in this [Act], and neither the minor nor the minor's legal representative has any right, power, duty, or authority with respect to the custodial property except as provided in this [Act].

(c) By making a transfer, the transferor incorporates in the disposition all the provisions of this [Act] and grants to the custodian, and to any third person dealing with a person designated as custodian, the respective powers, rights, and immunities provided in this [Act].

§ 12. Care of Custodial Property

(a) A custodian shall:

(1) take control of custodial property;

(2) register or record title to custodial property if appropriate; and

(3) collect, hold, manage, invest, and reinvest custodial property.

(b) In dealing with custodial property, a custodian shall observe the standard of care that would be observed by a prudent person dealing with property of another and is not limited by any other statute restricting investments by fiduciaries. If a custodian has a special skill or expertise or is named custodian on the basis of representations of a special skill or expertise, the custodian shall use that skill or expertise. However, a custodian, in the custodian's discretion and without liability to the minor or the minor's estate, may retain any custodial property received from a transferor.

(c) A custodian may invest in or pay premiums on life insurance or endowment policies on (i) the life of the minor only if the minor or the minor's estate is the sole beneficiary, or (ii) the life of another person in whom the minor has an insurable interest only to the extent that the minor, the minor's estate, or the custodian in the capacity of custodian, is the irrevocable beneficiary.

(d) A custodian at all times shall keep custodial property separate and distinct from all other property in a manner sufficient to identify it clearly as custodial property of the minor. Custodial property consisting of an undivided interest is so identified if the minor's interest is held as a tenant in common and is fixed. Custodial property subject to recordation is so identified if it is recorded, and custodial property subject to registration is so identified if it is either registered, or held in an account designated, in the name of the custodian, followed in substance by the words: "as a custodian for ______ (name of minor) under the [Name of Enacting State] Uniform Transfers to Minors Act."

(e) A custodian shall keep records of all transactions with respect to custodial property, including information necessary for the preparation of the minor's tax returns, and shall make them available for inspection at reasonable intervals by a parent or legal representative of the minor or by the minor if the minor has attained the age of 14 years.

§ 13. Powers of Custodian

(a) A custodian, acting in a custodial capacity, has all the rights, powers, and authority over custodial property that unmarried adult owners have over their own property, but a custodian may exercise those rights, powers, and authority in that capacity only.

(b) This section does not relieve a custodian from liability for breach of Section 12.

§ 14. Use of Custodial Property

(a) A custodian may deliver or pay to the minor or expend for the minor's benefit so much of the custodial property as the custodian considers advisable for the use and benefit of the minor, without court order and without regard to (i) the duty or ability of the custodian personally or of any other person to support the minor, or (ii) any other income or property of the minor which may be applicable or available for that purpose.

(b) On petition of an interested person or the minor if the minor has attained the age of 14 years, the court may order the custodian to deliver or pay to the minor or expend for the minor's benefit so much of the custodial property as the court considers advisable for the use and benefit of the minor.

(c) A delivery, payment, or expenditure under this section is in addition to, not in substitution for, and does not affect any obligation of a person to support the minor.

§ 15. Custodian's Expenses, Compensation, and Bond

(a) A custodian is entitled to reimbursement from custodial property for reasonable expenses incurred in the performance of the custodian's duties.

(b) Except for one who is a transferor under Section 4, a custodian has a non-cumulative election during each calendar year to charge reasonable compensation for services performed during that year.

(c) Except as provided in Section 18(f), a custodian need not give a bond.

§ 16. Exemption of Third Person From Liability

A third person in good faith and without court order may act on the instructions of or otherwise deal with any person purporting to make a transfer or purporting to act in the capacity of a custodian and, in the absence of knowledge, is not responsible for determining:

(1) the validity of the purported custodian's designation;

(2) the propriety of, or the authority under this [Act] for, any act of the purported custodian;

(3) the validity or propriety under this [Act] of any instrument or instructions executed or given either by the person purporting to make a transfer or by the purported custodian; or

(4) the propriety of the application of any property of the minor delivered to the purported custodian.

§ 17. Liability to Third Persons

(a) A claim based on (i) a contract entered into by a custodian acting in a custodial capacity, (ii) an obligation arising from the ownership or control of custodial property, or (iii) a tort committed during the custodianship, may be asserted against the custodial property by proceeding against the custodian in the custodial capacity, whether or not the custodian or the minor is personally liable therefor.

(b) A custodian is not personally liable:

(1) on a contract properly entered into in the custodial capacity unless the custodian fails to reveal that capacity and to identify the custodianship in the contract; or

(2) for an obligation arising from control of custodial property or for a tort committed during the custodianship unless the custodian is personally at fault.

(c) A minor is not personally liable for an obligation arising from ownership of custodial property or for a tort committed during the custodianship unless the minor is personally at fault.

§ 18. Renunciation, Resignation, Death, or Removal of Custodian; Designation of Successor Custodian

(a) A person nominated under Section 3 or designated under Section 9 as custodian may decline to serve by delivering a valid disclaimer [under the Uniform Disclaimer of Property Interests Act of the Enacting State] to the person who made the nomination or to the transferor or the transferor's legal representative. If the event giving rise to a transfer has not occurred and no substitute custodian able, willing, and eligible to serve was nominated under Section 3, the person who made the nomination may nominate a substitute custodian under Section 3; otherwise the transferor or the transferor's legal representative shall designate a substitute custodian at the time of the transfer, in either case from among the persons eligible to serve as custodian for that kind of property under Section 9(a). The custodian so designated has the rights of a successor custodian.

(b) A custodian at any time may designate a trust company or an adult other than a transferor under Section 4 as successor custodian by executing and dating an instrument of designation before a subscribing witness other than the successor. If the instrument of designation does not contain or is not accompanied by the resignation of the custodian, the designation of the successor does not take effect until the custodian resigns, dies, becomes incapacitated, or is removed.

(c) A custodian may resign at any time by delivering written notice to the minor if the minor has attained the age of 14 years and to the successor custodian and by delivering the custodial property to the successor custodian.

(d) If a custodian is ineligible, dies, or becomes incapacitated without having effectively designated a successor and the minor has attained the age of 14 years, the minor may designate as successor custodian, in the manner prescribed in subsection (b), an adult member of the minor's family, a conservator of the minor, or a trust company. If the minor has not attained the age of 14 years or fails to act within 60 days after the ineligibility, death, or incapacity, the conservator of the minor becomes successor custodian. If the minor has no conservator or the conservator declines to act, the transferor, the legal representative of the transferor or of the custodian, an adult member of the minor's family, or any other interested person may petition the court to designate a successor custodian.

(e) A custodian who declines to serve under subsection (a) or resigns under subsection (c), or the legal representative of a deceased or incapacitated custodian, as soon as practicable, shall put the custodial property and records in the possession and control of the successor custodian. The successor custodian by action may enforce the obligation to deliver custodial property and records and becomes responsible for each item as received.

(f) A transferor, the legal representative of a transferor, an adult member of the minor's family, a guardian of the person of the minor, the conservator of the minor, or the minor if the minor has attained the age of 14 years may petition the court to remove the custodian for cause and to designate a successor custodian other than a transferor under Section 4 or to require the custodian to give appropriate bond.

§ 19. Accounting by and Determination of Liability of Custodian

(a) A minor who has attained the age of 14 years, the minor's guardian of the person or legal representative, an adult member of the minor's family, a transferor, or a transferor's legal representative may petition the court (i) for an accounting by the custodian or the custodian's legal representative; or (ii) for a determination of responsibility, as between the custodial property and the custodian personally, for claims against the custodial property unless the responsibility has been adjudicated in an action under Section 17 to which the minor or the minor's legal representative was a party.

(b) A successor custodian may petition the court for an accounting by the predecessor custodian.

(c) The court, in a proceeding under this [Act] or in any other proceeding, may require or permit the custodian or the custodian's legal representative to account.

(d) If a custodian is removed under Section 18(f), the court shall require an accounting and order delivery of the custodial property and records to the successor custodian and the execution of all instruments required for transfer of the custodial property.

§ 20. Termination of Custodianship

The custodian shall transfer in an appropriate manner the custodial property to the minor or to the minor's estate upon the earlier of:

(1) the minor's attainment of 21 years of age with respect to custodial property transferred under Section 4 or 5;

(2) the minor's attainment of [majority under the laws of this State other than this [Act]] [age 18 or other statutory age of majority of Enacting State] with respect to custodial property transferred under Section 6 or 7; or

(3) the minor's death.

§ 21. Applicability

* * *

§ 22. Effect on Existing Custodianships

* * *

§ 23. Uniformity of Application and Construction

This [Act] shall be applied and construed to effectuate its general purpose to make uniform the law with respect to the subject of this [Act] among states enacting it.

§ 24. Short Title

This [Act] may be cited as the "[Name of Enacting State] Uniform Transfers to Minors Act."

---

1) *Benefits*

Simplicity. The process of making a transfer under the UTMA is quick and straight forward. Therefore, in most cases, the gift can be made with minimal, or no, legal, transaction, or drafting costs.

Tax Savings to Donor. UTMA transfers qualify for the gift tax annual exclusion and, to that extent, escape the generation-skipping transfer tax as well.

Expires on 21st Birthday. Custodial property is not subject to the donee's unrestricted control until the donee is 21 years old, as opposed to 18 years old under the UGMA and most states' guardianship laws.

2) *Drawbacks*

Lack of Flexibility. Transfers made under the UTMA may not be made with any conditions nor are provisions maintaining the custodianship past the beneficiary's twenty-first birthday permitted.

Lack of Power of Appointment. Gifts held by a custodian are not subject to a donee's power of appointment. Consequently, if the donee dies before reaching age 21, the property is distributed to the donee's estate. If the donee dies while still a minor or dies between the ages of 18 and 21 without having executed a valid will, the gifted property will pass by intestacy, often back to the donor parent.

Possible Inclusion in Client's Gross Estate. Custodial property may be included in the donor's gross estate if the donor dies while serving as the custodian before the donee reaches age 21. Estate of Prudowsky v. Commissioner, 55 T.C. 890 (1971), *aff'd per curiam*, 465 F.2d 62 (7th Cir. 1972).

LOCATE

Has the Uniform Transfers to Minors Act been adopted in your state? Perhaps your state has either the 1956 or 1966 version of the predecessor of this uniform act called the Uniform Gifts to Minors Act.

NOTES AND QUESTIONS

1. When would you recommend that your client make an inter vivos or testamentary gift to a custodian rather than creating a traditional trust?

2. While in the hands of the custodian, an item of property earned $1,000. Who is responsible for the tax on this income, the custodianship as a legal entity, the custodian personally, or the minor?

3. Custodian holds a parcel of real property for Minor. In the middle of winter, Plaintiff slips, falls, and is seriously injured on ice which accumulated on the sidewalk in front of the property. Is the property liable for Plaintiff's damages? Is either Custodian or Minor personally liable? See § 17 of the Act. Does the resolution of this question give you an additional reason to consider custodianships for certain high-risk property?

4. Why do you think the drafters selected age 21 as the age of adulthood rather than age 18?

DRAFT

Prepare a will provision leaving property to a custodian of a minor beneficiary.

c. Trust

Under most circumstances, your client will want to avoid the necessity of a court-appointed estate guardian for the client's child and will want to exercise greater control than allowed in a custodianship. Accordingly, it is normally far superior to establish a trust for the minor child. All of the benefits of a trust discussed in Chapter 2(D) are then available to the client. Several different methods are available to make gifts to minors in trust.

Revocable Trust. A gift to a minor made through the use of a revocable trust allows the client to retain complete control over the property. At any point and for any or even no reason at all, the client may simply take back the gift. This flexibility comes with a price, however. Gifts to revocable trusts are ignored for tax purposes and the property is treated as if owned by the client. The client gets no annual exclusion and is still taxed on the income earned by the trust property. Nonetheless, this tool may be appropriate for situations where the parent is ill or absent and property is transferred to provide for the care and education of the minor during that period.

Irrevocable Trust—Discretionary Income Distribution. The client may establish an irrevocable trust which does not distribute the corpus to the beneficiary until he or she reaches some pre-determined age, and leaves the income distribution to the discretion of the trustee. This technique provides a great deal of flexibility regarding trust distributions. However, the opportunity to qualify any amount of the gift for the annual exclusion is normally lost.

I.R.C. § 2503(b) Irrevocable Trust With Mandatory Income Distribution. A client may make a gift to an irrevocable trust and still benefit from the annual exclusion as long as there is a present gift of the property's income interest. Up to the annual exclusion amount of the actuarial value of this income interest is eligible for the annual exclusion if all income must be distributed to the donee at least annually and the trustee does not have the right to withhold income or distribute principal to others. Only the value of the income stream qualifies for the exclusion and thus the value of the remainder is subject to transfer taxes. If the beneficiary is a minor, the minor may need a guardian to manage the income distributions.

I.R.C. § 2503(c) "Minor's" Trust. If the donor satisfies the requirements of this tax code provision, the donor may make gifts to a trust for a person under 21 years old which still qualify for the annual exclusion. This technique is discussed in Chapter 4(B)(4)(a), note 6.

***Crummey* Trust**. Through use of the *Crummey* trust technique, gifts to an irrevocable trust for the benefit of a minor can qualify for the annual exclusion, even if the distributions from that trust are completely discretionary. By granting the beneficiary, or the beneficiary's guardian, the power to withdraw the transfer during a specified reasonable period of time, the transfer is regarded as a gift of a present interest which thus qualifies it for the annual exclusion. Of course, the client anticipates that this withdrawal power will never be exercised. Despite complexities in both creation and administration, *Crummey* trusts allow clients to set specific distribution restrictions and still use the annual exclusion. See Chapter 4(I)(2).

1) Benefits

Reduces Need For Guardianship. Because gifts made to a trust will be held and controlled by the trustee according to the terms of the trust, there is no need for a guardian to be appointed for the minor. In the situation presented by the mandatory income distribution type trust, the minor's need for a guardian can be avoided by making distributions under the UTMA.

Provides Flexibility and Control. Making a gift in trust allows the client to exercise the greatest amount of flexibility and control possible under the various transfer methods. The client can set limitations or conditions on distributions and termination as long as they are not illegal or against public policy.

Prevents Mandatory Distribution at Majority. Unlike outright gifts and custodial situations, a trust permits the trustee to manage and control trust property long after the beneficiary reaches adulthood. The client thus has greater reassurance that the property will be competently managed and that the beneficiary cannot squander it or use it for frivolous purposes.

Protects Assets From Beneficiary's Creditors. By including a spendthrift provision, the client can, under the law of most states, prevent the beneficiary's creditors from reaching trust property.

Creates Tax Savings. Though not all transfers to a trust qualify for the annual exclusion, transfers to a trust, as long as it is irrevocable, can easily be structured to keep the gifted property out of the donor's gross estate. Further, inclusion of *Crummey* withdrawal rights permits the donor to obtain the annual exclusion without sacrificing flexibility.

2) Drawbacks

Costs, Both in Money and Time. Trusts are the most complicated and expensive of the methods of making gifts to minors. The costs of drafting the documents, paying a trustee to administer the trust property, and filing tax returns may make the use of a trust impractical under the circumstances, especially for relatively low valued gifts.

Annual Exclusion May Not Be Available. Gifts made in trust are not considered gifts of a present interest because the beneficiary has no immediate right to the property. Because only present interest gifts qualify for the annual exclusion, gifts made to a trust generally do not qualify. Although use of *Crummey* withdrawal rights or mandatory income distribution provisions can solve this problem, the use of these techniques can bring additional complications and expense to the situation.

B. CLIENT WITH CHILD OR POTENTIAL CHILD FROM ALTERNATIVE REPRODUCTION TECHNOLOGIES

According to the Centers of Disease Control and Prevention, approximately 10% of American women between the ages 15 and 44 have difficulty getting or staying pregnant. In total, infertility affects approximately 6.1 million American women. Further, approximately 7.1% of American married couples are infertile. Accordingly, a significant number of your clients may have or may be interested in having a child who is born via reproductive techniques that involve more than the traditional two people. Examples of these methodologies include (1) *artificial insemination* (donated semen artificially introduced into the mother's vagina or uterus), (2) *in vitro fertilization* (donated egg and donated semen combined in a laboratory with the resulting embryo transferred to a donee), (3) *gamete intrafallopian transfer* (donated egg and donated sperm combined in a donee's fallopian tube), and (4) *embryo lavage and transfer* (fertilized egg removed from the donor and transferred to the donee's uterus).

Several options exist regarding the parentage of children born as a result of these techniques. The legal father could be (1) the supplier of the genetic material (sperm), (2) the husband of the supplier of the female genetic material (egg), or (3) the husband of the woman who gestates the child. Likewise, the legal mother could be (1) the supplier of the female genetic material, (2) the wife of the man who supplies the male genetic material, or (3) the woman who gestates the child even though this woman did not supply any genetic material (a surrogate mother).

Jurisdictions have taken a variety of approaches to deal with these matters. Because artificial insemination is a relatively old technique which has successfully been practiced on humans since 1770, many states have statutes directly on point. Most of these statutes provide that the sperm donor is not the father. The father is typically the husband of the woman who receives the donated sperm. There is less uniformity with the other techniques resulting from their newness and the social and political issues they raise. Some states use these statutes to legislate family values by providing for parentage resolutions only in cases where the donee is married and both husband and wife consent. Most of the existing legislation is not extensive or is designed to address issues of child support rather than estate planning concerns.

ASTRUE v. CAPATO

Supreme Court of the United States, 2012
___ U.S. ___, 132 S.Ct. 2021, 182 L.Ed.2d 887.

Justice GINSBURG delivered the opinion of the Court.

Karen and Robert Capato married in 1999. Robert died of cancer less than three years later. With the help of in vitro fertilization, Karen gave birth to twins 18 months after her husband's death. Karen's application for Social Security survivors benefits for the twins, which the Social Security Administration (SSA) denied, prompted this litigation. The technology that made the twins' conception and birth possible, it is safe to say, was not contemplated by Congress when the relevant provisions of the Social Security Act (Act) originated (1939) or were amended to read as they now do (1965).

Karen Capato, respondent here, relies on the Act's initial definition of "child" in 42 U.S.C. § 416(e): " '[C]hild' means ... the child or legally adopted child of an [insured] individual." Robert was an insured individual, and the twins, it is uncontested, are the biological children of Karen and Robert. That satisfies the Act's terms, and no further inquiry is in order, Karen maintains. The SSA, however, identifies subsequent provisions, § 416(h)(2) and (h)(3)(C), as critical, and reads them to entitle biological children to benefits only if they qualify for inheritance from the decedent under state intestacy law, or satisfy one of the statutory alternatives to that requirement.

We conclude that the SSA's reading is better attuned to the statute's text and its design to benefit primarily those supported by the deceased wage earner in his or her lifetime. And even if the SSA's longstanding interpretation is not the only reasonable one, it is at least a permissible construction that garners the Court's respect under Chevron U.S.A. Inc. v. Natural Resources Defense Council, Inc., 467 U.S. 837, 104 S.Ct. 2778, 81 L.Ed.2d 694 (1984).

I

Karen Capato married Robert Capato in May 1999. Shortly thereafter, Robert was diagnosed with esophageal cancer and was told that the chemotherapy he required might render him sterile. Because the couple wanted children, Robert, before undergoing chemotherapy, deposited his semen in a sperm bank, where it was frozen and stored. Despite Robert's aggressive treatment regime, Karen conceived naturally and gave birth to a son in August 2001. The Capatos, however, wanted their son to have a sibling.

Robert's health deteriorated in late 2001, and he died in Florida, where he and Karen then resided, in March 2002. His will, executed in Florida, named as beneficiaries the son born of his marriage to Karen and two children from a previous marriage. The will made no provision for children conceived after Robert's death, although the Capatos had told their lawyer they wanted future offspring to be placed on a par with existing children. Shortly after Robert's death, Karen began in vitro fertilization using her husband's frozen sperm. She conceived in January 2003 and gave birth to twins in September 2003, 18 months after Robert's death.

Karen Capato claimed survivors insurance benefits on behalf of the twins. The SSA denied her application, and the U.S. District Court for the District of New Jersey affirmed the agency's decision. See App. to Pet. for Cert. 33a (decision of the Administrative Law Judge); id., at 15a (District Court opinion). In accord with the SSA's construction of the statute, the District Court determined that the twins would qualify for benefits only if, as § 416(h)(2)(A) specifies, they could inherit from the deceased wage earner under state intestacy law. Robert Capato died domiciled in Florida, the court found. Under that State's law, the court noted, a child born posthumously may inherit through intestate succession only if conceived during the decedent's lifetime. Id., at 27a–28a.

The Court of Appeals for the Third Circuit reversed. Under § 416(e), the appellate court concluded, "the undisputed biological children of a deceased wage earner and his widow" qualify for survivors benefits without regard to state intestacy law. 631 F.3d 626, 631 (2011). Courts of Appeals have divided on the statutory interpretation question this case presents. Compare ibid. and Gillett–Netting v. Barnhart, 371 F.3d 593, 596–597 (C.A.9 2004) (biological but posthumously conceived child of insured wage earner and his widow qualifies for benefits), with Beeler v. Astrue, 651 F.3d 954, 960–964 (C.A.8 2011), and Schafer v. Astrue, 641 F.3d 49, 54–63 (C.A.4 2011) (post-humously conceived child's qualification for benefits depends on intestacy law of State in which wage earner was domiciled). To resolve the conflict, we granted the Commissioner's petition for a writ of certiorari. 565 U.S. ___, 132 S.Ct. 576, 181 L.Ed.2d 419 (2011).

II

Congress amended the Social Security Act in 1939 to provide a monthly benefit for designated surviving family members of a deceased insured wage earner. "Child's insurance benefits" are among the Act's family-protective measures. 53 Stat. 1364, as amended, 42 U.S.C. § 402(d). An applicant qualifies for such benefits if she meets the Act's definition of "child," is unmarried, is below specified age limits (18 or 19) or is under a disability which began prior to age 22, and was dependent on the insured at the time of the insured's death. § 402(d)(1).

To resolve this case, we must decide whether the Capato twins rank as "child[ren]" under the Act's definitional provisions. Section 402(d) provides that "[e]very child (as defined in section 416(e) of this title)" of a deceased insured individual "shall be entitled to a child's insurance benefit." Section 416(e), in turn, states: "The term 'child' means (1) the child or legally adopted child of an individual, (2) a stepchild [under certain circumstances], and (3) . . . the grandchild or stepgrandchild of an individual or his spouse [who meets certain conditions]."

The word "child," we note, appears twice in § 416(e)'s opening sentence: initially in the prefatory phrase, "[t]he term 'child' means . . . ," and, immediately thereafter, in subsection (e)(1) ("child or legally adopted child"), delineating the first of three beneficiary categories. Unlike § 416(e)(2) and (3), which specify the circumstances under which stepchildren and grandchildren qualify for benefits, § 416(e)(1) lacks any elaboration. Compare § 416(e)(1) (referring simply to "the child . . . of an individual") with, e.g., § 416(e)(2) (applicant must have been a stepchild for at least nine months before the insured individual's death).

A subsequent definitional provision further addresses the term "child." Under the heading "Determination of family status," § 416(h)(2)(A) provides: "In determining whether an applicant is the child or parent of [an] insured individual for purposes of this subchapter, the Commissioner of Social Security shall apply [the intestacy law of the insured individual's domiciliary State]."

An applicant for child benefits who does not meet § 416(h)(2)(A)'s intestacy-law criterion may nonetheless qualify for benefits under one of several other criteria the Act prescribes. First, an applicant who "is a son or daughter" of an insured individual, but is not determined to be a "child" under the intestacy-law provision, nevertheless ranks as a "child" if the insured and the other parent went through a marriage ceremony that would have been valid but for certain legal impediments. § 416(h)(2)(B). Further, an applicant is deemed a "child" if, before death, the insured acknowledged in writing that the applicant is his or her son or daughter, or if the insured had been decreed by a court to be the father or mother of the applicant, or had been ordered to pay child support. § 416(h)(3)(C)(i). In addition, an applicant may gain "child" status upon proof that the insured individual was the applicant's parent and "was living with or contributing to the support of the applicant" when the insured individual died. § 416(h)(3)(C)(ii).

The SSA has interpreted these provisions in regulations adopted through notice-and-comment rulemaking. The regulations state that an applicant may be entitled to benefits "as a natural child, legally adopted child, stepchild, grandchild, stepgrandchild, or equitably adopted child." 20 CFR § 404.354. Defining "[w]ho is the insured's natural child," § 404.355, the regulations closely track 42 U.S.C. § 416(h)(2) and (h)(3). They state that an applicant may qualify for insurance benefits as a "natural child" by meeting any of four conditions: (1) the applicant "could inherit the insured's personal property as his or her natural child under State inheritance laws"; (2) the applicant is "the insured's natural child and [his or her parents] went through a ceremony which would have resulted in a valid marriage between them except for a legal impediment"; (3) before death, the insured acknowledged in writing his or her parentage of the applicant, was decreed by a court to be the applicant's parent, or was ordered by a court to contribute to the applicant's support; or (4) other evidence shows that the insured is the applicant's "natural father or mother" and was either living with, or contributing to the support of, the applicant. 20 CFR § 404.355(a) (internal quotation marks omitted).

As the SSA reads the statute, 42 U.S.C. § 416(h) governs the meaning of "child" in § 416(e)(1). In other words, § 416(h) is a gateway through which all applicants for insurance benefits as a "child" must pass. * * *

III

Karen Capato argues, and the Third Circuit held, that § 416(h), far from supplying the governing law, is irrelevant in this case. Instead, the Court of Appeals determined, § 416(e) alone is dispositive of the controversy. 631 F.3d, at 630–631. Under § 416(e), "child" means "child of an [insured] individual," and the Capato twins, the Third Circuit observed, clearly fit that definition: They are undeniably the children of Robert Capato, the insured wage earner, and his widow, Karen Capato. Section 416(h) comes into play, the court reasoned, only when "a claimant's status as a deceased wage-earner's child is in doubt." Id., at 631. That limitation, the court suggested, is evident from § 416(h)'s caption: "Determination of family status." Here, "there is no family status to determine," the court said, id., at 630, so § 416(h) has no role to play.

In short, while the SSA regards § 416(h) as completing § 416(e)'s sparse definition of "child," the Third Circuit considered each subsection to control different situations: § 416(h) governs when a child's family status needs to be determined; § 416(e), when it does not. When is there no need to determine a child's family status? The answer that the Third Circuit found plain: whenever the claimant is "the biological child of a married couple." Id., at 630.

We point out, first, some conspicuous flaws in the Third Circuit's and respondent Karen Capato's reading of the Act's provisions, and then explain why we find the SSA's interpretation persuasive.

A

Nothing in § 416(e)'s tautological definition (" 'child' means ... the child ... of an individual") suggests that Congress understood the word "child" to refer only to the children of married parents. The dictionary definitions offered by respondent are not so confined. See Webster's New International Dictionary 465 (2d ed.1934) (defining "child" as, inter alia, "[i]n Law, legitimate offspring; also, sometimes, esp. in wills, an adopted child, or an illegitimate offspring, or any direct descendant, as a grandchild, as the intention may appear"); Merriam–Webster's Collegiate Dictionary 214 (11th ed.2003) ("child" means "son or daughter," or "descendant"). See also Restatement (Third) of Property § 2.5(1) (1998) ("[a]n individual is the child of his or her genetic parents," and that may be so "whether or not [the parents] are married to each other"). Moreover, elsewhere in the Act, Congress expressly limited the category of children covered to offspring of a marital union. See § 402(d)(3)(A) (referring to the "legitimate ... child" of an individual). Other contemporaneous statutes similarly differentiate child of a marriage ("legitimate child") from the unmodified term "child." See, e.g., Servicemen's Dependents Allowance Act of 1942, ch. 443, § 120, 56 Stat. 385 (defining "child" to include "legitimate child," "child legally adopted," and, under certain conditions, "stepchild" and "illegitimate child" (internal quotation marks omitted)).

Nor does § 416(e) indicate that Congress intended "biological" parentage to be prerequisite to "child" status under that provision. As the SSA points out, "[i]n 1939, there was no such thing as a scientifically proven biological relationship between a child and a father, which is ... part of the reason that the word 'biological' appears nowhere in the Act." Reply Brief 6. Notably, a biological parent is not necessarily a child's parent under law. Ordinarily, "a parent-child relationship does not exist between an adoptee and the adoptee's genetic parents." Uniform Probate Code § 2–119(a), 8 U.L.A. 55 (Supp.2011) (amended 2008). Moreover, laws directly addressing use of today's assisted reproduction technology do not make biological parentage a universally determinative criterion. See, e.g., Cal. Fam.Code Ann. § 7613(b) (West Supp.2012) ("The donor of semen ... for use in artificial insemination or in vitro fertilization of a woman other than the donor's wife is treated in law as if he were not the natural father of a child thereby conceived, unless otherwise agreed to in a writing signed by the donor and the woman prior to the conception of the child."); Mass. Gen. Laws, ch. 46, § 4B (West 2010) ("Any child born to a married woman as a result of artificial insemination with the consent of her husband, shall be considered the legitimate child of the mother and such husband.").

We note, in addition, that marriage does not ever and always make the parentage of a child certain, nor does the absence of marriage necessarily mean that a child's parentage is uncertain. An unmarried couple can agree that a child is theirs, while the parentage of a child born during a marriage may be uncertain. See Reply Brief 11 ("Respondent errs in treating 'marital' and 'undisputed' as having the same meaning.").

Finally, it is far from obvious that Karen Capato's proposed definition—"biological child of married parents," see Brief for Respondent 9—would cover the posthumously conceived Capato twins. Under Florida law, a marriage ends upon the death of a spouse. See Price v. Price, 114 Fla. 233, 235, 153 So. 904, 905 (1934). If that law applies, rather than a court-declared preemptive federal law, the Capato twins, conceived after the death of their father, would not qualify as "marital" children.

B

Resisting the importation of words not found in § 416(e)—"child" means "the biological child of married parents," Brief for Respondent 9—the SSA finds a key textual cue in § 416(h)(2)(A)'s opening instruction: "In determining whether an applicant is the child ... of [an] insured individual for purposes of this subchapter," the Commissioner shall apply state intestacy law. (Emphasis added.) Respondent notes the absence of any cross-reference in § 416(e) to § 416(h). Brief for Respondent 18. She overlooks, however, that § 416(h) provides the crucial link. The "subchapter" to which § 416(h) refers is Subchapter II of the Act, which spans §§ 401 through 434. Section 416(h)'s reference to "this subchapter" thus includes both §§ 402(d) and 416(e). Having explicitly complemented § 416(e) by the definitional provisions contained in § 416(h), Congress had no need to place a redundant cross-reference in § 416(e). See Schafer, 641 F.3d, at 54 (Congress, in § 416(h)(2)(A), provided "plain and explicit instruction on how the determination of child status should be made"; on this point, the statute's text "could hardly be more clear.").

The original version of today's § 416(h) was similarly drafted. It provided that, "[i]n determining whether an applicant is the ... child ... of [an] insured individual for purposes of sections 401–409 of this title, the Board shall apply [state intestacy law]." 42 U.S.C. § 409(m) (1940 ed.) (emphasis added). Sections 401–409 embraced §§ 402(c) and 409(k), the statutory predecessors of 42 U.S.C. §§ 402(d) and 416(e) (2006 ed.), respectively.

Reference to state law to determine an applicant's status as a "child" is anything but anomalous. Quite the opposite. The Act commonly refers to state law on matters of family status. For example, the Act initially defines "wife" as "the wife of an [insured] individual," if certain conditions are satisfied. § 416(b). Like § 416(e), § 416(b) is, at least in part, tautological (" 'wife' means the [insured's] wife"). One must read on, although there is no express cross-reference, to § 416(h) (rules on "[d]etermination of family status") to complete the definition. Section § 416(h)(1)(A) directs that, "for purposes of this subchapter," the law of the insured's domicile determines whether "[the] applicant and [the] insured individual were validly married," and if they were not, whether the applicant would nevertheless have "the same status" as a wife under the State's intestacy law. (Emphasis added.) The Act similarly defines the terms "widow," "husband," and "widower." See § 416(c), (f), (g), (h)(1)(A).

Indeed, as originally enacted, a single provision mandated the use of state intestacy law for "determining whether an applicant is the wife, widow, child, or parent of [an] insured individual." 42 U.S.C. § 409(m) (1940 ed.). All wife, widow, child, and parent applicants thus had to satisfy the same criterion. To be sure, children born during their parents' marriage would have readily qualified under the 1939 formulation because of their eligibility to inherit under state law. But requiring all "child" applicants to qualify under state intestacy law installed a simple test, one that ensured benefits for persons plainly within the legislators' contemplation, while avoiding congressional entanglement in the traditional state-law realm of family relations.

Just as the Act generally refers to state law to determine whether an applicant qualifies as a wife, widow, husband, widower, 42 U.S.C. § 416(h)(1) (2006 ed.), child or parent, § 416(h)(2)(A), so in several sections (§ 416(b), (c), (e)(2), (f), (g)), the Act sets duration-of-relationship limitations. * * * Time limits also qualify the statutes of several States that accord inheritance rights to posthumously conceived children. See Cal. Prob.Code Ann. § 249.5(c) (West Supp.2012) (allowing inheritance if child is in utero within two years of parent's death); Colo.Rev.Stat. Ann. § 15–11–120(11) (2011) (child in utero within three years or born within 45 months); Iowa Code Ann. § 633.220A(1) (West Supp.2012) (child born within two years); La.Rev.Stat. Ann. § 9:391.1(A) (West 2008) (child born within three years); N.D. Cent.Code Ann. § 30.1–04–19(11) (Lexis 2001) (child in utero within three years or born within 45 months). See also Uniform Probate Code § 2–120(k), 8 U.L.A. 58 (Supp.2011) (treating a posthumously conceived child as "in gestation at the individual's death," but only if specified time limits are met). No time constraints attend the Third Circuit's ruling in this case, under which the biological child of married parents is eligible for survivors benefits, no matter the length of time between the father's death and the child's conception and birth. See Tr. of Oral Arg. 36–37 (counsel for Karen Capato acknowledged that, under the preemptive federal rule he advocated, and the Third Circuit adopted, a child born four years after her father's death would be eligible for benefits).

The paths to receipt of benefits laid out in the Act and regulations, we must not forget, proceed from Congress' perception of the core purpose of the legislation. The aim was not to create a program "generally benefiting needy persons"; it was, more particularly, to "provide ... dependent members of [a wage earner's] family with protection against the hardship occasioned by [the] loss of [the insured's] earnings." Califano v. Jobst, 434 U.S. 47, 52, 98 S.Ct. 95, 54 L.Ed.2d 228 (1977). We have recognized that "where state intestacy law provides that a child may take personal property from a father's estate, it may reasonably be thought that the child will more likely be dependent during the parent's life and at his death." Mathews v. Lucas, 427 U.S. 495, 514, 96 S.Ct. 2755, 49 L.Ed.2d 651 (1976). Reliance on state intestacy law to determine who is a "child" thus serves the Act's driving objective. True, the intestacy criterion yields benefits to some children outside the Act's central concern. Intestacy laws in a number of States, as just noted, do provide for inheritance by posthumously conceived children, * * * and under federal law, a child conceived shortly before her father's death may be eligible for benefits even though she never actually received her father's support. It was nonetheless Congress' prerogative to legislate for the generality of cases. It did so here by employing eligibility to inherit under state intestacy law as a workable substitute for burdensome case-by-case determinations whether the child was, in fact, dependent on her father's earnings.

Respondent argues that on the SSA's reading, natural children alone must pass through a § 416(h) gateway. Adopted children, stepchildren, grandchildren, and step-grandchildren, it is true, are defined in § 416(e), and are not further defined in § 416(h). Respondent overlooks, however, that although not touched by § 416(h), beneficiaries described in § 416(e)(2) and (e)(3) must meet other statutorily prescribed criteria. In short, the Act and regulations set different eligibility requirements for adopted children, stepchildren, grandchildren, and stepgrandchildren, see 20 CFR §§ 404.356–404.358, but it hardly follows that applicants in those categories are treated more advantageously than are children who must meet a § 416(h) criterion.

The SSA's construction of the Act, respondent charges, raises serious constitutional concerns under the equal protection component of the Due Process Clause. Brief for Respondent 42; see Weinberger v. Wiesenfeld, 420 U.S. 636, 638, n. 2, 95 S.Ct. 1225, 43 L.Ed.2d 514 (1975). She alleges: "Under the government's interpretation . . . , posthumously conceived children are treated as an inferior subset of natural children who are ineligible for government benefits simply because of their date of birth and method of conception." Brief for Respondent 42–43.

Even the Courts of Appeals that have accepted the reading of the Act respondent advances have rejected this argument. See 631 F.3d, at 628, n. 1 (citing Vernoff v. Astrue, 568 F.3d 1102, 1112 (C.A.9 2009)). We have applied an intermediate level of scrutiny to laws "burden[ing] illegitimate children for the sake of punishing the illicit relations of their parents, because 'visiting this condemnation on the head of an infant is illogical and unjust.' "Clark v. Jeter, 486 U.S. 456, 461, 108 S.Ct. 1910, 100 L.Ed.2d 465 (1988) (quoting Weber v. Aetna Casualty & Surety Co., 406 U.S. 164, 175, 92 S.Ct. 1400, 31 L.Ed.2d 768 (1972)). No showing has been made that posthumously conceived children share the characteristics that prompted our skepticism of classifications disadvantaging children of unwed parents. We therefore need not decide whether heightened scrutiny would be appropriate were that the case. Under rational-basis review, the regime Congress adopted easily passes inspection. As the Ninth Circuit held, that regime is "reasonably related to the government's twin interests in [reserving] benefits [for] those children who have lost a parent's support, and in using reasonable presumptions to minimize the administrative burden of proving dependency on a case-by-case basis." Vernoff, 568 F.3d, at 1112 (citing Mathews, 427 U.S., at 509, 96 S.Ct. 2755).

IV

As we have explained, § 416(e)(1)'s statement, "[t]he term 'child' means . . . the child . . . of an individual," is a definition of scant utility without aid from neighboring provisions. See Schafer, 641 F.3d, at 54. That aid is supplied by § 416(h)(2)(A), which completes the definition of "child" "for purposes of th[e] subchapter" that includes § 416(e)(1). Under the completed definition, which the SSA employs, § 416(h)(2)(A) refers to state law to determine the status of a posthumously conceived child. The SSA's interpretation of the relevant provisions, adhered to without deviation for many decades, is at least reasonable; the agency's reading is therefore entitled to this Court's deference under Chevron, 467 U.S. 837, 104 S.Ct. 2778, 81 L.Ed.2d 694.

Chevron deference is appropriate "when it appears that Congress delegated authority to the agency generally to make rules carrying the force of law, and that the agency interpretation claiming deference was promulgated in the exercise of that authority." United States v. Mead Corp., 533 U.S. 218, 226–227, 121 S.Ct. 2164, 150 L.Ed.2d 292 (2001). Here, as already noted, the SSA's longstanding interpretation is set forth in regulations published after notice-and-comment rulemaking. See supra, at 6–7. Congress gave the Commissioner authority to promulgate rules "necessary or appropriate to carry out" the Commissioner's functions and the relevant statutory provisions. See 42 U.S.C. §§ 405(a), 902(a)(5). The Commissioner's regulations are neither "arbitrary or capricious in substance, [n]or manifestly contrary to the statute." Mayo Foundation for Medical Ed. and Research v. United States, 562 U.S. ___, ___, 131 S.Ct. 704, 711, 178 L.Ed.2d 588 (2011) (internal quotation marks omitted). They thus warrant the Court's approbation. See Barnhart v. Walton, 535 U.S. 212, 217–222, 225, 122 S.Ct. 1265, 152 L.Ed.2d 330 (2002) (deferring to the Commissioner's "considerable authority" to interpret the Social Security Act).

V

Tragic circumstances—Robert Capato's death before he and his wife could raise a family—gave rise to this case. But the law Congress enacted calls for resolution of Karen Capato's application for child's insurance benefits by reference to state intestacy law. We cannot replace that reference by creating a uniform federal rule the statute's text scarcely supports.

For the reasons stated, the judgment of the Court of Appeals for the Third Circuit is reversed, and the case is remanded for further proceedings consistent with this opinion.

It is so ordered.

LOCATE

What provisions are made under your state's law for children conceived as a result of alternative reproduction techniques?

NOTES AND QUESTIONS

1. Sam's sperm fertilizes Eve's egg in a test tube and the resulting embryo is implanted in Irene's womb with the consent of Irene's husband, Hal. A healthy child, Pat, is born. A provision of Sam's will reads, "I leave all my property to my children." Will Pat share under this provision?

2. (Same facts as question 1.) A provision of Eve's will reads, "I leave all my property to my children." Will Pat share under this provision?

3. (Same facts as question 1.) A provision of Irene's will reads, "I leave all my property to my children." Will Pat share under this provision?

4. (Same facts as question 1.) A provision of Hal's will reads, "I leave all my property to my children." Will Pat share under this provision?

5. (Same facts as question 1.) What precautions would you take in planning Sam's estate? Eve's estate? Irene's estate? Hal's estate?

6. Sperm, eggs, and embryos may be frozen by a process called *cryopreservation* and used years or even decades later as the genetic source material for a new life. How do you account for the possibility that your client could have a child many years after the client's death? See James E. Bailey, *An Analytical Framework for Resolving the Issues Raised by the Interaction Between Reproductive Technology and the Law of Inheritance*, 47 DEPAUL L. REV. 743 (1998); Emily McAllister, *Defining the Parent–Child Relationship in an Age of Reproductive Technology: Implications for Inheritance,* 29 REAL PROP., PROB. & TR. J. 55 (1994); Robert J. Kerekes, *My Child ... But Not My Heir: Technology, the Law, and Post–Mortem Conception*, 31 REAL PROP., PROB. & TR. J. 213 (1996).

7. Thirty hours after Bruce died, Gaby had sperm removed from Bruce's dead body. The sperm was then frozen. Fifteen months later, the sperm was used to make Gaby pregnant and a healthy baby was born. See *Sperm Taken From Corpse Used to Conceive Child*, SAN JOSE MERCURY NEWS, Mar. 27, 1999, at 3B. If Bruce had left a will leaving half of his estate to his children, will the new addition to the family share in this gift?

8. A task force consisting of New York attorneys, physicians, and ethicists recommended that the birth mother always be considered the legal mother even if the child is not biologically related to this woman. In addition, they recommended that sperm should not be harvested from a deceased or comatose man unless the man gave advance consent or a court has issued the appropriate order. See Julie Brienza, *Assisted Reproductive Technology Studied by New York Task Force*, TRIAL, July 1998, at 109. Do you agree with these recommendations?

9. May sperm, eggs, or embryos be the subject matter of a testamentary gift? See Hecht v. Superior Court, 16 Cal.App.4th 836, 20 Cal.Rptr.2d 275 (1993); John Dwight Ingram, *In Vitro Fertilization: Problems and Solutions,* 98 DICK. L. REV. 67 (1993). May a gift of other property be made contingent on the donee using the donated genetic material to create life?

10. If you feel like making your brain ache, think about how the possibility of having children after death impacts traditional Rule Against Perpetuities analysis. See Les A. McCrimmon, *Gametes, Embryos and the Life in Being: The Impact of Reproductive Technology on the Rule Against Perpetuities*, 34 REAL PROP., PROB. & TR. J. 697 (2000).

11. North Dakota has adopted the 1988 Uniform Status of Children of Assisted Conception Act. Alabama, Delaware, New Mexico, North Dakota, Oklahoma, Texas, Utah, Washington, and Wyoming have adopted the 2000 or 2002 version of the Uniform Parentage Act and the Act is being considered by the legislatures in several other states.

12. For additional information, see Michael K. Elliott, *Tales of Parenthood From the Crypt: The Predicament of the Posthumously Conceived Child*, 39 REAL PROP., PROB. & TR. J. 47 (2004); Laura D. Heard, Comment, *A Time to be Born, A Time to Die: Alternative Reproduction and Texas Probate Law*, 17 ST. MARY'S L.J. 927 (1986); John A. Robertson, *In the Beginning: The Legal Status of Early Embryos*, 76 VA. L. REV. 437 (1990); Stephanie F. Schultz, *Surrogacy Arrangements: Who Are the "Parents" of a Child Born Through Artificial Reproductive Techniques?*, 22 OHIO N.U. L. REV. 273 (1995).

C. CLIENT WITH PHYSICALLY OR MENTALLY CHALLENGED BENEFICIARY

A disabled person is entitled to substantial government benefits. For example, the federal government provides regular cash payments through the Supplemental Security Income (SSI) program for food, clothing, and shelter. Medicaid covers the person's health care expenses. (See Chapter 6(E).) The person may also qualify for food stamps and subsidized housing. State or local governments may provide even more assistance. However, government benefits are reduced or eliminated if the disabled individual has other resources. "[A] secure financial future means getting the most from available state and federal entitlement programs and using personal and family resources to provide cushion essential for a comfortable life. For the [estate planner], the challenge will be to assess the [beneficiary's] long-term needs and to structure [the estate plan] so that government entitlements are not compromised and the family's private resources are used to maximize financial security and enhance quality of life." Charles R. Robert, *Estate Planning for Families With Handicapped Children*, COMPLEAT LAW., Fall 1986, at 51, 53.

LAWRENCE A. FRIEDMAN, SPECIAL NEEDS ESTATE PLANNING*

New Jersey Lawyer, August 2010, at 38.

Estate plans for clients with disabled loved ones should address the usual factors that arise when drawing any competent estate plan. These include naming initial and contingent beneficiaries, minimizing taxes, apportioning taxes among beneficiaries, designating fiduciaries, according fiduciary powers, and designing trusts. However, a panoply of other considerations also arise when an estate beneficiary may have serious disabilities.

Special Estate Planning Considerations

While some people with serious disabilities have very successful careers (e.g. Franklin Roosevelt, Stephen Hawking, and Richard Pryor),

* This article was originally published in the August 2010 issue of New Jersey Lawyer Magazine, a publication of the New Jersey State Bar Association, and is reprinted here with permission and with the permission of Lawrence A. Friedman, Esq., Friedman Law, Bridgewater, New Jersey, www.specialneedsnj.com.

this article focuses on estate planning to benefit individuals who cannot support themselves due to serious disabilities. They come in all shapes, sizes, and stations in life. While some have debilitating conditions that lead to government placements in group homes or other facilities, others live in the community in similar manner to those without disabilities. Thus, an individual with severe mental retardation or autism may not be likely to travel or live alone. However, parents of a person with schizophrenia, bipolar disorder, paraplegia or mild retardation may expect to fund a home, vehicle, entertainment, and other typical quality of life items, as well as disability-specific needs like accessibility modifications and aides.

Paradoxically, the higher a person with disabilities functions, the more he or she is likely to need financial help from a parent's estate. This is because government aid typically covers only basic necessities. Thus, it is common for parents to fund a home for a son or daughter who is highly intelligent but cannot work because of schizophrenia or bipolar disorder. However, unless an estate plan is sensitive to this need, the disabled child likely will be forced from the home when the parents die. Even lower-functioning individuals who reside in government-funded group homes, supervised apartments, and other placements once they cease to reside with their parents, still may benefit from privately funded luxuries, case management, and advocacy.

In developing estate plans for clients with disabled loved ones, a lawyer must consider both the intended beneficiary's likely needs and whether or not public programs will meet them. By preserving eligibility for government aid, an estate plan can address the supplemental needs government agencies do not fund. In contrast, a poorly designed estate plan can disqualify a disabled beneficiary for government benefits that fund essential support and activities. Because some providers do not accept private payment, this may lead to a client's child with disabilities losing residential and vocational placements. A well-drawn estate plan, however, will make amounts available for needs and wants government aid does not cover while qualifying a disabled beneficiary for public programs.

Ask the Client

Do not rely on clients to volunteer whether a loved one has serious disabilities. Ask about the client's family, but recognize that some clients may be in denial or ashamed of a relative's impairments. For instance, 'Junior' Soprano described one of Tony Soprano's uncles as "slow," when he obviously had developmental disabilities, probably mental retardation. Similarly, clients may consider mental illness or addiction as a character failing rather than a disease, or characterize a client as 'lazy' when he or she actually is mentally disabled. Unfortunately, it is also common for people with some disabilities to forego government aid because they refuse to admit to mental impairments. Consequently, estate planners sometimes must read between the lines. Where it isn't clear whether or not an individual with disabilities (especially a young child) may be able to work, it is prudent to plan for the worst and hope for the best.

It also is important to ascertain the kind of disability involved, and refer the client to appropriate sources for aid. For instance, specialized programs may be available for people with developmental disabilities, traumatic brain injury, or other less common conditions. Because these benefits may be targeted toward comparatively limited groups, clients may not even realize help is available. Thus, clients may be surprised to learn that an honor high school student who suffers a debilitating head trauma may qualify for aid from the Division of Developmental Disabilities despite being born without disabilities. Similarly, many parents do not realize that their children with delays may be eligible for early intervention and supplemental education benefits.

Needs may differ substantially depending on the kind and extent of impairment. Different government benefits may be available depending on whether or not a person has been disabled since childhood or worked for a time before becoming disabled. Estate planners also should determine what (if any) government benefits a disabled beneficiary receives, and consider if he or she may qualify for other aid as well. For instance, a child who currently does not receive benefits may qualify at age 18, and benefits may increase or change when a parent dies or retires.

Government Benefits

Government benefits provide cash payments, healthcare, subsidized housing, group homes, other disabilities-oriented housing, psychiatric hospitalization, special education, vocational services, personal needs, long-term care, counseling, and other aid for people with serious disabilities. Most programs either are limited to disabled people with only nominal savings and incomes, or require participants with means to pay for goods and services that otherwise would be provided at little or no cost. Nearly all amounts (including gifts, inheritances, insurance, IRAs, and retirement benefits) count against financial caps.

People who cannot work, rarely exceed financial eligibility limitations on their own, unless they are married or worked previously. However, all but the smallest gifts, inheritances, and death benefits are likely to exceed government aid financial caps. Consequently, people with serious disabilities should not normally be outright beneficiaries. Clearly, estate planners who are oblivious to government benefit eligibility requirements may easily disqualify a disabled person from crucial government aid. In addition to being wasteful, disqualification can prove catastrophic because some government programs cannot readily be replaced privately. Although Medicare and some other programs do not base eligibility on finances, it is still advisable to plan with qualification limits for the more common finance-based disability benefits in mind, because a person who does not receive such aid now may need it later.

Ignoring disability issues in estate planning may lead to unpleasant consequences for the lawyer as well. Obviously, a malpractice claim may be brought against a lawyer whose estate plan disqualifies a client's child or grandchild for valuable disability aid, and lawyers *40 have been disciplined for egregiously impairing government benefit qualification.1 Therefore, to serve clients and the lawyer's own interest as well, estate planners either should develop expertise in special needs planning or consult a special needs lawyer when an estate-planning client has loved ones with serious disabilities.

Special/Supplemental Needs Trusts

Outright payments generally disqualify a person with serious disabilities for government benefits that base qualification on finances. Even if eligibility can be restored, benefits can be temporarily stopped, some prior benefits may have to be repaid, and other negative consequences may ensue. For instance, outright receipt of an inheritance, insurance death benefit, or IRA may trigger an immediate state claim for over a million dollars to reimburse years of group home residence. In addition, to retain government aid a beneficiary may have to agree to Medicaid repayment down the road. In contrast, a quality special needs plan could avoid any repayment obligation.

Most programs that limit participation by finances count only amounts that an applicant can access for support, which may constitute food, shelter, medical care, or general basic needs, depending on the program. Therefore, to avoid jeopardizing eligibility or giving rise to repayment obligations, never give an individual with serious disabilities outright distributions or support rights from a trust or anyone else. Instead, amounts to benefit an individual with serious disabilities should be paid into trust.

A trust to supplement government disability benefits often is called an SNT, which stands for special needs trust, supplemental needs trust, or supplemental benefits trust, depending on the lawyer's language preference. Regardless of terminology, an SNT is a trust that leaves distributions within trustee discretion, which can be extremely broad or more limited, depending on the client's wishes.

To keep from jeopardizing government aid, an SNT must not mandate distributions or give the beneficiary a right to force the SNT to distribute. For instance, where distributions are tied to an ascertainable standard, such as health and support, a trust has an obligation to pay for those items and the trust can be disqualifying. It is particularly important to preclude courts from construing an SNT as having an implied obligation to fund the beneficiary's support. Of course, special requirements may apply, depending on benefit programs and circumstances.

Nevertheless, SNTs need not be unduly limiting. For example, an SNT can pay for furniture, equipment, transportation, travel, clothes, professionals, accessibility items, entertainment, education, and nearly anything else.

Thoughtfully designed SNTs are drawn with the particular client's needs in mind, and will not be unduly limiting. For instance, parents who own their child's townhouse probably want their SNT to continue to fund housing expenses, even if government aid may be reduced by nominal amounts. Therefore, a cookie-cutter SNT that prohibits payments for shelter or expenditures that could cause a reduction in government aid would frustrate the parents' intent. Instead, the SNT should permit funding the child's shelter but minimize any resulting reduction of benefits.

Because paying basic needs like housing costs or food can jeopardize government aid when not done properly, the trustee must administer the SNT with government benefit rules in mind. Even the best-drafted SNT can disqualify a beneficiary for government programs when administered poorly. Therefore, an SNT trustee should consult counsel before funding basic needs or providing cash or valuables to a beneficiary.

Beneficiary and third-party assets should not be combined in the same SNT, because an SNT that contains a beneficiary's assets may be required to repay Medicaid upon the beneficiary's death, and meet other requirements detrimental to the interest of the beneficiary. Neither would apply where the SNT is funded only by third parties. For this reason, a separate SNT should be drawn to hold a disabled person's personal injury recovery and other receipts.

Conclusion

Special needs planning involves the full panoply of considerations that go into designing any quality estate plan, but it also raises daunting considerations unique to individuals who need financial help because of disabilities. Concerns and solutions vary with the type and extent of disability and family circumstances, but SNTs are an integral part of most plans. However, to serve clients well SNTs must be tailored to individual circumstances and goals. Although special needs estate planning can involve broad challenges, it can prove particularly rewarding to reassure a worried client that options are available to provide for a vulnerable loved one after the client passes on.

NOTE

For further information, see Scott Gardner, Comment, *Supplemental Needs Trusts: A Means to Conserve Family Assets and Provide Increased Quality of Life for the Disabled Family Member,* 32 DUQ. L. REV. 555 (1994); L. MARK RUSSELL, ET AL., PLANNING FOR THE FUTURE: PROVIDING A MEANINGFUL LIFE FOR A CHILD WITH A DISABILITY AFTER YOUR DEATH (1993); JOHN J. REGAN, ENTITLEMENTS (rev. ed. 1994); A. Frank Johns, *Preserving Assets With Supplemental Needs Trusts*, TRIAL, Nov. 1998, at 90.

D. CLIENT WHO SEEKS CREDITOR PROTECTION

ALEXANDER A. BOVE, JR., THE MECHANICS OF ESTABLISHING AN OFFSHORE TRUST*

American Bar Association, Section of Real Property Probate and Trust Law Asset Protection Planning Committee, Spring Symposium April 2005 (revised March 2012).

There seems to be no shortage of articles and even treatises on offshore asset protection trusts. Just about every facet of the subject seems to have been exhaustively covered, except, perhaps, how to actually set one up. Once an advisor has determined that offshore is the place to go for his client, what comes next? This article offers a practical overview of the steps to be taken from beginning to end in establishing an offshore trust. Of course, it is not possible to anticipate every set of circumstances or every glitch that could arise, but there should be enough here for the "novice" to successfully complete his first offshore venture.

The Decision To Go Offshore

Unfortunately, many advisors and perhaps even a greater number of clients believe that the menu of asset protection planning consists of one item: offshore trusts. This is simply not so, and any advisor who thinks that is way off the mark. There are many other options and combinations of options that may all be carried out domestically. Therefore, the first order of business for the advisor is to ascertain the level of the client's need for asset protection and, based on this, and in light of the extent and nature of the client's assets and personal and business circumstances, determine just what type of asset protection plan is indicated.

Everyone wants a plan to protect what she has accumulated, but certainly not everyone needs to go offshore to do it. Sometimes, protection is merely a case of securing or increasing a client's liability insurance coverage, or operating a business in a different form, such as a limited liability company or a corporation. And even for non-business assets, it may be possible to obtain protection of assets by establishing a trust in any one of the twelve states that have adopted legislation permitting self-settled discretionary domestic trusts, such as Alaska, Delaware, Nevada, or South Dakota, or through limited discretion self-settled trusts in any of the other forty-six states.

Only after all domestic plans have been considered and it is decided that they do not provide the degree of protection desired nor suitable for the particular client should the decision be made to go offshore. And when is that? In most cases, when:

(a) there are substantial liquid assets to be protected (upwards of $1 million);

---

* Reprinted with permission of Alexander A. Bove, Jr.

(b) there is a strong indication that because of the type of exposure this client has to potential claims, and because the history or trend of that type of claim suggests that judgments or settlements would be considerable (e.g., medical malpractice), a creditor would be inclined to diligently attack any assets held in the U.S.;

(c) the client has been thoroughly advised of the extensive reporting requirements associated with offshore trusts and the penalties for failure to comply with such requirements, and

(d) the advisor has concluded, after adequate due diligence, that an offshore trust is the appropriate and best plan for the client.

Due Diligence

There is growing concern over the ethical exposure and personal liability of an advisor who actively assists a client in making a fraudulent conveyance. While the certainty and extent of any such liability is not at all clear, it is generally accepted that an advisor should not knowingly advise or assist a client in making such a conveyance. But how would the advisor know whether the client advised him fully of the client's circumstances, particularly with respect to pending, threatened, or expected claims? The answer is, it is very difficult and sometimes impossible, especially if the client conceals information. Therefore, the advisor should undertake reasonable efforts to determine as much as he can about the client's situation, which should include the requirement that the client produce a current personal financial statement prepared by the client's accountant, an affidavit (from the client) relating to the statement and to all other representations he has made to the advisor, and possibly an electronic search for cases referencing the client as a named defendant.

Even after it is determined that the client has no threatened, pending, or expected claims against her, most advisors recommend that the client transfer no more than one-third to one-half of her total liquid assets to the offshore trust. This is to avoid a subsequent creditor's claim that the client did not retain enough funds to pay her anticipated liabilities as they came due, and therefore she made the transfer with the intention of prejudicing such creditors. If there is a claim that has already been made against the client, this does not mean she cannot protect her assets for other purposes. If the amount of the claim is known, the client can retain an amount adequate to cover the claim and transfer to the trust an amount in excess of the claim. Some attorneys who utilize offshore trusts, instead recommend transferring all of the assets that are earmarked for the offshore trust (not all of the client's assets) into the offshore trust but acknowledging the existing claim and providing in the trust that in the event a judgment is ultimately rendered against the client on this claim, the trustee may pay the judgment from trust funds. This author does not use or favor such an arrangement.

Your Place or Mine? Selecting a Jurisdiction

One of the most puzzling and, in some cases, daunting questions facing the uninitiated asset protection advisor is, where to establish the trust? We read and hear about so many jurisdictions, from the exotic, such as Vanuatu, to the legendary, such as (quite undeservedly) the Cayman Islands, and a large number of in-betweens. Selecting a jurisdiction could be a time-consuming task if every time an advisor prepared an offshore trust he was required to research the respective law and compare the key issues of all prospective jurisdictions. In fact, it would really be out of the question. Fortunately, we have the advantage of the research, mistakes made, and experience of the many advisors who have gone before us leaving a valuable, narrowed-down list of the more accepted and widely-used jurisdictions, chosen largely because of their favorable laws and attitude towards asset protection trusts, as well as their stability.

Although most advisors use common law jurisdictions because of the recognition of trust law and similarity of the legal system, some favor a civil law jurisdiction, such as Liechtenstein. Liechtenstein has adopted trust law by statute (1926) and is internationally respected for the protection given its family foundation (Stiftung). It often follows that creditors who find they must initiate their action in that jurisdiction and conduct all proceedings in German and must also post a cash bond of ten percent of the amount of the lawsuit, are often discouraged from pursuing the claim.

The select jurisdiction list is generally arrived at by considering and comparing the important criteria of each jurisdiction as applied to the operation and survival of the asset protection trust. For instance, after considering the easy items, like location, language, communications, government stability, common vs. civil law, and time difference, one must consider the more serious questions, such as whether foreign judgments are recognized and the period of limitations for fraudulent conveyances. In the more favorable (and therefore most popular) jurisdictions, such as the Cook Islands, the Bahamas, and Gibraltar, the courts will not recognize a U.S. judgment, and the period of limitations for fraudulent conveyance purposes is two years, or less. For instance, under Gibraltar law, if the transfer to the trust did not render the settlor insolvent (the burden of proof being on the attacker in an action brought in that jurisdiction), then there is no waiting period–the protection of those trust assets is immediate. And in the Cook Islands, a creditor attacking the trust must prove beyond a reasonable doubt that the settlor intended to defraud that particular creditor in order to reach trust assets.

It should be noted that even in those jurisdictions which are not necessarily at the top of the veteran asset protection advisor's list, e.g., Isle of Man, Jersey, or Bermuda, there is a certain amount of inherent asset protection value due to the fact that the assets are not in the U.S., and a creditor is forced to undertake legal proceedings in the jurisdiction governing the administration of the trust. This can be expensive and time-consuming, and often unproductive, especially if the situs of the trust is changed before the creditor can engage local counsel and be heard by the local court.

In sum, unless you have selected a particular jurisdiction through your own research, it is probably best to consider as possible candidates those jurisdictions which are generally accepted as the two or three "first choices" by the experienced asset protection bar. Which of those few you select may depend on the client's particular circumstances, confidence in a particular trustee desire to travel to that location, or general comfort level.

The Trustee

Once we know where the trust is to be sitused, it should be an easy matter locating a trustee to act for the trust. It should be, but it isn't. If you choose the Cook Islands, for example, how do you know where to begin? Make a few calls? If you do you'll have to do it between the hours of ? and ?, because they are ? hours behind us. And if you choose the Bahamas because they are so much closer and the time zone is more convenient, it is important you may want to interview a few trustees before you choose. For one thing, you'll find the fee schedules for trustees there can be quite different from one to another. Furthermore, you will find that some trustees have a policy of refusing to sign or file any documents with the U.S. government (i.e., The IRS). This poses a serious problem because of the U.S. requirement that the trustee of a foreign trust provide information for and sign form 3520 A (Annual Return of Foreign Trust with U.S. Beneficiaries) each year. Failure of the trustee to comply will cause a penalty to be imposed on the settlor of the trust, forcing the settlor herself to file the form.

In general, corporate trustees in any of the common offshore jurisdictions charge origination and set-up fees ranging from $3,500 to $10,000, and annual fees around the same, but this usually does not include the fees for managing the trust funds or the fees for the "protector" (discussed in the following section). Management fees are usually additional and depend on the amount being managed. It is not unusual to have a money manager and a trustee, unlike the typical U.S. case, and in fact, it is fairly common to have a trustee in one jurisdiction and the funds managed by a money manager in another jurisdiction.

You should also be sure that arrangements are clear as to when and to whom investment reports and trustee's accounts are to be sent out. The client should receive quarterly reports of the investment and trustee activities without fail. It can be very upsetting, to say the least, to a client when she fails to get information on the status of her funds situated four thousand or more miles away (including confirmation that they are still there!). When this does not happen, it is easy to conjure up an image of the offshore banker dressed in shorts and docksiders sailing off in a schooner with the client's money neatly stacked beside him.

One way to find candidates for trustee is to ask other advisors who have used trustees in the particular jurisdiction; this is usually the best referral source, since they would hardly recommend any with whom they had a bad experience. Another way is to use a professional publication that advertises and/or lists trustees and fiduciaries in the several offshore jurisdictions. Such publications include "The OFC Report" and "The IFC Review." In addition to articles of interest on the various "offshore financial centers", they contain a list of professionals, including trustees, in all of the listed jurisdictions with full contact information. If you locate a trustee in this way you should ask that they give you professional references (e.g., U.S. attorneys) that you may call.

The Protector

Most offshore trusts provide for the appointment of a protector. This is an individual (or a company) that acts "outside" the trust but who can have authority ranging from veto powers over proposed trust distributions, to removal and replacement of trustees, to additions or deletions of beneficiaries, and more. A newcomer to the field would be wise to not to get carried away with giving extensive powers to the protector, since, in some cases, depending on the selection of protector, there can be unanticipated tax ramifications.

A good understanding of the protector's role and a careful selection of the protector can be critical to the successful operation of the trust. In many cases, the client herself may want to be the protector since acting in that position gives her extensive control over the trust. It also gives a U.S. court the opportunity to order the client/protector to remove the offshore trustee and appoint a U.S. trustee which would bring the trust under the jurisdiction of a U.S. court. Failure to comply with such an order could subject the client to a contempt of court charge and possibly jail until the order is carried out. Many offshore planners, including this author, believe it is a good general rule to avoid naming any U.S. protector. It is not unusual to name an attorney or accountant in the foreign jurisdiction. Although the fees, of course, will vary with the extent of the services required, a typical fee is $1,500 annually.

The Documents

So, we have a client, we have a need for an offshore protective trust, we have a jurisdiction, and a trustee. Now all we need is a trust. Drafting an asset protection trust is not something you can do without some tutoring or, more typically, a model to work from. Although most common law trusts have numerous "standard" provisions, the offshore asset protection trust has many provisions that are quite uncommon to the typical trust and therefore would likely be omitted by the inexperienced draftsman of offshore trusts.

For instance, offshore trusts typically contain a "flee clause", allowing the trustee, in the event of an anticipated attack on the trust, to change the trust situs and its governing law before the attack occurs. Also, such trusts usually have an "anti-duress" provision, which permits the trustee to totally ignore an otherwise legal request for a distribution if the trustee believes that the request was made under some form of duress (such as a court order to repatriate the funds). And since appointment of a protector is typically provided for in the trust, the trust will have extensive provisions covering the protector's powers and the trustee's responsibilities in dealing with the protector. Also important are the provisions relating to removal of the protector (if desired) and appointment of a successor protector.

Remember, the offshore asset protection trust is an irrevocable, self-settled spendthrift trust. The client should retain no powers that a court might order her to carry out and which could in any way favor a U.S. creditor of the client, such as a power to remove and replace a trustee or a protector. Nevertheless, flexibility can be built in through a combination of powers residing in the trustee and the protector, and not the client. Many of the offshore trustees will provide a form of the trust document that is acceptable to them, and although this may be a good place to start it is certainly not a good place to finish. Furthermore, be aware that, unlike U.S. trust companies, many offshore trust companies actually charge a fee, usually in the vicinity of $1,500, to provide a sample trust. There are also form books you may use, which are very helpful.

Typically, the offshore trust will hold a substantial part of the U.S. settlor's assets, and even though offshore protective trusts are generally tax neutral from an income tax standpoint, they are not from an estate tax standpoint, so it is very important that the trust include the appropriate U.S. estate tax provisions necessary to carry out the client's estate plan. Such provisions are generally not included in the model forms provided by the offshore trusts. In addition, it is critical that the provisions of the offshore plan be coordinated with the provisions of other documents in the client's estate plan. Lastly, in such trusts the settlor should retain a special testamentary power of appointment; otherwise, the transfer to the trust could be a taxable gift.

Note also that the trust is not the only document that will be required by the offshore trustee. Before the trustee will accept the trust, it will also require a personal financial statement for the client, certified to be true and up to date by the client, the client's accountant, attorney, or other professional, a character reference from the attorney or from a bank including a statement as to the source of the client's funds, and an affidavit of solvency and claims status from the client. (See a sample affidavit at the end of this article). If the client advises the trustee of particular claims pending or brought against her, the trustee may want the trust to provide an exception for the claims (allowing them to be paid from the trust) or may require assurances and verification that the client has retained assets outside the trust adequate to cover the particular claims.

Putting the Show on the Road

Now we should be ready to put our money where our trust is. In the usual case, some "seed" money, say $5,000, will be sent (often wired) to the offshore trustee to open the trust account. Shortly thereafter, the balance of funds and/or securities will follow. As noted earlier, discussions with and selection of the trustee would normally include arrangements for management of the funds or the portfolio either by the trustee or by a money manager separate from the trustee. Occasionally, clients wish to continue to manage their own funds, and this can be done through various means, but in serious asset protection plans it should not be done by leaving the funds with a U.S. broker. This is not impossible, as explained below, but it does leave the funds vulnerable to a court order. Nevertheless, it is appropriate to note here that some asset protection plans are designed so that the funds and the portfolio in fact remain in the U.S. to be managed by the client until trouble strikes, at which time they are (hopefully) whisked away to the safe offshore jurisdiction before the creditor can gain access. Here is how that arrangement usually works:

After establishing and nominally funding her offshore asset protection trust, the trustee of that trust would establish a single member LLC in a foreign jurisdiction, such as Nevis Client would transfer the assets to be protected to the Nevis LLC, while the trustee (as the sole member of the LLC) would name Client as the manager, allowing Client to manage the assets locally. When the suit hits the fan, the trustee would immediately remove Client as the manager and, depending on the nature and strength of the suit, would either continue to manage some or all of the assets here, but in serious cases or real threats, would simply move the assets offshore, time permitting, or immediately reduce them all to cash and wire the cash offshore. The latter could be done in a matter of a few days. Removing Client from all of these dealings reduces, if not eliminates, exposure to attacking the transfer as a fraudulent transfer.

Advise Client of Filing Requirements

One of the unique features of our U.S. tax system when compared with the rest of the world is the tracking of income (and almost everything else) through a person's social security or other tax ID number. Banks, brokers, and other financial parties will not deal with any U.S. person without a "tax ID" number. This enables those parties to report to the IRS all income and capital transactions relating to the person with that tax number, and the IRS, in turn, can track the reporting; so if a person fails to report bank interest, for example, he'll certainly hear from the IRS about it.

The rest of the world, however, works a little differently. There is no such thing as a social security number, and in just about all of the jurisdictions where an offshore trust may be established, there is little or no tax. Therefore, to the offshore jurisdiction it is of no consequence that the trust account generates income or gains, and until January 1, 2001, such jurisdictions reported nothing to the IRS. Because of this situation, the IRS believed that huge amounts of offshore income, particularly in trust accounts, went unreported by U.S. persons who were settlors of such trusts, despite the fact that they were fully subject to tax on the income. On the basis of this information, Congress passed laws in 1996 (as part of The Small Business Jobs Protection Act, Pub. L. 104–188) and 1997 (as part of the Taxpayer Relief Act, Pub. L. 105–34) requiring a U.S. person who makes a transfer to a foreign trust and/or who received any distributions from a foreign trust, to report such transactions to the IRS. Failure to report as required subjects the U.S. person to substantial penalties (for instance, thirty-five percent of the amount transferred or distributed).

Accordingly, an advisor would be remiss and perhaps even exposed to liability if he prepared and helped establish an offshore trust for a client but failed to advise the client of her obligations to report to the federal government on account of the trust and the trust accounts, and the need to appoint a U.S. agent for the trust. As a matter of course, then, advisors who establish these trusts should advise the client in writing of the filing requirements and forms to be filed. For more information on reporting requirements, advisors may wish to refer to IRS notice 97–34, and the instructions to IRS Forms 3520, 3520 A, 8832, 8938, and TD F 90–22.1.

Summary

Establishing an offshore trust for a client involves some new areas of law and unique considerations, especially in the provisions that are customarily included in such trusts. Nevertheless, an experienced estate-planning advisor should be able to adapt and competently handle such a project, after some research on the more unique issues, such as jurisdiction, after study of the legal and tax forms involved, and after consultation with other professionals in the field. Further, as in all complex tax matters, it is essential to thoroughly advise the client of his ongoing responsibilities with respect to the project.

Recent developments reflect an increased willingness of courts to enforce spendthrift provisions in domestic asset protection trusts, that is, trusts in which the settlor and beneficiary are the same person and which contain a spendthrift provision prohibiting the settlor/beneficiary's creditors from reaching the property in the trust. At least thirteen states including Alaska, Colorado, Delaware, Missouri, Nevada,, New Hampshire, Oklahoma, Rhode Island, South Dakota, Tennessee, Utah, Virginia, and Wyoming have changed their statutes to authorize self-settled spendthrift trusts, sometime called Domestic Asset Protection Trusts. A primary motivating factor behind this change in the law is to reduce the flow of assets out of these states to offshore trusts in foreign countries such as the Cook Islands, the Caymans, and Barbados. These nations have made a lucrative business out of acting as sanctuaries for settlors who wish to protect their assets with self-settled trusts.

ALASKA STATUTES

§ 34.40.110 Restricting Transfers of Trust Interests

(a) A person who in writing transfers property in trust may provide that the interest of a beneficiary of the trust, including a beneficiary who is the settlor of the trust, may not be either voluntarily or involuntarily transferred before payment or delivery of the interest to the beneficiary by the trustee. Payment or delivery of the interest to the beneficiary does not include a beneficiary's use or occupancy of real property or tangible personal property owned by the trust if the use or occupancy is in accordance with the trustee's discretionary authority under the trust instrument. A provision in a trust instrument that provides the restrictions described in this subsection is considered to be a restriction that is a restriction on the transfer of the transferor's beneficial interest in the trust and that is enforceable under applicable nonbankruptcy law within the meaning of 11 U.S.C. 541(c)(2) (Bankruptcy Code), as that paragraph reads on September 15, 2004, or as it may be amended in the future. In this subsection,

(1) "property" includes real property, personal property, and interests in real or personal property;

(2) "transfer" means any form of transfer, including deed, conveyance, or assignment.

(b) If a trust contains a transfer restriction allowed under (a) of this section, the transfer restriction prevents a creditor existing when the trust is created or a person who subsequently becomes a creditor from satisfying a claim out of the beneficiary's interest in the trust, unless the creditor is a creditor of the settlor and

(1) the creditor establishes by clear and convincing evidence that the settlor's transfer of property in trust was made with the intent to defraud that creditor, and a cause of action or claim for relief with respect to the fraudulent transfer complies with the requirements of (d) of this section; however, a settlor's expressed intention to protect trust assets from a beneficiary's potential future creditors is not evidence of an intent to defraud;

(2) the trust, except for an eligible individual retirement account trust, provides that the settlor may revoke or terminate all or part of the trust without the consent of a person who has a substantial beneficial interest in the trust and the interest would be adversely affected by the exercise of the power held by the settlor to revoke or terminate all or part of the trust; in this paragraph, "revoke or terminate" does not include a power to veto a distribution from the trust, a testamentary nongeneral power of appointment or similar power, or a right to receive a distribution of income or principal under (3)(A), (B), (C), or (D) of this subsection;

(3) the trust, except for an eligible individual retirement account trust, requires that all or a part of the trust's income or principal, or both, must be distributed to the settlor; however, this paragraph does not apply to a settlor's right to receive the following types of distributions, which remain subject to the restriction provided by (a) of this section until the distributions occur:

(A) income or principal from a charitable remainder annuity trust or charitable remainder unitrust; in this subparagraph, "charitable remainder annuity trust" and "charitable remainder unitrust" have the meanings given in 26 U.S.C. 664 (Internal Revenue Code) as that section reads on October 8, 2003, and as it may be amended;

(B) a percentage of the value of the trust each year as determined from time to time under the trust instrument, but not exceeding the amount that may be defined as income under AS 13.38 or under 26 U.S.C. 643(b) (Internal Revenue Code) as that subsection reads on October 8, 2003, and as it may be amended;

(C) the transferor's potential or actual use of real property held under a qualified personal residence trust within the meaning of 26 U.S.C. 2702(c) (Internal Revenue Code) as that subsection reads on September 15, 2004, or as it may be amended in the future; or

(D) income or principal from a grantor retained annuity trust or grantor retained unitrust that is allowed under 26 U.S.C. 2702 (Internal Revenue Code) as that section reads on September 15, 2004, or as it may be amended in the future; or

(4) at the time of the transfer, the settlor is in default by 30 or more days of making a payment due under a child support judgment or order.

(c) The satisfaction of a claim under (b)(1)-(4) of this section is limited to that part of the trust for which a transfer restriction is not allowed under (b)(1)-(4) of this section, and an attachment or other order may not be made against the trustee with respect to a beneficiary's interest in the trust or against property that is subject to a transfer restriction, except to the extent that a transfer restriction is determined not to be allowed under (b)(1)-(4) of this section.

(d) A cause of action or claim for relief with respect to a fraudulent transfer of a settlor's assets under (b)(1) of this section is extinguished unless the action under (b)(1) of this section is brought by a creditor of the settlor who

(1) is a creditor of the settlor before the settlor's assets are transferred to the trust, and the action under (b)(1) of this section is brought within the later of

(A) four years after the transfer is made; or

(B) one year after the transfer is or reasonably could have been discovered by the creditor if the creditor

(i) can demonstrate, by a preponderance of the evidence, that the creditor asserted a specific claim against the settlor before the transfer; or

(ii) files another action, other than an action under (b)(1) of this section, against the settlor that asserts a claim based on an act or omission of the settlor that occurred before the transfer, and the action described in this sub-subparagraph is filed within four years after the transfer; or

(2) becomes a creditor subsequent to the transfer into trust, and the action under (b)(1) of this section is brought within four years after the transfer is made.

(e) If a trust contains a transfer restriction allowed under (a) of this section, the transfer restriction prevents a creditor existing when the trust is created, a person who subsequently becomes a creditor, or another person from asserting any cause of action or claim for relief against a trustee of the trust or against others involved in the preparation or funding of the trust for conspiracy to commit fraudulent conveyance, aiding and abetting a fraudulent conveyance, or participation in the trust transaction. Preparation or funding of the trust includes the preparation and funding of a limited partnership or a limited liability company if interests in the limited partnership or limited liability company are subsequently transferred to the trust. The creditor and other person prevented from asserting a cause of action or claim for relief are limited to recourse against the trust assets and the settlor to the extent allowed under AS 34.40.010.

(f) A transfer restriction allowed under (a) of this section and enforceable under (b) of this section applies to a settlor who is also a beneficiary of the trust even if the settlor serves as a co-trustee or as an advisor to the trustee under AS 13.36.375 if the settlor does not have a trustee power over discretionary distributions.

(g) A transfer restriction allowed under (a) of this section and enforceable under (b) of this section applies to a beneficiary who is not the settlor of the trust, whether or not the beneficiary serves as a sole trustee, a co-trustee, or an advisor to the trustee under AS 13.36.375.

(h) A transfer restriction is allowed under (a) of this section and is enforceable under (b) of this section even if the settlor has the authority under the terms of the trust instrument to

(1) appoint a trustee, a trust protector under AS 13.36.370, or an advisor under AS 13.36.375;

(2) remove a trustee or trust protector and appoint a replacement trustee or trust protector who is not a related or subordinate party; in this paragraph, "related or subordinate party" has the meaning given in 26 U.S.C. 672(c) (Internal Revenue Code); or

(3) remove an advisor and appoint a replacement advisor.

(i) A settlor whose beneficial interest in a trust is subject to a transfer restriction that is allowed under (a) of this section may not benefit from, direct a distribution of, or use trust property except as may be stated in the trust instrument. An agreement or understanding, express or implied, between the settlor and the trustee that attempts to grant or permit the retention of greater rights or authority than is stated in the trust instrument is void.

(j) A settlor who creates a trust that names the settlor as a beneficiary and whose beneficial interest is subject to a transfer restriction allowed under (a) of this section shall sign a sworn affidavit before the settlor transfers assets to the trust. The affidavit must state that

(1) the settlor has full right, title, and authority to transfer the assets to the trust;

(2) the transfer of the assets to the trust will not render the settlor insolvent;

(3) the settlor does not intend to defraud a creditor by transferring the assets to the trust;

(4) the settlor does not have any pending or threatened court actions against the settlor, except for those court actions identified by the settlor on an attachment to the affidavit;

(5) the settlor is not involved in any administrative proceedings, except for those administrative proceedings identified on an attachment to the affidavit;

(6) at the time of the transfer of the assets to the trust, the settlor is not currently in default of a child support obligation by more than 30 days;

(7) the settlor does not contemplate filing for relief under the provisions of 11 U.S.C. (Bankruptcy Code); and

(8) the assets being transferred to the trust were not derived from unlawful activities.

(k) Notwithstanding another provision of the law of this state, an action, including an action to enforce a judgment entered by a court or other body having adjudicative authority, may not be brought at law or in equity for an attachment or other provisional remedy against property of a trust subject to this section or to avoid a transfer of property to a trust that is the subject of this section unless the action is brought under (b)(1) of this section and within the limitations period of (d) of this section. A court of this state has exclusive jurisdiction over an action brought under a cause of action or claim for relief that is based on a transfer of property to a trust that is the subject of this section.

(*l*) If a trust has a transfer restriction allowed under (a) of this section, in the event of the divorce or dissolution of the marriage of a beneficiary of the trust, the beneficiary's interest in the trust is not considered property subject to division under AS 25.24.160 or 25.24.230 or a part of a property division under AS 25.24.160 or 25.24.230. Unless otherwise agreed to in writing by the parties to the marriage, this subsection does not apply to a settlor's interest in a self-settled trust with respect to assets transferred to the trust

(1) after the settlor's marriage; or

(2) within 30 days before the settlor's marriage unless the settlor gives written notice to the other party to the marriage of the transfer.

(m) If a trust contains a transfer restriction allowed under (a) of this section, the transfer restriction prevents a creditor existing when the trust is created or a person who subsequently becomes a creditor from satisfying a claim out of the interest of a beneficiary, including a beneficiary who is the settlor of the trust, even if

(1) the beneficiary has the right to receive through the exercise of a person's discretion, whether or not the exercise of the discretion is governed by a standard, a distribution of income, principal, or both principal and interest, from the trust; in this paragraph, "person" includes a trustee who is the settlor, unless the settlor is the beneficiary; or

(2) the settlor potentially will receive or actually receives income or principal to pay, in whole or in part, income taxes due on the income of the trust, if the potential or actual receipt of income or principal will be or is made under a provision in the trust instrument that expressly provides for the payment of the taxes and if the potential or actual receipt of income or principal would be the result of a trustee's acting in the trustee's discretion or under a mandatory direction in the trust instrument; a distribution to pay income taxes that is made under a discretionary or mandatory provision in a governing instrument under this paragraph may be made by direct payment to a taxing authority.

(n) In this section,

(1) "eligible individual retirement account trust" means an individual retirement account under 26 U.S.C. 408(a) or an individual retirement plan under 26 U.S.C. 408A(b) (Internal Revenue Code), as those sections read on September 13, 2006 or as they may be amended in the future, that is in the form of a trust, if a trust company or bank with its principal place of business in this state is the trustee or custodian;

(2) "settlor" means a person who transfers real property, personal property, or an interest in real or personal property, in trust.

§ 13.36.035 Court Jurisdiction; Choice of Law.

* * *

(c) A provision that the laws of this state govern the validity, construction, and administration of the trust and that the trust is subject to the jurisdiction of this state is valid, effective, and conclusive for the trust if

(1) some or all of the trust assets are deposited in this state and are being administered by a qualified person; in this paragraph, "deposited in this state" includes being held in a checking account, time deposit, certificate of deposit, brokerage account, trust company fiduciary account, or other similar account or deposit that is located in this state;

(2) a trustee is a qualified person who is designated as a trustee under the governing instrument or by a court having jurisdiction over the trust;

(3) the powers of the trustee identified under (2) of this subsection include or are limited to

(A) maintaining records for the trust on an exclusive basis or a nonexclusive basis; and

(B) preparing or arranging for the preparation of, on an exclusive basis or a nonexclusive basis, an income tax return that must be filed by the trust; and

(4) part or all of the administration occurs in this state, including physically maintaining trust records in this state. * * *

UNIFORM PROBATE CODE

Section 6–102. Liability of Nonprobate Transferees for Creditor Claims and Statutory Allowances.

(a) In this section, "nonprobate transfer" means a valid transfer effective at death, other than a transfer of a survivorship interest in a joint tenancy of real estate, by a transferor whose last domicile was in this State to the extent that the transferor immediately before death had power, acting alone, to prevent the transfer by revocation or withdrawal and instead to use the property for the benefit of the transferor or apply it to discharge claims against the transferor's probate estate.

(b) Except as otherwise provided by statute, a transferee of a nonprobate transfer is subject to liability to any probate estate of the decedent for allowed claims against decedent's probate estate and statutory allowances to the decedent's spouse and children to the extent the estate is insufficient to satisfy those claims and allowances. The liability of a nonprobate transferee may not exceed the value of nonprobate transfers received or controlled by that transferee.

(c) Nonprobate transferees are liable for the insufficiency described in subsection (b) in the following order of priority:

(1) a transferee designated in the decedent's will or any other governing instrument, as provided in the instrument;

(2) the trustee of a trust serving as the principal nonprobate instrument in the decedent's estate plan as shown by its designation as devisee of the decedent's residuary estate or by other facts or circumstances, to the extent of the value of the nonprobate transfer received or controlled;

(3) other nonprobate transferees, in proportion to the values received.

(d) Unless otherwise provided by the trust instrument, interests of beneficiaries in all trusts incurring liabilities under this section abate as necessary to satisfy the liability, as if all of the trust instruments were a single will and the interests were devises under it.

(e) A provision made in one instrument may direct the apportionment of the liability among the nonprobate transferees taking under that or any other governing instrument. If a provision in one instrument conflicts with a provision in another, the later one prevails.

(f) Upon due notice to a nonprobate transferee, the liability imposed by this section is enforceable in proceedings in this State, whether or not the transferee is located in this State.

(g) A proceeding under this section may not be commenced unless the personal representative of the decedent's estate has received a written demand for the proceeding from the surviving spouse or a child, to the extent that statutory allowances are affected, or a creditor. If the personal representative declines or fails to commence a proceeding after demand, a person making demand may commence the proceeding in the name of the decedent's estate, at the expense of the person making the demand and not of the estate. A personal representative who declines in good faith to commence a requested proceeding incurs no personal liability for declining.

(h) A proceeding under this section must be commenced within one year after the decedent's death, but a proceeding on behalf of a creditor whose claim was allowed after proceedings challenging disallowance of the claim may be commenced within 60 days after final allowance of the claim.

(i) Unless a written notice asserting that a decedent's probate estate is nonexistent or insufficient to pay allowed claims and statutory allowances has been received from the decedent's personal representative, the following rules apply:

(1) Payment or delivery of assets by a financial institution, registrar, or other obligor, to a nonprobate transferee in accordance with the terms of the governing instrument controlling the transfer releases the obligor from all claims for amounts paid or assets delivered.

(2) A trustee receiving or controlling a nonprobate transfer is released from liability under this section with respect to any assets distributed to the trust's beneficiaries. Each beneficiary to the extent of the distribution received becomes liable for the amount of the trustee's liability attributable to assets received by the beneficiary.

Comment

1. Added to the Code in 1998, this section clarifies that the recipients of nonprobate transfers can be required to contribute to pay allowed claims and statutory allowances to the extent the probate estate is inadequate. The maximum liability for a single nonprobate transferee is the value of the transfer. Values are determined under subsection (b) as of the time when the benefits are "received or controlled by that transferee." This would be the date of the decedent's death for nonprobate transfers made by means of a revocable trust, and date of receipt for other nonprobate transfers. Two or more transferees are severally liable for the portion of the liability based on the value of the transfers received by each.

This section replaces Section 6–107 of the original Code, and its 1989 sequel, 6–215. To the extent a deceased party's probate estate was insufficient, these sections made a deceased party's interest in multiple-name accounts in financial institutions passing outside probate liable for the deceased party's statutory allowances and creditor claims. Assets passing at death by revocable trust or TOD asset registration agreements were not covered by these sections. Also, Section 6–201(b) of the original Code and its 1989 sequel, 6–101(b), provided merely that the section did not limit any other rights that might exist. Neither section created any rights.

If there are no probate assets, a creditor or other person seeking to use this Section 6–102 would first need to secure appointment of a personal representative to invoke Code procedures for establishing a creditor's claim as "allowed." The use of probate proceedings as a prerequisite to gaining rights for creditors against nonprobate transferees has been a feature of UPC Article VI since originally approved in 1969. It works well in practice. The Article III procedures for opening estates, satisfying probate exemptions, and presenting claims are very efficient.

2. Section 6–102 replaces 6–215 with coverage designed to extend the principle of 6–215 to transfers at death by revocable trust, TOD security registration agreements and similar death benefits not insulated from decedents' creditors or statutory allowances by other legislation. The initial clause of subsection (b), "Except as otherwise provided by statute," is designed to prevent a conflict with and to clarify that this section does not supersede existing legislation protecting death benefits in life insurance, retirement plans or IRAs from claims by creditors.

If a state's insurance laws do not exempt or protect a particular insurance death benefit, the insured's creditors would not be able to establish a "nonprobate transfer" under (a) except to the extent of any cash surrender value generated by premiums paid by the insured that the insured could have obtained immediately before death. Note, also, that (i)(1) would protect a life insurance company that paid a death benefit before receiving written notice from the decedent's personal representative.

3. The definition of "nonprobate transfer" in subsection (a) includes revocable transfers by a decedent; it does not include a transfer at death incident to a decedent's exercise or non-exercise of a presently exercisable general power of appointment created by another person. The drafters decided against including such powers even though presently exercisable general powers of appointment are subject to the Code's augmented estate provisions dealing with protection of a surviving spouse from disinheritance. Spousal protection against disinheritance by the other spouse supports the institution of marriage; creditors are better able to fend for themselves than financially disadvantaged surviving spouses. In addition, a presently exercisable general power of appointment created by another person is commonly viewed as a provision in the trust creator's instrument designed to provide flexibility in the estate plan rather than as a gift to the donee.

4. The required ability to revoke or otherwise prevent a nonprobate transfer at death that is vital to application of subsection (a) is described as a "power," a word intended by the drafters to signify legal authority rather

than capacity or practical ability. This corresponds to the definition in Code Section 2–201(6).

5. The exclusion of "a survivorship interest in a joint tenancy of real estate" from the definition of "nonprobate transfer" in subsection (a) is contrary to the law of some states (e.g., South Dakota) that allow an insolvent decedent's creditors to reach the share the decedent could have received prior to death by unilateral severance of the joint tenancy. The law in most other states is to the contrary. By excluding real estate joint tenancies, stability of title and ease of title examination is preserved. Moreover, real estate joint tenancies have served for generations to keep the share of a couple's real estate owned by the first to die out of probate and away from estate creditors. This familiar arrangement need not be disturbed incident to expanding the ability of decedents' creditors to reach newly recognized nonprobate transfers at death.

No view is expressed as to whether a survivorship interest in personal or intangible property registered in two or more names as joint tenants with right of survivorship would come within 6–102(a). The outcome might depend on who originated the registration and whether severance by any co-owner acting alone was possible immediately preceding a co-owner's death.

6. A feature of replaced Section 6–215 that was clarified by a 1991 technical amendment protected a survivor beneficiary of a joint account from liability to the probate estate of a deceased co-depositor for funds in the account owned by the survivor prior to decedent's death. Subsection (a) continues this protection by use of the language "valid transfer effective at death ... by a transferor ... [who] had power, acting alone, to prevent the transfer by revocation or withdrawal and instead use the property for the benefit of the transferor...." Section 6–211 and related sections of the Code make it clear that parties to a joint and survivor account separately own values in the account in proportion to net contributions. Hence, a surviving joint account depositor who had contributed to the balance on deposit prior to the death of the other party is subject to the remedies described in this section only to the extent of new account values gained through survival of the decedent.

7. Transferees of nonprobate transfers subject to the possible liability described in subsection (b) include trustees of revocable trusts to the extent assets transferred to the trust before death were subject to the decedent's sole power to revoke. Such assets would be valued as of the date of death. While the trustee of an irrevocable trust, or of a trust that may be revoked only by the settlor and another person would ordinarily not be subject to this section, this section could apply if the trust is named as a beneficiary of a nonprobate transfer, such as of securities registered in TOD form. Under subsection (b), such a transfer would involve a possibility of trust liability based on the value of the TOD transfer as of the time of its receipt. Liability under this section incurred by a trustee is a trust liability for which the trustee does not incur personal liability except as provided by Section 3–808(b).

8. Trusts and non-trust recipients of nonprobate transfers incur liability in the order prescribed in subsection (c). Note that either a revocable or an irrevocable trust might be designated devisee of a pour-over provision that

would make the trust the "principal non-probate instrument in the decedent's estate plan" and, consequently, make it liable under subsection (c)(2) ahead of other nonprobate transferees to the extent of values acquired by a transfer at death as described in subsection (a). Note, too, that nothing would pass to the receptacle trust by the pour-over devise if all probate estate assets are used to discharge statutory allowances and claims. However, the fact that the trust was designated to receive a pour-over devise signals that the trust probably includes the equivalent of a residuary clause measuring benefits by available assets and signaling probable intention of the settlor that residuary benefits should abate to pay the settlor's debts prior to other trust gifts.

9. The abatement order among classes of beneficiaries of trusts specified by subsection (d) applies to all trusts subject to liability to the extent of nonprobate transfers received or administered whether or not the trust instrument is the principal nonprobate instrument in the decedent's estate plan. The drafters decided against a cross-reference to the Code's abatement provision, Section 3–902, in part because that section deals with intestate and partially intestate estates as well as estates governed by wills. Note, too, that trusts for successive beneficiaries also will be governed by income and principal accounting rules that will serve to resolve some abatement issues.

10. Subsection (e) recognizes that a number of separate instruments and transactions, executed at different times and with or without internal references linking them to other documents, may constitute the paperwork describing succession to a decedent's assets by probate and nonprobate methods. By authorizing control of abatement among gifts made by various transfers at death by the last executed instrument, the subsection permits a simple, last-minute override of earlier directions concerning a decedent's wishes regarding priorities among successors. Thus, a will or trust amendment can correct or avoid liquidity and abatement problems discovered prior to death. The expression "block buster will" was coined by estate planners in the mid 70's to refer to interest in legislation enabling a later will to override death benefits by any nonprobate transfer device. This subsection meets some of the goals of advocates of this legislation.

11. Subsection (f) builds on the principle employed in the Code's augmented estate provisions (UPC §§ 2–201–2–214) in relation to nonprobate transfers made to persons in other states, possibly by transactions governed by laws of other states. The underlying principle is that the law of a decedent's last domicile should be controlling as to rules of public policy that override the decedent's power to devise the estate to anyone the decedent chooses. The principle is implemented by subjecting donee recipients of the decedent to liability under the decedent's domiciliary law, with the belief that judgments recovered in that state following appropriate due process notice to defendants in other states will be accorded full faith and credit by courts in other states should collection proceedings be necessary.

12. The first and third sentences of subsection (g) are identical to sentences from former Section 6–215, which this section replaces. The second sentence is new. It reflects sensitivity for the dilemma confronting a probate fiduciary who, acting as required of a fiduciary, concludes that the costs and risks associated with a possible recovery from a nonprobate transferee out-

weigh the probable advantages to the estate and its claimants. A creditor whose claim has been allowed but remains unsatisfied and whose demand for a proceeding has been turned down by the estate fiduciary may proceed at personal risk in efforts to enforce the estate claim against the nonprobate beneficiary. This is so because the last two sentences of (g) shift the risk of unrecoverable costs from the decedent's estate to the claimant who undertakes collection efforts on behalf of the decedent's estate. Any recovery of costs should be used to reimburse the claimant who bore the risk of loss for the proceeding. A personal representative tempted to decline a demand for a proceeding should note that the "good faith" standard of this subsection must be determined in light of the fiduciary responsibility imposed by Section 3–703.

13. Subparagraph (h) meshes with time limits in the Code's sections governing allowance and disallowance of claims. See Sections 3–804 and 3–806.

14. Subsection (i)(1) is designed to protect issuers of TOD security registrations who make payments or delivery to designated death beneficiaries before receiving notice from the decedent's probate estate of a probable insolvency. These entities are not "transferees" subject to liability under (b), but they might incur legal or other costs if the beneficiaries request payment in spite of warning notices from estate fiduciaries.

Subsection (i)(2) is designed to enable trustees handling nonprobate transfers to distribute trust assets in accordance with trust terms if a warning of probable estate insolvency has not been received. Beneficiaries receiving distributions from a trustee take subject to personal liability in the amount and priority of the trustee based on the value distributed.

NOTES AND QUESTIONS

1. In most states where self-settled spendthrift trusts are not allowed, transfers to the trust under which the settlor is a potential beneficiary are not completed gifts for tax purposes. The reasoning for this outcome is that the settlor's creditors are still able to reach the trust assets. See Treas. Reg. § 25.2511–2(b). Would the transfer be complete in states like Alaska which protect self-settled spendthrift trusts from the settlor's creditors? Would the trust property also be excluded from the settlor's gross estate? See Priv. Ltr. Rul. 98–37–007 and Phyllis C. Smith, *The Estate and Gift Tax Implications of Self-Settled Domestic Asset Protection Trusts: Can You Really Have Your Cake and Eat It Too?*, 44 NEW ENG. L. REV. 25 (Fall 2009) (asserting that it is appropriate to include certain trust property in the settlor's gross estate for estate tax purposes).

2. For additional information on domestic self-settled spendthrift trusts, see David G. Shaftel, *Domestic Asset Protection Trusts: Key Issues and Answers*, 30 ACTEC J. 10 (2004); Charles D. Fox IV & Michael J. Huft, *Asset Protection and Dynasty Trusts*, 37 REAL PROP., PROB. & TR. J. 287 (2002); Christopher M. Reimer, *The Undiscovered Country: Wyoming's Emergence as a Leading Trust Situs Jurisdiction*, 11 WYO. L. REV. 165 (2011).

3. "Experts estimate that Americans now have more than $1 trillion in assets offshore and illegally evade between $40 billion and $70 billion in U.S. taxes each year through the use of offshore tax schemes...." John C. McDougal, *International Estate & Tax Planning 2011: Planning for the International Private Client,* Practicing Law Institute (2011) at 287 (citing *The Enablers, The Tools and Secrecy: Hearing on Tax Haven Abuses Before the Permanent Subcomm. on Investigations*, p. 1 (2006)).

4. One of the "creditors" a client may be trying avoid is a spouse's claim upon divorce. Offshore trusts may be especially effective in this situation because their trustees are usually not bound by judgments of United States courts. Would you be subject to ethics sanctions if you assisted a client to move his or her assets offshore primarily to avoid future claims of a spouse? See Debra Baker, *Island Castaway*, A.B.A. J., Oct. 1998, at 54 (explaining the difficulty in drawing the line between assisting a client and perpetrating a fraud).

5. Denyse and Michael sold products such as the Aquabell (a water-filled dumbbell), Talking Pet Tag, and KenKut (a plastic wrap dispenser) by way of late night television commercials. They created a limited liability company to give investors the opportunity to share in their profits. In actuality, the investment was a Ponzi scheme. Eventually, the Federal Trade Commission enjoined their activities and ordered Denyse and Michael to repatriate any assets held for their benefit outside of the United States, including those held in an irrevocable trust under the law of the Cook Islands. Following the provisions of the trust designed to frustrate attacks by United States courts, the Cook Island trustee refused to repatriate the assets. The district court found that Denyse and Michael were in contempt of court and they were later taken into custody because they had not purged themselves of the contempt. The appellate court affirmed the lower court's injunction, contempt order, and subsequent incarceration in Federal Trade Commission v. Affordable Media, LLC, 179 F.3d 1228 (9th Cir. 1999).

6. For a comprehensive treatment of foreign trust law, see WALTER H. DIAMOND & DOROTHY B. DIAMOND, INTERNATIONAL TRUST LAWS AND ANALYSIS (most recent edition).

7. Special considerations arise when a debtor dies during the pendancy of a bankruptcy action. For a review of the bankruptcy-probate interface, see Gregory M. McCoskey, *Death and Debtors: What Every Probate Lawyer Should Know About Bankruptcy*, 34 REAL PROP., PROB. & TR. J. 669 (2000).

E. CLIENT WHO WANTS TRUST OF PERPETUAL DURATION

Under the law of most states, the Rule Against Perpetuities prohibits trusts in which the ability to ascertain the identity of the beneficiaries in whom equitable title will vest is delayed beyond a specified period of time. At common law, and still in many states today, this time is twenty-one years after the death of some life in being at the time of the creation of the interest, plus a period of gestation. For irrevocable inter vivos trusts, the time period starts to run when the settlor declares the trust or conveys the property to the trust. If the settlor can revoke the inter vivos trust, the period begins to run when the trust is no longer revocable which is usually when the settlor dies. If the trust is testamentary, the clock begins to run when the settlor dies.

The application of the Rule Against Perpetuities is restricted in many cases. Most, if not all, jurisdictions limit the application of the Rule to private trusts; certainty in vesting is not required for trusts in which all beneficial interests are charitable. Some states reject the common law approach of voiding the beneficiary's interest if there is any possibility, no matter how unlikely it may be, that a contingency could occur that would delay vesting beyond the perpetuities period. Instead, they adopted a *wait and see* approach and look at how vesting actually occurs instead of how it could occur. Other jurisdictions lengthen the period or permit the courts to reform the trust using *cy pres*, that is, the court may modify the trust to make it fit within the Rule while still carrying out the settlor's intent as closely as possible. Many states have enacted the Uniform Statutory Rule Against Perpetuities Act (also found in UPC §§ 2–901 to 2–905) which combines many of these reforms such as a 90 year time period from the time of the grant (rather than the death of the lives in being) plus wait-and-see and deferred-reformation components.

About one-half of the states have completely abolished or substantially reformed the Rule with regard to trusts, but not necessarily with regard to other types of transfers. In these states, settlors may create *dynasty* or *perpetual trusts* which last indefinitely and restrict benefits to remote descendants of the settlor. The decision to abolish the Rule in these states was, at least in part, an economic decision to encourage wealthy settlors to bring their property into these states, establish trusts, employ local trustees and attorneys, and pay local taxes. For an extensive discussion of the reasons why the Rule is fading in popularity, see Joel C. Dobris, *The Death of the Rule Against Perpetuities, or the RAP Has No Friends—An Essay*, 35 REAL PROP., PROB. & TR. J. 601 (2000).

NOTES

1. For a discussion of how to create dynasty trusts in states which still retain the Rule Against Perpetuities, see Stephen M. Margolin & Mitchell D. Weinstein, *Dynasty Trusts and the Rule Against Perpetuities*, 87 ILL. B.J. 134 (1999).

2. Clients considering the creation of a dynasty trust in a state which has abolished the Rule Against Perpetuities may want to enhance their benefits by selecting a state which also has no fiduciary income tax. See Thomas H. Foye, *Using South Dakota Law for Perpetual Trusts*, PROB. & PROP., Jan./Feb. 1998, at 17.

F. ILLITERATE CLIENT

A new client comes to your office and hires you to prepare a will to dispose of the person's sizable estate. During your meeting, the client seems to be of average intelligence and appears in all respects to be "normal." However, something unusual happens at one of your conferences. You hand the client a draft of the will and after flipping the pages, the client says, "It looks all right to me; I trust you." You become insistent and explain that you want the client to read the will carefully to make certain it correctly disposes of the estate. At this point your client, obviously quite embarrassed, admits to you that the client cannot read or write except to make a signature.

Although this situation is less likely to occur today in our highly educated society than it was a hundred years ago, it is probably more common than we care to admit. As of February 2011, the ProLiteracy report that over 63 million Americans cannot read well enough to follow a bus schedule or read to their children This means that, on average and assuming your client mix is representative of the general population, at least one out of five of your adult clients will be functionally illiterate.

The courts in the United States have generally not exacted any educational standard on testators. In Oliver v. Williams, 381 S.W.2d 703 (Tex. Civ. App. 1964), the court was confronted with a situation where the testator's testamentary capacity was in dispute because, among other things, he was unable to read or write although he could sign his own name. The court stated that "[t]he test is not whether the person who has made testamentary disposition of his property possesses a high order of intelligence * * *. The lack of education or proof of illiteracy has little, if any, bearing on the mental capacity to make a will." Id. at 709.

Thus, a testator's illiteracy is irrelevant as far as testamentary capacity is concerned, as long as the usual elements can be demonstrated. (Note that in some states, such as Louisiana, the ability to read may affect the capacity to execute some types of wills).

A testator must intend the very instrument executed to be his or her last will and testament. This indicates that a testator must know the contents of the document and intend those contents to be the testator's will. Testamentary intent is lacking if the testator has no knowledge of the actual text of the will. To justify the admission of a will of an illiterate person to probate, many jurisdictions require the proponent of the will to show that the testator had knowledge of the contents of the will. It is usually not necessary to show that the will was read to the testator provided other evidence shows the testator had knowledge of its contents.

For literate testators, the burden of showing that a testator knew the contents of the will is usually made easier by a general presumption that "[i]f a person of sound mind, able to read and write, and no way incapacitated to acquire knowledge of the contents of a paper, by exercising the faculties he has, signs a testamentary paper, and has it witnessed as required by the statute, then, upon proof of these facts, the will ought to be admitted to probate without further proof that the testator knew the contents of the paper, unless suspicion in someway be thrown upon it." Boyd v. Frost Nat'l Bank, 145 Tex. 206, 223, 196 S.W.2d 497, 507 (1946) (quoting Kelly v. Settegast, 68 Tex. 13, 2 S.W. 870 (1887)). The issue then raised is whether this presumption operates in the case of an illiterate testator. Some jurisdictions have applied the rebuttable presumption that the testator had knowledge of the contents of the will if the will was properly executed even in the case of the illiterate testator. Other jurisdictions, however, hold that no such presumption arises and that an affirmative showing is required.

You must determine whether your client is illiterate. But, how do you do so? Many illiterate people have learned to hide their shortcomings. Thus, illiteracy may be difficult to detect if you are not looking for it. If your client is illiterate, you must make sure the client knows the contents of the will and that such can be shown after his or her death. Although some privacy is sacrificed, a possible way of lessening probate problems would be to have the will read aloud during the execution ceremony. The witnesses should follow along as the will is read, hear the testator agree to the contents of the will, and then watch the testator sign the will. It may be good practice to have the witnesses sign a notarized transcript of the ceremony, including a statement of the testator's inability to read and agreement to what was read, or to have the entire will execution ceremony preserved on videotape.

QUESTION

What steps will you take to screen clients for potential functional illiteracy?

G. NON-ENGLISH SPEAKING CLIENT

You will be confronted with another special situation if you are employed by a client who is literate but not in English. Statistics show that about one out of ten people in the United States speak a language other than English as their primary language. There are two basic options available to the estate planner. First, the will could be drafted in the language of the testator's literacy, or second, the will could be written in English.

Courts generally hold that "it is no impediment to the probate of a will that it is written in a foreign language. [The statute] prescribing the requisites for a valid will, contains no provision requiring a will to be written in the English language. Nor is there any other article of the statute that prohibits the probating of a will written in a foreign language." Dieckow v. Schneider, 83 S.W.2d 417, 417 (Tex. Civ. App. 1935).

The main difficulty with foreign language wills is interpreting their contents. Portions of the will may be translated differently by different people. There is always a danger of "losing something in the translation," especially with languages from different language groups and with technical matters such as taxes. Perhaps the testator could obtain and approve an English translation of his or her will to help prevent such problems. Nonetheless, the best advice may be to obtain an English language will but make certain its contents accurately reflect the testator's disposition plans.

The situation where a will is written in a language which the testator cannot read is quite similar to that of the illiterate testator. The first issue is whether this has an adverse impact on testamentary capacity. The general rule is that testamentary capacity is not necessarily affected because the testator did not read or understand the language in which the will was written. The biggest problem, of course, is to show that the testator knew the contents of the document and intended those contents to guide the disposition of property upon death. You should take precautions, such as those discussed for illiterate testators, to help avoid will contest actions. Perhaps a translation of the will in the testator's native language which is approved by the testator would also be beneficial. But, problems could arise if there were inconsistencies between the two versions.

H. VISUALLY IMPAIRED CLIENT

There are over 1 million blind individuals over the age of 40 in the United States. See *Vision Problems in the U.S., Prevalence of Adult Vision Impairment and Age–Related Eye Disease in America,* Prevent Blindness America (2008). In addition, 3.6 million older Americans are visually impaired. See http://www.nei.nih.gov/eyedata/pbd_tables.asp. Accordingly, you should be alert to the issues which arise when a visually impaired individual wants to make a will. "It is well settled at the common law and under modern statutes that testamentary capacity, depending as it does, on soundness of mind and memory, is not affected by the fact that the testator is blind." Annotation, *Will of Blind Person,* 9 A.L.R. 1416, 1416 (1920). As long as a blind person otherwise has testamentary capacity, the fact that a person cannot see will not prevent the person from being able to execute a valid will. See Goldsmith v. Gates, 205 Ala. 632, 88 So. 861 (1921).

As with illiteracy and non-English speaking situations, there are difficulties in demonstrating that the blind testator knew the contents of the document which he or she executed. The blindness of the testator seems to rebut the presumption, otherwise arising from the due execution of a will, that the testator was aware of its contents. Accordingly, the proponent of the will has the burden of demonstrating that the blind testator knew the will's contents. When probate matters were governed by the ecclesiastical courts, it was necessary to show that the will was read to the blind testator. THOMAS ATKINSON, HANDBOOK OF THE LAW OF WILLS § 53 (1953). It is now, however, "well settled that the will of a blind person is valid though it is not read to him at the time of its execution. It is sufficient if he, in any manner, is aware of its contents." Annotation, *Will of Blind Person,* 9 A.L.R. 1416, 1417 (1920).

Thus, you must take steps before or during the execution of the will to ensure that there is evidence that the blind person was aware of the will's contents. Of course, reading the will to the blind testator in front of witnesses as they carefully follow along would be a good technique, just as it would be a good technique to use for an illiterate testator. Although you may use the same witnesses who attest to the will, there is no requirement to do so since the communication of contents to a blind testator is not a part of the execution procedure.

Many states require a will to be attested by witnesses in the presence of the testator. How is this requirement handled for a blind testator? Some courts that have ruled on this point "adhere to the general rational, and insist that the parties should have been so situated that testator could have seen if he had had vision." THOMAS ATKINSON, HANDBOOK OF THE LAW OF WILLS § 72, at 344 (1953). Other courts hold that it is "sufficient if the witnesses sign in such proximity to the testator that he can discern their presence by the use of his remaining senses." Annotation, *Will of Blind Person,* 9 A.L.R. 1416, 1418 (1920). Thus, if the testator can hear or touch the other witnesses, the attestation would be deemed done in the testator's presence. "Obviously a court should not be too strict in this regard, for a blind testator can seldom be certain from his other senses that the witnesses he has chosen are signing his will." THOMAS ATKINSON, HANDBOOK OF THE LAW OF WILLS § 72, at 344 (1953). Courts strive to avoid the fraud that could easily be perpetrated upon the blind testator but, on the other hand, are flexible enough so that a blind person is not precluded from executing an effective will.

You can take several measures to help ensure that the testamentary desires of a blind person are carried out.

- Read the will to the blind testator in front of witnesses.
- The blind testator could execute a Braille will if the testator reads Braille. Even if a normal print will were executed, a conformed unexecuted Braille copy might be useful.
- Videotape the will execution ceremony.

I. CLIENT WITH QUESTIONABLE CAPACITY

VIGNES v. WEISKOPF

Supreme Court of Florida, 1949.
42 So.2d 84.

THOMAS, JUSTICE.

The will of Daniel K. Weiskopf, executed 27 March 1947, was admitted to probate, but a codicil executed sixteen days before he died, 22

March 1948, was denied by the county judge for the reasons "among others, that it [was] * * * neither published nor declared [by him] to be his Codicil to his Last Will * * *," there was no evidence that the testator had read it or knew its contents, and it was signed by him during his last illness while he was not "possessed of testamentary capacity."

At the time of the presentation of the codicil for probate an ex parte hearing had been conducted by the county judge, and the order was predicated on the matters there developed. Then, upon a motion to revoke the order, further testimony was taken at a hearing where both appellant and appellees were represented by counsel.

At the conclusion of this second hearing the same judge opined that the testator at the time he consulted his secretary about the codicil and requested his counsel to be summoned, as well as at the time he signed the instrument, lacked testamentary capacity, did not know or understand the contents of the paper. He held the view, too, that the witnesses did not sign in the testator's "conscious presence."

The order was affirmed by the circuit court.

We now turn to the testimony taken on the two occasions, not with a view of weighing it or pitting out judgment against that of the court which heard it, but of determining whether there was substantial legal evidence to support the findings and whether the judge misapprehended its legal effect. This rule, announced in In re Donnelly's Estate, 137 Fla. 459, 188 So. 108, is at least one feature of the controversy on which counsel for the litigants seem to agree.

The testator's secretary, who had been in his service for twenty years, was called by his nurse who told her that Mr. Weiskopf wished to see her. She went to his bedside, where she found him apparently sleeping. He made no response when first she spoke to him, but after an interval, said, "I want a codicil. * * * $100,000 to Mrs. Vignes; you to get $30,000—ten, ten and ten." She continued: " * * * then he stopped. He seemed to be trying to break through * * *." After another pause he said: "I want to leave $100,000 to somebody, but I can't think who. Isn't that awful?" Then he kept repeating the question, "What else?" She endeavored to assist him by reviewing the contents of his original will with which, because of her position, she was familiar. At the end of this conference she called his attorney, as she had been directed, and "gave him some sketchy notes and remarks." Because of the incomplete nature of the instructions to him, the attorney questioned her "very carefully," and evidently urged her to communicate to him more definite information. She continued: "I went back in the room and tried to get Mr. Weiskopf to be more specific, and more in detail, but he did not say anything further. That is how the codicil got to be written."

The following day the attorney, accompanied by his wife, appeared at the testator's home, bringing with him the codicil which he had undertaken to prepare from the meager information given him by the secretary. The testator did not read it nor was it read to him. At the time, according to one of the witnesses to the codicil, his nurse, it was questionable whether he knew what he was signing. The wife testified that when her husband asked the testator if he desired the instrument read to him he declined and said he would read it later. The lawyer signed it; then at his request his wife and the nurse signed it also. It was immediately sealed and delivered to the secretary, who kept it until after the testator's death; so it is a fair deduction that he never did know exactly what it contained.

It is obvious that the testator was desperately, incurably ill and was in such pain that a great deal of medicine to relieve him of his suffering was being administered, such as phenobarbital, novatrine, demerol, cobra venom, and so forth.

There is ample support in the testimony to form a basis for the county judge's conclusion, and certainly it has not been demonstrated that he misapprehended its legal effect. The testator in the last throes of a deadly disease entertained the thought that he should revise his original will, but there is abundant proof that he had no clear idea, when he had his secretary call his attorney, what he intended to do, and no comprehension of what he had done when he had executed the codicil and ordered it sealed without being acquainted with its contents. There was evidence that he wished to make a bequest of $100,000 to Mrs. Vignes, the appellant; but there was evidence too that he wished to give the same amount to someone whom he could not recollect. It is certain that in a former will executed in 1945 he had devised $75,000 to Mrs. Vignes, then after giving her $50,000 the following year, had provided in the will now probated that she receive but $25,000. This leads to the conclusion that the amount he wished her to receive had been fixed in his mind two years before and confirmed a year later when it was reduced by the amount of the gift. The very reasonable doubt then presents itself whether in his last illness he proposed to raise the bequest to her to $100,000 or confused her name with the name of the person he wished to receive that bequest but whom he could not in his extremity recall.

This is illustrative of the situation as it existed 6 March 1948, and these circumstances, taken with the others we have detailed, such as the administration of narcotics, the hopeless physical condition of the testator, his lethargy, and the affirmative testimony to the effect that he probably did not comprehend what he was doing or had done, justified the order.

Much has been said in the arguments and written in the briefs about the conduct of the attorney who drafted the codicil and who appears now as counsel for the appellees. The inference is left with us that he was guilty of some duplicity because he prepared the codicil for Daniel Weiskopf and now represents those who would have it declared invalid. We have seen what his activities were with reference to preparing the codicil, bringing it to the sickbed of the testator, and having it acknowledged and witnessed. When it was presented to the county judge for probate he joined the other two witnesses in an oath that they were present when the testator subscribed his name to the instrument; that the testator did not read it; that its contents were not read to him nor made known to him, although the attorney "asked him to read it or have its contents made known to him but the testator replied, 'I will read it later' "; that the codicil was immediately sealed; that the seal was not thereafter broken until its deposit with the court; that the attorney received no reply from the testator when he asked him if he wished three subscribing witnesses to attest his execution; that the witnesses thereupon signed the paper at the request of the attorney; "that they verily [believed] that the testator did not know the contents of what he was signing nor did he at the time of the signing thereof have testamentary capacity."

Patently the purpose of this affidavit was to apprise the court at the first opportunity precisely what happened in the sickroom when the codicil was executed.

When the attorney was interrogated about his securing the execution and attestation of the codicil, which he was later to state in the oath had been witnessed without a direct request of the testator, by one who at the time lacked testamentary capacity he gave an answer which seems to us to have been quite sensible. He said simply, "I did the best I knew how."

It occurs to us that he would have been unfaithful to an old client had he not done his best to comply with the request to prepare the codicil and bring it to him. It is true that the information was incomplete, but there is evidence that he tried diligently at the time to have it clarified. When he reached his client's bedside there was good reason to believe, from the atmosphere there, that the client had not long to live and that he was probably not mentally alert, but these circumstances did not make it necessary that the attorney constitute himself a court to pass on the medical and legal question whether he was in fact capable of executing a valid codicil. That the question is debatable is demonstrated by the procedure which has taken its course in the county judge's court, the circuit court, and this court.

We are convinced that the lawyer should have complied as nearly as he could with the testator's request, should have exposed the true situation to the court, which he did, and should have then left the matter to that tribunal to decide whether in view of all facts surrounding the execution of the codicil it should be admitted to probate.

Had the attorney arrogated to himself the power and responsibility of determining the capacity of the testator, decided he was incapacitated, and departed, he would indeed have been subjected to severe criticism when, after the testator's death, it was discovered that because of his presumptuousness the last-minute effort of a dying man to change his will had been thwarted.

The appellant has cited to us law in support of the proposition that testimony of a witness to a will assailing the mental capacity of a testator is viewed with suspicion and given little weight, but there is no need for us to elaborate on that principle because we shall assume that the lower court gave the testimony of these particular witnesses only the weight to which it was, in all the circumstances, entitled, and even if the testimony of this particular class of witnesses be discounted, there appears no need for this court to interfere. We repeat that we are not undertaking to weigh the testimony, but only to determine whether the effect of the whole of it was misapprehended by the court.

As for the hint that the attorney who prepared the codicil acted improperly when he appeared for the appellees in this litigation, we have only to say that his conduct in this regard is utterly beside the points whether the instrument was properly executed and the testator at that time had testamentary capacity.

Affirmed.

MODEL RULES OF PROFESSIONAL CONDUCT—PRIOR TO 2002

Rule 1.14.

CLIENT UNDER A DISABILITY

(a) When a client's ability to make adequately considered decisions in connection with the representation is impaired, whether because of minority, mental disability or for some other reason, the lawyer shall, as far as reasonably possible, maintain a normal client-lawyer relationship with the client.

(b) A lawyer may seek the appointment of a guardian or other protective action with respect to a client only when the lawyer reasonably believes that the client cannot adequately act in the client's own interest.

MODEL RULES OF PROFESSIONAL CONDUCT—2002 REVISION

Rule 1.14.

CLIENT WITH DIMINISHED CAPACITY

(a) When a client's capacity to make adequately considered decisions in connection with a representation is diminished, whether because of minority, mental impairment or for some other reason, the lawyer shall, as far as reasonably possible, maintain a normal client-lawyer relationship with the client.

(b) When the lawyer reasonably believes that the client has diminished capacity, is at risk of substantial physical, financial or other harm unless action is taken and cannot adequately act in the client's own interest, the lawyer may take reasonably necessary protective action, including consulting with individuals or entities that have the ability to take action to protect the client and, in appropriate cases, seeking the appointment of a guardian ad litem, conservator or guardian.

(c) Information relating to the representation of a client with diminished capacity is protected by Rule 1.6. When taking protective action pursuant to paragraph (b), the lawyer is impliedly authorized under Rule 1.6(a) to reveal information about the client, but only to the extent reasonably necessary to protect the client's interests.

ACTEC COMMENTARY ON MRPC 1.14*

ACTEC COMMENTARIES ON MODEL RULES OF PROFESSIONAL CONDUCT, pages 132–134 (4th ed. 2006).

Testamentary Capacity. If the testamentary capacity of a client is uncertain, the lawyer should exercise particular caution in assisting the client to modify his or her estate plan. The lawyer generally should not prepare a will, trust agreement or other dispositive instrument for a client who the lawyer reasonably believes lacks the requisite capacity. On the other hand, because of the importance of testamentary freedom, the lawyer may properly assist clients whose testamentary capacity appears to be borderline. In any such case the lawyer should take steps to preserve evidence regarding the client's testamentary capacity.

In cases involving clients of doubtful testamentary capacity, the lawyer should consider, if available, procedures for obtaining court supervision of the proposed estate plan, including substituted judgment proceedings.

Lawyer Retained by Fiduciary for Person with Diminished Capacity. The lawyer retained by a person seeking appointment as a fiduciary or retained by a fiduciary for a person with diminished capacity, including a guardian, conservator or attorney-in-fact, stands in a lawyer-client relationship with respect to the prospective or appointed fiduciary. A lawyer who is retained by a fiduciary for a person with diminished capacity, but who did not previously represent the person with diminished capacity, represents only the fiduciary. Nevertheless, in such a case the lawyer for the fiduciary owes some duties to the person with diminished capacity. See ACTEC

Commentary on MRPC 1.2 (Scope of Representation and Allocation of Authority Between Client and Lawyer). If the lawyer represents the fiduciary, as distinct from the person with diminished capacity, and is aware that the fiduciary is improperly acting adversely to the person's interests, the lawyer may have an obligation to disclose, to prevent or to rectify the fiduciary's misconduct. See MRPC 1.2(d) (Scope of Representation and Allocation of Authority Between Client and Lawyer) (providing that a lawyer shall not counsel a client to engage, or assist a client, in conduct that the lawyer knows is criminal or fraudulent).

As suggested in the Commentary to MRPC 1.2 (Scope of Representation and Allocation of Authority Between Client and Lawyer), a lawyer who represents a fiduciary for a person with diminished capacity or who represents a person who is seeking appointment as such, should consider asking the client to agree that, as part of the engagement, the lawyer may

* Reprinted with permission of The American College of Trust and Estate Counsel.

disclose fiduciary misconduct to the court, to the person with diminished capacity, or to other interested persons.

Person with Diminished Capacity Who Was a Client Prior to Suffering Diminished Capacity and Prior to the Appointment of a Fiduciary. A lawyer who represented a client before the client suffered diminished capacity may be considered to continue to represent the client after a fiduciary has been appointed for the person. Although incapacity may prevent a person with diminished capacity from entering into a contract or other legal relationship, the lawyer who represented the person with diminished capacity at a time when the person was competent may appropriately continue to meet with and counsel him or her. Whether the person with diminished capacity is characterized as a client or a former client, the client's lawyer acting as counsel for the fiduciary owes some continuing duties to him or her. See Ill. Advisory Opinion 91–24 (1991) (summarized in the Annotations following the ACTEC Commentary on MRPC 1.6 (Confidentiality of Information). If the lawyer represents the person with diminished capacity and not the fiduciary, and is aware that the fiduciary is improperly acting adversely to the person's interests, the lawyer has an obligation to disclose, to prevent or to rectify the fiduciary's misconduct.

Wishes of Person with Diminished Capacity Who Is Under Guardianship or Conservatorship When the Fiduciary is the Client. A conflict of interest may arise if the lawyer for the fiduciary is asked by the fiduciary to take action that is contrary either to the previously expressed wishes of the person with diminished capacity or to the best interests of such person, as the lawyer believes those interests to be. The lawyer should give appropriate consideration to the currently or previously expressed wishes of a person with diminished capacity.

May Lawyer Represent Guardian or Conservator of Current or Former Client? The lawyer may represent the guardian or conservator of a current or former client, provided the representation of one will not be directly adverse to the other. See ACTEC Commentary on MRPC 1.7 (Conflict of Interest: Current Clients) and MRPC 1.9 (Duties to Former Clients). Joint representation would not be permissible if there is a significant risk that the representation of one will be materially limited by the lawyer's responsibilities to the other. See MRPC 1.7(a)(2) (Conflict of Interest: Current Clients). Because of the client's, or former client's, diminished capacity, the waiver option may be unavailable. See MRPC 1.0(e) (Terminology) (defining *informed consent*).

NOTES AND QUESTIONS

1. What special steps would you take if you concluded that your client, although borderline, does have testamentary capacity and is not under undue influence? See American College of Trust and Estate Counsel, Wills and Trusts Subcommittee of the Fiduciary Litigation Committee, *Contest Planning for the Client with Marginal Capacity—A Checklist of Strategical and Tactical Considerations and Options*, 12 ACTEC NOTES 251 (1997).

2. A person in the early stages of Alzheimer's disease may still have the capacity necessary to execute a valid will and other estate planning documents. See *In re Davidson*, 310 Ark. 639, 839 S.W.2d 214 (1992), and Robert P. Friedland & James J. McMonagle, *Crisis of Competence: Capacity to Execute Wills is Tenuous for Victims of Alzheimer's Disease*, A.B.A. J., May 1996, at 80 (recommending that the testator be examined and tested by an experienced psychiatrist or neurologist and that both the medical examination and the will execution ceremony be documented on videotape); A. Frank Johns, *Older Clients with Diminishing Capacity and Their Advance Directives*, 39 REAL PROP., PROB. & TR. J. 107 (2004).

3. For a comprehensive treatment of the concerns that arise with age-challenged individuals, see Lawrence A. Frolik, *"Old Age with Fears and Ills": Planning for the Very Old Client*, 38TH ANN. HECKERLING INST. ON EST. PLAN. ch. 18 (2004).

J. CLIENT WITH MARITAL PROBLEMS

Approximately one-half of all marriages in the United States end in divorce. Accordingly, divorce is one of the realities of a client's life that you must keep in mind during all stages of estate planning. Whenever a married client seeks estate planning advice, you should inquire as to the condition of the marriage. If divorce is looming on the horizon, you must take action to protect as much of the client's property as is legally possible from potential attacks by the soon-to-be ex-spouse. For example, beneficiary designations in wills, trusts, insurance policies, retirement plans, bank accounts, and like arrangements need to be changed immediately. Likewise, the client must revise fiduciary designations in wills, trusts, durable powers of attorney, and guardian self-declarations. Even if divorce does not appear imminent, you need to keep a watchful eye on the marriage just in case circumstances change.

Unfortunately, from the perspective of an estate planner, a person with marital problems is typically more concerned with child custody and the property settlement than with the disposition of property upon death and the naming of fiduciaries. Even after divorce, many people do not seek prompt assistance to revise their estate plans to reflect the tremendous change in circumstances. Thus, you will be frequently faced with administering the estate of a divorced person that was prepared while that person was married and which was based on the assumption that the marriage would still be intact.

LOCATE

What is the effect of (a) filing for divorce and (b) a final divorce decree on the following designations made by one spouse in favor of the other under the law of your state?

- Beneficiary of a will.
- Executor of an estate.

- Guardian of a minor child.
- Beneficiary of an inter vivos trust.
- Trustee of an inter vivos trust.
- Beneficiary of a life insurance policy.
- Beneficiary of a retirement plan.
- Party to or beneficiary of a multiple-party account.
- Safe deposit box entry authority.
- Property management agent.
- Health care agent.
- Guardian declaration.

NOTES AND QUESTIONS

1. Testator named Spouse as the primary will beneficiary and Stepchild as the alternate beneficiary to take if Spouse did not survive. Testator and Spouse are divorced. Testator died without changing the will. Assume that the applicable state law revokes gifts in favor of an ex-spouse. May Stepchild still take? See In re Group Life Ins. Proceeds of Mallory, 872 S.W.2d 800 (Tex. App. 1994).

2. The death of one spouse terminates a pending divorce action because the surviving spouse is now "unmarried" by operation of law. However, a pending annulment action may continue because its purpose is to determine if the parties were married in the first instance. See In re Marriage of Goldberg, 22 Cal.App.4th 265, 27 Cal.Rptr.2d 298 (1994).

3. What effect does taking an aggressive attitude toward altering a client's estate plan during times of marital difficulty have on the couple's reconciliation chances? Could your actions be the final blow that drives the couple apart forever?

4. For a discussion of the ethical problems of representing both spouses, see Chapter 8(I)(7).

K. CLIENT WITH A SPOUSAL EQUIVALENT

Traditionally, a surviving spouse was of the opposite sex from the deceased spouse because only individuals of different sexes could marry. There is a growing movement to permit individuals in same-sex relationships to marry and receive all the benefits of marriage, including the right to take under intestacy as a surviving spouse. In 2004, Massachusetts became the first state to make it legal for same-sex couples to marry followed in later years by states including Connecticut, Iowa, Maryland, New Hampshire, New York, Vermont, and Washington, as well as the District of Columbia.

A growing number of individuals are in committed relationships that are not evidenced by a formal marriage. These spousal equivalent relationships may exist between partners of different sexes or of the same sex. Is the surviving partner of one of these relationships entitled to inherit upon the death of the other partner?

If the partners are of opposite sexes, most states provide no inheritance rights to the surviving partner. Some states, however, recognize the concept of a *common law marriage* so that the surviving partner will be treated as a surviving spouse and be entitled to inherit even though the partners were not formally married. The requirements of a common law marriage typically include the partners (1) agreeing to be married, (2) living together as husband and wife, and (3) representing to others that they are married.

In addition, some states, such as California, allow opposite-sex unmarried couples to register as domestic partners if at least one partner is over age 62, which will then entitle the surviving partner to inherit the same share as a surviving spouse.

A few states permit same-sex partners to obtain inheritance rights via other means, such as by entering into a *civil union* (e.g., Delaware, Hawaii, Illinois, New Jersey, and Rhode Island) or registering as a *domestic partner* (e.g., California and Maine) or *reciprocal beneficiary*. If the partners satisfy the statutory formalities, the surviving partner typically is entitled to inherit the same share a surviving spouse would inherit.

FRANK S. BERALL, ESTATE PLANNING CONSIDERATIONS FOR UNMARRIED COHABITANTS*

31 EST. PLAN. 307 (2004).

ESTATE PLANNING

Estate planning for cohabiting unmarried couples should include a written contract (a cohabitation agreement) expressing the parties' intentions, similar to an antenuptial or postnuptial agreement. Estate planning for cohabiting unmarried couples is quite similar to planning for married ones. However, unmarried couples do not have the state law property rights and state and federal tax benefits available to spouses. Nonetheless, planning for unmarried couples may resemble planning for spouses if both parties are parents of all their children. It may also be similar to planning for remarried couples, one or both of whom have children from prior marriages.

If the couple does not expect to marry or have a common-law marriage in a state still recognizing one, their living together agreement should disclaim any intent that a legally recognized marriage arises from their cohabitation. Otherwise, their agreement may be unenforceable because it violates public policy.

No statement should be made that the parties are living together as husband and wife, to avoid the doctrine that the consideration for their contract is meretricious sexual services. In most states, consideration based on such sexual services between an unmarried couple will invalidate any agreement. But, merely holding themselves out as spouses does not necessarily imply sexual services. Furthermore, consideration based on business services alone is valid. Even homemaking services may be valid consideration in some states.

The parties' interests in each other's earnings and other income, as well as their property acquired by purchase, gift or inheritance before or during their relationship, their debts both owed before and incurred during their relationship, their understanding of how to share living expenses and household responsibilities, as well as bill paying and tax consequences should all be expressed, so as to preclude any court from later discerning some assumed intent or implied agreements.

Unless all property is kept separate, with provisions for any interest in the appreciation of one cohabitant's property resulting from the other's services or by acquisitions from third parties, there should be a stipulation in the agreement about commingled property and a statement as to the meaning of any change in ownership or purchase of joint property during the relationship.

If the couple lives in a jurisdiction where no support obligation exists between unmarried cohabitants, any such obligation should be either specified or waived, both during and after the relationship, while any intentions for post-separation support should be stated. Until recently, absent an enforceable contract for post-separation support, no entitlement existed.

Intentions about the division of property if the relationship terminates or one of the partners dies (while the cohabitants are still living together) should be expressed, both in the contract and in the couples' wills. California, Washington, Michigan, and New Hampshire will enforce such express contracts at death between people in a meretricious relationship.

Other matters to be included in the partnership agreement should be signature authority, recordkeeping, investment strategy, insurance, dispute resolution (whether arbitration is to apply), remedies for defaults, powers over one another's health care decisions, and the responsibility for domestic services. If children are contemplated in the relationship, there should be a separate agreement. Even if they are not contemplated, provisions concerning their custody and visitation rights and the rearing of unplanned children should be included in any agreement.

As in any estate planning, wills, possibly trusts and durable powers of attorney for both financial and health care purposes should be prepared for the couple and executed by them. In addition, the legal consequences of the way title is held to any real estate should be explained to the couple.

A practitioner may prepare an estate plan for both cohabitants, whether or not they are married, provided he warns them that any disclosure made to him by one of them will be told to the other. However, it is unwise to represent both cohabitants when preparing a living together agreement. During negotiation of the terms of any antenuptial, postnuptial or separation agreements, both parties should have separate counsel to avoid possible later claims of fraud, duress and invalidity of the agreement. And separate counsel should also be used in negotiating a living together agreement.

Acting as counsel for more than one party to any partnership agreement could lead to the representation of conflicting interests. This may create potential ethical problems, possibly resulting in unenforceability of the agreement and a malpractice claim. While representing both parties to a pre-or post-marital or separation agreement will almost always make the agreement subject to attack in later litigation, this is not necessarily true with a partnership agreement, even one drawn for same-or opposite-sex couples. Nevertheless, if the practitioner plans to represent both parties, written waivers of conflicts of interest—together with consents for financial disclosure—should be obtained from each one. Consents for financial disclosure are needed because financial information is confidential between unmarried couples.

Oral agreements present proof problems, but implied contracts may be found to exist by some courts. Oral agreements are like implied contracts and are probably unenforceable in many jurisdictions, despite inequitable results. But oral contracts based on mutual consideration have been enforced. Furthermore, as living together arrangements begin to appear more like traditional marriages, some courts may hold that an implied contract was made.

The following factors are considered: existence or absence of marital intent, how the status is represented to others, how title to property acquired during the relationship is taken, and other financial arrangements, such as joint bank accounts, sharing expenses and acquiring property jointly. All of these are some indication of an intent to pool earnings or share property. On the other hand, maintaining separate bank accounts, splitting expenses, acquiring property in separate names, and keeping records of separate property are all indications that the parties do not intend to pool resources. However, the foregoing of financial and other opportunities by one party and having mutual children are both indications of an implied contract.

WILLS, TRUSTS, AND ADOPTION

Unmarried couples should consider making each other the beneficiaries of their wills and trust instruments, contingent on the partner remaining as such and defining "partner" as "the person living with me at my death." Consider stating that a separation may not disqualify the bequest unless it is due to domestic disharmony. Separation due to a temporary relocation of one partner's job or the confinement of one partner to a hospital or extended care facility may not disqualify the bequest. If a fiduciary other than the surviving partner is named, that person or institution could determine if the surviving partner qualified at the first partner's death.

The class described as the partners' "children" or "descendants" should be carefully defined and broad enough to include all children whom the partners intend to benefit, even if not their biological ones. Using the children's names in a will or trust is wise. But referring to a class of "children" could also include "someone born to or adopted by my partner during the period that we have been partners." The class of descendants should be defined to include "children and more remote descendants of my children."

Adoption of a child or children of one unmarried partner by the other may be done to establish a legal relationship. Several states, including California, Illinois and New York, permit such adoptions by same-sex partners, while Florida and New Hampshire have statutes barring them.

Adoption of one partner by the other could be considered, thus making the adoptee an heir at law. While he or she could still be disinherited by a will, which he or she could contest, the adoption itself is irrevocable. But adult adoption is not available in all states, and some restrict adoption to close relatives.

Where permitted, an adult adoption would convert the absence of any legal status into a parent-child relationship between the parties, giving the surviving partner certain inheritance and other rights. These may eliminate other family members' rights in the deceased partner's estate.

If the adopting partner is the beneficiary of a trust passing property to his or her "descendants" at his or her death, adoption would bring the adopted partner within the definition of that class. However, the effect of adoption is to eliminate the adopted partner's rights in his or her biological family's estate. A better alternative, as indicated above would be naming the other partner as beneficiary under a will or revocable trust.

While a spouse cannot be entirely disinherited (because of the existence of dower, curtesy or elective share statutes in common law states and community property laws in those jurisdictions), an adoptee may be disinherited entirely. But, the adoptive relationship itself is ordinarily irrevocable.

ADDITIONAL CONSIDERATIONS

Avoid Joint Tenancy

Joint tenancy with right of survivorship (a form of ownership disfavored by the author of this article) may have some advantages for unmarried partners. But the presumption that where both names appear in the title, a right of survivorship exists between married joint tenants, [may] not apply to unmarried partners. The words "with a right of survivorship" [may have to] be used in the title. Gift tax problems could also arise. Under the estate tax, at the death of an unmarried joint tenant, there is a presumption that all contributions to acquire the joint property were made by the deceased joint tenant. Thus, there will be inclusion of the entire value of the joint property in the first decedent's estate, unless the survivor can prove contribution to rebut the presumption.

Alimony may be reduced or eliminated if a divorcee cohabits with another person. Following a divorce, cohabitation with someone else, if considered the equivalent of a remarriage, may result in reduction or even elimination of alimony, unless a provision to the contrary appears in a separation agreement incorporated in a divorce decree.

Tax Planning Techniques

The use of a grantor retained income trust (GRIT) can pass assets to a less wealthy unmarried partner at a reduced transfer cost, because the partner is not a family member within the definition of Chapter 14. That chapter eliminated the use of the GRIT technique for a remainder beneficiary who was a family member. Because Chapter 14 deals with transfers among traditional family members, other techniques formerly used before its enactment may still be used, since domestic partners and other unrelated parties are not in this category.

Accordingly, because an unmarried couple is unrelated, a GRIT could be used, with the grantor retaining all income from the trust for a fixed term, at the end of which the remainder would pass to the beneficiary. If the grantor died before the end of the trust term, the corpus would be includable in the grantor's estate. The creation of the trust would be a gift equal to the property's fair market value less the retained income interest.

The tax advantage of a GRIT is that if the rate of accounting income is lower than the IRS' assumed rate, there will be an overvaluation of the income interest and the remainder will be undervalued; thus, a very low discounted value for gift tax purposes will be obtained. Then, upon trust termination, the corpus (including appreciation) will pass transfer tax-free to the other partner.

While the prohibitions of Section 2702 restrict family members in the use of personal residence trusts to specially restricted qualified trusts (called QPRTs), domestic partners and other unrelated parties are able to use personal residence trusts where sales may be made between the grantor and the trust holding his or her residence. Consequently, the grantor may purchase the residence from the trust just prior to the end of the term and the remainder beneficiaries will receive the purchase price, without the grantor or the trust having to recognize gain or loss. On the other hand, if after expiration of the term, the residence remains in the grantor trust, it can be rented from the trustee to the grantor without taxable rental income. Furthermore, if the grantor pays rent based on the fair market value of the residence, the latter will be excluded from his or her gross estate, because his or her economic enjoyment ceases upon the payment of rent.

While domestic partners and others not related by blood or marriage may be considered natural objects of the transferor's bounty, and thus act like family members under Section 2703, the restrictions of Section 2704 should not apply to non-family arrangements, such as domestic partnerships. This will give an opportunity to obtain discounts by using partnerships, limited liability partnerships, limited liability corporations, and other similar entities.

Use of life insurance, possibly by having it acquired by an irrevocable trust for the benefit of one of the partners, and the making of annual exclusion gifts of $11,000 in 2004, should be considered by unmarried partners. Clients should also consider gift tax-free payments of tuition and medical expenses as well as the use of the applicable exclusion of $1.5 million (in 2004). The use of charitable remainder and charitable lead trusts are possibilities too, but since unmarried partners are not related, if there is more than a 37–1/2 year age difference between them, GST tax will be incurred on a large transfer. * * *

You must carefully plan for your client's spousal equivalent, be the partner of the same or opposite sex. Without proper estate planning, your client's partner will be totally omitted because the law does not include a non-spouse partner in any of its default plans. The partner will have no right to be involved in decisions regarding the property management or medical care of your client, will not take under intestacy, and may not get other benefits and protections that a spouse receives (e.g., homestead, exempt personal property, a family allowance, an unlimited marital deduction, employer-supplied benefits, etc.).

Please review Chapter 9(B) discussing will contest prevention techniques. You may use many of these techniques to protect an estate plan in favor of a spousal equivalent from attack.

NOTES AND QUESTIONS

1. Are you personally opposed to spousal equivalent relationships on moral, legal, or religious grounds? If yes, would you accept a client who is in such a relationship? If yes, do you think you could provide quality estate planning services despite your opposition to the client's lifestyle?

2. Each partner should have his or her own attorney to reduce claims of undue influence. See Jeffrey G. Sherman, *Undue Influence and the Homosexual Testator*, 42 UNIV. PITT. L. REV. 225 (1988).

3. For a discussion of the estate planning ramifications of a same-sex relationship, see Patricia A. Cain, *Same Sex Couples and the Federal Tax Laws,* 1 LAW & SEXUALITY 97 (1991); Jane A. Marquardt, *A Will—Not a Wish—Makes it So: Estate Planning Options for Same–Sex Couples*, FAM. ADVOC., Summer 1997, at 34.

L. CLIENT WITH CHRONIC ILLNESS

MARTIN M. SHENKMAN, ESTATE PLANNING STRATEGIES FOR CLIENTS LIVING WITH CHRONIC ILLNESSES*

It is no surprise that the population is aging. As but one illustration of this trend, in 2010, just under 2 percent of the U.S. population was age 85 and over. By 2050 that number is anticipated to increase to 4.3 percent, or over 19 million people, 6.2 million of whom have severe or moderate memory impairment. But this is only one component of the story. Chronic illness, contrary to common misconception, is not a challenge of only the elderly. 60% of those living with chronic illness are between the ages of 18 and 64. With approximately 120 million living with chronic illness, these issues affect a large number of clients.

These trends have profound implications to estate planners that extend far beyond the issues of Medicaid planning. In particular, the process of meeting with clients facing these challenges must be modified to better serve them.

How Client Symptoms Affect Meetings

There are a number of important differences in how estate planners and their staff should schedule and handle client meetings for clients with chronic illnesses. Most symptoms of a chronic illness, such as severe fatigue and chronic pain, are not readily observable. Only a very small percentage of those who are disabled by these symptoms utilize visible mobility aids. The reality is if you don't ask, in most cases, you cannot know what challenges a particular client faces.

For individuals who have never experienced a chronic illness or seen the affects of such illnesses firsthand, it is often difficult to comprehend the symptoms and the affect they have. For example, chronic fatigue is nothing like a healthy person having a "late night," and several cups of Joe will not have any impact on the person affected. Those living with chronic fatigue often describe it "as if I'm drowning in quicksand." Estate planners may witness a client living with chronic fatigue acting reasonably alert one minute and then becoming overwhelmed by fatigue the next.

Training Staff to Inquire Proactively

One problem most estate planners and their staff face when dealing with clients with chronic illnesses is the difficulty in determining if a client has a health challenge. To help address this issue, estate planning practices should implement a routine procedure of inquiring whether a

* Reprinted with the permission of Martin M. Shenkman who maintains the charitable website www.RV4TheCause.org which is a free website he uses to disseminate information on planning for chronic illness.

client needs special accommodations for any health or other challenges. For example, clients who struggle with fatigue may wish to book meetings at times of the day when they are more likely to be alert, and they can inform the attorney or staff if they need to limit their meeting times. For some clients with chronic illnesses, scheduling a series of shorter meetings rather than one longer meeting is much more beneficial and far less stressful.

It is also important to consider how the office itself can affect a client living with a chronic illness. For example, if conference rooms were recently painted or carpeted, the fumes, which might at most be annoying to most people, could trigger a flare-up for a client with COPD, resulting in severe consequences. Nearly 12 million Americans have been diagnosed as having COPD, and there may be another 12 million that have not been diagnosed but who are living with the disease.

Too many professionals simply assume that clients facing such challenges will communicate them, but this often is not the case. Some clients are embarrassed and others are calloused by the indifference they generally encounter. Practitioners should be proactive and ask directly and specifically about a client's health status and how they can accommodate any such challenges.

Recording Meetings and Other Options

Clients with chronic illness may struggle with cognitive fatigue, or dementia. A common cognitive symptom is difficulty in multitasking. A client may be extremely intelligent, but have difficulty doing multiple tasks at once, such as taking notes while listening to discussions with counsel. Having a record of the meeting might be essential for the client and attorney to be able to follow up on the meeting.

Recording the meeting is one way to keep a detailed record of everything discussed. The problem with recording a meeting, however, is that discussions of strategies and solutions that the attorney and client decided not to follow may confuse the client when he or she listens to the recording after the meeting. Another approach to addressing the cognitive impairment associated with many chronic illnesses is to suggest that the client bring a family member or friend to take notes for them during the meeting. An attorney may also choose to provide the client with a summary after the meeting.

Estate planners can also utilize technology during client meetings to help clients with chronic illnesses. Attorneys can use a smart board to project a meeting agenda on a large screen and modify the agenda as the meeting progresses. The enlargement that such a screen provides can make it much easier for clients with cognitive impairment to stay focused and aid clients with visual impairment. Vision impairment (blindness and low vision) ranks eighth in the list of conditions that limit a client's activity and is responsible for limiting the activities of 1.3 million people.

Regular Meetings for Clients with Chronic Illness

The premise of a review or update meeting can have far greater importance for a client with chronic illness. Every practitioner has undoubtedly advised every client of the need to return for an update meeting if circumstances or laws change, or in any event perhaps every three years. However, if the client's diagnosis includes growing cognitive challenges, meeting more regularly than every few years is vital.

Establishing annual meetings can help create a clear record of the client's wishes, and this record can be important for agents and others who may have to take over management of the client's affairs. As the client's disease progresses, estate planners should update the estate plan to reflect new developments. Practitioners should be wary of making any assumptions as to disease progression, however, as each client's experience of a disease is unique and may differ from other clients who have the same disease. Regular meetings can also help establish benchmarks as a disease may progress, and provide an opportunity to identify the potential for undue influence or abuse, which clients with significant challenges are more susceptible to.

Involving Others

Typically, estate planners hold client meetings with just the client present. Occasionally, another adviser or heir might join in. However, for clients facing chronic illness, broadening the scope of those in attendance during the meeting can often be very helpful. If the client faces challenges multi-tasking, another attendee can take notes. Many clients remain in denial of the scope and magnitude of their disease or suffer from depression. Depression can be a natural result of the disease process itself, a function of the client's reaction to the impact of the disease on their life, a result of the medication prescribed, or any combination of these. Having a family member or loved one attend estate planning meetings can benefit both the client and the attorney.

Regular meetings will greatly increase the likelihood that the client will pursue essential planning. If the client is accompanied by a caregiver, family members, or other loved ones at the meetings, these additional people can encourage follow-ups and address some of the emotional challenges and other impediments associated with the planning process. Involving others can be far more important for clients with chronic illness because the input and observations of others can be critical in how the client approaches and engages in the planning process.

Educating Agents and Others

For clients with progressive illnesses, involving children or others named as agents and fiduciaries (e.g., trustees under a living trust) before they have to assume an active role is a wonderful opportunity to "kick the estate planning tires" before the plan has to "drive." Involving these key individuals can provide a forum to educate the agents in advance, permit the client to express his or her wishes directly to those who will carry them out, and deal with practical and logistical issues that are often ignored.

For example, many clients have multiple bank and brokerage accounts. While simplification and consolidation is appropriate for all clients, numerous accounts can become a particular problem for a client facing the challenges of chronic illness, such as difficulties with executive function skills (e.g., balancing a check book because of cognitive impairment). Estate planners can suggest that the client consolidate and simplify financial holdings and can suggest the client bring his or her financial planner or wealth manager into the annual estate planning meeting. By involving the financial planner or wealth manager, the client and estate planner will receive tremendous help in keeping the client in control of his or her financial for as long as possible. Chronic illness disempowers the client. Creative and intelligent planning can empower the client.

Involving a Care Manager

Practitioners often find that involving a client's care manager can greatly aid the planning process. Care managers are typically licensed nurses, social workers, or allied professionals, and they can bridge a number of important gaps in the planning team and help facilitate the entire process. If the client is reticent to proceed because of denial, apathy, or other common issues associated with chronic illnesses, the care manager has the skill set to serve as the catalyst to move the planning process forward.

The client's competency is obviously critical to the execution of estate-planning documents. While the final determination of competency is a legal decision within the purview of counsel, having input from a care manager as to the clients psycho-social status, interpretation of medical letters and reports and the like can be of considerable help. The cognitive impacts of many chronic illnesses are enigmatic. Care-manager involvement can assure that the practitioner does not overlook significant issues and that a client who is competent to handle decisions is not unnecessarily giving up control. Practitioners must be careful to recognize the limitations of a care manager's expertise and to involve a neurologist or psychiatrist as appropriate.

Caregivers can also aid the client when it comes time to name agents for powers of attorney and health proxies and trustees for revocable trusts. While most clients view these assignments somewhat abstractly, these assignments are quite real for a client struggling with a chronic illness. Practitioners rarely meet the agents to be named and do not have the formal training to identify whether the designee is really an adequate candidate for the role even if such a meeting were to take place. A care manager, on the other hand, can often interview the client, caregiver, family, and others in a home setting and provide counsel with valuable input as to the client's proposed agents.

If a client is considering implementing tax planning strategies, a gift program will likely be involved. Further, if uncertainty surrounds the client's future competency to consummate gifts, especially sophisticated transfers, there may be an urgency to consummate such transfers as soon as possible. A care manager can provide a care plan to help determine the resources the client will likely to need for future care, and the attorney can use this input to help determine the appropriate extent of a gift program. The attorney can also use the caregiver's plan to support the fact that adequate resources were retained to mitigate against an IRS argument under Code Section 2036 or a fraudulent conveyance challenge. An estate planner may also consider including a mechanism in the estate plan that calls for a periodic review and report from an independent care manager. Such a report can provide important guidance to a trustee who is making investment and distribution decisions.

The National Association of Professional Geriatric Care Managers is a professional organization many care managers belong to and can provide practitioners valuable resources on finding and working with care managers.

At the heart of planning for clients with chronic illnesses is tailoring the planning and documents to address the client's unique challenges and needs. The process and concepts are not dramatically different from those used for all clients, but minor modifications can enable practitioners to better serve this large and growing base of clients.

NOTES AND QUESTIONS

1. Your estate planning advice encompasses additional concerns if your client has AIDS. Thus, should you ask each of your clients if he or she is HIV positive? If the client has not been recently tested, should you recommend a test before proceeding with the estate plan? Might you lose potential clients who are offended by these inquiries?

2. For additional information, see Emily Berendt & Laura Lynn Michaels, *Your HIV Positive Client: Easing the Burden on the Family Through Estate Planning,* 24 J. MARSHALL L. REV. 509 (1991).

M. CLIENT WITH PERSONAL PROPERTY CONCERNS

JOHN T. BERTEAU, STEPS TO AVOID BENEFICIARY CONFLICTS OVER BEQUESTS OF TANGIBLE PERSONAL PROPERTY*

12 EST. PLAN. 356 (1985).

The distribution of a decedent's tangible personal property can be a challenging problem for the estate planner. The nature of the property,

* "Steps to Avoid Beneficiary Conflicts Over Bequests of Tangible Personal Property," by John T. Berteau, published in Estate Planning, Volume 12, 1985. © 1985 by Thomson Reuters/WG&L. Reprinted with permission.

the client's desires, and the expectations of beneficiaries can combine to create difficult situations that require expert handling.

DEFINITIONS AND OWNERSHIP

* * * Few estate planners * * * intend a bequest of tangible personal property to include all of the decedent's money. Thus, estate planning documents should specifically exclude money from the definition of tangible personal property so that a court construction may be avoided and all concerned will understand that tangible personal property does not include money. * * *

AMBIGUITY AND IMPRECISION

* * * One of the simplest ways of disposing of tangible personal property is to simply state, "I give all of the assets which I own to my spouse, or if my spouse shall be deceased, then all of my estate shall be divided equally among my children." Such language will rarely be appropriate, however, since the distribution of tangible personal property under such a clause will cause taxable income to be distributed to the beneficiary. Under such a clause, the value of all assets distributed to a beneficiary during the taxable year of the estate are includable in the gross income of the beneficiary to the extent that the estate has distributable net income.[15] The early distribution of a car or other item of tangible personal property may cause the estate to lose the benefit of selecting the most appropriate tax bracket. If the decedent's estate is one which produces a substantial amount of income, someone is going to have the very unpleasant task of telling the widow (or other beneficiary) that when her husband's Mercedes (which she always considered to be "theirs") was distributed to her, she received ordinary income equal to its fair market value. If no cash or liquid assets were distributed to her during that fiscal year, she may have no money to pay the tax on this income.

If there is no surviving spouse, then, under the above form language, all of the estate goes to the decedent's children equally. There may be a serious question whether children are the proper beneficiaries of items of tangible personal property. A bequest to a minor of the Mercedes or of the decedent-entrepreneur's trucks from his moving business seems wholly inappropriate. If one or more of the children are deceased, many states provide by anti-lapse statutes that a bequest to the deceased child will be distributed to his or her then-living lineal descendants, per stirpes. This may cause personal items of sentimental value to the surviving children to be distributed to very young grandchildren who have no appreciation of the family history behind such items. Guardianships may further complicate the situation. * * *

Disposition of "all of the contents of my home" may also cause a great deal of confusion. Does this include cash, securities or passbooks found in the home? Generally, a gift of the contents of the decedent's home is

15. See Regs. 1.661(a)–2(f), 1.662(a)–3(b) and 1.663(a)–1.

limited to those things ordinarily identified with the home, but here again, circumstances may cause widely divergent interpretations. * * *

THE SPECIFIC BEQUEST

One of the most frequent methods of disposition of tangible personal property is by specific bequest, which avoids many of the problems outlined above. However, many times clients will bring to the estate planner a lengthy list of specific items of tangible personal property which they wish to have distributed to various beneficiaries. Such lists may be either clear and detailed or vague and general. The length of a list of specific bequests can greatly increase the length of the will and prove unnecessarily cumbersome in the administration of the decedent's estate. Frequently, such lists will not provide alternative dispositions, which will cause the planner to raise more questions and spend more time.

To the extent that the items are listed in the will, their description should be precise enough for an independent person readily to identify the assets. A simple disposition of "Grandmother Montgomery's wedding present" is a sure bet for problems. Other drafting concerns include the possibility that the intended beneficiary will predecease the client, causing anti-lapse problems, or the client will give the property away to another person or sell it prior to death, causing ademption problems.

Incorporation by Reference

Closely allied to the method of listing specific items in the will is the incorporation of an extrinsic document by reference. States treat such documents in three different ways. In some states, the rule of incorporation by reference has not been accepted, since the extrinsic document was not executed with the formalities required of a will and is therefore void as an attempted will substitute. Other states permit extraneous documents to be incorporated in the will by reference, provided the document is referred to in the will, is clearly identified, and is actually in existence at the time that the will is signed. While these requirements are reasonably straightforward, their application is more complicated. The necessity of showing that the document was in existence at the time the will was signed is a frequent problem. Also, the clear identification of the paper or separate writing is subject to challenge. * * *

Finally, some states permit the will to refer to a written statement or a list disposing of items of tangible personal property which are not otherwise specifically disposed of by the will.[16] The separate writing must be signed by the testator and describe the items and beneficiaries with reasonable certainty. Frequently, such a written statement may not dispose of money or property used in a trade or business. Of significance is that the writing may be in existence at the time the will is signed or it may come into existence at a later time. Such a statutory approach permits the testator to easily change the disposition of tangible personal

16. * * * UPC Section 2–513 (1977).

property and avoid the inconvenience of seeing an attorney to have the will changed.

Separate Writing Problems

Considerable caution needs to be exercised when using the separate writing, however. Not only are the problems of precise description more likely to occur when a layperson is describing the items, but also he or she may fail to provide for alternative dispositions. * * *

Additional difficulties may arise with separate writings. The testator may die leaving two (or more) separate writings, neither of which is dated or can be identified as the predecessor by any extrinsic evidence. The dispositions in the separate writings will likely be different and will undoubtedly produce litigation except among the most friendly of beneficiaries.

Since the separate writing does not have the formality of a will, it is much more likely to be lost or destroyed. The testator may inadvertently destroy it, or housekeepers or relatives may inadvertently destroy it. Persons reviewing the separate writing who are dissatisfied with the plan may not realize the dignity to which the statutes give such a separate writing and destroy it.

Finally, the separate writing may dispose of items of tangible personal property having great value. For example, jewelry, paintings or airplanes may all be disposed of by the separate writing. Since the separate writing need not have the formality of witnesses or be dated, considerable problems can arise when items worth substantial sums are disposed of by the decedent on a slip of paper. Where a separate writing is desirable, one solution to the problems encountered with this method is for the estate planner to review the client's first draft. This may provide an opportunity to correct errors and also provide a guide to the client in the future.

SELECTION METHODS

Occasionally, the client will request incorporation of a scheme by which the beneficiaries will have the right to make certain selections. Frequently, this will be done on a rotating basis, typically found where there are several children inheriting the tangible personal property when both parents are deceased. The choosing systems may be as varied as the imagination permits.

Rotation

One common method is to give the eldest child the first right to make a selection of an individual item of tangible personal property, then the next eldest child, and then continuing until all of the children have made a selection. The eldest child will then have the right to make a second selection or, alternatively, the order of selection will reverse and the youngest child will then have the first choice on the second round. While this system may have some appeal to the client, the professional should consider how it is going to work in practice. If there is a significant difference in value among the items, then this scheme may result in an unequal economic distribution. Questions may also arise concerning what items are included in a single choice. Is all of the silver to be included as a single item? What about the crystal where there are tall glasses, short glasses, wine glasses or other glasses all having the same pattern but in distinctive groups? If it is not convenient and feasible to have all of the children present at one time, then this type of round robin can cause an enormous delay in the distribution of the tangibles.

Family Auction

In the family auction method, beneficiaries (typically children) are given the right to spend portions of their inheritances as though it were a real expenditure at an auction in order to acquire items of tangible personal property. For example, assume that a child's share of the residue has a value of $50,000. The child can then use this amount to bid on certain items which he or she most desires. This has the practical effect that the children are most likely to get those items for which they have the strongest preference, since they are voting with dollars. However, placing the children in conflict with each other as they bid for items which have sentimental values far in excess of their dollar values may well seriously injure the family relationship.

Public Auction

Another alternative for the distribution of tangible personal property is the public auction. The property must be of sufficient quality and quantity to merit the expense of time and money involved in the public auction process. Also, if a local auction is impractical or inappropriate, select pieces of special value may need to be handled through a national auction firm.

LETTER OF INSTRUCTIONS

* * * Frequently, one of the best ways to assist a client in the disposition of the tangible personal property is to suggest that the client leave a letter of instruction to the children containing specific suggestions as to allocation of the tangible personal property. A non-binding, informal letter that provides suggestions to the children, with specific allocations of various articles, serves to provide some very real guidance at a time when that guidance is necessary. It can also provide the children with a sense of carrying out the deceased parent's wishes. Since the document is not legally binding, the formalities and the legalities necessary for separate writings noted above are not required. While this is an advantage, it is imperative to point out to the client that such a document does not have the force of law behind it, and the children may choose to vary the suggested plan of disposition.

When neither a spouse nor children survive, the disposition of the tangible personal property can create additional problems. Distribution may be more difficult because the beneficiaries may be unrelated or, if related, they may be so distantly related that the cooperative nature of the family unit is not available. (However, it may also be easier because frequently there is less emotional attachment to a particular item, which can be very much of a problem at the time of the death of a parent, when sensitivities are close to the surface.)

In this case, items of tangible personal property of substantial value should be specifically devised to named individuals. Where the items of tangible personal property are not of substantial monetary value, it may be wise to have most of the tangible personal property specifically bequeathed to a close friend or relative of the decedent; the client should provide a letter of instruction requesting distribution of these items to named individuals. The person entrusted to distribute tangibles to the intended beneficiaries generally may do so with no tax detriment. However, because of gift tax implications, if the tangible personal property will exceed $10,000 per beneficiary, a legally enforceable specific bequest will be a better choice.

A great deal of emphasis is necessary to point out that such a writing would not have the force of law behind it. The writing should be morally persuasive but not create a trust. Since the person to whom this tangible personal property is bequeathed may ignore the request and keep the assets, the decision to use this type of plan of distribution should be undertaken with caution. The client should be absolutely convinced that the individual selected will carry out the dispositive responsibilities in a trustworthy fashion. * * *

SECOND MARRIAGES

Among the special problems which arise is the disposition of tangible personal property owned by a client who has recently married for a second time. Special care is needed in drafting to leave the proper items to the children of the first marriage without leaving the second spouse in an empty home. While there are no simple solutions to this dilemma, one appears to work better than the others.

Generally, the tangible personal property may be divided into two categories. One category is made up of those items which have a very personal family feeling about them. The clients would like to be sure these will pass to the proper family members. Fortunately, these items are usually not numerous. The other category is a broad class of tangible personal property which includes those day-to-day items which are necessary for furnishing the home.

If the clients have a valid prenuptial or postnuptial agreement, then they are presumably free to deal with their tangible personal property as they wish. Thus, each can designate which items of tangible personal property are to go to their respective families. This should be done in writing and should be signed by both of the spouses to indicate a recognition that the items on the list are, in fact, the sole property of the designated spouse. This tangible personal property may be bequeathed to the family members using one of the suggested methods set forth above. The remaining tangible personal property not designated as specifically belonging to either party may be considered joint. Each of the spouses, as a result, can be assured that the specific personal items of tangible personal property will pass to their chosen beneficiaries. At the same time the surviving spouse, with whom they have accumulated possessions over the course of their second marriage, will not be inconvenienced by having the first deceased spouse's children remove everything.

Occasionally, rather than provide for immediate distribution, clients will request that the surviving spouse be given the right to live in the furnished home during the balance of the surviving spouse's life. The estate planner may be asked to create a life estate for the benefit of the surviving spouse upon the death of the first spouse not only in the residence but also in all the furniture and furnishings. A life estate in such items of tangible personal property is impractical, despite its apparent simplicity.

PACKING EXPENSES, ETC.

Regardless of the method of disposition selected, the planner and client should address the problem of who bears the cost of packing, shipping and insuring of the bequeathed items of tangible personal property. It may be argued that the beneficiary receiving the gift should be willing to pay for the cost of receiving it. It may also be argued that the executor has a responsibility to administer and settle an estate, and since it is necessary to deliver the gifts in order to settle the estate, the estate has the responsibility for these costs. In those states where this responsibility is not defined, a specific provision in the will should state who shall bear the cost of packing and shipping in accordance with the testator's wishes. Even in states where the law is settled, it may be desirable to set forth very briefly where the responsibility is to lie, since the responsibility for packing, shipping and insuring estate assets imposed by the statutory or case law of the jurisdiction may not be in accord with the client's wishes, and the client may wish to vary or modify these provisions.

LOCATE

Does your state permit a separate writing to dispose of items of tangible personal property not otherwise provided for in a testator's will? If yes, what are the requirements for the instrument's validity?

NOTES AND QUESTIONS

1. Mr. Berteau emphatically warns against using a provision leaving all property to a surviving spouse because distributions may be deemed taxable income to the spouse. Can you alleviate this problem if your client really wants all personal property to pass to the spouse?

2. Testator's valid will states, "I leave my cedar chest and all of its contents to Beneficiary." Assume that Testator dies owning only one cedar chest so there is no problem ascertaining the bequeathed item. When Testator executed the will, the chest was empty. When Testator died, the chest contained $10,000 in cash, a sealed envelope marked "Testator," a sealed envelope marked "James Picard," and a sealed envelope marked in Testator's own handwriting, "I leave this envelope to Clark Lane." What is the proper distribution of this property?

3. For additional information, see Nancy G. Henderson, *Drafting Dispositive Provisions in Wills (Part 2)*, PRAC. LAW., July 1997, at 15, 25–28.

4. Unlike many testators who are very concerned about the disposition of heirloom items, beneficiaries may not really care. Beneficiaries might rather liquidate the heirlooms and receive cash. Why? See Joyce Cohen, *Heirlooms Get Passed On—To Highest Bidder*, USA TODAY, Aug. 13, 2004, at 5D.

N. CLIENT WITH PROPERTY IN OTHER JURISDICTIONS

1. BASIC RULES

a. Personal Property Succession

"[U]nless changed by statute, it is well settled that movable property, wherever situated, will be distributed as provided by the whole law in force at the place where the decedent was domiciled at the time of his death." PETER HAY, PATRICK J. BORCHERS, SYMEON C. SYMEONIDES, EUGENE F. SCOLES, CONFLICT OF LAWS § 20.3, at 1114 (4th ed. 2004).

b. Real Property Succession

"It is a doctrine firmly established that the law of a state in which the land is situated controls and governs * * * its passage in case of intestacy." Clarke v. Clarke, 178 U.S. 186, 20 S.Ct. 873, 44 L.Ed. 1028 (1900).

c. Testamentary Disposition of Personal Property

"When a person dies leaving movable property in one or more states, and leaves a will directing its disposition, the law of the state of the decedent's domicile at the time of death is of primary importance in deciding questions about the will." PETER HAY, PATRICK J. BORCHERS, SYMEON C. SYMEONIDES, EUGENE F. SCOLES, CONFLICT OF LAWS § 20.9, at 1125 (4th ed. 2004).

d. Testamentary Disposition of Real Property

"The question of the form in which the will must be executed to pass land is determined by the whole law of the situs since the will operates as a conveyance or transfer." Id. § 20.6, at 1118.

UNIFORM PROBATE CODE

1993 Act.

Section 2–506. Choice of Law as to Execution.

A written will is valid if executed in compliance with Section 2–502 or 2–503 or if its execution complies with the law at the time of execution of the place where the will is executed, or of the law of the place where at the time of execution or at the time of death the testator is domiciled, has a place of abode, or is a national.

Comment

This section permits probate of wills in this state under certain conditions even if they are not executed in accordance with the formalities of Section 2–502 or 2–503. Such wills must be in writing but otherwise are valid if they meet the requirements for execution of the law of the place where the will is executed (when it is executed in another state or country) or the law of testator's domicile, abode or nationality at either the time of execution or at the time of death. Thus, if testator is domiciled in state 1 and executes a typed will merely by signing it without witnesses in state 2 while on vacation there, the Court of this state would recognize the will as valid if the law of either state 1 or state 2 permits execution by signature alone. Or if a national of Mexico executes a written will in this state which does not meet the requirements of Section 2–502 but meets the requirements of Mexican law, the will would be recognized as validly executed under this section. The purpose of this section is to provide a wide opportunity for validation of expectations of testators.

LOCATE

Does your state have a savings statute? If yes, how does it operate?

NOTE

See generally G. Warren Whitaker & Michael J. Parets, *My Client Married an Alien: Ten Things Everyone Should Know About International Estate Planning*, PROB. & PROP., Mar./Apr. 2004, at 24.

2. INTERNATIONAL ESTATE PLANNING

STUART B. DORSETT, INTERNATIONAL ESTATE PLANNING: WHAT TO DO WHEN YOUR ESTATE CROSSES THE BORDER*

December 16, 2010.

The term "international estate planning" may conjure up images of offshore trusts in the Cayman Islands or numbered bank accounts in Switzerland, but multi-national tax and fiduciary law issues affect not only ultra-wealthy international jet-setters, but also anyone who is a resident non-citizen, who is married to a non-citizen, or who has property located in more than one country.

There are two basic estate planning issues that need to be addressed if you reside in the United States:

- Planning for distribution of property at death. You should have a Last Will and Testament to direct how your property will be distributed after your death. Alternatively, a Revocable "Living" Trust Agreement may be used for this purpose and has the added benefit of avoiding probate with the Clerk of Court. In either case, the document should (a) designate the individual or corporate fiduciary who will administer your estate or trust after your death, (b) clearly identify the beneficiaries who will receive your property, and (c) include appropriate trust arrangements for any beneficiary who is incompetent or too young to receive property outright.
- Planning for incapacity. You also need to plan for the possibility that you may become incapacitated prior to death. You should have a Durable General Power of Attorney in which a third party (either an individual or a corporate fiduciary) is named as your "attorney-in-fact" to handle your personal and financial affairs in the event you become incapacitated. Similarly, you should have a Health Care Power of Attorney naming one or more trusted individuals to make health care decisions for you if you cannot communicate your intent. You also may want a so-called "Living Will" which expresses your wishes concerning end-of-life decisions.

Although your need for these basic estate planning documents is unaffected by your nationality, certain special considerations apply if you are a foreign national, are married to a foreign national, or have property located in a foreign country:

Non-Tax Considerations in International Estate Planning

If you are a foreign national or you have property located in a foreign country, unique non-tax considerations affecting your estate plan include the following:

- A will or trust prepared under the laws of the United States may not be effective to dispose of your property that is located in another country. Accordingly, if you have such property, you likely will need a will or trust prepared under the laws of that country, particularly if your foreign property consists of real estate.
- You might like to name family members residing in your foreign home country as executor, trustee, or attorney-in-fact under your U.S. estate planning documents. Typically, there are no legal prohibitions on a foreign individual serving in these roles in the United States, but logistical issues and language barriers can make such service impracticable, which amplifies the importance of naming back-up fiduciaries.

- A U.S. court will have initial jurisdiction over the guardianship of minor children and will require a local resident to serve as guardian. While it is possible to transfer guardianship to an individual in another country, the process is not simple and straightforward.

Federal Tax Considerations in International Estate Planning*

If you are a resident non-citizen or a citizen who owns property in another country, you must consider the impact of both U.S. and foreign estate tax laws. An estate tax is a "transfer tax" which taxes the right of a decedent to transfer wealth to other individuals. In the United States, if the tax applies, it is due generally nine months after the date of death.

Three factors control the application of U.S. estate tax laws: citizenship, residency, and situs (or location) of property. U.S. citizens are subject to estate taxation on their property located worldwide, not just their property located in the United States. This worldwide taxation scheme creates a real risk of double taxation, as property located in a foreign country may be subject to the estate tax of both the foreign country and the United States. Although many countries have tax treaties with the United States that avoid double taxation on income, only a few countries have tax treaties that avoid double taxation on estates.

The U.S. estate tax was repealed for the year 2010. However, barring congressional and presidential action prior to January 1, 2011, the federal estate tax will be reinstated automatically on that date. Therefore, as matters stand now, beginning in 2011, three basic estate tax principles will apply for both U.S. citizens and resident non-citizens:

- The unlimited "marital deduction" will allow property to pass to a surviving spouse tax-free. However, this deduction will be available only for spouses who are U.S. citizens. If your spouse is a non-citizen, the marital deduction may be claimed only if the property passes into a Qualified Domestic Trust ("QDOT") with a U.S. trustee. A QDOT will distribute all of its income to your surviving spouse and may permit distributions of its principal to your spouse, but any principal distributions will be subject to federal estate taxation as if the property was part of your taxable estate. At your spouse's subsequent death, all remaining trust property will be subject to estate tax at your tax rate, not your spouse's tax rate.
- The unlimited charitable deduction will avoid taxation on any property passing to a qualified charitable organization. Note, however, that most foreign charitable organizations will not qualify for the charitable deduction.
- The "applicable exclusion amount" will be the amount of property that can pass free of estate tax to all other beneficiaries (regardless of the beneficiaries' domicile or citizenship). Starting in 2011, the exclusion will be $1,000,000 (although it is possible that the Congress that will convene in 2011 will change the exclusion). If the value of all of a decedent's property is above the applicable exclu-

sion amount, the portion of the value above the applicable exclusion amount will be taxed at 55%.

If you are a resident non-citizen, you are subject to the same estate tax rules as U.S. citizens, including taxation on your worldwide property. For purposes of the U.S. estate tax laws, residency means domicile, which is a different, and more subjective, standard than the federal income tax concept of a resident alien. U.S. "domicile" has two components: physical presence in the United States and the intent to remain in the United States indefinitely. Proof of U.S. domicile is fact specific to your particular circumstances and requires a consideration of the following factors:

- Whether your entry into the United States was pursuant to a permanent resident visa;
- Whether you obtained a green card and a social security number;
- The amount and location of your property;
- Whether you have filed tax returns in the United States and/or your home country;
- The amount of your international travel and the duration of your stays in the United States;
- Whether you have obtained a U.S. driver's license;
- The immigration history of your family;
- The size, value, and type of your home in the United States;
- Your motivations for being in the United States; and,
- Your group affiliations and involvement in community affairs.

Federal Estate Tax Planning Techniques for U.S. Citizens and Resident Non–Citizens

If the combined value of your and your spouse's estates will be less than the applicable exclusion amount ($1,000,000 in 2011), you need not be concerned about the effect of U.S. estate tax laws. However, if you are a resident non-citizen, you need to consider whether your home country's estate tax system will be triggered. Similarly, if you are a U.S. citizen who has property located in a foreign country, you need to determine whether such property is subject to taxation by that country.

If your and your spouse's combined estates exceed the applicable exclusion amount, your estate planning documents should create trusts to utilize both spouses' exclusions which, in 2011, will allow a married couple to protect up to $2,000,000 of property from U.S. estate tax. In addition, both individuals and married couples may use lifetime gifts to reduce their taxable estates. Such gifts may utilize an annual exclusion of $13,000 per year per donee and a $1,000,000 lifetime gift tax exemption (for all gifts not qualifying for the annual exclusion), and may take the form of gifts of cash, securities, and real estate, or may be used to fund life insurance policies. Often, irrevocable trusts are used to receive and hold the gifted property.

Federal Estate Tax Planning for Non–Resident Non–Citizens

If you are a non-resident non-citizen ("NRNC"), you are not subject to the U.S. system of estate taxation on your worldwide property. Rather, U.S. estate taxes are imposed only on your property legally located in the United States, including:

- Real estate located in the United States;
- Stock in a U.S. corporation;
- Deposits in U.S. banks;
- Debt obligations of U.S. residents to you;
- Intangible personal property if issued by, or enforceable against, a U.S. resident, a U.S. corporation, or a U.S. governmental unit (but not proceeds from a life insurance policy, even if issued by a U.S. insurance company); and,
- Tangible personal property located in the United States (for example, cars and artwork).

If you are an NRNC, virtually all of your property located in the United States will be subject to federal estate tax at a 55% rate because the available exemption for NRNCs is only $60,000. Accordingly, if you are an NRNC, most estate tax planning techniques will involve the transformation of your U.S. property into foreign property through the use of foreign holding companies, foreign partnerships, foreign trusts, annuities, and life insurance contracts.

Conclusion

In today's global society, international boundaries are blurred more and more on business, financial, and personal levels. As a result, the fiduciary and tax laws of foreign countries impact virtually all individuals with a foreign connection, not just those with large estates. If either you or your spouse is not a U.S. citizen, or if you have property located in a foreign country regardless of your citizenship, you must include consideration of international law in your estate planning if you want the maximum amount of your property to be distributed as you intend after your death.

NOTES AND QUESTIONS

1. For a current list of United States inheritance, estate, and death tax conventions, see JEFFREY A. SCHOENBLUM, MULTISTATE AND MULTINATIONAL ESTATE PLANNING Appendix F (3rd ed. 2006 & most recent Supp.).

2. On August 2, 1991, the United States Senate ratified the Convention Providing a Uniform Law of the Form of an International Will. Federal implementing legislation would enhance the effectiveness of this convention. Has any such legislation been introduced or enacted? Note that, as of the end of 2010, approximately 18 states have enacted the Uniform International Wills Act or its counterpart in the U.P.C. §§ 2–1001 to 2–1010. These states

include: Alaska, California, Colorado, Connecticut, Delaware, District of Columbia, Hawaii, Illinois, Michigan, Minnesota, Montana, New Hampshire, New Mexico, North Dakota, Oklahoma, Oregon, Pennsylvania, and Virginia.

3. The Senate may also consider a 1988 Hague Convention entitled the Law Applicable to Succession to Estates of Deceased Persons which covers intestacy matters. See Jeffrey A. Schoenblum, *Choice of Law and Succession to Wealth: A Critical Analysis of the Ramifications of the Hague Convention on Succession to Decedents' Estates,* 32 VA. J. INT'L L. 83 (1991).

4. For a discussion of the special considerations with respect to Canada, see Wolfe D. Goodman, *Estate Planning Across the Canadian–United States Border,* TR. & EST., Feb. 1993, at 67; Wolfe D. Goodman, *Cross-Border Estate Planning: The Canada–United States Income Tax Convention*, PROB. & PROP., July/Aug. 1996, at 45.

O. CLIENT OWNING A PET ANIMAL

Pet animals play an extremely significant role in the lives of many individuals. People own pets for a variety of reasons—they love animals, they enjoy engaging in physical activity with the animal such as playing ball or going for walks, and they enjoy the giving and receiving of attention and unconditional love. Research indicates that pet ownership positively impacts the owner's life by lowering blood pressure, reducing stress and depression, lowering the risk of heart disease, shortening the recovery time after a hospitalization, and improving concentration and mental attitude. See *A Dog's Life (or Cat's) Could Benefit Your Own*, SAN ANTONIO EXPRESS-NEWS, May 18, 1998, at 1B (explaining how some insurance companies lower life insurance rates for older owners of pets).

Over two-thirds of pet owners treat their animals as members of their families. See Cindy Hall & Suzy Parker, *USA Snapshots—What We Do For Our Pets*, USA TODAY, Oct. 18, 1999, at 1D. Twenty percent of Americans have even altered their romantic relationships over pet disputes. See Andre Mouchard, *Book Prepares Pet Owners For Loss of Their Loved Ones*, SAN JOSE MERCURY NEWS, Mar. 16, 1999, at 2E. Pet owners are extremely devoted to their animal companions with 80% bragging about their pets to others, 79% allowing their pets to sleep in bed with them, 37% carrying pictures of their pets in their wallets, and 31% taking off of work to be with their sick pets. See Hall & Parker, supra. During the December 1999 holiday season, the average pet owner spent $95 on gifts for pets. See Anne R. Carey & Marcy E. Mullins, *USA Snapshots—Surfing For Man's Best Friend*, USA TODAY, Dec. 16, 1999, at B1

The number of individuals who own animals is staggering. As many as 33.9 million households in the United States own dogs and 28.3 million own cats. See Richard Mendelson, *Carving Out Your Niche*, A.B.A. J., May 1997, at 48, 50. In addition to these traditional pets, Americans also own a wide variety of other animals. For example, there are 11 million households with fish, six million with birds, five million with small animals such as hamsters and rabbits, and three million with reptiles. See Gregory

Potts, *Pampered Pets Prove Profitable*, J. REC. (Oklahoma City), July 6, 1999.

The love owners have for their pets transcend death as documented by studies revealing that between 12% and 27% of pet owners include their pets in their wills. The popular media frequently reports cases which involve pet owners who have a strong desire to care for their beloved companions. See Anne R. Carey & Marcy E. Mullins, *USA Snapshots—Man's Best Friend?*, USA TODAY, Dec. 2, 1999, at 1B (12%); Elys A. McLean, *USA Snapshots—Fat Cats—and Dogs*, USA TODAY, June 28, 1993, at 1D (27%); *Vital Statistics*, Health, Oct. 1998, at 16 (18%). Billionaire Leona Helmsley left $12 million in her will to a trust to benefit her white Maltese named Trouble. Singer Dusty Springfield's will made extensive provisions for her cat, Nicholas. The will instructed that Nicholas' bed be lined with Dusty's nightgown, Dusty's recordings be played each night at Nicholas' bedtime, and that Nicholas be fed imported baby food. *Dusty's Cool Fat Cat*, PEOPLE, Apr. 19, 1999, at 11. Doris Duke, the sole heir to Baron Buck Duke who built Duke University and started the American Tobacco Company, left $100,000 in trust for the benefit of her dog. See Walter Scott, *Personality Parade*, PARADE MAG., Sept. 11, 1994, at 2; *In re Estate of Duke*, No. 4440/93, slip op. (N.Y. Sur. Ct. N.Y. County July 31, 1997) (upholding trust and quoting relevant provisions of Duke's will). Natalie Schafer, the actress who portrayed Lovey on the television program *Gilligan's Island*, provided that her fortune be used for the benefit of her dog. See Beverly Williston, *Gilligan's Lovey Leaves It All to Her Dog*, SAN ANTONIO STAR, Apr. 28, 1991, at 5. The wills of well-known individuals who are still alive may also contain pet provisions. For example, actress Betty White is reported as having written a will which leaves her estate estimated at $5 million for the benefit of her pets. See *Betty White Leaves $5M to Her Pets*, SAN ANTONIO STAR, Nov. 4, 1990, at 25. Likewise, Oprah Winfrey's will purportedly mandates that her dog live out his life in luxury. See Janet Charlton, *Star People*, SAN ANTONIO STAR, Mar. 3, 1996, at 2.

Will the legal system permit animal owners to accomplish their goal of providing after-death care for their pets? The common law courts of England looked favorably on gifts to support specific animals. See *In re Dean*, 41 Ch. D. 552 (1889). This approach, however, did not cross the Atlantic. "Historically, the approach of most American courts towards bequests for the care of specific animals has not been calculated to gladden the hearts of animal lovers." Barbara W. Schwartz, *Estate Planning for Animals*, 113 TR. & EST. 376, 376 (1974). Attempted gifts in favor of specific animals usually failed for a variety of reasons such as for being in violation of the rule against perpetuities because the measuring life was not human or for being an unenforceable honorary trust because it lacked a human or legal entity as a beneficiary who would have standing to enforce the trust.

The persuasiveness of these two traditional legal grounds for prohibiting gifts in favor of pet animals is waning under modern law. Courts and legislatures have been increasingly likely to permit such arrangements by applying a variety of techniques and policies. In 1990, the National Conference of Commissioners on Uniform State Laws added a section to the Uniform Probate Code to validate "a trust for the care of a designated domestic or pet animal and the animal's offspring." Unif. Prob. Code § 2–907, cmt. (1990). Likewise, Section 408 of the Uniform Trust Code completed in 2000 provides that a "trust may be created to provide for the care of an animal alive during the settlor's lifetime." Almost all states have adopted one of these uniform provisions or legislation with a similar purpose.

The primary goal of the pet owner's attorney is to carry out the pet owner's intent to the fullest extent allowed under applicable law. Accordingly, the attorney should select a method which has the highest likelihood of working successfully to provide for the pet after its owner's death. (The pet owner should also determine if any special arrangements need to be made to care for the pet if the owner becomes disabled. These instructions may be included in a durable power of attorney.)

I. PREPARE SHORT TERM PLAN

The owner should take four important steps to assure that the animal will receive proper care immediately upon the owner being unable to look after the animal. The owner should carry an "animal card" in the owner's wallet or purse. This card should contain information about the pet such as its name, type of animal, location where housed, and special care instructions along with the information necessary to contact someone who can obtain access to the pet. If the owner is injured or killed, emergency personnel will recognize that an animal is relying on the owner's return for care and may notify the named person or take other steps to locate and provide for the animal. The animal card will help assure that the animal survives to the time when the owner's plans for the pet's long-term care take effect.

Next the owner should prepare an "animal document." The document should contain the same information as on the animal card and perhaps additional details as well. The owner should keep the animal document in the same location where the pet owner keeps his or her estate planning documents. The benefit of this technique is basically the same as for carrying the animal card, that is, an enhanced likelihood that the owner's desires regarding the pet will be made known to the appropriate person in a timely manner.

Third, the owner should provide signage regarding the pets on entrances to the owner's dwelling. These notices will alert individuals entering the house or apartment that pets are inside. The signage is also important during the owner's life to warn others who may enter the dwelling (e.g., police, fire fighters, inspectors, meter readers, friends) about the pets. See M. Keith Branyon, *What Do You Do With Four–Legged Beneficiaries*, STATE BAR OF TEXAS, LEGAL ASSISTANTS DIVISION, LAU SEMINAR (2001). The Humane Society of the United States recommends and supplies self-stick door/window signs for emergency workers and emergency contacts stickers for the inside of the dwelling which provide information about the pet owner, veterinarian, neighbors familiar with the pets, emergency pet caregivers, pet sitters, etc.

Finally, the owner should consider including special instructions pertaining to the pet in the owner's durable power of attorney. These instructions should authorize the agent to care for the pet and to spend the owner's money on the pet's care (day-to-day, veterinarian, etc.). The owner may also wish to grant the agent the power to place the pet with a long-term caregiver. For a sample form drafted to comply with New Hampshire law, see *Durable Power of Attorney for Pet Care*, ElderPet, University of New Hampshire. See also *Providing for Your Pet's Future Without You*, 69 TEX. B.J. 1025 (2006).

II. MAKE CONDITIONAL GIFT TO PET'S CARETAKER, IN TRUST

The most predictable and reliable method to provide for a pet animal is for the owner to create an enforceable inter vivos or testamentary trust in favor of a human beneficiary and then require the trustee to make distributions to the beneficiary to cover the pet's expenses provided the beneficiary is taking proper care of the pet. This technique avoids the two traditional problems with gifts to benefit pet animals. The actual beneficiary is a human and thus there is a beneficiary with standing to enforce the trust and there is a human measuring life for rule against perpetuities purposes. Even if the owner lives in a state which enforces animal trusts, the conditional gift in trust may provide for more flexibility and a greater likelihood of the owner's intent being carried out. For example, some states limit the duration of an animal trust to 21 years. If a long-lived animal is involved, the trust may end before the animal dies.

A wide variety of factors and considerations come into play in drafting a trust to carry out the pet owner's desires.

A. *Determine Whether to Create Inter Vivos or Testamentary Trust*

The pet owner must initially determine whether to create an inter vivos trust or a testamentary trust. An inter vivos trust takes effect immediately and thus will be in operation when the owner dies thereby avoiding the delay between the owner's death and the probating of the will and subsequent functioning of the trust. Funds may not be available to provide the pet with proper care during this delay period. The pet owner can also make changes to the inter vivos trust more easily than to a testamentary trust which requires the execution of a new will or codicil.

On the other hand, the inter vivos trust may have additional start-up costs and administration expenses. A separate trust document would be needed and the owner would have to part with property to fund the trust. The inter vivos trust, could, however, be nominally funded and revocable. Additional funding could be tied to a nonprobate asset, such as a bank account naming the trustee (in trust) as the pay on death payee or a life insurance policy naming the trustee (in trust) as the beneficiary, to provide the trust with immediate funds after the owner's death. If appropriate, the pet owner could provide additional property by using a pour over provision in the owner's will.

B. Designate Trust Beneficiary/Animal Caretaker

The pet owner must thoughtfully select a caretaker for the animal. This person becomes the actual beneficiary of the trust who has standing to enforce the trust if the trustee fails to carry out its terms. Thus, the caretaker should be sufficiently savvy to understand the basic functioning of a trust and his or her enforcement rights.

It is of utmost importance for the pet owner to locate a beneficiary/caretaker who is willing and able to care for the animal in a manner that the owner would find acceptable. The prospective caretaker should be questioned before being named to make certain the caretaker will assume the potentially burdensome obligation of caring for the pet, especially when the pet is in need of medical care or requires special attention as it ages. The pet and the prospective caretaker should meet and spend quality time together to make sure they, and the caretaker's family, get along harmoniously with each other.

The pet owner should name several alternate caretakers should the owner's first choice be unable to serve for the duration of the pet's life. To prevent the pet from ending up homeless, the owner may authorize the trustee to select a good home for the pet should none of the named individuals be willing or able to accept the animal. The trustee should not, however, have the authority to appoint him-or herself as the caretaker as such an appointment would eliminate the checks and balances aspect of separating the caregiver from the money provider.

C. Nominate Trustee

As with the designation of the caretaker, the pet owner needs to select the trustee with care and check with the trustee before making a nomination. The trustee, whether individual or corporate, must be willing to administer the property for the benefit of the animal and to expend the time and effort necessary to deal with trust administration matters. If the pet owner has sufficient funds, a stipend for the trustee may be appropriate. The pet owner should name alternate trustees should the named trustee be unable to serve until the trust terminates. In addition, an alternate trustee may have standing to remove the original trustee from office should the original trustee cease to administer the trust for the benefit of the pet.

D. Bequeath Animal to Trustee, in Trust

The pet owner should bequeath the animal to the trustee, in trust, with directions to deliver custody of the pet to the beneficiary/caretaker. If the owner has left animal instructions in an animal card or document, the animal may actually already be in the possession of the caretaker.

E. *Determine Amount of Other Property to Transfer to Trust*

The pet owner should carefully compute the amount of property necessary to care for the animal and to provide additional payments, if any, for the caretaker and the trustee. Many factors will go into this decision such as the type of animal, the animal's life expectancy, the standard of living the owner wishes to provide for the animal, and the need for potentially expensive medical treatment. Adequate funds should also be included to provide the animal with proper care, be it an animal-sitter or a professional boarding business, when the caretaker is an vacation, out-of-town on business, receiving care in a hospital, or is otherwise temporarily unable to personally provide for the animal.

The size of the owner's estate must also be considered. If the owner's estate is relatively large, the owner could transfer sufficient property so the trustee could make payments primarily from the income and use the principal only for emergencies. On the other hand, if the owner's estate is small, the owner may wish to transfer a lesser amount and anticipate that the trustee will supplement income with principal invasions as necessary.

The pet owner must avoid transferring an unreasonably large amount of money or other property to the trust because such a gift is likely to encourage heirs and remainder beneficiaries of the owner's will to contest the arrangement. The pet owner should determine the amount which is reasonable for the care of the animals and fund the trust accordingly. Even if the owner has no desire to benefit family members, friends, or charities until the demise of the animal, the owner should not leave his or her entire estate for the animal's benefit. If the amount of property left to the trust is unreasonably large, the court may reduce the amount to what it considers to be a reasonable amount. See, e.g., *Templeton Estate*, 4 Fiduciary 2d 172, 175 (Pa. Orphans' Ct. 1984) (applying "inherent power to reduce the amount involved ... to an amount which is sufficient to accomplish [the owner's] purpose"); *Lyon Estate*, 67 Pa. D. & C. 2d 474, 482–83 (Orphan's Ct. 1974) (reducing the amount left for the animal's care based on the supposition that the owner mistook how much money would be needed to care for the animals). Cf. Unif. Prob. Code § 2–907(c)(6) (1993) (authorizing the court to reduce amount if it "substantially exceeds the amount required" to care for the animal).

F. *Describe Desired Standard of Living*

The owner should specify the type of care the beneficiary is to give the animal and the expenses for which the caretaker can expect reimbursement from the trust. Typical expenses would include food, housing, grooming, medical care, and burial or cremation fees. The pet owner may also want to include more detailed instructions. Alternatively, the owner may leave the specifics of the type of care to the discretion of the trustee. If the pet owner elects to do so, the pet owner should seriously consider providing the caretaker with general guidelines to both (1) avoid claims that the caretaker is expending an unreasonable amount on the animal and (2) prevent the caretaker from expending excessive funds. For example, in the case of *In re Rogers*, 100 Ariz. 214, 412 P.2d 710, 710–11 (1966), the court determined that the caretaker was acting in an unreasonable manner when he purchased an automobile to transport the dog while stating that it was a matter of opinion whether the purchase of a washing machine to launder the dog's bed clothing was reasonable.

G. Specify Distribution Method

The owner should specify how the trustee is to make disbursements from the trust. The simplest method is for the owner to direct the trustee to pay the caretaker a fixed sum each month regardless of the actual care expenses. If the care expenses are less than the distribution, the caretaker enjoys a windfall for his or her efforts. If the care expenses are greater than the distribution, the caretaker absorbs the cost. The caretaker may, however, be unable or unwilling to make expenditures in excess of the fixed distribution that are necessary for the animal. Thus, the owner should permit the trustee to reimburse the caretaker for out-of-pocket expenses exceeding the normal distribution.

Alternatively, the owner could provide only for reimbursement of expenses. The caretaker would submit receipts for expenses associated with the animal on a periodic basis. The trustee would review the expenses in light of the level of care the pet owner specified and reimburse the caretaker if the expenses are appropriate. Although this method may be in line with the owner's intent, the pet owner must realize that there will be additional administrative costs and an increased burden on the caretaker to retain and submit receipts.

H. Establish Additional Distributions for Caretaker

The owner should determine whether the trustee should make distributions to the caretaker above and beyond the amount established for the animal's care. An owner may believe that the addition of the animal to the caretaker's family is sufficient, especially if the trustee will reimburse the caretaker for all reasonable care expenses. On the other hand, the animal may impose a burden on the caretaker and thus additional distributions may be appropriate to encourage the caretaker to continue as the trust's beneficiary. In addition, the caretaker may feel more duty bound to provide good care if the caretaker is receiving additional distributions contingent on providing the animal with appropriate care.

I. Limit Duration of Trust

The duration of the trust should not be linked to the life of the pet. The measuring life of a trust must be a human being unless state law has enacted specific statutes for animal trusts or has modified or abolished the rule against perpetuities. For example, the pet owner could establish the trust's duration as 21 years beyond the life of the named caretakers and trustees with the possibility of the trust ending sooner if the pet dies within the 21 year period.

J. Designate Remainder Beneficiary

The pet owner should clearly designate a remainder beneficiary to take any remaining trust property upon the death of the pet. Otherwise, court involvement will be necessary with the most likely result being a resulting trust for the benefit of the owner's successor's in interest. See *Willett v. Willett*, 197 Ky. 663, 247 S.W. 739, 741 (1923) (noticing that the pet owner neglected to provide for the distribution of the remaining trust property upon the pet's death and thus the property would pass through intestate succession). The pet owner must be cautioned not to leave the remaining trust property to the caretaker because the caretaker would then lack a financial motive to care for the animal and thus might accelerate its death to gain immediate access to the trust corpus. The pet owner may also want to authorize the trustee to terminate the trust before the pet's death "if the remaining principal is small and suitable arrangements have been made for the care of the animals." Frances Carlisle & Paul Franken, *Drafting Trusts for Animals*, N.Y. L.J., Nov. 13, 1997, at 1.

The pet owner may wish to consider naming a charity which benefits animals as the remainder beneficiary. "Hopefully the charity would want to assure the well-being of the animals and an added advantage is that the Attorney General would be involved to investigate if any misappropriation of funds by the trustee occurred." Id. The pet owner must precisely state the legal name and location of the intended charitable beneficiary so the trustee will not have difficulty ascertaining the appropriate recipient of the remainder gift.

K. Identify Animal to Prevent Fraud

The pet owner should clearly identify the animal which is to receive care under the trust. If this step is not taken, an unscrupulous caretaker could replace a deceased, lost, or stolen animal with a replacement so that the caretaker may continue to receive benefits. For example, there is a report that "[a] trust was established for a black cat to be cared for by its deceased owner's maid. Inconsistencies in the reported age of the pet tipped off authorities to fact that the maid was on her third black cat, the original long since having died." Torri Still, *This Attorney is for the Birds*, RECORDER (San Francisco), at 4 (Mar. 22, 1999).

The pet owner may use a variety of methods to identify the animal. A relatively simple and inexpensive method is for the trust to contain a detailed description of the animal including any unique characteristics such blotches of colored fur and scars. Veterinarian records and pictures of the animal would also be helpful. A professional could tattoo the pet with an alpha-numeric identifier. A tattoo, however, could later cause problems for the pet because a pet thief could mutilate the pet to remove the tattoo, such as cutting off an ear or leg, if the pet's primary function is breeding. A more sophisticated procedure is for the pet owner to have a microchip implanted in the animal. The trustee can then have the animal scanned to verify that the animal the caretaker is minding is the same animal. Of course, an enterprising caretaker could surgically remove the microchip and have it implanted in another physically similar animal. The best, albeit expensive, method to assure identification is for the trustee to retain a sample of the animal's DNA before turning the animal over to the caretaker and then to run periodic comparisons between the retained sample and new samples from the animal.

A pet owner, however, may be less concerned with providing for the animals owned at the time of will execution, but rather wants to arrange for the care of the animals actually owned at time of death. "It would be onerous for [the owner] to execute a new trust instrument or will whenever a new animal joins the family." Carlisle & Franken, at 1. In this situation, the owner may wish to describe the animals as a class instead of by individual name or specific description.

L. Require Trustee to Inspect Animal on Regular Basis

The owner should require the trustee to make regular inspections of the animal to determine its physical and psychological condition. T he inspections should be at random times so the caretaker does not provide the animal with extra food, medical care, or attention merely because the caretaker knows the trustee is coming. The inspections should take place in the caretaker's home so the trustee may observe first-hand the environment in which the animal is being kept.

M. Provide Instructions for Final Disposition of Animal

The pet owner should include instructions for the final disposition of the animal when the animal dies. The will of one pet owner is reported as containing the following provision: "[U]pon the death of my pets they are to be embalmed and their caskets to be placed in a Wilbert Vault at Pine Ridge Cemetery." *The Last Laugh—Wills With a Sense of Humor*, FAM. ADVOC., Summer 1981, at 60, 62. The owner may want the animal to be buried in a pet cemetery or cremated with the ashes either distributed or placed in an urn. The cost for a pet burial ranges from $250 to $1,000 while pet cremations are significantly less expensive. A memorial for the pet may also be created for viewing on a variety of Internet sites.

III. CONSIDER OUTRIGHT CONDITIONAL GIFT

An outright gift of the animal coupled with a reasonable sum to care for the animal which is conditioned on the beneficiary taking proper care of the animal is a simpler but less predictable method. Both drafting and administrative costs may be reduced if the owner does not create a trust. Only if the pet owner's estate is relatively modest, should this technique be considered because there is a reduced likelihood of the owner's intent being fulfilled because there is no person directly charged with ascertaining that the animal is receiving proper care. Although the owner may designate a person to receive the property if the pet is not receiving proper care, such person might not police the caretaker sufficiently, especially if the potential gift-over amount is small or the alternate taker does not live close enough to the caretaker to make first-hand observations of the animal.

If the owner elects this method, the owner needs to decide if the condition of taking care of the pet is a condition precedent or a condition subsequent. If the owner elects a condition precedent, the caretaker receives the property only if the caretaker actually cares for the animal. Thus, if the animal were to predecease the owner, the caretaker would not benefit from the gift. On the other hand, the owner could create a condition subsequent so that the gift vests in the caretaker and is only divested if the caretaker fails to provide proper care. The owner should expressly state what happens to the gift if the pet predeceases its owner. In the absence of express language, the caretaker would still receive a condition subsequent gift but not one based on a condition precedent. See *In re Andrews's Will*, 34 Misc.2d 432, 228 N.Y.S.2d 591, 594 (Sur. Ct. 1962) (holding that the beneficiary received the legacy even though the pet died before the testator because the condition was subsequent).

IV. FOLLOW APPLICABLE STATUTE, IF ANY

If the pet owner is domiciled in a state with a statute authorizing the creation of enforceable trusts for animals, as compared to states whose statutes merely authorize such arrangements, the owner may desire to create an enforceable trust under the statute rather than using the conditional gift technique. Although the exact concerns will depend on the particular statute involved, many considerations will be the same as those for the conditional gift method. The effectiveness of this technique may be compromised if after executing the will, the pet owner moves and then dies domiciled in another state which does not have a similar statute.

V. CONSIDER OUTRIGHT GIFT TO VETERINARIAN OR ANIMAL SHELTER

A simple option available to the pet owner is to leave the pet and sufficient property for its care to a veterinarian or animal shelter. This alternative will not, however, appeal to most pet owners who do not like the idea of the pet living out its life in a clinic or shelter setting. The animal would no longer be part of a family and is not likely to receive the amount and quality of special attention that the pet would receive in a traditional home. Nonetheless, this option may be desirable if the owner is unable to locate an appropriate caretaker for the animal.

VI. CONSIDER GIFT TO LIFE CARE CENTER

In exchange for an inter vivos or testamentary gift, various organizations promise to provide care for an animal for the remainder of the animal's life. The amount of the payment often depends on the type of animal, age of animal, and age of pet owner. One of the nation's most notable life care centers is the Stevenson Companion Animal Life–Care Center located at Texas A & M University.

VII. AVOID HONORARY TRUSTS

Pet owners should avoid honorary trusts and related techniques be they judicially or statutorily authorized. If state law validates trusts for specific animals by using the honorary trust doctrine, the trustee will be permitted to carry out the owner's intent and provide care for the pet. The owner's heirs and beneficiaries would probably be unable to successfully contest the trustee's use of the property for the pet. However, the trustee cannot be forced to use the property for the pet because honorary trusts are unenforceable. If the trustee refuses to carry out the pet owner's intent, the trust property simply passes to the remainder beneficiaries or the owner's successors in interest. The owner's desire to care for the animal may go unsatisfied. In addition, the income tax ramifications of honorary trusts may not be as favorable as other arrangements. See Rev. Rul. 76–486, 1976–2 C.B. 192 (explaining income tax treatment of income earned by trusts for pet animals).

LOCATE

What is the law of your state regarding gifts to pet animals?

NOTES AND QUESTIONS

1. Family members and friends can be a source of tremendous support but they may also let you down in a variety of ways ranging from minor betrayals to orchestrating your own death. Pet animals, however, have a much better track record in providing unconditional love and steadfast loyalty. It is not surprising that a pet owner often wants to assure that his or her trusted companion is well-cared for after the owner's death.

2. For a detailed treatment of estate planning to provide for pet animals, see Gerry W. Beyer, *Pet Animals—What Happens When Their Humans Die?*, 40 SANTA CLARA L. REV. 617 (2000), from which portions of this section are adapted. See also BARRY SELTZER & GERRY W. BEYER, FAT CATS & LUCKY DOGS: HOW TO LEAVE (SOME OF) YOUR ESTATE TO YOUR PET (2010) and http://www.professorbeyer.com/Articles/Animals.html.

P. CLIENT WITH DESIRE TO REGULATE SURVIVOR'S CONDUCT

GERRY W. BEYER AND STEVEN F. CARVEL, MANIPULATING THE CONDUCT OF BENEFICIARIES WITH CONDITIONAL GIFTS

EST. PLAN. DEV. TEX. PROF., June 2001, at 1.

We may preserve and transfer the fruits of lifelong struggle as we see fit to those we select. Though not constitutionally provided, this privilege, often mistaken as a right, is taken for granted. Indeed, to proclaim otherwise would threaten the western ideal of a productive way of life. If upon death, the yield of a life of labor could not pass to our survivors as we see fit, any surplus would be of no use in securing a better life for our family and friends. This would create no incentive for industriousness beyond present need. As a result, the ability to transfer property at death and prescribe the terms upon which it should be enjoyed is recognized by law. Further, this privilege of free testation is proclaimed to be almost inseparable from the American concept of property ownership. Free testation, though long established, may be compromised when donors place conditions upon their gifts.

Some conditions are relatively benign such as a provision requiring property to be held in trust until the beneficiary reaches a specified age. However, testators and settlors may use conditions to control or influence nuances of the beneficiary's behavior. For example, a testator left his house and $30,000 to his wife on the condition that she smoke five cigarettes per day for the rest of her life to get even for her disdain of his practice. See *Widow Fumes at Order to Start Smoking*, San Antonio Express–News, Sept. 10, 1993, at 6A. Will the court force a beneficiary to engage in a dangerous habit to receive the property? If not, would the wife get the property free of the condition or would the property pass under other provisions of the testator's will? What about a will provision providing $500 per month for the police officer who gives the most traffic tickets to motorists for double-parking? *Dead Man Had Will, Way to Get Double–Parkers*, Wash. Post, Aug. 25, 1998, at A2. This article explores conditional gifts and focuses on how to increase the likelihood that the court will enforce the conditions.

A. Forces acting against conditional gifts

The testator may condition a specified gift on the occurrence or non-occurrence of a stated event, the conduct of the beneficiary, or the truth of a given statement. Conditional gifts are generally upheld unless they are against public policy or violate some rule of law. See *In re Kasschau*, 11 S.W.3d 305 (Tex. App.—Houston [14th Dist.] 1999, no writ). Many forces may act to make the enforcement of a conditional gift problematic.

1. Illegality

Courts do not enforce provisions that require the beneficiary to take illegal action as a condition to receiving a benefit. Some courts set such conditions aside and allow the beneficiary to take the gift as if the condition did not exist while other courts simply void the gift and return the benefit to the donor or the donor's successors in interest. The same holds true for conditions that are deemed to be unconstitutional.

2. Violation of Public Policy

Public policy dictates that courts cannot enforce provisions in wills and trust that injure the public at large or have the potential to do so. Many conditions that are not illegal per se are invalidated on public policy grounds as such provisions may be deleterious to the public welfare. Courts may also use public policy arguments to justify invalidating provisions when they can find no settled reason, other than that such provisions are manifestly unfair or unreasonable.

3. Insufficiency in Drafting

For a condition to be upheld by a court, not only must the will or trust demonstrate the donor's intent to create a conditional gift, but the instrument should also demonstrate "proper" intent. In addition, though a particular condition may arguably violate public policy, it could still be upheld based on the finding of "good" intent. For example, a court upheld a condition providing for the support of the testator's daughter if she became divorced or outlived her husband. *Hunt v. Carroll*, 157 S.W.2d 429 (Tex. Civ. App.—Beaumont 1941, writ dism'd). Arguably the condition is against public policy because it provides for a benefit upon divorce or survival of a spouse, both of which could result from behavior that society seeks to discourage. However, because the donor's intent was to provide support for the beneficiary if the beneficiary found herself without the support of a spouse, the court upheld the provision. Accordingly, an effective conditional provision must clearly demonstrate the donor's admirable intent although the condition could be subject to a contrary interpretation.

Courts look unfavorably on a condition when the donor does not provide a consequence for an unsatisfied condition. Courts may construe the failure of the donor to consider the ramifications of an unsatisfied condition as reflecting a lack of true intent for the gift to be unsuccessful if the condition is not met. Courts may set aside provisions that do not provide an adequate consequence, such as a gift over or the return of the property to the donor's estate, and allow the beneficiary to take as if the condition never existed.

Courts have a hierarchy of favoritism regarding the particular phrasing of conditions in terms of the condition's potential influence and effect on a beneficiary. Conditions that do not exert a strong continuing influence, that is, ones that are unlikely to influence a beneficiary's behavior past the point in time the benefit is initially disclosed, are not seen as having the potentially unreasonable effect of causing a person to continually alter his or her behavior. As a result, these conditions stand a better chance of being upheld.

A condition precedent is one upon which the vesting of the estate is contingent. *Deviney v. NationsBank*, 993 S.W.2d 443 (Tex. App.—Waco 1999, pet. denied). Stated another way, a condition precedent is an event that must occur before the beneficiary can receive the benefit. For example, a provision providing for a gift to a daughter if she is married at the time of the donor's death is a condition precedent. If the daughter is indeed married, the condition will be satisfied. The condition precedent must be measured as of a certain date. Additionally, because many beneficiaries find out about a condition precedent only after the time at which satisfaction of the condition is determined, i.e., at the execution of the will or death of the donor, such a provision cannot influence a beneficiary's future behavior. A condition precedent is favored because courts see it as not exerting a continuing influence on the beneficiary.

A condition subsequent is a condition that, if it occurs, divests the beneficiary of a benefit already received. *Deviney v. NationsBank*, 993 S.W.2d 443 (Tex. App.—Waco 1999, pet. denied). An example of a condition subsequent is a devise of property to a son "so long as alcohol is not consumed on the premises, but if alcohol is sold, my heirs may reenter and terminate the estate." If the son were to hold a wine tasting event on the premises, then he would lose his benefit. Because the beneficiary has already received the benefit, the fear of losing this benefit is likely to provide strong motivation to comply with the condition. For this reason, courts view the condition subsequent as exerting a strong continuing influence and are more likely to strike such a provision because of its possible perverse influence.

B. Types of conditions

1. Restraints on marriage

Marriage is often seen as the foundation of the family unit and therefore one of the pillars upon which our society is based. Because of the importance of marriage, Texas courts generally have found restraints on marriage unenforceable whether resulting from a promise not to marry or a condition forfeiting rights in case of marriage. See *Southwestern Bell Tel. Co. v. Gravitt*, 551 S.W.2d 421 (Tex. Civ. App.—San Antonio 1976, writ denied). Further, the United States Supreme Court has found marriage to be a constitutional right as an aspect of liberty protected by the Due Process Clause of the Constitution. *Zablocki v. Redhail*, 343 U.S. 374 (1978). Any limitation on the right to marry would seem unconstitutional and therefore unenforceable by courts, as the government actors enforcing provisions in wills and trusts. Interestingly, in spite of these policies, some conditional limitations on marriage, especially those where the dominant motive is to provide support for an unmarried or suddenly separated, divorced, or single-by-death beneficiary, are upheld.

Provisions providing for no benefit should a beneficiary marry for the first time, though seemingly in violation of public policy, are upheld in a majority of jurisdictions, including Texas. See *Hunt v. Carroll*, 157 S.W.2d 429 (Tex. Civ. App.—Beaumont 1941, writ dism'd). Usually decisions supporting such conditions are based on the donor's intent not violating public policy. The testator usually intends to provide support for the beneficiary until such beneficiary finds a spouse to support him or her. Many times this type of condition is not meant as an impediment to marriage, though logically, if the benefit of receipt outweighs the benefit of marriage, the condition may quickly become an impediment to marriage. While not an enlightened view of marriage, the courts may still uphold such provisions.

Conditions requiring a beneficiary to marry within a particular category of individuals based on religion, ethnicity, or some other easily recognized delineation are generally upheld. Courts usually apply a reasonableness analysis based on the effect the provision has on the available "pool" of potential mates and the size of the pool remaining after the condition takes effect. Generally speaking, as the pool of potential candidates grows smaller, the provision's risks becoming unreasonable and therefore invalid. See *In re Rosenthal's Will*, 127 N.Y.S.2d 778 (N.Y. App. Div. 1954).

Slightly reducing the pool of potential mates is reasonable because a sufficient number of satisfactory candidates for marriage remain. For example, former vice-presidential candidate Joseph Lieberman was asked to administer an uncle's will that contained provisions discussing the disinheritance of two beneficiaries for marrying outside the Jewish faith. Phil Kuntz & Bob Davis, *A Beloved Uncle's Will Tests Diplomatic Skills of Joseph Lieberman*, Wall St. J., Aug. 25, 2000, at A1. These conditions would likely be valid. The reasoning of courts upholding provisions restricting "some" marriages is that the restraint is narrow and reasonable because it leaves an ample pool of acceptable partners. See *In re Rosenthal's Will*, 127 N.Y.S.2d 778 (N.Y. App. Div. 1954). This same reasoning holds true if a particular person is excluded, as there are many other potential candidates in the remaining pool. *Id.*

If a provision greatly reduces the number of potential candidates remaining in the pool, the provision is unreasonable because it becomes more and more unlikely that a suitable partner remains in the pool. If the condition permits marriage only to a single named individual, the restraint narrows the pool of prospective partners greatly. Accordingly, courts treat the condition as a general restraint on marriage and usually refuse to enforce the condition.

Provisions providing for benefit only if a marriage occurs after a certain designated age, in an attempt to prevent marriage until a certain maturity level is reached, are considered valid. Courts usually find that these provisions do not prevent marriage, but instead seek to protect the beneficiary from making a hasty or imprudent decision to marry at a young age.

Provisions requiring that a beneficiary not marry until a very high age, seventy for example, present a unique facet to the issue. Courts would likely find such a high age requirement to be of unreasonable duration, as it would continue throughout most of a person's life. Such a provision also unreasonably reduces the potential partners in two ways. First, many potential partners of similar age would likely already be married or perhaps disinterested in marriage. Second, the number of non age-appropriate partners (those willing to marry outside their own age group) is proportionately quite small in the absence of other motivating factors.

Provisions requiring the consent of a designee before marriage, such as requiring parental consent, have been found to be valid. See *Pacholder v. Rosenheim*, 99 A.2d 672 (Md. 1916). As with the requirement of attaining a certain age, such conditions protect the beneficiary from hasty decision-making. The donor should name a designee who has no financial stake in the outcome. The designee's decision can be based on criteria established by the donor or it may be left up to the designee's personal discretion.

A provision requiring marriage as a condition to receiving a benefit is unlikely to be struck down because it fosters what courts consider to be a useful purpose. (Unless perhaps, it is phrased as follows, "I leave my estate to my spouse on the condition that my spouse remarries, so there will be at least one person who regrets my death.") Courts consider that such a provision has the effect of inducing an act beneficial to society. This type of provision is generally meant to provide support in the event of marriage and possibly to increase the attractiveness of a beneficiary to a potential spouse. Arguably, such a provision may induce imprudent decision-making on the part of the beneficiary, such as getting married only to receive the benefit. In addition, it is important to indicate the number of times the beneficiary may get married to receive a distribution. In one case, the settlor instructed the trustee to pay the beneficiary $250,000 when he got married; he got married 13 times. J. Peder Zane, *Six Feet Under and Overbearing*, N.Y. Times, Mar. 12, 1995, § 4, at 5.

Provisions requiring a person to remain married to his or her original spouse are often struck down. The requirement that a beneficiary remain in an untenable relationship has, from early case law, been found to be repugnant and against public policy. *Knost v. Knost*, 129 S.W. 665 (Mo. Ct. App. 1910).

A provision requiring that a beneficiary be married at the time of a donor's death is merely a fact whose existence is determined at a particular time. Courts reason that a beneficiary is unlikely to be aware of such a provision and therefore there is no influence of a potential beneficiary's actions. *Foote v. Foote*, 76 S.W.2d 194 (Tex. Civ. App.—San Antonio 1934, writ ref'd). Provisions of this type are generally found to be reasonable when phrased appropriately as a condition precedent rather than a condition subsequent, therefore lessening the continuing influence of the testator on the beneficiary.

In Texas and a majority of jurisdictions, conditions divesting a beneficiary of a gift when the beneficiary remarries have been upheld. In Texas, such a provision has been recognized as early as 1858. *Little v. Birdwell*, 21 Tex. 597 (1858). Because one marriage has already taken place, reasonableness standards regarding general restraints do not apply. See *Haring v. Shelton*, 114 S.W. 389 (Tex. Civ. App.—Houston 1908, writ denied). Also, a testator's desire to compel fidelity to the former relationship has been considered valid. See *In re Lambert's Estate*, 46 N.Y.S.2d 905 (N.Y. App. Div. 1944). However, perhaps the most compelling reason is the intent to provide for the offspring of the original marriage between the donor and the beneficiary. See *Haring v. Shelton*, 114 S.W. 389 (Tex. Civ. App.—Houston 1908, writ denied). If the spouse remarries, it is likely that assets derived from the first marriage may be used for the benefit of persons arising outside of the original marriage. Further, it is likely that the fruits of the first marriage may pass by gift or intestacy to offspring of a second marriage. Courts have considered the contemplation of these occurrences as valid reasons to uphold conditions preventing the remarriage of a spouse. *Foote v. Foote*, 76 S.W.2d 194 (Tex. Civ. App.—San Antonio 1934, rehearing denied).

2. Conditions encouraging divorce or separation

As a general rule, conditions that a beneficiary must be divorced to receive a benefit have been found to be contrary to public policy. Courts, recognizing the importance of the family unit in an organized, harmonious society, seek to protect the familial bond from injurious outside influences. In Texas, however, a provision requiring divorce as a precursor to receipt of a benefit was upheld where the testator's dominant motive was to provide support for the beneficiary if the beneficiary became divorced or widowed. *Hunt v. Carroll*, 157 S.W.2d 429 (Tex. Civ. App.—Beaumont 1941, writ ref'd). When deviating from the norm, it is necessary that proper intent, i.e., the intent to provide support if the beneficiary loses the support of a spouse, be shown and that the provision be drafted carefully to demonstrate this good intent.

A provision in a will requiring the death or demise of a beneficiary's spouse to receive a benefit could conceivably be invalidated. Such a provision, arguably encouraging the hastening of a spouse's demise, would be against public policy as well as void for illegality. However, Texas courts have upheld the condition based on a finding that the donor's intent was shown to provide for a beneficiary outliving a spouse instead of becoming destitute upon losing the support of the spouse. *Ellis v. Birkhead*, 71 S.W. 31 (Tex. Civ. App. 1902, writ ref'd).

For a provision requiring a beneficiary to cease to support or live with spouse to be upheld, it would likely require careful drafting coupled with clearly communicated intent to provide support should the beneficiary happen to end a relationship with a spouse.

3. Conditions involving religion

As might be expected, attempts to influence a beneficiary's choice of religion are fairly common. These provisions often run afoul of constitutional rights, namely the freedom of religion.

The rights to freedom of religion and to be free from religious persecution are tenets upon which our nation is founded. Accordingly, conditions attempting to limit a person's freedom of religion, a fundamental constitutional right, are generally not upheld.

Requirements that a child be raised in a particular faith have been upheld though they may be contested on the grounds of interference with freedom of religion. Courts upholding such provisions cite a child's ability to choose his or her own religion when old enough to make an informed decision. See *In re Estate of Laning*, 339 A.2d 520 (N.J. Sup. Ct. App. Div. 1975).

4. Conditions involving behavior

Another major area where a donor attempts to control the actions of beneficiaries is that of personal behavior. Often such conditions are intended to correct some unacceptable trait or prevent the occurrence of some proscribed act. However, this is not always the case. Some donors attempt to force beneficiaries to behave in ways they would not ordinarily act. Remember the earlier example requiring a beneficiary to smoke five cigarettes a day as a condition to a gift. In Texas and a majority of jurisdictions, such provisions regarding behavior, provided they are not illegal, in violation of public policy, or immoral, are upheld as within a donor's right. See Paul A. Meints, *Value-Based Estate Planning: Using Trusts to Promote and Reward Behavior*, 87 Ill. B.J. 138 (1999).

A condition that a beneficiary be drug or alcohol free is a frequent modern condition. It is well settled in a majority of jurisdictions that such provisions are valid because they not only promote public policy, but also operate for the welfare of the beneficiary, which is within the donor's prerogative.

A condition that a beneficiary not be involved in criminal activity would likely be upheld because it promotes public policy and public welfare.

The requirement that a beneficiary attain a certain level of education is common in modern will and trust provisions. Again, such provisions promote public policy and public welfare because society encourages education and productivity.

Requirements of attaining a certain age, and hopefully commensurate maturity, before receiving a benefit are also common and generally upheld. Immature beneficiaries often squander gifts due to lack of the sophistication and responsibility which usually comes with age. However, if the prescribed age is high, seventy-five, for example, courts might invalidate the restriction as operating for an unreasonable duration. Of course, the evidence may show that the donor's intent was to provide for a donee in old age.

5. Other personal conduct

Courts have not established bright line rules regarding differing attempts by donors to influence the conduct of beneficiaries. These conditions must be evaluated on a case by case basis.

A Texas court invalidated a clause in a will providing that a the gift would revert to others if the beneficiary gave any portion of the gift to certain named relatives. *Barmore v. Darragh*, 231 S.W. 472 (Tex. Civ. App.—Austin 1921), rev'd on other grounds, 242 S.W. 714 (Tex. Com. App. 1922). The court cited the importance of communication among family members as sufficient public policy on which to invalidate the clause.

A Texas court determined that a condition requiring that a beneficiary not join the military was within the prerogative of the donor to promote the welfare of the beneficiary. *Van Hoose v. Moore*, 441 S.W.2d 597 (Tex. Civ. App.—Amarillo 1969, writ ref'd n.r.e.).

A provision requiring a beneficiary to assume or carry on a family name has been found valid in a number of states. While not specifically addressed in Texas, other jurisdictions have found such a provision to be within the testator's right to attach any lawful conditions to a gift.

6. Character

Benefits conditioned upon subjective standards as "good character" have a greater chance of being upheld if the donor appoints a neutral and detached designee to make a determination of the satisfaction of a condition. Failure to provide standards or appoint a designee whose discretion is to be used may invalidate the condition as being too vague to enforce.

7. Residence

Provisions prescribing the location of a residence often involve minor beneficiaries who have been orphaned. In such instances, a condition requiring a minor beneficiary to reside with certain relatives should they become orphaned is likely to be upheld. Alternatively, provisions dictating the residence of adult beneficiaries may be found to violate the constitutionally recognized right to travel.

A provision requiring a child to live with a person other than a surviving parent is likely to be found contrary to public policy as it is against the constitutionally recognized rights of parental control.

C. Drafting suggestions

Proper drafting should be able to overcome almost all impediments to the enforceability of conditional gifts. Keeping in mind the types of possible restrictions a donor may impose on a beneficiary coupled with common forces acting against these conditional provisions, an attorney can enhance the likelihood of the court upholding a conditional gift. See generally Harriet Lang Chappell, *Conditional Bequests: Control from Beyond the Grave*, Prob. & Prop., Mar./Apr. 1988, at 7, 8.

1. Reveal testator's intent

By gaining clear insight into a testator's intent and wishes, courts are less likely to strike down a provision as mean-spirited or pointless and more likely to uphold the contentious provision as the wish of the testator. The donor's intent should be set out in the document creating the gift because courts will first look within the four corners of the document for the necessary intent. Language making the gift conditional must be clearly communicated. Precatory, non-binding language must be avoided. It is necessary that the intention be of the type which courts are willing to accept and enforce. So-called "good" intent is especially necessary when creating conditions that are likely to be challenged.

2. Create Condition Precedent

The phrasing of a condition can exert influence on a court's position depending upon the continuing influence that a donor is exerting on a beneficiary. Whenever possible, a condition should be expressed as a condition precedent that causes an interest to vest upon the happening of an event. These conditions are seen by courts as not exerting a continuing influence on a beneficiary, and therefore are more likely to be carried out. Courts view a condition subsequent as exerting a strong continuing influence and thus are more likely to be struck down.

3. Include the consequences of a failed condition

Because courts consider the donor's failure to provide for the disposition of the property if the condition is not satisfied, conditional gifts should clearly state the ramifications of the condition not being satisfied. The will or trust should provide for the gift to pass to another party or revert to the donor upon failure of the condition.

Perhaps the most successful and motivating gift over provides for the property to pass to an individual or organization detestable to the original beneficiary. The thought of someone the beneficiary despises receiving the benefit as the result of the beneficiary's failure to meet the condition may provide incentive for the beneficiary to comply with the condition.

4. Consider the implications of impossibility of performance

A donor should also take into consideration the possibility that performance or satisfaction of the condition may become impossible. For example, the gift may be conditioned on the beneficiary caring for a pet animal which died prior to the testator's death. The donor should indicate what should happen to the gift in this eventuality; is performance excused permitting the beneficiary to take the gift or does the property pass to someone else?

5. Anticipate attack on condition as being contrary to public policy

Improperly worded conditions that conflict with public policy could render a conditional gift susceptible to a successful challenge. Conditions should be carefully considered and any which are potentially in conflict with public policy or any other negating force should be carefully worded to document the intent necessary to defeat such a challenge.

6. Providing objective standards for conditions

Conditions that include ambiguous standards for measuring completion might be considered impossible to fulfill and therefore void. Whenever possible, clearly articulated quantitative guidelines indicating the successful completion of a condition should be included in the will or trust.

7. Specifying who will determine subjective standards

A discretionary designee whose responsibility it is to determine whether subjective standards have been met should be neutral and have nothing to gain from the failure of the provision. Further, to lend credence to such a condition, a discretionary designee should be of good reputation.

8. Include a no contest clause

The donor may include a no contest or *in terrorem* clause providing that if the beneficiary contests the conditional gift then the beneficiary is automatically removed as a beneficiary. If enforced, such a clause may render a conditional gift virtually incontestable because beneficiaries have nothing to gain and everything to lose. It must be noted, however, that courts may set aside such a provision if a challenge to the validity of the conditional gift is based upon good faith or probable cause. For a detailed treatment of no contest clauses, see Gerry W. Beyer, et al., *The Fine Art of Intimidating Disgruntled Beneficiaries With In Terrorem Clauses*, 51 SMU L. Rev. 225 (1998).

D. Conclusion

Conditional bequests may be an effective way to carry out a testator's or settlor's intent. Courts uphold a wide array of conditions as long as they are phrased appropriately, not contrary to public policy, and not illegal. Some provisions not meeting these criteria might still endure if the instrument contains an effective no-contest clause. Whether to provide incentive for accomplishment, motivation for achievement, protection for the naive, or revenge from the grave, well-drafted conditional gifts may survive to do the bidding of the dead.

NOTES AND QUESTIONS

1. In the case of *In re Feinberg*, 235 Ill.2d 256, 335 Ill.Dec. 863, 919 N.E.2d 888 (Ill. 2009), the Illinois Supreme Court upheld an inheritance condition based on marrying within the Jewish faith. The court summarized this case as follows:

> Max Feinberg, who died in 1986, left a wife, Erla, two adult children, and five grandchildren. He had executed a will that created trusts from which his widow would receive income during her lifetime. At her death, the trust assets were to be combined, and half of these assets were to be held in trust for the benefit of the grandchildren during their lifetimes, provided they had not married out of the Jewish faith, in which case they were to be "deemed deceased" on the date of such a marriage. Shares of such "deceased" grandchildren would revert to the settlor's two children. Between 1990 and 2001, all of the five grandchildren married.
>
> Distribution of decedent's assets did not go according to this original plan, however, because Max also gave his widow a limited lifetime power of appointment as to his descendants which she exercised in 1997. Instead of lifetime trusts, she directed that, at the time of her death, fixed $250,000 sums be given to each of her two children and to each of her five grandchildren. She provided, however, that, as to the latter, her husband's religious-restriction clause must be complied with. Erla died in

2003. By this time, although all the grandchildren had married, only one had complied with the religious restriction.

This situation resulted in several different proceedings which were consolidated in the circuit court of Cook County. The religious-restriction clause was invalidated there as contrary to public policy, and the appellate court affirmed.

In reaching a different result, the Illinois Supreme Court found that the issue is not Max's original scheme of lifetime trusts for the grandchildren, but the distribution which was authorized by Erla, giving out fixed sums at the time of her death. The supreme court declined to hold the religious-restriction clause void. The grandchildren had no vested interests and Erla had merely created a condition precedent that operated on the date of her death to determine who was qualified to take. The supreme court said Erla was free to make a distribution in favor of grandchildren whose lifestyles were approved of over other grandchildren who made choices which were disapproved of.

The judgment of the appellate court was reversed, and the cause was remanded to the circuit court for further proceedings.

See Helen W. Gunnarsson, *Illinois Supreme Court upholds Jewish-marriage clause in trust provision*, 97 ILL. BAR J. 549 (2009).

2. Testator's will created a life estate in certain property for Wife with the remainder to his children. Daughter would receive her share outright only if she was unmarried when Wife died; otherwise, the property would be held in trust for her benefit. Is this provision valid? See *Hall v. Eaton*, 259 Ill.App.3d 319, 197 Ill.Dec. 583, 631 N.E.2d 805 (1994).

3. Testator's will contained the following provision:

> Because I believe that people should pay for their arrogant disobedience of our laws and their lack of manners and their selfishness, I give and bequeath the sum of $500 to the most conscientious police officer, each month for ten months, who gives the most traffic tickets to motorists who double-park, thereby causing law-abiding motorists to break the law by crossing the double yellow line.

Is this provision enforceable? See *Dead Man Had Will, Way to Get Double–Parkers*, WASH. POST, Aug. 25, 1998, at A2.

4. Evaluate the validity of the following gift: "I leave my entire estate to my spouse on the condition that my spouse remarry, so there will be at least one person who regrets my death." This language is adapted from the will of Heinrich Heine, a German poet who died in 1856.

5. For a detailed analysis of how to construct an estate plan to influence the behavior of the beneficiaries in a positive manner and the potential problems that can arise from creating an incentive trust, see Judy Barber, *The Psychology of Conditional Giving: What's the Motivation?*, 21 PROB. & PROP., Dec. 2007, at 57; Edward F. Koren, *Incentive Trusts and Beyond: Settlors' Intent and the Fiduciary Conundrum* (pt. 1), KOREN EST. & PERS. FIN. PLAN., Apr. 2009; Bruce L. Stout, *Incentive Trusts: A Potential Tool for Every Estate Plan*, W. VA. LAW., July/Sept. 2009, at 28; Joshua C. Tate, *Conditional*

Love: Incentive Trusts and the Inflexibility Problem, 41 REAL PROP. PROB. & TR. J. 445, Fall 2006, at 465–66, 488–91.

Q. CLIENT WHO ACQUIRES SUDDEN WEALTH

JOHN K. O'MEARA, ESTATE PLANNING CONCERNS FOR THE PROFESSIONAL ATHLETE*

3 MARQ. SPORTS L.J. 85, 85–86 (1992) (revised October 2011).

For most people, the creation stage of estate planning takes many years with early emphasis on creating enough wealth to enable the estate owner to enjoy the fruits of his or her efforts. For a successful professional athlete, the creation stage is quite short. The early emphasis is on the preservation and protection of the wealth that has been accumulated while the athlete is relatively young. Although many of the estate planning considerations and techniques used in the more conventional case of an estate owner who has accumulated his or wealth over a long time are applicable to the professional athlete, the relative youth of the athlete forces a different perspective on the advisor. Planning strategies that require irrevocable decisions assume a much longer time horizon and may not be as palatable as the same strategies are to the estate owner who is advanced in years. In addition, while the amount of wealth accumulated by the professional athlete may be substantial, the need to rely on that wealth to maintain a desirable lifestyle could extend for an extended time period.

The relative inexperience of the professional athlete in managing wealth is also an important consideration in advising the athlete. In fact, the sudden acquisition of large amounts of wealth can often result in a state of shock. As such, the athlete may not comprehend the necessity of planning to preserve and protect the wealth suddenly acquired. The estate planning advisor should work with the other members of the investment and financial planning team in order to conceive an estate plan consistent with the personal financial goals of the athlete.

The role of the estate planning advisor on the team should be clearly defined. In general, the estate planner is not the financial or investment advisor, insurance agent, accountant or banker. Rather, the estate planner's role is to focus on the preservation of wealth, the reduction of taxation, and the ultimate transfers of wealth in a carefully structured plan tailored to the individual's personal, family, financial and, possibly, charitable goals. The objective of the estate planner should be to assist the athlete in realizing both lifetime and at death goals from a tax and non-tax perspective. The estate planner can achieve this objective only by working with the athlete to coordinate accounting and investment decisions that will fit into a comprehensive plan.

* Reprinted with permission.

NOTE

Mr. O'Meara's discussion also applies to individuals who achieve rapid wealth by other means such as by winning a lottery, receiving a large inheritance, suddenly becoming a successful actor or actress, or obtaining a large personal injury award.

LOTTERY PLAYERS AND WINNERS*

The case of the lottery winner requires special planning. Here is an example of what may happen without proper planning, both when purchasing the ticket and upon discovering it is a winner. In May 1995, Johnny Ray Brewster won $12.8 million in the Texas lottery. Johnny died of a heart attack ten months later after receiving only one annual payment of $463,320. Johnny's sister, Penny, was the sole beneficiary of his estate which included as its primary asset the right to the remaining lottery payments. The estimated federal estate tax totaled approximately $3.5 million. Because the estate did not yet have these funds, the IRS agreed to a ten year payment plan with annual payments of approximately $482,000, that is, $18,680 *more* than the annual lottery payments. Under this arrangement, Penny would need to put $18,680 of her own money toward the taxes for ten years. Only in the eleventh year, would Penny finally be able to benefit from her brother's lucky ticket. See *Lotto Texas Heirs Cry For Help With Federal Tax Bills*, SAN ANTONIO EXPRESS-NEWS, July 12, 1996, at 6B. Luckily for Penny, the Lottery Commission allowed the estate to cash in the remainder of the prize at its present value. *Commission Moves to Aid Estate Handle Large Inheritance Tax Bill*, SAN ANTONIO EXPRESS-NEWS, Aug. 29, 1996, at 20A.

The Consequences of Winning—The Important Preliminary Decisions

An eager and excited lottery winner may quickly claim lottery winnings. However, a prudent winner has important decisions to make before accepting the prize. The holder of a winning ticket should use the claim period to evaluate and select the best options.

1. Who Owns the Ticket?

The threshold question is "who owns the winning ticket?" Lottery tickets are often purchased with (1) pooled funds of friends or colleagues or (2) the community property of a husband and wife. Therefore, it is possible that more than one person "owns" the winning ticket. In such situations, the potential owners of the winning ticket must determine whether they were in a partnership-type relationship at the time of the purchase of the winning ticket. If a partnership existed, then the potential owners must determine whether the winning ticket was purchased on behalf of the partnership.

* Adapted from Gerry W. Beyer & Jessica Petrini, *Lottery Players and Winners: Estate Planning for the Optimistic and the Lucky*, EST. PLAN. DEV. TEX. PROF. (Aug. 2000).

For example, assume that A and B are unmarried, significant others who live together. Although they each have their own bank accounts, they share in the household expenses. A and B have a custom and practice of buying lottery tickets every Monday. They always elect the lump sum payment. Sometimes A and B are together when the tickets are purchased. Sometimes it is agreed beforehand that either A or B will pick up the tickets on a Monday after work. Regardless of who buys the ticket, it is understood by both A and B that the ticket "belongs" to them both and that any prize money awarded will be split equally between them. On one particular Monday, A and B agree that B will purchase their weekly ticket on his way home from work. He pays with a dollar bill from his own wallet. Much to A and B's delight, the ticket is a winner. So, who owns the ticket? A individually, B individually, or A and B together equally?

Courts typically focus on the facts and circumstances surrounding the purchase of a lottery ticket, including the intent and understanding of the parties at the time of purchase, to determine ownership of the proceeds of a winning ticket for tax purposes. See *Estate of Winkler v. Commissioner*, 73 T.C.M. (CCH) 1657 (1997). If a taxpayer purchased a lottery ticket with the intent and understanding that the proceeds would be shared with others, the courts have treated the proceeds of the ticket as income to all the recipients rather than as income to just the purchaser. See *Solomon v. Commissioner*, 25 T.C. 936 (1956).

2. Who Accepts the Prize?

a. Trust Arrangement for Individual Winners—The best entity to form for an individual winner is a revocable trust. See Kimberly Adams Colgate, *Win, Lose or Draw: The Tax Ramifications of Winning a Major Lottery*, 10 COOLEY L. REV. 275, 293 (1993) (providing extensive discussion of this technique which forms the basis of the discussion in this section). The lottery winner should create a revocable trust and apply for an employer identification number. The winner should then transfer the ticket into the trust and the trustee should redeem it for the benefit of the trust.

The winner receives a variety of benefits by creating a revocable trust. (1) Probate of the lottery proceeds will be avoided. Instead, the remaining payments are distributed to the beneficiaries according to the terms of the trust instrument. (2) No transfer occurs for gift tax purposes when the winner places the ticket in the revocable trust. (3) The transfer of the ticket prior to redemption is unlikely to trigger compliance with the special procedures needed to assign lottery winnings. (4) The settlor-winner may amend the trust without the approval of the lottery commission. With this freedom to amend, the settlor may later decide to relinquish his or her power to revoke a certain percent interest of the trust, thereby reducing the settlor's taxable estate by that percentage. For example, the settlor could relinquish his/her power to revoke a two percent interest in both the trust income and principal, making someone else the irrevocable beneficiary of that two percent interest. The two percent interest would then be distributed and taxable to that irrevocable beneficiary. By making the complete transfer of a two percent interest in trust property, a taxable gift is triggered, however, as long as the settlor lives three years after relinquishing the right to revoke the two percent interest, his/her estate would include only ninety-eight percent of the value of the future lottery payments.

b. The Family or Group Partnership—Spouses and family members who make it a regular practice to pool their money to purchase lotto tickets should seriously consider forming a partnership entity before claiming their winnings. See Linda Suzzanne Griffin, *The Lottery: A Practical Discussion on Advising the Lottery Winner*, FLA. BAR J., Apr. 1998, at 84. If one person were to accept the prize individually on behalf of a group or multiple winners, only that individual, or that individual's estate will receive checks. Therefore, when multiple "winners" are involved, it is important to establish an entity to serve as the recipient of the lottery proceeds on behalf of all winners.

Placing the lottery winnings in joint name with someone other than a spouse is not a wise idea. The full fair market value of jointly owned property is included in the taxable estate of the first joint tenant to die, except to the extent that the surviving joint tenant(s) can prove they contributed to the acquisition of the property or that there is a joint tenancy between the spouses. I.R.C. § 2040(a). By establishing an entity to serve as the recipient of the lottery proceeds, an outright, clear division of ownership is achieved preventing any joint tenancy issues that may arise when the first joint tenant dies. If the joint tenancy is with a spouse, however, there is an automatic division of the property, causing only 50% of the fair market value of the property to be included in the estate of the first joint tenant to die, regardless of who provided contributions. Nonetheless, even spouses would be prudent to use an entity.

Consequences of Winning—Income, Gift and Estate Tax Liabilities

1. Income Tax Liability

Lottery winnings are taxable income. I.R.C. §§ 61 & 74(a). A lottery winner has income only upon the receipt of a winnings check because most lottery winners are cash basis calendar year taxpayers. See *Lavery v. Commissioner*, 158 F.2d 859, 860 (7th Cir. 1946). If a lottery winner elects to receive a lump sum payment of the present value of the winnings, the winner must report the entire amount of the lump sum payment as income. On the other hand, a winner who elects the option to receive annual payments is taxed only on the amount received with each annual installment rather than the total present value of all future lottery distributions. A lottery winner is not in "actual receipt" of future winnings because the winner has not yet received the checks. Moreover, a lottery winner is not in "constructive receipt" of his or the future winnings because future winnings cannot be reduced to the taxpayer's current possession or enjoyment.

2. Gift Tax Liability

A gift by a lottery ticket purchaser of a ticket or lottery proceeds to someone other than the purchaser may be a taxable transfer. I.R.C. § 2501. When lottery players purchase tickets jointly, it is important for them to execute a separate ownership agreement or partnership agreement *before* accepting the prize and to accept the prize as a group or partnership, not individually. If the players wish to distribute winnings unequally, they should execute a written partnership agreement detailing the proportions *prior* to purchasing the winning ticket. By taking these steps, the players may reduce the likelihood of the I.R.S. successfully contending that one person purchased the ticket and then made a taxable gift of the proceeds to another individual. In Priv. Ltr. Rul. 92–17–004 (April 24, 1992), the issue was whether a separate ownership agreement signed after winning created a gift tax liability because the sole official lottery winner gave a one-half interest in the winnings to a co-player. The I.R.S. determined that the underlying separate ownership agreement merely reflected the true intentions of the parties and that each party possessed equal ownership interests in the ticket from the inception. Accordingly, the ownership agreement acted to shift one-half of the winning proceeds without incurring any gift tax. See also *Estate of Winkler v. Commissioner*, 73 T.C.M. (CCH) 1657 (1997).

3. Estate Tax Liability

Quite possibly the most ominous potential tax liability facing a lottery winner is the federal estate tax upon the winner's death. The value at the time of death of all the winner's property, real or personal, tangible or intangible, wherever situated is included in the winner's gross estate. I.R.C. § 2031(a). Consequently, the gross estate includes any lottery proceeds the winner has already received but has not yet spent as well as the present value of future lottery payments.

For the winner who elects the lump sum option, gross estate valuation is straight forward. Generally, only funds the winner has not spent or given away are in the winner's gross estate. The winner has no future lottery payments to worry about because the winner has already received all lottery distributions.

If the winner elected to receive annual payments, the value of the estate includes the present value of the winner's right to future payments. The actual computation of the present value is somewhat complex and there is uncertainty regarding the appropriate computation method. See *Shackleford v. United States*, 262 F.3d 1028 (9th Cir. 2001); *Gribauskas v. Commissioner*, 342 F.3d 85 (2d Cir. 2003); and *Cook Estate v. Commissioner*, 349 F.3d 850 (5th Cir. 2003). See also Linda S. Griffin & Richard V. Harrison, *Florida State Lottery Tax and Estate Planning Issues*, FLA. B.J., Jan. 1996, at 74 (1996); Ja Lee Kao, *Valuing Future Lottery Winnings for Estate Tax Purposes: Estate of Shackleford v. United States*, 52 TAX LAW. 609 (1999).

The valuation process results in the imposition of estate tax for the net present value of lottery payments outstanding at the time of a decedent's death. The problem, however, for a deceased winner's heirs and beneficiaries, is that this money is not actually in the estate. The estate cannot accelerate the payments even though the estate tax is currently due. How can an estate pay such a tax? Perhaps the heir or beneficiaries could assign the proceeds to a company who purchases lottery annuities, pay the tax, and hopefully have funds remaining for themselves. The fewer payments the winner receives before dying, the greater the tax liability and consequentially the greater the hardship imposed on the winner's successors in interest.

Tax Planning For Lottery Winners

1. Income Tax

A winner should not accept a prize as a single individual if more than one person has rights to a winning ticket. The winner may thus avoid being assessed a tax on more than the winner's own portion of the proceeds.

2. Gift Tax

a. Make Annual Exclusion Gifts— Every lottery winner may give up to $13,000 per year (as of 2012) to an unlimited number of donees without incurring gift tax liability. I.R.C. § 2503(b)(1). Annual exclusion gifts will not augment the winner's gross estate and the winner has no liability for tax on any appreciation or income which accrues after making the gift.

Annual exclusion gifts are a very effective way of depleting a winner's estate and should be used aggressively as a tax saving strategy, unless, of course, the winner needs or wants the winnings for other purposes. To qualify for the annual exclusion, the donor must give a "present interest." Gifts of future interests in property, such as gifts in trust, are not covered by the annual exclusion unless special steps are taken (e.g., a § 2503(c) minor's trust or a *Crummey* trust).

If a lottery winner is married, the winner can join with his or her spouse and the two can combine their annual exclusion amounts and make gift tax free gifts of $26,000 instead of $13,000.

b. Contribute to Education and Medical Care—All payments that a lottery winner makes for another person's educational or medical expenses are not subject to the federal gift tax. I.R.C. § 2503(e). There is no limit on the amount of these gifts or on the number of donees. The lottery winner and the donee do not need to be related for this exclusion from gift tax to apply.

c. Consider Intraspousal Gift—A gift of lottery proceeds from one spouse to another is generally deductible and thus is not subject to federal gift tax. I.R.C. § 2523(a). By making inter vivos and testamentary gifts to a spouse, a lottery winner can essentially eliminate all of his or her gift and estate tax liability (to the extent of the winner's share of the lottery proceeds) by use of the unlimited marital deduction. Remember, however, that this technique increases the size and potential tax liability of the surviving spouse's estate. (Note that in some states, lottery winnings are community property, regardless of whether the ticket was purchased with community funds or a spouse's separate property. See *Dixon v. Sanderson*, 72 Tex. 359, 10 S.W. 535 (1888).)

d. Make Charitable Gifts—All gifts to qualified charities are totally deductible when computing the gift tax. I.R.C. § 2522. The lottery winner must make certain the recipient's use of the property for religious, charitable, scientific, literary, or educational purposes is sufficiently charitable to qualify the gift for charitable deduction treatment.

e. Beware of the Generation Skipping Transfer Tax—Lottery winners should be aware that the generation-skipping transfer (GST) tax is imposed on certain inter vivos and at-death transfers to non-spouse donees who are more than one generation younger than the lottery winner. I.R.C. §§ 2601–2663.

C. Estate Tax

a. Elect Lump Sum Payment— The most tax-sound strategy for the lottery winner will often be to elect to take the lump sum present value lottery payment. A lump sum payment may seem a significant sacrifice of lottery winnings, however, the annual payments essentially equal what the winner would receive in the lump sum with the added appreciation from investment by the local lottery commission. Lottery winners may take the lump sum payment and invest the money wisely. Moreover, with a lump sum distribution, the lottery winner may control the method of investment. It is indeed possible that the investments a winner makes on his or her own could lead to a much better appreciation than the commission's investments.

For estate tax purposes, the lump sum arrangement will prevent the lottery winner's successors in interest from assuming a terribly burdensome death tax obligation. The winner's estate will have the money with which to pay the estate tax. Liquidity problems are avoided.

The winner must also consider the non-tax benefits of a lump sum payment. A lottery winner never knows when he or she may need to access the winnings for emergency or other purposes. With the lump sum arrangement, the funds are always within the winner's grasp. With annual payments, a winner is unable to accelerate payments, regardless of the emergency, unless a court mercifully grants a voluntary assignment request. (Caveat: An imprudent lottery winner could furiously spend a lump sum payment; measured distributions enforce a budget on a spendthrift lottery winner.)

b. Execute a Will—A lottery winner may maximize at-death deductions such as the marital and charitable deductions by executing an appropriate will. By planning ahead, a lottery winner may control the distribution of property to beneficiaries and may be able to structure marital trusts and bypass arrangements to greatly lessen the estate tax burden.

c. Purchase Life Insurance—Life insurance is a very effective technique to provide the funds necessary to pay the estate tax on either the remaining proceeds of a lump sum distribution or the present value of future lottery proceeds. See M. Eldridge Blanton, III, *Who Gets a Dead Man's Gold? The Dilemma of Lottery Winnings Payable to a Decedent's Estate*, 28 U. RICH. L. REV. 443 (1994). Generally, the proceeds of a life insurance policy made payable to the lottery winner's beneficiaries are not treated as the beneficiaries' taxable income. I.R.C. § 101(a)(1). Moreover, by placing the policy in an irrevocable life insurance trust, or by otherwise divesting him-or herself of the incidents of ownership of the policy, the lottery winner can ensure that the proceeds of the policy will not be subject to estate tax in the winner's estate. I.R.C. § 2042.

d. Consider the Marital Deduction Along With Bypass Planning—Any winnings that pass to the lottery winner's spouse via will or intestacy are generally deductible and thus not subject to federal estate tax. I.R.C. § 2056(a). Like all marital deduction gifts, a gift of lump sum or future lottery winnings to a spouse increases the size and potential estate tax liability of the surviving spouse's estate. Accordingly, the lottery winner should consider making outright gifts of any unused applicable credit amount to others, creating a bypass trust, or otherwise taking the steps necessary so that the winner does not waste his or her applicable credit amount.

e. Make Charitable Gifts—All at-death transfers to qualified charities are totally deductible when computing the federal estate tax. I.R.C. § 2055. The lottery winner must make certain the recipient's use of the property for religious, charitable, scientific, literary, or educational purposes is sufficiently charitable to qualify the transfer for charitable deduction treatment.

f. Beware of the Generation Skipping Transfer Tax—The lottery winner must also be alert to transfers which may trigger the GST tax and take steps necessary to reduce GST liability.

R. DIGITAL ASSETS*

Digital assets include "any online account that you own or any file that you store on your computer or that you store in the cloud." Posting of Nathan Lustig to Entrustet HIWI Blog, *Digital Estate Planning: What are Digital Assets?* (Apr. 19, 2010). Online accounts include, but are not limited to: email accounts like Gmail, Yahoo!, and Hotmail; pictures stored online at Flickr, Picasa, Shutterfly, or Kodak EasyShare; videos or documents on YouTube, GoogleDocs, or Scribd; websites or blogs such as Typepad, Blogger, or WordPress; online banking, investment, and credit

* Adapted from Gerry W. Beyer & Kerri M. Griffin, *Estate Planning for Digital Assets*, EST. PLAN. DEV. TEX. PROF., April 2011, at 1.

card accounts; PayPal; domain names from GoDaddy or Network Solutions; Web-hosting accounts; social networking accounts such as Facebook, Myspace, Twitter, and LinkedIn; online shopping accounts such as eBay or Amazon; virtual businesses; online auction houses; avatars on World of Warcraft or Second Life; professional and personal data backups; and online bill payment accounts for loans, insurance, utilities, and website hosting. Examples of the types of files many clients store on their computers include personal and business letters and other documents, photographs, videos, artwork, and music. While many of these assets do not have monetary value, many of them may have sentimental value to family members. Thus, every category of digital assets needs to be considered when drafting an estate plan.

I. Importance to Planning for Digital Assets

A. To Make Things Easier on Executors and Family Members

If your clients are smart about their online life, they have many different usernames and passwords for their accounts. This is the only way to secure identities, but this devotion to protecting sensitive personal information can wreak havoc on families upon incapacity or death. Andrea Coombes, *You Need an Online Estate Plan*, WALL ST. J. July 19, 2009 [hereinafter Coombes]. Consider A & E's Hoarders, a show that reveals the lives of people who cannot part with their belongings and have houses full of floor-to-ceiling stacks of junk as a result. While most of us find this disgusting, are we not also committing the same offense online when we create multiple e-mail accounts, social networking accounts, websites, Twitter accounts, eBay accounts, online bill-paying arrangements, and more? Sorting through a deceased's online life for the important things can be just as daunting as cleaning out the house of a hoarder.

To make matters worse, the rights of executors, agents, guardians, and beneficiaries with regard to digital assets are muddy. Although a few states such as Connecticut, Idaho, Indiana, Oklahoma, and Rhode Island have statutes on point, it is still unclear if these law conflicts with service agreements. Thus, family members may have to go to court for legal authority to gain access to these accounts. See *Who Owns Your E–Mails?*, BBC NEWS, Jan. 11, 2005 (parents of L/Cpl Justin Ellsworth fought Yahoo! for access to their son's email). Even after gaining legal authority, the company running the online account still may not acquiesce to a family member's authority without a battle. See Coombes.

This process is complicated further if someone is incapacitated rather than deceased because that person will continue to have expenses that a deceased person would not have. Without passwords, a power of attorney alone may not be enough for the agent to pay these expenses. If no power of attorney is in place, a guardian may have to be appointed to access these accounts, and some companies will still require a specific court order on top of that before they release account information. Id.

B. To Prevent Identity Theft

In addition to needing access to online accounts for personal reasons and closing probate, family members need this information quickly so that a deceased's identity is not stolen. Until authorities update their databases regarding a new death, criminals can open credit cards, apply for jobs under a dead person's name, and get state identification cards. There are methods of protecting a deceased's identity, but they all involve having access to the deceased's online accounts. See Aleksandra Todorova, *Dead Ringers: Grave Robbers Turn to ID Theft,* WALL ST. J., Aug. 4, 2009.

C. To Prevent Losses to the Estate

Some digital assets may be of value that can be lost if they go undiscovered for too long. Consider the case of Leonard Bernstein who died in 1990 leaving the manuscript for his memoir entitled Blue Ink on his computer in a password protected file. To this day, no one has been able to break the password and access what may be a very interesting and valuable document. Helen W. Gunnarsson, *Plan for Administering Your Digital Estate,* 99 ILL. B.J. 71 (2011).

Electronic bills for loans, insurance, and website hosting need to be discovered quickly and paid to prevent cancellations. See Maimes. This concern is augmented further if the deceased or incapacitated ran an online business and is the only person with access to incoming orders, the servers, corporate bank accounts, and employee payroll accounts. See Tamara Schweitzer, *Passing on Your Digital Data*, Inc., Mar. 1, 2010 [hereinafter Schweitzer]. Bids for items advertised on eBay may go unanswered and lost forever.

D. To Avoid Losing the Deceased's Story

Most digital assets are not inherently valuable, but are valuable to family members who extract meaning from what the deceased leaves behind. Historically, people kept special pictures, letters, and journals in shoeboxes or albums for future heirs. Today, this material is stored on computers or online and is often never printed. Personal blogs and Twitter feeds have replaced physical diaries and e-mails have replaced letters. Without alerting family members that these assets exist, and without telling them how to get access to them, the story of the life of the deceased may be lost forever. This is not only a tragedy for family members, but also possibly for future historians who are losing pieces of history in the digital abyss. Rob Walker, *Cyberspace When You're Dead*, N.Y. TIMES, Jan. 5, 2011 [hereinafter Walker].

For more active online lives, this concern may also involve preventing spam from infiltrating a loved one's website or blog site. Comments from friends and family are normally welcomed, but it is jarring to discover the comment thread gradually infiltrated with links for "cheap Ugg boots." Id. "It's like finding a flier for a dry cleaner stuck among flowers on a grave, except that it is much harder to remove." Id. In the alternative, family members may decide to delete the deceased's website against the deceased's wishes simply because those wishes were not expressed to the family. Id.

E. To Prevent Unwanted Secrets from Being Discovered

Sometimes people do not want their loved ones discovering private emails or messages. They may contain hurtful secrets, or maybe just inside jokes and personal rantings. Without designating appropriate people to take care of certain accounts, the wrong person may come across this type of information.

II. Deceased–User Policies

Many online account providers have vague policies regarding the fate of online accounts after the user's death, or no policies at all. Some of the more popular online accounts, along with their current deceased-user policies, are described below:

- Facebook: Family members can either remove the deceased's account or "memorialize" it. Memorializing means the account continues, other Facebook members can interact with the deceased's wall, all status updates and contact information are deleted, access is restricted to confirmed friends, and future log-ins are prevented. Section 5 of Facebook's Privacy Policy (last visited Mar. 10, 2011).
- Hotmail: Family members can either delete the deceased's account or receive a CD–ROM of the contents of the email account after providing Hotmail with a copy of a death certificate, paperwork stating that the family member is an executor or has a power of attorney, a photocopy of the family member's government-issued identification, and a document answering specific verification questions. If these documents are not provided to Hotmail within six months, the account will be deleted forever. Hotmail needs thirty days to process and validate these documents. Windows Live Solution Center, How to Request Data from a Deceased User's Account? (last visited Mar. 10, 2011).
- Gmail/Google: Family members can gain access to the deceased user's account in the same manner as required by Hotmail, with the additional requirement of providing an email correspondence between the family member and the account owner. Gmail Help, Accessing a Deceased Person's Mail (last visited Mar. 10, 2011).
- LinkedIn: Family members can memorialize the deceased's account, meaning that profile access is restricted and messaging functionality is removed. Family members can also close the account. Section 3D of LinkedIn's Privacy Policy (last visited Mar. 10, 2011).
- MySpace: Family members can delete, remove content from, or preserve the deceased's MySpace profile after providing proof of death, the deceased's MySpace ID, and proof of relation to the deceased. MySpace Help, How Can I Delete or Access a Deceased User's Profile? (last visited Mar. 10, 2011).

- Twitter: Family members can either remove the deceased's account or receive an archive of the deceased's tweets after providing Twitter with their relationship to the deceased, the deceased's username, and a link to a public obituary. Twitter Help Center, How to Contact Twitter About a Deceased User (last visited Mar. 10, 2011).
- Yahoo! Mail: Family members cannot access the deceased's account unless a court has ordered its release. However, family members can close the account by providing Yahoo! with a copy of a death certificate. Yahoo! Terms of Service #27 (last visited Mar. 10, 2011).

III. Planning For Digital Assets

A. Placing Digital Asset Information in a Will or Trust

Be cautious when entering information about digital assets into a will, remembering that once the will is admitted to probate, it becomes public information. Further, if a client actually wishes to pass on a digital asset rather than the information of how to deal with the asset, a will may not do the trick if the asset is one that will no longer exist upon death. Naming a digital executor in a will would be fine, as well as specifying beneficiaries of specific digital assets should your client wish to do so. See Maimes. Referencing a separate document that contains detailed account information would be better than placing this information in the will itself.

A trust is a more desirable place for account information because it would not become part of the public record. If the value of the digital assets is substantial, a digital asset trust may be created for digital property. The trust can be the owner of the assets and will survive death, enabling others to access the information. Id.

B. Drafting a Separate Document with Digital Asset Information

Due to the privacy issues involved with placing this information in a will, drafting a separate document with all of the information may be a better idea. Have your clients make a list of all their online accounts, passwords, security questions and answers, whether the accounts have monetary value, and special instructions for locating specific assets or information. They also need to designate which assets they want deleted versus which ones they want passed on to family members and who they want to take care of such business. This document can be printed or stored on a computer, USB flash drive, or in a cloud with remote access. Deborah L. Jacobs, *Six Ways to Store Securely the Keys to Your Online Financial Life*, FORBES, Feb. 15, 2011. If a client doesn't want to design his own looseleaf system, he can use a tool that does it for him, such as the Beneficiary Book. Id.

Giving a family member this information while alive and well can backfire on your clients. For example, if a client gives his daughter his online banking information to pay his bills while he is sick, siblings may accuse her of misusing the funds. See Deborah L. Jacobs, *When Others Need The Keys To Your Online Kingdom*, N.Y. TIMES, May 20, 2009 [hereinafter Jacobs]. Further, a dishonest family member would be able to steal your client's money undetected. If you decide that a separate document with digital asset information is the best route for your clients, this document should be kept with your client's will and durable power of attorney in a safe place. The document can be delivered to the client's executor upon the client's death or agent upon the client's incapacity.

C. Use Online Afterlife Companies

Recently, entrepreneurs recognizing the need for digital estate planning have created companies that offer services to assist in planning for digital assets. These companies offer a variety of services to assist clients in storing information about digital assets as well as notes and emails that clients wish to send post-mortem. As an estate planning attorney, you may find this additional service to be valuable and recommend one to your clients. Many companies also allow users to create memorial websites for loved ones. Different sites allow different content, including pictures, notes, videos, and audio recordings.

IV. Obstacles To Planning For Digital Assets

A. Safety Concerns

Clients may be hesitant to place all of their usernames, passwords, and other information in one place. We have all been warned, "Never write down your passwords." This document could fall into the hands of the wrong person, leaving your client exposed. One option to safeguard against this is to have your clients create two documents; one with usernames and one with passwords. The documents can be stored in different locations or given to different family members. With an online afterlife management company or an online password vault, clients may worry that the security system could be breached, leaving them completely exposed. See Jacobs. The same concern is present if your client chooses to place all this information in one document.

B. Hassle

Another obstacle to planning for digital assets is that it is an unwanted burden. Digital asset information is constantly changing and stored on a variety of devices (e.g., desktop computers, laptop computers, smart phones, cameras, iPads, CDs, DVDs, and flashdrives). A client may open new email accounts, new social networking or gaming accounts, or change passwords routinely. Documents with this information must be revised and accounts at online afterlife management companies must be updated frequently. For the clients who wish to keep this information in a document, tell them to update the document quarterly and save it to a USB flash drive or in the cloud, making sure that a family member knows where to locate it. See Schweitzer.

C. Uncertain Reliability of Online Afterlife Management Companies

Afterlife management companies come and go; their life is dependent upon the whims and attention spans of their creators and creditors. Lack of sustained existence of all of these companies make it hard, if not impossible, to determine whether this market will remain viable. Clients may not want to spend money to save digital asset information when they are unsure about the reliability of the companies. See Walker.

D. Overstatement of Online Afterlife Management Companies Abilities

Some of these companies purport to distribute digital assets to beneficiaries. Explain to your clients that these companies cannot do this legally, and that they need a will to transfer assets, no matter what kind. Using these companies to store information to make the probate process easier is fine, but they cannot be used to avoid probate altogether. David Shulman, an estate planner in Florida, stated that he "would relish the opportunity to represent the surviving spouse of a decedent whose eBay business was 'given away' by Legacy Locker to an online friend in Timbuktu." David Shulman, *Estate Planning for Your Digital Life, or, Why Legacy Locker is a Big Fat Lawsuit Waiting to Happen*, SOUTH FLORIDA ESTATE PLANNING LAW, Mar. 21, 2009.

V. Conclusion

Despite the complications surrounding planning for digital assets, clients need to understand the ramifications of failing to do so. Estate planners need to understand that this is not a trivial consideration and that it is a developing area of law. Cases will arise regarding terms of service agreements, rights of beneficiaries, and the success of online afterlife management companies. More states are likely to enact legislation regarding rights over digital assets of the deceased and a uniform law may be needed. Estate planners need to be aware of new developments. Until then, some elementary form of planning for these assets will have to do.

S. LOYALTY PROGRAM BENEFITS*

In today's highly competitive business environment, there are numerous options for customers to make the most of their travel and spending habits, especially if they are loyal to particular providers. Airlines have created programs in which frequent flyers accumulate "miles" or "points" they may use towards free or discounted trips. Some credit card companies offer users an opportunity to earn "cash back" on their purchases or accumulate "points" which the card holder may then use for discounted merchandise, travel, or services. Retail stores often allow shoppers to

* Adapted from Gerry W. Beyer & Mikela Bryant, *Rewards from the Grave: Keeping Loyalty Program Benefits in the Family*, EST. PLAN. DEV. TEX. PROF., July 2011, at 1.

accumulate benefits including discounts and credit vouchers. Some members of these programs accumulate a staggering amount of points or miles and then die without having "spent" them. For example, there are reports that "members of frequent-flyer programs are holding at least 3.5 trillion in unused miles." *Managing Your Frequent–Flyer Miles*, http://www.groco.com/readingroom/fin_frequentflyer.aspx (last visited June 19, 2011).

What happens to these accumulations of miles and reward points after the member of the program dies? Do they just disappear? Can these benefits be transferred upon death by will or could they pass by intestacy? Are they instead non-probate assets governed by the terms of the contract between the company and the customer? Each program is different and has varying rules, both formal and informal, regarding the transfer of benefits upon the death of the program member.

Preparing for the transfer of loyalty benefits hinges on the client's specific circumstances and the program involved. The estate planner should determine the following:

1. To what loyalty programs does the client belong?
2. Does the client have (or is likely to have) a sufficient accumulation of benefits to merit planning?
3. What is each program's formal policy for the transfer of benefits when a member dies?
4. Does the program have an informal method for the transfer of benefits upon a member's death?
5. Does the program have a policy for the transfer or gifting of miles or points during a member's life which may be a better option than delaying a possible transfer until the client's death?
6. Is the intended beneficiary a current member of the same program as the client?

The rules of the loyalty program to which the client belongs plays the key role in determining whether the accrued points may be transferred. Many customer loyalty programs do not allow transfer of accrued points upon death, but as long as the beneficiary knows the online login information of the member, it may be possible for the remaining benefits may be transferred or redeemed. However, some loyalty programs may view this redemption method as fraudulent or require that certain paperwork be filed before authorizing the redemption of remaining benefits. The drafting attorney should be aware of whether he or she even needs to include the method of point redemption in the estate plan. If the program allows anyone with access to the deceased member's online account to redeem unused points, it is important that the intended recipient have all the information needed to make the transfer such as the account number, user name, and password.

Not all is lost simply because a program's terms and conditions state on paper or online that benefits may not be transferred by will or other estate planning technique. For example, some frequent flier programs, even ones stating that miles are nontransferable, may have informal policies which allow the transfer of miles after a program member's death. Contacting the program's customer service department is the best way to determine what steps to take to make sure accrued miles stay in the family. It may be advisable for this step to be taken before the client dies so that all necessary information and forms are available to complete the transfer after death.

It is also important to know whether the program allows accrued miles or points to be transferred, shared, or gifted at any time during active membership. Program rules usually cover various methods a member may use to share or gift rewards to other members, or in some cases to buy rewards for non-members. These provisions offer the estate planning attorney methods of transferring unused rewards if the client is willing to part with the benefits during life.

Numerous airlines allow testamentary transfer of accrued miles if the miles could have been transferred under the programs terms and conditions during the life of the member. The likelihood that a testamentary transfer will be successful increases significantly when the intended beneficiary of the transfer is a member of the same program. If membership is free, or even if there is a small fee involved, it may be in the best interest of the client for potential beneficiaries to become members of the programs from which the testator wants to transfer miles or points. Though many of these transfers require payment of a service or processing fee, the fee is a small price to pay for ensuring that the client's wishes are met.

Loyalty program rules often change. Thus, a dispositive plan, be it inter vivos or testamentary, may not work as intended. Accordingly, a regular review of loyalty program rules is necessary to make certain the client's intent will be effectuated. The costs of conducting such a review must be balanced against the value of the benefits so that the expense of planning does not exceed the value of the benefits.

T. CLIENTS WHO OWN FIREARMS*

Many clients are proud owners of a variety of firearms and many children and grandchildren hope to inherit or purchase firearms in the future. In fact, a 2006 poll reported that 43% of Americans keep a gun in their home. *Americans By Slight Margin Say Gun In the Home Makes it Safer*, Gallup Poll, Oct. 20, 2006. Another study, conducted by the Bureau of Justice Statistics, found that 240,000 machine guns are registered with the Bureau of Alcohol Tobacco, Firearms, and Explosives. Through legislation, federal and state governments have tightened the reigns on the purchase, transfer, and ownership of weapons. Regulations with regard to machine guns and other similar weapons have received the most scrutiny and reform.

---

* Adapted from Gerry W. Beyer and Jessica B. Jackson, *What Estate Planners Need to Know About Firearms*, EST. PLAN. DEV. TEX. PROF., April 2010, at 1.

Estate planning professionals must familiarize themselves with national and state gun laws and use approved estate planning techniques to represent clients effectively who own or are interested in owning firearms. Failure to comply with national and state laws can lead to fines of up to $250,000 and 10 years in prison. 26 U.S.C. §§ 5861(d),(j) (2005); 26 U.S.C. § 5872 (2005); 49 U.S.C. §§ 781–788 (2003).

Congress enacted the National Firearms Act in 1934 under Congress' Sixteenth Amendment power of taxation and it largely governs the purchase, sale, transfer, use, and ownership of certain weapons. The $200 transfer tax dictated by the Act in 1934 remains in force today. http://www.atf.gov/firearms/nfa/.

The Alcohol Tobacco and Firearms division of the United States Department of Treasury provides resources on how to identify whether a weapon falls under NFA regulations. http://www.atf.gov/publications/download/p/atf-p–5320–8/atf-p–5320–8.pdf. NFA firearms include weapons such as machine guns, suppressors, short-barreled shotguns (sawed-off shotguns), and destructive devices (mortars, howitzers, grenade launchers). 27 C.F.R. 479 (2003). NFA firearms are also commonly referred to as "Title II weapons" because these firearms are defined in this title of the National Firearms Act and Gun Control Act. The most commonly owned NFA weapon is the machine gun.

Congress has amended and expanded the NFA as the political culture of our nation has evolved. For example, Congress enacted the following additional provisions to regulate firearms: the Gun Control Act of 1968 (GCA) and, most recently, the Firearm Owners' Protection Act (FOPA). The FOPA, although intended to protect Second Amendment rights, changed the GCA so severely that it made the transfer and ownership of machine guns illegal, subject to two exceptions:

- Transfer and possession of machine guns by government agencies (18 U.S.C. § 921 (1986)); and
- Transfer and possession of machine guns that were lawfully possessed in compliance with the NFA at the time of the prohibition in 1986 (House Amend. 777 to H.R. 4332).

The second exception protects any legal transfer of machine guns lawfully possessed in 1986, whether through sale or inheritance.

Unlawful possession of NFA firearms, be it actual or constructive, comes with strictly enforced criminal penalties and a no tolerance policy. As previously mentioned, the NFA authorizes a fine of up to $250,000, up to ten years in prison, and the forfeiture of the weapon and any "vessel, vehicle, or aircraft" used to conceal or convey the firearm. Therefore, the seemingly tedious procedures and processes that accompany ownership of an NFA weapon are important and relevant for any estate that contains one or more of these weapons.

Although the federal government has a comprehensive framework established to regulate the rights associated with certain firearms, state and local governments are not prohibited from imposing additional restrictions.

Transfer of a Title II NFA firearm to an individual is a long and tedious process. Because improper transfer can result in major fines and jail time, a personal representative must take the transfer of these weapons very seriously. Chapter 9 of the NFA Handbook describes the necessary steps to transfer NFA firearms. The NFA defines transfer as "selling, assigning, pledging, leasing, loaning, giving away, or otherwise disposing of" an NFA firearm. Although the definition of transfer is fairly general, it only lawfully applies to NFA weapons that are registered to the transferor in the National Firearm Register and Transfer Record. Transferring, possessing, or receiving an NFA weapon that is not legally registered is a criminal act. Once a weapon has been determined registered, the administrative steps of transfer are as follows: completing ATF Form 4, paying of required taxes, and obtaining a signed law enforcement certification from the Chief Law Enforcement Officer of your jurisdiction. ATF NATIONAL FIREARMS ACT HANDBOOK 59–66 (Rev. Apr. 2009), http://www.atf.gov/publications/download/p/atf-p-5320-8/atf-p-5320-8.pdf. Form 4 can be downloaded from http://www.atf.gov/forms/firearms/. Applicants must submit duplicate forms with original signatures. An individual transferee must attach (1) a 2'' x 2'' photograph of the frontal view of the transferee taken within 1 year prior to the date of the application, and (2) two properly completed FBI Forms FD–258.

Individual ownership of an NFA weapon may put your client's family at risk due to the doctrine of constructive possession. When an individual owns an NFA weapon, that individual, and only that individual may possess the firearm. *United States v. Turnbough*, No. 96–2531, 1997 WL 264475 (7th Cir. May 14, 1997), is the landmark constructive possession case. Although the case is not specific to an NFA firearm, the principles and issues are identical to those confronted with NFA firearms. Mr. Turnbough kept an illegal firearm in the home he shared with his girlfriend and his girlfriend's daughter. The court ruled that "the government may establish constructive possession by demonstrating the defendant exercised ownership, dominion, or control over the premises in which the contraband is concealed." The court does not require that the defendant exercised ownership, dominion, or control over the actual contraband itself. To be charged with and convicted of constructive possession or any violation of the NFA, the prosecution is not required to prove intent. Something as simple as a spouse knowing the access code to the gun safe can lead to prosecution of both the spouse and the weapon owner. This is particularly important to understand due to the criminal penalties associated with unauthorized possession.

Another common dilemma relates to the transfer of NFA weapons in a person's estate following death or incapacity. Because the registration information compiled in the National Firearms Registry and Transfer record is tax information, the personal representative of an estate is the only person to whom this information may be disclosed. Any unregistered firearms should be handed over to law enforcement immediately and cannot be retroactively registered by the estate. For registered firearms, the executor is responsible for completing the necessary steps to register the firearm to him/herself. The estate planner should discuss these requirements with clients when determining who to name as the executor of their will.

Although technically the personal representative unlawfully possesses the firearm until the registration is cleared, ATF does allow the personal representative a reasonable amount of time to complete the transfer. Generally, the process should be completed prior to the end of probate. The personal representative is wholly responsible for the firearm registered to the decedent, therefore, the weapon should remain in the personal representative's custody and control. Although the personal representative may seek advice and support from a federally licensed firearms owner or dealer, he or she may not transfer the firearm to the licensee. If the personal representative were to transfer the firearm to a licensee for consignment or safekeeping, the personal representative would be criminally liable, because even consignment and safekeeping are transfers subject to the requirements of the NFA. However, the personal representative may seek assistance from a licensee to identify potential purchasers.

Although this process is burdensome for a personal representative, the benefit of a probate transfer is that the transfer is exempt from the $200 tax when transferred to a will beneficiary or, if the owner died intestate, an heir. ATF Form 5 is used when applying for a tax-exempt transfer to a beneficiary or heir. These procedures are the same as a transfer to any other individual. If the firearm is to be transferred out of the estate, the transfer is no longer tax-exempt and the transfer is subject to the requirements of ATF Form 4. If the firearm is unserviceable then the transfer is tax-exempt. ATF, TRANSFERS OF NATIONAL FIREARMS ACT FIREARMS IN DECEDENTS' ESTATES 1 (2006).

The solution to most of the obstacles associated with acquiring an NFA weapon as an individual is simple. The National Firearms Act defines "individual" to include corporations, trusts, and other similar legal entities. Because it is lawful to transfer a registered NFA firearm to an individual, barring any specific state legislation stating otherwise, it follows that you can transfer a registered NFA firearm to a trust–a "gun trust." If drafted properly, an NFA Gun Trust should give guidance to the grantor, trustee(s), and beneficiaries of the trust to avoid any NFA violations. 27 C.F.R. § 479.11 (2003).

The Gun Trust expedites the purchase of firearms as well as provides a comprehensive estate plan to maintain ownership and ease transfer at death. Additional benefits of the gun trust include (1) ease of administration as no finger prints, photos, or law enforcement certification are required; (2) the ability of anyone acting as a trustee lawfully to possess the firearms held in trust; (3) removal of the weapons from probate proceedings; and (4) subject to the Rule Against Perpetuities, the trust continues to protect a client's assets if the transfer of NFA firearms is later prohibited. Although a traditional trust may satisfy the purchase requirements and even expedite the process, it will not provide for the complexities of the future nor comprehensively protect against unlawful possession in case of death or incapacity.

When creating a Gun Trust, it is important to help clients think through the specifics of their situation. Ultimately, this process requires your client to determine their present and future goals and with whom these goals relate. Sometimes it can be difficult to determine how someone would like property handled at death or incapacity, but it is important so that the trust can outline specific instructions and powers for the trustee in case of unplanned events. Considering that NFA weapons cannot be transferred like traditional personal property, without proper trust creation, the risk of criminal penalties and confiscation is significant.

Basic underlying principles of trust formation apply to the creation of a Gun Trust. When determining the people to involve, keep in mind that your client cannot be named as the only beneficiary if your client is also the sole trustee as then no trust will actually be created. Therefore, if the trust purchases a firearm, your client will be deemed an individual illegally possessing an NFA firearm. Also, be weary of including too many people in the trust because anyone designated as a trustee is free to use the firearms. This presents significant risks because each trustee is jointly and severally liable for all of the actions of co-trustees under the partnership issues addressed in the NFA.

One of the most important steps in creating a Gun Trust is determining the powers, duties, and other terms in the trust. Because the duties and terms are so drastically different from the traditional purposes for trust arrangements, it is ill-advised to include other assets in an NFA Gun Trust. Additional assets would only create confusion and unnecessary risk for the client.

A generic Gun Trust is almost impossible to create because of the variety of circumstances that present themselves in each client's life. But, there are a few key elements that should always be addressed. An NFA Gun Trust must include the following information to determine necessary actions to ensure proper transfer upon death or incapacity: whether it is permissible in the jurisdiction to transfer the items, whether the items are legal in the state to where they will be transferred, whether the beneficiary is legally able to be in possession of or use the items, and whether the successor trustee is given the ability to determine whether the beneficiary is mature and responsible enough to have control of the firearms. David M. Goldman, *How is a NFA Gun Trust Different than a Revocable Trust?* July 15, 2009, http://www.guntrustlawyer.com/2009/07/how-is-a-nfa-gun-trust-differe.html.

Clients may be tempted to use forms they find on the Internet or in bookstores to create a trust. Although this is risky conduct with regard to any property, there are substantial risks involved when NFA weapons are included in the trust property. For example, a significant number of these forms, when used for NFA weapons, fail to create a valid trust. If the trust does not legally exist, regardless of whether the ATF approved the transfer to the trust, your client, as an individual, would be deemed to be in unlawful possession of the firearm and would be subject to the penalties the NFA imposes. If a valid trust were formed, but exists with the terms of a generic trust instrument, the transfer of the weapon may be lawful but other problems may arise. Traditional trusts do not address death or incapacity with regard to firearms and often instruct trustees to transfer the property in ways that create liability to the beneficiary, puts the assets as risk of seizure, and put both the trustee and beneficiary at risk of violating the NFA. David M. Goldman, *BATFE Seeks to Seize NFA Firearms from an Invalid Quicken Trust*, May 22, 2009, http://www.guntrustlawyer.com/2009/05/batfe-seeks-to-seize-nfa-firea.html.

Another short cut clients may be tempted to take is to use a free NFA Gun Trust Form provided by their gun dealer. Typically, gun dealers are not attorneys nor are they well versed in estate planning techniques. Therefore, not only are these forms inadequate in establishing even the most basic of trusts, they will not create the kind of trust necessary to protect NFA firearms.

There is a plethora of issues that can arise when using generic forms to create a trust consisting of NFA weapons. Most trust forms are set up for one settlor and one trustee. If you were to form an NFA Gun Trust under those limitations, you would completely defeat the trust's potential to protect against constructive possession. Another common issue with generic forms is that they create revocable trusts. Considering that the trust is the registered owner of the firearm, revocation of the trust would lead to unlawful possession by anyone possessing the firearms owned by the revoked trust. Traditional revocable trusts also risk being revoked by someone acting under the settlor's power of attorney. Sub-trusts for children are often created by these forms and should not be for NFA weapons because of their restrictive nature and the possibility that a minor may end up illegally owning the firearms. The language used in trust forms with regard to trust property usually permits the trustee to buy, sell, lease, or alter the property. If a trustee were to act according to the trust and without following protocol, the trustee would be subject to criminal penalties.

Although not a complete list of issues involving generic trust forms, it should be clear that the risks associated with making a mistake or improperly forming the trust agreement are severe. Remember, ATF approval of a purchase by a trust does not shield purchasers if a problem with the trust is later discovered. Basically, ATF assumes the validity of the trust but in no way guarantees the validity of the trust. David M. Goldman, *Why Do I Need an NFA Trust?*, Oct. 6, 2009, http://www.guntrustlawyer.com/2009/10/why-do-i-need-an-nfa-firearms.html.

U. OTHER SPECIAL CIRCUMSTANCES

1. CLIENT UNABLE TO SIGN

Your client may be unable to sign estate planning documents because of an injury or a muscular or neurological disease. Most statutes permit proxy signatures on wills and other documents provided the proxy signs in the presence of and by the direction of the person unable to sign. See, e.g., U.P.C. § 2–502(a)(2). In addition, the term signature is usually broadly defined or interpreted to include a mark or other symbol which a person executes or adopts with the present intent to authenticate the document. See generally THOMAS E. ATKINSON, LAW OF WILLS § 64 (1953). Professor Atkinson also suggested that "[t]he best form of signature by proxy is to write the testator's name 'by ______ (the proxy),' and perhaps following this with a statement that it was written by testator's direction and in his presence."

QUESTION

Would you take any additional steps to document a proxy signature? If yes, what would you do?

LOCATE

What are the rules in your state regarding proxy signatures on wills, powers of attorney, living wills, and other estate planning documents?

2. CLIENT UNABLE TO SPEAK AND/OR HEAR

You may communicate with a client who cannot speak and/or hear through sign language or in writing. You may consider having a sign language interpreter present during your meetings with the client. However, the introduction of a third-party into the interview raises confidentiality issues as well as fears that the translation may not be accurate. The situation is analogous to the non-English speaking client discussed in Chapter 10(G). Although somewhat tedious, you may decide to conduct all communications in writing or via a TDD–TYY device to assure privacy and accuracy.

3. CLIENT WITH RELIGIOUS REQUIREMENTS

Clients who adhere to certain religious faiths may have a strong desire for their wills to comply with their religious tenets. Compliance may be a simple such as the inclusion certain language in the will. On the other hand, compliance may be difficult because of the differences between state law and the requirements of the client's religion. See Omar T. Mohammedi, *Shaiah-Compliant Wills*, PROB. & PROP., Jan./Feb. 2011, at 58.

4. ATTORNEY AS SOLE PRACTITIONER

What happens if you are a sole practitioner when you die? "The going concern or goodwill value of your business would rapidly diminish. A forced sale of your business assets * * * will sacrifice the sale price and impair your family's long-term security. And if your cases are not handled appropriately, your estate may be subject to malpractice claims." Teddar S. Brooks, *Have You Taken Care of Your Tomorrow?,* COMPLEAT LAW., Winter 1989, at 37. "Anticipating the death of an attorney presents some challenges unlike those that face other businesses." Richard A. Sugar, *Death of a Lawyer—Duty to Client, Heirs, and Country*, 83 ILL. B.J. 116 (1995).

NOTES AND QUESTIONS

1. What types of issues must you address in planning for the estate of a sole practitioner?

2. What special steps would you take to resolve these issues?

3. Assume you represent the estate of a deceased sole practitioner. As you sort through the attorney's files, you find several original wills and various other original estate planning documents. What should you do with them?

CHAPTER 11

DOCUMENT PREPARATION, EXECUTION, AND RELATED MATTERS

■ ■ ■

A. INTRODUCTION

You must have a firm grasp of all relevant law to prepare an effective estate plan. The most sophisticated and contest-proof plan, however, is useless if the documents are not properly prepared and executed. Many estate plans fail because of careless mistakes made in the office or by sloppy document execution, safekeeping, or review. Before studying the materials in this chapter, please review the basic principles of document drafting discussed in Chapter 1(E).

B. DOCUMENT FORMATTING

1. ORGANIZATION OF BASIC WILL

Estate planning documents should be clearly and logically organized. Frequent use of descriptive headings aids in the understandability of the documents. Below is a sample format for a basic will which includes a testamentary trust. Remember, this example is just a suggestion. Different situations may call for different arrangements of provisions. In addition, your personal style affects how you organize your documents.

1. **Exordium**

   The introductory clause is usually unlabeled and contains the following items:

   a. Client's name, including a.k.a. names, e.g., names Client used prior to marriage, names Client used during previous marriages, nicknames, etc. The term "nee" is often used to indicate the last name which a married woman used prior to marriage, that is, her family or maiden name.

   b. Client's current residence (city, county, and state).

   c. Statement that this document is Client's will.

   d. Express revocation of prior wills and codicils.

e. Social security number. Client's social security number will be useful during the administration process to track down assets, obtain other benefits, and complete probate forms.

2. Description of Client's Family

This section is used to explain Client's family tree and whether the indicated relatives were alive or deceased at the time Client executed the will.

a. Marital status, e.g., name of Client's current spouse (if any) and when married; names of any ex-spouses and when divorced.

b. Descendants (children, grandchildren, etc.), including birth dates.

c. Parents.

d. Siblings.

e. Other relevant family information on a case-by-case basis.

f. Identifying information. To aid Client's executor in locating family members, you may want to include the current city and state of residence of each listed person.

3. General Provisions

This section contains provisions as appropriate under state law and Client's situation. Below are some examples of provisions typically included in this section of the will.

a. Definitions of key words used in the will. Define any terms used in the will which may cause controversy if left undefined. For example, if Client makes a class gift to "children" or "grandchildren," you should carefully explain whether Client intends to include adopted individuals, individuals born out of wedlock, or individuals born as the result of alternative reproduction technologies. In addition, Client should specify the age by which an adopted grandchild needs to be adopted by Client's child to fall within the class. Definitions, especially if extensive, may also be placed as a separate section immediately after the exordium.

b. Survival period, that is, the length of time a beneficiary must outlive Client to take under the will.

c. Express disinheritance. If Client wishes to make certain an heir does not take any portion of the estate, even if by chance Client dies partially intestate, express disinheritance is appropriate if local law recognizes negative will provisions. If Client fears that an as yet unknown person may claim paternity, a statement such as, "I expressly disinherit any child of mine whom I have not expressly listed by name in Article [ ]," may be included.

d. Treatment of omitted (pretermitted) children. An after-born or after-adopted child may be entitled to a statutory forced share. Client needs to decide whether Client wants these individuals to share in the estate.

e. Effect of marital problems. Provisions in favor of an ex-spouse are automatically revoked upon divorce unless the will provides otherwise in most states. However, merely filing for divorce is not treated as a divorce and will not revoke any provisions of the will unless the will expressly so states.

f. No contest (*in terrorem*) provision. A no contest provision may prevent heirs who are also beneficiaries of the will (but who are not receiving as much as they would under intestacy) from contesting the will. Note that the clause may be unenforceable if the contestant has probable cause for instituting the proceedings and brings them in good faith.

g. Satisfaction. Client should indicate whether transfers Client subsequently makes to a beneficiary offset gifts made in the will.

h. Disposition of disclaimed property.

i. Contractual nature of will. Client should state whether the will is executed pursuant to a contract. If yes, the material provisions of that contract should be set out.

j. Rule Against Perpetuities savings clause.

k. Anatomical gifts. Although anatomical gifts may be made by will, it is not prudent because Client's will may not be found and read until long after the time for making usable gifts has passed. Thus, Client should execute a separate document. Nonetheless, confirmation in a will may be helpful if the family is unsure about Client's intent.

l. Body disposition instructions. Although body disposition instructions may be stated in a will, they will not be effective unless the will is found immediately after death. Thus, if permitted under state law, it is better practice for Client to use a separate document or appoint an agent to control the disposition.

4. Settlement of Estate Obligations

The exact contents of this section of Client's will depends on the extent to which state law gives a person the opportunity to effect the satisfaction of estate obligations. The following topics should be covered:

a. Exoneration. Do beneficiaries of specific gifts receive only Client's equity in the gifted item or are mortgages, security interests, and other debts against the property paid from other estate assets?

b. Abatement. If Client wishes to change the state's abatement order if Client's estate is not sufficient to satisfy all gifts, Client should include an express abatement order.

c. Apportionment (or non-apportionment) of estate taxes.

5. Distribution of Property

Several techniques may be used to structure the dispositive provisions. The most common are listed below. Note that these methods are often combined in the same will.

a. By type of gift, e.g., begin with specific gifts, follow with the general gifts, and conclude with the residuary gift.

b. By identity of survivors, e.g., "I leave all my property to my spouse. If my spouse does not survive me, I leave all my property to my children."

c. By whether certain conditions are satisfied, e.g., "If all my children are at least twenty-five years old at the time of my death, I leave all my property to them in equal shares. If at least one of my children is under age twenty-five at the time of my death, I leave all my property to the Education and Support Trust created in Article V of this will."

The following issues must be addressed by the dispositive provisions if not already covered by general provisions applicable to all gifts:

a. Ademption.

b. Satisfaction.

c. Asset value changes.

d. Death of beneficiary before Client, including effect of the state's anti-lapse statute.

6. Testamentary Trust

This outline may also be used as a basic guide if you are preparing an inter vivos trust provided you address additional concerns such as the property Client wishes to transfer to the trust and whether Client may revoke the trust. Unless Client is creating the trust for tax purposes, Client probably wants to retain the power to revoke.

a. Conditions of creation.

b. Indication of which jurisdiction's law governs the trust.

c. Designation of trustees and alternates.

d. Whether bond is required.

e. Method of determining the trustee's compensation.

f. Identification of the beneficiaries.

g. Explanation of when the trustee may make distributions during the trust's existence, e.g., upon what conditions or contingencies, for what purposes, upon the discretion of the trustee, etc.

h. Events causing the trust to terminate.

i. Distribution of remaining trust property upon termination.

j. Rule Against Perpetuities savings clause.

k. The trustee's investment and administrative powers. Extensive trustee powers may be provided by state statute. If Client wishes the trustee to retain any particular item in the trust (e.g., a family heirloom or the family home) without regard to diversification or its wisdom as an prudent investment, Client should include an express provision permitting the retention.

l. Principal and income allocation instructions. To make it easier for non-corporate trustees to administer the trust, Client may permit the trustee to allocate receipts and expenses in whatever way the trustee determines is reasonable and equitable. This provision is less likely to be used if Client names a professional or corporate trustee because they have the expertise and bookkeeping systems to make the allocation in accordance with applicable principal and income legislation.

m. Spendthrift provision to protect the beneficiary's interest in the trust from the beneficiary's creditors and to prevent the beneficiary from transferring the interest.

n. Exculpatory clause for ordinary negligence.

7. Administration

Below are examples of provisions typically found in the administration section of the will.

a. Nomination of the executor and alternates.

b. Whether bond is required.

c. Method of determining the executor's compensation.

d. Type of administration, if subject to Client's control under state law.

e. Powers and duties of the executor.

f. Exculpatory clause for ordinary negligence.

g. Administrative provisions to secure favorable tax treatment.

8. Guardian of Person and Guardian/Conservator of the Estate of Minor Children

Guardian appointments are typically effective only upon the death of the surviving parent. Many states permit guardian and conservator appointments by way of a separate document as well as in a will.

9. Testimonium

This clause contains Client's signature and should also include an indication of the number of pages in the will and the date of execution.

10. Attestation

The attestation clause contains the witnesses' signatures and should also state the number of pages in the will and the date of attestation.

11. Self-Proving Affidavit

Most states authorize the use of a self-proving affidavit to expedite the probate of the will. The statutes typically contain the appropriate form language.

QUESTION

What changes, additions, or deletions would you make to this outline? Why?

2. INTERNAL INTEGRATION

Each estate planning document should fit neatly together as a unified instrument. By taking proper precautions, you may reduce the chance of fraudulent page insertion and also make it easier to show that the pages present when the client signed are the same pages now being used. Below are some methods to assure the continuity of the instrument and the interrelationship among all its pages.

- The testator and the witnesses initial each page.
- All handwriting on the will is in a color of ink other than black so the difference between the original and a photocopy is readily discernable. The testimonium and attestation clauses should specifically state the color of ink the testator and the witnesses used to sign the will. Some law firms include special chemical markers in their inks so the will can easily be traced. In addition, some individuals actually have their DNA mixed with the ink to enhance the likelihood of a positive identification.
- All pages are securely fastened together. Once the pages are connected, they should not be disconnected. Courts have considered multiple staple holes in a document to be evidence of improper page substitution. See Mahan v. Dovers, 730 S.W.2d 467 (Tex. App. 1987).
- The will is numbered using *ex toto* pagination, that is, by using the "page [current page number] of [total number of pages]" format.
- All pages are the same type of paper and uniform in size and color.
- The will is prepared with a consistent typeface scheme. For example, suspicions of page substitution are likely to arise if one page is printed in Arial while all of the other pages are in Times New Roman. Some law firms use custom designed fonts that include unique characteristics that are visible under high magnification.
- The same printer toner, ink-jet cartridge or typewriter ribbon is used for all of the pages of the will.
- Blank space is avoided. If the testator needs to conclude a provision before the end of the page, some indication of that fact should be

included in the will. For example, language such as the following could be included immediately after the text on the "short" page: "Article IV(C) ends here; Article V begins on the next page. The space below is intentionally left blank."

- The testator does not conclude each page with the end of a sentence. To avoid having a "loose-leaf will" which makes it easy for pages to be removed and inserted, the testator should have sentences that begin on one page and are carried over to the following page.

QUESTION

What other steps would you suggest to enhance internal integration?

3. PROFESSIONAL APPEARANCE

Estate planning documents should look professional. Do not crowd the printing on the pages, be sure the documents are printed in a readable font, use a good quality paper, avoid smudges and wrinkles, etc. Many estate planners place the executed documents in decorative covers or staple them to a thicker page, traditionally blue in color ("blue-backing").

C. FORMS*

*"Forms * * * are probably God's gift to lawyers."*[1]

1. SOURCES OF FORMS

a. Forms You Develop

Over time, you will develop your own set of forms based on prior experience. When a new document is needed, you will use your previously prepared documents as a starting point for drafting the new instrument.

b. Form Books

Many commercial publishers market single volume or multi-volume sets of books containing estate planning forms. You may search these books to locate the forms which match, as nearly as possible, the instrument you need to prepare. These forms then serve as models or samples for drafting the new instrument.

---

* Portions of this section are adapted from 1 GERRY W. BEYER, STATUTORILY ENACTED ESTATE PLANNING FORMS: DEVELOPMENT, EXPLANATION, ANALYSIS, STUDIES, COMMENTARY, AND RECOMMENDATIONS 25–64 (1990).

1. Sam S. Griffin, *Less Technical Legal Forms*, 19 PROC. IDAHO ST. B. 26, 26 (1944). For a less dramatic statement, see Florida Bar v. American Legal & Business Forms, Inc., 274 So.2d 225, 227 (Fla. 1973) ("[t]he printing and sale of legal forms * * * has been an aid to attorneys").

LOCATE

What are the popular form books used by estate planners in your state? Which ones do you like best? Least? Why?

c. Computer Generated Forms

You may prepare and store forms in computer usable formats. Commercial publishers also market computer programs to assist you in document preparation. Some programs supply only the text of forms much like traditional form books. Other programs will prompt you to enter relevant information and then use that data to select and print a suitable form, inserting individualized information at the appropriate locations. Features of sophisticated programs include interactive advice and analysis, citations and links to additional resource material, regular updates, the ability to use information entered for one document as the basis for an entire array of estate planning documents, and visual aids such as pie charts and graphs. For a comprehensive review of nine major programs, see Joseph G. Hodges, Jr. & Jason E. Havens, *Deftly Drafting Estate Planning Documents*, PROB. & PROP., July/Aug. 2004, at 35.

LOCATE

1. What document assembly programs are commonly used by attorneys in your community?

2. Many software publishers supply free demo programs to law students (prospective purchasers). Obtain several of these programs and perform a critical comparison by looking at factors such as ease of use, accuracy, understandability, and whether the publisher supplies regular updates. Which program, if any, would you purchase for your practice?

d. Pre-printed Forms

Commonly used forms, especially those of the fill-in-the-blank variety, are printed by commercial publishers, bar associations, and public service organizations in a ready-to-use format. In addition, you may obtain some forms, especially those relating to procedural matters, directly from the clerk's office at the courthouse.

e. Statutorily Supplied Forms

Statutes frequently provide the text of estate planning forms which you may reproduce as contained in the statute or incorporate into documents by reference. California, Maine, Michigan, and Wisconsin have enacted statutory fill-in-the-blank forms for wills and Massachusetts and New Mexico have adopted the Uniform Statutory Will Act which permits the testator to incorporate various provisions into a will by reference. See Gerry W. Beyer, *Statutory Will Methodologies—Incorporated Forms vs. Fill–In Forms: Rivalry or Peaceful Coexistence,* 94 DICK. L. REV. 231 (1990).

Although only a few states have statutory fill-in forms for wills, most states have forms for at least one of the following documents: self-proving affidavit, durable power of attorney for property management, durable power of attorney for health care, living will, self-designation of guardian, burial instructions.

LOCATE

What statutory forms are available in your state?

NOTES AND QUESTIONS

1. Legal scholars, practitioners, and the bench have praised and criticized statutory fill-in forms. They vigorously debate their value and effect on both the legal and non-legal communities. What are the potential advantages and disadvantages of these forms? See Gerry W. Beyer, *Statutory Fill-in Will Forms—The First Decade: Theoretical Constructs and Empirical Findings,* 72 OR. L. REV. 769 (1993).

2. For cases involving statutory wills, see Estate of Perry, 51 Cal. App.4th 440, 58 Cal.Rptr.2d 797 (1996) (holding that a statutory will failing to meet statutory requirements may still be admitted to probate if it complies with the general requirements for execution of wills); Estate of Smith v. Smith, 61 Cal.App.4th 259, 71 Cal.Rptr.2d 424 (1998) (requiring statutory will to be admitted to probate despite terms inapplicable to testator giving rise to contestants' claim of mistake because there was sufficient evidence that testator intended the instrument to be her will).

f. Public Records

Many estate planning documents must be filed on the public record. Thus, you may visit the local courthouse, review filed documents, and adapt what you find to your own use.

2. BENEFITS OF USING FORMS

a. Reduction in Preparation Time

Using previously prepared estate planning forms is an efficient method for reducing the time and effort you must expend to draft a document. You may save a great amount of time with forms that need or permit little or no original material, e.g., a living will based on a statutory form. Even if you must prepare new material, such as the dispositive provisions of a will, drafting time is significantly reduced by using a form as a starting point.

Considerable clerical time is also saved through the use of estate planning forms. Pre-printed or computer-generated forms with blanks for the insertion of relevant information permit your secretary to complete forms rapidly. With the development of computers capable of storing and swiftly retrieving practically unlimited quantities of text, the speed at which forms may be assembled and printed has dramatically increased.

b. Lower Cost of Legal Services

As a direct result of the professional and clerical time saved through proper use of estate planning forms, you can lower the cost of your legal services. This reduction in cost produces widespread benefits. Individuals who could not previously afford estate planning services may now be able to reap the benefits of a planned estate and individuals who can afford to pay higher prices are less burdened by legal expenses.

c. Increased Predictability of Results

Because forms contain standardized provisions, you may safely rely on the content of each form being the same every time that form is used. You must still use care, of course, when adapting the form to particular situations. This uniformity improves your ability to predict the results which will automatically flow from the use of the form.

d. Lessened Opportunity for Error

By using a well-designed form, you decrease the chance of undetected clerical and legal errors. "If every paper drawn * * * had to be prepared de novo * * * the possibility of error, such as the accidental omission by a stenographer of a line or two, which would easily pass unnoticed in signing and serving a formal paper, would be greatly multiplied." *The Legal Blank*, 30 Law Notes 124, 124 (1926). Forms also serve as checklists so you do not inadvertently omit or misstate essential terms.

e. Decreased Opportunity for Litigation

As already mentioned, prudent use of forms increases the predictability of results and lessens the opportunity for error. As a consequence, there should be less litigation involving estate planning matters. Since you are relieved from concerns about form, you may "concentrate on any legal questions which may be involved in the matter of substance to be filled into the blank." *Advantages of Uniform Land Mortgage Act*, 30 Law Notes 123, 124 (1926) (statement made in support of passage of Uniform Land Mortgage Act). This reduces the chances of a problem arising after it is too late to take corrective measures short of litigation because you may give greater attention to substantive matters.

QUESTION

What are the additional benefits of using estate planning forms?

3. POTENTIAL DIFFICULTIES IN USING LEGAL FORMS

Although the benefits of estate planning forms are great, their use is subject to inherent difficulties as well as abuse.

a. Lack of Individualization

Estate planning forms are generic in nature; they are not designed with any particular client in mind. A form, especially one which is pre-printed with blanks to be filled in, may be difficult to customize to the facts of your client. No two cases are exactly alike and a form may be too rigid to permit the individualized adjustments needed in a particular situation.

b. Improper Selection

You must exercise great care in selecting the proper form because use of the wrong form could have disastrous effects on the estate plan. Improper selection (e.g., selecting the wrong template in a computer will drafting program) could result from mere inadvertence or haste. Improper selection may also be due to an attorney's ignorance as to which form should be used. This could occur when an attorney who is unfamiliar with estate planning leafs through a form book and picks a form that to the untrained eye appears proper but which yields unexpected results. Selection problems also arise because of the differences in law among the states. A form meeting the requirements of one state may fail to meet the requirements of another. Likewise, choosing a form that you have used for years with excellent results may suddenly cause difficulties if you are unaware of recent legislative changes or judicial decisions.

c. Improper Completion

A form, no matter how simple or artfully drafted, may be improperly completed. Improper completion may stem from the attorney's lack of understanding on how to complete the form, especially if the attorney is not familiar with estate planning matters. Improper completion may also occur subsequent to the document's execution if spaces originally left empty are filled in. This could be done by a client who is unaware of the consequences of altering the original document. Alternatively, someone determined to obtain an advantage by improper means could perform the completion.

Inappropriate completion defeats the client's intent by creating problems that are often difficult and costly to correct. In some situations, the discovery of the errors will come so late that a remedy is not available; for example, defects in a will may not be discovered until after the testator's death.

d. Carelessness Encouraged

Using prepared forms, for the most part, requires less effort and is faster than drafting a form entirely from scratch. Desire for increased efficiency may cause some attorneys to become lax in their use of forms. A form may be used because the lawyer does not "care to take the time to think through a transaction and develop [his or her] own paperwork" rather than because it is best suited to the task at hand. PETER B. BROIDA, A GUIDE TO MERIT SYSTEMS PROTECTION BOARD LAW & PRACTICE ch. 19, § B

(1987). Similarly, a form may be used without sufficient research into the validity and effect of the form under current case and statutory law. Naturally, such carelessness will often lead to undesired results.

e. Potential for Abuse by Attorneys

Despite their specialized training, attorneys may improperly select and complete an estate planning form or may be too hurried to ascertain whether a particular form is appropriate and to make the required changes. Proper selection of a form requires detailed knowledge of substantive law and facts of the particular transaction. Lawyers may misplace their trust in forms merely because they have "the halo of publication." JACOB A. RABKIN & MATTHEW H. JOHNSON, CURRENT LEGAL FORMS WITH TAX ANALYSIS ix (1988) (noting that forms are good tools for good lawyers, not substitutes for good lawyers). Such lack of ordinary and reasonable care may subject lawyers to malpractice liability. In addition, the bar may discipline attorneys for failing to act with reasonable diligence.

Prepared forms also give unscrupulous attorneys a technique for taking advantage of naive clients. Clients who need estate planning documents may not realize that their attorneys are merely using forms taken from a book or generated by a computer program that required little or no original effort to prepare. Attorneys may bill for their time as if the documents had been drafted especially for these clients and the clients may pay their attorneys without suspecting the fraud perpetrated upon them.

NOTES AND QUESTIONS

1. What other difficulties can you see with using "canned" estate planning forms?

2. Since forms play a vital part in the estate planning process, what steps will you take to be sure forms are properly used in your office? See Maureen B. Collins, *Using Forms Effectively and Efficiently*, 85 ILL. B.J. 337 (1997).

D. COMMON DRAFTING ERRORS

1. INACCURATE REFLECTION OF CLIENT'S INTENT

The estate planning document may not accurately reflect the client's intent for a variety of reasons.

a. Failure to Gather Sufficient Information

You must conduct a very detailed client interview and compile a vast array of data before preparing the estate plan. Please review Chapter 8(D). Failure to obtain relevant facts makes it difficult or impossible to draft an adequate estate plan. A client may not reveal certain important information merely because the attorney did not ask; the client may not realize the material's significance. On the other hand, the client may be embarrassed by certain facts and be reluctant to reveal them (e.g., a child born out of wedlock). Use of detailed client interview forms and checklists will increase the likelihood of discovering relevant information.

b. Believing Client Without Independent Verification

A client unskilled in legal matters may inadvertently (or even intentionally) mislead the estate planner. To avoid unexpected surprises, you should ask for supporting documentation whenever possible regarding family matters (e.g., marriages, divorces, birth of children, adoptions), ownership of assets (e.g., deeds, stock certificates, bonds), employee benefits (e.g., retirement plans, bonus plans, annuities), bank accounts (e.g., statements, passbooks, certificates of deposit, account contracts, signature cards), debts (e.g., promissory notes, deeds of trust, mortgages), life insurance (e.g., policies and beneficiary designations), and other relevant matters (e.g., powers of attorney, directives to physicians).

Clients frequently believe that documents have a particular effect when in actuality they do not. A simple example is instructive. The client tells you that he has a large certificate of deposit in his name and his best friend's name. The client explains he wants this certificate to pass to his friend, rather than to his family under his will. He assures you that the certificate is in survivorship form and you do not independently verify this assertion. When the client dies, you discover that the friend's name was either not on the certificate or that the certificate lacked survivorship language. The friend goes away empty-handed and the client's intent is frustrated.

c. Neglecting Communications With Client

You must be aware of the importance of maintaining communication with the client both during and after the preparation of the estate plan. During the estate planning process, the client may have questions or wish to make changes; this is often the case once a client begins thinking seriously about the disposition of family heirlooms. You are more likely to prepare an intent-reflecting estate plan if you promptly return telephone calls and answer letters. Please review Chapter 8(F).

d. Failure to Act Timely

An estate plan should be completed in a timely fashion. Obviously, this is true if the client is elderly or seriously ill. Prompt estate planning is also necessary even if a client is young and in perfect health at the time of the initial interview; the person could have a fatal automobile accident or heart attack on the way home. You may want to have the client execute a simple will, even a holographic one, at the time of the initial interview to accomplish at least a portion of the client's estate planning objectives. A one page will leaving all the client's property to the surviving spouse and appointing the spouse as executor is often a desirable alternative to intestacy.

e. Failure to Document Unusual Requests

If a client makes an estate planning decision that you fear may appear suspicious to others or might be viewed as evidence of your negligence, special precautions are necessary. For example, a married individual may want to leave the entire estate to the spouse or more than the applicable exclusion amount to a non-spouse and thus incur, or cause the surviving spouse to incur, federal estate tax liability which could easily have been avoided. You should explain the potential outcomes to the client in writing and then have the client sign a copy of the writing acknowledging that the client is aware of the ramifications of the decision.

f. Failure to Recognize Circumstances Increasing the Likelihood of a Contest

You must always be on guard when drafting instruments which may supply incentive for someone to contest a will or other estate planning document. Please review Chapter 9(A).

g. Poor Proofreading of Documents

Many mistakes in estate planning documents are the result of poor proofreading. In a fast-paced office, time pressure may appear to restrict your opportunity to review carefully the documents. Under no circumstances should a client sign an estate planning document without both the client and the attorney carefully reading and studying the final draft. It may also be advisable for another attorney to review the documents. Major errors (e.g., a misplaced decimal point in a legacy or the omission of an important provision) as well as seemingly minor errors (a misspelling of a beneficiary's name) may be the focus of later litigation.

2. OMISSIONS

Problems often arise when important provisions are missing from an estate planning document. The law may have provided the client the ability to control how a particular situation is handled but if the instrument is silent, we may never know what the client would have wanted. Likewise, failure to plan for a contingency which actually occurs places the resolution thereof out of the client's control. Please review Chapter 2 paying particular attention to the following concepts.

- Ademption.
- Lapse.
- Exoneration.
- Satisfaction.
- Survival.

- Abatement.
- Pretermitted children.
- Adopted children.
- Children born out of wedlock.
- Rule Against Perpetuities.
- Type of administration.
- Identity of personal representative and alternates.
- Bond of personal representative.
- Compensation of personal representative.
- Tax matters, especially marital deduction, special use valuation, generation skipping tax, apportionment of taxes, etc.
- Divorce.
- Spendthrift provisions.

3. AMBIGUITIES

Ambiguity is one of the most frequent causes of will litigation. You must exercise care to phrase the will clearly and precisely. Choose words to avoid doubt as to their intended meaning. If you use potentially ambiguous language, unambiguous definitions should be included. Be especially leery of using the following words and phrases: "cash," "money," "funds," "personal property," "issue," and "heirs." The descriptions of specific gifts and designations of beneficiaries should be precise.

NOTES AND QUESTIONS

1. Testator's will gives "$100,000 to both of my children with the remainder to Most Excellent Law School." The distributable estate consists of $500,000. How is the estate divided assuming both children are alive?

2. Testator's will states, "I leave $20,000 to Susan and $40,000 to Maria. I also leave her all my shares in Huge Corporation." Who receives the stock? Would your answer change if you knew Testator had only two children, Susan and Maria, and that the stock was worth approximately $20,000?

4. PRECATORY LANGUAGE

Instructions in a will regarding the disposition of property must be mandatory to be enforceable. Precatory language, such as "I wish," "I would like," and "I recommend," is normally considered suggestive in nature and not binding on the beneficiary. Precatory language has no place in a will. If your client wishes to express non-mandatory desires, a separate non-testamentary document or videotape should be used. If the testator insists on placing such language in the will, you should add language indicating that the suggestions are merely precatory and are not binding.

NOTES AND QUESTIONS

1. Can you think of other types of drafting errors? If yes, what are they?

2. What steps will you take to avoid these problems?

3. For further information, see Susan F. Bloom, *The Need For a Will: Preresiduary Considerations and Common Drafting Errors,* 182 PLI/EST 7 (1988); Myles J. Laffey, *Common Drafting Errors*, 13 QUINNIPIAC PROB. L.J. 57 (1998); Nancy G. Henderson, *Drafting Dispositive Provisions in Wills (Part 1),* PRAC. LAW., June 1997, at 33; Debra Baker, *Where There's a Will, There's a Way to Make Mistakes*, A.B.A. J., May 1998, at 60.

E. SELECTING WITNESSES*

Little thought is usually given to the selection of witnesses. Typically, witnesses are individuals who merely by chance are available at the time of document execution, e.g., secretaries, paralegals, law clerks, delivery persons, etc. In most cases, this practice is not harmful, e.g., a self-proving affidavit eliminates the necessity for finding the witnesses to a will and the vast majority of wills are uncontested. The situation is considerably different, however, if a contest arises and the testimony of the witnesses regarding capacity or the details of the execution ceremony is crucial.

This section discusses some of the factors you should consider when selecting witnesses to a will. As you have seen, other estate planning documents may also need to be witnessed. Generally, the concerns with respect to witnesses for these instruments are the same as for wills. However, the enabling legislation for a particular document may impose additional requirements or restrictions on the individuals who may serve as witnesses. You must be certain to comply with the statutory mandates.

1. WITNESSES FAMILIAR WITH TESTATOR

"The jury is likely to give little weight to the testimony of a witness who never saw the testator before or after the execution of the will, and whose opportunity to form a conclusion was limited to the single brief occasion." M.K. WOODWARD & ERNEST E. SMITH, III, PROBATE AND DECEDENTS' ESTATES § 336, at 278 (17 Tex. Prac. 1971). Accordingly, if you anticipate a will contest, it is prudent to select witnesses previously acquainted with the testator, such as personal friends, co-workers, and business associates. These people are more likely to remember the ceremony and provide testimony about how the testator acted at the relevant time. In addition, they can compare the testator's conduct at the ceremony with how the testator acted at a time when the contestants concede that the testator had capacity.

The witnesses should not be will beneficiaries, heirs or other relatives of the testator either by consanguinity or affinity, creditors, or anyone else

* This section is adapted from Gerry W. Beyer, *Drafting in Contemplation of Will Contests,* in AMERICAN BAR ASSOCIATION, ESTATE AND TRUST LITIGATION: DRAFTING IN CONTEMPLATION OF CONTESTS; THE TRIAL; AND THE JUDICIAL PERSPECTIVE—A VIEW FROM THE BENCH (1991).

with a financial interest in the estate. Most states have statutes addressing the effect of a witness-beneficiary scenario on the validity of the will or the validity of certain gifts.

Considerable debate exists regarding the wisdom of having health care providers serve as witnesses or attend the will execution ceremony. The doctors and nurses who care for the testator appear well-qualified to testify about the testator's condition. During cross-examination, however, details about the testator's illness may come out that would not otherwise have been discovered. This additional information may prove sufficient to sway the fact-finder to conclude the testator lacked capacity. The danger is heightened if the doctor is a psychiatrist. "The very presence of a psychiatrist may be seized upon by the contestant as indicative of doubt as to testamentary capacity and, by adroit handling, may be caused to operate adversely to the proponent." Leon Jaworski, *The Will Contest,* 10 BAYLOR L. REV. 87, 93 (1958).

2. SUPERNUMERARY WITNESSES

Although attested wills in most states require only two witnesses, extra witnesses may be advisable if a contest is likely. The additional witnesses provide a greater pool of individuals who may be alive, available, and able to recollect the ceremony and the testator's condition.

3. YOUTHFUL AND HEALTHY WITNESSES

You should select witnesses who are younger than the testator and in good health. Although it is no guaranty, the use of young healthy witnesses increases the likelihood that they will be available (alive and competent) to testify if a will contest arises.

4. TRACEABLE WITNESSES

The proponent of a will who is charged with locating attesting witnesses to counter a will contest is often faced with a difficult task. Witnesses may move out of the city, state, or country. In addition, witnesses may change their names. For example, a female witness may marry and adopt her husband's name, a married female may divorce and retake her maiden name, or a witness may enter the federal witness relocation program and assume a new identity. To increase the chance of locating crucial witnesses, select witnesses who appear easy to trace, e.g., individuals with close family, friendship, business, educational, or political ties with the local community. To assist in the location process, the witnesses should write their social security numbers on the will. Note, however, that some witnesses may balk at the prospect of placing their numbers on documents which are likely to become public record in the future.

5. WITNESSES WHO WOULD FAVORABLY IMPRESS THE COURT AND JURY

You should carefully evaluate the personal characteristics of the witnesses. The witnesses should be people who would "make a good impression on the court and jury—substantial people of strong personality who speak convincingly and with definiteness." Leon Jaworski, *The Will Contest,* 10 BAYLOR L. REV. 87, 91 (1958).

NOTES AND QUESTIONS

1. What other qualifications are desirable in a witness?

2. It is easier to find someone if attempted contact is made at least once a year because the United States Postal Service will forward mail and, for a small fee, provide the sender with a corrected address. If you wait years, or decades, to find the witnesses (i.e., until the testator dies), you may need to hire expensive search services to locate them. Do you have a duty to keep track of witnesses on a regular basis?

F. EXECUTION PROCEDURE*

One of the most crucial stages of a client's estate plan is the will execution ceremony—the point at which the client memorializes desires regarding at-death distribution of property. Unfortunately, attorneys may handle this key event in a casual or sloppy fashion. There are even reports of attorneys mailing or hand-delivering unsigned wills to clients along with will execution instructions. Some attorneys may allow law clerks or paralegals to supervise a will execution ceremony. This practice is questionable not only because it raises the probability of error, but because the delegation of responsibility may be considered a violation of professional conduct rules proscribing the aiding of a non-lawyer in the practice of law. An unprofessional or unsupervised ceremony may provide the necessary ammunition for a will contestant successfully to challenge a will.

Since the earliest recognition of the power of testation, some type of ceremony has accompanied the exercise of that power. Will ceremonies have helped demonstrate that the testator was not acting in a casual, haphazard, whimsical, or capricious manner by furnishing proof that the testator deliberated about testamentary desires and had a fixed purpose in mind when making the will. The ceremonies also have provided evidence that the will was actually made by the testator, by impressing the act on the minds of witnesses.

A proper ceremony, coupled with sensitive and tactful counseling by the attorney during the entire estate planning process, may make it easier for clients to cope with the inevitability of death. Unfortunately, attorneys

* Portions of this section are adapted from Gerry W. Beyer, *The Will Execution Ceremony—History, Significance, and Strategies,* 29 S. TEX. L. REV. 413 (1988).

have been accused of showing "little concern about the therapeutic counseling that goes on in an 'estate planning' client's experience." Thomas Shaffer, *The "Estate Planning" Counselor and Values Destroyed by Death,* 55 IOWA L. REV. 376, 376 (1969). You need to remember that many clients make only one will during the client's entire life and that the psychological effects of confronting death are strong. Even if you conduct scores of will ceremonies each year, you must not lose sight of the client's emotions and the psychological benefits that may be obtained through client interviews and will ceremonies.

One commentator has somewhat humorously summarized the psychological benefits of the ceremony as follows:

> When a client comes in to do something about his estate planning problem, he wants a lot of things. He wants solace because he is thinking about the day when he will not be here. He wants approval of what he has done and what he proposes to do. And he wants something else he almost never gets—a ceremony. Now, life offers very few opportunities for high ceremony. Birth is not a very good time. It is too laborious. Marriage is handled in rather a spectacular style. Nobody has been able to do much with divorce on the ceremonial side. For death, there is a ceremony, but it is hard for a decedent to be there to enjoy it. He is the principal.
>
> The estate planning process * * * ought to be a high ceremonial occasion because a client should be getting great intangible satisfactions about these significant decisions that he has made that were embodied in the instruments he leaves behind.

Estate Planning for Human Beings, 3 U. MIAMI INST. ON EST. PLAN. § 69.1902 (P. Heckerling ed. 1969) (statement of Dean Willard H. Pedrick, panelist).

The client's testamentary desires will be effectuated only if all formalities are satisfied. The reporters are filled with cases in which a testator had the requisite legal and testamentary capacity and intent, but where a defect in the ceremony caused the will to fail. A properly conducted will execution ceremony helps assure compliance with the various formalities required for a valid will as well as impressing the event on the witnesses' minds.

When errors with the will execution ceremony are discovered during the testator's lifetime, the testator's only loss is the cost of having another will prepared and executed. This is normally not the type of situation where malpractice liability is litigated. The attorney may be able to avoid becoming a defendant by simply having the will re-executed without cost to the client and providing appropriate apologies for the inconvenience. Of course, if tax benefits were lost because of the error, the attorney's liability could be significantly greater.

Errors in the ceremony, however, often do not manifest themselves until after the client's death. At that time, the testator's estate probably could sue the negligent attorney. In a suit by the testator's estate, however, the only damages would be the attorney's fees paid for drafting the will since there would be no other diminution of the estate funds caused by the error. Accordingly, if there is a flaw in the will execution ceremony causing the will to be ineffective and that flaw can be traced to the conduct of the attorney in charge of the ceremony, it is the intended beneficiaries who now find themselves short-changed that are apt to bring a malpractice action.[1] These actions can be avoided with proper ceremonies.

This section suggests a comprehensive step-by-step format for a proper will execution ceremony. Although the procedure meets or exceeds the requirements of most common law states, the format must be adapted to the statutory and case law of each state. The basic structure of this will ceremony may also be used to formulate execution procedures for other estate planning documents.

1. PRIOR TO THE CEREMONY

a. Proofread Will

Before the client arrives for the will execution ceremony, you should carefully proofread the will for errors such as misspellings, omissions, erasures, and overstrikes. To reduce the number of inadvertent errors, it is advisable for another attorney to review the will. All errors should be carefully corrected and a new original prepared; interlineations, markouts, erasures, and correction fluid should not be used.

b. Assure Internal Integration of Will

Please review the discussion in Chapter 11(B)(2).

c. Review Will With Client

You should review the final draft of the will with the client to confirm that the client understands the will and that it comports with the client's intent. The client should have adequate time to read the will to confirm that corrections to prior drafts have been made and to determine that no unauthorized provisions have inadvertently crept into the will.

d. Explain Ceremony to Client

You should explain the mechanics of the will execution ceremony to the testator in language the testator understands. Avoid legal jargon because the client may be too embarrassed to admit a lack of understanding. It is helpful for the client to know how the ceremony will proceed and what is expected, e.g., to answer certain questions.

1. Whether or not privity is required for a malpractice action is discussed in Chapter 8(J).

2. THE CEREMONY

a. Select Appropriate Location

The will execution ceremony should take place in pleasant surroundings. A conference room works well, as does a large office with appropriate tables and chairs. The client should be comfortable and at ease with the ceremony. A relaxed client is more likely to present a better image to the witnesses.

b. Avoid Interruptions

The ceremony should be free of interruptions. Thus, your secretaries should hold all your telephone calls and receive instructions not to interfere with the ceremony. Once the ceremony begins, no one should enter or leave the room until the ceremony is completed. Interruptions disrupt the flow of the ceremony and may cause you to inadvertently omit a key element.

c. Gather Participants

You will gather the testator, two or three disinterested witnesses, and a notary at the appropriate location. As a precaution against claims of overreaching and undue influence, no one else should be present under normal circumstances.

d. Seat Participants Strategically

Seat the participants so each can easily observe and hear the others. You should be conveniently located near the participants to make certain the proper pages are signed in the correct places.

e. Make General Introductions

You should introduce all participants. Although it may be advisable to use witnesses already known to the client, it is a common practice for attorneys to recruit anyone who is around to serve as the witnesses.[2] Accordingly, it is important to impress the identity of the testator on the witnesses so they will be able to remember the ceremony should their testimony later be needed.

f. Explain Ceremony

You should explain that the will execution ceremony is about to commence and its importance. Although most states do not require publication, i.e., for the witnesses to know the type of document being witnessed, it is useful for the witnesses to know the document is a will should their testimony be needed later. In addition, publication may be required for the self-proving affidavit.

g. Establish Testamentary Capacity

If you anticipate a will contest, it is especially important to establish each element of testamentary capacity during the ceremony. You should

2. The selection of witnesses is discussed in Chapter 11(E).

engage the testator in a discussion designed to cover these elements, e.g., the testator should demonstrate that the testator knows the testator is executing a will disposing of property upon death and that the testator knows the general nature and extent of the testator's property as well as the natural objects of the testator's bounty.

h. Establish Testamentary Intent

You should direct questions in substantially the following form to the testator to demonstrate testamentary intent.

- [Testator's name], is this your will?
- Have you carefully read this will and do you understand it?
- Do you wish to make any additions, deletions, corrections, or other changes to your will?
- Does this will dispose of your property at your death in accordance with your desires?
- Do you request [witnesses' names] to witness the execution of your will?

i. Conduct Will Execution

The following steps should be followed when the testator executes the will.

- All writing on the will should be in blue ink to make an obvious distinction between the original and a photocopy. The will's testimonium and attestation clauses should indicate that the testator and the witnesses used blue ink.
- Testator initials each page of the will, except the last page, at the bottom or in the margin to reduce later claims of page substitution.
- Testator completes the testimonium clause by filling in the date and the location of the ceremony.
- Testator signs the will at the end. The testator should sign as the testator usually does when executing legal documents to prevent a contest based on forgery.
- You should pay close attention to make certain everything is written in the proper locations.
- The witnesses should watch the testator sign the will so that they may testify to the signing.

j. Conduct Attestation by Witnesses

The following procedure should be used for the witnesses' attestation.

- One of the witnesses reads the attestation clause aloud to help impress the will execution ceremony on the minds of the witnesses.

- Each witness initials every page, except the page with the attestation clause, at the bottom or in the margin. This helps reduce claims of page substitution.
- One of the witnesses dates the attestation clause to provide additional evidence of when the execution occurred.
- Each witness signs the attestation clause and writes the witness's address. Having the addresses on the will may be helpful should it later become necessary to locate the witnesses.
- You carefully watch to make certain everything is written in the proper locations.
- The testator observes the witnesses signing the will.
- The witnesses observe each other signing.

k. Declare Will Executed

After the attestation is finished, you should declare that the will is executed. A clear demarcation between the actual will ceremony and the completion of the self-proving affidavit is important because a proper will is usually a prerequisite to an effective self-proving affidavit.

l. Complete Self–Proving Affidavit

If state law permits a will to be self-proved, the appropriate affidavit should now be completed. The completion of the self-proving affidavit should include the following steps. Note that many states permit the self-proving affidavit to be included as part of the will so that only one set of signatures is required. If this is the case in your state, you will need to integrate these steps into the execution and attestation.

- You should explain the purpose and effect of a self-proving affidavit, i.e., to make probate easier and more efficient by allowing the will to be admitted without the testimony of witnesses.
- The notary takes the oath of the testator and witnesses.
- The notary asks the testator and witnesses to swear or affirm to the items required by state law. You should prepare a list of questions for the notary to ask the testator and witnesses modeled after the language of the affidavit which is normally found in a statutory form. This serves to impress the ceremony on the witnesses better than if they are merely asked to read and sign the affidavit.
- Neither you nor the notary should coax or otherwise suggest answers to these questions.
- The testator and witnesses sign the affidavit.
- The notary signs the affidavit and affixes the appropriate seal or stamp.
- If required by state law, the notary records the ceremony in the notary's record book.

m. Conclude Ceremony

You should indicate that the will execution ceremony is now complete. If other estate planning documents, such as a durable power of attorney, living will, or trust, are needed in the estate plan, it is convenient to execute them at the same time because these other documents often require witnesses, notarization, or self-proving affidavits.

3. AFTER THE CEREMONY

a. Confirm Testator's Intent

You should talk with the testator to confirm that the testator understood what just happened and that the testator does not have second thoughts about the disposition plan.

b. Make Copies of Will

You should photocopy the executed will for your file so that you may review it on a periodic basis to determine whether revisions are needed due to a change in the law or the testator's circumstances. In addition, the copy of the executed will is useful evidence of the will's contents if the original cannot be produced after death and there is sufficient evidence to overcome the presumption of revocation that often arises when the original is not located. Each copy should be clearly stamped, "copy."

c. Discuss Safekeeping of Original Will

This topic is covered in Chapter 11(H).

d. Destroy or Preserve Prior Will

See Chapter 9(B)(8) which discusses the wisdom of destroying or retaining the testator's prior will.

e. Provide Testator With Post–Will Instructions

You should provide your client with a list of post-will instructions containing at least the following:

- Discussion of the need to reconsider the will should the client's circumstances change due to births, adoptions, deaths, divorces, marriages, changes in feelings toward beneficiaries and heirs, significant changes in size or composition of estate, changes in state of domicile, retirement, etc.
- Explanation that mark-outs, interlineations, and other informal changes are usually insufficient to change the will.
- Instructions regarding safekeeping of the original will.
- Statement that the will must be reviewed if relevant state or federal tax laws change.

LOCATE

What are the will execution formalities mandated by law in your state?

QUESTIONS

1. Does the procedure outlined in this section meet the requirements of your state? What steps would you add or subtract? Why?

2. Should the testator reveal the contents of the testator's new will to family members? Why or why not?

DRAFT

1. When you start your career as an estate planner, you may find it difficult to remember all of the will execution steps during the excitement of the actual ceremony. After you are experienced, ceremonies become routine and you may simply forget steps. To avoid these problems, prepare a checklist you would use each time you supervise a will execution ceremony.

2. If your state authorizes self-proving affidavits, prepare the list of questions the notary should ask the testator and the witnesses.

3. Outline the steps for the execution of other estate planning documents under the law of your state.

G. VIDEO-RECORDING THE WILL EXECUTION CEREMONY

Modern video technology provides you with an inexpensive, convenient, and reliable method of preserving evidence of the will execution ceremony and its important components. A properly prepared videotape or DVD may be used to establish testamentary capacity, testamentary intent, compliance with will formalities, the contents of the will, lack of undue influence or fraud, and the correct interpretation or construction of the will.

The admissibility of a video depends generally on the following considerations: (1) relevance; (2) fairness and accuracy; (3) the exercise of judicial discretion as to whether the probative value of the recording outweighs the prejudice or possible confusion it may cause; and (4) other evidentiary considerations such as the presence of hearsay. A video of the will execution ceremony may easily be admitted under these standards. A video is not subject to the vagaries of a witness' fading memory, and it presents a more comprehensive and accurate view of the testator and the testator's condition at the time of will execution than does a piecemeal tendering into evidence of witnesses' testimony.

Although jurisdictions differ and courts do not always enumerate a complete list of foundation elements, there is basic agreement that seven elements must be established before a video is admitted into evidence: (1)

proper functioning of equipment; (2) competency of equipment operator; (3) accuracy of recording; (4) proper preservation of recording; (5) lack of alteration; (6) accurate identification of participants; and (7) making of recording voluntarily.

A video of the will execution ceremony has many potential advantages. It is highly accurate unlike witnesses whose memories and impressions fade with the passage of time. The video improves the ability of the court or jury to evaluate the testator's condition by preserving valuable non-verbal evidence such as demeanor, voice tone and inflection, facial expressions, and gestures. The video may also have psychological benefits for both the testator and the survivors. The testator may feel more confident that the intended dispositive plan will take effect and the survivors may gain solace from viewing the testator delivering a final message.

Despite the significant benefits of a will execution video, there are several potential problems. In some cases, steps may be taken to reduce or eliminate these problems, while in other situations the prudent decision would be to forego recording the ceremony.

Although a situation may otherwise seem appropriate for video-recording the will execution ceremony, you may be hesitant to expose the testator to the court. An accurate picture of the testator may lead a judge or jury to conclude that the testator was incompetent or unduly influenced. Similarly, the testator's outward appearance may prejudice some individuals because of, for example, the testator's age, sex, race, physical challenge, or annoying habits.

If the testator's appearance is "poor," you may decide to forego video-recording the ceremony. If the video is made and turns out badly, several difficult issues arise. Should the recording be erased? If the recording is retained, will it aid the will contestant if shown? What response is proper if during the deposition stage of a will contest you are asked whether the will execution ceremony was video-recorded? What can you do to prevent the potentially damaging recording's introduction short of perjury? There are few, if any, good answers to these questions.

There is always a possibility that the video of the will execution ceremony will be altered. The alteration could be accidental but careful storage procedures greatly reduce these risks. Recent reports have, however, raised the concern that the videotapes and DVDs may simply deteriorate over time.

Intentional alteration through skillful editing and dubbing may also occur, although videotapes and DVDs are more difficult to alter than written documents. Anyone with correction tape or fluid, scissors, a photocopier, and a bit of evil ingenuity can alter a written document. However, more sophisticated equipment and skills are required to make undetectable changes to a video. Use of a continuous display time-date generator along with a storage method requiring a documented chain of custody significantly reduces the possibility of tampering.

GLINN v. PETERSON

Supreme Court of Nebraska, 1989.
232 Neb. 105, 439 N.W.2d 516.

GRANT, JUSTICE.

The parties to this action are the five sons of the decedent, Bessie I. Peterson. Appellants, Francis J. Glinn, Marvin L. Peterson, and Dale I. Peterson (contestants), filed a "Petition for Formal Probate of Will and Formal Appointment of Personal Representative" in the county court for Arthur County, seeking the admission to probate of Mrs. Peterson's last will and testament, executed September 6, 1972, and objecting to a codicil to the will, executed January 16, 1985. Appellees, Eldon J. Peterson and Donald R. Peterson (proponents), are the proponents of the codicil, and Eldon Peterson apparently had offered the will and codicil for informal probate. Contestants' petition alleged, in part, that Mrs. Peterson executed the codicil as the result of undue influence on the part of Eldon Peterson and that Mrs. Peterson lacked testamentary capacity when she executed the codicil. All parties conceded the validity of the 1972 will. * * *

The will and codicil were received in evidence during the proponents' case in chief, and proponents then rested. After the close of the contestants' case, the district court sustained proponents' motion for a directed verdict on the issue of undue influence and directed a verdict for the proponents on that issue. The proponents then presented rebuttal testimony. At the close of all the evidence, the district court overruled both parties' motions for directed verdict on the remaining issue of testamentary capacity, and that issue was submitted to the jury. The jury returned a verdict for the proponents on the issue of testamentary capacity. The contestants timely appealed and assign as errors in this court the actions of the trial court in (1) granting the proponents' motion for directed verdict on the issue of undue influence and (2) failing to grant contestants' motion for directed verdict on the issue of testamentary capacity in that the proponents did not prove by a preponderance of the evidence that Mrs. Peterson had testamentary capacity at the time she executed the codicil. We affirm.

The record shows the following. Marvin, Dale, Eldon, and Donald Peterson are the sons of the decedent and her late husband John Peterson. Francis Glinn is Mrs. Peterson's son by a previous marriage. The family lived on John Peterson's 14,000–acre livestock ranch in Arthur County while the five sons were growing up and attending high school.

All of Mrs. Peterson's five sons worked on the ranch while they were in high school. Donald, Dale, and Marvin Peterson all attended college.

Appellant Francis Glinn testified that he returned to work on the ranch for 3 years after leaving the merchant marine in 1946. For the past 30 years, Glinn has operated his own livestock ranch 9 miles north of Keystone, Nebraska.

Appellant Dale Peterson testified that he attended Kearney State College after graduating from high school in 1948, and continued to work on the family ranch during college vacation. He decided to leave the ranch because "there didn't seem to be enough for all of us there." Dale formerly taught in Hastings. He currently resides in Omaha and teaches at Metropolitan Community College.

Appellant Marvin Peterson, the youngest son, testified that he had full responsibility for the ranch from the time he graduated from high school in 1957 until 1959, when Eldon returned from the Army. Marvin attended the University of Nebraska in 1959 and worked on the ranch during summer vacations until he graduated with an engineering degree in 1964. He lives in Ponca City, Oklahoma, and is employed as an engineer.

Appellee Donald Peterson is the oldest son of Bessie and John Peterson and works as a chemical engineer in Columbus, Nebraska. He testified that he worked on the ranch during college vacations and, even after college, has returned regularly to help with branding cattle.

Appellee Eldon Peterson, the second-youngest son, did not go to college, but stayed on the ranch with his father and mother. Marvin Peterson admitted that Eldon was on the family ranch "everyday of his life" except the time he spent in the Army. John Peterson was semiretired in 1959 when Eldon returned from the Army, and Eldon assumed management of the ranch at that time.

When John Peterson died in 1968 at the age of 78, he devised one-half of the ranchland to his wife, and undivided interests in the other half to his sons, Marvin, Dale, Eldon, and Donald, subject to Eldon's option to purchase the land at a price designated in John Peterson's will. Francis Glinn received a legacy of $10,000 cash from John Peterson.

Eldon and his mother continued the cattle operation on an equal partnership basis. At the time of Mrs. Peterson's death in January 1985, Eldon owned three-fourths and she owned one-fourth of the 14,000-acre ranch.

Mrs. Peterson had medical problems for many years, beginning with the removal of her left kidney in 1956. On September 6, 1972, Mrs. Peterson executed her last will and testament, devising equal shares of her real and personal property to her five sons, subject to Eldon Peterson's option to purchase certain farm and ranchland. The will named Delbert O. Cole as executor and Keith County Bank & Trust Company as substitute executor of the will.

Mrs. Peterson remained on the ranch after her husband's death and kept house for Eldon until 1982, when she had a stroke and was placed in a nursing home. After the stroke, her left side was essentially paralyzed, but she was sometimes able to walk with the help of a physical therapist. Eldon visited his mother at least once a week during the time she was in the nursing home. The other Peterson sons lived some distance away, but also visited their mother on a somewhat regular basis, two or three times a year. Appellant Glinn, who operated his own ranch north of Keystone, testified he visited his mother "probably a half a dozen times" in 3 years.

Several witnesses testified during the contestants' case as to Mrs. Peterson's physical and mental state after her stroke. Nursing home personnel testified that Mrs. Peterson was "alert" during 1982 and 1983. During that period, she could feed herself, wheel herself in her wheelchair, write letters, watch television, use the telephone, and hold conversations. She apparently suffered a renal failure in the fall of 1984. A nurse's aide testified that by December 1984 Mrs. Peterson was "somewhat alert, [but] wasn't totally alert." There is evidence that Mrs. Peterson sometimes was disoriented as to time, that she made errors in her correspondence, and that her letters to relatives did not totally make sense.

A doctor examined Mrs. Peterson on January 5, 1985, in the Ogallala hospital emergency room. She had been diagnosed as diabetic some time prior to this examination. He testified that in January 1985 Mrs. Peterson had very erratic blood pressure and gross intestinal bleeding. She was taking a variety of medications, complained of weakness, and was unable to eat. The doctor did not give Mrs. Peterson an orientation test. He was of the opinion that a person in her condition taking these medications might possibly have trouble with clear thinking, but was unable to form an opinion as to whether Mrs. Peterson had the necessary testamentary capacity on January 5 to make a will or codicil.

During the last month of her life, Mrs. Peterson sometimes appeared depressed and withdrawn, and often cried. She had difficulty eating, lost weight, slept frequently, and lost interest in her appearance. She told the nurse's aides she believed she was going to die. Like other elderly patients, however, Mrs. Peterson had "good days and bad days." Nursing home employees testified that on a good day, she was cheerful and able to respond.

In early December 1984, Eldon Peterson told his mother's attorney, James A. Lane, that Mrs. Peterson wanted to see him at the nursing home to discuss a change in her will. Neil Williams, a partner of Lane's, testified that Mrs. Peterson, not Eldon, was their client, although Williams did meet with Eldon once or twice to get a list of machinery. Williams also researched the issue of testamentary capacity and prepared a memorandum to Lane, his senior partner, about topics that should be covered when interviewing Mrs. Peterson. Williams testified that he participated in a conference with Mrs. Peterson and assisted in drafting the codicil.

On January 16, 1985, Mrs. Peterson executed the codicil to her will, changing the provisions of her will by devising to Eldon Peterson all her livestock and household goods. The codicil also modified the will in nominating Eldon Peterson as personal representative of the estate. The codicil did not modify the will in any other respect.

Mrs. Peterson's execution of the codicil, and the signing by the witnesses to the codicil, was videotaped at the nursing home. Eldon

Peterson was not present, but arrived at the nursing home after the codicil was signed. The conversation between Lane and Mrs. Peterson before the execution of the codicil also was videotaped. In that conversation, Mrs. Peterson was asked about the extent of her property, about the time of her husband's death, and about the time of a fire that destroyed her home. When asked why she wanted to leave all her cattle to Eldon, she stated that Eldon "took care of me all these years. He's been good to me, and he's a good manager." She wanted to give Eldon her household goods because "he paid for most of them" after the fire. In response to other questions, Mrs. Peterson indicated she realized that under the terms of the codicil Eldon would receive a larger share than the other children, but that "[Eldon] worked harder.... And he stayed there at home when none of the rest of them did." She further stated that she wanted to change her will, signed the codicil, and said, "I'm doing it because I want to."

Mrs. Peterson died on January 25, 1985, at the age of 81.

We review this probate case for error appearing on the record. * * *

Contestants first contend that the trial court erred in granting the proponents' motion for directed verdict on the issue of undue influence.

In order to successfully contest a will or codicil on the ground of undue influence, the contesting parties must prove by a preponderance of the evidence that (1) the testator was subject to undue influence, (2) there was an opportunity to exercise such influence, (3) there was a disposition to exercise such influence, and (4) the result was clearly the effect of such influence. * * * Not every exercise of influence will vitiate a will. Undue influence sufficient to defeat a will is such manipulation as destroys the free agency of the testator and substitutes another's purpose for that of the testator. * * *

In granting proponents' motion for directed verdict on the issue of undue influence, the district court determined that the evidence presented by the contestants, when taken in a light most favorable to the contestants, established that while Mrs. Peterson was vulnerable to undue influence because of her age and health, and Eldon had an opportunity to exercise undue influence because he saw his mother once a week, there was no evidence at all to suggest that Eldon was disposed to exercise undue influence or that the codicil was clearly the effect of such influence. Rather, the terms of the codicil reflected Mrs. Peterson's recognition of the special business relationship she had with Eldon for 17 years. That relationship was not shared with any of her other children.

After reviewing the record, we determine that the trial court did not err in granting the proponents' motion for directed verdict on the issue of undue influence.

The contestants also contend that the district court erred in overruling their motion for directed verdict on the issue of testamentary capacity, made at the close of the proponents' rebuttal testimony.

One possesses testamentary capacity if she understands the nature of her act in making a will or codicil thereto, knows the extent and character of her property, knows and understands the proposed disposition of her property, and knows the natural objects of her bounty. * * * Testamentary capacity is tested by the state of the testator's mind at the time the will or codicil is executed. * * *

Several of the contestants' witnesses testified to Mrs. Peterson's general decline during 1984 and that she had good days and bad days during the last month of her life. Mrs. Peterson had not discussed the terms of her will or the codicil with any of the witnesses other than attorneys Lane and Williams.

Only three of the contestants' witnesses specifically recalled seeing Mrs. Peterson on the day the codicil was executed. Teresa Gibson, a nurse's aide, recalled seeing attorneys and video equipment at the nursing home on January 16, 1985. Gibson testified that she stood in an open doorway and watched some of the videotaping. She observed that Mrs. Peterson was in her wheelchair, with her head down and her eyes closed, and appeared to be asleep. Dora Caudy, the laundry supervisor at the nursing home, testified that she had been asked to witness the codicil, but was reluctant to do so because, "I just didn't think that she knew what she was doing." The jury saw the videotape of the signing of the codicil, and by its verdict, it is apparent that it gave little weight to this testimony. Our examination of the videotape on this appeal leads to the same conclusion.

During the videotaped conversation, Mrs. Peterson stated her age as 79 rather than 81 and made mistakes regarding the year her house burned down and the year her husband died. She misstated that the ranch consisted of 1,400 acres but corrected herself, agreeing that the ranch was 14,000 acres. She was aware that she owned a one-fourth interest in the ranch and knew generally the extent of her cattle holdings. Mrs. Peterson also was aware that she held certificates of deposit, but did not know the exact amount of money so held. She stated that Eldon told her everything about the business. When naming her sons, she had to be reminded of Marvin, but she knew where all her sons lived and knew their occupations. Mrs. Peterson acknowledged that her stroke affected the use of her left arm but said, "It didn't hurt my head any."

Due to the manner in which the case was tried on the issue of testamentary capacity, the bulk of proponents' evidence was presented in their rebuttal case. Lane, an attorney of 47 years' experience, testified that at the time of this trial, more than 50 percent of his practice involved probate work, and that he had drafted over 4,000 wills or codicils during the course of his career. Lane met with Mrs. Peterson on January 13, 14, 15, and 16. During those meetings, she had contemplated disinheriting Glinn, but decided not to do so. Mrs. Peterson told Lane she wanted to give Eldon her interest in the cattle because she was grateful for all Eldon had done for her and was worried about the burden it would be for him to raise the cash to buy cattle from the estate. She also requested that the codicil name Eldon as personal representative. Lane testified he was of the opinion that on January 16, 1985, Mrs. Peterson knew generally the extent of her property, knew what was in the codicil, knew what she was doing in the codicil with the property, and knew the purposes of a codicil. Williams, who was present during the videotaping, also testified that Mrs. Peterson had the capacity to execute the codicil.

Rebuttal witness Charley Simineo, the nursing home administrator on January 16, 1985, witnessed the codicil. At the time of trial, Simineo was employed as health/medical facilities coordinator for the State of Wyoming. He holds a bachelor's degree in gereology from the University of Northern Colorado in Greeley. Simineo testified that it was common for elderly people to mix dates, years, and periods of time between occurrences. He was aware that Mrs. Peterson had this problem, but was of the opinion that it would not affect her mental capacity. Simineo also was of the opinion that on January 16, 1985, Mrs. Peterson knew the natural objects of her bounty, the extent and nature of her property, and the nature of her signing the codicil, and understood the proposed disposition of her property in the codicil. He further testified that Caudy, a witness called by the contestants, had not been asked to witness the codicil, as she had testified.

Appellee Donald Peterson was not present at the nursing home on January 16 but, based on his review of the videotape, was of the opinion that on January 16 his mother knew the members of her family, that she knew in general what she owned, that she knew she was executing a codicil that changed her will, and that she knew what the codicil was for. Donald Peterson obviously was testifying against his own personal financial interest, in that the codicil reduced his share of his mother's estate. Donald testified that his mother had a close relationship with Eldon and that some time after her will was executed she "made a very special point of telling me that she was going to take care of Eldon because he was considerate of her needs and wishes and she appreciated it. I have known it for years, what she intended to do." He testified that he became a proponent of the codicil when, "Finally it got to the point that only due, my mother's reputation ... I felt duty-bound, there was nothing I could do but to agree to help support what she wanted to do."

The testimony relating to the issue of testamentary capacity was not such that reasonable minds could draw but one conclusion therefrom. The trial court properly overruled both contestants' and proponents' motions for directed verdict and submitted the issue to the jury. The evidence was sufficient to establish by a preponderance that Mrs. Peterson understood the nature of her act, knew generally the extent and character of her property, knew and understood the proposed disposition of her property, and knew the natural objects of her bounty. The errors assigned are without merit.

The judgment of the district court is affirmed.

AFFIRMED.

TRAUTWEIN v. O'BRIEN

Court of Appeals of Ohio, Franklin County, 1989.
1989 WL 2149.

BURKHART, JUDGE.

Plaintiff, Frances Cherry Trautwein, appeals from the decision of the probate court in directing a verdict in favor of the defendants in an action to contest the validity of the purported will and codicil of William K. O'Brien, deceased. Plaintiff raises only one assignment of error as follows:

"The trial court committed prejudicial error in granting the defendants' motion for directed verdict."

Plaintiff challenges the validity of Codicil One to the Last Will and Testament of William K. O'Brien dated September 30, 1983, and the Last Will and Testament of William K. O'Brien dated September 14, 1983. The complaint alleged lack of testamentary capacity and undue influence.

"Testamentary capacity exists when the testator has sufficient mind and memory:

"First, to understand the nature of the business in which he is engaged;

"Second, to comprehend generally the nature and extent of his property;

"Third, to hold in his mind the names and identity of those who have natural claims upon his bounty;

"Fourth, to be able to appreciate his relation to the members of his family." Niemes v. Niemes (1917), 97 Ohio St. 145, paragraph four of the syllabus.

Applying the requirements of *Niemes* to the evidence presented in this case, we conclude that the trial court erred in sustaining defendants' motion for a directed verdict.

Civ.R. 50 provides that a directed verdict may be granted on the evidence when the trial court, after construing the evidence most strongly in favor of the party against whom the motion is directed, finds upon the determinative issues that reasonable minds could come to but one conclusion upon the evidence submitted and that conclusion is adverse to such party.

This court having reached the conclusion that the probate court erred in directing the jury to return a verdict for the defendants, we next consider the record evidence most favorable to the plaintiff, as the rule requires.

As noted in plaintiff's brief at page ten, the most compelling evidence presented on the issue of testamentary capacity in the trial court was a videotape of the testator at the execution of the purported will. That tape discloses a man near the end of his life suffering the debilitating effects of a series of severe strokes; a man who at times appears totally detached from the proceedings. Viewing the tape clearly reveals the testator's inability to comprehend all that was going on about him. Certainly, one would seriously question his ability to dispose of several million dollars in estate assets by means of a complicated will and trust arrangement. Further, it is apparent from the tape that the whole proceeding was directed and controlled by the decedent's attorney. Mr. O'Brien's total participation was prompted by the use of leading questions. The tape further shows that the decedent lacked an accurate understanding of the extent of his property and holdings, his estimates ranging from five to eight million dollars.

While we have not considered all the evidence regarding the physical and mental condition of the decedent relevant to testamentary capacity, we are of the opinion that what we have considered is sufficient to indicate that the granting of defendants' motion for a directed verdict was erroneous.

In addition to the lack of testamentary capacity, plaintiff claims that the testator was unduly influenced in the making of the purported will. In our view, this issue was also one for the jury's determination.

Undue influence is established when it is shown that: (1) the testator was susceptible; (2) another had the opportunity to exert influence; (3) improper influence exerted or attempted; and (4) result showing the effect of such influence. West v. Henry (1962), 173 Ohio St. 498.

That the testator in the case under review was susceptible cannot be seriously questioned. He was advanced in years, in extreme ill health and totally dependent on defendants for care. Defendants had every opportunity to exert their influence. They completely surrounded the testator in his final days isolating him from plaintiff. From these facts, it could be inferred that defendants exercised their opportunity to influence. Their improper activity resulted in a new will increasing their inheritance and disinheriting plaintiff.

While the facts in the case sub judice may not be sufficient to establish undue influence, they do present a question upon which reasonable minds could reach different conclusions.

It is the conclusion of this court that there was presented in the trial court credible evidence of a substantial character requiring the trial court to overrule defendants' motion for a directed verdict.

Therefore, plaintiff's assignment of error is sustained, and the judgment of the Franklin County Common Pleas Court, Probate Division, is reversed, and this cause is remanded to that court for further proceedings consistent herewith.

Judgment reversed and cause remanded.

INDIANA PROBATE CODE

§ 29–1–5–3.2 Videotape

Subject to the applicable Indiana Rules of Trial Procedure, a videotape may be admissible as evidence of the following:

(1) The proper execution of a will.

(2) The intentions of a testator.

(3) The mental state or capacity of a testator.

(4) The authenticity of a will.

(5) Matters that are determined by a court to be relevant to the probate of a will.

LOUISIANA CODE OF CIVIL PROCEDURE

Art. 2904. Admissibility of videotape of execution of testament

A. In a contradictory trial to probate a testament under Article 2901 or an action to annul a probated testament under Article 2931, and provided the testator is sworn by a person authorized to take oaths and the oath is recorded on the videotape, the videotape of the execution and reading of the testament by the testator may be admissible as evidence of any of the following:

(1) The proper execution of the testament.

(2) The intentions of the testator.

(3) The mental state or capacity of the testator.

(4) The authenticity of the testament.

(5) Matters that are determined by a court to be relevant to the probate of the testament.

B. For purposes of this Article, "videotape" means the visual recording on a magnetic tape, film, videotape, compact disc, digital versatile disc, digital video disc, or by other electronic means together with the associated oral record.

NOTES AND QUESTIONS

1. What is your opinion of the wisdom of video-recording the execution ceremony? Do you think its potential benefits outweigh the additional cost and possible problems?

2. What procedure would you follow if you wanted to video-record the will execution ceremony? See Gerry W. Beyer, *Videotaping the Will Execution Ceremony—Preventing Frustration of the Testator's Final Wishes,* 15 ST. MARY'S L.J. 1, 27–37 (1983).

3. Indiana and Louisiana are so far the only states to enact legislation specifically addressing the use of video-recordings in the probate process. In 1989, a survey was taken of Indiana probate judges to obtain their reaction to videotaped will executions. After reviewing the data, the surveyors stated that "it would be safe to conclude that videotape captured rave reviews in the Indiana probate courts. These survey results indicate that one may be securely optimistic in predicting videotape's increasing significance in the probate arena." Gerry W. Beyer & William R. Buckley, *Videotape and the Probate Process: The Nexus Grows,* 42 OKLA. L. REV. 43, 69 (1989).

4. Several other states, including New Jersey, New York, and Texas, have considered will videotape legislation. See id. at 70–74.

5. Should the execution of other types of estate planning documents be videotaped? See William R. Buckley, *Videotaping Living Wills: Dying Declarations Brought to Life,* 22 VAL .U.L. REV. 39 (1987).

H. SAFEKEEPING OF DOCUMENTS

Determining the proper custodian of the original will and other estate planning documents is a difficult task, especially if you anticipate a contest. There are three main factors in determining who should retain the documents.

(1) Availability to Client. The client should have ready access to the documents so the client may review them, revoke them, show them to others, etc.

(2) Protection. The documents must be protected from unintended destruction. The feared destruction could be from an accident or natural disaster (e.g., fire, flood, earthquake, hurricane, etc.) or from evil conduct by someone who would prefer the document not to exist (e.g., a disinherited heir).

(3) Locatable. The documents need to be kept in a location where they can be found when needed, e.g., upon incapacity (durable power of attorney), when in a terminal condition (living will), or upon death (will).

NOTES AND QUESTIONS

1. Evaluate each of the following possible repositories for estate planning documents. Analyze the pros and cons of each option. Also remember that different documents may call for different safekeeping methods.

a. Client, either at client's home or in client's safe deposit box.

b. Drafting attorney.

c. Key person named in document, e.g., executor or agent.

d. Appropriate court.

2. If the client elects to have you retain an original document, give the client a detailed receipt for the document which also explains where the original will be kept and how to retrieve it. See James E. Brill, *Will Vaults—*

Profit Centers or Malpractice Traps, 42 REAL EST., PROB. & TR. L. REP.19 (2004) (advocating that the attorney should, "Never. Never. Never." retain a client's original will).

I. REVIEW OF ESTATE PLAN

1. RIGHT OR DUTY

AMERICAN BAR ASSOCIATION, FORMAL OPINION 210

March 15, 1941.

An attorney may properly advise a client for whom he has drawn a will of the advisability of reexamining the will periodically and may from time to time send notices to the client advising him of changes in law or fact which may defeat the client's testamentary purpose, unless the attorney has reason to believe that he has been supplanted by another attorney.

CANON INTERPRETED: PROFESSIONAL ETHICS 27

A member calls attention to the effect on testamentary dispositions of subsequent changes in general economic conditions, of changes in the attitude or death of named fiduciaries in a will, of the removal of the testator to a different jurisdiction where different laws of descent may prevail, of changes in financial conditions, family relationship and kindred matters, and then inquires whether it is proper for the lawyer who drew the will to call attention of the testator from time to time to the importance of going over his will.

The committee's opinion was stated by Mr. Houghton, Messrs. Phillips, Drinker, Brown, Miller, Brand, and Jackson concurring.

The inquiry presents the question as to whether such action on the part of a lawyer is solicitation of legal employment and so to be condemned.

Many events transpire between the date of making the will and the death of the testator. The legal significance of such occurrences are often of serious consequence, of which the testator may not be aware, and so the importance of calling the attention of the testator thereto is manifest.

It is our opinion that where the lawyer has no reason to believe that he has been supplanted by another lawyer, it is not only his right, but it might even be his duty to advise his client of any change of fact or law which might defeat the client's testamentary purpose as expressed in the will.

Periodic notices might be sent to the client for whom a lawyer has drawn a will, suggesting that it might be wise for the client to reexamine his will to determine whether or not there has been any change in his situation requiring a modification of his will.

2. CONTRACTUAL LIMITATION

Estate planners often include language in their employment contracts indicating that they have no duty to review the estate plan. That is, the client is hiring the attorney for a "one-shot deal" and there is no continuing relationship between the attorney and the client.

NOTES AND QUESTIONS

1. How will you deal with your estate planning clients, i.e., will they be in a continuing relationship or merely a one-time arrangement? Why?

2. Here is a sample contract provision from Larry W. Gibbs, *Contract for Legal Services*, STATE BAR OF TEXAS, THE BUILDING BLOCKS OF AN ESTATE PLAN, Ch. 1, at 9:

> The engagement evidenced by this contract is limited to the time prescribed by this contract and to the scope of the service to be provided as described by this contract. There is no implied representation that Attorney can or will provide any further service beyond the engagement period and scope of service without [ ] first negotiating a new contract in writing. Any change as to scope of work or extension of the engagement period must be in writing to be binding. Attorney will be reasonably available to Client during the engagement period.

Do you like this provision? How would you improve it?

3. SCOPE OF ESTATE PLAN REVIEW

EDWARD F. KOREN, ESTATE, TAX AND PERSONAL FINANCIAL PLANNING*

2 Est. Tax & Pers. Fin. Plan. § 15:21 (updated 2012).

Estate planning never should be just a "one shot" process, unless the client's death is imminent. Changes likely will occur in the client's asset composition or estate size, the needs of the intended beneficiaries, or the law impacting upon the plan. Thus, the planner should suggest to the client that the status of the plan be reviewed on a periodic basis—for example, every three to five years—to ensure that the plan is still appropriate for the circumstances. In many instances it will be, and all that is involved is a conference, but the plan to meet changing circumstances (some of which, like legal or tax changes, may occur without the client's knowledge).

In some instances, the client's relationship with the planner will be such that the updating process occurs continually. If there is an ongoing relationship, it may be incumbent upon the planner to monitor the estate plan on an almost continual basis, suggesting revisions where changed circumstances become apparent. But in most instances, the planner will

* Reprinted with permission of Thomson Reuters.

not undertake this responsibility, often because the client is unwilling to pay for this kind of monitoring. Computerization may permit better review of documents in the future, and when major changes in the law occur, the planner may wish to provide an almost blanket notification of the changes to clients, both as a service, and also as a potential means of business generation. It should be made clear to the client, however, that such a review is not part of the plan unless an additional fee is paid, so that it is the client's responsibility to seek the periodic review, rather than that of the planner.

CHAPTER 12

AFTER CLIENT'S DEATH

■ ■ ■

A. INTRODUCTION

THOMAS L. SHAFFER, CAROL ANN MOONEY & AMY JO BOETTCHER, THE PLANNING AND DRAFTING OF WILLS AND TRUSTS*

Ch. 2, pages 35, 38–48 (5th ed. 2007).

A probate client comes to a law office in mourning. That means two things: First, the property owner has died; what is left is memory and property, and the property—so far as the law is concerned—has a new owner. The probate process is provided or imposed, by the state, to allow the new owner to take over with authority, and with a minimum fuss. And, second, the person who now comes to the law office, the new owner, may be undertaking a frightening adventure—a second adolescence that is as involuntary and as painful as first adolescence was. The adventure is an intense form of the social task a person has after losing a job or being the victim of violent crime. The realities of it have to do with commitment and the loss of commitment, sorrow, alarm, anger, guilt, and an irrational searching for what is lost and will not come back. It is a sad, scary business, even if it is also an adventure. Professional assistance, for such a person, from a lawyer, is possible; it should be hopeful; and it is sometimes not given when needed. * * *

A widow (to take the female survivor of a marriage as the prototypical, more common case)[4] is within four weeks of the loss of her husband when she first sees a probate lawyer. She is in the midst of deep feelings of searching and finding; both feelings come and go. "The most characteristic feature of grief is not prolonged depression but acute and episodic 'pangs.' A pang of grief is an episode of severe and psychological pain. At such time the lost person is strongly missed and the survivor sobs or cries aloud for him" (Parkes). She (or he) is yearning and protesting, in a pattern of behavior that lies deep in our biological history. Parkes invokes

4. The life expectancy of an adult woman remains longer than the life expectancy of an adult man, although the gap is narrowing. Most survivors of marriage are widows.

Konrad Lorenz's aggression studies, especially the behavior of a greylag goose that has lost its mate. The situation is characterized by aimless search and calls for help. "The value of such behavior for the survival of both individual and species is obvious, crying and searching both making it more likely that the lost one will be recovered." The cry is also a cry for help—help in searching, help from pain and danger, protection even from oneself. The emotions involved are grief (at loss), fear (at danger, because the protector is gone), and restlessness that leads to the sort of hyperactivity any experienced probate lawyer can tell you about—unnecessary concern about technical transfer questions, compulsive telephone calls, too much worrying about whether the doors are locked.

Parkes quotes Lindemann's description: "The activity throughout the day of the severely bereaved person shows remarkable changes. There is no retardation of action and speech; quite to the contrary, there is a rush of speech, especially when talking about the deceased. There is restlessness, inability to sit still, moving about in an aimless fashion, continually searching for something to do. There is, however, at the same time, a painful lack of capacity to initiate and maintain normal patterns of activity."

The experience may also be characterized by a trick of visual memory in which the lost person is "found"; these may go so far as clear, waking hallucinations, and will often include visual images and dreams. The feelings are typically accompanied by a physical sense of dread, loss of appetite, sleeplessness, and a compulsion to return and remain at physical sites where the lost person often was, and where, somehow in the psyche, he might again be found. This resembles what Parkes calls "home valency." The individual who has lost one source of emotional security is likely to remain near or return to other people, or to familiar places.

The searching part of the normal grief reaction tends to become a search for mitigation, for some relief from the pain of loss. Searching may be expressed in string attachment to things—photographs, furniture, even (some widows report) a bolster or pillow which can be touched or held, as the lost person was. There is also a tendency to "find" the lost person in intensified religious practice or spiritualism. Where guilt is a significant factor, Parkes says, these intense social indicia of grief may last an abnormally and disablingly long time. In virtually all cases the weeks and months of bereavement are deeply, steadily painful.

Parkes found that widows and widowers *want* to talk about their feelings:

"At the outset I had some misgivings about the entire project," he said. "It was not my wish to intrude upon private grief and I was quite prepared to abandon the study if it seemed that my questions were going to cause unnecessary pain. In fact, discussion of the events leading up to the husband's death and of the widow's reaction to them did cause pain, and it was quite usual for widows to break down and cry at some time during our first interview; but . . . they did not regard this as a harmful experience. On the contrary, the majority seemed grateful for the opportunity to talk freely about the disturbing problems and feelings that preoccupied them."

When he did not impose time limits, he found that "the first interview usually lasted from two to three hours, not because I had planned it that way but because the widow needed that amount of time if she was to 'talk through' the highly charged experiences that were on her mind. Once she found that I was not going to be embarrassed or upset by her grief she seemed to find the interview therapeutic.... I had no sense of intrusion after the first few minutes of the initial contact."

Bereaved people who are inhibited from free expression of their feelings are more inclined to suffer the worst effects of bereavement—depression, deterioration in health, prolonged disability. The idea that proper behavior for a mourner is control, and avoidance of contact with mounting sorrow, is a stupid idea and a harmful convention. It robs our "civilized" funeral rituals of much of their value. It seems also to excuse the insensitivity of a probate lawyer who lets himself be a bureaucrat instead of a counselor. What is significant for lawyers is the fact that these feelings are not as intense at the time of the funeral ritual (within a week, at most, of death in our culture) as they are when the bereaved person get involved in "settling the estate": "The peak of pangs of grief ... tends to be reached during the second week of bereavement. The 'bold face' put on for the funeral can then no longer be maintained and there is a need for someone [lawyer?] to take over many of the accustomed roles and responsibilities of the bereaved person, thereby setting him or her free to grieve. The person who is most valued at this is ... the person who ... quietly gets on with day-to-day ... tasks and makes few demands upon the bereaved. * * *"

The normal period of intensity for the bereaved begins from two to six weeks after the death of the lost person and continues for six months to a year. Many of the indicia of grief (most notably the visual image of the dead person) increase during most of this period. The period of grief occurs after the usual officers of bereavement—undertaker and clergy—have come and gone, and usually after related medical attention has been withdrawn. Probate lawyers are more likely to be around than any other professionals who preside over death in our culture. It is during this period, the probate period, that the bereaved person has finally to accept the fact of death. Until the initial several days of numbness pass the client is likely to *deny* death. "I just didn't want ... to talk about it," one of Parkes' widowers said, "because the more they talked the more they'd make me believe she was dead." This period of numbness is chronologically over at about the time the probate lawyers appears; the material realities of survival—need for material support, bank accounts, registration of automobiles, and early probate procedures—contribute to the dawning clarity of the consequences of death. * * *

HELPFUL HINTS

The *first* principle of legal counseling in probate work is to provide *a place and an interpersonal climate* in which feelings can be freely and fully expressed. Parkes's advice for the clergy seems to be transferable: "The role of the visiting clergyman is similar to that of any other friendly person who wishes the bereaved person well and would like to be of help. He too should be prepared to show by his manner and acceptance of grief and particularly acceptance of the bitter anger against God and man that is likely to be expressed. He will not help matters by returning to anger, by meeting emotion with dogma or agony with glib assurance. He will help best by listening and, if invited to do so, by trying to collaborate with the bereaved person in an honest attempt to 'get things straight'.... It is tempting to hide behind ... 'easy' answers and avoid involvement by too readily prescribing 'magical' solutions to grief. Nobody can provide the one thing the bereaved person seeks—the lost person back again. But an honest acknowledgement of helplessness in this respect may make the visitor more acceptable than a spurious omniscience."

A *second* principle relates to the possible development of *dependence* on a counselor, to what psychiatry usually talks about as "projection," "transference," or "distortion." If a client is searching for the dead person, it is reasonable to suppose that some "displacement" may occur—that the client will "find" the lost person in someone who can bring out feelings in the client that resemble the feelings he had toward the lost person. We believe that this often happens—and are supported in that belief, in at least a general sense, by popular psychology and by the curious line of litigated cases that involve a bereaved widower (widow) who gives all of his property to his lawyer or physician. (Both professions have been, as they should be, stern with members who take advantage of such situations.)

Openness is probably the best solution to this tendency to overdependence. The Rogerian school of thought (named for the author and psychotherapist Carl Rogers) claims that clients will not develop dependence if their feelings are expressed and accepted without being judged. The Rogerian theory turns on the difference between *accepting* what somebody does and *approving* (or disapproving) of it. Other schools of counseling agree that dependence will become less dangerous if it is kept in the open, and that would seem to involve identifying it when it is present and talking to the client about it.

G.M. Gazda, in the book *Human Relations Development* (1973), points out the challenge in practicing non-judgmental legal counseling: The counselor tries to get as close as possible to a frame of reference she will *never fully understand*. Even with the help of perceptive specialists such as Parkes, a lawyer can never be sure she understands how her client sees things. "It is impossible ... to be the other person," Gazda says. "The best we can do amounts to reasonably correct but approximate understandings," and requires *caution* in making guesses, being "open-minded in appraising others," tentative in forming conclusions. "At best we have a limited understanding of the unique person with whom we are communicating."

Gazda recommends phrases such as these for the times when conversation with the client seems to be going well:

You feel....

From your point of view....

It seems to you....

In your experience....

From where you stand....

As you see it....

You think....

You believe....

What I hear is....

You're....

I'm picking up that you....

You figure....

You mean....

Notice that phrases such as these—rather than lawyers' *questions*—are both (i) ways to show that you hear what the client is saying and (ii) invitations to the client to correct your misunderstandings. They are probably the most efficient way to "get the facts" in a short period of time, because they encourage the client to speak openly, in the client's words, and from the client's frame of reference.

If the conversation is not going so well, if you feel that you are not understanding your client or that your client is not as forthcoming as he might be, Gazda suggests some cautious intrusions into the client's frame of reference:

Could it be that....

I wonder if....

I'm not sure I'm with you, but....

Would you buy this idea....

Correct me if I'm wrong, but....

Is it possible that....

From where I stand, you're saying....

You appear to be feeling....

It appears you....

Perhaps you are feeling....

I'm not sure I'm with you; do you mean....

It seems that you....

As I heard it, you....

Let me see if I understand; you....

I get the impression that....

I guess that you're....

This second list of suggestions is worth thought and discussion, or, even better, worth *practice*: Try saying these tings out loud and notice how any one of them can sound about right or all wrong. The difficulty Gazda proposes to meet here is the appearance of obstacles to communication; the perception, by the lawyer, that obstacles are appearing is the difference between the first list and the second. The two risks you take in tackling the problem of perceived obstacles, with phrases such as those in the second list, are: (i) that you will come across as if you were a parent talking to a child; and (ii) that you will come across as being devious. ("Aren't you really pretty tired, little boy? Don't you really want to go to bed now?") Any of Gazda's corrective phrases can, with the right tone and inflection, say in effect: "I'm having trouble understanding you; I need your help." Or, with the wrong tone and inflection, any one of these phrases can come across as saying either that the client is not performing up to snuff or that the client is suffering form a disability that the lawyer understands and the client doesn't understand.

A *third* principle is that disabling grief is least likely to develop, and the bereavement experience most likely to result in a healthy, new, and self-reliant identity, when the dying person and her likely survivors have prepared for the loss of death. Death may be unavoidable and even unpredictable, but it is foreseeable, notably so for clients who are being cared for by hospice agencies and AIDS ministries. Parkes disapproves of our refusal to talk to dying people about death, and of our false notion that they will feel better if they and everyone around them try to deny that death is at hand: "The wife who has shared her thoughts and plans with her dying husband and with others, who has begun to anticipate what life without him will be like, and who has made adequate preparation for managing practical affairs, is in a far better position to cope with bereavement than one who has pretended that her husband is going to survive until it is too late for her to prepare for anything. When both know that there are others around who will help her through the period of adjustment [the family lawyer, for example], it is easier for them to face the situation and, having faced it, to enjoy what remains of their time together."

Fourth: The goal of counseling in this situation is competence. A time comes, for example, when a young widow says (or thinks) that she does not need to remarry in order to rebuild her life. "I have far more peace of mind and acceptance now than I have had since Dwight's death," one you widow said. "And I can accept his death more philosophically, if that is the word to be used. We must live our lives here on earth. The future is rather nebulous. In my acceptance I am more content. I still have up and down days, but these are to be expected. Life is worth living."

Part of competence is social confidence. "Primitive" cultures, with funeral rituals that often extend for months or even years, show more wisdom than we do about the difference between physical death and social death. Social death can occur even before physical death, but, for us, it typically occurs after. It occurs after those who were close to the dead person have made the fact of loss real to themselves and have rebuilt their relationships so that they can go on without the dead person. "Primitive" societies institutionalize this reality by delaying the final disposition of the corpse until social adjustments have been given time to develop. We don't do that. The probate process may be the best we have. Our analogue for the final funeral procession may be the probate judge's order discharging the personal representative and closing the dead person's estate.

NOTE

For additional discussion on the importance of taking into account how a client is affected by the grief process, see Victoria J. Koch, *The Specter of Death—Bereaved Clients Require Sensitivity and Emotional Support From Lawyers*, A.B.A. J., Nov. 1998, at 82.

B. IMMEDIATE CONCERNS

1. ACTIONS TO TAKE IF CONTACTED IMMEDIATELY

If you are contacted immediately before or after the decedent's death, you may need to assist with a variety of matters.

- Did the decedent execute a living will?
- Did the decedent make an anatomical gift?
- If the decedent did not make an anatomical gift, may your client so consent? If yes, does your client want to?
- Did the decedent leave instructions for the final disposition of the decedent's body?
- Did the decedent purchase a pre-paid funeral?
- Did the decedent purchase a burial plot or crematorium niche?
- If the decedent did not make arrangements, you may need to help the client make funeral plans, prepare the obituary, notify friends and relatives of the death, etc.
- Suggest that the decedent's family change the decedent's answering machine and voice-mail greetings.

NOTE

Please review Chapter 7.

2. OBTAIN PRELIMINARY INFORMATION

You need to resist the urge to gather all relevant information at the first meeting with a probate client. As you have already read, this is a time of high stress for the client. Focus only on the essential information.

3. DETERMINE CLIENT'S EMOTIONAL NEEDS

Although you are a "counselor," you are probably not a trained psychologist. If you believe the client is having more than normal difficulty coping with the death, you should consider suggesting professional grief counseling.

LOCATE

Prepare a list of professionals in your area who are qualified to provide grief counseling services.

4. DETERMINE CLIENT'S FINANCIAL NEEDS

What is your client's financial situation? Does the client have enough cash to cover utility bills, pay the rent or mortgage, buy food and medicine, etc.? You may need to help the client collect readily available non-probate assets such as survivorship accounts and life insurance proceeds. You should also be prepared to help the client apply for assistance from the local, state, and federal governments, both for "earned" benefits such as social security and veterans' benefits and "unearned" assistance such as welfare and food stamps.

LOCATE/DRAFT

Prepare a step-by-step checklist for your client to use if the client decides to apply for governmental assistance.

5. DETERMINE NEEDS OF DECEDENT'S PROPERTY

The decedent's property may be of such a nature that it will rapidly decline in value or suffer other losses if there is a gap in management. You may need to seek some type of temporary or accelerated administration.

LOCATE

What types of temporary or accelerated administration are available in your state to preserve the value of a decedent's estate prior to opening a formal estate administration?

6. DISCUSS FEES

Although it may seem insensitive, you must discuss fees at the initial meeting and, if you are hired, obtain a written fee agreement. Please review Chapter 8(G); most of the discussion relating to fees for preparing an estate plan is also relevant to determining the fee for administration services.

DRAFT

Prepare a checklist for the initial meeting with the client. See Rainer R. Weigel, *Master Probate Checklist,* 10 PROB. NOTES 78 (1984).

C. INFORMATION AND DOCUMENT COLLECTION

1. LOCATING THE WILL

If the person who contacts you regarding the administration does not have the decedent's will, you may need to conduct a thorough search to find it, especially if you have evidence that the decedent executed a will. Here are some places to look.

- Decedent's residence (search carefully as wills are often hidden).
- Decedent's office.
- Safe deposit box (many states have statutes allowing rapid access to a decedent's safe deposit box to locate certain documents, such as a will, burial plot deed, or life insurance policy).
- Decedent's attorney.
- Decedent's family members.
- Decedent's friends.
- Decedent's employer.
- Clerk of the court.

LOCATE

1. Does your state permit rapid access to a safe deposit box to locate a will? If yes, what is the procedure?

2. Does your state have a method which a person may use to deposit a will with the court for safekeeping? If yes, how does it operate? In which court records would you search for the will?

3. Does your state require the custodian of a decedent's will to deposit it with the court upon learning of the decedent's death?

2. GATHERING INFORMATION

a. Types of Information Needed

The type of information you need falls into three main categories. First, you need information about the decedent's family. In most cases, the client will be a family member of the deceased so this information should be easy to obtain. If not, you may need to hire a professional tracing service. Second, you need to locate all of the decedent's assets. A close family member may have this information but sometimes even a surviving spouse will not know the true extent of the deceased spouse's property. Third, you need information about the decedent's liabilities. During the administration process, creditors are entitled to notice and thus you will eventually get this information directly from them. Of course, it is better for you to have this information from the beginning so you can give the client a better estimate of administration costs and the amount to which the client may be entitled.

LOCATE

Contact several tracing services. Compare their fees and services. Which one would you hire to track down missing beneficiaries or heirs?

b. Sources of Information

If you are extremely fortunate, the client may have compiled all the relevant information for you already. See LYNN MCPHELIMY, IN THE CHECKLIST OF LIFE: A WORKING BOOK TO HELP YOU LIVE AND LEAVE THIS LIFE! (2d ed. 1997). In most cases, however, you need to use your detective skills. You may find valuable information by searching in many of the same places in which a will may be found. You should also screen the decedent's incoming mail carefully for hints regarding assets (e.g., bank statements, brokerage statements, real estate tax bills, corporate reports, etc.) and liabilities (bills from various creditors).

D. ETHICAL DUTIES TO DECEASED CLIENT

SWIDLER & BERLIN v. UNITED STATES

Supreme Court of the United States, 1998.
524 U.S. 399, 118 S.Ct. 2081, 141 L.Ed.2d 379.

CHIEF JUSTICE REHNQUIST delivered the opinion of the Court.

Petitioner, an attorney, made notes of an initial interview with a client shortly before the client's death. The Government, represented by the Office of Independent Counsel, now seeks his notes for use in a criminal investigation. We hold that the notes are protected by the attorney-client privilege.

This dispute arises out of an investigation conducted by the Office of the Independent Counsel into whether various individuals made false statements, obstructed justice, or committed other crimes during investigations of the 1993 dismissal of employees from the White House Travel Office. Vincent W. Foster, Jr., was Deputy White House Counsel when the firings occurred. In July, 1993, Foster met with petitioner James Hamilton, an attorney at petitioner Swidler & Berlin, to seek legal representation concerning possible congressional or other investigations of the firings. During a 2–hour meeting, Hamilton took three pages of handwritten notes. One of the first entries in the notes is the word "Privileged." Nine days later, Foster committed suicide.

In December 1995, a federal grand jury, at the request of the Independent Counsel, issued subpoenas to petitioners Hamilton and Swidler & Berlin for, inter alia, Hamilton's handwritten notes of his meeting with Foster. Petitioners filed a motion to quash, arguing that the notes were protected by the attorney client privilege and by the work product privilege. The District Court, after examining the notes in camera, concluded they were protected from disclosure by both doctrines and denied enforcement of the subpoenas.

The Court of Appeals for the District of Columbia Circuit reversed. In re Sealed Case, 124 F.3d 230 (1997). While recognizing that most courts assume the privilege survives death, the Court of Appeals noted that holdings actually manifesting the posthumous force of the privilege are rare. Instead, most judicial references to the privilege's posthumous application occur in the context of a well recognized exception allowing disclosure for disputes among the client's heirs. Id., at 231–232. It further noted that most commentators support some measure of posthumous curtailment of the privilege. Id., at 232. The Court of Appeals thought that the risk of posthumous revelation, when confined to the criminal context, would have little to no chilling effect on client communication, but that the costs of protecting communications after death were high. It therefore concluded that the privilege was not absolute in such circumstances, and that instead, a balancing test should apply. Id., at 233–234. It thus held that there is a posthumous exception to the privilege for communications whose relative importance to particular criminal litigation is substantial. Id., at 235. While acknowledging that uncertain privileges are disfavored, * * * the Court of Appeals determined that the uncertainty introduced by its balancing test was insignificant in light of existing exceptions to the privilege. * * * The Court of Appeals also held that the notes were not protected by the work product privilege. * * *

We granted certiorari * * * and we now reverse.

The attorney client privilege is one of the oldest recognized privileges for confidential communications. * * * Upjohn Co. v. United States, 449 U.S. 383, 389, 101 S.Ct. 677, 682, 66 L.Ed.2d 584 (1981); Hunt v. Blackburn, 128 U.S. 464, 470, 9 S.Ct. 125, 127, 32 L.Ed. 488 (1888). The privilege is intended to encourage "full and frank communication between attorneys and their clients and thereby promote broader public interests in the observance of law and the administration of justice." Upjohn, supra, at 389, 101 S.Ct. at 682. The issue presented here is the scope of that privilege; more particularly, the extent to which the privilege survives the death of the client. Our interpretation of the privilege's scope is guided by "the principles of the common law ... as interpreted by the courts ... in the light of reason and experience." Fed.Rule Evid. 501; * * *.

The Independent Counsel argues that the attorney-client privilege should not prevent disclosure of confidential communications where the client has died and the information is relevant to a criminal proceeding. There is some authority for this position. * * *

But other than these two decisions, cases addressing the existence of the privilege after death—most involving the testamentary exception—uniformly presume the privilege survives, even if they do not so hold. * * * Several State Supreme Court decisions expressly hold that the attorney-client privilege extends beyond the death of the client, even in the criminal context. * * *

Such testamentary exception cases consistently presume the privilege survives. See, e.g., United States v. Osborn, 561 F.2d 1334, 1340 (C.A.9 1977); De Loach v. Myers, 215 Ga. 255, 259–260, 109 S.E.2d 777, 780–781 (1959); Doyle v. Reeves, 112 Conn. 521, 152 A. 882 (1931); Russell v. Jackson, 9 Hare. 387, 68 Eng. Rep. 558 (V.C.1851). They view testamentary disclosure of communications as an exception to the privilege: "[T]he general rule with respect to confidential communications ... is that such communications are privileged during the testator's lifetime and, also, after the testator's death unless sought to be disclosed in litigation between the testator's heirs." Osborn, 561 F.2d, at 1340. The rationale for such disclosure is that it furthers the client's intent. Id., at 1340, n. 11.[2]

Indeed, in Glover v. Patten, 165 U.S. 394, 406–408, 17 S.Ct. 411, 416, 41 L.Ed. 760 (1897), this Court, in recognizing the testamentary exception, expressly assumed that the privilege continues after the individual's death. The Court explained that testamentary disclosure was permissible because the privilege, which normally protects the client's interests, could be impliedly waived in order to fulfill the client's testamentary intent. Id., at 407–408, 17 S.Ct., at 416 (quoting Blackburn v. Crawfords, 3 Wall. 175, 18 L.Ed. 186 (1865), and Russell v. Jackson, supra).

---

2. About half the States have codified the testamentary exception by providing that a personal representative of the deceased can waive the privilege when heirs or devisees claim through the deceased client (as opposed to parties claiming against the estate, for whom the privilege is not waived). See, e.g., Ala.Rule Evid. 502 (1996); Ark.Code Ann. § 16–41–101, Rule 502 (Supp.1997); Neb.Rev.Stat. § 27–503, Rule 503 (1995). These statutes do not address expressly the continuation of the privilege outside the context of testamentary disputes, although many allow the attorney to assert the privilege on behalf of the client apparently without temporal limit. See, e.g., Ark.Code Ann. § 16–41–101, Rule 502(c) (Supp.1997). They thus do not refute or affirm the general presumption in the case law that the privilege survives. California's statute is exceptional in that it apparently allows the attorney to assert the privilege only so long as a holder of the privilege (the estate's personal representative) exists, suggesting the privilege terminates when the estate is wound up. See Cal.Code Evid.Ann. §§ 954, 957 (West 1995). But no other State has followed California's lead in this regard.

The great body of this caselaw supports, either by holding or considered dicta, the position that the privilege does survive in a case such as the present one. Given the language of Rule 501, at the very least the burden is on the Independent Counsel to show that "reason and experience" require a departure from this rule.

The Independent Counsel contends that the testamentary exception supports the posthumous termination of the privilege because in practice most cases have refused to apply the privilege posthumously. He further argues that the exception reflects a policy judgment that the interest in settling estates outweighs any posthumous interest in confidentiality. He then reasons by analogy that in criminal proceedings, the interest in determining whether a crime has been committed should trump client confidentiality, particularly since the financial interests of the estate are not at stake.

But the Independent Counsel's interpretation simply does not square with the caselaw's implicit acceptance of the privilege's survival and with the treatment of testamentary disclosure as an "exception" or an implied "waiver." And the premise of his analogy is incorrect, since cases consistently recognize that the rationale for the testamentary exception is that it furthers the client's intent, see, e.g., Glover, supra. There is no reason to suppose as a general matter that grand jury testimony about confidential communications furthers the client's intent.

Commentators on the law also recognize that the general rule is that the attorney-client privilege continues after death. See, e.g., 8 Wigmore, Evidence § 2323 (McNaughton rev. 1961); Frankel, The Attorney–Client Privilege After the Death of the Client, 6 Geo.J.Legal Ethics 45, 78–79 (1992); 1 J. Strong, McCormick on Evidence § 94, p. 348 (4th ed. 1992). Undoubtedly, as the Independent Counsel emphasizes, various commentators have criticized this rule, urging that the privilege should be abrogated after the client's death where extreme injustice would result, as long as disclosure would not seriously undermine the privilege by deterring client communication. See, e.g., C. Mueller & L. Kirkpatrick, 2 Federal Evidence § 199, at 380–381 (2d ed. 1994); Restatement (Third) of the Law Governing Lawyers § 127, Comment d (Proposed Final Draft No. 1, Mar. 29, 1996). But even these critics clearly recognize that established law supports the continuation of the privilege and that a contrary rule would be a modification of the common law. See, e.g., Mueller & Kirkpatrick, supra, at 379; Restatement of the Law Governing Lawyers, supra, § 127, Comment c; 24 C. Wright & K. Graham, Federal Practice and Procedure § 5498, p. 483 (1986).

Despite the scholarly criticism, we think there are weighty reasons that counsel in favor of posthumous application. Knowing that communications will remain confidential even after death encourages the client to communicate fully and frankly with counsel. While the fear of disclosure, and the consequent withholding of information from counsel, may be reduced if disclosure is limited to posthumous disclosure in a criminal context, it seems unreasonable to assume that it vanishes altogether. Clients may be concerned about reputation, civil liability, or possible harm to friends or family. Posthumous disclosure of such communications may be as feared as disclosure during the client's lifetime.

The Independent Counsel suggests, however, that his proposed exception would have little to no effect on the client's willingness to confide in his attorney. He reasons that only clients intending to perjure themselves will be chilled by a rule of disclosure after death, as opposed to truthful clients or those asserting their Fifth Amendment privilege. This is because for the latter group, communications disclosed by the attorney after the client's death purportedly will reveal only information that the client himself would have revealed if alive.

The Independent Counsel assumes, incorrectly we believe, that the privilege is analogous to the Fifth Amendment's protection against self-incrimination. But as suggested above, the privilege serves much broader purposes. Clients consult attorneys for a wide variety of reasons, only one of which involves possible criminal liability. Many attorneys act as counselors on personal and family matters, where, in the course of obtaining the desired advice, confidences about family members or financial problems must be revealed in order to assure sound legal advice. The same is true of owners of small businesses who may regularly consult their attorneys about a variety of problems arising in the course of the business. These confidences may not come close to any sort of admission of criminal wrongdoing, but nonetheless be matters which the client would not wish divulged.

The contention that the attorney is being required to disclose only what the client could have been required to disclose is at odds with the basis for the privilege even during the client's lifetime. In related cases, we have said that the loss of evidence admittedly caused by the privilege is justified in part by the fact that without the privilege, the client may not have made such communications in the first place. * * * This is true of disclosure before and after the client's death. Without assurance of the privilege's posthumous application, the client may very well not have made disclosures to his attorney at all, so the loss of evidence is more apparent than real. In the case at hand, it seems quite plausible that Foster, perhaps already contemplating suicide, may not have sought legal advice from Hamilton if he had not been assured the conversation was privileged.

The Independent Counsel additionally suggests that his proposed exception would have minimal impact if confined to criminal cases, or, as the Court of Appeals suggests, if it is limited to information of substantial importance to a particular criminal case. However, there is no case authority for the proposition that the privilege applies differently in criminal and civil cases, and only one commentator ventures such a suggestion, see Mueller & Kirkpatrick, supra, at 380–381. In any event, a client may not know at the time he discloses information to his attorney whether it will later be relevant to a civil or a criminal matter, let alone whether it will be of substantial importance. Balancing ex post the importance of the information against client interests, even limited to criminal cases, introduces substantial uncertainty into the privilege's application. For just that reason, we have rejected use of a balancing test in defining the contours of the privilege. * * *

In a similar vein, the Independent Counsel argues that existing exceptions to the privilege, such as the crime-fraud exception and the testamentary exception, make the impact of one more exception marginal. However, these exceptions do not demonstrate that the impact of a posthumous exception would be insignificant, and there is little empirical evidence on this point. The established exceptions are consistent with the purposes of the privilege, * * * while a posthumous exception in criminal cases appears at odds with the goals of encouraging full and frank communication and of protecting the client's interests. A "no harm in one more exception" rationale could contribute to the general erosion of the privilege, without reference to common law principles or "reason and experience."

Finally, the Independent Counsel, relying on cases such as United States v. Nixon, 418 U.S. 683, 710, 94 S.Ct. 3090, 3108, 41 L.Ed.2d 1039 (1974), and Branzburg v. Hayes, 408 U.S. 665, 92 S.Ct. 2646, 33 L.Ed.2d 626 (1972), urges that privileges be strictly construed because they are inconsistent with the paramount judicial goal of truth seeking. But both Nixon and Branzburg dealt with the creation of privileges not recognized by the common law, whereas here we deal with one of the oldest recognized privileges in the law. And we are asked, not simply to "construe" the privilege, but to narrow it, contrary to the weight of the existing body of caselaw.

It has been generally, if not universally, accepted, for well over a century, that the attorney-client privilege survives the death of the client in a case such as this. While the arguments against the survival of the privilege are by no means frivolous, they are based in large part on speculation—thoughtful speculation, but speculation nonetheless—as to whether posthumous termination of the privilege would diminish a client's willingness to confide in an attorney. In an area where empirical information would be useful, it is scant and inconclusive.

Rule 501's direction to look to "the principles of the common law as they may be interpreted by the courts of the United States in the light of reason and experience" does not mandate that a rule, once established, should endure for all time. * * * But here the Independent Counsel has simply not made a sufficient showing to overturn the common law rule embodied in the prevailing caselaw. Interpreted in the light of reason and experience, that body of law requires that the attorney client privilege prevent disclosure of the notes at issue in this case. The judgment of the Court of Appeals is

Reversed.

JUSTICE O'CONNOR, with whom JUSTICE SCALIA and JUSTICE THOMAS join, dissenting.

MODEL RULES OF PROFESSIONAL CONDUCT

Rule 1.6

CONFIDENTIALITY OF INFORMATION

(a) A lawyer shall not reveal information relating to the representation of a client unless the client gives informed consent, the disclosure is impliedly authorized in order to carry out the representation or the disclosure is permitted by paragraph (b).

(b) A lawyer may reveal information relating to the representation of a client to the extent the lawyer reasonably believes necessary:

(1) to prevent reasonably certain death or substantial bodily harm;

(2) to prevent the client from committing a crime or fraud that is reasonably certain to result in substantial injury to the financial interests or property of another and in furtherance of which the client has used or is using the lawyer's services;

(3) to prevent, mitigate or rectify substantial injury to the financial interests or property of another that is reasonably certain to result or has resulted from the client's commission of a crime or fraud in furtherance of which the client has used the lawyer's services;

(4) to secure legal advice about the lawyer's compliance with these Rules;

(5) to establish a claim or defense on behalf of the lawyer in a controversy between the lawyer and the client, to establish a defense to a criminal charge or civil claim against the lawyer based upon conduct in which the client was involved, or to respond to allegations in any proceeding concerning the lawyer's representation of the client; or

(6) to comply with other law or a court order.

GUIDANCE OPINION NUMBER 91–4*

Philadelphia Bar Association Professional Guidance Committee, March 1991.
1991 WL 160101.

You have asked the Committee whether you may disclose the contents of an earlier Will to the Testator's children. We understand the facts to be as follows.

You prepared the earlier Will for Testator and retained the original for safekeeping. This Will named you as Executor and one of the Testator's children as alternate. Testator moved to another state, where he later consulted a different attorney and executed a new Will, revoking all earlier Wills. You continued to represent Testator concerning some other matters in Pennsylvania. Upon his death, Testator's new Will was probated. Unlike the earlier Will, it contained no gift for any of the Testator's children or other family members. Apparently, Testator had told one or more of the children that he had made a Will with you. One of the children and an attorney representing all of the children have asked you to disclose the contents of the earlier Will to them. The children's attorney has threatened you with suit if you refuse.

You wish to know whether you may disclose the contents of the Will to the children or their attorney. You wish further to know whether the propriety of the disclosure is affected by the earlier Will's provision appointing you and one of the children as Executor and alternate.

Rules 1.6(a) and (d) of the Rules of Professional Conduct state: (a) A lawyer shall not reveal information relating to representation of a client unless the client consents after consultation, except for disclosures that are impliedly authorized in order to carry out the representation, and except as stated in paragraphs (b) and (c). (d) The duty not to reveal information relating to representation of a client continues after the client-lawyer relationship has terminated.

The mandatory language of Rule 1.6(a) prohibits you from disclosing the contents of the Will to the children or their attorney, as your client, the Testator, has not authorized you to do so. The earlier Will constitutes confidential information relating to your representation of the Testator, and your duty not to reveal its contents continues even after your client's death. (Since the children learned from the Testator that the earlier Will existed, we do not address whether you may properly reveal the existence of an earlier Will when contacted by a family member.) Confidentiality is not affected by the provisions in the earlier Will naming you and a child as Executor and alternate. This inchoate representation was eliminated when the new Will revoked the earlier Will. This opinion does not address whether a court of competent jurisdiction may order you to produce the earlier Will, or whether applicable substantive law would allow the personal representative to waive the attorney client privilege.

CAVEAT: The foregoing opinion is advisory only and is based upon the facts set forth above. The opinion is not binding on the Disciplinary Board of the Supreme Court of Pennsylvania or any court. It carries only such weight as an appropriate reviewing authority may choose to give it.

ACTEC COMMENTARY ON MRPC 1.6*

ACTEC COMMENTARIES ON MODEL RULES OF PROFESSIONAL CONDUCT, page 73 (4th ed. 2006).

Obligation After Death of Client. In general, the lawyer's duty of confidentiality continues after the death of a client. Accordingly, a lawyer ordinarily should not disclose confidential information following a client's

* Reprinted with permission of the American College of Trust and Estate Counsel.

death. However, if consent is given by the client's personal representative, or if the decedent had expressly or impliedly authorized disclosure, the lawyer who represented the deceased client may provide an interested party, including a potential litigant, with information regarding a deceased client's dispositive instruments and intent, including prior instruments and communications relevant thereto. A lawyer may be impliedly authorized to make appropriate disclosure of client confidential information that would promote the client's estate plan, forestall litigation, preserve assets, and further family understanding of the decedent's intention. Disclosures should ordinarily be limited to information that the lawyer would be required to reveal as a witness.

E. ESTATE ADMINISTRATION

1. GOALS AND PURPOSES

When a person dies, some type of formal process is required for two main reasons. First, successors in interest need proof that they are indeed the new owners of the decedent's property by virtue of being heirs under the state's intestacy law or by being beneficiaries under the decedent's valid will. Procedures to establish title are relatively simple and often do not require a full estate administration. Second, the decedent's creditors need to be paid. In a sense, death is like going bankrupt. Estate administration assures that creditors get paid to the fullest extent possible. However, state statutes often shield a portion of the decedent's estate from the claims of creditors to protect the decedent's surviving spouse and minor children.

An estate administration begins with the personal representative collecting all of the decedent's probate assets. The personal representative preserves this property and manages it in a fiduciary capacity. The personal representative then pays the creditors and if property still remains, distributes it to the appropriate heirs or beneficiaries. The details of estate administration vary tremendously among the states.

NOTES

1. Please review Chapter 2(C).

2. A letter to the administrator of unclaimed property of each state in which the decedent lived may reveal additional estate property. See J. Brooke Spotswood, *Laying Claim to Decedent's Unclaimed Property,* PROB. & PROP., Jan./Feb. 1993, at 46 (includes sample letter).

2. SELECTING TYPE OF ADMINISTRATION

State law may provide options regarding the type of administration available. Selecting the appropriate method may reduce cost and increase the speed and convenience of the administration process. A particular type of administration may (1) be specified in the will, (2) be agreed to by the heirs or beneficiaries, (3) need court approval, or (4) be selected at the personal representative's discretion.

Administration methods break down into four main types. (1) Temporary—to preserve the estate until a formal administration is opened or during a will contest. (2) Short Form—for low value or simple estates. (3) Dependent—a heavily court supervised proceeding. (4) Independent, Informal, or Non-intervention—where the personal representative can take most actions without specific court approval.

LOCATE

What different types of administration are available in your state and when are they available? How would you decide which method to suggest to your client?

3. BASIC STEPS

The specifics of estate administration vary tremendously among the states. Below is a list of steps common to most administrations.

- Initiate proceedings with a proper applicant, e.g., heir, beneficiary, or creditor.
- File appropriate documents with the court that has both jurisdiction and venue.
- Cite interested parties, e.g., posting, publication, mail, or personal service. Some states allow an ex parte probate.
- Attend court hearing on application.
- Qualify personal representative by having this person take the oath of office and, unless waived or otherwise not required, post bond.
- Obtain letters testamentary or letters of administration.
- Give notice to creditors to submit claims.
- Prepare inventory and appraisement of estate assets.
- Set aside homestead, exempt personal property, and the family allowance.
- Pay creditors according to statutory priority.
- Complete tax returns: (1) the decedent's final federal income tax return no later than 3½ months after the close of the decedent's taxable year (normally April 15 of the year after the year in which the decedent died); (2) the estate's income tax return no later than 3½ months following the end of each of the estate's fiscal years; (3) the decedent's last federal gift tax return (usually April 15 of the year after the year in which the decedent died); (4) the federal estate tax return usually due nine months after the decedent's death; and (5) state tax returns according to local law.

- Provide appropriate reports and accountings.
- Distribute what is left to heirs or beneficiaries.
- Close the estate.

LOCATE

Prepare an outline of the administration procedure in your state using the above format as a guide.

4. COSTS

Costs of estate administration include (1) filing and court fees, (2) personal representative fees, unless waived in will, (3) bond, unless not needed, and (4) attorneys fees.

5. ENVIRONMENTAL LIABILITY

The decedent's property may include contaminated property which would make the owner or operator personally liable for the costs of cleaning up the property under the federal Comprehensive Environmental Response, Compensation, and Liability Act of 1980, 42 U.S.C. §§ 9601 et seq. (CERCLA), and the Resource Conservation and Recovery Act of 1976, 42 U.S.C. §§ 6901 et seq. (RCRA). Several courts held that fiduciaries, such as personal representatives and trustees, were personally liable for the cleanup costs if estate assets were insufficient. See, e.g., Castlerock Estates, Inc. v. Estate of Markham, 871 F.Supp. 360 (N.D. Cal. 1994) (executor); City of Phoenix v. Garbage Servs. Co., 827 F.Supp. 600 (D. Ariz. 1993) (testamentary trustee). The result of these cases made the act of serving as a personal representative problematic if the decedent owned real property which even potentially could be shown to be contaminated.

Congress amended CERCLA and RCRA in 1996 to alleviate this problem. Under current law, a person is liable for costs associated with property held in a fiduciary capacity only up to the value of the assets that are held in the fiduciary capacity. 42 U.S.C. § 9607(n)(1) & 42 U.S.C. 6991(h)(9). In addition, a fiduciary will not be liable for administering a "facility that was contaminated before the fiduciary relationship began." U.S.C. § 9607(n)(4)(H). Accordingly, the risk of personal liability for serving as a personal representative has been reduced, but not eliminated. The fiduciary may still be personally liable under a variety of situations. For example, liability attaches if the fiduciary's negligence causes or contributes to the contamination. 42 U.S.C. § 9607(n)(3).

NOTE

For further information on the personal representative's potential environmental liability, see Robert D. Bannon & Alexandra Laboutin Bannon, *Congress Passes Fiduciary Exemption From Environmental Liability*, 22 AC-

TEC NOTES 222 (1996); Baxter Dunaway & Andrew C. Cooper, *Good News for Lenders and Fiduciaries*, PROB. & PROP., May/June 1997, at 49.

Appendix A

Federal Gift Tax Return and Instructions

■ ■ ■

1. Gift Tax Return—Form 709

Form **709** | **United States Gift (and Generation-Skipping Transfer) Tax Return** | OMB No. 1545-0020

Department of the Treasury
Internal Revenue Service

(For gifts made during calendar year 2011)
▶ See instructions.

2011

Part 1—General Information

1 Donor's first name and middle initial	2 Donor's last name	3 Donor's social security number
4 Address (number, street, and apartment number)		5 Legal residence (domicile)
6 City, state, and ZIP code		7 Citizenship (see instructions)

		Yes	No
8	If the donor died during the year, check here ▶ ☐ and enter date of death ______, ______.		
9	If you extended the time to file this Form 709, check here ▶ ☐		
10	Enter the total number of donees listed on Schedule A. Count each person only once. ▶		
11a	Have you (the donor) previously filed a Form 709 (or 709-A) for any other year? If "No," skip line 11b		
b	If the answer to line 11a is "Yes," has your address changed since you last filed Form 709 (or 709-A)?		
12	**Gifts by husband or wife to third parties.** Do you consent to have the gifts (including generation-skipping transfers) made by you and by your spouse to third parties during the calendar year considered as made one-half by each of you? (See instructions.) (If the answer is "Yes," the following information must be furnished and your spouse must sign the consent shown below. **If the answer is "No," skip lines 13–18 and go to Schedule A.**)		
13	Name of consenting spouse — 14 SSN		
15	Were you married to one another during the entire calendar year? (see instructions)		
16	If 15 is "No," check whether ☐ married ☐ divorced or ☐ widowed/deceased, and give date (see instructions) ▶		
17	Will a gift tax return for this year be filed by your spouse? (If "Yes," mail both returns in the same envelope.)		
18	**Consent of Spouse.** I consent to have the gifts (and generation-skipping transfers) made by me and by my spouse to third parties during the calendar year considered as made one-half by each of us. We are both aware of the joint and several liability for tax created by the execution of this consent.		

Consenting spouse's signature ▶ **Date** ▶

Part 2—Tax Computation

1	Enter the amount from Schedule A, Part 4, line 11	1	
2	Enter the amount from Schedule B, line 3	2	
3	Total taxable gifts. Add lines 1 and 2	3	
4	Tax computed on amount on line 3 (see *Table for Computing Gift Tax* in instructions)	4	
5	Tax computed on amount on line 2 (see *Table for Computing Gift Tax* in instructions)	5	
6	Balance. Subtract line 5 from line 4	6	
7	Maximum unified credit (see instructions)	7	
8	Enter the unified credit against tax allowable for all prior periods (from Sch. B, line 1, col. C)	8	
9	Balance. Subtract line 8 from line 7. Do not enter less than zero	9	
10	Enter 20% (.20) of the amount allowed as a specific exemption for gifts made after September 8, 1976, and before January 1, 1977 (see instructions)	10	
11	Balance. Subtract line 10 from line 9. Do not enter less than zero	11	
12	Unified credit. Enter the smaller of line 6 or line 11	12	
13	Credit for foreign gift taxes (see instructions)	13	
14	Total credits. Add lines 12 and 13	14	
15	Balance. Subtract line 14 from line 6. Do not enter less than zero	15	
16	Generation-skipping transfer taxes (from Schedule C, Part 3, col. H, Total)	16	
17	Total tax. Add lines 15 and 16	17	
18	Gift and generation-skipping transfer taxes prepaid with extension of time to file	18	
19	If line 18 is less than line 17, enter **balance due** (see instructions)	19	
20	If line 18 is greater than line 17, enter **amount to be refunded**	20	

Attach check or money order here.

Sign Here

Under penalties of perjury, I declare that I have examined this return, including any accompanying schedules and statements, and to the best of my knowledge and belief, it is true, correct, and complete. Declaration of preparer (other than donor) is based on all information of which preparer has any knowledge.

May the IRS discuss this return with the preparer shown below (see instructions)? ☐ Yes ☐ No

▶ Signature of donor — Date

Paid Preparer Use Only

Print/Type preparer's name	Preparer's signature	Date	Check ☐ if self-employed	PTIN
Firm's name ▶			Firm's EIN ▶	
Firm's address ▶			Phone no.	

For Disclosure, Privacy Act, and Paperwork Reduction Act Notice, see the instructions for this form. Cat. No. 16783M Form **709** (2011)

Form 709 (2011) Page 2

SCHEDULE A **Computation of Taxable Gifts** (Including transfers in trust) (see instructions)

A Does the value of any item listed on Schedule A reflect any valuation discount? If "Yes," attach explanation . . . . Yes ☐ No ☐

B ☐ ◄ Check here if you elect under section 529(c)(2)(B) to treat any transfers made this year to a qualified tuition program as made ratably over a 5-year period beginning this year. See instructions. Attach explanation.

Part 1—Gifts Subject Only to Gift Tax. Gifts less political organization, medical, and educational exclusions. (see instructions)

A Item number	B • Donee's name and address • Relationship to donor (if any) • Description of gift • If the gift was of securities, give CUSIP no. • If closely held entity, give EIN	C	D Donor's adjusted basis of gift	E Date of gift	F Value at date of gift	G For split gifts, enter ½ of column F	H Net transfer (subtract col. G from col. F)
1							

Gifts made by spouse —*complete* ***only*** *if you are splitting gifts with your spouse and he/she also made gifts.*

Total of Part 1. Add amounts from Part 1, column H . . . . ►

Part 2—Direct Skips. Gifts that are direct skips and are subject to both gift tax and generation-skipping transfer tax. You must list the gifts in chronological order.

A Item number	B • Donee's name and address • Relationship to donor (if any) • Description of gift • If the gift was of securities, give CUSIP no. • If closely held entity, give EIN	C 2632(b) election out	D Donor's adjusted basis of gift	E Date of gift	F Value at date of gift	G For split gifts, enter ½ of column F	H Net transfer (subtract col. G from col. F)
1							

Gifts made by spouse —*complete* ***only*** *if you are splitting gifts with your spouse and he/she also made gifts.*

Total of Part 2. Add amounts from Part 2, column H . . . . ►

Part 3—Indirect Skips. Gifts to trusts that are currently subject to gift tax and may later be subject to generation-skipping transfer tax. You must list these gifts in chronological order.

A Item number	B • Donee's name and address • Relationship to donor (if any) • Description of gift • If the gift was of securities, give CUSIP no. • If closely held entity, give EIN	C 2632(c) election	D Donor's adjusted basis of gift	E Date of gift	F Value at date of gift	G For split gifts, enter ½ of column F	H Net transfer (subtract col. G from col. F)
1							

Gifts made by spouse —*complete* ***only*** *if you are splitting gifts with your spouse and he/she also made gifts.*

Total of Part 3. Add amounts from Part 3, column H . . . . ►

(If more space is needed, attach additional sheets of same size.) Form **709** (2011)

Form 709 (2011) Page **3**

Part 4—Taxable Gift Reconciliation

1	Total value of gifts of donor. Add totals from column H of Parts 1, 2, and 3	1	
2	Total annual exclusions for gifts listed on line 1 (see instructions)	2	
3	Total included amount of gifts. Subtract line 2 from line 1	3	
Deductions (see instructions)			
4	Gifts of interests to spouse for which a marital deduction will be claimed, based on item numbers ____________ of Schedule A . . 4		
5	Exclusions attributable to gifts on line 4 . . . 5		
6	Marital deduction. Subtract line 5 from line 4 . . . 6		
7	Charitable deduction, based on item nos. ________ less exclusions . 7		
8	Total deductions. Add lines 6 and 7	8	
9	Subtract line 8 from line 3	9	
10	Generation-skipping transfer taxes payable with this Form 709 (from Schedule C, Part 3, col. H, Total)	10	
11	**Taxable gifts.** Add lines 9 and 10. Enter here and on page 1, Part 2—Tax Computation, line 1	11	

Terminable Interest (QTIP) Marital Deduction. (See instructions for Schedule A, Part 4, line 4.)

If a trust (or other property) meets the requirements of qualified terminable interest property under section 2523(f), and:

a. The trust (or other property) is listed on Schedule A, and

b. The value of the trust (or other property) is entered in whole or in part as a deduction on Schedule A, Part 4, line 4, then the donor shall be deemed to have made an election to have such trust (or other property) treated as qualified terminable interest property under section 2523(f).

If less than the entire value of the trust (or other property) that the donor has included in Parts 1 and 3 of Schedule A is entered as a deduction on line 4, the donor shall be considered to have made an election only as to a fraction of the trust (or other property). The numerator of this fraction is equal to the amount of the trust (or other property) deducted on Schedule A, Part 4, line 6. The denominator is equal to the total value of the trust (or other property) listed in Parts 1 and 3 of Schedule A.

If you make the QTIP election, the terminable interest property involved will be included in your spouse's gross estate upon his or her death (section 2044). See instructions for line 4 of Schedule A. If your spouse disposes (by gift or otherwise) of all or part of the qualifying life income interest, he or she will be considered to have made a transfer of the entire property that is subject to the gift tax. See *Transfer of Certain Life Estates Received From Spouse* in the instructions.

12 Election Out of QTIP Treatment of Annuities

☐ ◄ Check here if you elect under section 2523(f)(6) **not** to treat as qualified terminable interest property any joint and survivor annuities that are reported on Schedule A and would otherwise be treated as qualified terminable interest property under section 2523(f). See instructions. Enter the item numbers from Schedule A for the annuities for which you are making this election ► ____________

SCHEDULE B Gifts From Prior Periods

If you answered "Yes" on line 11a of page 1, Part 1, see the instructions for completing Schedule B. If you answered "No," skip to the Tax Computation on page 1 (or Schedule C, if applicable). See instructions for recalculation of the column C amounts. Attach calculations.

A Calendar year or calendar quarter (see instructions)	B Internal Revenue office where prior return was filed	C Amount of unified credit against gift tax for periods after December 31, 1976	D Amount of specific exemption for prior periods ending before January 1, 1977	E Amount of taxable gifts
1 Totals for prior periods	1			

2	Amount, if any, by which total specific exemption, line 1, column D is more than $30,000	2	
3	Total amount of taxable gifts for prior periods. Add amount on line 1, column E and amount, if any, on line 2. Enter here and on page 1, Part 2—Tax Computation, line 2	3	

(If more space is needed, attach additional sheets of same size.)

Form **709** (2011)

Form 709 (2011) Page 4

SCHEDULE C Computation of Generation-Skipping Transfer Tax

Note. Inter vivos direct skips that are completely excluded by the GST exemption must still be fully reported (including value and exemptions claimed) on Schedule C.

Part 1—Generation-Skipping Transfers

A Item No. (from Schedule A, Part 2, col. A)	B Value (from Schedule A, Part 2, col. H)	C Nontaxable portion of transfer	D Net Transfer (subtract col. C from col. B)
1			
Gifts made by spouse (for gift splitting only)			

Part 2—GST Exemption Reconciliation (Section 2631) and Section 2652(a)(3) Election

Check here ▶ ☐ if you are making a section 2652(a)(3) (special QTIP) election (see instructions)

Enter the item numbers from Schedule A of the gifts for which you are making this election ▶ ______________

1	Maximum allowable exemption (see instructions)	1	
2	Total exemption used for periods before filing this return	2	
3	Exemption available for this return. Subtract line 2 from line 1	3	
4	Exemption claimed on this return from Part 3, column C total, below	4	
5	Automatic allocation of exemption to transfers reported on Schedule A, Part 3 (see instructions)	5	
6	Exemption allocated to transfers not shown on line 4 or 5, above. **You must attach a "Notice of Allocation."** (see instructions)	6	
7	Add lines 4, 5, and 6	7	
8	Exemption available for future transfers. Subtract line 7 from line 3	8	

Part 3—Tax Computation

A Item No. (from Schedule C, Part 1)	B Net transfer (from Schedule C, Part 1, col. D)	C GST Exemption Allocated	D Divide col. C by col. B	E Inclusion Ratio (Subtract col. D from 1.000)	F Maximum Estate Tax Rate	G Applicable Rate (multiply col. E by col. F)	H Generation-Skipping Transfer Tax (multiply col. B by col. G)
1					35% (.35)		
					35% (.35)		
					35% (.35)		
					35% (.35)		
					35% (.35)		
					35% (.35)		
Gifts made by spouse (for gift splitting only)							
					35% (.35)		
					35% (.35)		
					35% (.35)		
					35% (.35)		
					35% (.35)		
					35% (.35)		
Total exemption claimed. Enter here and on Part 2, line 4, above. May not exceed Part 2, line 3, above			**Total generation-skipping transfer tax.** Enter here; on page 3, Schedule A, Part 4, line 10; and on page 1, Part 2—Tax Computation, line 16				

(If more space is needed, attach additional sheets of same size.)

Form 709 (2011)

2. Gift Tax Return Instructions

Instructions for Form 709

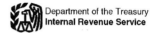

Department of the Treasury
Internal Revenue Service

United States Gift (and Generation-Skipping Transfer) Tax Return

For gifts made during calendar year 2011.

Section references are to the Internal Revenue Code unless otherwise noted.

For Disclosure, Privacy Act, and Paperwork Reduction Act Notice, see below.

For Gifts Made After	and Before	Use Revision of Form 709 Dated
- - - - -	January 1, 1982	November 1981
December 31, 1981	January 1, 1987	January 1987
December 31, 1986	January 1, 1989	December 1988
December 31, 1988	January 1, 1990	December 1989
December 31, 1989	October 9, 1990	October 1990
October 8, 1990	January 1, 1992	November 1991
December 31, 1992	January 1, 1998	December 1996
December 31, 1997	- - - - -	*

* Use the corresponding annual form.

What's New

- File Form 709 for 2011 gifts by April 17, 2012. The due date is April 17, instead of April 15, because April 15 is a Sunday and April 16 is the Emancipation Day holiday in the District of Columbia.
- The annual gift exclusion for 2011 remains $13,000. See *Annual Exclusion*, later.
- For gifts made to spouses who are not U.S. citizens, the annual exclusion has increased to $136,000. See *Nonresident Aliens*, later.
- The top rate for gifts and generation-skipping transfers is now 35%. See *Table for Computing Gift Tax*, later.
- The unified credit for 2011 is $1,730,800. See *Table of Unified Credits*, later.
- Section 302(d)(2) of the Tax Relief, Unemployment Insurance Reauthorization, and Job Creation Act of 2010 (Pub. L. 111-312) mandates that any unified credit allocated to gifts made in prior periods be redetermined using current gift tax rates. See instructions for column C in *Schedule B. Gifts From Prior Periods*, below, for more details.
- The applicable exclusion amount now may consist of a basic exclusion amount of $5,000,000 that, starting in 2012, will be indexed for inflation, and, in the case of a surviving spouse, the unused exclusion amount of a predeceased spouse (who died after December 31, 2010). The executor of the predeceased spouse's estate must have elected on a timely and complete Form 706 to allow the donor to use the predeceased spouse's unused exclusion amount.
- The IRS has created a page on IRS.gov for information about Form 709 and its instructions, at *www.irs.gov/form709*. Information about any future developments affecting Form 709 (such as legislation enacted after we release it) will be posted on that page.

Photographs of Missing Children

The IRS is a proud partner with the National Center for Missing and Exploited Children. Photographs of missing children selected by the Center may appear in instructions on pages that would otherwise be blank. You can help bring these children home by looking at the photographs and calling 1-800-THE-LOST (1-800-843-5678) if you recognize a child.

General Instructions

Purpose of Form

Use Form 709 to report the following:

- Transfers subject to the federal gift and certain generation-skipping transfer (GST) taxes and to figure the tax due, if any, on those transfers and
- Allocation of the lifetime GST exemption to property transferred during the transferor's lifetime. (For more details, see *Part 2—GST Exemption Reconciliation*, later, and Regulations section 26.2632-1.)

CAUTION *All gift and GST taxes must be computed and filed on a calendar year basis. List all reportable gifts made during the calendar year on one Form 709. This means you must file a separate return for each calendar year a reportable gift is given (for example, a gift given in 2011 must be reported on a 2011 Form 709). Do not file more than one Form 709 for any one calendar year.*

How To Complete Form 709

1. Determine whether you are required to file Form 709.
2. Determine what gifts you must report.
3. Decide whether you and your spouse, if any, will elect to split gifts for the year.
4. Complete lines 1 through 18 of Part 1, page 1.
5. List each gift on Part 1, 2, or 3 of Schedule A, as appropriate.
6. Complete Schedule B, if applicable.
7. If the gift was listed on Part 2 or 3 of Schedule A, complete the necessary portions of Schedule C.
8. Complete Schedule A, Part 4.
9. Complete Part 2 on page 1.
10. Sign and date the return.

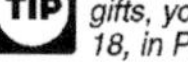

Remember, if you are splitting gifts, your spouse must sign line 18, in Part 1–General Information.

Who Must File

In general. If you are a citizen or resident of the United States, you must file a gift tax return (whether or not any tax is ultimately due) in the following situations.

- If you gave gifts to someone in 2011 totalling more than $13,000 (other than to your spouse), you probably must file Form 709. But see *Transfers Not Subject to Gift Tax* and *Gifts to Spouse*, later, for more information on specific gifts that are not taxable.
- Certain gifts, called future interests, are not subject to the $13,000 annual exclusion and you must file Form 709 even if the gift was under $13,000. See *Annual Exclusion*, later.
- A husband and wife may not file a joint gift tax return. Each individual is responsible for his or her own Form 709.
- You must file a gift tax return to split gifts with your spouse (regardless of their amount) as described in *Part 1—General Information*.
- If a gift is of community property, it is considered made one-half by each spouse. For example, a gift of $100,000 of community property is considered a gift of $50,000 made by each spouse, and each spouse must file a gift tax return.
- Likewise, each spouse must file a gift tax return if they have made a gift of property held by them as joint tenants or tenants by the entirety.
- Only individuals are required to file gift tax returns. If a trust, estate, partnership, or corporation makes a gift, the individual beneficiaries, partners, or stockholders are considered donors and may be liable for the gift and GST taxes.

• The donor is responsible for paying the gift tax. However, if the donor does not pay the tax, the person receiving the gift may have to pay the tax.
• If a donor dies before filing a return, the donor's executor must file the return.

Who does not need to file. If you meet all of the following requirements, you are not required to file Form 709:
• You made no gifts during the year to your spouse,
• You did not give more than $13,000 to any one donee, and
• All the gifts you made were of present interests.

Gifts to charities. If the only gifts you made during the year are deductible as gifts to charities, you do not need to file a return as long as you transferred your entire interest in the property to qualifying charities. If you transferred only a partial interest, or transferred part of your interest to someone other than a charity, you must still file a return and report all of your gifts to charities.

If you are required to file a return to report noncharitable gifts and you made gifts to charities, you must include all of your gifts to charities on the return.

Transfers Subject to the Gift Tax

Generally, the federal gift tax applies to any transfer by gift of real or personal property, whether tangible or intangible, that you made directly or indirectly, in trust, or by any other means.

The gift tax applies not only to the free transfer of any kind of property, but also to sales or exchanges, not made in the ordinary course of business, where value of the money (or property) received is less than the value of what is sold or exchanged. The gift tax is in addition to any other tax, such as federal income tax, paid or due on the transfer.

The exercise or release of a general power of appointment may be a gift by the individual possessing the power. General powers of appointment are those in which the holders of the power can appoint the property under the power to themselves, their creditors, their estates, or the creditors of their estates. To qualify as a power of appointment, it must be created by someone other than the holder of the power.

The gift tax may also apply to forgiving a debt, to making an interest-free or below market interest rate loan, to transferring the benefits of an insurance policy, to certain property settlements in divorce cases, and to giving up of some amount of annuity in exchange for the creation of a survivor annuity.

Bonds that are exempt from federal income taxes are not exempt from federal gift taxes.

Sections 2701 and 2702 provide rules for determining whether certain transfers to a family member of interests in corporations, partnerships, and trusts are gifts. The rules of section 2704 determine whether the lapse of any voting or liquidation right is a gift.

Gifts to your spouse. You must file a gift tax return if you made any gift to your spouse of a terminable interest that does not meet the exception described in *Life estate with power of appointment*, or if your spouse is not a U.S. citizen and the total gifts you made to your spouse during the year exceed $136,000.

You must also file a gift tax return to make the Qualified Terminable Interest Property (QTIP) election described under *Line 12. Election Out of QTIP Treatment of Annuities*.

Except as described above, you do not have to file a gift tax return to report gifts to your spouse regardless of the amount of these gifts and regardless of whether the gifts are present or future interests.

Transfers Not Subject to the Gift Tax

Three types of transfers are not subject to the gift tax. These are:
• Transfers to political organizations,
• Payments that qualify for the educational exclusion, and
• Payments that qualify for the medical exclusion.

These transfers are not "gifts" as that term is used on Form 709 and its instructions. You need not file a Form 709 to report these transfers and should not list them on Schedule A of Form 709 if you do file Form 709.

Political organizations. The gift tax does not apply to a transfer to a political organization (defined in section 527(e)(1)) for the use of the organization.

Educational exclusion. The gift tax does not apply to an amount you paid on behalf of an individual to a qualifying domestic or foreign educational organization as tuition for the education or training of the individual. A qualifying educational organization is one that normally maintains a regular faculty and curriculum and normally has a regularly enrolled body of pupils or students in attendance at the place where its educational activities are regularly carried on. See section 170(b)(1)(A)(ii) and its regulations.

The payment must be made directly to the qualifying educational organization and it must be for tuition. No educational exclusion is allowed for amounts paid for books, supplies, room and board, or other similar expenses that are not direct tuition costs. To the extent that the payment to the educational organization was for something other than tuition, it is a gift to the individual for whose benefit it was made, and may be offset by the annual exclusion if it is otherwise available.

Contributions to a qualified tuition program (QTP) on behalf of a designated beneficiary do not qualify for the educational exclusion. See *Line B—Qualified Tuition Programs (529 Plans or Programs)*.

Medical exclusion. The gift tax does not apply to an amount you paid on behalf of an individual to a person or institution that provided medical care for the individual. The payment must be to the care provider. The medical care must meet the requirements of section 213(d) (definition of medical care for income tax deduction purposes). Medical care includes expenses incurred for the diagnosis, cure, mitigation, treatment, or prevention of disease, or for the purpose of affecting any structure or function of the body, or for transportation primarily for and essential to medical care. Medical care also includes amounts paid for medical insurance on behalf of any individual.

The medical exclusion does not apply to amounts paid for medical care that are reimbursed by the donee's insurance. If payment for a medical expense is reimbursed by the donee's insurance company, your payment for that expense, to the extent of the reimbursed amount, is not eligible for the medical exclusion and you are considered to have made a gift to the donee of the reimbursed amount.

To the extent that the payment was for something other than medical care, it is a gift to the individual on whose behalf the payment was made and may be offset by the annual exclusion if it is otherwise available.

The medical and educational exclusions are allowed without regard to the relationship between you and the donee. For examples illustrating these exclusions, see Regulations section 25.2503-6.

Qualified disclaimers. A donee's refusal to accept a gift is called a *disclaimer*. If a person makes a qualified disclaimer of any interest in property, the property will be treated as if it had never been transferred to that person. Accordingly, the disclaimant is not regarded as making a gift to the person who receives the property because of the qualified disclaimer.

Requirements. To be a qualified disclaimer, a refusal to accept an interest in property must meet the following conditions.

1. The refusal must be in writing.
2. The refusal must be received by the donor, the legal representative of the donor, the holder of the legal title to the property disclaimed, or the person in possession of the property within 9 months after the later of:
   a. the day the transfer creating the interest is made or
   b. the day the disclaimant reaches age 21.
3. The disclaimant must not have accepted the interest or any of its benefits.
4. As a result of the refusal, the interest must pass without any direction from the disclaimant to either:
   a. the spouse of the decedent or
   b. a person other than the disclaimant, and

5. The refusal must be irrevocable and unqualified.

The 9-month period for making the disclaimer generally is determined separately for each taxable transfer. For gifts, the period begins on the date the transfer is a completed transfer for gift tax purposes.

Annual Exclusion

The first $13,000 of gifts of present interest to each donee during the calendar year is subtracted from total gifts in figuring the amount of taxable gifts. For a gift in trust, each beneficiary of the trust is treated as a separate donee for purposes of the annual exclusion.

All of the gifts made during the calendar year to a donee are fully excluded under the annual exclusion if they are all gifts of present interest and they total $13,000 or less.

Note. For gifts made to spouses who are not U.S. citizens, the annual exclusion has been increased to $136,000, provided the additional (above the $13,000 annual exclusion) $123,000 gift would otherwise qualify for the gift tax marital deduction (as described in the line 4 instructions discussed later).

A gift of a future interest cannot be excluded under the annual exclusion.

A gift is considered a present interest if the donee has all immediate rights to the use, possession, and enjoyment of the property or income from the property.

A gift is considered a future interest if the donee's rights to the use, possession, and enjoyment of the property or income from the property will not begin until some future date. Future interests include reversions, remainders, and other similar interests or estates.

A contribution to a QTP on behalf of a designated beneficiary is considered a gift of a present interest.

A gift to a minor is considered a present interest if all of the following conditions are met:

1. Both the property and its income may be expended by, or for the benefit of, the minor before the minor reaches age 21;
2. All remaining property and its income must pass to the minor on the minor's 21st birthday; and
3. If the minor dies before the age of 21, the property and its income will be payable either to the minor's estate or to whomever the minor may appoint under a general power of appointment.

The gift of a present interest to more than one donee as joint tenants qualifies for the annual exclusion for each donee.

Nonresident Aliens

Nonresident aliens are subject to gift and GST taxes for gifts of tangible property situated in the United States. Under certain circumstances, they are also subject to gift and GST taxes for gifts of intangible property. See section 2501(a).

If you are a nonresident alien who made a gift subject to gift tax, you must file a gift tax return where:

- You gave any gifts of future interests,
- Your gifts of present interests to any donee other than your spouse total more than $13,000, or
- Your outright gifts to your spouse who is not a U.S. citizen total more than $136,000.

Transfers Subject to the GST Tax

You must report on Form 709 the GST tax imposed on *inter vivos* direct skips. An *inter vivos* direct skip is a transfer made during the donor's lifetime that is:

- Subject to the gift tax,
- Of an interest in property, and
- Made to a skip person. (See *Gifts Subject to Both Gift and GST Taxes.*)

A transfer is subject to the gift tax if it is required to be reported on Schedule A of Form 709 under the rules contained in the gift tax portions of these instructions, including the split gift rules. Therefore, transfers made to political organizations, transfers that qualify for the medical or educational exclusions, transfers that are fully excluded under the annual exclusion, and most transfers made to your spouse are not subject to the GST tax.

Transfers subject to the GST tax are described in further detail in the instructions.

CAUTION *Certain transfers, particularly transfers to a trust, that are not subject to gift tax and are therefore not subject to the GST tax on Form 709 may be subject to the GST tax at a later date. This is true even if the transfer is less than the $13,000 annual exclusion. In this instance, you may want to apply a GST exemption amount to the transfer on this return or on a Notice of Allocation. For more information, see* Part 2—GST Exemption Reconciliation *and* Part 3—Indirect Skips.

Transfers Subject to an Estate Tax Inclusion Period (ETIP)

Certain transfers that are direct skips receive special treatment. If the transferred property would have been includible in the donor's estate if the donor had died immediately after the transfer (for a reason other than the donor having died within 3 years of making the gift), the direct skip will be treated as having been made at the end of the ETIP rather than at the time of the actual transfer.

For example, if A transferred her house to her granddaughter, B, but retained the right to live in the house until her death (a retained life estate), the value of the house would be includible in A's estate if she died while still holding the life estate. In this case, the transfer to B is a completed gift (it is a transfer of a future interest) and must be reported on Part 1 of Schedule A. The GST portion of the transfer would not be reported until A died or otherwise gave up her life estate in the house.

Report the gift portion of such a transfer on Schedule A, Part 1, at the time of the actual transfer. Report the GST portion on Schedule A, Part 2, but only at the close of the ETIP. Use Form 709 only to report those transfers where the ETIP closed due to something other than the donor's death. (If the ETIP closed as the result of the donor's death, report the transfer on Form 706, United States Estate (and Generation-Skipping Transfer) Tax Return.)

If you are filing this Form 709 solely to report the GST portion of transfers subject to an ETIP, complete the form as you normally would with the following exceptions:

1. Write "ETIP" at the top of page 1;
2. Complete only lines 1 through 6, 8, and 9 of Part 1—General Information;
3. Complete Schedule A, Part 2, as explained in the instructions for that schedule;
4. Complete Schedule C. Complete Column B of Schedule C, Part 1, as explained in the instructions for that schedule;
5. Complete only lines 10 and 11 of Schedule A, Part 4; and
6. Complete Part 2—Tax Computation.

Section 2701 Elections

The special valuation rules of section 2701 contain three elections that you must make with Form 709.

1. A transferor may elect to treat a qualified payment right he or she holds (and all other rights of the same class) as other than a qualified payment right.
2. A person may elect to treat a distribution right held by that person in a controlled entity as a qualified payment right.
3. An interest holder may elect to treat as a taxable event the payment of a qualified payment that occurs more than 4 years after its due date.

The elections described in (1) and (2) above must be made on the Form 709 that is filed by the transferor to report the transfer that is being valued under section 2701. The elections are made by attaching a statement to Form 709. For information on what must be in the statement and for definitions and other details on the elections, see section 2701 and Regulations section 25.2701-2(c).

The election described in (3) above may be made by attaching a statement to the Form 709 filed by the recipient of the qualified payment for the year the payment is received. If the election is made on a timely filed return, the taxable event is deemed to occur on the date the qualified payment is received. If it is made on a late filed return, the taxable event is deemed to occur on the first day of the month immediately preceding the month in which the return is filed. For information on what must be in the statement and for definitions and other details on this election, see section 2701 and Regulations section 25.2701-4(d).

All of the elections may be revoked only with the consent of the IRS.

When To File

Form 709 is an annual return.

Generally, you must file the Form 709 no earlier than January 1, but not later than April 15, of the year after the gift was made. However, for gifts made in 2011, the due date of the Form 709 is April 17, 2012, because April 15, 2012, is a Sunday and April 16, 2012, is a legal holiday in the District of Columbia. See section 7503.

If the donor died during 2011, the executor must file the donor's 2011 Form 709 not later than the earlier of:

- The due date (with extensions) for filing the donor's estate tax return, or
- April 17, 2012, or the extended due date granted for filing the donor's gift tax return.

Extension of Time To File

There are two methods of extending the time to file the gift tax return. Neither method extends the time to pay the gift or GST taxes. If you want an extension of time to pay the gift or GST taxes, you must request that separately. (See Regulations section 25.6161-1.)

By extending the time to file your income tax return. Any extension of time granted for filing your calendar year 2011 federal income tax return will also automatically extend the time to file your 2011 federal gift tax return. Income tax extensions are made by using Form 4868, Application for Automatic Extension of Time To File U.S. Individual Income Tax Return, or Form 2350, Application for Extension of Time To File U.S. Income Tax Return. You may only use these forms to extend the time for filing your gift tax return if you are also requesting an extension of time to file your income tax return.

By filing Form 8892. If you do not request an extension for your income tax return, use Form 8892, Application for Automatic Extension of Time To File Form 709 and/or Payment of Gift/Generation-Skipping Transfer Tax, to request an automatic 6-month extension of time to file your federal gift tax return. In addition to containing an extension request, Form 8892 also serves as a payment voucher (Form 8892-V) for a balance due on federal gift taxes for which you are extending the time to file. For more information, see Form 8892.

Where To File

File Form 709 at the following address:

Department of the Treasury
Internal Revenue Service Center
Cincinnati, OH 45999

See the Caution under Lines 12 – 18. Split Gifts, *later, before you mail the return.*

Adequate Disclosure

CAUTION *To begin the running of the statute of limitations for a gift, the gift must be adequately disclosed on Form 709 (or an attached statement) filed for the year of the gift.*

In general, a gift will be considered adequately disclosed if the return or statement includes the following:

- A full and complete Form 709.
- A description of the transferred property and any consideration received by the donor;
- The identity of, and relationship between, the donor and each donee;
- If the property is transferred in trust, the trust's employer identification number (EIN) and a brief description of the terms of the trust (or a copy of the trust instrument in lieu of the description); and
- Either a qualified appraisal or a detailed description of the method used to determine the fair market value of the gift.

See Regulations section 301.6501(c)-1(e) and (f) for details, including what constitutes a qualified appraisal, the information required if no appraisal is provided, and the information required for transfers under sections 2701 and 2702.

Penalties

Late filing and late payment. Section 6651 imposes penalties for both late filing and late payment, unless there is reasonable cause for the delay.

Reasonable cause determinations. If you receive a notice about penalties after you file Form 709, send an explanation and we will determine if you meet reasonable cause criteria. Do **not** attach an explanation when you file Form 709.

There are also penalties for willful failure to file a return on time, willful attempt to evade or defeat payment of tax, and valuation understatements that cause an underpayment of the tax. A substantial valuation understatement occurs when the reported value of property entered on Form 709 is 65% or less of the actual value of the property. A gross valuation understatement occurs when the reported value listed on the Form 709 is 40% or less of the actual value of the property.

Return preparer. Penalties may also be applied to tax return preparers, including gift tax return preparers.

The Small Business and Work Opportunity Tax Act of 2007 extended section 6694 income tax return preparer penalties to all tax return preparers, including gift tax return preparers. Now, gift tax return preparers who prepare any return or claim for refund with an understatement of tax liability due to willful or reckless conduct can be penalized $5,000 or 50% of the income received (or income to be received), whichever is greater, for each return. See section 6694, its regulations, and Ann. 2009-15, 2009-11 I.R.B. 687 (available at *www.irs.gov/pub/irs-irbs/irb09-11.pdf*) for more information.

Joint Tenancy

If you buy property with your own funds and the title to the property is held by yourself and a donee as joint tenants with right of survivorship and if either you or the donee may give up those rights by severing your interest, you have made a gift to the donee in the amount of half the value of the property.

If you create a joint bank account for yourself and a donee (or a similar kind of ownership by which you can get back the entire fund without the donee's consent), you have made a gift to the donee when the donee draws on the account for his or her own benefit. The amount of the gift is the amount that the donee took out without any obligation to repay you.

If you buy a U.S. savings bond registered as payable to yourself or a donee, there is a gift to the donee when he or she cashes the bond without any obligation to account to you.

Transfer of Certain Life Estates Received From Spouse

If you received a qualified terminable interest (see *Line 12. Election Out of QTIP Treatment of Annuities,* later) from your spouse for which a marital deduction was elected on your spouse's estate or gift tax return, you will be subject to the gift tax (and GST tax, if applicable) if you dispose of all or part of your life income interest (by gift, sale, or otherwise).

Generally, the entire value of the property transferred less:

1. The amount you received (if any) for the life income interest, and
2. The amount (if any) determined after the application of section 2702, valuing certain retained interests at zero, for the life income interest you retained after the transfer,

will be treated as a taxable gift.

That portion of the property's value that is attributable to the remainder interest is a gift of a future interest for which no annual exclusion is allowed. To the extent you made a gift of the life income interest, you may claim an annual exclusion, treating the person to whom you transferred the interest as the donee for purposes of figuring the annual exclusion.

Specific Instructions

Part 1—General Information

Lines 4 and 6. Address. Enter your current mailing address.

Foreign address. If your address is outside of the United States or its possessions or territories, enter the information as follows: city, province or state, and name of country. Follow the country's practice for entering the postal code. Do not abbreviate the country name.

Line 5. Legal residence (domicile). In general, your legal residence (also known as your domicile) is acquired by living in a place, for even a brief period of time, with no definite present intention of moving from that place.

Enter the state of the United States (including the District of Columbia) or a foreign country in which you legally reside or are domiciled at the time of the gift.

Line 7. Citizenship. Enter your citizenship.

The term "citizen of the United States" includes a person who, at the time of making the gift:

- Was domiciled in a possession of the United States,
- Was a U.S. citizen, and
- Became a U.S. citizen for a reason other than being a citizen of a U.S. possession or being born or residing in a possession.

A nonresident alien includes a person who, at the time of making the gift:

- Was domiciled in a possession of the United States,
- Was a U.S. citizen, and
- Became a U.S. citizen only because he or she was a citizen of a possession or was born or resided in a possession.

Lines 12–18. Split Gifts

CAUTION *A married couple may not file a joint gift tax return. However, if after reading the instructions below, you and your spouse agree to split your gifts, you should file both of your individual gift tax returns together (that is, in the same envelope) to help the IRS process the returns and to avoid correspondence from the IRS.*

If you and your spouse agree, all gifts (including gifts of property held with your spouse as joint tenants or tenants by the entirety) either of you make to third parties during the calendar year will be considered as made one-half by each of you if:

- You and your spouse were married to one another at the time of the gift;
- If divorced or widowed after the gift, you did not remarry during the rest of the calendar year;
- Neither of you was a nonresident alien at the time of the gift; and
- You did not give your spouse a general power of appointment over the property interest transferred.

If you transferred property partly to your spouse and partly to third parties, you can only split the gifts if the interest transferred to the third parties is ascertainable at the time of the gift.

The consent is effective for the entire calendar year; therefore, all gifts made by both you and your spouse to third parties during the calendar year (while you were married) must be split.

If the consent is effective, the liability for the entire gift tax of each spouse is joint and several.

If you meet these requirements and want your gifts to be considered made one-half by you and one-half by your spouse, check the "Yes" box on line 12; complete lines 13 through 17; and have your spouse sign the consent on line 18.

If you are not married or do not wish to split gifts, skip to Schedule A.

Line 15. If you were married to one another for all of 2011, check the "Yes" box and skip to line 17. If you were married for only part of the year, check the "No" box and go to line 16. If you were divorced or widowed after you made the gift, you cannot elect to split gifts if you remarried before the end of 2011.

Line 16. Check the box that explains the change in your marital status during the year and give the date you were married, divorced, or widowed, or the date the donor spouse died.

Consent of Spouse

Your spouse must sign the consent for your gift-splitting election to be valid. The consent may generally be signed at any time after the end of the calendar year. However, there are two exceptions.

1. The consent may not be signed after April 15 following the end of the year in which the gift was made. But, if neither you nor your spouse has filed a gift tax return for the year on or before that date, the consent must be made on the first gift tax return for the year filed by either of you.
2. The consent may not be signed after a notice of deficiency for the gift tax for the year has been sent to either you or your spouse.

The executor for a deceased spouse or the guardian for a legally incompetent spouse may sign the consent.

When the Consenting Spouse Must Also File a Gift Tax Return

In general, if you and your spouse elect gift splitting, then both spouses must file his or her own, individual, gift tax return.

However, only one spouse must file a return if the requirements of either of the exceptions below are met. In the exceptions below, "gifts" means gifts (or parts of gifts) that do not qualify for the political organization, educational, or medical exclusions.

Exception 1. During the calendar year:

- Only one spouse made any gifts,
- The total value of these gifts to each third-party donee does not exceed $26,000, and
- All of the gifts were of present interests.

Exception 2. During the calendar year:

- Only one spouse (the donor spouse) made gifts of more than $13,000 but not more than $26,000 to any third-party donee,
- The only gifts made by the other spouse (the consenting spouse) were gifts of not more than $13,000 to third-party donees other than those to whom the donor spouse made gifts, and
- All of the gifts by both spouses were of present interests.

If either of the above exceptions is met, only the donor spouse must file a return and the consenting spouse signifies consent on that return.

Specific instructions for *Part 2—Tax Computation* are discussed later. Because you must complete Schedules A, B, and C to fill out *Part 2*, you will find instructions for these schedules below.

Schedule A. Computation of Taxable Gifts

Do not enter on Schedule A any gift or part of a gift that qualifies for the political organization, educational, or medical exclusions. In the instructions below, "gifts" means gifts (or parts of gifts) that do not qualify for the political organization, educational, or medical exclusions.

Line A. Valuation Discounts

If the value of any gift you report in either Part 1, Part 2, or Part 3 of Schedule A includes a discount for lack of marketability, a minority interest, a fractional interest in real estate, blockage, market absorption, or for any other reason, answer "Yes" to the question at the top of Schedule A. Also, attach an explanation giving the basis for the claimed discounts and showing the amount of the discounts taken.

Line B. Qualified Tuition Programs (529 Plans or Programs)

If in 2011, you contributed more than $13,000 to a QTP on behalf of any one person, you may elect to treat up to $65,000 of the contribution for that person as if you had made it ratably over a 5-year period. The election allows you to apply the annual exclusion to a portion of the contribution in each of the 5 years, beginning in 2011. You can make this election for as many separate people as you made QTP contributions.

You can only apply the election to a maximum of $65,000. You must report all of your 2011 QTP contributions for any single person that exceed $65,000 (in addition to any other gifts you made to that person).

For each of the 5 years, you report in Part 1 of Schedule A one-fifth (20%) of the amount for which you made the election. In column E of Part 1 (Schedule A) list the date of the gift as the calendar year for which you are deemed to have made the gift (that is, the year of the current Form 709 you are filing). Do not list the actual year of contribution for subsequent years.

However, if in any of the last 4 years of the election, you did not make any other gifts that would require you to file a Form 709, you do not need to file Form 709 to report that year's portion of the election amount.

Example. In 2011, D contributed $85,000 to a QTP for the benefit of her son. D elects to treat $65,000 of this contribution as having been made ratably over a 5-year period. Accordingly, for 2011, D reports the following:

$20,000	(the amount of the contribution that exceeded $65,000)
+ $13,000	(the 1/5 portion from the election)
$33,000	the total gift to her son listed in Part 1 of Schedule A for 2011

In 2012, D gives a gift of $20,000 cash to her niece and no other gifts. On her 2012 Form 709, D reports in Part 1 of Schedule A the $20,000 gift to her niece and a $13,000 gift to her son (the one-fifth portion of the 2011 gift that is treated as made in 2012). In column E of Part 1 (Schedule A), D lists "2012" as the date of the gift.

D makes no gifts in 2013, 2014, or 2015. She is not required to file Form 709 in any of those years to report the one-fifth portion of the QTP gift, because she is not otherwise required to file Form 709.

You make the election by checking the box on line B at the top of Schedule A. The election must be made for the calendar year in which the contribution is made. Also attach an explanation that includes the following:
- The total amount contributed per individual beneficiary,
- The amount for which the election is being made, and
- The name of the individual for whom the contribution was made.

If you are electing gift splitting, apply the gift-splitting rules before applying these rules. Each spouse would then decide individually whether to make this QTP election.

Contributions to QTPs do not qualify for the education exclusion.

How To Complete Parts 1, 2, and 3

After you determine which gifts you made in 2011 that are subject to the gift tax, list them on Schedule A. You must divide these gifts between:

1. Part 1—those subject only to the gift tax (gifts made to nonskip persons—see *Part 1—Gifts Subject Only to Gift Tax*),
2. Part 2—those subject to both the gift and GST taxes (gifts made to skip persons—see *Gifts Subject to Both Gift and GST Taxes* and *Part 2—Direct Skips*), and
3. Part 3—those subject only to the gift tax at this time but which could later be subject to GST tax (gifts that are indirect skips, see *Part 3—Indirect Skips*).

If you need more space, attach a separate sheet using the same format as Schedule A.

Use the following guidelines when entering gifts on Schedule A:

- *Enter a gift only once—in Part 1, Part 2, or Part 3;*
- *Do not enter any gift or part of a gift that qualified for the political organization, educational, or medical exclusion;*
- *Enter gifts under "Gifts made by spouse" only if you have chosen to split gifts with your spouse and your spouse is required to file a Form 709 (see* Part 1—General Information, Lines 12–18. Split Gifts *); and*
- *In column F, enter the full value of the gift (including those made by your spouse, if applicable). If you have chosen to split gifts, that one-half portion of the gift is entered in column G.*

Gifts to Donees Other Than Your Spouse

You must always enter all gifts of future interests that you made during the calendar year regardless of their value.

No gift splitting. If the total gifts of present interests to any donee are more than $13,000 in the calendar year, then you must enter all such gifts that you made during the year to or on behalf of that donee, including those gifts that will be excluded under the annual exclusion. If the total is $13,000 or less, you need not enter on Schedule A any gifts (except gifts of future interests) that you made to that donee. Enter these gifts in the top half of Part 1, 2, or 3, as applicable.

Gift splitting elected. Enter on Schedule A the entire value of every gift you made during the calendar year while you were married, even if the gift's value will be less than $13,000 after it is split in Column G of Part 1, 2, or 3 of Schedule A.

Gifts made by spouse. If you elected gift splitting and your spouse made gifts, list those gifts in the space below "Gifts made by spouse" in Part 1, 2, or 3. Report these gifts in the same way you report gifts you made.

Gifts to Your Spouse

Except for the gifts described below, you do not need to enter any of your gifts to your spouse on Schedule A.

Terminable interest. Terminable interests are defined in the instructions to *Part 4, line 4*. If all the terminable interests you gave to your spouse qualify as life estates with power of appointment (defined under *Life estate with power of appointment*), you do not need to enter any of them on Schedule A.

However, if you gave your spouse any terminable interest that does not qualify as a life estate with power of appointment, you must report on Schedule A all gifts of terminable interests you made to your spouse during the year.

Charitable remainder trusts. If you make a gift to a charitable remainder trust and your spouse is the only noncharitable beneficiary (other than yourself), the interest you gave to your spouse is not considered a terminable interest and, therefore, should not be shown on Schedule A. See section 2523(g)(1). For definitions and rules concerning these trusts, see section 2056(b)(8)(B).

Future interest. Generally, you should not report a gift of a future interest to your spouse unless the future interest is also a terminable interest that is required to be reported as described above. However, if you gave a gift of a future interest to your spouse and you are required to report the gift on Form 709 because you gave the present interest to a donee other than your spouse, then you should enter the entire gift, including the future interest given to your spouse, on Schedule A. You should use the rules under *Gifts Subject to Both Gift and GST Taxes*, below, to determine whether to enter the gift on Schedule A, Part 1, Part 2, or Part 3.

Spouses who are not U.S. citizens. If your spouse is not a U.S. citizen and you gave him or her a gift of a future interest, you must report on Schedule A all gifts to your spouse for the year. If all gifts to your spouse were present interests, do not report on Schedule A any gifts to your spouse if the total of such gifts for the year does not exceed $136,000 and all gifts in excess of $13,000 would qualify for a marital deduction if your spouse were a U.S. citizen (see the instructions for Schedule A, Part 4, line 4). If the gifts exceed $136,000, you must report all of the gifts even though some may be excluded.

Gifts Subject to Both Gift and GST Taxes

Definitions

Direct skip. The GST tax you must report on Form 709 is that imposed only on *inter vivos* direct skips. An "*inter vivos* direct skip" is a transfer that is:
- Subject to the gift tax,
- Of an interest in property, and
- Made to a skip person.

All three requirements must be met before the gift is subject to the GST tax.

A gift is "subject to the gift tax" if you are required to list it on Schedule A of Form 709. However, if you make a nontaxable gift (which is a direct skip) to a trust for the benefit of an individual, this transfer is subject to the GST tax unless:

1. During the lifetime of the beneficiary, no corpus or income may be distributed to anyone other than the beneficiary and
2. If the beneficiary dies before the termination of the trust, the assets of the trust will be included in the gross estate of the beneficiary.

Note. If the property transferred in the direct skip would have been includible in the donor's estate if the donor died immediately after the transfer, see *Transfers Subject to an Estate Tax Inclusion Period (ETIP).*

To determine if a gift "is of an interest in property" and "is made to a skip person," you must first determine if the donee is a "natural person" or a "trust" as defined below.

Trust. For purposes of the GST tax, a *trust* includes not only an ordinary trust, but also any other arrangement (other than an estate) that although not explicitly a trust, has substantially the same effect as a trust. For example, a *trust* includes life estates with remainders, terms for years, and insurance and annuity contracts. A transfer of property that is conditional on the occurrence of an event is a transfer in trust.

Interest in property. If a gift is made to a *natural person,* it is always considered a gift of an interest in property for purposes of the GST tax.

If a gift is made to a trust, a natural person will have an *interest in the property* transferred to the trust if that person either has a present right to receive income or corpus from the trust (such as an income interest for life) or is a permissible current recipient of income or corpus from the trust (for example, possesses a general power of appointment).

Skip person. A donee, who is a natural person, is a *skip person* if that donee is assigned to a generation that is two or more generations below the generation assignment of the donor. See *Determining the Generation of a Donee,* below.

A donee that is a trust is a skip person if all the interests in the property transferred to the trust (as defined above) are held by skip persons.

A trust will also be a skip person if there are no interests in the property transferred to the trust held by any person, and future distributions or terminations from the trust can be made only to skip persons.

Nonskip person. A *nonskip person* is any donee who is not a skip person.

Determining the Generation of a Donee

Generally, a generation is determined along family lines as follows:

1. If the donee is a lineal descendant of a grandparent of the donor (for example, the donor's cousin, niece, nephew, etc.), the number of generations between the donor and the descendant (donee) is determined by subtracting the number of generations between the grandparent and the donor from the number of generations between the grandparent and the descendant (donee).
2. If the donee is a lineal descendant of a grandparent of a spouse (or former spouse) of the donor, the number of generations between the donor and the descendant (donee) is determined by subtracting the number of generations between the grandparent and the spouse (or former spouse) from the number of generations between the grandparent and the descendant (donee).
3. A person who at any time was married to a person described in (1) or (2) above is assigned to the generation of that person. A person who at any time was married to the donor is assigned to the donor's generation.
4. A relationship by adoption or half-blood is treated as a relationship by whole-blood.

A person who is not assigned to a generation according to (1), (2), (3), or (4) above is assigned to a generation based on his or her birth date as follows:

1. A person who was born not more than 12½ years after the donor is in the donor's generation.
2. A person born more than 12½ years, but not more than 37½ years, after the donor is in the first generation younger than the donor.
3. Similar rules apply for a new generation every 25 years.

If more than one of the rules for assigning generations applies to a donee, that donee is generally assigned to the youngest of the generations that would apply.

If an estate, trust, partnership, corporation, or other entity (other than governmental entities and certain charitable organizations and trusts, described in sections 511(a)(2) and 511(b)(2), as discussed below) is a donee, then each person who indirectly receives the gift through the entity is treated as a donee and is assigned to a generation as explained in the above rules.

Charitable organizations and trusts, described in sections 511(a)(2) and 511(b)(2), and governmental entities are assigned to the donor's generation. Transfers to such organizations are therefore not subject to the GST tax. These gifts should always be listed in Part 1 of Schedule A.

Charitable Remainder Trusts

Gifts in the form of charitable remainder annuity trusts, charitable remainder unitrusts, and pooled income funds are not transfers to skip persons and therefore are not direct skips. You should always list these gifts in Part 1 of Schedule A even if all of the life beneficiaries are skip persons.

Generation Assignment Where Intervening Parent Is Deceased

If you made a gift to your grandchild and at the time you made the gift, the grandchild's parent (who is your or your spouse's or your former spouse's child) is deceased, then for purposes of generation assignment, your grandchild is considered to be your child rather than your grandchild. Your grandchild's children will be treated as your grandchildren rather than your great-grandchildren.

This rule is also applied to your lineal descendants below the level of grandchild. For example, if your grandchild is deceased, your great-grandchildren who are lineal descendants of the deceased grandchild are considered your grandchildren for purposes of the GST tax.

This special rule may also apply in other cases of the death of a parent of the transferee. If property is transferred to a descendant of a parent of the transferor and that person's parent (who is a lineal descendant of the parent of the transferor) is deceased at the time the transfer is subject to gift or estate tax, then for purposes of generation assignment, the individual is treated as if he or she is a member of the generation that is one generation below the lower of:

- The transferor's generation or
- The generation assignment of the youngest living ancestor of the individual who is also a descendant of the parent of the transferor.

The same rules apply to the generation assignment of any descendant of the individual.

This rule does not apply to a transfer to an individual who is not a lineal descendant of the transferor if the transferor at the time of the transfer has any living lineal descendants.

If any transfer of property to a trust would have been a direct skip except for this generation assignment rule, then the rule also applies to transfers from the trust attributable to such property.

Ninety-day rule. For assigning individuals to generations for purposes of the GST tax, any individual who dies no later than 90 days after a transfer occurring by reason of the death of the transferor is treated as having predeceased the transferor. The 90-day rule applies to transfers occurring on or after July 18, 2005. See Regulations section 26.2651-1(a)(2)(C)(iii) for more information.

Examples

The GST rules can be illustrated by the following examples.

Example 1. You give your house to your daughter for her life with the remainder then passing to her children. This gift is made to a "trust" even though there is no explicit trust instrument. The interest in the property transferred (the present right to use the house) is transferred to a nonskip person (your daughter). Therefore, the trust is not a skip person because there is an interest in the transferred property that is held by a nonskip person, and the gift is not a direct skip. The transfer is an indirect skip, however, because on the death of the daughter, a termination of her interest in the trust will occur that may be subject to the GST tax. See the instructions for *Part 3—Indirect Skips* for a discussion of how to allocate GST exemption to such a trust.

Example 2. You give $100,000 to your grandchild. This gift is a direct skip that is not made in trust. You should list it in Part 2 of Schedule A.

Example 3. You establish a trust that is required to accumulate income for 10 years and then pay its income to your grandchildren for their lives and upon their deaths distribute the corpus to their children. Because the trust has no current beneficiaries, there are no present interests in the property transferred to the trust. All of the persons to whom the trust can make future distributions (including distributions upon the termination of interests in property held in trust) are skip persons (that is, your grandchildren and great-grandchildren). Therefore, the trust itself is a skip person and you should list the gift in Part 2 of Schedule A.

Example 4. You establish a trust that pays all of its income to your grandchildren for 10 years. At the end of 10 years, the corpus is to be distributed to your children. Since for this purpose interests in trusts are defined only as present interests, all of the interests in this trust are held by skip persons (the children's interests are future interests). Therefore, the trust is a skip person and you should list the entire amount you transferred to the trust in Part 2 of Schedule A even though some of the trust's ultimate beneficiaries are nonskip persons.

Part 1—Gifts Subject Only to Gift Tax

List in Part 1 gifts subject only to the gift tax. Generally, all of the gifts you made to your spouse (that are required to be listed, as described earlier), to your children, and to charitable organizations are not subject to the GST tax and should, therefore, be listed only in Part 1.

Group the gifts in four categories:

- Gifts made to your spouse,
- Gifts made to third parties that are to be split with your spouse,
- Charitable gifts (if you are not splitting gifts with your spouse), and
- Other gifts.

If a transfer results in gifts to two or more individuals (such as a life estate to one with remainder to the other), list the gift to each separately.

Number and describe all gifts (including charitable, public, and similar gifts) in the columns provided in Schedule A.

Column B

Describe each gift in enough detail so that the property can be easily identified, as explained below.

For real estate, give:

- A legal description of each parcel;
- The street number, name, and area if the property is located in a city; and
- A short statement of any improvements made to the property.

For bonds, give:

- The number of bonds transferred;
- The principal amount of each bond;
- Name of obligor;
- Date of maturity;
- Rate of interest;
- Date or dates when interest is payable;
- Series number, if there is more than one issue;
- Exchanges where listed or, if unlisted, give the location of the principal business office of the corporation; and
- CUSIP number. The CUSIP number is a nine-digit number assigned by the American Banking Association to traded securities.

For stocks:

- Give number of shares;
- State whether common or preferred;
- If preferred, give the issue, par value, quotation at which returned, and exact name of corporation;
- If unlisted on a principal exchange, give the location of the principal business office of the corporation, the state in which incorporated, and the date of incorporation;
- If listed, give principal exchange; and
- CUSIP number.

For interests in property based on the length of a person's life, give the date of birth of the person. If you transfer any interest in a closely held entity, provide the EIN of the entity.

For life insurance policies, give the name of the insurer and the policy number.

Clearly identify in the description column which gifts create the opening of an ETIP as described under *Transfers Subject to an Estate Tax Inclusion Period (ETIP)*. Describe the interest that is creating the ETIP. An allocation of GST exemption to property subject to an ETIP that is made prior to the close of the ETIP becomes effective no earlier than the date of the close of the ETIP. See *Schedule C. Computation of GST Tax*.

Column D. Donor's Adjusted Basis of Gifts

Show the basis you would use for income tax purposes if the gift were sold or exchanged. Generally, this means cost plus improvements, less applicable depreciation, amortization, and depletion.

For more information on adjusted basis, see Pub. 551, Basis of Assets.

Columns E and F. Date and Value of Gift

The value of a gift is the fair market value (FMV) of the property on the date the gift is made (valuation date). The FMV is the price at which the property would change hands between a willing buyer and a willing seller, when neither is forced to buy or to sell, and when both have reasonable knowledge of all relevant facts. FMV may not be determined by a forced sale price, nor by the sale price of the item in a market other than that in which the item is most commonly sold to the public. The location of the item must be taken into account whenever appropriate.

The FMV of a stock or bond (whether listed or unlisted) is the mean between the highest and lowest selling prices quoted on the valuation date. If only the closing selling prices are available, then the FMV is the mean between the quoted closing selling price on the valuation date and on the trading day before the valuation date. If there were no sales on the valuation date, figure the FMV as follows:

1. Find the mean between the highest and lowest selling prices on the nearest trading date before and the nearest trading date after the valuation date. Both trading dates must be reasonably close to the valuation date.
2. Prorate the difference between mean prices to the valuation date.
3. Add or subtract (whichever applies) the prorated part of the difference to or from the mean price figured for the nearest trading date before the actual valuation date.

If no actual sales were made reasonably close to the valuation date, make the same computation using the mean between the bona fide bid and the asked prices instead of sales prices. If actual sales prices or bona fide bid and asked prices are available within a reasonable period of time before the valuation date but not after the valuation date, or vice versa, use the mean between the highest and lowest sales prices or bid and asked prices as the FMV.

Stock of close corporations or inactive stock must be valued on the basis of net worth, earnings, earning and dividend capacity, and other relevant factors.

Generally, the best indication of the value of real property is the price paid for the property in an arm's-length transaction on or before the valuation date. If there has been no such transaction, use the comparable sales method. In comparing similar properties, consider differences in the date of the sale, and the size, condition, and location of the properties, and make all appropriate adjustments.

The value of all annuities, life estates, terms for years, remainders, or reversions is generally the present value on the date of the gift.

Sections 2701 and 2702 provide special valuation rules to determine the amount of the gift when a donor transfers an equity interest in a corporation or partnership (section 2701) or makes a gift in trust (section 2702). The rules only apply if, immediately after the transfer, the donor (or an applicable family member) holds an applicable retained interest in the corporation or partnership, or retains an interest in the trust. For details, see sections 2701 and 2702, and their regulations.

Column G. Split Gifts

Enter an amount in this column only if you have chosen to split gifts with your spouse.

Split Gifts—Gifts Made by Spouse

If you elected to split gifts with your spouse and your spouse has given a gift(s) that is being split with you, enter in this area of Part 1 information on the gift(s) made by your spouse. If only you made gifts and you are splitting them with your spouse, do not make an entry in this area.

Generally, if you elect to split your gifts, you must split all gifts made by you and your spouse to third-party donees. The only exception is if you gave your spouse a general power of appointment over a gift you made.

Supplemental Documents

To support the value of your gifts, you must provide information showing how it was determined.

For stock of close corporations or inactive stock, attach balance sheets, particularly the one nearest the date of the gift, and statements of net earnings or operating results and dividends paid for each of the 5 preceding years.

For each life insurance policy, attach Form 712, Life Insurance Statement.

Note for single premium or paid-up policies. In certain situations, for example, where the surrender value of the policy exceeds its replacement cost, the true economic value of the policy will be greater than the amount shown on line 59 of Form 712. In these situations, report the full economic value of the policy on Schedule A. See Rev. Rul. 78-137, 1978-1 C.B. 280 for details.

If the gift was made by means of a trust, attach a certified or verified copy of the trust instrument to the return on which you report your first transfer to the trust. However, to report subsequent transfers to the trust, you may attach a brief description of the terms of the trust or a copy of the trust instrument.

Also attach any appraisal used to determine the value of real estate or other property.

If you do not attach this information, Schedule A must include a full explanation of how value was determined.

Part 2—Direct Skips

List in Part 2 only those gifts that are currently subject to both the gift and GST taxes. You must list the gifts in Part 2 in the chronological order that you made them. Number, describe, and value the gifts as described in the instructions for Part 1.

If you made a transfer to a trust that was a direct skip, list the entire gift as one line entry in Part 2.

Column C. 2632(b) Election

If you elect under section 2632(b)(3) to not have the automatic allocation rules of section 2632(b) apply to a transfer, enter a check in column C next to the transfer. You must also attach a statement to Form 709 clearly describing the transaction and the extent to which the automatic allocation is not to apply. Reporting a direct skip on a timely filed Form 709 and paying the GST tax on the transfer will qualify as such a statement.

How to report generation-skipping transfers after the close of an ETIP. If you are reporting a generation-skipping transfer that was subject to an ETIP (provided the ETIP closed as a result of something other than the death of the transferor; see Form 706), and you are also reporting gifts made during the year, complete Schedule A as you normally would with the following changes.

Report the transfer subject to an ETIP on Schedule A, Part 2.

Column B. In addition to the information already requested, describe the interest that is closing the ETIP; explain what caused the interest to terminate; and list the year the gift portion of the transfer was reported and its item number on Schedule A that was originally filed to report the gift portion of the ETIP transfer.

Column E. Give the date the ETIP closed rather than the date of the initial gift.

Columns F, G, and H. Enter "N/A" in these columns.

The value is entered only in Column B of Part 1, Schedule C. See *Column B* above.

Split Gifts—Gifts Made by Spouse

See this heading under Part 1.

Part 3—Indirect Skips

Some gifts made to trusts are subject only to gift tax at the time of the transfer but later may be subject to GST tax. The GST tax could apply either at the time of a distribution from the trust, at the termination of the trust, or both.

Section 2632(c) defines indirect skips and applies special rules to the allocation of GST exemption to such transfers. In general, an indirect skip is a transfer of property that is subject to gift tax (other than a direct skip) and is made to a GST trust. A GST trust is a trust that could have a generation-skipping transfer with respect to the transferor, unless the trust provides for certain distributions of trust corpus to nonskip persons. See section 2632(c)(3)(B) for details.

List in Part 3 those gifts that are indirect skips as defined in section 2632(c) or may later be subject to GST tax. This includes indirect skips for which election (2), described below, will be made in the current year or has been made in a previous year. You must list the gifts in Part 3 in the chronological order that you made them.

Column C. 2632(c) Election

Section 2632(c) provides for the automatic allocation of the donor's unused GST exemption to indirect skips. This section also sets forth three different elections you may make regarding the allocation of exemption.

Election 1. You may elect not to have the automatic allocation rules apply to the current transfer made to a particular trust.

Election 2. You may elect not to have the automatic rules apply to both the current transfer and any and all future transfers made to a particular trust.

Election 3. You may elect to treat any trust as a GST trust for purposes of the automatic allocation rules.

See section 2632(c)(5) for details.

When to make an election. Election (1) is timely made if it is made on a timely filed gift tax return for the year the transfer was made or was deemed to have been made.

Elections (2) and (3) may be made on a timely filed gift tax return for the year for which the election is to become effective.

To make one of these elections, check column C next to the transfer to which the election applies. You must also attach an explanation as described below. If you are making election (2) or (3) on a return on which the transfer is not reported, simply attach the statement described below.

If you are reporting a transfer to a trust for which election (2) or (3) was made on a previously filed return, do not make an entry in column C for that transfer and do not attach a statement.

Attachment. You must attach a statement to Form 709 that describes the election you are making and clearly identifies the trusts and/or transfers to which the election applies.

Split Gifts—Gifts Made by Spouse

See this heading under Part 1.

Part 4—Taxable Gift Reconciliation

Line 2

Enter the total annual exclusions you are claiming for the gifts listed on Schedule A. See *Annual Exclusion*, later. If you split a gift with your spouse, the annual exclusion you claim against that gift may not be more than the smaller of your half of the gift or $13,000.

Deductions

Line 4. Marital deduction

Enter all of the gifts to your spouse that you listed on Schedule A and for which you are claiming a marital deduction. Do not enter any gift that you did not include on Schedule A. On the dotted line on line 4, indicate which numbered items from Schedule A are gifts to your spouse for which you are claiming the marital deduction.

Do not enter on line 4 any gifts to your spouse who was not a U.S. citizen at the time of the gift.

You may deduct all gifts of nonterminable interests made during the year that you entered on Schedule A regardless of amount, and certain gifts of terminable interests as outlined below.

Terminable interests. Generally, you cannot take the marital deduction if the gift to your spouse is a terminable interest. In most instances, a terminable interest is nondeductible if someone other than the donee spouse will have an interest in the property following the termination of the donee spouse's interest. Some examples of terminable interests are:

- A life estate,
- An estate for a specified number of years, or
- Any other property interest that after a period of time will terminate or fail.

If you transfer an interest to your spouse as sole joint tenant with yourself or as a tenant by the entirety, the interest is not considered a terminable interest just because the tenancy may be severed.

Life estate with power of appointment. You may deduct, without an election, a gift of a terminable interest if all four requirements below are met:

1. Your spouse is entitled for life to all of the income from the entire interest;
2. The income is paid yearly or more often;
3. Your spouse has the unlimited power, while he or she is alive or by will, to appoint the entire interest in all circumstances; and
4. No part of the entire interest is subject to another person's power of appointment (except to appoint it to your spouse).

If either the right to income or the power of appointment given to your spouse pertains only to a specific portion of a property interest, the marital deduction is allowed only to the extent that the rights of your spouse meet all four of the above conditions. For example, if your spouse is to receive all of the income from the entire interest, but only has a power to appoint one-half of the entire interest, then only one-half qualifies for the marital deduction.

A partial interest in property is treated as a specific portion of an entire interest only if the rights of your spouse to the income and to the power are a fractional or percentile share of the entire property interest. This means that the interest or share will reflect any increase or decrease in the value of the entire property interest. If the spouse is entitled to receive a specified sum of income annually, the capital amount that would produce such a sum will be considered the specific portion from which the spouse is entitled to receive the income.

Election to deduct qualified terminable interest property (QTIP). You may elect to deduct a gift of a terminable interest if it meets requirements (1), (2), and (4) above, even though it does not meet requirement (3).

You make this election simply by listing the qualified terminable interest property on Schedule A and deducting its value from Schedule A, Part 4, line 4. You are presumed to have made the election for all qualified property that you both list and deduct on Schedule A. You may not make the election on a late filed Form 709.

Line 5

Enter the amount of the annual exclusions that were claimed for the gifts you listed on line 4.

Line 7. Charitable Deduction

You may deduct from the total gifts made during the calendar year all gifts you gave to or for the use of:

- The United States, a state or political subdivision of a state or the District of Columbia for exclusively public purposes;
- Any corporation, trust, community chest, fund, or foundation organized and operated only for religious, charitable, scientific, literary, or educational purposes, or to prevent cruelty to children or animals, or to foster national or international amateur sports competition (if none of its activities involve providing athletic equipment unless it is a qualified amateur sports organization), as long as no part of the earnings benefits any one person, no substantial propaganda is produced, and no lobbying or campaigning for any candidate for public office is done;
- A fraternal society, order, or association operating under a lodge system, if the transferred property is to be used only for religious, charitable, scientific, literary, or educational purposes, including the encouragement of art and the prevention of cruelty to children or animals; or
- Any war veterans' organization organized in the United States (or any of its possessions), or any of its auxiliary departments or local chapters or posts, as long as no part of any of the earnings benefits any one person.

On line 7, show your total charitable, public, or similar gifts (minus annual exclusions allowed). On the dotted line, indicate which numbered items from the top of Schedule A are charitable gifts.

Line 10. GST Tax

If GST tax is due on any direct skips reported on this return, the amount of that GST tax is also considered a gift and must be added to the value of the direct skip reported on this return.

If you entered gifts on Part 2, or if you and your spouse elected gift splitting and your spouse made gifts subject to the GST tax that you are required to show on your Form 709, complete Schedule C, and enter on line 10 the total of Schedule C, Part 3, column H. Otherwise, enter zero on line 10.

Line 12. Election Out of QTIP Treatment of Annuities

Section 2523(f)(6) creates an automatic QTIP election for gifts of joint and survivor annuities where the spouses are the only possible recipients of the annuity prior to the death of the last surviving spouse.

The donor spouse can elect out of QTIP treatment, however, by checking the box on line 12 and entering the item number from Schedule A for the annuities for which you are making the election. Any annuities entered on line 12 cannot also be entered on line 4 of Schedule A, Part 4. Any such annuities that are not listed on line 12 must be entered on line 4 of Part 4, Schedule A. If there is more than one such joint and survivor annuity, you are not required to make the election for all of them. Once made, the election is irrevocable.

Schedule B. Gifts From Prior Periods

If you did not file gift tax returns for previous periods, check the "No" box on page 1 of Form 709, line 11a of *Part 1—General Information* and skip to *Part 2—Tax Computation* on the same page. (However, be sure to complete Schedule C, if applicable.) If you filed gift tax returns for previous periods, check the "Yes" box on line 11a and complete Schedule B by listing the years or quarters in chronological order as described below. If you need more space, attach a separate sheet using the same format as Schedule B.

Column A. If you filed returns for gifts made before 1971 or after 1981, show the calendar years in column A. If you filed returns for gifts made after 1970 and before 1982, show the calendar quarters.

Column B. In column B, identify the IRS office where you filed the returns. If you have changed your name, be sure to list any other names under which the returns were filed. If there was any other variation in the names under which you filed, such as the use of full given names instead of initials, please explain.

Column C. To determine the amount of the unified credit used for gifts made after 1976, use the *Worksheet for Form 709 Schedule B, Column C (Unified Credit Allowable for Prior Gifts)*, below, unless your prior gifts total $500,000 or less.

Prior gifts totaling $500,000 or less. In column C, enter the amount of unified credit actually applied in the prior period.

Prior gifts totaling over $500,000. See *Redetermining the Unified Credit,* below.

Column D. In column D, enter the amount of specific exemption claimed for gifts made in periods ending before January 1, 1977.

Column E. In column E, show the correct amount (the amount finally determined) of the taxable gifts for each earlier period.

See Regulations section 25.2504-2 for rules regarding the final determination of the value of a gift.

Redetermining the Unified Credit.

Beginning with the earliest year in which taxable gifts that used unified credit were made, redetermine the unified credit amount for each quarter/year as follows:

Column	*Instructions for Worksheet for Form 709 Schedule B, Column C (Unified Credit Allowable for Prior Periods).*
(a) Period.	Beginning with the earliest year in which taxable gifts were made, enter the quarter/year of the prior gift(s).
(b) Taxable Gifts for Current Period.	Enter all taxable gifts. Enter all pre-1977 gifts together on the pre-1977 row.
(c) Taxable Gifts for Prior Periods.	Enter the amount from column (d) of the ***previous*** row.
(d) Cumulative Taxable Gifts Including Current Period.	Enter the sum of column (b) and column (c) from the current row.
(e) Tax Based on 2011 Rates on Gifts for Prior Periods.	Enter the amount from column (f) of the ***previous*** row.
(f) Tax Based on 2011 Rates on Cumulative Gifts Including Current Period.	Enter the tax based on the amount in column (d) of the current row using the *Table for Computing Gift Tax*, below.
(g) Tax on Gifts for Current Period.	Subtract the amount in column (e) from the amount in column (f) for the current row.
(h) Maximum Unified Credit Available for Current Period (based on 2011 Rates).	Enter the amount from the *Table of Unified Credits (as recalculated using 2011 tax rates).* **Note.** The entry in each row of column (h) must be reduced by 20 percent of the amount allowed as a specific exemption for gifts made after September 8, 1976, and before January 1, 1977 (but no more than $6,000).
(i) Unified Credit Allowable in Prior Periods.	Enter the sum of column (i) and column (k) from the ***previous*** row.
(j) Available Credit in Current Period.	Subtract column (i) from column (h) for the current row.
(k) Credit Allowable.	Enter the lesser of column (g) or column (j) for the current row. Enter the column (k) amount on Schedule B, column C.
Repeat this process for each prior year with taxable gifts. Do not enter less than zero.	

Worksheet for Form 709 Schedule B, Column C (Unified Credit Allowable for Prior Periods).
Keep for your records.

Use this worksheet to figure amounts for Schedule B, column C.										
(a) Period	**(b) Taxable Gifts for Current Period**	**(c) Taxable Gifts for Prior Periods**[1]	**(d) Cumulative Taxable Gifts Including Current Period** *(Col. (b) + Col. (c))*	**(e) Tax Based on 2011 Rates on Gifts for Prior Periods** *(Col. (c))*[2]	**(f) Tax Based on 2011 Rates on Cumulative Gifts Including Current Period** *(Col. (d))*	**(g) Tax on Gifts for Current Period** *(Col. (f) - Col. (e))*	**(h) Maximum Unified Credit Available for Current Period (based on 2011 rates)**[3]	**(i) Unified Credit Allowable in Prior Periods**[4]	**(j) Available Credit in Current Period** *(Col. (h) - Col. (i))*	**(k) Credit Allowable** *(lesser of Col. (g) and Col. (j))*
Pre-1977										
Total Unified Credit Used for Prior Gifts:										

[1] Column (c): Enter amount from column (d) of the ***previous*** row.
[2] Column (e): Enter amount from column (f) of the ***previous*** row.
[3] Column (h): Enter amount from the Table of Unified Credit. (For each row in column (h), subtract 20 percent of any amount allowed as a specific exemption for gifts made after September 8, 1976, and before January 1, 1977.)
[4] Column (i): Enter the sum of column (i) and column (k) from the ***previous*** row.

Example 1. Prior Years Unified Credit Recalculation (for Form 709 Schedule B, Column C)
(Three post-1976 years involved. All have the same maximum unified credit available. Tentative tax equals available unified credit.)

Use this worksheet to figure amounts for Schedule B, Column C.										
(a) Period	**(b) Taxable Gifts for Current Period**	**(c) Taxable Gifts for Prior Periods[1]**	**(d) Cumulative Taxable Gifts Including Current Period** *(Col. (b) + Col. (c))*	**(e) Tax Based on 2011 Rates on Gifts for Prior Periods** *(Col. (c))*[2]	**(f) Tax Based on 2011 Rates on Cumulative Gifts Including Current Period** *(Col. (d))*	**(g) Tax on Gifts for Current Period** *(Col. (f) - Col. (e))*	**(h) Maximum Unified Credit Available for Current Period (based on 2011 rates)[3]**	**(i) Unified Credit Allowable in Prior Periods[4]**	**(j) Available Credit in Current Period** *(Col. (h) - Col. (i))*	**(k) Credit Allowable** *(lesser of Col. (g) and Col. (j))*
Pre-1977										
2005	500,000	0	500,000	0	155,800	155,800	330,800	0	330,800	155,800
2007	300,000	500,000	800,000	155,800	260,800	105,000	330,800	155,800	175,000	105,000
2009	200,000	800,000	1,000,000	260,800	330,800	70,000	330,800	260,800	70,000	70,000
Total Unified Credit Used for Prior Gifts :										330,800

[1] Column (c): Enter amount from column (d) of the ***previous*** row.
[2] Column (e): Enter amount from column (f) of the ***previous*** row.
[3] Column (h): Enter amount from the Table of Unified Credits. (For each row in column (h), subtract 20 percent of any amount allowed as a specific exemption for gifts made after September 8, 1976, and before January 1, 1977.)
[4] Column (i): Enter the sum of column (i) and column (k) from the ***previous*** row.

Example 2. Prior Years Unified Credit Recalculation (for Form 709 Schedule B, Column C)
(Three post-1976 years involved. All have the same maximum unified credit available. Tentative tax exceeds available unified credit.)

Use this worksheet to figure amounts for Schedule B, Column C.										
(a) Period	**(b) Taxable Gifts for Current Period**	**(c) Taxable Gifts for Prior Periods[1]**	**(d) Cumulative Taxable Gifts Including Current Period** *(Col. (b) + Col. (c))*	**(e) Tax Based on 2011 Rates on Gifts for Prior Periods** *(Col. (c))*[2]	**(f) Tax Based on 2011 Rates on Cumulative Gifts Including Current Period** *(Col. (d))*	**(g) Tax on Gifts for Current Period** *(Col. (f) - Col. (e))*	**(h) Maximum Unified Credit Available for Current Period (based on 2011 rates)[3]**	**(i) Unified Credit Allowable in Prior Periods[4]**	**(j) Available Credit in Current Period** *(Col. (h) - Col. (i))*	**(k) Credit Allowable** *(lesser of Col. (g) and Col. (j))*
Pre-1977										
2004	800,000	0	800,000	0	260,800	260,800	330,800	0	330,800	260,800
2007	300,000	800,000	1,100,000	260,800	365,800	105,000	330,800	260,800	70,000	70,000
2009	200,000	1,100,000	1,300,000	365,800	435,800	70,000	330,800	330,800	0	0
Total Unified Credit Used for Prior Gifts :										330,800

[1] Column (c): Enter amount from column (d) of the ***previous*** row.
[2] Column (e): Enter amount from column (f) of the ***previous*** row.
[3] Column (h): Enter amount from the Table of Unified Credits. (For each row in column (h), subtract 20 percent of any amount allowed as a specific exemption for gifts made after September 8, 1976, and before January 1, 1977.)
[4] Column (i): Enter the sum of column (i) and column (k) from the ***previous*** row.

Example 3. Prior Years Unified Credit Recalculation (for Form 709 Schedule B, Column C)
(Gifts made during 6 consecutive years with different maximum unified credits available.)

Use this worksheet to figure amounts for Schedule B, Column C.										
(a) Period	**(b) Taxable Gifts for Current Period**	**(c) Taxable Gifts for Prior Periods[1]**	**(d) Cumulative Taxable Gifts Including Current Period** *(Col. (b) + Col. (c))*	**(e) Tax Based on 2011 Rates on Gifts for Prior Periods** *(Col. (c))*[2]	**(f) Tax Based on 2011 Rates on Cumulative Gifts Including Current Period** *(Col. (d))*	**(g) Tax on Gifts for Current Period** *(Col. (f) - Col. (e))*	**(h) Maximum Unified Credit Available for Current Period (based on 2011 rates)** [3]	**(i) Unified Credit Allowable in Prior Periods[4]**	**(j) Available Credit in Current Period** *(Col. (h) - Col. (i))*	**(k) Credit Allowable** *(lesser of Col. (g) and Col. (j))*
Pre-1977	100,000		100,000		23,800					
1977 qtr. 1	100,000	100,000	200,000	23,800	54,800	31,000	6,000	0	6,000	6,000
1977 qtr. 3	100,000	200,000	300,000	54,800	87,800	33,000	30,000	6,000	24,000	24,000
1978 qtr. 1	100,000	300,000	400,000	87,800	121,800	34,000	34,000	30,000	4,000	4,000
1979 qtr. 1	100,000	400,000	500,000	121,800	155,800	34,000	38,000	34,000	4,000	4,000
1980 qtr. 1	100,000	500,000	600,000	155,800	190,800	35,000	42,500	38,000	4,500	4,500
1981 qtr. 1	100,000	600,000	700,000	190,800	225,800	35,000	47,000	42,500	4,500	4,500
1982	100,000	700,000	800,000	225,800	260,800	35,000	62,800	47,000	15,800	15,800
Total Unified Credit Used for Prior Gifts :										62,800

[1] Column (c): Enter amount from column (d) of the ***previous*** row.
[2] Column (e): Enter amount from column (f) of the ***previous*** row.
[3] Column (h): Enter amount from the Table of Unified Credits. (For each row in column (h), subtract 20 percent of any amount allowed as a specific exemption for gifts made after September 8, 1976, and before January 1, 1977.)
[4] Column (i): Enter the sum of column (i) and column (k) from the ***previous*** row.

Example 4. Prior Years Unified Credit Recalculation (for Form 709 Schedule B, Column C)
(Pre-1977 gifts plus 3 post-1976 years: Earlier years' gifts exceed unified credit then available. Last gift made after unified credit increased.)

Use this worksheet to figure amounts for Schedule B, Column C.										
(a) Period	**(b) Taxable Gifts for Current Period**	**(c) Taxable Gifts for Prior Periods[1]**	**(d) Cumulative Taxable Gifts Including Current Period** *(Col. (b) + Col. (c))*	**(e) Tax Based on 2011 Rates on Gifts for Prior Periods** *(Col. (c))*[2]	**(f) Tax Based on 2011 Rates on Cumulative Gifts Including Current Period** *(Col. (d))*	**(g) Tax on Gifts for Current Period** *(Col. (f) - Col. (e))*	**(h) Maximum Unified Credit Available for Current Period (based on 2011 rates)** [3]	**(i) Unified Credit Allowable in Prior Periods[4]**	**(j) Available Credit in Current Period** *(Col. (h) - Col. (i))*	**(k) Credit Allowable** *(lesser of Col. (g) and Col. (j))*
Pre-1977	200,000		200,000		54,800					
1987	600,000	200,000	800,000	54,800	260,800	206,000	190,800	0	190,800	190,800
1999	200,000	800,000	1,000,000	260,800	330,800	70,000	208,300	190,800	17,500	17,500
2002	100	1,000,000	1,000,100	330,800	330,835	35	330,800	208,300	122,500	35
Total Unified Credit Used for Prior Gifts :										208,335

[1] Column (c): Enter amount from column (d) of the ***previous*** row.
[2] Column (e): Enter amount from column (f) of the ***previous*** row.
[3] Column (h): Enter amount from the Table of Unified Credits. (For each row in column (h), subtract 20 percent of any amount allowed as a specific exemption for gifts made after September 8, 1976, and before January 1, 1977.)
[4] Column (i): Enter the sum of column (i) and column (k) from the ***previous*** row.

Example 5. Current Year Gift with Prior Years Unified Credit Recalculation (for Form 709 Schedule B, Column C) (Three post-1977 years involved, with 3 different maximum unified credits available.)

Use this worksheet to figure amounts for Schedule B, Column C.

(a) Period	(b) Taxable Gifts for Current Period	(c) Taxable Gifts for Prior Periods[1]	(d) Cumulative Taxable Gifts Including Current Period *(Col. (b) + Col. (c))*	(e) Tax Based on 2011 Rates on Gifts for Prior Periods *(Col. (c))*[2]	(f) Tax Based on 2011 Rates on Cumulative Gifts Including Current Period *(Col. (d))*	(g) Tax on Gifts for Current Period *(Col. (f) - Col. (e))*	(h) Maximum Unified Credit Available for Current Period (based on 2011 rates)[3]	(i) Unified Credit Allowable in Prior Periods[4]	(j) Available Credit in Current Period *(Col. (h) - Col. (i))*	(k) Credit Allowable *(lesser of Col. (g) and Col. (j))*
Pre-1977										
1990	700,000	0	700,000	0	225,800	225,800	190,800	0	190,800	190,800
2003	200,000	700,000	900,000	225,800	295,800	70,000	330,800	190,800	140,000	70,000
2009	500,000	900,000	1,400,000	295,800	470,800	175,000	330,800	260,800	70,000	70,000
Total Unified Credit Used for Prior Gifts :										330,800
2011	1,000,000	1,400,000	2,400,000	470,800	820,800	350,000	1,730,800	330,800	1,400,000	350,000
Total Unified Credit Remaining:										680,800

[1] Column (c): Enter amount from column (d) of the ***previous*** row.
[2] Column (e): Enter amount from column (f) of the ***previous*** row.
[3] Column (h): Enter amount from the Table of Unified Credits. (For each row in column (h), subtract 20 percent of any amount allowed as a specific exemption for gifts made after September 8, 1976, and before January 1, 1977.)
[4] Column (i): Enter the sum of column (i) and column (k) from the ***previous*** row.

Table of Unified Credits (as Recalculated for 2011 Rates)

Period	Recalculated Unified Credit
1977 (Quarters 1 and 2)	$6,000
1977 (Quarters 3 and 4)	$30,000
1978	$34,000
1979	$38,000
1980	$42,500
1981	$47,000
1982	$62,800
1983	$79,300
1984	$96,300
1985	$121,800
1986	$155,800
1987 through 1997	$190,800
1998	$199,550
1999	$208,300
2000 and 2001	$217,050
2002 through 2010	$330,800
2011	$1,730,800

Schedule C. Computation of GST Tax

Part 1—Generation-Skipping Transfers

You must enter in Part 1 all of the gifts you listed in Part 2 of Schedule A, in that order and using those same values.

Column B

If you are reporting a generation-skipping transfer that occurred because of the close of an ETIP, complete column B for such transfer as follows:

1. If the GST exemption is being allocated on a timely filed (including extensions) gift tax return, enter the value as of the close of the ETIP.

2. If the GST exemption is being allocated on a late filed (past the due date including extensions) gift tax return, enter the value as of the date the gift tax return was filed.

Column C

You are allowed to claim the gift tax annual exclusion currently allowable for your reported direct skips (other than certain direct skips to trusts—see *Note* below), using the rules and limits discussed earlier for the gift tax annual exclusion. However, you must allocate the exclusion on a gift-by-gift basis for GST computation purposes. You must allocate the exclusion to each gift to the maximum allowable amount and in chronological order, beginning with the earliest gift that qualifies for the exclusion. Be sure that you do not claim a total exclusion of more than $13,000 per donee.

Note. You may not claim any annual exclusion for a transfer made to a trust unless the trust meets the requirements discussed under *Part 2—Direct Skips.*

Part 2—GST Exemption Reconciliation

Line 1

Every donor is allowed a lifetime GST exemption. The amount of the exemption for 2011 is $5,000,000. For transfers made through 1998, the GST exemption was $1 million. The exemption amounts for 1999 through 2012 are as follows:

Year	Amount
1999	$1,010,000
2000	$1,030,000
2001	$1,060,000
2002	$1,100,000
2003	$1,120,000
2004 and 2005	$1,500,000
2006, 2007, and 2008	$2,000,000
2009	$3,500,000
2010 and 2011	$5,000,000
2012	$5,120,000

In general, each annual increase can only be allocated to transfers made (or appreciation occurring) during or after the year of the transfer.

Example. A donor made $1,750,000 in GSTs through 2005, and allocated all $1,500,000 of the exemption to those transfers. In 2011, the donor makes a $207,000 taxable generation-skipping transfer. The donor can allocate $207,000 of exemption to the 2011 transfer but cannot allocate the $3,293,000 of unused 2011 exemption to pre-2011 transfers.

However, if in 2005, the donor made a $1,750,000 transfer to a trust that was not a direct skip, but from which generation-skipping transfers could be made in the future, the donor could allocate the increased exemption to the trust, even though no additional transfers were made

Table for Computing Gift Tax

Column A	Column B	Column C	Column D
Taxable amount over	Taxable amount not over—	Tax on amount in Column A	Rate of tax on excess over amount in Column A
- - - - -	$10,000	- - - - -	18%
$10,000	20,000	$1,800	20%
20,000	40,000	3,800	22%
40,000	60,000	8,200	24%
60,000	80,000	13,000	26%
80,000	100,000	18,200	28%
100,000	150,000	23,800	30%
150,000	250,000	38,800	32%
250,000	500,000	70,800	34%
500,000	- - - - - - -	155,800	35%

to the trust. See Regulations section 26.2642-4 for the redetermination of the applicable fraction when additional exemption is allocated to the trust.

You should keep a record of your transfers and exemption allocations to make sure that any future increases are allocated correctly.

Enter on line 1 of Part 2 the maximum GST exemption you are allowed. This will not necessarily be the highest indexed amount if you made no generation-skipping transfers during the year of the increase.

The donor can apply this exemption to *inter vivos* transfers (that is, transfers made during the donor's life) on Form 709. The executor can apply the exemption on Form 706 to transfers taking effect at death. An allocation is irrevocable.

In the case of *inter vivos* direct skips, a portion of the donor's unused exemption is automatically allocated to the transferred property unless the donor elects otherwise. To elect out of the automatic allocation of exemption, you must file Form 709 and attach a statement to it clearly describing the transaction and the extent to which the automatic allocation is not to apply. Reporting a direct skip on a timely filed Form 709 and paying the GST tax on the transfer will prevent an automatic allocation.

Special QTIP election. If you elect QTIP treatment for any gifts in trust listed on Schedule A, then on Schedule C you may also elect to treat the entire trust as non-QTIP for purposes of the GST tax. The election must be made for the entire trust that contains the particular gift involved on this return. Be sure to identify the item number of the specific gift for which you are making this special QTIP election.

Line 5

Enter the amount of GST exemption you are applying to transfers reported in Part 3 of Schedule A.

Section 2632(c) provides an automatic allocation to indirect skips of any unused GST exemption. The unused exemption is allocated to indirect skips to the extent necessary to make the inclusion ratio zero for the property transferred. You may elect out of this automatic allocation as explained in the instructions for Part 3.

Line 6

Notice of allocation. You may wish to allocate GST exemption to transfers not reported on this return, such as a late allocation.

To allocate your exemption to such transfers, attach a statement to this Form 709 and entitle it "Notice of Allocation." The notice must contain the following for each trust (or other transfer):

- Clear identification of the trust, including the trust's EIN, if known;
- If this is a late allocation, the year the transfer was reported on Form 709;
- The value of the trust assets at the effective date of the allocation;
- The amount of your GST exemption allocated to each gift (or a statement that you are allocating exemption by means of a formula such as "an amount necessary to produce an inclusion ratio of zero"); and
- The inclusion ratio of the trust after the allocation.

Total the exemption allocations and enter this total on line 6.

Note. Where the property involved in such a transfer is subject to an ETIP because it would be includible in the donor's estate if the donor died immediately after the transfer (other than by reason of the donor having died within 3 years of making the gift), an allocation of the GST exemption at the time of the transfer will only become effective at the end of the ETIP. For details, see *Transfers Subject to an Estate Tax Inclusion Period (ETIP)*, previously, and section 2642(f).

Part 3—Tax Computation

You must enter in Part 3 every gift you listed in Part 1 of Schedule C.

Column C

You are not required to allocate your available exemption. You may allocate some, all, or none of your available exemption, as you wish, among the gifts listed in Part 3 of Schedule C. However, the total exemption claimed in column C may not exceed the amount you entered on line 3 of Part 2 of Schedule C.

You may enter an amount in column C that is greater than the amount you entered in column B.

Column D

Carry your computation to three decimal places (for example, "1.000").

Part 2—Tax Computation (Page 1 of Form 709)

Lines 4 and 5

To compute the tax for the amount on line 3 (to be entered on line 4) and the tax for the amount on line 2 (to be entered on line 5), use the *Table for Computing Gift Tax*, earlier.

Line 7

The maximum unified credit amount is the tentative tax on the applicable exclusion amount. For gifts made in 2011, the applicable exclusion amount equals:

- The basic exclusion amount of $5,000,000, PLUS
- Any deceased spousal unused exclusion (DSUE) amount.

If you are a citizen or resident of the United States, you must apply any available unified credit against gift tax. If you are not eligible to use a DSUE amount from a predeceased spouse, enter $1,730,800 on Line 7. Nonresident aliens may not claim the unified credit and should enter zero on line 7.

Deceased spousal unused exclusion amount. If you are a citizen or resident of the United States and your spouse died after December 31, 2010, you may be eligible to use your deceased spouse's unused exclusion amount. The executor of your spouse's estate must have elected on the 2011 Form 706 to allow you to use the unused exclusion amount. See instructions for Form 706, Part 4, Line 4. If the executor of your spouse's estate made this election, attach the 2011 Form 706 for your spouse's estate and a calculation of the DSUE amount. For more information on calculating the DSUE amount, see the instructions for Form 706, Part 4, Line 3. See also section 2010(c)(4).

Note. You may only use the DSUE amount, if any, of the spouse who most recently predeceased you; if the spouse who most recently predeceased you had no DSUE amount or the deceased spouse's estate did not effectively elect to allow you to use the DSUE amount, you may not apply the DSUE amount of any other predeceased spouse.

Determine the tentative tax on the applicable exclusion amount using the rates in *Table for Computing Gift Tax*, above, and enter the result on Line 7.

Line 10

Enter 20% of the amount allowed as a specific exemption for gifts made after September 8, 1976, and before January 1, 1977. (These amounts will be among those listed in Schedule B, column D, for gifts made in the third and fourth quarters of 1976.)

Line 13

Gift tax conventions are in effect with Australia, Austria, Denmark, France, Germany, Japan, and the United Kingdom. If you are claiming a credit for payment of foreign gift tax, figure the credit on an attached sheet and attach evidence that the foreign taxes were paid. See the applicable convention for details of computing the credit.

Line 19

Make your check or money order payable to "United States Treasury" and write the donor's social security number on it. You may not use an overpayment on Form 1040 to offset the gift and GST taxes owed on Form 709.

Signature

As a donor, you must sign the return. If you pay another person, firm, or corporation to prepare your return, that person must also sign the return as preparer unless he or she is your regular full-time employee.

Third-party designee. If you want to allow the return preparer (listed on the bottom of page 1 of Form 709) to discuss your 2011 Form 709 with the IRS, check the "Yes" box to the far right of your signature on page 1 of your return.

If you check the "Yes" box, you (and your spouse, if splitting gifts) are authorizing the IRS to call your return preparer to answer questions that may arise during the processing of your return. You are also authorizing the return preparer of your 2011 Form 709 to:

- Give the IRS any information that is missing from your return,
- Call the IRS for information about the processing of your return or the status of your payment(s),
- Receive copies of notices or transcripts related to your return, upon request, and
- Respond to certain IRS notices about math errors, offsets, and return preparation.

You are not authorizing your return preparer to receive any refund check, to bind you to anything (including any additional tax liability), or otherwise represent you before the IRS. If you want to expand the authorization of your return preparer, see Pub. 947, Practice Before the IRS and Power of Attorney.

The authorization will automatically end three years from the date of filing Form 709. If you wish to revoke the authorization before it ends, see Pub. 947.

Disclosure, Privacy Act, and Paperwork Reduction Act Notice. We ask for the information on this form to carry out the Internal Revenue laws of the United States. We need the information to figure and collect the right amount of tax. Form 709 is used to report (1) transfers subject to the federal gift and certain GST taxes and to figure the tax, if any, due on those transfers, and (2) allocations of the lifetime GST exemption to property transferred during the transferor's lifetime.

Our legal right to ask for the information requested on this form is found in sections 6001, 6011, 6019, and 6061, and their regulations. You are required to provide the information requested on this form. Section 6109 requires that you provide your identifying number.

Generally, tax returns and return information are confidential, as stated in section 6103. However, section 6103 allows or requires the Internal Revenue Service to disclose or give such information shown on your Form 709 to the Department of Justice to enforce the tax laws, both civil and criminal, and to cities, states, the District of Columbia, and U.S. commonwealths or possessions for use in administering their tax laws. We may also disclose this information to other countries under a tax treaty, to federal and state agencies to enforce federal nontax criminal laws, or to federal law enforcement and intelligence agencies to combat terrorism.

We may disclose the information on your Form 709 to the Department of the Treasury and contractors for tax administration purposes; and to other persons as necessary to obtain information which we cannot get in any other way for purposes of determining the amount of or to collect the tax you owe. We may disclose the information on your Form 709 to the Comptroller General to review the Internal Revenue Service. We may also disclose the information on your Form 709 to Committees of Congress; federal, state, and local child support agencies; and to other federal agencies for the purpose of determining entitlement for benefits or the eligibility for, and the repayment of, loans.

If you are required to but do not file a Form 709, or do not provide the information requested on the form, or provide fraudulent information, you may be charged penalties and be subject to criminal prosecution.

You are not required to provide the information requested on a form that is subject to the Paperwork Reduction Act unless the form displays a valid OMB control number. Books or records relating to a form or its instructions must be retained as long as their contents may become material in the administration of any Internal Revenue law.

The time needed to complete and file this form will vary depending on individual circumstances. The estimated average time is:

Recordkeeping	52 min.
Learning about the law or the form	1 hr., 53 min.
Preparing the form	1 hr., 58 min.
Copying, assembling, and sending the form to the IRS	1 hr., 3 min.

If you have comments concerning the accuracy of these time estimates or suggestions for making this form simpler, we would be happy to hear from you. You can write to the Internal Revenue Service, Tax Products Coordinating Committee, SE:W:CAR:MP:T:M:S, 1111 Constitution Ave. NW, IR-6526, Washington, DC 20224. Do not send the tax form to this office. Instead, see *Where To File*, previously.

APPENDIX B

FEDERAL ESTATE TAX RETURN AND INSTRUCTIONS

■ ■ ■

1. Estate Tax Return—Form 706

Form **706** (Rev. August 2011)
Department of the Treasury Internal Revenue Service

United States Estate (and Generation-Skipping Transfer) Tax Return

Estate of a citizen or resident of the United States (see instructions). To be filed for decedents dying after December 31, 2010, and before January 1, 2012.

OMB No. 1545-0015

Part 1—Decedent and Executor

1a Decedent's first name and middle initial (and maiden name, if any)	1b Decedent's last name		2 Decedent's social security no.
3a County, state, and ZIP code, or foreign country, of legal residence (domicile) at time of death	3b Year domicile established	4 Date of birth	5 Date of death
6a Name of executor (see instructions)	6b Executor's address (number and street including apartment or suite no.; city, town, or post office; state; and ZIP code) and phone no.		
6c Executor's social security number (see instructions)	Phone no.		
7a Name and location of court where will was probated or estate administered			7b Case number

8 If decedent died testate, check here ▶ ☐ and attach a certified copy of the will. 9 If you extended the time to file this Form 706, check here ▶ ☐

10 If Schedule R-1 is attached, check here ▶ ☐

Part 2—Tax Computation

1	Total gross estate less exclusion (from Part 5—Recapitulation, item 12)	1	
2	Tentative total allowable deductions (from Part 5—Recapitulation, item 22)	2	
3a	Tentative taxable estate (before state death tax deduction) (subtract line 2 from line 1)	3a	
b	State death tax deduction	3b	
c	Taxable estate (subtract line 3b from line 3a)	3c	
4	Adjusted taxable gifts (total taxable gifts (within the meaning of section 2503) made by the decedent after December 31, 1976, other than gifts that are includible in decedent's gross estate (section 2001(b)))	4	
5	Add lines 3c and 4	5	
6	Tentative tax on the amount on line 5 from Table A in the instructions	6	
7	Total gift tax paid or payable with respect to gifts made by the decedent after December 31, 1976. Include gift taxes by the decedent's spouse for such spouse's share of split gifts (section 2513) only if the decedent was the donor of these gifts and they are includible in the decedent's gross estate (see instructions)	7	
8	Gross estate tax (subtract line 7 from line 6)	8	
9	Maximum unified credit (applicable credit amount) against estate tax (see instructions) — 9		
10	Adjustment to unified credit (applicable credit amount). (This adjustment may not exceed $6,000. See instructions.) — 10		
11	Allowable unified credit (applicable credit amount) (subtract line 10 from line 9)	11	
12	Subtract line 11 from line 8 (but do not enter less than zero)	12	
13	Credit for foreign death taxes (from Schedule P). (Attach Form(s) 706-CE.) — 13		
14	Credit for tax on prior transfers (from Schedule Q) — 14		
15	Total credits (add lines 13 and 14)	15	
16	Net estate tax (subtract line 15 from line 12)	16	
17	Generation-skipping transfer (GST) taxes payable (from Schedule R, Part 2, line 10)	17	
18	Total transfer taxes (add lines 16 and 17)	18	
19	Prior payments. Explain in an attached statement	19	
20	Balance due (or overpayment) (subtract line 19 from line 18)	20	

Under penalties of perjury, I declare that I have examined this return, including accompanying schedules and statements, and to the best of my knowledge and belief, it is true, correct, and complete. Declaration of preparer other than the executor is based on all information of which preparer has any knowledge.

Sign Here

▶ Signature of executor ▶ Date

▶ Signature of executor ▶ Date

Paid Preparer Use Only

Print/Type preparer's name	Preparer's signature	Date	Check ☐ if self-employed	PTIN
Firm's name ▶			Firm's EIN ▶	
Firm's address ▶			Phone no.	

For Privacy Act and Paperwork Reduction Act Notice, see instructions. Cat. No. 20548R Form **706** (Rev. 8-2011)

Form 706 (Rev. 8-2011)

Estate of:	Decedent's social security number

Part 3—Elections by the Executor

Please check the "Yes" or "No" box for each question (see instructions).
Note. Some of these elections may require the posting of bonds or liens.

			Yes	No
1	Do you elect alternate valuation?	1		
2	Do you elect special-use valuation? If "Yes," you must complete and attach Schedule A-1.	2		
3	Do you elect to pay the taxes in installments as described in section 6166? If "Yes," you must attach the additional information described in the instructions. **Note. By electing section 6166, you may be required to provide security for estate tax deferred under section 6166 and interest in the form of a surety bond or a section 6324A lien.**	3		
4	Do you elect to postpone the part of the taxes attributable to a reversionary or remainder interest as described in section 6163?	4		

Part 4—General Information **(Note.** Please attach the necessary supplemental documents. **You must attach the death certificate.)** (See instructions)

Authorization to receive confidential tax information under Regs. sec. 601.504(b)(2)(i); to act as the estate's representative before the IRS; and to make written or oral presentations on behalf of the estate if return prepared by an attorney, accountant, or enrolled agent for the executor:

Name of representative (print or type)	State	Address (number, street, and room or suite no., city, state, and ZIP code)

I declare that I am the ☐ attorney/ ☐ certified public accountant/ ☐ enrolled agent (you must check the applicable box) for the executor and prepared this return for the executor. I am not under suspension or disbarment from practice before the Internal Revenue Service and am qualified to practice in the state shown above.

Signature	CAF number	Date	Telephone number

1 Death certificate number and issuing authority (attach a copy of the death certificate to this return).

2 Decedent's business or occupation. If retired, check here ▶ ☐ and state decedent's former business or occupation.

3 Marital status of the decedent at time of death (see instructions if more than one marriage):
- ☐ Married
- ☐ Widow or widower—Name, SSN, and date of death of deceased spouse ▶
- ☐ Single
- ☐ Legally separated
- ☐ Divorced—Date divorce decree became final ▶

Explanation:

4a Surviving spouse's name	4b Social security number	4c Amount received (see instructions)

5 Individuals (other than the surviving spouse), trusts, or other estates who receive benefits from the estate (do not include charitable beneficiaries shown in Schedule O) (see instructions).

Name of individual, trust, or estate receiving $5,000 or more	Identifying number	Relationship to decedent	Amount (see instructions)
All unascertainable beneficiaries and those who receive less than $5,000 ▶			
Total			

Please check the "Yes" or "No" box for each question.		Yes	No
6	Does the gross estate contain any section 2044 property (qualified terminable interest property (QTIP) from a prior gift or estate) (see instructions)?		
7a	Have federal gift tax returns ever been filed? If "Yes," please attach copies of the returns, if available, and furnish the following information:		
b	Period(s) covered / 7c Internal Revenue office(s) where filed		
8a	Was there any insurance on the decedent's life that is not included on the return as part of the gross estate?		
b	Did the decedent own any insurance on the life of another that is not included in the gross estate?		

(continued on next page)

Page 2

Form 706 (Rev. 8-2011)

Part 4—General Information *(continued)*

	If you answer "Yes" to any of questions 9–16, you must attach additional information as described in the instructions.	Yes	No
9	Did the decedent at the time of death own any property as a joint tenant with right of survivorship in which **(a)** one or more of the other joint tenants was someone other than the decedent's spouse, and **(b)** less than the full value of the property is included on the return as part of the gross estate? If "Yes," you must complete and attach Schedule E		
10a	Did the decedent, at the time of death, own any interest in a partnership (for example, a family limited partnership), an unincorporated business, or a limited liability company; or own any stock in an inactive or closely held corporation?		
b	If "Yes," was the value of **any** interest owned (from above) discounted on this estate tax return? If "Yes," see the instructions on reporting the total accumulated or effective discounts taken on Schedule F or G		
11	Did the decedent make any transfer described in section 2035, 2036, 2037, or 2038? (see the instructions) If "Yes," you must complete and attach Schedule G		
12a	Were there in existence at the time of the decedent's death any trusts created by the decedent during his or her lifetime?		
b	Were there in existence at the time of the decedent's death any trusts not created by the decedent under which the decedent possessed any power, beneficial interest, or trusteeship?		
c	Was the decedent receiving income from a trust created after October 22, 1986, by a parent or grandparent?		
	If "Yes," was there a GST taxable termination (under section 2612) on the death of the decedent?		
d	If there was a GST taxable termination (under section 2612), attach a statement to explain. Provide a copy of the trust or will creating the trust, and give the name, address, and phone number of the current trustee(s).		
e	Did the decedent at any time during his or her lifetime transfer or sell an interest in a partnership, limited liability company, or closely held corporation to a trust described in question 12a or 12b?		
	If "Yes," provide the EIN number for this transferred/sold item. ▶		
13	Did the decedent ever possess, exercise, or release any general power of appointment? If "Yes," you must complete and attach Schedule H		
14	Did the decedent have an interest in or a signature or other authority over a financial account in a foreign country, such as a bank account, securities account, or other financial account?		
15	Was the decedent, immediately before death, receiving an annuity described in the "General" paragraph of the instructions for Schedule I or a private annuity? If "Yes," you must complete and attach Schedule I		
16	Was the decedent ever the beneficiary of a trust for which a deduction was claimed by the estate of a pre-deceased spouse under section 2056(b)(7) and which is not reported on this return? If "Yes," attach an explanation		

Part 5—Recapitulation

Item number	Gross estate		Alternate value	Value at date of death
1	Schedule A—Real Estate	1		
2	Schedule B—Stocks and Bonds	2		
3	Schedule C—Mortgages, Notes, and Cash	3		
4	Schedule D—Insurance on the Decedent's Life (attach Form(s) 712)	4		
5	Schedule E—Jointly Owned Property (attach Form(s) 712 for life insurance)	5		
6	Schedule F—Other Miscellaneous Property (attach Form(s) 712 for life insurance)	6		
7	Schedule G—Transfers During Decedent's Life (att. Form(s) 712 for life insurance)	7		
8	Schedule H—Powers of Appointment	8		
9	Schedule I—Annuities	9		
10	Total gross estate (add items 1 through 9)	10		
11	Schedule U—Qualified Conservation Easement Exclusion	11		
12	Total gross estate less exclusion (subtract item 11 from item 10). Enter here and on line 1 of Part 2—Tax Computation	12		

Item number	Deductions		Amount
13	Schedule J—Funeral Expenses and Expenses Incurred in Administering Property Subject to Claims	13	
14	Schedule K—Debts of the Decedent	14	
15	Schedule K—Mortgages and Liens	15	
16	Total of items 13 through 15	16	
17	Allowable amount of deductions from item 16 (see the instructions for item 17 of the Recapitulation)	17	
18	Schedule L—Net Losses During Administration	18	
19	Schedule L—Expenses Incurred in Administering Property Not Subject to Claims	19	
20	Schedule M—Bequests, etc., to Surviving Spouse	20	
21	Schedule O—Charitable, Public, and Similar Gifts and Bequests	21	
22	Tentative total allowable deductions (add items 17 through 21). Enter here and on line 2 of the Tax Computation	22	

Page 3

Form 706 (Rev. 8-2011)

Estate of:	Decedent's social security number

SCHEDULE A—Real Estate

- For jointly owned property that must be disclosed on Schedule E, see instructions.
- Real estate that is part of a sole proprietorship should be shown on Schedule F.
- Real estate that is included in the gross estate under section 2035, 2036, 2037, or 2038 should be shown on Schedule G.
- Real estate that is included in the gross estate under section 2041 should be shown on Schedule H.
- If you elect section 2032A valuation, you must complete Schedule A and Schedule A-1.

Item number	Description	Alternate valuation date	Alternate value	Value at date of death
1				
Total from continuation schedules or additional sheets attached to this schedule				
TOTAL. (Also enter on Part 5—Recapitulation, page 3, at item 1.)				

(If more space is needed, attach the continuation schedule from the end of this package or additional sheets of the same size.)

Schedule A—Page 4

Form 706 (Rev. 8-2011)

Estate of:	Decedent's social security number

SCHEDULE A-1—Section 2032A Valuation

Part 1. Type of Election (Before making an election, see the checklist in the instructions.):

☐ **Protective election (Regulations section 20.2032A-8(b)).** Complete Part 2, line 1, and column A of lines 3 and 4. (see instructions)

☐ **Regular election.** Complete all of Part 2 (including line 11, if applicable) and Part 3. (see instructions)

Before completing Schedule A-1, see the instructions for the information and documents that must be included to make a valid election.

The election is not valid unless the agreement (that is, *Part 3. Agreement to Special Valuation Under Section 2032A):*

- Is signed by each qualified heir with an interest in the specially valued property and
- Is attached to this return when it is filed.

Part 2. Notice of Election (Regulations section 20.2032A-8(a)(3))

Note. All real property entered on lines 2 and 3 must also be entered on Schedules A, E, F, G, or H, as applicable.

1 Qualified use—check one ▶ ☐ Farm used for farming, or
☐ Trade or business other than farming

2 Real property used in a qualified use, passing to qualified heirs, and to be specially valued on this Form 706.

A Schedule and item number from Form 706	B Full value (without section 2032A(b)(3)(B) adjustment)	C Adjusted value (with section 2032A (b)(3)(B) adjustment)	D Value based on qualified use (without section 2032A(b)(3)(B) adjustment)
Totals			

Attach a legal description of all property listed on line 2.
Attach copies of appraisals showing the column B values for all property listed on line 2.

3 Real property used in a qualified use, passing to qualified heirs, but not specially valued on this Form 706.

A Schedule and item number from Form 706	B Full value (without section 2032A(b)(3)(B) adjustment)	C Adjusted value (with section 2032A (b)(3)(B) adjustment)	D Value based on qualified use (without section 2032A(b)(3)(B) adjustment)
Totals			

If you checked "Regular election," you must attach copies of appraisals showing the column B values for all property listed on line 3.

(continued on next page) **Schedule A-1—Page 5**

Form 706 (Rev. 8-2011)

4 Personal property used in a qualified use and passing to qualified heirs.

A Schedule and item number from Form 706	**B** Adjusted value (with section 2032A (b)(3)(B) adjustment)	**A (continued)** Schedule and item number from Form 706	**B (continued)** Adjusted value (with section 2032A (b)(3)(B) adjustment)
		"Subtotal" from Col. B, below left	
Subtotal		**Total adjusted value** . . .	

5 Enter the value of the total gross estate as adjusted under section 2032A(b)(3)(A). ▶

6 **Attach a description of the method used to determine the special value based on qualified use.**

7 Did the decedent and/or a member of his or her family own all property listed on line 2 for at least 5 of the 8 years immediately preceding the date of the decedent's death? . . . . ☐ **Yes** ☐ **No**

8 Were there any periods during the 8-year period preceding the date of the decedent's death during which the decedent or a member of his or her family:

		Yes	No
a	Did not own the property listed on line 2?		
b	Did not use the property listed on line 2 in a qualified use?		
c	Did not materially participate in the operation of the farm or other business within the meaning of section 2032A(e)(6)?		

If "Yes" to any of the above, you must attach a statement listing the periods. If applicable, describe whether the exceptions of sections 2032A(b)(4) or (5) are met.

9 **Attach affidavits describing the activities constituting material participation and the identity and relationship to the decedent of the material participants.**

10 Persons holding interests. Enter the requested information for each party who received any interest in the specially valued property. **(Each of the qualified heirs receiving an interest in the property must sign the agreement, to be found on Part 3 of this Schedule A-1, and the agreement must be filed with this return.)**

	Name	Address
A		
B		
C		
D		
E		
F		
G		
H		

	Identifying number	Relationship to decedent	Fair market value	Special-use value
A				
B				
C				
D				
E				
F				
G				
H				

You must attach a computation of the GST tax savings attributable to direct skips for each person listed above who is a skip person. (see instructions)

11 **Woodlands election.** Check here ▶ ☐ if you wish to make a Woodlands election as described in section 2032A(e)(13). Enter the schedule and item numbers from Form 706 of the property for which you are making this election ▶

You must attach a statement explaining why you are entitled to make this election. The IRS may issue regulations that require more information to substantiate this election. You will be notified by the IRS if you must supply further information.

Schedule A-1—Page 6

Form 706 (Rev. 8-2011)

Part 3. Agreement to Special Valuation Under Section 2032A

Estate of:	Decedent's social security number

There cannot be a valid election unless:

- The agreement is executed by each one of the qualified heirs and
- The agreement is included with the estate tax return when the estate tax return is filed.

We (list all qualified heirs and other persons having an interest in the property required to sign this agreement)

____

____,

being all the qualified heirs and ____

____,

being all other parties having interests in the property which is qualified real property and which is valued under section 2032A of the Internal Revenue Code, do hereby approve of the election made by ____________________________________,

Executor/Administrator of the estate of ____,

pursuant to section 2032A to value said property on the basis of the qualified use to which the property is devoted and do hereby enter into this agreement pursuant to section 2032A(d).

The undersigned agree and consent to the application of subsection (c) of section 2032A of the Code with respect to all the property described on Form 706, Schedule A-1, Part 2, line 2, attached to this agreement. More specifically, the undersigned heirs expressly agree and consent to personal liability under subsection (c) of 2032A for the additional estate and GST taxes imposed by that subsection with respect to their respective interests in the above-described property in the event of certain early dispositions of the property or early cessation of the qualified use of the property. It is understood that if a qualified heir disposes of any interest in qualified real property to any member of his or her family, such member may thereafter be treated as the qualified heir with respect to such interest upon filing a Form 706-A, United States Additional Estate Tax Return, and a new agreement.

The undersigned interested parties who are not qualified heirs consent to the collection of any additional estate and GST taxes imposed under section 2032A(c) of the Code from the specially valued property.

If there is a disposition of any interest which passes, or has passed to him or her, or if there is a cessation of the qualified use of any specially valued property which passes or passed to him or her, each of the undersigned heirs agrees to file a Form 706-A, and pay any additional estate and GST taxes due within 6 months of the disposition or cessation.

It is understood by all interested parties that this agreement is a condition precedent to the election of special-use valuation under section 2032A of the Code and must be executed by every interested party even though that person may not have received the estate (or GST) tax benefits or be in possession of such property.

Each of the undersigned understands that by making this election, a lien will be created and recorded pursuant to section 6324B of the Code on the property referred to in this agreement for the adjusted tax differences with respect to the estate as defined in section 2032A(c)(2)(C).

As the interested parties, the undersigned designate the following individual as their agent for all dealings with the Internal Revenue Service concerning the continued qualification of the specially valued property under section 2032A of the Code and on all issues regarding the special lien under section 6324B. The agent is authorized to act for the parties with respect to all dealings with the Service on matters affecting the qualified real property described earlier. This includes the authorization:

- To receive confidential information on all matters relating to continued qualification under section 2032A of the specially valued real property and on all matters relating to the special lien arising under section 6324B;
- To furnish the Internal Revenue Service with any requested information concerning the property;
- To notify the Internal Revenue Service of any disposition or cessation of qualified use of any part of the property;
- To receive, but not to endorse and collect, checks in payment of any refund of Internal Revenue taxes, penalties, or interest;
- To execute waivers (including offers of waivers) of restrictions on assessment or collection of deficiencies in tax and waivers of notice of disallowance of a claim for credit or refund; and
- To execute closing agreements under section 7121.

(continued on next page)

Form 706 (Rev. 8-2011)

Part 3. Agreement to Special Valuation Under Section 2032A *(continued)*

Estate of:	Decedent's social security number

• Other acts (specify) ▶ ______

By signing this agreement, the agent agrees to provide the Internal Revenue Service with any requested information concerning this property and to notify the Internal Revenue Service of any disposition or cessation of the qualified use of any part of this property.

Name of Agent	Signature	Address

The property to which this agreement relates is listed in Form 706, United States Estate (and Generation-Skipping Transfer) Tax Return, and in the Notice of Election, along with its fair market value according to section 2031 of the Code and its special-use value according to section 2032A. The name, address, social security number, and interest (including the value) of each of the undersigned in this property are as set forth in the attached Notice of Election.

IN WITNESS WHEREOF, the undersigned have hereunto set their hands at ______,

this ______ day of ______.

SIGNATURES OF EACH OF THE QUALIFIED HEIRS:

Signature of qualified heir	Signature of qualified heir
Signature of qualified heir	Signature of qualified heir
Signature of qualified heir	Signature of qualified heir
Signature of qualified heir	Signature of qualified heir
Signature of qualified heir	Signature of qualified heir
Signature of qualified heir	Signature of qualified heir

Signatures of other interested parties

Signatures of other interested parties

Form 706 (Rev. 8-2011)

Estate of:	Decedent's social security number

SCHEDULE B—Stocks and Bonds

(For jointly owned property that must be disclosed on Schedule E, see instructions.)

Item number	Description, including face amount of bonds or number of shares and par value for identification. Give CUSIP number. If trust, partnership, or closely held entity, give EIN	CUSIP number or EIN, where applicable	Unit value	Alternate valuation date	Alternate value	Value at date of death
1						
Total from continuation schedules (or additional sheets) attached to this schedule						
TOTAL. (Also enter on Part 5—Recapitulation, page 3, at item 2.)						

(If more space is needed, attach the continuation schedule from the end of this package or additional sheets of the same size.)

Form 706 (Rev. 8-2011)

Estate of:

Decedent's social security number

SCHEDULE C—Mortgages, Notes, and Cash

(For jointly owned property that must be disclosed on Schedule E, see instructions.)

Item number	Description	Alternate valuation date	Alternate value	Value at date of death
1				
Total from continuation schedules (or additional sheets) attached to this schedule . . .				
TOTAL. (Also enter on Part 5—Recapitulation, page 3, at item 3.)				

(If more space is needed, attach the continuation schedule from the end of this package or additional sheets of the same size.)

Form 706 (Rev. 8-2011)

Estate of:	Decedent's social security number

SCHEDULE D—Insurance on the Decedent's Life

You must list all policies on the life of the decedent and attach a Form 712 for each policy.

Item number	Description	Alternate valuation date	Alternate value	Value at date of death
1				
Total from continuation schedules (or additional sheets) attached to this schedule . . .				
TOTAL. (Also enter on Part 5—Recapitulation, page 3, at item 4.)				

(If more space is needed, attach the continuation schedule from the end of this package or additional sheets of the same size.)

Schedule D—Page 11

Form 706 (Rev. 8-2011)

Estate of:	Decedent's social security number

SCHEDULE E—Jointly Owned Property

(If you elect section 2032A valuation, you must complete Schedule E and Schedule A-1.)

PART 1. Qualified Joint Interests—Interests Held by the Decedent and His or Her Spouse as the Only Joint Tenants (Section 2040(b)(2))

Item number	Description. For securities, give CUSIP number. If trust, partnership, or closely held entity, give EIN	CUSIP number or EIN, where applicable	Alternate valuation date		Alternate value	Value at date of death
1						
	Total from continuation schedules (or additional sheets) attached to this schedule					
1a	Totals			1a		
1b	Amounts included in gross estate (one-half of line **1a**)			1b		

PART 2. All Other Joint Interests

2a State the name and address of each surviving co-tenant. If there are more than three surviving co-tenants, list the additional co-tenants on an attached sheet.

	Name	Address (number and street, city, state, and ZIP code)
A.		
B.		
C.		

Item number	Enter letter for co-tenant	Description (including alternate valuation date if any). For securities, give CUSIP number. If trust, partnership, or closely held entity, give EIN	CUSIP number or EIN, where applicable	Percentage includible		Includible alternate value	Includible value at date of death
1							
		Total from continuation schedules (or additional sheets) attached to this schedule					
2b		Total other joint interests			2b		
3		**Total includible joint interests** (add lines 1b and 2b). Also enter on Part 5—Recapitulation, page 3, at item 5			3		

(If more space is needed, attach the continuation schedule from the end of this package or additional sheets of the same size.)

Form 706 (Rev. 8-2011)

Estate of: | Decedent's social security number

SCHEDULE F—Other Miscellaneous Property Not Reportable Under Any Other Schedule

(For jointly owned property that must be disclosed on Schedule E, see instructions)
(If you elect section 2032A valuation, you must complete Schedule F and Schedule A-1.)

		Yes	No
1	Did the decedent own any works of art, items, or any collections whose artistic or collectible value at date of death exceeded $3,000? . . . . . If "Yes," submit full details on this schedule and attach appraisals.		
2	Has the decedent's estate, spouse, or any other person received (or will receive) any bonus or award as a result of the decedent's employment or death? . . . . . If "Yes," submit full details on this schedule.		
3	Did the decedent at the time of death have, or have access to, a safe deposit box? . . . . . If "Yes," state location, and if held jointly by decedent and another, state name and relationship of joint depositor. If any of the contents of the safe deposit box are omitted from the schedules in this return, explain fully why omitted.		

Item number	Description. For securities, give CUSIP number. If trust, partnership, or closely held entity, give EIN	CUSIP number or EIN, where applicable	Alternate valuation date	Alternate value	Value at date of death
1					
	Total from continuation schedules (or additional sheets) attached to this schedule . . .				
	TOTAL. (Also enter on Part 5—Recapitulation, page 3, at item 6.)				

(If more space is needed, attach the continuation schedule from the end of this package or additional sheets of the same size.)

Schedule F—Page 13

Form 706 (Rev. 8-2011)

Estate of:

Decedent's social security number

SCHEDULE G—Transfers During Decedent's Life

(If you elect section 2032A valuation, you must complete Schedule G and Schedule A-1.)

Item number	Description. For securities, give CUSIP number. If trust, partnership, or closely held entity, give EIN	Alternate valuation date	Alternate value	Value at date of death
A.	Gift tax paid or payable by the decedent or the estate for all gifts made by the decedent or his or her spouse within 3 years before the decedent's death (section 2035(b))	X X X X X		
B.	Transfers includible under section 2035(a), 2036, 2037, or 2038:			
1				
	Total from continuation schedules (or additional sheets) attached to this schedule . . .			
	TOTAL. (Also enter on Part 5—Recapitulation, page 3, at item 7.)			

SCHEDULE H—Powers of Appointment

(Include "5 and 5 lapsing" powers (section 2041(b)(2)) held by the decedent.)
(If you elect section 2032A valuation, you must complete Schedule H and Schedule A-1.)

Item number	Description	Alternate valuation date	Alternate value	Value at date of death
1				
	Total from continuation schedules (or additional sheets) attached to this schedule			
	TOTAL. (Also enter on Part 5—Recapitulation, page 3, at item 8.)			

(If more space is needed, attach the continuation schedule from the end of this package or additional sheets of the same size.)

Schedules G and H—Page 14

Form 706 (Rev. 8-2011)

Estate of:	Decedent's social security number

SCHEDULE I—Annuities

Note. Generally, no exclusion is allowed for the estates of decedents dying after December 31, 1984 (see instructions).

		Yes	No
A	Are you excluding from the decedent's gross estate the value of a lump-sum distribution described in section 2039(f)(2) (as in effect before its repeal by the Deficit Reduction Act of 1984)? . . . . If "Yes," you must attach the information required by the instructions.		

Item number	Description. Show the entire value of the annuity before any exclusions	Alternate valuation date	Includible alternate value	Includible value at date of death
1				
	Total from continuation schedules (or additional sheets) attached to this schedule . . .			
	TOTAL. (Also enter on Part 5—Recapitulation, page 3, at item 9.)			

(If more space is needed, attach the continuation schedule from the end of this package or additional sheets of the same size.)

Schedule I—Page 15

Form 706 (Rev. 8-2011)

Estate of:	Decedent's social security number

SCHEDULE J—Funeral Expenses and Expenses Incurred in Administering Property Subject to Claims

Note. Do not list expenses of administering property not subject to claims on this schedule. To report those expenses, see instructions.

If executors' commissions, attorney fees, etc., are claimed and allowed as a deduction for estate tax purposes, they are not allowable as a deduction in computing the taxable income of the estate for federal income tax purposes. They are allowable as an income tax deduction on Form 1041, U.S. Income Tax Return for Estates and Trusts, if a waiver is filed to waive the deduction on Form 706 (see Instructions for Form 1041).

Item number	Description	Expense amount	Total amount
	A. Funeral expenses:		
1			
	Total funeral expenses . . . . ▶		
	B. Administration expenses:		
	1 Executors' commissions—amount estimated/agreed upon/paid. (Strike out the words that do not apply.)		
	2 Attorney fees—amount estimated/agreed upon/paid. (Strike out the words that do not apply.) . . .		
	3 Accountant fees—amount estimated/agreed upon/paid. (Strike out the words that do not apply.) . .		
	4 Miscellaneous expenses:	Expense amount	
	Total miscellaneous expenses from continuation schedules (or additional sheets) attached to this schedule		
	Total miscellaneous expenses . . . . ▶		
	TOTAL. (Also enter on Part 5—Recapitulation, page 3, at item 13.) . . . . ▶		

(If more space is needed, attach the continuation schedule from the end of this package or additional sheets of the same size.)

Schedule J—Page 16

Form 706 (Rev. 8-2011)

Estate of:	Decedent's social security number

SCHEDULE K—Debts of the Decedent, and Mortgages and Liens

Item number	Debts of the Decedent—Creditor and nature of claim, and allowable death taxes	Amount unpaid to date	Amount in contest	Amount claimed as a deduction
1				
	Total from continuation schedules (or additional sheets) attached to this schedule			
	TOTAL. (Also enter on Part 5—Recapitulation, page 3, at item 14.)			

Item number	Mortgages and Liens—Description	Amount
1		
	Total from continuation schedules (or additional sheets) attached to this schedule	
	TOTAL. (Also enter on Part 5—Recapitulation, page 3, at item 15.)	

(If more space is needed, attach the continuation schedule from the end of this package or additional sheets of the same size.)

Form 706 (Rev. 8-2011)

Estate of:	Decedent's social security number

SCHEDULE L—Net Losses During Administration and Expenses Incurred in Administering Property Not Subject to Claims

Item number	Net losses during administration (**Note.** Do not deduct losses claimed on a federal income tax return.)	Amount
1		
	Total from continuation schedules (or additional sheets) attached to this schedule	
	TOTAL. (Also enter on Part 5—Recapitulation, page 3, at item 18.)	

Item number	Expenses incurred in administering property not subject to claims. (Indicate whether estimated, agreed upon, or paid.)	Amount
1		
	Total from continuation schedules (or additional sheets) attached to this schedule	
	TOTAL. (Also enter on Part 5—Recapitulation, page 3, at item 19.)	

(If more space is needed, attach the continuation schedule from the end of this package or additional sheets of the same size.)

Form 706 (Rev. 8-2011)

Estate of:	Decedent's social security number

SCHEDULE M—Bequests, etc., to Surviving Spouse

			Yes	No
1	Did any property pass to the surviving spouse as a result of a qualified disclaimer? . . . . If "Yes," attach a copy of the written disclaimer required by section 2518(b).	1		
2a	In what country was the surviving spouse born?			
b	What is the surviving spouse's date of birth?			
c	Is the surviving spouse a U.S. citizen?	2c		
d	If the surviving spouse is a naturalized citizen, when did the surviving spouse acquire citizenship?			
e	If the surviving spouse is not a U.S. citizen, of what country is the surviving spouse a citizen?			
3	**Election Out of QTIP Treatment of Annuities.** Do you elect under section 2056(b)(7)(C)(ii) not to treat as qualified terminable interest property any joint and survivor annuities that are included in the gross estate and would otherwise be treated as qualified terminable interest property under section 2056(b)(7)(C)? (see instructions) . .	3		

Item number	Description of property interests passing to surviving spouse. For securities, give CUSIP number. If trust, partnership, or closely held entity, give EIN			Amount
A1	QTIP property:			
B1	All other property:			
	Total from continuation schedules (or additional sheets) attached to this schedule			
4	**Total** amount of property interests listed on Schedule M		4	
5a	Federal estate taxes payable out of property interests listed on Schedule M . . .	5a		
b	Other death taxes payable out of property interests listed on Schedule M	5b		
c	Federal and state GST taxes payable out of property interests listed on Schedule M	5c		
d	Add items 5a, 5b, and 5c		5d	
6	Net amount of property interests listed on Schedule M (subtract 5d from 4). Also enter on Part 5—Recapitulation, page 3, at item 20		6	

(If more space is needed, attach the continuation schedule from the end of this package or additional sheets of the same size.)

Form 706 (Rev. 8-2011)

Estate of: | Decedent's social security number

SCHEDULE O—Charitable, Public, and Similar Gifts and Bequests

		Yes	No
1a	If the transfer was made by will, has any action been instituted to contest or have interpreted any of its provisions affecting the charitable deductions claimed in this schedule? . . . . If "Yes," full details must be submitted with this schedule.		
b	According to the information and belief of the person or persons filing this return, is any such action planned? . If "Yes," full details must be submitted with this schedule.		
2	Did any property pass to charity as the result of a qualified disclaimer? . . . . If "Yes," attach a copy of the written disclaimer required by section 2518(b).		

Item number	Name and address of beneficiary	Character of institution	Amount
1			
Total from continuation schedules (or additional sheets) attached to this schedule			

3	Total			3	
4a	Federal estate tax payable out of property interests listed above	4a			
b	Other death taxes payable out of property interests listed above	4b			
c	Federal and state GST taxes payable out of property interests listed above .	4c			
d	Add items 4a, 4b, and 4c			4d	
5	Net value of property interests listed above (subtract 4d from 3). Also enter on Part 5—Recapitulation, page 3, at item 21			5	

(If more space is needed, attach the continuation schedule from the end of this package or additional sheets of the same size.)

Form 706 (Rev. 8-2011)

Estate of:	Decedent's social security number

SCHEDULE P—Credit for Foreign Death Taxes

List all foreign countries to which death taxes have been paid and for which a credit is claimed on this return.

If a credit is claimed for death taxes paid to more than one foreign country, compute the credit for taxes paid to one country on this sheet and attach a separate copy of Schedule P for each of the other countries.

The credit computed on this sheet is for the ______________________________ (Name of death tax or taxes)

______________________________ imposed in ______________________________ (Name of country)

Credit is computed under the ______________________________ (Insert title of treaty or "statute")

Citizenship (nationality) of decedent at time of death

(All amounts and values must be entered in United States money.)

1 Total of estate, inheritance, legacy, and succession taxes imposed in the country named above attributable to property situated in that country, subjected to these taxes, and included in the gross estate (as defined by statute) .	1	
2 Value of the gross estate (adjusted, if necessary, according to the instructions)	2	
3 Value of property situated in that country, subjected to death taxes imposed in that country, and included in the gross estate (adjusted, if necessary, according to the instructions)	3	
4 Tax imposed by section 2001 reduced by the total credits claimed under sections 2010 and 2012 (see instructions)	4	
5 Amount of federal estate tax attributable to property specified at item 3. (Divide item 3 by item 2 and multiply the result by item 4.)	5	
6 Credit for death taxes imposed in the country named above (the smaller of item 1 or item 5). Also enter on line 13 of Part 2—Tax Computation	6	

SCHEDULE Q—Credit for Tax on Prior Transfers

Part 1. Transferor Information

	Name of transferor	Social security number	IRS office where estate tax return was filed	Date of death
A				
B				
C				

Check here ▶ ☐ if section 2013(f) (special valuation of farm, etc., real property) adjustments to the computation of the credit were made (see instructions).

Part 2. Computation of Credit (see instructions)

Item	Transferor			Total A, B, & C
	A	B	C	
1 Transferee's tax as apportioned (from worksheet, (line 7 ÷ line 8) × line 35 for each column) . . .				
2 Transferor's tax (from each column of worksheet, line 20)				
3 Maximum amount before percentage requirement (for each column, enter amount from line 1 or 2, whichever is smaller)				
4 Percentage allowed (each column) (see instructions)	%	%	%	
5 Credit allowable (line 3 × line 4 for each column) .				
6 TOTAL credit allowable (add columns A, B, and C of line 5). Enter here and on line 14 of Part 2—Tax Computation				

Form 706 (Rev. 8-2011)

SCHEDULE R—Generation-Skipping Transfer Tax

Note. To avoid application of the deemed allocation rules, Form 706 and Schedule R should be filed to allocate the GST exemption to trusts that may later have taxable terminations or distributions under section 2612 even if the form is not required to be filed to report estate or GST tax.

The GST tax is imposed on taxable transfers of interests in property located outside the United States as well as property located inside the United States. (see instructions)

Part 1. GST Exemption Reconciliation (Section 2631) and Section 2652(a)(3) (Special QTIP) Election

You no longer need to check a box to make a section 2652(a)(3) (special QTIP) election. If you list qualifying property in Part 1, line 9 below, you will be considered to have made this election. See instructions for details.

1	Maximum allowable GST exemption	1	
2	Total GST exemption allocated by the decedent against decedent's lifetime transfers	2	
3	Total GST exemption allocated by the executor, using Form 709, against decedent's lifetime transfers	3	
4	GST exemption allocated on line 6 of Schedule R, Part 2	4	
5	GST exemption allocated on line 6 of Schedule R, Part 3	5	
6	Total GST exemption allocated on line 4 of Schedule(s) R-1	6	
7	Total GST exemption allocated to *inter vivos* transfers and direct skips (add lines 2–6)	7	
8	GST exemption available to allocate to trusts and section 2032A interests (subtract line 7 from line 1)	8	
9	Allocation of GST exemption to trusts (as defined for GST tax purposes):		

A Name of trust	B Trust's EIN (if any)	C GST exemption allocated on lines 2–6, above (see instructions)	D Additional GST exemption allocated (see instructions)	E Trust's inclusion ratio (optional—see instructions)
9D Total. May not exceed line 8, above		9D		

10	GST exemption available to allocate to section 2032A interests received by individual beneficiaries (subtract line 9D from line 8). You must attach special-use allocation schedule (see instructions)	10	

Schedule R—Page 22

Form 706 (Rev. 8-2011)

Estate of:	Decedent's social security number

Part 2. Direct Skips Where the Property Interests Transferred Bear the GST Tax on the Direct Skips

Name of skip person	Description of property interest transferred	Estate tax value

1	Total estate tax values of all property interests listed above	1	
2	Estate taxes, state death taxes, and other charges borne by the property interests listed above	2	
3	GST taxes borne by the property interests listed above but imposed on direct skips other than those shown on this Part 2 (see instructions)	3	
4	Total fixed taxes and other charges (add lines 2 and 3)	4	
5	Total tentative maximum direct skips (subtract line 4 from line 1)	5	
6	GST exemption allocated	6	
7	Subtract line 6 from line 5	7	
8	GST tax due (divide line 7 by 3.857143)	8	
9	Enter the amount from line 8 of Schedule R, Part 3	9	
10	**Total GST taxes payable by the estate** (add lines 8 and 9). Enter here and on line 17 of Part 2—Tax Computation	10	

Schedule R—Page 23

Form 706 (Rev. 8-2011)

Estate of:

Decedent's social security number

Part 3. Direct Skips Where the Property Interests Transferred Do Not Bear the GST Tax on the Direct Skips

Name of skip person	Description of property interest transferred	Estate tax value

1	Total estate tax values of all property interests listed above	**1**	
2	Estate taxes, state death taxes, and other charges borne by the property interests listed above . .	**2**	
3	GST taxes borne by the property interests listed above but imposed on direct skips other than those shown on this Part 3 (see instructions)	**3**	
4	Total fixed taxes and other charges (add lines 2 and 3)	**4**	
5	Total tentative maximum direct skips (subtract line 4 from line 1)	**5**	
6	GST exemption allocated	**6**	
7	Subtract line 6 from line 5	**7**	
8	GST tax due (multiply line 7 by .35). Enter here and on Schedule R, Part 2, line 9	**8**	

SCHEDULE R-1
(Form 706)
(Rev. August 2011)
Department of the Treasury
Internal Revenue Service

Generation-Skipping Transfer Tax

Direct Skips From a Trust
Payment Voucher

OMB No. 1545-0015

Executor: File one copy with Form 706 and send two copies to the fiduciary. Do not pay the tax shown. See instructions for details.
Fiduciary: See instructions for details. Pay the tax shown on line 6.

Name of trust		Trust's EIN
Name and title of fiduciary	Name of decedent	
Address of fiduciary (number and street)	Decedent's SSN	Service Center where Form 706 was filed
City, state, and ZIP code	Name of executor	
Address of executor (number and street)	City, state, and ZIP code	
Date of decedent's death	Filing due date of Schedule R, Form 706 (with extensions)	

Part 1. Computation of the GST Tax on the Direct Skip

Description of property interests subject to the direct skip		Estate tax value
1 Total estate tax value of all property interests listed above	1	
2 Estate taxes, state death taxes, and other charges borne by the property interests listed above	2	
3 Tentative maximum direct skip from trust (subtract line 2 from line 1)	3	
4 GST exemption allocated	4	
5 Subtract line 4 from line 3	5	
6 **GST tax due from fiduciary** (divide line 5 by 3.857143). **(See instructions if property will not bear the GST tax.)**	6	

Under penalties of perjury, I declare that I have examined this document, including accompanying schedules and statements, and to the best of my knowledge and belief, it is true, correct, and complete.

Signature(s) of executor(s) Date

Date

Signature of fiduciary or officer representing fiduciary Date

Schedule R-1—Page 25

Instructions for the Trustee

Introduction

Schedule R-1 (Form 706) serves as a payment voucher for the Generation-Skipping Transfer (GST) tax imposed on a direct skip from a trust, which you, the trustee of the trust, must pay. The executor completes the Schedule R-1 (Form 706) and gives you two copies. File one copy and keep one for your records.

How to pay

You can pay by check or money order.

- Make it payable to the "United States Treasury."
- Make the check or money order for the amount on line 6 of Schedule R-1.
- Write "GST Tax" and the trust's EIN on the check or money order.

Signature

You must sign the Schedule R-1 in the space provided.

What to mail

Mail your check or money order and the copy of Schedule R-1 that you signed.

Where to mail

Mail to the Department of the Treasury, Internal Revenue Service Center, Cincinnati, OH 45999.

When to pay

The GST tax is due and payable 9 months after the decedent's date of death (shown on the Schedule R-1). You will owe interest on any GST tax not paid by that date.

Automatic extension

You have an automatic extension of time to file Schedule R-1 and pay the GST tax. The automatic extension allows you to file and pay by 2 months after the due date (with extensions) for filing the decedent's Schedule R (shown on the Schedule R-1).

If you pay the GST tax under the automatic extension, you will be charged interest (but no penalties).

Additional information

For more information, see section 2603(a)(2) and the Instructions for Form 706, United States Estate (and Generation-Skipping Transfer) Tax Return.

Form 706 (Rev. 8-2011)

Estate of:	Decedent's social security number

SCHEDULE U—Qualified Conservation Easement Exclusion

Part 1. Election

Note. The executor is deemed to have made the election under section 2031(c)(6) if he or she files Schedule U and excludes any qualifying conservation easements from the gross estate.

Part 2. General Qualifications

1 Describe the land subject to the qualified conservation easement (see instructions) ____________

2 Did the decedent or a member of the decedent's family own the land described above during the 3-year period ending on the date of the decedent's death? . . . . ☐ Yes ☐ No

3 Describe the conservation easement with regard to which the exclusion is being claimed (see instructions).

Part 3. Computation of Exclusion

4	Estate tax value of the land subject to the qualified conservation easement (see instructions) .			4	
5	Date of death value of any easements granted prior to decedent's death and included on line 10 below (see instructions)	5			
6	Add lines 4 and 5	6			
7	Value of retained development rights on the land (see instructions)	7			
8	Subtract line 7 from line 6	8			
9	Multiply line 8 by 30% (.30)	9			
10	Value of qualified conservation easement for which the exclusion is being claimed (see instructions)	10			
	Note. If line 10 is less than line 9, continue with line 11. If line 10 is equal to or more than line 9, skip lines 11 through 13, enter ".40" on line 14, and complete the schedule.				
11	Divide line 10 by line 8. Figure to 3 decimal places (for example, ".123")	11			
	Note. If line 11 is equal to or less than .100, stop here; the estate does not qualify for the conservation easement exclusion.				
12	Subtract line 11 from .300. Enter the answer in hundredths by rounding any thousandths up to the next higher hundredth (that is, .030 = .03, but .031 = .04)	12			
13	Multiply line 12 by 2	13			
14	Subtract line 13 from .40	14			
15	Deduction under section 2055(f) for the conservation easement (see instructions)	15			
16	Amount of indebtedness on the land (see instructions)	16			
17	Total reductions in value (add lines 7, 15, and 16)			17	
18	Net value of land (subtract line 17 from line 4)			18	
19	Multiply line 18 by line 14			19	
20	Enter the smaller of line 19 or the exclusion limitation (see instructions). Also enter this amount on item 11, Part 5—Recapitulation, page 3			20	

Form 706 (Rev. 8-2011) (Make copies of this schedule before completing it if you will need more than one schedule.)

Estate of: | Decedent's social security number

CONTINUATION SCHEDULE

Continuation of Schedule ______
(Enter letter of schedule you are continuing.)

Item number	Description. For securities, give CUSIP number. If trust, partnership, or closely held entity, give EIN.	Unit value (Sch. B, E, or G only)	Alternate valuation date	Alternate value	Value at date of death or amount deductible
TOTAL. (Carry forward to main schedule.)					

2. Estate Tax Return Instructions

Instructions for Form 706

(Rev. August 2011)

For decedents dying after December 31, 2010, and before January 1, 2012

United States Estate (and Generation-Skipping Transfer) Tax Return

Section references are to the Internal Revenue Code unless otherwise noted.

Prior Revisions of Form 706

For Decedents Dying and After	Before	Use Revision of Form 706 Dated
December 31, 1998	January 1, 2001	July 1999
December 31, 2000	January 1, 2002	November 2001
December 31, 2001	January 1, 2003	August 2002
December 31, 2002	January 1, 2004	August 2003
December 31, 2003	January 1, 2005	August 2004
December 31, 2004	January 1, 2006	August 2005
December 31, 2005	January 1, 2007	October 2006
December 31, 2006	January 1, 2008	September 2007
December 31, 2007	January 1, 2009	August 2008
December 31, 2008	January 1, 2010	September 2009
December 31, 2009	January 1, 2011	July 2011

Contents **Page**

Contents **Page**

What's New

- Use this revision of Form 706 only for the estates of decedents who died in calendar year 2011.
- The Tax Relief, Unemployment Insurance Reauthorization and Job Creation Act of 2010 (Act) included several provisions affecting the 2011 Form 706. They are:

  a. Estates, generation-skipping transfers (GST), and lifetime gifts all have a maximum tax rate of 35%.

  b. The credit for transfers made by gift is reunified with the credit for transfers made at death. Both will receive a combined unified credit of $1,730,800 (basic exclusion amount of $5,000,000) under section 2010.

  c. The applicable exclusion amount now may consist of a basic exclusion amount of $5,000,000 and, in the case of a surviving spouse, the unused exclusion amount of a predeceased spouse (who died after December 31, 2010). A timely and complete Form 706 filed for the predeceased spouse's estate is required, even if there is no tax due, to allow the surviving spouse to use the last predeceased spouse's unused exclusion amount. See instructions for *Part 2—Tax Computation*, line 9 and *Part 4—General Information*, line 3 and line 4.

  d. If the estate chooses not to allow the surviving spouse to take into account, for estate and gift tax purposes, the decedent's unused exclusion amount, then do one of the following: attach a statement to the Form 706 indicating that the estate is not making the election under section 2010(c)(5) or enter "No Election Under Section 2010(c)(5)" across the top of the first page of Form 706.

  e. Prior gifts must be calculated at the rate in effect at the decedent's date of death. See *Worksheet TG—Taxable Gifts Reconciliation, Line 4 Worksheet*, and *Line 7 Worksheet* (Unified Credit Allowable for Prior Periods), below.
- Various dollar amounts and limitations in the Form 706 are indexed for inflation. For decedents dying in 2011, the following amounts are applicable:

  a. The ceiling on special-use valuation is $1,020,000.

  b. The amount used in figuring the 2% portion of estate tax payable in installments is $1,360,000.

The IRS will publish amounts for future years in annual revenue procedures.

- Executors must provide documentation of their status.
- The IRS has created a page on IRS.gov for information about Form 706 and its instructions, at *www.irs.gov/form706*. Information about any future developments affecting Form 706 (such as legislation enacted after we release it) will be posted on that page.

Reminders

In 2008, we added a worksheet to help executors figure how much of the estate tax may be paid in installments under section 6166. See *Determine how much of the estate tax may be paid in installments under section 6166*, below.

General Instructions

Purpose of Form

The executor of a decedent's estate uses Form 706 to figure the estate tax imposed by Chapter 11 of the Internal Revenue Code. This tax is levied on the entire taxable estate and not just on the share received by a particular beneficiary. Form 706 is also used to figure the generation-skipping transfer (GST) tax imposed by Chapter 13 on direct skips (transfers to skip persons of interests in property included in the decedent's gross estate).

Which Estates Must File

For decedents dying in 2011, Form 706 must be filed by the executor for the estate of every U.S. citizen or resident:

a. Whose gross estate, plus adjusted taxable gifts and specific exemption, is more than $5,000,000; or,

b. Whose executor wants to make the election to permit the decedent's surviving spouse to use the decedent's unused exclusion amount, regardless of the size of the decedent's gross estate. See instructions for Part 4, line 4.

To determine whether you must file a return for the estate, add:

1. The adjusted taxable gifts (as defined in section 2503) made by the decedent after December 31, 1976;
2. The total specific exemption allowed under section 2521 (as in effect before its repeal by the Tax Reform Act of 1976) for gifts made by the decedent after September 8, 1976; and
3. The decedent's gross estate valued at the date of death.

If you determine filing a return for the estate is not required, you nonetheless should file a return if you intend to elect to allow the decedent's surviving spouse to use the decedent's unused exclusion amount for estate and gift tax purposes. See instructions for line 4, *Part 4—General Information*, below, and section 2010(c)(4) and (c)(5).

Gross Estate

The gross estate includes all property in which the decedent had an interest (including real property outside the United States). It also includes:

- Certain transfers made during the decedent's life without an adequate and full consideration in money or money's worth,
- Annuities,
- The includible portion of joint estates with right of survivorship (see instructions for Schedule E),
- The includible portion of tenancies by the entirety (see instructions for Schedule E),
- Certain life insurance proceeds (even though payable to beneficiaries other than the estate) (see instructions for Schedule D),
- Property over which the decedent possessed a general power of appointment,
- Dower or curtesy (or statutory estate) of the surviving spouse, and
- Community property to the extent of the decedent's interest as defined by applicable law.

For more specific information, see the instructions for Schedules A through I.

U.S. Citizens or Residents; Nonresident Noncitizens

File Form 706 for the estates of decedents who were either U.S. citizens or U.S. residents at the time of death. For estate tax purposes, a resident is someone who had a domicile in the United States at the time of death. A person acquires a domicile by living in a place for even a brief period of time, as long as the person had no intention of moving from that place.

File Form 706-NA, U.S. Estate (and Generation-Skipping Transfer) Tax Return, for the estates of nonresident alien decedents (decedents who were neither U.S. citizens nor U.S. residents at the time of death).

Residents of U.S. Possessions

All references to citizens of the United States are subject to the provisions of sections 2208 and 2209, relating to decedents who were U.S. citizens and residents of a U.S. possession on the date of death. If such a decedent became a U.S. citizen only because of his or her connection with a possession, then the decedent is considered a nonresident alien decedent for estate tax purposes, and you should file Form 706-NA. If such a decedent became a U.S. citizen wholly independently of his or her connection with a possession, then the decedent is considered a U.S. citizen for estate tax purposes, and you should file Form 706.

Executor

The term "executor" means the executor, personal representative, or administrator of the decedent's estate. If none of these is appointed, qualified, and acting in the United States, every person in actual or constructive possession of any property of the decedent is considered an executor and must file a return.

Executors must provide documentation proving their status. Documentation will vary, but may include documents such as a certified copy of the will or a court order designating the executor(s). A statement by the executor attesting to their status is insufficient.

When To File

You must file Form 706 to report estate and/or GST tax within 9 months after the date of the decedent's death. If you are unable to file Form 706 by the due date, you may receive an extension of time to file. Use Form 4768, Application for Extension of Time To File a Return and/or Pay U.S. Estate (and Generation-Skipping Transfer) Taxes, to apply for an automatic 6-month extension of time to file.

Private delivery services. You can use certain private delivery services designated by the IRS to meet the "timely mailing as timely filing/paying" rule for tax returns and payments. These private delivery services include only the following:

- DHL Express (DHL): DHL Same Day Service.
- Federal Express (FedEx): FedEx Priority Overnight, FedEx Standard Overnight, FedEx 2Day, FedEx International Priority, FedEx International First.
- United Parcel Service (UPS): UPS Next Day Air, UPS Next Day Air Saver, UPS 2nd Day Air, UPS 2nd Day Air A.M., UPS Worldwide Express Plus, and UPS Worldwide Express.

The private delivery service can tell you how to get written proof of the mailing date.

Where To File

File Form 706 at the following address:

Department of the Treasury
Internal Revenue Service Center
Cincinnati, OH 45999

Paying the Tax

The estate and GST taxes are due within 9 months after the date of the decedent's death. You may request an extension of time for payment by filing Form 4768. You may also elect under section 6166 to pay in installments or under section 6163 to postpone the part of the tax attributable to a reversionary or remainder interest. These elections are made by checking lines 3 and 4 (respectively) of Part 3—Elections by the Executor, and attaching the required statements.

If the tax paid with the return is different from the balance due as figured on the return, explain the difference in an attached statement. If you have made prior payments to the IRS, attach a statement to Form 706 including these facts.

Paying by check. Make the check payable to the "United States Treasury." Please write the decedent's name, social security number (SSN), and "Form 706" on the check to assist us in posting it to the proper account.

Signature and Verification

CAUTION *If there is more than one executor, all listed executors are responsible for the return. However, it is sufficient for only one of the co-executors to sign the return.*

All executors are responsible for the return as filed and are liable for penalties provided for erroneous or false returns.

If two or more persons are liable for filing the return, they should all join together in filing one complete return. However, if they are unable to join in making one complete return, each is required to file a return disclosing all the information the person has about the estate, including the name of every person holding an interest in the property and a full description of the property. If the appointed, qualified, and acting executor is unable to make a complete return, then every person holding an interest in the property must, on notice from the IRS, make a return regarding that interest.

The executor who files the return must, in every case, sign the declaration on page 1 under penalties of perjury.

Generally, anyone who is paid to prepare the return must sign the return in the space provided and fill in the "Paid Preparer Use Only" area. See section 7701(a)(36)(B) for exceptions.

In addition to signing and completing the required information, the paid preparer must give a copy of the completed return to the executor.

Note. A paid preparer may sign original or amended returns by rubber stamp, mechanical device, or computer software program.

Amending Form 706

If you find that you must change something on a return that has already been filed, you should:

- File another Form 706;
- Enter "Supplemental Information" across the top of page 1 of the form; and
- Attach a copy of pages 1, 2, and 3 of the original Form 706 that has already been filed.

If you have already been notified that the return has been selected for examination, you should provide the additional information directly to the office conducting the examination.

Supplemental Documents

Note. You must attach the death certificate to the return.

If the decedent was a citizen or resident of the United States and died testate, attach a certified copy of the will to the return. If you cannot obtain a certified copy, attach a copy of the will and an explanation of why it is not certified. Other supplemental documents may be required as explained below. Examples include Forms 712, Life Insurance Statement; 709, United States Gift (and Generation-Skipping Transfer) Tax Return; and 706-CE, Certificate of Payment of Foreign Death Tax; trust and power of appointment instruments; and state certification of payment of death taxes. If you do not file these documents with the return, the processing of the return will be delayed.

If the decedent was a U.S. citizen but not a resident of the United States, you must attach the following documents to the return:

1. A copy of the inventory of property and the schedule of liabilities, claims against the estate, and expenses of administration filed with the foreign court of probate jurisdiction, certified by a proper official of the court;
2. A copy of the return filed under the foreign inheritance, estate, legacy, succession tax, or other death tax act, certified by a proper official of the foreign tax department, if the estate is subject to such a foreign tax; and
3. If the decedent died testate, a certified copy of the will.

Rounding Off to Whole Dollars

You may show the money items on the return and accompanying schedules as whole-dollar amounts. To do so, drop any amount less than 50 cents and increase any amount from 50 cents through 99 cents to the next higher dollar.

Penalties

Late filing and late payment. Section 6651 provides for penalties for both late filing and for late payment unless there is reasonable cause for the delay. The law also provides for penalties for willful attempts to evade payment of tax. The late filing penalty will not be imposed if the taxpayer can show that the failure to file a timely return is due to reasonable cause.

Reasonable cause determinations. If you receive a notice about penalties after you file Form 706, send an explanation and we will determine if you meet reasonable cause criteria. Do not attach an explanation when you file Form 706. Explanations attached to the return at the time of filing will not be considered.

Valuation understatement. Section 6662 provides a 20% penalty for the underpayment of estate tax that exceeds $5,000 when the under-payment is attributable to valuation understatements. A valuation understatement occurs when the value of property reported on Form 706 is 65% or less of the actual value of the property.

This penalty increases to 40% if there is a gross valuation under-statement. A gross valuation under-statement occurs if any property on the return is valued at 40% or less of the value determined to be correct.

Penalties also apply to late filing, late payment, and underpayment of GST taxes.

Return preparer. Estate tax return preparers, who prepare any return or claim for refund which reflects an understatement of tax liability due to willful or reckless conduct, are subject to a penalty of $5,000 or 50% of the income derived (or income to be derived), whichever is greater, for the preparation of each such return. See section 6694, the regulations thereunder, and Ann. 2009-15, 2009-11 I.R.B. 687 (available at *www.irs.gov/pub/irs-irbs/irb09-11.pdf*) for more information.

Obtaining Forms and Publications To File or Use

Internet. You can access the IRS website 24 hours a day, 7 days a week at *IRS.gov* to:

- Download forms, instructions, and publications;
- Order IRS products online;
- Research your tax questions online;
- Search publications online by topic or keyword; and
- Sign up to receive local and national tax news by email.

Other forms that may be required.

- Form SS-5, Application for Social Security Card.

• Form 706-CE, Certificate of Payment of Foreign Death Tax.
• Form 706-NA, United States Estate (and Generation-Skipping Transfer) Tax Return, Estate of nonresident not a citizen of the United States.
• Form 709, United States Gift (and Generation-Skipping Transfer) Tax Return.
• Form 712, Life Insurance Statement.
• Form 2848, Power of Attorney and Declaration of Representative.
• Form 4768, Application for Extension of Time To File a Return and/or Pay U.S. Estate (and Generation-Skipping Transfer) Taxes.
• Form 4808, Computation of Credit for Gift Tax.
• Form 8821, Tax Information Authorization.
• Form 8822, Change of Address.

Additional Information. The following publications may assist you in learning about and preparing Form 706:
• Publication 559, Survivors, Executors, and Administrators.
• Publication 910, IRS Guide to Free Tax Services.
• Publication 950, Introduction to Estate and Gift Taxes.

Note. For information about release of nonresident U.S. citizen decedents' assets using transfer certificates under Regulation 20.6325-1, write to:

Internal Revenue Service
Cincinnati, OH 45999
Stop 824G

Specific Instructions

You must file the first three pages of Form 706 and all required schedules. File Schedules A through I, as appropriate, to support the entries in items 1 through 9 of Part 5—Recapitulation.

IF . . .	THEN . . .
you enter zero on any item of the Recapitulation,	you need not file the schedule (except for Schedule F) referred to on that item.
you claim an exclusion on item 11,	complete and attach Schedule U.
you claim any deductions on items 13 through 21 of the Recapitulation,	complete and attach the appropriate schedules to support the claimed deductions.
you claim credits for foreign death taxes or tax on prior transfers,	complete and attach Schedule P or Q.
there is not enough space on a schedule to list all the items,	attach a Continuation Schedule (or additional sheets of the same size) to the back of the schedule; (see the Continuation Schedule at the end of Form 706); photocopy the blank schedule before completing it, if you will need more than one copy.

Also consider the following:
• Form 706 has 28 numbered pages. The pages are perforated so that you can remove them for copying and filing.
• Number the items you list on each schedule, beginning with the number "1" each time, or using the numbering convention as indicated on the schedule (for example, Schedule M).
• Total the items listed on the schedule and its attachments, Continuation Schedules, etc.
• Enter the total of all attachments, Continuation Schedules, etc., at the bottom of the printed schedule, but do not carry the totals forward from one schedule to the next.
• Enter the total, or totals, for each schedule on page 3, *Part 5—Recapitulation.*
• Do not complete the "Alternate valuation date" or "Alternate value" columns of any schedule unless you elected alternate valuation on line 1 of *Part 3—Elections by the Executor.*
• When you complete the return, staple all the required pages together in the proper order.

Part 1—Decedent and Executor

Line 2

Enter the SSN assigned specifically to the decedent. You cannot use the SSN assigned to the decedent's spouse. If the decedent did not have an SSN, the executor should obtain one for the decedent by filing Form SS-5, with a local Social Security Administration office.

Line 6a. Name of Executor

If there is more than one executor, enter the name of the executor to be contacted by the IRS. List the other executors' names, addresses, and SSNs (if applicable) on an attached sheet.

Line 6b. Executor's Address

Use Form 8822 to report a change of the executor's address.

Line 6c. Executor's Social Security Number

Only individual executors should complete this line. If there is more than one executor, all should list their SSNs on an attached sheet.

Part 2—Tax Computation

In general, the estate tax is figured by applying the unified rates shown in Table A to the total of transfers both during life and at death, and then subtracting the gift taxes, as refigured based on the date of death rates. See *Worksheet TG, Line 4 Worksheet,* and *Line 7 Worksheet.*

Table A — Unified Rate Schedule

Column A Taxable amount over	Column B Taxable amount not over	Column C Tax on amount in Column A	Column D Rate of tax on excess over amount in Column A
$0	$10,000	$0	18%
$10,000	20,000	$1,800	20%
20,000	40,000	3,800	22%
40,000	60,000	8,200	24%
60,000	80,000	13,000	26%
80,000	100,000	18,200	28%
100,000	150,000	23,800	30%
150,000	250,000	38,800	32%
250,000	500,000	70,800	34%
500,000	- - - -	155,800	35%

Worksheet TG and Line 4 Worksheet

Worksheet TG—Taxable Gifts Reconciliation

(To be used for lines 4 and 7 of the Tax Computation)

	a. Calendar year or calendar quarter	b. Total taxable gifts for period (see Note)	**Note.** For the definition of a taxable gift, see section 2503. Follow Form 709. That is, include only the decedent's one-half of split gifts, whether the gifts were made by the decedent or the decedent's spouse. In addition to gifts reported on Form 709, you must include any taxable gifts in excess of the annual exclusion that were not reported on Form 709.			
Gifts made after June 6, 1932, and before 1977			c. Taxable amount included in col. b for gifts included in the gross estate	d. Taxable amount included in col. b for gifts that qualify for "special treatment of split gifts" described below	e. Gift tax paid by decedent on gifts in col. d	f. Gift tax paid by decedent's spouse on gifts in col. c
	1. Total taxable gifts made before 1977					
Gifts made after 1976						
2. Totals for gifts made after 1976						

Line 4 Worksheet—Adjusted Taxable Gifts Made After 1976

1. Taxable gifts made after 1976. Enter the amount from Worksheet TG, line 2, column b		1
2. Taxable gifts made after 1976 reportable on Schedule G. Enter the amount from Worksheet TG, line 2, column c.	2	
3. Taxable gifts made after 1976 that qualify for "special treatment." Enter the amount from Worksheet TG, line 2, column d	3	
4. Add lines 2 and 3		4
5. Adjusted taxable gifts. Subtract line 4 from line 1. Enter here and on Part 2—Tax Computation, line 4.		5

Note. You must complete *Part 2—Tax Computation.*

Line 1

If you elected alternate valuation on line 1, *Part 3—Elections by the Executor,* enter the amount you entered in the "Alternate value" column of item 12 of *Part 5—Recapitulation.* Otherwise, enter the amount from the "Value at date of death" column.

Line 3b. State Death Tax Deduction

CAUTION *The estates of decedents dying after December 31, 2004, will be allowed a deduction for state death taxes, instead of a credit. The state death tax credit was repealed as of January 1, 2005.*

You may take a deduction on line 3b for estate, inheritance, legacy, or succession taxes paid as the result of the decedent's death to any state or the District of Columbia.

You may claim an anticipated amount of deduction and figure the federal estate tax on the return before the state death taxes have been paid. However, the deduction cannot be finally allowed unless you pay the state death taxes and claim the deduction within 4 years after the return is filed, or later (see section 2058(b)) if:

- A petition is filed with the Tax Court of the United States,
- You have an extension of time to pay, or
- You file a claim for refund or credit of an overpayment which extends the deadline for claiming the deduction.

Note. The deduction is not subject to dollar limits.

If you make a section 6166 election to pay the federal estate tax in installments and make a similar election to pay the state death tax in installments, see section 2058(b) for exceptions and periods of limitation.

If you transfer property other than cash to the state in payment of state inheritance taxes, the amount you may claim as a deduction is the lesser of the state inheritance tax liability discharged or the fair market value (FMV) of the property on the date of the transfer. For more information on the application of such transfers, see the principles discussed in Revenue Ruling 86-117, 1986-2 C.B. 157, prior to the repeal of section 2011.

You should send the following evidence to the IRS:

1. Certificate of the proper officer of the taxing state, or the District of Columbia, showing the:

   a. Total amount of tax imposed (before adding interest and penalties and before allowing discount),

   b. Amount of discount allowed,

   c. Amount of penalties and interest imposed or charged,

   d. Total amount actually paid in cash, and

   e. Date of payment.

2. Any additional proof the IRS specifically requests.

You should file the evidence requested above with the return, if possible. Otherwise, send it as soon after you file the return as possible.

Line 6

To figure the tentative tax on the amount on line 5, use *Table A — Unified Rate Schedule*, above, and put the result on this line.

Lines 4 and 7

Three worksheets are provided to help you figure the entries for these lines.

Line 7 Worksheet (Unified Credit Allowable for Prior Periods) *Keep for Your Records* 

Line 7 Worksheet – Tax on Gifts Made After 1976

(a) Period	(b) Taxable Gifts for the Current Period	(c) Total Taxable Gifts for Prior Periods[1]	(d) Cumulative Taxable Gifts Including Current Period. *(Col. (b) + Col. (c))*	(e) Tax Based on 2011 Rates on Gifts from Prior Periods *(Col. (c))*[2]	(f) Tax Based on 2011 Rates on Cumulative Gifts Including Current Period *(Col. (d))*	(g) Tax on Gifts for Current Period *(Col. (f) – Col. (e))*	(h) Maximum Unified Credit Available for Current Period (based on 2011 rates)[3]	(i) Unified Credit Allowable in Prior Periods[4]	(j) Available Credit in Current Period *(Col. (h) – Col. (i))*	(k) Credit Allowable *(Lesser of Col. (g) and Col. (j))*	(l) Tax Payable for Current Period *(Col. (g) – Col. (k))*
Pre-1977											

1. Total gift taxes payable on gifts made after 1976 (add all amounts in column (l)).	1.	
2. Gift taxes paid by the decedent on gifts that qualify for "special treatment." Enter the amount from Worksheet TG, line 2, column e.	2.	
3. Subtract line 2 from 1.	3.	
4. Gift tax paid by decedent's spouse on split gift included on Schedule G. Enter amount from Worksheet TG, line 2, column (f).	4.	
5. Add lines 3 and 4. Enter here and on Part 2—Tax Computation, line 7.	5.	

[1] Column (c): Enter amount from column (d) of the ***previous*** row.
[2] Column (e): Enter amount from column (f) of the ***previous*** row.
[3] Column (h): Enter amount from the Table of Unified Credits. (For each row in column (h), subtract 20 percent of any amount allowed as a specific exemption for gifts made after September 8, 1976, and before January 1, 1977.)
[4] Column (i): Enter the sum of column (l) and column (k) from the ***previous*** row.

You need not file these worksheets with your return but should keep them for your records. *Worksheet TG—Taxable Gifts Reconciliation* allows you to reconcile the decedent's lifetime taxable gifts to figure totals that will be used for the Line 4 Worksheet and the Line 7 Worksheet.

You must have all of the decedent's gift tax returns (Form 709) before you complete *Worksheet TG—Taxable Gifts Reconciliation.* The amounts you will enter on *Worksheet TG* can usually be derived from the filed returns that were subject to tax. However, if any of the returns were audited by the IRS, you should use the amounts that were finally determined as a result of the audits.

In addition, you must make a reasonable inquiry as to the existence of any gifts in excess of the annual exclusion made by the decedent (or on behalf of the decedent under a power of attorney) for which no Forms 709 were filed. Include the value of such gifts in column b of *Worksheet TG.* The annual exclusion per donee for 1977 through 1981 was $3,000, $10,000 for 1981 through 2001, $11,000 for 2002 through 2005, and $12,000 for 2006 through 2008. For 2009, 2010, and 2011, the annual exclusion for gifts of present interest is $13,000 per donee.

How to complete line 7 worksheet

Column (a). Beginning with the earliest year in which taxable gifts were made, enter the quarter/year of the prior gift(s).

Column (b). Enter all taxable gifts. Enter all pre-1977 gifts on the pre-1977 row.

Column (c). Enter the amount from column (d) of the ***previous*** row.

Column (d). Enter the sum of column (b) and column (c) from the current row.

Column (e). Enter the amount from column (f) of the ***previous*** row.

Column (f). Enter the tax based on the amount in column (d) of the current row from *Table A — Unified Rate Schedule* above.

Column (g). Subtract the amount in column (e) from the amount in column (f) for the current row.

Column (h). Enter the amount from the *Table of Unified Credits (as recalculated using 2010 rates).*

Note. The entries in each row of column (h) must be reduced by 20 percent of the amount allowed as a specific exemption for gifts made after September 8, 1976, and before January 1, 1977 (but no more than $6,000).

Column (i). Enter the sum of column (i) and column (k) from the ***previous*** row.

Column (j). Subtract the amount in column (i) from the amount in column (h).

Column (k). Enter the lesser of column (g) and column (j) for the current row.

Column (l). Subtract the amount in column (k) from the amount in column (g) to determine any tax due. Enter result in column (l).

Repeat for each year in which taxable gifts were made.

For examples of how to use the Line 7 Worksheet, see the examples in the 2010 Instructions for Form 709, United States Gift (and Generation-Skipping Transfer) Tax Return, schedule B, column C (Unified Credit Allowable for Prior Periods). Add a column to the right of column (k) to determine the tax payable for the current period (column (g) minus column (k)).

Table of Unified Credits (as Recalculated for 2011 Rates)	
Period	Unified Credit
1977 (Quarters 1 and 2)	$6,000
1977 (Quarters 3 and 4)	$30,000
1978	$34,000
1979	$38,000
1980	$42,500
1981	$47,000
1982	$62,800
1983	$79,300
1984	$96,300
1985	$121,800
1986	$155,800
1987 through 1997	$190,800
1998	$199,550
1999	$208,300
2000 and 2001	$217,050
2002 through 2010	$330,800
2011	$1,730,800

Note. In figuring the line 7 amount, do not include any tax paid or payable on gifts made before 1977. The line 7 amount is a hypothetical figure used to calculate the estate tax.

Special treatment of split gifts. These special rules apply only if:
- The decedent's spouse predeceased the decedent;
- The decedent's spouse made gifts that were "split" with the decedent under the rules of section 2513;
- The decedent was the "consenting spouse" for those split gifts, as that term is used on Form 709; and
- The split gifts were included in the decedent's spouse's gross estate under section 2035.

If all four conditions above are met, do not include these gifts on line 4 of the Tax Computation and do not include the gift taxes payable on these gifts on line 7 of the Tax Computation. These adjustments are incorporated into the worksheets.

Line 9. Maximum Unified Credit (applicable credit amount)

The maximum unified credit (applicable credit amount) is the tentative tax on the applicable exclusion amount. For estates of decedents dying in 2011, the applicable exclusion amount equals:

- The basic exclusion amount of $5,000,000, PLUS
- The deceased spousal unused exclusion amount (DSUE amount), in the case of a decedent having a predeceased spouse dying in 2011.

See also instructions for line 3, *Part 4—General Information*, below, and section 2010(c)(5).

Line 10. Adjustment to Unified Credit (applicable credit amount)

If the decedent made gifts (including gifts made by the decedent's spouse and treated as made by the decedent by reason of gift splitting) after September 8, 1976, and before January 1, 1977, for which the decedent claimed a specific exemption, the unified credit (applicable credit amount) on this estate tax return must be reduced. The reduction is figured by entering 20% of the specific exemption claimed for these gifts.

Note. The specific exemption was allowed by section 2521 for gifts made before January 1, 1977.

If the decedent did not make any gifts between September 8, 1976, and January 1, 1977, or if the decedent made gifts during that period but did not claim the specific exemption, enter zero.

Line 15. Total Credits

Generally, line 15 is used to report the total of credit for foreign death taxes (line 13) and credit for tax on prior transfers (line 14).

However, you may also use line 15 to report credit taken for federal gift taxes imposed by Chapter 12 of the Code, and the corresponding provisions of prior laws, on certain transfers the decedent made before January 1, 1977, that are included in the gross estate. The credit cannot be more than the amount figured by the following formula:

$$\frac{\text{Gross estate tax minus (the sum of the state death taxes and unified credit)}}{\text{Value of gross estate minus (the sum of the deductions for charitable, public, and similar gifts and bequests and marital deduction)}} \times \text{Value of included gift}$$

When taking the credit for pre-1977 federal gift taxes:
- Include the credit in the amount on line 15 and
- Identify and enter the amount of the credit you are taking on the dotted line to the left of the entry space for line 15 on page 1 of Form 706 with a notation, "section 2012 credit."

For more information, see the regulations under section 2012. This computation may be made using Form 4808. Attach a copy of a completed Form 4808 or the computation of the credit. Also, attach all available copies of Forms 709 filed by the decedent to help verify the amounts entered on lines 4 and 7, and the amount of credit taken (on line 15) for pre-1977 federal gift taxes.

Canadian marital credit. In addition to using line 15 to report credit for federal gift taxes on pre-1977 gifts, you may also use line 15 to claim the Canadian marital credit, where applicable.

When taking the marital credit under the 1995 Canadian Protocol:
- Include the credit in the amount on line 15 and
- Identify and enter the amount of the credit you are taking on the dotted line to the left of the entry space for line 15 on page 1 of Form 706 with a notation, "Canadian marital credit."

Also, attach a statement to the return that refers to the treaty, waives QDOT rights, and shows the computation of the marital credit. See the 1995 Canadian income tax treaty protocol for details on figuring the credit.

Part 3—Elections by the Executor

Note. For decedents dying in 2011, the election to allow the decedent's surviving spouse to use the decedent's unused exclusion amount is made by filing a timely and complete Form 706. See instructions for line 4, *Part 4—General Information*, below and section 2010(c)(4) and (c)(5).

Line 1. Alternate Valuation

See the example showing the use of Schedule B where the alternate valuation is adopted.

Unless you elect at the time you file the return to adopt alternate valuation as authorized by section 2032, you must value all property included in the gross estate on the date of the decedent's death. Alternate valuation cannot be applied to only a part of the property.

You may elect special-use valuation (line 2) in addition to alternate valuation.

You may not elect alternate valuation unless the election will decrease both the value of the gross estate and the sum (reduced by allowable credits) of the estate and GST taxes payable by reason of the decedent's death for the property includible in the decedent's gross estate.

You elect alternate valuation by checking "Yes" on line 1 and filing Form 706. You may make a protective alternate valuation election by checking "Yes" on line 1, writing the word "protective," and filing Form 706 using regular values.

Once made, the election may not be revoked. The election may be made on a late-filed Form 706 provided it is not filed later than 1 year after the due date (including extensions actually granted). Relief under sections 301.9100-1 and 301.9100-3 may be available to make an alternate valuation election or a protective alternate valuation election, provided a Form 706 is filed no later than 1 year after the due date of the return (including extensions actually granted).

If you elect alternate valuation, value the property that is included in the gross estate as of the applicable dates as follows:

- Any property distributed, sold, exchanged, or otherwise disposed of or separated or passed from the gross estate by any method within 6 months after the decedent's death is valued on the date of distribution, sale, exchange, or other disposition, whichever occurs first. Value this property on the date it ceases to form a part of the gross estate; for example, on the date the title passes as the result of its sale, exchange, or other disposition.
- Any property not distributed, sold, exchanged, or otherwise disposed of within the 6-month period is valued on the date 6 months after the date of the decedent's death.
- Any property, interest, or estate that is "affected by mere lapse of time" is valued as of the date of decedent's death or on the date of its distribution, sale, exchange, or other disposition, whichever occurs first. However, you may change the date of death value to account for any change in value that is not due to a "mere lapse of time" on the date of its distribution, sale, exchange, or other disposition.

The property included in the alternate valuation and valued as of 6 months after the date of the decedent's death, or as of some intermediate date (as described above) is the property included in the gross estate on the date of the decedent's death. Therefore, you must first determine what property was part of the gross estate at the decedent's death.

Interest. Interest accrued to the date of the decedent's death on bonds, notes, and other interest-bearing obligations is property of the gross estate on the date of death and is included in the alternate valuation.

Rent. Rent accrued to the date of the decedent's death on leased real or personal property is property of the gross estate on the date of death and is included in the alternate valuation.

Dividends. Outstanding dividends that were declared to stockholders of record on or before the date of the decedent's death are considered property of the gross estate on the date of death, and are included in the alternate valuation. Ordinary dividends declared to stockholders of record after the date of the decedent's death are not property of the gross estate on the date of death and are not included in the alternate valuation. However, if dividends are declared to stockholders of record after the date of the decedent's death so that the shares of stock at the later valuation date do not reasonably represent the same property at the date of the decedent's death, include those dividends (except dividends paid from earnings of the corporation after the date of the decedent's death) in the alternate valuation.

As part of each Schedule A through I, you must show:

1. What property is included in the gross estate on the date of the decedent's death;
2. What property was distributed, sold, exchanged, or otherwise disposed of within the 6-month period after the decedent's death, and the dates of these distributions, etc.

(These two items should be entered in the "Description" column of each schedule. Briefly explain the status or disposition governing the alternate valuation date, such as: "Not disposed of within 6 months following death," "Distributed," "Sold," "Bond paid on maturity," etc. In this same column, describe each item of principal and includible income);

3. The date of death value, entered in the appropriate value column with items of principal and includible income shown separately; and
4. The alternate value, entered in the appropriate value column with items of principal and includible income shown separately.

(In the case of any interest or estate, the value of which is affected by lapse of time, such as patents, leaseholds, estates for the life of another, or remainder interests, the value shown under the heading "Alternate value" must be the adjusted value; for example, the value as of the date of death with an adjustment reflecting any difference in its value as of the later date not due to lapse of time.)

Distributions, sales, exchanges, and other dispositions of the property within the 6-month period after the decedent's death must be supported by evidence. If the court issued an order of distribution during that period, you must submit a certified copy of the order as part of the evidence. The IRS may require you to submit additional evidence, if necessary.

If the alternate valuation method is used, the values of life estates, remainders, and similar interests are figured using the age of the recipient on the date of the decedent's death and the value of the property on the alternate valuation date.

Line 2. Special-Use Valuation of Section 2032A

In general. Under section 2032A, you may elect to value certain farm and closely held business real property at its farm or business use value rather than its fair market value (FMV). You may elect both special-use valuation and alternate valuation.

To elect this valuation, you must check "Yes" on line 2 and complete and attach Schedule A-1 and its required additional statements. You must file Schedule A-1 and its required attachments with Form 706 for this election to be valid. You may make the election on a late-filed return so long as it is the first return filed.

The total value of the property valued under section 2032A may not be decreased from FMV by more than $1,020,000 for decedents dying in 2011.

Real property may qualify for the section 2032A election if:

1. The decedent was a U.S. citizen or resident at the time of death;
2. The real property is located in the United States;
3. At the decedent's death, the real property was used by the decedent or a family member for farming or in a trade or business, or was rented for such use by either the surviving spouse or a lineal descendant of the decedent to a family member on a net cash basis;
4. The real property was acquired from or passed from the decedent to a qualified heir of the decedent;
5. The real property was owned and used in a qualified manner by the decedent or a member of the decedent's family during 5 of the 8 years before the decedent's death;
6. There was material participation by the decedent or a member of the decedent's family during 5 of the 8 years before the decedent's death; and
7. The qualified property meets the following percentage requirements:
   a. At least 50% of the adjusted value of the gross estate must consist of the adjusted value of real or personal property that was being used as a farm or in a closely held business and that was acquired from, or passed from, the decedent to a qualified heir of the decedent, and
   b. At least 25% of the adjusted value of the gross estate must consist of the adjusted value of qualified farm or closely held business real property.

For this purpose, adjusted value is the value of property determined without regard to its special-use value. The value is reduced for unpaid mortgages on the property or any indebtedness against the property, if the full value of the decedent's interest in the property (not reduced by such mortgage or indebtedness) is included in the value of the gross estate. The adjusted value of the qualified real and personal property used in different businesses may be combined to meet the 50% and 25% requirements.

Qualified Real Property

Qualified use. *Qualified use* means the use of the property as a farm for farming purposes or the use of property in a trade or business other than farming. Trade or business applies only to the active conduct of a business. It does not apply to passive investment activities or the mere passive rental of property to a person other than a member of the decedent's family. Also, no trade or business is present in the case of activities not engaged in for profit.

Ownership. To qualify as special-use property, the decedent or a member of the decedent's family must have owned and used the property in a qualified use for 5 of the last 8 years before the decedent's death. Ownership may be direct or indirect through a corporation, a partnership, or a trust.

If the ownership is indirect, the business must qualify as a closely held business under section 6166. The ownership, when combined with periods of direct ownership, must meet the requirements of section 6166 on the date of the decedent's death and for a period of time that equals at least 5 of the 8 years preceding death.

If the property was leased by the decedent to a closely held business, it qualifies as long as the business entity to which it was rented was a closely held business for the decedent on the date of the decedent's death and for sufficient time to meet the "5 in 8 years" test explained above.

Structures and other real property improvements. Qualified real property includes residential buildings and other structures and real property improvements regularly occupied or used by the owner or lessee of real property (or by the employees of the owner or lessee) to operate the farm or business. A farm residence which the decedent had occupied is considered to have been occupied for the purpose of operating the farm even when a family member and not the decedent was the person materially participating in the operation of the farm.

Qualified real property also includes roads, buildings, and other structures and improvements functionally related to the qualified use.

Elements of value such as mineral rights that are not related to the farm or business use are not eligible for special-use valuation.

Property acquired from the decedent. Property is considered to have been acquired from or to have passed from the decedent if one of the following applies:

- The property is considered to have been acquired from or to have passed from the decedent under section 1014(b) (relating to basis of property acquired from a decedent);
- The property is acquired by any person from the estate; or
- The property is acquired by any person from a trust, to the extent the property is includible in the gross estate.

Qualified heir. A person is a *qualified heir* of property if he or she is a member of the decedent's family and acquired or received the property from the decedent. If a qualified heir disposes of any interest in qualified real property to any member of his or her family, that person will then be treated as the qualified heir for that interest.

The term "member of the family" includes only:

- An ancestor (parent, grandparent, etc.) of the individual;
- The spouse of the individual;
- The lineal descendant (child, stepchild, grandchild, etc.) of the individual, the individual's spouse, or a parent of the individual; or
- The spouse, widow, or widower of any lineal descendant described above.

A legally adopted child of an individual is treated as a child of that individual by blood.

Material Participation

To elect special-use valuation, either the decedent or a member of his or her family must have materially participated in the operation of the farm or other business for at least 5 of the 8 years ending on the date of the decedent's death. The existence of material participation is a factual determination, but passively collecting rents, salaries, draws, dividends, or other income from the farm or other business does not constitute material participation. Neither does merely advancing capital and reviewing a crop plan and financial reports each season or business year.

In determining whether the required participation has occurred, disregard brief periods (that is, 30 days or less) during which there was no material participation, as long as such periods were both preceded and followed by substantial periods (more than 120 days) during which there was uninterrupted material participation.

Retirement or disability. If, on the date of death, the time period for material participation could not be met because the decedent had retired or was disabled, a substitute period may apply. The decedent must have retired on social security or been disabled for a continuous period ending with death. A person is disabled for this purpose if he or she was mentally or physically unable to materially participate in the operation of the farm or other business.

The substitute time period for material participation for these decedents is a period totaling at least 5 years out of the 8-year period that ended on the earlier of:

- The date the decedent began receiving social security benefits or
- The date the decedent became disabled.

Surviving spouse. A surviving spouse who received qualified real property from the predeceased spouse is considered to have materially participated if he or she was engaged in the active management of the farm or other business. If the surviving spouse died within 8 years of the first spouse's death, you may add the period of material participation of the predeceased spouse to the period of active management by the surviving spouse to determine if the surviving spouse's estate qualifies for special-use valuation. To qualify for this, the property must have been eligible for special-use valuation in the predeceased spouse's estate, though it does not have to have been elected by that estate.

For additional details regarding material participation, see Regulations section 20.2032A-3(e).

Valuation Methods

The primary method of valuing special-use value property that is used for farming purposes is the annual gross cash rental method. If comparable gross cash rentals are not available, you can substitute comparable average annual net share rentals. If neither of these are available, or if you so elect, you can use the method for valuing real property in a closely held business.

Average annual gross cash rental. Generally, the special-use value of property that is used for farming purposes is determined as follows:

1. Subtract the average annual state and local real estate taxes on actual tracts of comparable real property from the average annual gross cash rental for that same comparable property and
2. Divide the result in (1) by the average annual effective interest rate charged for all new Federal Land Bank loans.

The computation of each average annual amount is based on the 5 most recent calendar years ending before the date of the decedent's death. See *Effective interest rate* below.

Gross cash rental. Generally, gross cash rental is the total amount of cash received in a calendar year for the use of actual tracts of comparable farm real property in the same locality as the property being specially valued. You may not use:

- Appraisals or other statements regarding rental value or areawide averages of rentals, or
- Rents that are paid wholly or partly in-kind, and the amount of rent may not be based on production.

The rental must have resulted from an arm's-length transaction. Also, the amount of rent is not reduced by the amount of any expenses or liabilities associated with the farm operation or the lease.

Comparable property. Comparable property must be situated in the same locality as the specially valued property as determined by generally accepted real property valuation rules. The determination of comparability is based on all the facts and circumstances. It is often necessary to value land in segments where there are different uses or land characteristics included in the specially valued land.

The following list contains some of the factors considered in determining comparability:

- Similarity of soil;
- Whether the crops grown would deplete the soil in a similar manner;
- Types of soil conservation techniques that have been practiced on the two properties;
- Whether the two properties are subject to flooding;
- Slope of the land;
- For livestock operations, the carrying capacity of the land;
- For timbered land, whether the timber is comparable;
- Whether the property as a whole is unified or segmented. If segmented, the availability of the means necessary for movement among the different sections;
- Number, types, and conditions of all buildings and other fixed improvements located on the properties and their location as it affects efficient management, use, and value of the property; and
- Availability and type of transportation facilities in terms of costs and of proximity of the properties to local markets.

You must specifically identify on the return the property being used as comparable property. Use the type of descriptions used to list real property on Schedule A.

Effective interest rate. See Tables 2 and 3 of Revenue Ruling 2011-17, 2011-33 I.R.B. 160, available at *www.irs.gov/pub/irs-irbs/irb11-33.pdf*, for the average annual effective interest rates in effect for 2011.

Net share rental. You may use average annual net share rental from comparable land only if there is no comparable land from which average annual gross cash rental can be determined. Net share rental is the difference between the gross value of produce received by the lessor from the comparable land and the cash operating expenses (other than real estate taxes) of growing the produce that, under the lease, are paid by the lessor. The production of the produce must be the business purpose of the farming operation. For this purpose, produce includes livestock.

The gross value of the produce is generally the gross amount received if the produce was disposed of in an arm's-length transaction within the period established by the Department of Agriculture for its price support program. Otherwise, the value is the weighted average price for which the produce sold on the closest national or regional commodities market. The value is figured for the date or dates on which the lessor received (or constructively received) the produce.

Valuing a real property interest in closely held business. Use this method to determine the special-use valuation for qualifying real property used in a trade or business other than farming. You may also use this method for qualifying farm property if there is no comparable land or if you elect to use it. Under this method, the following factors are considered:

- The capitalization of income that the property can be expected to yield for farming or for closely held business purposes over a reasonable period of time with prudent management and traditional cropping patterns for the area, taking into account soil capacity, terrain configuration, and similar factors;
- The capitalization of the fair rental value of the land for farming or for closely held business purposes;
- The assessed land values in a state that provides a differential or use value assessment law for farmland or closely held business;
- Comparable sales of other farm or closely held business land in the same geographical area far enough removed from a metropolitan or resort area so that nonagricultural use is not a significant factor in the sales price; and
- Any other factor that fairly values the farm or closely held business value of the property.

Making the Election

Include the words "section 2032A valuation" in the "Description" column of any Form 706 schedule if section 2032A property is included in the decedent's gross estate.

An election under section 2032A need not include all the property in an estate that is eligible for special-use valuation, but sufficient property to satisfy the threshold requirements of section 2032A(b)(1)(B) must be specially valued under the election.

If joint or undivided interests (that is, interests as joint tenants or tenants in common) in the same property are received from a decedent by qualified heirs, an election for one heir's joint or undivided interest need not include any other heir's interest in the same property if the electing heir's interest plus other property to be specially valued satisfies the requirements of section 2032A(b)(1)(B).

If successive interests (that is, life estates and remainder interests) are created by a decedent in otherwise qualified property, an election under section 2032A is available only for that property (or part) in which qualified heirs of the decedent receive all of the successive interests, and such an election must include the interests of all of those heirs.

For example, if a surviving spouse receives a life estate in otherwise qualified property and the spouse's brother receives a remainder interest in fee, no part of the property may be valued under a section 2032A election.

Where successive interests in specially valued property are created, remainder interests are treated as being received by qualified heirs only if the remainder interests are not contingent on surviving a nonfamily member or are not subject to divestment in favor of a nonfamily member.

Protective Election

You may make a protective election to specially value qualified real property. Under this election, whether or not you may ultimately use special-use valuation depends upon values as finally determined (or agreed to following examination of the return) meeting the requirements of section 2032A.

To make a protective election, check "Yes" on line 2 and complete Schedule A-1 according to the instructions for *Protective election.*

If you make a protective election, you should complete the initial Form 706 by valuing all property at its FMV. Do not use special-use valuation. Usually, this will result in higher estate and GST tax liabilities than will be ultimately determined if special-use valuation is allowed. The protective election does not extend the time to pay the taxes shown on the return. If you wish to extend the time to pay the taxes, you should file Form 4768 in adequate time before the return due date.

If it is found that the estate qualifies for special-use valuation based on the values as finally determined (or agreed to following examination of the return), you must file an amended Form 706 (with a complete section 2032A election) within 60 days after the date of this determination. Complete the amended return using special-use values under the rules of section 2032A, and complete Schedule A-1 and attach all of the required statements.

Additional information

For definitions and additional information, see section 2032A and the related regulations.

Line 3. Section 6166 Installment Payments

If the gross estate includes an interest in a closely held business, you may be able to elect to pay part of the estate tax in installments under section 6166.

The maximum amount that can be paid in installments is that part of the estate tax that is attributable to the closely held business; see *Determine how much of the estate tax may be paid in installments under section 6166*, below. In general, that amount is the amount of tax that bears the same ratio to the total estate tax that the value of the closely held business included in the gross estate bears to the adjusted gross estate.

Bond or lien. The IRS may require that an estate furnish a surety bond when granting the installment payment election. In the alternative, the executor may consent to elect the special lien provisions of section 6324A, in lieu of the bond. The IRS will contact you regarding the specifics of furnishing the bond or electing the special lien. The IRS will make this determination on a case-by-case basis, and you may be asked to provide additional information.

If you elect the lien provisions, section 6324A requires that the lien be placed on property having a value equal to the total deferred tax plus 4 years of interest. The property must be expected to survive the deferral period, and does not necessarily have to be property of the estate. In addition, all of the persons having an interest in the designated property must consent to the creation of this lien on the property pledged.

Percentage requirements. To qualify for installment payments, the value of the interest in the closely held business that is included in the gross estate must be more than 35% of the adjusted gross estate (the gross estate less expenses, indebtedness, taxes, and losses—Schedules J, K, and L of Form 706 (do not include any portion of the state death tax deduction)).

Interests in two or more closely held businesses are treated as an interest in a single business if at least 20% of the total value of each business is included in the gross estate. For this purpose, include any interest held by the surviving spouse that represents the surviving spouse's interest in a business held jointly with the decedent as community property or as joint tenants, tenants by the entirety, or tenants in common.

Value. The value used for meeting the percentage requirements is the same value used for determining the gross estate. Therefore, if the estate is valued under alternate valuation or special-use valuation, you must use those values to meet the percentage requirements.

Transfers before death. Generally, gifts made before death are not included in the gross estate. However, the estate must meet the 35% requirement by both including in and excluding from the gross estate any gifts made by the decedent in the 3-year period ending on the date of death.

Passive assets. In determining the value of a closely held business and whether the 35% requirement is met, do not include the value of any passive assets held by the business. A passive asset is any asset not used in carrying on a trade or business. Any asset used in a qualifying lending and financing business is treated as an asset used in carrying on a trade or business; see section 6166(b)(10) for details. Stock in another corporation is a passive asset unless the stock is treated as held by the decedent because of the election to treat holding company stock as business company stock; see *Holding company stock*, below.

If a corporation owns at least 20% in value of the voting stock of another corporation, or the other corporation had no more than 45 shareholders and at least 80% of the value of the assets of each corporation is attributable to assets used in carrying on a trade or business, then these corporations will be treated as a single corporation, and the stock will not be treated as a passive asset. Stock held in the other corporation is not taken into account in determining the 80% requirement.

Interest in closely held business. For purposes of the installment payment election, an "interest in a closely held business" means:

- Ownership of a trade or business carried on as a proprietorship,
- An interest as a partner in a partnership carrying on a trade or business if 20% or more of the total capital interest was included in the gross estate of the decedent or the partnership had no more than 45 partners, or
- Stock in a corporation carrying on a trade or business if 20% or more in value of the voting stock of the corporation is included in the gross estate of the decedent or the corporation had no more than 45 shareholders.

The partnership or corporation must be carrying on a trade or business at the time of the decedent's death. For further information on whether certain partnerships or corporations owning real property interests constitute a closely held business, see Revenue Ruling 2006-34, 2006-26 I.R.B. 1171, available at *www.irs.gov/pub/irs-irbs/irb06-26.pdf*.

In determining the number of partners or shareholders, a partnership or stock interest is treated as owned by one partner or shareholder if it is community property or held by a husband and wife as joint tenants, tenants in common, or as tenants by the entirety.

Property owned directly or indirectly by or for a corporation, partnership, estate, or trust is treated as owned proportionately by or for its shareholders, partners, or beneficiaries. For trusts, only beneficiaries with present interests are considered.

The interest in a closely held farm business includes the interest in the residential buildings and related improvements occupied regularly by the

Line 3 Worksheet—Adjusted Gross Estate

1	What is the value of the decedent's interest in closely held business(es) included in the gross estate (less value of passive assets, as mentioned in section 6166(b)(9))?	______
2	What is the value of the gross estate (Form 706, page 3, Part 5, line 12)?	______
3	Add lines 17, 18, and 19 from Form 706, page 3, Part 5.	______
4	Subtract line 3 from line 2 to calculate the adjusted gross estate. . . .	______
5	Divide line 1 by line 4 to calculate the value the business interest bears to the value of the adjusted gross estate. For purposes of this calculation, carry the decimal to the sixth place; the IRS will make this adjustment for purposes of determining the correct amount. If this amount is less than 0.350000, the estate does not qualify to make the election under section 6166.	______
6	Multiply line 5 by the amount on line 16 of Form 706, page 1, Part 2. This is the maximum amount of estate tax that may be paid in installments under section 6166. (Certain GST taxes may be deferred as well; see section 6166(i) for more information.)	______

owners, lessees, and employees operating the farm.

Holding company stock. The executor may elect to treat as business company stock the portion of any holding company stock that represents direct ownership (or indirect ownership through one or more other holding companies) in a business company. A holding company is a corporation holding stock in another corporation. A business company is a corporation carrying on a trade or business.

In general, this election applies only to stock that is not readily tradable. However, the election can be made if the business company stock is readily tradable, as long as all of the stock of each holding company is not readily tradable.

For purposes of the 20% voting stock requirement, stock is treated as voting stock to the extent the holding company owns voting stock in the business company.

If the executor makes this election, the first installment payment is due when the estate tax return is filed. The 5-year deferral for payment of the tax, as discussed below under *Time for payment*, does not apply. In addition, the 2% interest rate, discussed below under *Interest computation*, will not apply. Also, if the business company stock is readily tradable, as explained above, the tax must be paid in five installments.

Determine how much of the estate tax may be paid in installments under section 6166. To determine whether the election may be made, you must calculate the adjusted gross estate. (See *Line 3 Worksheet—Adjusted Gross Estate* below.) To determine the value of the adjusted gross estate, subtract the deductions (Schedules J, K, and L) from the value of the gross estate.

To determine over how many installments the estate tax may be paid, please refer to sections 6166(a), (b)(7), (b)(8), and (b)(10).

Time for payment. Under the installment method, the executor may elect to defer payment of the qualified estate tax, but not interest, for up to 5 years from the original payment due date. After the first installment of tax is paid, you must pay the remaining installments annually by the date 1 year after the due date of the preceding installment. There can be no more than 10 installment payments.

Interest on the unpaid portion of the tax is not deferred and must be paid annually. Interest must be paid at the same time as and as a part of each installment payment of the tax.

Acceleration of payments. If the estate fails to make payments of tax or interest within 6 months of the due date, the IRS may terminate the right to make installment payments and force an acceleration of payment of the tax upon notice and demand.

Generally, if any portion of the interest in the closely held business which qualifies for installment payments is distributed, sold, exchanged, or otherwise disposed of, or money and other property attributable to such an interest is withdrawn, and the aggregate of those events equals or exceeds 50% of the value of the interest, then the right to make installment payments will be terminated, and the unpaid portion of the tax will be due upon notice and demand. See section 6166(g).

Interest computation. A special interest rate applies to installment payments. For decedents dying in 2011, the interest rate is 2% on the lesser of:

- $476,000 or
- The amount of the estate tax that is attributable to the closely held business and that is payable in installments.

2% portion. The *2% portion* is an amount equal to the amount of the tentative estate tax (on $1,000,000 plus the applicable exclusion amount in effect) minus the applicable credit amount in effect. However, if the amount of estate tax extended under section 6166 is less than the amount figured above, the 2% portion is the lesser amount.

Inflation adjustment. The $1,000,000 amount used to calculate the 2% portion is indexed for inflation for the estates of decedents dying in a calendar year after 1998. For an estate of a decedent dying in calendar year 2011, the dollar amount used to determine the "2% portion" of the estate tax payable in installments under section 6166 is $1,360,000.

Computation. Interest on the portion of the tax in excess of the 2% portion is figured at 45% of the annual rate of interest on underpayments. This rate is based on the federal short-term rate and is announced quarterly by the IRS in the Internal Revenue Bulletin.

If you elect installment payments and the estate tax due is more than the maximum amount to which the 2% interest rate applies, each installment payment is deemed to comprise both tax subject to the 2% interest rate and tax subject to 45% of the regular underpayment rate. The amount of each installment that is subject to the 2% rate is the same as the percentage of total tax payable in installments that is subject to the 2% rate.

The interest paid on installment payments is not deductible as an administrative expense of the estate.

Making the election. If you check this line to make a final election, you must attach the notice of election described in Regulations section 20.6166-1(b). If you check this line to make a protective election, you must attach a notice of protective election as described in Regulations section 20.6166-1(d). Regulations section 20.6166-1(b) requires that the notice of election is made by attaching to a timely filed estate tax return the following information:

- The decedent's name and taxpayer identification number as they appear on the estate tax return;
- The amount of tax that is to be paid in installments;
- The date selected for payment of the first installment;
- The number of annual installments, including first installment, in which the tax is to be paid;
- The properties shown on the estate tax return that are the closely held business interest (identified by schedule and item number); and
- The facts that formed the basis for the executor's conclusion that the estate qualifies for payment of the estate tax in installments.

You may also elect to pay certain GST taxes in installments. See section 6166(i).

Line 4. Reversionary or Remainder Interests

For details of this election, see section 6163 and the related regulations.

Part 4—General Information

Authorization

Completing the authorization will authorize one attorney, accountant, or enrolled agent to represent the estate and receive confidential tax information, but will not authorize the representative to enter into closing agreements for the estate.

Note. If you wish to represent the estate, you must complete and sign the authorization.

If you wish to authorize persons other than attorneys, accountants, and enrolled agents, or if you wish to authorize more than one person to receive confidential information or represent the estate, you must complete and attach Form 2848. You must also complete and attach Form 2848 if you wish to authorize someone to enter into closing agreements for the estate. Filing a completed Form 2848 with this return may expedite processing of the Form 706.

If you wish only to authorize someone to inspect and/or receive confidential tax information (but not to represent you before the IRS), complete and file Form 8821.

Line 3

Enter the marital status of the decedent at the time of death by checking the appropriate box and providing the requested information. If the decedent had more than one marriage in his or her lifetime, on the Explanation line provide the name and SSN of each former spouse, the date(s) the marriage ended, and specify whether the marriage ended by annulment, divorce decree, or death of spouse (to the extent the information was not already provided above). Also, if the prior marriage ended in death and the predeceased spouse died after December 31, 2010, indicate on the Explanation line whether the executor of the estate of the predeceased spouse elected to allow the decedent to use the deceased spouse's unused exclusion amount. If the executor of the predeceased spouse's estate made the election, attach to the return the predeceased spouse's Form 706 and a calculation of the deceased spousal unused exclusion amount (DSUE amount). For more information, see section 2010(c)(4).

For estates of decedents dying in 2011, the DSUE amount equals the lesser of:

1. The basic exclusion amount of $5,000,000, or
2. The basic exclusion amount of $5,000,000, MINUS the amount in line 5, *Part 2—Tax Computation*, of the last predeceased spouse's Form 706 (but not below zero).

Note. The election to use the DSUE amount applies to the most recent predeceased spouse of the decedent.

Line 4

Complete line 4 whether or not there is a surviving spouse and whether or not the surviving spouse received any benefits from the estate. If there was no surviving spouse on the date of decedent's death, enter "None" in line 4a and leave lines 4b and 4c blank. The value entered in line 4c need not be exact. See the instructions for "Amount" under line 5 below.

Note. The executor is considered to have elected to allow the surviving spouse to use the decedent's unused exclusion amount by filing a timely and complete Form 706.

Note. If the estate chooses not to allow the surviving spouse to take into account, for estate and gift tax purposes, the decedent's unused exclusion amount, then do one of the following:

- Attach a statement to the Form 706 indicating that the decedent's estate is not making the election under section 2010(c)(5); or,
- Enter "No Election under Section 2010(c)(5)" across the top of the first page of Form 706.

Alternatively, if the filing of a Form 706 is not otherwise required for the decedent's estate, not filing a timely and complete Form 706 will effectively prohibit the surviving spouse's use of the decedent's unused exemption.

Line 5

Name. Enter the name of each individual, trust, or estate that received (or will receive) benefits of $5,000 or more from the estate directly as an heir, next-of-kin, devisee, or legatee; or indirectly (for example, as beneficiary of an annuity or insurance policy, shareholder of a corporation, or partner of a partnership that is an heir, etc.).

Identifying number. Enter the SSN of each individual beneficiary listed. If the number is unknown, or the individual has no number, please indicate "unknown" or "none." For trusts and other estates, enter the EIN.

Relationship. For each individual beneficiary, enter the relationship (if known) to the decedent by reason of blood, marriage, or adoption. For trust or estate beneficiaries, indicate "TRUST" or "ESTATE."

Amount. Enter the amount actually distributed (or to be distributed) to each beneficiary including transfers during the decedent's life from Schedule G required to be included in the gross estate. The value to be entered need not be exact. A reasonable estimate is sufficient. For example, where precise values cannot readily be determined, as with certain future interests, a reasonable approximation should be entered. The total of these distributions should approximate the amount of gross estate reduced by funeral and administrative expenses, debts and mortgages, bequests to surviving spouse, charitable bequests, and any federal and state estate and GST taxes paid (or payable) relating to the benefits received by the beneficiaries listed on lines 4 and 5.

All distributions of less than $5,000 to specific beneficiaries may be included with distributions to unascertainable beneficiaries on the line provided.

Line 6. Section 2044 Property

If you answered "Yes," these assets must be shown on Schedule F.

Section 2044 property is property for which a previous section 2056(b)(7) election (QTIP election) has been made, or for which a similar gift tax election (section 2523) has been made. For more information, see the instructions for Schedule F, below.

Line 8. Insurance Not Included in the Gross Estate

If you answered "Yes" to either 8a or 8b, for each policy you must complete and attach Schedule D, Form 712, and an explanation of why the policy or its proceeds are not includible in the gross estate.

Line 10. Partnership Interests and Stock in Close Corporations

If you answered "Yes" on line 10a, you must include full details for partnerships (including family limited partnerships), unincorporated businesses, and limited liability companies on Schedule F (Schedule E if the partnership interest is jointly owned). You must also include full details for fractional interests in real estate on Schedule A, and full details for stock of inactive or close corporations on Schedule B.

Value these interests using the rules of Regulations section 20.2031-2 (stocks) or 20.2031-3 (other business interests).

A *close corporation* is a corporation whose shares are owned by a limited number of shareholders. Often, one family holds the entire stock issue. As a result, little, if any, trading of the stock takes place. There is, therefore, no established market for the stock, and those sales that do occur are at irregular intervals and seldom reflect all the elements of a representative transaction as defined by FMV.

Line 12. Trusts

If you answered "Yes" on either line 12a or line 12b, you must attach a copy of the trust instrument for each trust.

You must complete Schedule G if you answered "Yes" on line 12a and Schedule F if you answered "Yes" on line 12b.

Line 14. Foreign Accounts

Check "Yes" on line 14 if the decedent at the time of death had an interest in or signature or other authority over a financial account in a foreign country, such as a bank account, securities account, an offshore trust, or other financial account.

Part 5—Recapitulation

Gross Estate

Items 1 through 10. You must make an entry in each of items 1 through 9.

If the gross estate does not contain any assets of the type specified by a given item, enter zero for that item. Entering zero for any of items 1 through 9 is a statement by the executor, made under penalties of perjury, that the

Schedule A–Example 1

In this example, alternate valuation is not adopted; the date of death is January 1, 2011.				
Item Number	**Description**	**Alternate Valuation Date**	**Alternate Value**	**Value at date of death**
1	House and lot, 1921 William Street, NW, Washington, DC (lot 6, square 481). Rent of $8,100 due at the end of each quarter, February 1, May 1, August 1, and November 1. Value based on appraisal, copy of which is attached.			$550,000
	Rent due on item 1 for quarter ending November 1, 2010, but not collected at date of death			8,100
	Rent accrued on Item 1 for November and December 2010			5,400
2	House and lot, 304 Jefferson Street, Alexandria, VA (lot 18, square 40). Rent of $1,800 payable monthly. Value based on appraisal, copy of which is attached			375,000
	Rent due on Item 2 for December 2010, but not collected at death			1,800

gross estate does not contain any includible assets covered by that item.

Do not enter any amounts in the "Alternate value" column unless you elected alternate valuation on line 1 of Part 3—Elections by the Executor on page 2 of the Form 706.

Which schedules to attach for items 1 through 9. You must attach:

- Schedule F to the return and answer its questions even if you report no assets on it;
- Schedules A, B, and C if the gross estate includes any (1) Real Estate, (2) Stocks and Bonds, or (3) Mortgages, Notes, and Cash, respectively;
- Schedule D if the gross estate includes any life insurance or if you answered "Yes" to question 8a of *Part 4—General Information;*
- Schedule E if the gross estate contains any jointly owned property or if you answered "Yes" to question 9 of Part 4;
- Schedule G if the decedent made any of the lifetime transfers to be listed on that schedule or if you answered "Yes" to question 11 or 12a of Part 4;
- Schedule H if you answered "Yes" to question 13 of Part 4; and
- Schedule I if you answered "Yes" to question 15 of Part 4.

Exclusion

Item 11. Conservation easement exclusion. You must complete and attach Schedule U (along with any required attachments) to claim the exclusion on this line.

Deductions

Items 13 through 21. You must attach the appropriate schedules for the deductions you claim.

Item 17. If item 16 is less than or equal to the value (at the time of the decedent's death) of the property subject to claims, enter the amount from item 16 on item 17.

If the amount on item 16 is more than the value of the property subject to claims, enter the greater of:

- The value of the property subject to claims or
- The amount actually paid at the time the return is filed.

In no event should you enter more on item 17 than the amount on item 16. See section 2053 and the related regulations for more information.

Schedule A—Real Estate

If the total gross estate contains any real estate, you must complete Schedule A and file it with the return. On Schedule A, list real estate the decedent owned or had contracted to purchase. Number each parcel in the left-hand column.

Describe the real estate in enough detail so that the IRS can easily locate it for inspection and valuation. For each parcel of real estate, report the area and, if the parcel is improved, describe the improvements. For city or town property, report the street and number, ward, subdivision, block and lot, etc. For rural property, report the township, range, landmarks, etc.

If any item of real estate is subject to a mortgage for which the decedent's estate is liable, that is, if the indebtedness may be charged against other property of the estate that is not subject to that mortgage, or if the decedent was personally liable for that mortgage, you must report the full value of the property in the value column. Enter the amount of the mortgage under "Description" on this schedule.

Schedule A–Example 2

In this example, alternate valuation is adopted; the date of death is January 1, 2011				
Item Number	**Description**	**Alternate Valuation Date**	**Alternate Value**	**Value at date of death**
1	House and lot, 1921 William Street, NW, Washington, DC (lot 6, square 481). Rent of $8,100 due at the end of each quarter, February 1, May 1, August 1, and November 1. Value based on appraisal, copy of which is attached. Not disposed of within 6 months of date of death	7/1/11	$535,000	$550,000
	Rent due on item 1 for quarter ending November 1, 2010, but not collected until February 1, 2011	2/1/11	8,100	8,100
	Rent accrued on Item 1 for November and December 2010, collected on February 1, 2011	2/1/11	5,400	5,400
2	House and lot, 304 Jefferson Street, Alexandria, VA (lot 18, square 40). Rent of $1,800 payable monthly. Value based on appraisal, copy of which is attached. Property exchanged for farm on May 1, 2011	5/1/11	369,000	375,000
	Rent due on Item 2 for December 2010, but not collected until February 1, 2011	2/1/11	1,800	1,800

The unpaid amount of the mortgage may be deducted on Schedule K.

If the decedent's estate is not liable for the amount of the mortgage, report only the value of the equity of redemption (or value of the property less the indebtedness) in the value column as part of the gross estate. Do not enter any amount less than zero. Do not deduct the amount of indebtedness on Schedule K.

Also list on Schedule A real property the decedent contracted to purchase. Report the full value of the property and not the equity in the value column. Deduct the unpaid part of the purchase price on Schedule K.

Report the value of real estate without reducing it for homestead or other exemption, or the value of dower, curtesy, or a statutory estate created instead of dower or curtesy.

Explain how the reported values were determined and attach copies of any appraisals.

Schedule A-1—Section 2032A Valuation

The election to value certain farm and closely held business property at its special-use value is made by checking "Yes" on Form 706, Part 3—Elections by the Executor, line 2. Schedule A-1 is used to report the additional information that must be submitted to support this election. In order to make a valid election, you must complete Schedule A-1 and attach all of the required statements and appraisals.

For definitions and additional information concerning special-use valuation, see section 2032A and the related regulations.

Part 1. Type of Election

Estate and GST tax elections. If you elect special-use valuation for the estate tax, you must also elect special-use valuation for the Generation-Skipping Transfer (GST) tax and *vice versa.*

You must value each specific property interest at the same value for GST tax purposes that you value it at for estate tax purposes.

Protective election. To make the protective election described in the separate instructions for Part 3—Elections by the Executor, line 2, you must check this box, enter the decedent's name and social security number in the spaces provided at the top of Schedule A-1, and complete *Part 2. Notice of Election,* line 1 and lines 3 and 4, column A. For purposes of the protective election, list on line 3 all of the real property that passes to the qualified heirs even though some of the property will be shown on line 2 when the additional notice of election is subsequently filed. You need not complete columns B through D of lines 3 and 4. You need not complete any other line entries on Schedule A-1. Completing Schedule A-1 as described above constitutes a Notice of Protective Election as described in Regulations section 20.2032A-8(b).

Part 2. Notice of Election

Line 10. Because the special-use valuation election creates a potential tax liability for the recapture tax of section 2032A(c), you must list each person who receives an interest in the specially valued property on Schedule A-1. If there are more than eight persons who receive interests, use an additional sheet that follows the format of line 10. In the columns "Fair market value" and "Special-use value," you should enter the total respective values of all the specially valued property interests received by each person.

GST Tax Savings

To figure the additional GST tax due upon disposition (or cessation of qualified use) of the property, each "skip person" (as defined in the instructions to Schedule R) who receives an interest in the specially valued property must know the total GST tax savings on all of the interests in specially valued property received. This GST tax savings is the difference between the total GST tax that was imposed on all of the interests in specially valued property received by the skip person valued at their special-use value and the total GST tax that would have been imposed on the same interests received by the skip person had they been valued at their FMV.

Because the GST tax depends on the executor's allocation of the GST exemption and the grandchild exclusion, the skip person who receives the interests is unable to figure this GST tax savings. Therefore, for each skip person who receives an interest in specially valued property, you must attach worksheets showing the total GST tax savings attributable to all of that person's interests in specially valued property.

How to figure the GST tax savings. Before figuring each skip person's GST tax savings, you must complete Schedules R and R-1 for the entire estate (using the special-use values).

For each skip person, you must complete two Schedules R (Parts 2 and 3 only) as worksheets, one showing the interests in specially valued property received by the skip person at their special-use value and one showing the same interests at their FMV.

If the skip person received interests in specially valued property that were shown on Schedule R-1, show these interests on the Schedule R, Parts 2 and 3 worksheets, as appropriate. Do not use Schedule R-1 as a worksheet.

Completing the special-use value worksheets. On Schedule R, Parts 2 and 3, lines 2 through 4 and 6, enter -0-.

Completing the fair market value worksheets.

- *Schedule R, Parts 2 and 3, lines 2 and 3, fixed taxes and other charges.* If valuing the interests at their FMV (instead of special-use value) causes any of these taxes and charges to increase, enter the increased amount (only) on these lines and attach an explanation of the increase. Otherwise, enter -0-.
- *Schedule R, Parts 2 and 3, line 6—GST exemption allocation.* If you completed Schedule R, Part 1, line 10, enter on line 6 the amount shown for the skip person on the line 10 special-use allocation schedule you attached to Schedule R. If you did not complete Schedule R, Part 1, line 10, enter -0- on line 6.

Total GST tax savings. For each skip person, subtract the tax amount on line 10, Part 2 of the special-use value worksheet from the tax amount on line 10, Part 2 of the fair market value worksheet. This difference is the skip person's total GST tax savings.

Part 3. Agreement to Special Valuation Under Section 2032A

The agreement to special valuation by persons with an interest in property is required under section 2032A(a)(1)(B) and (d)(2) and must be signed by all parties who have any interest in the property being valued based on its qualified use as of the date of the decedent's death.

An interest in property is an interest that, as of the date of the decedent's death, can be asserted under applicable law so as to affect the disposition of the specially valued property by the estate. Any person who at the decedent's death has any such interest in the property, whether present or future, or vested or contingent, must enter into the agreement. Included are owners of remainder and executory interests; the holders of general or special powers of appointment; beneficiaries of a gift over in default of exercise of any such power; joint tenants and holders of similar undivided interests when the decedent held only a joint or undivided interest in the property or when only an undivided interest is specially valued; and trustees of trusts and representatives of other entities holding title to, or holding any interests in the property. An heir who has the power under local law to challenge a will and thereby affect disposition of the property is not, however, considered to be a person with an interest in property under section 2032A solely by reason of that right. Likewise, creditors of an estate are not such persons solely by reason of their status as creditors.

If any person required to enter into the agreement either desires that an agent act for him or her or cannot legally bind himself or herself due to infancy or other incompetency, or due to death before the election under section 2032A is timely exercised, a representative authorized by local law to bind the person in an agreement of this nature may sign the agreement on his or her behalf.

The IRS will contact the agent designated in the agreement on all matters relating to continued qualification under section 2032A of the specially valued real property and on all matters relating to the special lien arising under section 6324B. It is the duty of the agent as attorney-in-fact for the parties with interests in the specially valued property to furnish the IRS with any requested information and to notify the IRS of any disposition or cessation of qualified use of any part of the property.

Checklist for Section 2032A Election

CAUTION *If you are going to make the special-use valuation election on Schedule A-1, please use this checklist to ensure that you are providing everything necessary to make a valid election.*

To have a valid special-use valuation election under section 2032A, you must file, in addition to the federal estate tax return, (a) a notice of election (Schedule A-1, Part 2), and (b) a fully executed agreement (Schedule A-1, Part 3). You must include certain information in the notice of election. To ensure that the notice of election includes all of the information required for a valid election, use the following checklist. The checklist is for your use only. Do not file it with the return.

☐ Does the notice of election include the decedent's name and social security number as they appear on the estate tax return?

☐ Does the notice of election include the relevant qualified use of the property to be specially valued?

☐ Does the notice of election describe the items of real property shown on the estate tax return that are to be specially valued and identify the property by the Form 706 schedule and item number?

☐ Does the notice of election include the FMV of the real property to be specially valued and also include its value based on the qualified use (determined without the adjustments provided in section 2032A(b)(3)(B))?

☐ Does the notice of election include the adjusted value (as defined in section 2032A(b)(3)(B)) of (a) all real property that both passes from the decedent and is used in a qualified use, without regard to whether it is to be specially valued, and (b) all real property to be specially valued?

☐ Does the notice of election include (a) the items of personal property shown on the estate tax return that pass from the decedent to a qualified heir and that are used in qualified use and (b) the total value of such personal property adjusted under section 2032A(b)(3)(B)?

☐ Does the notice of election include the adjusted value of the gross estate? (See section 2032A(b)(3)(A).)

☐ Does the notice of election include the method used to determine the special-use value?

☐ Does the notice of election include copies of written appraisals of the FMV of the real property?

☐ Does the notice of election include a statement that the decedent and/or a member of his or her family has owned all of the specially valued property for at least 5 years of the 8 years immediately preceding the date of the decedent's death?

☐ Does the notice of election include a statement as to whether there were any periods during the 8-year period preceding the decedent's date of death during which the decedent or a member of his or her family did not (a) own the property to be specially valued, (b) use it in a qualified use, or (c) materially participate in the operation of the farm or other business? (See section 2032A(e)(6).)

☐ Does the notice of election include, for each item of specially valued property, the name of every person taking an interest in that item of specially valued property and the following information about each such person: (a) the person's address, (b) the person's taxpayer identification number, (c) the person's relationship to the decedent, and (d) the value of the property interest passing to that person based on both FMV and qualified use?

☐ Does the notice of election include affidavits describing the activities constituting material participation and the identity of the material participants?

☐ Does the notice of election include a legal description of each item of specially valued property?

(In the case of an election made for qualified woodlands, the information included in the notice of election must include the reason for entitlement to the Woodlands election.)

Any election made under section 2032A will not be valid unless a properly executed agreement (Schedule A-1, Part 3) is filed with the estate tax return. To ensure that the agreement satisfies the requirements for a valid election, use the following checklist:

☐ Has the agreement been signed by each qualified heir having an interest in the property being specially valued?

☐ Has every qualified heir expressed consent to personal liability under section 2032A(c) in the event of an early disposition or early cessation of qualified use?

☐ Is the agreement that is actually signed by the qualified heirs in a form that is binding on all of the qualified heirs having an interest in the specially valued property?

☐ Does the agreement designate an agent to act for the parties to the agreement in all dealings with the IRS on matters arising under section 2032A?

☐ Has the agreement been signed by the designated agent and does it give the address of the agent?

Schedule B—Stocks and Bonds

TIP *Before completing Schedule B, see the examples illustrating the alternate valuation dates being adopted and not being adopted, below.*

If the total gross estate contains any stocks or bonds, you must complete Schedule B and file it with the return.

On Schedule B, list the stocks and bonds included in the decedent's gross estate. Number each item in the left-hand column.

Note. Unless specifically exempted by an estate tax provision of the Code, bonds that are exempt from federal income tax are not exempt from estate tax. You should list these bonds on Schedule B.

Public housing bonds includible in the gross estate must be included at their full value.

If you paid any estate, inheritance, legacy, or succession tax to a foreign country on any stocks or bonds included in this schedule, group those stocks and bonds together and label them "Subjected to Foreign Death Taxes."

List interest and dividends on each stock or bond on a separate line.

Indicate as a separate item dividends that have not been collected at death and are payable to the decedent or the estate because the decedent was a stockholder of record on the date of death. However, if the stock is being traded on an exchange and is selling ex-dividend on the date of the decedent's death, do not include the amount of the dividend as a separate item. Instead, add it to the ex-dividend quotation in determining the FMV of the stock on the date of the decedent's death. Dividends declared on shares of stock before the death of

Schedule B Examples

Example showing use of Schedule B where the alternate valuation is not adopted; date of death, January 1, 2011

Item number	Description, including face amount of bonds or number of shares and par value where needed for identification. Give CUSIP number. If trust, partnership, or closely held entity, give EIN.	CUSIP number or EIN, where applicable	Unit value	Alternate valuation date	Alternate value	Value at date of death
1	$60,000-Arkansas Railroad Co. first mortgage 4%, 20-year bonds, due 2012. Interest payable quarterly on Feb. 1, May 1, Aug. 1, and Nov. 1; N.Y. Exchange	XXXXXXXXX	100	-------	$-------	$ 60,000
	Interest coupons attached to bonds, item 1, due and payable on Nov. 1, 2010, but not cashed at date of death . .		-------	-------	-------	600
	Interest accrued on item 1, from Nov. 1, 2010, to Jan. 1, 2011		-------	-------	-------	400
2	500 shares Public Service Corp., common; N.Y. Exchange	XXXXXXXXX	110	-------	-------	55,000
	Dividend on item 2 of $2 per share declared Dec. 10, 2010, payable on Jan. 9, 2011, to holders of record on Dec. 30, 2010		-------	-------	-------	1,000

Example showing use of Schedule B where the alternate valuation is adopted; date of death, January 1, 2011

Item number	Description, including face amount of bonds or number of shares and par value where needed for identification. Give CUSIP number. If trust, partnership, or closely held entity, give EIN.	CUSIP number or EIN, where applicable	Unit value	Alternate valuation date	Alternate value	Value at date of death
1	$60,000-Arkansas Railroad Co. first mortgage 4%, 20-year bonds, due 2012. Interest payable quarterly on Feb. 1, May 1, Aug. 1, and Nov. 1; N.Y. Exchange	XXXXXXXXX	100	------	$------	$ 60,000
	$30,000 of item 1 distributed to legatees on Apr. 1, 2011 . .		99	4/1/11	29,700	------
	$30,000 of item 1 sold by executor on May 1, 2011		98	5/1/11	29,400	------
	Interest coupons attached to bonds, item 1, due and payable on Nov. 1, 2010, but not cashed at date of death. Cashed by executor on Feb. 2, 2011		------	2/2/11	600	600
	Interest accrued on item 1, from Nov. 1, 2010, to Jan. 1, 2011. Cashed by executor on Feb. 2, 2011		------	2/2/11	400	400
2	500 shares Public Service Corp., common; N.Y. Exchange	XXXXXXXXX	110	------	------	55,000
	Not disposed of within 6 months following death		90	7/1/11	45,000	------
	Dividend on item 2 of $2 per share declared Dec. 10, 2010, paid on Jan. 9, 2011, to holders of record on Dec. 30, 2010		------	1/9/11	1,000	1,000

the decedent but payable to stockholders of record on a date after the decedent's death are not includible in the gross estate for federal estate tax purposes and should not be listed here.

Description

Stocks. For stocks, indicate:
- Number of shares;
- Whether common or preferred;
- Issue;
- Par value where needed for identification;
- Price per share;
- Exact name of corporation;
- Principal exchange upon which sold, if listed on an exchange; and
- Nine-digit CUSIP number (defined below).

Bonds. For bonds, indicate:
- Quantity and denomination;
- Name of obligor;
- Date of maturity;
- Interest rate;
- Interest due date;
- Principal exchange, if listed on an exchange; and
- Nine-digit CUSIP number.

If the stock or bond is unlisted, show the company's principal business office.

If the gross estate includes any interest in a trust, partnership, or closely held entity, provide the employer identification number (EIN) of the entity in the description column on Schedules B, E, F, G, M, and O, where applicable. You must also provide the EIN of the estate (if any) in the description column on the above-noted schedules, where applicable.

The CUSIP (Committee on Uniform Security Identification Procedure) number is a nine-digit number that is assigned to all stocks and bonds traded on major exchanges and many unlisted securities. Usually, the CUSIP number is printed on the face of the stock certificate. If you do not have a stock certificate, the CUSIP may be found on the broker's or custodian's statement or by contacting the company's transfer agent.

Valuation

List the FMV of the stocks or bonds. The FMV of a stock or bond (whether listed or unlisted) is the mean between the highest and lowest selling prices quoted on the valuation date. If only the closing selling prices are available, then the FMV is the mean between the quoted closing selling price on the valuation date and on the trading day before the valuation date.

If there were no sales on the valuation date, figure the FMV as follows:

1. Find the mean between the highest and lowest selling prices on the nearest trading date before and the nearest trading date after the valuation date. Both trading dates must be reasonably close to the valuation date.
2. Prorate the difference between the mean prices to the valuation date.
3. Add or subtract (whichever applies) the prorated part of the difference to or from the mean price figured for the nearest trading date before the valuation date.

If no actual sales were made reasonably close to the valuation date, make the same computation using the mean between the *bona fide* bid and asked prices instead of sales prices. If actual sales prices or *bona fide* bid and asked prices are available within a reasonable period of time before the valuation date but not after the valuation date, or *vice versa*, use the mean between the highest and lowest sales prices or bid and asked prices as the FMV.

For example, assume that sales of stock nearest the valuation date (June 15) occurred 2 trading days before (June 13) and 3 trading days after (June 18). On those days, the mean sale prices per share were $10 and $15, respectively. Therefore, the price of $12 is considered the FMV of a share of stock on the valuation date. If, however, on June 13 and 18, the mean sale prices per share were $15 and $10, respectively, the FMV of a share of stock on the valuation date is $13.

If only closing prices for bonds are available, see Regulations section 20.2031-2(b).

Apply the rules in the section 2031 regulations to determine the value of inactive stock and stock in close corporations. Attach to Schedule B complete financial and other data used to determine value, including balance sheets (particularly the one nearest to the valuation date) and statements of the net earnings or operating results and dividends paid for each of the 5 years immediately before the valuation date.

Securities reported as of no value, of nominal value, or obsolete should be listed last. Include the address of the company and the state and date of the incorporation. Attach copies of correspondence or statements used to determine the "no value."

If the security was listed on more than one stock exchange, use either the records of the exchange where the security is principally traded or the composite listing of combined exchanges, if available, in a publication of general circulation. In valuing listed stocks and bonds, you should carefully check accurate records to obtain values for the applicable valuation date.

If you get quotations from brokers, or evidence of the sale of securities from the officers of the issuing companies, attach to the schedule copies of the letters furnishing these quotations or evidence of sale.

Schedule C—Mortgages, Notes, and Cash

Complete Schedule C and file it with your return if the total gross estate contains any:
- Mortgages,
- Notes, or
- Cash.

List on Schedule C:
- Mortgages and notes payable **to the decedent** at the time of death.
- Cash the decedent had at the date of death.

Note. Do not list mortgages and notes payable **by the decedent** on Schedule C. (If these are deductible, list them on Schedule K.)

List the items on Schedule C in the following order:

1. Mortgages;
2. Promissory notes;
3. Contracts by decedent to sell land;
4. Cash in possession; and
5. Cash in banks, savings and loan associations, and other types of financial organizations.

What to enter in the "Description" column:
For mortgages, list:
- Face value,
- Unpaid balance,
- Date of mortgage,
- Name of maker,
- Property mortgaged,
- Date of maturity,
- Interest rate, and
- Interest date.

Example to enter in "Description" column: "Bond and mortgage of $50,000, unpaid balance: $17,000; dated: January 1, 1992; John Doe to Richard Roe; premises: 22 Clinton Street, Newark, NJ; due: January 1, 2012; interest payable at 10% a year—January 1 and July 1."

For promissory notes, list in the same way as mortgages.

For contracts by the decedent to sell land, list:
- Name of purchaser,
- Contract date,
- Property description,
- Sale price,
- Initial payment,
- Amounts of installment payment,
- Unpaid balance of principal, and
- Interest rate.

For cash on hand, list such cash separately from bank deposits.

For cash in banks, savings and loan associations, and other types of financial organizations, list:
- Name and address of each financial organization,

• Amount in each account,
• Serial or account number,
• Nature of account—checking, savings, time deposit, etc., and
• Unpaid interest accrued from date of last interest payment to the date of death.

Note. If you obtain statements from the financial organizations, keep them for IRS inspection.

Schedule D—Insurance on the Decedent's Life

If you are required to file Form 706 and there was any insurance on the decedent's life, whether or not included in the gross estate, you must complete Schedule D and file it with the return.

Insurance you must include on Schedule D. Under section 2042, you must include in the gross estate:
• Insurance on the decedent's life receivable by or for the benefit of the estate; and
• Insurance on the decedent's life receivable by beneficiaries other than the estate, as described below.

The term "insurance" refers to life insurance of every description, including death benefits paid by fraternal beneficiary societies operating under the lodge system, and death benefits paid under no-fault automobile insurance policies if the no-fault insurer was unconditionally bound to pay the benefit in the event of the insured's death.

Insurance in favor of the estate. Include on Schedule D the full amount of the proceeds of insurance on the life of the decedent receivable by the executor or otherwise payable to or for the benefit of the estate. Insurance in favor of the estate includes insurance used to pay the estate tax, and any other taxes, debts, or charges that are enforceable against the estate. The manner in which the policy is drawn is immaterial as long as there is an obligation, legally binding on the beneficiary, to use the proceeds to pay taxes, debts, or charges. You must include the full amount even though the premiums or other consideration may have been paid by a person other than the decedent.

Insurance receivable by beneficiaries other than the estate. Include on Schedule D the proceeds of all insurance on the life of the decedent not receivable by, or for the benefit of, the decedent's estate if the decedent possessed at death any of the following incidents of ownership, exercisable either alone or in conjunction with any person or entity.

Incidents of ownership in a policy include:
• The right of the insured or estate to its economic benefits;
• The power to change the beneficiary;
• The power to surrender or cancel the policy;
• The power to assign the policy or to revoke an assignment;
• The power to pledge the policy for a loan;
• The power to obtain from the insurer a loan against the surrender value of the policy; and
• A reversionary interest if the value of the reversionary interest was more than 5% of the value of the policy immediately before the decedent died. (An interest in an insurance policy is considered a reversionary interest if, for example, the proceeds become payable to the insured's estate or payable as the insured directs if the beneficiary dies before the insured.)

Life insurance not includible in the gross estate under section 2042 may be includible under some other section of the Code. For example, a life insurance policy could be transferred by the decedent in such a way that it would be includible in the gross estate under section 2036, 2037, or 2038. See the instructions to Schedule G for a description of these sections.

Completing the Schedule

You must list every insurance policy on the life of the decedent, whether or not it is included in the gross estate.

Under "Description," list:
• The name of the insurance company, and
• The number of the policy.

For every life insurance policy listed on the schedule, you must request a statement on Form 712, Life Insurance Statement, from the company that issued the policy. Attach the Form 712 to the back of Schedule D.

If the policy proceeds are paid in one sum, enter the net proceeds received (from Form 712, line 24) in the value (and alternate value) columns of Schedule D. If the policy proceeds are not paid in one sum, enter the value of the proceeds as of the date of the decedent's death (from Form 712, line 25).

If part or all of the policy proceeds are not included in the gross estate, you must explain why they were not included.

Schedule E—Jointly Owned Property

If you are required to file Form 706, you must complete Schedule E and file it with the return if the decedent owned any joint property at the time of death, whether or not the decedent's interest is includible in the gross estate.

Enter on this schedule all property of whatever kind or character, whether real estate, personal property, or bank accounts, in which the decedent held at the time of death an interest either as a joint tenant with right to survivorship or as a tenant by the entirety.

Do not list on this schedule property that the decedent held as a tenant in common, but report the value of the interest on Schedule A if real estate, or on the appropriate schedule if personal property. Similarly, community property held by the decedent and spouse should be reported on the appropriate Schedules A through I. The decedent's interest in a partnership should not be entered on this schedule unless the partnership interest itself is jointly owned. Solely owned partnership interests should be reported on Schedule F, "Other Miscellaneous Property Not Reportable Under Any Other Schedule."

Part 1. Qualified joint interests held by decedent and spouse. Under section 2040(b)(2), a joint interest is a qualified joint interest if the decedent and the surviving spouse held the interest as:
• Tenants by the entirety, or
• Joint tenants with right of survivorship if the decedent and the decedent's spouse are the only joint tenants.

Interests that meet either of the two requirements above should be entered in Part 1. Joint interests that do not meet either of the two requirements above should be entered in Part 2.

Under "Description," describe the property as required in the instructions for Schedules A, B, C, and F for the type of property involved. For example, jointly held stocks and bonds should be described using the rules given in the instructions to Schedule B.

Under "Alternate value" and "Value at date of death," enter the full value of the property.

Note. You cannot claim the special treatment under section 2040(b) for property held jointly by a decedent and a surviving spouse who is not a U.S. citizen. You must report these joint interests on Part 2 of Schedule E, not Part 1.

Part 2. All other joint interests. All joint interests that were not entered in Part 1 must be entered in Part 2.

For each item of property, enter the appropriate letter A, B, C, etc., from line 2a to indicate the name and address of the surviving co-tenant.

Under "Description," describe the property as required in the instructions for Schedules A, B, C, and F for the type of property involved.

In the "Percentage includible" column, enter the percentage of the total value of the property that you intend to include in the gross estate.

Generally, you must include the full value of the jointly owned property in the gross estate. However, the full value should not be included if you can show that a part of the property originally belonged to the other tenant or tenants and was never received or acquired by the other tenant or tenants from the decedent for less than adequate and full consideration in money or money's worth, or unless you can show that any part of the property was acquired with consideration originally belonging to the surviving joint tenant or tenants. In this case, you may exclude from the value of the property an amount proportionate to the consideration furnished by the other tenant or tenants. Relinquishing or promising to relinquish dower, curtesy, or statutory estate created instead of dower or curtesy, or other marital rights in the decedent's property or estate is not consideration in money or money's worth. See the Schedule A instructions for the value to show for real property that is subject to a mortgage.

If the property was acquired by the decedent and another person or persons by gift, bequest, devise, or inheritance as joint tenants, and their interests are not otherwise specified by law, include only that part of the value of the property that is figured by dividing the full value of the property by the number of joint tenants.

If you believe that less than the full value of the entire property is includible in the gross estate for tax purposes, you must establish the right to include the smaller value by attaching proof of the extent, origin, and nature of the decedent's interest and the interest(s) of the decedent's co-tenant or co-tenants.

In the "Includible alternate value" and "Includible value at date of death" columns, you should enter only the values that you believe are includible in the gross estate.

Schedule F—Other Miscellaneous Property

You must complete Schedule F and file it with the return.

On Schedule F, list all items that must be included in the gross estate that are not reported on any other schedule, including:

- Debts due the decedent (other than notes and mortgages included on Schedule C);
- Interests in business;
- Any interest in an Archer medical savings account (MSA) or health savings account (HSA), unless such interest passes to the surviving spouse; and
- Insurance on the life of another (obtain and attach Form 712, for each policy).

Note (for single premium or paid-up policies). In certain situations, for example, where the surrender value of the policy exceeds its replacement cost, the true economic value of the policy will be greater than the amount shown on line 59 of Form 712. In these situations, you should report the full economic value of the policy on Schedule F. See Revenue Ruling 78-137, 1978-1 C.B. 280 for details.

- Section 2044 property (see *Decedent Who Was a Surviving Spouse* below);
- Claims (including the value of the decedent's interest in a claim for refund of income taxes or the amount of the refund actually received);
- Rights;
- Royalties;
- Leaseholds;
- Judgments;
- Reversionary or remainder interests;
- Shares in trust funds (attach a copy of the trust instrument);
- Household goods and personal effects, including wearing apparel;
- Farm products and growing crops;
- Livestock;
- Farm machinery; and
- Automobiles.

Interests. If the decedent owned any interest in a partnership or unincorporated business, attach a statement of assets and liabilities for the valuation date and for the 5 years before the valuation date. Also, attach statements of the net earnings for the same 5 years. Be sure to include the EIN of the entity. You must account for goodwill in the valuation. In general, furnish the same information and follow the methods used to value close corporations. See the instructions for Schedule B.

All partnership interests should be reported on Schedule F unless the partnership interest, itself, is jointly owned. Jointly owned partnership interests should be reported on Schedule E.

If real estate is owned by the sole proprietorship, it should be reported on Schedule F and not on Schedule A. Describe the real estate with the same detail required for Schedule A.

Valuation discounts. If you answered "Yes" to Part 4—General Information, line 10b for any interest in miscellaneous property not reportable under any other schedule owned by the decedent at the time of death, attach a statement that lists the item number from Schedule F and identifies the total accumulated discount taken (that is, XX.XX%) on such interest.

If you answered "Yes" to line 10b for an interest in a limited liability company owned by the decedent at the time of death, attach a statement that lists the item number from Schedule F and identifies the effective discount taken on such interest.

Example of effective discount:

a	Pro-rata value of limited liability company (before any discounts)	$100.00
b	Minus: 10% discounts for lack of control	(10.00)
c	Marketable minority interest value (as if freely traded minority interest value)	$90.00
d	Minus: 15% discount for lack of marketability	(13.50)
e	Non-marketable minority interest value	$76.50

Calculation of effective discount:

(**a** minus **e**) divided by **a** = effective discount
($100.00 - $76.50) ÷ $100.00 = 23.50%

Note. The amount of discounts are based on the factors pertaining to a specific interest and those discounts shown in the example are for demonstration purposes only.

If you answered "Yes" to line 10b for any transfer(s) described in (1) through (5) in the Schedule G instructions (and made by the decedent), **attach a statement to Schedule G** which lists the item number from that schedule and identifies the total accumulated discount taken (that is, XX.XX%) on such transfer(s).

Line 1. If the decedent owned at the date of death works of art or items with collectible value (for example, jewelry, furs, silverware, books, statuary, vases, oriental rugs, coin or stamp collections), check the "Yes" box on line 1 and provide full details. If any item or collection of similar items is valued at more than $3,000, attach an appraisal by an expert under oath and the required statement regarding the appraiser's qualifications (see Regulations section 20.2031-6(b)).

Decedent Who Was a Surviving Spouse

If the decedent was a surviving spouse, he or she may have received qualified terminable interest property (QTIP) from the predeceased spouse for which the marital deduction was elected either on the predeceased spouse's estate tax return or on a gift tax return, Form 709. The election was available for gifts made and decedents dying after December 31, 1981. List such property on Schedule F.

If this election was made and the surviving spouse retained his or her interest in the QTIP property at death, the full value of the QTIP property is includible in his or her estate, even though the qualifying income interest terminated at death. It is valued as of the date of the surviving spouse's death, or alternate valuation date, if applicable. Do not reduce the value by any annual exclusion that may have applied to the transfer creating the interest.

The value of such property included in the surviving spouse's gross estate is treated as passing from the surviving spouse. It therefore qualifies for the charitable and marital deductions on the surviving spouse's estate tax return if it meets the other requirements for those deductions.

For additional details, see Regulations section 20.2044-1.

Schedule G—Transfers During Decedent's Life

Complete Schedule G and file it with the return if the decedent made any of the transfers described in (1) through (5) below, or if you answered "Yes" to question 11 or 12a of Part 4—General Information.

Report the following types of transfers on this schedule:

IF...	AND...	THEN...
the decedent made a transfer from a trust,	at the time of the transfer, the transfer was from a portion of the trust that was owned by the grantor under section 676 (other than by reason of section 672(e)) by reason of a power in the grantor,	for purposes of sections 2035 and 2038, treat the transfer as made directly by the decedent.
		Any such transfer within the annual gift tax exclusion is not includible in the gross estate.

1. **Certain gift taxes (section 2035(b)).** Enter at item A of Schedule G the total value of the gift taxes that were paid by the decedent or the estate on gifts made by the decedent or the decedent's spouse within 3 years of death.

The date of the gift, not the date of payment of the gift tax, determines whether a gift tax paid is included in the gross estate under this rule. Therefore, you should carefully examine the Forms 709 filed by the decedent and the decedent's spouse to determine what part of the total gift taxes reported on them was attributable to gifts made within 3 years of death.

For example, if the decedent died on July 10, 2010, you should examine gift tax returns for 2010, 2009, 2008, and 2007. However, the gift taxes on the 2007 return that are attributable to gifts made on or before July 10, 2007, are not included in the gross estate.

Attach an explanation of how you figured the includible gift taxes if you do not include in the gross estate the entire gift taxes shown on any Form 709 filed for gifts made within 3 years of death. Also attach copies of any pertinent gift tax returns filed by the decedent's spouse for gifts made within 3 years of death.

2. **Other transfers within 3 years of death (section 2035(a)).** These transfers include only the following:

- Any transfer by the decedent with respect to a life insurance policy within 3 years of death; or
- Any transfer within 3 years of death of a retained section 2036 life estate, section 2037 reversionary interest, or section 2038 power to revoke, etc., if the property subject to the life estate, interest, or power would have been included in the gross estate had the decedent continued to possess the life estate, interest, or power until death.

These transfers are reported on Schedule G, regardless of whether a gift tax return was required to be filed for them when they were made. However, the amount includible and the information required to be shown for the transfers are determined:

- For insurance on the life of the decedent using the instructions to Schedule D (attach Forms 712);
- For insurance on the life of another using the instructions to Schedule F (attach Forms 712); and
- For sections 2036, 2037, and 2038 transfers, using paragraphs (3), (4), and (5) of these instructions.

3. **Transfers with retained life estate (section 2036).** These are transfers by the decedent in which the decedent retained an interest in the transferred property. The transfer can be in trust or otherwise, but excludes *bona fide* sales for adequate and full consideration.

Interests or rights. Section 2036 applies to the following retained interests or rights:

- The right to income from the transferred property;
- The right to the possession or enjoyment of the property; and
- The right, either alone or with any person, to designate the persons who shall receive the income from, or possess or enjoy, the property.

Retained annuity, unitrust, and other income interests in trusts. If a decedent transferred property into a trust and retained or reserved the right to use such property, or the right to an annuity, unitrust, or other interest in such trust for the property decedent so transferred for decedent's life, any period not ascertainable without reference to the decedent's death, or for a period that does not, in fact, end before the decedent's death, then the decedent's right to use the property or the retained annuity, unitrust, or other interest (whether payable from income and/or principal) is the retention of the possession or enjoyment of, or the right to the income from, the property for purposes of section 2036. See Regulations section 20.2036-1(c)(2).

Retained voting rights. Transfers with a retained life estate also include transfers of stock in a controlled corporation after June 22, 1976, if the decedent retained or acquired voting rights in the stock. If the decedent retained direct or indirect voting rights in a controlled corporation, the decedent is considered to have retained enjoyment of the transferred property. A corporation is a *controlled corporation* if the decedent owned (actually or constructively) or had the right (either alone or with any other person) to vote at least 20% of the total combined voting power of all classes of stock. See section 2036(b)(2). If these voting rights ceased or were relinquished within 3 years of the decedent's death, the corporate interests are included in the gross estate as if the decedent had actually retained the voting rights until death.

The amount includible in the gross estate is the value of the transferred property at the time of the decedent's death. If the decedent kept or reserved an interest or right to only a part of the transferred property, the amount includible in the gross estate is a corresponding part of the entire value of the property.

A retained life estate does not have to be legally enforceable. What matters is that a substantial economic benefit was retained. For example, if a mother transferred title to her home to her daughter but with the informal understanding that she was to continue living there until her death, the value of the home would be includible in the mother's estate even if the agreement would not have been legally enforceable.

4. **Transfers taking effect at death (section 2037).** A transfer that takes effect at the decedent's death is one under which possession or enjoyment can be obtained only by surviving the decedent. A transfer is not treated as one that takes effect at the decedent's death unless the decedent retained a reversionary interest (defined below) in the property that immediately before the decedent's death had a value of more than 5% of the value of the transferred property. If the transfer was made before October 8, 1949, the reversionary interest must have arisen by the express terms of the instrument of transfer.

A *reversionary interest* is generally any right under which the transferred property will or may be returned to the decedent or the decedent's estate. It also includes the possibility that the transferred property may become subject to a power of disposition by the decedent. It does not matter if the right arises by the express terms of the instrument of transfer or by operation of law. For this purpose, reversionary interest does not include the possibility that the income alone from the property may return to the decedent or become subject to the decedent's power of disposition.

5. **Revocable transfers (section 2038).** The gross estate includes the value of transferred property in which the enjoyment of the transferred property was subject at decedent's death to any change through the exercise of a power to alter, amend, revoke, or terminate. A decedent's power to change the beneficiaries and to hasten or increase any beneficiary's enjoyment of the property are examples of this.

It does not matter whether the power was reserved at the time of the transfer, whether it arose by operation of law, or whether it was later created or conferred. The rule applies regardless of the source from which the power was acquired, and regardless of whether the power was exercisable by the decedent alone or with any person (and regardless of whether that person had a substantial adverse interest in the transferred property).

The capacity in which the decedent could use a power has no bearing. If the decedent gave property in trust and was the trustee with the power to revoke the trust, the property would be included in his or her gross estate. For transfers or additions to an irrevocable trust after October 28, 1979, the transferred property is includible if the decedent reserved the power to remove the trustee at will and appoint another trustee.

If the decedent relinquished within 3 years of death any of the includible powers described above, figure the gross estate as if the decedent had actually retained the powers until death.

Only the part of the transferred property that is subject to the decedent's power is included in the gross estate.

For more detailed information on which transfers are includible in the gross estate, see the Estate Tax Regulations.

Special Valuation Rules for Certain Lifetime Transfers

Sections 2701 through 2704 provide rules for valuing certain transfers to family members.

Section 2701 deals with the transfer of an interest in a corporation or partnership while retaining certain distribution rights, or a liquidation, put, call, or conversion right.

Section 2702 deals with the transfer of an interest in a trust while retaining any interest other than a qualified interest. In general, a qualified interest is a right to receive certain distributions from the trust at least annually, or a noncontingent remainder interest if all of the other interests in the trust are distribution rights specified in section 2702.

Section 2703 provides rules for the valuation of property transferred to a family member but subject to an option, agreement, or other right to acquire or use the property at less than FMV. It also applies to transfers subject to restrictions on the right to sell or use the property.

Finally, section 2704 provides that in certain cases, the lapse of a voting or liquidation right in a family-owned corporation or partnership will result in a deemed transfer.

These rules have potential consequences for the valuation of property in an estate. If the decedent (or any member of his or her family) was involved in any such transactions, see sections 2701 through 2704 and the related regulations for additional details.

How To Complete Schedule G

All transfers (other than outright transfers not in trust and *bona fide* sales) made by the decedent at any time during life must be reported on Schedule G, regardless of whether you believe the transfers are subject to tax. If the decedent made any transfers not described in these instructions, the transfers should not be shown on Schedule G. Instead, attach a statement describing these transfers by listing:

- The date of the transfer,
- The amount or value of the transferred property, and
- The type of transfer.

Complete the schedule for each transfer that is included in the gross estate under sections 2035(a), 2036, 2037, and 2038 as described in the Instructions for Schedule G.

In the "Item number" column, number each transfer consecutively beginning with "1." In the "Description" column, list the name of the transferee and the date of the transfer, and give a complete description of the property. Transfers included in the gross estate should be valued on the date of the decedent's death or, if alternate valuation is adopted, according to section 2032.

If only part of the property transferred meets the terms of section 2035(a), 2036, 2037, or 2038, then only a corresponding part of the value of the property should be included in the value of the gross estate. If the transferee makes additions or improvements to the property, the increased value of the property at the valuation date should not be included on Schedule G. However, if only a part of the value of the property is included, enter the value of the whole under the column headed "Description" and explain what part was included.

Attachments. If a transfer, by trust or otherwise, was made by a written instrument, attach a copy of the instrument to Schedule G. If the copy of the instrument is of public record, it should be certified; if not of public record, the copy should be verified.

Schedule H—Powers of Appointment

Complete Schedule H and file it with the return if you answered "Yes" to question 13 of Part 4—General Information.

On Schedule H, include in the gross estate:

- The value of property for which the decedent possessed a general power of appointment (defined below) on the date of his or her death and
- The value of property for which the decedent possessed a general power of appointment that he or she exercised or released before death by disposing of it in such a way that if it were a transfer of property owned by the decedent, the property would be includible in the decedent's gross estate as a transfer with a retained life estate, a transfer taking effect at death, or a revocable transfer.

With the above exceptions, property subject to a power of appointment is not includible in the gross estate if the decedent released the power completely and the decedent held no interest in or control over the property.

If the failure to exercise a general power of appointment results in a lapse of the power, the lapse is treated as a release only to the extent that the value of the property that could have been appointed by the exercise of the lapsed power is more than the greater of $5,000 or 5% of the total value, at the time of the lapse, of the assets out of which, or the proceeds of which, the exercise of the lapsed power could have been satisfied.

Powers of Appointment

A *power of appointment* determines who will own or enjoy the property subject to the power and when they will own or enjoy it. The power must be created by someone other than the decedent. It does not include a power created or held on property transferred by the decedent.

A power of appointment includes all powers which are, in substance and effect, powers of appointment regardless of how they are identified and regardless of local property laws. For example, if a settlor transfers property in trust for the life of his wife, with a power in the wife to appropriate or consume the principal of the trust, the wife has a power of appointment.

Some powers do not in themselves constitute a power of appointment. For example, a power to amend only administrative provisions of a trust that cannot substantially affect the beneficial enjoyment of the trust property or income is not a power of appointment. A power to manage, invest, or control assets, or to allocate receipts and disbursements, when exercised only in a fiduciary capacity, is not a power of appointment.

General power of appointment. A *general power of appointment* is a power that is exercisable in favor of the decedent, the decedent's estate, the decedent's creditors, or the creditors of the decedent's estate, except:

1. A power to consume, invade, or appropriate property for the benefit of the decedent that is limited by an ascertainable standard relating to health, education, support, or maintenance of the decedent.
2. A power exercisable by the decedent only in conjunction with:
   a. the creator of the power or
   b. a person who has a substantial interest in the property subject to the power, which is adverse to the exercise of the power in favor of the decedent.

A part of a power is considered a general power of appointment if the power:

1. May only be exercised by the decedent in conjunction with another person and
2. Is also exercisable in favor of the other person (in addition to being exercisable in favor of the decedent, the decedent's creditors, the decedent's estate, or the creditors of the decedent's estate).

The part to include in the gross estate as a general power of appointment is figured by dividing the value of the property by the number of persons (including the decedent) in favor of whom the power is exercisable.

Date power was created. Generally, a power of appointment created by will is considered created on the date of the testator's death.

A power of appointment created by an *inter vivos* instrument is considered created on the date the instrument takes effect. If the holder of a power exercises it by creating a second power, the second power is considered as created at the time of the exercise of the first.

Attachments

If the decedent ever possessed a power of appointment, attach a certified or verified copy of the instrument granting the power and a certified or verified copy of any instrument by which the power was exercised or released. You must file these copies even if you contend that the power was not a general power of appointment, and that the property is not otherwise includible in the gross estate.

Schedule I—Annuities

You must complete Schedule I and file it with the return if you answered "Yes" to question 15 of Part 4—General Information.

Enter on Schedule I every annuity that meets all of the conditions under *General,* below, and every annuity described in paragraphs (a) through (h) of *Annuities Under Approved Plans,* even if the annuities are wholly or partially excluded from the gross estate.

For a discussion regarding the QTIP treatment of certain joint and survivor annuities, see the Schedule M, line 3 instructions.

General

These rules apply to all types of annuities, including pension plans, individual retirement arrangements, purchased commercial annuities, and private annuities.

In general, you must include in the gross estate all or part of the value of any annuity that meets the following requirements:

- It is receivable by a beneficiary following the death of the decedent and by reason of surviving the decedent;
- The annuity is under a contract or agreement entered into after March 3, 1931;
- The annuity was payable to the decedent (or the decedent possessed the right to receive the annuity) either alone or in conjunction with another, for the decedent's life or for any period not ascertainable without reference to the decedent's death or for any period that did not in fact end before the decedent's death; and
- The contract or agreement is not a policy of insurance on the life of the decedent.

Note. A *private annuity* is an annuity issued from a party not engaged in the business of writing annuity contracts, typically a junior generation family member or a family trust.

An annuity contract that provides periodic payments to a person for life and ceases at the person's death is not includible in the gross estate. Social security benefits are not includible in the gross estate even if the surviving spouse receives benefits.

An annuity or other payment that is not includible in the decedent's or the survivor's gross estate as an annuity may still be includible under some other applicable provision of the law. For example, see *Powers of Appointment* and the Instructions for *Schedule G—Transfers During Decedent's Life,* above. See also Regulations section 20.2039-1(e).

If the decedent retired before January 1, 1985, see *Annuities Under Approved Plans,* below, for rules that allow the exclusion of part or all of certain annuities.

Part Includible

If the decedent contributed only part of the purchase price of the contract or agreement, include in the gross estate only that part of the value of the annuity receivable by the surviving beneficiary that the decedent's contribution to the purchase price of the annuity or agreement bears to the total purchase price.

For example, if the value of the survivor's annuity was $20,000 and the decedent had contributed three-fourths of the purchase price of the contract, the amount includible is $15,000 ($^3/_4$ × $20,000).

Except as provided under *Annuities Under Approved Plans,* contributions made by the decedent's employer to the purchase price of the contract or agreement are considered made by the decedent if they were made by the employer because of the decedent's employment. For more information, see section 2039.

Definitions

Annuity. An *annuity* consists of one or more payments extending over any period of time. The payments may be equal or unequal, conditional or unconditional, periodic or sporadic.

Examples. The following are examples of contracts (but not necessarily the only forms of contracts) for annuities that must be included in the gross estate:

1. A contract under which the decedent immediately before death was receiving or was entitled to receive, for the duration of life, an annuity with payments to continue after death to a designated beneficiary, if surviving the decedent.
2. A contract under which the decedent immediately before death was receiving or was entitled to receive, together with another person, an annuity payable to the decedent and the other person for their joint lives, with payments to continue to the survivor following the death of either.
3. A contract or agreement entered into by the decedent and employer

under which the decedent immediately before death and following retirement was receiving, or was entitled to receive, an annuity payable to the decedent for life. After the decedent's death, if survived by a designated beneficiary, the annuity was payable to the beneficiary with payments either fixed by contract or subject to an option or election exercised or exercisable by the decedent. However, see *Annuities Under Approved Plans*, below.

4. A contract or agreement entered into by the decedent and the decedent's employer under which at the decedent's death, before retirement, or before the expiration of a stated period of time, an annuity was payable to a designated beneficiary, if surviving the decedent. However, see *Annuities Under Approved Plans* below.

5. A contract or agreement under which the decedent immediately before death was receiving, or was entitled to receive, an annuity for a stated period of time, with the annuity to continue to a designated beneficiary, surviving the decedent, upon the decedent's death and before the expiration of that period of time.

6. An annuity contract or other arrangement providing for a series of substantially equal periodic payments to be made to a beneficiary for life or over a period of at least 36 months after the date of the decedent's death under an individual retirement account, annuity, or bond as described in section 2039(e) (before its repeal by P.L. 98-369).

Payable to the decedent. An annuity or other payment was payable to the decedent if, at the time of death, the decedent was in fact receiving an annuity or other payment, with or without an enforceable right to have the payments continued.

Right to receive an annuity. The decedent had the right to receive an annuity or other payment if, immediately before death, the decedent had an enforceable right to receive payments at some time in the future, whether or not at the time of death the decedent had a present right to receive payments.

Annuities Under Approved Plans

The following rules relate to whether part or all of an otherwise includible annuity may be excluded. These rules have been repealed and apply only if the decedent either:

- On December 31, 1984, was both a participant in the plan and in pay status (for example, had received at least one benefit payment on or before December 31, 1984) and had irrevocably elected the form of the benefit before July 18, 1984, or
- Had separated from service before January 1, 1985, and did not change the form of benefit before death.

The amount excluded cannot exceed $100,000 unless either of the following conditions is met:

- On December 31, 1982, the decedent was both a participant in the plan and in pay status (for example, had received at least one benefit payment on or before December 31, 1982) and the decedent irrevocably elected the form of the benefit before January 1, 1983, or
- The decedent separated from service before January 1, 1983, and did not change the form of the benefit before death.

Approved Plans

Approved plans may be separated into two categories:

- Pension, profit-sharing, stock bonus, and other similar plans and
- Individual retirement arrangements (IRAs), and retirement bonds.

Different exclusion rules apply to the two categories of plans.

Pension, etc., plans. The following plans are approved plans for the exclusion rules:

a. An employees' trust (or a contract purchased by an employees' trust) forming part of a pension, stock bonus, or profit-sharing plan that met all the requirements of section 401(a), either at the time of the decedent's separation from employment (whether by death or otherwise) or at the time of the termination of the plan (if earlier);

b. A retirement annuity contract purchased by the employer (but not by an employees' trust) under a plan that, at the time of the decedent's separation from employment (by death or otherwise), or at the time of the termination of the plan (if earlier), was a plan described in section 403(a);

c. A retirement annuity contract purchased for an employee by an employer that is an organization referred to in section 170(b)(1)(A)(ii) or (vi), or that is a religious organization (other than a trust), and that is exempt from tax under section 501(a);

d. Chapter 73 of Title 10 of the United States Code; or

e. A bond purchase plan described in section 405 (before its repeal by P.L. 98-369, effective for obligations issued after December 31, 1983).

Exclusion rules for pension, etc., plans. If an annuity under an "approved plan" described in (a) through (e) above is receivable by a beneficiary other than the executor and the decedent made no contributions under the plan toward the cost, no part of the value of the annuity, subject to the $100,000 limitation (if applicable), is includible in the gross estate.

If the decedent made a contribution under a plan described in (a) through (e) above toward the cost, include in the gross estate on this schedule that proportion of the value of the annuity which the amount of the decedent's contribution under the plan bears to the total amount of all contributions under the plan. The remaining value of the annuity is excludable from the gross estate subject to the $100,000 limitation (if applicable). For the rules to determine whether the decedent made contributions to the plan, see Regulations section 20.2039-1(c).

IRAs and retirement bonds. The following plans are approved plans for the exclusion rules:

f. An individual retirement account described in section 408(a),

g. An individual retirement annuity described in section 408(b), or

h. A retirement bond described in section 409(a) (before its repeal by P.L. 98-369).

Exclusion rules for IRAs and retirement bonds. These plans are approved plans only if they provide for a series of substantially equal periodic payments made to a beneficiary for life, or over a period of at least 36 months after the date of the decedent's death.

Subject to the $100,000 limitation, if applicable, if an annuity under a "plan" described in (f) through (h) above is receivable by a beneficiary other than the executor, the entire value of the annuity is excludable from the gross estate even if the decedent made a contribution under the plan.

However, if any payment to or for an account or annuity described in paragraph (f), (g), or (h) above was not allowable as an income tax deduction under section 219 (and was not a rollover contribution as described in section 2039(e) before its repeal by P.L. 98-369), include in the gross estate on this schedule that proportion of the value of the annuity which the amount not allowable as a deduction under section 219 and not a rollover contribution bears to the total amount paid to or for such account or annuity. For more information, see Regulations section 20.2039-5.

Rules applicable to all approved plans. The following rules apply to all approved plans described in paragraphs (a) through (h) above.

If any part of an annuity under a "plan" described in (a) through (h) above is receivable by the executor, it is generally includible in the gross estate to the extent that it is receivable by the executor in that capacity. In general, the annuity is receivable by the executor if it is to be paid to the executor or if there is an agreement (expressed or implied) that it will be applied by the beneficiary for the benefit of the estate (such as in discharge of the estate's liability for death taxes or debts of the decedent, etc.) or that its distribution will be governed to any extent by the terms of the decedent's will or the laws of descent and distribution.

If data available to you does not indicate whether the plan satisfies the requirements of section 401(a), 403(a), 408(a), 408(b), or 409(a), you may obtain that information from the IRS office where the employer's principal place of business is located.

Line A. Lump Sum Distribution Election

Note. The following rules have been repealed and apply only if the decedent:

- On December 31, 1984, was both a participant in the plan and in pay status (for example, had received at least one benefit payment on or before December 31, 1984) and had irrevocably elected the form of the benefit before July 18, 1984, or
- Had separated from service before January 1, 1985, and did not change the form of benefit before death.

Generally, the entire amount of any lump sum distribution is included in the decedent's gross estate. However, under this special rule, all or part of a lump sum distribution from a qualified (approved) plan will be excluded if the lump sum distribution is included in the recipient's income for income tax purposes.

If the decedent was born before 1936, the recipient may be eligible to elect special "10-year averaging" rules (under repealed section 402(e)) and capital gain treatment (under repealed section 402(a)(2)) in figuring the income tax on the distribution. For more information, see Pub. 575, Pension and Annuity Income. If this option is available, the estate tax exclusion cannot be claimed unless the recipient elects to forego the "10-year averaging" and capital gain treatment in figuring the income tax on the distribution. The recipient elects to forego this treatment by treating the distribution as taxable on his or her income tax return as described in Regulations section 20.2039-4(d). The election is irrevocable.

The amount excluded from the gross estate is the portion attributable to the employer contributions. The portion, if any, attributable to the employee-decedent's contributions is always includible. Also, you may not figure the gross estate in accordance with this election unless you check "Yes" on line A and attach the name, address, and identifying number of the recipients of the lump sum distributions. See Regulations section 20.2039-4.

How To Complete Schedule I

In describing an annuity, give the name and address of the grantor of the annuity. Specify if the annuity is under an approved plan.

IF . . .	THEN . . .
the annuity is under an approved plan,	state the ratio of the decedent's contribution to the total purchase price of the annuity.
the decedent was employed at the time of death and an annuity as described in *Definitions, Annuity, Example 4*, above, became payable to any beneficiary because the beneficiary survived the decedent,	state the ratio of the decedent's contribution to the total purchase price of the annuity.
an annuity under an individual retirement account or annuity became payable to any beneficiary because that beneficiary survived the decedent and is payable to the beneficiary for life or for at least 36 months following the decedent's death,	state the ratio of the amount paid for the individual retirement account or annuity that was not allowable as an income tax deduction under section 219 (other than a rollover contribution) to the total amount paid for the account or annuity.
the annuity is payable out of a trust or other fund,	the description should be sufficiently complete to fully identify it.
the annuity is payable for a term of years,	include the duration of the term and the date on which it began.
the annuity is payable for the life of a person other than the decedent,	include the date of birth of that person.
the annuity is wholly or partially excluded from the gross estate,	enter the amount excluded under "Description" and explain how you figured the exclusion.

Schedule J—Funeral Expenses and Expenses Incurred in Administering Property Subject to Claims

General. You must complete and file Schedule J if you claim a deduction on item 13 of Part 5—Recapitulation.

On Schedule J, itemize funeral expenses and expenses incurred in administering property subject to claims. List the names and addresses of persons to whom the expenses are payable and describe the nature of the expense. **Do not list expenses incurred in administering property not subject to claims on this schedule. List them on Schedule L instead.**

The deduction is limited to the amount paid for these expenses that is allowable under local law but may not exceed:

1. The value of property subject to claims included in the gross estate, plus
2. The amount paid out of property included in the gross estate but not subject to claims. This amount must actually be paid by the due date of the estate tax return.

The applicable local law under which the estate is being administered determines which property is and is not subject to claims. If under local law a particular property interest included in the gross estate would bear the burden for the payment of the expenses, then the property is considered property subject to claims.

Unlike certain claims against the estate for debts of the decedent (see the instructions for Schedule K), you cannot deduct expenses incurred in administering property subject to claims on both the estate tax return and the estate's income tax return. If you choose to deduct them on the estate tax return, you cannot deduct them on a Form 1041, U.S. Income Tax Return for Estate and Trusts, filed for the estate. Funeral expenses are only deductible on the estate tax return.

Funeral expenses. Itemize funeral expenses on line A. Deduct from the expenses any amounts that were reimbursed, such as death benefits payable by the Social Security Administration and the Veterans Administration.

Executors' commissions. When you file the return, you may deduct commissions that have actually been paid to you or that you expect will be paid. You may not deduct commissions if none will be collected. If the amount of the commissions has not been fixed by decree of the proper court, the deduction will be allowed on the final examination of the return, provided that:

- The Estate and Gift Tax Territory Manager is reasonably satisfied that the commissions claimed will be paid;
- The amount entered as a deduction is within the amount allowable by the laws of the jurisdiction where the estate is being administered; and
- It is in accordance with the usually accepted practice in that jurisdiction for estates of similar size and character.

If you have not been paid the commissions claimed at the time of the final examination of the return, you must support the amount you deducted with an affidavit or statement signed under the penalties of perjury that the amount has been agreed upon and will be paid.

You may not deduct a bequest or devise made to you instead of commissions. If, however, the decedent fixed by will the compensation payable to you for services to be rendered in the administration of the estate, you may deduct this amount to the extent it is not more than the compensation allowable by the local law or practice.

Do not deduct on this schedule amounts paid as trustees' commissions whether received by you acting in the capacity of a trustee or by a separate trustee. If such amounts were paid in administering property not subject to claims, deduct them on Schedule L.

Note. Executors' commissions are taxable income to the executors. Therefore, be sure to include them as income on your individual income tax return.

Attorney fees. Enter the amount of attorney fees that have actually been paid or that you reasonably expect to be paid. If, on the final examination of the return, the fees claimed have not been awarded by the proper court and paid, the deduction will be allowed provided the Estate and Gift Tax Territory Manager is reasonably satisfied that the amount claimed will be paid and that it does not exceed a reasonable payment for the services performed, taking into account the size and character of the estate and the local law and practice. If the fees claimed have not been paid at the time of final examination of the return, the amount deducted must be supported by an affidavit, or statement signed under the penalties of perjury, by the executor or the attorney stating that the amount has been agreed upon and will be paid.

Do not deduct attorney fees incidental to litigation incurred by the beneficiaries. These expenses are charged against the beneficiaries personally and are not administration expenses authorized by the Code.

Interest expense. Interest expenses incurred after the decedent's death are generally allowed as a deduction if they are reasonable, necessary to the administration of the estate, and allowable under local law.

Interest incurred as the result of a federal estate tax deficiency is a deductible administrative expense. Penalties are not deductible even if they are allowable under local law.

Note. If you elect to pay the tax in installments under section 6166, you may not deduct the interest payable on the installments.

Miscellaneous expenses. Miscellaneous administration expenses necessarily incurred in preserving and distributing the estate are deductible. These expenses include appraiser's and accountant's fees, certain court costs, and costs of storing or maintaining assets of the estate.

The expenses of selling assets are deductible only if the sale is necessary to pay the decedent's debts, the expenses of administration, or taxes, or to preserve the estate or carry out distribution.

Schedule K—Debts of the Decedent and Mortgages and Liens

You must complete and attach Schedule K if you claimed deductions on either item 14 or item 15 of Part 5—Recapitulation.

Income vs. estate tax deduction. Taxes, interest, and business expenses accrued at the date of the decedent's death are deductible both on Schedule K and as deductions in respect of the decedent on the income tax return of the estate.

If you choose to deduct medical expenses of the decedent only on the estate tax return, they are fully deductible as claims against the estate. If, however, they are claimed on the decedent's final income tax return under section 213(c), they may not also be claimed on the estate tax return. In this case, you also may not deduct on the estate tax return any amounts that were not deductible on the income tax return because of the percentage limitations.

Debts of the Decedent

List under "Debts of the Decedent" only valid debts the decedent owed at the time of death. List any indebtedness secured by a mortgage or other lien on property of the gross estate under the heading "Mortgages and Liens." If the amount of the debt is disputed or the subject of litigation, deduct only the amount the estate concedes to be a valid claim. Enter the amount in contest in the column provided.

Generally, if the claim against the estate is based on a promise or agreement, the deduction is limited to the extent that the liability was contracted *bona fide* and for an adequate and full consideration in money or money's worth. However, any enforceable claim based on a promise or agreement of the decedent to make a contribution or gift (such as a pledge or a subscription) to or for the use of a charitable, public, religious, etc., organization is deductible to the extent that the deduction would be allowed as a bequest under the statute that applies.

Certain claims of a former spouse against the estate based on the relinquishment of marital rights are deductible on Schedule K. For these claims to be deductible, all of the following conditions must be met:

- The decedent and the decedent's spouse must have entered into a written agreement relative to their marital and property rights.
- The decedent and the spouse must have been divorced before the decedent's death and the divorce must have occurred within the 3-year period beginning on the date 1 year before the agreement was entered into. It is not required that the agreement be approved by the divorce decree.
- The property or interest transferred under the agreement must be transferred to the decedent's spouse in settlement of the spouse's marital rights.

You may not deduct a claim made against the estate by a remainderman relating to section 2044 property. Section 2044 property is described in the instructions to line 6.

Include in this schedule notes unsecured by mortgage or other lien and give full details, including:

- Name of payee,
- Face and unpaid balance,
- Date and term of note,
- Interest rate, and
- Date to which interest was paid before death.

Include the exact nature of the claim as well as the name of the creditor. If the claim is for services performed over a period of time, state the period covered by the claim.

Example. Edison Electric Illuminating Co., for electric service during December 2010, $150.

If the amount of the claim is the unpaid balance due on a contract for the purchase of any property included in the gross estate, indicate the schedule and item number where you reported the property. If the claim represents a joint and separate liability, give full facts and explain the financial responsibility of the co-obligor.

Property and income taxes. The deduction for property taxes is limited to the taxes accrued before the date of the decedent's death. Federal taxes on income received during the decedent's lifetime are deductible, but taxes on income received after death are not deductible.

Keep all vouchers or original records for inspection by the IRS.

Allowable death taxes. If you elect to take a deduction for foreign death taxes under section 2053(d) rather than a credit under section 2014, the deduction is subject to the limitations described in section 2053(d) and its regulations. If you have difficulty figuring the deduction, you may request a computation of it. Send your request within a reasonable amount of time before the due date of the return to:

Department of the Treasury
Commissioner of Internal Revenue
Washington, DC 20224.

Attach to your request a copy of the will and relevant documents, a statement showing the distribution of the estate under the decedent's will, and a computation of the state or foreign death tax showing any amount payable by a charitable organization.

Mortgages and Liens

List under "Mortgages and Liens" only obligations secured by mortgages or other liens on property that you included in the gross estate at its full value or at a value that was undiminished by the amount of the mortgage or lien. If the debt is enforceable against other property of the estate not subject to the mortgage or lien, or if the decedent was personally liable for the debt, you must include the full value of the property subject to the mortgage or lien in the gross estate under the appropriate schedule and may deduct the mortgage or lien on the property on this schedule.

However, if the decedent's estate is not liable, include in the gross estate only the value of the equity of redemption (or the value of the property less the amount of the debt), and do not deduct any portion of the indebtedness on this schedule.

Notes and other obligations secured by the deposit of collateral, such as stocks, bonds, etc., also should be listed under "Mortgages and Liens."

Description

Include under the "Description" column the particular schedule and item number where the property subject to the mortgage or lien is reported in the gross estate.

Include the name and address of the mortgagee, payee, or obligee, and the date and term of the mortgage, note, or other agreement by which the debt was established. Also include the face amount, the unpaid balance, the rate of interest, and date to which the interest was paid before the decedent's death.

Schedule L—Net Losses During Administration and Expenses Incurred in Administering Property Not Subject to Claims

You must complete Schedule L and file it with the return if you claim deductions on either item 18 or item 19 of Part 5—Recapitulation.

Net Losses During Administration

You may deduct only those losses from thefts, fires, storms, shipwrecks, or other casualties that occurred during the settlement of the estate. You may deduct only the amount not reimbursed by insurance or otherwise.

Describe in detail the loss sustained and the cause. If you received insurance or other compensation for the loss, state the amount collected. Identify the property for which you are claiming the loss by indicating the particular schedule and item number where the property is included in the gross estate.

If you elect alternate valuation, do not deduct the amount by which you reduced the value of an item to include it in the gross estate.

Do not deduct losses claimed as a deduction on a federal income tax return or depreciation in the value of securities or other property.

Expenses Incurred in Administering Property Not Subject to Claims

You may deduct expenses incurred in administering property that is included in the gross estate but that is not subject to claims. You may only deduct these expenses if they were paid before the section 6501 period of limitations for assessment expired.

The expenses deductible on this schedule are usually expenses incurred in the administration of a trust established by the decedent before death. They may also be incurred in the collection of other assets or the transfer or clearance of title to other property included in the decedent's gross estate for estate tax purposes, but not included in the decedent's probate estate.

The expenses deductible on this schedule are limited to those that are the result of settling the decedent's interest in the property or of vesting good title to the property in the beneficiaries. Expenses incurred on behalf of the transferees (except those described above) are not deductible. Examples of deductible and nondeductible expenses are provided in Regulations section 20.2053-8(d).

List the names and addresses of the persons to whom each expense was payable and the nature of the expense. Identify the property for which the expense was incurred by indicating the schedule and item number where the property is included in the gross estate. If you do not know the exact amount of the expense, you may deduct an estimate, provided that the amount may be verified with reasonable certainty and will be paid before the period of limitations for assessment (referred to above) expires. Keep all vouchers and receipts for inspection by the IRS.

Schedule M—Bequests, etc., to Surviving Spouse (Marital Deduction)

General

You must complete Schedule M and file it with the return if you claim a deduction on Part 5—Recapitulation, item 20.

The marital deduction is authorized by section 2056 for certain property interests that pass from the decedent to the surviving spouse. You may claim the deduction only for property interests that are included in the decedent's gross estate (Schedules A through I).

Note. The marital deduction is generally not allowed if the surviving spouse is not a U.S. citizen. The marital deduction is allowed for property passing to such a surviving spouse in a *qualified domestic trust (QDOT)* or if such property is transferred or irrevocably assigned to such a trust before the estate tax return is filed. The executor must elect QDOT status on the return. See the instructions that follow for details on the election.

Property Interests That You May List on Schedule M

Generally, you may list on Schedule M all property interests that pass from the decedent to the surviving spouse and are included in the gross estate. However, you should not list any *nondeductible terminable interests* (described below) on Schedule M unless you are making a QTIP election. The property for which you make this election must be included on Schedule M. See *Qualified terminable interest property*, below.

For the rules on common disaster and survival for a limited period, see section 2056(b)(3).

You may list on Schedule M only those interests that the surviving spouse takes:

1. As the decedent's legatee, devisee, heir, or donee;
2. As the decedent's surviving tenant by the entirety or joint tenant;
3. As an appointee under the decedent's exercise of a power or as a taker in default at the decedent's nonexercise of a power;
4. As a beneficiary of insurance on the decedent's life;
5. As the surviving spouse taking under dower or curtesy (or similar statutory interest); and
6. As a transferee of a transfer made by the decedent at any time.

Example—Listing Property Interests on Schedule M

Item number	Description of property interests passing to surviving spouse. For securities, give CUSIP number. If trust, partnership, or closely held entity, give EIN.	Amount
	All other property:	
B1	One-half the value of a house and lot, 256 South West Street, held by decedent and surviving spouse as joint tenants with right of survivorship under deed dated July 15, 1975 (Schedule E, Part I, item 1)	$182,500
B2	Proceeds of Metropolitan Life Insurance Company policy No. 104729, payable in one sum to surviving spouse (Schedule D, item 3)	200,000
B3	Cash bequest under Paragraph Six of will	100,000

Property Interests That You May Not List on Schedule M

You should not list on Schedule M:

1. The value of any property that does not pass from the decedent to the surviving spouse;
2. Property interests that are not included in the decedent's gross estate;
3. The full value of a property interest for which a deduction was claimed on Schedules J through L. The value of the property interest should be reduced by the deductions claimed with respect to it;
4. The full value of a property interest that passes to the surviving spouse subject to a mortgage or other encumbrance or an obligation of the surviving spouse. Include on Schedule M only the net value of the interest after reducing it by the amount of the mortgage or other debt;
5. Nondeductible terminable interests (described below); or
6. Any property interest disclaimed by the surviving spouse.

Terminable Interests

Certain interests in property passing from a decedent to a surviving spouse are referred to as *terminable interests.* These are interests that will terminate or fail after the passage of time, or on the occurrence or nonoccurrence of a designated event. Examples are: life estates, annuities, estates for terms of years, and patents.

The ownership of a bond, note, or other contractual obligation, which when discharged would not have the effect of an annuity for life or for a term, is not considered a terminable interest.

Nondeductible terminable interests. A terminable interest is nondeductible. Unless you are making a QTIP election, a terminable interest should not be entered on Schedule M if:

1. Another interest in the same property passed from the decedent to some other person for less than adequate and full consideration in money or money's worth; and
2. By reason of its passing, the other person or that person's heirs may enjoy part of the property after the termination of the surviving spouse's interest.

This rule applies even though the interest that passes from the decedent to a person other than the surviving spouse is not included in the gross estate, and regardless of when the interest passes. The rule also applies regardless of whether the surviving spouse's interest and the other person's interest pass from the decedent at the same time.

Property interests that are considered to pass to a person other than the surviving spouse are any property interest that: (a) passes under a decedent's will or intestacy; (b) was transferred by a decedent during life; or (c) is held by or passed on to any person as a decedent's joint tenant, as appointee under a decedent's exercise of a power, as taker in default at a decedent's release or nonexercise of a power, or as a beneficiary of insurance on the decedent's life.

For example, a decedent devised real property to his wife for life, with remainder to his children. The life interest that passed to the wife does not qualify for the marital deduction because it will terminate at her death and the children will thereafter possess or enjoy the property.

However, if the decedent purchased a joint and survivor annuity for himself and his wife who survived him, the value of the survivor's annuity, to the extent that it is included in the gross estate, qualifies for the marital deduction because even though the interest will terminate on the wife's death, no one else will possess or enjoy any part of the property.

The marital deduction is not allowed for an interest that the decedent directed the executor or a trustee to convert, after death, into a terminable interest for the surviving spouse. The marital deduction is not allowed for such an interest even if there was no interest in the property passing to another person and even if the terminable interest would otherwise have been deductible under the exceptions described below for life estates, life insurance, and annuity payments with powers of appointment. For more information, see Regulations sections 20.2056(b)-1(f) and 20.2056(b)-1(g), Example (7).

If any property interest passing from the decedent to the surviving spouse may be paid or otherwise satisfied out of any of a group of assets, the value of the property interest is, for the entry on Schedule M, reduced by the value of any asset or assets that, if passing from the decedent to the surviving spouse, would be nondeductible terminable interests. Examples of property interests that may be paid or otherwise satisfied out of any of a group of assets are a bequest of the residue of the decedent's estate, or of a share of the residue, and a cash legacy payable out of the general estate.

Example. A decedent bequeathed $100,000 to the surviving spouse. The general estate includes a term for years (valued at $10,000 in determining the value of the gross estate) in an office building, which interest was retained by the decedent under a deed of the building by gift to a son. Accordingly, the value of the specific bequest entered on Schedule M is $90,000.

Life estate with power of appointment in the surviving spouse. A property interest, whether or not in trust, will be treated as passing to the surviving spouse, and will not be treated as a nondeductible terminable interest if: (a) the surviving spouse is entitled for life to all of the income from the entire interest; (b) the income is payable annually or at more frequent intervals; (c) the surviving spouse has the power, exercisable in favor of the surviving spouse or the estate of the surviving spouse, to appoint the entire interest; (d) the power is exercisable by the surviving spouse alone and (whether exercisable by will or during life) is exercisable by the surviving spouse in all events; and (e) no part of the entire interest is subject to a power in any other person to appoint any part to any person other than the surviving spouse (or the surviving spouse's legal representative or relative if the surviving spouse is disabled. See Revenue Ruling 85-35, 1985-1 C.B. 328). If these five conditions are satisfied only for a specific portion of the entire interest, see the section 2056(b) regulations to determine the amount of the marital deduction.

Life insurance, endowment, or annuity payments, with power of

appointment in surviving spouse. A property interest consisting of the entire proceeds under a life insurance, endowment, or annuity contract is treated as passing from the decedent to the surviving spouse, and will not be treated as a nondeductible terminable interest if: (a) the surviving spouse is entitled to receive the proceeds in installments, or is entitled to interest on them, with all amounts payable during the life of the spouse, payable only to the surviving spouse; (b) the installment or interest payments are payable annually, or more frequently, beginning not later than 13 months after the decedent's death; (c) the surviving spouse has the power, exercisable in favor of the surviving spouse or of the estate of the surviving spouse, to appoint all amounts payable under the contract; (d) the power is exercisable by the surviving spouse alone and (whether exercisable by will or during life) is exercisable by the surviving spouse in all events; and (e) no part of the amount payable under the contract is subject to a power in any other person to appoint any part to any person other than the surviving spouse. If these five conditions are satisfied only for a specific portion of the proceeds, see the section 2056(b) regulations to determine the amount of the marital deduction.

Charitable remainder trusts. An interest in a charitable remainder trust will not be treated as a nondeductible terminable interest if:

1. The interest in the trust passes from the decedent to the surviving spouse, and
2. The surviving spouse is the only beneficiary of the trust other than charitable organizations described in section 170(c).

A *charitable remainder trust* is either a charitable remainder annuity trust or a charitable remainder unitrust. (See section 664 for descriptions of these trusts.)

Election To Deduct Qualified Terminable Interests (QTIP)

You may elect to claim a marital deduction for qualified terminable interest property or property interests. You make the QTIP election simply by listing the qualified terminable interest property on Schedule M and inserting its value. You are presumed to have made the QTIP election if you list the property and insert its value on Schedule M. If you make this election, the surviving spouse's gross estate will include the value of the qualified terminable interest property. See the instructions for Part 4—General Information, line 6, for more details. **The election is irrevocable.**

If you file a Form 706 in which you do not make this election, you may not file an amended return to make the election unless you file the amended return on or before the due date for filing the original Form 706.

The effect of the election is that the property (interest) will be treated as passing to the surviving spouse and will not be treated as a nondeductible terminable interest. All of the other marital deduction requirements must still be satisfied before you may make this election. For example, you may not make this election for property or property interests that are not included in the decedent's gross estate.

Qualified terminable interest property. *Qualified terminable interest property* is property (a) that passes from the decedent, and (b) in which the surviving spouse has a qualifying income interest for life.

The surviving spouse has a *qualifying income interest for life* if the surviving spouse is entitled to all of the income from the property payable annually or at more frequent intervals, or has a usufruct interest for life in the property, and during the surviving spouse's lifetime no person has a power to appoint any part of the property to any person other than the surviving spouse. An annuity is treated as an income interest regardless of whether the property from which the annuity is payable can be separately identified.

Amendments to Regulations sections 20.2044-1, 20.2056(b)-7, and 20.2056(b)-10 clarify that an interest in property is eligible for QTIP treatment if the income interest is contingent upon the executor's election even if that portion of the property for which no election is made will pass to or for the benefit of beneficiaries other than the surviving spouse.

The QTIP election may be made for all or any part of qualified terminable interest property. A partial election must relate to a fractional or percentile share of the property so that the elective part will reflect its proportionate share of the increase or decline in the whole of the property when applying section 2044 or 2519. Thus, if the interest of the surviving spouse in a trust (or other property in which the spouse has a qualified life estate) is qualified terminable interest property, you may make an election for a part of the trust (or other property) only if the election relates to a defined fraction or percentage of the entire trust (or other property). The fraction or percentage may be defined by means of a formula.

Election to Deduct Qualified Terminable Interest Property Under Section 2056(b)(7). If a trust (or other property) meets the requirements of qualified terminable interest property under section 2056(b)(7), and

a. The trust or other property is listed on Schedule M and

b. The value of the trust (or other property) is entered in whole or in part as a deduction on Schedule M,

then unless the executor specifically identifies the trust (all or a fractional portion or percentage) or other property to be excluded from the election, the executor shall be deemed to have made an election to have such trust (or other property) treated as qualified terminable interest property under section 2056(b)(7).

If less than the entire value of the trust (or other property) that the executor has included in the gross estate is entered as a deduction on Schedule M, the executor shall be considered to have made an election only as to a fraction of the trust (or other property). The numerator of this fraction is equal to the amount of the trust (or other property) deducted on Schedule M. The denominator is equal to the total value of the trust (or other property).

Qualified Domestic Trust Election (QDOT)

The marital deduction is allowed for transfers to a surviving spouse who is not a U.S. citizen only if the property passes to the surviving spouse in a qualified domestic trust (QDOT) or if such property is transferred or irrevocably assigned to a QDOT before the decedent's estate tax return is filed.

A QDOT is any trust:

1. That requires at least one trustee to be either an individual who is a citizen of the United States or a domestic corporation;
2. That requires that no distribution of corpus from the trust can be made unless such a trustee has the right to withhold from the distribution the tax imposed on the QDOT;
3. That meets the requirements of any applicable regulations; and
4. For which the executor has made an election on the estate tax return of the decedent.

Note. For trusts created by an instrument executed before November 5, 1990, paragraphs 1 and 2 above will be treated as met if the trust instrument requires that all trustees be individuals who are citizens of the United States or domestic corporations.

You make the QDOT election simply by listing the qualified domestic trust or the entire value of the trust property on Schedule M and deducting its value. You are presumed to have made the QDOT election if you list the trust or trust property and insert its value on

Schedule M. **Once made, the election is irrevocable.**

If an election is made to deduct qualified domestic trust property under section 2056A(d), provide the following information for each qualified domestic trust on an attachment to this schedule:

1. The name and address of every trustee;
2. A description of each transfer passing from the decedent that is the source of the property to be placed in trust; and
3. The employer identification number (EIN) for the trust.

The election must be made for an entire QDOT trust. In listing a trust for which you are making a QDOT election, **unless you specifically identify the trust as not subject to the election, the election will be considered made for the entire trust.**

The determination of whether a trust qualifies as a QDOT will be made as of the date the decedent's Form 706 is filed. If, however, judicial proceedings are brought before the Form 706's due date (including extensions) to have the trust revised to meet the QDOT requirements, then the determination will not be made until the court-ordered changes to the trust are made.

Election to Deduct Qualified Domestic Trust Property Under Section 2056A. If a trust meets the requirement of a qualified domestic trust under section 2056A(a), the return is filed no later than 1 year after the time prescribed by law (including extensions), and the entire value of the trust or trust property is listed and entered as a deduction on Schedule M, then unless the executor specifically identifies the trust to be excluded from the election, the executor shall be deemed to have made an election to have the entire trust treated as qualified domestic trust property.

Line 1

If property passes to the surviving spouse as the result of a qualified disclaimer, check "Yes" and attach a copy of the written disclaimer required by section 2518(b).

Line 3

Section 2056(b)(7) creates an automatic QTIP election for certain joint and survivor annuities that are includible in the estate under section 2039. To qualify, only the surviving spouse can have the right to receive payments before the death of the surviving spouse.

The executor can elect out of QTIP treatment, however, by checking the "Yes" box on line 3. **Once made, the election is irrevocable.** If there is more than one such joint and survivor annuity, you are not required to make the election for all of them.

If you make the election out of QTIP treatment by checking "Yes" on line 3, you cannot deduct the amount of the annuity on Schedule M. If you do not elect out, you must list the joint and survivor annuities on Schedule M.

Listing Property Interests on Schedule M

List each property interest included in the gross estate that passes from the decedent to the surviving spouse and for which a marital deduction is claimed. This includes otherwise nondeductible terminable interest property for which you are making a QTIP election. Number each item in sequence and describe each item in detail. Describe the instrument (including any clause or paragraph number) or provision of law under which each item passed to the surviving spouse. If possible, show where each item appears (number and schedule) on Schedules A through I.

In listing otherwise nondeductible property for which you are making a QTIP election, unless you specifically identify a fractional portion of the trust or other property as not subject to the election, the election will be considered made for all of the trust or other property.

Enter the value of each interest before taking into account the federal estate tax or any other death tax. The valuation dates used in determining the value of the gross estate apply also on Schedule M.

If Schedule M includes a bequest of the residue or a part of the residue of the decedent's estate, attach a copy of the computation showing how the value of the residue was determined. Include a statement showing:

- The value of all property that is included in the decedent's gross estate (Schedules A through I) but is not a part of the decedent's probate estate, such as lifetime transfers, jointly owned property that passed to the survivor on decedent's death, and the insurance payable to specific beneficiaries;
- The values of all specific and general legacies or devises, with reference to the applicable clause or paragraph of the decedent's will or codicil. (If legacies are made to each member of a class, for example, $1,000 to each of decedent's employees, only the number in each class and the total value of property received by them need be furnished);
- The date of birth of all persons, the length of whose lives may affect the value of the residuary interest passing to the surviving spouse; and
- Any other important information such as that relating to any claim to any part of the estate not arising under the will.

Lines 5a, 5b, and 5c. The total of the values listed on Schedule M must be reduced by the amount of the federal estate tax, the federal GST tax, and the amount of state or other death and GST taxes paid out of the property interest involved. If you enter an amount for state or other death or GST taxes on line 5b or 5c, identify the taxes and attach your computation of them.

Attachments. If you list property interests passing by the decedent's will on Schedule M, attach a certified copy of the order admitting the will to probate. If, when you file the return, the court of probate jurisdiction has entered any decree interpreting the will or any of its provisions affecting any of the interests listed on Schedule M, or has entered any order of distribution, attach a copy of the decree or order. In addition, the IRS may request other evidence to support the marital deduction claimed.

Schedule O—Charitable, Public, and Similar Gifts and Bequests

General

You must complete Schedule O and file it with the return if you claim a deduction on item 21 of Part 5—Recapitulation.

You can claim the charitable deduction allowed under section 2055 for the value of property in the decedent's gross estate that was transferred by the decedent during life or by will to or for the use of any of the following:

- The United States, a state, a political subdivision of a state, or the District of Columbia, for exclusively public purposes;
- Any corporation or association organized and operated exclusively for religious, charitable, scientific, literary, or educational purposes, including the encouragement of art, or to foster national or international amateur sports competition (but only if none of its activities involve providing athletic facilities or equipment, unless the organization is a qualified amateur sports organization) and the prevention of cruelty to children and animals, as long as no part of the net earnings benefits any private individual and no substantial activity is undertaken to carry on propaganda, or otherwise attempt to influence legislation or participate in any political campaign on behalf of any candidate for public office;
- A trustee or a fraternal society, order or association operating under the lodge system, if the transferred property is to be used exclusively for religious, charitable, scientific, literary, or educational purposes, or for the prevention of cruelty to children or

animals, and no substantial activity is undertaken to carry on propaganda or otherwise attempt to influence legislation, or participate in any political campaign on behalf of any candidate for public office;

- Any veterans organization incorporated by an Act of Congress or any of its departments, local chapters, or posts, for which none of the net earnings benefits any private individual; or
- A foreign government or its political subdivision when the use of such property is limited exclusively to charitable purposes.

For this purpose, certain Indian tribal governments are treated as states and transfers to them qualify as deductible charitable contributions. See Revenue Procedure 2008-55, on page 768 of 2008-39 I.R.B., *www.irs.gov/pub/irs-irbs/irb08-39.pdf*, as modified and supplemented by subsequent revenue procedures, for a list of qualifying Indian tribal governments.

You may also claim a charitable contribution deduction for a qualifying conservation easement granted after the decedent's death under the provisions of section 2031(c)(9).

The charitable deduction is allowed for amounts that are transferred to charitable organizations as a result of either a qualified disclaimer (see *Line 2. Qualified Disclaimer* below) or the complete termination of a power to consume, invade, or appropriate property for the benefit of an individual. It does not matter whether termination occurs because of the death of the individual or in any other way. The termination must occur within the period of time (including extensions) for filing the decedent's estate tax return and before the power has been exercised.

The deduction is limited to the amount actually available for charitable uses. Therefore, if under the terms of a will or the provisions of local law, or for any other reason, the federal estate tax, the federal GST tax, or any other estate, GST, succession, legacy, or inheritance tax is payable in whole or in part out of any bequest, legacy, or devise that would otherwise be allowed as a charitable deduction, the amount you may deduct is the amount of the bequest, legacy, or devise reduced by the total amount of the taxes.

If you elected to make installment payments of the estate tax, and the interest is payable out of property transferred to charity, you must reduce the charitable deduction by an estimate of the maximum amount of interest that will be paid on the deferred tax.

For split-interest trusts (or pooled income funds), enter in the "Amount" column the amount treated as passing to the charity. Do not enter the entire amount that passes to the trust (fund).

If you are deducting the value of the residue or a part of the residue passing to charity under the decedent's will, attach a copy of the computation showing how you determined the value, including any reduction for the taxes described above.

Also include:

- A statement that shows the values of all specific and general legacies or devises for both charitable and noncharitable uses. For each legacy or devise, indicate the paragraph or section of the decedent's will or codicil that applies. If legacies are made to each member of a class (for example, $1,000 to each of the decedent's employees), show only the number of each class and the total value of property they received;
- The date of birth of all life tenants or annuitants, the length of whose lives may affect the value of the interest passing to charity under the decedent's will;
- A statement showing the value of all property that is included in the decedent's gross estate but does not pass under the will, such as transfers, jointly owned property that passed to the survivor on decedent's death, and insurance payable to specific beneficiaries; and
- Any other important information such as that relating to any claim, not arising under the will, to any part of the estate (that is, a spouse claiming dower or curtesy, or similar rights).

Line 2. Qualified Disclaimer

The charitable deduction is allowed for amounts that are transferred to charitable organizations as a result of a qualified disclaimer. To be a qualified disclaimer, a refusal to accept an interest in property must meet the conditions of section 2518. These are explained in Regulations sections 25.2518-1 through 25.2518-3. If property passes to a charitable beneficiary as the result of a qualified disclaimer, check the "Yes" box on line 2 and attach a copy of the written disclaimer required by section 2518(b).

Attachments

If the charitable transfer was made by will, attach a certified copy of the order admitting the will to probate, in addition to the copy of the will. If the charitable transfer was made by any other written instrument, attach a copy. If the instrument is of record, the copy should be certified; if not, the copy should be verified.

Value

The valuation dates used in determining the value of the gross estate apply also on Schedule O.

Schedule P—Credit for Foreign Death Taxes

General

If you claim a credit on line 13 of Part 2—Tax Computation, you must complete Schedule P and file it with the return. You must attach Form(s) 706-CE to support any credit you claim.

If the foreign government refuses to certify Form 706-CE, you must file it directly with the IRS as instructed on the Form 706-CE. See Form 706-CE for instructions on how to complete the form and for a description of the items that must be attached to the form when the foreign government refuses to certify it.

The credit for foreign death taxes is allowable only if the decedent was a citizen or resident of the United States. However, see section 2053(d) and the related regulations for exceptions and limitations if the executor has elected, in certain cases, to deduct these taxes from the value of the gross estate. For a resident, not a citizen, who was a citizen or subject of a foreign country for which the President has issued a proclamation under section 2014(h), the credit is allowable only if the country of which the decedent was a national allows a similar credit to decedents who were U.S. citizens residing in that country.

The credit is authorized either by statute or by treaty. If a credit is authorized by a treaty, whichever of the following is the most beneficial to the estate is allowed:

- The credit figured under the treaty;
- The credit figured under the statute; or
- The credit figured under the treaty, plus the credit figured under the statute for death taxes paid to each political subdivision or possession of the treaty country that are not directly or indirectly creditable under the treaty.

Under the statute, the credit is authorized for all death taxes (national and local) imposed in the foreign country. Whether local taxes are the basis for a credit under a treaty depends upon the provisions of the particular treaty.

If a credit for death taxes paid in more than one foreign country is allowable, a separate computation of the credit must be made for each foreign country. The copies of Schedule P on which the additional computations are made should be attached to the copy of Schedule P provided in the return.

The total credit allowable for any property, whether subjected to tax by one or more than one foreign country, is limited to the amount of the federal estate tax attributable to the property.

The anticipated amount of the credit may be figured on the return, but the credit cannot finally be allowed until the foreign tax has been paid and a Form 706-CE evidencing payment is filed. Section 2014(g) provides that for credits for foreign death taxes, each U.S. possession is deemed a foreign country.

Convert death taxes paid to the foreign country into U.S. dollars by using the rate of exchange in effect at the time each payment of foreign tax is made.

If a credit is claimed for any foreign death tax that is later recovered, see Regulations section 20.2016-1 for the notice required within 30 days.

Limitation Period

The credit for foreign death taxes is limited to those taxes that were actually paid and for which a credit was claimed within the later of the 4 years after the filing of the estate tax return, or before the date of expiration of any extension of time for payment of the federal estate tax, or 60 days after a final decision of the Tax Court on a timely filed petition for a redetermination of a deficiency.

Credit Under the Statute

For the credit allowed by the statute, the question of whether particular property is situated in the foreign country imposing the tax is determined by the same principles that would apply in determining whether similar property of a nonresident not a U.S. citizen is situated within the United States for purposes of the federal estate tax. See the instructions for Form 706-NA.

Computation of Credit Under the Statute

Item 1. Enter the amount of the estate, inheritance, legacy, and succession taxes paid to the foreign country and its possessions or political subdivisions, attributable to property that is:

- Situated in that country,
- Subjected to these taxes, and
- Included in the gross estate.

The amount entered at item 1 should not include any tax paid to the foreign country for property not situated in that country and should not include any tax paid to the foreign country for property not included in the gross estate. If only a part of the property subjected to foreign taxes is both situated in the foreign country and included in the gross estate, it will be necessary to determine the portion of the taxes attributable to that part of the property. Also, attach the computation of the amount entered at item 1.

Item 2. Enter the value of the gross estate, less the total of the deductions on items 20 and 21 of Part 5—Recapitulation.

Item 3. Enter the value of the property situated in the foreign country that is subjected to the foreign taxes and included in the gross estate, less those portions of the deductions taken on Schedules M and O that are attributable to the property.

Item 4. Subtract any credit claimed on line 15 for federal gift taxes on pre-1977 gifts (section 2012) from line 12 of Part 2—Tax Computation, and enter the balance at item 4 of Schedule P.

Credit Under Treaties

If you are reporting any items on this return based on the provisions of a death tax treaty, you may have to attach a statement to this return disclosing the return position that is treaty based. See Regulations section 301.6114-1 for details.

In general. If the provisions of a treaty apply to the estate of a U.S. citizen or resident, a credit is authorized for payment of the foreign death tax or taxes specified in the treaty. Treaties with death tax conventions are in effect with the following countries: Australia, Austria, Canada, Denmark, Finland, France, Germany, Greece, Ireland, Italy, Japan, Netherlands, Norway, South Africa, Switzerland, and the United Kingdom.

A credit claimed under a treaty is in general figured on Schedule P in the same manner as the credit is figured under the statute with the following principal exceptions:

- The *situs* rules contained in the treaty apply in determining whether property was situated in the foreign country;
- The credit may be allowed only for payment of the death tax or taxes specified in the treaty (but see the instructions above for credit under the statute for death taxes paid to each political subdivision or possession of the treaty country that are not directly or indirectly creditable under the treaty);
- If specifically provided, the credit is proportionately shared for the tax applicable to property situated outside both countries, or that was deemed in some instances situated within both countries; and
- The amount entered at item 4 of Schedule P is the amount shown on line 12 of Part 2—Tax Computation, less the total of the credits claimed for federal gift taxes on pre-1977 gifts (section 2012) and for tax on prior transfers (line 14 of Part 2—Tax Computation). (If a credit is claimed for tax on prior transfers, it will be necessary to complete Schedule Q before completing Schedule P.) For examples of computation of credits under the treaties, see the applicable regulations.

Computation of credit in cases where property is situated outside both countries or deemed situated within both countries. See the appropriate treaty for details.

Schedule Q—Credit for Tax on Prior Transfers

General

You must complete Schedule Q and file it with the return if you claim a credit on Part 2—Tax Computation, line 14.

The term "transferee" means the decedent for whose estate this return is filed. If the transferee received property from a transferor who died within 10 years before, or 2 years after, the transferee, a credit is allowable on this return for all or part of the federal estate tax paid by the transferor's estate for the transfer. There is no requirement that the property be identified in the estate of the transferee or that it exist on the date of the transferee's death. It is sufficient for the allowance of the credit that the transfer of the property was subjected to federal estate tax in the estate of the transferor and that the specified period of time has not elapsed. A credit may be allowed for property received as the result of the exercise or nonexercise of a power of appointment when the property is included in the gross estate of the donee of the power.

If the transferee was the transferor's surviving spouse, no credit is allowed for property received from the transferor to the extent that a marital deduction was allowed to the transferor's estate for the property. There is no credit for tax on prior transfers for federal gift taxes paid in connection with the transfer of the property to the transferee.

If you are claiming a credit for tax on prior transfers on Form 706-NA, you should first complete and attach Part 5—Recapitulation from Form 706 before figuring the credit on Schedule Q from Form 706.

Section 2056(d)(3) contains specific rules for allowing a credit for certain transfers to a spouse who was not a U.S. citizen where the property passed outright to the spouse, or to a qualified domestic trust.

Property

The term "property" includes any interest (legal or equitable) of which the transferee received the beneficial ownership. The transferee is considered the beneficial owner of property over which the transferee received a general power of appointment. Property does not include interests to which the transferee received only a bare legal title, such as that of a trustee. Neither does it include an interest in property over which the transferee received a power of

Worksheet for Schedule Q—Credit for Tax on Prior Transfers

Part I Transferor's tax on prior transfers

Item	Transferor (From Schedule Q) A	B	C	Total for all transfers (line 8 only)
1. Gross value of prior transfer to this transferee				
2. Death taxes payable from prior transfer				
3. Encumbrances allocable to prior transfer				
4. Obligations allocable to prior transfer. .				
5. Marital deduction applicable to line 1 above, as shown on transferor's Form 706 . . .				
6. **TOTAL.** Add lines 2, 3, 4, and 5 . . .				
7. **Net value of transfers.** Subtract line 6 from line 1.				
8. **Net value of transfers.** Add columns A, B, and C of line 7.				
9. Transferor's taxable estate.				
10. Federal estate tax paid.				
11. State death taxes paid				
12. Foreign death taxes paid				
13. Other death taxes paid.				
14. **TOTAL taxes paid.** Add lines 10, 11, 12, and 13				
15. **Value of transferor's estate.** Subtract line 14 from line 9				
16. Net federal estate tax paid on transferor's estate				
17. Credit for gift tax paid on transferor's estate with respect to pre-1977 gifts (section 2012)				
18. Credit allowed transferor's estate for tax on prior transfers from prior transferor(s) who died within 10 years before death of decedent . .				
19. **Tax on transferor's estate.** Add lines 16, 17, and 18				
20. Transferor's tax on prior transfers ((line 7 ÷ line 15) × line 19 of respective estates). .				

Part II Transferee's tax on prior transfers

Item				Amount
21. Transferee's actual tax before allowance of credit for prior transfers (see instructions)			21	
22. Total gross estate of transferee from line 1 of the Tax Computation, page 1, Form 706.			22	
23. Net value of all transfers from line 8 of this worksheet			23	
24. Transferee's reduced gross estate. Subtract line 23 from line 22			24	
25. Total debts and deductions (not including marital and charitable deductions) (line 3b of Part 2—Tax Computation, page 1 and items 17, 18, and 19 of the Recapitulation, page 3, Form 706)	25			
26. Marital deduction from item 20, Recapitulation, page 3, Form 706 (see instructions).	26			
27. Charitable bequests from item 21, Recapitulation, page 3, Form 706 . .	27			
28. Charitable deduction proportion ([line 23 ÷ (line 22 − line 25)] × line 27)	28			
29. Reduced charitable deduction. Subtract line 28 from line 27.	29			
30. Transferee's deduction as adjusted. Add lines 25, 26, and 29			30	
31. (a) Transferee's reduced taxable estate. Subtract line 30 from line 24			31(a)	
(b) Adjusted taxable gifts			31(b)	
(c) Total reduced taxable estate. Add lines 31(a) and 31(b)			31(c)	
32. Tentative tax on reduced taxable estate.	32			
33. (a) Post-1976 gift taxes paid	33(a)			
(b) Unified credit (applicable credit amount)	33(b)			
(c) Section 2012 gift tax credit.	33(c)			
(d) Section 2014 foreign death tax credit .	33(d)			
(e) Total credits. Add lines 33(a) through 33(d)	33(e)			
34. Net tax on reduced taxable estate. Subtract line 33(e) from line 32.			34	
35. Transferee's tax on prior transfers. Subtract line 34 from line 21			35	

appointment that is not a general power of appointment. In addition to interests in which the transferee received the complete ownership, the credit may be allowed for annuities, life estates, terms for years, remainder interests (whether contingent or vested), and any other interest that is less than the complete ownership of the property, to the extent that the transferee became the beneficial owner of the interest.

Maximum Amount of the Credit

The maximum amount of the credit is the smaller of:

1. The amount of the estate tax of the transferor's estate attributable to the transferred property or
2. The amount by which:

a. An estate tax on the transferee's estate determined without the credit for tax on prior transfers exceeds

b. An estate tax on the transferee's estate determined by excluding from the gross estate the net value of the transfer.

If credit for a particular foreign death tax may be taken under either the statute or a death duty convention, and on this return the credit actually is taken under the convention, then no credit for that foreign death tax may be taken into consideration in figuring estate tax (a) or estate tax (b), above.

Percent Allowable

Where transferee predeceased the transferor. If not more than 2 years elapsed between the dates of death, the credit allowed is 100% of the maximum amount. If more than 2 years elapsed between the dates of death, no credit is allowed.

Where transferor predeceased the transferee. The percent of the maximum amount that is allowed as a credit depends on the number of years that elapsed between dates of death. It is determined using the following table:

Period of Time Exceeding	Not Exceeding	Percent Allowable
-----	2 years	100
2 years	4 years	80
4 years	6 years	60
6 years	8 years	40
8 years	10 years	20
10 years	-----	none

How To Figure the Credit

A worksheet for Schedule Q is provided to allow you to figure the limits before completing Schedule Q. Transfer the appropriate amounts from the worksheet to Schedule Q as indicated on the schedule. You do not need to file the worksheet with your Form 706, but you should keep it for your records.

Cases involving transfers from two or more transferors. Part I of the worksheet and Schedule Q enable you to figure the credit for as many as three transferors. The number of transferors is irrelevant to Part II of the worksheet. If you are figuring the credit for more than three transferors, use more than one worksheet and Schedule Q, Part I, and combine the totals for the appropriate lines.

Section 2032A additional tax. If the transferor's estate elected special-use valuation and the additional estate tax of section 2032A(c) was imposed at any time up to 2 years after the death of the decedent for whom you are filing this return, check the box on Schedule Q. On lines 1 and 9 of the worksheet, include the property subject to the additional estate tax at its FMV rather than its special-use value. On line 10 of the worksheet, include the additional estate tax paid as a federal estate tax paid.

How To Complete the Schedule Q Worksheet

Most of the information to complete Part I of the worksheet should be obtained from the transferor's Form 706.

Line 5. Enter on line 5 the applicable marital deduction claimed for the transferor's estate (from the transferor's Form 706).

Lines 10 through 18. Enter on these lines the appropriate taxes paid by the transferor's estate.

If the transferor's estate elected to pay the federal estate tax in installments, enter on line 10 only the total of the installments that have actually been paid at the time you file this Form 706. See Revenue Ruling 83-15, 1983-1 C.B. 224, for more details. Do not include as estate tax any tax attributable to section 4980A, before its repeal by the Taxpayer Relief Act of 1997.

Line 21. Add lines 11 (allowable unified credit) and 13 (foreign death taxes credit) of Part 2—Tax Computation to the amount of any credit taken (on line 15) for federal gift taxes on pre-1977 gifts (section 2012). Subtract this total from Part 2—Tax Computation, line 8. Enter the result on line 21 of the worksheet.

Line 26. If you figured the marital deduction using the unlimited marital deduction in effect for decedents dying after 1981, for purposes of determining the marital deduction for the reduced gross estate, see Revenue Ruling 90-2, 1990-1 C.B. 169. To determine the "reduced adjusted gross estate," subtract the amount on line 25 of the Schedule Q Worksheet from the amount on line 24 of the worksheet. If community property is included in the amount on line 24 of the worksheet, figure the reduced adjusted gross estate using the rules of Regulations section 20.2056(c)-2 and Revenue Ruling 76-311, 1976-2 C.B. 261.

Schedules R and R-1—Generation-Skipping Transfer Tax

Introduction and Overview

Schedule R is used to figure the generation-skipping transfer (GST) tax that is payable by the estate. Schedule R-1 is used to figure the GST tax that is payable by certain trusts that are includible in the gross estate.

The GST tax that is to be reported on Form 706 is imposed only on "direct skips occurring at death." Unlike the estate tax, which is imposed on the value of the entire taxable estate regardless of who receives it, the GST tax is imposed only on the value of interests in property, wherever located, that actually pass to certain transferees, who are referred to as "skip persons."

For purposes of Form 706, the property interests transferred must be includible in the gross estate before they are subject to the GST tax. Therefore, the first step in figuring the GST tax liability is to determine the property interests includible in the gross estate by completing Schedules A through I of Form 706.

The second step is to determine who the skip persons are. To do this, assign each transferee to a generation and determine whether each transferee is a "natural person" or a "trust" for GST purposes.

The third step is to determine which skip persons are transferees of "interests in property." If the skip person is a natural person, anything transferred is an interest in property. If the skip person is a trust, make this determination using the rules under *Interest in property* below. These first three steps are described in detail under the main heading, *Determining Which Transfers Are Direct Skips* below.

The fourth step is to determine whether to enter the transfer on Schedule R or on Schedule R-1. See the rules under the main heading, *Dividing Direct Skips Between Schedules R and R-1.*

The fifth step is to complete Schedules R and R-1 using the *How To Complete* instructions for each schedule.

Determining Which Transfers Are Direct Skips

Effective dates. The rules below apply only for the purpose of determining if a transfer is a direct skip that should be reported on Schedule R or R-1 of Form 706.

In general. The GST tax is effective for the estates of decedents dying after October 22, 1986.

Irrevocable trusts. The GST tax will not apply to any transfer under a trust that was irrevocable on September 25, 1985, but only to the extent that the transfer was not made out of corpus added to the trust after September 25, 1985. An addition to the corpus after that date will cause a proportionate part of future income and appreciation to be subject to the GST tax. For more information, see Regulations section 26.2601-1(b)(1)(ii).

Mental disability. If, on October 22, 1986, the decedent was under a mental disability to change the disposition of his or her property and did not regain the competence to dispose of property before death, the GST tax will not apply to any property included in the gross estate (other than property transferred on behalf of the decedent during life and after October 21, 1986). The GST tax will also not apply to any transfer under a trust to the extent that the trust consists of property included in the gross estate (other than property transferred on behalf of the decedent during life and after October 21, 1986).

Under a mental disability means the decedent lacked the cognitive ability or competence to execute an instrument governing the disposition of his or her property, regardless of whether there was an adjudication of incompetence or an appointment of any other person charged with the care of the person or property of the transferor.

If the decedent had been adjudged mentally incompetent, a copy of the judgment or decree must be filed with this return.

If the decedent had not been adjudged mentally incompetent, the executor must file with the return a certification from a qualified physician stating that in his opinion the decedent had been mentally incompetent at all times on and after October 22, 1986, and that the decedent had not regained the competence to modify or revoke the terms of the trust or will prior to his death or a statement as to why no such certification may be obtained from a physician.

Direct skip. The GST tax reported on Form 706 and Schedule R-1 is imposed only on direct skips. For purposes of Form 706, a *direct skip* is a transfer that is:

- Subject to the estate tax,
- Of an interest in property, and
- To a skip person (defined below).

All three requirements must be met before the transfer is subject to the GST tax. A transfer is subject to the estate tax if you are required to list it on any of Schedules A through I of Form 706. To determine if a transfer is of an interest in property and to a skip person, you must first determine if the transferee is a natural person or a trust as defined below.

Trust. For purposes of the GST tax, a trust includes not only an ordinary trust (as defined in *Special rule for trusts other than ordinary trusts*), but also any other arrangement (other than an estate) which, although not explicitly a trust, has substantially the same effect as a trust. For example, a trust includes life estates with remainders, terms for years, and insurance and annuity contracts.

Substantially separate and independent shares of different beneficiaries in a trust are treated as separate trusts.

Interest in property. If a transfer is made to a natural person, it is always considered a transfer of an interest in property for purposes of the GST tax.

If a transfer is made to a trust, a person will have an interest in the property transferred to the trust if that person either has a present right to receive income or corpus from the trust (such as an income interest for life) or is a permissible current recipient of income or corpus from the trust (that is, may receive income or corpus at the discretion of the trustee).

Skip person. A transferee who is a natural person is a *skip person* if that transferee is assigned to a generation that is two or more generations below the generation assignment of the decedent. See *Determining the generation of a transferee* below.

A transferee who is a trust is a skip person if all the interests in the property (as defined above) transferred to the trust are held by skip persons. Thus, whenever a non-skip person has an interest in a trust, the trust will not be a skip person even though a skip person also has an interest in the trust.

A trust will also be a skip person if there are no interests in the property transferred to the trust held by any person, and future distributions or terminations from the trust can be made only to skip persons.

Non-skip person. A *non-skip person* is any transferee who is not a skip person.

Determining the generation of a transferee. Generally, a generation is determined along family lines as follows:

1. Where the beneficiary is a lineal descendant of a grandparent of the decedent (that is, the decedent's cousin, niece, nephew, etc.), the number of generations between the decedent and the beneficiary is determined by subtracting the number of generations between the grandparent and the decedent from the number of generations between the grandparent and the beneficiary.

2. Where the beneficiary is a lineal descendant of a grandparent of a spouse (or former spouse) of the decedent, the number of generations between the decedent and the beneficiary is determined by subtracting the number of generations between the grandparent and the spouse (or former spouse) from the number of generations between the grandparent and the beneficiary.

3. A person who at any time was married to a person described in (1) or (2) above is assigned to the generation of that person. A person who at any time was married to the decedent is assigned to the decedent's generation.

4. A relationship by adoption or half-blood is treated as a relationship by whole-blood.

5. A person who is not assigned to a generation according to (1), (2), (3), or (4) above is assigned to a generation based on his or her birth date, as follows:

a. A person who was born not more than 12½ years after the decedent is in the decedent's generation.

b. A person born more than 12½ years, but not more than 37½ years, after the decedent is in the first generation younger than the decedent.

c. A similar rule applies for a new generation every 25 years.

If more than one of the rules for assigning generations applies to a transferee, that transferee is generally assigned to the youngest of the generations that would apply.

If an estate, trust, partnership, corporation, or other entity (other than certain charitable organizations and trusts described in sections 511(a)(2) and 511(b)(2)) is a transferee, then each person who indirectly receives the property interests through the entity is treated as a transferee and is assigned to a generation as explained in the above rules. However, this look-through rule does not apply for the purpose of determining whether a transfer to a trust is a direct skip.

Generation assignment where intervening parent is deceased. A special rule may apply in the case of the death of a parent of the transferee. For terminations, distributions, and transfers after December 31, 1997, the existing rule that applied to grandchildren of the decedent has been extended to apply to other lineal descendants.

If property is transferred to an individual who is a descendant of a parent of the transferor, and that individual's parent (who is a lineal descendant of the parent of the transferor) is deceased at the time the transfer is subject to gift or estate tax, then for purposes of generation assignment, the individual is treated as if he or she is a member of the generation that is one generation below the lower of:

- The transferor's generation or
- The generation assignment of the youngest living ancestor of the individual, who is also a descendant of the parent of the transferor.

The same rules apply to the generation assignment of any descendant of the individual.

This rule does not apply to a transfer to an individual who is not a lineal descendant of the transferor if the transferor has any living lineal descendants.

If any transfer of property to a trust would have been a direct skip except for this generation assignment rule, then the rule also applies to transfers from the trust attributable to such property.

Ninety-day rule. For purposes of determining if an individual's parent is deceased at the time of a testamentary transfer, an individual's parent who dies no later than 90 days after a transfer occurring by reason of the death of the transferor is treated as having predeceased the transferor. The 90-day rule applies to transfers occurring on or after July 18, 2005. See Regulations section 26.2651-1, for more information.

Charitable organizations. Charitable organizations and trusts described in sections 511(a)(2) and 511(b)(2) are assigned to the decedent's generation. Transfers to such organizations are therefore not subject to the GST tax.

Charitable remainder trusts. Transfers to or in the form of charitable remainder annuity trusts, charitable remainder unitrusts, and pooled income funds are not considered made to skip persons and, therefore, are not direct skips even if all of the life beneficiaries are skip persons.

Estate tax value. Estate tax value is the value shown on Schedules A through I of this Form 706.

Examples. The rules above can be illustrated by the following examples:

1. Under the will, the decedent's house is transferred to the decedent's daughter for her life with the remainder passing to her children. This transfer is made to a "trust" even though there is no explicit trust instrument. The interest in the property transferred (the present right to use the house) is transferred to a non-skip person (the decedent's daughter). Therefore, the trust is not a skip person because there is an interest in the transferred property that is held by a non-skip person. The transfer is not a direct skip.

2. The will bequeaths $100,000 to the decedent's grandchild. This transfer is a direct skip that is not made in trust and should be shown on Schedule R.

3. The will establishes a trust that is required to accumulate income for 10 years and then pay its income to the decedent's grandchildren for the rest of their lives and, upon their deaths, distribute the corpus to the decedent's great-grandchildren. Because the trust has no current beneficiaries, there are no present interests in the property transferred to the trust. All of the persons to whom the trust can make future distributions (including distributions upon the termination of interests in property held in trust) are skip persons (for example, the decedent's grandchildren and great-grandchildren). Therefore, the trust itself is a skip person and you should show the transfer on Schedule R.

4. The will establishes a trust that is to pay all of its income to the decedent's grandchildren for 10 years. At the end of 10 years, the corpus is to be distributed to the decedent's children. All of the present interests in this trust are held by skip persons. Therefore, the trust is a skip person and you should show this transfer on Schedule R. You should show the estate tax value of all the property transferred to the trust even though the trust has some ultimate beneficiaries who are non-skip persons.

Dividing Direct Skips Between Schedules R and R-1

TIP *Report all generation-skipping transfers on Schedule R unless the rules below specifically provide that they are to be reported on Schedule R-1.*

Under section 2603(a)(2), the GST tax on direct skips from a trust (as defined for GST tax purposes) is to be paid by the trustee and not by the estate. Schedule R-1 serves as a notification from the executor to the trustee that a GST tax is due.

For a direct skip to be reportable on Schedule R-1, the trust must be includible in the decedent's gross estate.

If the decedent was the surviving spouse life beneficiary of a marital deduction power of appointment (or QTIP) trust created by the decedent's spouse, then transfers caused by reason of the decedent's death from that trust to skip persons are direct skips required to be reported on Schedule R-1.

If a direct skip is made "from a trust" under these rules, it is reportable on Schedule R-1 even if it is also made "to a trust" rather than to an individual.

Similarly, if property in a trust (as defined for GST tax purposes) is included in the decedent's gross estate under section 2035, 2036, 2037, 2038, 2039, 2041, or 2042 and such property is, by reason of the decedent's death, transferred to skip persons, the transfers are direct skips required to be reported on Schedule R-1.

Special rule for trusts other than ordinary trusts. An *ordinary trust* is a trust as defined in Regulations section 301.7701-4(a) as "an arrangement created by a will or by an *inter vivos* declaration whereby trustees take title to property for the purpose of protecting or conserving it for the beneficiaries under the ordinary rules applied in chancery or probate courts." Direct skips from ordinary trusts are required to be reported on Schedule R-1 regardless of their size unless the executor is also a trustee (see *Executor as trustee*, below).

Direct skips from trusts that are trusts for GST tax purposes but are not ordinary trusts are to be shown on Schedule R-1 only if the total of all tentative maximum direct skips from the entity is $250,000 or more. If this total is less than $250,000, the skips should be shown on Schedule R. For purposes of the $250,000 limit, "tentative maximum direct skips" is the amount you would enter on line 5 of Schedule R-1 if you were to file that schedule.

A liquidating trust (such as a bankruptcy trust) under Regulations section 301.7701-4(d) is not treated as an ordinary trust for the purposes of this special rule.

If the proceeds of a life insurance policy are includible in the gross estate and are payable to a beneficiary who is a skip person, the transfer is a direct skip from a trust that is not an ordinary trust. It should be reported on Schedule R-1 if the total of all the tentative maximum direct skips from the company is $250,000 or more. Otherwise, it should be reported on Schedule R.

Similarly, if an annuity is includible on Schedule I and its survivor benefits are payable to a beneficiary who is a skip person, then the estate tax value of the annuity should be reported as a direct skip on Schedule R-1 if the total tentative maximum direct skips from the entity paying the annuity is $250,000 or more.

Executor as trustee. If any of the executors of the decedent's estate are trustees of the trust, then all direct skips for that trust must be shown on Schedule R and not on Schedule R-1 even if they would otherwise have been required to be shown on Schedule R-1. This rule applies even if the trust has other trustees who are not executors of the decedent's estate.

How To Complete Schedules R and R-1

Valuation. Enter on Schedules R and R-1 the estate tax value of the property interests subject to the direct skips. If you elected alternate valuation (section 2032) and/or special-use valuation (section 2032A), you must use the alternate and/or special-use values on Schedules R and R-1.

How To Complete Schedule R

Part 1. GST Exemption Reconciliation

Part 1, line 6 of both Parts 2 and 3, and line 4 of Schedule R-1 are used to allocate the decedent's GST exemption. This allocation is made by filing Form 706 and attaching a completed Schedule R and/or R-1. Once made, the allocation is irrevocable. You are not required to allocate all of the decedent's GST exemption. However, the portion of the exemption that you do not allocate will be allocated by the IRS under the deemed allocation at death rules of section 2632(e).

For transfers made through 1998, the GST exemption was $1 million. The current GST exemption is $5,000,000. The exemption amounts for 1999 through 2010 are as follows:

Year of transfer	GST exemption
1999	1,010,000
2000	1,030,000
2001	1,060,000
2002	1,100,000
2003	1,120,000
2004 and 2005	1,500,000
2006, 2007, and 2008	2,000,000
2009	3,500,000
2010	5,000,000

The amount of each increase can only be allocated to transfers made (or appreciation that occurred) during or after the year of the increase. The following example shows the application of this rule:

Example. In 2003, G made a direct skip of $1,120,000 and applied her full $1,120,000 of GST exemption to the transfer. G made a $450,000 taxable direct skip in 2004 and another of $90,000 in 2006. For 2004, G can only apply $380,000 of exemption ($380,000 inflation adjustment from 2004) to the $450,000 transfer in 2004. For 2006, G can apply $90,000 of exemption to the 2006 transfer, but nothing to the transfer made in 2004. At the end of 2006, G would have $410,000 of unused exemption that she can apply to future transfers (or appreciation) starting in 2007.

Special QTIP election. In the case of property for which a marital deduction is allowed to the decedent's estate under section 2056(b)(7) (QTIP election), section 2652(a)(3) allows you to treat such property for purposes of the GST tax as if the election to be treated as qualified terminable interest property had not been made.

The 2652(a)(3) election must include the value of all property in the trust for which a QTIP election was allowed under section 2056(b)(7).

If a section 2652(a)(3) election is made, then the decedent will, for GST tax purposes, be treated as the transferor of all the property in the trust for which a marital deduction was allowed to the decedent's estate under section 2056(b)(7). In this case, the executor of the decedent's estate may allocate part or all of the decedent's GST exemption to the property.

You make the election simply by listing qualifying property on line 9 of Part 1.

Line 2. These allocations will have been made either on Forms 709 filed by the decedent or on Notices of Allocation made by the decedent for *inter vivos* transfers that were not direct skips but to which the decedent allocated the GST exemption. These allocations by the decedent are irrevocable.

Also include on this line allocations deemed to have been made by the decedent under the rules of section 2632. Unless the decedent elected out of the deemed allocation rules, allocations are deemed to have been made in the following order:

1. To *inter vivos* direct skips and
2. Beginning with transfers made after December 31, 2000, to lifetime transfers to certain trusts, by the decedent, that constituted indirect skips that were subject to the gift tax.

For more information, see section 2632.

Line 3. Make an entry on this line if you are filing Form(s) 709 for the decedent and wish to allocate any exemption.

Lines 4, 5, and 6. These lines represent your allocation of the GST exemption to direct skips made by reason of the decedent's death. Complete Parts 2 and 3 and Schedule R-1 before completing these lines.

Line 9. Line 9 is used to allocate the remaining unused GST exemption (from line 8) and to help you figure the trust's inclusion ratio. Line 9 is a Notice of Allocation for allocating the GST exemption to trusts as to which the decedent is the transferor and from which a generation-skipping transfer could occur after the decedent's death.

If line 9 is not completed, the deemed allocation at death rules will apply to allocate the decedent's remaining unused GST exemption, first to property that is the subject of a direct skip occurring at the decedent's death, and then to trusts as to which the decedent is the transferor. If you wish to avoid the application of the deemed allocation rules, you should enter on line 9 every trust (except certain trusts entered on Schedule R-1, as described below) to which you wish to allocate any part of the decedent's GST exemption. Unless you enter a trust on line 9, the unused GST exemption will be allocated to it under the deemed allocation rules.

If a trust is entered on Schedule R-1, the amount you entered on line 4 of Schedule R-1 serves as a Notice of Allocation and you need not enter the trust on line 9 unless you wish to allocate more than the Schedule R-1, line 4 amount to the trust. However, you must enter the trust on line 9 if you wish to allocate any of the unused GST exemption amount to it. Such an additional allocation would not ordinarily be appropriate in the case of a trust entered on Schedule R-1 when the trust property passes outright (rather than to another trust) at the decedent's death. However, where section 2032A property is involved, it may be appropriate to allocate additional exemption amounts to the property. See the instructions for line 10 below.

To avoid application of the deemed allocation rules, Form 706 and Schedule R should be filed to allocate the exemption to trusts that may later have taxable terminations or distributions under section 2612 even if the form is not required to be filed to report estate or GST tax.

Line 9, column C. Enter the GST exemption included on lines 2 through 6 of Part 1 of Schedule R, and discussed above, that was allocated to the trust.

Line 9, column D. Allocate the amount on line 8 of Part 1 of Schedule R in line 9, column D. This amount may be allocated to transfers into trusts that are not otherwise reported on Form 706. For example, the line 8 amount may be allocated to an *inter vivos* trust established by the decedent during his or her lifetime and not included in the gross estate. This allocation is made by identifying the trust on line 9 and making an allocation to it using column D. If the trust is not included in the gross estate, value the trust as of the date of death. You should inform the trustee of each trust listed on line 9 of the total GST exemption you allocated to the trust. The trustee will need this information to figure the GST tax on future distributions and terminations.

Line 9, column E. Trust's inclusion ratio. The trustee must know the trust's inclusion ratio to figure the trust's GST tax for future distributions and terminations. You are not required to inform the trustee of the inclusion ratio and may not have enough information to figure it. Therefore, you are not required to make an entry in column E. However, column E and the worksheet below are provided to assist you in figuring the inclusion ratio for the trustee if you wish to do so.

You should inform the trustee of the amount of the GST exemption you allocated to the trust. Line 9, columns C and D may be used to figure this amount for each trust.

Note. This worksheet will figure an accurate inclusion ratio only if the decedent was the only settlor of the trust. You should use a separate worksheet for each trust (or separate share of a trust that is treated as a separate trust).

WORKSHEET (inclusion ratio):

1	Total estate and gift tax value of all of the property interests that passed to the trust	______
2	Estate taxes, state death taxes, and other charges actually recovered from the trust	______
3	GST taxes imposed on direct skips to skip persons other than this trust and borne by the property transferred to this trust	______
4	GST taxes actually recovered from this trust (from Schedule R, Part 2, line 8 or Schedule R-1, line 6)	______
5	Add lines 2 through 4	______
6	Subtract line 5 from line 1	______
7	Add columns C and D of line 9 . .	______
8	Divide line 7 by line 6	______
9	Trust's inclusion ratio. Subtract line 8 from 1.000	______

Line 10. Special-use allocation. For skip persons who receive an interest in section 2032A special-use property, you may allocate more GST exemption than the direct skip amount to reduce the additional GST tax that would be due when the interest is later disposed of or qualified use ceases. See Schedule A-1, above, for more details about this additional GST tax.

Enter on line 10 the total additional GST exemption available to allocate to all skip persons who received any interest in section 2032A property. Attach a special-use allocation schedule listing each such skip person and the amount of the GST exemption allocated to that person.

If you do not allocate the GST exemption, it will be automatically allocated under the deemed allocation at death rules. To the extent any amount is not so allocated, it will be automatically allocated to the earliest disposition or cessation that is subject to the GST tax. Under certain circumstances, post-death events may cause the decedent to be treated as a transferor for purposes of Chapter 13.

Line 10 may be used to set aside an exemption amount for such an event. You must attach a schedule listing each such event and the amount of exemption allocated to that event.

Parts 2 and 3

Use Part 2 to figure the GST tax on transfers in which the property interests transferred are to bear the GST tax on the transfers. Use Part 3 to report the GST tax on transfers in which the property interests transferred do not bear the GST tax on the transfers.

Section 2603(b) requires that unless the governing instrument provides otherwise, the GST tax is to be charged to the property constituting the transfer. Therefore, you will usually enter all of the direct skips on Part 2.

You may enter a transfer on Part 3 only if the will or trust instrument directs, by specific reference, that the GST tax is not to be paid from the transferred property interests.

Part 2, Line 3. Enter zero on this line unless the will or trust instrument specifies that the GST taxes will be paid by property other than that constituting the transfer (as described above). Enter on line 3 the total of the GST taxes shown on Part 3 and Schedule(s) R-1 that are payable out of the property interests shown on Part 2, line 1.

Part 2, Line 6. Do not enter more than the amount on line 5. Additional allocations may be made using Part 1.

Part 3, Line 3. See the instructions to Part 2, line 3 above. Enter only the total of the GST taxes shown on Schedule(s) R-1 that are payable out of the property interests shown on Part 3, line 1.

Part 3, Line 6. See the instructions to Part 2, line 6 above.

How To Complete Schedule R-1

Filing due date. Enter the due date of Form 706. You must send the copies of Schedule R-1 to the fiduciary before this date.

Line 4. Do not enter more than the amount on line 3. If you wish to allocate an additional GST exemption, you must use Schedule R, Part 1. Making an entry on line 4 constitutes a Notice of Allocation of the decedent's GST exemption to the trust.

Line 6. If the property interests entered on line 1 will not bear the GST tax, multiply line 6 by 35% (0.35).

Signature. The executor(s) must sign Schedule R-1 in the same manner as Form 706. See *Signature and Verification.*

Filing Schedule R-1. Attach to Form 706 one copy of each Schedule R-1 that you prepare. Send two copies of each Schedule R-1 to the fiduciary.

Schedule U—Qualified Conservation Easement Exclusion

CAUTION *If at the time of the contribution of the conservation easement, the value of the easement, the value of the land subject to the easement, or the value of any retained development right was different than the estate tax value, you must complete a separate computation in addition to completing Schedule U.*

Use a copy of Schedule U as a worksheet for this separate computation. Complete lines 4 through 14 of the worksheet Schedule U. However, the value you use on lines 4, 5, 7, and 10 of the worksheet is the value for these items as of the date of the contribution of the easement, not the estate tax value. If the date of contribution and the estate tax values are the same, you do not need to do a separate computation.

After completing the worksheet, enter the amount from line 14 of the worksheet on line 14 of Schedule U. Finish completing Schedule U by entering amounts on lines 4, 7, and 15 through 20, following the instructions below for those lines. At the top of Schedule U, enter "worksheet attached." Attach the worksheet to the return.

Under section 2031(c), you may elect to exclude a portion of the value of land that is subject to a qualified conservation easement. You make the election by filing Schedule U with all of the required information and excluding the applicable value of the land that is subject to the easement on Part 5—Recapitulation, page 3, at item 11. To elect the exclusion, you must include on Schedule A, B, E, F, G, or H, as appropriate, the decedent's interest in the land that is subject to the exclusion. You must make the election on a timely filed Form 706, including extensions.

The exclusion is the lesser of:

- The applicable percentage of the value of land (after certain reductions) subject to a qualified conservation easement or
- $500,000.

Once made, the election is irrevocable.

General Requirements

Qualified Land

Land may qualify for the exclusion if all of the following requirements are met:

• The decedent or a member of the decedent's family must have owned the land for the 3-year period ending on the date of the decedent's death.
• No later than the date the election is made, a qualified conservation easement on the land has been made by the decedent, a member of the decedent's family, the executor of the decedent's estate, or the trustee of a trust that holds the land.
• The land is located in the United States or one of its possessions.

Member of Family

Members of the decedent's family include the decedent's spouse; ancestors; lineal descendants of the decedent, of the decedent's spouse, and of the parents of the decedent; and the spouse of any lineal descendant. A legally adopted child of an individual is considered a child of the individual by blood.

Indirect Ownership of Land

The qualified conservation easement exclusion applies if the land is owned indirectly through a partnership, corporation, or trust, if the decedent owned (directly or indirectly) at least 30% of the entity. For the rules on determining ownership of an entity, see *Ownership rules* below.

Ownership rules. An interest in property owned, directly or indirectly, by or for a corporation, partnership, or trust is considered proportionately owned by or for the entity's shareholders, partners, or beneficiaries. A person is the beneficiary of a trust only if he or she has a present interest in the trust. For additional information, see the ownership rules in section 2057(e)(3).

Qualified Conservation Easement

A *qualified conservation easement* is one that would qualify as a qualified conservation contribution under section 170(h). It must be a contribution:
• Of a qualified real property interest,
• To a qualified organization, and
• Exclusively for conservation purposes.

Qualified real property interest. A *qualified real property interest* is any of the following:
• The entire interest of the donor, other than a qualified mineral interest;
• A remainder interest; or
• A restriction granted in perpetuity on the use that may be made of the real property. The restriction must include a prohibition on more than a *de minimis* use for commercial recreational activity.

Qualified organization. A *qualified organization* includes:
• Corporations and any community chest, fund, or foundation, organized and operated exclusively for religious, charitable, scientific, testing for public safety, literary, or educational purposes, or to foster national or international amateur sports competition, or for the prevention of cruelty to children or animals, without net earnings benefitting any individual shareholder and without activity with the purpose of influencing legislation or political campaigning, which

a. Receives more than one-third of its support from gifts, contributions, membership fees, or receipts from sales, admissions fees, or performance of services, or

b. Is controlled by such an organization.
• Any entity that qualifies under section 170(b)(1)(A)(v) or (vi).

Conservation purpose. An easement has a *conservation purpose* if it is for:
• The preservation of land areas for outdoor recreation by, or for the education of, the public;
• The protection of a relatively natural habitat of fish, wildlife, or plants, or a similar ecosystem; or
• The preservation of open space (including farmland and forest land) where such preservation is for the scenic enjoyment of the general public, or under a clearly delineated federal, state, or local conservation policy and will yield a significant public benefit.

Specific Instructions

Line 1

If the land is reported as one or more item numbers on a Form 706 schedule, simply list the schedule and item numbers. If the land subject to the easement is only part of an item, however, list the schedule and item number and describe the part subject to the easement. See the Instructions for Schedule A—Real Estate for information on how to describe the land.

Line 3

Using the general rules for describing real estate, provide enough information so the IRS can value the easement. Give the date the easement was granted and by whom it was granted.

Line 4

Enter on this line the gross value at which the land was reported on the applicable asset schedule on this Form 706. Do not reduce the value by the amount of any mortgage outstanding. Report the estate tax value even if the easement was granted by the decedent (or someone other than the decedent) prior to the decedent's death.

Note. If the value of the land reported on line 4 was different at the time the easement was contributed than that reported on Form 706, see the *Caution* at the beginning of the Schedule U Instructions.

Line 5

The amount on line 5 should be the date of death value of any qualifying conservation easements granted prior to the decedent's death, whether granted by the decedent or someone other than the decedent, for which the exclusion is being elected.

Note. If the value of the easement reported on line 5 was different at the time the easement was contributed than at the date of death, see the *Caution* at the beginning of the Schedule U Instructions.

Line 7

You must reduce the land value by the value of any development rights retained by the donor in the conveyance of the easement. A development right is any right to use the land for any commercial purpose that is not subordinate to and directly supportive of the use of the land as a farm for farming purposes.

Note. If the value of the retained development rights reported on line 7 was different at the time the easement was contributed than at the date of death, see the *Caution* at the beginning of the Schedule U Instructions.

You do not have to make this reduction if everyone with an interest in the land (regardless of whether in possession) agrees to permanently extinguish the retained development right. The agreement must be filed with this return and must include the following information and terms:

1. A statement that the agreement is made under section 2031(c)(5);
2. A list of all persons in being holding an interest in the land that is subject to the qualified conservation easement. Include each person's name, address, tax identifying number, relationship to the decedent, and a description of their interest;
3. The items of real property shown on the estate tax return that are subject to the qualified conservation easement (identified by schedule and item number);
4. A description of the retained development right that is to be extinguished;
5. A clear statement of consent that is binding on all parties under applicable local law:

a. To take whatever action is necessary to permanently extinguish the retained development rights listed in the agreement and

b. To be personally liable for additional taxes under section 2031(c)(5)(C) if this agreement is not implemented by the earlier of:

• The date that is 2 years after the date of the decedent's death or
• The date of sale of the land subject to the qualified conservation easement;

6. A statement that in the event this agreement is not timely implemented, that they will report the additional tax on whatever return is required by the IRS and will file the return and pay the additional tax by the last day of the 6th month following the applicable date described above.

All parties to the agreement must sign the agreement.

For an example of an agreement containing some of the same terms, see Part 3 of Schedule A-1 (Form 706).

Line 10

Enter the total value of the qualified conservation easements on which the exclusion is based. This could include easements granted by the decedent (or someone other than the decedent) prior to the decedent's death, easements granted by the decedent that take effect at death, easements granted by the executor after the decedent's death, or some combination of these.

Use the value of the easement as of the date of death, even if the easement was granted prior to the date of death. But, if the value of the easement was different at the time the easement was contributed than at the date of death, see the Caution *at the beginning of the Schedule U Instructions.*

Explain how this value was determined and attach copies of any appraisals. Normally, the appropriate way to value a conservation easement is to determine the FMV of the land both before and after the granting of the easement, with the difference being the value of the easement.

You must reduce the reported value of the easement by the amount of any consideration received for the easement. If the date of death value of the easement is different from the value at the time the consideration was received, you must reduce the value of the easement by the same proportion that the consideration received bears to the value of the easement at the time it was granted. For example, assume the value of the easement at the time it was granted was $100,000 and $10,000 was received in consideration for the easement. If the easement was worth $150,000 at the date of death, you must reduce the value of the easement by $15,000 ($10,000/$100,000 × $150,000) and report the value of the easement on line 10 as $135,000.

Line 15

If a charitable contribution deduction for this land has been taken on Schedule O, enter the amount of the deduction here. If the easement was granted after the decedent's death, a contribution deduction may be taken on Schedule O, if it otherwise qualifies, as long as no income tax deduction was or will be claimed for the contribution by any person or entity.

Line 16

You must reduce the value of the land by the amount of any acquisition indebtedness on the land at the date of the decedent's death. Acquisition indebtedness includes the unpaid amount of:

- Any indebtedness incurred by the donor in acquiring the property;
- Any indebtedness incurred before the acquisition if the indebtedness would not have been incurred but for the acquisition;
- Any indebtedness incurred after the acquisition if the indebtedness would not have been incurred but for the acquisition and the incurrence of the indebtedness was reasonably foreseeable at the time of the acquisition; and
- The extension, renewal, or refinancing of acquisition indebtedness.

Continuation Schedule

When you need to list more assets or deductions than you have room for on one of the main schedules, use the Continuation Schedule at the end of Form 706. It provides a uniform format for listing additional assets from Schedules A through I and additional deductions from Schedules J, K, L, M, and O.

Please remember to:

- Use a separate Continuation Schedule for each main schedule you are continuing. Do not combine assets or deductions from different schedules on one Continuation Schedule.
- Make copies of the blank schedule before completing it if you expect to need more than one.
- Use as many Continuation Schedules as needed to list all the assets or deductions.
- Enter the letter of the schedule you are continuing in the space at the top of the Continuation Schedule.
- Use the *Unit value* column **only** if continuing Schedule B, E, or G. For all other schedules, use this space to continue the description.
- Carry the total from the Continuation Schedules forward to the appropriate line on the main schedule.

If continuing	Report	Where on Continuation Schedule
Schedule E, Pt. 2	*Percentage includible*	*Alternate valuation date*
Schedule K	*Amount unpaid to date*	*Alternate valuation date*
Schedule K	*Amount in contest*	*Alternate value*
Schedules J, L, M	*Description of deduction continuation*	*Alternate valuation date* **and** *Alternate value*
Schedule O	*Character of institution*	*Alternate valuation date* **and** *Alternate value*
Schedule O	*Amount of each deduction*	*Amount deductible*

Privacy Act and Paperwork Reduction Act Notice. We ask for the information on this form to carry out the Internal Revenue laws of the United States. You are required to give us the information. We need it to ensure that you are complying with these laws and to allow us to figure and collect the right amount of tax. Subtitle B and section 6109, and the regulations require you to provide this information.

You are not required to provide the information requested on a form that is subject to the Paperwork Reduction Act unless the form displays a valid OMB control number. Books or records relating to a form or its instructions must be retained as long as their contents may become material in the administration of any Internal Revenue law. Generally, tax returns and return information are confidential as required by section 6103. However, section 6103 allows or requires the Internal Revenue Service to disclose information from this form in certain circumstances. For example, we may disclose information to the Department of Justice for civil or criminal litigation, and to cities, states, the District of Columbia, and U.S. commonwealths or possessions for use in administering their tax laws. We may also disclose this information to other countries under a tax treaty, to federal and state agencies to enforce federal nontax criminal laws, or to federal law enforcement and intelligence agencies to combat terrorism. Failure to provide this information, or providing false information, may subject you to penalties.

The time needed to complete and file this form and related schedules will vary depending on individual circumstances. The estimated average times are:

Form	Recordkeeping	Learning about the law or the form	Preparing the form	Copying, assembling, and sending the form to the IRS
706	1 hr., 25 min.	1 hr., 50 min.	3 hr., 42 min.	48 min.
Schedule A	- - - -	15 min.	12 min.	20 min.
Schedule A-1	33 min.	31 min.	1 hr., 15 min.	1 hr., 3 min.
Schedule B	19 min.	9 min.	16 min.	20 min.
Schedule C	19 min.	1 min.	13 min.	20 min.
Schedule D	6 min.	6 min.	13 min.	20 min.
Schedule E	39 min.	6 min.	36 min.	20 min.
Schedule F	26 min.	8 min.	18 min.	20 min.
Schedule G	26 min.	21 min.	12 min.	13 min.
Schedule H	26 min.	6 min.	12 min.	13 min.
Schedule I	13 min.	30 min.	15 min.	20 min.
Schedule J	26 min.	6 min.	16 min.	20 min.
Schedule K	13 min.	9 min.	18 min.	20 min.
Schedule L	13 min.	4 min.	15 min.	20 min.
Schedule M	13 min.	34 min.	25 min.	20 min.
Schedule O	19 min.	12 min.	21 min.	20 min.
Schedule P	6 min.	15 min.	18 min.	13 min.
Schedule Q	- - - -	12 min.	15 min.	13 min.
Worksheet for Schedule Q	6 min.	6 min.	58 min.	20 min.
Schedule R	19 min.	45 min.	1 hr., 10 min.	48 min.
Schedule R-1	6 min.	46 min.	35 min.	20 min.
Schedule U	19 min.	26 min.	29 min.	20 min.
Continuation Schedule	19 min.	1 min.	13 min.	20 min.

If you have comments concerning the accuracy of these time estimates or suggestions for making this form simpler, we would be happy to hear from you. You can write to the Internal Revenue Service, Tax Products Coordinating Committee, SE:W:CAR:MP:T:M:S, 1111 Constitution Ave. NW, IR-6526, Washington, DC 20224. Do not send the tax form to this address. Instead, see *Where To File*.

Index

■

Checklist for Completing Form 706

To ensure a complete return, review the following checklist before filing Form 706.

Attachments . . .

- ☐ Death Certificate
- ☐ Certified copy of the will—if decedent died testate, you must attach a certified copy of the will. If not certified, explain why.
- ☐ Appraisals—attach any appraisals used to value property included on the return.
- ☐ Copies of all trust documents where the decedent was a grantor or a beneficiary.
- ☐ Form 2848 or 8821, if applicable.
- ☐ Copy of any Form(s) 709 filed by the decedent.
- ☐ Form 712, if any policies of life insurance are included on the return.
- ☐ Form 706-CE, if claiming a foreign death tax credit.

Have you . . .

- ☐ Signed the return at the bottom of page 1?
- ☐ Had the preparer sign, if applicable?
- ☐ Obtained the signature of your authorized representative on Part 4, page 2?
- ☐ Entered a Total on all schedules filed?
- ☐ Made an entry on every line of the Recapitulation, even if it is a zero?
- ☐ Included the CUSIP number for all stocks and bonds?
- ☐ Included the EIN of trusts, partnerships, and closely held entities?
- ☐ Included the first 3 pages of the return and all required schedules?
- ☐ Completed Schedule F? It must be filed with all returns.
- ☐ Completed Part 4, line 4, on page 2, if there is a surviving spouse?
- ☐ Completed and attached Schedule D to report insurance on the life of the decedent, even if its value is not included in the estate?
- ☐ Included any QTIP property received from a predeceased spouse?
- ☐ Entered the decedent's name, SSN, and "Form 706" on your check or money order?
- ☐ Included a copy of the predeceased spouse's Form 706 if this estate applies the deceased spousal unused exclusion (DSUE) amount?
- ☐ Attached a statement to the Form 706 or entered "No Election under Section 2010(c)(5)" across the top of page 1, if the estate elects not to transfer any deceased spousal unused exclusion (DSUE) amount to the surviving spouse?

INDEX

References are to Pages

References are to Pages

References are to Pages

References are to Pages

References are to Pages

†